# WORD
# BIBLICAL
# COMMENTARY

**General Editors**
David A. Hubbard †
Glenn W. Barker †

**Old Testament Editor**
John D. W. Watts

**New Testament Editor**
Ralph P. Martin

# WORD

# BIBLICAL

# COMMENTARY

Volume 52

## Revelation 1–5

## DAVID E. AUNE

**THOMAS NELSON**
*Since 1798*

NASHVILLE   DALLAS   MEXICO CITY   RIO DE JANEIRO   BEIJING

Word Biblical Commentary
Revelation 1–5
Copyright © 1997 by Word, Incorporated

**Library of Congress Cataloging-in-Publication Data**
Main entry under title:

Word biblical commentary.

Includes bibliographies.
1. Bible—Commentaries—Collected works.
BS491.2.W67      22.2 '7      81–71768
ISBN 10: 0-8499-0251-7 (v. 52) AACR2
ISBN 13: 978-0-8499-0251-2

*Printed in Colombia*

The author's own translation of the Scripture text appears in italic type under the heading *Translation*.

10 11 12  QWB  09  08  07

*To*
*Peder and Inger Borgen*
*and*
*Martin and Marianne Hengel*

# Contents

# Editorial Preface

The launching of the *Word Biblical Commentary* brings to fulfillment an enterprise of several years' planning. The publishers and the members of the editorial board met in 1977 to explore the possibility of a new commentary on the books of the Bible that would incorporate several distinctive features. Prospective readers of these volumes are entitled to know what such features were intended to be; whether the aims of the commentary have been fully achieved time alone will tell.

First, we have tried to cast a wide net to include as contributors a number of scholars from around the world who not only share our aims but are in the main engaged in the ministry of teaching in university, college, and seminary. They represent a rich diversity of denominational allegiance. The broad stance of our contributors can rightly be called evangelical, and this term is to be understood in its positive, historic sense of a commitment to Scripture as divine revelation and the truth and power of the Christian gospel.

Then, the commentaries in our series are all commissioned and written for the purpose of inclusion in the *Word Biblical Commentary*. Unlike several of our distinguished counterparts in the field of commentary writing, there are no translated works, originally written in a non-English language. Also, our commentators were asked to prepare their own rendering of the original biblical text and to use those languages as the basis of their own comments and exegesis. What may be claimed as distinctive with this series is that it is based on the biblical languages, yet it seeks to make the technical and scholarly approach to the theological understanding of Scripture understandable by—and useful to—the fledgling student, the working minister, and colleagues in the guild of professional scholars and teachers as well.

Finally, a word must be said about the format of the series. The layout, in clearly defined sections, has been consciously devised to assist readers at different levels. Those wishing to learn about the textual witnesses on which the translation is offered are invited to consult the section headed *Notes*. If the readers' concern is with the state of modern scholarship on any given portion of Scripture, they should turn to the sections on *Bbiliography* and *Form/Structure/Setting*. For a clear exposition of the passage's meaning and its relevance to the ongoing biblical revelation, the *Comment* and concluding *Explanation* are designed expressly to meet that need. There is therefore something for everyone who may pick up and use these volumes.

If these aims come anywhere near realization, the intention of the editors will have been met, and the labor of our team of contributors rewarded.

General Editors: *David A. Hubbard*†
*Glenn W. Barker*†
Old Testament: *John D. W. Watts*
New Testament: *Ralph P. Martin*

# Author's Preface

Serious research on this commentary began in 1982–83, when I spent the academic year at the University of Trondheim, as a Fulbright guest professor in the Department of Religious Studies. Professor Peder Borgen was my host, and I am grateful to him and his wife, Inger, for the kindness, hospitality, and friendship shown to my family and me during that exciting year. Work on the commentary was all but completed some twelve years later in 1994–95 at the University of Tübingen, where I continued my research as the recipient of an Alexander von Humboldt Forschungspreis. Professor Martin Hengel (whom I first met when he gave a lecture at the University of Trondheim in the spring of 1983) was my host, and my wife and I experienced the gracious hospitality of the Hengels and Professor and Mrs. Peter Stuhlmacher on many occasions. I must also express my appreciation to Dr. Jörg Frey, Professor Hengel's research assistant, for his ready help in dealing with many practical details at the Theologicum in Tübingen. Since the years at Trondheim and Tübingen were critical for the commencement and completion of this commentary, I have dedicated it in gratitude to the Borgens and the Hengels. I am, of course, profoundly grateful both to the Council for International Exchange of Scholars for the Fulbright award and to the Alexander von Humboldt Stiftung for the award of a Forschungspreis, as well as to Loyola University Chicago for providing me with a subsidized leave of absence during the 1994–95 academic year.

A number of colleagues and students have made important contributions to this commentary. Colleagues who have read and offered critiques of portions of the commentary include Professors Lee Levine of Hebrew University, Jan Willem van Henten of the University of Amsterdam, and Bruce Metzger of Princeton Theological Seminary. Some of the material that found its way into the commentary was originally formulated and delivered as lectures at the University of Aberdeen (February 1983), the University of Oslo and the Baptist Theological Seminary in Oslo (March 1983), Washington University (February 1990), and the University of Utrecht (March 1995). I also profited greatly by participating in various seminars on Revelation, including the Seminar on Early Christian Apocalypticism (1983–87), chaired by Professor Adela Yarbro Collins, the Seminar on Reading the Apocalypse (1991–97), chaired by Professor David Barr, both under the auspices of the Society of Biblical Literature, and the Seminar on Apocalyptic in the New Testament, chaired by a succession of scholars including Professors Traugott Holtz, Elizabeth Schüssler Fiorenza, Charles H. Giblin, and Jens Taeger, under the auspices of the Studiorum Novi Testamenti Societas. Three graduate research assistants, Peter Sibilio (spring 1994), Paul Hartog (fall 1995), and Kevin McCruden (Spring 1997), have waded through countless pages of text and saved me from hundreds of errors.

My own interest in Revelation began in connection with earlier work on issues relating to early Christiain prophecy that came to fruition in a book entitled *Prophecy in Early Christianity and the Ancient Mediterranean World* (Grand Rapids, MI:

Eerdmans, 1983). It seemed a natural continuation of that interest to focus on a detailed study of the Revelation of John. I am grateful for the confidence that Professor Ralph Martin had in my work, which led to the issuing of the contract that made this commentary part of the Word Biblical Commentary series.

The writing of a commentary on any book of the Bible is a daunting task, particularly so in the case of the Revelation of John. Though the bibliography of books and articles on Revelation is enormous (extensive as the bibliographies in this commentary are, they are far from exhaustive), I am particularly indebted to the rich and creative commentaries of Wilhelm Bousset and R. H. Charles, and to the very detailed and painstaking textual work of H. C. Hoskier and Josef Schmid. In the words of J. W. v. Goethe:

> Seh iche die Werke der Meister an,
> So seh ich das, was sie getan;
> Betracht ich meine Siebensachen,
> Seh ich, was ich hätt sollen machen.

The *Notes* sections in this commentary contain discussions of the grammar and text of Revelation. Readers who have a special interest in the text of Revelation are urged to read Section 6 of the *Introduction,* where a full explanation of the many abbreviations of manuscripts and families of manuscripts can be found.

DAVID E. AUNE

*April 1997*
*Loyola University Chicago*

# Abbreviations

## A. General Abbreviations

| | | | |
|---|---|---|---|
| abs. | absolute | n.d. | no date |
| acc. | accusative | neut. | neuter |
| adj. | adjective, adjectival | no. | number |
| adv. | adverb, adverbial | nom. | nominative |
| aor. | aorist | n.s. | new series |
| Aram. | Aramaic | NT | New Testament |
| ca. | *circa*, about | obj. | object, objective |
| cent. | century | OL | Old Latin |
| cf. | *confer,* compare | OT | Old Testament |
| chap(s). | chapter(s) | par. | parallel |
| d. | deceased | pass. | passive |
| dat. | dative | PEnteux | *Enteuxeis* Papyri (Cairo) |
| DSS | Dead Sea Scrolls | pf. | perfect |
| ed. | editor, edited by | PGiss | Giessen Papyri |
| e.g. | *exempli gratia,* for example | PKöln | Kölner Papyri |
| ET | English translation | pl. | plural |
| et. al. | *et alii,* and others | plupf. | pluperfect |
| fem. | feminine | poss. | possessive |
| fig. | figure | POxy | Oxyrhynchus Papyri |
| fl. | *floruit,* flourished | prep. | preposition |
| fol. | folio | PRoss | Papyri russischer und georgischer Sammlungen |
| FS | *Festschrift,* volume written in honor of | | |
| fut. | future | ptcp. | participle |
| gen. | genitive | PWash | Washington University Papyri |
| Gk. | Greek | | |
| *hap. leg.* | *hapax legomenon,* sole occurrence | repr. | reprint |
| | | rev. | revised, reviser, revision |
| Heb. | Hebrew | sc. | *scilicet,* namely |
| id. | *idem,* the same | ser. | series |
| i.e. | *id est,* that is | sing. | singular |
| imper. | imperative | s.v. | *sub verbo,* under the word |
| impf. | imperfect | tr. | translator, translated by, translation |
| ind. | indicative | | |
| inf. | infinitive | UP | University Press |
| lit. | literally | v, vv | verse, verses |
| LXX | Septuagint | *var. lect.* | *varia(e) lectio(nes),* "variant reading(s)" |
| masc. | masculine | | |
| MS(S) | manuscript(s) | vol. | volume |
| MT | Masoretic Text | x | times (2x = two times) |
| n. | note | | |

## B. Abbreviations for Translations and Paraphrases

| | | | |
|---|---|---|---|
| ASV | American Standard Version, American Revised Version (1901) | NEB | New English Bible |
| | | NIV | New International Version |
| | | NRSV | New Revised Standard Version |
| AV | Authorized Version = KJV | | |
| KJV | King James Version (1611) = AV | REB | Revised English Bible |
| | | RSV | Revised Standard Version |
| NASB | New American Standard Bible | | |

## C. Abbreviations of Commonly Used Periodicals, Reference Works, and Serials

| | | | |
|---|---|---|---|
| *AAA* | R. A. Lipsius and M. Bonnet (eds.), *Acta Apostolorum Apocrypha* | AramBib | Aramaic Bible (Wilmington, DE: Glazier) |
| | | *ARW* | *Archiv für Religionswissenschaft* |
| AB | Anchor Bible | *AsSeign* | *Assemblées du Seigneur* |
| *ABD* | D. N. Freedman (ed.), *Anchor Bible Dictionary*, 6 vols. | ATANT | Abhandlung zur Theologie des Alten und Neuen Testaments |
| *AC* | *Antike und Christentum* | | |
| *AcCl* | *Acta Classica* | *ATR* | *Anglican Theological Review* |
| *AD* | I. J. Gelb et al. (eds), *The Assyrian Dictionary of the Oriental Institute of the University of Chicago*, 21 vols. | AUSDDS | Andrews University Seminary Doctoral Dissertation Series |
| | | *AUSS* | *Andrews University Seminary Studies* |
| *AHI* | G. I. Davies (ed.), *Ancient Hebrew Inscriptions: Corpus and Concordance* | *BA* | *Biblical Archaeologist* |
| | | BAGD | W. Bauer, W. F. Arndt, F. W. Gingrich, and F. W. Danker, *A Greek-English Lexicon of the NT*, 2nd ed. |
| *AJA* | *American Journal of Archaeology* | | |
| AJBI | Annual of the Japanese Biblical Institute | | |
| *AJP* | *American Journal of Philology* | *BAR* | *Biblical Archaeologist Reader* |
| ALUOS | Annual of Leeds University Oriental Society | *BARev* | *Biblical Archaeology Review* |
| | | BARevSup | *BARev* Supplementary Series |
| AnBib | Analecta biblica | *BASOR* | *Bulletin of the American Schools of Oriental Research* |
| AnBoll | Analecta Bollandiana | | |
| *ANEP* | J. B. Pritchard (ed.), *The Ancient Near East in Pictures* | BASORSup | *BASOR* Supplementary Studies |
| *ANET* | J. B. Pritchard (ed.), *Ancient Near Eastern Texts* | Bauer-Aland | W. Bauer, *Griechisch-deutsches Wörterbuch zum den Schriften des Neuen Testaments und der frühchristlichen Literatur*, 6th ed., rev. K. and B. Aland |
| *ANRW* | *Aufsteig und Niedergang der römischen Welt* | | |
| ANTF | Arbeiten zur neutestamentlichen Textforschung | *BCH* | *Bulletin de Correspondance Hellénique* |
| AOB | Acta Orientalia Beligica | BDB | F. Brown, S. R. Driver, and C. A. Briggs, *Hebrew and English Lexicon of the OT* |
| *AOT* | H. F. D. Sparks (ed.), *The Apocryphal Old Testament* | | |

| | | | |
|---|---|---|---|
| BDF | F. Blass, A. Debrunner, and R. W. Funk, *A Greek Grammar of the NT* | CBQ | *Catholic Biblical Quarterly* |
| | | CBQMS | Catholic Biblical Quarterly—Monograph Series |
| BDR | F. Blass, A. Debrunner, and F. Rehkopf, *Grammatik des neutestamentlichen Griechisch* (1984) | CCL | Corpus Christianorum, Series Latina |
| | | CH | *Church History* |
| | | Checklist | J. F. Oates, R. S. Bagnall, W. H. Willis, and K. A. Worp, *Checklist of Editions of Greek Papyri and Ostraca*, 3rd ed. |
| BETL | Bibliotheca ephemeridum theologicarum lovaniensium | | |
| BG | W. C. Till (ed.), *Die gnostischen Schriften des koptischen Papyrus Berolinensis 8502* | CIG | *Corpus Inscriptionum Graecarum*, 4 vols. |
| | | CIJ | *Corpus Inscriptionum Judaicarum* |
| BGBE | Beiträge zur Geschichte der biblischen Exegese | CIL | *Corpus Inscriptionum Latinarum* |
| BHS | *Biblia hebraica stuttgartensia* | CIMRM | M. J. Vermaseren (ed.), *Corpus Inscriptionum et Monumentorum Religionis Mithraicae*, 2 vols. |
| BHT | Beiträge zur historischen Theologie | | |
| Bib | *Biblica* | | |
| BibLeb | *Bibel und Leben* | | |
| BibReal | K. Galling (ed.), *Biblisches Reallexikon*, 2nd ed. | CJ | *Classical Journal* |
| | | CMIR | J. R. Cayón, *Compendio de las Monedas del Imperio Romano*, 2 vols. |
| BJRL | *Bulletin of the John Rylands University Library of Manchester* | | |
| | | ConBOT | Coniectanea biblica, Old Testament |
| BJS | Brown Judaic Studies | | |
| BK | *Bibel und Kirche* | ConNT | Coniectanea neotestamentica |
| BMC | H. Mattingly, *Coins of the Roman Empire in the British Museum* | CP | *Classical Philology* |
| | | CPJ | V. A. Tcherikover, A. Fuks, and M. Stern (eds.), *Corpus Papyrorum Judaicorum*, 3 vols. |
| BMI | *British Museum Inscriptions* | | |
| BN | *Biblische Notizen* | | |
| BR | *Biblical Research* | | |
| BSac | *Bibliotheca Sacra* | CQ | *Classical Quarterly* |
| BT | *The Bible Translator* | CQR | *Church Quarterly Review* |
| BTB | *Biblical Theology Bulletin* | CREBM | H. Mattingly and R. A. G. Carson, *Coins of the Roman Empire in the British Museum*, 6 vols. |
| BurH | *Buried History* | | |
| BVC | *Bible et vie chrétienne* | | |
| BWANT | Beiträge zur Wissenschaft vom Alten und Neuen Testament | | |
| | | CRINT | Compendia Rerum Iudaicarum ad Novum Testamentum |
| ByzNeugrJb | *Byzantinisch-neugriechische Jahrbücher* | | |
| | | CSCA | *California Studies in Classical Antiquity* |
| BZ | *Biblische Zeitschrift* | | |
| BZAW | Beihefte zur ZAW | CSCO | Corpus scriptorum christianorum orientalium |
| BZNW | Beihefte zur ZNW | | |
| CAH | *Cambridge Ancient History* | | |

| | | | |
|---|---|---|---|
| CSEL | Corpus scriptorum ecclesiasticorum latinorum | ETR | *Études théologiques et religieuses* |
| | | EvQ | *Evangelical Quarterly* |
| | | EvT | *Evangelische Theologie* |
| CTM | *Concordia Theological Monthly* | EWNT | H. Balz and G. Schneider (eds.), *Exegetisches Wörterbuch zum Neuen Testament*, 3 vols. |
| CTQ | *Concordia Theological Quarterly* | | |
| CTR | *Criswell Theological Review* | | |
| | | ExpTim | *Expository Times* |
| DACL | F. Cabrol (ed.), *Dictionnaire d'archéologie chrétienne et la liturgie*, 15 vols. | | |
| | | FHJA | C. R. Holladay (ed.), *Fragments from Hellenistic Jewish Authors*, 4 vols. |
| DBSup | *Dictionnaire de la Bible, Supplément* | | |
| | | FNT | *Filologia Neotestamentaria* |
| DCH | D. J. A. Clines (ed.), *The Dictionary of Classical Hebrew* | FOTL | The Forms of the Old Testament Literature |
| | | FrGrHist | F. Jacoby (ed.), *Die Fragmente der griechischen Historiker* |
| DDD | K. van der Toorn, B. Becking, and P. W. van der Horst (eds.), *Dictionary of Deities and Demons in the Bible* | | |
| | | FRLANT | Forschungen zur Religion und Literatur des Alten und Neuen Testaments |
| | | FuF | *Forschungen und Fortschritte* |
| DJD | Discoveries in the Judaean Desert | FVS | H. Diels and W. Kranz, *Die Fragmente der Vorsokratiker*, 3 vols. |
| DJPA | M. Sokoloff, *A Dictionary of Jewish Palestinian Aramaic of the Byzantine Period* | | |
| | | GCS | Griechischen christlichen Schriftsteller |
| DSD | *Dead Sea Discoveries* | | |
| DTT | *Dansk teologisk tidsskrift* | GELS | J. Lust, E. Eynikel, and K. Hauspie, *A Greek-English Lexicon of the Septuagint* |
| EDNT | H. Balz and G. Schneider (eds.), *Exegetical Dictionary of the New Testament*, 3 vols. | | |
| | | GGR | M. P. Nilsson, *Geschichte der griechischen Religion*, vol. 1, 3rd ed. (1967); vol. 2, 2nd ed. (1961) |
| EEC | Angelo Di Berardino (ed.), *Encyclopedia of the Early Church*, 2 vols. | | |
| | | GHÅ | *Göteborgs Högskolas Årsskrift* |
| EncJud | *Encyclopedia Judaica*, 16 vols. | GKC | *Gesenius' Hebrew Grammar*, ed. E. Kautzsch, tr. A. E. Cowley |
| EncRel | M. Eliade (ed.), *The Encyclopedia of Religion* | | |
| | | GNS | Good News Studies |
| EPRO | Études préliminaires aux religions orientales dans l'empire romain | GRBS | *Greek, Roman, and Byzantine Studies* |
| ERE | J. Hastings (ed.), *Encyclopedia of Religion and Ethics* | GTJ | *Grace Theological Journal* |
| ErFor | Erträge der Forschung | HAT | Handbuch zum Alten Testament |
| ESAR | T. Frank (ed.), *An Economic Survey of Ancient Rome*, 5 vols. | | |
| | | HCNT | M. E. Boring, K. Berger, and C. Colpe, *Hellenistic Commentary to the NT* |
| ETL | *Ephemerides theologicae lovanienses* | | |

| | | | |
|---|---|---|---|
| HDA | H. Bächtold-Stäubli with E. Hoffmann-Krayer (eds.), *Handwörterbuch des deutschen Aberglaubens* | JAOS | *Journal of the American Oriental Society* |
| | | JBL | *Journal of Biblical Literature* |
| | | JE | *Jewish Encyclopedia* |
| HDR | Harvard Dissertations in Religion | JETS | *Journal of the Evangelical Theological Society* |
| HeyJ | *Heythrop Journal* | JHS | *Journal of Hellenic Studies* |
| HibJ | *Hibbert Journal* | JIGRE | W. Horbury and D. Noy (eds.), *Jewish Inscriptions of Graeco-Roman Egypt* |
| HNT | Handbuch zum Neuen Testament | | |
| HSCP | *Harvard Studies in Classical Philology* | JJS | *Journal of Jewish Studies* |
| | | JMS | *Journal of Mithraic Studies* |
| HSM | Harvard Semitic Monographs | JNES | *Journal of Near Eastern Studies* |
| | | JP | *Journal of Philology* |
| HSS | Harvard Semitic Studies | JQR | *Jewish Quarterly Review* |
| HTR | *Harvard Theological Review* | JR | *Journal of Religion* |
| HTS | Harvard Theological Studies | JRS | *Journal of Roman Studies* |
| HUCA | *Hebrew Union College Annual* | JSJ | *Journal for the Study of Judaism in the Persian, Hellenistic and Roman Period* |
| IBM | *Ancient Greek Inscriptions in the British Museum*, 4 vols. | JSNT | *Journal for the Study of the New Testament* |
| IDB | G. A. Buttrick (ed.), *Interpreter's Dictionary of the Bible,* 4 vols. | JSNTSup | Journal for the Study of the New Testament— Supplement Series |
| IDBSup | Supplementary Volume to IDB | JSOT | *Journal for the Study of the Old Testament* |
| IEJ | *Israel Exploration Journal* | | |
| I. Eph. | H. Wankel (ed.), *Die Inschriften von Ephesos,* IGSK, 8 vols. | JSOTSup | Journal for the Study of the Old Testament— Supplement Series |
| IGRom | R. Cagnat et al., *Inscriptiones Graecae ad res Romanas pertinentes,* 4 vols. | JSP | *Journal for the Study of the Pseudepigrapha* |
| | | JSPSup | Supplement to *JSP* |
| IGSK | Inschriften griechischer Städte aus Kleinasien | JSS | *Journal of Semitic Studies* |
| | | JTC | *Journal for Theology and the Church* |
| IM | *Istanbuler Mitteilungen* | | |
| Int | *Interpretation* | JTS | *Journal of Theological Studies* |
| ISBE | G. W. Bromiley (ed.), *International Standard Bible Encyclopedia*, rev., 4 vols. | KAT | Kommentar zum Alten Testament |
| ITQ | *Irish Theological Quarterly* | KAV | Kommentar zu den Apostolischen Vätern |
| JAAR | *Journal of the American Academy of Religion* | KB³ | L. Koehler and W. Baumgartner, *Hebräisches und Aramäisches Lexikon zum Alten Testament,* 3rd ed., 4 vols. |
| JAC | Jahrbuch für Antike und Christentum | | |
| JAF | *Journal of American Folklore* | | |
| | | KD | *Kerygma und Dogma* |

| | | | |
|---|---|---|---|
| *Kleine Pauly* | K. Ziegler and W. Sontheimer, *Der Kleine Pauly: Lexikon der Antike*, 5 vols. | | *Excavations in the Holy Land*, 4 vols. |
| | | *NedTTs* | *Nederlands theologisch tijdschrift* |
| | | *Neot* | *Neotestamentica* |
| *LB* | *Linguistica Biblica* | Nestle-Aland[26] | E. Nestle, K. Aland, et al. (eds.), *Novum Testamentum Graece*, 26th ed. |
| LCL | Loeb Classical Library | | |
| *LexÄgypt* | W. Helck and E. Otto (eds.), *Lexikon der Ägyptologie* | | |
| *LIMC* | *Lexicon Iconographicum Mythologiae Classicae* | Nestle-Aland[27] | E. Nestle, K. Aland, et al. (eds.), *Novum Testamentum Graece*, 27th ed. |
| Louw-Nida | J. P. Louw and E. A. Nida, *Greek-English Lexicon of the New Testament Based on Semantic Domains*, 2 vols. | *Neuer Wettstein* | G. Strecker and U. Schnelle (eds.), *Neuer Wettstein: Texte zum Neuen Testament aus Griechentum und Hellenismus:* vol. 2/2. *Texte zur Briefliteratur und zur Johannes-apokalypse* |
| *LQHR* | *London Quarterly and Holburn Review* | | |
| *LR* | *Lutherische Rundschau* | | |
| LSJ | H. G. Liddell, R. Scott, H. S. Jones, and R. McKenzie, *A Greek-English Lexicon*, 9th ed. | *New Docs* | G. H. R. Horsley and S. R. Llewelyn (eds.), *New Documents Illustrating Early Christianity* |
| | | *NGM* | *National Geographic Magazine* |
| *MAMA* | W. M. Calder and J. M. R. Cormack (eds.), *Monumenta Asiae Minoris Antiqua* | NHS | Nag Hammadi Studies |
| | | NICNT | New International Commentary on the New Testament |
| *MDAIRA* | *Mitteilungen des deutschen archaeologischen Instituts, Römische Abteilung* | *NIDNTT* | C. Brown (ed.), *The New International Dictionary of New Testament Theology* |
| MeyerK | H. A. W. Meyer, Kritischexegetischer Kommentar über das Neue Testament | *NKZ* | *Neue kirchliche Zeitschrift* |
| | | *NorTT* | *Norsk Teologisk Tidsskrift* |
| | | *NovT* | *Novum Testamentum* |
| | | NovTSup | Novum Testamentum, Supplements |
| *MGWJ* | *Monatsschrift für Geschichte und Wissenschaft des Judentums* | *NRT* | *La nouvelle revue théologique* |
| | | *NTA* | E. Hennecke and W. Schneemelcher (eds.), *New Testament Apocrypha*, rev. ed. |
| *MIR* | I. G. Mazzini, *Monete Imperiale Romane*, 4 vols. | | |
| MM | J. H. Moulton and G. Milligan, *The Vocabulary of the Greek Testament* | NTAbh | Neutestamentliche Abhandlungen |
| | | NTOA | Novum Testamentum et Orbis Antiquus |
| *MQ* | *McCormick Quarterly* | | |
| *Mus* | *Le Muséon* | *NTS* | *New Testament Studies* |
| | | NumenSup | Supplements to *Numen* |
| NCB | New Century Bible | *NumZ* | *Numismatische Zeitschrift* |
| *NEAEHL* | E. Stern (ed.), *The New Encyclopedia of Archaeological* | OBO | Orbis biblicus et orientalis |

| | | | |
|---|---|---|---|
| OCD² | Oxford Classical Dictionary, 2nd ed. (1975) | RevThom | Revue thomiste |
| OGIS | W. Dittenberger, Orientis Graeci Inscriptiones Selectae, 2 vols. | RGRW | Religions in the Graeco-Roman World (formerly EPRO) |
| OLD | P. G. W. Glare (ed.), Oxford Latin Dictionary | RHPR | Revue d'histoire et de philosophie religieuses |
| OrChr | Oriens christianus | RHR | Revue de l'histoire des religions |
| ORPB | Oberrheinisches Pastoralblat | RIC | H. Mattingly, E. A. Sydenham, et al., Roman Imperial Coinage, 8 vols. |
| OTP | J. H. Charlesworth (ed.), The Old Testament Pseudepigrapha | RivB | Rivista biblica |
| OTS | Oudtestamentische Studiën | RMP | Rheinisches Museum für Philologie |
| OTS | Old Testament Studies | RQ | Römische Quartalschrift für christliche Altertumskunde und Kirchengeschichte |
| PAAJR | Proceedings of the American Academy of Jewish Research | RSR | Recherches de science religieuse |
| PDM | H. D. Betz (ed.), The Greek Magical Papyri in Translation, including the Demotic Spells | RVV | Religionsgeschichtliche Versuche und Vorarbeiten |
| PG | J.-P. Migne, Patrologia graeca | SBFLA | Studii Biblici Franciscani Liber Annuus |
| PGL | G. H. W. Lampe (ed.), A Patristic Greek Lexicon | SBL | Society of Biblical Literature |
| PGM | K. Preisendanz (ed.), Papyri graecae magicae, 2nd ed., 2 vols. | SBLDS | SBL Dissertation Series |
| | | SBLMS | SBL Monograph Series |
| PL | J.-P. Migne, Patrologia latina | SBT | Studies in Biblical Theology |
| PW | Pauly-Wissowa, Real-Encyclopädie der classischen Altertumswissenschaft | SC | Sources chrétiennes |
| | | SCHNT | Studia ad corpus hellenisticum Novi Testamenti |
| PWSup | Supplement to PW | ScrT | Scripta Theologica |
| | | SEÅ | Svensk exegetisk årsbok |
| RAC | Reallexikon für Antike und Christentum | SE | Studia Evangelica 1, 2, 3 (= TU 73 [1959], 87 [1964], 88 [1964], 102 [1968], 103 [1968], 112 [1973]) |
| RÄRG | H. Bonnet (ed.), Reallexikon der ägyptischen Religionsgeschichte, 2nd ed. | | |
| | | SD | Studies and Documents |
| RB | Revue biblique | SEG | Supplementum Epigraphicum Graecum |
| RBén | Revue bénédictine | | |
| RCT | Revista Catalana de Teologia | SGU | Studia Graeca Upsaliensia |
| RE | Realencyklopädie für protestantische Theologie und Kirche | SIG | W. Dittenberger (ed.), Sylloge Inscriptionum Graecarum, 3rd ed., 4 vols. |
| REG | Revue des études grecques | SJLA | Studies in Judaism in Late Antiquity |
| ResQ | Restoration Quarterly | | |
| RevExp | Review and Expositor | SJT | Scottish Journal of Theology |
| RevistB | Revista bíblica | SKI | Studien zu Kirche und Israel |
| RevQ | Revue de Qumran | | |

| | | | |
|---|---|---|---|
| SNT | Studien zum Neuen Testament | *TGL* | H. Stephanus, *Thesaurus Graecae Linguae* |
| SNTSMS | Society for New Testament Studies Monograph Series | *THAT* | E. Jenni and C. Westermann (eds.), *Theologisches Handwörterbuch zum Alten Testament* |
| *SO* | *Symbolae osloenses* | | |
| *SPA* | *Studia Philonica Annual* | THKNT | Theologischer Handkommentar zum Neuen Testament |
| *SPap* | *Studia papyrologica* | | |
| SPB | Studia postbiblica | | |
| *SR* | *Studies in Religion/Sciences religieuses* | *TLNT* | C. Spicq, *Theological Lexicon of the New Testament*, tr. J. D. Ernst, 3 vols. |
| *ST* | *Studia theologica* | | |
| STDJ | Studies on the Texts of the Desert of Judah | *TLZ* | *Theologische Literaturzeitung* |
| Str-B | [H. Strack and] P. Billerbeck, *Kommentar zum Neuen Testament aus Talmud und Midrash* | *TPQ* | *Theologisch-praktische Quartalschrift* |
| | | *TQ* | *Theologische Quartalschrift* |
| | | *TRE* | *Theologische Realenzyklopädie* |
| | | *TRu* | *Theologische Rundschau* |
| *StudP* | *Studia Patristica* | *TS* | *Theological Studies* |
| SUNT | Studien zur Umwelt des Neuen Testaments | *TSK* | *Theologische Studien und Kritiken* |
| *SVF* | J. von Arnim, *Stoicorum Veterum Fragmenta*, 4 vols. | *TT* | *Theologisk Tijdskrift* |
| | | *TThQ* | *Tübinger theologische Quartalschrift* |
| SVTG | Septuaginta: Vetus Testamentum Graecum | *TTZ* | *Trierer theologische Zeitschrift* |
| | | TU | Texte und Untersuchungen |
| *TAPA* | *Transactions of the American Philological Association* | *TWAT* | G. J. Botterweck, H. Ringgren, and H.-J. Fabry (eds.), *Theologisches Wörterbuch zum Alten Testament* |
| *TBA* | *Tübinger Beiträge zur Altertumswissenshaft* | | |
| *TBei* | *Theologische Beiträge* | | |
| *TBl* | *Theologische Blätter* | *TWNT* | G. Kittel and G. Friedrich (eds.), *Theologisches Wörterbuch zum Neuen Testament* |
| *TCGNT*[1] | B. M. Metzger, *A Textual Commentary on the Greek New Testament* | | |
| *TCGNT*[2] | B. M. Metzger, *A Textual Commentary on the Greek New Testament*, 2nd ed. | *TynBul* | *Tyndale Bulletin* |
| | | *TZ* | *Theologische Zeitschrift* |
| *TDNT* | G. Kittel and G. Friedrich (eds.), *Theological Dictionary of the New Testament*, 10 vols. | UBSGNT[3] | K. Aland et al. (eds.), United Bible Societies *Greek New Testament*, 3rd ed. |
| *TDOT* | G. J. Botterweck and H. Ringgren (eds.), *Theological Dictionary of the Old Testament* | UBSGNT[4] | K. Aland et al. (eds.), United Bible Societies *Greek New Testament*, 4th ed. |
| | | *VC* | *Vigiliae Christianae* |
| TextsS | Texts and Studies | *VCaro* | *Verbum caro* |
| *TGl* | *Theologie und Glaube* | *VD* | *Verbum domini* |

| | | | |
|---|---|---|---|
| *VoxEv* | *Vox Evangelica* | *ZAW* | *Zeitschrift für die alttestamentliche Wissenschaft* |
| *VT* | *Vetus Testamentum* | | |
| VTG | Vetus Testamentum Graecum | *ZNW* | *Zeitschrift für die neutestamentliche Wissenschaft* |
| VTSup | Supplements to *Vetus Testamentum* | | |
| | | *ZPE* | *Zeitschrift für Papyrologie und Epigraphie* |
| WBC | Word Biblical Commentary | | |
| WHort | B. F. Westcott and F. J. A. Hort, *The New Testament in the Original Greek* | *ZRGG* | *Zeitschrift für Religions- und Geistesgeschichte* |
| | | *ZST* | *Zeitschrift für systematische Theologie* |
| WMANT | Wissenschaftliche Monographien zum Alten und Neuen Testament | *ZTK* | *Zeitschrift für Theologie und Kirche* |
| *WO* | *Die Welt des Orients* | *ZVS* | *Zeitschrift für vergleichende Sprachforschung* |
| *WTJ* | *Westminster Theological Journal* | | |
| WUNT | Wissenschaftliche Untersuchungen zum Neuen Testament | *ZWT* | *Zeitschrift für wissenschaftliche Theologie* |
| | | *ZZ* | *Zeichen der Zeit* |
| *ZASA* | *Zeitschrift für Ägyptische Sprache und Altertumskunde* | | |

## D. Abbreviations for Books of the Bible with Aprocrypha

### OLD TESTAMENT

| | | | |
|---|---|---|---|
| Gen | 1–2 Kgs | Cant | Obad |
| Exod | 1–2 Chr | Isa | Jonah |
| Lev | Ezra | Jer | Mic |
| Num | Neh | Lam | Nah |
| Deut | Esth | Ezek | Hab |
| Josh | Job | Dan | Zeph |
| Judg | Ps(s) | Hos | Hag |
| Ruth | Prov | Joel | Zech |
| 1–2 Sam | Eccl | Amos | Mal |

### NEW TESTAMENT

| | | | |
|---|---|---|---|
| Mark | 1–2 Cor | 1–2 Thess | Jas |
| Luke | Gal | 1–2 Tim | 1–2 Pet |
| John | Eph | Titus | 1–2–3 John |
| Acts | Phil | Philem | Jude |
| Rom | Col | Heb | Rev |

## APOCRYPHA

| 1 Kgdms | 1 Kingdoms | | (Wisdom of Jesus the |
|---------|-----------|---|---|
| 2 Kgdms | 2 Kingdoms | | son of Sirach) |
| 3 Kgdms | 3 Kingdoms | Bar | Baruch |
| 4 Kgdms | 4 Kingdoms | Ep Jer | Epistle of Jeremiah |
| 1–2 Esdr | 1–2 Esdras | S Th Ch | Song of the Three |
| Tob | Tobit | | Children (or Young Men) |
| Jdt | Judith | Sus | Susanna |
| Add Esth | Additions to | Bel | Bel and the Dragon |
| | Esther | Pr Azar | Prayer of Azariah |
| 4 Ezra | 4 Ezra | 1 Macc | 1 Maccabees |
| Wis | Wisdom of | 2 Macc | 2 Maccabees |
| | Solomon | 3 Macc | 3 Maccabees |
| Sir | Ecclesiasticus | 4 Macc | 4 Maccabees |

## E. Abbreviations of Pseudepigrapha and Early Jewish Literature

| *Adam and Eve* | *Books of Adam and Eve* or | *Jos. As.* | *Joseph and Aseneth* |
|---|---|---|---|
| | *Vita Adae et Evae* | *Jub.* | *Jubilees* |
| *Apoc. Abr.* | *Apocalypse of Abraham* | *Mart. Isa.* | *Martyrdom of Isaiah* |
| *2–3 Apoc. Bar.* | Syriac, Greek *Apocalypse* | *Par. Jer.* | *Paraleipomena Jeremiou* or |
| | *of Baruch* | | *4 Baruch* |
| *Apoc. Sedr.* | *Apocalypse of Sedrach* | *Pr. Man.* | *Prayer of Manassis* |
| *Apoc. Zeph.* | *Apocalypse of Zephaniah* | *Pss. Sol.* | *Psalms of Solomon* |
| *Bib. Ant.* | Ps.-Philo, *Biblical* | *Sib. Or.* | *Sibylline Oracles* |
| | *Antiquities* | *T. Job* | *Testament of Job* |
| *1–2–3 Enoch* | Ethiopic, Slavonic, | *T. Mos.* | *Testament of Moses* |
| | Hebrew *Enoch* | | *(Assumption of Moses)* |
| *Ep. Arist.* | *Epistle of Aristeas* | *T. 12 Patr.* | *Testaments of the Twelve* |
| Jos. *Ag. Ap.* | Josephus *Against Apion* | | *Patriarchs* |
| *Ant.* | *The Jewish Antiquities* | *T. Levi* | *Testament of Levi* |
| *J. W.* | *The Jewish War* | *T. Benj.* | *Testament of Benjamin* |
| *Life* | *The Life* | *T. Reub.* | *Testament of Reuben*, etc. |

## F. Abbreviations of Dead Sea Scrolls

| CD | Cairo (Genizah text of the) | Mur | Wadi Murabba'at texts |
|---|---|---|---|
| | *Damascus* (*Document*) | p | pesher (commentary) |
| Hev | Nahal Hever texts | Q | Qumran |
| 8 Hev XIIgr | Greek Scroll of the Minor | 1Q, 2Q, 3Q, etc. | Numbered caves of |
| | Prophets from Nahal | | Qumran |
| | Hever | QL | Qumran literature |
| Mas | Masada texts | 1QapGen | *Genesis Apocryphon* of |
| MasShirShabb | *Songs of Sabbath Sacrifice*, or | | Qumran Cave 1 |
| | *Angelic Liturgy* from | 1QH | *Hôdāyôt* (*Thanksgiving* |
| | Masada | | *Hymns*) from Qumran |
| Mird | Khirbet Mird texts | | Cave 1 |

| | |
|---|---|
| 1QpHab | *Pesher on Habakkuk* from Qumran Cave 1 |
| 1QM | *Milḥāmāh* (*War Scroll*) |
| 1QS | *Serek hayyaḥad* (*Rule of the Community, Manual of Discipline*) |
| 1QSa | Appendix A (*Rule of the Congregation*) to 1QS |
| 1QSb | Appendix B (*Blessings*) to 1QS |
| 3Q15 | *Copper Scroll* from Qumran Cave 3 |
| 4QFlor | *Florilegium* (or *Eschatological Midrashim*) from Qumran Cave 4 |
| 4QMess ar | Aramaic "Messianic" text from Qumran Cave 4 |
| 4QMMT | *Miqsat Maʿaseh Torah* from Qumran Cave 4 |
| 4QPhyl | Phylacteries from Qumran Cave 4 |
| 4QPrNab | *Prayer of Nabonidus* from Qumran Cave 4 |
| 4QPssJosh | *Psalms of Joshua* from Qumran Cave 4 |
| 4QShirShabb | *Songs of Sabbath Sacrifice*, or *Angelic Liturgy* from Qumran Cave 4 |
| 4QTestim | *Testimonia* text from Qumran Cave 4 |
| 4QTLevi | *Testament of Levi* from Qumran Cave 4 |
| 11QMelch | *Melchizedek* text from Qumran Cave 11 |
| 11QShirShabb | *Songs of Sabbath Sacrifice*, or *Angelic Liturgy* from Qumran Cave 11 |
| 11QTemple | *Temple Scroll* from Qumran Cave 11 |
| 11QpaleoLev | Copy of Leviticus in paleo-Hebrew script from Qumran Cave 11 |
| 11QtgJob | *Targum of Job* from Qumran Cave 11 |

## G. Philo

| | |
|---|---|
| *Abr.* | *De Abrahamo* |
| *Aet.* | *De aeternitate mundi* |
| *Agr.* | *De agricultura* |
| *Cher.* | *De cherubim* |
| *Conf.* | *De confusione linguarum* |
| *Congr.* | *De congressu eruditionis gratia* |
| *Decal.* | *De decalogo* |
| *Det.* | *Quod deterius potiori insidiari solet* |
| *Ebr.* | *De ebrietate* |
| *Flacc.* | *In Flaccum* |
| *Fug.* | *De fuga et inventione* |
| *Gig.* | *De gigantibus* |
| *Hyp.* | *Hypothetica/Apologia pro Iudaeis* |
| *Jos.* | *De Josepho* |
| *Leg.* | *De legatione ad Gaium* |
| *Leg. All.* | *Legum allegoriarum* |
| *Mig.* | *De migratione Abrahami* |
| *Mos.* | *De vita Mosis* |
| *Mut.* | *De mutatione nominum* |
| *Op.* | *De opificio mundi* |
| *Plant.* | *De plantatione* |
| *Post.* | *De posteritate Caini* |
| *Praem.* | *De praemiis et poenis* |
| *Prov.* | *De providentia* |
| *Quaest. in Gn.* | *Questiones et solutiones in Genesin* |
| *Quaest. in Ex.* | *Questiones et solutiones in Exodum* |
| *Quis Her.* | *Quis rerum divinarum heres sit* |
| *Quod Deus* | *Quod Deus sit immutabilis* |
| *Quod Omn. Prob.* | *Quod omnis Probus Liber sit* |
| *Sac.* | *De Sacrificiis Abelis et Caini* |
| *Sob.* | *De sobrietate* |
| *Som.* | *De somniis* |
| *Spec. Leg.* | *De specialibus legibus* |
| *Virt.* | *De virtute* |
| *Vit. Cont.* | *De vita contemplativa* |

## H. Abbreviations of Early Christian Literature

| | | | |
|---|---|---|---|
| Acts Pil. | Acts of Pilate | Justin Apol. | Justin 1 Apology |
| Acts Scill. | Acts of the Scillitan Martyrs | 2 Apol. | 2 Apology |
| Apoc. Pet. | Apocalypse of Peter | Dial. | Dialogue with Trypho |
| Apost. Const. | Apostolic Constitutions | Mart. Agape | The Martyrdom of Agape, |
| Asc. Isa. | Ascension of Isaiah | | Irene, Chione, Companions |
| Barn. | Barnabas | Mart. Apollo- | The Martyrdom |
| 1–2 Clem. | 1–2 Clement | nius | of Apollonius |
| Corp. Herm. | Corpus Hermeticum | Mart. Carpus | Martyrdom of Saints |
| Did. | Didache | | Carpus, Papylus, and |
| Diogn. | Diognetus | | Agathonice |
| Ep. Lugd. | Epistula ecclesiarum apud | Mart. Dasius | The Martyrdom of Dasius |
| | Lugdunum et Viennam = | Mart. Fruct. | The Martyrdom of Bishop |
| | Letter of the Churches of Lyons | | Fructuosus and his |
| Eusebius | Eusebius Historia | | Deacons, Augurius and |
| Hist. ecc. | Ecclesiastica | | Eulogius |
| Praep. | Praeparatio evangelica | Mart. Julius | The Martyrdom of Julius the |
| Gos. Eb. | Gospel of the Ebionites | | Veteran |
| Gos. Heb. | Gospel of the Hebrews | Mart. Justin | The Martyrdom of Saints |
| Gos. Naass. | Gospel of the Naassenes | | Justin, Chariton, Charito, |
| Gos. Pet. | Gospel of Peter | | Evelpistus, Hierax, |
| Herm. Mand. | Hermas Mandate(s) | | Paeon, Liberian, and |
| Sim. | Similitude(s) | | Their Community |
| Vis. | Vision(s) | Mart. Mont. | Martyrdom of Saints |
| Ign. Eph. | Ignatius Letter to the | | Montanus and Lucius |
| | Ephesians | Mart. | The Martyrdom of Perpetua |
| Magn. | Letter to the Magnesians | Perpetua | and Felicitas |
| Phld. | Letter to the Philadelphians | Mart. Pionius | The Martyrdom of Pionius |
| Pol. | Letter to Polycarp | Mart. Pol. | The Martyrdom of Polycarp |
| Rom. | Letter to the Romans | Odes Sol. | Odes of Solomon |
| Smyrn. | Letter to the Smyrnaeans | Pol. Phil. | Polycarp, Letter to the |
| Trall. | Letter to the Trallians | | Philippians |
| Iren. Adv. | Irenaeus Against | Prot. Jas. | Protevangelium of James |
| Haer. | All Heresies | Tert. De | Tertullian, On the |
| Jos. Ag. Ap. | Josephus Against Apion | Praesc, Haer. | Proscribing of Heretics |
| Ant. | The Jewish Antiquities | Test. Forty | The Testament of the Forty |
| J.W. | The Jewish War | Martyrs | Martyrs of Sebaste |
| Life | The Life | | |

## I. Abbreviations of Targumic Material

| | | | |
|---|---|---|---|
| Tg. Onq. | Targum Onqelos | Tg. Neof. | Targum Neofiti I |
| Tg. Neb. | Targum of the Prophets | Tg. Ps.-J. | Targum Pseudo-Jonathan |
| Tg. Ket. | Targum of the Writings | Tg. Esth. I, II | First or Second Targum of Esther |
| Tg. Isa. | Targum of Isaiah | Tg. Ezek. | Targum of Ezekiel |

## J. Abbreviations of Nag Hammadi Tractates

| | | | |
|---|---|---|---|
| *Acts Pet. 12 Apost.* | Acts of Peter and the Twelve Apostles | *Marsanes* | *Marsanes* |
| | | *Melch.* | *Melchizedek* |
| *Allogenes* | *Allogenes* | *Norea* | *Thought of Norea* |
| *Ap. Jas.* | *Apocryphon of James* | *On Bap. A–B–C* | *On Baptism A–B–C* |
| *Ap. John* | *Apocryphon of John* | | |
| *Apoc. Adam* | *Apocalypse of Adam* | *On Euch A–B* | *On Eucharist A–B* |
| *1–2 Apoc. Jas.* | *1–2 Apocalypse of James* | | |
| *Apoc. Paul* | *Apocalypse of Paul* | *Orig. World* | *On the Origin of the World* |
| *Apoc. Pet.* | *Apocalypse of Peter* | *Paraph. Shem* | *Paraphrase of Shem* |
| *Asclepius* | *Asclepius 21–29* | *Pr. Paul* | *Prayer of the Apostle Paul* |
| *Auth. Teach.* | *Authoritative Teaching* | *Pr. Thanks.* | *Prayer of Thanksgiving* |
| *Dial. Sav.* | *Dialogues of the Savior* | *Sent. Sextus* | *Sentences of Sextus* |
| *Disc. 8–9* | *Discourse on the Eight and Ninth* | *Soph. Jes. Chr.* | *Sophia of Jesus Christ* |
| | | *Steles Seth* | *Three Steles of Seth* |
| *Ep. Pet. Phil.* | *Letter of Peter to Philip* | *Teach. Silv.* | *Teachings of Silvanus* |
| *Eugnostos* | *Eugnostos the Blessed* | *Testim. Truth* | *Testimony of Truth* |
| *Exeg. Soul* | *Exegesis on the Soul* | *Thom. Cont.* | *Book of Thomas the Contender* |
| *Gos. Eg.* | *Gospel of the Egyptians* | | |
| *Gos. Phil.* | *Gospel of Philip* | *Thund.* | *Thunder, Perfect Mind* |
| *Gos. Thom.* | *Gospel of Thomas* | *Treat. Res.* | *Treatise on Resurrection* |
| *Gos. Truth* | *Gospel of Truth* | *Treat. Seth* | *Second Treatise of the Great Seth* |
| *Great Pow.* | *Concept of Our Great Power* | | |
| *Hyp. Arch.* | *Hypostasis of the Archons* | *Tri. Trac.* | *Tripartite Tractate* |
| *Hypsiph.* | *Hypsiphrone* | *Trim. Prot.* | *Trimorphic Protennoia* |
| *Interp. Know.* | *Interpretation of Knowledge* | *Val. Exp.* | *A Valentinian Exposition* |
| | | *Zost.* | *Zostrianos* |

## K. Manuscripts of Revelation

**Andr or Andreas**  Andreas, or Andrew, a bishop of Caesarea in Cappadocia, wrote a commentary on Revelation, ca. A.D. 600 (J. Schmid, ed., *Studien*, part 1: *Der Apokalypse-Kommentar des Andreas von Kaisareia*). "Andreas" means that the reading is in the text of Schmid. "Andr," when followed by a letter, e.g., "a," refers to a group of Andreas MSS (listed in the *Introduction*, Section 6: Text); when a letter is followed by a superscript number, e.g., Andreas $f^{051}$, only that MS in the group has the reading; when a letter is followed by a super script prefixed with a minus sign, e.g., $f^{-2023}$, only that MS in the group lacks the reading.

**Apringius**  Apringius of Beja, a Spanish biblical interpreter (mid-sixth century A.D.) who wrote a commentary on Revelation; portions on Rev 1:5–7; 18:7–22:20 survive.

**Arethas**  Arethas (ca. 850–944), a native of the Peloponnesus who became the bishop of Caesarea in 902, wrote a commentary on Revelation that was a revision of the commentary of Andreas of Caesarea.

arm
Armenian version of the NT; F. C. Conybeare, *Armenian Version*. arm[1] = Bodleian Codex (Conybeare, 115–134, appendix 1–189); arm[2] = British Museum Codex (Conybeare, 135–37); arm[3] = Bibliotheque Nationale (Conybeare, 135–37)); arm[4] = Armenian Convent Codex (Conybeare, 95–114).

Beatus
Beatus of Liebana, d. 798, was a Spanish abbot who compiled a commentary on Revelation, chiefly from the now lost commentary of Tyconius. The Tyconian text of Beatus is printed in Vogels, *Untersuchungen*, 194–208. For the modern critical edition of Beatus, *Commentarius in Apocalypsin*, see Romero-Pose, *Sancti Beati*.

bo
Bohairic version of Coptic NT.

Byz
Byzantine family of MSS. When followed by an arabic numeral and superscript arabic numbers, e.g., Byz 1[920 1859], this refers to family 1 of the Byzantine recension (as described by Schmid, *Studien*), and specifically to MSS 920 and 1859 within that family.

Byzantine
When most MSS in the Byzantine, or Koine, recension support a reading, the designation is spelled out in full.

Compl.
Complutensian group of MSS.

cop
Coptic version of the NT; used when the Sahidic (sa) and Bohairic (bo) agree.

eth
Variants discussed by J. Hofmann, *Die äthiopische Johannes-Apokalypse*.

eth[comm]
Commentaries on the Ethiopic version of Revelation published by R. W. Cowley, *Ethiopian Orthodox*.

Fulgentius
Bishop of Ruspe in North Africa (A.D. 468–533); Latin text of Revelation in Vogels, *Untersuchungen*, 217–19.

Irenaeus[Lat]
Irenaeus, bishop of Lyons, died ca. A.D. 200; evidence for his use of the Old Latin version is collected in Sanday-Turner, *Nouum Testamentum*.

Oecumenius
Greek bishop of Tricca (early seventh century) and author of a commentary on Revelation; see in H. C. Hoskier, ed., *Oecumenius*. As used in the *Notes*, Oecumenius refers to the reading in Hoskier's text, while the citation of a particular MS with a superlinear number, e.g., Oecumenius[2053], refers to a specific MS.

Prom
*De promissionibus et praedictionibus dei*, anonymous composition with Latin quotations from Revelation (in Vogels, *Untersuchungen*, 215–17).

sa
Sahidic version of the NT.

syr            Syriac version of the NT.

TR             The so-called *Textus Receptus*, "Received Text," of the NT, consisting of
               Erasmus' edition of the Greek NT of 1516 based largely on minuscule
               codex 1 (twelfth–thirteenth century) of the NT.

Tyc            Tyconius, died ca. A.D. 400, was a Donatist who wrote a commentary
               on Revelation, which exists only in fragments and excerpts. Tyc[1] = Turin
               fragments of Tyconius (first edited by the Benedictines of Monte Cassino in
               the third volume of the *Spicilegium Casinense* [reproduced in Vogels,
               *Untersuchungen,* 179–82] but more recently edited by F. Lo Bue, *Tyconius*),
               containing only Rev 2:18–4:1; 7:16–12:6; Tyc[2] = Tyconius text of the Ps.-
               Augustine Homily (Vogels, *Untersuchungen,* 182–90); Tyc[3] = Tyconius text of
               the *Summa Dicendorum* of Beatus (Vogels, *Untersuchungen,* 190–93).

Victorinus     Victorinus of Petovium (died ca. 304 B.C.) wrote the first commentary on
               Revelation; see in J. Haussleiter, ed., *Victorinus.*

vg             Vulgate: *Biblia sacra iuxta Vulgatam versionem,* ed. R. Weber.


**Note:** Some textual notes and numbers are drawn from the apparatus criticus of *Novum Testamentum Graece,* ed. E. Nestle, K. Aland, et al., 26th ed. (Stuttgart: Deutsche Bibelgesellschaft, 1979); from *Novum Testamentum Graece,* ed. E. Nestle, K. Aland, et al., 27th ed. (Stuttgart: Deutsche Bibelgesellschaft, 1994), designated Nestle-Aland[26] and Nestle-Aland[27]; and from *The Greek New Testament,* ed. K. Aland, M. Black, C. Martini, B. M. Metzger, and A. Wikgren. 4th ed. (New York: United Bible Societies, 1994), designated UBSGNT[4]. These three identical editions of the Greek New Testament are the bases for the *Translation* sections.

# Commentary Bibliography

Alford, H. "Apocalypse of John." In *The Greek Testament*. Chicago: Moody, 1958. 4:544–750. **Allo, E. B.** *L'Apocalypse du Saint Jean*. Paris: Gabalda, 1933. **Beasley-Murray, G. R.** *Revelation*. Rev. ed. NCB. London: Marshall, Morgan & Scott, 1978. **Beckwith, I. T.** *The Apocalypse of John*. New York: Macmillan, 1919. **Behm, J.** *Die Offenbarung des Johannes*. Göttingen: Vandenhoeck & Ruprecht, 1935. **Böcher, O.** *Die Johannesapokalypse*. 2nd ed. ErFor 41. Darmstadt: Wissenschaftliche Buchgesellschaft, 1980. **Boring, M. E.** *Revelation*. Interpretation. Louisville: John Knox, 1989. **Bousset, W.** *Die Offenbarung Johannis*. 6th ed. Kritisch-exegetischer Kommentar zum Neuen Testament 16. Göttingen: Vandenhoeck & Ruprecht, 1906. ———. *Die Offenbarung Johannis*. 5th ed. Kritisch-exegetischer Kommentar zum Neuen Testament 16. Göttingen: Vandenhoeck & Ruprecht, 1896. **Caird, G. B.** *A Commentary on the Revelation of St. John the Divine*. Harper's/Black's New Testament Commentaries. New York: Harper & Row, 1966. **Charles, R. H.** *A Critical and Exegetical Commentary on the Revelation of St. John*. 2 vols. Edinburgh: T. & T. Clark, 1920. **Delebecque, É.** *L'Apocalypse de Jean*. Paris: Mame, 1992. **Eichhorn, J. G.** *Commentarius in Apocalypsin Joannis*. 2 vols. Göttingen: Dieterich, 1791. **Ford, J. M.** *Revelation: Introduction, Translation and Commentary*. AB 38. Garden City, NY: Doubleday, 1965. **Giblin, C. H.** *The Book of Revelation: The Open Book of Prophecy*. GNS 34. Collegeville, MN: Liturgical, 1991. **Giesen, H.** *Johannes-Apokalypse*. 2nd ed. Stuttgarter kleiner Kommentar NT 18. Stuttgart: Katholisches Bibelwerk, 1989. **Glasson, T. F.** *The Revelation of John*. CBC. Cambridge: Cambridge UP, 1965. **Hadorn, D. W.** *Die Offenbarung des Johannes*. THKNT 18. Leipzig: Deichert, 1928. **Harrington, W. J.** *Revelation*. Sacra Pagina 16. Collegeville: Liturgical, 1993. **Hendricksen, W.** *More Than Conquerors*. Grand Rapids, MI: Baker, 1944. **Hengstenberg, E. W.** *The Revelation of St. John*. Edinburgh: T. & T. Clark, 1851. **Hort, F. J. A.** *The Apocalypse of St John I–III*. London: Macmillan, 1908. **Kiddle, M.,** and **Ross, M. K.** *The Revelation of St. John*. London: Hodder & Stoughton, 1946. **Kraft, H.** *Die Offenbarung des Johannes*. HNT 16a. Tübingen: Mohr-Siebeck, 1974. **Krodel, G. A.** *Revelation*. Augsburg Commentary on the New Testament. Minneapolis: Augsburg, 1989. **Ladd, G. E.** *A Commentary on the Revelation of John*. Grand Rapids, MI: Eerdmans, 1972. **Lange, J. P.** *Die Offenbarung des Johannes*. 2nd ed. Bielefield/Leipzig:Velhagen und Klasing, 1878. **Lohmeyer, E.** *Die Offenbarung des Johannes*. 3rd ed. HNT 16. Tübingen: Mohr-Siebeck, 1970. **Lohse, E.** *Die Offenbarung des Johannes*. Göttingen: Vandenhoeck & Ruprecht, 1976. **Loisy, A.** *L'Apocalypse de Jean*. Paris: Nourry, 1923. **Moffatt, J.** "The Revelation of St. John the Divine." In *The Expositor's Greek Testament*, ed. W. R. Nicoll. London: Hodder & Stoughton, 1910. 5:297–494. **Mounce, R. H.** *The Book of Revelation*. NICNT. Grand Rapids, MI: Eerdmans, 1977. **Müller, U. B.** *Die Offenbarung des Johannes*. Gütersloh: Mohn, 1984. **Prigent, P.** *L'Apocalypse de Saint Jean*. 2nd ed. Geneva: Labor et Fides, 1988. **Rissi, M.** "The Revelation of St. John the Divine: Introduction and Exegesis." In *The Interpreter's Bible*, ed. G. A. Buttrick et al. New York; Nashville: Abingdon, 1957. 12:345–613. **Roloff, J.** *Die Offenbarung des Johannes*. Zürcher Bibelkommentare NT 18. Zürich: Theologischer, 1984. ———. *The Revelation of John*. Tr. J. E. Alsup. Continental Commentaries. Minneapolis: Fortress, 1993 (hereafter Roloff, ET). **Romero-Pose, E.** *Sancti Beati a Liebana Commentarius in Apocalypsin*. 2 vols. Rome: Typis Officinae Polygraphicae, 1985. **Rowland, C.** *Revelation*. Epworth Commentaries. London: Epworth, 1993. **Spitta, F.** *Die Offenbarung des Johannes*. Halle: Waisenhaus, 1889. **Stuart, M.** *Commentary on the Apocalypse*. 2 vols. Andover: Allen, Morrill and Wardwell, 1845. **Sweet, J. P. M.** *Revelation*. Philadelphia: Westminster, 1979. **Swete, H. B.** *The Apocalypse of John*. 3rd ed. London: Macmillan, 1908. **Talbert, C. H.** *The Apocalypse: A Reading of the Revelation of John*. Louisville: Westminster John Knox, 1994. **Völter, D.** *Die Offenbarung Johannis neu untersucht und erläutert.* 2nd ed. Strassburg: Heitz & Mundel, 1911. **Weiss, J.,** and **Heitmüller, W.** "Die Offenbarung des Johannes." In *Die Schriften des Neuen Testaments.* 3rd ed. Göttingen: Vandenhoeck & Ruprecht, 1920. 4:229–319. **Wikenhauser, A.** *Die Offenbarung Johannes.* 3rd. ed. Das Neue Testament 9. Regensburg: Pustet, 1959. **Zahn, T.** *Die Offenbarung des Johannes.* 1st to 3rd ed. 2 vols. Kommentar zum Neuen Testament 18. Leipzig; Erlangen: Deichert, 1924.

# General Bibliography

**Abbott, E. A.** *Johannine Grammar.* London: Adam & Charles Black, 1906. **Aberbach, M.,** and **Grossfeld, B.** *Targum Onkelos to Genesis.* New York: Ktav, 1982. **Abrahams, I.** *Studies in Pharisaism and the Gospels.* 1924. Repr. New York: Ktav, 1967. **Aejmelaeus, A.** *Parataxis in the Septuagint: A Study of the Renderings of the Hebrew Coordinate Clauses in the Greek Pentateuch.* Helsinki: Suomalainen Tiedeakatemia, 1982. **Albright, W. F.** *Archaeology and the Religion of Israel.* Baltimore: Johns Hopkins UP, 1956. ———. *Yahweh and the Gods of Canaan.* Garden City, NY: Doubleday, 1969. **Alföldi, A.** "Die Ausgestaltung des monarchischen Zeremoniells am römischen Kaiserhofe." *MDAIRA* 49 (1934) 1–118. ———. *Die monarchische Repräsentation im römischen Kaiserreiche.* Darmstadt: Wissenschaftliche Buchgesellschaft, 1970. **Allen, J. H.,** and **Greenough, J. B.** *A Latin Grammar: Founded on Comparative Grammar.* Rev. ed. Boston: Ginn and Heath, 1884. **Andersen, F. I.** *The Sentence in Biblical Hebrew.* The Hague: Mouton, 1974. ——— and **Freedman, D. N.** *Amos.* New York: Doubleday, 1989. **Attridge, H. W.** *The Epistle to the Hebrews.* Philadelphia: Fortress, 1989. ———. *First-Century Cynicism in the Epistles of Heraclitus.* HTS 29. Missoula, MT: Scholars, 1976. ———, ed. *Nag Hammadi Codex I (The Jung Codex).* NHS 22. Leiden: Brill, 1985. ———, ed. *Nag Hammadi Codex I (The Jung Codex) Notes.* NHS 23. Leiden: Brill, 1985. ——— and **Oden, R. A.** *Philo of Byblos: The Phoenician History.* CBQMS 9. Washington, DC: The Catholic Biblical Association, 1981. ——— and **Oden, R. A.** *The Syrian Goddess (De Dea Syria).* Missoula, MT: Scholars, 1976. **Audet, J.-P.** *La Didachè: Instructions des Apôtres.* Paris: Gabalda, 1958. **Aune, D. E.** "The Apocalypse of John and Graeco-Roman Revelatory Magic." *NTS* 33 (1987) 481–501. ———. "Charismatic Exegesis in Early Judaism and Early Christianity." In *The Pseudepigrapha and Early Biblical Interpretation,* ed. J. H. Charlesworth and C. A. Evans. Sheffield: JSOT, 1993. 126–50. ———. *The New Testament in Its Literary Environment.* Philadelphia: Westminster, 1987. ———. "The Odes of Solomon and Early Christian Prophecy." *NTS* 28 (1982) 435–60. ———. "Prolegomena to the Study of Oral Tradition in the Hellenistic World." In *Jesus and the Oral Gospel Tradition,* ed. H. Wansbrough. JSNTSup 64. Sheffield: Sheffield Academic, 1991. 59–106. ———. *Prophecy in Early Christianity and the Ancient Mediterranean World.* Grand Rapids, MI: Eerdmans, 1983. **Avigad, N.** *Beth She'arim: Report on the Excavations during 1953–1958.* Vol. 3. New Brunswick, NJ: Rutgers UP, 1976. **Bailey, C.** *Titi Lucreti Cari De Rerum Natura Libri Sex.* 3 vols. Oxford: Clarendon, 1947. **Baillet, M.** *Qumran Grotte 4.* Vol. 3. DJD 7. Oxford: Clarendon, 1982. **Bakker, W. F.** *The Greek Imperative: An Investigation into the Aspectual Differences between the Present and Aorist Imperatives in Greek Prayer from Homer up to the Present Day.* Amsterdam: Hakkert, 1966. **Balsdon, J. P. V. D.** *Romans and Aliens.* Chapel Hill: University of North Carolina, 1979. **Barr, J.** *The Semantics of Biblical Language.* Oxford: Oxford UP, 1961. **Barrett, C. K.** *The Gospel According to St. John.* 2nd ed. London: SPCK, 1978. **Barton, J.** *Oracles of God: Perceptions of Ancient Prophecy in Israel after the Exile.* New York: Oxford UP, 1988. **Bauckham, R. J.** *The Climax of Prophecy: Studies on the Book of Revelation.* Edinburgh: T. & T. Clark, 1993. ———. *Jude, 2 Peter.* WBC 50. Waco, TX: Word, 1983. ———. *The Theology of the Book of Revelation.* Cambridge: Cambridge UP, 1993. **Bauer, W.,** and **Paulsen, H.** *Die Briefe des Ignatius von Antiochia und des Polykarp von Smyrna.* 2nd ed. HNT 18. Tübingen: Mohr-Siebeck, 1985. **Baumgarten, A. I.** *The Phoenician History of Philo of Byblos: A Commentary.* Leiden: Brill, 1981. **Beale, G. K.** *The Use of Daniel in Jewish Apocalyptic Literature and in the Revelation of John.* Lanham: University Press of America, 1984. **Beck, R.** *Planetary Gods and Planetary Orders in the Mysteries of Mithras.* EPRO 109. Leiden: Brill, 1988. **Bell, A. A.** "The Date of John's Apocalypse." *NTS* 25 (1978) 98–99. **Benoit, P., Milik, J. T.,** and **Vaux, R. de.** *Les Grottes de Muraba'at.* DJD 2. Oxford: Clarendon, 1961. **Berger, A.** *Encyclopedic Dictionary of Roman Law.* Philadelphia: American Philosophical Society, 1953. **Berger, K.** *Die Amen-Worte Jesu: Eine Untersuchung zum Problem der Legitimation in apokalyptischer Rede.* BZNW 39. Berlin: de Gruyter, 1970. ———. *Formgeschichte des Neuen Testaments.* Heidelberg: Quelle & Meyer, 1984. **Bergman, J.** *Ich bin Isis: Studien zum memphitischen Hintergrund der griechischen Isisaretalogien.* Lund: Berlingska Boktryckeriet, 1968. **Bergmeier, R.** "'Jerusalem, du hochgebaute Stadt." *ZNW* 75 (1984) 86–106. **Berlin, A.** *Zephaniah.* AB 25A. New York: Doubleday, 1994. **Beskow, P.** *Rex Gloriae: The Kingship of Christ in the Early Church.* Stockholm: Almqvist & Wiksell, 1962. **Betz, H. D.** *Galatians: A Commentary on Paul's Letter to the Churches in Galatia.* Philadelphia: Fortress, 1979. ———. *Lukian von Samosata und das Neue Testament: Relgionsgeschichtliche und Paränetische Parallelen.* Berlin: Akademie, 1961. ———, ed. *The Greek Magical Papyri in Translation Including the Demotic Spells.* 2nd ed. Chicago: University of Chicago, 1992. ———, ed. *Plutarch's Ethical Writings and Early Christian Literature.* Leiden: Brill, 1978. ———, ed. *Plutarch's Theological Writings and Early Christian Literature.* Leiden: Brill, 1975. **Beyer, K.** *Die aramäischen Texte vom Toten Meer.* Göttingen: Vandenhoeck & Ruprecht, 1984. ———. *Die aramäischen Texte vom Toten Meer: Ergänzungsband.* Göttingen: Vandenhoeck & Ruprecht, 1994. ———. *Semitische Syntax im Neuen Testament.* Göttingen: Vandenhoeck & Ruprecht, 1962. **Beyerlin, J.** *Near Eastern Religious Texts Relating to the Old Testament.* Philadelphia: Westminster, 1978. **Bietenhard, H.** *Die himmlische Welt im Urchristentum und Spätjudentum.* Tübingen: Mohr-Siebeck, 1951. ———. *Der Tosefta-Traktat Sota: Hebräischer Text mit kritischem Apparat, Übersetzung, Kommentar.* Bern; Frankfurt am Main; New York: Lang, 1986. **Bihlmeyer, K.** *Die apostolischen Väter.* 2nd ed. Part 1. Tübingen: Mohr-Siebeck, 1956. ———. *Die apostolischen Väter: Neubearbeitung der funkschen Ausgabe.* 2nd ed. Ed. W. Schneemelcher. Tübingen: Mohr-Siebeck, 1956. **Birt, T.** *Das antike Buchwesen in seinem Verhältnis zur Literatur.* Berlin: W. Hertz, 1882. **Black, M.** *An Aramaic Approach to the Gospels and Acts.* 3rd ed. Oxford: Clarendon, 1967. ———. *The Book of Enoch or 1 Enoch: A New English Edition with Commentary and Textual Notes.* Leiden: Brill, 1985. ———. *The Scrolls and Christian Origins.* London: Thomas Nelson, 1961. ———, ed. *Apocalypsis Henochi Graeci.* Leiden: Brill, 1970. **Blomqvist, J.** *Das sogennante KAI adversitivum: Zur Semantik einer griechischen Partikel.* SGU 13. Stockholm, 1979. **Blümner, H.** *The Home Life of the Ancient Greeks.* Tr. A. Zimmern. New York: Cooper Square, 1966. **Böcher, O.** "Johanneisches in der Apokalypse des Johannes." *NTS* 27 (1981) 310–21. ———. *Kirche in Zeit und Endzeit: Aufsätze zur Offenbarung des Johannes.* Neukirchen: Neukirchener, 1983. **Bodenmann, R.** *Naissance d'une Exégèse: Daniel dans l'Église ancienne de trois premiers siècles.* BGBE 28. Tübingen: Mohr-Siebeck, 1986. **Böhlig, A., Wisse, F.,** and **Labib, P.** *Nag Hammadi Codices II,2 and IV,2: The Gospel of the Egyptians.* NHS 4. Leiden: Brill, 1975. **Boll, F.** *Aus der Offenbarung Johannis: Hellenistische Studien zum Weltbild der Apokalypse.* Leipzig; Berlin: Teubner, 1914. **Bömer, F.** *Untersuchungen über die Religion der Sklaven in Griechenland und Rom.* 4 vols. Wiesbaden: Steiner, 1958–63. ———. *Untersuchungen über die Religion der Sklaven in Griechenland und Rom. Dritter Teil: Die wichtigsten Kulte der Griechischen Welt.* 2nd ed. with P. Herz. Stuttgart: Steiner, 1990. **Bonner, C.** *Studies in Magical Amulets Chiefly Graeco-Egyptian.* Ann Arbor: University of Michigan, 1950. **Bornkamm, G.** "Die Komposition der apokalyptischen Visionen in der Offenbarung Johannis." *ZNW* 36 (1937) 132–49. **Borsch, F. H.** *The Christian and Gnostic Son of Man.* SBT 2nd ser. 14. London: SCM, 1970. **Bouché-Leclerq, A.** *Histoire de la divination dans l'antiquité.* 4 vols. 1879–82. Repr. Aalen: Scientia, 1978. **Boulluec, A. Le,** and **Sandevoir, P.** *L'Exode.* Vol. 2 of *La Bible d'Alexandrie.* Paris: Cerf, 1980. **Bousset, W.** *Textkritische Studien zum Neuen Testament.* TU 11/4. Leipzig: Hinrichs, 1894. ——— and **Gressmann, H.** *Die Religion des Judentums im späthellenistischen Zeitalter.* 4th ed. Tübingen: Mohr-Siebeck, 1966. **Bowersock, G.** *Augustus and the Greek World.* Oxford: Clarendon, 1965. **Bowker, J.** *The Targums and Rabbinic Literature.* Cambridge: Cambridge UP, 1969. **Bratcher, R. G.,** and **Hatton, H. A.** *A Handbook on the Revelation to John.* New York: United Bible Societies, 1993. **Braude, W. G.** *The Midrash on Psalms.* 2 vols. New Haven, CT: Yale UP, 1959. **Brenk, F. E.** *In Mist Apparelled: Religious Themes in Plutarch's Moralia and Lives.* Leiden: Brill, 1977. **Brettler, M. Z.** *God*

*Is King: Understanding an Israelite Metaphor.* JSOTSup 76. Sheffield: JSOT, 1989. **Briscoe, J.** *A Commentary on Livy, Books XXXIV–XXXVI.* Oxford: Clarendon, 1981. **Brown, R. E.** *The Epistles of John: A New Translation with Introduction and Commentary.* AB 30. Garden City, NY: Doubleday, 1982. ———. *The Gospel according to John.* 2 vols. Garden City, NY: Doubleday, 1966–70. **Bruce, F. F.** "The Spirit in the Apocalypse." In *Christ and Spirit in the New Testament.* FS C. F. D. Moule, ed. B. Lindars and S. Smalley. Cambridge: Cambridge UP, 1973. 333–44. **Bultmann, R.** *Die Geschichte der synoptischen Tradition.* 8th ed. Göttingen: Vandenhoeck & Ruprecht, 1970. ———. *Die Geschichte der synoptischen Tradition: Ergänzungsheft.* Rev. G. Theissen and P. Vielhauer. 4th ed. Göttingen: Vandenhoeck & Ruprecht, 1971. ———. *The History of the Synoptic Tradition.* Tr. J. Marsh. New York: Harper & Row, 1963. **Burkert, W.** *Ancient Mystery Cults.* Cambridge: Harvard UP, 1987. ———. *Greek Religion.* Tr. J. Raffan. Cambridge: Harvard UP, 1985. ———. *Homo Necans: The Anthropology of Ancient Greek Sacrificial Ritual and Myth.* Tr. P. Bing. Berkeley; Los Angeles: University of California Press, 1983. ———. *Structure and History in Greek Mythology and Ritual.* Berkeley: University of California, 1979. **Burney, C. F.** *The Aramaic Origin of the Fourth Gospel.* Oxford: Clarendon, 1922. **Burton, E. DeW.** *Syntax of the Moods and Tenses in New Testament Greek.* 3rd ed. Edinburgh: T. & T. Clark, 1898. **Buttmann, A.** *A Grammar of the New Testament Greek.* Andover: Warren F. Draper, 1878. **Cadbury, H. J.** *The Making of Luke-Acts.* London: SPCK, 1958. **Caley, E. R.** *Orichalcum and Related Ancient Alloys: Origin, Composition and Manufacture, with Special Reference to the Coinage of the Roman Empire.* New York: American Numismatic Society, 1964. **Carr, W.** *Angels and Principalities.* SNTSMS 42. Cambridge: Cambridge UP, 1981. **Casson, L.** *The Periplus Maris Erythraei Text: with Introduction, Translation and Commentary.* Princeton: Princeton UP, 1989. **Cathcart, K. J.,** and **Gordon, R. P.** *The Targum of the Minor Prophets: Translated, with a Critical Introduction, Apparatus, and Notes.* AramBib 14. Wilmington, DE: Glazier, 1989. **Charles, R. H.** *The Book of Enoch.* 2nd ed. Oxford: Clarendon, 1912. ———. *The Greek Versions of the Testaments of the Twelve Patriarchs.* Oxford: Clarendon, 1908. ———. *Studies in the Apocalypse: Being Lectures Delivered before the University of London.* Edinburgh: T. & T. Clark, 1913. **Chilton, B. D.** *The Isaiah Targum: Introduction, Translation, Apparatus, Notes.* AramBib. Wilmington, DE: Glazier, 1987. **Chilver, G. E. F.** *A Historical Commentary on Tacitus' Histories I and II.* Oxford: Clarendon, 1979. **Clemen, C. C.** *Religionsgeschichtliche Erklärung des Neuen Testaments.* Giessen: Töpelmann, 1924. **Collins, J. J.** *The Apocalyptic Vision of the Book of Daniel.* Missoula, MT: Scholars, 1977. ———. *Daniel: A Commentary on the Book of Daniel.* Minneapolis: Fortress, 1993. ———. *The Sibylline Oracles of Egyptian Judaism.* Missoula, MT: Scholars, 1972. **Comblin, J.** *Le Christ dans l'Apocalypse.* Paris; Tournai: Desclée, 1965. **Conybeare, F. C.** *The Armenian Version of Revelation.* London: The Text and Translation Society, 1907. ——— and **Stock, St. G.** *Grammar of Septuagint Greek.* 1905. Repr. Peabody, MA: Hendrickson, 1988. **Conzelmann, H.** *1 Corinthians: A Commentary on the First Epistle to the Corinthians.* Tr. J. W. Leitch; ed. G. W. MacRae. Philadelphia: Fortress, 1975. ———. *An Outline of the Theology of the New Testament.* Tr. J. Bowden. New York; Evanston, IL: Harper & Row, 1969. **Copely, F. O.** *Vergil, The Aeneid.* 2nd ed. Indianapolis: Bobbs-Merrill, 1975. **Copenhaver, B. P.** *Hermetica: The Greek Corpus Hermeticum and the Latin Asclepius in a New English Translation with Notes and Introduction.* Cambridge: Cambridge UP, 1992. **Court, J.** *Myth and History in the Book of Revelation.* Atlanta: John Knox, 1979. **Cousar, C. B.** *A Theology of the Cross: The Death of Jesus in the Pauline Letters.* Minneapolis: Fortress, 1990. **Cowley, A.** *Aramaic Papyri of the Fifth Century B.C.* Oxford: Clarendon, 1923. **Cowley, R. W.** *The Traditional Interpretation of the Apocalypse of St John in the Ethiopian Orthodox Church.* Cambridge: Cambridge UP, 1983. **Cranfield, C. E. B.** *Romans.* 2 vols. Edinburgh: T. & T. Clark, 1975–79. **Crossan, J. D.** *In Fragments: The Aphorisms of Jesus.* San Francisco: Harper & Row, 1983. **Cullmann, O.** *Early Christian Worship.* Tr. A. S. Todd and J. B. Torrance. London: SCM, 1953. **Cumont, F.** *The Mysteries of Mithra.* New York: Dover, 1956. ———. *Oriental Religions in Roman Paganism.* New York: Dover, 1956. ———. *Recherches sur le Symbolisme Funéraire des Romains.* Paris: Geuthner, 1942. **Cuss, D.** *Imperial*

*Cult and Honorary Terms in the New Testament.* Fribourg: The University Press, 1974. **Dalman, G.** *Aramäisch-Neuhebräisches Handwörterbuch zu Targum, Talmud und Midrasch.* 2nd ed. Göttingen: Vandenhoeck & Ruprecht, 1938. ———. *Die Worte Jesu mit Berücksichtigung des nachkanonischen jüdischen Schrifttums und der Aramäischen Sprache.* 2nd ed. 1930. Repr. Darmstadt: Wissenschaftliche Buchgesellschaft, 1965. **Daniel, R. W.,** and **Maltomini, F.** *Supplementum Magicum.* Vol. 1. Papyrologica Coloniensia 16.1. Oppladen: Westdeutscher, 1990. Vol. 2. Papyrologica Coloniensia 16.2. Oppladen: Westdeutscher, 1992. **Daniélou, J.** *The Theology of Jewish Christianity.* Tr. J. A. Baker. London: Darton, Longman & Todd, 1964. **Danker, F. W.** *Benefactor: Epigraphic Study of a Graeco-Roman and New Testament Semantic Field.* St. Louis: Clayton, 1982. **Davies, P. R.** *1QM, the War Scroll from Qumran: Its Structure and History.* Rome: Biblical Institute, 1977. ———. *The Damascus Covenant.* JSOTSup 25. Sheffield: JSOT, 1983. **Davies, W. D.** *Paul and Rabbinic Judaism: Some Rabbinic Elements in Pauline Theology.* Rev. ed. New York; Evanston: Harper & Row, 1955. ——— and **Allison, D. C., Jr.** *A Critical and Exegetical Commentary on the Gospel according to Saint Matthew.* 2 vols. ICC. Edinburgh: T. & T. Clark, 1988, 1991. **Day, J.** *God's Conflict with the Dragon and the Sea.* Cambridge: Cambridge UP, 1985. **Debord, P.** *Aspects Sociaux et économiques de la vie religieuse dans l'Anatolie greco-romaine.* Leiden: Brill, 1982. **Deichgräber, R.** *Gotteshymnus und Christushymnus in der frühen Christenheit: Untersuchungen zu Form, Sprache und Stil der frühchristlichen Hymnen.* Göttingen: Vandenhoeck & Ruprecht, 1967. **Deissmann, A.** *Bible Studies.* Edinburgh: T. & T. Clark, 1901. ———. *Light from the Ancient East.* New York; London: Hodder & Stoughton, 1910. **Delatte, A.** *Anecdota Atheniensia.* Paris, Champion, 1927. ——— and **Derchain, Ph.** *Les intailles magiques gréco-égyptiennes.* Paris: Bibliothèque Nationale, 1964. **Delling, G.** *Jüdische Lehre und Frömmigkeit in den Paralipomena Jeremiae.* BZAW 100. Berlin: Töpelmann, 1967. ———. *Worship in the New Testament.* Tr. P. Scott. Philadelphia: Westminster,1962. **Delobel, J.** "Le texte de l'Apocalypse: Problemes de méthode." In *L'Apocalypse,* ed. J. Lambrecht. 151–66. **Denis, A.-M.** *Concordance Grecque des Pseudépigraphes d'ancien Testament: Concordance, Corpus des textes, Indices.* Louvain-la-Neuve: Université Catholique de Louvain, 1987. ———. *Fragmenta Pseudepigraphorum quae supersunt Graeca.* Leiden: Brill, 1970. **Deniston, J. D.** *The Greek Particles.* 2nd ed. Oxford: Clarendon, 1954. ———. *Greek Prose Style.* Oxford: Clarendon, 1952. **Dexinger, F.** *Henochs Zehnwochenapokalypse und offene Probleme der Apokalyptikforschung.* SPB 29. Leiden: Brill, 1977. **Dibelius, M.,** and **Greeven, H.** *James: A Commentary on the Epistle of James.* Tr. M. A. Williams. Philadelphia: Fortress, 1976. **Dick, K.** *Der schriftstellerische Plural bei Paulus.* Halle: Niemeyer, 1900. **Dieterich, A.** *Abraxas: Studien zur Religionsgeschichte.* Leipzig: Teubner, 1891. ———. *Eine Mithrasliturgie.* 2nd ed. Leipzig; Berlin: Teubner, 1910. **Diobouniotis, C.,** and **Harnack, A.** *Der Scholien-Kommentar des Origenes zur Apokalypse-Johannis.* TU 38/3. Leipzig: Hinrichs, 1911. **Dodd, C. H.** *According to the Scriptures.* Digswell Place: James Nisbet, 1952. ———. *The Interpretation of the Fourth Gospel.* Cambridge: Cambridge UP, 1965. **Dogniez, C.,** and **Harl, M.** *Le Deutéronome.* La Bible d'Alexandrie 5. Paris: Cerf, 1992. **Doran, R.** *Temple Propaganda: The Purpose and Character of 2 Maccabees.* CBQMS 12. Washington DC: Catholic Biblical Association, 1981. **Dornseiff, F.** *Das Alphabet in Mystik und Magie.* 2nd ed. Leipzig; Berlin: Teubner, 1925. **Dothan, M.** *Hammath Tiberias: Early Synagogues and the Hellenistic and Roman Remains.* Jerusalem: Israel Exploration Society, 1983. **Doudna, J. C.** *The Greek of the Gospel of Mark.* Philadelphia: Society of Biblical Literature, 1961. **Dover, K. J.** *Greek Popular Morality.* Berkeley; Los Angeles: University of California, 1974. **Dunn, J. D. G.** *Romans.* 2 vols. WBC 38A–B. Waco, TX: Word, 1988. **Durham, J. I.** *Exodus.* WBC 3. Waco, TX: Word, 1987. **Durling, R. J.** *A Dictionary of Medical Terms in Galen.* SAM 5. Leiden: Brill, 1993. **Eckhardt, K. A.** *Der Tod des Johannes.* Berlin: de Gruyter, 1961. **Ehrenberg, V.,** and **Jones, A. H. M.** *Documents Illustrating the Reigns of Augustus and Tiberius.* 2nd ed. Oxford: Clarendon, 1976. **Eisenman, R. H.,** and **Wise, M.** *The Dead Sea Scrolls Uncovered.* Rockport: Element, 1992. **Eissfeldt, O.** *The Old Testament: An Introduction.* Tr. P. R. Ackroyd. New York; Evanston, IL: Harper & Row, 1965. **Eitrem, S.** *Papyri Osloenses.* Fasc. 1: *Magical Papyri.* Oslo:

Dybwad, 1925. ———. *Some Notes on the Demonology in the New Testament.* 2nd ed. Oslo: Universitetsforlaget, 1966. **Eliade, M.** *The Sacred and the Profane: The Nature of Religion.* Tr. W. R. Trask. New York: Harper & Row, 1959. **Elliott, J. H.** *A Home for the Homeless: A Sociological Exegesis of I Peter.* Philadelphia: Fortress, 1981. **Engelmann, H.** *The Delian Aretalogy of Sarapis.* Leiden: Brill, 1975. **Enslin, M. S.,** and **Zeitlin, S.** *The Book of Judith.* Leiden: Brill, 1972. **Epstein, I.,** ed. *Babylonian Talmud.* 27 vols. London: Soncino, 1935–60. **Evans, C. A, Webb, R. L.,** and **Wiebe, R. A.** *Nag Hammadi Texts and the Bible: A Synopsis and Index.* Leiden: Brill, 1993. **Fanning, B. M.** *Verbal Aspect in New Testament Greek.* Oxford: Clarendon, 1990. **Farrer, A.** *A Rebirth of Images: The Making of St John's Apocalypse.* Albany: State University of New York, 1986. **Fee, G.** *The First Epistle to the Corinthians.* Grand Rapids, MI: Eerdmans, 1987. **Fekkes, J.** *Isaiah and Prophetic Traditions in the Book of Revelation.* JSNTSup 93. Sheffield: JSOT, 1994. **Ferrar, W. J.,** ed. and tr. *Eusebius, The Proof of the Gospel.* 2 vols. New York: Macmillan, 1920. **Festugière, A.-J.** *La révélation d'Hermès Trismégiste.* 4 vols. Paris: J. Gabalda, 1950–54. **Fiedler, P.** *Die Formel "Und Siehe" im Neuen Testament.* Munich: Kosel, 1969. **Field, F.** *Origenis Hexaplorum quae supersunt; sive Veterum Interpretum Graecorum in totus Veius Testamentum Fragmenta.* 2 vols. Oxford: Clarendon, 1875. **Finegan, J.** *The Archaeology of the New Testament.* Princeton: Princeton UP, 1969. **Finley, M. I.** *The Ancient Economy.* Berkeley; Los Angeles: University of California, 1985. ———. *The World of Odysseus.* Rev. ed. New York: Penguin, 1979. **Fitzmyer, J. A.** *The Gospel according to Luke.* 2 vols. Garden City, NY: Doubleday, 1979–83. **Fontenrose, J.** *The Delphic Oracle: Its Responses and Operations with a Catalogue of Responses.* Berkeley; Los Angeles: University of California, 1978. ———. *Didyma: Apollo's Oracle, Cult, and Companions.* Berkeley: University of California, 1988. **Forestell, J. T.** *Targumic Traditions and the New Testament.* Chico, CA: Scholars, 1979. **Fraenkel, E.** *Aeschylus, Agamemnon.* Oxford: Clarendon, 1950. ———. *Horace.* Oxford: Clarendon, 1957. **Frank, T.,** ed. *An Economic Survey of Ancient Rome.* 6 vols. Baltimore: Johns Hopkins, 1933–40. **Fraser, P. M.,** and **Matthews, E.** *A Lexicon of Greek Personal Names.* Vol. 1: *The Aegean Islands, Cyprus, Cyrenaica.* Oxford: Clarendon, 1987. **Freedman, H.,** ed. *Midrash Rabbah.* 10 vols. 3rd ed. London; New York: Soncino, 1983. **Friesen, S. J.** *Twice Neokoros: Ephesus, Asia and the Cult of the Flavian Imperial Family.* Leiden: Brill, 1993. **Frisk, H.** *Griechisches Etymologisches Wörterbuch.* 3 vols. Heidelberg: Winter, 1960. ———. *Le Périple de la Mer Érythrée suivi d'une étude sur la tradition et la langue.* Göteborg: Elander, 1927. **Frost, S. B.** *Old Testament Apocalyptic.* London: Epworth, 1952. **Fustel de Coulanges, N. D.** *The Ancient City.* Baltimore: Johns Hopkins UP, 1980. **Gallop, D.** *Plato, Phaedo: Translated with Notes.* Oxford: Clarendon, 1975. **García Martínez, F.** *The Dead Sea Scrolls Translated.* Leiden: Brill, 1994. ———. *Qumran and Apocalyptic: Studies on the Aramaic Texts from Qumran.* Leiden: Brill, 1994. **Geissen, A.** *Der Septuaginta-Text des Buches Daniel nach dem Kölner Teil des Papyrus 967: Kap. V-XII.* Bonn: Habelt, 1968. **Georgi, D.** *Die Gegner des Paulus im 2. Korintherbrief.* WMANT 11. Neukirchen: Neukirchener, 1964. **Gibson, J. C. L.** *Canaanite Myths and Legends.* 2nd ed. Edinburgh: T. & T. Clark, 1978. ———. *Hebrew and Moabite Inscriptions.* Vol. 1 of *Textbook of Syrian Semitic Inscriptions.* Oxford: Clarendon, 1973. **Giet, S.** *L'Apocalypse et l'Histoire.* Paris: Presses universitaires de France, 1957. **Gignac, F. T.** *A Grammar of the Greek Papyri of the Roman and Byzantine Periods.* 2 vols. Milan: Cisalpino-Goliardica, 1976–81. **Ginzberg, L.** *The Legends of the Jews.* Philadelphia: Jewish Publication Society of America, 1909. **Gollinger, H.** *Die Kirche in der Bewährung: Eine Einführung in die Offenbarung des Johannes.* Aschaffenburg: Pattloch, 1973. **Goodenough, E. R.** *Jewish Symbols in the Greco-Roman Period.* 12 vols. New York: Bollingen Foundation, 1953–65. ———. "The Menorah among Jews of the Roman World." *HUCA* 23 (1950–51) 449–92. **Goodspeed, E. J.** *Problems of New Testament Translation.* Chicago: University of Chicago, 1945. **Gow, A. S. F.,** and **Page, D. L.** *The Greek Anthology: The Garland of Philip and Some Contemporary Epigrams.* Vol. 1. Cambridge: Cambridge UP, 1968. **Grant F. C.,** ed. *Hellenistic Religions: The Age of Syncretism.* New York: Liberal Arts, 1953. **Grant, R. M.** *Early Christianity and Society.* New York: Harper & Row, 1977. **Grese, W. C.** *Corpus Hermeticum XII and Early Christian Literature.* SCHNT 5.

Leiden: Brill, 1979. **Gressmann, H.** *Altorientalische Texte zum Alten Testament.* 2nd ed. Berlin; Leipzig: de Gruyter, 1926. **Griffiths, J. G.** *Apuleius of Madauros, The Isis-Book (Metamorphoses, Book XI).* Leiden: Brill, 1975. **Gross, W.** *Die Pendenskonstruktion im biblischen Hebräisch.* St. Ottilien: EOS, 1987. **Grossfeld, B.** *The First Targum to Esther.* New York: Sepher-Hermon, 1983. ———. *The Targum Sheni to the Book of Esther.* New York: Sepher-Hermon, 1994. ———. *The Two Targums of Esther.* AramBib 18. Wilmington, DE: Glazier, 1991. ———, tr. *The Targum Onqelos to Leviticus and The Targum Onqelos to Numbers.* AramBib 8. Wilmington, DE: Glazier, 1988. **Grotius, H.** *Annotationes in Novum Testamentum.* 8 vols. Groningen: Zuidema, 1830. **Gruenwald, I.** *Apocalyptic and Merkavah Mysticism.* Leiden: Brill, 1980. **Guelich, R. A.** *Mark 1–8:26.* WBC 34A. Dallas: Word, 1989. **Gunkel, H.** *Schöpfung und Chaos in Urzeit und Endzeit: Eine religionsgeschichtliche Untersuchung über Gen 1 und Ap Joh 12.* Göttingen: Vandenhoeck & Ruprecht, 1921. ———. *Zum religionsgeschichtlichen Verständnis des Neuen Testaments.* Göttingen: Vandenhoeck & Ruprecht, 1903. **Guthrie, D.** *New Testament Introduction.* Downers Grove, IL: Inter-Varsity Press, 1970. **Hachlili, R.** *Ancient Jewish Art and Archaeology in the Land of Israel.* Leiden: Brill, 1988. **Hadas, M.** *The Third and Fourth Books of Maccabees.* New York: Harper & Brothers, 1953. **Hadas-Lebel, M.** *Jérusalem contre Rome.* Paris: Cerf, 1990. **Haelst, J. van.** *Catalogue des papyrus littéraires Juifs et Chrétiens.* Paris: Publications de la Sorbonne, 1976. **Haenchen, E.** *A Commentary on the Gospel of John.* 2 vols. Hermeneia. Philadelphia: Fortress, 1984. **Hafemann, S. J.** *Paul, Moses, and the History of Israel.* WUNT 81. Tübingen: Mohr-Siebeck, 1995. ———. *Suffering and the Spirit: An Exegetical Study of II Cor. 2:14–3:3 within the Context of the Corinthian Correspondence.* WUNT 2/19. Tübingen: Mohr-Siebeck, 1986. **Hahn, F.** "Die Rede von der Parusie des Menschensohnes Markus 13." In *Jesus und der Menschensohn,* ed. R. Pesch and R. Schnackenburg. Freiburg: Herder & Herder, 1975. ———. *Mission in the New Testament.* London: SCM, 1965. **Hals, R. M.** *Ezekiel.* FOTL 19. Grand Rapids, MI: Eerdmans, 1989. **Hands, A. R.** *Charities and Social Aid in Greece and Rome.* Ithaca, NY: Cornell UP, 1968. **Hannestad, N.** *Roman Art and Imperial Policy.* Aarhus: Aarhus UP, 1988. **Hanson, A. T.** *The Wrath of the Lamb.* London: S.P.C.K., 1957. **Hanson, P. D.** *The Dawn of Apocalyptic.* Philadelphia: Fortress, 1975. **Haran, M.** *Temples and Temple-Service in Ancient Israel.* Oxford: Clarendon, 1978. **Hare, D. R. A.** *The Son of Man Tradition.* Minneapolis: Fortress, 1990. **Harnisch, W.** *Verhängnis und Verheißung der Geschichte: Untersuchungen zum Zeit- und Geschichtsverständnis im 4. Buch Esra und in der syr. Baruchapokalypse.* FRLANT 97. Göttingen: Vandenhoeck & Ruprecht, 1969. **Harrington, D. J.,** and **Saldarini, A. J.** *Targum Jonathan of the Former Prophets: Introduction, Translation and Notes.* AramBib 10. Wilmington, DE: Glazier, 1987. **Harrington, W. J.** *Understanding the Apocalypse.* Washington, DC; Cleveland: Corpus Books, 1969. **Harvey, W. W.** *Sanci Irenaei Episcopi Lugdunensis Libros quinque adversus Haereses.* 2 vols. Cambridge: Typis Academicis, 1857. **Hatch, E.** *Essays in Biblical Greek.* Oxford: Oxford UP, 1889. **Haussleiter, J.** *Victorinus Episcopi Petavionensis Opera.* Leipzig: Freytag, 1916. **Hay, D. M.** *Glory at the Right Hand: Psalm 110 in Early Christianity.* Nashville: Abingdon, 1973. **Hayward, R.** *The Targum of Jeremiah: Translated, with a Critical Introduction, Apparatus, and Notes.* AramBib 12. Wilmington, DE: Glazier, 1987. **Heidel, A.** *The Gilgamesh Epic and Old Testament Parallels.* 2nd ed. Chicago: University of Chicago, 1949. **Heiler, F.** *Prayer: A Study in the History and Psychology of Religion.* Tr. S. McComb. London; New York: Oxford UP, 1932. **Heinemann, J.** *Prayer in the Talmud.* Berlin; New York: de Gruyter, 1977. **Helbing, R.** *Die Kasussyntax der Verba bei den Septuaginta: Ein Beitrag zur Hebraismenfrage und zur Syntax der Κοινή.* Göttingen: Vandenhoeck & Ruprecht, 1928. **Hellholm, D.** "The Problem of Apocalyptic Genre and the Apocalypse of John." In *Early Christian Apocalypticism: Genre and Social Setting,* ed. A. Yarbro Collins. *Semeia* 36 (1986) 13–64. ———, ed. *Apocalypticism in the Mediterranean World and the Near East.* Tübingen: Mohr-Siebeck, 1983. **Hemer, C. J.** *The Letters to the Seven Churches of Asia in Their Local Setting.* JSNTSup 11. Sheffield: JSOT, 1986. **Hengel, M.** *The Charismatic Leader and His Followers.* New York: Crossroad, 1981. ———. *The Zealots: Investigations into the Jewish Freedom Movement in the Period from Herod I until 70 A.D.* Tr. D. Smith.

Edinburgh: T. & T. Clark, 1989. **Hercher, R.** *Epistolographi graeci.* 1873. Repr. Amsterdam: Hocker, 1965. **Heubeck, A., West, S.,** and **Hainsworth, J. B.** *A Commentary on Homer's Odyssey.* Vol. 1. Oxford: Clarendon, 1988. **Hilhorst, A.** *Sémitismes et Latinismes dans le Pasteur d'Hermas.* Nijmegen: Dekker and Van de Vegt, 1976. **Hill, D.** *New Testament Prophecy.* Atlanta: John Knox, 1979. ———. "Prophecy and Prophets in the Revelation of St. John." *NTS* 18 (1971–72) 401–18. **Hillers, D.** *Treaty-Curses and the Old Testament Prophets.* Rome: Pontifical Biblical Institute, 1964. **Himmelfarb, M.** *Ascent to Heaven in Jewish and Christian Apocalypses.* New York; Oxford: Oxford UP, 1993. ———. *Tours of Hell: An Apocalyptic Form in Jewish and Christian Literature.* Philadelphia: University of Pennsylvania, 1983. **Hobbs, T. R.** *2 Kings.* WBC 13. Waco, TX: Word, 1985. **Hofmann, J.** *Die äthiopische Johannes-Apokalypse kritisch Untersucht.* CSCO 297. Louvain: Secrétariat du CorpusSCO, 1969. **Holladay, W. L.** *Jeremiah 1.* Philadelphia: Fortress, 1986. **Hollander, H. W.,** and **Jonge, M. de.** *The Testaments of the Twelve Patriarchs: A Commentary.* Leiden: Brill, 1985. **Holmberg, B.** *Sociology and the New Testament.* Minneapolis: Fortress, 1990. **Holtz, T.** *Die Christologie der Apokalypse des Johannes.* 2nd ed. Berlin: Akademie, 1971. **Hopfner, T.** *Griechisch-Ägyptischer Offenbarungszauber.* 2 vols. Leipzig: Haessel, 1921–24. **Horgan, M. P.** *Pesharim: Qumran Interpretations of Biblical Books.* CBQMS 8. Washington, DC: Catholic Biblical Association of America, 1979. **Horst, J.** *Proskynein: Zur Anbetung im Urchristentum nach ihrer religionsgeschichtlichen Eigenart.* Gütersloh: Bertelsmann, 1932. **Horst, P. W. van der.** *Ancient Jewish Epitaphs.* Kampen: Kok Pharos, 1991. **Hoskier, H. C.** *The Complete Commentary of Oecumenius on the Apocalypse.* Ann Arbor: University of Michigan, 1928. ———. *Concerning the Date of the Bohairic Version Covering a Detailed Examination of the Text of the Apocalypse.* London: Quaritch, 1911. ———. *Concerning the Text of the Apocalypse.* 2 vols. London: Quaritch, 1929. **Houtman, C.** *Der Himmel im Alten Testament: Israels Weltbild und Weltanschauung.* Oudtestamentische Studiën 30. Leiden: Brill, 1993. **Hurtado, L.** *One God, One Lord: Early Christian Devotion and Ancient Jewish Monotheism.* London: SCM, 1988. **Hvalvik, R.** *The Struggle for Scripture and Covenant: The Purpose of the Epistle of Barnabas and Jewish-Christian Competition in the Second Century.* WUNT 2/82. Tübingen: Mohr-Siebeck, 1996. **Isbell, C. D.** *Corpus of the Aramaic Incantation Bowls.* SBLDS 17. Missoula, MT: Scholars, 1975. **Jacobson, H.** *The Exagoge of Ezekiel.* Cambridge: Cambridge UP, 1983. **James, M. R.** *The Psalms of Solomon.* Cambridge: Cambridge UP, 1891. **Jastrow, M.** *A Dictionary of the Targumim, the Talmud Babli and Yerushalmi and the Midrashic Literature.* 2 vols. New York: Ktav, 1950. **Jellicoe, S.** *The Septuagint and Modern Study.* 1968. Repr. Winona Lake, IN: Eisenbrauns, 1989. **Jeremias, A.** *Babylonisches im Neuen Testament.* Leipzig: Hinrichs, 1905. **Jeremias, C.** *Die Nachtgeschichte des Sacharja.* FRLANT 117. Göttingen: Vandenhoeck & Ruprecht, 1977. **Jeremias, Joachim.** *The Eucharistic Words of Jesus.* New York: Scribner's Sons, 1966. ———. *Jerusalem in the Time of Jesus.* Tr. F. H. and C. H. Cave. Philadelphia: Fortress, 1969. ———. *The Parables of Jesus.* Rev. ed. New York: Scribner, 1964. ———. *The Prayers of Jesus.* Philadelphia: Fortress, 1978. ———. *New Testament Theology.* New York: Scribner's Sons, 1971. ——— and **Strobel, A.** *Die Briefe an Timotheus und Titus, Der Brief an die Hebräer.* 12th ed. Göttingen: Vandenhoeck & Ruprecht, 1981. **Jeremias, Jörg.** *Theophanie: Die Geschichte einer alttestamentlichen Gattung.* WMANT 10. 2nd ed. Neukirchen: Neukirchener, 1977. **Johannessohn, J.** *Der Gebrauch der Kasus und der Präpositionen in der Septuaginta.* Berlin: Friedrich-Wilhelms-Universität, 1910. **Jones, A. H. M.** *The Cities of the Eastern Roman Provinces.* Oxford: Clarendon, 1937. ———. *The Greek City from Alexander to Justinian.* Oxford: Clarendon, 1940. **Jones, C. P.** *The Roman World of Dio Chrysostom.* Cambridge: Harvard UP, 1978. **Jonge, M. de.** *The Testaments of the Twelve Patriarchs: A Critical Edition of the Greek Text.* Leiden: Brill, 1978. **Jörns, K.-P.** *Das hymnische Evangelium: Untersuchungen zu Aufbau, Funktion und Herkunft der hymnischen Stücke in der Johannesoffenbarung.* Gütersloh: Mohn, 1971. **Joüon, P.** *A Grammar of Biblical Hebrew.* 3 vols. Rome: Pontifical Biblical Institute, 1991. **Kahn, C. H.** *The Art and Thought of Heraclitus: An Edition of the Fragments with Translation and Commentary.* Cambridge: Cambridge UP, 1979. **Karrer, M.** *Die Johannesoffenbarung* *als Brief: Studien zu ihrem literarischen, historischen und theologischen Ort.* Göttingen: Vandenhoeck & Ruprecht, 1986. **Kaufmann, Y.** *The Religion of Israel: From Its Beginnings to the Babylonian Exile.* Tr. M. Greenberg. Chicago: University of Chicago, 1960. **Kavanagh, M. A.** *Apocalypse 22:6–21 as Concluding Liturgical Dialogue.* Rome: Pontifical Gregorian University, 1984. **Keel, O.** *Die Welt der altorientalischen Bildsymbolik und das Alte Testament.* Zürich: Benziger; Neukirchen: Neukirchener, 1972. **Kees, H.** *Der Götterglaube im alten Aegypten.* Leipzig: Hinrichs, 1941. **Kilmer, A. D., Crocker, R. L., and Brown, R. R.** *Sounds from Silence: Recent Discoveries in Ancient Near Eastern Music.* Berkeley: Bit Enki, 1976. **Klein, M. L.** *The Fragment-Targums of the Pentateuch according to their Extant Sources.* AnBib 76. 2 vols. Rome: Biblical Institute, 1980. **Klein, R.** *1 Samuel.* WBC 10. Waco, TX: Word, 1983. **Kloppenborg, J. S.** *The Formation of Q: Trajectories in Ancient Wisdom Collections.* Philadelphia: Fortress, 1987. **Knibb, M. A.** *The Ethiopic Book of Enoch: A New Edition in the Light of the Aramaic Dead Sea Fragments.* 2 vols. Oxford: Clarendon Press, 1978. ———. *The Qumran Community.* Cambridge: Cambridge UP, 1987. **Koch, G., and Sichtermann, H.** *Römische Sarkophage.* Munich: Beck, 1982. **Koch, K.** *The Growth of the Biblical Tradition.* New York: Scribner's Sons, 1969. **Koep, L.** *Das himmlische Buch in Antike und Christentum: Eine religionsgeschichtliche Untersuchung zur altchristlichen Bildersprache.* Bonn: Hanstein, 1952. **Koester, H.** *Introduction to the New Testament.* 2 vols. Philadelphia: Fortress, 1982. **Korpel, M. C. A.** *A Rift in the Clouds: Ugaritic and Hebrew Descriptions of the Divine.* Münster: UGARIT-Verlag, 1990. **Kraabel, A. T.** "Judaism in Western Asia Minor under the Roman Empire, with a Preliminary Study of the Jewish Community at Sardis, Lydia." Diss., Harvard, 1968. **Kraeling, C. H.** *The Synagogue.* The Excavations at Dura Europas 8/1. New Haven, CT: Yale UP, 1956. **Kraus, H.-J.** *Theology of the Psalms.* Tr. K. Crim. Minneapolis: Augsburg, 1986. ———. *Worship in Israel: A Cultic History of the Old Testament.* Richmond: John Knox, 1966. **Krause, M., and Labib, P.** *Die drei Versionen des Apokryphon des Johannes.* Wiesbaden: Harrassowitz, 1962. **Krauss, F. B.** *An Interpretation of the Omens, Portents, and Prodigies Recorded by Livy, Tacitus, Suetonius.* Philadelphia: University of Pennsylvania, 1930. **Krauss, S.** *Talmudische Archäologie.* Leipzig: Fock, 1910–12. **Kreitzer, L. J.** *Jesus and God in Paul's Eschatology.* Sheffield: JSOT, 1987. **Kroll, J.** *Die Lehren des Hermes Trismegistos.* 2nd ed. Münster: Aschendorff, 1928. **Kropp, A. M.** *Ausgewählte Koptische Zaubertexte.* 3 vols. Bruxelles: Égyptologique Reine Élisabeth, 1930–31. **Krüger, G., and Ruhbach, G.** *Ausgewählte Märtyrerakten.* 4th ed. Tübingen: Mohr-Siebeck, 1965. **Kuhn, P.** *Offenbarungsstimmen im Antiken Judentum: Untersuchungen zur Bat Qol und verwandten Phänomenen.* Texte und Studien zum Antiken Judentum 20. Tübingen: Mohr-Siebeck, 1989. **Kuhnen, H.-P.** *Nordwest-Palästina in hellenistisch-römischer Zeit: Bauten und Gräber im Karmelgebiet.* Weinheim: VCH Verlagsgesellschaft, 1987. **Kühner, R. and Gerth, B.** *Ausführliche Grammatik der griechischen Sprache: Satzlehre.* 2 vols. 3rd ed. Hannover: Hahsche, 1898–1904. **Kümmel, W. G.** *Introduction to the New Testament.* Rev. ed. Tr. H. C. Kee. Nashville: Abingdon, 1975. **Lambrecht, J.,** ed. *L'Apocalypse johannique et l'Apocalyptique dans le Nouveau Testament.* Leuven: Leuven UP, 1980. **Lancellotti, A.** *Uso delle forme verbali nell'Apocalisse alla luce ella sintassi ebraica.* Assisi: Studio Teologico "Porziuncola," 1964. **Lange, N. M. R. de.** *Origen and the Jews.* Cambridge: Cambridge UP, 1976. **Lattimore, R.** *Themes in Greek and Latin Epitaphs.* Urbana: University of Illinois, 1962. **Laughlin, T. C.** *Solecisms of the Apocalypse.* Princeton: C. S. Robinson, 1902. **Lauterbach, J. Z.** *Mekilta De-Rabbi Ishmael.* 3 vols. Philadelphia: Jewish Publication Society of America, 1935. **Leaney, A. R. C.** *The Rule of Qumran and Its Meaning.* Philadelphia: Westminster, 1966. **Lee, D.** "The Narrative Asides in the Book of Revelation." Diss., Chicago Theological Seminary, 1990. **Levey, S. H.** *The Targum of Ezekiel: Translated, with a Critical Introduction, Apparatus, and Notes.* AramBib 13. Wilmington, DE: Glazier, 1987. **Levy, J.** *Wörterbuch über die Talmudim und Midraschim.* 4 vols. Darmstadt: Wissenschaftliche Buchgesellschaft, 1963. **Lieberman, S.** *Hellenism in Jewish Palestine.* New York: The Jewish Theological Seminary of America, 1962. **Liebeschuetz, J. H. W. G.** *Antioch: City and Imperial Administration in the Later Roman Empire.* Oxford: Clarendon, 1972. ———. *Continuity and Change in Roman Religion.* Oxford:

Clarendon, 1979. **Lifshitz, B.** *Donateurs et fondateurs dans les synagogues juives.* Paris: Gabalda, 1967. **Lightfoot, J.** *Horae Hebraicae et Talmudicae.* 4 vols. Oxford UP, 1959. **Lightfoot, J. B.** *The Apostolic Fathers: Clement, Ignatius, and Polycarp.* Two parts in 5 vols. London: Macmillan, 1889–90. **Lindars, B.** *Jesus Son of Man: A Fresh Examination of the Son of Man Sayings in the Gospels in the Light of Recent Research.* Grand Rapids, MI: Eerdmans, 1983. ———. *New Testament Apologetic: The Doctrinal Significance of the Old Testament Quotations.* London: SCM, 1961. **Lindblom, J.** *Gesichte und Offenbarungen: Vorstellungen von göttlichen Weisungen und übernatürlichen Erscheinungen im ältesten Christentum.* Lund: Gleerup, 1968. **Lindemann, A.** *Die Clemensbriefe.* HNT 17. Tübingen: Mohr-Siebeck, 1992. ———. *Paulus im ältesten Christentum.* BHT 58. Tübingen: Mohr-Siebeck, 1979. **Ljungvik, H.** *Beiträge zur Syntax der spätgriechischen Volkssprache.* Uppsala: Almqvist & Wiksell; Leipzig: Harrassowitz, 1932. **Lo Bue, F.** *The Turin Fragments of Tyconius' Commentary on Revelation,* ed. G. G. Willis. Cambridge: Cambridge UP, 1963. **Lohse, E.** *Colossians and Philemon.* Philadelphia: Fortress, 1971. **Louw, J. P.** "On Greek Prohibitions." *AcCl* 2 (1959) 43–57. **Lücke, F.** *Versuch einer vollständigen Einleitung in die Offenbarung des Johannes oder Allgemeine Untersuchungen über die apokalyptischen Literatur überhaupt und die Apokalypse des Johannes insbesondere.* 2nd ed. Bonn, 1852. **Luterbacher, F.** *Der Prodigienglaube und Prodigienstil der Römer.* Burgdorf: Langlois, 1880. **MacDonald, D. R.,** ed. *The Acts of Andrew and The Acts of Andrew and Matthias in the City of the Cannibals.* Atlanta: Scholars, 1990. **Mach, M.** *Entwicklungsstadien des jüdischen Engelglaubens in vorrabbinischer Zeit.* Tübingen: Mohr-Siebeck, 1992. **Macho, A. D.** *Neophyti: Targum Palestinense Ms de la Biblioteca Vaticana.* Vol. 1. Madrid; Barcelona: Consejo Superior de Investigaciones Científicas, 1968. **MacMullen, R.** *Paganism in the Roman Empire.* New Haven, CT: Yale UP, 1981. **Magie, D.** *Roman Rule in Asia Minor to the End of the Third Century after Christ.* 2 vols. Princeton: Princeton UP, 1950. **Maher, M.** *Targum Pseudo-Jonathan: Genesis.* AramBib 1b. Wilmington, DE: Glazier, 1992. **Maier, J.** *The Temple Scroll.* JSOTSup 34. Sheffield: JSOT, 1985. **Malherbe, A. J.** *Social Aspects of Early Christianity.* 2nd ed. Philadelphia: Fortress, 1983. **Malina, B. J.** *On the Genre and Message of Revelation: Star Visions and Sky Journeys.* Peabody, MA: Hendrickson, 1995. **Maloney, E. C.** *Semitic Interference in Marcan Syntax.* Chico, CA: Scholars, 1981. **Marcovich, M.,** ed. *Hippolytus Refutatio Omnium Haeresium.* Patristische Texte und Studien 25. Berlin; New York: de Gruyter, 1986. **Martin, J.** *Commodiani Carmina.* CCL 128. Turnholti: Typographi Brepols Editores Pontificii, 1960. **Mason, H. J.** *Greek Terms for Roman Institutions: A Lexicon and Analysis.* Toronto: Hakkert, 1974. **Mateos, J.** *El Aspecta Verbal en el Neuevo Testamento.* Madrid: Ediciones Cristiandad, 1977. **Matthiae, K.,** and **Schönert-Geiss, E.** *Münzen aus der urchristlichen Umwelt.* Berlin: Evangelische, 1981. **Maurer, C.** *Ignatius von Antiochien und das Johannesevangelium.* Zürich: Zwingli, 1949. **Mayser, E.** *Satzlehre.* Vol. 2/3 of *Grammatick der griechischen Papyri aus der Ptolemäerzeit.* Berlin; Leipzig: de Gruyter, 1934. **Mazzaferri, F. D.** *The Genre of the Book of Revelation from a Source-critical Perspective.* BZNW 54. Berlin; New York: de Gruyter, 1989. **McDonald, M. F.,** tr. *Lactantius: The Divine Institutes.* Washington, DC: The Catholic University of America, 1964. **McKay, K. L.** *Greek Grammar for Students: A Concise Grammar of Classical Attic with Special Reference to Aspect in the Verb.* Canberra: Australian National University, 1974. **McNamara, M.** *The New Testament and the Palestinian Targum to the Pentateuch.* Rome: Pontifical Biblical Institute, 1966. ———. *Targum and Testament.* Grand Rapids, MI: Eerdmans, 1972. ———. *Targum Neofiti 1: Leviticus.* Collegeville: Liturgical, 1994. ——— and **Clarke, E. G.** *Targum Neofiti 1: Numbers.* AramBib 4. Wilmington, DE: Glazier, 1995. ———, **Hayward, R.,** and **Maher, M.** *Targum Neofiti 1: Exodus and Targum Pseudo-Jonathan: Exodus.* AramBib 2. Wilmington, DE: Glazier, 1984. ———, **Hayward, R.,** and **Maher, M.** *Targum Neofiti 1: Leviticus and Targum Pseudo-Jonathan: Leviticus.* AramBib 3. Wilmington, DE: Glazier, 1994. **Meiggs, R.,** and **Lewis, D.** *A Selection of Greek Historical Inscriptions to the End of the Fifth Century B.C.* Oxford: Clarendon, 1969. **Mellor, R.** ΘΕΑ 'ΡΩΜΗ: *The Worship of the Goddess Roma in the Greek World.* Göttingen: Vandenhoeck & Ruprecht, 1975. **Ménard, J. E.** *L'Évangile de Vérité: Rétroversion Grecque et Commentaire.* Paris: Letouzey & Ané, 1962.

————. *L'Évangile selon Thomas.* Montélimar: Marsanne, 1974. **Merk, A.,** ed. *Novum Testament: Graece et Latine.* 10th ed. Rome: Pontifical Biblical Institute, 1984. **Meshorer, Y.** *Jewish Coins of the Second Temple Period.* Tr. I. H. Levine. Tel-Aviv: Am Hassefer, 1967. **Metzger, B. M.** *Breaking the Code: Understanding the Book of Revelation.* Nashville: Abingdon, 1993. ————. *Manuscripts of the Greek Bible.* New York; Oxford: Oxford UP, 1981. ————. *The Text of the New Testament: Its Transmission, Corruption and Restoration.* 2nd. ed. New York: Oxford UP, 1968. ————. *A Textual Commentary on the Greek New Testament:* Stuttgart: United Bible Societies, 1975. **Meyer, E.** *Ursprung und Anfänge des Christentums.* 3 vols. 1923. Repr. Darmstadt: Wissenschaftliche Buchgesellschaft, 1962. **Michaels, J. R.** *1 Peter.* WBC 49. Waco, TX: Word, 1988. ————. *Interpreting the Book of Revelation.* Grand Rapids, MI: Baker, 1992. **Milik, J. T.** *The Books of Enoch: Aramaic Fragments of Qumran Cave 4.* Oxford: Clarendon, 1976. **Millar, F.** *The Emperor in the Roman World (31 B.C.–A.D. 337).* Ithaca, NY: Cornell UP, 1977. ————. *The Roman Near East 31 B.C.–A.D. 337.* Cambridge: Harvard UP, 1993. **Miller, A. M.** *From Delos to Delphi: A Literary Study of the Homeric Hymn to Apollo.* Leiden: Brill, 1986. **Minear, P. S.** *I Saw a New Earth: An Introduction to the Visions of the Apocalypse.* Washington DC; Cleveland: Corpus, 1968. **Mitchell, S.** *Anatolia: Land, Men, and Gods in Asia Minor.* 2 vols. Oxford: Clarendon, 1993. **Mommsen, T.** *Römisches Staatsrecht.* 3rd ed. Graz: Akademische Druck- und Verlagsanstalt, 1952. ———— and **Krueger, P.** *The Digest of Justinian.* Tr. and ed. Alan Watson. 4 vols. Philadelphia: University of Pennsylvania, 1985. **Montgomery, J. A.** *Aramaic Incantation Texts from Nippur.* Philadelphia: The University Museum, 1909. ————. *A Critical and Exegetical Commentary on the Book of Daniel.* Edinburgh: T. & T. Clark, 1927. **Moore, C. A.** *Judith: A New Translation with Introduction and Commentary.* AB 40. Garden City, NY: Doubleday, 1985. **Moore, G. F.** *Judaism in the First Centuries of the Christian Era: The Age of the Tannaim.* 3 vols. Cambridge: Harvard UP, 1927. **Moran, H. E.** *The Consolations of Death in Ancient Greek Literature.* Washington, DC: The Catholic University of America, 1917. **Morenz, S.** *Egyptian Religion.* Tr. A. E. Keep. Ithaca, NY: Cornell UP, 1973. **Morgan, M. A.,** tr. *Sepher ha-Razim: The Book of the Mysteries.* Chico, CA: Scholars, 1983. **Moule, C. F. D.** *An Idiom-Book of New Testament Greek.* 2nd ed. Cambridge: Cambridge UP, 1959. **Moulton, J. H.** *A Grammar of New Testament Greek.* 3 vols. Edinburgh: T. & T. Clark, 1908–76. ————. *Prolegomena.* Vol. 1 of *A Grammar of New Testament Greek.* 3rd ed. Edinburgh: T. & T. Clark, 1908. ———— and **Howard, W. F.** *Accidence and Word-Formation.* Vol. 2 of *A Grammar of New Testament Greek.* Edinburgh: T. & T. Clark, 1928. **Mowinckel, S.** *Offersang og Sangoffer.* Oslo: Universitetsforlaget, 1951. ————. *The Psalms in Israel's Worship.* 2 vols. New York; Nashville: Abingdon, 1967. **Müller, U. B.** "Literarische und formgeschichtliche Bestimmung der Apokalypse des Johannes als einem Zeugnis frühchristlicher Apokalyptic." In *Apocalypticism,* ed. D. Hellholm. 599–620. ————. *Messias und Menschensohn in jüdischen Apokalypsen und in der Offenbarung des Johannes.* SNT 6. Gütersloh: Mohn, 1972. ————. *Prophetie und Predigt im Neuen Testament: Formgeschichtliche Untersuchungen zur urchristlichen Prophetie.* Gütersloh: Mohn, 1975. ————. *Zur frühchristlichen Theologiegeschichte: Judenchristentum und Paulinismus in Kleinasien an der Wende vom ersten zum zweiten Jahrhundert n. Chr.* Gütersloh: Mohn, 1976. **Muraoka, T.** *A Greek-English Lexicon of the Septuagint (Twelve Prophets).* Louvain: Peeters, 1993. **Mussies, G.** *Dio Chrysostom and the New Testament.* Leiden: Brill, 1972. ————. "Identification and Self-Identification of Gods in Classical and Hellenistic Times." In *Knowledge of God in the Graeco-Roman World,* ed. R. van den Broek, T. Baarda, and J. Mansfeld. EPRO 112. Leiden: Brill, 1988. 1–18. ————. *The Morphology of Koine Greek as Used in the Apocalypse of John: A Study in Bilingualism.* Leiden: Brill, 1971. **Musurillo, H.** *The Acts of the Christian Martyrs.* Oxford: Clarendon, 1972. **Myers, J. M.** *I and II Esdras.* AB 42. Garden City, NY: Doubleday, 1974. **Nachmanson, E.** *Partitives Subjekt im Griechischen.* Göteborg: Elanders Boktryckeri, 1942. **Nauck, A.** *Tragicorum graecorum fragmenta.* Leipzig: Teubner, 1856. **Naveh, J.,** and **Shaked, S.** *Amulets and Magic Bowls: Aramaic Incantations of Late Antiquity.* Jerusalem: Magnes; Leiden: Brill, 1985. **Newsom, C.** *Songs of the Sabbath Sacrifice: A Critical Edition.* Atlanta: Scholars, 1985. **Nickelsburg, G. W. E.** *Jewish Literature between* *the Bible and the Mishnah*. Philadephia: Fortress, 1981. **Niederwimmer, K.** *Die Didache*. KAV 1. Göttingen: Vandenhoeck & Ruprecht, 1989. **Niggemeyer, J.-H.** *Beschwörungsformeln aus dem 'Buch der Geheimnisse' (Sefär ha-razîm)*. Hildesheim; New York: Olms, 1975. **Nock, A. D.** *Essays on Religion and the Ancient World*, ed. Z. Stewart. 2 vols. Oxford: Clarendon, 1972. ———— and **Festugière, A.-J.** *Hermès Trismégiste*. 4 vols. Paris: Société d'Édition 'Les Belles Letters,' 1954–60. **Norden, E.** *Agnostos Theos: Untersuchungen zur Formengeschichte religiöser Rede*. Darmstadt: Wissenschaftliche Buchgesellschaft, 1956. **Nussbaum, M.** *The Therapy of Desire: Theory and Practice in Hellenistic Ethics*. Princeton: Princeton UP, 1994. **Odelain, O.**, and **Séguineau, R.** *Lexikon der Biblischen Eigennamen*. Düsseldorf: Patmos; Neukirchen: Neukirchener, 1981. **Olyan, S. M.** *A Thousand Thousands Served Him: Exegesis and the Naming of Angels in Ancient Judaism*. Tübingen: Mohr-Siebeck, 1993. **Palmer, L. R.** *The Greek Language*. Atlantic Highlands, NJ: Humanities, 1980. **Parker, R.** *Miasma: Pollution and Purification in Early Greek Religion*. Oxford: Clarendon, 1983. **Pax, E.** *Epiphaneia: Ein religionsgeschichtlier Beitrag zur biblischen Theologie*. Munich: Münchener Theologische Studien, 1955. **Peerbolte, L. J. L.** *The Antecedents of Antichrist: A Traditio-Historical Study of the Earliest Christian Views on Eschatological Opponents*. Leiden: Peerbolte, 1995. **Perrin, M.** *Lactance: Épitomé des Institutions Divines*. SC 335. Paris: Cerf, 1987. **Perrin, N.** *Rediscovering the Teaching of Jesus*. New York; Evanston, IL: Harper & Row, 1967. **Pesch, R.** *Das Markus-evangelium*. 2 vols. Freiburg: Herder, 1977. ————. *Naherwartungen: Tradition und Redaktion in Mk 13*. Düsseldorf: Patmos, 1968. **Peterson, E.** *Εἷς Θεός: Epigraphische, formgeschichtliche und religionsgeschichtliche Untersuchungen*. Göttingen: Vandenhoeck & Ruprecht, 1926. **Pétrement, S.** *A Separate God: The Christian Origins of Gnosticism*. San Francisco: Harper & Row, 1990. **Petzl, G.** *Die Inschriften von Smyrna*. Part 1: *Grabinschriften, postume Ehrungen, Grabepigramme. Inschriften griechischer Städte aus Kleinasien*, vol. 23. Bonn: Habelt, 1982. ————. *Die Inschriften von Smyrna*. Part 2, vol. 2. Bonn: Habelt, 1990. **Philipp, H.** *Mira et Magica: Gemmen im ägyptischen Museum der staatlichen Museen, preussischer Kulturbesitz Berlin-Charlottenburg*. Mainz am Rhein: von Zabern, 1986. **Philonenko, M.** *Joseph et Aséneth*. Leiden: Brill, 1968. **Pietersma, A.** *The Apocryphon of James and James the Magician*. RGRW 119. Leiden: Brill, 1994. **Pohlenz, M.** *Vom Zorne Gottes: Eine Studie über den Einfluss der griechischen Philosophie auf das alte Christentum*. FRLANT 12. Göttingen: Vandenhoeck & Ruprecht, 1909. **Pollitt, J. J.** *Art in the Hellenistic Age*. Cambridge: Cambridge UP, 1986. **Porten, B.** *Archives from Elephantine: The Life of an Ancient Jewish Military Colony*. Berkeley; Los Angeles: University of California, 1968. ———— and **Yardeni, A.** *Textbook of Aramaic Documents from Ancient Egypt*. 3 vols. Jerusalem: Hebrew University, 1986–93. **Porter, S. E.** *Verbal Aspect in the Greek of the New Testament with Reference to Tense and Mood*. Frankfurt/M.; Berne; New York: Lang, 1978. **Qimron, E.**, and **Strugnell, J.** *Qumran Cave 4*. Vol. V: *Miqsat Maʿase ha-Torah*. DJD 10. Oxford: Clarendon, 1994. **Rad, G. von.** *Old Testament Theology*. 2 vols. New York; Evanston, IL: Harper & Row, 1962–65. ————. *Wisdom in Israel*. Nashville; New York: Abingdon, 1972. **Radermacher, L.** *Neutestamentliche Grammatik*. 2nd ed. Tübingen: Mohr-Siebeck, 1925. **Rahlfs, A.** *Septuaginta: Id est Vetus Testamentum graece iuxta LXX interpretes*. 8th ed. 2 vols. Stuttgart: Würtembergische Bibelanstalt, 1935. **Ramsay, W. M.** *The Cities of St. Paul: Their Influence on His Life and Thought*. London: Hodder and Stoughton, 1907. ————. *The Letters to the Seven Churches*. London: Hodder & Stoughton, 1904. **Reader, W. W.** "Die Stadt Gottes in der Johannesapokalypse." Diss., Göttingen, 1971. **Rehm, B.** *Die Pseudoklementinen*. Vol. 1: *Homilien*. GCS. Berlin: Akademie, 1953. **Reichelt, G.** *Das Buch mit den sieben Siegeln in der Apokalypse des Johannes*. Göttingen: Georg-August-Universität zu Göttingen, 1975. **Reichelt, H.** *Angelus Interpres-Texte in der Johannes-Apokalypse*. Frankfurt am Main: Lang, 1994. **Reicke, B.** *The New Testament Era: The World of the Bible from 500 B.C. to A.D. 100*. Philadelphia: Fortress, 1968. ————. *Die zehn Worte in Geschichte und Gegenwart*. BGBE 13. Tübingen: Mohr-Siebeck, 1973. **Rendtorff, R.** *Studien zur Geschichte des Opfers im alten Israel*. Neukirchen: Neukirchener, 1967. **Reynolds, J.** *Aphrodisias and Rome*. London: Society for the Promotion of Roman Studies, 1982. ———— and **Tannenbaum, R.** *Jews and*

*Godfearers at Aphrodisias.* Cambridge: Cambridge Philological Society, 1987. **Rijksbaron, A.** *The Syntax and Semantics of the Verb in Classical Greek: An Introduction.* Amsterdam: Gieben, 1984. **Rissi, M.** *The Future of the World: An Exegetical Study of Revelation 19.11–22.15.* SBT 23. Naperville, IL: Allenson, n.d. ———. *Die Hure Babylon und die Verführung der Heiligen: Eine Studie zur Apokalypse des Johannes.* BWANT 136. Stuttgart: Kohlhammer, 1995. ———. "The Kerygma of the Revelation to John." *Int* 22 (1968) 3–17. ———. *Zeit und Geschichte.* Zürich: Zwingli, 1952. **Robert, L.** *Nouvelles inscriptions de Sardes.* Paris: Librairie d'Amérique et d'Orient, 1964. **Robertson, A. T.** *A Grammar of the Greek New Testament in the Light of Historical Research.* Nashville: Broadman, 1934. **Robinson, J. A. T.** *Redating the New Testament.* Philadelphia: Westminster, 1976. **Robinson, J. M.,** ed. *The Nag Hammadi Library.* Rev. ed. San Francisco: Harper & Row, 1988. **Roloff, J.** *Das Kerygma und der irdische Jesus: Historische Motive in den Jesus-Erzählungen der Evangelien.* Göttingen: Vandenhoeck & Ruprecht, 1970. **Romero-Pose, E.,** ed. *Sancti Beati a Liebana Commentarius in Apocalipsin.* Rome: Typis officinae polygraphicae, 1985. **Rordorf, W.,** and **Tuilier, A.** *La Doctrine des douze Apôtres (Didachè).* SC 248. Paris: Cerf, 1978. **Roscher, W. H.** *Ausführliches Lexikon der griechischen und römischen Mythologie.* 6 vols. Leipzig: Teubner, 1884–1937. **Rosenthal, F.** *A Grammar of Biblical Aramaic.* Wiesbaden: Harrassowitz, 1963. **Rostovtzeff, M.** *The Social and Economic History of the Roman Empire.* 2nd ed. by P. M. Fraser. 2 vols. Oxford: Clarendon, 1957. **Roueché, C.** *Aphrodisias in Antiquity.* London: Society for the Promotion of Roman Studies, 1989. **Ruckstuhl, E.,** and **Dschulnigg, P.** *Stilkritik und Verfasserfrage im Johannesevangelium.* Göttingen: Vandenhoeck & Ruprecht; Freiburg: Universitätsverlag, 1991. **Rudolf, K.** *Gnosis: The Nature and History of Gnosticism.* Tr. R. McL. Wilson. San Francisco: Harper & Row, 1983. **Rusam, F.** "Hymnische Formeln in Apokalypse 1." Diss., Christian-Albrechts-Universität zu Kiel, 1970. **Russell, D. S.** *The Method and Message of Jewish Apocalyptic.* Philadelphia: Westminster, 1964. **Rydbeck, L.** *Fachprosa, Vermeintliche Volkssprache und Neues Testament.* Uppsala: Berlingska Boktryckeriet, 1967. **Sanday, W.,** and **Headlam, A. C.** *Romans.* 5th ed. Edinburgh: T. & T. Clark, 1902. ——— and **Turner, C. H.** *Nouum Testamentum Sancti Irenaei Episcopi Lugdunensis.* Old-Latin Biblical Texts 7. Oxford: Clarendon, 1923. **Sanders, E. P.** *Jesus and Judaism.* Philadelphia: Fortress, 1985. **Sanders, J. T.** *The New Testament Christological Hymns: Their Historical Religious Background.* SNTSMS 15. Cambridge: Cambridge UP, 1971. **Sandnes, K. O.** *Paul—One of the Prophets? A Contribution to the Apostle's Self-Understanding.* WUNT 2/43. Tübingen: Mohr-Siebeck, 1991. **Satake, A.** *Die Gemeindeordnung in der Johannesapokalypse.* WMANT 21. Neukirchen: Neukirchener, 1966. **Sattler, W.** "Das Buch mit sieben Siegeln: Studien zum literarischen Aufbau der Offenbarung Johannis." *ZNW* 20 (1921) 231–40. **Sauter, F.** *Der römische Kaiserkult bei Martial und Statius.* Stuttgart; Berlin: Kohlhammer, 1934. **Schäfer, P.** *Synopse zur Hekhalot-Literatur.* Tübingen: Mohr-Siebeck, 1981. **Schiffman, L. H.,** and **Swartz, M. D.** *Hebrew and Aramaic Incantation Texts from the Cairo Genizah: Selected Texts from Taylor-Schechter Box K1.* Sheffield: Sheffield Academic, 1992. **Schlatter, A.** *Das Alte Testament in der johanneischen Apokalypse.* Gütersloh: Bertelsmann, 1912. **Schlier, H.** *Der Brief an die Galater.* 12th ed. Göttingen: Vandenhoeck & Ruprecht, 1962. **Schmid, J.** *Studien zur Geschichte des griechischen Apokalypse-Textes.* 2 vols. Munich: Zink, 1955. **Schmidt, C.,** and **MacDermot, V.** *The Books of Jeu and the Untitled Text in the Bruce Codex.* NHS 13. Leiden: Brill, 1978. ——— and **MacDermot, V.** *Pistis Sophia.* NHS 9. Leiden: Brill, 1978. ——— and **Till, W.** *Koptisch-gnostische Schriften.* Vol. 1: *Die Pistis Sophia, Die beiden Bücher des Jeu, Unbekanntes altgnostisches Werk.* GCS 13. 3rd ed. Berlin: Akademie, 1962. **Schmidt, F.** *Le Testament grec d'Abraham.* Tübingen: Mohr-Siebeck, 1986. **Schnackenburg, R.** *The Gospel according to St. John.* 3 vols. Vol. 1: New York: Herder & Herder, 1968; Vol. 2: New York: Seabury, 1980; Vol. 3: New York: Crossroad, 1982. **Schoedel, W. R.** *Ignatius of Antioch: A Commentary on the Letters of Ignatius of Antioch.* Philadelphia: Fortress, 1985. **Schowalter, D. N.** *The Emperor and the Gods: Images from the Time of Trajan.* HDR 28. Minneapolis: Fortress, 1993. **Schrenk, G.** *Die Weissagung über Israel im Neuen Testament.* Zürich: Gotthelf, 1951. **Schröder, S.** *Plutarchs Schrift*

*De Pythiae oraculis. Text, Einleitung und Kommentar.* Stuttgart: Teubner, 1990. **Schürer, E.** *The History of the Jewish People in the Age of Jesus Christ.* 4 vols. Ed. G. Vermes, F. Millar, and M. Goodman. Edinburgh: T. & T. Clark, 1973–87. **Schüssler Fiorenza, E.** "Apokalypsis and Propheteia: The Book of Revelation in the Context of Early Christian Prophecy." In *L'Apocalypse johannique et l'Apocalyptique dans le Nouveau Testament,* ed. J. Lambrecht. Leuven: Leuven UP, 1980. 105–28. ———. *The Book of Revelation: Justice and Judgment.* Philadelphia: Fortress, 1985. ———. "Composition and Structure of the Book of Revelation." *CBQ* 39 (1977) 344–66. ———. "The Eschatology and Composition of the Apocalypse." *CBQ* 30 (1968) 564. ———. *Priester für Gott: Studien zum Herrschafts- und Priestermotiv in der Apokalypse.* NTAbh 7. Münster: Aschendorf, 1972. ———. "The Quest for the Johannine School: The Apocalypse and the Fourth Gospel." *NTS* 23 (1976–77) 402–27. **Schwemer, A. M.** "Studien zu den frühjüdischen Prophetenlegenden: Vitae Prophetarum." 2 vols. Diss., Tübingen, 1993. **Scott, W.** *Hermetica: The Ancient Greek and Latin Writings Which Contain Religious or Philosophic Teachings Ascribed to Hermes Trismegistus.* 4 vols. 1924–36. Repr. Boston: Shambhala, 1985. **Scullard, H. H.** *Festivals and Ceremonies of the Roman Republic.* Ithaca, NY: Cornell UP, 1981. **Sellin, E.,** and **Fohrer, G.** *Introduction to the Old Testament.* Tr. D. E. Green. Nashville: Abingdon, 1968. **Shepherd, M. H.** *The Paschal Liturgy and the Apocalypse.* Richmond: John Knox, 1960. **Sherk, R. K.** *Roman Documents from the Greek East: Senatus Consulta and Epistulae to the Age of Augustus.* Baltimore: Johns Hopkins UP, 1969. **Sherwin-White, A. N.** *The Letters of Pliny: A Historical and Social Commentary.* Oxford: Clarendon, 1966. **Simon, M.** *Verus Israel: A Study of the Relations between Christians and Jews in the Roman Empire (A.D. 135–425).* Oxford: Oxford UP, 1986. **Simpson, M.,** tr. *Gods and Heroes of the Greeks: The Library of Apollodorus.* Amherst: University of Massachusetts, 1976. **Skarsaune, O.** *The Proof from Prophecy: A Study in Justin Martyr's Proof-Text Tradition: Text-Type, Provenance, Theological Profile.* NovTSup 56. Leiden: Brill, 1987. **Skehan, W., Ulrich, E.,** and **Sanderson, J. E.** *Qumran Cave 4.* Vol. 4: *Palaeo-Hebrew and Greek Biblical Manuscripts.* DJD 9. Oxford: Clarendon, 1992. **Skutsch, O.** *The Annals of Quintus Ennius.* Oxford: Clarendon, 1985. **Smalley, S. S.** *Thunder and Love: John's Revelation and John's Community.* Milton Keynes: Nelson Word, 1994. **Smith, J. Z.** "The Prayer of Joseph." In *Religions in Antiquity,* ed. J. Neusner. NumenSup 14. Leiden: Brill, 1968. 253–94. **Smith, K. F.** *The Elegies of Albius Tibullus.* New York: American Book Company, 1913. **Smith, M.** *Tannaitic Parallels to the Gospels.* SBLMS 6. 2nd ed. Philadelphia: Society of Biblical Literature, 1968. **Smyth, H. W.** *Greek Grammar.* Rev. G. M. Messing. Cambridge: Harvard UP, 1956. **Soden, H. F. von.** *Text mit Apparat.* Part 2 of *Die Schriften des Neuen Testaments in ihrer ältesten erreichbaren Textgestalt.* Göttingen: Vandenhoeck & Ruprecht, 1913. **Söder, R.** *Die apokryphen Apostelgeschichten und die romanhafte Literatur der Antike.* Stuttgart: Kohlhammer, 1932. **Soisalon-Soininen, I.** *Die Infinitive in der Septuagints.* Helsinki: Suomalainen Tiedeakatemia, 1965. **Sokolowski, F.** *Lois sacrées de l'Asie Mineure.* Paris: de Boccard, 1955. **Sollamo, R.** *Renderings of Hebrew Semiprepositions in the Septuagint.* Helsinki: Suomalainen Tiedeakatemia, 1979. **Souza Nogueira, P. A. de.** "Der Widerstand gegen Rom in der Apokalypse des Johannes: Eine Untersuchung zur Tradition des Falls von Babylon in Apokalypse 18." Diss., Heidelberg, 1991. **Spengel, L.** *Rhetores Graeci.* 3 vols. Leipzig: Teubner, 1853–56. **Sperber, A.** *The Bible in Aramaic.* 4 vols. Leiden: Brill, 1959–73. **Spicq, C.** *Notes de lexicographie Néo-testamentaire.* 3 vols. Göttingen: Vandenhoeck & Ruprecht, 1978–82. **Stegemann, W.** *Zwischen Synagoge und Obrigkeit: Zur historischen Situation der lukanischen Christen.* Göttingen: Vandenhoeck & Ruprecht, 1991. **Stengel, P.** *Die griechischen Kultusaltertümer.* 3rd ed. Munich: Beck, 1920. **Stone, M. E.** *Fourth Ezra: A Commentary on the Book of Fourth Ezra.* Minneapolis: Fortress, 1990. **Stoneman, R.** *Palmyra and Its Empire: Zenobia's Revolt against Rome.* Ann Arbor: University of Michigan, 1992. **Strobel, A.** "Apokalypse des Johannes." In *Theologische Realenzyklopädie.* Vol. 3. New York; Berlin: de Gruyter, 1978. **Stroker, W. D.** *Extracanonical Sayings of Jesus.* Atlanta: Scholars, 1989. **Stuckenbruck, L. T.** *Angel Veneration and Christology: A Study in Early Judaism and the Apocalypse of John.* Tübingen: Mohr-Siebeck, 1995.

**Stuhlmann, R.** *Das eschatologische Maß im Neuen Testament.* Göttingen: Vandenhoeck & Ruprecht, 1983. **Swartz, M. D.** *Mystical Prayer in Ancient Judaism: An Analysis of Maʿaseh Merkavah.* Tübingen: Mohr-Siebeck, 1992. **Swete, H. B.** *Introduction to the Old Testament in Greek.* Cambridge: Cambridge UP, 1914. **Tagawa, K.** *Miracles et Évangile: la pensée personelle de l'évangeliste Marc.* Paris: Presses universitaires de France, 1966. **Tajra, H. W.** *The Martyrdom of St. Paul: Historical and Judicial Context, Traditions and Legends.* WUNT 2/67. Tübingen: Mohr-Siebeck, 1994. **Taylor, L. R.** *The Divinity of the Roman Emperor.* Middletown: American Philological Association, 1931. **Tcherikover, V.** *Hellenistic Civilisation and the Jews.* Philadelphia: Jewish Publication Society of America, 1961. **Thackeray, H. St. J.** *A Grammar of the Old Testament in Greek.* Cambridge: Cambridge UP, 1909. ———. *Josephus the Man and the Historian.* New York: Ktav, 1967. **Thayer, J. H.** *A Greek-English Lexicon of the New Testament.* Grand Rapids, MI: Zondervan, n.d. **Theisohn, J.** *Der auserwählte Richter: Untersuchungen zur traditionsgeschichtlicher Ort der Menschensohngestalt der Bilderreden des Äthiopisch Henoch.* Göttingen: Vandenhoeck & Ruprecht, 1976. **Theissen, G.** *The Gospels in Context: Social and Political History in the Synoptic Tradition.* Minneapolis: Fortress, 1991. ———. *The Miracle Stories of the Early Christian Tradition.* Philadelphia: Fortress, 1983. **Thompson, L. L.** *The Book of Revelation: Apocalypse and Empire.* New York: Oxford UP, 1990. **Thompson, S.** *The Apocalypse and Semitic Syntax.* SNTSMS 52. Cambridge: Cambridge UP, 1985. ———. *Motif-Index of Folk-Literature.* 6 vols. 1932–34. Repr. Bloomington: Indiana UP, 1983. **Tischendorf, C.** *Novum Testamentum Graece.* 8th ed. 2 vols. Leipzig: Giesecke & Devrient, 1872. **Tödt, H. E.** *The Son of Man in the Synoptic Tradition.* Tr. D. M. Barton. Philadelphia: Westminster, 1965. **Toit, A. du.** "Vilification as a Pragmatic Device in Early Christian Epistolography." *Bib* 75 (1994) 403–12. **Torrey, C. C.** *The Apocalypse of John.* New Haven: Yale UP, 1958. **Touilleux, P.** *L'Apocalypse et les cultes de Domitien et de Cybèle.* Paris: Librairie Orientaliste Paul Geuthner, 1935. **Tov, E.** *The Greek Minor Prophets Scroll from Nahal Ḥever (8HevXIIgr, The Seiyal Collection I).* DJD 8. Oxford: Clarendon, 1990. **Trebilco, P.** *Jewish Communities in Asia Minor.* SNTSMS 69. Cambridge: Cambridge UP, 1991. **Tromp, J.** *The Assumption of Moses: A Critical Edition with Commentary.* Leiden: Brill, 1992. **Turner, N.** *Grammatical Insights into the New Testament.* Edinburgh: T. & T. Clark, 1965. ———. *Style.* Vol. 4 of *A Grammar of New Testament Greek,* ed. J. H. Moulton. Edinburgh: T. & T. Clark, 1976. ———. *Syntax.* Vol. 3 of *A Grammar of New Testament Greek,* ed. J. H. Moulton. Edinburgh: T. & T. Clark, 1963. **Ulrichsen, J. H.** *Die Grundschrift der Testamente der zwölf Patriarchen: Eine Untersuchung zu Umfang, Inhalt und Eigenart der ursprünglichen Schrift.* Uppsala: Almqvist & Wiksel, 1991. **Urbach, E. E.** *The Sages: Their Concepts and Beliefs.* Cambridge: Harvard UP, 1987. **VanderKam, J. C.** *The Book of Jubilees: A Critical Text.* CSCO 510; Scriptores Aethiopici 87. Louvain: Peeters, 1989. ———. *Enoch and the Growth of an Apocalyptic Tradition.* CBQMS 16. Washington, DC: Catholic Biblical Society of America, 1984. **Vanhoye, A.** "L'utilisation du livre d'Ézéchiel dans l'Apocalypse. *Bib* 43 (1962) 436–76. **Vanni, U.** *L'Apocalisse: Ermeneutica, Esegesi, Teologia.* Bologna: Edizioni Dehoniane, 1988. ———. *La struttura letteraria dell'Apocalisse.* 2nd ed. Napoli: Morcelliana, 1980. **Vaux, R. de.** *Ancient Israel: Its Life and Institutions.* Tr. J. McHugh. New York: McGraw-Hill, 1961. **Vermaseren, M. J.** *Mithraica III: The Mithraeum at Marino.* EPRO 16. Leiden: Brill, 1982. ———. *Mithras the Secret God.* London: Chatto & Windus, 1963. **Vermes, G.** *The Dead Sea Scrolls in English.* 3rd rev. and aug. ed. London: Penguin, 1987. ———. *Jesus the Jew.* New York: Macmillan, 1973. **Vermeule, C. C.** *Roman Imperial Art in Greece and Asia Minor.* Cambridge: Harvard UP, 1968. **Vermeule, E.** *Aspects of Death in Early Greek Art and Poetry.* Berkeley: University of California, 1979. **Versnel, H. S.** "Religious Mentality in Ancient Prayer." In *Faith, Hope and Worship: Aspects of Religious Mentality in the Ancient World.* Leiden: Brill, 1981. 1–64. ———. *Triumphus: An Inquiry into the Origin, Development and Meaning of the Roman Triumph.* Leiden: Brill, 1970. **Vielhauer, P.** *Geschichte der urchristlichen Literatur.* Berlin; New York: de Gruyter, 1975. **Vischer, E.** *Die Offenbarung Johannis: eine jüdische Apokalypse in christlicher Bearbeitung.* TU 2/3. Leipzig: Hinrichs, 1886. **Vlastos, G.** *Socrates: Ironist and Moral Reformer.* Cambridge: Cambridge UP, 1991. **Vogels, H. J.** *Untersuchungen zur Geschichte der lateinischen Apokalypse-Übersetzung.* Düsseldorf: Schwann, 1920. **Vögtle, A.** *Das Neue Testament und die Zukunft des Kosmos.* Düsseldorf: Patmos, 1970. ———. *Die Tugend- und Lasterkataloge im Neuen Testament.* NTAbh 16. Münster: Aschendorff, 1936. **Völter, D.** *Die Entstehung der Apokalypse.* 2nd ed. Freiburg: Mohr-Siebeck, 1882. **Volz, P.** *Die Eschatologie der jüdischen Gemeinde.* Tübingen: Mohr-Siebeck, 1934. **Vos, L. A.** *The Synoptic Traditions in the Apocalypse.* Kampen: Kok, 1965. **Votaw, C. W.** *The Use of the Infinitive in Biblical Greek.* Chicago: Votaw, 1896. **Vuyst, J. de.** *De structuur van de apokalyps.* Kampen: Kok, 1968. **Walbank, F. W.** *A Historical Commentary on Polybius.* 3 vols. Oxford: Clarendon, 1957–79. **Watson, A.,** ed. *The Digest of Justinian.* Philadelphia: University of Pennsylvania, 1985. **Weber, R.** ed., *Biblia sacra iuxta Vulgatam versionem.* 2 vols. Stuttgart: Deutsche Bibelgesellschaft, 1969. **Wehr, L.** *Arznei der Unsterblichkeit: Die Eucharistie bei Ignatius von Antiochien und im Johannesevangelium.* NTAbh 18. Münster: Aschendorff, 1987. **Weiser, A.** *The Psalms: A Commentary.* Philadelphia: Westminster, 1962. **Weiss, B.** *Die Johannes-Apokalypse: Textkritische Untersuchungen und Textherstellung.* TU 7.1. Leipzig: Hinrichs, 1892. **Weiss, H.-F.** *Untersuchungen zur Kosmologie des hellenistischen und palästinischen Judentums.* TU 97. Berlin: Akademie, 1966. **Weiss, J.** *Der erste Korintherbrief.* 8th ed. Göttingen: Vandenhoeck & Ruprecht, 1910. ———. *Die Offenbarung des Johannes: Ein Beitrag zur Literatur- und Religionsgeschichte.* Göttingen: Vandenhoeck & Ruprecht, 1904. **Wellhausen, J.** *Analyse der Offenbarung Johannis.* Berlin: Weidmann, 1907. **Wellmann, M.,** ed. *Pedanii Dioscurides Anazarbei, De material medica libri quinque.* 3 vols. Berlin: Weidmann, 1958. **Wengst, K.** *Schriften des Urchristentums: Didache (Apostellehre), Barnabasbrief, Zweiter Klemensbrief, Schrift an Diognet.* Munich: Kösel, 1984. **Werner, E.** *The Sacred Bridge: Liturgical Parallels in Synagogue and Early Church.* New York: Columbia UP, 1959. **West, M. L.** *Hesiod, Theogony: Edited with Prolegomena and Commentary.* Oxford: Clarendon, 1966. **Westcott, B. F.,** and **Hort, F. J. A.** *Introduction to the New Testament in the Original Greek.* New York: Harper, 1882 (\*indicates pages in the Appendix). **Westermann, C.** *Genesis: A Commentary.* Tr. J. J. Scullion. 3 vols. Minneapolis: Augsburg, 1984–86. ———. *The Praise of God in the Psalms.* Tr. K. R. Crim. Richmond: John Knox, 1965. **Wettstein, J. J.** *Novum Testamentum Graecum.* 2 vols. 1752. Repr. Graz: Akademische Druck- und Verlaganstalt, 1962. **Weyland, W. G. J.** *Omwerkings en Compilatie-Hypothesen toegepast op de Apokalypse van Johannes.* Groningen: Wolters, 1888. **White, R. J.** *The Interpretation of Dreams: Oneirocritica by Artemidorus.* Park Ridge, NJ: Noyes, 1975. **Wilken, R. L.** *The Christians as the Romans Saw Them.* New Haven; London: Yale UP, 1984. **Williams, F.** *Callimachus, Hymn to Apollo: A Commentary.* Oxford: Clarendon, 1978. **Wilson, W. T.** *The Mysteries of Righteousness: The Literary Composition and Genre of the Sentences of Pseudo-Phocylides.* Tübingen: Mohr-Siebeck, 1994. **Winer, G. B.** *A Treatise on the Grammar of New Testament Greek.* Tr. W. F. Moulton. 3rd ed. rev. Edinburgh: T. & T. Clark, 1882. **Winston, D.** *The Wisdom of Solomon.* Garden City, NY: Doubleday, 1979. **Wissowa, G.** *Religion und Kultus der Römer.* 2nd ed. Munich: Beck, 1912. **Witt, R. E.** *Isis in the Graeco-Roman World.* Ithaca, NY: Cornell UP, 1971. **Wolff, C.** *Jeremia im frühjudentum und Urchristentum.* TU 118. Berlin: Akademie, 1976. **Wülker, L.** *Die geschichtliche Entwicklung des Prodigienwesens bei den Römern: Studien zur Geschichte und Überlieferung der Staatsprodigien.* Leipzig: Glausch, 1903. **Yarbro Collins, A.** *The Combat Myth in the Book of Revelation.* Missoula, MT: Scholars, 1975. ———. *Crisis and Catharsis: The Power of the Apocalypse.* Philadelphia: Westminster, 1984. ———. "The Political Perspective of the Revelation to John." *JBL* 96 (1977) 241–56. ———. "The 'Son of Man' Tradition and the Book of Revelation." In *The Messiah: Developments in Earliest Judaism and Christianity,* ed. J. H. Charlesworth. Minneapolis: Fortress, 1992. 536–68. **Ysebaert, J.** *Die Amtsterminologie im Neuen Testament und in der Alten Kirche: Eine lexicographische Untersuchung.* Breda: Eureia, 1994. **Zahn, T.** *Ignatii et Polycarpi Epistolae Marytia Fragmenta.* Vol. 2 of *Patrum Apostolicorum Opera.* Leipzig: Hinrichs, 1876. ———. *Introduction to the New Testament.* 3 vols. Grand Rapids, MI: Kregel, 1953. ———, ed. *Forschungen zur Geschichte des neutestamentlichen Kanons und der altkirchlichen Literatur.* Erlangen: Deichert, 1891. **Zazoff,**

**P.** *Die antike Gemmen.* Munich: Beck, 1983. **Zerwick, M.** *Biblical Greek.* Tr. J. Smith, S.J. Rome: Pontifical Biblical Institute, 1963. ———— and **Grosvenor, M.** *A Grammatical Analysis of the Greek New Testament.* 2 vols. Rome: Biblical Institute, 1974. **Ziegler, J.,** ed. *Duodecim prophetae.* VTG 13. Göttingen: Vandenhoeck & Ruprecht, 1943. ————, ed. *Ezechiel.* Septuaginta: VTG 16/1. Göttingen: Vandenhoeck & Ruprecht, 1952. ————, ed. *Susanna, Daniel, Bel et Draco.* VTG 16/2. Göttingen: Vandenhoeck & Ruprecht, 1954. **Ziegler, K.-H.** *Die Beziehungen zwischen Rom und dem Partherreich.* Wiesbaden: Steiner, 1964. **Zimmerli, W.** *Ezekiel.* Tr. R. E. Clements. 2 vols. Philadelphia: Fortress, 1979–83.

# Introduction

## Section 1: Authorship

### Bibliography

**Aune, D. E.** "The Prophetic Circle of John of Patmos and the Exegesis of Revelation 22:16." *JSNT* 37 (1989) 103–16. ―――. "The Social Matrix of the Apocalypse of John." *BR* 26 (1981) 16–32. **Bacon, W. B.** "The Elder John in Jerusalem." *ZNW* 26 (1927) 187–202. **Balz, H. R.** "Anonymität und Pseudepigraphie im Urchristentum." *ZTK* 66 (1969) 403–36. **Barrett, C. K.** *The Gospel according to St John.* 2nd ed. Philadelphia: Westminster, 1978. **Beasley-Murray, G. R.** "The Relation of the Fourth Gospel to the Apocalypse." *EvQ* 18 (1946) 173–86. **Becker, J.** "Erwägungen zu Fragen der neutestamentlichen Exegese." *BZ* 13 (1969) 99–102. **Bernard, J. H.** *A Critical and Exegetical Commentary on the Gospel according to St. John.* 2 vols. Edinburgh: T. & T. Clark, 1928. **Böcher, O.** "Johanneisches in der Apokalypse des Johannes." *NTS* 27 (1981) 310–21. ―――. "Das Verhältnis der Apokalypse des Johannes zum Evangelium des Johannes." In *L'Apocalypse*, ed. J. Lambrecht. 289–301. **Booth, W. C.** *The Rhetoric of Fiction.* 2nd ed. Chicago: University of Chicago, 1983. **Carpenter, J. E.** *The Johannine Writings: A Study of the Apocalypse and the Fourth Gospel.* London: Constable, 1927. **Cullmann, O.** *The Johannine Circle.* Tr. J. Bowden. Philadelphia: Westminster, 1976. **Culpepper, R. A.** *The Johannine School: An Evaluation of the Johannine-School Hypothesis Based on an Investigation of the Nature of Ancient Schools.* Missoula, MT: Scholars, 1975. ―――. *John, the Son of Zebedee: The Life of a Legend.* Columbia: University of South Carolina, 1994. **Dibelius, M.** *Geschichte der urchristlichen Literatur.* Munich: Kaiser, 1975. **Dunkerley, R.** "The Five Johns." *LQHR* 30 (1961) 292–98. **Eckhardt, K. A.** *Der Tod des Johannes als Schlüssel zum Verständnis der Johanneischen Schriften.* Berlin: de Gruyter, 1961. **Frey, J.** "Erwägungen zum Verhältnis der Johannesapokalypse zu den übrigen Schriften des Corpus Johanneum." In *Die johanneische Frage: Ein Lösungsversuch*, ed. M. Hengel. Tübingen: Mohr-Siebeck, 1993. 326–49. **Gunther, J. J.** "The Elder John, Author of Revelation." *JSNT* 11 (1981) 3–20. **Heitmüller, W.** "Zur Johannes-Tradition." *ZNW* 15 (1914) 189–209. **Helmbold, A.** "A Note on the Authorship of the Apocalypse." *NTS* 8 (1961–62) 77–79. **Hengel, M.** *The Johannine Question.* Tr. J. Bowden. London: SCM; Philadelphia: Trinity, 1989. **Hort, F. J. A.** *The Apocalypse of St John I–III.* London: Macmillan, 1908. **Körtner, U. H. J.** *Papias von Hierapolis: Ein Beitrag zur Geschichte des frühen Christentums.* Göttingen: Vandenhoeck & Ruprecht, 1983. **Kürzinger, J.** *Papias von Hierapolis und die Evangelien des Neuen Testaments.* Regensburg: Pustet, 1983. **Lightfoot, J. B.** "The Later School of St John." In *Essays on the Work Entitled Supernatural Religion.* London; New York: Macmillan, 1889. 217–50. **Maier, G.** *Die Johannesoffenbarung und die Kirche.* WUNT 25. Tübingen: Mohr-Siebeck, 1981. **Osborne, E. F.** *Justin Martyr.* Tübingen: Mohr-Siebeck, 1973. **Preisker, H.** "Das Evangelium des Johannes als erster Teil eines apokalyptischen Doppelwerkes." *TBl* 15 (1936) 185–92. **Sanders, J. N.** "St John on Patmos." *NTS* 9 (1962–63) 75–85. **Schnelle, U.** "Die johanneische Schule." In *Bilanz und Perspektiven gegenwärtiger Auslegung des Neuen Testaments.* FS G. Strecker, ed. F. W. Horn. BZNW 75. Berlin; New York: de Gruyter, 1995. 198–217. **Schüssler Fiorenza, E.** "Apokalypsis and Propheteia: The Book of Revelation in the Context of Early Christian Prophecy." In *L'Apocalypse*, ed. J. Lambrecht. 105–28. ―――. "The Quest for the Johannine School: The Apocalypse and the Fourth Gospel." *NTS* 23 (1976–77) 402–27. **Smalley, S. S.** "John's Revelation and John's Community." *BJRL* 69 (1987) 549–71. ―――. *Thunder and Love: John's Revelation and John's Community.* Milton

Keynes: Word, 1994. **Stonehouse, N. B.** *The Apocalypse in the Ancient Church: A Study in the History of the New Testament Canon.* Goes: Oosterbaan & Le Cointre, 1929. **Strecker, G.** "Die Anfänge der johanneischen Schule." *NTS* 32 (1986) 31–47. ———. "Chiliasmus und Doketismus in der johanneischen Schule." *KD* 38 (1992) 30–46. ———. *Die Johannesbriefe.* Göttingen: Vandenhoeck & Ruprecht, 1989. **Taeger, J.-W.** *Johannesapokalypse und johanneischer Kreis: Versuch einer traditionsgeschichtlichen Ortbestimmung am Paradigma der Lebenswasser-Thematik.* BZNW 51. Berlin; New York: de Gruyter, 1989. **Trevett, C.** "The Other Letters to the Churches of Asia: Apocalypse and Ignatius of Antioch." *JSNT* 37 (1989) 117–35. **Vanni, U.** "L'Apocalypse johannique: État de la question." In *L'Apocalypse,* ed. J. Lambrecht. 21–46. **Weizäcker, C.** *Das apostolische Zeitalter der christlichen Kirche: Die Apokalypse.* 2nd ed. Freiburg, 1890. **Westcott, B. F.** *A General Survey of the History of the Canon of the New Testament.* 6th ed. Grand Rapids, MI: Baker, 1980.

## I. INTRODUCTION

The problem of the authorship of various biblical writings has been a traditional focus in introductions to the Old and New Testaments, as well as in the introductory chapters of biblical commentaries. More recently, however, the issue of authorship has become a less pressing matter for several reasons: (1) Many biblical books, in both the OT and the NT, are *anonymous* (e.g., all four of the canonical Gospels were originally anonymous; the later addition of titles reflects the views and educated guesses of the mid-second century A.D.), and there is little hope of linking these compositions with known historical figures. The phenomenon of anonymity in ancient literature suggests that ancients, in contrast to moderns, had very different attitudes toward the literary task, involving less distance between the author and the community he or she represents than is the case in the modern West.

(2) The identification of the author of a biblical book, from the mid-second century on, has often been a task more theologically than historically motivated. In the early church there was a pronounced tendency to link early religious writings to apostles or those closely associated with them because of their authority as founders as well as because of their traditional link to the historical Jesus. Apostolicity eventually was used as a major criterion of authenticity and canonicity, usually for compositions already widely accepted as possessing an authority on a par with that of the OT. Critical scholarship from the eighteenth century on has been willing to bracket theological issues and to use historical criticism as a control for understanding and assessing the witness of the biblical text for the Christian church.

(3) Ancient authors exhibit various degrees of creativity, but the value that many biblical authors placed on earlier traditions, whether written or oral, was such that they might more appropriately be designated "author-editors" rather than simply "authors." The person who gave final form to Revelation, for example, should be considered such an "author-editor." (4) Many biblical writings have gone through so many stages of rewriting and revision (in the case of some OT books this process took centuries) that the concept of "authorship" is problematic, unless one refers to the last "author-editor" or, more speculatively, to earlier "author-editors" (e.g., "Matthew" was the author-editor of the first Gospel, who used an earlier writing now designated "Q," the so-called "Sayings Source," which was in turn shaped by an unknown author-editor). It is quite likely, for example, that sections of Revelation were shaped by earlier writers but finally incorporated into the book that we now possess by John, the final author-editor. In some instances, therefore, the use of

source criticism is a necessary part of the "authorship" issue. (5) Many books of the Bible, particularly in the NT, are pseudonymous; that is, they are written under the names of people more prominent and authoritative than the actual author. Pseudonymous authorship was such a widespread ancient literary phenomenon that it is not particularly helpful to label these productions as "forgeries" using modern moralistic categories. Since nearly all Jewish and Christian apocalypses were pseudonymous (with the possible exceptions of Revelation and the *Shepherd of Hermas*), it is not unthinkable that Revelation itself is pseudonymous. (6) From a historical perspective, even if the authorship of a specific biblical book can be determined, so little is known or can be known about such authors that little light is actually shed on the composition itself. That in itself, of course, is not a valid reason for avoiding the authorship issue.

(7) All biblical books, particularly those with an epistolary character, are written communications that link an author to an audience within the setting of a particular historical, social, and cultural context, so that all of these factors should be taken into consideration as a basis for interpreting the text. (8) Modern literary criticism, however, has made us aware that what we meet in a text is not the author himself or herself but rather the *implied* author, i.e., the author as he or she has chosen, consciously or unconsciously, to reveal himself or herself in the written text (Booth, *Fiction*, 74–75). (9) By the same token, the audience envisaged by the creator of a text is not the real audience but the *implied* audience, i.e., the audience as conceptualized in literary terms by the author. This insight is particularly important for interpreting Revelation, which does not fit in easily with what is known of Christianity in Asia Minor toward the end of the first century and beginning of the second century A.D. This may mean that the author of Revelation, perhaps like Ignatius of Antioch, projected his own conceptions upon his audiences.

## II. INTERNAL EVIDENCE

The author of Revelation tells us four times that his name is "John" (1:1, 4, 9; 22:8). This repetition of the author's name, together with the frequent use of first-person singular verb forms that regularly punctuate the vision narratives, serves to emphasize his role as a witness to the revelatory visions he narrates, a phenomenon with parallels in other Jewish apocalypses (Dan 7:2, 15; 8:1; 9:2; 10:2; 4 Ezra 2:33, 42; 3:1; *3 Apoc. Bar.* 1:1, 7; 4:1, 9; 5:1 [the name "Baruch" occurs even more frequently in the Slavonic version]). The repetition of the name of the ostensible author was doubtless part of a legitimation strategy in pseudonymous compositions, particularly apocalypses. Since Revelation is an apocalypse, it would be natural for a modern interpreter to assume that the name "John" is a pseudonym (Weizäcker, *Zeitalter,* 78; Becker, *BZ* 13 [1969] 101–2; Vanni, "L'Apocalypse," 28 n. 6; Strecker, *KD* 38 [1992] 33; Vielhauer and Strecker in Schneemelcher, *NTA* 2:586; Dunkerley, *LQHR* 30 [1961] 298). It is striking that the name "John" only appears in the framework of Revelation (1:1–3:21; 22:6–21) and not in the main part of the composition (4:1–22:5), a feature that may suggest that the first edition of Revelation was anonymous or, more likely, pseudonymous (see *Introduction*, Section 5: Source Criticism).

Apart from suggesting that the bearer is Jewish, the name "'John" reveals little, for the name "John" (Greek: Ἰωάννης), a grecized form of the Hebrew name יֹהָנָן

*yôḥānān,* "Yoḥanan," is a theophoric name meaning "Yahweh is [or 'has been'] gracious" (2 Kgs 25:3; 1 Chr 26:3; Ezra 10:6; Neh 6:18; 12:22; Jer 40:8) that was relatively common among ancient Jews (for details, see *Comment* on 1:1). The author also calls himself a "servant" of God (1:1), an OT title of honor, and a "brother" of those he addresses (1:9). That he did not further identify himself does not necessarily indicate that he was the only person of this name generally known to Christians in the Roman province of Asia. Revelation is framed as a letter, and the person who carried the letter would presumably make it clear to the recipients who the author was. There is insufficient internal evidence to suppose that this "John" either was or pretended to be John of Ephesus, the author of the Gospel and Letters of John (contra Zahn, *Introduction* 3:428). However, it does suggest that he was well known to the recipients of the book.

Whether or not the book is pseudonymous, there is strong evidence to suggest that the author was a Palestinian Jew: (1) The author has an impressive familiarity with the OT, to which he alludes more than a hundred times; many allusions indicate a knowledge of the Hebrew text of the OT (exclusively, according to Charles, 1:lxvi), while others suggest a familiarity with Greek versions of the OT as well. (2) The author writes using a type of the literary genre, apocalypse, that was at home in early Palestinian Judaism. No known examples of Jewish apocalypses originated in the eastern or western Diaspora, nor did the genre survive long in early Christianity once it had moved outside the boundaries of Palestine. (3) The author exhibits familiarity with the Jewish temple and cult in Jerusalem (8:3–4; 11:1–2, 19), and perhaps even with the pre-A.D. 70 topography of Jerusalem itself (see *Comment* on 11:8). (4) Several sections of Revelation focus either on Palestine (Harmageddon is named in 16:16) or on Jerusalem, either not named clearly (11:2, 8; 20:9) or named as the transformed heavenly city (3:12; 21:2, 10), and on the temple in Jerusalem (11:1–2). (5) The author writes in a distinctive type of Semitizing Greek that clearly suggests he is not a native Greek speaker but rather a native speaker of Aramaic and perhaps even Hebrew (Mussies, *Morphology,* 352–53). (6) This in turn reinforces the notion that the author was a Palestinian Jew, probably a refugee from Palestine in the aftermath of the first Jewish revolt of A.D. 66–73 (Charles, 1:xxxix). Following that revolt, many Jews fled Palestine (Jos. *Ant.* 20.256), some of whom attempted to export revolution to the Diaspora (*J. W.* 7.410–19). Many thousands of Jews were sold into slavery in various parts of the western Diaspora. Jewish Christians had earler been forced to leave Jerusalem for Judea and Samaria (Acts 8:1) and later were compelled to leave Palestine for the Diaspora (Acts 11:29).

### III. EXTERNAL EVIDENCE

Several known early Christian figures named "John" have been proposed as the author of Revelation, including (1) John the son of Zebedee, the brother of James, and a disciple of Jesus, (2) John the Elder, (3) Cerinthus, (4) John Mark, and (5) John the Baptist. The last two suggestions have convinced very few scholars, however, and will therefore not be considered in any detail. John Mark was suggested as a possible author of Revelation by Dionysius of Alexandria (Eusebius *Hist. eccl.* 7.25.15), only to be immediately dismissed, and John the Baptist has been seriously suggested only by Ford (28–46, 50–56). Dionysius of Alexandria was sure that the author's name was "John," since that claim is made in Rev 1:9; 22:7–8, but he was unsure which "John" this might be (Eusebius *Hist. eccl.* 7.25.11–14). He eliminated John the Apostle and John Mark and finally suggested that the author was one of the two Johns buried at Ephesus (Eusebius *Hist. eccl.* 7.25.12–16). Papias had earlier distinguished between John the Apostle and the Presbyter John (Eusebius *Hist. eccl.* 3.39.4), though some have denied that he really meant what he seems to say (Zahn, *Introduction* 2:452; Smalley, *Thunder,* 38). We shall briefly consider only the first three proposals listed above.

*1. John the Apostle.* The first clear testimony that the apostle John, the son of Zebedee, was the author of Revelation is found in Justin *Dial.* 81.4, who wrote ca. A.D. 155 (see Eusebius *Hist. eccl.* 4.18.8):

> And further, there was a certain man with us, whose name was John, one of the apostles of Christ, who prophesied, by a revelation that was made to him, that those who believe in our Christ would dwell a thousand years in Jerusalem; and that thereafter the general, and in short, the eternal resurrection and judgment of all men would likewise take place.

After the middle of the second century, this conviction was widely disseminated throughout the ancient church (Irenaeus *Adv. haer.* 4.20.11; Tertullian *Adv. Marc.* 3.14.3; 3.24.4; Clement of Alexandria *Quis Dives* 42; *Strom.* 6.106; *Paed.* 2.108, 119; Hippolytus *De antichristo* 36–42; Eusebius *Hist. eccl.* 3.18.1). Elsewhere Revelation is associated with "John," but he is not more closely identified (Irenaeus *Adv. haer.* 1.26.3; 4.14.2; 5.26.1). Eusebius also preserved the opinions of the elder Gaius and Dionysius bishop of Alexandria, both of whom doubted Revelation's apostolic origin (*Hist. eccl.* 7.25). Similarly, Tertullian reports that Marcion did not regard John as the author of the Apocalypse (*Adv. Marc.* 4.5). However, the author does not call himself an apostle and even refers to the Twelve Apostles as founder figures of the past (18:20; 21:14; cf. Eph 2:20), suggesting that he is not one of their number. No internal evidence (see above) suggests any connection between the author and an apostle of the same name. Further, John the Apostle was thought to be the author not only of Revelation but also of the Gospel and Letters of John (Irenaeus attributes the Gospel to John the disciple in *Adv. haer.* 3.1.1; 3.11.1; 3.16.5; he attributes 1 John to him in *Adv. haer.* 3.16.5, 8 and 2 John to him in *Adv. haer.* 1.16.3; 3.16.8; see Jerome *De vir. illustr.* 9).

Papias of Hierapolis (ca. A.D. 60–130) is a shadowy figure from the first quarter of the second century A.D. about whom little is known. He composed a work in five volumes called "Interpretations of the Sayings of the Lord" (Λογίων κυριακῶν ἐξηγήσεις), which survives in fragments. Thirteen fragments have been collected in Bihlmeyer (*Väter* 133–40), twenty-two fragments have been collected by Körtner (*Papias,* 43–71), and twenty-five fragments have been collected in Kürzinger (*Papias,* 89–138), including three from Armenian texts published by F. Siegert ("Unbeachtete Papiaszitzate bei armenischen Schriftstellern," *NTS* 27 [1981] 605–14). Papias is first mentioned ca. A.D. 180 by Irenaeus (*Adv. haer.* 5.33.4), who describes him as an "auditor of the apostle John" (Ἰωάννου μὲν ἀκουστής), a companion of Polycarp, and an "ancient man" (ἀρχαῖος ἀνήρ), i.e., a younger contemporary of John and a contemporary of Polycarp. A number of scholars think that Papias was acquainted with Revelation (Bousset [1906] 19–20; Maier, *Kirche,* 62 n. 243). Haenchen (*John* 1:10) even speculates without any firm basis that Papias "probably believed that John the son of Zebedee was the author of the Apocalypse."

Revelation is the only book in the NT to which Justin specifically refers (*Dial.* 81.4). Written ca. A.D. 155, this reference also contains the earliest extant claim that the author was John the Apostle. There are a number of other allusions to Revelation in Justin (Osborne, *Justin Martyr,* 137): He refers (1) to the coming Messiah who has been "pierced" in Rev 1:7; see Zech 12:10; John 19:27 (*Dial.* 32.2; 64.7; 118.1), (2) to the aliases and punishment of Satan mentioned in Rev 20:2–3 (*1 Apol.* 28.1), (3) to the thousand years during which believers will live in Jerusalem in Rev 20:4 (*Dial.* 80.5; 81.4), (4) to the new heaven mentioned in Rev 21:1 (*Dial.* 131.6), and (5) to the destruction of death in Rev 21:4 (*Dial.* 45.5). In view of these allusions, it is striking that there is just one possible allusion to the Gospel of John (3:3, 5), in *1 Apol.* 61.4, though even this may actually be derived from a baptismal liturgy (Osborne, *Justin Martyr,* 137). Melito of Sardis (late second century A.D.) reportedly wrote a book entitled *On the the Devil and the Apocalypse of John* (Eusebius *Eccl. hist.* 4.26.2; Jerome *Vir. ill.* 24), of which only the title is known.

Among the Western witnesses to Revelation is the Letter of the Churches of Lyons and Vienne (*Ep. Lugd.*), preserved in Eusebius *Hist. eccl.* 5.1.3–5.3.3, written in A.D. 177 to the churches of Asia and Phrygia shortly after a persecution in Lyons (Musurillo, *Acts,* xx–xxii, 62–89). In *Ep. Lugd.* 58 we find this statement: "that the Scriptures might be fulfilled [ἵνα ἡ γραγὴ πληρωθῇ] 'Let the wicked be wicked and the righteous perform righteousness'" (a free quotation of Rev 22:11 in a variant attested in A 2030 fam 1611[2050] Oecumenius[2062txt] ; see *Notes* on 22:11).

Eusebius reports that Dionysius of Alexandria (d. A.D. 264–65) wrote a treatise in two books entitled *On the Promises,* in which he attempted to refute Nepos, a deceased Egyptian bishop who had written a work entitled *Refutation of the Allegorists,* i.e., an attack against people like Dionysius who, Nepos thought, did not interpret the OT promises literally enough (*Hist. eccl.* 7.24). Since Nepos appealed to the Revelation of John to justify his views, Dionysius devoted the second book of *On the Promises* to a discussion of Revelation (*Hist. eccl.* 3.28.3; 7.24.3). Dionysius does not reject Revelation as incomprehensible, or ascribe it to Cerinthus as some earlier authors had, but suggests that its apparent obscurity suggests a deeper and more profound meaning (Eusebius *Hist. eccl.* 7.25.1–5). Thus Dionysius suggests that Revelation, no less than the OT, must be interpreted allegorically. Dionysius accepts the fact that the author's name was John but argues largely on the basis of language and style that it could not be the same person who wrote the Gospel and Letters of John (*Hist. eccl.* 7.25.6–8). There were many beside John the Apostle named "John," he argues (*Hist. eccl.* 7.25.12–16). While Dionysius finds common language and themes in the Gospel and 1 John, he finds little in common between those Johannine writings and Revelation (*Hist. eccl.* 7.25.22):

> But the Apocalypse is completely different from, and alien to, these books [the Gospel and Letters of John]. It has no connection or affinity with them in any way; it hardly has, so to say, even a syllable in common with them.

A number of scholars have found it more plausible to argue that John the Apostle was the author of Revelation rather than of the Fourth Gospel (Beasley-Murray, 33; Barrett, *John,* 62, 133–34; Brown, *John* 1:cii). Bernard (*John* 1:lxiv–lxviii) proposed that John the Apostle wrote Revelation and that the Presbyter (who wrote 2 and 3 John and belonged to the outer circle of Jesus' disciples) was his disciple, and it was he who wrote the Gospel and Letters. Helmbold (*NTS* 8 [1961–62] 77–79) suggests that the statement found in Rev 1:19 ("Now write what you have seen, what is, and what is to happen after this") is cited in *Ap. John* (2.1.16–17; 4.3.10–12) and that, since the author is said to be John the brother of James and the son of Zebedee, this constitutes an early (ca. A.D. 150) link between Revelation and John the Apostle. Unfortunately, the widespread use of the past-present-future prophetic formula makes it difficult to prove that *Ap. John* is in fact dependent on Rev 1:19. While there are still a number of conservative scholars who would like to attribute Revelation to John the son of Zebedee (Mounce, 31; Smalley, *Thunder,* 37–40), there appears to be little actual evidence that can be adduced in support of this traditional view.

2. *John the Elder.* Knowledge of the figure of John the Elder, as distinct from John ben Zebedee the disciple and apostle, is based on a statement in Eusebius (*Hist. eccl.* 3.29.2–4), attributed to Papias of Hierapolis, writing ca. A.D. 120:

> And if anyone chanced to come who had actually been a follower of the elders, I would enquire as to the discourses of the elders, what Andrew or what Peter said, or what Philip, or what Thomas or James, or what John or Matthew or any other of the Lord's disciples [said]; and the things which Aristion and John the elder, disciples of the Lord, say.

Eusebius understood this statement to refers to *two* Johns, John the disciple and John the elder, and regarded the first as the author of the Gospel and the second as the author of Revelation (Eusebius *Hist. eccl.* 7.25.12–16), while some dispute the existence of John the Elder, ascribing him to a misreading of the text of Papias by Eusebius and many subsequent scholars (Zahn, *Introduction* 2:452; Smalley, *Thunder,* 38). Hengel (*Johannine Question,* 127) suggests that John the Elder might have written Revelation in A.D. 68–70 and that it was then reworked by his pupils following his death late in the first century. Or, he asks, was it in fact a pseudepigraphic work by a student (*Johannine Question,* 127)?

3. *Cerinthus.* The Alogoi in Asia Minor opposed the Montanists during the second half of the second century A.D. and rejected both the authority and the authenticity of the Fourth Gospel and Revelation, attributing the latter to Cerinthus (Epiphanius *Haer.* 51.3–6). Gaius (late second to early third century), a Roman presbyter who was the contemporary of Zephyrinus (198–217) the bishop of Rome, wrote a dialogue against the Montanist Proclus, of which just a few fragments are preserved in quotations found in Eusebius (*Hist. eccl.* 2.25.5–7; 3.28.1–2; 3.31.4; 6.20.3). Gaius apparently thought that Revelation was really written by Cerinthus, who in turn pretended that it was written by an apostle (Eusebius *Hist. eccl.* 3.28.2). Gaius was opposed by Hippolytus, though what relationship Gaius may have had with the Alogoi, if any, is unknown (Eusebius *Hist. eccl.* 3.28.1–2). Westcott (*Canon,* 278) correctly considered this "a mere arbitrary hypothesis," since some ancient Christians regarded the theology of Revelation as false, and for this reason they could not consider the book to be apostolic. Though Cerinthus is often designated a "Gnostic," this label reveals very little since he was also a millennarian, and it was this that made him a candidate for the authorship of Revelation.

## IV. THE SOCIAL IDENTITY OF "JOHN"

Although the author does not explicitly designate himself a prophet, his description of the book he is writing as a "prophecy" (1:3) and a "prophetic book"

(22:7, 10, 18, 19) clearly carries that implication. Further, the commission with which the book begins in 1:9–20 and the second commission in 10:1–11, which is modeled primarily after part of the narrative of call of Ezekiel in Ezek 2:8–3:3, are functionally analogous to the prophetic call narratives in OT prophetic books and early Jewish apocalypses (Jer 1:4–10; Isa 6:1–13; Ezek 1:1–3:11; Isa 40:1–11; see *1 Enoch* 14:8–25). In Rev 10:11 the author is enjoined to "prophesy again against many peoples and nations and languages and kings." He comes closest to identifying himself as a prophet in the words he attributes to the revelatory angel in 22:9, "I am your fellow servant, and of your brothers the prophets." John, it appears, is one of a number of prophets who may have constituted a prophetic circle or guild. This is confirmed in 22:16, where John associates himself with a group whose task is the communication of revelation to the churches (Schüssler Fiorenza, "Apocalypsis," 120–21; Aune, *BR* 26 [1981] 19; id., *JSNT* 37 [1989] 103–16): "I Jesus sent my angel to testify these things to you [ὑμῖν] for the churches." John refers several times to "prophets" as an identifiable group (22:6, 9), sometimes mentioned along with such other apparently distinct groups as "saints" and "apostles" (11:18; 16:6; 18:20, 24; 22:6). The primary reference is probably to *Christian* prophets, though some of these passages could conceivably include OT prophets as well, since John probably did not distinguish between the two. John is arguably a member of a prophetic guild, perhaps functioning as a master prophet. It is possible that the public reading of Revelation explicitly intended by the author (1:3; 22:18) was intended to replace a public address to the communities by a local prophet (see Minear, *New Earth*, 5; Aune, *Prophecy*, 274).

Prophetic guilds led by master prophets are religious phenomena found in both ancient Israel and early Christianity. There is considerable evidence in the OT for the existence of prophetic schools (called "sons of the prophets"), which sometimes practiced group prophecy and were led by master prophets given the title "father" (Aune, *Prophecy*, 83). Elisha led one such school (1 Kgs 20:35; 2 Kgs 2:3, 5, 7, 15; 4:1–38). Even classical prophets such as Isaiah had disciples (Isa 8:16–18), who were probably responsible for writing down, collecting, and editing the masters' oracles into the complex and layered books that bear their names. The odist of the *Odes of Solomon* may represent a group of inspired singers, perhaps as their leader, who constituted a distinct group within the community (see *Odes Sol.* 7:16b–20; Aune, *NTS* 28 [1982] 448–49).

## V. THE PROBLEM OF THE JOHANNINE CONNECTION

The *Corpus Johanneum* consists of five NT compositions that are attributed to John (generally understood by the ancient church to be John the Apostle, the son of Zebedee): the Gospel of John, 1, 2, and 3 John, and the Revelation of John. Critical scholars have long agreed that the linguistic and theological differences between the Gospel of John and Revelation are so striking that the same author could not have written both works (Lohse, 4–7; Kraft, 9–11). Further, many critical scholars doubt that John the son of Zebedee is the author of *any* of the compositions in the *Corpus Johanneum*, though some connect him with earlier stages of the composition of the Gospel and the Letters (Smalley, *Thunder*, 16). There are four typical approaches to the problem of the authorship of the *Corpus Johanneum*: (1) The apostle John was the author of the Fourth Gospel but not the author of

Revelation. (2) The apostle John was the author of Revelation but not of the Fourth Gospel. (3) The apostle John wrote both Revelation and the Fourth Gospel but wrote the first nearly a generation before the second. (4) The apostle John was an emigrant from Palestine to Ephesus, where different pupils wrote the Apocalypse, the Epistles of John, and the Gospel of John (Barrett, *John*, 113). Revelation has often been connected with Johannine tradition through the hypothesis of a Johannine "circle" or "school," though there is little internal evidence to support that supposition.

By the end of the nineteenth century, there was nearly unanimous agreement among critical scholars that the author of Revelation and the author of the Gospel of John could not be the same person. At the same time, the five compositions of the *Corpus Johanneum* were widely thought to have originated within a common group, perhaps constituted by disciples of John the Apostle (Culpepper, *School*, 1–5). Nevertheless, the connection between Revelation and the rest of the *Corpus Johanneum* was maintained by proposing that it was written in whole or in part by one or more students of the Fourth Evangelist. Evidence for the existence of a Johannine school or Johannine circle was based in part on the view held by a number of scholars that despite the linguistic and conceptual similarities between the Fourth Gospel and 1 John, they were not written by the same person (Brown, *Epistles*, 19–30). Further, many scholars both ancient and modern have doubted the common authorship of all three Johannine letters (Brown, *Epistles*, 14–19). The real question is whether it is meaningful to link Revelation in any significant way with the so-called Johannine school (Culpepper, *Johannine School*, 263). The most detailed discussion of this issue is that of Frey ("Erwägungen," 326–429), whose careful consideration of a wide range of evidence leads him to see tentative links between the Johannine Gospel and Letters, on the one hand, and Revelation, on the other, at the level of the final editing of Revelation. He even flirts with the notion that Revelation is pseudonymous (425–26). It is valid to ask whether there is any connection between the *Corpus Johanneum* and Revelation apart from the use of the name "John," which was original with Revelation but was secondarily added to the titles of the Gospel and Letters of John (the connection is doubted by Strecker, *KD* 38 [1992] 31). Even those who link Revelation with the Johannine school think that it is peripheral to that school (Hengel, *Johannine Question*, 126–27; Schnelle, "Schule," 200–201). What Weizäcker considered the close relationship between the Gospel of John and Revelation led him to propose that both originated within the Johannine school, though neither was written by the apostle John himself (*Zeitalter*, 502–5). Charles (1:xxix) regarded Revelation as the product of the Johannine school: "the two writers [of John and Revelation] were related to each other, either as master and pupil, or as pupils of the same master, or as members of the same school." Dibelius regarded John of Ephesus as the founder of the Johannine circle and the author of Revelation (*Geschichte*, 76). According to Caird (4), "it is certain that they all came from the same geographical, cultural, and theological setting, if not from the one hand." Beasley-Murray (36) favors the view that the authors of John and Revelation were both disciples of John the son of Zebedee.

If the Gospel of John and Revelation were written at very nearly the same time, i.e., the last decade of the first century A.D., then the linguistic and theological differences suggest either that there is no literary or traditional relationship between the two works or that both works are dependent on earlier traditions, perhaps stemming from a Johannine circle, that were developed in distinctive ways (Böcher, *NTS* 27 [1981] 318–19). However, if the two compositions originated with members of the "Johannine school," it makes sense to regard Revelation as the earlier of the two, with the Fourth Gospel representing considerable modifications, particularly in the area of eschatology (Hadorn, 225). Thus Hadorn (221) dates Revelation ca. A.D. 70, while he places the Fourth Gospel ca. A.D. 92 or 93.

## VI. SUMMARY

While the final author-editor of Revelation was named "John," it is not possible to identify him with any other early Christian figures of the same name, including John the son of Zebedee or the shadowy figure of John the Elder. The otherwise unknown author of Revelation in its final form was probably a Palestinian Jew who had emigrated to the Roman province of Asia, perhaps in connection with the first Jewish revolt in A.D. 66–70. He regarded himself as a Christian prophet and his composition as a prophetic book, and he was well acquainted with the Christian congregations in Roman Asia to which he addressed the final version of his book. Though Revelation has been linked with the other Johannine writings in the NT, there are in fact very few features that suggest that this author was part of the Johannine community in any meaningful sense.

## Section 2: Date

### Bibliography

**Arnold, C. F.** *Die neronische Christenverfolgung.* Leipzig, 1888. **Barnard, L. W.** "Clement of Rome and the Persecution of Domitian." *NTS* 10 (1963–64) 251–60. **Barnes, T. D.** "Legislation against the Christians." *JRS* 58 (1968) 32. **Bell, A. J.** "The Date of John's Apocalypse: The Evidence of Some Roman Historians Reconsidered." *NTS* 25 (1978) 93–102. **Benko, S.** "The History of the Roman Empire." In *The Catacombs and the Colosseum: The Roman Empire as the Setting of Primitive Christianity,* ed. S. Benko and J. J. O'Rourke. Valley Forge, PA: Judson, 1971. 37–80. **Bishop, J.** *Nero: The Man and the Legend.* London: Hale, 1964. **Borleffs, J. W. P.** "Institutum Neronianum." *VC* 6 (1952) 129–45. **Chase, S. H.** "The Date of the Apocalypse: The Evidence of Irenaeus." *JTS* 8 (1907) 431. **Culpepper, R. A.** *John, the Son of Zebedee: The Life of a Legend.* Columbia: University of South Carolina, 1994. **Dibelius, M.** "Rom und die Christen im ersten Jahrhundert." In *Botschaft und Geschichte: Gesammelte Aufsätze.* Tübingen: Mohr-Siebeck, 1956. 2:177–228. **Eckhardt, K. A.** *Der Tod des Johannes als Schlüssel zum Verständnis der Johanneischen Schriften.* Berlin: de Gruyter, 1961. **Ely, F. H.** "The Date of the Apocalypse: The Evidence of Irenaeus." *JTS* 8 (1907) 431–35. **Freudenberger, R.** *Das Verhalten der römischen Behörden gegen die Christen im 2. Jahrhundert.* Munich: Beck, 1967. **Gentry, K. L.** *Before Jerusalem Fell: Dating the Book of Revelation.* Tyler, TX: Institute for Christian Economics, 1989. **Hardy, E. G.** *Christianity and the Roman Government.* London: Allen & Unwin, 1925. **Hort, F. J. A.** *The Apocalypse of John I–III.* London: Macmillan, 1908. **Hunzinger, C.-H.** "Babylon als Deckname für Rom und die Datierung des 1 Petrusbriefes." In *Gottes Wort und Gottes Land,* ed. H. G. Reventlow. Göttingen: Vandenhoeck & Ruprecht, 1965. 67–77. **Jones, B.** *Domitian and the Senatorial Order.* Philadelphia: American Philosophical Society, 1979. ———. "Domitian's Attitude to the Senate." *AJP* 94 (1973) 79–91. ———. *The Emperor Domitian.* London; New York: Routledge, 1992. **Keresztes, P.** *Imperial Rome and the Christians.* Vol. 1. Lanham, NY; London: University Press of America, 1989. ———. "The Jews, the Christians, and Emperor Domitian." *VC* 27 (1973) 1–28. **Klauck, H.-J.** "Das Sendschreiben nach Pergamon und der Kaiserkult in der Johannesoffenbarung." *Bib* 73 (1992) 153–82. **Krauss, S.** "Die Schonung von Öl und Wein in der Apokalypse." *ZNW* 10 (1909) 81–89. **Krodel, G.** "Persecution and Toleration of Christianity until Hadrian." In *The Catacombs and the Colosseum: The Roman Empire as the Setting of Primitive Christianity*, ed. S. Benko and J. J. O'Rourke. Valley Forge, PA: Judson, 1971. 255–67. **Kuhn, K. G.** "Βαβυλών." *TDNT* 1:514–17. **Levick, B.** "Domitian and the Provinces." *Latomus* 41 (1982) 50–73. **Lightfoot, J. B.** *Biblical Essays.* London; New York: Macmillan, 1893. ———. *Essays on the Work Entitled Supernatural Religion.* London; New York: Macmillan, 1889. **McDermott, W. C.**, and **Orentzel, A.** "Silius Italicus and Domitian." *AJP* 98 (1977) 23–34. **Milburn, R. L.** "The Persecution of Domitian." *CQR* 139 (1944–45) 154–64. **Millar, F.** "The Imperial Cult and the Persecutions." In *Le culte des souverains dans l'Empire Romain*, ed. W. den Boer. Geneva: Vandoeuvres, 1972. 145–75. **Newmann, B. C.** "The Fallacy of the Domitian Hypothesis." *NTS* 10 (1963–64) 133–39. **Pleket, H.** "Domitian, the Senate and the Provinces." *Mnemosyne* 7 (1961) 296–315. **Prigent, P.** "Au Temps de l'Apocalypse: I. Domitien." *RHPR* 54 (1974) 455–83. **Robinson, J. A. T.** *Redating the New Testament.* Philadelphia: Westminster, 1976. **Rogers, R.** "A Group of Domitianic Treason Trials." *CP* 55 (1960) 19–23. **Rordorf, W.** "Die neronische Christenverfolgung im Spiegel der apokryphen Paulusakten." *NTS* 28 (1982) 365–74. **St. Croix, G. E. M.** "Why Were the Early Christians Persecuted?" In *Studies in Ancient Society*, ed. M. I. Finley. London: Routledge and Kegan Paul, 1974. 210–49. **Scott, K.** "Statius' Admiration of Domitian." *TAPA* 54 (1933) 247–59. **Smallwood, E. M.** "Domitian's Attitude toward the Jews and Judaism." *CP* 51 (1956) 1–13. **Stolt, J.** "Om dateringen af Apokalypsen." *DTT* 40 (1977) 202–7. **Szelest, H.** "Domitian and Martial." *Eos* 62 (1974) 105–14. **Thompson, L. L.** *The Book of Revelation: Apocalypse and Empire.* New York: Oxford UP, 1990. ———. "Domitian and the Jewish Tax." *Historia* 31 (1982) 329–42. ———. "*Domitianus Dominus:* A Gloss on Statius *Silvae* 1.6.82." *AJP* 105 (1984) 469–75. **Ulrichsen, J. H.** "Die sieben Häupter und die zehn Hörner: Zur Datierung der Offenbarung des Johannes." *ST* 39 (1985) 1–20. **Vessey, D.** "Pliny, Martial, and Silius Italicus." *Hermes* 102 (1974) 109–16. **Waters, K.** "The Character of Domitian." *Phoenix* 18 (1964) 49–77. ———. "Traianus Domitiani Continuator." *AJP* 90 (1969) 385–405. **Wilson, J. C.** "The Problem of the Domitianic Date of Revelation." *NTS* 39 (1993) 587–605. **Yarbro Collins, A.** *Crisis and Catharsis: The Power of the Apocalypse.* Philadelphia: Westminster, 1984. ———. "Dating the Apocalypse of John." *BR* 26 (1981) 33–45. ———. "Myth and History in the Book of Revelation: The Problem of Its Date." In *Traditions in Transformation: Turning Points in Biblical Faith*, ed. B. Halpern and J. D. Levenson. Winona Lake, IN: Eisenbrauns, 1981. 377–403.

## I. INTRODUCTION

There are two different major opinions concerning the date when Revelation was written. From the late second century A.D. until the nineteenth century, and again (after the interval of a century of criticism) in the twentieth century, the prevailing opinion has been that Revelation was written toward the end of the reign of the Roman emperor Domitian (A.D. 81–96), i.e., ca. A.D. 95 (a summary of the research representing these two views is presented in Robinson, *Redating*, 224–25; Wilson, *NTS* 39 [1993] 587–97). During much of the nineteenth century, however, the prevailing view held that Revelation was written between A.D. 64 (in response to the Neronian persecution) and A.D. 70, i.e., the destruction of Jerusalem (Lightfoot, *Essays*, 132; id., *Biblical Essays*, 52; Hort, x). The critical tide turned toward the beginning of the twentieth century, when major commentators again began to date Revelation toward the end of the reign of Domitian (Swete, xcix–cvi; Beckwith, 197–208; Charles, 1:xci–xcvii). During the last half of the twentieth century, most scholars concerned with the question expressed support for the Domitianic date (Böcher, 41; id., *NTS* 27 [1981] 318; Yarbro Collins,

*Crisis,* 54–83; id., *BR* 26 [1981] 33–45; Müller, 40–42; Roloff, 16–19; Koester, *Introduction* 2:250–51; Hemer, *Letters,* 2–5), while a minority still argue for the earlier date (Eckhardt, *Johannes,* 71; Stolt, *DTT* 40 [1977] 202–7; Bell, *NTS* 25 [1978] 93–102; Wilson, *NTS* 39 [1993] 597–605; Rowland, 17).

The position taken in this commentary is that *both* views contain aspects of the correct solution, since it appears that while the final edition of Revelation was completed toward the end of the reign of Domitian (or, more likely, during the early part of the reign of Trajan), the first edition of the book was composed as much as a generation earlier based on written and oral apocalyptic traditions that reach back into the decade of the A.D. 60s, if not somewhat earlier.

Though most ancient Christian authors, apparently dependent on Irenaeus, thought that Revelation was written toward the end of the reign of Domitian, a few have suggested it was written earlier, during the reign of Claudius, Nero, or Galba, while others thought that it was written after the death of Domitian, during the reign of Trajan (the ancient evidence is summarized in Swete, xcix–c; Charles, 1:xci–xciii).

## II. External Evidence

1. Polycarp, writing to the Philippians before A.D. 155 (the year of his martyrdom), claims that when Paul wrote Philippians no Smyrneans had yet been evangelized (Pol. *Phil.* 5:3, *non autem nondum cognoveramus,* "we had not yet known him [i.e., the Lord]"). This bit of information, if true, suggests a *terminus a quo* for the composition of Revelation. Though the exact year when Paul's letter to the Philippians was written and the place where it was written cannot be determined with any confidence, if Paul wrote from prison in Ephesus, the date would range from 53 to 55, and if he wrote from prison in Caesarea, the date would range from 56 to 58 (Kümmel, *Introduction,* 332). This means that the congregation in Smyrna, first mentioned in Rev 1:11; 2:8, could have been founded no earlier than ca. A.D. 52–55 (Hemer, *Letters,* 66), and perhaps as late as A.D. 60–64 (Charles, 1:xciv). It is possible that during Paul's two-year stay at Ephesus (Acts 19:10), the Christian community at Smyrna was founded (cf. Acts 19:26), though it must be admitted that nothing concrete is known about the founding of the Christian community at Smyrna.

2. Revelation was written before or near the time of the second Jewish revolt led by Bar Kosiba (A.D. 132–35), since Justin Martyr, who places the setting for his extended discussion with Trypho the Jew shortly after the revolt of Bar Kosiba (*Dial.* 1.3; 9.3), also explicitly mentions that John wrote Revelation at some undetermined point in the past (*Dial.* 81.4).

3. The view that Revelation was written toward the end of the reign of Domitian was expressed by the Christian heresiologist Irenaeus, writing about A.D. 180 (*Adv. haer.* 5.30.3, the Greek version of which is preserved in two different passages in Eusebius *Hist. eccl.* 3.18.3; 5.30.3):

εἰ δὲ ἔδει ἀναφανδὸν ἐν τῷ νῦν καιρῷ κηρύττεσθαι τοὔνομα αὐτου, δι' ἐκείνου ἂν ἐρρέθη τοῦ καὶ τὴν ἀποκάλυψιν ἑορακότος. οὐδὲ γὰρ πρὸ πολλοῦ χρόνου ἑωράθη, ἀλλὰ σχεδὸν ἐπὶ τῆς ἡμετέρας γενεᾶς, πρὸς τῷ τέλει τῆς Δομετιανοῦ ἀρχῆς.

But if it had been necessary to announce his name plainly at the present time, it would have been spoken by him who saw the apocalypse. For [he or it] was not seen long ago but almost in our own time, at the end of the reign of Domitian.

Wettstein (*Novum Testamentum Graecum* 2:746) suggested that ἐρρέθη, "it was spoken," should be emended to ἐγράφη, "it was written." Another critical issue here is to determine the logical subject of ἐωράθη, which could be "it" and refer to τὴν ἀποκάλυψιν, "the Apocalypse," or "he" and refer to τοῦ καὶ τὴν ἀποκάλυψιν ἑορακότος, "the one who also saw the Apocalypse," i.e., John of Patmos. Stolt (*DTT* 40 [1977] 202–7; following Wettstein, *Novum Testamentum Graecum* 2:746) has argued that "the one who saw the Apocalypse" is the logical subject of ἐωράθη and has proposed that what Irenaeus had in mind was to comment on *how long* the author of Revelation had lived, not on *when* he had written Revelation. This is in fact a view argued by various scholars since Wettstein (Chase, *JTS* 8 [1907] 31–32; G. Edmundson, *The Church in Rome in the First Century* [1913] 164–65). Stolt thinks that the book itself was written much earlier, i.e., during the reign of Claudius, A.D. 37–54. Stolt's argument (accepted by Karrer, *Brief*, 18 n. 6) assumes that the Latin translation of Irenaeus *Adv. haer.* 5.30.3 is corrupt (the Latin text reads [Harvey, *Haereses* 2:410]: *si oporteret manifeste praesenti tempore praeconari nomen ejus, per ipsum utique dictum fuisset qui et apocalypsim viderat: neque enim ante multum temporis visum est, sed pene sub nostro saeculo ad finem Domitiani imperii*). Here *visum est* cannot refer to the person (but rather to the *nomen* of the Antichrist), and if the Apocalypse itself was meant, it should have been *visa est*. Further, the passive verb ἐωράθη, "he/she/ it was seen," does not appear to be the most appropriate way to describe the length of a person's life; it is much more likely that ἐωράθη means "it [i.e., 'the Apocalypse'] was seen," referring to the time when the Apocalypse was "seen" by John of Patmos (Robinson, *Redating*, 221). A second problem is whether Irenaeus made this statement based on some firm tradition or he was expressing his own opinion. One argument for construing his comment as based on a fixed tradition is that in two other places he claims that John the Apostle lived to the time of Domitian's successor Trajan, A.D. 98–117 (*Adv. haer.* 2.22.5; 3.3.4; both passages are quoted in Eusebius *Hist. eccl.* 3.23.3–4), in disagreement with what he says in *Adv. haer.* 5.30.3. There is also the issue that some traditions that Irenaeus confidently claims originated with John very probably did not (cf. *Adv. haer.* 5.33.3, where the fabulous fruitfulness of the eschatological era is described; see Aune, "Oral Tradition," 80–83). Eusebius expresses the view that Revelation was written in the fourteenth year of Domitian, i.e., in A.D. 95 (*Chronicon, PG* XIX.551–52).

The opinion of Irenaeus was widely accepted in the ancient church (Origen *Hom. in Matt.* 16.6; Victorinus *Comm. in Apoc.* 10.11; 17.10; Ps.-Augustine *Quaest. Vetus et Novum Test.* 76.2; Jerome *De virr. illustr.* 9). Clement of Alexandria relates a story that he claims has been transmitted by oral tradition and that refers to the departure of John the Apostle from the Island of Patmos after the death of "the tyrant" (*Quis div. salv.* 42; also preserved in Eusebius *Hist. eccl.* 3.23.5–19). While Clement neglects to specify which tyrant he has in mind, Eusebius understands the tyrant to be Domitian. If the tyrant was Domitian, John's departure from Patmos must have occurred after A.D. 96, the year when Domitian was murdered (Suetonius *Dom.* 18). The same tradition is found in Eusebius (*Hist. eccl.* 3.20.8–9), where he mentions that, upon the death of Domitian, his decrees were annulled by the senate and those who had their property confiscated and were banished were restored; the apostle John was one of these, and he took up residence in Ephesus. Similarly in the *Chronicle*, Eusebius lists the following events for the fourteenth year of Domitian: "Persecution of Christians and under him the apostle John is banished to Patmos and sees his Apocalypse, as Irenaeus mentions."

4. Epiphanius of Salamis (ca. 315–403) placed the exile and return of John during the reign of Claudius, A.D. 41–54 (*Haer.* 51.13.33; *PG* XLI.909–10, 949–50). John's exile to Patmos is set during the reign of Nero in the title of two Syriac versions of Revelation. Similarly, Theophylact, the bishop of Achrida during the eleventh century A.D., also places John's exile during the reign of Nero in the preface to his commentary on the Gospel of John (*PG* CXXIII.1133–34).

5. Irenaeus preserves the tradition that John the Apostle, widely regarded in the ancient church as the author of Revelation, lived until the reign of Trajan, A.D. 98–117 (*Adv. haer.* 2.22.5; 3.3.4; both passages are quoted in Eusebius *Hist. eccl.* 3.23.3–4). This could suggest that Revelation was completed as late as the reign of Trajan.

## III. INTERNAL EVIDENCE

Since most ancient apocalypses were written pseudonymously, their authors rarely reveal the specific circumstances in response to which they wrote. Two of the earliest Christian apocalypses, Revelation and Hermas, are probably exceptions to this rule, for they do not appear to be pseudonymous and their authors do not seem to conceal the purposes for which they were writing. In Rev 22:10, in fact, the author reverses a literary device used in Daniel (see *Comment* on 22:10): "Do not seal up the words of the prophecy of this book for the time is near." The visions incorporated into Revelation, on the contrary, are intended to be read by Christians contemporaneous with the author, and it is clear that the proclamations to the seven churches in Rev 2–3 reveal a relatively close acquaintance with the specific circumstances of each of the Christian communities addressed (Hemer, *Letters;* Court, *Myth and History,* 20–42).

1. References to the temple and Jerusalem in Rev 11 have often been used to support a date for the composition of Revelation before A.D. 70 (see the discussion in Yarbro Collins, *Crisis,* 64–69). Rev 11:1–2 appears to presuppose that the temple in Jerusalem is still standing and that while the court outside the temple will be occupied by the Gentiles for forty-two months, the temple precinct itself will remain inviolable:

> I was given a reed, like a staff, with these instructions: "Go and measure the temple of God including the sanctuary and count those who worship within it. But exclude the courtyard outside the temple and do not measure it, for the Gentiles will be permitted to keep the holy city under subjection for forty-two months."

While this appears to reflect the existence of the Herodian temple and can be taken to reflect the situation that existed just prior to the fall of Jerusalem and the temple in A.D. 70 (Robinson, *Redating,* 238–42; Wilson, *NTS* 39 [1993] 604–5), it has also been construed as a spiritualized reinterpretation of a prophetic or apocalyptic fragment that originated before the end of the second Jewish revolt in A.D. 66–70 (the view of Wellhausen [*Analyse*] and others; see *Form/Structure/Setting* under 11:1–14). Rev 11:8 appears to refer to a street or square in Jerusalem that could only have existed until A.D. 70; this passage appears to reflect the author's knowledge of pre-A.D. 70 topography in Jerusalem. The destruction of Jerusalem in Rev 11:13 is caused by a great earthquake in which seven thousand people died, one tenth of the population. Since this is not how the historical Jerusalem actually fell in A.D. 70, it has been argued that this text originated before A.D. 70 (Robinson, *Redating*, 239–40). If these three passages are interpreted literally, they suggest that Revelation was written before A.D. 70, when both Jerusalem and the temple were destroyed by the Romans under Titus.

2. The name "Babylon," which occurs six times in Revelation (14:6; 16:19; 17:4; 18:2, 10, 21), is clearly a symbol for Rome. "Babylon" is also used as a symbol for Rome in Jewish apocalyptic literature, but in every case the apocalypses that used this symbol were written *after* A.D. 70 (4 Ezra 3:1–2; 28–31; *2 Apoc. Bar.* 10:1–3; 11:1; 67:7; *Sib. Or.* 5.143, 159). Babylon is an appropriate symbol for Rome because, just as Babylon captured Jerusalem and destroyed the temple in 587 B.C. (2 Kgs 25), so Rome captured and destroyed Jerusalem and the temple in A.D. 70. The use of "Babylon" as a symbol for Rome points to a date after A.D. 70 (Yarbro Collins, *BR* 26 [1981] 35).

3. In Rev 13 there are three references to a mortal wound suffered by the Beast that was nevertheless healed. In Rev 13:3 it is said that one of the seven heads of the Beast from the Sea appeared fatally wounded, but the Beast was healed (see *Comment* on 13:3). According to Rev 13:12, the Beast had a mortal wound but was healed, while in Rev 13:14 it is said that the Beast was wounded by the sword but lived. None of these references states that the Beast, or one of its seven heads, died as a result of the wound, or that the wound was self-inflicted (the historical Nero committed suicide). There is wide agreement among scholars that these are references to Nero, who committed suicide on 9 June 68; however, there were later rumors that he returned from the dead or that he did not actually die (see *Comment* on 13:3). It is not likely that the Nero *redivivus* or Nero *redux* myth was widely circulated until the end of the first century A.D. (Beckwith, 207).

4. Rev 17:9b–11 is a text that many scholars have used to solve the problem of the date of Revelation:

> The seven heads are seven mountains upon which the woman is seated. They are also seven kings, five of whom have fallen, one is living, the other has not yet come. When he comes he can remain for only a short while. The Beast which was and is not, he is the eighth and is one of the seven and is headed for destruction.

While this text seems relatively clear, scholars have interpreted it in a bewildering number of ways (for surveys see Beckwith, 704–8; Yarbro Collins, *Crisis,* 58–64). Following the assumption that Rev 17:9b–11 refers to Roman history, it is logical to assume that if one begins to calculate the seven kings or emperors beginning with Julius Caesar (see *Excursus 17B: Alternate Ways of Counting the Roman Emperors*) and *includes* the three short-term emperors who reigned briefly in A.D. 68–69, then Galba (October 68 to 15 January 69) would be the "other," i.e., the seventh emperor who would appropriately be said to reign "for only a short time." However, if one begins counting with Julius Caesar but *excludes* the three emperors who reigned briefly in A.D. 68–69 (as many scholars do), then Claudius would be the fifth emperor and Nero (13 October 54 to 9 June 68) the sixth emperor, the "one [who] is living" (Wilson, *NTS* 39 [1993] 599), and Vespasian (1 July 69 to 23 June 79) would be the "other," the seventh emperor who will reign "for only a short while" (though in fact Vespasian ruled for eleven years). On the other hand, if one begins with Augustus as the first of the kings who have fallen. and if one includes the three emperors who reigned briefly during the tumultuous years A.D. 68–69, then the fifth emperor would be Nero, the "one [who] is living" would be Galba, and the "other" who will reign "for only a short while" would be Otho (5 January 69 to 16 April 69). However, if the three emperors of A.D. 68–69 are excluded, Nero would be the fifth emperor, the "one [who] is living" would be Vespasian, and the "other" who will reign "for only a short while" would be Titus (23 June 79 to 13 September 81), who was apparently known to be in ill health (Plutarch *De tuenda san. praec.* 123d). Since the phrase "one is living" seems to refer to the emperor whose reign was contemporaneous with the composition of Rev 17:9–11, the main options are Nero or Galba (Weiss-Heitmüller, 302; Beckwith, 704; Bishop, *Nero*, 173; Wilson, *NTS* 39 [1993] 605), while the questionable procedure of omitting the three so-called interregnum emperors would point to either Vespasian (A.D. 69–79) or Titus (A.D. 79–81).

There is wide agreement among scholars that the Beast who is identified as the eighth king who "is one of the seven" (17:11) is Nero *redivivus* (Lohse, 95), but it is not immediately evident which (if any) of the seven should be identified with Nero. Yarbro Collins argued that the reference in Rev 13:3 to the fact that one of the seven heads of the Beast from the Sea had a mortal wound must refer to Nero, and that therefore one of the seven heads that are kings in Rev 17 must also refer to Nero, while the eighth king referred to in Rev 17:11 must refer to Nero returned from the dead (*BR* 26 [1981] 35–36; *Crisis*, 59).

Although each of the four ways of calculating the seven emperors just discussed places the composition of Revelation from 54 (the beginning of the reign of Nero) to 79 (the end of the reign of Vespasian), there have been several ways in which scholars convinced of a Domitianic date for Revelation have used Rev 17:9–11 as evidence for a late first-century date, sometimes working back from Domitian to ensure that the calculation ends up with the appropriate emperor: (a) The author used an earlier source reflected in Rev 17:9–11 (from the reigns of the emperors Nero through Vespasian) and updated it (Meyer, *Christentum* 3:525–26 n. 4; Roloff [ET] 199; this option is also considered by Lohse, 95). (b) The author used Rev 17:9–11 as a *vaticinium ex eventu*, i.e., a means of antedating his book, written during the late first century, to an earlier period (Wikenhauser, 131). (c) The author used the source reflected in Rev 17:9–11 but did not update it (Bousset [1906] 478–80; Charles, 2:69). (d) The author began to count emperors with Gaius Caligula, who ruled A.D. 37–54 (Strobel, "Abfassung," 437–45; Lohse, 95; Prigent, 261; Ulrichsen, *ST* 39 [1985] 1–20), the first emperor after the crucifixion and resurrection of Jesus Christ, so that Otho would be the fifth emperor, and Vitellius (2 January 69 to 21 or 22 December 69) would be the sixth emperor, who is the "one [who] is living," while the "one who is coming" would be Vespasian. Or, if we discount the three emperors of A.D. 68–69, Titus would be the fifth emperor, while Domitian would be the sixth emperor, the "one [who] is living ," while Nerva would be the one to reign for a short while. (e) What seems to have become the most popular view in the late twentieth century is that the seven emperors do not refer to literal emperors at all but rather symbolize a complete (but perhaps unknown) number of rulers, since the beast with *seven* horns is a traditional image that fortuitously corresponds to the Roman tradition of *seven* kings preceding the foundation of the Republic in 509 B.C. (Beckwith, 704–8; Kiddle-Ross, 350–51; Lohmeyer, 143; Beasley-Murray, 256–57;

Caird, 218–19; Lohse, 95; Guthrie, *Introduction,* 959; Mounce, 315; Sweet, 257; Harrington, 172; Giblin, 164–65; Bauckham, *Climax,* 406–7). (f) A very different interpretation, which goes back at least to Andreas of Caesarea, is the view that the seven kings represent successive kingdoms. Andreas proposed the following list of kingdoms, each of which he associated with an individual king (*Comm. in Apoc.* 17.9; Schmid, *Studien* 1:186–88): [1] Assyria (Ninus), [2] Media (Arbakus), [3] Babylon or Chaldea (Nebuchadnezzar), [4] Persia (Cyrus), [5] Macedonia (Alexander), [6] the old Roman empire (Romulus), [7] the new Roman empire (Constantine), followed by [8] the kingdom of the Antichrist. Variations on this scheme have been proposed by modern commentators (Zahn, *Introduction* 3:441–42; Alford, 4:710–11; Hendricksen, 204; Ladd, 229).

5. The historical situation of the seven churches in Roman Asia reflected in Rev 2–3 has provided a variety of arguments for the Domitianic date of Revelation (Guthrie, *Introduction,* 954–56; Hemer, *Letters,* 2–5). (a) Some have argued that the deteriorated condition of the seven churches in Roman Asia suggests a date later rather than earlier in the first century (Beckwith, 207), though this obviously depends on the standard of behavior against which these Christian congregations are measured. (b) Rev 3:17 ("For you say, 'I am rich . . . and need nothing'") has been linked to Laodicea's rebuilding after the earthquake during the reign of Nero (ca. A.D. 60–61) without accepting imperial assistance (Ramsay, *Letters,* 428). The wealth of the Laodicean congregation, if taken literally, would more likely have occurred toward the end of the first century rather than during the reign of Nero (or shortly thereafter). However, both lines of argument are capable of a variety of interpretations, so that a firm date late in the first century A.D. cannot be based on these arguments.

6. Rev 6:6 has been connected to an edict issued by Domitian in A.D. 92 restricting provincial viticulture (Suetonius *Dom.* 7.2; 14.2; see the detailed discussion in the *Comment* on 6:6). This edict ordered half the vineyards in the provinces to be destroyed and prohibited the planting of new vineyards in Italy. The opposition to this edict in Roman Asia was so violent that the edict was rescinded before its provisions could be enacted. Rostovtzeff (*History* 1:201) regarded the vine edict as an imperial attempt to encourage the production of wheat during a severe famine that occurred during the reign of Domitian. According to Suetonius, this occurred "on the occasion of a plentiful wine crop coinciding with a scarcity of grain" (*Dom.* 7.2). While many NT scholars have used this allusion to argue that Revelation was written ca. A.D. 93 (Bousset [1906] 135; Hemer, *Letters,* 158), others have argued that the famine conditions may reflect other times and places. Krauss (*ZNW* 10 [1909] 83–89), for example, reads Rev 6:6 against the background of the end of the second Jewish revolt in A.D. 70.

7. The phenonenon of emperor worship is presupposed in those passages in Revelation where the worship of the Beast is emphasized, particularly where those who worship the Beast are branded with his name on their right hand or forehead (13:4, 15–16; 14:9–11; 15:2; 16:2; 19:20; 20:4). That such a procedure is unknown from any other historical sources suggests that the author has blended tradition with reality. Even though the emperor cult had its beginnings with Julius Caesar and was developed in the provinces during the reign of Augustus, a number of scholars have argued that the demands of the imperial cult were particularly strong during the reign of Domitian, proving an appropriate setting for the dating of

Revelation toward the end of the first century A.D. (Swete, civ–cv; Charles, 1:xciv; Beckwith, 201). The significance of the imperial cult in the persecution of Christians, however, has frequently been overemphasized. The main concern of the emperors and their representatives was that people should sacrifice to the cults of the gods, while the deified emperors were often tangential or subordinate to these cults, and distinctions were normally made between the gods and the deified emperors (S. R. F. Price, *Rituals and Power: The Roman Imperial Cult in Asia Minor* [Cambridge: Cambridge UP, 1984] 221–22; see *Excursus 13E: The Roman Imperial Cult in Asia Minor*).

8. In describing the twelve foundations of the New Jerusalem, the author says that on them were inscribed "the twelve names of the twelve apostles of the Lamb" (21:14). This passage is often referred to in discussions of the authorship of Revelation, for here the twelve apostles are referred to as figures of the past, revered founders of the church, suggesting that the author could not have been one of their number. Rev 21:14 may also shed light on the *date* of Revelation. It is not usually recognized that the phrase οἱ δώδεκα ἀπόστολοι, "the twelve apostles," is a rare phrase in the NT, occurring elsewhere only in Matt 10:2 in a closely parallel phrase (τῶν δὲ δώδωκα ἀποστόλων τὰ ὀνόματα, "the names of the twelve apostles"). Elsewhere in the NT οἱ δώδεκα ἀπόστολοι occurs only as *variae lectiones* in Luke 9:1; 22:14 (the parallel phrase οἱ δώδεκα μαθηταί occurs in Matt 10:1; 11:1, and as *variae lectiones* in Matt 20:17; 26:20). While it is true that Luke is the first author to systematically restrict the title ἀπόστολος to the twelve disciples, J.-A. Bühner is incorrect when he claims that the expression "the twelve apostles" occurs in Luke-Acts (*EDNT* 1:144). The phrase οἱ δώδεκα ἀπόστολοι also occurs in both the short and long titles of the *Didache* (short title: Διδαχὴ τῶν δώδεκα ἀποστόλων, "Teaching of the Twelve Apostles"; long title: Διδαχὴ κυρίου διὰ τῶν δώδεκα ἀποστόλων τοῖς ἔθνεσιν, "Teaching of the Lord through the Twelve Apostles to the Nations"), though this was probably added at a relatively late date, i.e., the mid-second century or later. The phrase οἱ δώδεκα ἀπόστολοι is not attested earlier than ca. A.D. 80–95, for there is consensus that this is the most likely period within which the Gospel of Matthew was written (Kümmel, *Introduction*, 119–20; Davies-Allison, *Matthew* 1:127–38). The phrase οἱ δώδεκα, "the Twelve," was a technical term that originated before Easter (cf. 1 Cor 15:5) and is used with some frequency in the synoptic Gospels (T. Holtz, *EDNT* 1:363), while οἱ ἀπόστολοι, "the apostles," originated later, since the adjectival use of δώδεκα in the phrase οἱ δώδεκα ἀπόστολοι means the *twelve* apostles, not other apostles (here δώδεκα points to the existing technical phrase οἱ δώδεκα). Since the earliest attestation of the phrase οἱ δώδεκα ἀπόστολοι, "the twelve apostles," is not earlier than A.D. 80, the use of the same phrase in Rev 21:14 suggests a date later rather than earlier in the first century.

9. Until very recently the internal evidence of a situation of repression and persecution of Christians by Roman authorities was combined with the external evidence for a persecution of Christians by Domitian to place the composition of Revelation in a very specific historical and temporal setting, i.e., the end of Domitian's reign, ca. A.D. 95. Therefore, we shall begin with a discussion of the evidence for the persecution of Christians during the reign of Domitian, whether official or unofficial, and then consider the character of Domitian and his reign.

While there is some information in Rev 2–3 about the persecution of Christians in Asia Minor, it is striking that the persecutors mentioned are neither pagans nor representative of the Roman government, but Jews (2:9–10; cf. 3:9). The church at Smyrna is warned that some of its members will be imprisoned, and they are urged to be faithful to death (2:10). While the reason for these imprisonments is not mentioned, the authorities responsible must either be municipal authorities in Roman Asia (i.e., Greek citizens of particular cities) or Roman administrative authorities. The author names a single martyr, Antipas of Pergamon, but it is unclear how he met his death or who was responsible for it (lynch law? official Roman trial and execution?). It appears, at any rate, that his death lies in the relatively distant past (2:13). Rev 2–3, then, does not reflect a persecution of Christians sponsored by Rome or Roman authorities, nor does it contain any allusions to the imperial cult (Charles, 1:44; Smalley, *Thunder,* 44). Klauck's attempt to find evidence of the imperial cult in the proclamation to Pergamon in Rev 2:12–17 is hardly convincing (*Bib* 73 [1992] 153–82). Charles used this negative finding to suggest that the proclamations of Rev 2–3 were written *earlier* than the rest of Revelation, during the reign of Vespasian, but were revised by John to make them suitable for incorporation into a work written during the reign of Domitian (Charles, 1:xciv–xcv, 43–45). The diametrically opposed position taken in this commentary is that Rev 2–3 was written *later* than the bulk of the book (see *Introduction,* Section 5: Source Criticism).

There is more evidence for the persecution of Christians in the rest of Revelation. There are a number of references to "blood" and "death," particularly regarding the execution or lynching of Christians: (a) Rev 6:9–11 describes the cry for vengeance of those "who had been slain for the word of the God and for the witness they had borne." This passage suggests that many had died as martyrs for their faith and that some time had elapsed since their deaths. This is very probably a reference to a persecution that occurred not in Asia Minor (a single martyr from this region, Antipas of Pergamon, is mentioned in Rev 2:13) but rather in Rome, allegorically represented by a whore "drunk with the blood of the saints and the blood of the martyrs of Jesus" (17:6), i.e., to the Neronian persecution in Rome (Zahn, *Introduction* 2:165–73; 2:409–10). (b) 12:11: "They conquered him through the blood of the Lamb and through the word of their testimony," a passage suggesting that conquest is an ironical metaphor for martyrdom. (c) 14:13: "Blessed are the dead who from now on die in the Lord." (d) 16:6: "because they have shed the blood of the saints and prophets, you have given them blood to drink." (e) 17:6: the Great Harlot is depicted as drunk "with the blood of the saints and the blood of the witnesses to Jesus." (f) 18:24: "And in you was found the blood of prophets and saints, and of all who have been slaughtered on earth." (g) The innumerable multitude in white robes depicted in Rev 7:9 consists of those who have come out of (i.e., died in) the great tribulation (7:14). (h) John tells his readers that he shares the tribulation and kingdom and patient endurance (1:9), obviously reflecting social and perhaps political pressure against Christians. (i) The two prophetic witnesses described in Rev 11:3–13 are killed by the Beast (11:7–8). (j) Rev 20:4 refers to those who had been beheaded for their testimony to Jesus and for the word of God. (k) The Beast from the Sea is allowed to make war on the saints and conquer them (13:7).

These and other passages in Revelation reflect either instances of Christian suffering that have occurred in the past or the prophetic expectation that such suffering will occur in the future, or perhaps a combination of the two. If the references cited above are taken to refer to past suffering, it is far from clear when or where this persecution occurred.

The persecution of Christians in Rome under Nero is reported in Tacitus *Annals* 15.38, 44 (cf. Suetonius *Nero* 16.2; curiously, the punishment of Christians is not mentioned in connection with the Great Fire in Suetonius *Nero* 38). In the aftermath of the great fire in Rome in July of A.D. 64, Nero (according to Tacitus) placed the blame on Christians. Many Christians who were arrested revealed the names of many more, with the result that there were hundreds of arrests. Christians were dressed in animal skins and torn to pieces by dogs, they were crucified, and at night crucified victims were set afire to light Nero's games. Strangely enough, though no other early Christian writer used this episode to further blacken the name of Nero, the veracity of Tacitus' account must be accepted (R. Martin, *Tacitus* [Berkeley; Los Angeles: University of California, 1981] 182–83; J. Beaujeu, "L'incendie de Rome en 64 et les Chrétiens," *Latomus* 19 [1960] 65–80, 219–311). According to the *Acts of Paul* 11.2 (Hennecke-Schneemelcher, *NTA* 2:384; Lipsius-Bonnet, *AAA* 1:110), "He [Nero] issued a decree [διάταγμα] to this effect, that all who were found to be Christians and soldiers of Christ should be put to death." However, in this text as well there is no attempt to relate this decree to the great fire. While the so-called *institutum Neronianum* is mentioned by Tertullian (*Ad nationes* 1.7; n.b. that he was familiar with the *Acts of Paul;* cf. *De bapt.* 17.4; Rordorf, *NTS* 28 [1982] 366–67), *there is no other mention of a formal condemnation of Christians by Nero in either Roman or Christian literature.* Sulpicius Severus (*Chr.* 2.29) does mention an edict of Nero that was the basis for the persecution of Christians. Peter and Paul were both reportedly executed under the reign of Nero (*Asc. Isa.* 4:2–3; Eusebius *Hist. eccl.* 2.4–5; 3.1); according to Epiphanius (*Pan.* 27.6.6), it occurred in Nero's twelfth year, i.e., A.D. 66. The earliest reference is *1 Clem.* 5, where the fact of their death but neither the date nor the circumstances are mentioned.

The most complete collection of the alleged evidence for the persecution of Christians under Domitian was collected by J. B. Lightfoot (*Apostolic Fathers* 1/1, 104–15) and accepted without much discussion by many commentators on Revelation (Swete, lxxxv; Ramsay, *Letters,* 91–92; Beckwith, 204; Charles, 1:xcv). Metzger even claims that "The first emperor who tried to compel Christians to participate in Caesar worship was Domitian" (*Code,* 16). Melito of Sardis, writing to the emperor Marcus Aurelius in the mid-second century A.D. (Eusebius *Hist. eccl.* 4.26.9 [LCL tr.]), claimed that

> The only emperors who were ever persuaded by malicious men to slander our teaching were Nero and Domitian, and from them arose the lie, and the unreasonable custom [ἀλόγῳ συνηθείᾳ] of falsely accusing Christians.

This apologetic strategy suggests that most emperors were basically good and just men who were able to withstand the bad advice of their advisors. This text does not claim that either Nero or Domitian actively persecuted Christians, even though they are said to have slandered Christian teaching. Similarly, in Philostratus *Vita Apoll.* 8.5, Apollonius condemns the advisers of Domitian for the problems involving the cities, the army, and the senate. The "unreasonable custom" of Melito appears to have been transformed into the *institutum Neronianum* of Tertullian (*Ad nat.* 1.7.8–9; *Apol.* 5.3–4), a legendary embellishment that transformed the sporadic and scattered persecution of Christians into the supposedly formal official policies of Nero and Domitian (Millar, *Emperor,* 555).

Evidence for a Domitianic persecution is also said to be found in various other Christian and Greco-Roman writers, including *1 Clem.* 1:1, Suetonius (*Dom.* 15), Dio Cassius (67.14), Hegesippus (Eusebius *Hist. eccl.* 3.19–20), Melito of Sardis (Eusebius *Hist. eccl.* 4.26.5–11), and Tertullian (*Apol.* 5.4). These texts actually provide evidence for *three* different kinds of repression attributed to Domitian: (a) his conflict with the Roman senatorial class, (b) his persecution of Jews (Dio Cassius 67.14; Eusebius *Hist. eccl.* 3.19–20), and (c) his persecution of Christians (Hegesippus in Eusebius *Hist. eccl.* 3.19; Tertullian *Apol.* 5.4). The latter two authors agree that, while Domitian began like Nero, he stopped his persecution of Christians and recalled those whom he had banished. The historical problem is whether Domitian himself actually rescinded orders banishing various people or they were rescinded by his successor Nerva.

There is some evidence to suggest that Domitian was hostile to Judaism. The Roman historian Cassius Dio (late second to early third century A.D.) mentions that Domitian executed his nephew, the consul Flavius Clemens, and banished his wife, Flavia Domitilla, on the charge of atheism because they (like many others) either converted to Judaism or were very close to doing so (67.13.1–3). Eusebius, however, considered Flavius Clemens and Flavia Domitilla to be Christians (*Hist. eccl.* 3.18.4), an example of how Domitian's persecution of Christians was intensified in retrospect (Millar, *Emperor,* 555).

We may conclude by expressing our agreement with the following judgment of Ste. Croix, a Roman social historian ("Early Christians," 211):

> We know of no persecution by the Roman government until 64, and there was no general persecution until that of Decius. Between 64 and 250 there were only isolated, local persecutions; and even if the total number of victims was quite considerable (as I think it probably was), most individual outbreaks must usually have been quite brief.

It is striking that Irenaeus, the first author to date the composition of Revelation to the reign of Domitian, failed to mention that Domitian persecuted Christians (Irenaeus *Adv. haer.* 5.30.3; Eusebius *Hist. eccl.* 3.18; see Newman, *NTS* 10 [1963–64] 138).

The Domitianic date for Revelation has often been justified by correlating the evidence for the persecution of Christians within the book with the view widely held among ancient authors, both pagan and Christian, that Domitian was a detestable autocrat and incompetent ruler whose principate was a reign of terror. Eusebius of Caesarea, for example, after describing the great cruelty of Domitian by having a "multitude" (πλῆθος) of prominent Romans executed without trial and by banishing and confiscating the property of "countless others" (μυρίους τε ἄλλους), claims that Domitian finally showed himself to be Nero's successor by persecuting the Christian church (*Hist. eccl.* 3.17).

Much of the Latin literary evidence that presented this image of Domitian was the product of a relatively tight circle of politician-writers associated with the senatorial aristocracy with which Domitian was frequently in conflict: Pliny the Younger (ca. A.D. 61–112), Tacitus (ca. A.D. 56–115), and Suetonius (ca. A.D. 69–125). The propagandistic views of this circle, and of later writers who accepted their party line (e.g., Flavius Philostratus, born ca. A.D. 170, and Dio Cassius, late second century to mid-third century A.D.), have been widely accepted (a list of the "standard" sources for Domitian and his reign is found in L. L. Thompson, *Revelation*, 97, and the image of Domitian they created is described on 97–101, summarized in what follows). Modern historians have often accepted as fact the distortions of these Roman historians of the imperial period (e.g., Benko, "History," 65–68). These writers tended to characterize the reign of Domitian as one of *saevitia*, "savageness, violence, ferocity" (Dio Cassius 67.1.1; 67.4.2; Pliny *Ep.* 1.12.6–8; 3.11.3; 7.27.14). Pliny describes Domitian's "reign of terror" September to December of A.D. 93 (Sherwin-White, *Letters*, 242) with these words (*Pan.* 90.5–7 [LCL tr.]):

> Both of us [Pliny and Cornutus Tertullus] had suffered from that robber [he confiscated property] and assassin of every honest man through the massacre of our friends, as the hot breath of his falling thunderbolt passed close by our heads.

Domitian was also characterized as power-hungry (Suetonius *Dom.* 1.3; Dio Cassius 65.2.3), a plotter against Titus (Tacitus *Hist.* 4.52; Suetonius *Titus* 9.3; *Dom.* 2.3; Dio Cassius 66.26.2), insane (Suetonius *Dom.* 3.1; Dio Cassius 65.9.4–5), tyrannical (Pliny *Ep.* 4.11.6; Suetonius *Dom.* 1.3; 12.3), dissimulating (Dio Cassius 67.2.6), a murderer (Pliny *Pan.* 48.3–5), a thief (Suetonius *Dom.* 12.1; Dio Cassius 67.4.5), and a sex fiend (Tacitus *Hist.* 4.2; 4.68; *Agricola* 7; Suetonius *Dom.* 22.1; Dio Cassius 67.6.3). During his reign as emperor, his military successes were pitiful and overblown (Dio Cassius 67.3.5), he had a system of informers (*delatores*) who brought false charges of treason against the opposition (Pliny *Pan.* 33.3–4; Tacitus *Agricola* 2–3), and his reign was an economic disaster (Suetonius *Dom.* 12.1).

The character of Domitian and his reign has been subject to reevaluation in recent years in the light of a careful consideration of epigraphical evidence. It has become clear that Tacitus, Pliny, and Suetonius, together with other writers involved in politics during the late first and early second century A.D., distorted nearly every aspect of Domitian's career and achievements (L. L. Thompson, *Revelation*, 101–9). For an assessment of Tacitus' character assassination of Domitian in the *Agricola, Germania,* and *Histories,* see R. Martin, *Tacitus* (Berkeley: University of California, 1981) 45–48, 55–56, 91–93. Other Latin writers, contemporaries of Domitian, present a much different image (Quintilian, Frontinus, Statius, Martial, and Silius Italicus). They emphasize Domitian's military successes (Quintilian *Inst.* 10.1.91; Silius Italicus *Pun.* 3.607) and his modesty (Martial 8.15, 78; Statius *Silvae* 3.3.171; 4.3.159). For a more objective characterization of Domitian and his reign, see L. L. Thompson, *Revelation*, 102–9.

Domitian's execution of a number of Roman senators was very probably motivated by the fact that in many cases these senators had conspired against him and were put on trial for treason (Roger, *CP* 55 [1960] 19–23; Pleket, *Mnemosyne* 7 [1961] 299). Domitian found himself in conflict with the senate, and apparently tried to bypass the senate as a governmental institution. Why did members of the senatorial class conspire against Domitian? There are several apparent reasons (Pleket, *Mnemosyne* 7 [1961] 299–303): (a) Several crises that arose toward the end of Domitian's reign encouraged him to take decisive and unilateral action. (b) Domitian lacked the tactfulness of some of his predecessors (Rostovtzeff, *History*

1:118–19). (c) He was dissatisfied with the way in which the senate ran the provinces, for he was concerned with the welfare of lower- as well as upper-class provincials (primarily validated by epigraphic evidence; cf. Pleket, *Mnemosyne* 7 [1961] 304–8, but cf. Levick, *Latomus* 4 [1982] 51–60, for a carefully qualified reassessment of these inscriptions). Domitian's attitude toward the provinces can be characterized by the assessment of Suetonius (*Dom.* 8.2 [LCL tr.]):

> He took such care to exercise restraint over the city officials and the governors of the provinces, that at no time were they more honest or just, whereas after his time we have seen many of them charged with all manner of offences.

This emphasis on Domitian's concern for justice is echoed in a few other authors, such as Statius (*Silvae* 5.2.91–92) and Frontinus (*Strat.* 2.11.7; cf. Levick, *Latomus* 4 [1982] 64). After Domitian's death, provincial governors began extorting money again, as evidence from Pliny reveals (Pleket, *Mnemosyne* 7 [1961] 301 n. 4). In the view of Levick (*Latomus* 4 [1982] 50),

> If the senate lost power during his [Domitian's] principate, that was to the advantage of the provincials, in particular of provincials of the humbler class, whose interests Domitian had at heart; indeed, it was concern for their welfare that helped bring him into conflict with the senate and with ruling circles in the cities.

Opposition to Domitian may well have been galvanized by the ideal of the Stoic and Cynic conception of kingship (summarized by Rostovtzeff, *History* 1:120; cf. Pleket, *Mnemosyne* 4 [1982] 311):

> The main points are these: the emperor is selected by divine providence and acts in full agreement with the supreme god; during life he is not himself a god; he regards his power, not as a personal privilege, but as a duty; his life is toil, not pleasure; he is the father and benefactor of his subjects, not their master; his subjects are free men, not slaves; his subjects just love him, and he must be both φιλοπολίτης and φιλοστρατιώτης; he must be πολεμικός, but also εἰρηνικός in the sense that nobody worth fighting is left; finally, he must be surrounded by friends (an allusion to the senate) who ought to have a share in the management of all the affairs of the state, being free and noble men.

## IV. Conclusions

The *external evidence* for the date of Revelation centers on the date proposed by Irenaeus (*Adv. haer.* 5.30.3; Eusebius *Hist. eccl.* 3.18.3; 5.30.3); i.e., Revelation was "seen" toward the end of the reign of Domitian (ca. A.D. 95), though there are some dissenting voices suggesting earlier and later dates. The *internal evidence* is mixed, and each of the nine points made above will now be summarized: (1) The references to Jerusalem and the temple in Revelation are ambiguous since they can be construed as referring to the pre-A.D. 70 period, though there is evidence in the text that these references were given an interpretive overlay that may have arisen years after the destruction of Jerusalem and the temple in A.D. 70. (2) The use of the name "Babylon" for Rome in Revelation seems to require a post-A.D. 70 date, with a date as late as A.D. 95 seeming not unreasonable. (3) The legend of Nero *redux* or *redivivus*, upon which the author-editor of Revelation seems to depend, is attested as early as A.D. 69, though a later date for the widespread currency of this legend seems required. (4) Rev 17:9c–11, with its reference to seven kings, understood literally, points to a date of composition during the short reign of Galba (A.D. 68) or Vespasian (A.D. 69–79), though if understood symbolically could be construed to point to any emperor subsequent to Nero. (5) The situation of the seven churches produces ambiguous evidence that could be dated from the early 70s to the late 90s A.D. (6) The vine edict of Domitian, which many scholars have seen reflected in Rev 6:6 and have used to date Revelation to A.D. 93, is not clearly reflected in that passage. (7) The phenomenon of emperor worship in the provinces began with Augustus and continued well after Trajan. The view that the imperial cult was particularly emphasized during the reign of Domitian is not confirmed by the evidence. (8) The use of the phrase "the twelve apostles" in Rev 21:14 is not attested before A.D. 80 and suggests a date in the late 80s or early 90s A.D. (9) Since there is no reason to suppose that a particularly strong opposition to Christianity was manifest during the reign of Domitian, there is therefore no reason to insist that the persecution experience apparently reflected in Revelation occurred during the reign of Domitian.

## Section 3: Genre

### Bibliography

Attridge, H. W. "Greek and Latin Apocalypses." *Semeia* 14 (1979) 159–86. Aune, D. E. "The Apocalypse of John and the Problem of Genre." *Semeia* 36 (1986) 65–96. Berger, K. "Apostelbrief und apostolische Rede: Zum Formular frühchristlicher Briefe." *ZNW* 65 (1974) 190–231. Betz, H. D. "On the Problem of the Religio-Historical Understanding of Apocalypticism." *JTC* 6 (1969) 134–56. ———. "The Problem of Apocalyptic Genre in Greek and Hellenistic Literature: The Case of the Oracle of Trophonius." In *Apocalypticism*, ed. D. Hellholm. 577–97. Blevins, J. L. "The Genre of Revelation." *RevExp* 77 (1980) 393–408. ———. *Revelation as Drama.* Nashville: Abingdon, 1984. ———. "The Revelation to John: Its Dramatic Structure and Message." *Int* 9 (1955) 436–53. Boring, M. E. "The Apocalypse as Christian Prophecy: A Discussion of the Issues Raised by the Book of Revelation for the Study of Early Christian Prophecy." In *Society of Biblical Literature 1974 Seminar Papers*, ed. G. MacRae. Cambridge, MA: Society of Biblical Literature, 1974. 2:43–62. Brewer, R. R. "The Influence of Greek Drama on the Apocalypse of John." *ATR* 18 (1936) 74–92. Carmignac, J. "Qu'est-ce que l'Apocalyptique? Son emploi à Qumran." *RevQ* 10 (1979) 3–33. Collins, J. J. *The Apocalyptic Imagination: An Introduction to the Jewish Matrix of Christianity.* New York: Crossroad, 1984. ———. "The Genre Apocalypse in Hellenistic Judaism." In *Apocalypticism*, ed. D. Hellholm. 531–48. ———. "Genre, Ideology and Social Movements in Jewish Apocalypticism." In *Mysteries and Revelations: Studies since the Uppsala Colloquium*, ed. J. J. Collins and J. H. Charlesworth. Sheffield: Sheffield Academic, 1991. 13–32. ———. "Introduction: Toward the Morphology of a Genre." *Semeia* 14 (1979) 1–20. ———. "The Jewish Apocalypses." *Semeia* 17 (1979) 21–49. ———. "Pseudonymity, Historical Reviews and the Genre of the Revelation of John." *CBQ* 39 (1977) 329–43. Dijkstra, M. "Prophecy by Letter (Jeremiah XXIX 24–32)." *VT* 33 (1983) 319–22. Doty, W. G. "The Concept of Genre in Literary Analysis." In *Society of Biblical Literature 1972 Proceedings*, ed. L. C. McGaughy. Missoula, MT: Scholars, 1972. 1:413–48. Glasson, T. F. "What Is Apocalyptic?" *NTS* 27 (1981) 98–105. Goodspeed, E. J. *New Solutions of New Testament Problems.* Chicago: University of Chicago, 1927. Grudem, W. *The Gift of Prophecy in 1 Corinthians.* Washington, DC: University Press of America, 1982. Hahn, F. "Die Sendschreiben der Johannesapokalypse: Ein Beitrag zur Bestimmung prophetischer Redeformen." In *Tradition und Glaube*, ed. G. Jeremias, H.-

W. Kuhn, and H. Stegemann. Göttingen: Vandenhoeck & Ruprecht, 1971. 357–94. **Hanson, J. S.** "Dreams and Visions in the Graeco-Roman World and Early Christianity." In *Aufstieg und Niedergang der römischen Welt*, ed. W. Haase. Berlin; New York: de Gruyter, 1980. II, 23/2: 1395–1427. **Hartman, L.** "Survey of the Problem of Apocalyptic Genre." In *Apocalypticism*, ed. D. Hellholm. 329–43. **Hellholm, D.** "The Problem of Apocalyptic Genre and the Apocalypse of John." *Semeia* 36 (1986) 13–64. ———. *Das Visionenbuch des Hermas als Apokalypse: Formgeschichtliche und texttheoretische Studien zu einer literarischen Gattung.* Lund: Gleerup, 1980. **Hill, D.** "Christian Prophets as Teachers or Instructors in the Church." In *Prophetic Vocation in the New Testament and Today*, ed. J. Panagopoulos. Leiden: Brill, 1977. 108–30. ———. *New Testament Prophecy.* Richmond: John Knox, 1979. ———. "Prophecy and Prophets in the Revelation of St. John." *NTS* 18 (1971–72) 401–18. **Himmelfarb, M.** "The Experience of the Visionary and Genre in the Ascension of Isaiah 6–11 and the Apocalypse of Paul." *Semeia* 36 (1986) 97–111. **Jones, B. W.** "More about the Apocalypse as Apocalyptic." *JBL* 87 (1968) 325–27. **Kallas, J.** "The Apocalypse—an Apocalyptic Book?" *JBL* 86 (1967) 69–80. **Karrer, M.** *Die Johannesoffenbarung als Brief: Studien zu ihrem literarischen, historischen und theologischen Ort.* Göttingen: Vandenhoeck & Ruprecht, 1986. **Koch, K.** *The Rediscovery of Apocalyptic.* Naperville, IL: Allenson, n.d. **Kuykendall, R. M.** *The Literary Genre of the Book of Revelation.* Ann Arbor: University Microfilms, 1986. **Ladd, G. E.** "The Revelation and Jewish Apocalyptic." *EvQ* 29 (1957) 94–100. **Loenertz, R. J.** *The Apocalypse of St. John.* London: Sheed and Ward, 1947. **Malina, B. J.** *On the Genre and Message of Revelation: Star Visions and Sky Journeys.* Peabody, MA: Hendrickson, 1995. **Mathewson, D.** "Revelation in Recent Genre Criticism: Some Implications for Interpretation." *Trinity Journal* 13 (1992) 193–213. **Mazzaferri, F. D.** *The Genre of the Book of Revelation from a Source-critical Perspective.* BZNW 54. Berlin; New York: de Gruyter, 1989. **Osiek, C.** "The Genre and Function of the Shepherd of Hermas." *Semeia* 36 (1986) 113–21. **Pardee, D.** *Handbook of Ancient Hebrew Letters.* Chico, CA: Scholars, 1982. **Riddle, D. W.** "From Apocalypse to Martyrology." *ATR* 9 (1927) 260–80. ———. *The Martyrs: A Study in Social Control.* Chicago: University of Chicago, 1931. **Sanders, E. P.** "The Genre of Palestinian Jewish Apocalypses." In *Apocalypticism*, ed. D. Hellholm. 447–59. **Schmidt, J. M.** *Die jüdische Apokalyptik: Die Geschichte ihrer Erforschung von den Anfängen bis zu den Textfunden von Qumran.* Neukirchen: Neukirchener, 1963. **Schüssler Fiorenza, E.** "Apokalypsis and Propheteia: The Book of Revelation in the Context of Early Christian Prophecy." In *L'Apocalypse*, ed. J. Lambrecht. 105–28. **Smith, J. Z.** "Wisdom and Apocalyptic." In *Religious Syncretism in Antiquity: Essays in Conversation with Geo Widengren*, ed. B. A. Pearson. Missoula, MT: Scholars, 1975. 131–56. **Smith, M.** "On the History of ΑΠΟΚΑΛΥΠΤΩ and ΑΠΟΚΑΛΥΨΙΣ." In *Apocalypticism*, ed. D. Hellholm. 9–20. **Soden, W. von.** "Verkündung des Gotteswillens durch prophetisches Wort in den altbabylonischen Briefen aus Mari." *WO* 1 (1947–52) 397–403. **Stone, M.** "Lists of Revealed Things in the Apocalyptic Literature." In *Magnalia Dei: The Mighty Acts of God.* FS G. E. Wright, ed. F. M. Cross, W. E. Lemke, and P. D. Miller, Jr. Garden City, NY: Doubleday, 1976. 414–52. ———. *Scriptures, Sects and Visions: A Profile of Judaism from Ezra to the Jewish Revolts.* Philadelphia: Fortress, 1980. **Vouga, F.** *Geschichte des frühen Christentums.* Tübingen; Basel: Franke, 1994. **Woude, A. S. van der.** "The Book of Nahum: A Letter Written in Exile." *OTS* 20 (1977) 108–26. **Yarbro Collins, A.** "The Early Christian Apocalypses." *Semeia* 14 (1979) 61–103.

## I. The Problem of Genre

Genre criticism is that aspect of comparative literature that attempts to understand a literary work in relation to other similar works, both diachronically and synchronically. A literary genre consists of a group of texts that exhibit a coherent and recurring pattern of features constituted by the interrelated elements of form, content, and function (Hellholm, *Semeia* 36 [1986] 13–17). Definitions of "genre" exhibit wide variations, because they are based largely on intuitive or phenomenological judgments that certain groups of texts have closer affinities with one another than texts that appear to belong to other groups. Doty ("Genre," 1:439–40) reveals the lack of specificity that has characterized discussions of genre:

> Generic definitions ought not be restricted to any one particular feature (such as form, content, etc.), but they ought to be widely enough constructed to allow one to conceive of a genre as a congeries of (a limited number of) factors. The cluster of traits charted may include: authorial intention, audience expectancy, formal units used, structure, use of sources, characterizations, sequential action, primary motifs, institutional setting, rhetorical patterns, and the like.

This list of possible generic features that could be incorporated into a definition of genre indicates that abstract definitions of genre applicable to all literary texts are not really very useful. Progress in genre definition depends on the extent to which particularly close groupings of affiliated texts are generically analyzed.

Revelation has been generically categorized in a variety of ways, the most common of which are as a *letter*, as a *prophetic book*, and as an *apocalypse*, and we shall consider each of these categories in turn.

## II. REVELATION AS A LETTER

Revelation clearly has a formal epistolary framework in 1:4–5 and 22:21 and contains separate proclamations, often labeled "letters," addressed to each of the seven churches of the Roman province of Asia (Rev 2:1–3:22). The Canon Muratori 57–59 recognized the epistolary character of Revelation, which is understood to mean that the seven individual churches to whom John wrote, when taken together, represent the universal Church: *Et Iohannes enim in Apocalypse, licit septem ecclesis scribat, tamen omnibus dicit,* "For John too, though he wrote to seven churches in the Apocalypse, nevertheless speaks to all." Here it is likely that the unknown author has in mind not only the seven "letters" of Rev 2–3 but primarily the address in 1:4 (Karrer, *Brief,* 20–21). Though the epistolary form of Revelation is occasionally mentioned in the ancient church (e.g., Dionysius of Corinth as quoted in Eusebius *Hist. eccl.* 7.25.9–10), recognition of that fact was accorded little or no interpretive significance.

Since almost any ancient literary form or genre could be bracketed with the opening and/or the closing formulaic features of the letter form (*Barnabas* is arguably an example of the former [Hvalvik, *Barnabas,* 72–75], Hebrews of the latter), the crucial issue is whether the epistolary features of Revelation constitute merely a superficial or secondary formal feature essentially external to the body of Revelation (a widespread view; e.g., Swete, xli; Yarbro Collins, *Semeia* 14 [1979] 70–71). Yet even if the epistolary frame of Revelation is readily detachable from the body of the composition, the function of the epistolary framework still requires discussion. It is quite possible, for example, that John placed Revelation within an epistolary guise to facilitate its reading within the setting of Christian worship (Vanni, *La struttura letteraria,* 114–15), a precedent already long established by the Pauline letters (cf. Col 4:16), as analyses of the liturgical design of their concluding sections have suggested.

The possibility should not be overlooked that Revelation might exhibit other, more substantive, generic features of the letter genre that have penetrated more deeply into the body of Revelation. F. Lücke (*Offenbarung*, 375–77) was one of the first to maintain that Revelation as a whole has an epistolary character, though this is subordinated through the inclusion of extensive sections with an apocalyptic character so that the epistolary and apocalyptic elements stand in mutual tension (cf. Karrer, *Brief,* 23–24). Charles also maintained that "the whole Book from 1.4 to its close is in fact an Epistle" (1:8), a claim frequently made but never adequately supported by an analysis of the text. Karrer has indeed attempted to rectify this situation by interpreting the epistolary character of the whole of Revelation. Despite the wide-ranging character of his analysis and interpretation of Revelation, his analysis is not successful. It is precisely the body of ancient letters, whether in Hebrew, Aramaic, Greek, or Latin, that has proven most resistant to analysis.

There are many examples from the ancient world of the use of letters to communicate divine revelation, i.e., oracles or prophecies (Aune, *Prophecy,* 72–73; references to prophetic letters in the ancient Near East, other than those discussed below, are found in Dijkstra, *VT* 33 [1983] 321 n. 2). With some justification, then, one can speak of "prophetic letters" or "oracular letters." The discovery of the royal archives of the ancient kingdom of Mari revealed cuneiform documents in Akkadian covering the period ca. 1800–1760 B.C.

> Some of these included cuneiform letters containing advice to king Zimri-Lin from the gods of Mari sent to him by "prophets" (H. B. Huffmon, "Prophecy in the Mari Letters," *BA* 31 [1968] 101–24; F. Ellermeier, *Prophetie in Mari und Israel* [Herzberg: Erwin Jungfer, 1968]; E. Noort, *Untersuchungen zum Gottesbescheid in Mari* [Neukirchen: Neukirchener, 1977]; for a bibliography and a selection of translations, see W. Beyerlin, *Near Eastern Religions Relating to the Old Testament,* tr. J. Bowden [Philadelphia: Westminster, 1978]).

> A collection of five texts written on ostraca with a similar function has survived from Hellenistic Egypt, ca. A.D. 168 (T. C. Skeat and E. G. Turner, "An Oracle of Hermes Trismegistos at Saqqara," *Journal of Egyptian Archaeology* 54 (1968) 199–208; the five texts were published the next year in *Sammelbuch griechischer Urkunden aus Ägypten* 10 [1969] 159–60, no. 10574; texts B and E are translated below). The five texts include rough and final drafts of a letter to the king. One of the rough drafts (text B) reads:

> Regarding the matters disclosed to me by the thrice-great god Hermes concerning oracles for the sovereign, I wish to announce that (the insurgent) Egyptians will quickly be defeated and that the king is to advance immediately to the Thebaid.

The final draft is formulated in epistolary form:

> To King Ptolemy and to King Ptolemy the Brother and to Queen Cleopatra the Sister, greetings. Horus the priest of Isis at the sanctuary of Sebenutos in the city of Isis wishes to make an announcement about certain oracles to the sovereigns, that (the insurgent) Egyptians will be defeated quickly and that the king is to advance immediately to the Thebaid.

Yet these ancient texts from Mari and Hellenistic Egypt provide evidence only that prophetic or oracular advice could be communicated in epistolary as well as oral form. There is no clear evidence that the epistolary format influenced the form and content of the message.

Two of the tractates in the *Corpus Hermeticum* (XIV and XVI) present themselves as written treatises, one sent by Hermes Trismegistus to an absent Asclepius (*Corp. Herm.* XIV) and the other sent by Asclepius to an absent King Ammon (*Corp. Herm.* XVI). Despite their quasi-epistolary function, these revelatory treatises contain no epistolary formulas either at the beginning or at the end. The claim that these revelatory treatises were written by Hermes and Asclepius, respectively, is simply a device to account for the written existence of these documents.

Prophetic letters are occasionally found in the OT and early Jewish literature (cf. Berger, *ZNW* 65 [1974] 212–19). 2 Chr 21:12–15 (cf. Jos. *Ant.* 9.99–101) contains a letter attributed to Elijah the prophet containing an announcement of judgment introduced with the traditional prophetic messenger formula "thus says the Lord." Most of these "prophetic" letters are associated with Jeremiah and his scribe Baruch (Jer 29:4–23[LXX: 36:4–23], 24–28[LXX: 36:24–28], 30–32[LXX 36:30–32]; Dijkstra argues that Jer 29:24–32 is a single letter; *2 Apoc. Bar.* 77:17–19; 78–87; Ep Jer [LXX]; *Par. Jer.* 6:15–7:4; 7:24–35). The letters in Jer 29, like the letter of Elijah in 2 Chr 21:12–15, are all prophetic oracles in epistolary form introduced with prophetic rather than epistolary formulas (Pardee, *Handbook,* 175–78, 181); unaccountably, Pardee omits consideration of Jer 29:30–32 in his otherwise complete discussion of Hebrew letter fragments in the OT. A. S. van der Woude (*OTS* 20 [1977] 108–26) has argued that the prophecy of Nahum in its original form was mediated by letter (the term סֵפֶר *sēper* in the superscription can mean "letter"). Elsewhere in early Jewish literature the association of divine revelation with epistolary form is found in *1 Enoch* 91–108, the so-called Epistle of Enoch. The Greek text of *1 Enoch* 100:6 refers to the entire composition as an Ἐπιστολὴ Ἐνώχ, "The Epistle of Enoch" (cf. Milik, *Enoch,* 47–57; though see Black, *Enoch,* 283, for appropriate qualifications). After discussing the phenomenon of the prophetic letter as a constituent form included in larger literary forms in the OT and early Jewish literature, K. Berger observes that "The letters of Revelation are therefore primarily to be regarded as exemplars of the *Gattung* of the prophetic letter which never died out completely" (Berger, *ZNW* 65 [1974] 214). Berger does not, however, suggest that this prophetic-letter tradition served as a literary model for the whole of Revelation. However, the great diversity in form and content exhibited in the "prophetic letters" ascribed to Elijah, Jeremiah, Baruch, and the more problematic Epistle of Enoch argue against the supposition of a unified prophetic-letter tradition or genre in early Judaism. His proposal, therefore, sheds no real light either on the "letters" in Rev 2–3 or on the total epistolary form of Revelation (Karrer, *Brief,* 49–59). Further, after examining the Hellenistic, Christian, and Gnostic texts that are in any way comparable to Revelation, Karrer concludes that while Revelation moves within the context of the epistolary form of communication and within the possibilities inherent in ancient apocalyptic and revelatory literature, it was directly influenced by none of these contemporary "parallel" literary phenomena (Karrer, *Brief,* 66).

Since the final compilation of Revelation was completed in the Roman province of Asia at the end of the first century A.D., the potential influence of Paulinism is a factor that must be considered. Karrer, who interprets the epistolary character of Revelation within the context of the Pauline epistolary tradition, argues that the epistolary prescript (1:4–5) and postscript (22:21) are dependent on Pauline models (*Brief,* 73–74), though John has modified these formulas in a distinctive way (for a contrary view, see *Comments* on 1:4–5; 22:21).

E. J. Goodspeed proposed that the collection of seven Pauline letters (Romans, Corinthians, Galatians, Philippians, Colossians, Thessalonians, and Philemon) with Ephesians as a pseudonymous "cover letter" provided a model for John's collection of seven letters introduced by a cover letter consisting of Rev 1:4–20 (*New Solutions*, 21–28). The influence of the ten Pauline letters, including Ephesians (to count them separately), is seen in the salutation in Rev 1:4 (*New Solutions*, 24–25). In fact, the composition of Revelation serves to establish the *terminus ad quem* for the collection of the Pauline corpus, ca. A.D. 90 (*New Solutions*, 87).

### III. REVELATION AS PROPHECY

The problem of the relationship between prophecy and apocalyptic is part of the larger complex issue of the degree of continuity or discontinuity thought to exist between apocalyptic and antecedent Israelite religious and literary traditions (see Aune, *Prophecy*, 112–14). In some respects, the dichotomy between prophecy and apocalyptic is a false one, since neither "prophecy" nor "apocalypse" designates a static type of literature; rather, each represents a spectrum of texts composed over centuries. The biblical material analogous to later apocalypses has been designated "proto-apocalyptic" (Stone, *Scriptures*, 46; see P. D. Hanson, *Dawn*, for an analysis of several "proto-apocalyptic" OT texts). Since many of the features of Jewish apocalyptic literature between 200 B.C. and A.D. 100 (see below under IV. Revelation as an Apocalypse) have demonstrable roots both in Israelite OT prophetic and in wisdom literature as well as in a variety of other mythic traditions from the ancient Near East, it is appropriate to see Jewish apocalypticism in the context of the syncretistic influences of the second temple period.

Within the context of an increased interest in early Christian prophecy in recent years (survey in Aune, *Prophecy*, 1–14), a number of scholars have argued for the prophetic character of Revelation, often using typologies that distinguish prophecy from apocalyptic (T. M. Crone, *Early Christian Prophecy: A Study of Its Origin and Function* [Baltimore: St. Mary's UP, 1973] 247–63; Boring, "Apocalypse," 43–62; Schüssler Fiorenza, "Apokalypsis and Propheteia," 105–28; Aune, *Prophecy*, 174–288). The prophetic character of the proclamations to the seven churches in Rev 2–3 has been particularly emphasized (Hahn, "Sendschreiben," 357–94; Müller, *Prophetie und Predigt*, 47–107; Aune, *Prophecy*, 275–79). While the author-editor never refers to himself directly as a prophet, he does describe his vision report as a prophetic book (Rev 1:3; 22:7, 10, 18, 19), and he does use the verb προφητεύειν in 10:11 to refer to his prophetic task: "Then I was told, 'You must again prophecy against peoples and nations and languages and many kings.'" Further, Rev 1:9–20 and 10:1–11 have frequently been considered prophetic call narratives (though this view is problematic), and there appear to be a number of oracles, presumably originating with the original author, that have been inserted at various points in Revelation (Aune, *Prophecy*, 279–88).

A detailed form-critical analysis of the seven proclamations of Rev 2–3 was carried out by Müller (*Prophetie und Predigt*, 47–107) in the context of a more comprehensive analysis of prophetic speech forms in the NT. Müller argues that the form of the proclamations is primarily determined by the structures of oral prophecy. Disregarding the steotyped framework of each proclamation, Müller focuses on the body of the proclamations and identifies two basic forms of prophetic speech, the parenetic sermon of repentance (*Bussparaklese*) and the sermon of salvation (*Heilspredigt*). The parenetic sermon of repentance is more characteristic of Rev 2–3, and Müller locates the basic form in 2:1–7: (1) accusation (v 4), (2) admonition (v 5a), and (3) conditional threat of judgment (v 5b). With many variations, Müller finds this form in 2:12–17, 18–29; 3:1–6, 14–22. The proclamation or sermon of salvation is found, according to Müller, in relatively pure form in 2:8–11, and in combination with the parenetic sermon of repentance in 3:1–6. In discussing the history of the basic form of the parenetic sermon of repentance, Müller traces it back to early Judaism, through John the Baptist (Matt 3:7–10; Luke 3:7–9), to the speech of admonition found in apocalyptic texts (e.g., *1 Enoch* 91:3–10; *Jub.* 7:20–29; 36:3–11).

A number of scholars have not only emphasized the prophetic vocation of the author of Revelation but have pushed this insight too far by insisting that John was not simply one early Christian prophet among others but a unique prophet with more in common with OT prophecy than with early Christian prophetic traditions (Friedrich, *TDNT* 6:849–50, 853; Hill, *NTS* 18 [1971–72] 406–11, 415–16; id., "Christian Prophets," 119–22; Grudem, *Prophecy*, 106–9). Vielhauers speaks vaguely of the author's "authentic prophetic consciousness" (Hennecke-Schneemelcher, *NTA* 2:607). This is frequently expressed in terms of the unparalleled authority assumed by the author (Friedrich, *TDNT* 6:849; Hill, *Prophecy*, 87–89) and the use he made of the OT (Hill, *NTS* 18 [1971–72] 401–18).

In an extensive monograph, Mazzaferri (*Genre*) has pushed this perspective even further by arguing that Revelation is not an apocalypse at all but belongs rather to the genre of OT prophetic writings. The author analyzes what he claims are the generic features of "classical prophecy" (*Genre*, 85–156) and of "classical apocalyptic" (*Genre*, 157–84) and concludes that generically Revelation belongs with the former rather than the latter. He analyzes the genre of classical prophecy under the rubrics of form, content, and function (summary in *Genre*, 154). *Form:* Classical prophecy includes the call (the divine confrontation), the introductory word, and the commission. Verbal revelation includes both threatening and benevolent oracles, while nonverbal proclamation involves action and sign language. *Content:* The content of classical prophecy includes call and vision reports, as well as threatening and benevolent oracles and theology. The oracles are conditional rather than deterministic, and the possibility of full restoration under a new covenant is held out for those addressed by the prophet. *Function:* Prophets are the spokespersons of Yahweh, delivering to them his conditional word, sometimes threatening, sometimes benevolent. Mazzaferri also analyzes the genre of "classical apocalyptic" in terms of form, content, and function (summary in *Genre*, 181–84): (1) *form:* pseudonymity and written form; (2) *content:* pseudo-prophecy, which sketches an eschatology with four complementary aspects: dualism, pessimism, determinism, and imminence; and (3) *function:* apocalypses that inform the audience of the imminence of the end and the deterministic purpose of God.

While Mazzaferri's emphasis on the conscious continuity between OT prophecy and Revelation has obvious merit because of the frequency with which the author alludes to prophetic texts, and sometimes even uses prophetic models in composing sections of his book, the generic descriptions of "classical prophecy" and "classical apocalyptic" are little more than caricatures of those texts (see the review by R. Morton, *CBQ* 53 [1991] 143–44).

## IV. REVELATION AS AN APOCALYPSE

### A. *Early Jewish Apocalypses*

The first ancient composition to be designated an "apocalypse" by its author was the book of Revelation, which begins with the phrase ἀποκάλυψις Ἰησοῦ Χριστοῦ, "the revelation of Jesus Christ" (1:1), later transformed into the title ἀποκάλυψις Ἰωάννου, "the Revelation of John" (see M. Smith, "History," 14, 19). Since 1822, when the term "apocalypse" was coined by the German scholar K. I. Nitzsch on the basis of Rev 1:1 (Schmidt, *Apokalyptik*, 98–99), it has been widely used as a generic designation for literary works that resemble the Revelation of John in both form and content. Most of the works that are considered Jewish apocalypses were written between 200 B.C. and A.D. 100. Daniel, particularly chaps. 7–12, usually considered the earliest apocalypse, is the only one included in the OT canon, though portions of other OT prophetic books contain proto-apocalyptic features and sections (Isa 24–27; 56–66; Ezek 38–39; Joel 3–4; Zech 9–14; see Hanson, *Apocalyptic*, 1–31). Other compositions widely regarded as apocalypses include *1 Enoch, 2 Enoch, 2 Baruch, 3 Baruch*, 4 Ezra, the *Apocalypse of Abraham*, the *Testament of Abraham*, and *T. Levi* 2–5 (Collins, *Apocalyptic*, 2–8; Koch, *Apocalyptic*, 18–23). *1 Enoch* is the longest and most complex of these apocalypses, for it is a composite of at least five apocalypses that were gradually assembled over the centuries: (1) *1 Enoch* 1–36, the "Book of the Watchers," perhaps the oldest part of the work, dating back to the early second century B.C.; (2) *1 Enoch* 37–71, the "Similitudes of Enoch," probably the latest part of the work, dating to the late first century A.D.; (3) *1 Enoch* 72–82, the "Book of Heavenly Luminaries"; (4) *1 Enoch* 83–90, the "Animal Apocalypse"; and (5) *1 Enoch* 91–105, the "Apocalypse of Weeks" (on the complexity of *1 Enoch*, see Nickelsburg, *Jewish Literature*, 46–55, 90–94, 145–51, 214–23; Collins, *Apocalyptic*, 33–67, 142–54).

### B. *Competing Definitions*

Perhaps the most common, though not completely satisfactory, way of describing apocalyptic literature has been the enumeration of what are perceived to be the common *literary* features of the genre (Vielhauer in Hennecke-Schneemelcher, *NTA* 2:545–55; Russell, *Apocalyptic*, 104–39; Koch, *Apocalyptic*, 23–28; see the summary of earlier research in Kuykendall, *Genre*, 72–102): pseudonymity (Russell, *Apocalyptic*, 127–39; Aune, *Prophecy*, 109–10), reports of visions, reviews of history presented as prophecies, number speculation, the figure of the *angelus interpres*, "the interpreting angel," the tendency to make frequent allusions to the OT, and the tendency to incorporate a variety of literary forms (testaments, laments, hymns, woes, visions). The more characteristic *religious* and *ideological* features of apocalypses include imminent eschatology, pessimism, dualism (spatial, temporal, ethical), determinism, esotericism, bizarre imagery, an emphasis on individual, transcendent salvation, and an emphasis on the disclosure of detailed knowledge of both the sacred and the profane aspects of the universe.

The traditional way of defining apocalypses through lists of traits, however, is not completely satisfactory for several reasons (see Kuykendall, *Genre*, 102–12): (1) The virtualities of apocalypses, their essential features, are not distinguished from optional elements that are present in some apocalypses but absent from others. (2)

Many of the characteristics on such lists are also found in other ancient literary genres (Sanders, "Genre," 449; Stone, "Lists," 440). (3) Some of the compositions widely considered to be apocalypses do not exhibit many of the proposed traits of apocalypses. (4) The usual lists of traits leave out features that are present in apocalypses, such as the interest in cosmology, astrology, demonology, botany, zoology, and pharmacy (Betz, *JTC* 6 [1969] 135–36).

Perhaps the most influential definition of the apocalypse genre is that proposed by J. J. Collins, who chaired the Apocalypse Group of the SBL Genres Project (*Semeia* 14 [1979] 9; *Apocalyptic*, 4):

"Apocalypse" is a genre of revelatory literature with a narrative framework, in which a revelation is mediated by an otherworldly being to a human recipient, disclosing a transcendent reality which is both temporal, insofar as it envisages eschatological salvation, and spatial, insofar as it involves another, supernatural world.

This definition, describing the core elements of the genre, is related to a master paradigm Collins has proposed, which contains a lengthy list of the constituent features of ancient apocalypses, divided into the following major categories, each of which describes an aspect of the form or content of apocalypses (*Semeia* 14 [1979] 6–8):

MANNER OF REVELATION (Form)
| | |
|---|---|
| 1. | Medium by which the revelation is communicated |
| 1.1. | Visual revelation has two forms |
| 1.1.1. | Visions |
| 1.1.2. | Epiphanies |
| 1.2. | Auditory revelation often clarifies the visual |
| 1.2.1. | Discourse |
| 1.2.2. | Dialogue |
| 1.3. | Otherworldly journey |
| 1.4. | Writing (revelation in a heavenly book) |
| 2. | Otherworldly mediator |
| 3. | Human recipient |
| 3.1. | Pseudonymity |
| 3.2. | Disposition of recipient |
| 3.3. | Reaction of recipient |

TEMPORAL AXIS (Content)
| | |
|---|---|
| 4. | Protology (matters concerning beginning) |
| 4.1. | Cosmogony |
| 4.2. | Primordial events |
| 5. | History is reviewed as either |
| 5.1. | Recollection of past or |
| 5.2. | *Ex eventu* prophecy |
| 6. | Present salvation through knowledge (Gnostic) |
| 7. | Eschatological crisis |
| 7.1. | Persecution |
| 7.2. | Other eschatological upheavals |
| 8. | Eschatological judgment or destruction |
| 8.1. | The wicked or the ignorant |
| 8.2. | The world |

Further, in addition to the core definition and the master paradigm of elements that are frequently, but not always, found in individual apocalypses, Collins proposes two main types of apocalypses, those with an otherworld journey (Type I) and those without an otherworldly journey (Type II). Each type may be further specified by one of three features: (1) those with a review of history, (2) those with cosmic or political eschatology, and (3) those with only personal eschatology.

Collins' definition, master paradigm, and typological grouping focus on the generic dimensions of *form* and *content*. On the relationship of the dimension of *function* to generic definition, Collins observes (*Semeia* 14 [1979] 1–2):

> Further, while a complete study of a genre must consider function and social setting, neither of these factors can determine the definition. At least in the case of ancient literature our knowledge of function and setting is often extremely hypothetical and cannot provide a firm basis for generic classification. The only firm basis which can be found is the identificaiton of recurrent elements which are explicitly present in the texts.

Part of the problem, of course, is the fact that the groups who produced apocalypses (if indeed apocalypses are not the products of individual scribes) are not known to us (Stone, *Scriptures,* 114); that is, the *Sitze im Leben* of apocalypses are unknown (Collins, *Apocalyptic,* 17–19).

This definition of the apocalypse genre is one of the more complete and systematic attempts to define the genre at the pragmatic level. It has not gone without criticism. David Hellholm, who insists that the three interrelated generic features of form, content, and function must be integrated for a useful definition of particular genre (Hellholm, *Semeia* 36 [1986] 26), accepts Collins' definition as a paradigmatically established definition but proposes adding a statement dealing explicitly with *function:* "intended for a group in crisis with the purpose of exhortation and/or consolation by means of divine authority" (Hellholm, *Semeia* 36 [1986] 27).

Hartman and Sanders have criticized Collins' definition from different perspectives. Hartman ("Survey," 329–43) lists four groups of genre constituents: (1) linguistic and stylistic constituents, (2) propositional constitutents, (3) illocutionary features, and (4) socio-linguistic function. Hartman thinks that in dealing with propositional constituents one must not only consider such features as plot, themes, and motifs (as Collins does) but also take into consideration the hierarchic structure and literary interrelations of those elements. Another critic of Collins' definition is Sanders, who discusses the difficulties of using the term "genre" as an appropriate designation for entire literary works when applied to texts that are compilations ("Genre," 447–59). He points out that Collins does not consider *1 Enoch* 91–104 an apocalypse, even though he categorizes other sections of *1 Enoch* as apocalypses. Similarly, he claims, Collins considers only *Jub.* 23 to be an apocalypse, not the rest of the composition, while other scholars (notably J. Carmignac, *RevQ* 10 [1979] 3–33) consider the entire document to be an apocalypse. Sanders concludes that "a lot of the material is left out of the description. The questions of the whole and the parts of composite works still leave problems for students of genre" ("Genre," 454). He further objects that the enumeration of the basic features for defining a genre proposed by Doty ("Genre," 413–48) has little relationship to the elements included by Collins (Sanders, "Genre," 454–55). This criticism, however, wrongly assumes that Doty's synthesis of generically salient literary features is something other than an eclectic summary of possibilities.

One must conclude that the definition of the genre apocalypse proposed by J. J. Collins represents an important step forward in research on the genre of ancient apocalypses, though two problematic features have surfaced in critical reactions: (1) the problem of the *function* of the genre and (2) the problem of the hierarchical arrangement of various generically salient features of apocalypses.

The work of David Hellholm, referred to above, constitutes another important step forward in genre research and complements the work of J. J. Collins. Hellholm utilizes text-linguistic methodology but is well aware that language has paradigmatic as well as syntagmatic relations. He therefore argues that the paradigmatic approach to the definition of the genre of apocalypses by such scholars as J. J. Collins be supplemented by a syntagmatic approach (*Semeia* 36 [1986] 33). Hellholm must make this concession since formal linguistic structures (syntagmatics) *have no intrinsic meaning* (pragmatics), and it is difficult to imagine a generic definition that ignored text-pragmatics. In his macro-syntagmatic approach to the analysis of generic structures, Hellholm proposes two necessary and complementary steps in text analysis: (1) division of the text into hierarchically arranged communication levels (the text-pragmatic aspect) and (2) division of the text into hierarchical text sequences (the text-semantic aspect). The communication levels are of two types, those external to the text (between the sender and receiver, author and readers), and those internal to the text (between *dramatis personae*). Text sequences are signaled by several types of markers: (1) changes in "world" (earth; heaven), (2) episode markers indicating time and change of time, localization and relocalization, (3) changes in the grouping of actors, (4) renominalization (an actor referred to by a pronoun is reintroduced with a noun or name), and (5) adverbs and conjunctions that relate clauses to each other. Communication levels and text sequences together constitute the generic structure of the text. Hellholm has analyzed two apocalypses using this text-linguistic approach, the *Shepherd of Hermas* (*Visionenbuch*, 11–13) and the Revelation of John (*Semeia* 36 [1986] 43–44). Hellholm presents six hierarchical communication levels in his analysis of the Revelation of of John (*Semeia* 36 [1986] 43–44):

Level 1:     Between the author and the general Christian audience
             (1:1–3; 22:18–19)

| Level 2 | Between the author and the more specified group of seven churches (1:4) |
| Level 3: | Between otherworldly mediators and the author (Jesus himself in 1–3; angelic revealers or Jesus Christ in the rest of the book) |
| Level 4: | Between the "heavenly scroll" and the author (6:1–22:5) |
| Level 5: | Between the otherworldly mediators and the author within the "heavenly scroll" |
| Level 6: | Between God himself on the throne and the author within the "heavenly scroll" with the divine command to the author to write down the words of the Supreme Divinity (22:5–8) |

Hellholm finds that the most profoundly embedded text at the functional communication level coincides with the sixth, i.e., the highest, grade of the macrostructure of the Revelation of John. This most embedded text is Rev 21:5b–8, a passage that Hellholm claims expresses the central message of Revelation:

"Behold, I am making everything new." He also said, "Write, for this message is trustworthy and true." He also said to me, "It is finished. I am the Alpha and the Omega, the Beginning and the End. I will freely give some water to the one who is thirsty, from the well of living water. The one who conquers will inherit these things, for I will be his God and he will be my son. But as for the cowards and unfaithful and the abominable and murderers and the immoral and sorcerers and idolaters and all who lie, they will experience the lake which burns with fire and sulphur, which is the second death."

This analysis leads Hellholm to draw three major conclusions (*Semeia* 36 [1986] 45–46): (1) The first conclusion concerns *virtuality:* the phenomenon of the most profoundly embedded text as the bearer of the central message of an apocalypse is an invariable feature of the genre. (2) The second conclusion concerns *function:* the reason for the hierarchic embedment of texts centers on the matter of the *authorization* of the message. (3) Third, he concludes there is a direct relationship between communication embedment on the *pragmatic* level and the content on the *semantic* level. The message of Revelation is the promise to those who conquer that they will live with God in his new world and the threat that the cowardly and unfaithful will be separated from God (the "second death").

Hellholm's complex text-linguistic approach to defining the apocalypse genre invites some criticism (see Aune, *Semeia* 36 [1986] 73–74). First, his claim that *pragmatics* (communication embedment and illocutions) and *semantics* meet at the center of the communication hierarchy of Revelation (*Semeia* 36 [1986] 46) is neither an obvious nor a necessary move but is apparently based on the need to attribute meaning to profoundly embedded texts. Second, the role assigned to the "heavenly scroll" of Rev 5 in Hellholm's analysis is not based exclusively on text-linguistic features but is imposed on the text. Third, the analysis of two "apocalypses," Revelation and the *Shepherd of Hermas,* is a slim basis on which to characterize a genre.

## C. The Definition of Genre for This Commentary

Descriptions of literary genres should deal with each of the three interrelated features of form, content, and function. For that reason the definition of the apocalyptic genre, with special reference to Revelation, will be defined in the following manner (for a more extensive discussion see Aune, *Semeia* 36 [1986] 86–91): (1) *Form:* an apocalypse is a first-person prose narrative, with an episodic structure consisting of revelatory visions often mediated to the author by a supernatural revealer, so structured that the central revelatory message constitutes a literary climax, and framed by a narrative of the circumstances surrounding the purported revelatory experience. (2) *Content:* the communication of a transcendent, usually eschatological, perspective on human experiences and values. (3) *Function:* (a) to legitimate the transcendent authorization of the message, (b) by mediating a reactualization of the original revelatory experience through a variety of literary devices, structures, and imagery, which function to "conceal" the message that the text purposes to "reveal," so that (c) the recipients of the message will be encouraged to continue to pursue, or if necessary to modify, their thinking and behavior in conformity with transcendent perspectives.

## D. Revelation as an Apocalypse

The majority of scholars maintain that Revelation belongs to the literary genre apocalypse. While Revelation is certainly framed as a letter (1:4–6; 22:21), this is clearly an optional compositional feature that has not exerted any noticeable generic effects on the rest of the composition. Further, Revelation contains a variety of shorter literary forms held together by the encompassing features of the apocalypse genre (Yarbro Collins, *Semeia* 14 [1979] 70). The largest unit of text in 4:1–22:9 consists of a complex otherworldly journey, and thus conforms to J. J. Collins' Type IIb: Apocalypses with Otherworldly Journeys with Cosmic and/or Political Eschatology (Yarbro Collins' denial [*Semeia* 14 (1979) 71] that the otherworldly journey in Revelation is generically insignificant is not convincing). While such otherworldly journeys occur in other apocalypses (*1 Enoch* 1–36; *2 Enoch; T. Levi* 2–5; *Apocalypse of Ezra; Asc. Isa.* 6–11), they never occur in OT prophetic books. Revelation, however, is distinguished by the fact that another extensive section in 1:9–3:22 consists of an epiphany of the exalted Christ that involves no otherworldly journey.

Using J. J. Collins' master paradigm given in complete form above, I propose to provide an inventory of those aspects of Revelation that fit the categories proposed in the paradigm to highlight the extent to which Revelation resembles other apocalypses.

MANNER OF REVELATION (Form)

### 1.1.1. Visions

While Rev 1:9–22:9, formally considered, constitutes a single vision report (Hanson, "Visions," 1422), it is customary to regard 4:1–22:9 (just where the main vision section ends is debated) as the main section of Revelation, which consists of an otherworldly journey. Nevertheless, since the location or vantage point of the seer oscillates (often abruptly) between earth and heaven, the otherworldly journey motif has been used to introduce a series of discrete visions or revelatory narratives (11:3–13, for example, belongs to the latter category), which suggests a conscious editorial attempt to create an apocalypse. Within Rev 4:1–22:9, the journey to heaven in 4:1 is the only explicit reference to an otherworldly journey (there is no subsequent reference to the seer's return to earth). This larger section is explicitly constructed of twelve shorter vision reports (10:1–11; 11:19–12:17; 13:1–18; 14:1, 6–11; 15:1–16:21; 17:1–18; 18:1–24; 19:11–21; 20:1–15; 21:1–8; 21:9–22:9). These include two horizontal journeys from one place on earth to a mysterious location elsewhere on the earth (17:1–18; 21:9–22:9).

### 1.1.2. Epiphanies
Rev 1:9–3:22 constitutes an earthly epiphany of the exalted Christ, which consists of two parts, the epiphany itself in 1:9–20, consisting of many symbolic features, and the dictation of seven proclamations to the seven Christian communities to whom the entire book is addressed in 2:1–3:22.

### 1.2. Auditions
Like most Jewish apocalypses, auditions frequently accompany visions in Revelation as the juxtaposed phrases "I saw" and "I heard" indicate, though such auditions are not frequently used to interpret the visions. Some segments appear to be exclusively auditions (11:15–18; 14:2–5; 14:13; 19:1–8). Auditory elements in the visions often exhibit specific forms (Yarbro Collins, *Semeia* 14 [1979] 70): doxologies (5:13; 7:12), acclamations (4:11; 5:9–10, 12), victory songs (12:10–12; 14:8; 19:1–2, 3), beatitudes (14:13; 16:15; 19:9; 20:6).

### 1.2.1. Discourse
Uninterrupted speeches by the mediators of revelation occur frequently in apocalypses. While the presence of discourse material in Revelation is largely restricted to the seven proclamations of the exalted Christ to the seven Christian communities in 2:1–3:22, there is also a relatively short discourse attributed to God in 21:5–8 that is of central significance for understanding the purpose and function of Revelation.

### 1.2.2. Dialogue
While dialogical sections are quite common in both Jewish and Christian apocalypses, they are relatively rare in Revelation. There is a short dialogue between one of the twenty-four elders and the seer in 7:13–17 and a much longer dialogue between one of the bowl angels and the seer in 17:6b–18.

### 1.3. Otherworldly journey
Rev 4:1–22:9, the main vision-report section of the book, begins with an otherworldly journey to the heavenly court; the vantage point of the seer oscillates unpredictably between heaven and earth. While the heavenly perspective of the seer is maintained from 4:1 to 9:21, thereafter the perspective changes unpredictably. In 10:1–11, the vision of the mighty angel with the open scroll is presented from an earthly perspective, as are 11:1–13; 12:1–6, 13–17; 13:1–18; 14:1–5, 6–7, 8, 9–11. A heavenly perspective is found in 14:14–16, 17–20; 15:1–16:21; 19:1–8, 11–21; 20:1–15; 21:1–8; 21:9–22:9). Nowhere is it stated, however, that the seer returns to earth.

### 1.4. Writing
There are two otherworldly writings that are the focus of two narrative segments of Revelation. The first is the scroll sealed with seven seals, which is the explicit focus of 5:1–8:1, and the second is the open scroll in the hand of the mighty angel,

which the seer is commanded to eat in 10:2, 8–11 (see relevant sections of the commentary for a discussion of the significance of these scrolls).

## 2. Otherworldly mediator

The framework of Revelation makes use of the traditional apocalyptic figure of the *angelus interpres,* "the interpreting angel" (1:2; 22:8–16), though that heavenly mediator is not explicitly mentioned anywhere else in the book. One of the bowl angels plays the role of the *angelus interpres* in 17:1–18, where he carries on an interpretive dialogue with the seer. Another bowl angel provides the seer with a guided tour of the New Jerusalem in 21:9–22:6, though he provides no commentary on what is seen. This angelic mediator may be identified with the *angelus interpres* in 22:8–16, though that identification is uncertain. The exalted Christ functions as a mediator of revelation in the title of the book (1:1) and in the epiphany of Christ in 1:9–3:22. Since the "voice like a trumpet" that invites the seer to heaven in 4:1 seems to refer to the voice of the exalted Christ in 1:10, Christ is formally placed in the position of the primary mediator in 4:1–22:9, though this is not maintained.

## 3. Human recipient

The recipient of revelation identifies himself simply as "John" (1:1, 4, 9; 22:8), and the audience is frequently reminded through the repeated use of the first person (typically in phrases such as καὶ εἶδον, "then I saw") that the seer has experienced the revelatory visions that are narrated in such detail.

### 3.1. Pseudonymity

Although all Jewish apocalypses are pseudonymous, it appears that Revelation is not, and for this reason some scholars have argued that it is not an apocalypse (Jones, *JBL* 87 [1968] 325–27; Mazzaferri, *Genre,* 377; see the discussion below under E. Dissenting Voices).

### 3.2. Disposition of recipient

The setting for the vision report of 1:9–22:9 is found in 1:9–10, where the author identifies himself as John, who shares with his readers the experience of persecution for the sake of Jesus and who is on the island of Patmos. The revelation that the seer received occurred on the Lord's day, when he was in a state of ecstasy (see *Comment* on 1:10).

### 3.3. Reaction of recipient

When the seer experienced the epiphany of Christ (1:9–20), he fainted dead away (1:17). He weeps when no one is found worthy to open the book with seven seals (5:4–5) and expresses amazement when he sees the allegorical figure of the Whore seated on the scarlet beast (17:6). On two occasions in the narrative, he attempts to worship the angelic mediator but each time is rebuked (19:10; 22:8–9).

TEMPORAL AXIS (Content)

## 4. Protology

It is probable that the expulsion of Satan and his angels from heaven following their rebellion, mentioned in 12:7–9, reflects the old Jewish myth of the origin of evil in the world through the fall of Satan. The hymnic commentary in 12:10–12, however, transforms this ostensibly protological event into an eschatological event.

### 4.1. Cosmogony

While there is no description of the origins of the world in Revelation, there are occasional declarations (usually in hymnic contexts) that God is the creator of all that exists (4:11; 10:6; 14:7) and that Christ was somehow prior to creation (3:14).

### 4.2. Primordial events

The war in heaven, which can be construed as a protological event, results in the defeat and expulsion of Satan and his angels (12:7–9).

### 5. History, reviewed as either
### 5.1. Recollection of past or

The only clear mention of political history in Revelation is the allusive reference to the seven kings in 17:9–11, where the author refers to the sixth king as his contemporary, i.e., "one is now living." While some have read this passage as *ex eventu* history, it is likely that the author has reinterpreted an older prophecy. The remainder of Rev 17, however, belongs to the sphere of prophecy, with the prediction of the war of the Beast and the ten kings against the Lamb (vv 12–14) and the attack of the Beast and the ten kings against Rome (vv 15–18).

### 5.2. *Ex eventu* prophecy
See above under 5.1.

### 6. Present salvation through knowledge (limited to Gnostic apocalypses).

### 7. Eschatological Crisis
### 7.1. Persecution

There are many references in Revelation to the suffering of Christians. The imprisonment and death of Christians from Smyrna are anticipated in 2:10, while the execution or lynching of Antipas of Pergamon is mentioned in 2:13. Rev 6:9–11 describes the cry for vengeance for those "who had been slain for the word of the God and for the witness they had borne," while Rome is allegorically represented by a whore "drunk with the blood of the saints and the blood of the martyrs of Jesus" (17:6). For other references to persecution, see Rev 1:9; 7:9, 14; 11:3–13; 12:11; 13:7; 14:13; 16:6; 18:24; 20:4.

### 7.2. Other eschatological upheavals

A complex series of eschatological punishments is unleashed with the opening of the seven seals (6:1–8:1), the sounding of the seven trumpets (8:2–9:21; 11:15–18), and the pouring out of the seven bowls (15:1–16:21). These upheavals culminate in the destruction of Babylon (18:1–19:10).

### 8. Eschatological judgment or destruction
### 8.1. The wicked

The Beast and ten allied kings make war on the Lamb but are conquered by him in 17:12–14 (a doublet of 19:17–21). Rome is destroyed in an act of divine vengeance (18:1–24). The army led by the Beast and the False Prophet is defeated and killed by the Rider on the White Horse (19:21). The dead of all social stations will stand before the great white throne of God for judgment in accordance with their deeds, and those whose names are not recorded in the Book of Life will be throne into the lake of fire (20:11–15). All the cowardly, the faithless, the polluted, the murderers, the fornicators, the sorcerers, the idolaters, and all liars will be cast into the lake of fire, the second death (21:8).

### 8.2. The world

John's vision of a new heaven and a new earth is predicated upon the destruction of the first heaven and the first earth (21:1). Earth and heaven are said to have fled from the presence of God (20:11).

### 8.3. Otherworldly beings

The Beast and the False Prophet are defeated and cast into the lake of fire by the Rider on the White Horse (19:20), and Satan is ultimately defeated and thrown into the lake of fire where he, with the Beast and the False Prophets, will be eternally tormented (20:10).

### 9. Eschatological salvation may involve
### 9.1. Cosmic transformation

The destruction of the first heaven and the first earth is followed by the creation of a new heaven and a new earth (21:1). The New Jerusalem, representing the presence of God in the midst of his people on a transformed earth, will descend from heaven (21:2–4) and is described in 21:9–22:5.

### 9.2. Personal salvation may take the form of
### 9.2.1. Resurrection

Those who had died for their testimony to Jesus returned to life and reigned with Christ for a thousand years in the first resurrection (20:4–6), while the general resurrection is mentioned in 20:11–15. Referring to Christ under the traditional title of the "firstborn from the dead" naturally implies the resurrection of all believers (1:5), though resurrection is never explicitly made one of the promises that conclude the seven proclamations.

### 9.2.2. Other forms of afterlife

Those who conquer are promised the fruit of the tree of life in the paradise of God (2:7; 22:14) and are assured that they will wear white robes (3:5), a metaphor for eternal life, be given a place with the exalted Christ on his throne (3:22), and have access to the New Jerusalem (22:14). The righteous will dwell with God, and he will abolish all sorrow, death, and suffering (7:13–17; 21:3–4; 22:3–5).

SPATIAL AXIS (Content)

### 10. Otherworldly elements
### 10.1. Otherworldly regions

Though Revelation reflects the ancient Jewish cosmology of heaven, earth, and underworld (see *Comment* on 5:3), the seer tells us a great deal about heaven but reveals little of the underworld. The heavenly world is represented primarily by the heavenly court, where God presides surrounded by a variety of supernatural beings who are characteristically engaged in the worship of God (4:1–5:14; 7:9–17; 8:2–5; 11:16–18; 12:10–12; 15:1–16:1; 19:1–8).

### 10.2. Otherworldly beings

The vision narratives of Revelation are populated with a complex array of supernatural beings arranged in two competitive hierarchies, one headed by God and the other by Satan. The exalted Christ, who has a special and unique relationship to God, has an even more central role in the framework of Revelation than does God the Father (1:9–3:22; 22:12–21), though his role, Lamb, Messiah, and Rider on the White Horse, is curiously varied and certainly less prominent in the main section 4:1–22:9 (5:1–8:1; 11:15; 12:4–5; 14:1–5; 17:14; 19:11–21; 20:4–6). The heavenly court and its denizens are frequently the focus of vision narratives, including the seven spirits of God (4:5), the four cherubim (4:6b–10; 5:6, 14; 7:11; 14:3), the twenty-four elders (4:4, 10; 5:5–14; 7:11; 11:16; 14:3; 19:4), a variety of individual angelic beings that function in various ways (7:1; 8:3–9:21; 10:1–11), and an innumerable host of angelic beings (5:11; 7:11). Satan plays a central role in the narratives as the chief antagonist known by various names and forms including Devil, Satan, the great dragon, the ancient serpent, the deceiver of the whole world (12:9). Satan's second in command is the Beast (11:7; 13:1–10; 16:13), who is an infernal being thought of sometimes as incarnate in the Roman empire and other times as one of the Roman emperors (17:7–11). The third member of this unholy trinity is the Beast from the Land (13:11–17), also referred to as the False Prophet (16:13; 19:20; 20:10). Satan also has his host of angels (12:7–9), which can apparently be represented as a horde of demonic locusts (9:3–11).

PARENESIS BY REVEALER (Content)

### 11. Parenesis

Parenesis, i.e., moral exhortation, is comparatively rare in Jewish apocalypses. One of the few clear examples is *1 Enoch* 94:3–5 (see Lebram, "Piety," in *Apocalypticism*, ed. D. Hellholm, 93), but parenesis does occur in isolated sections of Revelation, i.e., in the framing sections 1:1–3:22; 22:10–21. The seer's emphasis on "keeping" or "obeying" (τηρεῖν) the commands written in Revelation (1:3; 22:7, 8), or "keeping my words" (2:26), and obeying "my [i.e., the exalted Christ's] words" (3:8, 10[2x]), is therefore applicable *only* to the material found in Rev 1:1–3:22; 22:10–21. In the First Edition of Revelation, it is the words of *God* that must be obeyed, though it is never specified exactly what these words of God are or entail. In 4:1–22:5, for instance, we meet the idea of "obeying the commands of God" (12:17; 14:12) and of "keeping one's garments" (16:15), though 14:12 and 16:15 are probably editorial expansions (see *Comments* on those passages). It is also important to note that there is actually very little of a hortatory or parenetic nature in 4:1–22:5 that can appropriately be said to be "obeyed," though exhortation is an important part of 2:1–3:22; 22:10–21. Hortatory features found in 2:1–3:22; 22:6–21 include: (a) the necessity of remaining firm in the faith, i.e., by "conquering" (2:7, 11b, 17b, 26; 3:5, 12, 21); (b) the importance of "remembering" their previous state (2:5a; 3:3a) or of becoming "awake" (3:2; 16:15; the last passage is an expansion), coupled with the necessity of repentance in order to regain those earlier standards (2:5a; 3:3a, 19b), reinforced with the threat of judgment (2:5b, 16; 3:3b); (c) the exhortation not to fear what they will suffer, even to the point of death (2:10). (d) the importance of endurance or holding fast (2:25; 3:11; 13:10c; 14:12a; the last two passages are expansions; see *Comments*); (e) instruction that the righteous should continue to do right and the holy should continue to be holy (22:11).

CONCLUDING ELEMENTS (Form)

12. Instructions to recipient
At the conclusion of Revelation, the seer is instructed not to seal "the words of this prophetic book, for the time is near" (22:10), an allusion to Dan 12:4, 9, where the opposite is enjoined.

## E. Dissenting Voices

Though most scholars maintain that Revelation belongs to the generic category "apocalypse," there are some dissenting voices. Kallas (*JBL* 86 [1967] 69–80) has argued that the hallmark of apocalyptic was a particular attitude toward suffering. In contrast to the ancient Israelite-Jewish view that suffering comes from God, the authors of apocalypses took the diametrically opposed view that suffering is malicious, vindictive, and arbitrary and comes from the cosmic forces opposed to God (*JBL* 86 [1967] 74). Since this view of suffering is not found in Revelation, it is not an apocalypse. However, not only has Kallas oversimplified the theology of suffering in Jewish apocalyptic literature and Revelation (Jones, *JBL* 87 [1968] 325–26); he has also fallen into the trap of arbitrarily selecting a feature of apocalyptic and elevating it to the status of the central, indispensable feature of the apocalypse genre (Collins, *Semeia* 14 [1979] 12). Further, Kallas does not suggest an alternative generic category for Revelation.

If all apocalypses are pseudonymous and Revelation is not pseudonymous, so the argument goes, then Revelation is not an apocalypse (Jones, *JBL* 87 [1968] 325–27; Mazzaferri, *Genre,* 377). This is yet another position that arbitrarily isolates one generic feature and elevates it to the status of the *sine qua non* of apocalyptic. There are several flaws in this neat syllogism, however. First, and most obvious, Revelation is a *Christian* apocalypse, not a *Jewish* apocalypse, and there is another Christian apocalypse, the *Shepherd of Hermas,* which is not pseudonymous. Second, the syllogism raises pseudonymity to the level of an indispensable or invariable characteristic, a judgment that is based on an overly rigid conception of the nature of literary genres (pseudonymity was certainly not limited to apocalypses). Third, even though modern scholars think to distinguish between pseudonymous and real authorship using criteria not intrinsic to the apocalypses (or other literary genres) under investigation, it is far from evident that ancient readers would have made (or been capable of making) such discriminating judgments. Fourth, pseudonymity was used with a whole range of literary genres in antiquity, though admittedly not as thoroughly and consistently as in the case of Jewish apocalypses.

Finally, there is the curious view of Malina, who rejects the generic category "apocalypse" as an anachronistic conception that originated in the nineteenth century and has been projected back into the ancient world by scholars (*Revelation*, 10–12). Malina, who also rejects the category "eschatology" as anachronistic, has categorized Revelation as *astral prophecy*, a specific type of the astronomical and astrological literature of antiquity. "Astral prophecy," he observes, "refers to those ancient narratives reporting the interaction of prophets and seers with star-related, celestial personages and the outcomes of that interaction" (*Revelation*, 19; see also 25–26). Malina's strategies include reading far more astrological lore into Revelation than is actually there and nudging some OT prophetic books and other Jewish "apocalypses" into more explicitly astrological contexts. However, the fact that the term "apocalypse" was used in the title of ancient revelatory compositions suggests that it is not merely a modern construct (Collins, *Apocalyptic*, 3).

## V. Revelation as a Prophetic Apocalypse

That there are compositions that include apocalyptic sections but cannot themselves be categorized as apocalypses (e.g., Dan 7–12; *Jub.* 23; *T. Levi* 2–5; *T. Abr.* 10–15) suggests that it is not unreasonable to regard Revelation as a similar *mixtum compositum*. That is, the First Edition of Revelation (4:1–22:9) is clearly an apocalypse, while the expansions that were added in the Second Edition (1:1–3:22; 22:10–21) have a more clearly prophetic character (see *Introduction*, Section 5: Source Criticism). The sequence of literary forms in Revelation in its present state conforms to no known ancient literary conventions. Since the author rarely provides signals anticipating what he will do next, the readers either had no way to anticipate what would occur next or were in fact as surprised as modern readers by new turns in the narrative. Since Revelation, whatever else it may be, certainly belongs to the category of ancient revelatory literature, it is worth pondering whether the original readers would have thought that such abrupt literary moves were consonant with their understanding of the appropriate ways of narrating divine revelation.

As a literary form, an apocalypse seems a somewhat outmoded and inappropriate theological vehicle written during the last decade of the first century A.D. for Christian communities with a mixed ethnic heritage, though it was still apparently a viable literary form within Judaism as the production of both 4 Ezra and *2 Apocalypse of Baruch* suggests. Apart from Hermas *Vis.* 1–4 and perhaps Mark 13, the apocalyptic genre was not adopted in Christian circles. The dating of Revelation in the last decade of the first century A.D., therefore, is somewhat anomalous and has led some scholars to speak of a "renaissance" of apocalyptic in Asia Minor (see Vouga, *Geschichte*, 219–24) or of a "renewal" of apocalypticism in the Pauline churches (Koester, *Introduction* 2:241–61). The production of Revelation, however, is consistent with the hypothesis that the author was himself nourished on Jewish apocalypticism and regarded the apocalyptic genre as an entirely appropriate literary vehicle to communicate his theological agenda.

In Revelation, the literary forms that had come to be associated with either apocalyptic or prophetic literary traditions (but not both) have been synthesized through juxtaposition. At this juncture, it is critical to define what the terms "prophecy" and "apocalyptic" mean in this context. Perhaps the most significant way in which prophecy can be differentiated from apocalyptic is *sociologically*. In contrast to apocalypticism, prophecy does not rigidly distinguish between the righteous and the wicked but rather assumes that the wicked may repent and change their ways and that the righteous require admonition, censure, and exhortation to encourage them to remain faithful or to repent and return to the fold. Apocalypticism, on the other hand (i.e., the religious ideology within the context of which apocalypses were written), is a perspective generally thought to have been espoused by an oppressed minority that clearly distinguished the righteous from the wicked and anticipated an eschatological dénouement, in which the righteous would be rewarded and the wicked punished. By placing apocalyptic traditions within a prophetic framework (Rev 1–3; 22:10–20) and by juxtaposing apocalyptic with prophetic elements throughout the entire composition, the author appears to have attempted to give a new lease on life to apocalyptic traditions that could not and did not long retain their vitality in early Christianity because of their indissoluble association with nationalistic myths connected with the royal ideology of ancient Israel. Apocalypses, the primary repository of apocalyptic traditions, were largely scribal phenomena perforce divorced from real settings because of their pseudepigraphical character. This suprahistorical perspective of apocalyptic literature generally appears to have been mitigated in the Revelation of John through the incorporation of prophetic concerns that have a distinctly historical orientation. The Revelation of John is one of the few apocalypses for which the author, audience, and setting are generally known because they are not concealed in the work itself, though that setting is not reflected in the hardcore, genre-bound apocalyptic sections of the work.

## Section 4: Literary Structure

### Bibliography

**Allo, E. B.** "La structure de l'Apocalypse de S. Jean." *RB* 8 (1911) 481–501. **Barr, D. L.** "The Apocalypse as a Symbolic Transformation of the World: A Literary Analysis." *Int* 38 (1984) 39–50. ———. "The Apocalypse of John as Oral Enactment." *Int* 40 (1986) 243–56. ———. "Elephants and Holograms: From Metaphor to Methodology in the Study of John's Apocalypse." In *1986 SBL Seminar Papers*, ed. K. H. Richards. Atlanta: Scholars, 1986. **Bauckham, R.** "Structure and Composition." In *The Climax of Prophecy: Studies in the Book of Revelation*. Edinburgh: T. & T. Clark, 1993. 1–37. **Bogaert, P.** *Apocalypse de Baruch: Introduction, Traduction du Syriaque et Commentaire*. SC 144–45. Paris: Cerf, 1969. **Bornkamm, G.** "Die Komposition der apokalyptischen Visionen in der Offenbarung Johannis." *ZNW* 36 (1938) 132–49. **Bowman, W. J.** "The Revelation to John: Its Dramatic Structure and Message." *Int* 9 (1955) 436–53. **Brandenburger, E.** *Die Verborgenheit Gottes im Weltgeschehen: Das literarische und theologische Problem des 4. Esrabuches*. Zürich: Theologischer, 1981. **Farrer, A.** *A Rebirth of Images: The Making of St. John's Apocalypse*. 1949. Repr. Albany: State University of New York, 1986. **Geiger, A.,** and **Sorg, J.** *Offenbarung Jesu Christi: Eine Darstellung ihres Aufbaues*. Stuttgart: Degerloch, 1947. **Genette, G.** *Narrative Discourse: An Essay in Method*. Tr. J. E. Lewin. Ithaca: Cornell UP, 1980. **Giblin, C. H.** "Recapitulation and the Literary Coherence of John's Apocalypse." *CBQ* 56 (1994) 81–95. ———. "Revelation 11.1–13: Its Form, Function, and Contextual Integration." *NTS* 30 (1984) 433–59. ———. "Structural and Thematic Correlations in the Theology of Revelation 16–22." *Bib* 55 (1974) 487–504. **Hahn, F.** "Zum Aufbau der Johannesoffenbarung." In *Kirche und Bibel*. FS B. E. Schick, ed. A. Winter et al. Paderborn: Schöningh, 1979. 145–54. **Lambrecht, J.** "A Structuration of Rev 4,1–22,5." In *L'Apocalypse*, ed. J. Lambrecht. 77–104. **Murphy, F. J.** *The Structure and Meaning of Second*

*Baruch.* SBLDS 78. Atlanta: Scholars, 1985. **Rousseau, F.** *L'Apocalypse et le milieu prophétique du Nouveau Testament: Structure et préhistoire du texte.* Paris: Desclée, 1971. **Schmidt, P. W.** *Anmerkungen über die Komposition der Offenbarung Johannis.* Freiburg, 1891. **Schüssler Fiorenza, E.** "Composition and Structure of the Book of Revelation." *CBQ* 39 (1977) 344–66. ———. "The Eschatology and Composition of the Apocalypse." *CBQ* 30 (1968) 537–69. **Smith, C. R.** "The Structure of the Book of Revelation in Light of Apocalyptic Literary Conventions." *NovT* 36 (1994) 373–93. **Studerus, R.** "Zum Aufbau der Apokalypse." *TPQ* 3 (1963) 29–35. **Vanni, U.** *La struttura letteraria dell'Apocalisse.* 2nd ed. Breschia: Morcelliana, 1980. **Vuyst, J. de.** *De structuur van de Apokalyps.* Kampen: Kok, 1968. **White, R. F.** "Reexamining the Evidence for Recapitulation in Revelation 20:1–10." *WJT* 51 (1989) 319–44. **Willett, T. M.** *Eschatology in the Theodicies of 2 Baruch and 4 Ezra.* JSPSup 4. Sheffield: JSOT, 1989.

## I. Introduction

The problem of the literary analysis of Revelation, despite many proposals, remains a matter on which there is no general consensus among scholars. This should not be surprising, however, since consensus on most issues is a fleeting phenomenon among biblical scholars. In this case, there are several obvious reasons for this disagreement. First, while there are a number of linguistic features that might point to aspects of the structure of the text, they may be construed in a variety of ways. Second, tightly organized sections of material are juxtaposed with what appear to be more loosely constructed sections of text that are usually regarded as digressions. For whatever reason, the literary structure of Revelation is more intricate than that of nearly every other ancient apocalypse. This structural complexity suggests that Revelation was not written over a period of a few days, weeks, or even months, but rather was the product of years of apocalyptic-prophetic proclamation, writing, and reflection, including the appropriation and adaptation of a variety of types and forms of earlier traditional material, both written and oral.

## II. Approaching the Problem of Structure

### A. *Recapitulation Theory*

One of the central problems in analyzing the central section of Revelation, particularly from 6:1 to 19:10, is the determination of whether various sections recapitulate earlier sections (e.g., the plagues unleased by the seven trumpets and seven bowls have many similarities) or the author intends to present a chronological sequence of eschatological events in a manner consistent with a history-of-salvation perspective.

Victorinus of Pettau proposed that the seven bowl plagues (15:1–16:21) do not chronologically follow the seven trumpet plagues (8:6–11:15) as part of a continuous series but are actually parallel accounts of the same events, which they recapitulate in another form. Among subsequent interpreters, the narrative of the seven seals (6:1–8:1) was also regarded as another version of the events narrated in the seven trumpet plagues and the seven bowl plagues; i.e., these sections were regarded as parallel accounts of the same events (Giblin, *CBQ* 56 [1994] 81).

A. Yarbro Collins has proposed that the principle of recapitulation is evident in five cycles of visions (*Combat Myth,* 32–44): (1) the seven seals (6:1–8:5), (2) the seven trumpets (8:2–11:19), (3) seven unnumbered visions (12:1–15:4), (4) the seven bowls (15:1–16:21), with the Babylon appendix (17:1–19:10), and (5) seven unnumbered visions (19:11–21:8), with the Jerusalem appendix (21:9–22:5). Motifs that regularly occur or are recapitulated in these five cycles include: (a) persecution, (b) the punishment of the nations, (c) the triumph of God, the Lamb, and/or the faithful. Further, the second cycle of visions recapitulates the first. Recapitulation is not unique to Revelation, she argues (*Combat Myth*, 43–44), but is found in other compositions with eschatological concerns such as *Sib. Or.* 3 and 5, the visions of Dan 7–10, and 4 Ezra 3:1–9:22.

R. F. White, focusing on a more restricted part of Revelation (*WJT* 51 [1989] 319–44), argues that the relationship between Rev 20:1–10 and 19:11–21 is one of recapitulation rather than one of progression. He advances three arguments for this view: (1) the discrepancy between the events narrated in 19:11–21 and 20:1–3, (2) the recapitulation of 19:11–21 (the Armageddon revolt) in 20:7–10 (the Gog-Magog revolt), and (3) the motif of angelic ascent and descent in Revelation. This solves a theological problem for White, who argues that 20:1–6 is a vision sequence that does not narrate events following the second coming of Christ but rather recapitulates events before it.

C. H. Giblin, after briefly surveying aspects of earlier theories of recapitulation, argues that recapitulation occurs primarily in the plot line of Rev 4–22, which consists of the coherent, progressively enunciated holy war of God on behalf of his harassed people. The structure of Revelation from this perspective consists of a *beginning* (4:1–8:6), a *middle*, the second stage of the major vision (8:7–15:8), and an *end*, the vision of the "kingdom come" (16:1–22:11). Giblin emphasizes that interpreters must avoid historicizing any aspects of John's vision of the end by interpreting them as specific factual events of history.

In the brief survey of opinion given above, it is evident that "recapitulation" is defined in very different ways by different commentators. Victorinus thought that the seven bowls provided a fuller account of the eschatological events at the end of the world than did the seven trumpets. For him, these eschatological events were events that would actually occur in history at some indeterminate future time. A. Yarbro Collins (*Combat Myth*), on the other hand, is centrally concerned with similar patterns of motifs that are observable throughout various sections of Revelation. The term "recapitulation" does not seem appropriate for this kind of repetition. Just because the book of Judges uses a stereotyped outline to narrate the experience of premonarchic Israel in terms of recurring cycles of national apostasy, enslavement, repentance, and deliverance (see Judg 2:11–23) does not mean that each cycle should be designated a "recapitulation" of the others. Finally, C. H. Giblin (*CBQ* 56 [1994] 81–95), with typical sensitivity to the literary structure of Revelation, redefines recapitulation in terms of a plot line that recurs throughout the central section of the book. But a recurring plot line, which can be another way of viewing the cyclic pattern of the narratives in Judges, does not constitute "recapitulation" in the classic sense.

In deciding whether recapitulation is an appropriate category for analyzing the structure of Revelation, of central importance is the relationship between *story* (the events narrated) and *narrative* (the narrative text itself). To borrow terminology from narratologist Gerard Genette (*Narrative Discourse*), Revelation is a weak *homodiegetic* narrative; that is, the narrator is present as a character in the story but only in a secondary role as bystander, observer, and witness. Most of Revelation formally consists of a single extensive vision report, which begins at 1:9 and continues to 22:20. This artificial literary unity has been imposed on numerous discrete units that have been paratactically linked together in an apparently chronological order; i.e., if the phenomenon of recapitulation is present, it lacks any clear formal literary indications of its presence or (perhaps more likely) belongs to an earlier level of composition than that now extant in Revelation. John occasionally links major segments of text together in artificial chronological sequence using the temporal phrase "after these things" (4:1; 7:1, 9; 15:5; 18:1; 19:1). More frequently (nearly forty times) he uses the paratactic phrase καὶ εἶδον, "and I saw," usually intending temporal sequence and appropriately translated by the RSV as "*then* I saw." The reason the author has cemented diverse materials and traditions together into a single formal vision is not simply because he wants to relate the visions in the order in which he saw them (as Hermas) or because he wants to develop a theme (4 Ezra) but primarily because he intends the visions themselves to constitute *a single chronological narrative of the eschatological events that will soon begin to unfold.* That is, he wants to present his own eschatological scenario. This means that no form of the recapitulation theory is valid for the present text of Revelation. That does not mean, however, that many of the constituent visions and traditions used as sources by the author could not have referred to essentially the same eschatological events from different perspectives and used variegated imagery. This is evident from the fact that the *circumstances* of the visionary experience (a reference to the person, place, and time of the dream or vision), a uniform introductory feature of the vision-report form, is found only in 1:9–10. The internal analysis of Revelation, however, makes it clear that a number of visions have been set within the larger literary framework of 1:9–22:20. Rev 1:10–3:22, for example, is a visionary experience set in this world (several apocalypses similarly omit otherworldly journeys; e.g., Dan 7–12; *1 Enoch* 85–90 [Animal Apocalypse]; *1 Enoch* 93; 91:12–17 [Apocalypse of Weeks]; *2 Baruch;* 4 Ezra; *Jub.* 23; and *Shepherd of Hermas* consist only of visions on earth), while Rev 4:1 begins a radical change of venue with a vision report following an ascent to heaven (many other apocalypses include such otherworldly journeys, e.g., *1 Enoch* 1–36; *1 Enoch* 37–71; *1 Enoch* 72–82 [Heavenly Luminaries]; *2 Enoch*). The barely perceptible change of scene from heaven to earth (cf. the earthly perspectives of the visions in 17:1ff.; 19:11ff.; 21:9ff.) is a further indication that separate visions have been linked together within a larger literary framework. The originally discrete existence of these earthly visions is further suggested by the reference to John's being transported "in the spirit" (17:3; 21:10). Further, the author has imposed various linguistic devices to segment individual visions into separate scenes (phrases such as "and I saw," "then I saw," and "then I looked" are used to segment larger sequences into separate scenes; cf. 13:1, 11; 14:1, 6, 14; 15:1).

## B. The Series of Seven

The author was preoccupied with the symbolic significance of the number seven (commonly understood to signify completeness), which he used fifty-four

times. One of the ways in which this concern with the number seven is expressed
is in the author's explicit mention of groupings of seven: *seven* churches (1:4a, 11,
20), *seven* spirits before the throne (1:4b), *seven* golden menorahs (1:12, 20; 2:1),
*seven* stars (1:16, 20; 2:1; 3:1), *seven* flaming torches (4:5), representing the *seven*
spirits of God (3:1; 4:5; 5:6), the Lamb with *seven* horns and *seven* eyes (5:6), *seven*
angels who stand before God (8:2), the *seven* thunders (10:3–4), the great red
dragon with *seven* heads (12:3; 13:1; 17:3, 7, 9). The author also includes other
groups of seven that he does not explicitly enumerate, such as the seven
beatitudes (1:3; 14:13; 16:15; 19:9; 20:6; 22:7, 10, 14) and the sevenfold use of the
varied fourfold phrase "every tribe and tongue and people and nation" (5:9; 7:9;
10:11; 11:9; 13:7; 14:6; 17:5).

More important in the present context, the author uses four groups of seven to
structure major portions of the narrative: *seven* proclamations (2:1–3:22), *seven*
seals (5:1–8:1), *seven* trumpets (8:2–11:18), and *seven* bowls (15:1–16:21). A number of scholars, struck by the use of heptads as a structuring device, have tried to
identify further heptads. Farrer, for example, proposed that Revelation should be
divided into six sections, each of which is based on the number seven (*Images*, 45):
(1) the seven messages (1–3), (2) the seven seals (4–7), (3) the seven trumpets
(8:2–11:14), (4) seven unnumbered visions (11:15–14:20), (5) seven bowls (15–
18), (6) seven unnumbered visions (19–22). This analysis, however, is not completely convincing. The recurrence of the adjective "unnumbered" is suspicious
because the author-editor was perfectly able to include explicit heptads when it
suited him. Further, it is not self-evident that 11:15–14:20 and 19–22 each contain
precisely *seven* visions; there is more than one way of dividing up each of these
sections of text. Farrer includes Rev 17–18 as the conclusion of Rev 15–16, though
there is little warrant in the text for doing so. Then too, he does not recognize the
explicit parallels that the author set up between 17:1–19:10 and 21:9–22:9, leading
him to ignore these structures in dividing up the text. Farrer's analysis was revised
by Yarbro Collins (*Combat Myth*, 13–29), who proposed a similar division of eight
main parts by including a prologue and epilogue:

1. Prologue (1:1–8)
2. The seven messages (1:9–3:22)
3. The seven seals (4:1–8:5)
4. The seven trumpets (8:2–11:19)
5. Seven unnumbered visions (12:1–15:4)
6. The seven bowls (15:1–16:21)
        Babylon appendix (17:1–19:10)
7. Seven unnumbered visions (19:11–21:8)
        Jerusalem appendix (21:9–22:5)
8. Epilogue (22:6–21)

Again, the use of the designation "unnumbered" is somewhat disquieting, since the
author-editor is perfectly able to use the number seven explicitly when he wishes
to. Further, the two appendices in 17:1–19:10 and 21:9–22:5 are extensive sections
of text that Yarbro Collins apparently cannot integrate into the overall structure of
Revelation.

It is important to recognize that three of the heptads, the seven seals (5:1–8:1), the seven trumpets (8:2–11:18), and the seven bowls (15:1–16:21), exhibit a special structural relationship identified by Vanni (*Struttura letteraria*) and accepted by such scholars as J. Lambrecht ("Structuration") and C. H. Giblin (*Bib* 55 [1974] 487–504). The seventh seal (8:1), which is separated from the sixth seal by an excursus on the protection of the 144,000 in 7:1–17, contains within itself all the plagues of the seven trumpets and seven bowls that follow. Further, the seventh trumpet, again separated from the sixth trumpet by 10:1–11:13, contains within itself the plagues of the following seven bowls. The seventh bowl is not separated from the sixth bowl; it, with the series of divinely caused plagues inflicted on the people of the world, ends with the decisive announcement "It is done!" (16:17).

The author's elaborate use of the number seven in Revelation is explicable given the frequency with which the apocalyptic literary tradition generally uses the number seven as a structuring principle. 4 Ezra is arranged in seven sections (Brandenburger, *Verborgenheit Gottes*, 95–98; cf. Willett, *Eschatology*, 54–65): (1) 3:1–5:20; (2) 5:21–6:34; (3) 6:35–9:25; (4) 9:26–10:59; (5) 11:1–12:51; (6) 13:1–58; (7) 14:1–48 (chaps. 1–2; 15–16 are later Christian additions, sometimes designated 5 Ezra and 6 Ezra, respectively). Similarly, many scholars hold the opinion that 2 *Baruch* is also arranged in seven sections (Murphy, *Structure*, 11–29; cf. Bogaert, *Baruch* 1:62; Willett, *Eschatology*, 80–95): (1) 1:1–9:2 [Bogaert: 1:1–12:4]; (2) 10:1–20:6 [Bogaert: 13:1–20:6]; (3) 21:1–34:1; (4) 35:1–47:1; (5) 47:2–52:7; (6) 53:1–77:17; (7) 77:18–87:1 (the letter in the last section is probably an integral part of the text). The *Sepher ha-Razim*, a Jewish magical handbook from the third or fourth century A.D., also has a sevenfold structure, based on a description of each of the seven heavens (Morgan, tr., *Sepher ha-Razim*, 6–7).

The chief interpretive problem is whether the consequences of the opening of the seven seals, the blowing of the seven trumpets, and the pouring out of the seven bowls represent imaginative descriptions of essentially the same eschatological events described in different ways (the recapitulation theory) or they should be understood as presenting the linear unfolding of an eschatological scenario culminating in the dénouement of the New Jerusalem.

## C. Rev 17:1–19:10 and 21:9–22:9 as Paired Angelic Revelations

The structure of Rev 17:1–22:9 is dominated by two angelic revelations in 17:1–19:10 and 21:9–22:9, which frame 19:11–21:8, a structure that is quite different from those used by the author-editor in Rev 1–16. Rev 17:1–19:10 and 21:9–22:9 have been carefully and convincingly analyzed as paired angelic revelations by Giblin (*Bib* 55 [1974] 487–504). The striking parallel structures of these two texts are evident in the following synoptic comparison of the parallel texts that frame these units, i.e., Rev 17:1–3; 19:9–10 and 21:9–10; 22:6–9:

| *Rev 17:1–19:10* | *Rev 21:9–22:9* |
|---|---|
| 17:1 καὶ ἦλθεν εἷς ἐκ τῶν ἑπτὰ | 21:9 καὶ ἦλθεν εἷς ἐκ τῶν ἑπτὰ |
| Then came one of the seven | Then came one of the seven |
| | |
| ἀγγέλων τῶν ἐχόντων τὰς ἑπτὰ | ἀγγέλων τῶν ἐχόντων τὰς ἑπτὰ |
| angels with the seven | angels with the seven |

φιάλας
bowls

φιάλας τῶν γεμόντων τῶν ἑπτὰ
bowls full of the seven

πληγῶν τῶν ἐσχάτων
last plagues

καὶ ἐλάλησεν μετ᾽ ἐμου λέγων·
and spoke with me saying,

καὶ ἐλάλησεν μετ᾽ ἐμου λέγων·
and spoke to me saying,

δεῦρο, δείξω σοι
Come, I will show you

δεῦρο, δείξω σοι
Come, I will show you

τὸ κρίμα τῆς πόρνης τῆς μεγάλης
the judgment of the great Whore

τὴν νύμφην τὴν γυναῖκα τοῦ ἀρνίου.
the bride the wife of the Lamb.

17:3 καὶ ἀπήνεγκέν με
He then transported me

21:10 καὶ ἀπήνεγκέν με
He then transported me

εἰς ἔρημον
to the desert

ἐν πνεύματι.
in prophetic ecstasy.

ἐν πνεύματι
in prophetic ecstasy

ἐπὶ ὄρος μέγα καὶ ὑψηλόν,
to a great and high mountain,

καὶ εἶδον
Then I saw . . .

καὶ ἔδειξέν μοι
Then he showed me . . .

[Body of vision]

[Body of vision]

19:9b καὶ λέγει μοι·
Then he said to me

22:6 καὶ εἶπέν μοι·
Then he said to me

οὗτοι οἱ λόγοι ἀληθινοὶ
These are the true words

οὗτοι οἱ λόγοι πιστοὶ καὶ ἀληθινοί . . .
These words are trustworthy and true . . .

τοῦ θεοῦ εἰσιν . . .
of God . . .

22:8b καὶ ὅτε ἤκουσα καὶ ἔβλεψα,
And when I heard and saw this,

19:10 καὶ ἔπεσα ἔμπροσθεν
Then I fell before

ἔπεσα προσκυνῆσαι ἔμπροσθεν
I fell to worship before

τῶν ποδῶν αὐτοῦ
his feet

τῶν ποδῶν τοῦ ἀγγέλου
the feet of the angel

τοῦ δεικνύοντός μοι ταῦτα.
who showed me these things.

| | |
|---|---|
| προσκυνῆσαι αὐτῷ.<br>to worship him. | |
| καὶ λέγει μοι·<br>but he said to me, | καὶ λέγει μοι·<br>but he said to me, |
| ὅρα μή·<br>Don't do that! | ὅρα μή·<br>Don't do that! |
| σύνδουλός σού εἰμι<br>I am a fellow servant with you | σύνδουλός σού εἰμι<br>I am a fellow servant with you |
| καὶ τῶν ἀδελφῶν σου τῶν ἐχόντων<br>and your brothers who maintain | καὶ τῶν ἀδελφῶν σου τῶν προφητῶν<br>and your brothers the prophets |
| τὴν μαρτυρίαν Ἰησοῦ·<br>the witness to Jesus. | |
| | καὶ τῶν τηρούντων τοὺς λόγους<br>and who keep the commands |
| | τοῦ βιβλίου τούτου·<br>of this book. |
| τῷ θεῷ προσκύνησον.<br>Worship God! | τῷ θεῷ προσκύνησον.<br>Worship God! |

The strikingly close parallels between these framing units indicate that the author has chosen to depart from the use of seven as an organizing principle for major textual units and instead has preferred this very different structure for linking several discrete shorter units of text into a unified whole. It seems probable that since both texts are introduced by referring to an angelic guide who is explicitly said to be one of the seven bowl angels (17:1; 21:9), the final editing of these texts took place after the section on the seven bowl plagues in Rev 15:1–16:20 had been completed. Further, since the parallels between 17:1–19:10 and 21:9–22:9 involve only the beginning and ending sections of both textual units, it is likely that the texts they frame were composed earlier (and independently) of those frameworks and that the author-editor used these framing structures to weld together originally discrete material. It also appears likely, in my view, that Rev 21:9–22:9 was consciously structured in imitation of 17:1–19:10 (rather than the reverse), but only *after* Rev 21:5–22:2 had been inserted between 21:3–4 and 22:3–5 (on 21:5–22:2 as an insertion, see III. Source-Critical Analysis, under *Form/Structure/Setting* for Rev 21:1–8).

## D. Heavenly Throne-Room Scenes

Revelation often punctuates the visionary narrative with scenes set in the heavenly court. The first and longest such scene is found in Rev 4:1–5:14, and six similar scenes follow in 7:9–17; 8:1–4; 11:15–18; 14:1–5; 15:2–8; 19:1–10. Most of the hymns and hymnic fragments in Revelation are placed in these literary settings (4:8c, 11; 5:9b–10, 12b, 13b; 7:10b, 12; 11:15b, 17–18; 15:3b–4; 19:1b–2, 3, 5b, 6b–8). While all of the heavenly throne scenes contain hymnic elements, only two hymns (12:10b–12; 16:5b–7b) are not set in the context of heavenly throne-room scenes. Since these hymnic sections usually provide commentary on the narrative vision contexts in which they are embedded, the primary reason the author introduced throne scenes was to serve as literary contexts for hymnic commentary; thus they are extremely important in any structural analysis of Revelation.

## E. The Scrolls of Revelation 5 and 10

A number of scholars have regarded the scroll with seven seals, first mentioned in Rev 5:1, as a clue to the structure of all or part of Revelation. While a brief summary of the contents of the scroll could be read on the outside, the contents themselves could presumably be revealed only after all the seals had been broken (the seventh seal is broken in 8:1). Bornkamm (*ZNW*36 [1938] 132–49) has argued that the scroll with seven seals covers 8:2–22:6. After the seven seals have been opened (6:1–8:1), the contents of the scroll are revealed with the seven trumpets (8:2–14:20) and the seven bowls (15:1–16:21), which are a recapitulation of the seven trumpets.

However, the text of Rev 5:1–8:1, which narrates the breaking of the seven seals by the Lamb, contains no explicit indication of the contents of the scroll. Nevertheless, there has been a good deal of speculation about the contents of the scroll, which some see as identical with the little scroll of Rev 10 (Mazzaferri, *Genre*, 265–79), while others see no real connection between the two scrolls. Narrow descriptions of the content of the scroll of Rev 5 are restricted to all or part of the narrative in Revelation. Schüssler Fiorenza, for example, argues that the scroll narrates the eschatological punishments inflicted on the world by the will of God (*CBQ* 30 [1968] 564), while Bornkamm has proposed that the scroll is essentially identical with what John has been commissioned to write to the seven churches (*ZNW*36 [1938] 132–49). A broader description of the scroll is that it is a "book of destiny" consisting of God's predetermined plan for human beings and the world (variously described by Swete, 75; Caird, 72; Beasley-Murray, 120; Lohse, 41–42) or the foreordained eschatological plan of God, which cannot be known until the period of fulfillment, a biblical tradition reflected in Ezek 2:9–10; Dan 8:26; 12:9; *Jub.* 32:20–22; *1 Enoch* 81:2–3. It has been argued that, if the scroll contains a narrative of eschatological events that are put in motion by the breaking of the seven seals, the contents of the scroll begin to be actualized with the opening of the first seal in 6:1 and extend either to 8:1 (the opening of the seventh seal) or even further into the book (Bousset [1960] 254–55; Charles, 1:135; Hadorn, 75; Lohmeyer, 53; G. Schrenk, *TDNT* 1:619; H.-P. Müller, "Die himmlische Ratsversammlung: Motivgeschichtliches zu Apc 5:1–5," *ZNW*54 [1963] 255). Some consider Rev 6:1–22:6 to be essentially a transcript of the scroll (Staritz, "Offenbarung," 166; Holtz, *Christologie,* 35). Since the author describes his composition as a prophetic βιβλίον (1:11; 22:7, 9, 18–19), some have identified the entire work as the scroll with seven seals, though it is explicitly said that John's prophetic book should not be sealed (22:10). Others argue that the contents of the scroll cannot begin to be actualized until all seven seals have been broken, an event that does not occur until 8:1, so that the contents of the scroll are only revealed beginning with 8:2 (Beckwith, 263–64; Bornkamm, *ZNW* 36 [1938] 132–49; Jeremias, *TDNT* 4:872 n. 250; Strobel, "Apokalypse," *TRE* 3:178–79). Hellholm, who regards the form of the scroll as a doubly written legal document, neatly combines these two views by arguing that 6:1–7:17 is the *scriptura exterior* that summarizes the content of the scroll, while 8:1–22:5 is the *scriptura interior*, i.e., an account of the content of the scroll ("Genre," 48–53). The problem with this view is that this scroll is never given to the narrator to transcribe, as is the case with most heavenly books that are featured in revelatory narratives, and the scroll is never mentioned again after 8:1. An important clue for the contents of the scroll is found in Ezek 2:9–10, the model for this passage, in which the contents of the scroll shown to Ezekiel are described as "words of mourning, lamentation, and woe," i.e., the message of divine judgment that the prophet will announce. This may refer to the prophet's proclamation of the coming judgment on Israel (Ezek 4–24) and on the nations (Ezek 25–32).

Since the scroll with seven seals was the central focus of the throne scene in Rev 5, and the opening of each of the seals was the structuring device for the first series of seven plagues in 6:1–8:1, it is important to ask whether the author intends the audience to identify this scroll with the open scroll of Rev 10. Several scholars have recently argued forcefully for this identification (Mazzaferri, *Genre*, 265–79; Bauckham, "Conversion," in *Climax*, 243–57). Since the revelation that John's prophecy is intended to communicate is contained in the scroll he received in Rev 10, so the argument runs, the real content of the scroll is only revealed following Rev 10.

However, there are several strong arguments against identifying the scrolls of Rev 5 and 10: (1) A weighty syntactical argument *against* their identity is the fact that while τὸ βιβλίον in 10:8 has an anaphoric article (referring back to the synonymous βιβλαρίδιον in 10:2), the term βιβλαρίδιον introduced in 10:2 is anarthrous and therefore cannot refer to the βιβλίον of Rev 5. (2) The scroll in Ezekiel is open, while the scroll in Rev 5 is sealed with seven seals, which are gradually opened (6:1–8:1), while the scroll in Rev 10 is brought down from heaven to the seer opened (10:2a). (3) The mission of John, as described in 10:11, is to "prophesy again *against* peoples and nations and languages and many kings," not *to* them (see *Comment* on 10:11).

Whether or not the scrolls of Rev 5 and 10 are the same, the question still remains, "Does the scroll in Rev 10 contain any or all of the following visionary narrative beginning with Rev 11?" Since the scroll with seven seals provides the structure, if not the content, of Rev 6:1–8:1, it is worth considering whether the same is true for the little open scroll of Rev 10. Since the author provides no clear literary indications that might aid in the solution of this problem, the answers to this question are necessarily speculative. The content of the scroll in Rev 10 has been identified with the following segments of Revelation: (1) Rev 10–11 (G. Bornkamm, "Komposition der apokalyptischen Visionen in der Offenbarung Johannis," in *Studien zu Antike und Urchristentum: Gesammelte Aufsätze* [Munich: Kaiser, 1959] 217); (2) Rev 11:1–13 (Charles, 1:260, 269; Schrenk, *TDNT* 1:618; Lohmeyer, 87, 89; Lohse, 60–61); (3) Rev 11:1–15:4 (Schüssler Fiorenza, *CBQ* 30 [1968] 565–66; id., *CBQ* 39 [1977] 363); (4) Rev 12:1–22:5 (Bousset [1906] 312); (5) Rev 12 or 17 (Yarbro Collins, *Combat Myth*, 26); (6) Rev 15:1–22:9 (Giblin, *NTS* 30 [1984] 455 n. 10); and (7) Rev 20–22 (Beasley-Murray, 82).

## III. THE STRUCTURE OF REVELATION

Revelation consists of two major sections: (1) 1:9–3:22, which centers on a theophany of the exalted Christ, and (2) 4:1–22:9, a series of episodic vision narratives introduced with a heavenly journey. Both of these sections are placed within a single extended vision narrative (1:9–22:9), for 4:1 does not really interrupt this narrative but rather introduces a new phase, the heavenly journey of the seer. These major sections are framed by a prologue (1:1–8) and an epilogue (22:6–21). The fact that the second major section and the epiloque overlap exposes the limitations of a linear outline for conveying the complex structure of a composition such as Revelation, where segments of the text can serve as transitions, concluding the previous unit and introducing the next. It is the structure of this main part of Revelation that is the most problematic, and there is little agreement among scholars regarding the structure of this extensive textual unit.

The two main sections of Revelation are strikingly unequal in size. The first section is a theophany, which centers on John's visionary commission to address proclamations to the seven churches dictated by the exalted Christ (1:9–3:22). The second section is much longer and is unified in relatively cumbersome ways (4:1–22:9). The first part of this section (4:1–16:21) is unified by the eschatological framework provided by the seven seals, the seven trumpets, and the seven bowls. The second part of this section is unified by the paired angelic revelations (17:1–19:10 and 21:9–22:9) that frame 19:11–21:8.

The following outline is abbreviated and includes larger segments of the text. A more detailed outline of each section can be found at the beginning of each textual unit listed in the *Contents* under the heading of *Form/Structure/Setting*, where it will be followed by a relatively detailed literary analysis. The task of outlining Revelation in minute detail reveals a host of compositional problems that shorter outlines miss. These problems will be discussed in sections dealing with the literary analysis of each major textual unit.

The inscription
I. Prologue (1:1–8)
   A. Title: The revelation of Jesus Christ (1:1–2)
   B. Beatitude (1:3)
   C. Epistolary prescript (1:4–5c)
   D. Doxology (1:5d–6)
   E. Two prophetic oracles (1:7–8)
II. John's vision and commission (1:9–3:22)
   A. Vision of "one like a son of man" (1:9–20)
   B. Proclamations to the seven churches (2:1–3:22)
      1. The proclamation to Ephesus (2:1–7)
      2. The proclamation to Smyrna (2:8–11)
      3. The proclamation to Pergamon (2:12–17)
      4. The proclamation to Thyatira (2:18–29)
      5. The proclamation to Sardis (3:1–6)
      6. The proclamation to Philadelphia (3:7–13)
      7. The proclamation to Laodicea (3:14–22)
III. The disclosure of God's eschatological plan (4:1–22:9)

A. John's heavenly ascent (4:1–2a)
B. The sovereignty of God, the investiture of the Lamb, and the first six seals (4:2b–7:17)
1. The vision of the heavenly throne room (4:2b–5:14)
   a. The heavenly worship of God (4:2b–11)
   b. The investiture of the Lamb (5:1–14)
2. The Lamb breaks the first six seals (6:1–17)
   a. The first four seal visions (6:1–8)
   b. The fifth seal (6:9–11)
   c. Vision of the sixth seal (6:12–17)
3. The protective sealing of the 144,000 (7:1–17)
   a. The sealing of the 144,000 (7:1–8)
   b. Vision of a triumphant throne in the heavenly throne room (7:9–17)
C. The seventh seal and the first six trumpets (8:1–11:14)
1. The seventh seal (8:1)
2. Vision of the first six trumpets (8:2–9:21)
   a. Prologue: the third throne-room scene (8:2–6)
      (1) Commission of the seven angels (8:2)
      (2) Metaphor of the incense offering: the prayers of the saints for revenge are heard by God (8:3–5)
      (3) The seven trumpet angels prepare to sound their trumpets (8:6)
   b. The first four trumpets (8:7–12)
      (1) The first trumpet plague (8:7)
      (2) The second trumpet plague (8:8–9)
      (3) The third trumpet plague (8:10–11)
      (4) The fourth trumpet plague (8:12)
   c. The last three trumpets or the three woes (8:13–9:21)
      (1) Introduction to the the last three trumpets as the three woes (8:13)
      (2) The fifth trumpet, or first woe: demonic locusts (9:1–12)
      (3) The sixth trumpet, or second woe: a demonic cavalry (9:13–21)
3. The angel and the little scroll (10:1–11)
   a. The introduction of "another mighty angel" (10:1–3b)
      (1) Description of the mighty angel (10:1–2a)
      (2) The actions of the mighty angel (10:2b–3b)
   b. The episode of the seven thunders (10:3c–4)
   c. The stance and oath of the mighty angel (10:5–7)
   d. The eating of the scroll: a symbolic commission to prophecy (10:8–11)
4. The temple and the two witnesses (11:1–14)
   a. The command to measure the temple (11:1–2)
   b. The careers of the two witnesses (11:3–13)
      (1) Their mission and authority (11:3–6)
      (2) The fate of the two witnesses (11:7–10)
      (3) The ultimate triumph of the two witnesses (11:11–12)
      (4) Concluding scene of judgment and repentance (11:13)
   c. The second and third woes (11:14)

2. Sayings of the exalted Christ (22:12–13)
3. Beatitude (22:14–15)
4. Concluding attestation of the exalted Jesus (22:16)
5. Invitation to the water of life (22:17)
6. Jesus addresses conditional curses to those who hear this book (22:18–19)
7. Jesus, who attests this revelation, promises to return soon (22:20a)
8. Responses of the author (22:20b)
  B. Epistolary postscript (22:21)
The subscription

## Section 5: Source Criticism

*Bibliography*

**Aejmelaeus, A.** *Parataxis in the Septuagint: A Study of the Renderings of the Hebrew Coordinate Clauses in the Greek Pentateuch.* Helsinki: Suomalainen Tiedeakatemia, 1982. **Ashton, J.** *Understanding the Fourth Gospel.* Oxford: Clarendon, 1991. **Aune, D. E.** "Intertextuality and the Genre of the Apocalypse." In *SBL 1991 Seminar Papers.* Atlanta: Scholars, 1991. 142–60. **Bauckham, R.** *The Climax of Prophecy: Studies on the Book of Revelation.* Edinburgh: T. & T. Clark, 1993. **Bergmeier, R.** "Altes und Neues zur 'Sonnenfrau am Himmel' (Apk 12): Religionsgeschichtliche und quellenkritische Beobachtungen zu Apk 12.1–17." *ZNW* 73 (1982) 97–109. ———. "Die Buchrolle und das Lamm (Apk 5 und 10)." *ZNW* 76 (1985) 225–42. ———. "Die Erzhure und das Tier: Apk 12,18 und 17f. Eine quellen- und redaktionskritische Analyse." *ANRW* II, 25/5:3899–3916. ———. "'Jerusalem, du hochgebaute Stadt.'" *ZNW* 75 (1984) 86–106. **Boismard, M. É.** "'L'Apocalypse,' ou 'les apocalypses' de S. Jean." *RB* 56 (1949) 507–27. ———. "Notes sur L'Apocalypse." *RB* 59 (1952) 161–81. **Brekelmans, C. H. W.** "Een nieuwe theorie over de Apokalyps?" *Studia Catholica* 26 (1951) 113–19. **Charles, R. H.** *A Critical and Exegetical Commentary on the Revelation of St. John.* 2 vols. Edinburgh: T. & T. Clark, 1920. **Fekkes, J.** *Isaiah and Prophetic Traditions in the Book of Revelation.* JSNTSup 93. Sheffield: JSOT, 1994. **Gaechter, P.** "The Original Sequence of Apocalypse 20–22." *TS* 10 (1949) 485–521. ———. "The Role of Memory in the Making of the Apocalypse." *TS* 9 (1948) 419–52. **Giblin, C. H.** "Revelation 11.1–13: Its Form, Function, and Contextual Integration." *NTS* 30 (1984) 433–59. **Lee, J. A. L.** "Some Features of the Speech of Jesus in Mark's Gospel." *NovT* 27 (1985) 1–26. **Lohse, E.** "The Revelation of John and Pauline Theology." In *The Future of Early Christianity,* ed. B. A. Pearson. Minneapolis: Fortress, 1991. 358–66. **Lust, J.** "Ezek 36–40 in the Oldest Greek Manuscript." *CBQ* 43 (1981) 517–33. ———. "The Order of the Final Events in Revelation and in Ezekiel." In *L'Apocalypse,* ed. J. Lambrecht. 179–83. **Mazzaferri, F. D.** *The Genre of the Book of Revelation from a Source-Critical Perspective.* BZNW 54. Berlin; New York: de Gruyter, 1989. **Moore, S. D.** "Are the Gospels Unified Narratives?" In *1987 SBL Seminar Papers,* ed. K. H. Richards. Atlanta: Scholars, 1987. 443–58. ———. *Literary Criticism and the Gospels: The Theoretical Challenge.* New Haven; London: Yale UP, 1989. **Müller, U. B.** *Messias und Menschensohn in jüdischen Apokalypsen und in der Offenbarung des Johannes.* Gütersloh: Mohn, 1972. **Reader, W. W.** "Die Stadt Gottes in der Johannesapokalypse." Diss., Göttingen, 1971. **Rousseau, F.** *L'Apocalypse et le milieu prophétique du Nouveau Testament: Structure et préhistoire du texte.* Tournai: Desclée; Montréal: Bellarmin, 1971. **Sabatier, A.** *Les origines littéraires et la composition de l'Apocalypse de S. Jean.* Paris, 1888. **Spitta, F.** *Die Offenbarung des Johannes.* Halle: Waisenhaus, 1889. **Stierlin, H.** *La vérité sur l'Apocalypse: Essai de Reconstitution des Textes Originels.* Paris: Buchet/Chaster, 1972. **Vanhoye, A.** "L'utilisation du livre d'Ézéchiel dans l'Apocalypse." *Bib* 43 (1962) 436–76. **Vischer, E.** *Die Offenbarung Johannis:*

*Eine jüdische Apokalypse in christlicher Bearbeitung.* TU 2/3. Leipzig: Hinrichs, 1886. **Vos, L. A.** *The Synoptic Traditions in the Apocalypse.* Kampen: Kok, 1965. **Vouga, F.** *Geschichte des frühen Christentums.* Tübingen; Basel: Francke, 1994. **Wahlde, U. C. von.** *The Earliest Version of John's Gospel: Recovering the Gospel of Signs.* Wilmington: Glazier, 1989. ———. "A Redactional Technique in the Fourth Gospel." *CBQ* 38 (1976) 520–33. **Weber, H. E.** "Zum Verständnis der Offenbarung Johannis." In *Ausschrift und Geschichte: Theologische Abhandlungen Adolf Schlatter zu seinem 70. Geburtstage.* Stuttgart: Calwer, 1922. 47–64. **Weiss, J.** *Die Offenbarung des Johannes.* Göttingen: Vandenhoeck & Ruprecht, 1904.

## I. INTRODUCTION

More source-critical analyses of the Apocalypse of John have been proposed than for any other NT composition. Most of these proposals were made during the heyday of biblical source criticism, the approximately fifty-year period from ca. 1875 to 1925, when scholars exhibited boundless self-confidence in their ability to dissect biblical compositions into constituent sources. Since the middle of the twentieth century, however, relatively few comprehensive analyses of the sources of Revelation have been attempted. The source-critical proposals of Boismard, Stierlin, Rousseau, Bergmeier, and Ford are exceptions, though none of these proposals has met with any significant measure of acceptance outside very limited circles. In contrast, many source-critical theories have been proposed for the Fourth Gospel, which exhibits a far less problematic structure than Revelation (for brief reviews, see Ashton, *Understanding*, 76–90; von Wahlde, *Earliest Version*, 17–25).

More recently (particularly in American and Italian NT scholarship), the increasing currency of literary-critical methods that presuppose the unity of the literary texts under investigation has implicitly raised the question of the validity and utility of the source-critical method itself. Influenced by comparatively recent developments in literary criticism, a number of NT scholars have approached the Gospels from the perspectives of *composition criticism,* with its holistic approach to the theology of biblical narrative literature, and *narrative criticism,* with its broader concern for more comprehensive literary issues than simply the theology of the biblical narratives, the focus of both redaction and composition criticism (see Moore, *Literary Criticism,* 3–13). Since both of these newer forms of literary criticism often privilege the narrative unity of literary compositions, they have little use for source criticism.

> For a critique of the holistic preoccupation of narrative critics of the Gospels, see Stephen D. Moore, "Are the Gospels Unified Narratives?" in *1987 SBL Seminar Papers,* ed. K. H. Richards (Atlanta: Scholars, 1987) 443–58; id., *Literary Criticism,* 51–55. Moore's critique of the presupposition of the literary unity of the Gospels is made from the perspective of his own deconstructionist program. A holistic literary-critical approach to Revelation is advocated by L. L. Thompson, *Revelation,* 37–52.

Source criticism, however, has benefited from the relatively recent development of a new emphasis in literary criticism, *intertextuality,* a way of reading a text that sees it as part of a nexus of other texts and cultural systems, whether in the horizon of the author or of the readers (see Aune, "Intertextuality," 142–60).

In the present context, it is not my intention to defend the source-critical method. It needs no defense. Like any other critical method, it has strengths and weaknesses as well as limitations. The source-critical approach to apocalyptic literature in particular is justified, at least in part, because one of the major literary characteristics of the surviving Jewish and Christian apocalypses is that most of them have been subjected to a series of more or less extensive revisions and frequently reflect the use of earlier literary sources. Much of this literature was not simply copied so much as it was revised and rewritten. In analyzing such specific compositions as the Revelation of John and the *Shepherd of Hermas,* therefore, no holistic reading of these texts can entirely ignore the complex prehistory of the composition by papering over the many inconsistencies and seams that are present in them. Several examples, about which most scholars agree, will illustrate this point. Daniel, the oldest Jewish apocalypse, consists of two quite separate sections, 1–6 and 7–12; only the latter part can be considered an apocalypse (Collins, *Comm. Daniel,* 24–38). Further, the additions to the Hebrew-Aramaic Daniel found in the LXX indicate that the book continued to expand in its Greek form with the additions of the Prayer of Azariah and the Song of the Three Young Men (inserted after 3:23), the story of Susanna (placed before Dan 1 in the Theodotian version but after Dan 12 in the LXX and the Vulgate), and the tale of Bel and the Dragon, which concludes the book in the LXX and Theodotion. The longest Jewish apocalypse, *1 Enoch,* is in fact a combination of at least five different Jewish apocalypses (Nickelsburg, *Jewish Literature,* 46–55, 90–94, 145–51). *2 Enoch* exists in two quite different versions, the long recension and the short recension (F. I. Andersen in Charlesworth, *OTP* 1:91–100), and the *Testament of Abraham* also exists in two quite different recensions (E. P. Sanders in Charlesworth, *OTP* 1:871–80). There are also many instances of Christian interpolations in Jewish apocalypses, since the latter were preserved exclusively in Christian circles (Ford, 22–26). The *Shepherd of Hermas,* the oldest Christian apocalypse after Revelation, seems to have undergone extensive amplifications, so that the present text (which has not survived in complete form in Greek) came into existence in stages from A.D. 90 to 150. These examples could be multiplied many times over and clearly indicate that texts that had not (yet) been regarded as sacred were often subject to elaborate reworking and reformulation.

During the nineteenth and early twentieth centuries, NT critics proposed numerous source theories in which the hypothetical documents out of which Revelation was fashioned were identified; the way in which they were combined was described, and the later literary glosses added to the composition were isolated. Since the middle of the twentieth century, a reaction has set in against some of the excesses that characterized the source criticism of Revelation (and other biblical writings), with the result that there is a widespread tendency to regard Revelation as a composition that exhibits internal unity and coherence and to regard source-critical proposals as unnecessary if not perverse.

## II. THE UNITY AND HOMOGENEITY OF REVELATION

### A. *The Emphasis on Unity*

Writing in 1922, H. E. Weber expressed the opinion that the many source-critical theories of Revelation that had been proposed in the nineteenth and early twentieth centuries had failed. Convinced of the linguistic and structural unity of Revelation, he wrote with an almost audible sigh of relief: "A unified book!" ("Verständnis," 47–48).

In a similar vein, but much more recently, Mazzaferri (*Genre*, 37) has made this judgment: "the unity of the book has survived all attacks, and enjoys all but outright support today." It is worth noting that the term "attacks" is based on a martial image that assumes that those who propose source theories of Revelation are to be regarded as "enemies," a patently ridiculous assumption. The unity of Revelation has recently been emphasized by Bauckham (*Climax*, 1 n. 1):

> The more Revelation is studied in detail, the more clear it becomes that it is not simply a literary unity, but actually *one of the most unified works in the New Testament* [emphasis mine]. The evidence discussed in this chapter should be sufficient to refute theories which divide the book into disparate sources.

The term "unified" here is used in a problematic way, however. Revelation is largely a narrative composition (and in this respect comparable only to the Gospels and Acts in the NT), but it does not possess the kind of narrative unity often presupposed by narrative critics. There is, for example, little or no continuity in the *dramatis personae* that appear in the embedded episodic narratives in the text (see below). What Revelation does possess is a plethora of literary devices linking the various parts of the text together, though not always in a completely successful manner. Revelation is a "unity" because the author has worked diligently, even ingeniously, at the task of linking units of texts that were not originally designed to fit together. In my view, then, the literary unity and coherence of Revelation have been exaggerated, though they certainly exist in some levels of composition.

Some NT scholars analyze Revelation and see the forest, while others see the trees. However, a comprehensive and satisfactory literary approach to Revelation must deal with the literary manifestations of *both* unity and disunity. The assumption of narrative unity of a text like Revelation is in part the revival of the so-called fallacy of authorial intention, i.e., the view that the meaning of a literary work is identical with the intention of the author (see Moore, "Unified Narratives," 446–52). According to Moore, "Narratology does not privilege or emphasize the *unity* of individual literary works" ("Unified Narratives," 453). Moore distinguishes the approach of narratologists from biblical scholars who use narrative criticism as a tool to recover the unity of the biblical narrative ("Unified Narratives," 453–54):

> It is not with the unity of the given narrative that these writers [narratologists] are concerned but with the final unity of the narrative *theories* which they are advancing. In narrative criticism the priorities are reversed. It is the unity of the individual (biblical) text that is prized, and the critic dips at random into the reservoir of narrative theory.

According to Moore ("Unified Narratives," 456), biblical scholars have traditionally conceived of the biblical text as

> ... an objective, independent entity, possessed of stable, inherent, discoverable properties. It is an entity which embodies a more or less recoverable authorial purpose, a purpose which represents the text's primary meaning, and (in case of recent gospel scholarship, for example) is its primary source of unity.

In recent years biblical scholars have increasingly adopted the methods of nonbiblical literary criticism. Biblical scholars who now practice narrative criticism argue that while historical criticism tended to dissect and fragment biblical compositions, narrative criticism opens up the possibility of assuming the unity of the text and of reading such narrative texts on their own terms as unified stories. L. L. Thompson, a NT scholar influenced by narrative criticism, approaches the text of Revelation both as a coherent, integrated whole and as a work that is not autonomous but rather exhibits reciprocal relations with other social, political, psychological, historical, literary, and religious structures and contexts (*Revelation,* 2). Thompson is therefore concerned with two issues, the wholeness of Revelation (*Revelation,* 37–91) and the reciprocal relationship of Revelation with the cultural structures within which it was composed (*Revelation,* 95–201). However, when Thompson speaks of the "linguistic unity" or "unity of language" of Revelation (*Revelation,* 37–52), he is not referring to the language and style of Revelation (which he does not even discuss). Rather, he has in view the more strictly literary uses of language and therefore focuses on *narrative* unity, *metaphoric* unity, unity evident in the author's use of *OT images, patterns,* and *allusions,* and unity exhibited by the *language of worship* (*Revelation,* 53–73). In discussing all of these uses of language in Revelation, however, Thompson assumes rather than demonstrates that these various literary features exhibit the unity of the composition. Since it is difficult to understand how *disunity* would manifest itself in each of these literary features, the supposition of unity wins by default.

The many apparent inconsistencies and problems in analyzing the structure of Revelation have engendered a number of attempts to isolate the sources used by the author and the ways in which these sources were adapted to the final composition. The linguistic peculiarities of this book have also encouraged the formulation of a variety of analyses and hypotheses.

## B. Linguistic Homogeneity

In recent years it has been claimed that analysis of language and style indicates that the linguistic peculiarities of Revelation are not restricted to particular sections of the composition but permeate the book. If true, this means that there is no firm linguistic or stylistic basis on which to base theories of the existence of extensive earlier sources by different authors that have somehow been combined to form Revelation in its present state. It appears, however, that the linguistic and stylistic homogeneity of Revelation has been somewhat overstated, and this issue will be dealt with throughout the commentary at appropriate junctures. In a detailed study of the morphology of the Greek of Revelation, G. Mussies has discussed the linguistic character and peculiarities of Revelation and has concluded that the semitizing elements that reflect the linguistic interference of both Hebrew and Aramaic are not restricted to particular sections of the composition but are scattered uniformly throughout the book (Mussies, *Morphology,* 350–51). Though this judgment is somewhat exaggerated (i.e., Mussies includes no statistics justifying this judgment), it nevertheless suggests that there are no firm linguistic or stylistic bases that may be used to support various source-critical theories based on the supposition that extensive earlier sources by *different authors* have somehow been combined to form Revelation in its present state. The linguistic homogeneity of Revelation, then, casts doubt on the validity of all *compilation theories* (hypotheses that Revelation is the product of the combination of two or more relatively extensive apocalypses written by different authors), though it is less problematic for *revision theories* (a single extensive apocalyptic composition was subject to later editorial expansion by a different hand; either an original Jewish apocalypse was transformed into Revelation by a Christian editor, or an original Christian apocalypse was revised and augmented by a later editor or series of editors).

## C. The Homogeneity of OT Allusions

While there have been a number of significant studies that have focused on the use of the OT in Revelation, one of the most significant of such studies is the dissertation of J. Fekkes (*Prophetic Traditions*), who had the advantage of drawing on a number of previous studies on the use of the OT in Revelation and has produced a striking synthesis of such studies by summarizing the various thematic patterns of allusion to the OT that permeate the book. Further, he has clearly broken new ground by a very careful analysis of the dependence of the author of Revelation on Isaiah. Fekkes, however, regards the author as a masterful exegete of the OT, while in my view the author is less concerned with exegesis than with shaping his own theological message using OT style, language, and patterns of thought.

## III. MAJOR SOURCE-CRITICAL THEORIES

### A. Introduction

There are several approaches to understanding the final form of Revelation: (1) *compilation theories,* which propose that two or more originally separate apocalypses were combined together to form Revelation (F. Spitta; M. É. Boismard, *RB* 56 [1949] 507–27; F. Rousseau, *L'Apocalypse;* H. Stierlin, *La vérité*); (2) *revision theories,* which propose that a single extensive apocalyptic composition was subject to later editorial expansion; either an original Jewish apocalypse was transformed into Revelation by a Christian editor (E. Vischer, *Offenbarung*), or an original Christian apocalypse was revised and augmented by a later editor or series of editors (R. H. Charles), perhaps by a single author (H. Kraft; P. Prigent); and (3) *fragmentary theories,* which propose that various units of texts were joined together by John to form Revelation (J. Weiss; W. Bousset; P. Vielhauer, *Geschichte;* U. B. Müller, *Messias*).

### B. Compilation Theories

#### 1. M. É. BOISMARD (1949, 1952)

According to Boismard, the uniform style of Revelation is an argument against the supposition that the work is a combination of documents written by several authors and finally unified by a redactor. Boismard has proposed that the present text of Revelation is a compilation made up of two originally separate apocalypses, written at different times by a single author, which are largely parallel in structure and content. Text I was written after A.D. 70 (perhaps during the reign of Vespasian or the beginning of the reign of Domitian) in response to the crisis of idolatry and follows a coherent schema based on Ezekiel. Text II, on the other hand, was written during the reign of Nero in response to a situation of persecution and follows a coherent schema based on Dan 7 and Joel 3. Rev 1–3 was written after Texts I and

II because it contains material found in the two earlier apocalypses.

The content of Text I, according to Boismard, is as follows: (a) Announcement and Introduction of the Great Day of Wrath (4:1–9:21; 10:1, 2b, 5–7; 11:14–18). (b) The Great Day of Wrath: [1] Presentation of Babylon (17:1–9, 15–18), [2] Fall of Babylon (18:1–3), [3] The Elect Preserved (no parallel), [4] Lamentation over Babylon (18:9–13, 15–19, 21–24), [5] Song of Triumph (19:1–10). (c) The Messianic Reign (20:1–6). (d) The Eschatological Conflict (20:7–10). (e) The Judgment (20:13–15). (f) The Future Jerusalem (21:9–22:2; 22:6–15).

Text II, on the other hand, exhibits the following content, each unit of which is essentially parallel with the corresponding units in Text I: Prologue: The Swallowing of the Little Book (10:1, 2a, 3–4, 8–11). (a) Announcement and Introduction of the Great Day of Wrath (12:1–16:21). (b) The Great Day of Wrath: [1] Presentation of Babylon (17:10, 12–14), [2] Fall of Babylon (cf. 14:8), [3] The Elect Preserved (18:4–8), [4] Lamentations over Babylon (18:14, 22–23), [5] Song of Triumph (18:20 [cf. 16:5–7]). (c) (No parallel). (d) The Eschatological Conflict (19:11–20). (e) The Judgment (21:1–4; 22:3–5). (f) The Future Jerusalem (21:1–4; 22:3–5; 21:5–8). Appendix: The Two Witnesses (11:1–13, 19).

Boismard's proposals have been severely criticized by Brekelmans (*Studia Catholica* 26 [1951] 113–19), Vanni (*La struttura letteraria*, 76–83), and J.-P. Ruiz (*Ezekiel in the Apocalypse: The Transformation of Prophetic Language in Revelation 16:17–19:10* [Frankfurt: Lang, 1989] 38–54). Yet one of the strengths of Boismard's proposal is that a single author is responsible for the composition and combination of the two hypothetical apocalypses.

## 2. J. M. FORD (1965)

In her Anchor Bible Commentary of 1965, Professor Ford proposed a source-critical theory of Revelation that combines Jewish and Christian elements with a unique twist. Ford proposed that Revelation consists of two main sections: Rev 4:1–11:19 is a revelation to John the Baptist, while Rev 12:1–19:21 consists of a revelation to a disciple of John the Baptist. Rev 20–22, however, is particularly problematic, for it contains numerous aporias, and Ford has therefore chosen to follow, with slight modification, the textual rearrangement proposed by Gaechter (20:1–3; 21:9–22:2; 22:14–15; 20:4–6, 7–15; 21:1–4c; 22:3–5; 21:5a, 4d, 5b–7; 22:6–7a, 8–13, 7b, 17b, 18–19). In addition to these two main Jewish sections, Rev 1–3 and 22:16a, 20b, 21, were written by a disciple of John the Baptist who had become a follower of Jesus like those described in Acts 19:1–7 (39–41), a fact revealed by the distinctive christological and ecclesiological features in these sections, as well as by a characteristic vocabulary (41–46). Professor Ford has informed me (letter of 20 January 1995) that, in the revision of her Anchor Bible Commentary on Revelation currently in preparation, she has completely discarded her previous assessment of the sources. She now considers Revelation to be a unity, with the possible exception of the seven letters, and even these were an integral part of the original text.

## 3. F. ROUSSEAU (1971)

In his 1968 doctoral dissertation at the University of Montreal, F. Rousseau examined the structure and prehistory of Revelation. According to Rousseau, there are five redactional layers behind the present text of Revelation, the first two of which are Jewish and the last three Christian. The earliest layer is Jewish and is called the "Apocalypse of Three Calamities." It consists of 8:13; 9:1b–21 (less 9:13a, 14a); 11:1–2, 13–14 (less v 13c); 15:1; 6:9b–11bc; 16:1; 16:2ab, 10c–11, 3, 8–9, 12, 17–21, 5–7. The second layer, also of Jewish origin, is designated the "Apocalypse of the Double Heptad of Trumpets and Bowls." It absorbs the first and consists of Rev 4 (less vv 1, 4, 5b, 9–11); 8:2–13; 9; 10:1ab, 2b, 5b–6; 11:1–2, 13–14; 15:1; 6:9b–11bc; 15:5–8; 16 (less vv 13–16); 7:9–12 (less the mention of the Lamb and the Elders); 22:10–15. The third Christian layer absorbs the first two and is called the "Apocalypse of the Lamb" in Rev 4–11; 15–22. It consists of 1:1–3; 4 (less vv 1, 5b); 5–7 (less 5:6b); 8–11 (less 10:7; 11:15–19); 15–22 (less 15:2–4; 16:2c, 15; 19:10d–16; 21:1–8; 22:3–5, 16–21). The fourth layer, called the "Apocalypse of Letters," is independent of the first three and consists of 1:4ab; 1:9–3:22 (less two expressions in 3:1b, 14b); 21:1a, 2–4b; 22:3–5; 21:5–8. The final redaction links the "Apocalypse of the Lamb" with the "Apocalypse of Letters" and adds the large section in 12–14. It includes a number of finishing touches, and consists of 1:4c–8; 3:1b, 14b; 4:1, 5b; 5:6b; 10:7; 11:15–19; 12:1–14:20; 15:2–4; 16:2c, 15; 19:10d, 11–16; 21:1b, 2a, 3c, 4c, 9c; 22:3b, 6c, 16–21.

With one exception, each of these five layers of Revelation has an epilogue, which contains the following basic elements: (a) an attestation of the book, (b) a judgment of salvation and judgment, (c) a double exhortation (negative and positive), (d) a promise of recompense, and (e) an emphasis on the prophetic character of Revelation. The following chart lists the five basic features of each of the epilogues (see Kavanagh, *Liturgical Dialogue*, 36–37).

|               | I       | II      | III      | IV        | V        |
|---------------|---------|---------|----------|-----------|----------|
|               | 19:9–10 | 21:5c–8 | 22:6–9   | 22:10–15  | 22:16–21 |
| *Basic Element* |       |         |          |           |          |
| Attestation   | 9e      | 5e      | 6b       | 10bc      | 20a      |
| Judgment      | 10      | 6d–8    | 8–9      | 11, 14–15 | 17c–19   |
| Exhortation   |         |         |          |           |          |
|   Negative    | 10c     | 8       | 9b       | 10, 15    | 18–19    |
|   Positive    | 10d     | 6d–7    | 7b, 9c   | 14        | 17bcd    |
| Recompense    | 9c      | 6e–7    | 7ab      | 12, 14    | 17cd, 20b|
| Prophecy      | 10a     | ——      | 6c, 7b, 9c | 10b     | 18a, 19a |

These elements, however, are not always clearly present, as Kavanagh (*Liturgical Dialogue*, 37–38) demonstrates. Further, Rousseau's very complex analysis of the prehistory of Revelation has had a negligible influence on subsequent research and has not unexpectedly met with some severe criticism; see X. Jacques, *Novelle Revue Théologique* 95 (1973) 413–15; A. Moda, *Studia Patavina* 22 (1975) 209–11.

### 4. H. STIERLIN (1972)

Inspired by the work of M. É. Boismard, H. Stierlin has proposed the original existence of three separate "synoptic" apocalypses, which were preceded by the "Apocalypse of the Two Witnesses" and followed by the "Letters to the Seven

Churches." These five compositions were combined early in the second century A.D. to form Revelation. A brief summary of Stierlin's description of these five compositions follows:

a. The "Apocalypse of the Two Witnesses" (A.D. 68–69) consists of the following segments: Rev 11:3–5a, 6–8a, 9–13 (Stierlin, *La vérité*, 105–9).

b. The "First Apocalypse" (A.D. 70) consists of the following segments (Stierlin, *La vérité*, 110–22): (1) Introduction (22:16; 1:3ab), (2) Prologue of the Swallowed Book (10:1ac, 2a, 3–4, 8–11), (3) Measuring the Temple (11:1–2), (4) The Beast and Its Image (13:11–14a, 14c–18; 17:8; 14:9–11), (5) Vision of the Ark of the Covenant (11:19; 6:9–11), (6) Four Plagues Afflict the World (15:5–6, 7b–8; 16:1, 10a,b, 12, 3–7, 17b), (7) The Rider and the Vintage (19:11, 13a, 14, 15b–16, 19; 20:9; 14:17–20), (8) The End of the World (6:12b–14; 15:2–4), (9) Judgment of the Dead (20:13a, 4, 13c; 21:3–4; 22:5), (10) Speech of Christ (16b, 10–11; 19:9c).

c. The "Second Apocalypse" (written A.D. 79) consists of the following segments (Stierlin, *La vérité*, 123–40): (1) Introduction (22:6c–7), (2) The Theophany (4:1–4, 6b–8a, 9–11; 5:13–14a), (3) The Lamb and the 144,000 (14:1–3, 4b–5), (4) Combat between Michael and the Dragon (12:7–8, 9c–11), (5) The First Three Plagues (15:1ab; 16:2, 10c–11, 8–9, 17a, 21), (6) The Woman and the Beast (17:3–7, 9a, 18, 9b–10, 12–14), (7) The Judgment of Babylon (18:4–8; 16:18–20; 14:8; 18:20), (8) Lamentations over Babylon (18:14, 22–23; 19:4–5), (9) The Last Four Plagues (7:1; 8:7–10, 11b–12), (10) The Millennial Reign (20:1ac, 2b–d, 3e, 4c–5), (11) The Final Eschatological Battle (16:13–14, 16; 20:9c–10; 14:6–7), (12) The Judgment of the Dead (14:14, 15c–16; 20:12), (13) The New Jerusalem (21:1–2, 16ab, 11b, 12, 14, 21c–23; 19:9ab, 10), (14) Speech of Christ (21:6–8, 5c).

d. The "Third Apocalypse" (A.D. 88–96) consists of the following segments (Stierlin, *La vérité*, 141–69): (1) Introduction (1:1b–3 [portions only]), (2) The Theophany (4:1–8ac), (3) The Dragon Pursues the Woman (12:1–3b, 4c–6, 9ab, 4ab, 15–17), (4) The Sealed Book (5:1–11, 14b), (5) The Four Riders (6:18, 15–17), (6) Vision of the Beast (12:18e, 13:1–8), (7) The Judgment of Babylon (17:1–2, 18bc, 15, 12a, 16b–17; 18:21, 24, 1–3), (8) Lamentations over Babylon (18:9–13, 15–19; 19:1–3), (9) The 144,000 Elect (8:1b–5; 7:2, 3b–8), (10) The Plagues of the Trumpets (8:5, 13; 9:1–11a; 9:12–21; 11:14), (11) The End of Time and the Millennial Reign (10:1, 2bc, 5c–7; 20:1–2a, 3, 4cfg, 6–8; 19:17–18, 21b, 20ad; 11:15–18), (12) The Judgment of the Dead (20:11ab; 19:11d–12, 15a, 13b; 20:11cd, 13bc, 12, 15, 14), (13) The New Jerusalem (21:4d, 5ab; 19:6–8b; 21:9ac, 10–11a, 15, 16c–21b, 13, 12def; 22:1–4; 21:24–27; 22:8b–9), (14) Speech of Christ (22:12–13, 17, 14–15, 6a).

e. The Letters to the Seven Churches, written toward the beginning of the second century A.D., consists of the following segments (Stierlin, *La vérité*, 170–83): (1) Introduction (1:1ag, 2a), (2) Prologue (1:4–8), (3) Vision of the Son of Man (1:9–20), (4) To Ephesus (2:1–7), (5) To Smyrna (2:8–11), (6) To Pergamon (2:12–17), (7) To Thyatira (2:18–29), (8) To Sardis (3:1–6), (9) To Philadelphia (3:7–13), (10) To Laodicea (3:14–22), (11) Epilogue (22:20–21).

The subjective and extremely speculative character of Stierlin's source-critical analysis of Revelation means that the reconstruction of the five hypothetical sources is virtually worthless for scholarship. He has essentially atomized the text of Revelation into segments, which he then rearranges in what he proposes represents the original order of five separate documents. It is difficult to imagine how the final compiler could have accomplished such a radical rearrangement. While it is relatively certain that the (final) author of Revelation utilized sources, the incredibly complex way in which Stierlin proposes that the final document was compiled is difficult to justify. When ancients compiled sources into new compositions, they simply did not work in the way that Stierlin's reconstruction requires. Stierlin particularly focuses on the presence of doublets (e.g., 6:9–11 and 7:9–17; 12:6b and 12:14) and triplets (see *La vérité*, 232, Tableau III) as well as explanatory remarks (i.e., narrative asides), all of which he considers indicative of the combination of sources. The chief value in Stierlin's analysis is the sensitivity he exhibits toward the uneven character of the narrative and the fact that he recognizes that Revelation reflects compositional activity that took place over three decades.

## C. *Revision Theories*

### 1. R. H. CHARLES (1920)

While the definitive commentary on Revelation written by R. H. Charles in 1920 is not "recent," its importance for English scholarship on Revelation is such that a review of his complex source-critical theory is necessary. Charles suggested that John, the original author of Revelation, died when he had completed 1:1–20:3. Rev 20:4–22:21, which was already in existence in the form of a number of independent documents, was assembled and added to the original composition by an editor who was "a faithful but unintelligent disciple" of John the Apocalyptist (1:l–lv). According to Charles (2:144–54), this editor made a chaos of 20:4–22:21. However, the editor was more accomplished in Greek than the author, as exemplified by the construction in 20:11, τὸν καθήμενον ἐπ' αὐτοῦ, "the one sitting on it," and 21:5, ὁ καθήμενος ἐπὶ τοῦ θρόνου, "the one seated on the throne." This editor was responsible for about forty-three interpolations in the text, identifiable either because they clash with their context or because they violate the original author's linguistic style (1:lvii–lviii): 1:4c, 8, 14; 2:5, 22; 4:5, 6, 8; 5:8d, 11; 6:8bde; 8:2; 9:5c, 11c, 16b–17a, 19b; 11:5b; 14:32–42, 15–17 [here "the editor reaches the climax of his stupidity," 1:lii], 18; 15:1, 3, 6; 16:2c, 5a, 13b–14a, 19a; 17:9b, 15, 17; 18:13; 19:8b, 9b–10, 16; 20:4, 5, 11, 12, 13 [here "dishonesty has taken the part of incapacity," 1:lv], 14b; 21:6a; 22:12, 18b–19 [this section "exhibits the editor at his worst," 1:lv]).

In 20:4–22:21, according to Charles, the original author saw a vision of the future evangelization of the world by Christ and the glorified martyrs at the second coming, anticipated in 11:15; 15:4; 14:6–7. Through the editor's rearrangement, the millennial reign of Christ has no real significance, for when Christ and the glorified martyrs return to earth, they enjoy a dramatic but inconsequential victory, after which they sit on thrones in idleness for a thousand years (20:4–6). Since the text as it stands is both incoherent and self-contradictory, Charles identified a large number of dislocations in the text, which he has attempted to restore to their original order (2:144–54).

Charles has restored eleven "dislocated" passages to their original location (1:lix): (a) 2:27c after 2:26b; (b) 3:8bc before 3:8a; (c) 7:5c–6 after 7:8; (d) 11:18h after 11:18b; (e) 11:8g after 11:18c; (f) 13:5b after 13:6b; (g) 14:12–13 after 13:18; (h) 16:5b–7 after 19:4; (i) 16:15 after 3:3b; (j) 17:14–17 restored as 17:17, 16, 14; (k) 18:14–23 restored as 18:15–19, 21, 14, 22a–d, 23cd, 22e–h, 23ab, 20, 23–24.

Charles has also identified four lacunae in the text (1:lx–lxi): (a) several clauses in 16:10; (b) lost verses after 19:19a; (c) a line after 18:22a; (d) part of a couplet in 21:22.

In addition, Charles also identifies several Hebrew and Greek sources (1:lxii–lxv): (a) 7:1–3 (Hebrew source); (b) 7:4–8 (Hebrew source); (c) 11:1–13 (Greek source); (d) 12:1–17 (Greek source); and (e) 17:1–18:24 (Greek source), which was derived from two Hebrew sources, Source A (17:1c–2, 3b–6, 7, 18, 8–10; 18:2–23) and Source B (17:11, 12–13, 17, 16).

## 2. R. GAECHTER (1949)

Like Charles, Gaechter was struck by the numerous aporias in Rev 20–22, which he thought were the result of "blunders of memory" (*TS* 9 [1948] 114–52). Gaechter, like Charles, concluded that the two descriptions of the New Jerusalem in 21:1–4c and 21:9–22:2 exhibited discrepancies that suggested there were actually two New Jerusalems, one that exists in the present world and will last until the destruction of the first heaven and the first earth (21:9–22:2), which thereafter will be transformed into an eternal New Jerusalem (21:1–4c; 22:3–5); therefore, 21:9–22:2 should come before 21:1–4c; 22:3–5. Gaechter, therefore, reconstructed the original form of Rev 20–22 in the following way (*TS* 10 [1949] 485–521): (a) *the first triplet:* [1] 20:1–3 (the thousand-year chaining of Satan); [2] 21:9–22:2, 14–15 (the millennial Jerusalem); [3] 20:4–6 (the millennial rule of the martyrs with Christ); (b) *the second triplet:* [1] 20:7–10 (the release of Satan); [2] 11–15 (the last judgment); [3] 21:1–4c; 22:3–5; 21:5ab, 4d, 5c–8 (the eternal Jerusalem); and (c) *the third triplet:* [1] 22:10–13, 7b, 16bc, 17ab, 20 (the conclusion of the visions); [2] 22:21 (the conclusion of the epistle); [3] 22:18–19 (the conclusion of the book). While Gaechter deals only with the admittedly problematic final chapters of Revelation, his reconstruction of the text has strongly influenced the analysis of Ford (39).

## 3. H. KRAFT

Kraft, who provides a thumbnail sketch of his analysis of the composition of Revelation in *Offenbarung*, 11–15, tends to regard Revelation as essentially the work of a single author, though he is willing to entertain the possibility that Rev 2–3 (the letters to the seven churches) and Rev 21:9–22:5 (the description of the heavenly city) were added by a second hand. He thinks that it is impossible to consider Revelation the product of a unified literary plan (14), proposing that the author began with a first draft, which he later expanded. These expansions, however, disturbed the unity of the original conception and resulted in a work that in its present form is not well arranged. The original draft, he proposes, contained the seven-seals vision, later expanded by the addition of the seven-trumpets and the seven-bowls visions. At this point, the composition had a thematic focus on the sovereignty of God's actions in the world consisting of three series of seven plagues. However, several traditional components of eschatological expection were missing: the problem of the preservation of the righteous, the appearance of the eschatological prophets, the great eschatological tribulation, the onslaught of the heathen, and the gathering of the dispersed tribes. The author dealt with these issues through various insertions (*Einschüben*) into the original composition, such as the insertion of Rev 7 (the protective sealing of the righteous) after the sixth seal and Rev 11 (the two eschatological prophets) after the sixth trumpet. The author regarded the persecution under Domitian as the great eschatological tribulation and depicted the emperor as the agent of Satan on earth. He introduced a Satanic trinity (the Dragon, the Beast from the Sea, and the Beast from the Land = the False Prophet). The author thereby incorporated a dualistic drama in the second half of his work. This was later supplemented by the vision of the heavenly city (21:9–22:5), the letters to the seven churches (2:1–3:22), and finally various kinds of material at the beginning and end, including prophetic oracles, the protection formula (22:18–19), and other additions.

Though Kraft is somewhat vague about this, he thinks that Revelation went through three major phases, each indicated by a new conclusion. The first conclusion is now found in 19:1–10 (240–45), the second in 21:5b–8 (264–66), and the third and final conclusion in 22:6–21 (276–82). With regard to the problem of dating, Kraft thinks that the earlier part appeared between the summer of 97 and the spring of 98, based on Rev 13 and 17 (10, 222), while the seven letters of Rev 2–3 and the introductory and concluding sections were written between Trajan's death and the Jewish revolt in A.D. 114–15, i.e., ca. A.D. 110 (93).

### 4. P. PRIGENT (1988)

Prigent has proposed a theory of two editions of Revelation, a theory most recently expressed in an appendix to the second edition of his commentary on Revelation (371–73). The second edition differs only slightly from the first edition. The second edition consists of an insertion that consists mainly of the letters and begins in 1:19 and extends to the end of Rev 3. Rev 4:1 then picks up the threads of the narrative of the first edition. Further the second edition includes a second epilogue in 22:16–21. There are, in addition, a number of interpolations that also belong to the second edition (16:15; 21:25; 17:15). Prigent's analysis is perceptive and cautious and has several features in common with the theory proposed in this commentary (see below).

## D. *Fragmentary Theories*

The assumption that the author and editors of Revelation have incorporated an indeterminate number of pre-existing written sources into the composition has an important methodological advantage over the various compilation theories. Perhaps the major advantage is that Revelation is not approached with a proposal that can easily be foisted on individual textual units. Rather, each unit of text must be analyzed to see if there is evidence for the author's or the editor's use of sources, without the pressure of trying to fit these sources into some grand pattern.

### 1. W. BOUSSET (1906)

Although Bousset's discussion of the sources of Revelation was published early in this century (1906), his proposals have been extremely influential in subsequent discussions of the the source criticism of Revelation (particularly in German scholarship), and therefore a brief review of his approach is appropriate. According to Bousset, the author of Revelation incorporated a number of sources into various parts of his composition. Among the sections of Revelation that he thought reflected existing fixed documents are 7:1–8; 11:1–13 (a Jewish pamphlet from the time of the siege of Jerusalem); 12:1–17 (a vision of the Queen of Heaven, the Child, and the Dragon, derived from Eastern mythology); 13:11–18 (from the hand of the final redactor of Revelation; [1906] 379); 14:14–20; 17:1–18:24; 21:9–22:5 ([1906] 141; followed by P. Vielhauer, in Hennecke–Schneemelcher, *NTA* 2:622).

Bousset did not regard Rev 17 as a unity ([1906] 474) but proposed that behind it lay an older and a more recent version of the Nero *redivivus* legend; the more recent version represents the redaction of the earlier source ([1906] 414). This document was composed during the time of Vespasian, perhaps of Jewish origin ([1906] 415). To this source belong vv 1–7, 9–11, 15–18. Nero was the Beast who would return with the Parthian kings to destroy Rome ([1906] 414). The redactor added vv 8, 12–14 and several words and phrases in vv 6, 9, and 11 ([1906] 415). The notion of "Nero *redivivus*" was contributed by this redactor, as well as the conception of Nero as the Satanic counterpart of the Lamb ([1906] 415). Among the elements added ca. A.D. 100 were v 6 (καὶ ... ἐκ τοῦ αἵματος τῶν μαρτύρων Ἰησοῦ, "and ... with the blood of the witnesses to Jesus") and vv 8, 9b, 14–15 ([1906] 480).

### 2. R. BERGMEIER (1982–85)

In a series of articles published from 1982 through 1985, Bergmeier has provided source-critical analyses of major sections of Revelation (Rev 5; 10; 12; 17–18; 21:1–22:5).

a. In *ZNW* 73 (1982) 97–109, Bergmeier argues that Rev 12:7–12 (apart from v 11) is pure Jewish apocalyptic (*ZNW* 73 [1982] 98), a view also held by Charles (1:300, 307–8). The unity of the Jewish source behind Rev 12 is argued by Bergmeier (*ZNW* 73 [1982] 99) as well as by Müller (*Messias*, 168–69). Bergmeier argues that 12:1–6, 13–17 were originally a single source but that vv 5–7 were inserted by a Jewish (not a Christian) hand (*ZNW* 73 [1982] 100 n. 21). Vv 11, 17 are the only two traces of Christian tradition in the chapter. Though there are problems with interpreting the figure of the woman as Isis, Bergmeier nevertheless regards Rev 12 as a prime example of the Jewish use of non-Jewish mythical material.

b. In *ZNW* 75 (1984) 86–106, Bergmeier focuses on Rev 21:1–22:5 in its immediate context. He proposes an original cohesion of Rev 17, 18, and 21, which was divided for the insertion of a self-contained Jewish apocalypse, which now consists of 19:11–21:4 and 22:3–5. He considers Rev 22:5 to be clearly the concluding highpoint of this earlier Jewish apocalypse. Bergmeier identifies another self-contained Jewish source that has "the new world of God" as its central theme in 21:9–27 and 22:1–2, which he proposes was inserted between 21:1–4 and 22:3–5 (J. Weiss, 107, also argued that 21:1–4 and 22:3–5 were originally continuous). Bergmeier argues that the following passages are Christian redactional interpolations: 19:9a; 19:9c; 21:5b; 22:6a (all similar).

c. In *ZNW* 76 (1985) 225–42, Bergmeier argues that Rev 5 and 10 are doublets, the first based on Ezek 2:8–3:3 and the second on Ezek 1:1–3:15. The author took a Jewish vision, which he reproduced in Rev 10, and provided it with a Christian interpretation in Rev 5 (*ZNW* 76 [1985] 241). The voices of the seven thunders in Rev 10 must be sealed so that the Lamb can open the seven seals in Rev 5.

## IV. STAGES IN THE COMPOSITION OF REVELATION

### A. *Introduction*

The term "source criticism" is not really a satisfactory way of describing the analysis of Revelation that I now propose. A more appropriate description would be "the history of the composition of Revelation," or *diachronic composition criticism.* This designation suggests the significance of two important foci in the study of the text of Revelation: (1) the problem of understanding the *composition* of Revelation as the end product of (2) a literary *process,* which took place during a relatively extended period of time. My ultimate concern is not to atomize Revelation into a plethora of discrete textual units, each with a distinctive oral or literary history (though that in itself is a valid, if necessarily speculative, enterprise), but rather to try to understand how and why a single author, John of Patmos, brought Revelation into being.

The source criticism, or diachronic composition criticism, of Revelation should have three foci: (1) the identification and analysis of the various written and oral sources that have been incorporated into the final composition; (2) the analysis of the various stages of composition that have left telltale signs in the final composition; and (3) the reconstruction of the various theological perspectives that characterized the constituent sources of Revelation as well as the various editions of the book.

### B. *Criteria for Source-Critical Analysis*

Several principles can be elicited from past source-critical attempts to analyze Revelation: (1) The more complex the theory, the less convincing it will be, and the less credible it will ultimately appear. (2) Recent analyses of the linguistic and literary style of Revelation suggest that all *compilation theories,* that is, hypotheses that Revelation is the product of the lightly redacted combination of two or more relatively extensive apocalypses, are ultimately problematic. In a detailed study of the morphology of the Greek of Revelation, Gerard Mussies has argued that the linguistic peculiarities of Revelation are not restricted to particular sections of the composition but are scattered uniformly throughout the book (*Morphology,* 350–51). If so (even though Mussies' argument is somewhat exaggerated), this means that there is no firm linguistic or stylistic basis on which to base theories of extensive earlier sources by different authors that have somehow been combined to form Revelation in its present state. The linguistic and stylistic homogeneity of Revelation, however, has been somewhat overstated. (3) Since *revision theories* (a single extensive apocalyptic composition was subject to later editorial expansion; either an original Jewish apocalypse was transformed into Revelation by a Christian editor, or an original Christian apocalypse was revised and augmented by a later editor or series of editors) and *fragmentary theories* (which propose that various units of texts were joined together by John to form Revelation) are not mutually exclusive theories (they are, in fact, combined by R. H. Charles), it is possible that both theories can contribute to the unraveling of the various layers of tradition in Revelation. (4) Theories of *radical displacement* prove unpersuasive, not only because of their speculative character but also because they allow the critic to rewrite the text in the way in which he or she thinks it should have been written.

A number of criteria can be articulated for identifying sources and redactional interpolations in Revelation: (1) Seams in the structure of the text, i.e., abrupt transitions, the presence of parenthetical forms. (2) Apparent inconsistencies in the text. (3) Unnecessary repetitions. (4) Peculiar patterns in the presence or absence of the definite article, which may reveal the presence of textual units composed independently of each other. (5) The presence of "framing repetitions," a technique used to resume the original text sequence after an editorial insertion (e.g., Rev 12:9, 13 frame the insertion in vv 10–12); see von Wahlde, *CBQ* 38 (1976) 530–43. (6) Lexical items and phrases found concentrated in parts of a composition but missing from other parts. (7) Interpolations inserted in order to coordinate various segments of Revelation together by referring to what was mentioned earlier, or what will be mentioned later. (8) Since the introduction of new material that exhibits new theological perspectives sets such material in tension with previous material, the author of Revelation appears to have tried to *homogenize* the new combination of sources by interpolating the earlier edition with later perspectives; these interpolations introduce consistency of interpretation into Revelation, often in places where it was originally absent. (9) Strikingly Christian statements that are found in units of texts in which distinctively Christian features are otherwise missing may be regarded as interpolations. (10) Sections of Revelation that exhibit few or no interpolations or interpretive expansions may be considered among the latest sections of the text.

## C. Indications of Sources and Revision

The most striking literary characteristic in Revelation is the presence of approximately twelve relatively independent textual units that have little to do with their immediate contexts or indeed with the macronarrative of Revelation: (1) 7:1–17 (the Sealing of the 144,000), (2) 10:1–11 (the Angel with the Little Scroll), (3) 11:1–13 (the Two Witnesses), (4) 12:1–18 (the Woman, the Child, and the Dragon), (5) 13:1–18 (the Beasts from the Sea and the Land), (6) 14:1–20 (a pastiche of several visions and auditions: Lamb and the 144,000 [vv 1–5], three angelic revelations [vv 6–12], a parenetic audition [v 13], and the angelic harvest of the earth's grain and vintage [vv 14–20]), (7) 17:1–18 (the Whore of Babylon), (8) 18:1–24 (the Fall of Babylon), (9) 19:11–16 (the Rider on the White Horse), (10) 20:1–10 (the final defeat of Satan), (11) 20:11–15 (the judgment of the dead), and (12) 21:9–22:5 (the vision of the New Jerusalem). Each of these units is discussed in some detail in relevant parts of this commentary.

These twelve units of text are extremely diverse and provide the critic with evidence to suggest that they were formulated over a relatively extensive period of time, for a variety of purposes, and apparently with very different *Sitze im Leben*. Some of the relevant characteristics of these textual units are the following: (1) There is *little if any continuity in the dramatis personae* found in these episodes when they are compared (the figure of the Dragon, however, does link 11:19–12:17 with 13:1–18, but the Woman and the Child permanently disappear from view). The recognition of the discontinuity between these relatively extensive textual units suggests that they were not originally composed for the literary context to which they have been later adapted. Each of these discrete units exhibits a striking degree of narrative unity when analyzed individually, and they have been embedded by the author-editor in an eschatological macrostructure that provides Revelation with the overall conceptual and thematic unity that has justifiably impressed many readers. (2) The *paucity of substantive literary links* between these textual units strengthens the impression that they were initially independent of their present literary context. No significant links connect 7:1–8 with 10:1–11 and 11:1–13, for example, and few literary connections exist between the various other textual units listed above. Those that are present (e.g., the number 144,000 of 7:4; 14:1; the seven heads and ten horns of 12:3; 13:1; 17:3; the description of the Whore in 17:4 and the city in 18:16; the first mention of the Beast from the Abyss in 11:7) strike this critic as secondary expansions intended to unify the macrostructure of Revelation. (3) The *genre* and *literary style* of the various embedded text units exhibit greater diversity than one might expect of episodes written expressly for inclusion in their present literary position. Examples: Rev 7:4–8 is a census list. Rev 10:1–11 is a prophetic call narrative. Rev 11:1–13 lacks the typical features of a vision report (εἶδον is conspicuously absent) and is rather a prophetic narrative, which begins as a meditation on Zech 4:1–14, though that passage immediately disappears from view. Rev 17:1–18 is distinctive in several ways. It is the only text in Revelation in which the *angelus interpres* exercises the typical function of providing an allegorical explanation of the enigmatic details of a vision. Further, Rev 17 exhibits the form of an *ekphrasis*, i.e., an interpretive description of a work of art, a literary form found nowhere else in Revelation. This generic variety suggests that each of these text units was written for its own purpose and in its distinctive *Sitz im Leben*. (4) The *strong Jewish character* of several of these self-contained text units led earlier critics to assign them to Jewish apocalypses or fragments of Jewish apocalyptic literature that were later joined together to form the Revelation of John. Several of these text units reflect a hermeneutical shift in which Jewish traditions and conceptions have been reinterpreted as essentially Christian. In line with the proposal that I will outline below, it is probable that those text units that exhibit the most thoroughly Jewish character are in fact among the oldest parts of Revelation. In Rev 7:1–8, an Israelite tribal census list becomes Christianized through the later mention of the 144,000 followers of the Lamb in 14:1. In Rev 11:1–13, a prophetic narrative based on Jewish eschatological traditions involving Moses and Elijah has been lightly Christianized through the reference to the crucifixion of "their Lord" (11:8) and through the implicit parallel between their death, resurrection after three and one-half days, and ascension and that of Jesus. Rev 19:11–16, a narrative that virtually all interpreters regard as a depiction of the Parousia, does not reflect motifs typical of other Parousia traditions in early Christian literature.

## D. *The Hypothesis Proposed in This Commentary*

The Revelation of John reached its present literary form in two major stages, which I shall refer to as the "First Edition" and the "Second Edition." The First Edition consisted approximately of 1:7–12a and 4:1–22:5 and appears to have had a thoroughly apocalyptic orientation; it may well have been anonymous, perhaps even pseudonymous. The Second Edition added 1:1–3 (the title), 1:4–6 (the epistolary introduction and the doxology), 1:12b–3:22 (the commissioning vision of the exalted Christ and the dictated proclamations to the seven churches), 22:6–21 (a concluding epilogue and an epistolary conclusion), and several expansions or interpolations in the earlier sections of the text and had a strongly prophetic and parenetic orientation. While part of 1:1–6 may have stood in the First Edition, it has been so thoroughly rewritten and reformulated that it is now impossible to discriminate earlier from later elements. These two major editions represent the two primary stages in the composition of Revelation that are the easiest to detect.

The presence of these largely self-contained narrative units in Revelation can be explained in one of several ways: (1) The author wrote Revelation sequentially and composed each of these twelve text units expressly for the particular context in which each unit is now located (the view of Bauckham, *Climax,* 1–37). (2) The author-editor wrote Revelation sequentially, and at particular junctures he inserted a variety of written and oral sources from the material available to him, revising each unit so that it would fit the new literary context in which it was now set (Bousset [1906]). (3) The author-editor began with a varied collection of shorter and longer written apocalyptic documents (to which he apparently attached great value) that derived from a variety of sources. At some point in time he decided to design an encompassing literary narrative as a vehicle for embedding these texts in a comprehensive and inclusive eschatological scenario. (4) During a relatively extensive period of time (perhaps as many as twenty to thirty years; cf. Ramsay, *Letters,* 89), the author-editor composed a number of relatively independent, self-contained apocalyptic documents for a variety of purposes and intended for a variety of settings (some written, some oral), into which he incorporated a number of earlier traditions. Eventually the author-editor decided to place these documents, which required various degrees of revision, into a unifying literary context that became the Revelation of John, his apocalyptic *magnum opus.*

In options (1) and (2), the emphasis is on the author's decision to design a comprehensive, unified apocalyptic work, while in options (3) and (4) the emphasis is rather on the importance of the constituent units out of which Revelation was composed. In my view, option (4) is probably the closest to the truth. According to this view, the author enjoyed a lengthy career, which he began as a Jewish apocalyptist in Palestine, perhaps in the early 60s if not earlier. His Palestinian Jewish origin is assured by an intimate familiarity with the Hebrew text of the OT as well as the linguistic inference of both Hebrew and Aramaic on his distinctive Greek style. He may indeed have been one of the many Jews and Jewish Christians who were forced to flee in the wake of the second Jewish revolt (A.D. 66–73; cf. Trypho's flight from Palestine to Asia Minor because of the Bar Kosiba rebellion alluded to in Justin *Dial.* 1.3). It appears that he settled in the Roman province of Asia in southwest Asia Minor and carried out a ministry as a Jewish Christian prophet, perhaps as a leader of a group of Christian prophets, whose authority was accepted in several Christian congregations in that region. If it was in fact this Jewish rebellion that caused him to forsake his homeland, it is likely that the catastrophic chain of events during this period provided the occasion for at least some of the earlier visions included in Revelation. The fact that some scholars can confidently date Revelation to the late 60s while others with equal confidence favor the mid-90s of the first century A.D. is possible in part because internal evidence for *both* dates occurs within this complex and layered composition (see *Introduction,* Section 2: Date). Further, some portions of Revelation may exhibit a thoroughly *Jewish* character while other portions exhibit a thoroughly *Christian* character because the author moved from Judaism to Christianity at some point in his career or because he became increasingly influenced by particular theological developments in early Christianity. The changing theological perspectives of the author, according to this proposal, are reflected in the various compositional layers of Revelation that we shall discuss in some detail below.

It is not necessary for me to underscore the speculative character of this proposal, the most hypothetical part of which is the role of a single author who moved from the role of Jewish apocalyptist to Christian prophet and who regarded himself as virtually on an equal footing with the Israelite-Jewish prophets whose writings are included in the OT canon. There are several supportive arguments that give this proposal some plausibility, which I present in the form of a diachronic hypothesis of the composition of Revelation.

## 1. STAGES OF COMPOSITION

### a. Stage One: The Formation of the Self-Contained Textual Units

The twelve self-contained textual units in Rev 4:1–22:9 (mentioned above) were nearly all composed prior to their inclusion in this extensive compilation of vision reports and prophetic narratives, probably in the 50s and 60s of the first century A.D.: (1) 7:1–17 (the Sealing of the 144,000), (2) 10:1–11 (the Angel with the Little Scroll), (3) 11:1–13 (the Two Witnesses), (4) 12:1–17 (the Woman, the Child, and the Dragon), (5) 13:1–18 (the Beasts from the Sea and the Land), (6) 14:1–20 (a pastiche of several visions and auditions: Lamb and the 144,000 [vv 1–5], three angelic revelations [vv 6–12], a parenetic audition [v 13]), and the angelic harvest of the earth's grain and vintage [vv 14–20]), (7) 17:1–18 (the Whore of Babylon), (8) 18:1–24 (the Fall of Babylon), (9) 19:11–16 (the Rider on the White Horse), (10) 20:1–10 (the final defeat of Satan), (11) 20:11–15 (the judgment of the dead), and (12) 21:9–22:5 (the vision of the New Jerusalem). They represent a variety of apocalyptic-type compositions, though they are not "mini-apocalypses" in the sense that they do not exhibit the kind of relatively complete eschatological scenarios found, for example, in Mark 13 and parallels, Luke 17:20–37, and *Did.* 16. Further, each of these self-contained units was written or revised by John of Patmos comparatively early in his career as an apocalyptist, or revised by him in connection with the compilation of 4:1–22:9. P. Minear suggested that Revelation originated as a series of prophecies delivered to the seven congregations during worship (*New Testament Apocalyptic* [Nashville: Abingdon, 1981] 91).

As a rule, the authors and revisers of apocalypses were adept at marshaling an extensive array of apocalyptic themes and motifs, placing them within the framework of traditional eschatological scenarios, and show little hesitation to use and revise existing material (whether in oral or written form) in the process of composition. Since several of the self-contained textual units in Revelation exhibit a strikingly Jewish character, these may be revisions of existing texts (the idiosyncratic syntax of Revelation indicates that the author-editor characteristically reformulated the sources he used) or compositions that he produced early in his career. Yet other self-contained textual units appear to be largely his own composition. It is possible that the less overtly Christian text units originated either before the seer espoused Christianity or before he assimilated a distinctive Christian theological idiom. Therefore, these textual units should be regarded not as "intermissions" or "interludes" or "intercalations" in the larger narrative structure but rather as the focal set pieces for the sake of which the author-editor created a larger narrative structure. From the perspective of composition history, therefore, it is not appropriate to regard some of these textual units as "enlargements" (C. H. Giblin, *NTS* 30 [1984] 434–35) for the simple reason that they existed prior to the narrative structure in which they are embedded. The larger embedded textual units, to be sure, occasionally exhibit further literary expansions, indicating that themes and motifs from other textual units have been secondarily imported in order to provide a greater degree of homogeneity and literary unity to the entire composition. For the most part, there are very few indications of when and where each text unit was formulated, though there is certainly a strong geographical focus on the temple and Jerusalem in 11:1–13, which would fit a Palestinian provenance, even though both the temple and Jerusalem have arguably been dehistoricized and transformed into timeless, universal symbols (see *Comments* on 11:1–2; 11:8). There is also an apparent chronological reference in 17:10 to the sixth emperor who "now lives," but here too the tendency to dehistoricize the emperors and transform them into symbols makes the reference problematic (see *Comment* on 17:10 and *Introduction*, Section 2: Date).

### b. Stage Two: The Composition of the "First Edition"

The First Edition of Revelation was probably compiled about A.D. 70 (i.e., from A.D. 68 to 74), and the events leading up to and following the first Jewish revolt (A.D. 66–73) provided the *Sitz im Leben* for this apocalyptic writing. The twelve relatively self-contained text units mentioned above tend to share the same syntactical peculiarities, marking them as the product (i.e., the composition or the revision of an existing source) of a single author-editor, either alone or as the leading member of a circle of early Christian prophets. Rev 4:1–22:9 exhibits two major subdivisions based on formal literary considerations: (1) The formal organization of 4:1–16:21 is based on three apparently chronologically consecutive heptads: (a) the seven seals (4:1–8:1), (b) the seven trumpets (8:2–11:18), and (c) the seven bowls (15:1–16:21). Within this heptadic framework, the author-editor embedded six of the self-contained text units mentioned above. Three of these texts are embedded *within* the heptadic structures: 7:1–17 (the Sealing of the 144,000) is placed between the sixth and seventh seal (6:1–8:1); 10:1–11 (the Angel with the Little Scroll) and 11:1–13 (the Two Witnesses) are placed between the sixth and seventh trumpet (8:2–11:18). Three other text units are embedded in the heptadic structure by their placement between the seven trumpets (8:2–11:18) and the seven bowls (15:1–16:21): 12:1–18 (the Woman, the Child, and the Dragon), 13:1–18 (the Beasts from the Sea and the Land), and 14:1–20 (a miscellany of several visions and auditions). This sequence of three series of seven must be seen for what it is: the numerical and chronological framework chosen by the author-editor within which to embed the six textual units. (2) In the second major unit, Rev 17:1–22:9, the author-editor used a completely different formal structure: two framing angelic revelations that have striking formal similarities: 17:1–19:10 and 21:9–22:9. For various reasons (see *Form/Structure/Setting* on 17:1–18; 21:9–22:9), it is probable that 17:1–19:10 was compiled first and then later 21:9–22:9 was modeled after it. These two angelic revelations frame, and hence emphasize, 19:11–21:8, a section that deals with such concluding eschatological events as the coming of Christ from heaven to defeat the hosts opposed to God (19:11–21), the temporary imprisonment of Satan (20:1–3), the resurrection of the martyrs to share the thousand-year reign of Christ (20:4–6), the final defeat and punishment of Satan and the armies of Gog and Magog (20:7–10), the judgment of the dead (20:11–15), and the salvific promise of the New Jerusalem (21:1–8).

(1) *Textual Criteria for Distinguishing the First from the Second Edition.* There is, first of all, a clear literary seam in Rev 4:1 with important implications for the composition criticism of Revelation as a whole: "and the first voice which I heard like a trumpet speaking to me, saying 'Come up here and I will reveal to you what must happen after this.'" The "first voice" must be the voice in 1:10–11, which commanded John to write a book and send it to the seven churches. Is this "first voice" an angel or the exalted Christ? There is no evidence in 1:9–20 for distinguishing two speakers as some commentators have proposed, an angel in 1:11 and the exalted Christ in 1:19. My proposal is that in the First Edition, when John heard the voice like a trumpet behind him (1:10–11), upon turning around (1:12a) he was immediately summoned to ascend to heaven (4:1). The First Edition of Revelation consisted almost entirely of a heavenly ascent of the seer. It was only with the insertion of 1:12b–3:22, the vision of the exalted Christ (apparently on earth), followed by the dictation of the proclamations to the seven churches, that the ascent to heaven was delayed until 4:1. While the voice announces "I will reveal to you what must happen after this" (4:1), this mysterious "I" is immediately forgotten, though one might expect the voice to be the *angelus interpres* mentioned in 1:1 (and later in 22:8).

There are a great many features of each of these main sections of the text that occur only or primarily in one of two major sections of the text, either in the First Edition (1:7–12a; 4:1–22:5) or in the Second Edition (1:1–6; 1:12b–3:22; 22:6–21). In addition, there are a number of homogenizing expansions designed to link the later to the earlier sections of the text.

In general, there are few connecting links between the additions to Revelation in the Second Edition (i.e., 1:1–6, 12b–20, 2:1–3:22; 22:6–21) and the First Edition (1:7–12a; 4:1–22:5). Those that do exist are relatively superficial and apparently result from a conscious attempt on the part of the author-editor to forge a literary connection between the two sections. Even as conservative a critic as Ramsay thought that 2:1–3:22 was the last part of Revelation to be conceived and that it was inserted into the composition as an afterthought (*Letters,* 36–37). This is, of course, a negative argument, but it can be tested by analyzing the connections between Rev 1–3 and 4–22 proposed by those who insist that only a holistic reading of Revelation is valid.

The angelic mediator mentioned in 1:1 (where the definite article suggests that the author expects the readers to be familiar with this figure) is presented as the primary conduit through which John received his divine revelation, though this figure is explicitly mentioned again only in 22:8–9, 16. An angelic guide does appear in 17:1–18 (identified as one of the seven bowl angels in 17:1), and another angelic guide appears in 21:9–22:5 (again identified as one of the seven bowl angels in 22:9 but not explicitly connected with the angelic guide of 17:1–18). There is, in 22:6, however, a (not very successful) attempt to link the angelic guide of 21:9–22:5 to the angelic mediator mentioned in 1:1 and 22:8–9, 16.

Revelation describes itself as a "prophetic book," using various phrases such as οἱ λόγοι τῆς προφητείας, "the words of the prophecy" (1:3), οἱ λόγοι τῆς προφητείας τοῦ βιβλίου τούτου, "the words of the prophecy of this book" (22:7, 10, 18), and οἱ λόγοι τοῦ βιβλίου τῆς προφητείας ταύτης, "the words of the book of this prophecy" (22:19), but it is *never* referred to as such in Rev 4:1–22:5. Though the distinction between "prophecy" and "apocalyptic" is admittedly a modern one, there are legitimate distinctions that can be made between the two, and in the final edition of Revelation the author consciously plays the role of an early Christian prophet.

The emphasis on "keeping" or "obeying" (τηρεῖν) the commands written in Revelation (1:3; 22:7, 8), or "keeping my words" (2:26) and obeying "my [i.e., the exalted Christ's] words" (3:8, 10[2x]), are found only in Rev 1:1–3, 1:12b–3:22, and 22:5–21, where it is the words of *Jesus* that must be obeyed. In the earlier sections of the book, it is the words of *God* that must be obeyed. In 4:1–22:5, for instance, we meet the idea of "obeying the commands of God" (12:17; 14:12) and of "keeping one's garments" (16:15), though 14:12 and 16:15 are probably later insertions by the author-editor into an already formulated narrative (see *Comments* on those passages). It is also important to note that *there is actually very little of a hortatory or parenetic nature in 4:1–22:5 that can be "obeyed,"* though exhortation is an important part of 2:1–3:22; 22:6–21. The parenesis found in 2:1–3:22; 22:6–21 includes: (a) the necessity of remaining firm in the faith, i.e., by "conquering" (2:7, 11b, 17b, 26; 3:5, 12, 21), (b) the importance of "remembering" their previous state (2:5a; 3:3a) or of becoming "awake" (3:2; 16:15; the last passage is probably an interpolation or expansion), coupled with the necessity of repentance in order to regain those earlier standards (2:5a; 3:3a, 19b), reinforced with the threat of judgment (2:5b, 16; 3:3b); (c) encouragement not to fear what they will suffer, even to the point of death (2:10), (d) the importance of endurance or holding fast (2:25; 3:11; 13:10c; 14:12a; the last two passages are expansions; see *Comments*), (e) a statement that the righteous should continue to do right and the holy should continue to be holy (22:11).

There are also striking differences in the Christology of the earlier parts of Revelation when compared with that of the later framing sections. (a) God is referred to as "the Alpha and the Omega" in 1:8; 21:6, whereas the same title is applied to Christ in 22:13. (b) God is referred to as "the Beginning and the End" in 21:6, while this title is applied to Christ in 22:13 (cf. 3:14). (c) Jesus is called "the First and the Last" in 1:17; 2:8; 22:13, but this title is not used in the First Edition of the book. (d) The divine title "the one who is and who was and who is to come [ὁ ἐρχόμενος]" (1:4, 8; 4:8; cf. 11:15; 16:5) is applied exclusively to God and occurs primarily in the First Edition (1:4 is an exception). (e) Jesus alone is the subject of the verb ἔρχεσθαι, "come," in passages found in the Second Edition: 2:5, 16; 3:11; 22:7, 12, 20 (the exception in 16:15 is clearly a later insertion). (f) The expression ὁ χριστός, "Christ," occurs four times in Revelation, twice as a title in the phrase ὁ χριστὸς αὐτοῦ, "his Christ" (11:15; 12:10), and twice without modification as a title (20:4, 6). On the other hand, the anarthrous name Ἰησοῦς Χριστός, "Jesus Christ," occurs only in 1:1, 2, 5 (the Second Edition). (g) Rev 1:13–14 describes the exalted Jesus as if he were identical with the Ancient of Days in Dan 7:16, though this equation is found only in the later additions to the text of Revelation and has no counterpart in the earlier sections of the work. (h) The term ἀρνίον, "Lamb," the most common way of designating Jesus in Revelation, occurs twenty-eight times, but only within 4:1–22:5, the First Edition. (i) The term κύριος, "Lord," is used primarily of God (14x), usually in the phrase κύριος/κύριε ὁ θεός, "Lord"/"Lord God" (10x). However, the term κύριος, "Lord," is used of Jesus in the phrase "Lord

Jesus" in the Second Edition (22:20, 21). In the body of Revelation, this title is applied to Jesus in the phrase "Lord of lords" (17:14; 19:16), which elsewhere in Jewish and early Christian literature is used almost exclusively of the God of Israel. 17:14 appears to be an expansion based on 19:16 (used in a homogenizing way), or else *both* passages were interpolated simultaneously as part of the author's program for enhancing the Christology of Revelation in the Second Edition. The title "Lord" is also applied to Jesus in the expansion in 11:8 ("where also their Lord was crucified") and perhaps in the expansion in 14:13 ("Blessed are the dead who die *in the Lord*"). (j) The phrase "(who) lives for ever and ever" is used of Christ once in 1:18 in the First Edition, but of God four times in the First Edition (4:9, 10; 10:6; 15:7). (k) The resurrection of Jesus is referred to only in 1:5, 18; 2:8, all part of the Second Edition (the verbs most frequently used in the NT and other early Christian literature of the resurrection of Jesus, ἐγείρειν and ἀνίστημι [both meaning "to rise, arise"], are conspicuous by their absence).

There have been a number of discussions of the possible influences of the Synoptic sayings on the Revelation of John. In the only monograph devoted to this issue, Louis Vos identifies eight passages in which sayings of Jesus appear to have been used by the author (Vos, *Synoptic Traditions*): (1) Blessings on Hearing and Keeping (Rev 1:3a, cf. Luke 11:28), (2) the Parousia: Tribes Mourn (Rev 1:7; see Matt 24:30), (3) Having Ears, Let Him Hear (e.g., Rev 2:7, 11, 17; see, e.g., Matt 11:15; 13:9), (4) Watch: the Thief Comes (Rev 3:2–3, 16:15; see Matt 24:42–43 = Luke 12:39–40), (5) Confession before God (Rev 3:5c; see Matt 10:32 = Luke 12:8), (6) The Door, the Feast, and the Fellowship (Rev 3:20; see Mark 13:29; Matt 24:33; cf. Luke 12:35ff.), (7) Occupying Throne(s) with Christ (Rev 3:21; see Luke 22:28–30; Matt 19:28), and (8) the Saying of the Sword (Rev 13:10b; see Matt 26:52b). All of the sayings Vos identifies as somehow dependent on the Synoptic Jesus tradition are found in those sections of Revelation that we have identified as the Second Edition, with the exception of 1:7; 13:10; 16:15, the last two of which are arguably later interpolations by the author-editor (see *Comments* on those passages).

The peculiar use of the definite article also reveals interesting compositional patterns that seem to reflect the use and compilation of written sources. The noun ρομφαία, "sword" (the one projecting from the mouth of the exalted Christ), is anarthrous in 1:16 but has (as expected) the anaphoric article in 2:12, 16 (all part of the Second Edition). However, ρομφαία, "sword," occurs twice more in Revelation, but the first of these two occurrences is unexpectedly anarthrous in 19:15, while the second is (as expected) arthrous in 19:21 (both in the First Edition). This suggests that 1:12b–3:22 was composed independently of the textual unit found in 19:11–21 and, further, that the "sharp two-edged sword" that issues from the mouth of the exalted Christ was in all probability derived from the messianic imagery of 19:11–21; i.e., 19:11–21 was composed *before* all or part of 1:12b–3:22 was written.

The stereotypical formulas καὶ εἶδον, "and I saw" (32x), καί . . . εἶδον (7x), καὶ ἤκουσα, "and I heard" (15x), καὶ εἶδον καὶ ἤκουσα, "and I saw and heard" (2x), and καί . . . ἤκουσα (7x), used by the author to introduce both major and minor units of text, and μετὰ ταῦτα/τοῦτο εἶδον, "after this I saw" (5x), and μετὰ ταῦτα ἤκουσα, "after this I heard" (1x), used by the author to introduce major units of text, occur almost exclusively in 1:7–12a and 4:1–22:5. The exceptions are καί . . . εἶδον in 1:12b, 17, and καὶ ὅτε ἤκουσα καὶ ἔβλεψα, "and when I heard and saw," in 22:8.

There are few if any reflections of Pauline influence within Revelation as many scholars have recognized (e.g., Lindemann, *Paulus,* 233, 396). Two possible exceptions are the epistolary prescript (1:4–5a) and postscript (22:21), both part of the Second Edition. I say "possible" exceptions because of the widespread view that these Christian epistolary elements were created by Paul (this is the view, for example, of E. Lohse). Another possible Pauline influence is the use of the phrase ἐν κυρίῳ, "in the Lord," in 14:13, found almost exclusively in the Pauline corpus with the exception of this passage and Ignatius *Pol.* 8.3. In Rev 14:13, however, it is not certain whether κύριος, "Lord," refers to God or Christ, and it is probable that both v 12 and v 13, which interrupt a series of angelic revelations, are later interpolations or expansions by the author-editor.

Rev 14:12 is a parenetic saying introduced by ὧδε, "here, this is," which interrupts the narrative. There are three other such sayings in Revelation, each introduced by ὧδε (13:10, 18; 17:9). The similarities between 14:12 and 13:10 are extremely close:

> 14:12: ὧδε ἡ ὑπομονὴ τῶν ἁγίων ἐστιν.
> "This indicates that the perseverance of God's people involves . . ."
> 13:10: ὧδέ ἐστιν ἡ ὑπομονὴ καὶ πίστις τῶν ἁγίων.
> "This indicates that the endurance and faith of God's people are involved."

This verbal similarity suggests that 14:12 was drawn from 13:10 and functions as a homogenizing expansion. Rev 14:13 is a saying that consists of two parts: (a) an unidentified voice from heaven commanding the seer to write, and (b) the second of seven beatitudes in Revelation (1:3; 14:13; 16:15; 19:9; 20:6; 22:7, 14). This too appears to be a later expansion.

The absence of Pauline influence throughout the body of Revelation is reinforced by the two unusual uses of the active verb εὐαγγελίζειν, "to announce good news" (10:7; 14:6), and the unusual use of the noun εὐαγγέλιον, "good news, gospel," in the phrase εὐαγγελίζειν εὐαγγέλιον, "announce the good news" (14:6), where there is not only no trace of Pauline influence but also no trace of the conventional use of this verb and noun in other early Christian literature (see *Comments* on these passages for details). There are a number of motifs that occur in the First Edition that are either not carried over into the Second Edition, or else are included for the express purpose of homogenizing the two versions: (1) The phrase ἡ μαρτυρία Ἰησοῦ, "the witness of Jesus," occurs five times in the First Edition (1:9; 12:17; 19:10[2x]; 20:4), while the term μαρτυρία, "witness, testimony," occurs three times in the First Edition (6:9; 11:7; 12:11). In the Second Edition, the phrase ἡ μαρτυρία Ἰησοῦ Χριστοῦ, "the witness borne of Jesus," occurs in only 1:2, where it is used as part of the title and appears to have been derived from the use of that motif in the First Edition. (2) The divine title ὁ ὢν καὶ ὁ ἦν καὶ ὁ ἐρχόμενος, "the one who is and who was and who is coming," occurs just three times (1:4, 8; 4:8), while the variations of this title occur twice in the First Edition (11:17, κύριε ὁ θεὸς ὁ παντοκράτωρ, ὁ ὢν καὶ ὁ ἦν, "Lord God Almighty, the one who is and who was"; 16:5, ὁ ὢν καὶ ὁ ἦν, ὁ ὅσιος, "the one who is and who was, the holy one"). It appears more probable that the twofold title ὁ ὢν καὶ ὁ ἦν, "the one who is and who was," was expanded to a threefold title with the addition of καὶ ὁ ἐρχόμενος than the reverse.

The verb λαλεῖν, "to talk, to speak" occurs twelve times in Revelation, only in the First Edition, six times as part of the distinctive expression λαλεῖν μετ᾽ ἐμοῦ, "to speak with me" (1:12; 4:1; 10:8; 17:1; 21:9, 15; elsewhere in the NT only in Mark 6:50; John 4:27; 14:30, though it occurs with some frequency in Hermas [*Vis.* 1.4.3; 3.10.1; *Mand.* 11.2; *Sim.* 5.3.2; 5.4.5; 6.3.2; 9.1.1; 9.11.1]), and six times in a variety of other ways (10:3, 4[2x]; 13:5, 11, 15).

There are several grammatical features that tend to cluster in the First or Second Edition. (1) The dative of indirect object is placed before the verb only fifteen times in Revelation, ten times in the seven proclamations that are part of the Second Edition (2:1, 7, 8, 12, 17, 18, 24; 3:1, 7, 14) and five times elsewhere: (6:4; 7:2; 16:6 [probably an expansion]; 19:10; 22:9). (2) The preposition παρά, "beside," occurs just three times, only in Rev 2–3 (2:13, 28; 3:18). (3) The inferential particle οὖν, "indeed, therefore," occurs just six times, only in Rev 1–3 (1:19; 2:5, 16; 3:3[2x], 19).

There are a number of motifs that occur in the First Edition that tend to be missing in the Second Edition, just as there are a number of motifs found in the Second Edition that do not occur in the First Edition: (1) The verb μαρτυρεῖν, "to testify," occurs only in the Second Edition (1:2; 22:16, 18, 20). (2) The phrase ὁ γὰρ καιρὸς ἐγγύς (1:3) or ὁ καιρὸς γὰρ ἐγγύς, "for the time is near" (22:10), occurs only in the Second Edition. (3) Words with the βασιλ- stem occur only in the older portions of Revelation: (a) βασίλεια, "kingdom" (nine times: 1:6, 9; 5:10; 11:15; 12:10; 16:10; 17:12, 17, 18); (b) βασιλεύς, "king" (twenty-one times: 1:5; 6:15; 9:11; 10:11; 15:3; 16:12, 14; 17:2, 9, 12[2x], 14[2x], 18; 18:3, 9; 19:16[2x], 18, 19; 21:24); (c) βασιλεύειν, "to rule as king" (seven times: 5:10; 11:15, 17; 19:6; 20:4, 6; 22:5). (4) The important Christian term ἐκκλησία, "church," occurs twenty times in Revelation (1:4, 11, 20[2x]; 2:1, 7, 8, 11, 12, 17, 18, 23, 29; 3:1, 6, 7, 13, 14, 22; 22:16), but just once in the First Edition in an explanatory gloss (1:11). This distribution probably occurs because the royal ideology characteristic of Jewish apocalypses had its greatest impact on the First Edition and only minimal effect on the Second Edition. (5) The term ὑπομονή, "patience, endurance," occurs in the First Edition only in 1:9 in a very distinctive way, referring to the ὑπομονὴ ἐν Ἰησοῦ, "endurance in Jesus," whereas elsewhere in Revelation the term occurs only in Rev 2–3 (2:2, 3, 19; 3:10) and in two obvious interpolations in 13:10; 14:12. (6) The phrase ἔρχομαι τάχυ, "I am coming soon," attributed to Jesus, occurs only in the Second Edition (2:16; 3:11; 22:7, 12, 20; n.b. that the phrase ἔρχεται τάχυ, "he is coming soon," in 11:14 refers to the third woe).

(2) *Techniques Used to Unify the First Edition.* There are two primary ways in which the originally discrete units of text that the author assembled were forged into a relatively unified composition. I say "relatively unified," for if his redactional techniques are evident to modern analysis, it is obvious that he was not completely successful in his task. However, it is possible that the author-editor wanted to preserve the original units of text in as unaltered a form as possible. One method he used was the creation of an overall eschatological program or scenario in which each of the major textual units could play a part. A second method was the insertion of expansions or interpolations whereby themes and motifs originally found in only one section or in the very latest compositional levels were extended to the rest of the composition in order to produce cohesion, coherence, and unity.

(a) *The Overarching Eschatological Framework.* One of the central redactional motivations evident in the First Edition of 4:1–22:5 is the importance of creating a relatively consistent eschatological program into which earlier apocalyptic-type texts could be fitted. While the units of oral or written traditions out of which 4:1–

22:5 was created were certainly keyed to aspects of particular eschatological scenarios, the juxtaposition of each major textual unit with others required an overall sequential scheme to make the composition comprehensible. As a redactional principle in the analysis of Revelation, this suggests that passages in which the eschatological scheme forged by the author is most visible or most distinctive belong to a later state in composition. One clear example is 20:4–6, dealing with the millennial reign of resurrected martyrs. By inserting this textual unit, the final editor has harmonized those eschatologies that anticipated the resurrection at the beginning of the messianic kingdom with those that place the resurrection at the end of the messianic kingdom but at the beginning of the eternal kingdom of God.

(b) *Homogenizing Expansions.* In the author's attempt to link together the various textual units that he chose to place into a larger framework, he made extensive use of literary expansions (the term often used, "interpolations," is usually used when added by a different hand) to bind the (originally) loosely connected sections together.

[1] Explanatory Expansions. There are a number of explanatory additions that clarify various features in the text. These function in a variety of ways. One way is to introduce allegorical interpretations of various features of the visions. These are striking within the context of Revelation as a whole since allegorical elements, often prominent in apocalyptic dream and vision reports, are relatively rare in Revelation, occurring primarily in conjunction with the explanations of the *angelus interpres* in Rev 17. The following allegorical explanatory additions are found in Revelation: [a] In Rev 1:20 there is an allegorical explanation provided by the exalted Christ, functioning as his own *angelus interpres:* "As for the secret meaning of the seven stars which you saw in my right hand and the seven golden menorahs, the seven stars are the angels of the seven churches, and the seven menorahs are the seven churches." [b] Similarly, in Rev 4:5 there is an allegorical explanation inserted by the author-editor that interprets the seven torches of fire before the throne of God as "the seven spirits of God." [c] In Rev 5:6 the seven horns and seven eyes of the Lamb are interpreted as "the seven spirits of God sent to all the earth." [d] In Rev 5:8 the incense in the golden bowls held by the twenty-four elders is interpreted as "the prayers of the saints." Finally, there is the expansion in Rev 14:4–5, which does not introduce an allegorical interpretation but rather functions as an exposition on the identity on the 144,000: "These are those who have not polluted themselves with women, for they are chaste; they are those who follow the Lamb where he would go. These have been redeemed from humanity, the first-fruits for God and the Lamb, and in their mouths guile was not found. They are blameless."

[2] Analeptic Expansions, i.e., interpolated comments that refer to earlier events, persons, or things, thereby functioning to link originally heterogeneous sections of Revelation more closely and to introduce consistency: [a] 4:1, "The first voice which I heard like a trumpet," refers to 1:10. [b] In 9:4, reference is made to those with the seal of God on their foreheads mentioned in 7:3. [c] 13:12c, "whose mortal wound was healed," referring to 13:3, links 13:11–18 to 13:1–10. [d] The Dragon, a central character in Rev 12 (where he is mentioned eight times), is essentially extraneous to Rev 13, where he is introduced through two glosses in 13:2b, "The Dragon gave him [the Beast from the Sea] his power and throne and great authority," and 13:4a, "They worshiped the Dragon because he gave authority to the Beast." These two glosses link 13:1–10 to 12:1–17. [e] Rev 13:12c contains an interpolated explanatory phrase that

serves to link 13:11–18 to 13:1–10: "whose mortal wound was healed" (referring to 13:3). [f] A similar interpolated explanatory phrase occurs also in Rev 13:15c, "which was wounded by the sword and yet lived." [g] The clauses mentioning those who worshiped the Beast and his image or received its mark on their forehead and hand (14:11; 16:2; 20:4) refer back to these motifs in the narrative found in 13:4, 8, 12, 15, where they first occur. [h] The *angelus interpres* who appears in 17:1 is described as one of those "who had the seven bowls" (referring to 15:7; links 17:1–18 to 15:1–16:21). [i] In Rev 18:16 the description of the city is a doublet of the earlier description of the Whore in 17:4. [j] The *angelus interpres* who appears in 21:9 is described (like the angel in 17:1) as one of those "who had the seven bowls" (referring to 15:7, and functioning to link 21:9–22:5 to 15:1–16:21).

[3] Proleptic Expansions (i.e., interpolated comments that refer to events, persons, or things that occur *later* in the narrative, thereby functioning to link originally heterogeneous sections of Revelation more closely together and to introduce consistency). [a] In Rev 10:7 reference is made to the seventh angel who will blow his trumpet, an event that is narrated in 11:15–18. This reference serves to link the apparently extraneous material in 10:1–11 with the larger framework provided by the trumpet vision in 8:2–11:18. [b] Rev 11:7 introduces "the Beast that ascends from the bottomless pit," an anticipation of the narrative in 13:1–9. [c] In Rev 12:3 the great red dragon is described as having "seven heads and ten horns, and seven diadems upon his heads." No meaning is associated with the seven heads and ten horns, suggesting that this is an editorial attempt to tie the narrative in Rev 12 with subsequent vision narratives where the same features are mentioned (13:1) and interpreted (17:3, 7, 9, 12, 16). [d] In Rev 14:8, there is an abrupt angelic announcement that Babylon has fallen, an announcement that is repeated in varied form in Rev 18:2–3, where the subject of Babylon's fall is treated in great detail. [e] According to Rev 16:19b, God remembered to punish, i.e., "to give her the cup of wine, that is, his furious wrath," a theme picked up in 18:3 and developed in detail in that chapter. [f] The description of Christ in Rev 17:14 as "Lord of lords and King of kings" anticipates 19:16, from where it was probably derived: "King of kings and Lord of lords."

[4] Redactional links between textual units: [a] Rev 4:1 forms a secondary transition between 1:9–20 and 4:2–22:9. [b] 11:14a serves to link 10:1–11:13 with 9:13–21, while 11:14b introduces 11:15–18. [c] 11:19 forms a bridge between 11:15–18 and 12:1–17. [d] 12:18 forms a secondary transition between 12:1–17 and 13:1–18.

(c) *"Christianizing" Additions.* There are a number of "expansions" that many scholars have regarded as "christianizing" additions to an underlying Jewish text. In the period of formative Christianity (beginnings through the early second century), it is very difficult to label some texts clearly Jewish and other texts clearly Christian, since Christianity took many decades to develop a distinctive theological idiom. For this reason it is probably better to regard these so-called christianizing additions or expansions in light of the evolving theological perspective of the author-editor as well as in the light of the historical events and circumstances that made an impact on him.

[1] There are several instances in which the author has inserted references to "blood" or "death" referring particularly to the execution or lynching of Christians where such statements seem contextually inappropriate: [a] Rev 12:11, "They

conquered him through the blood of the Lamb and through the word of their testimony." [b] Rev 14:13, "Blessed are the dead who from now on die in the Lord." [c] Rev 16:6, "because they have shed the blood of the saints and prophets, you have given them blood to drink." [d] Rev 17:6, the Great Harlot is depicted as drunk "with the blood of the saints and the blood of the witnesses to Jesus." [e] Rev 18:24, "And in you was found the blood of prophets and saints, and of all who have been slaughtered on earth." These additions all reflect a *Sitz im Leben* of expected or actual situation of suffering and persecution.

[2] The term ἀρνίον, "Lamb," occurs twenty-nine times in Revelation, and in all but a single instance (13:11) is a symbol for Jesus. This christological title does not appear to belong to the earliest stratum of the material incorporated into Revelation but was introduced at a secondary stage in the formulation of the First Edition. This is suggested by the peculiar distribution of the term throughout Revelation. The figure of the Lamb dominates one major vision narrative in 5:1–6:17 and one extended vision description in 21:9–22:5. In addition, the Lamb is somewhat significant in the brief descriptions in 14:1–5 and 19:6–10. On the other hand, there are major textual units in which the Lamb either is not mentioned at all or else is mentioned in passages that appear to be expansions. The figure of the Lamb is essentially absent from the following major textual units: [a] 4:1–11, [b] 7:1–12 (with the exceptions of vv 9, 10, which appear to be interpretive expansions), [c] 11:1–18, [d] 12:1–17 (with the exception of v 11), [e] 13:1–18 (with the exception of v 8), [f] 15:1–16:21 (with the exception of 15:3), [g] 17:1–18 (with the exception of v 14), [h] 18:1–24, and [i] 19:11–21:8. One of the more frequent interpolative techniques of the author is the association of the Lamb with God, in which the figure of the Lamb is tangential or extraneous (the underlined portions appear to be expansions):

| | |
|---|---|
| 7:9: | "before the throne *and before the Lamb*" |
| 7:10: | "to our God, seated on the throne, *and to the Lamb*" |
| 22:1: | "the throne of God *and of the Lamb*" |
| 22:3: | "the throne of God *and of the Lamb*" |

The Lamb is similarly mentioned in an ancillary way in 15:3:

"the song of Moses, the servant of God, *and the song of the Lamb*"

The Lamb is mentioned tangentially in the motto found in 12:11:

*"They have conquered him by the blood of the Lamb and by the word of their testimony."*

[3] The four cherubim or "living creatures" (ζῷα) are mentioned twenty times in Revelation, primarily in 4:1–11 (7x) and 5:1–6:17 (9x). They are mentioned three more times (7:11; 14:3; 19:4; a single cherub is mentioned in 15:7), but always in ancillary passages that appear to be expansions (7:11; 14:3; 15:7; 19:4).

[4] The twenty-four elders are mentioned twelve times, primarily in 4:1–11 (2x) and 5:1–14 (5x), but also tangentially in 7:11, 13; 11:16; 14:3; 19:4. It is important to note that the twenty-four elders and the four cherubim are often placed in the same scene (as in 7:11; 14:3; 19:4).

(d) *Indications of Sutures in 4:1–22:5.* In Rev 17, the noun θηρίον, "Beast," occurs nine times, all arthrous with the exception of the first occurrence in 17:3, despite the fact that the θηρίον has already been introduced anarthrously in 13:1, and then with the anaphoric article twenty more times (13:2, 3, 4[3x], 12[2x], 14[2x], 15[3x], 17, 18; 14:9, 11; 15:2; 16:2, 10, 13) before the surprising anarthrous occurrence of θηρίον in 17:3. This clearly suggests a seam between Rev 13–16 and Rev 17. The picture is made more complex by the occurrence of the arthrous noun τὸ θηρίον, "the Beast," in Rev 11:7 (note that the second occurrence of θηρίον in 13:1 is anarthrous), the first occurrence of the term that has the article because (presumably) the author assumes that the readers are already familiar with the Beast. This further suggests that 11:4–13 was formulated in isolation from both 13–16 and 17. Indications of other literary seams are found in 4:1; 8:13; 11:14, 19; 12:18 (see *Comments* on those passages).

## c. Stage Three: The Formation of the "Second Edition"

The Second Edition of Revelation was completed during the last decade of the first century A.D., perhaps even after the turn of the century during the reign of Trajan (A.D. 98–117). The Second Edition exhibits a strikingly different theological character than the First Edition. This difference is clearly evident in the christological developments reflected in the Second Edition in which titles and attributes normally reserved for God in Judaism are applied to the exalted Christ. There are, to be sure, limits to this extension. Such titles as ὁ ὢν καὶ ὁ ἦν καὶ ὁ ἐρχόμενος, "the one who is and who was and who will come," and ὁ παντοκράτωρ, "the Almighty," are reserved for God alone (Beskow, *Rex Gloriae*, 136–41). The difference is also evident in the parenetic elements that characterize the additions to the Second Edition in 1:1–3; 1:12b–3:22; 22:6–21 (as well as the expansions in 13:9–10; 14:12–13; 16:15).

The proclamations of the exalted Christ in Rev 2:1–3:22 constitute the major literary addition of the Second Edition. One of the striking features of the literary analysis of 2:1–3:22 is that very few scholars have suggested that this highly patterned textual unit exhibits interpolations or that it was revised by a later editor. Spitta considered only 2:7 to be an interpolation (236–313), while Charles regarded 2:5, 22 as interpolations (1:lvii–lviii) and restored 2:27c after 2:26b, 3:8bc before 3:8a, and 16:15 after 3:3b (1:lix). On the basis of the principle enunciated above, the general absence of material in Rev 2–3 that lends itself to being considered interpolations suggests that this collection of seven proclamations was one of the last textual units to be added to the composition.

Together with the introductory (1:1–20) and concluding (22:5–21) sections of Revelation, 2:1–3:22 reflects no persecution on the part of the Roman state, nor is there any evidence for the imperial cult. The proclamations to Ephesus, Thyatira, Sardis, and Laodicea contain no mention of trouble caused in these churches either by Roman authorities or by local civic authorities. In the proclamation to Pergamon, mention is made of the execution of Antipas (2:13), and in Smyrna and Philadelphia, Christians have apparently experienced denunciation by local Jews (who are called a "synagogue of Satan" in 2:9; 3:9). The mention of the possibility of prison and the possibility of death in Smyrna (2:10) suggests that the local civic authorities are involved.

With the exception of 2:1, all the proclamations to the seven churches begin with the conjunction καί, "and," which superficially coheres well with the paratactic Hebraistic style used by the author. A larger percentage of clauses and sentences in Revelation (followed at some distance by Mark) are introduced with καί than is the case with any other early Christian composition.

In this connection, special mention should be made of the Gospel of Mark, which, after Revelation, has the next largest percentage of sentences that begin with καί in the NT. Of a total of 589 sentences in Mark, 369 sentences (62.64 percent) begin with καί (remarkably, Mark 13, the most apocalyptic section of Mark, contains 30 sentences, just 11 of which, or 36.6 percent, begin with καί).

It appears that Revelation and Mark have a distinctive paratactic style that makes exceptionally frequent use of καί as a discourse marker to begin new sentences, similar to the Greek style that characterizes the LXX.

The most characteristic feature of Hebrew syntax is the coordination of clauses with ן, "and," a word that is used at the beginning of 56 percent of all clauses in the Pentateuch, while in the LXX version of the Pentateuch 44 percent of all clauses begin with καί (Aejmelaeus, *Parataxis*, 32). Of a random group of texts originally composed in Greek, 17 percent of the clauses in 2 Macc begin with καί, 6 percent in *Ep. Arist.*, 6 percent in Epicurus, 8 percent in Polybius, 11 percent in Philodemus (Aejmelaeus, *Parataxis*, 32). In the LXX, ן is frequently translated with καί because it too does not specify the relationship between the clauses it connects. In the Hebrew Bible more than half of all clauses begin with ן. Since all clauses connected with ן do not function coordinately, the category of "logical subordination" is often invoked. The phenomenon of "logical subordination" is not limited to Hebrew, however, for Greek also uses καί to coordinate clauses formally even though some form of subordination must be understood (Ljungvik, *Beiträge zur Syntax*, 54–87). Aejmelaeus has calculated that of the 9,124 clauses in the Pentateuch beginning with ן, 6,961 or 76.3 percent are translated in the LXX with καί (*Parataxis*, 13).

While 245 (or 73.79 percent) of the 337 sentences in Revelation begin with καί, "and" (following the punctuation of Nestle-Aland[27], which is not without problems), only 9 (20.5 percent) of the 44 sentences in Rev 2–3 begin with καί. This stylistic difference between Rev 2–3 and the rest of the book is quite striking. Similarly, three of the seven occurrences of δέ, "and, but," in Revelation occur in Rev 2–3 (2:5, 16, 24); of the thirteen occurrences of ἀλλά, "but," in Revelation, eight occur in Rev 2–3 (2:4, 6, 9[2x], 14, 20; 3:4, 9), and of six occurrences of οὖν, "therefore," all occur in Rev 1–3 (1:19; 2:5, 16; 3:3[2x], 19).

In the LXX μέν paired with δέ, "on the one hand . . . on the other," does not occur at all in Joshua through 2 Kings, or in Ecclesiastes, Canticles, Jeremiah, and rarely elsewhere except for 1-2-3 Maccabees and Wisdom of Solomon (F. C. Conybeare and St. G. Stock, *Grammar of Septuagint Greek* [Boston: Ginn, 1905] 50 § 39). δέ, "but," occurs just *seven* times in Revelation (1:14; 2:5, 16, 24; 10:2; 19:12; 21:8), twice in the stereotyped expression εἰ δὲ μή, "but if not" (2:5, 16). δέ occurs three times in Rev 2–3 (2:5, 16, 24). In 1:14 and 19:12, δέ is used for emphasis when the seer focuses on the face of the exalted Christ. In 21:8, δέ is used adversatively at the beginning of a sentence describing the fate of sinners in contrast to that of the righteous, which is described in the preceding sentence. In Mark, on the other hand, 111 of 589 sentences begin with δέ. If sentences in Mark that begin with both καί and δέ are considered together, they total 480 sentences out of a total of 589, or 81.49 percent. The frequency with which καί is used as a discourse marker to begin sentences in the Apocalypse is quite different from the style of Mark.

The concentration of these stylistic features in Rev 2–3 suggests that the author is intentionally trying to write in a slightly more elevated style or at least in a higher linguistic register when composing the speeches of the exalted Christ (cf. the analogous phenomenon of the more elevated style of the speeches of Jesus in Mark argued by Lee, *NovT* 27 [1985] 1–26). Admittedly, the occasional use of δέ, ἀλλά, or οὖν does not at first sight appear to be elevated style when compared with the style of other NT authors, and there is a complete absence in Revelation of the usual contrastive particles μέν and δέ, which characterize most classical and Hellenistic authors. But when Revelation is taken on its own terms, these subtle variations suggest that John considered them to be a more elevated style of diction. Another possibility is that the stylistic differences between Rev 2–3 and the rest of the book may indicate the presence of a later addition to the work, perhaps by one who is not the author of the rest of Revelation.

A number of important parenetic terms are largely restricted to 2:1–3:22: (1) ἀγάπη, "love," occurs twice, in 2:4 and 2:19. (2) πίστις, "faith," occurs four times, twice in 2:1–3:22 (2:13, 19) and twice more in expansions (13:10; 14:12). (3) ὑπομονή, "endurance," is almost exclusively limited to 2:1–3:22 (2:2, 3, 19; 3:10), with the exception of two expansions (13:10; 14:12) and 1:9. (4) διακονία, "service," occurs just once, in 2:19.

## Section 6: Text

### Bibliography

**Aland, K.** "Die griechischen Handschriften des Neuen Testaments: Ergänzungen zur 'Kurzgefassten Liste' (Fortsetzungsliste VII)." In *Materialen zur neutestamentlichen Handschriftenkunde*, ed. K. Aland. ANTF 3. Berlin: de Gruyter, 1969. 1–53. ———. *Kurzgefasste Liste der griechischen Handschriften des Neuen Testaments*. 2nd ed. Berlin; New York: de Gruyter, 1994. ———. *Repertorium der griechischen christlichen Papyri*. Vol. 1: *Biblische Papyri*. Berlin; New York: de Gruyter, 1976. ——— and **Aland B.** *The Text of the New Testament*, tr. E. F. Rhodes. Leiden: Brill; Grand Rapids, MI: Eerdmans, 1987. **Beis, N.** "Die Kollation der Apokalypse Johannis mit dem Kodex 573 des Meteoronklosters [2329]." *ZNW* 13 (1912) 260–65. **Borger, R.** "NA²⁶ und die neutestamentliche Textkritik." *TRu* 52 (1987) 1–58. **Bousset, W.** *Textkritische Studien zum Neuen Testament*. TU 1/4. Leipzig: Hinrichs, 1894. **Comfort, P. W.** *Early Manuscripts and Modern Translations of the New Testament*. Wheaton, IL: Tyndale House, 1990. **Conybeare, F. C.** *The Armenian Version of Revelation*. London: Text and Translation Society, 1907. **Cowper, B. H.** *Novum Testamentum Graece ex Antiquissimo Codice Alexandrino*. London: Williams & Norgate, 1860. **Crum, W. E.,** and **Bell, H. I.** *Coptica III: Wadi Sarga: Coptic and Greek Texts from the Excavations Undertaken by the Byzantine Research Account*. Hauniae: Gyldendalske Boghandel-Nordisk, 1922. **Delobel, J.** "Le texte de l'Apocalypse: Problemes de méthode." In *L'Apocalypse*, ed. J. Lambrecht. 151–66. **Diobouniotis, C.,** and **Harnack, A.** *Der Scholien–Kommentar des Origenes zur Apokalypse Johannis*. TU 38. Leipzig: Hinrichs, 1911. **Ehrman, B. D.** "A Problem of Textual Circularity: The Alands on the Classification of New Testament Manuscripts." *Bib* 70 (1989) 377–88. **Elliott, J. K.** *A Bibliography of Greek New Testament Manuscripts*. SNTSMS 62. Cambridge: Cambridge UP, 1989. ———. "Manuscripts of the Book of Revelation Collated by H. C. Hoskier." *JTS* 40 (1989) 100–111. ———. *A Survey of Manuscripts Used in Editions of the Greek New Testament*. NovTSup 57. Leiden: Brill, 1987. **Haelst, J. van.** *Catalogue des papyrus littéraires Juifs et Chrétiens*. Paris: Publications de la Sorbonne, 1976. **Hagedorn, D.** "P.IFAO II 31: Johannesapokalypse 1,13–20." *ZPE* 92 (1992) 243–47. **Holly, D.** *Comparative Studies in Recent Greek New Testament Texts*. Subsidia Biblica 112. Rome: Pontifical Biblical Institute, 1983. **Hoskier, H. C.** *The Complete Commentary of Oecumenius on the Apocalypse*. Ann Arbor: University of Michigan, 1928. ———. *Concerning the Text of the Apocalypse*. 2 vols. London: Quaritch, 1929. **Kenyon, F. G.** *The Chester Beatty Biblical Papyri*.

Fasc. 3: *Pauline Epistles and Revelation: Text.* London: Emery Walker, 1936. ———. *The Chester Beatty Biblical Papyri.* Fasc. 3: *Revelation: Plates.* London: Emery Walker, 1936. **Lagrange, M. J.** "Les Papyrus Chester Beatty." *RB* 43 (1934) 490 (on Rev). **Lake, K.** *Codex Sinaiticus Petropolitanus: The New Testament.* Oxford: Clarendon, 1911. **Metzger, B.,** ed. *Annotated Bibliography of the Textual Criticism of the New Testament: 1914–39.* Copenhagen: Munksgaard, 1955. ———. *The Text of the New Testament: Its Transmission, Corruption, and Restoration.* 2nd ed. New York; Oxford: Oxford UP, 1968. ———, ed. *A Textual Commentary on the Greek New Testament.* Corrected ed. London; New York: United Bible Societies, 1975. **Schmid, J.** "Der Apokalypsetext des Chester Beatty Papyrus $\mathfrak{P}^{47}$." *ByzNeugrJb* 11 (1934–35) 81–108. ———. "Der Apokalypse-Text des Kodex 0207 (Papiri della Società Italiana 1166)." *BZ* 23 (1936–37) 187–89. ———. "Der Apokalypse-Text des Oikumenios." *Bib* 40 (1959) 935–42. ———. "Die handschriftliche Überlieferung des Apokalypse-Kommentars des Arethas von Kaisareia." *ByzNeugrJb* 17 (1939–43) 72–81. ———. "Neue griechische Apokalypsehandschriften." *ZNW* 59 (1968) 250–58. ———. "Oikumenios der Apokalypse-Ausleger und Oikumenios der Bischof von Trikka." *ByzNeugrJb* 14 (1937–38) 322–30. ———. *Studien zur Geschichte des Griechischen Apokalypse-Textes.* 3 vols. Munich: Zink, 1955–56. ———. "Unbeachtete Apokalypse-Handschriften." *TQ* 117 (1936) 149–87. ———. "Unbeachtete und unbekannte griechische Apokalypsehandschriften." *ZNW* 52 (1961) 82–88. ———. "Untersuchungen zur Geschichte des griechischen Apokalypsetextes: Der K-Text." *Bib* 17 (1936) 11–44, 167–201, 273–93, 429–60. ———. "Zur Textkritik der Apokalypse." *ZNW* 43 (1950–51) 112–28. ——— and **Spitaler, A.** "Zur Klärung des Ökumeniusproblems." *OrChr* 9 (1934) 208–18. **Schwartz, J.** "Papyrus et tradition manuscrite." *ZPE* 4 (1969) 175–82. **Skard, E.** "Zum Scholien-Kommentar des Origenes zur Apokalypse Johannis." *SO* 15–16 (1936) 204–8. **Soden, H. F. von.** "Der Apokalypse Text in dem Kommentar-Codex Messina 99 [2053]." *AJP* 35 (1914) 179–91. ———. *Text mit Apparat.* Part 2 of *Die Schriften des Neuen Testaments in ihrer ältesten erreichbaren Textgestalt.* Göttingen: Vandenhoeck & Ruprecht, 1913. **Tasker, R. V. G.** "The Chester Beatty Papyrus of the Apocalypse of John." *JTS* 50 (1949) 60–68. **Thompson, E. M.** *Facsimile of the Codex Alexandrinus.* Vol. 4: *New Testament and Clementine Epistles.* London, 1879. **Tischendorf, C.** *Codex Ephraemi Syri Rescriptus.* Leipzig: Tauchnitz, 1845. ———. *Monumenta Sacra Inedita:* Vol. 6. *Apocalypsis et Actus Apostolorum.* Leipzig: Hinrichs, 1869. **Treu, K.** *Die griechischen Handschriften des Neuen Testaments in der USSR: Eine systematische Auswertung der Texthandschriften in Leningrad, Moskau, Kiev, Odessa, Tbilisi und Erevan.* TU 91. Berlin: Akademie, 1966. **Turner, C. H.** "The Text of the Newly Discovered Scholia of Origen on the Apocalypse." *JTS* 13 (1912) 386–97. **Voicu, S. J.,** and **D'Alisera, S.** *Index in manuscriptorum graecorum edita specimina.* Rome: Borla, 1981. **Weiss, B.** *Die Johannes-Apokalypse: Textkritische Untersuchungen und Textherstellung.* TU 7. Leipzig: Hinrichs, 1891. **Westcott, B. F.,** and **Hort, F. J. A.** *Introduction to the New Testament in the Original Greek: With Notes on Selected Readings.* New York: Harper & Brothers, 1882. ———. *The New Testament in the Original Greek.* 2 vols. Cambridge; London, 1881. **Wisse, F.** *The Profile Method for Classifying and Evaluating Manuscript Evidence.* SD 44. Grand Rapids, MI: Eerdmans, 1982. **Zellweger, E.** *Das neue Testament im Lichte der Papyrusfunde.* Frankfurt am Main: Lang, 1985.

## I. INTRODUCTION

In 1891, Bernhard Weiss wrote: "The text of the Apocalypse is extraordinarily uncertain" (*Johannes-Apokalypse,* 1). While the task of reconstructing the original text of Revelation, like that of the rest of the books of the NT, is probably an unattainable goal, a great deal of progress has been made in NT textual criticism generally and in the textual criticism of Revelation since the days of Weiss. Because of the detailed and comprehensive studies published by H. C. Hoskier (*Concerning the Text*) in 1929, and by Josef Schmid (*Studien*) in 1955, more is known about the textual tradition of

Revelation today than about any other book of the NT. According to J. Schmid, "the history of the transmission of the Greek text of Revelation in its entirety has now become clear" (*ZNW* 59 [1968] 251). Not even the Gospel of Luke is an exception to this judgment, despite the recent publication edited by the American and British Committees of the International Greek New Testament Project, *The New Testament in Greek*, Vol. 3: *The Gospel according to St. Luke*, 2 vols. (Oxford: Clarendon, 1984–87).

One of the peculiarities in the textual transmission of Revelation results from its relatively late acceptance as a canonical NT text in many parts of the ancient church. The text of Revelation was transmitted in two quite different settings, in an ecclesiastical setting and as part of collections of miscellaneous documents. Copies of Revelation transmitted in the second way have been less subject to harmonistic and theological alterations.

## II. THE TEXTUAL EVIDENCE

There are five main types of evidence for the text of Revelation: (1) papyri (six fragments), (2) uncial MSS (eleven, some fragmentary; some complete), (3) minuscule MSS (293 currently known), (4) patristic quotations, and (5) translations. Each of these categories of evidence is discussed in some detail below. K. Aland (*Text*, 105–6, 155–56) has categorized the type of text represented by the papyri, uncials, and minuscules that preserve all or parts of the NT: Category I: MSS of special quality important for establishing the original text; Category II: MSS of special quality but with alien influences (usually from the Byzantine text); Category III: MSS of a distinctive character with an independent text, usually important for establishing the original text and reconstructing the history of the text; Category IV: MSS of the D text (irrelevant in Revelation); and Category V: MSS with purely or predominantly Byzantine text. Yet, according to Aland (*Text*, 159), "While these are *not* Byzantine witnesses they may be classed together with them here . . . because they contribute equally little of significance for textual criticism as defined here." These classifications, however, while occasionally noted in connection with some MSS, are mentioned occasionally but not relied upon in this commentary because the Alands have not proposed a convincing basis for sorting the MSS in this way (cf. Ehrman, *Bib* 70 [1989] 384–87; E. J. Epp, *Int* 44 [1990] 71–75).

### A. Papyri

The fragmentary papyrus witnesses to the text of Revelation are represented by just five fragments currently known:

1. $\mathfrak{P}^{18}$ (London British Museum Pap. 2053 = POxy viii.1079 = van Haelst nr. 559); containing Rev 1:4–7 (late third or early fourth century); agrees closely with A, and also with ℵ and C; categorized by Aland as Normal text; Category I (text in B. P. Grenfell, A. S. Hunt et al., *The Oxyrhynchus Papyri* [London: Egyptian Exploration Society, 1896– ] 8:13–14; convenient transcription of text in Charles, 2:447). This fragment was part of a papyrus roll, not a codex (van Haelst, *Catalogue*, no. 559; Aland, *Repertorium*, 238), and is one of the few examples of NT papyri extant in such a form (see $\mathfrak{P}^{98}$); the only other examples are $\mathfrak{P}^{13}$ and $\mathfrak{P}^{22}$ (see below). It must be observed, however, that van Haelst apparently considers only $\mathfrak{P}^{22}$ (POxy

1228) to be originally part of a roll and not simply an opistograph (i.e., a roll reused on the back and thus imposing the roll format on the new text).

2. $\mathfrak{P}^{24}$ (Andover-Newton Seminary OP 1230 = POxy 1230 = van Haelst nr. 562), Rev 5:5–8; 6:5–8 (early fourth century); text published in Grenfell and Hunt, *Oxyrhynchus Papyri* 10:18–19, who observed that it did not follow any single MS or group of MSS rigidly; agrees with ℵ and A; Aland: Category I; transcription in Charles, 1:448–49. For a detailed description, see Aland, *Repertorium*, 245.

3. $\mathfrak{P}^{43}$ (British Museum Pap. 2241 = P. Wadi Sarga 12 = van Haelst nr. 560), Rev 2:12–13; 15:8–16:2 (sixth or seventh century); Aland: Category II. Reconstructed text in Crum and Bell, *Coptica III*, 43–51; description in van Haelst, *Catalogue*, no. 560, and Aland, *Repertorium*, 267. Since the contents of Revelation on each side of this single sheet of papyrus are so distant from each other within Revelation, and since the writing on the verso goes in the opposite direction to that on the recto, this fragment may be from a *roll* not a codex (the editors think it is a roll, while P. L. Hedley, *CQR* 118 (1934) 227, regards it as part of a codex). This is significant in that NT texts written on papyrus rolls are very rare; the few examples include: $\mathfrak{P}^{13}$ (Heb 2:14–5:5; 10:8–22; 10:29–11:13; 11:28–12:17); $\mathfrak{P}^{18}$ (Rev 1:4–7); $\mathfrak{P}^{22}$ (John 15:25–16:2, 21–32). E. G. Turner, in his brief catalog of MSS, does not consider $\mathfrak{P}^{43}$ to be part of a papyrus roll (*The Typology of the Early Codex* [Philadelphia: University of Pennsylvania, 1977] 147). Crum and Bell further suggest the possibility that the original MS contained only extracts from Revelation used for a lectionary or other liturgical usage. This proposal, however, seems doubtful, since there are no other known instances in which Revelation was incorporated into a lectionary system. The text is exceedingly fragmentary but lacks several readings characteristic of the Byzantine tradition.

4. $\mathfrak{P}^{47}$ (Pap. Chester Beatty III = van Haelst nr. 565), Rev 9:10–17:2 (late third century; the second oldest extant MS witness to Revelation; see $\mathfrak{P}^{98}$ ). For a detailed description, see Aland, *Repertorium*, 277. $\mathfrak{P}^{47}$ has eighty singular readings, i.e., readings supported by no other MS of Revelation, and twenty-seven readings supported only by one or a very few minuscules. $\mathfrak{P}^{47}$ alone *never* preserves an original reading, while the single agreement of $\mathfrak{P}^{47}$ and ℵ preserves the original text in 9:20 (οὐδέ); cf. Schmid, *Studien* 2:114 n. 4. The agreements and disagreements that $\mathfrak{P}^{47}$ has with several important witnesses to the text indicate that it is closer to ℵ A C P than to 046 or the Textus Receptus (Kenyon, *Revelation*, xiii):

|         | Agreements with $\mathfrak{P}^{47}$ | Disagreements with $\mathfrak{P}^{47}$ |
|---------|---------|---------|
| ℵ       | 182     | 196     |
| A       | 167     | 209     |
| C       | 157     | 171     |
| P       | 164     | 188     |
| 046 (Q) | 146     | 232     |
| TR      | 129     | 249     |

5. $\mathfrak{P}^{85}$ (Strasbourg, Bibl. Nat. et Univ. P. gr. 2677 = van Haelst nr. 564), Rev 9:19–10:1, 5–9 (fourth or fifth century); Aland: Category II. For a detailed description, see Aland, *Repertorium*, 319. A reconstructed text of this fragmentary single page of a papyrus codex is found in Schwartz, *ZPE* 4 (1969) 181–82. $\mathfrak{P}^{85}$ exhibits close agreement with $\mathfrak{P}^{47}$ and with ℵ rather than with A and C.

6. 𝔓⁹⁸ (Kairo, French Institute for Oriental Archaeology, P. IFAO inv. 237b) (2nd cent. ?); see Hagedorn, *ZPE* 92 (1992) 243–47. This papyrus fragment of Rev 1:13–20 is probably the oldest witness to the text of Revelation extant and is part of a roll, a rare form for papyrus witnesses to the NT (see 𝔓¹⁸).

## B. *Uncials*

Among the 301 MS witnesses to the text of Revelation currently known, 11 are uncials, just 3 of which are complete (ℵ A and 046). Three others consist of a single page (0163, 0169, and 0207). Among the more important witnesses to the text of Revelation are several important uncial MSS that contain nearly the entire text of Revelation (the prefixed 0 before each number is a standard way of designating uncial or majuscule MSS, i.e., those written in capital letters). Unfortunately, the important NT MS B, Codex Vaticanus, concludes with Heb 9:14 (it also lacks 1–2 Timothy, Titus, and Philemon) and lacks the entire text of Revelation.

1. ℵ (01), Codex *Sinaiticus* (London British Museum Add. 3725), fourth century; Aland: Category I. ℵ alone probably preserves the original text of Revelation in about six instances (Schmid, *Studien* 2:114 n. 4): 2:5 (πέπτωκες); 9:3–4 (αὐτοῖς); 9:7 (ὅμοιοι); 18:12 (μαργαριτῶν); 19:20 (μετ' αὐτοῦ ὁ ψευδοπροφήτης); 22:11 (ῥυπανθήτω).

2. A (02), Codex *Alexandrinus* (London, British Museum, Royal 1 D. VIII), fifth century; Aland: Category I.

3. C (04), Codex *Ephraemi Syri Rescriptus* (Paris, Bibl. Nat., Gr. 9), fifth century. Aland: Category II (missing the following portions of Revelation: 1:1; 3:20–5:14; 7:14–17; 8:5–9:16; 10:10–11:3; 16:13–18:2; 19:5–21:21).

4. P (025), Codex *Porphyrianus* (Leningrad, Publ. Bibl., Gr. 225); contains apr, missing Rev 16:12 ὁδός–17:1 ἑπτά; 19:21 αὐ]τῶν–20:9 τήν²; 22:6 τάχει–end; ninth century; Aland: Category V; described in Treu, *Handschriften*, 101–4.

5. 046, earlier designated Q (Rome, Bibl. Vatic., Gr. 2066), complete, tenth century; Aland: Category V.

6. 051, earlier designated E (Athos, Pantokratoros, 44 ), Rev 11:15–13:1; 13:3–22:7; 22:15–21 (tenth century); Aland: Category III.

7. 052 (Athos, Panteleimonos, 99,2), Rev 7:16–8:12 (tenth century); Aland: Category V; Byzantine Text.

8. 0163 (Chicago, Oriental Institute of the University of Chicago, 9351; POxy 848), Rev 16:17–19 (fifth century); agrees with A; Aland: Category III (convenient transcription in Charles, 2:449).

9. 0169 (Princeton Theological Seminary, Pap. 5; POxy 1080), Rev 3:19–4:3 (fourth century), Aland: Category III; a photograph is found in Metzger, *Manuscripts of the Greek Bible*, 72–73, and a transcription is found in Charles, 2:448.

10. 0207 (Firenze, Bibl. Laurenziana, PSI 1166), Rev 9:2–15 (fourth century). A collation of this single page is found in Schmid, *BZ* 23 (1936–37) 187–89.

11. 0229 (previously at Firenze, Bibl. Laurenziana PSI 1296b), Rev 18:16–17; 19:4–6 (seventh–eighth century). Brief description in J. Schmid, *ZNW* 52 (1951) 83. A palimpsest written over a Coptic text. The text is near, but not identical, to that of ℵ. This text, along with several minuscules, suggests that the text represented by ℵ 𝔓⁴⁷ and Origen had a relatively wide distribution (cf. Schmid, *Studien* 2:109–46).

The Contents and Dates of Papyrus and Uncial Manuscripts of Revelation

| Century | MS | Contents | | | |
|---|---|---|---|---|---|
| II | 𝔓⁹⁸ | 1:13–20 | | | |
| III | 𝔓⁴⁷ | | 9:1 ....................... 17:2 | | |
| | 𝔓¹⁸ | 1:4–7 | | | |
| IV | 𝔓²⁴ | 5:5–8   6:5–8 | | | |
| | א | 1:1 ......................................................................................................... 22:21 | | | |
| | 0169 | 3:19–4:3 | | | |
| | 0207 | | 9:2–15 | | |
| IV/V | 𝔓⁸⁵ | | 9:19–10:1, 5–9 | | |
| V | A | 1:1 ......................................................................................................... 22:21 | | | |
| | C | 1:2–3:19        8:1–4 | 11:4–16:2 | 21:22–22:21 | |
| | | 6:1–7:13   9:17–10:9 | 18:3–19:4 | | |
| | 0163 | | 16:17–19 | | |
| VI | 𝔓⁴³ | 2:12–13 | 15:8–16:2 | | |
| VII | 0229 | | 18:16–17/19:4–6 | | |
| IX | 025 | 1:1 ............................. 16:11/17:2 ...... 19:20 | 20:10 ......... 22:5 | | |
| X | 046 | 1:1 ......................................................................................................... 22:21 | | | |
| | 051 | | 11:15–13:1 ... 13:3 ....................... 22:7 .... 22:15–21 | | |
| | 052 | 7:16–8:12 | | | |

## C. Minuscules

Most witnesses to the text of Revelation are minuscule MSS. Unlike the other books of the NT, through the work of Hoskier (*Concerning the Text,* 1929), and then Schmid (*Studien,* 1955), *all* the minuscule evidence for Revelation available at the time was considered in these two works (Wisse, *Profile Method,* 6 n. 23). The 293 minuscule MSS currently known are listed below (based on Aland, *Kurzgefasste Liste,* 61–202; Aland, "Fortsetzungsliste VII," 22–37), brought up to date by a list of the more recent minuscules sent to the author (on 10 February 1989 and 7 May 1997) by Professor Barbara Aland of the Institut für Neutestamentliche Textforschung at the Westfälische Wilhelms-Universität in Münster. Seven of them should not be considered legitimate parts of the Greek MS tradition of Revelation: 2449 is a handwritten MS in modern Greek, while 296, 1668, 2049, 2066, 2136, and 2619 are copies of the printed Textus Receptus (perhaps 2072 also). This list of minuscules includes the equivalent MS number assigned by H. C. Hoskier in his mammoth work *Concerning the Text of the Apocalypse,* 2 vols. (London: Quaritch, 1929). Though Hoskier's work is indispensable, it is difficult to use since he devised his own numerical system for coding the MSS. He does provide a table identifying each MS with the equivalent numbering system of Scrivener, old Gregory, new Gregory, and von Soden (*Text* 2:11–21), but many of his new Gregory numbers = Gregory-Aland (now the standard) are inaccurate. In instances where Hoskier has no equivalent to the Gregory number, the MS was either not used by him or unknown to him. There are 50 such MSS found in the list below. This list also includes an indication of which family the MS belongs to, so that the attestation of entire families of MSS can be included in the textual notes of the commentary without listing every member of each textual family. When a text of Revelation is found in a commentary, the Gregory number is followed by the letter "C." Of the 292 minuscules of Revelation (1277 does not actually contain Revelation), 98 are commentaries on Revelation, 50 are dated to specific years, 1 was copied in the ninth century, 8 in the tenth, 35 in the eleventh, 30 in the twelfth, 30 in the thirteenth, 58 in the fourteenth, 57 in the fifteenth, 40 in the sixteenth, 13 in the seventeenth, 5 in the eighteenth, and 2 in the nineteenth. The dating of some MSS is more ambiguous: 2 are dated to the ninth–tenth centuries, 1 to the tenth–eleventh, 1 to the eleventh–twelfth, 1 to the twelfth–thirteenth, 1 to the twelfth–fourteenth, 3 to the thirteenth–fourteenth, 2 to the fourteenth–fifteenth. Under the heading *Family,* 20 minuscules are graded according to Aland's MS categories (Aland, *Text,* 105–6, 155–56). MSS marked with an asterisk contain the entire NT. Under Textual Categories, note the following abbreviations: e = Gospels; a = Apostolos; p = Pauline letters; c = Catholic letters; r = Revelation. I have been saved from several errors by the list compiled by Elliott (*JTS* 40 [1989] 100–111).

| | Gregory No. | Hoskier No. | Content Date | Textual Categories & Families |
|---|---|---|---|---|
| 1. | 1C | 1 | 12th | Andr a |
| 2. | *18 | 51 | 1364 | Byz 2 |
| 3. | *35 | 17 | 11th | (Andr f); Andr/Byz 3; homily of John Chrysostom between Paul and Revelation |
| 4. | 42 | 13 | 11th | Byz 15 |
| 5. | 60 | 10 | 1297 | Andr/Byz 3 |
| 6. | *61 | 92 | 16th | Byz 16; Aland: Category III; Revelation written by last of four copyists |
| 7. | *69 | 14 | 15th | Byz 16 |
| 8. | 82C | 2 | 10th | Byz 17 |
| 9. | 88 | 99 | 12th | Andr i; Aland: Category III; Revelation added by later copyist |
| 10. | 91C | 4 | 11th | Arethas; Byz 18 |
| 11. | 93 | 19 | 11th | Byz 17 |
| 12. | 94C | 18 | 12th | Andr Ø; Aland: Category III or lower |
| 13. | 104 | 7 | 1087 | Andr/Byz 2a |
| 14. | 110 | 8 | 12th | Byz 12 |
| 15. | *141 | 40 | 13th | Byz 4 |
| 16. | *149 | 25 | 15th | Byz 11 |
| 17. | 172 | 87 | 13–14th | Andr/Byz 4b; Contains Praxapostolos and Revelation; three hands, Revelation by third |
| 18. | *175 | 20 | 10th | Arethas; Byz 18 |
| 19. | 177 | 82 | 11th | Byz 8 |
| 20. | *180 | 44 | 1273 | Byz 8 |
| 21. | 181 | 12 | 15th | Andr Ø; Aland: Category V; Praxapostolos 11th cent.; Revelation added in 15th |
| 22. | *201 | 94 | 1357 | Byz 11 |
| 23. | 203 | 107 | 1111 | Byz 9 |
| 24. | *205 | 88 | 15th | Andr g |
| 25. | *205copy | 101 | 15th | This MS is a copy of 205 |

| | | | | |
|---|---|---|---|---|
| 26. | *209 | 46 | 15th | Aland: Category III; Revelation added later |
| 27. | *218 | 33 | 13th | Byz 6 |
| 28. | *241 | 47 | 11th | Byz 17 |
| 29. | *242 | 48 | 12th | Arethas; Byz 18; Treu, *Handschriften*, 258–60 |
| 30. | 250C | 165 | 11th | Andr/Byz a |
| 31. | 254C | 251 | 14th | Andr Ø |
| 32. | 256 | 109 | 11th | Arethas; Byz 18 |
| 33. | *296 | 57 | 16th | Copy of printed TR |
| 34. | 314C | 6 | 11th | Byz 19 |
| 35. | 325 | 9 | 11th | Byz 14 |
| 36. | 336 | 16 | 15th | Andr/Byz 2b |
| 37. | 337 | 52 | 12th | Byz 8 |
| 38. | *339 | 83 | 13th | No longer extant |
| 39. | *367 | 23 | 1331 | Byz 15 |
| 40. | 368 | 84 | 15th | Byz 11 |
| 41. | 385 | 29 | 1407 | Byz 3; Praxapostolos; Revelation added by later hand after works of Chrysostom |
| 42. | *386 | 70 | 14th | Byz 11 |
| 43. | 424 | 34 | 11th | Andr/Byz 4a; Aland: Category III |
| 44. | 429 | 30 | 15th | Byz 3; Praxapostolos 14th; Revelation 15th on diff. paper |
| 45. | 432 | 37 | 15th | Andr/Byz 3 |
| 46. | 452 | 42 | 12th | Byz 9 |
| 47. | 456 | 75 | 10th | Byz 14 |
| 48. | 459 | 45 | 1092 | Andr/Byz 2a |
| 49. | 467 | 53 | 15th | Byz 9; copy of 452 |
| 50. | 468 | 55 | 13th | Byz 15 |
| 51. | 469 | 56 | 13th | Byz 17 |
| 52. | *498 | 97 | 14th | Byz 13 |
| 53. | *506 | 26 | 11th | Byz 9 |
| 54. | *517 | 27 | 11–12th | Byz 14 |
| 55. | *522 | 98 | 1515 | Byz 3 |
| 56. | *582 | 102 | 1334 | Andr/Byz 2b |
| 57. | 598 | — | 13th | Andr Ø |
| 58. | 616 | 156 | 1434 | Andr/Byz 4a |
| 59. | 617C | 74 | 11th | Arethas; Byz 18 |
| 60. | 620 | 180 | 12th | Andr/Byz 2b |
| 61. | 627 | 24 | 10th | Byz 12 |
| 62. | 628 | 69 | 14th | Andr/Byz 2b |
| 63. | 632 | 22 | 14th | Byz 17; (Andr g; commentary in margins); Praxapostolos written by two copyists (12th–13th cents.), Revelation added by third in 14th |
| 64. | *664 | 106 | 15th | Byz 19 |
| 65. | *680 | 104 | 14th | Andr/Byz 2a |
| 66. | *699 | 89 | 11th | Byz 17 |
| 67. | 743C | 123 | 14th | (Andr d) |
| 68. | *757 | 150 | 13th | Andr/Byz 3; Revelation by later hand |

| 69. | 792 | 113 | 13th | Close to Byzantine, though with 2643 (sister MS or copy of 4792) belongs to no family or subgroup of MSS |
|---|---|---|---|---|
| 70. | *808 | 149 | 12th | Byz 5 |
| 71. | *824 | 110 | 14th | Andr/Byz 3 |
| 72. | | | | |
| 73. | *886C | 117 | 1454 | Elliott, *JTS* 40 (1989) 111 n. 12: "Not a text." Aland: Below Category III |
| 74. | 911C | 95 | 12th | = 2040; 1:1–11:7 = Byz 1; 11:9–22:21 = fam 1006 |
| 75. | 919 | 125 | 12th | Byz 2 |
| 76. | 20 | 126 | 13th | Byz 1 |
| 77. | *922 | 151 | 1116 | Andr/Byz 2a |
| 78. | *935 | 153 | 14th | Byz 10; contains scholia of Andreas *Comm. in Apoc.* on 2:16–6:14. |
| 79. | *986 | 157 | 14th | Andr/Byz 3 |
| 80. | 1006 | 215 | 11th | fam 1006–1841–911–2040–2626; Rev 1–4 Byzantine; evidence for this text family in Hoskier, *Text* 1:435–37; Aland: Category II |
| 81. | 1064 | — | 18th | |
| 82. | *1072 | 160 | 14th | Andr/Byz 3 |
| 83. | *1075 | 161 | 14th | Andr/Byz 3 |
| 84. | *1094 | 182 | 14th | Arethas; Byz 19 |
| 85. | 1140 | — | 13th | Byz 17; 1:1–22:19; apr; Revelation (fol. 209–30) by later hand; Schmid, *ZNW* 52 (1961) 83 |
| 86. | 1248 | 250 | | Andr/Byz 3 |
| 87. | 1277 | 185 | 11th | Aland: Byzantine; Hoskier: Revelation absent |
| 88. | 1328 | 190 | 14th | Andr/Byz 3 |
| 89. | 1352b | 194 | 14th | Byz 6; eapr; Rev 2:10–end; Treu, *Handschriften,* 141–43 |
| 90. | *1384 | 191 | 11th | (Andr i); Andr/Byz 3 |
| 91. | *1424 | 197 | 9–10th | Byz 4 |
| 92. | *1503 | 192 | 1317 | Andr/Byz 3 |
| 93. | 1551 | 212 | 13th | Andr/Byz 3 |
| 94. | *1597 | 207 | 1289 | Byz 11 |
| 95. | 1611 | 111 | 12th | fam 1611–1854–2050–2329–2344 (2344 most valuable); Aland: Category II |
| 96. | *1617 | 223 | 15th | Andr/Byz 3 |
| 97. | *1626 | 226 | 15th | Aland: Byzantine |
| 98. | *1637 | 230 | 1328 | Andr/Byz 3 |
| 99. | *1652 | 231 | 16th | Schmid: "worthless"; 1:1–3 |
| 100. | *1668 | 235 | 11th | Copy of Printed TR |
| 101. | *1678C | 240 | 15th | Andr l; Close to $\mathfrak{P}^{47}$ ℵ; double commentary by Andreas and |

| | | | | Oecumenius (see 1778); commentary of Oecumenius only |
|---|---|---|---|---|
| 102. | 1685 | 198 | 1292 | Andr i |
| 103. | *1704 | 214 | 1541 | Byz 13 |
| 104. | 1719 | 210 | 1287 | Byz 4 |
| 105. | 1728 | 211 | 13th | Byz 10; Praxapostolos & Revelation; between Hebrews & Revelation are *Erotapokriseis* |
| 106. | 1732 | 220 | 1384 | Andr i; Andr/Byz 3 |
| 107. | 1733 | 221 | 14th | Andr/Byz 3 |
| 108. | 1734 | 222 | 1015 | Byz 10; contains scholia on Andreas *Comm. in Apoc.* on 2:16–6:14. |
| 109. | 1740 | 229 | 13th | Andr/Byz 3 |
| 110. | 1745 | 227 | 15th | Andr/Byz 3 |
| 111. | 1746 | 228 | 14th | Andr/Byz 3 |
| 112. | 1757 | — | 15th | Aland: Byzantine |
| 113. | 1760 | 199 | 10th | |
| 114. | 1769C | — | 14th | |
| 115. | 1771 | 1230 | 14th | Andr/Byz 3 |
| 116. | 1773C | — | 14th | Andr Ø; copy of 2038 |
| 117. | *1774 | 232 | 15th | Byz 3; *Listed by Hoskier, but not Aland, as containing Revelation |
| 118. | 1775C | 236 | 1847 | Schmid: "worthless"; 1:1–13; 4:4–7; 19:19–20 |
| 119. | 1776C | 237 | 1791 | Schmid: "worthless"; 1:1–13[comm]; unknown commentator |
| 120. | 1777C | 238 | 19th | Schmid: "worthless"; commentary not by Andreas |
| 121. | 1778C | 203 | 15th | Andr l; close to $\aleph$ and $\mathfrak{P}^{47}$; double commentary of Andreas and Oecumenius (commentary of Oecumenius only); see 1678 |
| 122. | *1780 | — | 13th | Byz 17 |
| 123. | *1785 | 195 | 13–14th | |
| 124. | 1795 | 196 | 12th | Byz 3 |
| 125. | 1806 | 205 | 14th | |
| 126. | 1824C | * | 17th | *Copy of 2062 (Hoskier, *Text*, 155) |
| 127. | 1828 | 124 | 12th | Andr/Byz 4b |
| 128. | 1841 | 127 | 9–10th | fam 1006 (Rev 1–4 Byzantine); Aland: Category II |
| 129. | 1849 | 128 | 1069 | Byz 3 |
| 130. | 1852 | 108 | 13th | Byz 17 |
| 131. | 1854 | 130 | 11th | fam 1611; Aland: Category II; close to $\mathfrak{P}^{47}$ $\aleph$ |
| 132. | 1857 | 131 | 13th | Byz 14; Praxapostolos 13th cent. on parchment, concluding on fol. 198 with a table of the first seven ecumenical councils. Revelation added 14th cent. on paper. Schmid, *ZNW* 52 (1961) 84. |
| 133. | 1859C | 219 | 14th | Byz 1 |

| 134. | 1862C | 132 | 9th | Andr/Byz 4b |
|---|---|---|---|---|
| 135. | 1864 | 242 | 12th | Andr/Byz 3 |
| 136. | 1865 | 244 | 13th | Andr/Byz 3 |
| 137. | 1870 | 133 | 11th | Byz 10; contains scholia from Andreas *Comm. in Apoc.* on 2:16–6:14 |
| 138. | 1872 | 134 | 12th | Byz 1 |
| 139. | 1876 | 135 | 15th | Andr i |
| 140. | 1888C | 4181 | 11th | Andr/Byz 4b |
| 141. | 1893 | 186 | 12th | Byz 5 |
| 142. | 1894 | 187 | 16th | Andr/Byz 3; Acts (11th cent.); Rev 16th cent. (later hand) |
| 143. | 1903 | 243 | 1636 | Andr/Byz 3 |
| 144. | 1918 | 39 | 14th | Andr/Byz 2b |
| 145. | 1934C | 64 | 11th | Arethas; Byz 18 |
| 146. | 1948 | 78 | 15th | Byz 11 |
| 147. | 1955 | 93 | 11th | Byz 3 |
| 148. | 1957 | 91 | 15th | Andr/Byz 3 |
| 149. | 2004 | — | 12th | Byz 2 |
| 150. | 2014C | 421 | 15th | (Andr i) |
| 151. | 2015C | 428 | 15th | (Andr i) |
| 152. | 2016 | 31 | 15th | Arethas; Byz 19 |
| 153. | 2017 | 32 | 15th | Arethas; Byz 17 |
| 154. | 2018C | 435 | 14th | Andr/Byz 4b |
| 155. | 2019C | 436 | 13th | |
| 156. | 2020C | 438 | 15th | (Andr l) |
| 157. | 2021 | 41 | 15th | Byz 9; copy of 452 |
| 158. | 2022C | 43 | 14th | Andr/Byz 4c |
| 159. | 2023C | 49 | 15th | Andr f; Andr/Byz 3; r; with patristic writings; Treu, *Handschriften*, 296–97 |
| 160. | 2024 | 50 | 15th | Byz 7; r; with collection of hagiographies; Treu, *Handschriften*, 297–98 |
| 161. | 2025 | 58 | 15th | Byz 11 |
| 162. | 2026C | 49 | 15th | Andr e |
| 163. | 2027 | 62 | 13th | Byz 1 |
| 164. | 2028C | 62 | 1422 | Andr c |
| 165. | 2029C | 63 | 16th | (Andr c); copy of 2028 |
| 166. | 2030 | 65 r | 12th | Aland: Category III; 16:20–22:21; identical with 2377; appended to patristic writings; Treu, *Handschriften*, 331–32 |
| 167. | 2031C | 67 | 1301 | Andr f |
| 168. | 2032C | 68 | 11th | Andr/Byz 4b |
| 169. | 2033C | 72 | 16th | (Andr c) |
| 170. | 2034C | 73 | 15th | (Andr i) |
| 171. | 2035C | 77 | 16th | Andr/Byz 3 |
| 172. | 2036C | 79 | 14th | Andr i |
| 173. | 2036C[copy] | 79 | 16th | Copy of 2036; (Andr i) |
| 174. | 2037C | 80 | 14th | Andr m |
| 175. | 2038C | 81 | 16th | Copy of 598 |
| 176. | 2039 | 90 | 12th | Byz 2 |
| | 2040 | 95 | | See 911 |

| | | | | |
|---|---|---|---|---|
| 177. | 2041 | 96 | 14th | Andr/Byz 3 |
| 178. | 2042C | 100 | 14th | Andr i |
| 179. | 2043C | 103 r | 15th | Andr i; Treu, *Handschriften*, 73–74 |
| 180. | 2044C | 136 | 1560 | Andr c |
| 181. | 2045C | 137 | 13th | Andr g |
| 182. | 2046C | 138 | 16th | Andr m |
| 183. | 2047C | 139 | 1543 | (Andr i) |
| 184. | 2048 | 140 | 11th | Byz 12 |
| 185. | 2049 | 141 | 16th | Copy of printed TR |
| 186. | 2050 | 143 | 1107 | fam 1611; Aland: Category II |
| 187. | 2051C | 144 | 16th | Andr d |
| 188. | 2052C | 145 | 16th | (Andr c) |
| 189. | 2053C | 146 | 13th | Oecumenius fam 2053–62; Aland: Category I (= A and C); actual *text* of Oecumenius found only in 2053; commentary only in 1678 1778 |
| 190. | 2054C | 147 | 15th | (Andr c) |
| 191. | 2055C | 148 | 15th | (Andr d) |
| 192. | 2056C | 120 | 14th | Andr f |
| 193. | 2057 | 121 | 15th | Andr e |
| 194. | 2058C | 122 | 14th | Oecumenius; Byz 13 |
| 195. | 2059C | 152 | 11th | Andr b |
| 196. | 2060C | 114 | 1331 | Andr h |
| 197. | 2061 | 154 | 15th | Andr/Byz 3 |
| 198. | 2062C | 55 | 13th | Oecumenius fam 2053; Aland: Category I; contains text and commentary only on Rev 1–2; 15–22; cf. 2350 (copy of 2062) |
| 199. | 2063C | 116 | 16th | (Andr f); no Revelation text; commentary only |
| 200. | 2064C | 158 | 16th | Andr d |
| 201. | 2065C | 159 | 15th | Andr n |
| 202. | 2066C | 118 | 1574 | (Andr n); text of Revelation copy of printed TR |
| 203. | 2067C | 119 | 15th | (Andr d) |
| 204. | 2068C | 162 | 16th | (Andr c) |
| 205. | 2069C | 163 | 15th | Andr c |
| 206. | 2070C | 164 | 1356 | Andr/Byz 4c |
| 207. | 2071C | 167 | 1622 | Andr g |
| 208. | 2072C | 168 | 1798 | Schmid: "worthless"; copy of printed TR? |
| 209. | 2073C | 169 | 14th | Andr f |
| 210. | 2074C | 170 | 10th | Andr i |
| 211. | 2075C | 171 | 14th | Byz 19 |
| 212. | 2076 | 172 | 16th | 1:1–11:17 = Byz 2; 11:18–22:21 copy of 2073 |
| 213. | 2077C | 174 | 1685 | Arethas; Byz 19 |
| 214. | 2078 | 176 | 16th | Byz 17; copy of 2436 |
| 215. | 2079 | 177 | 13th | Byz 7 |
| 216. | 2080 | 178 | 14th | Andr l |
| 217. | 2081C | 179 | 11th | Andr b |
| 218. | 2082 | 112 | 16th | (Andr i); copy of 2043 |
| 219. | 2083C | 184 | 1560 | (Andr c) |

| 220. | 2084 | 188 | 15th | Andr/Byz 4a |
|---|---|---|---|---|
| 221. | 2087 | 15 | 15th | |
| 222. | 2091C | 189 | 15th | (Andr e) |
| 223. | 2114C | 234 | 1676 | Modern Gk. tr. of Andreas commentary with text of Maximus of Pelop. |
| 224. | 2116C | 248 | 1687 | |
| 225. | *2136 | 247 eacpr | 17th | Copy of printed TR; bilingual Gk. & Slavonic; Treu, *Handschriften*, 260–61 |
| 226. | 2138 | 246 apr | 1072 | Byz 2; Treu, *Handschriften*, 328–31 |
| 227. | 2186C | 208 | 12th | Andr a |
| 228. | 2196 | 233 | 16th | Andr/Byz 3 |
| 229. | *2200 | 245 | 14th | Byz 2 |
| 230. | *2201 | — | | Elliott, *Bibliography*, xiii |
| 231. | 2254C | 216 | 16th | (Andr f); copy of 2073 |
| 232. | 2256 | 218 | 15th | Byz 1 |
| 233. | 2258 | 217 | 17th | Copy of 2076 |
| 234. | 2259C | 213 | 11th | (Andr b); contents: 13:14–14:15 |
| 235. | 2286C | 241 | 12th | Andr h |
| 236. | 2302C | 193 | 15th | Andr h |
| 237. | 2305C | 209 | 14th | Andr/Byz 4c |
| 238. | 2323 | 202? | 12–13th | Andr/Byz 3; contains four Gospels and Revelation written in one hand 2324? |
| 239. | 2329C | 200 | 10th | fam 1611; Aland: Category II; close to $\mathfrak{P}^{47}$ ℵ. According to Hoskier, *Text* 2:641, the text underlying 2329 was contemporary with the oldest uncial witnesses to Revelation. |
| 240. | 2344 | — | 11th | fam 1611; Aland: Category I (= A and C) |
| | 2349 | | | See 1795 |
| 241. | 2350C | 155 | 17th | Oecumenius; copy of 2062 |
| 242. | 2351C | 201 | 10th | 1:1–13:18; 14:3b–5a; with scholia of Origen; text printed and collated in Diobouniotis-Harnack, though with many errors; cf. Hoskier, *Text* 2:657 and C. H. Turner, *JTS* 13 (1912) 386–97; Aland: Category III |
| 243. | *2352C | 202 | ? | Andr/Byz 3 |
| 244. | 2361C | — | 16th | (Andr c); 4:10–5:6; 6:14–17 |
| 245. | 2377 | — | 14th | Aland: Category III; 13:10–14:4 = Byzantine; 19:21–20:6; 20:14–22:6; 22:6–21 = 2030 |
| 246. | 2402C | — | 16th | |
| 247. | 2403C | — | 16th | Oecumenius[comm]; 1–3, 15–22 |
| 248. | 2408C | — | 14th | 5:1–5 |
| 249. | 2419C | — | 13–14th | Arethas; Byz 19 |
| 250. | 2428C | — | 15th | Andr a; 1:1–17:12 |
| 251. | 2429C | — | 14th | Andr n; 1:1–21:12 |
| 252. | 2431C | — | 1332 | Andr/Byz 3 |
| 253. | 2432C | — | 14th | Andr n |

| | | | | |
|---|---|---|---|---|
| 254. | 2433C | — | 1736 | (Andr l); commentary based on catena of portions of Andreas and Oecumenius |
| 255. | 2434C | — | 13th | Andr/Byz 3; paper MS; Revelation precedes nonbiblical compositions. |
| 256. | 2435C | — | 1562–87 | (Andr d); 1:1–8:6 |
| 257. | 2436 | 206 | 1418 | Byz 17 |
| 258. | 2449 | — | 1684 | Modern Gk.; paper MS; not part of Gk. MS tradition of Revelation |
| 259. | 2493 | — | 14th | Andr/Byz 2a; paper MS; text of Revelation included on pp. 122–36 of hagiographical texts |
| 260. | *2494 | — | 1316 | Byzantine (J. Schmid, *ZNW* 52 [1961] 88) |
| 261. | *2495 | — | 14–15th | Aland: Category III |
| 262. | *2554 | — | 1434 | Aland: Byzantine |
| 263. | 2582 | — | 16th | |
| 264. | 2594C | — | 16th | Andr h; paper MS; description in J. Schmid, *ZNW* 59 (1968) 254 |
| 265. | *2595C | — | 15th | Byzantine text in Revelation that belongs to no particular subgroup (J. Schmid, *ZNW* 52 [1961] 88) |
| 266. | 2619 | — | 18th | Accurate copy of TR; paper MS; not part of Gk. MS tradition of Revelation |
| 267. | 2625 | — | 12th | Andr i; Schmid, *ZNW* 59 (1968) 252–53 |
| 268. | 2626 | — | 14th | Rev 5:1–18:2 = fam 1006; Rev 1–4 = Byzantine; paper MS Rev 1:1–18:2 |
| 269. | 2638C | — | 14th | Andr/Byz; described by J. Schmid, *ZNW* 59 (1968) 254; printed in J. C. Cramer, *Catenae Graecorum Patrum in NT* (Oxford, 1840) 8:497–582 |
| 270. | 2643 | — | 1289 | Close to Byzantine, though with 792 (sister MS or perhaps *Vorlage*) belongs to no family or subgroup of MSS; four Gospels and Revelation in same hand |
| 271. | 2648 | — | 15th | Content: Rev 19:11–21:9 |
| 272. | 2656 | — | 1650 | |
| 273. | 2663 | — | 16th | Paper MS; Revelation follows nonbiblical compositions |
| 274. | 2664 | — | 17th | Paper MS; Revelation follows nonbiblical compositions |
| 275. | 2667 | — | 16th | |
| 276. | 2669 | — | 16th | |
| 277. | 2672 | — | 15th | |
| 278. | 2681 | — | 17th | ℵ-text; J. Schmid, *ZNW* 59 (1968) 257 |
| 279. | 2716 | — | 14th | Aland: Byzantine |
| 280. | 2723 | — | 11th | Aland: Byzantine |
| 281. | 2743 | — | 16th | Andr i; paper MS |

| 282. | 2759 | — | 16th | |
| 283. | 2776 | — | 17th | |
| 284. | 2794 | — | 12th | Rev. 1:1–22:12 |
| 285. | 2814 | — | 12th | |
| 286. | 2821 | — | 14th | |
| 287. | 2824 | — | 14th | |
| 288. | 2843 | — | 16th | |
| 289. | 2845 | — | 15th | |
| 290. | 2846 | — | 12th | |
| 291. | 2847 | — | 1518 | |
| 292. | 2849 | — | 14/15th | |
| 293. | 2855 | — | 12th | Rev 12:12–13:13 |

## D.  Patristic Quotations

### Bibliography

**Achelis, H.** *Hippolyt's kleinere exegetische und homiletische Schriften.* Vol. 3 of *Hippolytus Werke.* GCS. Leipzig: Hinrichs, 1897. **Adams, A. W.,** ed. *Primasius Episcopus Hadrumetinus: Commentarius in Apocalypsin.* CCL 95. Turnhout: Brepols, 1985. **Brock, S. P.** "The Use of the Syriac Fathers for New Testament Textual Criticism." In *The Text of the New Testament in Contemporary Research: Essays on the* Status Quaestionis, ed. B. D. Ehrman and M. W. Holmes. Grand Rapids, MI: Eerdmans, 1995. 224–36. **Bruce, F. F.** "The Earliest Latin Commentary on the Apocalypse." *EvQ* 110 (1938) 352–66. **Diobouniotis, C.,** and **Harnack, A.** *Der Scholien-Kommentar des Origenes zur Apokalypse Johannis.* TU 38/3. Leipzig: Hinrichs, 1911. **Dulaey, M.** *Victorin de Poetovio, premier exégète latin.* 2 vols. Turnhout: Brepols, 1994. **Fee, G. D.** "The Use of the Greek Fathers for New Testament Textual Criticism." In *The Text of the New Testament in Contemporary Research: Essays on the* Status Quaestionis, ed. B. D. Ehrman and M. W. Holmes. Grand Rapids, MI: Eerdmans, 1995. 191–207. **Haussleiter, J.,** ed. *Victorini Episcopi Petavionensis Opera.* CSEL 49. Leipzig: Freytag, 1916. **Muncey, R. W.** *The New Testament Text of Saint Ambrose.* TextsS 4. Cambridge: Cambridge UP, 1959. **North, J. L.** "The Use of the Latin Fathers for New Testament Textual Criticism." In *The Text of the New Testament in Contemporary Research: Essays on the* Status Quaestionis, ed. B. D. Ehrman and M. W. Holmes. Grand Rapids, MI: Eerdmans, 1995. 208–23. **Romero-Pose, E.,** ed. *Sancti Beati a Liebana Commentarius in Apocalypsin.* 2 vols. Rome: Typis Officinae Polygraphicae, 1985. **Sanday, W.,** and **Turner, C. H.** *Nouum Testamentum Sancti Irenaei Episcopi Lugdunensis.* Old-Latin Biblical Texts 7. Oxford: Clarendon, 1923. **Skard, E.** "Zum Scholien-Kommentar des Origenes zur Apokalypse Johannis." *SO* 15–16 (1936) 204–8. **Turner, C. H.** "The Text of the Newly Discovered Scholia of Origen on the Apocalypse." *JTS* 13 (1912) 386–97. **Vogels, H. J.** *Untersuchungen zur Geschichte der lateinischen Apokalypse-Übersetzung.* Düsseldorf: Schwann, 1920. **Williams, J.** *The Illustrated Beatus: A Corpus of the Illustration of the Commentary on the Apocalypse.* 2 vols. London: Harvey Miller; Langhorne, PA: International Publishers Distributor, 1994.

Since there are quotations and allusions to Revelation in Christian writings of the second through the sixth centuries A.D. (and even later), these offer the potential of providing evidence for the text of Revelation centuries earlier than the vast majority of the extant MSS, most of which are minuscules from the tenth century and later. While quotations of Revelation in the Christian fathers are important, they are also problematic. Passages in Revelation that are quoted most extensively have also been subject to revision, so that they are made to conform to later text types. Shorter quotations, such as the lemmata in Hippolytus, are often less affected by scribal modification, since copyists do not tend to revise the text of Revelation that is being quoted. Quotations and allusions to Revelation in Christian writings from the second century on have yet to be adequately discussed by scholars interested in the subject.

## 1. GREEK AUTHORS

Papias was a millenarian who apparently knew and perhaps commented on the Revelation of John (Andreas, *Commentarius in Apocalypsin*, prol.), though no actual quotations of the text have been preserved in any the fragments of Papias. While some have argued that Hermas alluded to Revelation (B. F. Westcott, *A General Survey of the History of the Canon of the New Testament*, 6th ed. [London: Macmillan, 1889] 201), those "allusions" appear to consist largely of apocalyptic topoi rather than actual literary allusions to Revelation. Justin knew and alluded to Revelation (*Dial.* 81) but does not actually cite the text. Clear allusions to the text of Revelation begin to occur frequently toward the end of the second century in Irenaeus (*Adv. haer.* 5.35.2), Hippolytus (see below), Tertullian (*Adv. Marc.* 3.14), Clement of Alexandria (*Paed.* 2.10.108), and Origen (see below). Irenaeus of Lyons (ca. A.D. 130–200), in the millenarian tradition of Papias and Justin, knew and alluded several times to Revelation (the Latin and Greek allusions are catalogued in Sanday-Turner, *Nouum Testamentum*).

Hippolytus of Rome (ca. A.D. 170–236) was a prolific writer, and many of his works have survived in whole or in part. Hippolytus wrote a commentary on the Apocalypse, which is lost, though fragments have been preserved in the Apocalypse commentary of the Syrian Dionysius bar Salabi (died 1171). Particularly in his *Demonstratio de Christo et Antichristo* (*De Ant.*, in *Hippolytus Werke*, ed. H. Achelis), Hippolytus copied extensive sections of the Greek text of Revelation (Rev 11:3–7, in *De Ant.* 47; Rev 12:1–2, 4b–6, 13–17, in *De Ant.* 60 [followed by the repetition of key lemmata followed by interpretive comments]; Rev 13:11–18 in *De Ant.* 48 [followed by the repetition of lemmata followed by comments in 49–50]; Rev 17:1–18:24 in *De Ant.* 36–42; Rev 17:9 in *De Ant.* 29; Rev 20:6, 15 in *De Ant.* 65). There are just three Greek MSS of the *De Antichristo*, E from the fifteenth century, H from the tenth century, and R from the sixteenth century (in addition there are four MSS of an Old Slavonic translation). The two more recent MSS, E and R, exhibit frequent assimilation to particular text traditions, particularly Andreas, while the oldest MS, H, often preserves the original text of Hippolytus with some distinctive and valuable readings (many of these readings are cited in the *Notes* to the passages quoted by Hippolytus in this commentary). One interesting feature of Hippolytus' quotations is his omission of Rev 12:7–12 in his quotation of Rev 12:1–6, 13–17 in *De Ant.* 60 (n.b. that he alludes to Rev 12:10 in a rather free form in *Frag. in Gen.* 34, in *Hippolytus Werke*, ed. Achelis, 64). In his most extensive surviving work, *Refutatio omnium haeresium*, or *Philosophoumena*, Hippolytus alludes only a few times to Revelation, though in *Commentarium in Dan.* he quotes a few passages from Revelation *in extenso* (Rev 3:7 in *Comm. in Dan.* 4.34; Rev 5:1–10 in *Comm. in Dan.* 4.34; Rev 6:9–11 [in a most peculiar version] in *Comm. in Dan.* 4.22).

One particularly valuable work of the prolific Origen (ca. A.D. 185–251) is his scholia on the Apocalypse, existing in a single tenth-century MS and published in an *editio princeps* in 1911 by Diobouniotis and Harnack (*Der Scholien-Kommentar*). This work appears to have been largely neglected after it was first published, since only four articles on that work have appeared since 1911 (including those by Turner and Skard). Although the scholia are anonymous, Doubouniotis and Harnack attributed the work to Origen on the grounds of style and content, and that view has been largely accepted (Skard, *SO* 15–16 [1936] 204–8).

The tradition of Greek commentaries on Revelation began toward the end of the sixth century with the commentary by Oecumenius in twelve books (text in Hoskier, *Oecumenius*). Somewhat later in the sixth century the second commentary on Revelation was composed by Andreas of Caesarea, who occasionally cites Oecumenius without naming him and also cites earlier authors extensively, including Irenaeus, Hippolytus, Methodius, and Gregory Nazianzen (critical text in Schmid, *Studien*, vol. 1). The commentary of Andreas is preserved, in whole or in part, in more than forty MSS.

## 2. LATIN AUTHORS

The tradition of Latin commentaries on Revelation began with the commentary of Victorinus of Pettau (d. ca. 304), who suffered martyrdom under Diocletian (text in Haussleiter, *Victorinus*). His writings (a list of which is found in Jerome *Vir. illustr.* 74) were condemned as apocryphal by the sixth-century Decretum Gelasianum because of his acceptance of millenarianism. Jerome later rewrote the commentary of Victorinus and removed some of the offensive millenarian features. Tyconius (ca. A.D. 330–90), a Donatist lay exegete whose works were used extensively by Augustine, wrote an influential commentary on Revelation, which was lost by the ninth century. Some of the original portions of Tyconius' commentary are probably preserved in the anonymous Turin Fragments (text in F. Lo Bue, *Turin Fragments*) and the commentary on Revelation by Beatus of Liébana (d. 798), a Spanish abbot who compiled a commentary on Revelation primarily from the now lost commentary of Tyconius (the Tyconian text of Beatus is printed in Vogels, *Untersuchungen*, 194–208; for a modern critical edition of Beatus, see E. Romero-Pose, *Sancti Beati*). Primasius (sixth century A.D.), a bishop of Hadrumetum in North Africa, wrote a Latin commentary on Revelation ca. A.D. 540 (text in Migne, *PL* 68:407–936; Vogels, *Untersuchungen*, 19–36, 153–64; critical text in Adams, *Commentarius*) in which he preserved extensive fragments of the otherwise lost commentary of Tyconius, as well as liberal quotations from Augustine. He purified the parts of Tyconius that he borrowed from Donatist ideas and eliminated the more transparent anti-Roman references. Beatus of Liébana's work in twelve books, entitled *Commentarius in Apocalypsin*, is heavily dependent on earlier authors and works on Revelation in addition to Tyconius, including Irenaeus, Victorinus, Augustine, Ambrose, Fulgentius, Primasius, and Apringius. Twenty-six illustrated MSS of the Beatus commentary have survived (Williams, *The Illustrated Beatus*).

## E. *Versions*

### *Bibliography*

**Belsheim, J.** *Die Apostelgeschichte und die Offenbarung Johannis in einer alten lateinischen Übersetzung aus dem 'Gigas librorum' auf der königlichen Bibliothek zu Stockholm.* Christiania, 1879. **Birdsall, J. N.** "The Georgian Version of the Book of Revelation." *Mus* 91 (1978) 355–66. **Browne, G. M.** "An Old Nubian Fragment of Revelation." *SPap* 20 (1981) 73–82. **Buchanan, E. S.** *The Epistles and the Apocalypse from the Codex Harleianus.* London: David Nutt, 1912. ———. *The Four Gospels from the Codex Coreiensis, Together with Fragments of the Catholic Epistles, of the Acts and of the Apocalypse from the Fleury Palimpsest.* Oxford: Clarendon, 1907. **Conybeare, F. C.** *The Armenian Version of Revelation.* London: The Text and Translation Society, 1907. **Fischer, B.** "Die Neue Testament in lateinischer Sprache: Der gegenwärtige Stand seiner Erforschung und seine Bedeutung für die griechische Textgeschichte." In *Die alten Übersetzungen des Neuen Testaments, die Kirchenväterzitate und Lectionare,* ed. K. Aland. ANTF 5. Berlin; New York: de Gruyter, 1972. 1–92. **Goussen, H.** *Apocalypsis S. Joannis Apostoli, Versio Sahidica.* Leipzig, 1895. **Gwynn, J.** *The Apocalypse of John in a Syriac Version Hitherto Unknown.* 1897. Repr. Amsterdam: Philo, 1981. ———. *Liber Ardmachanus: The Book of Armagh.* Dublin, 1913. **Haussleiter, J.** "Die lateinische Apokalypse der alten afrikanischen Kirche." In *Forschungen zur Geschichte des neutestamentlichen Kanons und der altkirchlichen Literatur,* ed. T. Zahn. Erlangen: Deichert, 1891. 4:1–224. **Hofmann, J.** "Der arabische Einfluss in der äthiopischen Übersetzung der Johannes-Apokalypse; textkritische Untersuchung auf Grund von Handschriften." *OrChr* 43 (1959) 24–53; 44 (1960) 25–39. ———. *Die äthiopische Johannes-Apokalypse kritisch Untersucht.* CSCO 297. Louvain: Secrétariat du CSCO, 1969. ———. *Die äthiopisches Übersetzung des Johannes-Apokalypse.* 2 vols. CSCO 281, 282. Louvain: Secrétariat de CSCO, 1967. ———. "Beziehungen der sa'idischen zur äthiopischen Übersetzung der Johannes-Apokalypse." In *Neutestamentliche Aufsätze.* FS J. Schmid, ed. J. Blinzler et al. Regensburg: Pustet, 1963. 115–24. **Horner, G.,** ed. *The Coptic Version of the New Testament in the Northern Dialect, Otherwise Called Memphitic and Bohairic.* 4 vols. Oxford: Clarendon, 1898–1905. ———. *The Coptic Version of the New Testament in the Southern Dialect, Otherwise Called Sahidic and Thebaic.* 7 vols. Oxford: Clarendon, 1911–24. **Lefort, L. T.** "Une étrange récension de l'Apocalypse." *Mus* 43 (1930). **Metzger, B. M.** *The Early Versions of the New Testament: Their Origin, Transmission, and Limitations.* Oxford: Clarendon, 1977. **Mink, G.** "Die koptischen Versionen des Neuen Testaments." In *Die alten Übersetzungen des Neuen Testaments, die Kirchenväterzitate und Lektionare,* ed. K. Aland. ANTF 5. Berlin; New York: de Gruyter, 1972. 160–299. **Molitor, J.** "Das Neue Testament in georgischer Sprache." In *Die alten Übersetzungen des Neuen Testaments, die Kirchenväterzitate und Lectionare,* ed. K. Aland. ANTF 5. Berlin; New York: de Gruyter, 1972. 327. ———. "Zum armenischen Vorlage der altgeorgischen Version des 1. Johannesbriefes." *Handes Amsoreay* 75 (1961) 415–24. ———. "Zum Textcharakter der armenischen Apokalypse." *OrChr* 55 (1971) 90–148; 56 (1972) 1–48. **Morin, G.** "Un texte préhieronymien du cantique de l'Apocalypse xv, 3–4." *RBén* 26 (1909) 464–67. **Reichmann, V.** "Die Übersetzungen ins Lateinische: Die altlateinischen Übersetzungen des Neuen Testament." *TRE* 6:172–76. **Rönsch, H.** *Itala und Vulgata.* 1875. Repr. Munich: Aschendorff, 1965. **Schick, C.** "Per la questione del latino africano: Il linguaggio dei più antichi atti dei martiri e di altri documenti volgarizzanti." *Rendiconti Istituto Lombardo* 96 (1962) 191–234. **Soden, Hans F. von.** *Das Lateinische Neue Testament in Afrika zur Zeit Cyprians.* TU 33. Leipzig: Hinrichs, 1909. **Stonehouse, N. B.** *The Apocalypse in the Ancient Church.* Goes, Holland: Oosterbaan & Le Cointre, 1929. **Valgiglio, E.** *Le antiche versioni latine del Nuovo Testamento.* Naples: D'Auria, 1985. **Vööbus, A.** *The Apocalypse in the Harklean Version: A Facsimile Edition of Ms. Mardin Orth. 35, fol. 143r–159v, with an Introduction.* CSCO 400. Louvain: Louvain UP, 1978. ———. "New Data for the Solution of the Problem Concerning the Philoxenian

Version." In *Spiritus et Veritas*. FS K. Kundzinš. Eutin, 1953. 169–86. ————. "Versions."
*ISBE* 4:969–83. **Vogels, H. J.** *Untersuchung zur Geschichte der Lateinischen Apocalypse-Übersetzung.*
Düsseldorf: Schwann, 1920. **Wordsworth, J.,** and **White, H. J.** *Nouum Testamentum Domini
nostri Iesu Christi Latine secundum editionem Sancti Hieronymi ad codicum manuscriptorum fi-
dem.* 3 vols. Oxford: Clarendon, 1889–1954.

## 1. THE LATIN VERSIONS

*a. The Old Latin* (Vetus Latina) *Versions (it).* The Old Latin version of the Bible
is a general designation used to describe the Latin versions antedating the Latin
translation (Vulgate) of Jerome and others, toward the end of the fourth century
A.D. The earliest document from the Latin church, the *Acts of the Scillitan Martyrs*
(A.D. 180), also contains the first mention of the existence of the Pauline corpus,
presumably in a Latin version (*Acts Scill.* 12). The earliest quotations of the NT in
Latin are found in the voluminous works of Tertullian (fl. A.D. 200), who often
appears to have translated directly from Greek MSS, though there is evidence
that he used an existing Latin version for parts of the OT. The important early
evidence for the Old Latin version is found in the equally voluminous works of
Cyprian (ca. 200–258). The Old Latin translation of the NT very probably did
not originate as a single original translation but as several translations of parts of
the NT in several places in the western Mediterranean, specifically in Italy and
North Africa. The earliest date for the first translations is the first quarter of the
second century A.D. Hermann F. von Soden and his son Hans F. von Soden used
the sigla af (*afra*) and it (*itala*) to refer to the African and Italian (or European)
text types within the Old Latin. This use of the term *itala* goes back to Augustine,
who used it to designate a form of the text that was in circulation in Italy (*De
doctrina christiana* 2.15). The only Old Latin MS that contains Revelation and has
been associated with the *afra* text type is it[h] (Floriacensis; see below). Hans von
Soden has published an edition of the African Latin version of the NT that for
Revelation relies exclusively on it[h] and Cyprian (von Soden, *Das Lateinische Neue
Testament,* 577–88). H. J. Vogels considers the distinction between African and
European text types of Revelation questionable and provides evidence for at least
*three* separate translations of Revelation into Latin (*Apokalypse-Übersetzung,* 144–
49): (1) The dominant text type is that of Primasius (a sixth-century bishop of
Hadrumetum in North Africa), which is found in all African writers from Cyprian
to the sixth century A.D. (with the exception of it[h] and Cassiodorus). (2) The
Tyconius (ca. 330–390) text type is as old as that of Primasius (perhaps an earlier
stage of the Tyconius text type is represented by the Interpolator of Cyprian's
*Testimonia* and the Old Latin translation of Irenaeus). (3) The text type represented by it[g] is more similar to the text types found in European authors such as
Priscillian of Spain (ca. 340–87), Hilarius of Gaul (ca. 315–65), Ambrose of Milan
(ca. 339–97), and "Ambrosiaster" (late fourth century) than to the Primasius or
Tyconius text types.

There are thirteen Old Latin MSS containing Revelation in whole or in part
(a restricted list is found in Nestle-Aland[26], 716; a more complete list is found in
UBSGNT[3], xxxii–xxxiv): (1) Codex *Ardmachanus* (it[a]; siglum in UBSGNT[3] is it[ar];
Fischer, "Die Neue Testament," 61), ninth century (eapcr); ed. Gwynn, *Liber
Ardmachanus.* (2) Codex *Colbertinus* (it[c]; Fischer, "Die Neue Testament," 6),

twelfth–thirteenth centuries (eapcr). (3) Codex *Demidouianus* (it^dem; Fischer, "Die Neue Testament," 59), thirteenth century (apcr). (4) Codex *Diuionensis* (it^div), thirteenth century (pcr). (5) Codex *Sandermanensis* (it^gl; Fischer, "Die Neue Testament," 7), ninth century (eapcr). (6) Codex *Gigas* (it^gig; Fischer, "Die Neue Testament," 51), thirteenth century (epc: Vulgate; ar: Old Latin). (7) Codex *Floriacensis* (it^h; Fischer, "Die Neue Testament," 55), the Fleury palimpsest, fifth century (acr); ed. Buchanan, *Four Gospels* (contains 1:1–2:1; 8:7–9:12; 11:16–12:14; 14:15–16:5). (8) Codex *Hafnianus* (it^haf), tenth century (r). (9) Codex *Legionensis* (it^l; Fischer, "Die Neue Testament," 67), seventh century (eapcr). (10) Codex *Speculum* or Ps.-Augustine (it^m), fourth to ninth century (eapcr). (11) Codex *Perpinianensis* (it^p; Fischer, "Die Neue Testament," 54), thirteenth century (eapcr). (12) Liber Comicus *Toletanus* (it^t; Fischer, "Die Neue Testament," 56), eleventh century (acpr); ed. Morin, *Liber Comicus*. (13) Codex *Harleianus Londiniensis* (it^z; Fischer, "Die Neue Testament," 65), eighth century (pcr); ed. Buchanan, *Epistles and Apocalypse* (contains only 1:1–14:16a). The Wordsworth and White edition of the Vulgate made use of eight Old Latin MSS, primarily for comparative purposes in the critical apparatus (listed in Wordsworth-White, *Nouum Testamentum* 3:419): (1) it^c, (2) it^dem, (3) it^div, (4) it^gig, (5) it^h, (6) it^haf, (7) it^m, (8) it^t (see above).

   *b. The Vulgate (vg).* In A.D. 383 Pope Damasus commissioned Jerome to revise the entire Latin Bible because of the lack of uniformity that existed among the Old Latin translations. Jerome's revision of the Gospels was completed by A.D. 384, and he translated most of the OT from Hebrew and Aramaic, guided by Old Latin MSS, between A.D. 390 and 406. As the translation progressed, the new translation exhibited increasing reliance on the various Old Latin MSS that were used. Since scholars other than Jerome wrote the prefaces to the other books of the NT, it is uncertain which books in addition to the Gospels, if any, were translated by Jerome himself. Since the Vulgate was not immediately accepted by all (indeed, it did not achieve dominance until the ninth century), various MSS containing parts of Old Latin translations continued to be copied and used until well into the Middle Ages. Toward the middle of the sixth century, Cassiodorus (ca. 485–580), a monk from Vivarium in south Italy, made an ambitious attempt to compile a complete Latin Bible. Cassiodorus prepared three editions of the entire Bible: (1) the Old Latin Bible (nine volumes), (2) a single-volume edition, called the *Codex grandior,* consisting of Jerome's revision of the LXX, Jerome's version of the Gospels, and Old Latin versions of the rest of the NT, and (3) the Lesser Pandect, a version of the Bible relying entirely on the Vulgate. While the term *vulgata versio,* "the common version," had previously been used of the Septuagint and Old Latin versions, after the ninth century it was applied to Jerome's version. The best extant authority for the Vulgate is Codex *Amiatinus* (A), an eighth-century MS of the entire Bible. During the Middle Ages, as many as seven distinctive regional versions of the Vulgate developed, influenced to various extents by Old Latin MSS: the Italian, Spanish, Anglo-Saxon, Irish, Laguedoc, Gallic, and Swiss. The post-Tridentine (1546) efforts to produce a new version of the Vulgate culminated in the publication of the Clementine Vulgate in 1592, followed by corrected editions in 1593 and 1598. The modern Vulgate text of Wordsworth and White was based on Codex *Amiatinus.* The final fascicle of the Wordsworth and White version of the Vulgate, completed in 1954 by H. F. D. Sparks, was based on sixteen Vulgate MSS (listed in Wordsworth-White, *Nouum*

*Testament* 3:419): (1) A (Codex *Amiatinus*), seventh–eighth centuries, (2) C (Codex *Cauensis*), ninth century, (3) D (Codex *Ardmachanus*), ninth century, (4) F (Codex *Fuldensis*), sixth century, (5) G (Codex *Sangermanensis*), ninth century, (6) Q (Codex *Theodulfianus*), ninth century, (7) I (Codex *Iuueniani Uallicellanus* B), eighth–ninth centuries, (8) K (Codex *Karolinus*), ninth century, (9) O (Codex *Oxoniensis*) twelfth–thirteenth centuries, (10) P (Codex *Parisinus*), ninth century, (11) S (Codex *Triueriensis*), eighth century, (12) T (Codex *Toletanus*), eighth century, (13) U (Codex *Ulmensis*), ninth century, (14) V (Codex *Uallicellanus*), ninth century, (15) W (Codex *Sarisburiensis*), thirteenth century, (16) Z (Codex *Harleianus*), ninth century.

## 2. THE ARMENIAN VERSION (arm)

The number of extant Armenian MSS of the NT is second only to the number of MSS of the Latin Vulgate (Metzger, *Early Versions*, 157). Revelation was translated into Armenian in the fifth century A.D., even though the book itself was not accepted into the biblical canon until the twelfth century. Conybeare argued that the Armenian version of Revelation was based on a Latin text but was revised on the basis of Greek MSS, though more recently Molitor has argued that the Armenian version of Revelation was based on the Greek text (*OrChr* 56 [1972] 45–46). Conybeare has grouped the Armenian translations of Revelation into four classes, Arm[1], Arm[2], Arm[3], and Arm[4]. Hoskier reviewed the MS evidence and concluded that, apart from the most conservative text, Arm[4], the other Armenian MSS were hopelessly at variance. He concluded that "I think we should incur small loss if we consigned the whole thing (with the exception, of *arm* 4) to the bottom of the sea" (*Text* 1:xxv).

## 3. THE GEORGIAN VERSION

According to Birdsall (*Mus* 91 [1978] 355–66), Imnašvili's edition of the Georgian translation of Revelation is based on three MSS, two from the tenth and one from the twelfth century A.D. In these MSS there is a continuous text of Revelation, followed by a lemmatized commentary on the text. The colophons of all three MSS identify Euthymius (d. 1028) as the translator of the book. Although the format of these three MSS differs from known MSS containing the commentary on Revelation by Andreas of Caesarea, Birdsall (*Mus* 91 [1978] 361–62) argues that the Georgian text of Revelation is based on the Greek text, more specifically the text of the commentary of Andreas, heavily contaminated with Byzantine readings. Aland and Aland (*Text of the New Testament*, 201) maintain that the first Georgian NT was translated from Armenian, a view held by Molitor ("Das Neue Testament," 327) but seriously challenged (at least for Revelation) by Birdsall (*Mus* 91 [1978] 355–66).

## 4. THE COPTIC VERSIONS (cop^sa cop^bo)

Of the various dialects of Coptic attested by literary remains (Sahidic, Bohairic, Fayyumic, Achmimic, Sub-Achmimic, Middle Egyptian; see Metzger, *Early Versions*, 106), the Sahidic and Bohairic are of most significance for the textual criticism of Revelation. The Sahidic version (cop$^{sa}$), in the dialect of Upper Egypt, was in existence by the fourth, perhaps even the third, century A.D. (text in Horner, *Southern Dialect*, vol. 7, 1924). Revelation was not denied canonical status in the ancient Egyptian church. Though the Sahidic version of Revelation exists only in fragments, Horner was able to piece together a translation lacking only portions of 1:1–8, though Lefort discovered a MS containing 1:1–2:1 with several omissions. The weakness of this critical text, however, is precisely the fact that texts from different periods and origins have been pieced together. Only a few MSS preserve copies of Revelation in the Bohairic version (cop$^{bo}$), the dialect of Lower Egypt, or the delta region, and the liturgical language of the modern Coptic Orthodox Church (text in Horner, *Northern Dialect*, vol. 4, 1905). The beginnings of the Bohairic version probably date to the fourth century A.D.

### 5. THE ETHIOPIC VERSION (eth)

The extensive work by J. Hofmann on the Ethiopic text of Revelation means that this part of the Ethiopic version of the NT has been the one most thoroughly studied. The twenty-six MSS collated by Hofmann are all descendants from one common text type, made between A.D. 550 and 650. The extension of Christianity into Ethiopia occurred during the late fifth century through wandering Syrian monks. Since Revelation was not yet recognized in their NT canon, and was not of central importance for the evangelization of Ethiopia, it appeared in Ethiopic at a relatively late stage (Hofmann, "Beziehungen," 116–17). Four MSS date from the fifteenth century, four from the sixteenth, seven from the seventeenth, ten from the eighteenth, and one from the nineteenth (descriptions of each MS in Hofmann, *Die äthiopische Übersetzung*, CSCO 281, ii–ix). This translation was revised in accordance with Arabic versions, the first time in the fourteenth or fifteenth century, and the second perhaps in the sixteenth century (Hofmann, *OrChr* 43 [1959] 24–53). Hofmann argues against the view that the Ethiopic version was translated from Sahidic (maintained by Goussen, *Apocalypsis*, vii), with the following arguments for a Greek original ("Beziehungen," 117–19; *Die äthiopische Johannes-Apokalypse*, 19–37): (a) in several passages the Ethiopic follows the Greek in both form and word order (Rev 12:18; 13:7; 19:18), (b) the vocabulary is often dependent on that found in the Greek text, (c) the Ethiopic version uses transcriptions of Greek words in places where the Sahidic version has Coptic words (1:13: ποδήρη; 18:13: καὶ ῥεδῶν; cf. 1:13; 9:11; 21:19, 20), and (d) in a few places the Ethiopic can be construed only on the basis of the Greek text. The Sahidic version did, however, have an influence on the Ethiopic version, for there are several instances in which the Ethiopic departs from the Greek in such a way that a misunderstanding of the Sahidic is presupposed (Hofmann, "Beziehungen," 120–21). According to Hofmann, the Ethiopic version of Revelation was translated from a good Greek text exhibiting the following characteristics (Hofmann, *Die äthiopische Johannes-Apokalypse*, 65): (a) There is no discernible influence from the Andreas and Byzantine text types. (b) The Ethiopic agrees with the Greek MSS A and C at places that appear original. (c) There is no relationship with $\mathfrak{P}^{47}$. (d) There is some relationship between the Ethiopic version of Revelation and the text tradition represented by ℵ.

6. THE SYRIAC VERSIONS (syr[ph] syr[h]).

Because of its absence from the Syriac canon of the NT (Stonehouse, *Apocalypse,* 134–39), Revelation was not translated into Syriac until the sixth century A.D. The text of Revelation is preserved in only two Syriac versions, though the precise relationship between the two remains a matter of dispute. The oldest is the so-called Philoxenian (syr[ph]; for which Gwynn and Hoskier used the siglum syr S, and Charles and Schmid use the siglum syr[1]), made in A.D. 507–8 and named after the monophysite bishop Philoxenus of Mabbug (A.D. 485–523), who commissioned its translation by the chorepiscopos Polycarp from Greek MSS. According to Hoskier (*Apocalypse* 1:442–43), fam 1611[1854] has "sympathy" with syr[ph]. The Harklean (syr[h]; for which Gwynn and Hoskier used the siglum syr Σ, and Charles and Schmid use the siglum syr[2]) is based on the Philoxenian version, but the extent of the revision is a matter of dispute. The Harklean version was published in 616 by Thomas of Harkel. According to Hoskier (*Apocalypse* 1:363), 1611 represents the Greek text underlying syr[h].

## III. Text Types of Revelation

"In the Book of Revelation the textual scene and its history differs greatly from the rest of the New Testament" (Aland and Aland, *Text,* 242). Though Westcott and Hort (*NT in Greek* 2:109) found it difficult to distinguish between text types in Revelation because of the paucity of MSS and the absence of Revelation from Codex *Vaticanus* (which ends with Heb 9:15), J. Schmid has more recently distinguished four text types (Schmid, *Studien* 2:44–172).

A. The best group of textual witnesses is the so-called neutral text consisting of the early uncial MSS A and C, together with the thirteenth-century minuscule MS 2053, containing the text of Revelation accompanied by the lemmatized commentary of Oecumenius (Schmid, *Studien* 2:85–109). The text preserved in Codex *Alexandrinus* (A; fourth or fifth century) is widely regarded as the best MS of Revelation (B. Weiss, *Johannes-Apokalypse,* 96–103; Charles, 1:clx–xlxvi; J. Schmid, *Studien* 2:141; id., *ZNW* 59 [1968] 251), in spite of its relative inferiority elsewhere. Though A and C diverge from each other in seventy-three readings (Schmid, *Studien* 2:97–109), when they agree they are as valuable for restoring the original text of Revelation as are agreements between א and B for other parts of the NT (Westcott-Hort, *Intro.,* 260–62).

B. The next most valuable text tradition, closely related to A above, is that which consists of 𝔓[47] (the oldest MS witness to the text of Revelation), א (01), and the text of Origen as preserved in his scholia on Revelation, 2351 (Schmid, *Studien* 2:109–46; Diobouniotis-Harnack, *Der Scholien-Kommentar des Origenes*). Bousset was the first to recognize the close relationship between the text of Revelation in א and Origen (2351). There is widespread agreement among scholars that א is the least reliable of the old uncial texts of Revelation (B. Weiss, *Johannes-Apokalypse,* 157–58; Charles, 1:clxxii, clx–xlxvi).

C. The Andreas text, used by Andreas of Caesarea in Cappadocia, who wrote a commentary on Revelation between A.D. 563 and 614, represents a "younger" textual tradition, which has been examined in detail by J. Schmid. Further, the two tenth-century MSS that preserve the Georgian version of Revelation were apparently based on copies of the Andreas commentary, which antedate all of the surviving minuscule copies of that commentary (Birdsall, *Mus* 91 [1978] 362). Andreas did not revise the text himself, and the text that was transmitted through the copying of his commentary tended to retain its distinctiveness. Schmid (*Studien* 2:26) has proposed the following twelve groups of seventy-five MSS (he has ignored the MSS in parentheses as not useful in reconstructing the text):

a = 1 2186 2428
b = 2059 2081 (2259)
c = 2028 (2029) (2033) 2044 (2052) (2054) (2068) 2069 (2083) (2361)
d = (743) 2051 (2055) 2064 (2067) (2435)
e = 2026 2057 (2091)
f = 051 (an uncial) (35) (2023) 2031 2056 2073 (2254) (2063 has commentary but no text of Revelation)
g = 205 205$^A$ 209 2045 (2071) (632 has Byzantine text but Andreas commentary in margins)
h = 2060 2286 2302 2594
i = (88) (1384) 1685 (1732) (1876) (2014) (2015) (2034) 2036 (2036$^A$) 2042 2043 (2047) 2074 (2082, copy of 2043) (2066, Revelation text copied from the printed TR) 2625
l = 052 (an uncial) 1678 1778 (2020) 2080 (2433)
m = 2037 2046 (mixed text of c and i)
n = 2065 2429 2432

D. The Byzantine text. Here Schmid (*Studien* 2:27) lists eighty-seven MSS, not counting 2040 and the missing 3 and 83:
1. 920 1859 1872 2027 2256 (2040 = 911 [1:1–11:7 Byzantine])
2. 18 2039 2076 (2258, copy of 2076) 2138 919 2004 2200
3. 385 429 522 1849 1955 2349 (= 1795)
4. 141 1424 1719
5. 808 1893
6. 218 1352
7. 2024 2079
8. 177 180 337
9. 203 452 467 506 2021
10. 935 1728 1734 1870
11. 149 201 368 386 1597 1948 2025
12. 110 627 2048
13. 498 1704 2058
14. 325 456 517 1857
15. 42 367 468
16. 61 69 Q (046)
17. 82 93 699 1140 1780 1852 469 632 241 2436 2078 (3 and 83 are both missing)
18. 91 175 242 256 617 1934 2017 (Arethas text)
19. 39$^A$ 314 664 1094 2016 2075 2077 2419 (Arethas text)

E. There are, in addition, a number of minuscules that preserve four subgroups of mixed texts derived from the Andreas and Byzantine text types, indicated in the text by the siglum Andr/Byz. The problems of the canonical status of Revelation in the Eastern church make it doubtful whether there ever was any "official" Byzantine text of Revelation.

1.      Arethas text (see above 18 and 19 under Byzantine).

2.      Two groups, fam 104 and fam 336; J. Schmid, *ZNW*52 (1961) 86; a mixed text based on Andreas and Byzantine and generally worthless: (a) 104 459 680 922 2493; (b) 336 582 620 628 1918.

3.      Complutensian Group (thirty-seven MSS). This group was first identified by Hoskier (*Text* 1:8) as consisting of twenty-nine minuscules: 35 60 432 757 824 986 1072 1075 1248 1328 1503 1551 1617 1637 1733 1740 1745 1746 1771 1774 1864 1865 1894 1903 1957 2023 2035 2041 2352. Though none of these minuscules is identical with the text of Revelation in the Complutensian Polyglot, part of the first printed edition of the Greek NT completed on 10 January 1514 under the direction of Cardinal Francisco Ximénez de Cisneros (a list of the readings found only in the Complutensian text of Revelation is found in Hoskier, *Text* 1:88), the minuscules in this family are closely related to the Complutensian exemplar, assuming that a single MS was the basis for the text of Revelation. Schmid, who has expanded this group by including eight more MSS, speculates that the restricted number of MSS in this group, coupled with the fact that nearly half of them are located in libraries at Mount Athos, suggests that this group originated at that location (*ZNW*59 [1968] 252; the asterisk indicates the added minuscules): 35 60 432 757 824 986 1072 1075 1248 1238 *1384 1503 1551 1617 1637 *1652 *1732 1733 1740 1745 1746 1771 1774 1864 1865 1894 1903 1957 2023 2035 2041 *2061 *2196 *2323 2352 *2431 *2434.

4.      Family Ø consists of a group of thirteen MSS in three subgroups: (a) 250 424 616 2084 (offer archetype of Ø unaltered); (b) 172 1828 1862 1888 2018 2032; (c) 2070 2305 2022.

## IV. RESTORING THE ORIGINAL TEXT OF REVELATION

The peculiarities of the text and of the history of the transmission of the text of Revelation make the restoration of the most original form of the text (i.e., the text of the third century A.D.) a challenging task. In the Greek MS tradition of Revelation, there is no trace of the so-called Western text, which must have existed before the time of Origen and Dionysius of Alexandria. Revelation is missing from most "complete" minuscule copies of the NT, and where it is found it has often been added at a later time (Schmid, *Studien* 2:31–43). MSS of Revelation are often found in collections of nonbiblical writings (e.g., 2023, 2024, 2030, 2449, 2681, 2737, 2743), a situation that is most unusual for NT compositions other than Revelation. Since readings from Revelation were not incorporated into Christian liturgies, they are also absent from lectionary MSS. (1) In a way analogous to textual problems in the synoptic Gospels, the frequently repeated stereotypical phrases and patterns (cf. Schmid, *Studien* 2:226–30) have led to scribal attempts to harmonize and unify the differences between and among these passages. Some of the typical examples of such stereotypical expressions include (a) "because of the word of God and the testimony of Jesus" (1:2, 9; 6:9; 20:4), (b) "of the wine [ἐκ τοῦ οἴνου]" (14:8, 10; 16:19; 17:2; 18:3; 19:15), (c) "small and great" (11:18; 13:16; 19:5, 18); (d) "faithful and true" (3:14; 19:11; 21:5); (e) "lightning, rumbling, and thunder" (4:5; 8:5; 11:19; 16:18); (f) "from the east [ἀπὸ ἀνατολῆς]" (7:2; 16:12; 21:13); (g) "the book of life" (3:5; 10:2, 8, 9, 10; 13:8; 17:8; 20:12, 15; 21:27). For specific examples of parallel clauses that have been changed to exhibit greater conformity, see Rev 11:5.

The presence of linguistic peculiarities in Revelation (particularly solecisms and anacoloutha) means that a linguistic criterion must occupy an important place in choosing the most superior reading among the available variants. The Greek of Revelation exhibits many Semitisms (both Hebraisms and Aramaisms), i.e., Semitic idioms literally expressed in ungrammatical Greek. Later copyists often improved or softened the linguistic idiosyncrasies of Revelation.

Important discussions of the linguistic usage of Revelation include Schmid, *Studien* 2:173–251; Bousset (1906) 159–79; Charles, 1:cxvii–clix; Mussies, *Morphology;* Turner, *Style,* 145–59; and S. Thompson, *Syntax* (less useful because of an exaggerated emphasis on doubtful Semitisms). The utilization of the idiomatic Greek expressions in Revelation for the purposes of textual restoration, however, presupposes the stylistic consistency of the author. This presupposition, however, is not without problems (Schmid, *Studien* 2:7, criticizes Charles for rigidly applying the principle of linguistic consistency to Revelation; cf. Delobel, "Le texte de L'Apocalypse," 158–61).

## V. READINGS IN THIS COMMENTARY DIFFERING FROM NESTLE-ALAND [27]

| | |
|---|---|
| 1:6 | omit τῶν αἰώνων (bracketed in Nestle-Aland[27]) |
| 2:15 | omit τῶν before Νικολαϊτῶν (bracketed in Nestle-Aland[27]) |
| 4:4 | θρόνοι εἴκοσι τέσσαρες (Nestle-Aland[27] θρόνους . . .) |
| 4:7 | ἔχον (Nestle-Aland[27] ἔχων) |
| 4:8 | ἔχον (Nestle-Aland[27] ἔχων) |
| 5:6 | ἔχον (Nestle-Aland[27] ἔχων) |
| 5:6 | omit ἑπτά (bracketed in Nestle-Aland[27]) |
| 5:10 | βασιλεύουσιν (Nestle-Aland[27] βασιλεύσουσιν) |
| 6:17 | αὐτοῦ (Nestle-Aland[27] αὐτῶν) |
| 9:6 | εὕρωσιν (Nestle-Aland[27] εὑρήσουσιν) |
| 9:9 | εὕρωσιν (Nestle-Aland[27] εὑρήσουσιν) |
| 10:6 | omit ἐν before τῷ ζῶντι (Nestle-Aland[27] ἐν before τῷ ζῶντι) |
| 11:16 | οἱ before ἐνώπιον (Nestle-Aland[27] [οἱ]) |
| 14:13 | ἀπαρτὶ λέγει (Nestle-Aland[27] ἀπ᾽ ἄρτι ναὶ λέγει) |
| 14:16 | τὴν νεφέλην (Nestle-Aland[27] τῆς νεφέλης) |
| 14:18 | omit ἔξελθεν (bracketed in Nestle-Aland[27]) |
| 14:18 | ὁ before ἔχων (bracketed in Nestle-Aland[27]) |
| 16:4 | ἐγένοντο (Nestle-Aland[27] ἐγένετο) |
| 16:6 | ἔδωκας (Nestle-Aland[27] [δ]έδωκας) |
| 16:6 | πεῖν (Nestle-Aland[27] πιεῖν) |
| 17:3 | γέμον (Nestle-Aland[27] γέμον[τα]) |
| 17:3 | ἔχον (Nestle-Aland[27] ἔχων) |
| 17:10 | κράζουσι (Nestle-Aland[27] κράζουσιν) |
| 18:2 | omit καὶ φυλακὴ παντὸς θηρίου ἀκαθάρτου (bracketed in Nestle-Aland[27]) |
| 18:3 | πέπτωκαν (Nestle-Aland[27] πέπωκαν) |
| 18:16 | ἐν before χρυσίῳ (Nestle-Aland[27] [ἐν]) |
| 19:5 | καί[2] (Nestle-Aland[27] [και]) |
| 19:6 | omit ἡμῶν (Nestle-Aland[27] [ἡμῶν]) |

| | |
|---|---|
| 19:7 | δῶμεν (Nestle-Aland²⁷ δώσωμεν) |
| 19:9 | οἱ before ἀληθινοί (omitted in Nestle-Aland²⁷) |
| 19:11 | omit καλούμενος (Nestle-Aland²⁷ [καλούμενος] πιστός καὶ ἀληθινός) |
| 19:12 | ὡς (Nestle-Aland²⁷ [ὡς]) |
| 19:17 | omit ἐν before φωνῇ (Nestle-Aland²⁷ [ἐν]; Nestle-Aland²³ ἐν) |
| 20:4 | omit τά before χίλια (bracketed in Nestle-Aland²⁷) |
| 20:11 | insert αὐτοῦ after ἀπὸ τοῦ προσώπου |
| 21:12 | τὰ ὀνόματα (bracketed in Nestle-Aland²⁷) |
| 21:16 | στάδιους (Nestle-Aland²⁷ σταδίων) |
| 21:22 | ὁ before ναός² (omitted by Nestle-Aland²⁷) |
| 21:27 | omit ὁ before ποιῶν (bracketed by Nestle-Aland²⁷) |
| 22:11 | ῥυπαρευθήτω (Nestle-Aland²⁷ ῥυπάνθητω) |

## Section 7: Syntax

### Bibliography

**Aejmelaeus, A.** *Parataxis in the Septuagint: A Study of the Renderings of the Hebrew Coordinate Clauses in the Greek Pentateuch.* Helsinki: Suomalainen Tiedeakatemia, 1982. **Aerts, W. J.** *Periphrastica: An Investigation into the Use of* εἶναι *and* ἔχειν *as Auxiliaries or Pseudo-Auxiliaries in Greek from Homer up to the Present Day.* Amsterdam: Hakkert, 1965. **Argyle, A. W.** "The Genitive Absolute in Biblical Greek." *ExpTim* 69 (1957–58) 285. **Armstrong, D.** "The Ancient Greek Aorist as the Aspect of Countable Action." In *Tense and Aspect,* ed. P. J. Tedeschi and A. Zaenen. New York: Academic Press, 1981. 1–12. **Bakker, W. F.** *The Greek Imperative.* Amsterdam: Hakkert, 1966. ———. *Pronomen Abundans and Pronomen Coniunctum: A Contribution to the History of the Resumptive Pronoun with the Relative Clause in Greek.* Amsterdam: North-Holland, 1974. **Beyer, K.** *Semitische Syntax im Neuen Testament.* Göttingen: Vandenhoeck & Ruprecht, 1962. **Black, M.** *An Aramaic Approach to the Gospels and Acts.* 3rd ed. Oxford: Oxford UP, 1967. ———. "Some Greek Words with 'Hebrew' Meanings in the Epistles and Apocalypse." In *Biblical Studies.* FS W. Barclay, ed. J. R. McKay and J. F. Miller. London: Collins, 1976. 135–46. **Blomqvist, J.** *Greek Particles in Hellenistic Prose.* Lund: Gleerup, 1969. ———. *Das sogennante KAI adversativum: Zur Semantik einer griechischen Partikel.* SGU 13. Stockholm, 1979. **Bretscher, P. M.** "Syntactical Peculiarities in Revelation." *CTM* 16 (1945) 95–105. **Brunel, J.** *La Construction de l'Adjectif dans les Groupes nominaux du Grec.* Paris: Presses Universitaires de France, 1964. **Burney, C. F.** "A Hebraic Construction in the Apocalypse." *JTS* 22 (1921) 371–76. **Burton, E. D.** *Syntax of the Moods and Tenses in New Testament Greek.* 3rd ed. Edinburgh: T. & T. Clark, 1898. **Denniston, J. D.** *The Greek Particles.* 2nd ed. Oxford: Clarendon, 1954. **Dik, S. C.** *Coordination: Its Implications for the Theory of General Linguistics.* Amsterdam: Hakkert, 1968. **Doudna, J. C.** *The Greek of the Gospel of Mark.* SBLMS 12. Philadelphia: Society of Biblical Literature and Exegesis, 1961. **Dougherty, E. C. A.** "The Syntax of the Apocalypse." Diss., Catholic University of America, 1990. **Dover, K. J.** *Greek Word Order.* Cambridge: Cambridge UP, 1960. **Eriksson, K.** *Das Präsens Historicum in der nachklassischen griechischen Historiographie.* Lund: Ohlsson, 1943. **Fiedler, P.** *Die Formel "Und Siehe" im Neuen Testament.* Munich: Kösel, 1969. **Fillmore, C. J.** "The Case for Case." In *Universals in Linguistic Theory,* ed. E. Bach and R. Harms. New York: Holt, Rinehart and Winston, 1968. 1–88. **Gehman, H. S.** "The Hebraic Character of Septuagint Greek." *VT* 1 (1951) 81–90. ———. "Hebraisms of the Old Greek Version of Genesis." *VT* 3 (1953) 141–48. **Gonda, J.** "A Remark on 'Periphrastic' Constructions in Greek." *Mnemosyne* 12 (1959) 97–112. **Gonzaga, M.** "Paratactic καί in the New Testament." *CJ* 21 (1925–26) 580–86. **Goodwin, W. W.** *Syntax of the Moods and Tenses of the Greek Verb.* London: Macmillan, 1889. **Hartman, L.** *Testimonium Linguae: Participial Constructions in the Synoptic Gospels. A Linguistic Examination of*

*Luke 21:13.* ConNT 19. Lund: Gleerup; Copenhagen: Munksgaard, 1963. **Hellwig, A.** "Zur Funktion und Bedeutung der griechischen Partikeln." *Glotta* 52 (1974) 145–71. **Hilhorst, A.** *Sémitismes et Latinismes dans le Pasteur d'Hermas.* Nijmegen: Dekker & Van de Vegt, 1976. **Horsley, G. H. R.** "Divergent Views on the Nature of the Greek of the Bible." *Bib* 65 (1984) 393–403. ———. "The Fiction of 'Jewish Greek.'" In *New Documents Illustrating Early Christianity.* Vol. 5: *Linguistic Essays.* New South Wales: Macquarie UP, 1989. 5–40. **Jellicoe, S.** *The Septuagint and Modern Study.* Oxford: Oxford UP, 1968. **Johannessohn, M.** "Das biblische καὶ ἰδού in der Erzählung samt einer hebräischen Vorlage." *ZVS* 66 (1939) 145–95; 67 (1942) 30–84. ———. *Der Gebrauch der Kasus und der Präpositionen in der Septuaginta.* Berlin: Friedrich-Wilhelms-Universität, 1910. **Kilpatrick, G. D.** "The Order of Some Noun and Adjective Phrases in the New Testament." *NovT* 5 (1962) 111–14. **Kühner, R.,** and **Gerth, B.** *Ausführliche Grammatik der griechischen Sprache: Satzlehre.* 2 vols. 3rd ed. Hannover: Hahnsche, 1898–1904. **Lagercrantz, O.** "Eine Parataxe der griechischen Volkssprache." *Eranos* 14 (1915) 171–77. **Lancellotti, A.** "Il kai 'consecutivo' di predizione alla maniera del weqatalti ebraico nell'Apocalisse." *SBFLA* 32 (1982) 133–46. **Laughlin, T. C.** *The Solecisms of the Apocalypse.* Princeton, 1902. **Lee, J. A. L.** *Lexical Study of the Septuagint Version of the Pentateuch.* Chico, CA: Scholars, 1983. **Ljungvik, H.** *Beiträge zur Syntax der spätgriechischen Volkssprache.* Uppsala: Almqvist & Wiksell; Leipzig: Harrassowitz, 1932. **Louw, J. P.** "Die Semantiese Waarde von die Perfektum in Hellenistiese Grieks." *AcCl* 10 (1967) 23–32. ———. "Verbal Aspect in the First Letter of John." *Neot* 9 (1975) 98–104. **Maloney, E. C.** *Semitic Interference in Marcan Syntax.* Chico, CA: Scholars, 1981. **Martin, R. A.** *Syntactical Evidence of Semitic Sources in Greek Documents.* Missoula, MT: Scholars, 1964. **Mateos, J.,** and **Alepuz, M.** "El imperfecto sucesivo en el Nuevo Testamento." In A. Urban, J. Mateos, and M. Alepuz. *Estudios de Nuevo Testamento.* Vol. II: *Cuestiones de Gramatica y Lexico.* Madrid: Ediciones Cristiandad, 1977. **Mayser, E.** *Grammatik der griechischen Papyri aus der Ptolemäerzeit.* 2 vols., each in three parts. Leipzig: Teubner, 1906–34. **McKay, K. L.** "Aspect in Imperatival Constructions in NT Greek." *NovT* 27 (1985) 201–26. ———. "Further Remarks on the 'Historical Present' and Other Phenomena." *Foundations of Language* 11 (1974) 247–51. ———. *Greek Grammar for Students: A Concise Grammar of Classical Attic with Special Reference to Aspect in the Verb.* Canberra: Australian National University, 1974. ———. "On the Perfect and Other Aspects in NT Greek." *NovT* 23 (1981) 289–329. ———. "On the Perfect and Other Aspects in the Greek Non-Literary Papyri." *Bulletin of the Institute of Classical Studies* 27 (1980) 23–49. ———. "Syntax in Exegesis." *TynBul* 23 (1972) 39–57. ———. "The Use of the Greek Perfect Down to the End of the Second Century A.D." *Bulletin of the Institute of Classical Studies* 12 (1965) 1–21. **Montgomery, J. A.** "The Education of the Seer of the Apocalypse." *JBL* 45 (1926) 70–80. **Mussies, G.** "Greek as the Vehicle of Early Christianity." *NTS* 29 (1983) 356–69. ———. "The Greek of the Book of Revelation." In *L'Apocalypse,* ed. J. Lambrecht. 167–77. ———. *The Morphology of Koine Greek as Used in the Apocalypse of John: A Study in Bilingualism.* NovTSup 27. Leiden: Brill, 1971. ———. "The Use of Hebrew and Aramaic in the Greek NT." *NTS* 30 (1984) 416–32. **Newport, K. G. C.** "Semitic Influence on the Use of Some Prepositions in the Book of Revelation." *BT* 37 (1986) 328–34. ———. "Some Greek Words with Hebrew Meanings in the Book of Revelation." *AUSS* 26 (1988) 25–31. ———. "The Use of ἐκ in Revelation: Evidence of Semitic Influence." *AUSS* 24 (1986) 223–30. **Ozanne, C. G.** "The Language of the Apocalypse." *TynBul* 16 (1965) 3–9. **Porter, S. E.** "The Language of the Apocalypse in Recent Discussion." *NTS* 35 (1989) 582–603. ———. *Verbal Aspect in the Greek of the New Testament with Reference to Tense and Mood.* New York: Lang, 1989. **Poythress, V. S.** "Johannine Authorship and the Use of Intersentence Conjunctions in the Book of Revelation." *WTJ* 47 (1985) 329–36. ———. "The Use of Intersentence Conjunctions De, Oun, Kai, and Asyndeton in the Gospel of John." *NovT* 26 (1984) 312–40. **Regard, P. F.** *La phrase nominale dans la langue du Nouveau Testament.* Paris, 1918. **Reiser, M.** *Syntax und Stil des Markusevangeliums im Licht der hellenistischen Volksliteratur.* Tübingen: Mohr-Siebeck, 1984. **Rijksbaron, A.** *The Syntax and Semantics of the Verb in Classical Greek: An Introduction.* Amsterdam: Gieben, 1984. **Rochais, G.** "Le règne des mille ans et la second mort: origines et sens." *NRT* 103 (1981) 831–56. **Scott, R. B. Y.** *The Original Language of the Apocalypse.* Toronto: University of Toronto, 1928.

Sieg, Fr. "Eigentliche Präpositionen als gebundene Morpheme der Substantive im Evangelium nach Johannes und in der Offenbarung des Johannes (Eine Vergleichsanalyse)." *Filologia Neotestamentaria* 5 (1992) 135–66. **Silva, M.** *Biblical Words and Their Meaning: An Introduction to Lexical Semantics.* Grand Rapids, MI: Zondervan, 1983. ———. "Bilingualism and the Character of Palestinian Greek." *Bib* 61 (1980) 199. **Soisalon-Soininen, I.** "Gebrauch des *genetivus absolutus* in der Septuaginta." In *The Fifth World Congress of Jewish Studies.* Jerusalem: Magnes, 1973. 4:131–36. ———. "Der Gebrauch des Verbes ἔχειν in der Septuaginta." *VT* 28 (1978) 92–99. ———. *Die Infinitive in der Septuaginta.* Helsinki: Suomalainen Tiedeakatemia, 1965. ———. "Die Konstruktion des Verbs bei einem Neutrum Plural im griechischen Pentateuch." *VT* 29 (1979) 189–99. ———. "Renderings of Hebrew Comparative Expressions with *min* in the Greek Pentateuch." *Bulletin of the International Organization for Septuagint and Cognate Studies* 12 (1979) 27–42. ———. "Verschiedene Wiedergaben der hebräischen status-constructus-Verbindung im griechischen Pentateuch." *SEÅ* 41–42 (1976–77) 214–23. **Sollamo, R.** *Renderings of Hebrew Semiprepositions in the Septuagint.* Helsinki: Suomalainen Tiedeakatemia, 1979. **Stagg, F.** "The Abused Aorist." *JBL* 91 (1972) 222–31. **Tabachovitz, D.** *Die Septuaginta und das Neue Testament.* Lund: Gleerup, 1956. **Thackeray, H. St. J.** *A Grammar of the Old Testament in Greek.* Cambridge: Cambridge UP, 1909. **Thompson, S.** *The Apocalypse and Semitic Syntax.* SNTSMS 52. Cambridge: Cambridge UP, 1985. **Torrey, C. C.** *The Apocalypse of John.* New Haven: Yale UP, 1958. **Trenker, S.** *Le style KAI dans le recit oral attique.* Brussels, 1948. **Trudinger, L. P.** "Some Observations concerning the Text of the Old Testament in the Book of Revelation." *JTS* 17 (1966) 82–88. **Verdenius, W. J.** "Adversative καί Again." *Mnemosyne* 28 (1975) 189–90. **Voelz, J. W.** "The Language of the New Testament." *ANRW* II, 25/2:893–977. **Wifstrand, A.** "A Problem concerning Word Order in the New Testament." *ST* 3 (1949) 172–84. ———. *Die Stellung der enklitischen Personalpronomina bei der Septuaginta.* Lund: Gleerup, 1950. **Wilcox, M.** "Semitisms in the New Testament." *ANRW* II, 25/2:978–1029.

## I. Introduction

The Greek of Revelation is the most peculiar Greek in the NT, in part because it exhibits interference from Semitic languages, perhaps both Hebrew and Aramaic. The peculiarity of the language of Revelation encouraged many copyists to make "improvements" in the text, with the result that the problem of reconstructing the original text has been made very difficult. In some instances it appears that only a single MS (Alexandrinus or Sinaiticus) has preserved the original reading (e.g., Rev 13:10). In order to reconstruct the most original form of the text of Revelation, it is necessary to understand the patterns involved in the author's distinctive use of the Greek language. Further, a knowledge of the author's linguistic style is indispensable for the interpreter, since insight into his syntax provides an important first step in elucidating the meaning of Revelation. For this reason, many previous commentators on Revelation have thought it important to devote a special section of their commentaries to a discussion of the grammar of Revelation. Since the last extensive discussions of the grammar and style of Revelation within the context of a commentary were published by R. H. Charles in 1920 (1:cxvii–xlix) and by E.-B. Allo in 1933 (cxliv–clxx), it is important that these discussions be updated in the light of more recent work done in the area of Hellenistic philology in general and in the more specific area of the language of Revelation.

The Septuagint presents a special problem for the study of NT Greek. Since most of the books of the LXX include semantic and syntactical features that appear to be abnormal or atypical Greek, the character of Septuagintal Greek requires examination and explanation. There are two very different explanations for this phenomenon. One view emphasizes the fact the LXX is a translation into Greek from Hebrew in which the tendency to translate literally and woodenly has produced the distinctive language of the LXX (Deissmann, *Bible Studies,* 66–85; Thackeray, *Grammar,* 25ff.). The alternate view is that the Greek of the LXX is a form of Jewish-Greek spoken by those who translated it from Hebrew to Greek and by the Hellenistic Jewish communities of which they were part (Gehman, *VT* 1 [1951] 81–90; N. Turner, "The Unique Character of Biblical Greek," *VT* 5 (1955) 208–13).

The following discussion of the syntax of Revelation makes no attempt at completeness (the only complete analysis of the syntax of Revelation known to me is that of Dougherty, "The Syntax of the Apocalypse," completed in 1990). Rather, I have attempted to focus on select grammatical features of the text that are of particular importance for the exegesis and textual criticism of this work.

## II. THE ARTICLE

The definite article is always used with a word group that consists of article + substantive. By using the article, the author assumes (rightly or wrongly) that the reader knows the persons or things indicated by the substantive.

A. The article is regularly absent before proper names, including "Jesus," while θεός, "God," is regularly arthrous (cf. 1:1, 9, 11; 2:13, 20; 5:5; 2:14; 7:4; 21:12; 7:5–8; 11:8; 14:1; 15:3; 16:16; 9:14; Schmid, *Studien* 2:190–91).

B. The article is regularly used with classes of things that the author can assume are known to any reader. (1) *Celestial bodies.* The *generic* article is regularly used with ἥλιος, σελήνη, γῆ, θάλασσα, οὐράνος (Schmid, *Studien* 2:192). (a) ὁ ἀήρ, "the air." Twice in Revelation, both occurrences arthrous (9:2; 16:17). (b) οἱ ἀστέρες, "the stars" (6:13; 8:12; 12:4). (c) ὁ ἀστὴρ [ὁ λαμπρὸς] ὁ πρωϊνός, "the [bright] evening star" (2:28; 22:16). An apparent exception is found in 12:1, στέφανος ἀστέρων δώδεκα, "a crown of twelve stars," which is anarthrous because it refers to a specific group of twelve stars not known to the reader. When a particular star is referred to that is not known to the reader, it is anarthrous in its first occurrence (8:10; 9:1). Similarly, a group of seven stars unknown to the reader lacks the definite article when first mentioned (1:16). (d) ἡ γῆ, "the earth." All but one of the eighty-two occurrences of the term are arthrous (including all uses in prepositional phrases). The exception is 21:1, καὶ εἶδον οὐρανὸν καινὸν καὶ γῆν καινήν, "Then I saw a new heaven and a new earth." Since this is not the γῆ with which people are familiar but part of an entire new creation, it is anarthrous. (e) τὸ δένδρον, "the tree." There are four occurrences, two arthrous (7:3; 8:7) and two with the phrase πᾶν δένδρον, in which πᾶς modifying an anarthrous noun means "each, every" (BDR § 275.1). (f) ὁ ἥλιος, "the sun" (1:16; 6:12; 7:16; 8:12; 9:2; 10:1; 12:1; 16:8; 19:17; 21:23). There are two types of exceptions: [1] ἀπὸ ἀνατολῆς ἡλίου, literally "from the rising of the sun," i.e., "from the east" (7:2; 16:12), and [2] φωτὸς ἡλίου, "the light of the sun" (22:5). (g) τὸ μεσουράνημα, "the midheaven." This occurs three times in Revelation, all anarthrous in the phrase ἐν μεσουρανήματι (8:13; 14:6; 19:17). (h) ὁ οὐρανός, "the heaven." This noun occurs fifty-two times in Revelation, and always arthrous with one exception: καὶ εἶδον οὐρανὸν καίνον, "Then I saw a new heaven." The reason is simply that this is not the heaven with which people are familiar but an entirely new one, and therefore it is anarthrous (when referred to subsequently, an anaphoric article is used to refer to this heaven: 21:2, 10). (i) ὁ ποταμός, "the river." This noun occurs eight times, five of which are arthrous (8:10; 9:14; 12:16; 16:4, 12). ὡς ποταμόν (12:15) is anarthrous because of the comparative particle ὡς. In 22:1, καὶ ἔδειξέν μοι ποτομὸν ὕδατος ζωῆς, "and he showed me a river of the water of life." Since this is a very particular river unknown to the reader, it is anarthrous; the second reference to this river is arthrous (22:2). (j) ἡ σελήνη, "the moon." All four occurrences of this noun are arthrous (6:12; 8:12; 12:1; 21:23). (k) ὁ χόρτος, "the grass." This occurs twice in Revelation, once in arthrous form (9:4) and once in the phrase πᾶς χόρτος χλωρός, "all green grass" (8:7). When πᾶς is not enclosed in the article-substantive unit, it (usually) means "every" (BDR § 275.1; Moule, *Idiom-Book*, 93–95).

(2) *Parts of the body of humans, animals, and insects.* (a) ἡ δεξιὰ [χείρ], "the right [hand]" (1:16, 17, 20; 2:1; 5:1, 7; 10:2, 5; 13:16). (b) τὸ κέρας, "the horn." There are ten occurrences of this noun, four of which are arthrous (9:13; 13:1; 17:12, 16). In several other instances an anarthrous κέρας or κέρατα is the object of ἔχειν, either in participial form, ἔχων or ἔχον (5:6; 2:3; 13:1; 17:3), or as the object of the imperfect εἶχεν (13:11). Cf. 17:7: τοῦ ἔχοντος τὰς ἑπτὰ κεφαλὰς καὶ τὰ δέκα κέρατα, "with seven heads and ten horns." (c) ἡ κεφαλή, "the head." This noun has nineteen occurrences, fourteen of which are arthrous (1:14; 4:4; 9:7, 17; 10:1; 12:1, 3; 13:1, 3; 14:14; 17:7, 9; 18:19; 19:12). The exceptions are of two types: [1] ὡς κεφαλαί, "as heads" (9:17), and [2] anarthrous κεφαλαί as the object of a participial form of ἔχειν: ἔχουσαι κεφαλάς, "having heads" (9:19); ἔχων κεφαλάς, "having heads" (12:3); ἔχον κέρατα δέκα καὶ κεφαλὰς ἑπτά, "having ten horns and seven heads" (13:1); ἔχων κεφαλὰς ἑπτά καὶ κέρατα δέκα, "having seven heads and ten horns" (17:3); cf. τοῦ ἔχοντος τὰς ἑπτὰ κεφαλὰς καὶ τὰ δέκα κέρατα (17:7). (d) τὸ μέτωπον, "the forehead." This occurs eight times, always arthrous (7:3; 9:4; 13:16; 14:1, 9; 17:5; 20:4; 22:4). (e) ὁ μηρός, "the thigh." The single occurrence in 19:16 is arthrous. (f) ὁ ὀφθαλμός, "the eye." This noun occurs ten times in Revelation, all but once in the plural. Six occurrences are arthrous (1:14; 2:18; 3:18; 7:17; 19:12; 21:4). There are three types of exceptions: [1] in the phrase πᾶς ὀφθαλμός (1:7), where πᾶς with an anarthrous substantive means "each, every" (BDR § 275.1); [2] in the phrases γέμοντα ὀφθαλμῶν, "full of eyes" (4:6), and γέμουσιν ὀφθαλμῶν, "full of eyes" (4:8); and [3] in the phrase ἔχων κέρατα ἑπτὰ καὶ ὀφθαλμοὺς ἑπτά, "with seven horns and seven eyes." (g) ὁ πούς/οἱ πόδες, "the foot/the feet." The eleven occurrences are consistently arthrous. (h) αἱ δύο πτέρυγες, "the two wings" (12:13). (i) ἡ χείρ, "the hand" (6:5; 7:9; 9:20; 10:2, 5, 8, 10; 14:9, 14; 17:4; 20:1, 4). The two exceptions here are 8:4, ἐκ χειρὸς τοῦ ἀγγέλου, "from the hand of the angel," and 19:2, ἐκ χειρὸς αὐτῆς, "from her hand." In the case of 8:4, however, note 10:10, ἐκ τῆς χειρὸς τοῦ ἀγγέλλου, "from the hand of the angel," where, however, the phrase is used literally of taking the scroll "from the hand of the angel." The anarthrous phrases in 8:4; 19:2 have two explanations: [1] articles are optionally omitted from substantives in prepositional phrases (Smyth, *Grammar*, § 1128), and [2] ἐκ χειρός + genitive (pronoun or substantive) is a Septuagintism (BDR § 217.2) frequently found in the LXX in the forms ἐκ/ἀπὸ [τῆς] χειρός as a translation of the Hebrew semipreposition מִיַּד *miyyad*, "from the hand of" (Sollamo, *Hebrew Semiprepositions*, 194–98, 340–42). (j) τὸ πρόσωπον, "the face" (4:7; 7:11; 9:7; 10:1; 11:6; 20:11; 22:4). Exceptions are the prepositional phrase ἀπὸ προσώπου + genitive (6:16; 12:14; cf. 20:11: ἀπὸ τοῦ προσώπου) and the phrase ὡς πρόσωπα (9:7). The anarthrous ἀπὸ προσώπου can be explained, like ἐκ χειρός, in two ways: [1] the definite article is optionally missing from substantives in prepositional phrases, and [2] ἀπὸ προσώπου is a Septuagintism (BDR § 217.1) used frequently in the LXX to translate such Hebrew semiprepositions as מִפְּנֵי *mippĕnê* (194 times; cf. Sollamo,

*Semiprepositions*, 82–83), מלפני *milpĕnê*, "from before, from" (34 times; Sollamo, 96), and לפני *lipnê* (12 times; Sollamo, 33–34). Although Sollamo regards ἀπὸ προσώπου as a peculiarity of translation Greek, it is better to consider the phrase a Septuagintism than a Hebraism, since it occurs seven times in the NT (Acts 3:20; 5:31; 7:45; 2 Thess 1:9; Rev 6:16; 12:14; 20:11) and four times in the Apostolic Fathers (*Barn*. 6:9; 11:7; *1 Clem*. 4:8, 10).

(k) τὸ στόμα, "the mouth" (1:16; 2:16; 3:16; 9:17, 18, 19; 10:9, 10; 11:5; 12:15, 16[2x]; 13:2, 6; 14:5; 16:13[3x]; 19:15, 21). στόμα is always arthrous even in prepositional phrases. Two kinds of exceptions are: [1] ὡς στόμα, "like a mouth" (13:2), and [2] καὶ ἐδόθη αὐτῷ στόμα λαλοῦν, literally, "a mouth was given to him to speak," i.e., "he was permitted to speak."

C. When a noun (usually used with a preposition) that is usually arthrous governs a noun in the genitive, the noun is anarthrous on analogy with the construct state in Hebrew (Schmid, *Studien* 2:192–93).

D. In a series of substantives, the article is normally repeated with each substantive (6:15; 13:16). Examples to the contrary: 1:9; 5:12; 9:15; 11:9; 21:8 (Schmid, *Studien* 2:193). The article is not repeated in a series of substantives if a single person is described with several words.

E. The "Second Mention," or Anaphoric Article. When a concept or thing is first mentioned, if the author supposes that it is unknown to his readers, the article is omitted on first mention. When the concept or thing is mentioned again, since it is now known to the readers, the substantive is arthrous. The term "anaphoric" means "referring back," i.e., to the first anarthrous occurrence of the substantive. This use of the definite article can be helpful exegetically, since it can help distinguish, e.g., between different angels, groups of angels, or women mentioned in the narrative. The following nouns are anarthrous when first mentioned but are arthrous thereafter: (1) ἄγγελοι [τῶν ἑπτὰ ἐκκλησιῶν] (1:20; 2:1, 8, 12, 18; 3:1, 5, 7, 14). (2) ἀκρίς (9:3, 7). (3) ἀρνίον (5:6, 5:8, 12; 6:1, 16; 7:9, 10, 14, 17; 12:11; 13:8; 14:1, 4[2x], 10; 15:3; 17:14[2x]; 19:7, 9; 21:9, 14, 22, 23, 27; 22:1, 3). (4) ἄρσην (adjective used as substantive in 12:5, 13). (5) ἀστέρες ἑπτά (1:16, 20[2x]; 2:1; 3:1). (6) ἀστὴρ μέγας, "a great star" (8:10, 11). (7) ἀστήρ, "a star" (9:1). (8) βιβλαρίδιον (10:2, 8 [τὸ βιβλίον], 9, 10). (9) βιβλία (20:12[2x]). (10) βιβλίον (1:11; 22:7, 9, 10, 18[2x], 19[2x]). (11) γυνή (12:1, 4, 6, 13, 14, 15, 16, 17). (12) γυνή (17:3, 4, 6, 7, 9, 18). (13) ζῷα τέσσαρα (4:6, 7[4x], 8, 9; 5:6, 8, 11, 14; 6:1, 3, 5, 6, 7; 7:11; 14:3; 15:7; 19:4). (14) θεμέλιος (21:14, 19[2x]). (15) θηρίον a (13:1, 2, 3, 4[3x], 12[2x], 14[2x], 15[3x], 17, 18; 14:9, 11; 15:2; 16:2, 10, 13; it is problematic whether τὸ θηρίον in 19:19, 20[2x]; 20:4, 10 refers to θηρίον a or θηρίον β). (16) θηρίον β (17:3, 7, 8[2x], 11, 12, 13, 16, 17). (17) θρόνος (4:2[2x], 4[2x], 5[2x], 6[3x], 9, 10; 5:1, 6, 7, 11, 13; 6:16; 7:9, 10, 11[2x], 15[2x], 17; 8:3; 12:5; 14:3; 16:17; 19:4, 5). (18) θρόνοι εἴκοσι τέσσαρες (4:4[2x]; 11:16). (19) θρόνος μέγας λευκός (20:11, 12; 21:3, 5; 22:1, 3). (20) πληγαί (15:1, 6, 8; 16:9, 21[2x]). (21) πρεσβύτεροι εἴκοσι τέσσαρες (4:4, 10; 5:5, 6, 8, 11, 14; 7:11, 13; 11:16; 14:3; 19:4). (22) ῥομφαία a (1:16; 2:12, 16). (23) ῥομφαία β (19:15, 21). (24) σάλπιγγες ἑπτά (8:2, 6, 13; 9:14). (25) σφραγίδες ἑπτά (5:1, 2, 5, 9; 6:1, 3, 5, 7, 9, 12; 8:1). (26) σφραγίς (7:2; 9:4). (27) τέσσαρα ζῷα (4:6, 4:8, 9; 5:6, 8, 11, 14). (28) υἱός (is anarthrous in 12:5 and does not occur again). (29) ἑπτὰ φιάλας (15:7; 16:1, 2, 3, 4, 8, 10, 12, 17; 17:1; 21:9). (30) χάραγμα (13:6, 17; 14:11; 16:2; 19:20; 20:4). The exception is in 14:9: καὶ λάμβανει χάραγμα, "and he receives the mark." This is anarthrous because it is a unique mark.

F. Part of the style of apocalyptic literature is the use of already familiar persons and things drawn from stock apocalyptic imagery, which are introduced the first time with the article (Schmid, *Studien* 2:194–95; Mussies, *Morphology*, 187–88): (1) ἡ ἄβυσσος, "the abyss" (9:1, 2, 11; 11:7; 17:8 20:1, 3). (2) ἡ ἀνάστασις, "the resurrection" (20:5, 6). (3) οἱ ἑπτὰ ἄγγελοι οἳ ἐνώπιον τοῦ θεοῦ ἑστήκασιν, "the seven angels who stand before God" (8:2 [see *Notes*], 6, 8, 10, 12, 13; 9:1, 13, 14). (4) οἱ τέσσαρες ἄγγελοι οἳ δεδεμένοι ἐπὶ τῷ ποταμῷ τῷ μεγάλῳ Εὐφράτῃ, "the four angels who are bound at the great river Euphrates" (9:14). (5) ὁ ᾅδης, "Hades" (1:18; 6:8; 20:13, 14). (6) ὁ ἀετός, "the eagle" (12:14). (7) τῆς βίβλου τῆς ζωῆς, "the book of life" (3:5), or τὸ βιβλίον τῆς ζωῆς (13:8; 17:8; 20:12 [ἄλλο βιβλίον]; 21:27). (8) αἱ ἑπτὰ βρονταί, "the seven thunders" (10:3). (9) ἡ γυνή, "the wife of the Lamb" (19:7; 21:9). (10) ἡ εἰρήνη τῆς γῆς, "the peace of the earth" (6:4). (11) ὁ θάνατος, "Death" (1:18; 6:8; 20:13, 14). (12) τῆς θλίψεως τῆς μεγάλης, "the Great Tribulation" (7:14). (13) τὸ θηρίον, "the Beast" (11:7). (14) ἡ ἶρις, "the rainbow" (10:1). (15) ἡ κιβωτὸς τῆς διαθήκης, "the ark of the covenant" (11:19). (16) τὴν λίμνην τοῦ πυρός (19:20; 20:10, 14[2x], 15; 21:8). (17) οἱ δύο μάρτυρες μου, "my two witnesses" (11:3). (18) ἡ πλατεῖα τῆς πόλεως τῆς μεγάλης, "the street of the great city" (11:8). (19) τὰ ἑπτὰ πνεύματα, "the seven spirits" (1:4; 3:1; 4:5; 5:6). (20) ὁ πόλεμος, "the war" (16:14). (21) ἡ πορνή, "the whore" (17:1, 15, 16; 19:2). (22) τὸ τέκνον, "the child" (12:4). (23) ὁ υἱὸς τοῦ θεοῦ, "the son of God" (2:18). (24) τὸ φρέαρ τῆς ἀβύσσου, "the shaft of the abyss" (9:1). (25) ὁ χριστός (11:15; 12:10; 20:4, 6).

G. The article is used several times in Revelation with the substantive in the predicate nominative (1:17; 3:17; 4:5; 5:6, 8; 17:18; 18:23; 19:10; 20:14).

## III. PRONOUNS

### A. *The* Pronomen Abundans *and the Semitic Resumptive Pronoun*

Revelation contains several examples of the so-called *pronomen abundans,* that is, a personal or demonstrative pronoun that repeats the relative pronoun in a single relative clause. One example is Rev 3:8: ἰδοὺ δέδωκα ἐνώπιόν σου θύραν ἠνεῳγμένην, ἣν οὐδεὶς δύναται κλεῖσαι αὐτήν, literally "Behold, I have placed before you an open door which no one is able to shut it." This grammatical phenomenon has often been labeled a Semitism because both Hebrew and Aramaic have an indeclinable relative particle (called a *nota relationis*), אֲשֶׁר *ᵓšr* and דִי *dy*, each of which in itself is ambiguous and requires a personal or demonstrative pronoun (i.e., another anaphoric word) for clarification. The LXX version of Gen 28:13 is an example of a text literally translated from Hebrew into Greek: ἡ γῆ, ἐφ᾽ ἧς σὺ καθεύδεις ἐπ᾽ αὐτῆς, σοὶ δώσω αὐτὴν καὶ τοῦ σπέρματί σου, "As for the land [pendent nominative] *on which* you lie *upon it,* I will give it to you and your seed." There are only ten known instances of the *pronomen abundans* in Greek literature from Homer to the fourth century B.C. (Kühner-Gerth, *Satzlehre* 2:433–34 n. 2). The frequency of occurrence increases somewhat in Koine Greek, for there are some twenty-six examples of this phenomenon in post-classical Greek (aside from the LXX and the NT), including eleven in Polybius and seven in the papyri (these occurrences are analyzed in Bakker, *Pronomen Abundans,* 23–28). Bakker suggests that the *pronomen abundans* is used when an author wishes to place great emphasis on an antecedent or write with greater clarity. He further separates two idioms: (1) clauses that begin with a relative pronoun that is resumed by a personal pronoun and (2) clauses that begin with a noun that is resumed by a personal pronoun (Bakker, *Pronomens Abundans,*

22). An example of the latter is found in Rev 2:7, τῷ νικῶντι δώσω αὐτῷ, "to the one who conquers I will give to him" (cf. 2:17; 6:4).

There has been considerable scholarly disagreement regarding whether the *pronomen abundans* should be considered a Semitism. Those who approach the *pronomen abundans* from the perspective of Semitic philology consider it a Semitism, while others who find examples of it in the papyri and other Koine Greek deny that it is a Semitism and tend to consider it a vulgarism, i.e., a phenomenon at home in colloquial speech. It is currently regarded as a Greek idiom that must, however, because of its statistical frequency in the LXX and the NT, be considered a result of Semitic influence.

The *pronomen abundans* occurs frequently in the LXX (twenty-three times in Genesis alone; Bakker, *Pronomen Abundans*, 34). In the NT the *pronomen abundans* occurs less frequently, eighteen times in all (Bakker, *Pronomens Abundans*, 35, 39–42): four occurrences in Mark (1:7; 7:25; 9:3; 13:9), two in Luke (3:16 = Mark 1:7; 3:17 = Matt 3:11–12; plus two in *var. lect.* 8:12; 12:43 [MS D]), one each in Matt (3:11–12 = Luke 3:17) and John (1:27), and nine in Revelation (3:8; 7:2, 9; 12:6, 14; 13:8, 12; 17:9; 20:8). One further occurrence in Rev 20:11 (*var. lect.;* see *Notes* on 20:11) may be original. Two occurrences are found in *1 Clement* (21:9; 27:7, though the latter is a quotation from Ps 18:2–4). For example, in the phrase οἷς ἐδόθη αὐτοῖς, literally "to whom was given them" (Rev 7:2), the pronoun αὐτοῖς is resumptive or pleonastic and is considered by many to be the Hebraism אֲשֶׁר נִתַּן לָהֶם *'šr ntn lhm* (BDR § 297; Turner, *Syntax*, 325; Mussies, *Morphology*, 177), but is also an idiom used occasionally by native Greek writers (at least twenty-six times in Koine Greek, aside from the LXX and NT). In 7:2, this construction is a Semitism since it is *essential* (i.e., it occurs in a dependent relative clause).

In order to solve the problem of whether the instances of the *pronomen abundans* in the LXX and the NT are Semitisms, Bakker proposes a qualitative determinant: whether the relative clause in which a *pronomen abundans* occurs is *nonessential* (i.e., in an independent or parenthetical relative clause) or *essential* (i.e., in a subordinate relative clause that limits the meaning of the antecedent). In all Greek examples (apart from the LXX and the NT) they are nonessential, while in Hebrew and Aramaic sentences they are essential. While instances of the former can occur under Semitic influence (e.g., LXX Isa 1:21, in which a *pronomen abundans* in a nonessential clause occurs in a sentence in which the resumptive pronoun does not occur in Hebrew), this simply indicates an idiom at home in both languages (cf. other nonessential examples of *pronomen abundans*: Gen 10:13–14; 2 Macc 12:27). The *pronomen abundans* also occurs in essential clauses in Jewish literature originally written in Greek, i.e., under the influence of Semitic syntax (1 Esdr 3:5; 4:54, 63; 6:32; cf. Thackeray, *Grammar*, 46; Bakker, *Pronomen Abundans*, 38). Using this rule as a criterion, eight of the eighteen instances of *pronomen abundans* in the NT prove to be nonessential, i.e., to conform to the Greek rule (Mark 1:7 = Luke 3:16; Matt 3:11–12 = Luke 3:17; Gal 2:10; Rev 12:4; 20:8; cf. Bakker, *Pronomen Abundans*, 39–42).

## B. *Possessive Pronouns and Word Order*

In 302 instances in Revelation, a possessive pronoun in the genitive *follows* an articular noun, as opposed to just 11 occurrences of a personal pronoun in the genitive *preceding* an articular noun. Seven of these 11 instances occur in Rev 2–3 (2:9, 19; 3:1, 2, 8[2x], 18), while the other 4 instances occur in 10:9; 14:18; 18:5, 14.

## C. εἷς *as an Indefinite Pronoun*

The cardinal number εἷς, "one," is occasionally used in Revelation as an indefinite pronoun referring to a single indefinite person or thing, with a meaning similar to the indefinite pronoun τις, "a, a certain," and often used where τις would be appropriate (7:13; 8:13; 9:13; 18:21; 19:17; see Zerwick, *Greek,* § 155; BDR § 247.2; MM, 187). Mussies (*Morphology,* 183) maintains, I think correctly, that it is a different word from the εἷς ordinal number, which means "one" in contrast to more than one (e.g., Rev 17:12, 13, 17; 18:8, 10, 17, 19; 21:21). εἷς is used here and elsewhere in Revelation as an indefinite pronoun followed by the partitive genitive (5:5; 8:13; 9:13; 17:1; 21:9; cf. Matt 18:6; Luke 5:12, 17; 17:2; *1 Clem.* 46:8). This construction cannot be construed as a Hebraism since it has many parallels in pagan Greek (MM, 187), or as a pronominal adjective, i.e., as an indefinite article (8:13; 18:21; 19:17; cf. Mark 11:29); see Bauer-Aland, 466, 3b; BAGD, 231, 3b). In spite of the arguments that this is a Hebraism (Black, *Aramaic,* 104ff.; BDR § 247; Turner, *Syntax,* 195–96), it is not a Hebraism when followed by the partitive genitive.

## IV. ADJECTIVES

A. The possessive adjective ἐμός occurs just once in Revelation, in the noun cluster τοὺς ἐμοὺς δούλους (2:20). Possession is elsewhere indicated by possessive pronouns in the genitive of possession. Note that possive adjectives occur fifty-one times in the Gospel and Letters of John, a striking contrast in style between Revelation and the rest of the Johannine corpus.

B. The comparative adjective πλείονα in 2:19, a neuter accusative plural based on πολύς, "much, many," is the only comparative adjective in Revelation. Since there are also two superlatives in Revelation, τιμιωτάτου (18:12) and τιμιωτάτῳ (21:11), Mussies suggests the reason for the absence of comparative forms lies in the absence of comparison categories in the Hebrew and Aramaic adjective systems (*Morphology,* 138).

## V. CASES

In conventional discussions of Greek syntax, the discussion of cases is usually separated from the discussion of prepositions. The present discussion assumes that case relationships are part of the deep structure of all languages. C. J. Fillmore proposed this significant modification of conventional transformational grammar, which usually maintains that cases do not belong to deep structure but are rather part of the surface structure of a language; i.e., they are the inflexional realization of particular syntactical relationships. The conditions for selecting the appropriate case forms are essentially similar to the conditions for selecting the appropriate prepositions; in languages, such as Greek, that use case forms and prepositions *together,* they ought to be discussed together, though I will not attempt to do that in this brief treatment.

## A. Nominative

The nominative case occurs about 950 times in Revelation, most frequently as the subject of a verb or as the predicate of a nonverbal clause or of the verb εἶναι. The following uses of the nominative are more distinctive.

*1. Nominative Absolute.* The pendent nominative (*casus pendens*) or the nominative absolute is used to refer to the logical, though not the grammatical, subject of a sentence. The term *casus pendens,* however, is a broader term. In the English sentence "The man, here he comes," "man" is a pendent nominative that is left hanging syntactically at the beginning of the sentence. Similarly, in 10:8, ἡ φωνή, "the voice," is in the nominative but functions as a pendent nominative or nominative absolute, since it has no syntactical relationship to the following clauses. This type of *casus pendens* occurs frequently in the OT (W. Gross, *Die Pendenskonstruktion im biblischen Hebräisch* [St. Ottilien: Eos, 1987] 105–45). There are several examples in Revelation of a substantival participle constituting a pendent nominative standing before the main clause (2:26; 3:12, 21; 6:8; 21:7[*var. lect.*]). Rev 2:26 contains two substantival participles used as pendent nominatives: καὶ ὁ νικῶν καὶ ὁ τηρῶν ἄχρι τέλους τὰ ἔργα μου, δώσω αὐτῷ, "As for the one who conquers and keeps my works to the end, I will give him." In the phrase κάθημαι βασίλισσα καὶ χήρα in 18:7 ("I sit [as] queen and widow," or "I, a queen and widow, sit"), βασίλισσα καὶ χήρα are independent nominatives that refer to the speaker, though they are not grammatically the subject of the verb κάθημαι (Mussies, *Morphology;* BDR § 143; Robertson, *Greek,* 456–61). This construction is found in Greek (Moulton-Howard, *Accidence,* 425), Hebrew (GKC § 143; Lancellotti, *Sintassi Ebraica,* 83; Gross, *Pendenskonstruktion,* 105–44), and Aramaic (Black, *Aramaic,* 51–55), as well as many modern languages.

*2. Vocative Use of Nominative* (BDF § 147). In 4:11, ὁ κύριος and ὁ θεός, are articular nominatives used as vocatives (Schmid, *Studien* 2:205; see Dougherty, "Syntax," 79–80). There are eighteen other occurrences of this construction in Revelation (6:10; 12:12[2x]; 15:3[3x]; 18:4, 10[2x], 16, 19, 20[3x]; 19:5[4x]). In three of these instances the nominative is used in apposition to an initial vocative in the set phrase κύριε ὁ θεὸς ὁ παντοκράτωρ (11:17; 15:3; 16:7).

*3. Nominative of Apposition.* The nominative is used more than thirty times in Revelation in apposition with another nominative (1:8, 9; 2:1, 13, 18; 3:7[2x], 14; 4:8[2x]; 8:9; 12:1, 7, 9, 10; 14:3; 16:3; 17:5; 18:8[2x], 10, 21; 19:6; 20:14; 21:6, 22; 22:5, 6, 8, 13, 16[2x]; Dougherty, "Syntax," 80). In 2:13, the noun cluster ὁ μάρτυς μου ὁ πιστός μου is a nominative of apposition modifying the personal name Antipas, which, though indeclinable, nevertheless must be in the genitive case (Mussies, *Morphology,* 191). The nominative is used as a solecism in apposition to oblique cases in eight instances (1:5; 2:20; 3:12; 9:11, 14; 14:12; 19:16; 20:2; Dougherty, "Syntax," 81). Rev 1:5 is a striking example: ἀπὸ Ἰησοῦ Χριστοῦ, ὁ μάρτυς ὁ πιστός (where ὁ μάρτυς ὁ πιστός should be in the genitive; see Schmid, *Studien* 2:239). This irregular use of the nominative also occurs in 2:13; 20:2 (participles in the appositional nominative are found in 2:20; 3:12; *7:9; 8:9; 9:13; 14:12, *14; *21:12[2x]; asterisks indicate passages that have anarthrous participles).

*4. Parenthetical Nominative.* The phrase ὄνομα αὐτῷ, "his name," is found in Rev 6:8; 9:11, while a slightly different form of the parenthetical nominative occurs in 8:11 (BDR § 144; Turner, *Syntax,* 230).

5. *Special Problems.* (a) οὐαί + nominative (functioning as vocative) occurs in Rev 18:10, 16, 19. Since the Latin interjection *uae* could be used with the accusative as well as the dative (*OLD*, 2003), it is possible that the unique οὐαί + accusative in Rev 8:13; 12:12 is a Latinism. In the LXX, οὐαί is often used with the dative of the person or thing to whom the woe is directed as well as with articular nominatives used as vocatives. Occasionally οὐαί is used with ἐπί + the accusative in the LXX (Jer 10:19; 28:2[MT 51:2]; 31:1[MT 48:1]; Ezek 7:26).

## B. *Accusative (Dougherty, "Syntax," 114–39)*

The conventional uses of the accusative are expectedly found in Revelation: (1) The accusative of *direct object* of finite verbs, participles, and infinitives occurs frequently. (2) The *predicate* accusative, i.e., accusative as a predicate of the direct object of a verb, occurs seven times (1:6, καὶ ἐποίησεν ἡμᾶς βασιλείαν; 2:2, 9, 20; 3:9, 12; 5:10; Turner, *Syntax*, 147–48; BDF § 157). (3) The accusative as subject of an infinitive occurs twelve times (1:1; 2:9; 3:9; 4:1; 10:11; 11:5, 9; 13:10, 13; 17:10; 20:3; 22:6). (4) There are several examples of the accusative of apposition, usually to another accusative (9:11; 10:7; 11:18; 12:5; 13:6, 17; 15:1; 16:12; 18:12[2x], 13[12x]; 20:8[2x]; 21:2, 9, 10, 15) but once in apposition to a dative (11:18). (5) The *cognate* accusative occurs twice (16:9; 17:3). In 16:9, καῦμα μέγα is a cognate accusative dependent on ἐκαυματίσθησαν (Winer, *Grammar*, 281; Robertson, *Grammar*, 478; Turner, *Syntax*, 245; BDR § 153.2), which functions more specifically as an adverbial accusative of manner. In 17:6, the phrase ἐθαύμασα . . . θαῦμα μέγα, literally, "I was astonished with great astonishment," is an example of a cognate accusative (Winer, *Grammar*, 280–83; Robertson, *Grammar*, 478; Turner, *Syntax*, 245–46; BDR § 153.2). Since this construction is common in Greek, it is not quite correct to claim that this construction is more common in Semitic than Greek (as does Maloney, *Semitic Interference*, 189–90). (6) In 3:3, the accusative of *extent of time* occurs in the phrase ποίαν ὥραν (BDR § 161.6).

The use of various prepositions with the accusative provides distinctive variations in meaning. (1) μετά + accusative is used with a temporal meaning (1:19, μετὰ ταῦτα; 4:1[2x]; 7:1, 9; 9:12; 11:11; 15:5; 18:1; 19:1; 20:3). (2) Various prepositions + accusative indicate direction: (a) εἰς + accusative (e.g., 1:11[5x]; 2:10; 5:6; 6:13; 15:8; 17:3; 19:9; 20:3, 10, 14; 22:14), (b) ἐπί + accusative (e.g., 1:17; 2:24; 6:16; 7:1; 11:16; 13:16; 14:9, 16; 18:17; 21:10), (c) πρός + accusative (1:17; 3:20; 10:9; 12:12). (3) The *locative* use of the accusative occurs with ἐπί + accusative (e.g., 3:20, ἕστηκα ἐπὶ τὴν θύραν; 6:4; 13:1; 14:1, 14; 17:3, 5; 20:4, 11) and once with περί + accusative (15:6). (4) διά + accusative indicates *cause* (e.g., 1:9; 4:11; 6:9[2x] 7:15; 12:12; 18:8) and *means* (12:11; 13:14).

Special problems. In 10:7, the accusative phrase τοὺς ἑαυτοῦ δούλους τοὺς προφήτας following εὐηγγέλισεν is problematic, for normally the one to whom something is proclaimed is in the dative and that which is proclaimed in the accusative (e.g., Luke 1:19; 8:35), though in Luke-Acts there are several instances in which the one to whom the proclamation is made is in the accusative (Luke 3:18; Acts 8:25, 40; 13:32; 14:21; 16:10). Kraft (149), therefore, understands the accusative phrase τοὺς ἑαυτοῦ δούλους τοὺς προφήτας as an accusative of relation, arguing that the prophets are the content, not the recipients, of the revelation.

## C. Genitive

1. The *adnominal genitive* is the adjectival function of the genitive. The genitive case occurs about 1,200 times in Revelation, usually adnominally (indicating a relationship between two substantives). (a) The genitive of *possession* (e.g., 2:7; 3:14; 8:13; 16:13; frequently with a personal pronoun). (b) The *descriptive* or *qualitative* genitive. In this use, the word in the genitive modifies the word on which it depends like an attributive adjective, sometimes mistakenly referred to as the Hebraic genitive (Maloney, *Semitic Interference,* 165–69; Zerwick, *Greek,* § 40–41); some examples include 12:4, τῶν ἀστέρων τοῦ οὐρανοῦ; 13:1; 17:3, ὀνόματα βλασφημίας, "blasphemous names," a descriptive genitive that functions as an adjective modifying ὀνόματα (G. Mussies, *Morphology,* 96; BDR § 165.2; e.g., 1:3, 5; 2:18; 4:1, 7; 5:6; 8:10, 13; 13:3, ἡ πληγὴ τοῦ θανάτου αὐτοῦ, "his mortal wound"; 16:3). (c) The genitive of *material* or *content* (e.g., 6:6; 12:1; 14:19; 16:1; 18:12[8x];19:15, 20; 22:1; the author also uses ἐκ + genitive in the same way as in 18:12: πᾶν σκεῦος ἐκ ξύλου τιμιωτάτου; BDF § 167). (d) The genitive of *price* (6:6[2x]). (e) The genitive of *time* (2:13; 3:10; 6:17; 10:7; 11:6, 18; 14:7). (f) The *objective* genitive (more than sixty times, e.g., 1:5, 18[2x]; 2:13[3x]; 7:4; 12:10; 14:11, 12, 13; 20:1, 7, 8). While the possessive pronoun μου in the phrase τὴν πίστιν μου in 2:13 appears to be a genitive of possession, it is probably an objective genitive; the entire phrase then refers to the faith or loyalty of the Pergamene community to Christ, "(your) faith in me" (Bousset [1906] 212; Charles, 1:61). (g) The *subjective* genitive (ca. 130 times, e.g., 1:2, τὸν λόγον τοῦ θεοῦ; 5:8; 14:7; 16:21[2x]; 17:2; 18:1, 2, 3; 19:1, 7, 8; 22:5[2x]). It is not always clear whether the name "Jesus" should be construed as an objective or subjective genitive (e.g., 1:1, 2, 9; 12:17; 19:10[2x] 20:4). (h) The genitive of *source* or *origin.* This occurs some seventeen times, both as a simple genitive (2:16; 3:18; 18:18; 19:3; 22:7, 9, 10, 16, 18, 19 and also with ἐκ + genitive (5:5; 11:11; 15:8). (i) The genitive of *measure* or *quantity* (9:16, τῶν στρατευμάτων). (j) The *superlative* genitive (BDF § 185; Turner, *Syntax,* 210–16; Dougherty, "Syntax," 90–91). This is based on a Semitic construction (reflected in the Hebrew phrase שִׁיר הַשִּׁירִים *šîr haššîrîm,* which means "song of songs" or "most excellent song"; GKC § 133i); it occurs in fixed expressions such as εἰς [τοὺς] αἰῶνας [τῶν] αἰώνων (1:18; 4:9, 10; 5:13; 7:12; 10:6; 11:15; 14:11; 15:7; 19:3; 20:10; 22:5) and κύριος κυρίων καὶ βασιλεὺς βασιλέων (17:14; the two noun groups occur in reverse order in 19:16) or μυριάδες μυριάδων καὶ χιλιάδες χιλιάδων (5:11), and δισμυριάδες μυριάδων (9:16). (k) The *epexegetical* or *explanatory* genitive (e.g., 3:9; 9:16; 13:7; 14:8, 10; 15:2; 16:19; 17:2; 18:3; 19:5). In 9:16, the phrase τῶν στρατευμάτων τοῦ ἱππικοῦ, τοῦ ἱππικοῦ is a genitive of apposition, since it is identical with τῶν στρατευμάτων but is more specific.

(l) The *partitive genitive.* The final adnominal use of the genitive in Revelation, which I will discuss in some detail, is the *partitive genitive.* In many Indo-European languages, the partitive genitive may function as the subject or object of the verb. For example, the Russian phrase *Daj nam chleba,* literally "Give us *of* bread," really means "Give us [some] bread." The partitive genitive as the object of the verb, though now obsolete in English, does occur in archaic English, such as in Rev 2:17 in the AV: "To him that overcometh will I give to eat *of* the hidden manna." In classical Greek, the partitive genitive can function as the direct object if the action of the verb affects the object only in part (Smyth, *Greek Grammar*, 320); cf. *Iliad* 14.121: Ἀδρήστοιο δ᾽ ἔγημε θυγατρῶν, "He married one of the daughters of Adrastos" (see also Aristophanes *Vespae* 1428; Xenophon *Anabasis* 1.5.7; 4.5.35; 4.6.11; 4.6.15). In such instances, an indefinite singular or plural object, often τίνα/τί or τίνας/τίνα, "some," is understood. Thucydides 2.56 is particularly instructive because the passage contains three nearly parallel constructions: καὶ τῆς τε γῆς ἔτεμον, "and they ravaged (part) of the region" (56.6); ἔτεμον τῆς γῆς τὴν πολλήν, "they ravaged most of the region" (56.4); ἔτεμον τήν τε Τροζηνίδα γῆν, "they ravaged the region of Troezen" (56.5). These three phrases differ only in the quantity of territory ravaged: *some* of the territory, *most* of the territory, *all* of the territory. In Hellenistic Greek, ἀπό and ἐκ are commonly used with the partitive genitive (Moulton, *Prolegomena*, 72). In Hebrew, Syriac, and Arabic, a prepositional phrase introduced by מִן *min*, "from," can function as the subject or object of a verb (GKC, 382 n. 2, implies this when מִן *min* is used with the meaning "some," "something," and "one"; cf. 2 Chr 21:4; Lev 4:2; 1 Kgs 18:5; Exod 29:12; Black, *Aramaic*, 107–8; Johannessohn, *Gebrauch der Kasus*, 18). In the LXX, prepositional phrases introduced by מִן *min* and functioning as the subjects or objects of the verb are translated with ἐκ + the partitive genitive (2 Sam 11:7; 1 Macc 6:48; 10:37; 2 Macc 4:41) or with ἀπό + the partitive genitive (Gen 2:16, 17; 3:2, 3, 5, 12; 4:4; 27:28; 33:15; 40:17; Exod 17:5; 1 Macc 7:33; 8:8; 2 Macc 1:19). However, like the examples from classical Greek listed above, prepositional phrases introduced by מִן *min* that function as subjects or objects of the verb can also be translated in the LXX by the simple genitive (Johannessohn, *Gebrauch der Kasus*, 19); e.g., Exod 6:25, ἔλαβεν τῶν θυγατέρων Φουτιὴλ αὐτῷ γυναῖκα, "he took for himself (some) of the daughters of Phutiel as wives" (cf. Gen 30:14; 27:19, 31; Exod 29:20). Occasionally the simple partitive genitive object in the LXX represents a Hebrew accusative: Exod 2:1 (ἔλαβεν τῶν θυγατέρων Λευεί, "he married one of the daughters of Levi"); Joel 3:1–2 (quoted in Acts 2:17–18); cf. Gen 28:22; 45:18; 1 Macc 10:65; 11:23; 14:39; 2 Macc 2:1.

In Revelation, the partitive genitive is used as *object* of the verb in three distinct forms: [1] with the simple genitive, [2] with the preposition ἐκ + the genitive, and [3] with the preposition ἀπό + the genitive. The prepositions do not have any independent semantic value in either of the last two forms. They function only as optional indicators of case. The partitive genitive with ἀπό and ἐκ is more common in Hellenistic Greek, including the LXX and the NT, where it is often and incorrectly ascribed to Semitic influence (Black, *Aramaic*, 107–8). Moulton-Howard (*Accidence*, 432–33), who are more hesitant to ascribe this idiom to Semitic influence, provide examples from classical and Hellenistic writers. [1] The simple partitive genitive as object of the verb occurs only in Revelation at 2:17 in the phrase δώσω αὐτῷ τοῦ μάννα τοῦ κεκρυμμένου, "I will give him some of the hidden manna." Cf. also Rev 16:7, καὶ ἤκουσα τοῦ θυσιαστηρίου λέγοντες. This is one of the few examples in the NT of this usage (cf. Acts 21:36, συνῆλθον δὲ καὶ τῶν μαθητῶν, "But some of the disciples came with"). Examples of the simple partitive genitive as the object of the verb διδόναι occur in the LXX and NT: Gen 28:22; 30:14; 45:18; Num 27:20. [2] In Rev 2:10, the prepositional phrase ἐξ ὑμῶν, "from/of you," is a partitive genitive (perhaps intensified by the preposition ἐκ) that functions as the *object* of the periphrasis μέλλει βάλλειν, "will throw"; cf. BDR § 164. The author also uses ἐκ + partitive genitive as the object of διδόναι in 2:7; 21:6 (cf. 1 John 3:24; 4:13). There are examples of ἐκ + partitive genitive object in the LXX (Ruth 4:12; 1 Kgs 30:22;

Exek 16:17), in the NT (Matt 23:34 = Luke 11:49; Matt 25:8; John 1:16; 16:14, 15, 17; 2 John 4), and in early Christian literature (Hermas *Mand.* 2.4). In Rev 5:7, the prepositional phrase ἐκ τῆς δεξιᾶς τοῦ καθημένου ἐπὶ τοῦ θρόνου, "from the right hand of the one seated upon the throne," is a partitive genitive object of the verb εἴληφεν, "he took." Though John uses the partitive genitive as the subject or object of various verbs seven times (usually intensified by ἀπό or ἐκ; cf. 2:7, 10, 17; 5:9; 11:9; 21:6; 22:19), this usage is different because the implied object is not an indefinite plural but rather the scroll referred to in 5:1. In Rev 5:9, the partitive genitive phrase ἐκ πάσης φυλῆς κτλ, "[people] from every tribe etc.," functions as the object of the aorist verb ἠγόρασας, "you ransomed." Rev 14:10 has another partitive genitive functioning as the object of the verb: καὶ αὐτὸς πίεται ἐκ τοῦ οἴνου τοῦ θυμοῦ τοῦ θεοῦ, "and he will drink some of the wine which is the wrath of God." In Rev 21:6, the prepositional phrase ἐκ τῆς πηγῆς τοῦ ὕδατος τῆς ζωῆς, "from the well of living water," is a partitive genitive object of the verb δώσω, "I will give." Cf. 16:7 (*var. lect.*): καὶ ἤκουσα [ἐκ] τοῦ θυσιαστηρίου. [3] ἀπό + partitive genitive functions as the object of the verb once in 22:19, where the phrase ἀφελεῖ ἀπὸ τῶν λόγων τοῦ βιβλίου τῆς προφητείας ταύτης, literally, "to take away from the prophetic words of this book," is a partitive genitive functioning as the object of the verb ἀφέλῃ, "remove, expunge." In this case, an indefinite plural object, such as τινα, "anything," is presupposed. Examples in the LXX are found in Lev 18:21; 20:2, 3; 22:22; Deut 2:9; Dan 1:12, while examples in the NT occur in Mark 6:43; 12:2 = Luke 20:10; John 21:10; *Did.* 9:5. ἐκ + partitive genitive functions as the subject of the verb in Revelation only in 11:9, where the phrase ἐκ τῶν λαῶν κτλ, "[some] of the people etc.," is the subject of the verb βλέπουσιν, "see." ἐκ + the partitive genitive functions as the subject in John 16:17: εἶπαν οὖν ἐκ τῶν μαθητῶν αὐτοῦ, "Therefore some of his disciples said" (cf. Rev 11:9; see *Notes* on 11:9); Luke 21:16 (BDR § 164). In Mark 5:35, in the phrase ἔρχεται ἀπὸ τοῦ ἀρχισυναγώγου, "'someone came from the ruler of the synagogue," ἀπό + the partitive genitive functions as the subject of the verb ἔρχεται (the parallel is not reproduced in Matthew, and Luke 8:49 alters it to ἔρχεται τις παρὰ τοῦ ἀρχισυναγώγου, "someone came from the rule of the synagogue"); see also John 4:30; 7:40.

2. The *adverbial uses of the genitive* indicate the objects of certain verbs. (a) The *genitive absolute* is striking by its general absence from Revelation. It occurs only in 1:15 and possibly in 17:8 (the former is not mentioned by Dougherty, and the latter is denied; Dougherty, "Syntax," 94). The presence of the genitive absolute in Revelation is often denied altogether (Charles, 1:cxxxviii). Even though this construction consists of a participle normally linked to a noun or pronoun that is not the subject of the sentence, it is possible to omit either the noun or (more frequently) the pronoun with which the participle agrees (examples: Matt 17:14, ἐλθόντων; Acts 21:10, ἐπιμενόντων; Acts 21:31, ζητούντων; Smyth, *Greek Grammar*, § 2072; Moulton, *Prolegomena*, 74, 236; BDR § 423; Mayser, *Satzlehre*, § 157g). In 1:15, it is possible that the feminine pronoun αὐτῆς has been omitted from the feminine participle πεπυρωμένης. Yet to which noun in the sentence does πεπυρωμένης refer? Possibly to the feminine noun καμίνῳ, "oven, furnace," in which case the relevant clauses should be translated "like gleaming bronze in a smelter when it is burning." Yet this is semantically doubtful. On the other hand, if the difficult term χαλκολιβάνῳ is understood as a *feminine* noun, ἡ χαλκολίβανος (see *Comment* on 1:15), then the clauses make sense both syntactically and semantically: "like brass

when smelted in a furnace." The second possible genitive absolute occurs in 17:8, where the genitive plural participle βλεπόντων is problematic. Though it can be understood as a syntactical error for βλέποντες, perhaps influenced by the genitive plural relative pronoun ὧν (Buttmann, *Grammar,* 306; Bousset [1906] 406; Beckwith, 698; Charles, 2:68; Robertson, *Grammar,* 718–19; Schmid, *Studien* 2:247), it can more naturally be construed as a genitive absolute with αὐτῶν understood (B. Weiss, *Johannes-Apokalypse,* 207; Winer, *Grammar,* 260; BDR §§ 423.3, 9).

(b) The genitive of *apposition* (Dougherty, "Syntax," 94–95) includes titles and proper names (e.g., 5:5, ἐκ φυλῆς Ἰούδα; 3:12; 7:5[3x], 6[3x], 7[3x], 8[3x]; 15:3, 5, τῆς σκηνῆς [Bousset (1906) 394]; 16:4, 14; 19:15; 21:12; 22:9, 21), as well as one instance of numerals (21:16).

(c) The genitive of *association* using μετά + genitive as a substitute for the simple dative of association is a Hebraism (Hilhorst, *Sémitismes,* 94–100). The idiom λαλεῖν μετά + genitive is used in the sense of "to say something to someone"; i.e., the direct object of λαλεῖν is often unexpressed, and μετά + genitive functions as an indirect object (T. Zahn, *Der Hirt des Hermas Untersucht* [Gotha: Friedrich Andreas Perthes, 1868] 493). It is a Hebraism (Charles 1:108), resulting from a literal translation of the Hebrew phrase אֵת דבר *dibbēr 'et,* "to speak with" (BDB, 181). There is a tendency to use this expression of God or a divine envoy (true of all references in LXX Daniel and Theod Daniel), whereas λαλεῖν + dative is generally used of human speakers (Hilhorst, *Sémitismes,* 97). λαλεῖν πρός + accusative is another acceptable form of expression (cf. Theod Dan 9:11 with LXX Dan 9:11). The phrase λαλεῖν μετ' ἐμοῦ occurs six times in Revelation (1:12; 4:1; 10:8; 17:1; 21:9; 21:15), with the subject of the verb *always* a divine revealer. The phrase occurs ten times in Hermas (*Vis.* 1.4.3; 3.10.1; *Mand.* 6.2.3; 11.2; *Sim.* 5.3.2; 5.4.5; 6.1.5; 6.3.2; 9.1.1; 9.11.1), where again the subject is consistently a divine revealer, and five times in Daniel (LXX Dan 8:18; 9:22; 10:11, 15, 19; cf. Theod Dan 8:18; 9:22; 10:15, 19), where again the subject is always a divine revealer. Other NT examples include Mark 6:50; John 4:27(2x); 9:37; 14:30. Examples from LXX include Gen 35:13–15(3x); Num 11:17; Judg 6:17 (A & B); Ezek 3:10; 44:5.

(d) The genitive is used to indicate the object of verbs of perception and verbs meaning "fill, be full" (Dougherty, "Syntax," 92–93). The verb ἀκούειν is used transitively twenty-seven times in Revelation, eleven times with a genitive object (the voice heard: 3:20; 11:12; 14:13; 16:1; 21:3; the person heard: 6:1, 3, 5; 8:13; 16:5, 7). The verb γέμειν is used six times with a genitive of content (4:6, 8; 5:8; 15:7; 17:4; 21:9), a normal construction (BDF §§ 159.1, 172; BDR §172.2), but once with an accusative (17:3, perhaps reflecting Hebrew syntax; see *Note* 17:3.e-e.) and once with *both* a genitive and an accusative in 17:4: γέμον βδελυγμάτων καὶ τὰ ἀκάθαρτα (see *Note* 17:4.f-f.).

3. *Strings of genitives.* In 16:19 there is a concatenation of four genitives: τὸ ποτήριον τοῦ οἴνου τοῦ θυμοῦ τῆς ὀργῆς αὐτου (see J. H. Moulton, *A Grammar of New Testament Greek* [Edinburgh: T. & T. Clark, 1963] 3:218): τοῦ οἴνου, "wine," is a genitive of content; τοῦ θυμοῦ, "fury," is an appositive or epexegetic genitive; τῆς ὀργῆς, "wrath," is a genitive of quality (BDR § 165) or a so-called Hebraic genitive (Zerwick, *Biblical Greek,* § 40–41), which intensifies the meaning of θυμός; and αὐτοῦ, "his," is a genitive of possession. An even larger string of five genitives is found in Rev 19:15: τὴν ληνὸν τοῦ οἴνου τοῦ θυμοῦ τῆς ὀργῆς τοῦ θεοῦ τοῦ παντοκράτορος, "the wine press, representing the furious wrath of God the Almighty." This string of five genitives is the longest such string in Revelation (see

*Comment* under Rev 15:5). τοῦ οἴνου, "of the wine," is a descriptive genitive or genitive of quality functioning as an adjective modifying ληνός, "press, vat"; τοῦ θυμοῦ, "the wrath," is an appositive or epexegetical genitive; τῆς ὀργῆς, "the anger," is a qualitative genitive functioning as an adjective, which intensifies the meaning of θυμός; τοῦ θεοῦ, "God," is a possessive genitive; and τοῦ παντοκράτορος, "Almighty," is an appositive or epexegetical genitive.

4. *Special problems.* In 15:2, the noun phrase κιθάραι τοῦ θεοῦ is ambiguous. τοῦ θεοῦ could be a genitive of possession: "God's citharas," i.e., "citharas belonging to God." τοῦ θεοῦ could be an objective genitive: "citharas for the praise of God" (Bauer-Aland, 878; cf. LXX 1 Chr 16:42, καὶ ὄργανα τῶν ᾠδῶν τοῦ θεοῦ, "instruments of song for God"). Finally, τοῦ θεοῦ could be a Hebraic periphrasis for the superlative (e.g., Col 2:19; 2 Cor 1:12; 1 Thess 4:16; Jas 5:11; cf. Winer, *Grammar,* 309–10, who argues against this view). In Ps 36:7, for example, in the phrase צִדְקָתְךָ כְּהַרְרֵי־אֵל *sidqātkā kĕharrê-ʾēl,* literally "your righteousness (is) as the mountains of God," אֵל *ʾēl* is used to express the superlative height and grandeur of mountains, and the phrase can be construed as "your righteousness is like the lofty mountains" (REB).

## D. Dative

1. The dative of *indirect object.* This occurs frequently in Revelation with verbs of giving, δίδωμι (e.g., 1:1; 2:7, 10; 11:18) and ἀποδίδωμι (e.g., 18:6; 22:12), verbs of speaking, λέγω (e.g., 2:7; 6:11) and κράζω (e.g., 7:2; 14:15), and seventeen other verbs (Dougherty, "Syntax," 101–4), including γράφω, δεικνύω, and μαρτυρέω (22:16, 18). Though the verb αἰνεῖν normally takes a direct object in the accusative, in 19:5 it takes a dative of direct object, reflecting the Hebrew הוֹדָה לְ *hôdâ l-* or הִלֵּל לְ *hillēl l-* (BAGD, 23), reflected in the LXX and in Greco-Jewish literature about one hundred times (e.g., Jer 4:2; 20:13; 1 Chr 16:36; 23:5; 2 Chr 5:13; 7:3; 20:19; 2 Esdr 3:11; Sir 51:12; Dan 2:23; 4:34; see *Pss. Sol.* 5:1; 10:5; cf. *Notes* on 19:5).

2. The dative of *direct object* used with certain verbs. προσκυνέω uses the dative thirteen times to indicate a direct object (e.g., 4:10; 7:11; 13:4; 11:16; 13:4; 19:4), while the accusative is used six times (9:20; 13:8, 12; 14:9, 11; 20:4); see the discussion in *Note* 4:10.b.

3. Dative of *means* or *instrument.* In classical Greek, the locative use of ἐν + dative is used far more frequently than the instrumental use (Helbing, *Kasussyntax,* 146–47). The frequency of the instrumental use in the LXX and Jewish Greek literature suggests that it is a *stylistic* Hebraism representing constructions beginning with בְּ *b* (Hilhorst, *Sémitismes,* 82–88; BDR § 219). The simple dative of instrument is used twelve times in Revelation (e.g., 5:1; 8:8; 15:2; 17:4[3x]; 19:13; 21:16), though ἐν + dative is used thirty-three times (e.g., 1:5; 2:16, 27; 5:9; 13:10; 14:10; 16:8; 17:16; (Louw-Nida, § 90.6). The phrase ταῖς προσευχαῖς in 8:4 has been construed as a "sociative instrumental" (i.e., a dative of association) meaning "with the prayers" (Moulton, *Prolegomena,* 75; Robertson, *Grammar,* 529), while Swete (109), Bousset ([1906] 294), Beckwith (553), Charles (1:231), and Turner (*Syntax,* 238) construe the phrase as a *dativus commodi,* "in favor of," "in behalf of," "to help" their prayers. Moule (*Idiom-Book,* 43) suggests that this is a temporal dative that should be translated "simultaneously with the prayers." In Greek, a personal agent cannot be expressed by the simple dative (BDR § 195); instead this is expressed using ἐν +

dative. Examples are 19:2, ἥτις ἔφθειρεν τὴν γῆν ἐν τῇ πορνείᾳ αὐτῆς, "who corrupted the earth with her immorality," and 6:6, ἀποκτεῖναι ἐν ῥομφαίᾳ καὶ ἐν λιμῷ καὶ ἐν θανάτῳ, "to kill with the sword, and with famine and with disease."

4. The dative of advantage and disadvantage (*dativus commodi et incommodi*). In 13:14, ποιῆσαι εἰκόνα τῷ θηρίῳ, the dative τῷ θηρίῳ could be the dative of indirect object, "to make a cult statue *for* the Beast," but the context makes it clear that it is a *dativus commodi* and should be translated "to make a cult statue *in honor* of the Beast." The *dativus incommodi* is used in 2:5 in the phrase ἔρχομαί σοι (and 2:16), where ἔρχομαι πρός σε is expected (Moulton, *Prolegomena,* 75; see further 18:6).

5. The *locative* use of the dative (indicating the place where an action occurs). This is used with the simple dative just three times, in the fixed expression κύκλῳ τοῦ θρόνου (4:6; 5:11; 7:11; see Dougherty, "Syntax," 106), though the use of ἐν + dative to indicate the place where an action happens occurs frequently, while ἐπί + dative, παρά + dative, and πρός + dative occur rarely.

## E. *Vocative (the case of address)*

There are thirty-five vocatives and functional vocatives in Revelation. They occur in two distinct forms and in one combination of two forms: (1) Nine occur in the vocative case, including κύριε six times (7:14; 11:17; 15:3, 4; 16:7; 22:20) and one instance each of Βαβυλών, the nominative and vocative forms of which are morphologically indistinguishable (18:10), οὐρανέ (18:20), and Ἰησοῦ (22:20). (2) Fourteen occur in the articular nominative alone (4:11; 6:10; 12:12[2x]; 15:3; 18:4; 18:10[2x], 16, 19; 19:5[4x]). (3) Eleven occur as articular nominatives in apposition to a vocative (11:17[4x]; 15:3[2x]; 16:7[2x]; 18:20[3x]), three of these in the formulaic expression κύριε ὁ θεὸς ὁ παντοκράτωρ (11:17; 15:3; 16:7; n.b. that in the phrase κύριε παντοκράτωρ in *T. Abr.* [Greek rec.] 15:12; *Par. Jer.* 1:5; 9:6 and in κύριε παντοκράτορ ὁ θεός in *Prayer Man.* 2.22.12, παντοκράτωρ occurs in a vocative form morphologically indistinct from the nominative).

By the classical period there was no vocative form morphologically distinct from the nominative in all plurals and in feminine nouns in the first declension. The particle ὦ, commonly placed before the vocative in classical Greek, does not occur in Revelation, and in the rest of the NT it is found only seven times (Acts 27:1; Rom 2:1, 3; Gal 3:1; 1 Tim 6:11, 20; Jas 2:20). The articular nominative (*not* used in apposition to a morphologically distinct vocative) occurs just twenty times in the NT, out of a total of 636 vocatives and functional vocatives (Matt 11:26; Mark 15:34; Luke 10:21; 18:11, 13; John 19:3; 20:28; Eph 5:25; 6:1, 4, 5, 9; Col 3:18, 19, 20, 21, 22; 4:1; Heb 1:8; 10:7). The phrase ἀββά ὁ πατήρ occurs several times; ἀββά is a morphologically indistinct vocative and ὁ πατήρ is a nominative in apposition to it, which therefore functions as a vocative (Mark 14:36; Rom 8:15; Gal 4:6). Cf. Robertson, *Grammar,* 264, 461; BDR § 147.

The articular nominative can stand in apposition to a vocative in classical Greek (Smyth, *Grammar,* § 1287; McKay, *Grammar,* § 17; cf. Xenophon *Cyr.* 3.3.20, ὦ Κῦρε καὶ οἱ ἄλλοι Πέρσαι, "Cyrus and the rest of you Persians") and occurs frequently in the LXX (cf. 3 Kgdms 17:20 [κύριε, ὁ μάρτυς τῆς χήρας]; 17:21 [κύριε ὁ θεός]), probably because the Hebrew vocative is expressed with the article (Conybeare-Stock, *Septuagint,* 54). The stereotyped address κύριε ὁ θεός, "Lord God," also occurs frequently in certain early Jewish texts (*Jos. As.* 4:10; 8:3, 9; 11:7, 12:1; 13:12;

27:10; *Pss. Sol.* 5:1; *Apoc. Sedr.* 8:6, 7; *Pr. Man.* (Greek frag.) 22:13). Noteworthy in Revelation are two passages with strings of articular nominatives functioning as vocatives, e.g., Rev 18:20, εὐφραίνου ἐπ᾽ αὐτῇ οὐρανὲ καὶ οἱ ἅγιοι καὶ οἱ ἀπόστολοι καὶ οἱ προφῆται, "Rejoice over her, heaven and you saints and apostles and prophets!" In Rev 11:17, the formulaic address κύριε ὁ θεός ὁ παντοκράτωρ is immediately following by the equally formulaic vocatives ὁ ὢν καὶ ὁ ἦν and consists of a vocative (κύριε) followed by four nominative substantives in apposition to κύριε, each of which functions as a vocative.

## VI. PREPOSITIONS

### A. ἀνά + *Accusative (1x)*

The preposition ἀνά occurs once as part of the compound preposition ἀνὰ μέσον in the puzzling phrase τὸ ἀρνίον τὸ ἀνὰ μέσον τοῦ θρόνου ποιμανεῖ αὐτούς and appears to mean the same as ἐν μέσῳ (5:6[2x]).

### B. ἀπό + *Genitive (36x)*

1. ἀπό as a marker of agent is a relatively rare usage found once in Revelation (12:6, ἡτοιμασμένον ἀπὸ τοῦ θεοῦ, "prepared by God"; Louw-Nida, § 90.7).
2. ἀπό functions as a marker of instrument twice (9:18, ἀπὸ τῶν τριῶν πληγῶν τούτων ἀπεκτάνθησαν τὸ τρίτον τῶν ἀνθρώπων, "by these three plagues, a third of humanity was slain"; 18:15; Louw-Nida, § 90.11).
3. ἀπό + genitive functions as a marker of source of an implied event twice (1:4–5).
4. ἀπό indicates extension from or away from a source: "from, away from" (3:12, Ἰερουσαλὴμ ἡ καταβαίνουσα ἐκ τοῦ οὐρανοῦ ἀπὸ τοῦ θεοῦ; 7:2; 14:20, ἀπὸ σταδίων χιλίων ἑξακοσίων, "1,600 stadia away"; 16:12, 17; 19:5; 21:2, 10; Louw-Nida, § 84.3).
5. ἀπό functions as a marker of dissociation, implying a rupture from a former association (6:16, κρύψατε ἡμᾶς ἀπὸ προσώπου τοῦ καθημένου ἐπὶ τοῦ θρόνου καὶ ἀπὸ τῆς ὀργῆς τοῦ ἀρνίου; 9:6; 12:14; 14:3, 4; 18:14[2x]; 20:11; 22:19[2x]; Louw-Nida, § 89.122).
6. ἀπό functions three times as a marker of the extent of time from a point in the past (13:8, ἀπὸ καταβολῆς κόσμου; 16:18; 17:8; Louw-Nida, § 67.131).
7. ἀπό functions as a marker of location four times in 21:13: ἀπὸ ἀνατολῆς πυλῶνες τρεῖς . . . , "three gates on the east . . . ."
8. Special problem. ἀπό occurs with the nominative in 1:4: χάρις ὑμῖν καὶ εἰρήνη ἀπὸ ὁ ὢν καὶ ὁ ἦν καὶ ὁ ἐρχόμενος (see *Notes* on 1:4). Some have explained this solecism by proposing that ὁ ὢν καὶ ὁ ἦν καὶ ὁ ἐρχόμενος was a fixed divine title functioning as an indeclinable name.

### C. διά + *Genitive (2x), Accusative (16x)*

1. διά + genitive can function as a marker of intermediate agent: "through, by" (1:1, διὰ τοῦ ἀγγέλου αὐτου; Louw-Nida, § 90.4).
2. διά + genitive can function as a marker of the means whereby an event makes another event possible: "by means of, through, by" (21:24, περιπατήσουσιν τὰ ἔθνη διὰ τοῦ φωτὸν αὐτῆς; Louw-Nida, § 89.76; Dougherty, "Syntax," 273).
3. διά + accusative occurs eleven times as a marker of cause or reason, with focus

on instrumentality, either objects or events (6:9[2x]; 12:11[2], 12; 17:7, 15; 18:8, 10, 15; 20:4[2x]; Louw-Nida, § 89.26).

4. διά + accusative occurs once as a marker of benefaction, i.e., a person or thing benefited by an event or for whom an event occurs (1:9, διὰ τὸν λόγον τοῦ θεοῦ; Louw-Nida, § 90.38; cf. BDF § 222, where this usage is designated "purpose").

5. διά + accusative occurs three times as a marker of a participant constituting the cause or reason for an event or state (2:3, ἐβάστασας διὰ τὸ ὄνομά μου; 4:11; 12:11[1]; Louw-Nida, § 90.44).

6. διά + accusative occurs once as a marker of the means whereby one event makes another event possible (13:14, πλανᾷ τοὺς κατοικοῦντας ἐπὶ τῆς γῆς διὰ τὰ σημεῖα; Louw-Nida, § 89.76; cf. 2. above).

### D. εἰς + *Accusative (79x)*

1. Of the nearly eighty occurrences of εἰς in Revelation, there are forty-nine occurrences generally indicating *direction* (Dougherty, "Syntax," 270), including more discriminating meanings such as (a) extension toward a special goal (1:11[6x]; 6:13; 8:5, 7, 8; 9:1, 9; 10:5; 11:12; 12:4, 6, 9, 13, 14[2x]; 13:13; 14:19[1]; 16:1, 2, 3, 4, 16; 17:3; 18:21; 19:9, 17; 20:3; Louw-Nida, § 84.16); (b) extension toward a special goal that is inside an area (2:10, 22[1]; 6:15[2x]; 11:9; 14:19[2]; 15:8; 19:20; 20:10, 14, 15; 21:24, 26, 27; 22:14; Louw-Nida, § 84.22); (c) a position on the surface of an area (9:3; Louw-Nida, § 83.47).

2. εἰς also functions as a marker for *extent of time,* particularly in the stock expression εἰς τοὺς αἰῶνας τῶν αἰώνων (1:6, 18; 4:9, 10; 5:13; 7:12; 10:6; 11:15; 14:11; 15:7; 19:3; 20:10; 22:5) but also in the phrase οἱ ἄγγελοι οἱ ἡτοιμασμένοι εἰς τὴν ὥραν καὶ ἡμέραν καὶ μῆνα καὶ ἐνιαυτόν.

3. εἰς functions as a marker of a change of state or condition (2:22[2]; 8:11; 11:6; 13:3, 10[2x]; 16:19; 17:8, 11; Louw-Nida, § 62), three times with the verb ὑπάγειν (13:10[2]; 17:8, 11).

4. εἰς is used as a marker of intent, frequently with the implication of intended result (9:7; 13:6; 16:14; 20:8; 22:2; Louw-Nida, § 89.57).

5. There is a single instance where εἰς indicates the indirect object. In 17:17, the phrase ὁ θεὸς ἔδωκεν εἰς τὰς καρδίας αὐτῶν, literally, "God put it into their hearts," is a Septuagintism in which εἰς indicates the indirect object, reflecting the Hebrew phrase נתן אל לבו *nātan ʾel libbô* or נתן בלבו *nātan bĕlibbô*, with God as subject, found several times in the OT: Neh 2:12; 7:5 (where it is used of the divine guidance that Nehemiah received in planning to rebuild the walls of Jerusalem); Exod 36:2 ("every wise man in whose mind the Lord had put wisdom [נתן יהוה חכמה בלבו *nātan YHWH ḥokmâ bĕlibbô*]"); 1 Kgs 10:24; 2 Chr 9:23 (Solomon's wisdom "which God had put in his mind [אשר־נתן אלהים בלבו *ʾăšer-nātan ʾĕlōhîm bĕlibbô* ]"); in 1QpHab 2:8 (where the author claims that God has put understanding in the heart (ה)נתן אל נב[לבו בינ[ה *ntn ʾl blbw bynh;* following W. H. Brownlee, *The Midrash Pesher of Habakkuk,* SBLMS 24 [Missoula, MT: Scholars, 1979] 53) of the Teacher of Righteousness (i.e., revealed to him the true meaning of the biblical prophets); and 1QH 14:8 ("[I give Thee thanks,] O Adonai, who hast put understanding into the heart of Thy servant [הנותן בלב עב(דכה)בינה *hnwtn blb ʿb (dkh) bynh*]").

## E. ἐκ + *Genitive (134x)*

ἐκ is the most frequently used preposition in Revelation; it occurs 134 times (i.e., 14 times per 1,000 words). This frequency is even greater than in the Gospel of John, where ἐκ occurs 165 times (i.e., 11 per 1,000). These statistics can be compared with the frequency of ἐκ in Luke-Acts (4 times per 1,000) and in Paul (6 times per 1,000).

1. ἐκ [τῆς] χειρός + genitive. This construction functions as a compound preposition, which some have called a Hebraistic circumlocution for a preposition. In the LXX the phrases ἐκ/ἀπὸ [τοῦ] χειρός are frequently used to translate the Hebrew semipreposition מִיַּד *miyyad*, "from the hand of" someone, i.e., "from the power of" someone (Sollamo, *Hebrew Semiprepositions,* 194–98, 340–42). The noun χειρός is redundant so that the phrases ἐκ χειρός and ἀπὸ χειρός can be translated "by" or "from." ἐκ [τῆς] χειρός + genitive is a *phraseological* Hebraism found frequently in the LXX and Greco-Jewish literature (*1 Enoch* 106:3; *T. Abr.* [Rec. A] 4:10; *T. Sim.* 2:8; *T. Levi* 18:52; *T. Gad* 2:5; *Jos. As.* 12:11; 27:10, 11; 28:4; *Par. Jer.* 1:6; *T. Job* 26:4), several times in the NT (cf. Luke 1:71; Acts 12:11), and occasionally in the Apostolic Fathers (*Barn.* 2:5; *1 Clem.* 56:9 [both quotations from the LXX]; Robertson, *Grammar,* 649; BDF § 217.2; Turner, *Syntax,* 280; BDR § 217.2). The Hebraistic use of the phrase ἐκ [τῆς] χειρός τινος occurs just once in Revelation, in 19:2 (the two other occurrences of ἐκ χειρός + genitive in 8:4; 10:10 refer literally to hands). Although parts of the body are normally articular, the tendency in classical and Hellenistic Greek is to omit the article in prepositional phrases (Smyth, *Greek Grammar,* § 1128), a phenomenon encouraged by the fact that the OT Hebrew term מִיַּד *miyyad,* "from the hand," is anarthrous. A close parallel to Rev 19:2 is found in 2 Kgs 9:7 (cf. Charles, 2:119): καὶ ἐκδικήσεις τὰ αἵματα τῶ δούλων μου τῶν προφητῶν καὶ τὰ αἵματα πάντων τῶν δούλων κυρίου ἐκ χειρὸς Ιεζαβελ [מִיַּד אִיזָבֶל *miyyad 'îzābel*], "And you will avenge the deaths of my servants the prophets and the deaths of all the servants of the Lord caused by Jezebel." Newport (*AUSS* 24 [1986] 223–24) thinks that the NIV captures this idiomatic use of ἐκ χειρός: "He has avenged on her the blood of his servants." This is incorrect, however, since ἐκ χειρός in Rev 19:2 and in 2 Kgs 9:7 is used in a *causal* sense.

2. Partitive ἐκ. For ἐκ + partitive genitive as subject or object of the verb (2:7, 10; 3:9; 5:9; 11:9), see above under Case. In Revelation, partitive ἐκ is used frequently in the phrase εἷς ἐκ + genitive, "one of" (5:5; 6:1 [2x]; 7:13; 9:13; 13:3; 15:7; 17:1; 21:9). The simple partitive genitive follows εἷς in 4:8; 21:22. εἷς ἐκ + partitive genitive occurs nine times in the Synoptics (Mark 9:17; 14:18 = Matt 26:21; Matt 10:29 = Luke 12:6; Matt 18:12 = Luke 15:4; Matt 22:34; 27:48). In Matt 22:34 the phrase εἷς ἐξ αὐτῶν νομικός has a simple partitive in the parallel in Mark 12:28, εἷς τῶν γραμματέων, while Luke 10:25 reads νομικός τις. εἷς ἐκ + partitive genitive occurs eleven times in John (1:40; 6:8, 70, 71; 7:50; 11:49; 12:4 [textually problematic]; 13:21, 23; 18:26; 20:24). Despite the similarity to the Hebrew phrase אֶחָד מִן *'eḥād min,* literally, "one from," the partitive use of ἐκ is common in Hellenistic literature and should not be regarded as a Hebraism (contra Newport, *AUSS* 24 [1986] 228–29). The phrase occurs occasionally in Greco-Jewish literature (*1 Enoch* 89:42; *T. Abr.* [Rec. A] 6:5; *T. Levi* 15:4; *T. Naph.* 2:3; *T. Benj.* 2:3).

3. Causal use of ἐκ (Smyth, *Greek Grammar*, § 1678); cf. Rev 8:13; 16:11 (cf. LXX Exod 15:23; Prov 5:18). It is inappropriate to conclude that causal ἐκ in Revelation is a Hebraism (contra Newport, *AUSS* 24 [1986] 228).

4. ἐκ denoting agent (personal and impersonal). Personal agent is more frequently expressed with ὑπό + dative (Smyth, *Greek Grammar*, §§ 1493–94). There are several instances in Revelation of ἐκ used to indicate the agent of an action (2:9; 3:18; 8:11; 9:18). It is also used in the LXX (Gen 19:36).

5. ἐκ with genitive of material or content (18:12, καὶ πᾶν σκεῦος ἐκ ξύλου τιμιωτάτου, "and every vessel made of precious wood"; cf. Hos 13:2).

6. ἐκ + genitive can convey the idea of reason, cause, or occasion: 16:21, καὶ ἐβλασφήμησαν οἱ ἄνθρωποι τὸν θεὸν ἐκ τῆς πληγῆς τῆς χαλάζης, "People cursed God because of the hail plague" (Robertson, *Grammar*, 599; Louw-Nida, § 89.25).

7. In the phrase τὴν βλασφημίαν ἐκ τῶν λεγόντων, "the slander of those who say" (2:9), ἐκ + the genitive functions as a subjective genitive. Paul uses the subjective genitive in the phrase τὸ ἐξ ὑμῶν ζῆλος, "your zeal" (2 Cor 9:2), and the author-editor of Revelation shows a marked preference for ἐκ (BDR § 212).

8. ἐκ + genitive can be understood as a marker of dissociation meaning "independent from (someone or something)," "from," "independent of" (Louw-Nida, § 89.121), in the phrase τηρήσω ἐκ τῆς ὥρας τοῦ πειρασμοῦ (3:10; see *Comments*). τηρεῖν ἐκ + genitive occurs elsewhere in the NT only in John 17:15. Many scholars have insisted that ἐκ is a preposition of motion meaning "out from within," "out of," "forth from," and cannot mean a stationary position outside its object but is used only of situations and circumstances out of which someone or something is brought; it presupposes that the person in question was previously in the situation or circumstance (Robertson, *Grammar*, 598). However, there are numerous examples of ἐκ used of a position "outside," "beyond" (LSJ, 498–99), used to denote a position outside an object, with no prior existence within the object or any thought of emergence from the object; see *Iliad* 14.130; *Odyssey* 19.7; Herodotus 2.142; 3.83; 5.24; Josh 2:13; Pss 33:19[LXX 32:19]; 56:13[LXX 55:13]; Prov 21:23 (διατηρεῖν ἐκ); 23:14; Josephus *Ant.*12.407 (ῥύεσθαι ἐκ); 13.200 (ῥύεσθαι ἐκ); Acts 15:29; John 12:27; Heb 5:7; Jas 5:20.

9. In the phrase ἐκ τοῦ θανάτου τοῦ δευτέρου, "by the second death" (2:11), ἐκ + genitive is used in an instrumental sense (cf. MM, 190), or as the cause or agent of a passive verb.

10. Special problems. The phrase μετανοεῖν ἐκ + genitive, "to repent of," occurs five times in Revelation (2:21, 22; 9:20, 21; 16:11) but not in the rest of the NT, the LXX, or the Apostolic Fathers. Another rare occurrence in Greco-Jewish literature is in *T. Abr.* 12:13: μετανοήσωσιν ἐκ τῶν ἁμαρτιῶν αὐτῶν, "they might repent of their sins." However, the equivalent phrase μετανοεῖν ἀπό + genitive occurs with some frequency (LXX Jer 8:6; Acts 8:22; *1 Clem.* 8:3 (freely citing LXX Ezek 33:11 as μετανοήσατε, οἶκος Ἰσραήλ, ἀπὸ τῆς ἀνομίας ὑμῶν, "repent, house of Israel, of your iniquity," while LXX Ezek 33:11 actually reads ἀποστροφῇ ἀποστρέψατε ἀπὸ τῆς ὁδοῦ ὑμῶν, "turn away from your way"); Heb 6:1; *Jos. As.* 9:2; Justin *Dial.* 109.1; 121.3). Charles (1:71) suggests that μετανοεῖν ἐκ reflects the Hebrew שׁוב מן *šûb min*, "turn from," and K. G. C. Newport proposed that in Revelation μετανοεῖν ἐκ should be translated "turn away from" (*AUSS* 24 [1986] 225–26).

## F. ἐν + Dative (156x)

1. ἐν occurs 156 times in Revelation, always with the dative, more than half of these occurences in a *locative* sense (e.g., 2:7; 3:14; 11:19; 13:6; 14:5, 6, 10; 20:8, 12, 13).

2. ἐν is also used more than thirty times in Revelation as a marker of immediate instrument (1:5; 2:16, 27; 5:9; 6:8; 7:14; 8:7; 10:6; 16:10[2x] 15:1; 17:16; 19:2, 15[2x]).

3. ἐν is used several times as a marker indicating a point in time that is simultaneous with another point in time: "when" (1:10; 2:13; 9:6; 10:7; 11:13; 18:8; Louw-Nida, § 67.33; Dougherty, "Syntax," 269).

4. ἐν = εἰς. In Koine, ἐν is often used with verbs of motion where εἰς is expected (BAGD, 260 [I.6]; BDF § 218; BDR § 218.3). There is a single example in Revelation of the interchange of ἐν and εἰς in Rev 11:11 (Schmid, *Studien* 2:217; cf. *Notes* on 11:11). In most instances in the LXX, early Jewish Greek literature, and the NT, the preposition used with εἰσέρχεσθαι is εἰς. Occasionally ἐν is used with verbs of motion where εἰς is expected (BAGD, 260 [I.6]; BDF § 218; BDR § 218.3). Parallels to εἰσέρχεσθαι εἰς + accusative in Rev 11:11 occur but are not common: Luke 9:46, εἰσῆλθεν ἐν αὐτοῖς, "he entered into them"; *1 Clem.* 48:2, εἰσελθὼν ἐν αὐταῖς, "after entering into them [i.e., gates]" (an allusion to Ps 118:19[LXX 117:19]); *1 Clem.* 48:3; *Apoc. Mos.* 5:3: ἐν ᾧ εἰσήρχετο, "in which he used to enter"; *T. Abr.* [rec. A] 7:1; *T. Abr.* [rec. B] 9:3, 4; *T. Jude* 9:4; *3 Apoc. Bar.* 13:4; *Greek Apoc. Ezra* 1:6. Elsewhere the author of Revelation uses εἰσέρχεσθαι εἰς + accusative in 15:8; 21:27; 22:14; εἰσέρχεσθαι πρός + accusative occurs only in 3:20 (cf. Mark 15:43; Luke 1:28). In the LXX, εἰσέρχεσθαι is followed by εἰς + accusative (sometimes representing בּוֹא בְּ *bôʾ b*, e.g., Isa 26:20) and occasionally by the simple accusative (Helbing, *Kasussyntax*, 83; he has overlooked Ps 117:19). According to Winer, the use of ἐν with verbs of motion where εἰς is expected emphasizes the *result* of that motion, namely, *rest* (*Grammar*, 514–15).

## G. ἐπί + Genitive (57x), Dative (11x), Accusative (71x)

1. The author uses ἐπί with the genitive, dative, and accusative without distinguishing location *in* a place or movement *to* a place (Mussies, *Morphology* 100–101). In 12:1, ἐπί, "on, upon," with the genitive noun cluster τῆς κεφαλῆς αὐτῆς, "her head," has a meaning semantically identical with ἐπί + accusative; cf. v 3, ἐπὶ τὰς κεφαλὰς αὐτοῦ, "on her head." However, the participial phrase καθημεν- ἐπί occurs twenty-five times, and the author shows a tendency to use a genitive following καθημένου ἐπί (4:10; 5:1, 7; 6:16; 17:1; 19:18, 19, 21; exceptions: 19:18[*var. lect.*], καθημένων ἐπ' αὐτούς), a dative following καθημένῳ ἐπί (4:9; 5:13; 7:10; 19:4; exceptions: 6:4, καθημένῳ ἐπὶ αὐτόν; 14:15, τῷ καθημένῳ ἐπὶ τῆς νεφέλης), and an accusative following καθήμενος or καθήμενον ἐπί (4:2, 4; 6:2, 5; 11:16; 14:14; 17:3; 19:11; 20:11; exceptions: 7:15, ὁ καθήμενος ἐπὶ τοῦ θρόνου; 9:17, καθημένους ἐπ' αὐτῶν; 14:6, τοὺς καθημένους ἐπὶ τῆς γῆς; 14:16, ὁ καθήμενος ἐπὶ τῆς νεφέλης; 20:11, καθήμενον ἐπ' αὐτου; 21:5, ὁ καθήμενος ἐπὶ τῷ θρόνῳ). In a Christian magical silver lamella (thin metal sheet rolled up into a tube as a phylactery or charm), a series of invocations is made using the formula ἐπικαλοῦμαι τὸν καθήμενον ἐπί followed by the noun governed in the genitive (first five invocations), the accusative (the sixth invocation), and the dative (the seventh invocation), without any distinction in

meaning (A. H. de Villefosse, "Tablette magique de Beyrouth," in *Florilegium Melchior Vogüé* [Paris: Imprimerie Nationale, 1909] 287–95; cf. Bonner, *Magical Amulets*, 101–2; L. Robert, "Amulettes grecques," *Journal des Savants* [1981] 10–11).

2. ἐπί + accusative usually means resting at or on a place, yet in 13:16 ἐπί + genitive and ἐπί + accusative function synonymously following the verbal phrase "to place a mark" in the two phrases ἐπὶ τῆς χειρὸς αὐτῶν, "on their hand" (ἐπί + genitive), and ἐπὶ τὸ μέτωπον αὐτῶν, "on their forehead"(ἐπί + accusative).

3. ἐπί + accusative can indicate the object of mourning after verbs of mourning such as κόπτειν, κλαίειν, and πενθεῖν (1:7); see Helbing, *Kasussyntax*, 73): (1) κόπτειν (2 Kgdms 1:12; 11:26 [*var. lect.*]; LXX Zech 12:10); (2) κλαίειν (2 Kgdms 1:12; *T. Job* 43:11; 53:4; Luke 23:28[2x]; Rev 18:11); (3) πενθεῖν (LXX 1 Kgdms 16:1; 2 Kgdms 13:37; 14:2; 19:1; 2 Chr 35:24; 1 Esdr 9:2; 2 Esdr 10:6; Hos 10:5; Isa 66:10; *T. Reuben* 1:10; 3:15; Rev 18:11); (4) θρηνεῖν (LXX 2 Kgdms 3:33; 2 Chr 35:25; Lam 1:1; Ezek 32:16, 18); (5) στενάζειν (Ezek 26:16; 28:19). Though this is frequently judged a Hebraism, this is doubtful in view of POxy 1.115, lines 3ff.: ἔκλαυσα ἐπὶ τῶι εὐμοίρωι, "I mourned for the blessed one" (MM, 345). BAGD (289) construes ἐπί in the phrase κόψονται ἐπ᾽ αὐτον in terms of feelings or actions directed toward a person or thing.

4. Special problems. a. In 10:11, the phrase προφητεῦσαι ἐπὶ λαοῖς καὶ ἔθνεσιν καὶ γλώσσαις καὶ βασιλεῦσιν πολλοῖς is problematic (see *Comments*). ἐπί + dative (or accusative) can function as "a marker of opposition in a judicial or quasi-judicial context" and therefore mean "against" with the *dativus incommodi* (Louw-Nida, § 90.34). In LXX Jer 32:30 (MT 25:30) there is a parallel phrase: καὶ σὺ προφητεύσεις ἐπ᾽ αὐτοὺς τοὺς λόγους τούτους, "and you will prophesy these words *against* them" (reflecting the Hebrew idiom נָבָא עַל *nibbāʾ ʿal*, e.g., Jer 25:13, 14; Ezek 4:7; 11:4; 13:16; 25:2). On the other hand, ἐπί + genitive can mean "about, concerning" (Louw-Nida, § 90.23), so that the phrase in 10:11 can be construed to mean "to prophesy *about* the people."

b. In 12:17 there is a relatively rare use of ἐπί + dative following a verb of strong emotion: καὶ ὠργίσθη ὁ δράκων ἐπὶ τῇ γυναικί. This idiom can indicate the cause of the emotion (Helbing, *Kasussyntax*, 211; BDF § 196; BDR § 196.3); cf. LXX Gen 40:2; Num 31:14; 3 Kgdms 11:9; 4 Kgdms 19:28.

c. The use of ἐπί + dative in the phrase μαρτυρῆσαι ὑμῖν ταῦτα ἐπὶ ταῖς ἐκκλησίαις in Rev 22:16 is very awkward Greek (see *Notes* on 22:16). It can mean "to testify *for* [the benefit of] the churches" (see Louw-Nida, § 90.40, ἐπί + dative as a marker of persons *benefited* by an event, i.e., with the dative of advantage) or, less probably, "to testify *to* the churches" (Louw-Nida, § 90.57, ἐπί as "a marker of the experiencer, often with the implication of an action by a superior force or agency").

d. In Rev 5:1, the phrase ἐπὶ τὴν δεξιάν could mean "in the right hand," "on/upon the right hand" (Bousset [1906] 254), or "at the right side" (cf. LXX Ps 120:5, ἐπὶ χεῖρα δεξιάν, "at your right hand"; BAGD, 288); evidence for these possibilities is surveyed in R. Stefanovič, "The Background and Meaning of the Sealed Book of Revelation 5," Diss., Andrews University, 1995, 145–57. In the phrase ἐπὶ τὴν δεξιάν (a *lectio originalis* found only here in Revelation), ἐπί probably means "in," just as the phrase ἐπὶ τῆς δεξιᾶς μου in 1:20 (also found only here in Revelation) means "in my right hand," as the parallel ἐν τῇ δεξιᾷ χειρὶ αὐτοῦ, "in his right hand," in 1:16 indicates.

e. In 14:6, ἐπὶ τοὺς καθημένους (governed by εὐαγγελίσαι) functions as an equivalent to the dative of indirect object (though see 10:7, where εὐγγέλισεν is followed by the accusative τοὺς δούλους).

## H. κατά + *Genitive (3x), Accusative (6x)*

1. κατά+genitive occurs three times as a marker of opposition, with the possible implication of antagonism in the stereotyped phrase ἀλλὰ ἔχω κατὰ σοῦ (2:4, 14, 10; Louw-Nida, § 90.31).

2. κατά + accusative functions twice as a marker of distributive relations (4:8; 22:2; Louw-Nida, § 89.90).

3. κατά + accusative functions as a marker of relation involving similarity of process four times in the stereotyped phrase κατὰ τὰ ἔργα + possessive pronoun (2:23; 18:6; 20:12, 13; (Louw-Nida, § 89.8).

## I. μετά + *Genitive (40x), Accusative (11x)*

1. μετά + genitive is used as a marker of association involving instruments relative to an event: "with, having" (1:7, ἔρχεται μετὰ τῶν νεφελῶν; Louw-Nida, § 89.109).

2. μετά + genitive is used as a marker of associative relations, with the implication of being in the company of (τοὺς μοιχεύοντας μετ' αὐτῆς; 3:4, 20[2x], 21[2x]; 6:8; 12:9; 14:1, 4, 13; 17:2, 12, 14; 18:3, 9; 19:20; 20:4, 6; 21:3[2x]; 22:12; Louw-Nida, § 89.108).

3. μετά + genitive is used as a marker of associative relations involving persons who are connected with objects or events (22:12, ὁ μισθός μου μετ' ἐμοῦ).

4. μετά + genitive is used six times with the verb λαλέω to indicate the indirect object (1:12, ἐλάλει μετ' ἐμοῦ; 4:1; 10:8; 17:1; 21:9, 15; Dougherty, "Syntax," 274).

5. μετά + genitive is used as a marker of opposition and conflict implying interaction (2:16, πολεμήσω μετ' αὐτῶν; 11:7; 12:7, 17; 13:4, 7; 17:14; 19:19[2x]; Louw-Nida, § 90.32; Dougherty, "Syntax," 274–75).

6. μετά + accusative is used eleven times as a marker of a point of time closely associated with a prior point of time: "after" (1:19; 4:1[2x]; 7:1, 9; 9:12; 11:11; 15:5; 18:1; 19:1; 20:3; Louw-Nida, § 67.48).

## J. παρά + *Genitive (2x), Dative (1x)*

1. παρά + genitive is used as a marker of the agentive source of an activity (2:28, ὡς κἀγὼ εἴληφα παρὰ τοῦ πατρός μου; 3:18; Louw-Nida, § 90.14).

2. παρά+dative is used of a position within an area determined by other objects and distributed among such objects (2:13, ὃς ἀπεκτάνθη παρ' ὑμῖν; Louw-Nida, § 83.9).

## K. περί + *Accusative (1x)*

περί + accusative occurs once to indicate a position around an area, though not necessarily involving complete encirclement: "around" (15:6, περὶ τὰ στήθη χρυσᾶς; Louw-Nida, § 83:13).

*L.* πρός *+ Dative (1x), Accusative (7x)*

1. πρός + dative is used once of a position near another location or object (1:13, περιεζωσμένον πρὸς τοῖς μαστοῖς ζώνην χρυσᾶν, "clothed with a golden belt *around* his chest"; Louw-Nida, § 83.24).

2. πρός + accusative is used of extension toward a goal with the probability of some type of implied interaction or reciprocity: "to" (1:17, ἔπεσα πρὸς τοὺς πόδας αὐτοῦ; 3:20; 10:9; 12:5[2x], 12; Louw-Nida, § 84.18).

3. πρός + accusative is used as a marker of opposition, with the probable implication of a reaction or response to a previous event: "against" (13:6, βλασφημίας πρὸς τὸν θεόν; Louw-Nida, § 90.33; cf. Dougherty, "Syntax," 275).

*M.* ὑπό *+ Genitive (2x)*

ὑπό + genitive occurs just twice in Revelation, and in both instances functions as a marker of agent (6:8, 13; Louw- Nida, 1, § 90.1). ὑπό also occurs just twice in John (1:48; 14:21).

## VII. THE VERB

### A. *Introduction*

In most grammars of NT Greek, the *Aktionsart,* "kind of action" (e.g., linear, punctiliar, etc.), is regarded as expressed semantically in the morphological features of the various tenses: present, imperfect, future, aorist, perfect, and pluperfect. Following the application of recent developments in linguistics to the Greek verb, it appears that the "tense" forms in ancient Greek primarily reflect an author's or speaker's conception of a *process,* or *aspect,* rather than a reference to time. This means that the temporal reference of the various Greek tenses is relative, not absolute, i.e., that the tenses in Greek are semantically nontemporal. In Greek, therefore, *aspect* is expressed morphologically, while time or tense is expressed through the use of a variety of contextual temporal indicators.

There is, however, a pragmatic use of tenses through various kinds of contextual indicators. The pragmatic expression of tenses can be divided into five categories: past, present, future, omnitemporal (valid in past, present, and future time), and timeless (statement or action given no temporal limitation).

### B. *The Tenses of the Verb*

#### 1. THE PRESENT

a. *The historical present* is used in narrative functions in at least three ways (Rijksbaron, *Syntax,* 22–25): (1) it allows the speaker or writer to assume the role of an eyewitness, (2) it can draw attention to decisive actions in the narrative (Porter, *Verbal Aspect,* 149), and (3) as the annalistic present, it is used to enumerate a series of actions. The historic present occurs forty-three times in Revelation (5:5, 9; 6:16; 7:10; 9:10, 11; 9:17, 19[2x]; 10:9, 11; 12:2, 4, 6[2x], 14; 13:12[2x], 13, 14[2x], 16; 14:3, 4; 15:3; 16:21[2x]; 17:15; 18:11[3x]; 19:9[2x], 10, 11[2x], 15 [2x], 16; 21:5; 22:9, 10, 20). Most frequently (twelve times) this involves the verb λέγω "to say," in such phrases as καὶ λέγει (10:9; 17:15; 19:9[2x], 10; 21:5; 22:9, 10), λέγει (1:8; 5:5; 10:9; 22:20), and λέγουσιν (6:16; 10:11). Some ancient authors (e.g., Diodorus Siculus, first century B.C.) avoided historical presents altogether. In the NT the historical present occurs with great frequency in Mark (151 times, 72 using the verb λέγω; J. C. Hawkins, *Horae Synopticae: Contributions to the Study of the Synoptic Problem,* 2nd ed. [Oxford: Clarendon, 1909] 143–48) and with considerably less frequency in Matthew (78 times, 59 using the verb λέγω; Hawkins, *Horae Synopticae,* 148–49). Luke avoids the historical present (H. J. Cadbury, *The Style and Literary Method of Luke,* HTS 6 [Cambridge: Harvard UP, 1920] 158–59); there are just 12 in Luke, 7:40; 8:49; 11:37, 45; 13:8; 16:7, 23, 29; 17:37; 19:22; 24:12, 36, and 13 in Acts: 8:36; 10:11, 27, 31; 12:8; 19:35; 21:37; 22:2; 23:18; 25:5, 22, 24; 26:24 (Hawkins, *Horae Synopticae,* 149; cf. Fitzmyer, *Luke* 1:107). John has 164 instances of the historical present, 119 using the verb λέγω (J. J. O'Rourke, "The Historic Present in the Gospel of John," *JBL* 93 [1974] 585–90). In Hermas *Vis.* 1–5, the Christian apocalypse closest to Revelation chronologically, the historical present is used 84 times, most frequently with λέγω (38 times), φήμι (27 times), and βλέπω (9 times), and then with a variety of others verbs (ἄγει, 3.1.7; αἴρει, 2.2.1; ἀσπάζεται, 4.2.2; ἐγείρει, 3.2.4; ἐντέλλομαι, 5.5; ἐξεγείρει, 3.1.7; καθίζει, 3.2.4; προσκαλεῖται, *Vis.* 2.3.4).

b. *The futuristic present* (Dougherty, "Syntax," 298–300). There are many instances of the futuristic present in Revelation, a usage typically found in oracles (Herodotus 7.140, 141; BDR § 323; Turner, *Syntax,* 63). There are several instances in Revelation of the use of ἔρχεται as *futurum instans* (1:7; 2:5, 16; 3:11; 9:12; 11:14; 16:15; 22:7, 12, 20; the same usage occurs twenty-six times in the Fourth Gospel). Burney incorrectly regarded this use of ἔρχεται in John to be a Semitism (*Aramaic Origin,* 150–52); the juxtaposition of ἔρχεται with a verb in future tense is found in Matt 17:11, Luke 12:54–55, and John 14:3 (BDR § 323.1). ὑπάγει, which belongs to the same semantic field as ἔρχομαι, occurs in the futuristic present three times (13:10; 17:8, 11). Several other verbs are also used with future meaning: in 2:22, βάλλω, "to throw, cast," is a futuristic present, as the parallel used of the *future* indicative verb ἀποκτενῶ, "I will kill," in v 23 demonstrates; in 9:6, φεύγει is a futuristic present, as the preceding three future verbs demonstrate (Fanning, *Verbal Aspect,* 225); see also 11:9–10 (βλέπουσιν, ἀφίουσιν, χαίρουσιν, εὐφραίνονται, πέμψουσιν); 21:24 (περιπατήσουσιν); 22:5 (ἔσται, ἔχουσιν).

## 2. THE IMPERFECT

Revelation contains 40 occurrences of the imperfect (3.957 occurrences per 1,000 words), compared with 287 occurrences in John (18.309 times per 1,000 words), a statistically significant stylistic difference. Yet this number can be further reduced to just twenty occurrences (1:12; 2:14; 5:3, 4, 14; 6:8, 9; 7:9; 9:8, 9; 13:11[2x]; 14:3; 15:8; 16:10; 18:18, 19; 19:14; 21:15; *22:8), since the 17 imperfects formed from εἰμί, the 2 imperfects formed from μέλλω (3:2; 10:4), and the single imperfect formed from κεῖμαι (4:2) have no contrasting aorist forms and therefore must be regarded as having a neutral past tense. This can be broken down further into 5 imperfects formed from ἔχω (6:9; 9:8, 9; 13:11; 21:15), 4 from δύναμαι, the aorist form of which is avoided (5:3; 7:9; 14:3; 15:8), 2 from ἀκολουθέω (6:8; 19:14), 2 from λαλέω (1:12; 13:11), 2 from κράζω (18:18, 19), and 1 each from βλέπω, the aorist form of which is avoided (22:8), διδάσκω (2:14), κλαίω (5:4), λέγω (5:14), and μασάομαι (16:10).

The imperfect indicative and aorist indicative are primarily used in narrative texts. The historical present can also be used in narratives, but that is primarily a matter of stylistic preference (see above). The following statistics omit the imperfect forms of εἰμί, κεῖμαι, and μέλλω, since they have no contrasting aorist forms: Revelation contains 451 aorist indicatives (45.75 per 1,000 words) compared with 20 imperfects (2.63 per 1,000 words), a ratio of 22.5:1. This may be compared with John, with 834 aorist indicatives (53.2 per 1,000 words) compared with 166 imperfects (10.6 per 1,000 words), a ratio of 5:1. The stylistic difference is striking and further underscores the difference in authorship between Revelation and John. The other narrative texts in the NT exhibit a much greater utilization of the imperfect than does Revelation: Matthew has 936 aorist indicatives (50.972 per 1,000 words) compared with 103 imperfects (5.6 per 1,000), a ratio of 9:1. Mark has 534 aorist indicatives (47.2 per 1,000), compared with 237 imperfects (20.9 per 1,000), a ratio of 2.25:1. Luke-Acts has 2,084 aorist indicatives (54.89 per 1,000), compared with 592 imperfects (15.59 per 1,000), a ratio of 3.5:1.

The imperfect is sometimes used in a narrative context dominated by aorists to highlight or emphasize a particular action (e.g., 6:9, εἶχον; McKay, *Grammar*, 142–43).

### 3. THE FUTURE

The future indicative occurs 120 times in Revelation (see Dougherty, "Syntax," 305–9), reflecting the typical Hellenistic Greek uses of the future tense. Of particular interest is the fact that the future indicative is apparently used interchangeably with the aorist subjunctive clauses (Mussies, *Morphology*, 342). ἵνα + future indicative occurs twelve times in Revelation (though there are often textual variants): 2:10; 3:9[2x]; 6:4, 11; 8:3; 9:4, 5, 20; 13:12; 14:13; 22:14 (see *Notes* on 2:10), where the aorist subjunctive is expected. The tendency to use future indicatives instead of aorist subjunctives in ἵνα clauses and ὅταν clauses is particularly characteristic of MS A, where the phenomenon occurs eighteen times (2:22, 25; 3:9[2x]; 4:9, 10; 6:4, 11; 8:3; 9:4, 5, 20; 13:12; 14:13; 15:4; 17:17; 18:14; 22:14); see Mussies, *Morphology*, 322. ἵνα + future indicative is occasionally found in the LXX (Conybeare-Stock, *Septuagint*, § 106), and there is MS evidence for scribal wavering between the future indicative and the aorist subjunctive (cf. Gen 16:2, ἵνα τεκνοποιήσεις [*var. lect.*]; Gen 24:49, ἵνα ἐπιστρέψω εἰς δεξίαν; Deut 14:29, ἵνα εὐλογήσει [*var. lect.* MS A] σε ὁ θεὸς σου; 3 Kgdms 2:4, ἵνα στήσει [*var. lect.* MS A] κύριος τὸν λόγον αὐτοῦ; 2 Chr 18:15, ἵνα μὴ λαλήσεις [*var. lect.* MS A] πρὸς μέ; Prov 6:30, ἵνα ἐμπλήσει [*var. lect.* MS A] τὴν ψυχὴν πεινῶν; Lam 1:19, ἵνα ἐπιστρέψουσιν [*var. lect.* MS ℵ + εἰς] ψυχὰς αὐτῶν; 1 Esdr 4:50, ἵνα ... ἀφίουσι [*var. lect.* MS A]; Sus 28, ἵνα θανατώσουσιν; LXX Dan 3:96, ἵνα ... διαμελισθήσεται). In many cases, however, the future indicatives used in these ἵνα clauses are variants found only in A, a MS that exhibits the same preference in Revelation. There is also evidence for the use of ἵνα + future indicative in the papyri; cf. POxy VI.939, line 19: ἵνα σε εὐθυμότερον καταστήσω, "that I may make you more cheerful" (cf. POxy VII.1068, lines 5, 19; MM, 304). For later Christian authors, cf. *PGL*, 673.1. Part of the vacillation between the present indicative and aorist subjunctive is based on the confusion among ω = ου = ο (Gignac, *Grammar* 1:275–77, 211–14).

### 4. THE AORIST

The aorist is the primary tense used in the narration of past events, and this is the way in which it is primarily used in Revelation. There are several instances in Revelation in which the aorist indicative has a future meaning (10:7; 11:10; 15:1 [Lancellotti, *Sintassi Ebraica*, 56]; 21:4; see 11:2). There are several possible explanations: (1) The aorist can be used in a future sense (Radermacher, *Grammatik* [2], 152; Robertson, *Grammar*, 847; Burton, *Syntax*, § 50, speaks of a "proleptic" use of the aorist). (2) The aorist can be used like the Hebrew prophetic perfect, which presented future events as though they had already occurred (Fanning, *Verbal Aspect*, 274). (3) The phrase καὶ ἐτελέσθη (10:7), "and it was completed," could reflect the Hebrew waw consecutive, which when used with a perfect tense gives it a future meaning and should therefore be translated as if it read τελεσθήσεται (Allo, 141; Bousset [1906] 310; Beyer, *Semitische Syntax*, 69; S. Thompson, *Apocalypse*, 56; Lohmeyer, 86). (4) ἐτελέσθη in 10:7 could also be understood as reflecting the sense of a Hebrew or Aramaic perfect (S. Thompson, *Apocalypse*, 40; Mussies, *Morphology*, 337; Lancellotti, *Sintassi Ebraica*, 56). (5) ἐδόθη in Rev 11:2 may be an instance of the so-called aorist of divine decree; i.e., a future event that is certain because it has been predetermined by God is spoken of in a past tense (Fanning, *Verbal Aspect*, 274).

The aorist is sometimes used with perfective value (Dougherty, "Syntax," 311–12). The aorist indicative ἠγάπησα in Rev 3:9 has the force of a perfect (see 4:11, ἔκτισας; 11:17, εἴληφας; 14:18, ἤχμασαν; 18:3, ἐπόρνευσαν; ἐπλούτησαν). The phrase καὶ ἦλθον καὶ εἴληφεν, "then he came and took" (5:7), is one of several instances in Revelation in which an aorist and a perfect are closely linked (see 2:3, ἐβάστασας and κεκοπίακες; 3:3, εἴληφας and ἤκουσας; 7:14, εἴρηκα and εἶπεν; 8:5, εἴληφεν and ἐγέμισεν; 11:17, εἴληφας and ἐβασίλευσας; 18:3, πέπωκαν and ἐπόρνευσαν; 19:3, εἴρηκαν and ἀναβαίνει), which some regard as an aoristic use of the perfect (Fanning, *Verbal Aspect*, 302–3; Dougherty, "Syntax," 312).

### 5. THE PERFECT

In 5:7, ἦλθον is one of a number of aorists used in the context to narrate past events. In this case, however, the author has used perfect εἴληφεν to highlight and dramatize the action conveyed by this verb, as in Matt 13:46 (K. L. McKay, *TynBul* 23 [1972] 54–55; id., *Bulletin of the Institute of Classical Studies* 12 [1965] 16–17).

### 6. THE PLUPERFECT

The only occurrence of the pluperfect in Revelation is found in 7:11b. Here εἱστήκεισαν, literally "they had stood," does not function as an imperfect (contra Mussies, *Morphology*, 347), nor is there any reason to suppose that the perfect and pluperfect forms of ἵστημι are influenced by Hebrew (contra S. Thompson, *Apocalypse*, 73). Rather, εἱστήκεισαν refers to the position the angels had before they fell down to worship God; i.e., the pluperfect is used to indicate the state resulting from the completion of the verbal action existing in the past (Rijksbaron, *Syntax*, 36–37). Porter (*Verbal Aspect*, 221–22) views the pluperfect from an exclusively aspectual standpoint and defines it as stative, like the perfect, but with the added aspectual feature of remoteness. According to McKay (*NovT* 23 [1981] 322), the pluperfect "always signals a state (usually based on a previous action) which is either past or in some other way remote (e.g. unreal), irrespective of time. In narrative its use is parallel to that of the imperfect in filling in descriptive background to the events, and of course most perfect participles in narrative are replacements for clauses which would have had pluperfect verbs." In translating the εἱστήκεισαν as "who had been standing" (a substantival perfect participle in English), the appropriate verbal aspect is conveyed in English, even though the sentence has been turned into a relative clause.

## C. *The Participle*

### 1. THE GENITIVE ABSOLUTE

While the genitive absolute is characteristic of both classical and Hellenistic Greek, it is relatively infrequent in parts of the LXX translated from Hebrew (e.g., 1 Macc has only four genitive absolutes) but relatively frequent in parts of the LXX that were originally composed in Greek (e.g., it occurs eighty times in 2 Maccabees, twenty-seven times in 3 Maccabees, twenty-one times in 4 Maccabees); cf. Argyle, *ExpTim* 69 (1956–58) 285. The genitive absolute is completely missing from many parts of the LXX (Ruth, Canticles, Amos, Joel, Obadiah, Nahum, Habakkuk, Zephaniah, Haggai, Zechariah, Malachi, Judith), and rare in others (Genesis: 9; Exodus: 9; Leviticus: 7; Numbers: 5; Deuteronomy: 7; Joshua: 1; Judges: 1; 1 Kingdoms: 7; 2 Kingdoms: 6; 1 Chronicles: 2; 2 Chronicles: 3; Psalms: 4; Proverbs: 8; Ecclesiastes: 1; Sirach: 1; Job: 13; Wisdom: 13; Tobit: 3; Epistle of Jeremiah: 1; Hosea: 4; Isaiah: 4; Jeremiah: 8; Jonah: 1; Ezekiel: 2; Daniel: 6; cf. Argyle, *ExpTim* 69 [1957–58] 285). The genitive absolute occurs more frequently in the NT: Mark: 29; Matthew: 40; Luke: 35; Acts: 81; John: 12; Paul: 21; Hebrews: 13; Catholic Letters: 10.

In Revelation, the genitive absolute occurs in 1:15 (see the extensive discussion in *Note* 1:15.a.), and perhaps also in 17:8 and 19:20 (see *Notes*); BDR §§ 423.3, 10; cf. F. Rehkopf, "Grammitisches zum Griechischen des Neuen Testaments," in *Der Ruf Jesu und die Antwort der Gemeinde*, FS Joachim Jeremias, ed. E. Lohse (Göttingen: Vandenhoeck & Ruprecht, 1970) 214–19. Some scholars have denied that Revelation contains any instances of the genitive absolute (Charles, 1:cxxxviii).

### 2. PERIPHRASTIC PARTICIPLES

Periphrastic participles are more common in Hellenistic than in classical Greek and frequently occur in the NT. Periphrastic constructions are common in the LXX (Conybeare-Stock, *Septuagint*, § 72). Many consider the periphrastic constructions in the LXX and the NT to be Semitisms since they occur so frequently in Hebrew and Aramaic. Yet the periphrastic construction can hardly be a Semitism in Revelation, since it only occurs twice (see *Notes*): 1:18, ζῶν εἰμι; 3:2, γίνου γρηγορῶν). Periphrastic constructions were used for a variety of purposes (e.g., variation, avoidance of uncommon forms, e.g., ἦν δεδομένον in John 19:11 instead of the rare ἐδέδοτο). In general, they are intransitive and serve to describe a situation (Aerts, *Periphrastica*, 17). In Rev 1:18 in the phrase ἰδοὺ ζῶν εἰμι εἰς τοὺς αἰῶνας τῶν αἰώνων, the present participle ζῶν *could* be construed as an adjectival participle in the predicate position, but it is probably a periphrastic construction emphasizing the eternal state of the exalted Christ (ζῶν εἰμι, "I am in a state of being alive"), in contrast to the temporal situation described with the preceding phrase ἐγενόμην νεκρός (here νεκρός is an adjective in the predicate nominative), "I was dead" (Regard, *La phrase nominale*, 118; Aerts, *Periphrastica*, 69–70).

## D. The Infinitive

There are 101 anarthrous infinitives in Revelation but only a single example of an articular infinitive with a genitive article (Rev 12:7, τοῦ πολεμῆσαι; see *Notes* on 12:7), aside from a few *variae lectiones* (i.e., in 13:15, τοῦ ποιῆ[σαι] ὅσοι is read by 𝔓⁴⁷, and in 14:15 τοῦ θερίσαι is read by the TR). The following uses of the infinitive occur in Revelation: (1) Infinitive as subject of a verb (15 instances: 1:1; 4:1; 6:4; 7:2; 10:11; 11:5; 13:7[2x], 10, 14, 15; 16:8; 17:10; 20:3; 22:6). (2) Infinitive as object of a verb (45 instances: 1:19; 2:2, 7, 10[2x], 14[3x], 20[2x], 21; 3:2, 8, 10, 16, 18, 21; 5:3[3x]; 6:11, 17; 7:9; 8:13; 9:6, 20[3x]; 10:4, 7; 11:5[2x]; 12:2, 4, 5; 13:4, 13, 17[2x]; 14:3; 15:8; 17:8, 17[3x]; in 3 instances the infinitive introduces indirect discourse (2:9; 3:9; 10:9).

(3) The periphrastic infinitive uses μέλλειν with the present and aorist infinitive (Turner, *Syntax*, 89). The periphrastic combination μέλλειν + infinitive occurs in Revelation with the present infinitive nine times (2:10[2x], 3:10; 6:11; 8:13; 10:4, 7; 12:5; 17:8) and four times with the aorist infinitive (Rev 1:19, μέλλει γενέσθαι; 3:2, 16; 12:4). μέλλειν + future infinitive occurs just three times in the NT (Acts 11:28; 24:15; 27:10). In periphrastic constructions with μέλλειν + infinitive, the present infinitive occurs far more frequently than either the future or aorist infinitives (Schmid, *Studien* 2:98, 208). One reason for expressing future actions by means of the periphrastic construction using μέλλειν and a present, future, or aorist infinitive rather than a simple future indicative is that the former permits the user to make semantic, though not temporal, distinctions (Rijksbaron, *Syntax*, 33).

(4) Infinitive of result (two instances: 5:5; 16:9). (5) There are two instances of the epexegetical or explanatory infinitive in Revelation (11:6; 13:6) and one possible instance (16:19). In Rev 11:6, στρέφειν more closely defines the preceding clause, καὶ ἐξουσίαν ἔχουσιν ἐπὶ τῶν ὑδάτων (it can also be explained as an infinitive that complements a noun; see Votaw, *Infinitive*, 15–16). In Rev 13:6, βλασφημῆσαι specifies more precisely how the Beast blasphemed God, while in Rev 16:19 δοῦναι more closely defines the verb ἐμνήσθη (cf. Votaw, *Infinitive*, 14–15). (6) There are seventeen instances of the infinitive of purpose, though none use the accompanying particles ὥστε or ὡς (1:1, 12; 3:10, 18; 12:17; 13:6; 14:6; 16:14; 19:10, 19; 20:8[2x]; 22:6, 8, 12, 16; one infinitive of purpose is articular [τοῦ + infinitive in 12:7]). (7) Complementary infinitive used to limit nouns (ten instances: 6:8; 9:10; 11:6[3x]; 18[3x]; 13:5; 14:15) or adjectives (eight instances: 4:11; 5:2[2x], 4[2x], 9[2x], 12).

## E. Impersonal or Indefinite Verbs

There are as many as seven instances in Revelation in which third-person plural verbs are used in an impersonal or indefinite way (Mussies, *Morphology*, 231–32; S. Thompson, *Apocalypse*, 18–22; Rydbeck, *Fachprosa*, 27–45; BDF § 130; BDR § 130): (1) Rev 2:24, ὡς λέγουσιν, "as *they* say." (2) Rev 10:11, καὶ λέγουσίν μοι, "and *they* say to me." (3) Rev 12:6, ἵνα ἐκεῖ τρέφωσιν αὐτήν, "that *they* might sustain her there." (4) Rev 16:10, μασῶντο τὰς γλώσσας αὐτῶν ἐκ τοῦ πόνου, "people gnawed their tongues in anguish." (5) Rev 16:15, καὶ βλέπωσιν τὴν ἀσχημοσύνην αὐτοῦ, "and they will see his shame." (6) Rev 18:14, καὶ οὐκέτι οὐ μὴ αὐτὰ εὑρήσουσιν, "so that *they* will never find them again." (7) Rev 20:4, καὶ ἐκάθησαν ἐπ᾽ αὐτούς, "and *they* sat on them [i.e., 'thrones']."

These third-person plural verbs have no grammatical subject but have an indefinite character in that they do not appear to refer exclusively to the speaker(s), addressees, or known nonparticipants. They rather have a more general meaning that can often be conveyed best through the use of the indefinite pronoun τις, "one" (Mussies, *Morphology*, 231), or with such generic terms as οἱ ἄνθρωποι, "people."

Since the impersonal third-person plural was used as a substitute for the passive in both Hebrew and Aramaic (GKC § 144g; Rosenthal, *Aramaic*, § 181), the presence of impersonal (third-person) plural verbs in Greek texts of early Jewish or early Christian origin have often been considered Semitisms (Howard in Moulton-Howard, *Accidence*, 30, 447–48; Doudna, *Greek*, 66–70; Black, *Aramaic*, 126–28; Wilcox, "Semitisms," 127–28). Doudna (*Greek*, 66–67) has called attention to a number of impersonal third-person plural verbs in Daniel, which are translated in the LXX and Theodotion sometimes by a third-personal plural Greek verb and sometimes by a passive, e.g., Dan 2:13, וּבְעוֹ דָנִיֵּאל *wbʿw dnyal*, "and they sought Daniel" (LXX: ἐζητήθη δὲ ὁ Δανιήλ, "and Daniel was sought"; Theodotion: καὶ ἐζήτησαν Δανιήλ; "and they sought Daniel"). Impersonal third-person plural verbs occur frequently in some books of the NT, including Mark (1:32; 2:3; 5:35; 6:14; 7:32; 8:22; 10:13; 12:13; 13:26; 14:12; 15:27), Matthew (1:23; 5:15; 7:16; 9:2, 17; 10:19; 17:27; 24:9), Luke (6:44; 8:34–35; 12:11, 20, 48; 13:29; 14:35; 16:4, 9; 17:23, 27–28; 18:15, 33; 21:12, 16; 23:29–31), John (15:6; 20:2), Acts (3:2; 19:19; 23:28), 1 Cor 10:20, and Heb 10:1. In several instances Luke avoids third-person plurals in which the subject is not expressed in Mark (cf. Mark 3:32 and Luke 8:20; Mark 6:14 and Luke 9:7; Mark 6:43 and Luke 9:17; Mark 9:8 and Luke 9:36; Mark 14:12 and Luke 22:7; cf. Cadbury, *Style*, 150, 165).

In Greek, there are several ways of expressing an indefinite subject (Kühner-Gerth, *Satzlehre* 1:36A, 4): (1) τίς, (2) third-person singular passive verbs, (3) third-person plural verbs restricted to *verba dicendi*, "verbs of saying or speaking," dealing with facts of common knowledge (e.g., λέγουσι, φασί, ὀνομάζουσιν), (4) second-person singular optative or indicative with ἄν (in Latin the second-person hortatory subjunctive is used only of an indefinite subject; cf. *Allen and Greenough's New Latin Grammar*, ed. J. B. Greenough, G. L. Kittredge, A. A. Howard, and B. I. D'Ooge [New Rochelle, NY: Caratzas, 1979] 279). One of the primary reasons for regarding this mode of expression as a Semitism is that in many of the NT texts cited above, the verbs used are not restricted to *verba dicendi*. However, Rydbeck has provided a wealth of examples of the impersonal plural from both classical and Hellenistic Greek authors, demonstrating how common this idiom actually was in the writings of native speakers of ancient Greek (*Fachprosa*, 27–45). Rydbeck found many examples of impersonal third-person verbs in the first-century A.D. medical writer Dioscorides (M. Wellman, *Pedanii Dioscuridis Anazarbei de materia medica libri quinque*, 3 vols. [Berlin: Weidmann, 1906–14], cited by book, page, and line: 1.12.6, δολίζουσι [the passive form δολίζεται is used in 1.13.9]; 1.25.14; 1.28.8; 1.40.16; 1.59.21; 1.88.12; 2.127.12; 2.164.1; 2.171.10; 2.252.20; 2.226.6; 2.210.7–8). He demonstrates that the impersonal third-person plural was not limited in classical literature to *verba dicendi* (e.g., Thucydides 7.69; 2.11.5; 3.45.1; 4.130.2; Herodotus 2.106.2; 2.130.1; 6.119.2; Xenophon *Hellenica* 2.1.8; Plato *Theat.* 176D; *Symp.* 221B) and points out numerous examples from Hellenistic literature indicating the continuity between the classical and Hellenistic use of this idiom (Aristotle *Rhet.* 1377B, κρίνουσι; Plutarch *Alex.* 678D, δεικνύουσι; Antoninus Liberalis 19.2, μυθολογοῦσι; Cleomedes 2.9, ὁρίζονται; Hermogenes *Progym.* 1, ἀξιοῦσι; Rydbeck, *Fachprosa*, 31–36). His view that such impersonal plural verbs are almost exclusively restricted to the present indicative is determined by the fact that most of his examples are from expository writings (Dioscorides) or from speeches within historical writings. In narratives, such as most sections of Revelation, however, impersonal plural verbs can also be imperfect, aorist, and future indicatives. Rydbeck (*Fachprosa*, 41) does provide some exceptions, such as ὠβέλισαν (Origen *De orat.* 14.4) and ἐμακάριζον (Plutarch *De exilio* 604C). There are a number of clear instances in which *verba dicendi* are used in Greek as a substitute for or an equivalent to the passive. In introducing the substance of statements made by informants, Pausanias frequently used such impersonal plurals of *verba dicendi*, such as λέγουσι or φασίν, "they say" (e.g., λέγουσι: 1.27.7; 1.28.5; φασίν: 1.27.10; 1.34.2; 1.37.2), but he frequently varied this mode of expression by employing the passive forms λέγεται or φήμη, "it is said" (e.g., λέγεται: 1.19.3; 1.20.3; 1.21.1; 1.23.8; 1.26.5; 1.29.4; 1.34.2; φήμη: 1.26.6). Similarly, the impersonal third-person active indicative plurals that Rydbeck cites from Dioscorides oscillate between that idiom and the passive indicative (*Fachprosa*, 29–30).

While it is not impossible that some of these impersonal third-person plurals were influenced by the LXX or by Semitic sources (particularly in the synoptic Gospels), since the same idiom occurs with relative frequency in various types of prose during the classical and Hellenistic periods, this mode of expression must be considered idiomatic Greek. Thus ὡς λέγουσι, meaning "as people say," in Rev 2:24 is idiomatic Greek, as is καὶ λέγουσίν μοι, "I was told," in Rev 10:11. In Rev 12:6, the phrase ἵνα ἐκεῖ τρέφωσιν αὐτήν is best rendered in English by the passive: "that she might be nourished there." Rev 18:14 can also be best rendered by the passive in English: "So that they will never again be found." Rev 16:15 is best rendered by the indefinite form, "and people will see his shame," just as Rev 20:4 should be translated "and people sat on them [i.e., 'thrones']."

## VIII. PARTICLES AND PARATAXIS

*A. The Functions of* καί

A larger percentage of clauses and sentences in Revelation are introduced with καί than is the case with any other early Christian composition. Following the punctuation in Nestle-Aland[27] (which is not without problems), there are 337 sentences in Revelation. Of these, 245 sentences (73.79 percent) begin with καί. In this connection, special mention should be made of the Gospel of Mark, which, after Revelation in the NT, has the next largest percentage of sentences that begin with καί. Of a total of 589 sentences in Mark, 369 sentences (62.64 percent) begin with καί (remarkably, Mark 13, the most apocalyptic section of Mark, contains 30 sentences, just 11 of which, or 36.6 percent, begin with καί).

The most characteristic feature of Hebrew syntax is the coordination of clauses with ו *w*, "and," a word that is used at the beginning of 56 percent of all clauses in the Pentateuch, while in the LXX version of the Pentateuch 44 percent of all clauses begin with καί (Aejmelaeus, *Parataxis*, 32). Of a random group of texts originally composed in Greek, 17 percent of the clauses in 2 Maccabees begin with καί, 6 percent in *Epistle of Aristeas*, 6 percent in Epicurus, 8 percent in Polybius, and 11 percent in Philodemus (Aejmelaeus, *Parataxis*, 32). In the LXX, ו is frequently translated with καί because it too does not specify the relationship between the clauses it connects. In the Hebrew Bible more than half of all clauses begin with ו. Since all coordinate clauses connected with ו do not function coordinately, the category of "logical subordination" is often invoked. The phenomenon of "logical subordination" is not limited to Hebrew, however, for Greek also uses καί to coordinate clauses formally even though some form of subordination must be understood (Ljungvik, *Syntax*, 54–87). Aejmelaeus has calculated that of the 9,124 clauses in the Pentateuch beginning with ו, 6,961 or 76.3 percent are translated in the LXX with καί (*Parataxis*, 13). Comparing these statistics with those of the previous paragraph, it appears that Revelation and Mark have a distinctive paratactic style that makes exceptionally frequent use of καί as a discourse marker to begin new sentences, similar to the Greek style that characterizes the LXX.

The frequent use of the conjunction καί in narrative written in Greek is sometimes regarded as an indication of the presence of *translation* Greek from a Semitic original (Hebrew or Aramaic). A. I. Baumgarten flirts with this line of argument (along with that of the presence of Semitic poetic parallelism) in considering the view that the cosmogony preserved among the fragments of Philo of Byblos has been translated from a Semitic or, more specifically, a Phoenician document (*The Phoenician History of Philo of Byblos: A Commentary*, EPRO 89 [Leiden: Brill, 1981] 98, 128–30). He concludes, however, that such an argument is not compelling. While the high frequency of καί in Greek narrative is sometimes the result of translation Greek (as in the LXX), the frequent use of καί in both Revelation and Mark cannot be used as a decisive argument for the presence of translation Greek.

Paratactically, καί is frequently used in Revelation to coordinate independent clauses and to begin a new paragraph or sentence. That καί, like ו, is used so frequently means that it has *dependent semantic value;* i.e., it conveys very little semantic meaning apart from the context in which it is used (Dik, *Coordination*, 258–59, 267). Paratactic καί is also used to introduce logically subordinate clauses in Revelation in a great variety of ways. In the examples from Revelation cited below, the superscript numbers indicate which καί in the particular verse cited functions in that way.

1. καί can function simply as a discourse marker indicating the beginning of a new sentence or clause (Louw-Nida, 1:vi), and since it contains no semantic content, need not be translated. There are numerous instances of this use of καί in Revelation (see *Notes* on each passage): Rev 3:4; 4:5; 6:3, 8; 7:2, 13, 14; 8:1; 10:2, 4, 8; 11:3; 13:1, 12[1]; 14:1, 3; 16:21[1]; 17:3; 18:2; 19:5.

2. καί can introduce coordinate clauses that have an *adversative* function, i.e., καί *adversativum*, and can be translated "but" in the LXX (Gen 42:22; Exod 6:3; Lev 19:18; Deut 9:14; Aejmelaeus, *Parataxis*, 14–15) and in the NT (Mark 5:18–19, 26, 31; 6:19, 33; 7:24; 8:16; 9:18; 12:12, 19 ; 14:49, 56, 59; Reiser, *Syntax und Stil*, 111–

14; Maloney, *Semitic Interference,* 69–70). In the LXX Cant 1:5, the phrase μέλαινά εἰμι καὶ καλή (translated *nigra sum, sed formosa* in the Vulgate) can mean "I am black and beautiful" (i.e., black is beautiful) or (as with the Vulgate) "I am black *but* beautiful." The presence of καί *adversativum* in the LXX, and perhaps the NT, is often considered a Hebraism, though this phenomenon occurs in both classical and Hellenistic Greek (Denniston, *Particles,* 292–93). Blomqvist (*Adversativum*) argues that this is essentially a translation problem and that there is not a single clear example of καί *adversativum* in Greek sources written by native Greek speakers. He does, however, recognize the occurrence of καί *adversativum* in Rev 2:2, 9 (Blomqvist, *Adversativum,* 47). Blomqvist, however, overstates his case. The adversative use of καί is found in all periods and in all types of Greek literature (Kühner-Gerth, *Satzlehre* 2:248; Denniston, *Particles,* 292; BDR § 442.1). Examples from the classical period include (Verdenius, *Mnemosyne* 28 [1975] 189–90): *Iliad* 5.853; *Odyssey* 4.606 (Heubeck et al., *Odyssey,* 230); 14.169; Herodotus 1.3.5 (καὶ πρόκατε); *Prometheus Vinctus* 172, 271, 1007; Sophocles *Trachiniae* 1048; *Oedipus Coloneus* 6; Aristophanes *Nubes* 821; *Ranae* 1283; Thucydides 7.3.3 (καὶ ὁ Νικίας); 7.28.3 (καὶ ἐς φιλονικίαν); Aristotle *De caelo* 304B.22 (ἀνάγκη πλείω εἶναι καὶ πεπερασμένα). Similarly, Reiser provides numerous examples of καί *adversativum* from Hellenistic popular literature (*Syntax und Stil,* 111–16). Nonliterary Koine exhibits an increasing tendency to leave adversative relations unspecified (Blomqvist, *Adversativum,* 52–54). Louw-Nida (§ 91.12) see καί as sometimes functioning as a marker of emphasis involving surprise and unexpectedness, with the appropriate translation "and yet, then." While this usage is close to the function of καί *adversativum* described above, it is not identical.

There are numerous instances of καί *adversativum* in Revelation (see Aejmelaeus, *Parataxis,* 14–15; Denniston, *Particles,* 292–93, and *Notes* on each passage): 1:18; 2:2 (Blomqvist, *Adversativum,* 47), 9, 21; 3:1, 9, 17(3x); 9:4; 11:2, 9, 18 (Jörns, *Evangelium,* 164); 12:2; 13:11, 14; 16:9; 19:10; 20:11; 21:27.

3. Coordinate clause containing a *result* or *consequence,* i.e., the καί *consecutivum* (Gen 7:20; 42:18; Exod 4:21; Lev 9:6; Num 10:9; Deut 1:13; Aejmelaeus, *Parataxis,* 15–18). There are at least eighteen examples in Revelation (see Mussies, *Morphology,* 342; Aejmelaeus, *Parataxis,* 15–18, and *Notes* on each passage): 2:23, καὶ τὰ τέκνα αὐτῆς ἀποκτενῶ ἐν θανάτῳ καὶ γνώσονται πᾶσαι αἱ ἐκκλησίαι, "and I will strike her children dead with the plague *so that* all the churches will know"; 3:7(2x), 9, 18; 8:7, 8; 9:10; 14:10; 16:2, 3, 4, 10(2x), 12; 11:11, 13; 18:14; 20:10. Similar examples are found in the NT (cf. Zerwick, *Greek,* § 455; Ljungvik, *Syntax,* 82–83): Matt 5:15; 26:53; Mark 8:25; Luke 5:1; 11:44; 24:26; Rom 11:35. Examples in Revelation include 3:7[2,4], 9; 11:3[2]; 15:4; 16:2[3] (Moulton-Howard, *Accidence,* 422). PGM IV.3039–40: ὁρκίζω σε κατὰ τῆς σφραγίδος, ἧς ἔθετο Σολομὼν ἐπὶ τὴν γλῶσσαν τοῦ Ἰερεμίου, καὶ ἐλάλησεν, "I adjure you by the seal which Solomon placed on the tongue of Jeremiah *so that* [i.e., 'with the result that'] he spoke." Examples in Mark include 4:20; 5:15; 8:24, 34; 9:39 (Maloney, *Semitic Interference,* 69).

4. Coordinate clauses expressing *purpose* (Gen 27:21; Exod 30:20; Lev 14:36; Num 8:14; Deut 1:42; Aejmelaeus, *Parataxis,* 18–20). Final καί clauses sometimes have a verb in the subjunctive (Exod 8:4; Gen 29:8) or the imperative (Gen 1:9; Num 13:2). Examples include 11:11[3], καὶ ἔστησαν ἐπὶ τοὺς πόδας αὐτῶν, "*so that* they stood on their feet" (cf. 11:3[2]; 13:8[1]; 14:15[2]; 15:4[2]; 20:10[4]). "It seems that the use of the subjunctive and the imperative constituted for the translator a means of

exhibiting his understanding of the logical relations of the clauses without changing the whole structure" (Aejmelaeus, *Parataxis*, 20). καὶ ἵνα expresses purpose in Rev 6:2, 4; 13:17, though καί is used redundantly.

5. In instances when a clause provides the *temporal* point for a second clause in coordination, the second clause can be introduced by καί functioning as a temporal particle or adverb of time (καί = "when, while"); cf. Zerwick, *Greek*, § 455, e.g., Mark 15:25; Luke 19:43. Clauses so introduced sometimes function like a main clause expressing the main event (Gen 7:6; 19:23; 44:3; Exod 13:19; Num 15:32; Deut 4:30; Aejmelaeus, *Parataxis*, 20–21; treated as a Semitism, cf. Moulton-Howard, *Accidence*, 421–22). As a substitute for such temporal particles as εἶτα or τότε, καί can be translated "then" or "when" (Trenker, *Style*, 34; Reiser, *Syntax und Stil*, 119). NT examples include Matt 26:45; Mark 2:15; 4:27; 15:25 (on the Markan texts see Maloney, *Semitic Interference*, 69); Luke 19:43; 23:44; John 2:13; 4:35; 7:33. This use is also found in classical literature (Smyth, *Greek Grammar*, §§ 2169, 2876; Trenker, *Style*, 40–42; Ljungvik, *Syntax*, 84–85). Examples in Revelation include (see *Notes* on each passage) 5:1; 11:12³, καὶ ἀνέβησαν εἰς τὸν οὐρανὸν ἐν τῇ νεφέλῃ, καὶ ἐθεώρησαν αὐτούς οἱ ἐχθροὶ αὐτῶν, "and they ascended to heaven in a cloud while their enemies watched them"; 20:13. In Rev 10:7, καί follows an independent clause (protasis) and introduces a dependent clause (apodosis), and can therefore be translated "then": ὅταν μέλλῃ σαλπίζειν, καὶ ἐτελέσθη τὸ μυστήριον τοῦ θεοῦ, "when he will sound the trumpet, *then* the mystery of God has been fulfilled." The same phenomenon occurs in Rev 3:3 (the καί before εἰσελεύσομαι is probably original; see the *Notes* on 3:3 for the textual evidence); 6:12; 14:9–10; cf. Luke 1:59; 2:21; Acts 13:19; Phil 1:22; 2 Cor 2:2; Jas 4:15. There are many instances of this construction in Greek (*Iliad* 1.494; 5.897; 8.69; *Odyssey* 14.112; Thucydides 2.93.4; Hermetica 13.1 [Nock-Festugière, *Hermès Trismégiste* 2:219]; LSJ, 857, s.v. καί, B.3). The construction can also be the result of Semitic influence (LXX Gen 24:30; BDR § 442.5; Beyer, *Semitische Syntax*, 66–72, esp. 69).

6. A coordinate clause can represent a *subjective* clause. The only possible example in Revelation is found in 11:2 (see *Notes*): ὅτι ἐδόθη τοῖς ἔθνεσιν, καὶ τὴν πόλιν τὴν ἁγίαν πατήσουσιν, "because to trample upon the holy city was permitted for the Gentiles."

7. A coordinate clause can provide the reason, condition, or concession to the preceding clause (Gen 8:18; 24:56; 26:27; Num 11:26; Deut 4:42; 19:6; Aejmelaeus, *Parataxis*, 23–24). After וְ *w*, the most frequent connective particle in biblical Hebrew is כִּי *kî*, "for, because." In the OT, causal clauses are occasionally introduced by waw (GKC § 158), and καί is similarly used in the LXX as a causal particle (Aejmelaeus, *Parataxis*, 23–24). However, this use of καί cannot be considered a strict Semitism since it is also found in pagan Greek (Ljungvik, *Syntax*, 57–59). Charles (1:cxlviii) says that καί (= וְ) "introduces a statement of the condition under which the action denoted by ἐνίκησαν took place." Two OT examples are Gen 8:18; 26:27. Examples in Revelation include 11:5; 12:11³; 18:3; 19:3.

8. καί functions as a relative pronoun (= "who"); Mark 2:15 (Maloney, *Semitic Interference*, 69). Rev 20:4 (καὶ ἐκάθισαν = ἐφ᾽ οὓς ἐκάθισαν); cf. BDR § 442.12. The particle καί² functions in 8:2 as a relative pronoun and can therefore be translated "who" (Zerwick, *Greek*, § 455ε): καὶ εἶδον τοὺς ἑπτὰ ἀγγέλους οἳ ἐνώπιον τοῦ θεοῦ ἑστήκασιν, καὶ ἐδόθησαν αὐτοῖς ἑπτὰ σάλπιγγες, "Then I saw the seven angels who stand before God *who* were given trumpets." Further examples are found in Rev 1:1; 11:15; 17:2 (see *Notes*).

9. καί *epexegeticus.* καί can be used with an explanatory function meaning "that is to say" (BDF § 142.9; Zerwick, *Greek,* § 455). Examples from Hellenistic Greek include *Periplus Maris Rubri* 4 [Frisk, *Périple,* 2, line 13], 42 [Frisk, *Périple,* 14, line 18], 48 [Frisk, *Périple,* 16, line 12]. Examples of the explanatory καί in Revelation include (see *Notes* on each passage): 1:2, 14, 18, 19; 2:2¹, 27; 3:1; 10:7 [*var. lect.*]; 12:2; 13:12; 15:2; 18:13(2x); 19:16 (Beckwith, 733–34); 20:4 (Rochais, *NRT* 103 [1981] 839 n. 18); 21:16, 27.

10. There are three other uses of καί in the LXX, Greco-Jewish, and early Christian literature that do not occur in Revelation: (1) ויהי *wayĕhî,* translated καὶ ἐγένετο (Gen 4:8; 6:1; 39:13), καὶ ἐγενήθη (Deut 1:3), or simply καί (Exod 32:19); Aejmelaeus, *Parataxis,* 24–25. (2) והנה *wĕhinnēh,* translated καὶ ἰδού, "and behold," described by F. I. Andersen as a "surprise clause" (*Sentence,* 94–96). "A feature that is common to most cases is that the formula clause expresses something that can be seen, something immediate and often rather surprising" (Aejmelaeus, *Parataxis,* 27). (3) A coordinate clause can represent an *objective* clause (Gen 6:12; Exod 14:10; Aejmelaeus, *Parataxis,* 21–22).

## B. *The use of* δέ

In classical Greek, δέ is normally used at the beginning of sentences with much greater frequency than καί (just like written English tends to avoid beginning sentences with "and"), and δέ used as a continuative rarely connects single words (Denniston, *Particles,* xlviii, 162). While καί simply links clauses together, δέ tends to contrast the ideas in the clauses that it connects. In classical Greek it is usually preceded by μέν, though this became less common in Hellenistic Greek and does not occur in Revelation. In the LXX μέν paired with δέ does not occur at all in Joshua through 2 Kings, or in Ecclesiastes, Canticles, Jeremiah, and Ezekiel, and rarely elsewhere except for 1–2–3 Maccabees and Wisdom (Conybeare-Stock, *Septuagint,* § 39). δέ occurs just *seven* times in Revelation (1:14; 2:5, 16, 24; 10:2; 19:12; 21:8), twice in the stereotyped expression εἰ δὲ μή, "but if not" (2:5, 16). δέ occurs three times in Rev 2–3 (2:5, 16, 24). In 1:14; 19:12, δέ is used for emphasis when the seer focuses on the face of the exalted Christ. In 21:8, δέ is used adversatively at the beginning of a sentence describing the fate of sinners in contrast to that of the righteous, which is described in the preceding sentence. In Mark, on the other hand, 111 of 589 sentences begin with δέ; if sentences that begin both with καί and with δέ are considered together, they total 480 sentences out of a total of 589, or 81.49 percent. The frequency with which καί is used as a discourse marker to begin sentences in Revelation is quite different from the style of Mark.

## C. *Other conjunctions and connective particles*

(1) ἀλλά, the adversative particle, occurs thirteen times in Revelation. Eight of those occurrences are concentrated in Rev 2–3 (2:4, 6, 9[2x], 14, 20; 3:4, 9). (2) γάρ occurs sixteen times throughout Revelation, remarkable only for the relative paucity of its occurrence (1:3; 3:2; 9:19[2x]; 13:18; 14:4, 13; 16:14; 17:17; 19:8, 10; 21:1, 22, 23, 25; 22:10). (3) ἤ, a disjunctive conjunction, occurs five times (3:15; 13:16, 17[2x]; 14:9). (4) οὖν occurs six times in Revelation (1:19; 2:5, 16; 3:2[2x], 19), all in sections that belong to the Second Edition. (5) πλήν, an adversative

conjunction, occurs once in Revelation (2:25), in a section belonging to the Second Edition. (6) τε, the enclitic particle, occurs once in Rev 19:18.

## IX.  COORDINATE AND SUBORDINATE CLAUSES

The various types of coordinate and subordinate clauses can be organized and presented in terms of their *functions* (i.e., subject clauses, object clauses, relative clauses, purpose clauses, result clauses, conditional clauses, temporal clauses), or they can be organized and presented in terms of the particular *particles* used to introduce them (i.e., ὅτι clauses, ἵνα clauses, ὅταν clauses, etc.). The following discussion is limited to a few types of clauses in Revelation.

### A. ἵνα *clauses*

1. ἵνα can function like an infinitive in introducing subject clauses (9:5; 19:8) or object clauses (3:9; 13:15, 16); see Zerwick, *Greek*, § 406–8. In two instances ἵνα + subjunctive functions as a substitute for the infinitive (13:16; 19:8). The use of the infinitive as a substitute for ἵνα + indicative can be illustrated from Rev 13:12, where the phrase ποιεῖ . . . ἵνα προσκυνήσουσιν (𝔓⁴⁷ A C), reads ποιεῖ . . . προσκυνεῖν in ℵ. Further, in Rev 6:4, in the phrase ἐδόθη αὐτῷ λαβεῖν . . . καὶ ἵνα . . . σφάξουσιν, with ἵνα + future indicative is parallel to the infinitive λαβεῖν (B. Weiss, *Johannes-Apokalypse*, 172).

2. ἵνα in final clauses (Zerwick, *Greek*, § 340–42). There are twenty-five instances in which ἵνα + subjunctive functions as a final or purpose clause in Revelation (2:10, 21; 3:11, 18; 6:2; 7:1; 8:6, 12; 9:15; 11:6; 12:4, 6, 14, 15; 13:13, 15, 17; 16:12, 15; 18:4; 19:15, 18; 20:3; 21:15, 23). There is a tendency in the MS tradition of Revelation to waver between present indicative (which should be considered the more difficult reading since it occurs just a few times in ἵνα clauses in the rest of the NT) and aorist subjunctive, although the latter occurs more frequently in Revelation (forty times in Nestle-Aland²⁷). It is worth noting that MS A, the best extant witness to the text of Revelation, uses the future indicative sixteen times in ἵνα clauses (2:22, 25; 3:9[2x]; 6:4, 11; 8:3; 9:4, 5, 20; 13:12; 14:13; 15:4; 17:17; 18:14; 22:14) and twice in ὅταν clauses (4:9, 10); see Mussies, *Morphology*, 322. There was always a close relationship between the future indicative and the (aorist) subjunctive in Greek (BDR § 318), since both express unrealized expectation rather than fact (BDR § 363). The interchangeable use of the future indicative and the aorist subjunctive was further facilitated by their morphological similarities, particularly close in contract verbs ending in -οω and -αω.

3. ἵνα + future indicative occurs twelve times in Revelation (though there are often textual variants): 2:10; 3:9[2x]; 6:4, 11; 8:3; 9:4, 5, 20; 13:12; 14:13; 22:14 (see *Notes* on 2:10). In one striking instance, a ἵνα clause with a future indicative follows an aorist indicative (9:5, καὶ ἐδόθη αὐτοῖς . . . ἵνα βασανισθήσονται). Only eight other instances of ἵνα + future indicative occur in the rest of the NT (Luke 14:10; 20:10; John 7:3; Acts 21:24; 1 Cor 9:18; Gal 2:4; Eph 6:3; 1 Pet 3:1, ἵνα . . . κερδηθήσεται). MS A (as noted above) has a propensity to use the future indicatives as if they were aorist subjunctives (2:22, 25; 3:9[2x]; 4:9, 10; 6:4, 11; 8:3; 9:4, 5, 20; 13:12; 14:13; 15:4; 17:17; 18:14; 22:14; cf. Mussies, *Morphology*, 322). ἵνα + future indicative is occasionally found in the LXX (Conybeare-Stock, *Septuagint*, § 106), and there is MS evidence for

scribal wavering between the future indicative and the aorist subjunctive (cf. Gen 16:2, ἵνα τεκνοποιήσεις [*var. lect.*]; Gen 24:49, ἵνα ἐπιστρέψω εἰς δεξίαν; Deut 14:29, ἵνα εὐλογήσει [*var. lect.* MS A] σε ὁ θεὸς σου; 3 Kgdms 2:4, ἵνα στήσει [*var. lect.* MS A] κύριος τὸν λόγον αὐτοῦ; 2 Chr 18:15, ἵνα μὴ λαλήσεις [*var. lect.* MS A] πρὸς μέ; Prov 6:30, ἵνα ἐμπλήσει [*var. lect.* MS A] τὴν ψυχὴν πεινῶν; Lam 1:19, ἵνα ἐπιστρέψουσιν [*var. lect.* MS ℵ + εἰς] ψυχὰς αὐτῶν; 1 Esdr 4:50, ἵνα . . . ἀφίουσι [*var. lect.* MS A]; Sus 28, ἵνα θανατώσουσιν; LXX Dan 3:96, ἵνα . . . διαμελισθήσεται). In many cases, however, the future indicatives used in these ἵνα clauses are variants found only in A, a MS that exhibits the same preference in Revelation. There is also evidence for the use of ἵνα + future indicative in the papyri; cf. POxy VI.939, line 19, ἵνα σε εὐθυμότερον καταστήσω, "that I may make you more cheerful"; cf. POxy VII.1068, lines 5, 19 (MM, 304). For later Christian authors, cf. *PGL*, 673.1. S. Thompson (*Syntax,* 28) claims that when a future indicative follows ἵνα it is a literal translation of a Hebrew imperfect, though he admits that "in some places the Hellenistic blurring of subjunctive and indicative forms influenced certain copyists" (*Syntax,* 28). In view of this problem, his solution is certainly too dogmatic. Further, his list of examples from the LXX in which "in each case the Hebrew *imperfect* was being translated mechanically by the Greek future indicative" (*Syntax,* 28, 118 n. 58) contains many errors. It is worth noting that MS A, the best extant witness to the text of Revelation, uses the future indicative sixteen times in ἵνα clauses (2:22, 25; 3:9[2x]; 6:4, 11; 8:3; 9:4, 5, 20; 13:12; 14:13; 15:4; 17:17; 18:14; 22:14) and twice in ὅταν clauses (4:9, 10); see Mussies, *Morphology,* 322. Part of the vacillation between the present indicative and aorist subjunctive is based on the confusion among ω = ου = ο (Gignac, *Grammar* 1:275–77, 211–14).

4. ἵνα + present subjunctive occurs ten times in Revelation, five times in final or purpose clauses (3:18; 7:1; 11:6; 12:6, 14), twice in consecutive or result clauses (16:15[2x]), and once in apposition.

5. ἵνα + aorist subjunctive. According to Dougherty ("Syntax," 352), the aorist subjunctive occurs twenty-eight times in ἵνα clauses in Revelation, seventeen times in purpose clauses (2:10, 21; 3:11, 18[3x]; 6:2; 8:6; 9:15; 12:4, 15; 16:12; 18:4; 19:15, 18; 20:3; 21:15) and four times in result clauses (8:12; 13:15[2x]; 22:14). There is a tendency in the MS tradition to waver between present indicative (which should be considered the more difficult reading since it occurs just a few times in ἵνα clauses in the rest of the NT) and aorist subjunctive, although the latter occurs more frequently in Revelation (forty times in Nestle-Aland[27]). An unusual construction involving both the aorist subjunctive and the future indicative in a ἵνα clause is found in Rev 2:10, ἵνα πειρασθῆτε καὶ ἕξετε θλῖψιν ἡμερῶν δέκα, in which an aorist subjunctive (πειρασθῆτε) is followed by a future indicative (ἕξετε), both apparently dependent on the ἵνα (for a discussion of the textual problems, see *Notes* on 2:10). A parallel occurs in Eph 6:3, which alludes to two OT passages, Exod 20:12; Deut 5:16, and includes both an aorist subjunctive and a future indicative within a single ἵνα clause: ἵνα εὖ σοι γένηται [aorist subjunctive] καὶ ἔσῃ [future indicative] μακροχρόνιος ἐπὶ τῆς γῆς, "that it might be good for you and you might live long upon the earth." Although this saying is probably dependent on two LXX passages, Exod 20:12; Deut 5:16, in neither passage is ἵνα used with the future indicative. That means that the author of Ephesians, writing ca. A.D. 90, like the author of Revelation, uses two verbs dependent on ἵνα, an aorist subjunctive and a future indicative. A similar construction occurs in John 15:8: ἵνα καρπὸν πολύν φέρητε καὶ γενήσεσθε [*var. lect.* in ℵ A Ψ fam 13 Byzantine] ἐμοὶ μαθηταί, "that you

may bear much fruit and be my disciples." See also the modified LXX translation of Isa 6:10 in John 12:40, where the ἵνα clause includes three aorist subjunctives followed by a future indicative. Since it is not always easy to draw a hard and fast line between intention, anticipation, and will, there is inevitable overlap in the use of the indicative, subjunctive, and imperative (McKay, *Grammar*, 148). A similarly difficult construction in Rev 22:14 consists of a ἵνα clause with two verbs: ἵνα ἔσται ἡ ἐξουσία αὐτῶν ἐπὶ τὸ ξύλον τῆς ζωῆς καὶ τοῖς πυλῶσιν εἰσέλθωσιν εἰς τὴν πόλιν, "that access to the true of life will be theirs and they might enter into the city by the gates." The first verb (ἔσται) is a future indicative, while the second (εἰσέλθωσιν) is an aorist subjunctive. Here it is clear that the future indicative is used in a way similar to the aorist subjunctive (Zerwick, *Biblical Greek*, § 342) and that perhaps the author did not distinguish between these categories (Mussies, *Morphology*, 322).

6. ἵνα *epexegeticus*. When used in this way, ἵνα does not enter into the internal syntactic structure of the clause it marks (Louw-Nida, § 91.15). Cf. BDR § 394.3; cf. 1 John 5:3; John 15:8. In Rev 13:13 there is a possible example of ἵνα *epexegeticus* in the clause ἵνα καὶ πῦρ ποιῇ ἐκ τοῦ οὐρανοῦ καταβαίνειν, "even making fire come down from heaven" (RSV). This ἵνα clause is dependent on the phrase ποιεῖ σημεῖα μεγάλα, "he performs great signs." Mussies translates the phrase "and he does great signs, so that ['namely that'] he makes even fire to come down" (*Morphology*, 245). BDR § 391.5, however, construes this ἵνα clause as a *result* clause (cf. Matt 24:24).Other instances of ἵνα *epexegeticus* in Revelation include (see *Notes* on each passage): 11:6, where στρέφειν more closely defines the preceding clause καὶ ἐξουσίαν ἔχουσιν ἐπὶ τῶν ὑδάτων (it can also be explained as an infinitive that complements a noun; see Votaw, *Infinitive*, 15–16); 13:6, where βλασφημῆσαι specifies more precisely how the Beast blasphemed God; and 16:19, where δοῦναι more closely defines the verb ἐμνήσθη (cf. Votaw, *Infinitive*, 14–15).

## B. ὅτι *clauses*

ὅτι clauses in Revelation reflect typical Hellenistic Greek usage, for ὅτι clauses function in three typical ways (Dougherty, "Syntax," 432–33): (1) ὅτι *recitativum* introduces direct speech (3:17; 10:6), (2) ὅτι introduces causal clauses (e.g., 3:10, 17; 4:11; 5:4, 9; 7:17; 8:11; 11:2; 12:10; 16:5; 17:14; 18:3, 5, 7, 8, 10; 19:2[2x]), and (3) ὅτι also introduces object clauses (2:2, 4, 6, 14, 20, 23; 3:1[2x], 8, 9, 15, 17; 12:12, 13; 17:8; 18:7; n.b. that a disproportionate number of occurrences, twelve of sixteen, are found in the Second Edition).

## C. ὅταν *clauses*

There are eight ὅταν clauses (which are by definition temporal clauses) in Revelation, five with ὅταν + aorist subjunctive (9:5; 11:7; 12:4 [ἵνα ὅταν + two aorist subjunctive verbs]; 17:10; 20:7; there are eighty-seven such clauses elsewhere in the NT), two with ὅταν + present subjunctive (10:7; 18:9, both temporal clauses; this is a relatively common construction found elsewhere in the NT thirty-four times); one with the future indicative (4:9; this is a comparatively rare construction found only five times outside Revelation: Mark 12:23; Luke 13:28; 14:10; John 7:31; 15:26). In 10:7, scribes mistakenly thought that ἐτελέσθη (aorist indicative) was also governed by ὅταν, which they altered to τελεσθῇ (aorist subjunctive); see *Notes* on 10:7.

## D. *Other conjunctions*

Other conjunctions introducing a variety of clauses include temporal clauses: (a) ἄχρι + aorist subjunctive (7:3; 15:8; 20:3, 5), (b) ἕως (6:11), (c) ὁσάκις ἐάν (11:6).

## E. εἰ/ἐάν *clauses*

There are very few conditional clauses in Revelation, and they fall into just two categories, the first-class condition, in which the condition is assumed as real, and the third-class condition, in which the condition is assumed as possible. The first-class conditional sentences use εἰ + indicative in the protasis of conditional sentences eight times (11:5[2x]; 13:9, 10[2x]; 14:9–10, 11; 20:15), with the present indicative (11:5; 13:10; 14:10) or the present imperative (13:9) in the apodosis. In most of these protases, with the exception of Rev 11:5, the verb is in the present indicative or imperative. In Rev 11:5 it is used with the aorist subjunctive:

Protasis:  εἴ τις θελήσῃ αὐτοὺς ἀδικῆσαι
          If anyone wants to harm them

Apodosis:  οὕτως δεῖ αὐτὸν ἀποκτανθῆναι.
          it is necessary for them to die in such a way.

A protasis that consists of εἰ + subjunctive (see *Notes* on 11:5) is unusual but not impossible since εἰ began to be used in place of ἐάν increasingly in papyri from the second century A.D. on (Turner, *Syntax*, 116; cf. BDF § 372.3). This is, therefore, a third-class condition, in which the condition is assumed to be possible of realization. Elsewhere in Revelation, third-class conditions are exclusively formed with ἐάν + subjunctive in the protasis of six conditional sentences (2:5, 22; 3:3, 20; 22:18, 19).

## X. SEMITIC INTERFERENCE

## A. *Introduction*

The Greek of Revelation is not only difficult and awkward, but it also contains many lexical and syntactical features that no native speaker of Greek would have written. In his assessment of the language of Revelation, Dionysius of Alexandria (died ca. A.D. 264) observes of the author of Revelation (Eusebius *Hist. eccl.* 7.26) ". . . that his use of the Greek language is inaccurate, and he employs barbarous idioms [ἰδιώμασίν τε βαρβαρικοῖς] producing solecisms [σολοικίζοντα]." There are several possible explanations for this peculiar use of Greek: (1) Revelation is a translation of a work originally written in a Semitic language, Hebrew (Scott, *Apocalypse*) or Aramaic (Torrey, *Apocalypse*). (2) The author wrote in Greek but thought in Hebrew or Aramaic (Charles; Mussies, *Morphology*). (3) Biblical Hebrew served as a model for the language of Revelation (S. Thompson, *Apocalypse*, 1, 34, 53–57, 106–7). (4) The author was secondarily bilingual (i.e., he had no formal instruction in Greek; cf. Horsley, *New Docs* 5:24), and he was probably able to speak as well as write Greek; the Semitisms that undoubtedly exist in Revelation are the result of bilingual interference.

Methodologically, the problem of identifying Semitisms in literature written in Greek, particularly Revelation, is a difficult issue. It is important to distinguish various types of Hebraisms and Aramaisms: (1) semantic Semitisms, (2) lexical Semitisms, (3) phraseological Semitisms, (4) syntactic Semitisms, and (5) stylistic Semitisms (expressions and constructions possible in Greek but whose exceptionally frequent usage is more characteristic of Hebrew or Aramaic).

## B. *Various Constructions*

1. The use of the nominative in apposition to a substantive in an oblique case (Schmid, *Studien* 2:239–40). In 8:9, the substantival participle τὰ ἔχοντα, "those with" or "those having," is a solecism since it should modify the preceding noun τῶν κτισμάτων, "the creatures," but instead is a nominative in apposition to τῶν κτισμάτων (BDR § 136.1).

2. The participle λέγων/λέγοντες is indeclinable, reflecting the Hebrew term לֵאמֹר *lēʾmōr* (Schmid, *Studien* 2:240–41). In 5:12, for example, the masculine nominative plural participle λέγοντες, "chanting," is an anacolouthon (i.e., Hebraism), since grammatically it should modify the noun φωνήν, "voice," in 5:11 and so should have the form λέγουσαν (feminine singular accusative participle); see BDR § 136.

3. Pendent nominative (Schmid, *Studien* 2:241); see above under IV. Cases, A. Nominative.

4. *Pronomen abundans* (Schmid, *Studien* 2:241–42).

5. Participle in place of a finite verb (Schmid, *Studien* 2:242). In 9:19, the nominative plural feminine participle ἔχουσαι functions as a finite verb in this clause (Mussies, *Morphology,* 325); for further examples of participles used as finite verbs in Revelation, see 1:16; 4:2, 4; 10:2, 8; 14:1, 4; 21:14; participles formed from ἔχω are frequently used in this way (1:16; 4:7, 8; 6:2, 5; 9:17, 19; 10:2; 12:2; 19:12 [Mussies, *Morphology,* 325]; 21:12, 14 [Mussies, *Morphology,* 325]).

6. Participle continued through a finite verb (Schmid, *Studien* 2:242–43; see *Note* 3:8.a.). In Hebrew (and perhaps in Aramaic as well), the last in a series of coordinated participles can be replaced with a finite verb. This phenomenon is discussed in Charles, 1:cxliv–cxlvi; id., *Studies in the Apocalypse* [Edinburgh: T. & T. Clark, 1913] 89ff.; Burney, *JTS* 22 (1921) 371–76; Moulton-Howard, *Accidence,* 428–30; Mussies, *Morphology,* 326–28; S. Thompson, *Apocalypse,* 66–67; Turner, *Syntax,* 155. 13:11 contains a possible instance of two finite verbs coordinated with a preceding participle: ἀναβαῖνον … εἶχεν … ἐλάλει (Burney, *JTS* 22 [1921] 321ff.). Mussies, however, thinks that since this verse can be broken up into two sentences, the construction is probably not present (*Morphology,* 326–27).

7. καί used to introduce subordinate clauses (Schmid, *Studien* 2:243). Both Hebrew and Aramaic make frequent use of a type of subordinate clause introduced by ו *w* called the *circumstantial clause* (S. R. Driver, *A Treatise on the Use of the Tenses in Hebrew and Some Other Syntactical Questions* [Oxford: Clarendon, 1892] 195–211; GKC §§ 141e; 156; F. I. Andersen, *The Sentence in Biblical Hebrew* [The Hague: Mouton, 1974] 77–91; Black, *Aramaic,* 81–89; S. Thompson, *Apocalypse,* 92–94; BDR § 417; Turner, *Style,* 152). In both Hebrew and Aramaic, circumstantial clauses are introduced by ו, and followed by a noun or pronoun and then a verb. Such clauses describe a state *contemporaneous* with the action described by the verb in the main clause and can often be translated "now," "while," "although," "when" (GKC § 141e; Black,

*Aramaic,* 81); that is, circumstantial clauses frequently function in a temporal sense, though logical connections between two clauses can function in conditional, causal, and concessive ways as well. S. Thompson (*Apocalypse,* 94) exaggerates when he claims that "The primary un-Greek feature is the introductory καί used in the Semitic type clauses." As examples of Semitic circumstantial clauses in the NT, Black points to just three passages: Mark 1:19; 6:45 (MS D); Luke 13:28 (*Aramaic,* 83); his examples from Mark are disputed by V. Taylor (*The Gospel according to St. Mark,* 2nd ed. [London: Macmillan; New York: St. Martin's, 1966] 59). He further suggests that Luke's use of the phrase καὶ αὐτός at the beginning of sentences is translation Greek rendering circumstantial clauses (*Aramaic,* 83). This view is dubious, however, for only the *unemphatic* use of καὶ αὐτός can be considered a Semitism (Fitzmyer, *Luke* 1:120–21). Turner refers to eight instances of circumstantial clauses introduced by καί in Revelation, yet each is problematic since each begins with καὶ αὐτός, and in Revelation this phrase is always used emphatically: 3:20; 14:10, 17; 17:11; 18:6; 19:15(2x); 21:7 (*Style,* 152). None of Turner's examples appears to reflect the Semitic circumstantial clause: (a) 3:20 (acceptable Greek); (b) 14:10 (καί introduces apodosis of conditional sentence; cf. Charles, 2:16, 423 n. 2; Beyer, *Semitische Syntax,* 69); (c) 14:17 (this clause is introduced by the circumstantial participle ἔχων; the καὶ αὐτός following means "he *also,*" referring to the earlier mention of a sharp sickle); (d) 17:11 (καὶ αὐτός is emphatic and does not introduce a circumstantial clause; contra S. Thompson, *Apocalypse,* 93); (e) 18:6 (the clause is introduced with the comparative particle ὡς followed by an emphatic καὶ αὐτός; also rejected by Thompson, *Apocalypse,* 131 n. 42); (f) 19:15(2x) (the two clauses introduced by καὶ αὐτός, used emphatically, are both used to introduce a complex main clause consisting of two parallel clauses); (g) 21:7 (καὶ αὐτός used emphatically; acceptable Greek).

R. B. Y. Scott (*Apocalypse,* 11) suggests fourteen examples of the Hebraic circumstantial clause in Revelation (though *none* of his examples coincides with any of those found on Turner's list): 2:17, 18; 9:7, 8, 9, 17; 10:1; 12:1, 3; 13:1; 17:5, 14; 19:12; 21:12. Not unexpectedly, most of these examples are similarly doubtful: (a) 2:17 (καί is paratactic and introduces a clause that functions like a relative clause in describing the ψῆφος more closely); (b) 2:18 (simply a paratactic clause that moves from a description of the eyes to the description of the feet; contra S. Thompson, *Apocalypse,* 93); (c) to (f) 9:7, 8, 9, 17 (all paratactic elements of descriptions; with S. Thompson, *Apocalypse,* 131 n. 42); (g) 10:1 (again καί introduces a clause that is part of a description; against S. Thompson, *Apocalypse,* 93); (h) 12:1 (descriptive passage with syntax similar to 10:1; contra S. Thompson, *Apocalypse,* 93); (i) 12:3 (again a paratactic clause that is part of a more extensive description); (j) 13:1 (another paratactic clause that is part of a description); (k) 17:5 (again part of a description; S. Thompson, *Apocalyspe,* 131 n. 42, rejects 17:4, though R. B. Y. Scott, *Apocalypse,* cites 17:5); (l) 17:14 (acceptable Greek); (m) 19:12 (again part of a descriptive passage).

Moulton-Howard (*Accidence,* 423) list just three examples of circumstantial clauses introduced by καί in Revelation, all derived from Charles (1:cxlviii; 2:120, 417, 431), though again none of these references is found in the lists of Turner or Scott: Rev 12:11; 18:3; 19:3. In each of the instances cited by Moulton-Howard from Charles, the clause introduced by καί functions in a *causal manner,* i.e., as a specific alternative to the normally temporal focus of circumstantial clauses (causal clauses in Hebrew can be introduced by ו *w;* see GKC § 158; for LXX examples, see

Aejmelaeus, *Parataxis*, 23–24; for examples from pagan Greek, see Ljungvik, *Syntax*, 57–59).

Therefore, the *only* valid examples of Semitic circumstantial clauses in Revelation are the three cited by Charles. This brief review suggests that there are serious methodological and analytical problems when three scholars each list circumstantial clauses in Revelation but not a single example occurs on more than one list! Further, S. Thompson (*Apocalypse*, 92–94) sheds little light on the problem since he accepts all the examples suggested by Turner and rejects just five of Scott's examples and two of Turner's (18:6; 16:10, which appears to be an error for 14:10). This reveals an overeagerness to find Semitisms where none are to be found.

8. Infinitive used in place of a finite verb (Schmid, *Studien* 2:243–44).

9. On the *pronomen abundans*, see above under III. Pronouns. In 13:8, for example, οὗ οὐ γέγραπται τὸ ὄνομα αὐτοῦ, "whose name was not written," is an example of a resumptive pronoun (cf. 3:12; 7:2, 9; 13:12; 17:2; 20:8), which has often been regarded as a Semitism but can be found also in pagan Greek (Turner, *Syntax*, 325). Another instance occurs in 12:6; in the phrase ὅπου ἔχει ἐκεῖ τόπον, literally, "where she has a place there," ἐκεῖ is a resumptive adverb that looks like a Semitism since it is redundant in Greek (Mussies, *Morphology*, 177). Here the clause is *essential;* i.e., it is a dependent clause, a characteristic of the Semitic resumptive pronoun (Bakker, *Pronomen Abundans*, 41–42); cf. 12:14, however, where the clause is *nonessential* and conforms to possible Greek usage. The indeclinable personal pronoun אֲשֶׁר *'ǎšer,* "which," in Hebrew is frequently elucidated by means of the adverb שָׁם *šām,* "there." Though ὅπου occurs five times without a resumptive adverb in Revelation (2:13[2x]; 11:8; 14:4; 20:10) and once with a resumptive pronoun (17:9), this does not conflict with the author's style (as claimed by Charles,1:clviii n. 1), since exactly the same idiom occurs in the LXX Judg 18:18(B), ὅπου οὐκ ἔστιν ἐκεῖ, while in Judg 21:20(B), ὅπου occurs *without* a resumptive adverb. For two other examples of ὅπου and ἐκεῖ used resumptively, see Ruth 3:4; Eccl 9:10. The adverbs οὗ and ἐκεῖ are used resumptively in Gen 13:4, οὗ ἐποίησεν ἐκεῖ (שָׁם אֲשֶׁר־עָשָׂה *'ǎšer-ʿāšâ šam*), "where he made there"; cf. Gen 20:13, 21; 31:13; 40:30; Exod 21:13; 24:10; Judg 18:10(A); 19:26; Ruth 1:7; 1 Sam 9:10; 14:11; 23:22; 26:5; 29:4, 10; 2 Sam 2:23; 15:32; 1 Kgs 7:7; 8:47; 2 Kgs 19:32; 2 Chr 1:3; 6:37; 8:11; 1 Esdr 6:33; 2 Esdr 1:4; Jdt 5:19; Joel 3:7; Jer 13:7; 23:3, 8; Bar 2:4, 13, 29; Ezek 12:16; 28:25; 29:13; 36:20, 21, 22; 37:21, 25; 46:20, 24; Theod Dan 9:7).

10. The *passivum divinum* occurs with some frequency in Revelation. In 15:5, for example, the second aorist passive verb ἠνοίγη, "was opened" or "opened itself," a passive of divine activity (see *Comment* on 9:3), is also an example of parataxis, for a subordinate participle commonly used in hypotactic sentences would normally be expected here (cf. BDR § 471; Ljungvik, *Syntax*, 80). In 10:3–5, a series of statements is made using passive verbs (v 3, ἐδόθη, "was given"; v 4, ἐρρέθη, "were instructed"; v 5, ἐδόθη, "was given"), all in the *passive of divine activity,* which is essentially a circumlocution used for avoiding the direct mention of the activity of God (Dalman, *Die Worte Jesu*, 183; BDR § 130; Joachim Jeremias, *Theology*, 9–14; Perrin, *Jesus*, 189). For other examples of διδόναι in the passive of divine activity (similar to 10:3, 5), see Grk *1 Enoch* 25:4; 98:5 (ἐδόθη occurs three times in the Greek text, which is longer than the Ethiopic text); *T. Levi* 4:4; *T. Sim.* 6:6; *T. Iss.* 5:5, 8; *Vitae Prophetarum* 1:5[8]. Ordinarily, Hebrew and Aramaic do not make frequent use of the passive voice; the impersonal plural is often preferred. While the

*passivum divinum,* the passive of divine activity (a term coined by Jeremias), occurs frequently in the canonical Gospels (see Matt 5:4, παρακληθήσονται, "they will be comforted," i.e., "God will comfort them"; cf. Matt 5:6, 7, 9; Mark 2:5; Luke 22:16). According to Jeremias (*Euch.,* 202), it occurs only rarely in rabbinic literature. Jeremias held the view that the primary setting of the *passivum divinum* was *apocalyptic* (Jeremias, *Theology,* 9–14), a reason that the idiom occurs frequently in Revelation. However, C. Macholz ("Das *'passivum divinum,'* seine Anfänge im Alten Testament und der 'Hofstil,'" *ZNW* 81 [1990] 247–53) has shown that the use of the passive as a way of avoiding the mention of God as the subject of various actions is widely found in later strata of the OT (Gen 42:22, 28; Num 4:20, 26, 31, 35; 5:6, 10, 13, 16, 18, 26; 2 Kgs 18:30 = Isa 36:15; Ps 18:4 = 2 Sam 22:4; Ps 130:4; Dan 9:9; Neh 9:17), and in early Jewish literature as well (Sir 44:16, 18; 45:24; 46:8; 49:7).

## XI. AGREEMENT

### A. *Neuter plurals with singular and plural verb forms*

While in Hellenistic Greek generally there is a tendency to use third-person singular verb forms with plural neuter substantives, in Revelation plural neuter substantives that refer to *living beings* tend to be used with third-person plural verb forms. This is so in the two instances in which ζῷα is the subject of a verb (4:9; 5:14) and in the single instance in which ὄρνεα is the subject of a verb (19:21). In the fragments of Philo of Byblos, a late first-century A.D. Greco-Phoenician writer, however, ζῷα is always used with a third-person *singular* verb (Eusebius *Praep. evang.* 1.10.2; see in *Philo,* ed. Baumgarten, 807, lines 23, 24). In Rev 11:18, the plural noun τὰ ἔθνη is used with the third-person plural verb ὠργίσθησαν (*var. lect.* ὠργίσθη in $\mathfrak{P}^{47}$ ℵ*, certainly the result of scribal correction); see also 15:4; 18:23; 21:24 (cf. *T. Levi* 14:4; 18:9; *T. Ben.* 9:2; *Jos. As.* 15:7. Yet in 14:8 a third-person singular verb is used: πεπότικεν πάντα τὰ ἔθνη (*var. lect.* πεπότικαν in $\mathfrak{P}^{47}$ ℵ² fam 1611¹⁸⁵⁴ Primasius). The text is very problematic in 18:3, where Nestle-Aland²⁶ reads πέπωκαν πάντα τὰ ἔθνη, but which has a strongly attested *var. lect.* in another third-person plural verb πέπτωκα[σι]ν: ℵ A C fam 1006¹⁰⁰⁶¹⁸⁴¹ fam 1611¹⁸⁵⁴ 2030 Byzantine. See also in some sources the third-person singular verbs πεπότικεν (2042) and πέπτωκε[ν] (fam 1611¹⁸⁵⁴ Oecumenius²⁰⁵³); the options are schematized in Bousset, *Textkritische Studien,* 11.

### B. *Special problems*

1. In 1:11, the present participle λεγούσης, "saying," is in the genitive case because it has been attracted to the case of σάλπιγγος, "trumpet," which immediately precedes it; it should, however, be an accusative modifying φωνὴν μεγάλην, "a loud voice." An almost identical solecism occurs in *Mart. Pol.* alternate ending 5 (Musurillo, *Acts,* 20–21): "Irenaeus who was in Rome heard a voice like a trumpet-call saying [ἤκουσεν φωνὴν . . . ὡς σάλπιγγος λεγούσης]: 'Polycarp has suffered martyrdom.'" Here λεγούσης has been attracted to the case of σάλπιγγος. It is not impossible, however, that this wording has been influenced by Rev 1:11.

2. In 2:20, ἡ λέγουσα, "who calls," is the *lectio difficilior* because it is a solecism since it is a nominative of apposition that must be linked *semantically* with the accusative clause τὴν γυναῖκα Ἰεζάβελ, "that woman 'Jezebel,'" though *syntactically* it should have been in the accusative (Mussies, *Morphology,* 63).

3. In 9:12, ἔρχεται, "comes," is a singular, which is incongruent with the subject, δύο οὐαί, "two woes" (Schmid, *Studien* 2:246; see *Notes* on 9:12). B. Weiss (*Johannes-Apocalypse*, 181) thought that the author regarded οὐαί as a neuter plural noun that could take a third-person plural verb, but the author's use of the feminine gender in this same verse, ἡ οὐαί ἡ μία, invalidates that proposal. This difficulty was corrected by scribes who substituted the third-person plural form ἔρχονται. The solution lies in the fact that δύο is used here in a *multiplicative* sense, so that οὐαί can be regarded as a singular requiring a third-person singular verb.

4. In 9:14, λέγοντα, "announcing," is a masculine singular accusative participle modifying φωνὴν μίαν, "a voice" (feminine singular accusative), and so should have the form λέγουσαν. This is not the only place in Revelation where a feminine noun is modified by a *masculine* adjective or participle (see 4:1; 11:4, 15; 17:3). Occasionally in Hebrew the masculine gender is used to refer back to females or to feminine nouns in instances where no stress is placed on gender (Laughlin, *Solecisms*, 13–14; GKC §144a; cf. 110k). For examples in the MT of masculine pronouns referring to females, see Exod 1:21; 2:17; Num 36:6; Jdt 11:34; 21:12; 19:24; 1 Sam 6:7; 2 Sam 6:22; Ezek 23:49; Ruth 1:8. For examples of masculine pronouns referring to feminine nouns, see Exod 11:6; 22:25; Lev 6:8; 27:9; Num 3:27, 33; Deut 27:5; 1 Sam 10:18; Isa 34:17. In 10:8, λέγουσαν is a present feminine accusative participle that has been attracted to the feminine gender and accusative case of λαλοῦσαν (whereas it should have modified ἡ φωνή and taken the form of the present feminine *nominative* participle λέγουσα); the result is an anacolouthon (Mussies, *Morphology*, 100).

5. In the same verse, 9:14, the adjectival participle ὁ ἔχων (masculine nominative singular), "who has" or "with," is a nominative of apposition modifying the noun phrase τῷ ἕκτῳ ἀγγέλῳ (masculine dative singular), "the eighth angel," and should have had the form τῷ ἔχοντι, a masculine dative singular participle.

6. In 13:14, the masculine singular participle λέγων functions as a predicate adjective modifying the neuter singular noun θηρίον (13:11). This is clearly a solecism and also reflects the narrator's practice of modifying neuter nouns that symbolize men with adjectives, pronouns, and participles in the masculine gender (Mussies, *Morphology*, 138).

7. In 14:3, the substantival participle οἱ ἠγορασμένοι (masculine nominative plural perfect passive), "those who have been redeemed," is a solecism because it is a masculine nominative plural in apposition to αἱ ἑκατὸν τεσσεράκοντα τέσσαρες χιλιάδες, "the 144,000," a feminine nominative plural (the same solecism occurs in 7:4: χιλιάδες ἐσφραγισμένοι). The emphasis in οἱ ἠγορασμένοι is on the resulting state of the subjects, with less attention on the action that produced the condition (Fanning, *Verbal Aspect*, 160).

8. In the phrase τὴν λίμνην τοῦ πυρὸς τῆς καιομένης (19:20), the articular τῆς καιομένης appears to be a solecism that is congruent with the case of τοῦ πυρός (a neuter noun) rather than with τὴν λίμνην (a feminine noun), i.e., with the word the author considered the most important of the two nouns (see Mussies, *Morphology*, 139).

## C. Constructio ad Sensum

The so-called *constructio ad sensum* involves two major types of syntactical incongruity: (1) the use of a plural verb form with a collective, though grammatically singular, noun (BDR § 134; Schmid, *Studien* 2:231–32) and (2) the resumption or modification of neuter or feminine nouns with masculine pronouns or masculine attributive participles (Schmid, *Studien* 2:232–39).

1. Plural verbs form used with collective nouns: (a) 7:9, ὄχλος πολύς . . . ἑστῶτες, "a great *crowd* [singular] . . . *standing* [plural]." (b) 8:9, τὸ τρίτον τῶν πλοίων διεφθάρησαν, "a *third* [singular] of the ships *were destroyed* [plural]." (c) 9:18, ἀπεκτάνθησαν τὸ τρίτον τῶν ἀνθρώπων, "a *third* [singular] of the people *were killed* [plural]." (d) 13:3–4, ἐθαυμάσθη ὅλη ἡ γῆ . . . καὶ προσεκύνησαν τῷ δράκοντι, "The whole *earth* [singular] was amazed . . . and *they worshiped* [plural] the Dragon." (e) 18:4, ἐξέλθατε ὁ λαός μου ἐξ αὐτῆς, "*Come out* [plural] from her my *people* [singular]." (f) 19:1, ὄχλου πολλοῦ . . . λεγόντων, "a large *crowd* [singular] . . . *were saying* [plural]." (g) 19:6, ἤκουσα ὡς φωνὴν ὄχλου πολλοῦ ὡς φωνὴν ὑδάτων πολλῶν καὶ ὡς φωνὴν βροντῶν ἰσχυρῶν λεγόντων, "I heard something like the sound of a great *multitude* [singular], or like the sound of *many waters* [plural], or like the sound of *loud thunder* [plural] *saying* [plural]." Although several scholars deny that the last example is an instance of the *constructio ad sensum* (Schmid, *Studien* 2:231; Mussies, *Morphology*, 138), it nevertheless appears to be such, since despite the fact that the plural noun phrases ὑδάτων πολλῶν, "many waters [plural]," and βροντῶν ἰσχυρῶν, "loud thunderings [plural]," occur *between* ὄχλου πολλοῦ and λεγόντων, it is clear that it is neither the waters nor the thunder that is speaking, but the *multitude*. In spite of the intervening plural nouns, therefore, this construction is essentially parallel to that in 19:1 (see *Notes*). In most of these instances, there is MS evidence that scribes have tried to correct these constructions by making them congruent in number (cf. *Notes* on each passage). In each instance, however, the presence of the *constructio ad sensum* is probably the *lectio originalis*.

There are many other examples of this type of *constructio ad sensum* in the rest of the NT: Mark 9:15; Luke 2:13; 9:12; 19:37, τὸ πλῆθος τῆς μαθητῶν χαίροντες, "the multitude of disciples rejoicing"; John 12:12; Acts 5:16; 21:36. See also collective nouns that are the subjects of plural verbs in Matt 21:8; Luke 23:1 and collective nouns with plural predicates in John 7:49 (cf. Buttmann, *Grammar*, § 129; BDR § 134).

2. The resumption of neuter or feminine nouns sometimes occurs with masculine pronouns or masculine attributive participles. (a) A famous example of this phenomenon is found in Mark 13:14, where the τὸ βδέλυγμα [a *neuter* noun] τῆς ἐρημώσεως, "the Abomination of Desolation," is modified by the *masculine* participle ἑστηκότα, "standing," though the neuter participle ἕστος should be used (this solecism is corrected in Matt 24:15). A similarly striking grammatical error occurs in Rev 11:4, where the author matches the masculine nominative plural perfect participle ἑστῶτες, "standing," with the feminine nominative plural definite article αἱ. Since he is using the symbol of "the two olive trees" (αἱ δύο ἐλαῖαι, feminine nominative plural), he probably uses ἑστῶτες because he has in view the two men that the olive trees symbolize (οὗτοι εἰσιν); i.e., this is a *constructio ad sensum*. The error is somewhat softened by the prepositional phrase that separates αἱ from ἑστῶτες. (b) In 17:3, ἔχων, "with, having," is a solecism since it modifies θηρίον, "Beast" (neuter singular accusative), and should therefore have the form ἔχον (neuter singular nominative or accusative participle). If the masculine participle is original (see *Notes* on 17:3), this is also an example of John's tendency to use the nominative of apposition when modifying an oblique case, particularly with a participle (cf. ζῷον ἔχων in 4:7–8).

Revelation contains fifty-seven participles from ἔχω, all present active. Several of these are substantival participles used as nouns, usually in the form ὁ ἔχων, "the one who has" or "the one with" (2:11, 12, 17, 18, 29; 3:1, 6, 13, 22; 13:17, 18; 20:6), or οἱ ἔχοντες, "those who have" (18:19). There are eleven instances in which various forms of the present participle from ἔχω are apparently solecisms (1:16; 4:7, 8; 5:6; 8:9; 9:14; 10:2; 14:14, 18; 17:3; 21:14), but these passages are difficult to evaluate. In several cases ἔχων (present masculine singular nominative) occurs instead of ἔχον (present *neuter* singular nominative [or accusative]): 4:7, 8; 5:6; 17:3; 21:14. In these cases a glance at the textual evidence suggests that scribal error based on the confusion between ο and ω is responsible for many readings (Moulton, *Prolegomena*, 35; Smyth, *Grammar*, 27, 36; BDR § 28). In Rev 4:7, for example, 49 minuscules read ἔχων, while 119 read ἔχον (cf. Hoskier, *Text* 2:132).

Present participles formed from λέγω (which occur fifty-three times) are frequently used redundantly in Revelation following other verbs of saying and are incongruent with the cases of the nouns they should modify, i.e., anacoloutha (cf. Rev 4:8; 5:12; 11:15). Since λέγων modified ἡ φωνή, "the voice," it should be expressed as the feminine nominative form λέγουσα, "saying." These two features indicate that this is an intentional Hebraism on the part of the author in which the term לֵאמֹר *lē᾽môr*, "so as to say," is used to introduce direct speech corresponding to the more conventional Greek use of ὅτι, "that" (D. Tabachovitz, *Die Septuaginta und das Neue Testament* [Lund: Gleerup, 1956] 12–13, 18). There are numerous examples of the redundant use of λέγων in the LXX, often in the pattern ἀνηγγέλη/ἀπηγγέλη + dative + λέγοντες, "it was said to such-and-such saying" (Gen 22:20; 38:13; 38:4; Exod 18:6; 2 Kgdms 15:31; 3 Kgdms 1:51). Other examples illustrate anacoloutha in which λέγων/λέγοντες are incongruent with their antecedents. (a) Gen 15:1, 4, ἐγενήθη ῥῆμα κυρίου πρὸς Αβρααμ ἐν ὁράματι λέγων Μὴ φοβοῦ, "the word of the Lord came to Abraham in a vision saying, 'Do not fear.'" Here λέγων (a masculine singular nominative participle) should be congruent with ῥῆμα (neuter singular nominative), though the possibility of ο = ω makes it possible that λέγων could be pronounced like λέγον (neuter singular nominative participle). (b) Gen 22:20, Ἐγένετο δὲ μετὰ τὰ ῥήματα ταῦτα καὶ ἀνηγγέλη τῷ Αβρααμ λέγοντες, "And it came to pass after these things that Abraham was told saying." Here λέγοντες (masculine plural nominative participle) should modify the logical subject of the aorist passive verb ἀνηγγέλη, which however is *singular*. Another instance is Gen 45:16, Καὶ διεβοήθη ἡ φωνὴ εἰς τὸν οἶκον Φαραω λέγοντες, "And the report was announced to the house of Pharaoh, saying." Here λέγοντες (nominative plural masculine participle) should be λέγουσα (nominative singular feminine participle), since it modifies ἡ φωνή.

In Revelation there are fifty-three occurrences of present participles of the verb λέγω; twelve are solecisms (4:1, 8; 5:12, 13; 6:10; 11:15; 13:14; 14:7; 15:3; 19:1, 6, 17; details are found in the *Notes* to each of these passages), while forty-one are properly used in agreement with grammatical or logical antecedents.

### D. *Indeclinable* ὅ ἐστιν *and declinable* ὅς ἐστιν

Koine seems to prefer ὅ ἐστιν, an indeclinable formulaic phrase meaning "that is to say" (similar to *id est* in Latin) used without regard to the gender of the substantive in the antecedent clause to which it refers, or to the gender of the predicate in the relative clause that it introduces (BDR § 132; BDF § 132; BAGD, 584; Turner, *Syntax*, 48). The phrase ὅ ἐστιν is often used in explanations (Matt

1:23; Mark 12:42; 15:16; Heb 7:2). Frisk is incorrect when he claims that, in the NT, Revelation is alone in exhibiting examples of the use of the indeclinable form ὅ ἐστιν alongside the more usual ὅς ἐστιν (*Périple*, 90); compare 1 Pet 3:4 with Rev 3:22, and Col 1:1, 7, 15, 18, with Rev 1:24, 27. The indeclinable ὅ ἐστιν occurs once in Revelation (21:8; see *Notes*) and in a *var. lect.* in 20:2. The three other occurrences of ὅ ἐστιν are grammatically appropriate (2:7; 20:12; 21:17), and the author also uses other forms of the relative pronoun with the third-person singular and plural forms of εἰμι in a grammatically appropriate manner (5:6, 8; 21:12). As in Revelation, the author of the *Periplus Maris Erythraei* (middle of the first century A.D.; cf. Casson, *Periplus*, 6–7) uses both the indeclinable idiom ὅ ἐστιν (6; 14) and the declinable expression ὅς ἐστιν (24; 39); cf. Frisk, *Périple*, 90.

## Section 8: Vocabulary

*Bibliography*

**Denis, A.-M.** *Concordance Grecque des Pseudépigraphes d'Ancien Testament.* Louvain-la-Neuve: Université Catholique de Louvain, 1987. **Morgenthaler, R.** *Statistik des Neutestamentlichen Wortschatzes.* Zürich; Frankfurt am Main: Gotthelf, 1958. **Rehkopf, F.** *Septuaginta-Vokabular.* Göttingen: Vandenhoeck & Ruprecht, 1989.

Revelation has a vocabulary of 916 words (Morgenthaler, *Statistik*, 164). There are 128 words found only in Revelation in the NT, 31 of which are also not found in the LXX. These words are 13.97 percent of the author's vocabulary. Comparisons with other NT compositions indicates that this is not an exceptionally high rate of *hapax legomena:*

| Book | Vocabulary | Hapax Legomena | Percent |
| --- | --- | --- | --- |
| Matthew | 1,691 | 137 | 8.10 |
| Mark | 1,345 | 102 | 7.58 |
| Luke | 2,055 | 312 | 15.18 |
| John | 1,011 | 114 | 11.27 |
| Acts | 2,038 | 478 | 23.45 |
| Paul | 2,648 | 795 | 30.02 |
| Hebrews | 1,038 | 169 | 16.28 |
| Revelation | 916 | 128 | 13.97 |

Three terms are usually not included in the lists of words unique to Revelation, but should be included: (1) ὁ ἀμήν, (2) ὁ ἦν, and (3) σῶμα. Although the words themselves are found elsewhere in the NT, ὁ ἀμήν is a masculine noun (the neuter substantive τὸ ἀμήν is found elsewhere in the NT), ὁ ἦν is a unique locution, and σῶμα in Rev 18:13 means "slave," belonging to quite a different semantic domain from the usual meaning of σῶμα.

I. WORDS OCCURRING ONLY IN REVELATION IN THE NT (108)

1. ἀκμάζειν (1); 14:8; LXX 1
2. ἄκρατος (1); 14:10; LXX 3; Aristophanes *Equites* 85, 87

3.    ἀλληλουιά (4); 19:1, 3, 4, 6; LXX 0; Pseud 2
4.    ἄλφα (3); 1:8; 21:6; 22:13; LXX 1
5.    ἀμέθυστος (1); 21:20; LXX 3
6.    ἄμωμον (1); 18:13; LXX 0; Pseud 3
7.    ἄρκος (1); 13:2; LXX 16; Pseud 5
8.    βασανισμός (6); 9:5(2x); 14:11; 18:7, 10, 15; LXX 2; Alexis Comicus
      3.515
9.    βάτραχος (1); 16:13; LXX 14; Pseud 3
10.   βήρυλλος (1); 21:20; LXX 1
11.   βιβλαρίδιον (3); 10:2, 9, 10; LXX 0
12.   βότρυς (1); 14:18; LXX 12; Pseud 5
13.   βύσσινος (5); 18:12, 16; 19:8(2x), 14; LXX 17; Pseud 9
14.   διάδημα (3); 12:3; 13:1; 19:12; LXX 18; Pseud 13
15.   διαυγής (1); 21:21
16.   διπλοῦν (1); 18:6; LXX 0
17.   δισμυριάς (1); 9:16; LXX 0
18.   δράκων (13); 12:3, 4, 7(2x), 9, 13, 16, 17; 13:2, 4, 11; 16:13; 20:2; LXX 37;
      Pseud 18
19.   δωδέκατος (1); 21:20; LXX 27; Pseud 7
20.   ἐγχρίειν (1); 3:18; LXX 4
21.   ἐλεφάντινος (1); 18:12; LXX 11; Pseud 1
22.   ἐμεῖν (1); 3:16; LXX 1
23.   ἐνδώμησις (1); 21:18; LXX 0
24.   ἑξακόσιοι (2); 13:18; 14:20; LXX 79; Pseud 4
25.   ζεστός (3); 3:15(2x), 16; LXX 2
26.   ζηλεύειν (1); 3:19; LXX 0
27.   ἡμίωριον (1); 8:1; LXX 0
28.   θειώδης (1); 9:17; LXX 0
29.   θύϊνος (1); 18:12; LXX 1
30.   ἴασπις (4); 4:3; 21:11, 18, 19; LXX 3
31.   ἱππικός (1); 9:16; LXX 2
32.   ἶρις (2); 4:3; 10:1; LXX 1
33.   κατάθεμα (1); 22:3; LXX 0; Pseud 1
34.   κατασφραγίζειν (1); 5:1; LXX 3
35.   κατήγωρ (1); 12:10; LXX 0
36.   καῦμα (2); 7:16; 16:9; LXX 22
37.   κεραμικός (1); 2:27; LXX 1; Sannyrio Comicus 2.874
38.   κεραννύναι (3); 14:10; 18:6(2x); LXX 9
39.   κιθαρῳδός (2); 14:2; 18:22; LXX 0
40.   κιννάμωμον (1); 18:13; LXX 5; Pseud 4
41.   κλέμμα (1); 9:21; LXX 3
42.   κολλούριον or κολλύριον (1); 3:18; LXX 3
43.   κριθή (1); 6:6; LXX 43; Pseud 1
44.   κρυσταλλίζειν (1); 21:11; LXX 0
45.   κρύσταλλος (2); 4:6; 22:1; LXX 9; Pseud 5
46.   κυκλεύειν (1); 20:9; LXX 1; Pseud 1; *var. lect.* in John 10:24; Hermas *Sim.*
      9.9.6

47. κυκλόθεν (3); 4:3, 4, 8; LXX 94; Pseud 12
48. λιβανωτός (2); 8:3, 5; LXX 2; Pseud 1
50. λιπαρός (1); 18:14; LXX 3; Pseud 1
51. μάρμαρος (1); 18:12; LXX 1
52. μασᾶσθαι (1); 16:10; LXX 2
53. μεσουράνημα (3); 8:13; 14:6; 19:17; LXX 0
54. μέτωπον (8); 7:3; 9:4; 13:16; 14:1, 9; 17:5; 20:4; 22:4; LXX 7; Pseud 4
55. μηρός (1); 19:16; LXX 55
56. μουσικός (1); 18:22; LXX 17; Pseud 3
57. μυκᾶσθαι (1); 10:3; LXX (*var. lect.* 2)
58. μύλινος (1); 18:21; LXX 0
59. νεφρός (1); 2:23; LXX 30
60. ὄλυνθος (1); 6:13; LXX 1
61. ὀπώρα (1); 18:14; LXX 3; Pseud 2
62. ὅρμημα (1); 18:21; LXX 10
63. ὄρνεον (3); 18:2; 19:17, 21; LXX 39
64. οὐρά (5); 9:10(2x), 19(2x); 12:4; LXX 8; Pseud 5
65. πάρδαλις (1); 13:2; LXX 9; Pseud 6
66. πελεκίζεσθαι (1); 20:4; LXX 0
67. πέμπτος (4); 6:9; 9:1; 16:10; 21:20; LXX 62
68. πέτεσθαι (5); 4:7; 8:13; 12:14; 14:6; 19:17; LXX 17
69. πλήσσειν (1); 8:12; LXX 32
70. ποδήρης (1); 1:13; LXX 12; Pseud 2
71. ποταμοφόρητος (1); 12:15; LXX 0
72. πρωϊνός (2); 2:28; 22:16; LXX 13
73. πύρινος (1); 9:17; LXX 3; Pseud 14
74. πυρρός (2); 6:4; 12:3; LXX 8; Pseud 4
75. ῥέδη (1); 18:13; LXX 0
76. ῥυπαίνεσθαι (1); 22:11; LXX 0
77. σαλπιστής (1); 18:22; LXX 0
78. σάπφιρος (1); 21:19; LXX 12; Pseud 1
79. σάρδιον (2); 4:3; 21:20; LXX 7
80. σαρδόνυξ (1); 21:20; LXX 0
81. σεμίδαλις (1); 18:13; LXX 81; Pseud 7
82. σηρικός or σιρικός (1); 18:12; LXX 0
83. σμαρδάγδινος (1); 4:3; LXX 0
84. σμάραγδος (1); 21:19; LXX 11; Pseud 2
85. στρηνιᾶν (2); 18:7, 9; LXX (*var. lect.* 1)
86. στρῆνος (1); 18:3; LXX 1; Pseud 1; Nicostratus Comicus 5.84
87. ταλαντιαῖος (1); 16:21; LXX 0; Pseud 3
88. τετράγωνος (1); 21:16; LXX 13; Pseud 2
89. τιμιότης (1); 18:19; LXX 0
90. τόξον (1); 6:2; LXX 79; Pseud 9
91. τοπάζιον (1); 21:20; LXX 5
92. τρίχινος (1); 6:12; LXX 2
93. ὑακίνθινος (1); 9:17; LXX 27
94. ὑάκινθος (1); 21:20; LXX 36; Pseud 5

95.     ὑάλινος (3); 4:6; 15:2(2x); LXX 0; Aristophanes *Achar.* 74
96.     ὕαλος (2); 21:18, 21; LXX 1; *Periplus Maris Rubi* 16.23; 18.19 (ὕελος)
97.     φάρμακος (2); 21:8; 22:15; LXX 13; Pseud 1
98.     φιάλη (12); 5:8; 15:7; 16:1, 2, 3, 4, 8, 10, 12, 17; 17:1; 21:9; LXX 36; Pseud 9
99.     χάλαζα (4); 8:7; 11:19; 16:21(2x); LXX 37; Pseud 13
100.    χαλκηδών (1); 21:19; LXX 0
101.    χαλκολίβανον (2); 1:15; 2:18; LXX 0
102.    χαλκοῦς (1); 9:20; LXX 107
103.    χλιαρός (1); 3:16; LXX 0
104.    χοῖνιξ (2); 6:6(2x); LXX 3
105.    χρυσόλιθος (1); 21:20; LXX -ος: 1; -ον: 2; the neuter χρυσόλιθον occurs in *Periplus Maris Rubi* 13.8; 16.22; 18.18.22
106.    χρυσόπρασος (1); 21:20; LXX 0
107.    χρυσοῦν (2); 17:4; 18:16; LXX 10; Pseud 3
108.    Ὦ (3); 1:8; 21:6; 22:13; LXX 0

## II. Words Occurring Only in Revelation, but in Variant Readings
### (not counted in statistics)

1.      ἀκαθάρτης (1); Rev 17:4
2.      βιβλιδάριον (3); Rev 10:2, 8, 10
3.      διαφανής (1); Rev 21:21
4.      ἐμμέσῳ (6); Rev 1:13; 2:1; 4:6; 5:6; 6:6; 22:2
5.      ἡμίωρον (1); Rev 8:1 (εἰμιώρον] A)
6.      κατανάθεμα (1); Rev 21:3
7.      καῦμα (2); Rev 7:16; 16:9
8.      λευκοβύσσινον (1); Rev 19:4
9.      μαζός (1); Rev 1:13
10.     ὅμιλος (1); Rev 18:17
11.     περιρ(ρ)αίνειν (1); Rev 19:13
12.     ῥυπάν (1); Rev 22:11
13.     ῥυπαρεύειν (1); Rev 22:11
14.     σάρδινος (1); Rev 4:3 (late form of σάρδιον)
15.     τεσσαρακονταδύο (2); Rev 11:2; 13:5
16.     τεσσαρακοντατέσσαρες (1); Rev 21:17
17.     φαρμακεύς (1); Rev 21:8
18.     φάρμακον (1); Rev 9:21

## III. Proper Nouns Occurring Only in Revelation in NT (20)

1.      Ἀβαδδών (1); LXX 1
2.      Ἀντίπας (1); LXX 1
3.      Ἁρμαγεδών (1); LXX 0
4.      Ἄψινθος (2); LXX 0
5.      Ἀπολλύων (1) LXX 0
6.      Βαλάκ (1); LXX 42

7.     Γάδ (1); LXX frequently; Pseud 23
8.     Γώγ (1); LXX 11; Pseud 2
9.     Ἑλληνικός (1); LXX 8; Pseud 2
10.     Εὐφράτης (2); LXX 10; Pseud 9
11.     Ἰεζάβελ (1); LXX 20
12.     Ἰσσαχάρ (1); LXX 5
13.     Μαγώγ (1); LXX 5; Pseud 2
14.     Νικολαΐται (2); LXX 0
15.     Πάτμος (1); LXX 0
16.     Πέργαμος (2); LXX 0
17.     Ῥουβήν (1); LXX frequently
18.     Σάρδεις (3); LXX 0; Pseud 1
19.     Σμύρνα (2); LXX 1; Pseud 4
20.     Φιλαδέλφεια (2); LXX 0

# Revelation
# 1:1–5:14

# The Inscription

## Bibliography

**Hengel, M.** "The Titles of the Gospels and the Gospel of Mark." In *Studies in the Gospel of Mark.* Philadelphia: Fortress, 1985. 64–84, 162–83. **Metzger, B. M.** "Appendix III: Titles of the Books in the New Testament." In *The Canon of the New Testament.* Oxford: Clarendon, 1987. 301–4. **Munck, J.** "Evangelium Veritatis and Greek Usage as to Book Titles." *ST* 17 (1963) 133–38. **Nachmanson, E.** "Der griechische Buchtitel: Eine Beobachtungen." *GHÅ* 47 (1941) 1–52. **Oliver, R. P.** "The First Medicean MS of Tacitus and the Titulature of Ancient Books." *TAPA* 82 (1951) 232–61. **Thompson, E. M.** *A Handbook of Greek and Latin Paleography.* Chicago: Ares, 1966. **Tucker, G. M.** "Prophetic Superscriptions and the Growth of a Canon." In *Canon and Authority,* ed. G. W. Coats and B. O. Long. Philadelphia: Fortress, 1977. 56–70. **Turner, E. G.** *Greek Manuscripts of the Ancient World.* Oxford: Clarendon, 1971. **Wendel, C.** *Die griechisch-römische Buchbeschreibung vergleichen mit der des vorderen Orients.* Halle, Saale: Niemeyer, 1949. **Zilliacus, H.** "Boktiteln in antik litteratur." *Eranos* 36 (1938) 1–41.

## Translation

> The Revelation by [a] John

## Notes

a. Variants: (1) ἀποκάλυψις Ἰωάννου] ℵ C 181. (2) Ἰωάννου ἀποκάλυψις] fam 1611[1854] Byz 1[911 920] Byz 3[1955] Byz 8[177 180 337] Byz 12[110 627] Byz 17[82] Byz 18[175 617]. (3) ἀποκάλυψις Ἰωάννου τοῦ θεολόγου] 792 fam 1006[1006] Andr i[2042] Byz 13[498] Byz 14[325] Byz 16[61 69] Andr/Byz 2[680] Andr/Byz 3[1957 2035]. The original form of the title, reading (1), was transposed, as in reading (2), or expanded in various ways, as in reading (3), with the addition of "the theologian." Only two uncials contain the *subscriptio* ἀποκάλυψις Ἰωάννου, ℵ (in the form Ἀποκάλυψεις Ἰωάννου) and A, and one cursive: fam 1611[1854] (see *Comment* on Superscription following Rev 22:19).

## Comment

Ἀποκάλυψις Ἰωάννου. The genitive Ἰωάννου is the genitive of source or origin and therefore has been given the more specific designation of genitive of authorship. The problem of the title of Revelation must be considered in the context of ancient book titles generally. Titles could appear in three places in papyrus rolls: (1) it could appear as an external title written on a parchment label, or title tag, called a σίλλυβος, "label, tag," attached to the roll (Thompson, *Handbook,* 57; for examples, see POxy 301, 2396, 2433; pictured and described in Turner, *Greek Manuscripts,* 34); (2) the title was in some cases written at the beginning of the roll, though very few examples have survived; and (3) the title was almost always to be found at the end of the roll (Oliver, *TAPA* 82 [1951] 243; Thompson, *Handbook,* 58). The internal title at the beginning is called the *inscriptio* or "inscription," while a concluding title is designated the *subscriptio* or "subscription." MSS of Revelation contain examples of both. Yet whether the author gave his work a title originally is uncertain; titles were often regarded as superfluous for works intended for oral recitation (such as Revelation), for their "titles" were inherent in the opening lines (Nachmanson, *GHÅ* 47 [1941] 7–8). It is therefore relatively certain that the first sentence of the book in 1:1–2 was intended by the author to function as a title. Ancient books were cited both by their initial words and phrases and by (or in the absence of) a separately formulated title (Nachmanson, *GHÅ* 47 [1941] 31, 49–50). Yet it is clear that, in the period before the codex supplanted the use of the roll, titles when used had the simplest possible form (e.g., the title of the work in one word, if possible, and the author's name in the genitive) and every roll ended with a subscription or concluding title (Oliver, *TAPA* 82 [1951] 245, 248; Wendel, *Buchbeschreibung*, 24–29).

That Ἀποκάλυψις Ἰωάννου was the title of the book in the second century is clear from Canon Muratori 71–72: *apocalypses etiam Iohannis, et Petri, tantum recipimus,* "We also accept only the apocalypses of John and Peter," a passage that also indicates the generic use of ἀποκάλυψις as a designation for a literary form. Revelation could apparently also be referred to as simply ἀποκάλυψις, though in most texts Ἰωάννου seems implied (Irenaeus *Adv. haer.* 4.14.12; 4.30.4; 5.30.3; 5.35.2). Similarly, references in Tertullian presuppose the title *Apocalypsis Iohannis,* "Revelation of John" (*Adv. Marc.* 3.14.3: *Nam et apostolus Ioannes in Apocalypsi . . . ,* "Now the apostle John in the Apocalypse . . ."; 4.5.2: *Habemus et Ioannis alumnas ecclesias. Nam etsi Apocalypsis eius Marcion respuit . . . ,* "We have also churches which are nurselings of John's for although Marcion disallows his Apocalypse . . ."). During the second half of the second century A.D., the two-word title is found reflected in various authors. The Latin translation of Irenaeus has "Iohannis Apocalypsis" (*Adv. haer.* 1.26.3), while the title of a lost work of Melito of Sardis (died ca. A.D. 190) was Περὶ τοῦ διαβόλου καὶ τῆς Ἀποκάλυψεως Ἰωάννου, "Concerning the Devil and the Apocalypse of John" (Eusebius *Hist. eccl.* 4.26.2). No title is used in Justin *Dial.* 81.4, though when the author says Ἰωάννης . . . ἐν ἀποκαλύψει γενομένη αὐτῷ, "John . . . in a revelation which came to him," he may simply be paraphrasing the opening words of the book. The two-word title must have originally appeared as a subscription, and only after Revelation began to be copied in a codex was it moved to the beginning of the composition and used as an inscription, just as was the case with many other ancient compositions that began in the form of rolls and were copied in codex form. The more elaborate titles given to the author ("the holy," MSS 1, 2015, 2020; "the theologian and evangelist," MSS 2043, 2057, 2082) appeared only after the book began to be copied in codex form. The longest of these is probably MS 1775 (copied as late as 1847): "The revelation of the all-glorious evangelist, bosom-friend [of Jesus], virgin, beloved to Christ, John the theologian, son of Salome and Zebedee, but adopted son of Mary the mother of God, and Son of Thunder" (*TCGNT*[1], 729). The fact that ἀποκάλυψις alone stands as a title in A, while the subscription in A includes the author's name in the genitive, follows the ancient laconic convention of omitting even the author's name in titles within the roll itself (Oliver, *TAPA* 82 [1951] 248).

# I. Prologue (1:1–8)

## A. Title: The Revelation of Jesus Christ (1:1–2)
## B. Beatitude (1:3)

### Bibliography

**Balogh, J.** "'Voces Paginarum': Beiträge zur Geschichte des lauten Lesens und Schreibens." *Philologus* 82 (1927) 84–109, 202–40. **Becker, J.** "Erwägungen zu Frage der neutestamentlichen Exegese." *BZ* 13 (1969) 99–102. **Betz, H. D.** "The Beatitudes of the Sermon on the Mount (Matt. 5:3–12): Observations on Their Literary Form and Theological Significance." In *Essays on the Sermon on the Mount.* Tr. L. L. Welborn. Philadelphia: Fortress, 1985. 17–36. **Bieder, W.** "Die sieben Seligpreisungen in der Offenbarung des Johannes." *TZ* 10 (1954) 13–30. **Boismard, M. E.** "Rapprochements littéraires entre l'évangile de Luc et l'Apocalypse." In *Synoptische Studien.* Munich: Zink, 1953. 53–63. **Cruz, V. P.** "The Beatitudes of the Apocalypse: Eschatology and Ethics." In *Perspectives on Christology.* FS P. K. Jewett, ed. M. Shuster and R. Muller. Grand Rapids, MI: Zondervan, 1991. 269–83. **Dehandschutter, B.** "The Meaning of Witness in the Apocalypse." In *L'Apocalypse,* ed. J. Lambrecht. 283–88. **Delling, G.** "Die Attribute Jeremias und Baruchs." In *Jüdische Lehre und Frömmigkeit in den Paralipomena Jeremiae.* Berlin: Töpelmann, 1967. **Fehling, D.** "Zur Funktion und Formgeschichte des Proömiums in der älteren griechischen Prosa." In *ΔΩPHMA.* FS H. Diller, ed. S. Vourreris and A. Skiadas. Athens: Griechische Humanistische Gesellschaft, 1975. 61–75. **Gevaryahu, H. M. I.** "Biblical Colophons: A Source for the 'Biography' of Authors, Texts and Books." In *Congress Volume.* VTSup 28. Leiden: Brill, 1975. 42–59. **Gilliard, F. D.** "More Silent Reading in Antiquity: *Non Omne Verbum Sonabat.* " *JBL* 112 (1993) 689–94. **Hartman, L.** "Form and Message: A Preliminary Discussion of 'Partial Texts' in Rev 1–3 and 22,6ff." In *L'Apocalypse,* ed. J. Lambrecht. 129–49. **Hendrikson, G. L.** "Ancient Reading." *CJ* 25 (1929–30) 182–90. **Johnson, A. R.** "Apocalypse 1,3." *RSR* 24 (1934) 365–66. **Kees, K.** "Der berichtende Gottesdiener." *ZASA* 85 (1960) 138–43. **Knox, B. M. W.** "Silent Reading in Antiquity." *GRBS* 9 (1968) 421–35. **Köpstein, H.** "Zur Fortleben des Wortes δοῦλος und anderer Bezeichnungen für Slaven im Mittel- und Neugriechischen." In *Untersuchungen ausgewählten altgriechischen socialer Typenbegriffe,* ed. E. C. Welskopf. Vol. 3 of E. C. Welskopf, *Sociale Typenbegriffe im alten Griechenland und ihr Fortleben in den Sprachen der Welt.* Berlin: Akademie, 1981. 314–53. **Leskow, T.** "Redaktionsgeschichtliche Analyse von Micha 1–5." *ZAW* 84 (1972) 61–64. **Martin, D. B.** *Slavery as Salvation: The Metaphor of Slavery in Pauline Christianity.* New Haven: Yale UP, 1990. **Mazzaferri, F.** "*Martyria Iesou* Revisited." *BT* 39 (1988) 114–22. **McCartney, E. S.** "On Reading and Praying Audibly." *CP* 43 (1948) 184–87. **Pesch, R.** "Offenbarung Jesu Christi: Eine Auslegung von Apk. 1:1–3." *BibLeb* 11 (1970) 15–29. **Pleket, H. W.** "Religious History as the History of Mentality: The 'Believer' as Servant of the Deity in the Greek World." In *Faith, Hope and Worship: Aspects of Religious Mentality in the Ancient World.* Leiden: Brill, 1981. 152–92. **Roberts, C. H.,** and **Skeat, T. C.** *The Birth of the Codex.* London: Oxford UP (for The British Academy), 1983. **Sass, G.** "Zur Bedeutung von δοῦλος bei Paulus." *ZNW* 40 (1941) 24–32. **Sheppard, A. R. R.** "Pagan Cults of Angels in Roman Asia Minor." *Talanta* 12–13 (1980–81) 77–101. **Slusser, M.** "Reading Silently in Antiquity." *JBL* 111 (1992) 499. **Smith, M.** "On the History of ΑΠΟΚΑΛΥΠΤΩ and ΑΠΟΚΑΛΥΨΙΣ." In *Apocalypticism,* ed. D. Hellholm. 9–20. **Stanford, W. B.** *The Sound of Greek: Studies in the Greek Theory and Practice of Euphony.* Berkeley; Los Angeles: University of California, 1967. **Strecker, G.** "Chiliasmus und Doketismus in der johanneischen Schule." *KD* 38 (1992) 30–46. **Trites, A. A.** *The New Testament Concept of*

*Witness.* Cambridge: Cambridge UP, 1977. **Vanni, U.** "L'Apocalypse johannique: État de la question." In *L'Apocalypse,* ed. J. Lambrecht. 21–46. **Vassiliadis, P.** "The Translation of Martyria Iesou in Revelation." *BT* 36 (1985) 129–34.

## Translation

[1]*This is* [a] *a revelation from* [b] *Jesus Christ which God granted him to show to his* [c]*servants events which must quickly come to pass, which* [d] [e]*he made known* [e] *by sending his angel* [f]*to his servant* [f] *John,* [2]*who now bears witness* [a] *to all the visions he saw which is* [b] *the message from* [c] *God, that is,* [d] *the witness borne by* [e] *Jesus.* [3] [a]*How fortunate* [b] *is the one who reads aloud* [a] *and those who both* [c] *hear* [d] *these* [e] [f]*prophetic* [g]*words* [f] *and obey what is written herein,* [h] *for the time is near.*

## Notes

1.a. The phrase "this is" is supplied since the first sentence (vv 1–2) is incomplete, lacking a main verb.

1.b. Ἰησοῦ Χριστοῦ, "of Jesus Christ," can be either a subjective gen. (the revelation is *from* Jesus Christ), or an obj. gen. (the revelation is *about* Jesus Christ). The translation "from Jesus Christ" assumes that it is a subjective gen., a view supported by the next phrase in the text: ἥν [here the fem. acc. relative pronoun has been attracted to the gender of ἀποκάλυψις] ἔδωκεν αὐτῷ ὁ θεός, "which God granted him [i.e., 'Jesus Christ']."

1.c. Variant reading: insert ἅγιοις] ℵ*. The unmodified phrase οἱ δοῦλοι σου αὐτοῦ occurs in 11:18; 19:2, 5.

1.d. καί functions here as a relative pronoun; cf. Mark 2:15 (Maloney, *Marcan Syntax,* 69).

1.e-e. The subject of ἐσήμανεν is unclear, though it is logical to take God as the subject, since ἐσήμανεν is coordinate with ἔδωκεν. Many commentators, however, understand "Jesus Christ" as the subject (Beckwith, 419; Bousset [1906] 182; Charles, 1:6). Favoring the second view is the fact that Jesus Christ is referred to in the indirect obj. αὐτῷ in v 1, and there are several instances in Revelation in which an indirect obj. is used as the subject of the verb in the following clause (2:21; 12:14; 14:4; these, however, are all subordinate clauses).

1.f-f. Variant: (1) omit τῷ δούλῳ αὐτοῦ] fam 1611[1854] Andreas i[2074] 2351. (2) τοῦ δούλου αὐτοῦ] A. Reading (1) is an error of omission through homoioteleuton; the copyist skipped from the second to the third αὐτοῦ in this sentence. Reading (2) is a singular reading.

2.a. ἐμαρτύρησεν is analogous to an epistolary aorist; i.e., what the author writes in the present will be a past event from the perspective of the readers and so must be translated as a present tense (Allo, 2). For a similar use of the aorist in a prologue, see Thucydides 1.1.1: "Thucydides, an Athenian, is writing [ξυνέγραψε] about the war which the Peloponnesians and the Athenians fought with one another." Other examples: in a subscript from Trajan to the Smyrnaeans written ca. A.D. 100 (*SEG* 32:1202.5), ἔγραψα is used to mean "I am writing." For epistolary aorists in early Christian literature, such as ἔπεμψα, ἔγραψα, ἐπέστειλα, cf. 2 Cor 8:18, 22; 9:3; Eph 6:22; Phil 2:25, 28; Col 4:8; Philem 11; Heb 13:22; Pol. *Phil.* 13; Ign. *Eph.* 9:1; *Trall.* 12:3.

2.b. ὅσα εἶδεν, "all the visions he saw," a subordinate clause, is the obj. of ἐμαρτύρησεν, "he testifies," which can be translated "he testifies to all the visions he saw." Within the subordinate clause the correlative adj. ὅσα (neut. pl. acc. from ὅσος) functions as the obj. of the verb εἶδεν. The noun cluster τὸν λόγον τοῦ θεοῦ καὶ τὴν μαρτυρίαν Ἰησοῦ Χριστοῦ is also the obj. of the verb ἐμαρτύρησεν, so that the noun cluster and the subordinate clause are in apposition.

2.c. In the phrase τὸν λόγον τοῦ θεοῦ, the gen. τοῦ θεοῦ could be either an obj. gen. ("the message about God") or a subjective gen. ("the message from God"); the latter seems more appropriate in this revelatory context.

2.d. The καί here is epexegetical rather than correlative, so that "the word of God" and "the testimony of Jesus" are not two different things, but rather the second is an aspect of the first. See *Comment* on 1:2.

2.e. In the phrase τὴν μαρτυρίαν Ἰησοῦ Χριστοῦ, "Jesus Christ" could be either an obj. gen., and so be translated "the testimony *about* Jesus Christ" or "witness (unto death) to Jesus" (Vassiliadis, *BT* 36 [1985] 133), or a subjective gen., "the testimony borne *by* Jesus Christ"; in line with *Note* 2.c., the subjective gen. is also preferable here, particularly if the καί (*Note* 2.d.) is epexegetical. The phrase μαρτυρία Ἰησοῦ occurs five times in Revelation (1:2, 9; 12:17; 19:10; 20:4). In most instances in which a gen. is dependent on μαρτυρία in Revelation, the gen. is subjective (1:9; 11:17; 12:17; 19:10[2x]; 20:4).

3.a-a. Variant: (1) μακάριος ὁ ἀναγινώσκων] *lectio originalis*. (2) μακάριοι οἱ ἀναγινωσκόντες] fam 1611²³⁴⁴ Byz 17⁴⁶⁹ arab cop Victorinus (*beati qui legunt*); Ps.-Ambrose. Of the seven beatitudes in Revelation, the two in 14:13; 22:14 have a pl. form analogous to reading (2).

3.b. μακάριος means "happy, fortunate" rather than "blessed" in the sense that God has or will bless such a person; see Bratcher-Hatton, *Revelation*, 16; Louw-Nida, § 25.119.

3.c. In the phrase οἱ ἀκούοντες καὶ τηροῦντες, "those who hear . . . and keep," the definite article goes with both substantival ptcps. indicating that *both* refer to a single group (BDR § 276).

3.d. Variant: (1) καὶ οἱ ἀκούοντες] 2329. (2) καὶ ἀκούων] Oecumenius²⁰⁵³ ²⁰⁶² it vg^cl Apringius Beatus.

3.e. Variant: insert ταύτης after προφητείας] 1611 Oecumenius²⁰⁵³ ²⁰⁶² 2344 Andr/Byz 2a Andr/Byz 2b it^gig vg syr bo Victorinus (*huius prophetiae*); Primarius^mss Beatus.

3.f-f. In the phrase τοὺς λόγους τῆς προφητείας, τῆς προφητείας *could* be construed as a qualitative gen. used as a substitute for an adj. and therefore be translated "prophetic words" (cf. BDR § 165). Yet since the emphasis in this phrase is apparently on the gen. τῆς προφητείας, it is preferable to understand it as a gen. of *apposition* (i.e., τῆς προφητείας and τοὺς λόγους are different ways of referring to the same thing), which can then be translated "the words which constitute this prophecy." This is partly confirmed by the fact that all of the other occurrences of this phrase have the additional phrase τοῦ βιβλίου τούτου, "this book" (22:7, 10, 18), so that the entire noun cluster reads τοὺς λόγους τῆς προφητείας τοῦ βιβλίου τούτου, "the words which constitute this prophetic book," decidedly shifting the emphasis from τοὺς λόγους to τοῦ βιβλίου.

3.g. Variant: (1) τοὺς λόγους] A C 025 2351 Andreas Byzantine vg cop syr Victorinus Primasius TR. (2) τοὺς λόγους τούτους] C (singular reading). (3) τὸν λόγον] ℵ 046 1678 1854 Andr i²⁰⁴²Andr l Tischendorf, *NT Graece*. The external evidence is overwhelming in favor of reading (1), as is the internal evidence for τοὺς λόγους in parallels in 22:7, 10, 18.

3.h. The prep. phrase ἐν αὐτῇ, "in it," modifies the antecedent fem. noun προφητείας (cf. *Note* 1:3.b.). Given the normally subordinate character of the gen. to the noun that governs it, one might expect that τοὺς λόγους, "the words," should be the antecedent of the personal pronoun αὐτῇ (which, however, would then have to read ἐν αὐτοῖς). It is unlikely that it modifies ἀποκάλυψις, "revelation" (v 1), or μαρτυρίαν, "testimony" (v 2), since both refer to revelatory experiences rather than texts.

## *Form/Structure/Setting*

### I. OUTLINE

I. Prologue (1:1–8)
  A. Title: The revelation of Jesus Christ (vv 1–2)
    1. The transmission of the revelation (v 1)
      a. God granted the revelation to Jesus Christ (v 1b)
      b. Jesus Christ showed the revelation to his servants (v 1c)
    2. Content of the revelation: the events that must soon take place (v 1d)
    3. The revelatory role of John (v 1e–2)
      a. Jesus Christ made the revelation known
        (1) Means: by sending his angel
        (2) Destination: his servant John (v 1e)
      b. John testified to all that he saw (v 2)
        (1) To the word of God (v 2a)
        (2) To the testimony of Jesus Christ (v 2b)
  B. Beatitude (v 3)
    1. The one who reads the prophecy is blessed (v 3a)
    2. Those who hear and obey the prophecy are blessed (v 3b)

    a. Because they obey what is written in it
    b. Because the time is near

## II. LITERARY ANALYSIS

Rev 1:1–3 consists of two clearly defined literary forms, with vv 1–2 constituting the title of the book, clearly marked off from v 3, which is a beatitude introduced with the conventional term μακάριος, "blessed, fortunate." The literary relationship between these two units is problematic, for they are linked by some features but exhibit a degree of tension with respect to others. The features that link the two units together are the following: (1) The element of eschatological imminence, even though the phraseology is completely different, is emphasized in both units, expressed in v 1 with the phrase ἃ δεῖ γενέσθαι ἐν τάχει, "events that will quickly come to pass," and the concluding phrase of v 3, ὁ γὰρ καιρὸς ἐγγύς, "for the time is near" (Pesch, *BibLeb* 11 [1970] 16; Karrer, *Brief,* 86–87). (2) The emphasis on the product of divine revelation is described as τὸν λόγον τοῦ θεοῦ, "the word of God," and τὴν μαρτυρίαν Ἰησοῦ Χριστοῦ, "the witness borne by Jesus," in v 2a, and as τοὺς λόγους τῆς προφητείας, "the prophetic words," in v 3a. (3) Both vv 1–2 and v 3 are formulated in the third person. On the other hand, the following features reflect a literary tension between vv 1–2 and v 3: (1) In vv 1–2 the "revelation from Jesus Christ" is dynamically described as ἔδωκεν, "given," to him by God; δεῖξαι, "shown," to his (Jesus Christ's) servants; and ἐσήμανεν, "made known," to John by an angelic intermediary, which is described as having been εἶδεν, "seen," by John, while in v 3 the "prophetic words" are suddenly regarded not only as a written product but also as the book for which vv 1–3 provide the first introduction. (2) The *dramatis personae* of vv 1–2 include God, Jesus Christ, "his servants" (prophets or Christians generally), "his [Jesus Christ's] angel," and 'his servant John," while the *dramatis personae* in v 3 are vaguely identified as "the reader" and "those who hear and obey" what is read to them. There is no obvious connection, unless "his servants" are assumed to be identical with "those who hear and obey," or "the reader" is identified with "his servant John."

The *form* of this entire unit, however, linking two discrete units together as it does, has a few parallels in ancient literature. The entire literary unit is written in the third person, distinguishing it from the narrative that follows, which is formulated as a first-person account. A number of scholars have used this difference in person as an argument that the author of 1:4–3:22 is *not* the author of 1:1–3 (Völter, *Entstehung,* 8–9; Spitta, 10–19; J. Weiss, *Offenbarung,* 35). However, this ignores the fact that many ancient texts, including apocalypses, begin with a brief introductory section in the third person and then switch over to the first person (cf. Herodotus 1.1; Jer 1:1–3; *2 Apoc. Bar.* 1:1–2a; cf. Fehling, "Proömium," 61–75).

Hartman ("Form and Message," 132–33) has called attention to the similarities between *1 Enoch* 1:1–2 and Rev 1:1–3 (tr. Knibb, *Enoch*):

> The words of the blessing of Enoch
> according to which he blessed the chosen and righteous
> who must be present on the day of distress
> (which is appointed) for the removal of all the wicked and impious.
> And Enoch answered and said:

> (There was) a righteous man whose eyes were opened by the Lord,
> And he saw a holy vision in the heavens
> which the angels showed to me.
> And I heard everything from them,
> And I understood what I saw,
> but not for this generation,
> but for a distant generation which will come.

There is also a striking structural similarity between the title of *T. Sol.* (tr. Charlesworth, *OTP* 1:960, where the textual problems of this section are also discussed in notes):

> Testament of Solomon, Son of David, who reigned in Jerusalem, and subdued all the spirits of the air, of the earth, and under the earth; through (them) he also accomplished all the magnificent works of the Temple; (this tells) what their authorities are against men, and by what angels these demons are thwarted. Blessed are you, Lord God, who has given this authority to Solomon. Glory and power to you forever. Amen.

This title is in the third person, whereas the remainder of the book is in the first person, an arrangement similar to the relation of Rev 1:1–3 to the rest of Revelation. This title also concludes with a beatitude that is part of the introductory text unit, however, since it identifies the Lord God as the one through whom Solomon accomplished the deeds described in the first sentence. The brief doxology in the third sentence has no direct parallel in Rev 1:1–3, though a doxology is found in Rev 1:5b–6.

Rev 1:1–3 consists of six separate elements: (1) a summary designation of the character of the work itself, "This is a *revelation*," (2) with a subjective genitive indicating its source, "*from Jesus Christ*," (3) and an indication of its ultimate origin, "granted him *by God*," (4) a reference to the addressees, "to show [i.e., 'to reveal'] *to his servants*," and (5) a summary of the content of the revelation, "*what must quickly come to pass*." This is followed by (6) a statement of how the revelation was transmitted, "He made it known *by sending his angel*," (7) a statement of the recipient of this revelation, "*to his servant John*," (8) confirmation of the accomplishment of this task through the composition of the present book, "*who now bears witness* to the word of God and the testimony of Jesus" (i.e., by writing this book), and (9) the brief mention of how the revelation was received, "even to all that he *saw*." Finally, (10) a beatitude (in the form of an enthymeme) is pronounced on those who read, hear, and keep this revelatory message: "Blessed is the one who reads aloud and those who hear these prophetic words and keep what is written herein, for the time is near."

### III. LITERARY FORMS

*A. Book Title*

The first sentence in Revelation, as in many other ancient books, certainly functions as a title conveying a summary of the contents of the work and the name of the author (Nachmanson, *GHÅ* 47 [1941] 7–8; Kraft, 18). The titles, i.e., the introductory sentence(s) of several Jewish and Christian revelatory compositions have some similarity to the title of Revelation (Jer 1:1–2; Ezek 1:1–3; Amos 1:1; *1*

*Enoch* 1:1, probably modeled on Deut 33:1; *3 Apoc. Bar. praef.* 1–2). One example is the title of the Apocalypse of Weeks, which consists of *1 Enoch* 93:1–10; 91:12–17 (Black, *Enoch,* 287–89; J. C. VanderKam, *Enoch,* 142–49); the title is found in 93:1–3 (Milik, *Enoch,* 264):

> [And when he was transmitting his Epistle],
> Enoch [took up] his discourse, saying:
> ["Concerning the children of righteousness
> and about the elect of the world who have grown] up from a
> plant of truth [and of justice,
> behold, I will speak and will make (it) known unto you], my sons.

> I Enoch, have been shown [everything in a heavenly vision,
> and from] the word of the Watchers and Holy Ones I have known everything;
> [and in the heavenly tablets I] have read everything [and understood."

> And Enoch took up his discourse again and said . . . .

This highly stylized title has been preserved in an Aramaic fragment from Qumran (4QEn$^g$ 1 iii; cf. Milik, *Enoch,* 263–65 [Aramaic text and notes with English translation]); for analyses of this title see Dexinger, *Zehnwochenapokalypse,* 106–9; VanderKam, *Enoch,* 149–53). The present form of the title contains the following information: (1) The oral communication of Enoch's earlier revelatory experience is emphasized: "Enoch began to speak from the books" (a conception that frames the title but is absent from the Aramaic fragments; cf. Milik, *Enoch,* 264; in its place is the phrase "And Enoch took up his discourse" [מתלה חנוך נסב *nsb ḥnwk mtlh*]); yet the motif of oral presentation also forms the *center* of this chiastically arranged text in a synonymously parallel couplet: "I will speak these things to you and make (them) known to you." (2) The recipient through whom revelation is communicated is identified as Enoch twice in the framing statements and once in the central couplet as "I Enoch." (3) The immediate audience for the communication of Enoch's revelation is identified as "my children." (4) A threefold summary of the ultimate recipients of Enoch's revelation (three phrases for the same group, the "righteous") is presented: (a) "Concerning the sons of righteousness," (b) "and concerning the chosen of the world," (c) "and concerning the plant of righteousness and uprightness." (5) The threefold *source* of the revelation is identified (balancing the threefold summary of the ultimate recipients of the revelation mentioned above): (a) the *medium* of the revelation, "According to that which appeared to me in the heavenly vision," (b) the *mediators* of the revelation, "and (which) I know from the words of the holy angels," and (c) the *product* of the revelation, "and understand from the tablets of heaven."

## B. Beatitude

Rev 1:3 contains a *beatitude* or *makarism,* the first of seven in Revelation (14:13; 16:15; 19:9; 20:6; 22:7, 14). This makarism is distinctive in form, for it is structured as an enthymeme, i.e., as a two-part statement consisting of a protasis and an apodosis, with the apodosis introduced by γάρ, "for," providing the reason for the statement made in the protasis. On the form of the makarism, see Betz,

"Beatitudes," 22–33. Makarisms are frequently found in Greek oracles (Aune, *Prophecy,* 64), as well as in Jewish apocalyptic literature. Makarisms are found singly (like the seven in Revelation) or in series (as the nine in Matt 5:3–12, the four in Luke 6:20b–23, and the five in 4Q525 = 4QBéat frag. 2 ii 1–3). The makarism in Rev 1:3 is unique in that it is formulated in *both* the third person singular ("the one who reads") and the third person plural ("those who hear"), thereby providing a blessing upon the communication process itself. Yet the tristich in 20:6 also switches, though somewhat awkwardly from the third person singular in the first line (μακάριος καὶ ἅγιος ὁ ἔχων μέρος ἐν τῇ ἀναστάσει τῇ πρώτῃ, "How fortunate and holy is the one who has part in the first resurrection") to the third person plural in the third line (ἀλλ᾽ ἔσονται ἱερεῖς τοῦ θεοῦ, "but they will be priests of God"). This reveals that whether the beatitude is formulated in the singular or plural, it applies to all those who fulfill the requirement outlined in the protasis. Of the remaining beatitudes, those in 14:13; 19:9; 22:14 are formulated in the third person plural (i.e., μακάριοι οἱ, "How fortunate are those"), while 16:15; 22:7 are expressed in the third person singular (μακάριος ὁ, "How fortunate is the one"). Betz ("Beatitudes," 25) distinguishes four types of makarisms: (1) religious makarisms (e.g., Ps 1:1), (2) secular makarisms (one is praised for beauty, wealth, strength, etc.), (3) the makarism of the wise man (one is praised for wisdom and virtue), and (4) the satirical makarism (e.g., *1 Enoch* 103:5–6).

Variations of the kind of pronouncement found in Rev 1:3, whether in the form of a beatitude or not, were used in early Christianity either to introduce or (more commonly) to conclude readings that were presumed to represent the word of God. Though very little is known of Christian liturgy before ca. A.D. 150, Justin notes in *1 Apol.* 67 that after reading selections from the Gospels and the Prophets, "the president of the assembly verbally admonishes and invites all to imitate such examples of virtue." While this *could* allude to the delivery of a homily based on the readings, it could also describe the kind of liturgical formula found in Rev 1:3; 22:7. John 12:47 forms an editorial conclusion to the first half of the Fourth Gospel in which the written text of the words and deeds of Jesus are presented as the revelation of God in the context of the importance of "hearing" and "keeping" those words: "I do not judge anyone who hears [ἀκούσῃ] my words and does not keep [φυλάξῃ] them." Knowing the words of Jesus is combined with a beatitude pronounced upon those who do them in John 13:17, the beginning of the farewell discourses (the speech actually begins in 13:12b). References to hearing and doing the words of Jesus form the conclusion to both the Sermon on the Mount (Matt 7:24, 26) and the Sermon on the Plain (Luke 6:47, 49). Rev 22:7 forms part of the conclusion to the vision that John has narrated in which obedience is once again enjoined. Further, the conclusion of Hermas *Vis.* 5.5 uses the "read and keep" and "hear and keep" formulas in such a way that allusions to Luke 11:28 or Rev 1:3; 22:7 are improbable: "that you might *read* them continually and be able to *keep* them"; cf. 5.7, "If you then *hear* and *keep* them [commandments]." The form also occurs in *2 Clem.* 19:1–3, near the conclusions, where reference is made to *reading* the exhortations, followed by a beatitude pronounced on those who obey the commandments (μακάριοι οἱ τουτοῖς ὑπακούοντες τοῖς πρὸς τάγμασιν). These texts suggest the existence and widespread use of formulaic pronouncements, often incorporating beatitudes, emphasizing the benefits of obeying the word of God read or heard.

## Comment

**1a** Ἀποκάλυψις Ἰησοῦ Χριστοῦ, "This is a revelation from Jesus Christ." The term ἀποκάλυψις, "revelation" or "uncovering," occurs only here in Revelation, a feature that, together with other factors, suggests that 1:1–3 was prefixed to this document at the last stage of its redaction. Paul uses the term to refer to a revelatory experience that can be recited in a Christian assembly (1 Cor 14:6). John is not describing his composition as belonging to a literary type called "apocalypse," since he characterizes his work as a "prophecy" (1:3) or a "prophetic book" (22:7, 10, 18–19). On the basis of its occurrence in Rev 1:1, and particularly because the term became the title for John's composition, "Apocalypse" came to be applied to a literary report of visions similar to those narrated in Revelation (cf. Canon Muratori 71–72, which refers to *Apocalypsis . . . Johannis et Petri*, i.e., "the Apocalypses of John and Peter"; Hermas *Vis.* 5, title). By the third and fourth centuries A.D., pagans were using both ἀποκαλύπτειν and ἀποκάλυψις to refer to literary accounts of revelatory experiences, a usage probably not derived from Christianity or Judaism (Iamblichus *De myst.* 6.7.11; Synesius *Ep.* 54; cf. Smith, "History," 18).

**1b** ἣν ἔδωκεν αὐτῷ ὁ θεός, δεῖξαι τοῖς δούλοις αὐτοῦ ἃ δεῖ γενέσθαι ἐν τάχει, "which God granted him to reveal to his servants events which must quickly come to pass." The phrase "[the revelation] which God granted him [Christ]" is without parallel in the rest of the book and has a distinct Johannine ring: God is the ultimate source of revelation, and Christ, the agent of that revelation, transmits it to believers. There are several parallels in the Fourth Gospel, though expressed differently (NRSV): "I have made known to you everything that I have heard from my Father" (15:15; see also 1:18; 8:28; 12:49–50; 14:10; 17:8, 14). The role of the Son as the agent to whom and through whom God reveals himself is also found in the so-called Johannine Q pericope in Matt 11:25–27 = Luke 10:21–22. Yet in the phrase "all things have been handed over to me [πάντα μοι παρεδόθη] by my Father," πάντα probably refers to ἐξουσία, "authority" (see the parallels in Matt 28:18; John 3:35; 5:27; 13:3; 17:2; Dan 7:13; *1 Enoch* 69:27; *Corp. Herm.* 1.32). In *Corp. Herm.* 1.32, the phrase παρέδωκας αὐτῷ τὴν πᾶσαν ἐξουσίαν, "you have given over to him all authority," has often been understood as referring to secret knowledge of magic and the mysteries (Scott, *Hermetica,* 4:359–60; Norden, *Agnostos Theos,* 288–94; Copenhaver, *Hermetica,* 124). In both John and this Q pericope, the role of Jesus is conceptualized as a prophet who received revelations from God and transmits them to others. An analogous type of intermediary revelatory function is referred to in Plato *Rep.* II.363C, where it is said that the legendary Musaeus and his son "transmit a more excellent song than these from the gods to the righteous [παρὰ θεῶν διδόασι τοῖς δικαίοις]" (see Norden, *Agnostos Theos,* 290). In the Gnostic Naassene hymn preserved in Hippolytus *Ref.* 5.10.2, Jesus says "Therefore send me, Father . . . I will disclose all mysteries . . . and the hidden things of the holy way, awaking knowledge, I will impart." The term δείκνυναι occurs eight times in Revelation, and in all instances but this one the subject of the verb is the *angelus interpres,* "interpreting angel" (1:1; 4:1; 17:1; 21:9, 10; 22:1, 6, 8· see Reichelt, *Angelus,* 34–136, who focuses on the following passages in connection with the *angelus interpres* in Revelation: 1:1; 22:6; 17; 21:9–21; 9:9–10; 22:8–16).

In the phrase τοῖς δούλοις αὐτοῦ, "to his servants," the possessive pronoun αὐτοῦ refers to God rather than to Christ, as the close parallel in 22:6 makes clear. The term δοῦλος, "servant, slave," is used fourteen times in Revelation, three times literally (6:15; 13:16; 19:18; cf. the synonym σώματα in Rev 18:13 and *Comment* there) and eleven times metaphorically. These metaphorical uses of δοῦλος refer to Moses (15:3), to John himself (1:1²), to prophets (10:7; 11:18), but most frequently to Christians generally (1:1[2x]; 2:20; 7:3; 19:2, 5; 22:3, 6; see *TDNT* 2:273–77), though at least two of the references in the last category may refer to Christian prophets (1:1¹; 22:6; see Charles, 1:6), though the fact that the revelation is intended for those who hear it read aloud suggests that "servants" may rather mean *all* Christians (Beckwith, 419). Metaphorical uses of δοῦλος (and words belonging to the same semantic domain) are not uncommon in the Hellenistic world, though this conception was derived from the ancient Near East (Pleket, "Religious History," 159–71), since considering oneself a slave of a deity was not typically a Greek conception (Pleket, "Religious History," 170; Conzelmann, *1 Corinthians*, 128; attempts to argue the contrary cite very few parallels: see Martin, *Slavery*). A free person can be a δοῦλος, "slave," of a god in a strictly religious sense (Böhmer, *Sklaven* 2:111). In a third-century A.D. inscription from Macedonian Edessa, a woman named Strato transfers a vineyard over to the goddess Ma, and calls herself δούλη θεᾶς, "slave of the goddess" (Bömer, *Sklaven* 2:89; Pleket, "Religious History," 170). Philostratus has Apollonius of Tyana describe himself as a "servant [θεράπων] and companion of Asklepios" (Philostratus, *Vita Apoll.* 1.12). Sophocles has Teiresia the seer refer to himself as the δοῦλος of Apollo (*Oed.* 410). In Asia Minor there were many ἱερόδουλοι, "temple slaves," for which two synonyms are ἱεροὶ παῖδες, "sacred slaves," and τοῦ θεοῦ σώματα, "slaves of the god" (Debord, *Aspects Sociaux,* 83–90). The term δοῦλος, "servant," came to have religious associations in Greek language and culture through the influence of Near Eastern religious traditions (Köpstein, "δοῦλος," 341 n. 14). In the OT, a courtier or soldier was called a "servant" (עבד *'ebed* or δοῦλος) of the king (1 Sam 18:5, 30; 19:4; 2 Sam 14:19–20, 22), following ancient Near Eastern conventions (Jdt 3:2; 6:3; 11:4). By extension, this use was metaphorically applied to servants of *God*, conceptualized as the Great King (Gen 50:17). In the OT, the phrase "his [God's] servant Jacob" (Isa 48:20) refers to Israelites generally. Similarly, in Josephus the phrase "the servants of God, both the Jews and their leaders" (*Ant.* 11.90, 101) clearly refers to Jews generally. In Philo the phrase "servants of God" is also used of Jews generally, particularly of pious Jews (*Mig.* 45; cf. *Mut.* 46). Elsewhere in the NT the term "servants of Christ" is used of Christians generally (1 Cor 7:22; Gal 1:10; Eph 6:6; Col 4:12) and "servant/servants of God" (1 Pet 2:16). The term "servant" or, more literally, "slave" is not necessarily a term exclusively suggestive of lowliness and humility, though slaves customarily identify themselves as such, with their owner's name in the genitive, on papyrus tax receipts (*CPJ* 2:206.1; 207.1; 212.2; 229.1: "Thermauthos, a slave of Aninios, a centurion"; *SEG* 26:482.4 [second- or third-century A.D. grave epigram]: "Hilaros, slave of Caesar"; see Martin, *Slavery,* 47).

Rev 1:1; 22:6 (cf. also 22:16) are doublets, as the following synoptic comparison reveals:

| Rev 1:1a | Rev 22:6 |
|---|---|
| ὁ θεός<br>God | καὶ ὁ κύριος ὁ θεὸς<br>And the Lord, the God |
| | τῶν πνευμάτων τῶν προφητῶν<br>of the spirits of the prophets, |
| ἔδωκεν<br>gave | ἀπέστειλεν τὸν ἄγγελον<br>sent his angel |
| ἦν [ἀποκάλυψις]<br>it [revelation] | |
| αὐτῷ ['Ιησου Χριστοῦ]<br>to him | |
| δεῖξαι<br>to reveal | δεῖξαι<br>to reveal |
| τοῖς δούλοις αὐτοῦ<br>to his servants | τοῖς δούλοις αὐτοῦ<br>to his servants |
| ἃ δεῖ γενέσθαι ἐν τάχει<br>what must soon happen. | ἃ δεῖ γενέσθαι ἐν τάχει<br>what must soon happen. |

While the last few phrases are identical, the main difference lies in the inclusion of Jesus Christ in the revelatory chain (though Jesus is the exclusive revealer in another parallel passage in 22:16). Further, the parallels between 1:1 and 22:6 are closer than the synoptic comparison above indicates, for in 1:1c (see below), the phrase ἀποστείλας διὰ τοῦ ἀγγέλου αὐτοῦ, "by sending through his angel," is close to the phrase ἀπέστειλεν τὸν ἄγγελον, "sent his angel," in 22:6. The structure of 1:1 is relatively complex, as indicated by the presence of parallel clauses identified by H. Reichelt (*Angelus,* 39), though he presents them in logical rather than in actual order:

| | θεός<br>God | |
|---|---|---|
| ἔδωκεν<br>gave | | ἀποστείλας<br>by sending |
| 'Ιησοῦς Χριστός<br>Jesus Christ | | διὰ τοῦ ἀγγέλου αὐτοῦ<br>through his angel |
| δεῖξαι<br>to show | | ἐσήμανεν<br>he made known |
| τοῖς δούλος αὐτοῦ<br>to his servants | | τῷ δούλῳ αὐτοῦ 'Ιωάννῃ<br>to his servant John |

This comparison is instructive in that it reveals the equality that John recognized between himself and the Christians he was addressing.

**1c** καὶ ἐσήμανεν ἀποστείλας διὰ τοῦ ἀγγέλου αὐτοῦ τῷ δούλῳ αὐτοῦ Ἰωάννῃ, "which he made known by sending his angel to his servant John." The subject of the verb ἐσήμανεν, "he made known," is ambiguous; it could be either God or Jesus Christ, though the latter is logically more probable since the revelation was transmitted by God to Jesus Christ, and it must be Jesus Christ who then further communicates the revelation. The verb σημαίνειν, meaning "to indicate clearly" (Louw-Nida, § 33.153; see Acts 25:27), occurs only here in Revelation and appears to be in tension with the symbolic and enigmatic character of much of what follows. Yet σημαίνειν is used in prophetic or oracular contexts where the meaning of the prophecy or oracle is not completely clear; see the famous saying of Heraclitus about the Oracle of Delphi preserved in Plutarch *De Pyth. orac.* 404E: οὔτε λέγει, οὔτε κρύπτει, ἀλλὰ σημαίνει, "[Apollo] neither declares nor conceals but signifies" (Diels-Kranz, *FVS* 1:172; frag. B93). This refers to the fact that the Delphic oracle gave ambiguous advice using images and riddles and that such advice required interpretation (see Kahn, *Heraclitus,* 121–23). σημαίνειν is also used in other oracular or revelatory contexts. In Greek *1 Enoch* 106:13, σημαίνειν is used of the communication of a vision seen by Enoch, and in Greek *1 Enoch* 107:2, Enoch tells Methuselah to reveal the substance of Enoch's dream to Lamech (σήμανον Λάμεχ), that Lamech's child Noah is really his own child. In Ezekiel Trag. *Exagoge* 83, Raguel interprets a dream that Moses had by saying that καλόν σοι τοῦτ' ἐσήμηνεν θεός, "God signified this to you for good." In Acts 11:28 (see *TDNT* 7:264), a prophecy of Agabus is introduced with the phrase ἐσήμαινεν διὰ τοῦ πνεύματος, "he indicated through the Spirit." The verb σημαίνειν occurs three times in John, all in the context of Jesus "indicating" by what death he would die (John 12:33; 18:32; 21:19); i.e., Jesus predicted his death by using the phrase "lifted up" as an ambiguous description of his impending crucifixion. In Rev 1:1, σημαίνειν cannot mean "to indicate clearly." By using the term σημαίνειν, the author expresses the difficulty in understanding the revelation narrated in the text that follows, and perhaps even emphasizes the necessity of informed interpretation.

One characteristic feature of apocalyptic literature is the presence of a stock literary figure who functions as a supernatural mediator, an *angelus interpres,* "interpreting angel," who begins to appear in late OT prophecy (Ezek 40–48; Zech 1–6; Dan 7–12). This *angelus interpres* may have developed by analogy to revelatory dialogues between God and a human recipient of revelation, i.e., passages in which God himself provides an interpretation of a vision (Jer 1:11–13; Job 38–42:6). In later Jewish apocalyptic the *deus interpres* occurs in the same compositions as an *angelus interpres* (*Apoc. Abr.* 20–31; 2 *Apoc. Bar.* 22:1–30:5; 39:1–43:3; 50:1–51:16 [thereafter the *angelus interpres* appears]; 4 Ezra 8:37–9:25; 13:20–56; cf. Reichelt, *Angelus,* 11). Thereafter, with increasing frequency in early Jewish apocalyptic, that which the seer sees and hears, whether on earth or heaven, is explained by the *angelus interpres* through a question-and-answer dialogue. Examples include Uriel and Enoch in *1 Enoch* 21:5–10; Raphael and Enoch in *1 Enoch* 22:1–14; 26:1–27:5; Raguel and Enoch in *1 Enoch* 23:1–4; Michael and Enoch in *1 Enoch* 24:1–25:7; Uriel and Ezra in 4 Ezra 4:1–5:13; 5:31–6:34; 7:1–8:19 (for further references and discussion, see M. Mach, *Engelglaubens,* 142–44; H. Reichelt, *Angelus,* 34–136). In Revelation, however, the first appearance of an *angelus interpres* in the narrative is in 17:1–18, while the second appearance of possibly the same angelic guide is described in 21:9–22:5 (in both passages the angel is identified as one of the bowl angels of Rev 16, though it remains unclear whether the author intends the audience to understand that the *same* bowl angel is involved in both passages). The presence of the definite article with this first occurrence of the term ἄγγελος suggests that John had a very specific angel in mind, one whom he assumed was known to his audience, the angel primarily responsible for mediating divine revelation from God through Christ to John. It is curious that the notion of a single angelic guide responsible for mediating divine revelation to John is mentioned only in the prologue (1:1–8) and epilogue (22:6–21) and is contradicted by the variety of supernatural revealers found throughout the book (the exalted Christ, 1:9–20; 4:1; one of the twenty-four elders, 7:13–17; the bowl angel[s], 17:1–18; 21:9–22:5).

Evidence for a conception of supernatural ἄγγελοι who mediate divine revelation is also found in the Greco-Roman world (Michl, "Engel I (heidnisch)," *RAC* 5:53–60). The belief in angels began to gain currency in Hellenistic pagan beliefs by the first century A.D. if not somewhat earlier. In the Greek magical papyri, when a god or goddess is summoned, he or she occasionally sends ἄγγελοι in his or her place. In *PGM* XIII.608–11: εἰσελεύσεται ἄγγελος, καὶ λέγε τῷ ἀγγέλῳ . . . , "A messenger will enter, and tell that messenger . . ." In a spell directed to Selene-Hekate, the goddess is asked to "send forth your angel from among those who assist you" (*PGM* VII.891), and again "Hear my words and send forth your angel" (*PGM* VII.898). An inscription from Lydia from A.D. 164/5 concludes: "So the god [Men] gave orders through an angel [ὁ θεὸς οὖν ἐκέλευσε δι' ἀνγέλου] that the cloak should be sold and his powers written upon a stele" (Sheppard, *Talanta* 12–13 [1980–81] 92–93). (2) *PGM* VII.833–36: "Also you [do I call upon] as many of you angels [ἄγγελοι] who are placed under his power. Hence, I call upon you all that you may come quickly in this night and reveal to me clearly and firmly, concerning those matters I desire." (3) *PGM* VII.839–41: "Hence, I call upon you in this night, and may you reveal all things to me through dreams with accuracy, O angel ZIZAUBIO." (4) In *PGM* I.73–81, the practitioner is told that he will see a sign consisting of a star falling on his housetop that is actually an angel from whom he will learn the decisions of the gods (θεῶν δὲ βουλὰς). Other references to ἄγγελοι that appear to magicians include *PGM* I.172, 176; IV.3024–25, 3166; XII.118; XIII.73, 585. In *PGM* V.108–14, two phrases are parallel constructions, "I am Moses your prophet [προφήτης]," and "I am the angel [ἄγγελος] of Pharaoh Osoronnophris." Here the terms "prophet" and "angel" are synonyms. There are inscriptions from Anatolia that link "highest Zeus and the divine angel [Διὶ ὑψίστῳ καὶ θείῳ ἀνγέλῳ]," or "highest Zeus and the good angel," or "highest Zeus and the divine heavenly angel" (see Mitchell, *Anatolia* 2:45–46). These texts distinguish two divine beings, Zeus and an associated divine being, which should perhaps be interpreted as the heavenly messenger of Zeus.

In the phrase τῷ δούλῳ αὐτοῦ Ἰωάννῃ, "his servant John," δοῦλος (in addition to the associations of the term discussed above under *Comment* on 1:1b) may also be understood from the OT and early Jewish literature and in NT epistolary literature as a title of *honor* (Sass, *ZNW* 40 [1941] 30–32; Martin, *Slavery,* 51–60).

In the client-patron structure of society during the period of Roman Hellenism, a δοῦλος could function as the agent of his master, possessing a representative authority (Martin, *Slavery*, 58). The designation "servant of God," "his [i.e. 'God's'] servant," or "servant of the Lord" is used of famous OT figures such as Abraham (Ps 105:6, 42), Isaac (2 Macc 1:2; Pr Azar 12), Jacob (2 Macc 1:2; Bar 3:36), Moses (Josh 9:24; 14:7; 1 Kgs 8:56; Ps 105:26; 1 Chr 6:49; 2 Chr 24:9; Neh 10:29; Dan 9:11; Jos. *Ant.* 5.39; Bar 1:20; 2:28; 4QpDibHam; Rev 15:3), Joshua (Josh 24:29; Judg 2:8), David (1 Macc 4:30; 2 Esdr 3:23; 1QM 11:2), Hezekiah (2 Chr 32:16), Zerubbabel (1 Esdr 6:27), and Daniel (Dan 6:20). By the end of the first century A.D. the term δοῦλος had already become a common self-designation for Christian leaders in epistolary superscriptions (Rom 1:1; Phil 1:1; Titus 1:1; Jas 1:1; 2 Pet 1:1; Jude 1; cf. Rev 1:1[2]), a self-designation that gained stature by association with the term "apostle," clearly a title of honor (Rom 1:1; Titus 1:1; 2 Pet 1:1; see Martin, *Slavery*, 54–60). Martin argues that slaves in the world of Roman Hellenism were frequently upwardly mobile and that as agents of their masters they wielded a considerable degree of authority and power in the context of the patron-client structure of society (*Slavery*, 57–59). This convention is, incidentally, completely missing from the twelve Christian letters found in the heterogeneous collection of documents called the Apostolic Fathers. The term δοῦλος is also used to refer to Christian leaders in the parables of Jesus (Matt 18:23–35 [vv 23, 26, 27, 28, 32]; 21:33–51 [vv 34–36]; 24:45–51 [vv 45, 46, 48, 50]; Luke 12:41–46 [vv 43, 45, 46]; see Martin, *Slavery*, 52–53). In Acts 16:17, a girl who is possessed addresses Paul and Barnabas as "slaves [δοῦλοι] of the most high God," a designation intended to be understood positively. Just as "servant" is used as a self-designation by courtiers and supplicants of earthly kings, so the term "servant" is often used as a self-designation by those who pray to God (2 Sam 7:20; 1 Kgs 8:28; Ps 27:9; Dan 9:17; Sir 36:17; 2 Esdr 5:56; 7:102; 8:24; Luke 2:29). The author of the *Hôdāyôt* or Hymns of the Qumran Community, for example, referred to himself when addressing God in prayer as "thy servant" (1QH 13:18; 17:25; cf. 1QS 11:16). In the letter of Baruch to Jeremiah in *Par. Jer.* 6:19, Baruch uses the self-predication "servant of God" (cf. Baruch's prayer in 6:13, where he associates himself with "your [God's] servants"). Here the designation "servant of God" means one who subordinates himself or herself to God and lives obediently and humbly before God, and thus is a righteous or just person able to call confidently on the Lord in prayer (cf. Delling, "Attribute," 27). By referring to Christians generally as servants of God and himself as a servant of God, John places himself on the same plane as those to whom he is writing (H. Reichelt, *Angelus*, 42). His authority is not based on any superior social role he might have but rather is grounded in the revelation that he mediates to the Christian communities to whom he writes.

In the Greek magical papyri, the practitioner occasionally calls himself a δοῦλος, as in *PGM* XII.71, "the servant of the most high God [δοῦλός εἰμι τοῦ ὑψίστου θεοῦ]" (cf. Acts 16:17), and *PGM* XIII.637, "I am your servant [δοῦλός εἰμι σός]." In Rev 10:7; 11:18, prophets are called "servants of God." It has been suggested that the term δοῦλος has prophetic overtones for John (Kraft, 21–22, 50). Kraft suggests that the term ἄγγελος, "messenger," in Rev 1:1; 22:16, originally referred to John and emends τῷ δούλῳ αὐτοῦ Ἰωάννῃ, "to his servant John," in 1:1 to τοῦ δούλου αὐτοῦ Ἰωάννου, "his servant John," so that the entire prepositional phrase reads "through his messenger, his servant John." However, this view is doubtful

(Satake, *Gemeindeordnung*, 87–96). The technical phrase "my/thy servants the prophets" is frequently found in the OT (2 Kgs 9:7; 17:13, 23; 21:10; 24:2; Ezra 9:11; Jer 7:25; 25:4; 26:5; 29:19; 35:15; Ezek 38:17; Dan 9:6, 10; Amos 3:7; Zech 1:6); individual prophets are also singled out as "servants of God," such as Isaiah (2 Esdr 2:18) and Jeremiah (2 Esdr 2:18). The phrase "my/thy servants the prophets" also occurs occasionally in the Pseudepigrapha (1 Esdr 8:82; 2 Esdr 1:32; 2:1; Bar 2:20, 24) and several times in the Dead Sea Scrolls (1QpHab 2:9; 7:5; 1QS 1:3; 4QpHos[b] 2:5; 4QpDibHam 3:12). The Egyptian priest called "the servant of God" (*hem neter*) was uniformly translated into Greek using the term προφήτης, "prophet," because the *hem neter* was drawn from a priestly group from which an official spokesman was chosen to report oracular responses from a god; this priest was therefore called *hem neter wechem*, "the servant of God who reports" (Kees, *ZASA* 85 [1960] 138–43).

The author of Revelation tells us four times that his name is "John" (1:1, 4, 9; 22:8). Ἰωάννης is a Greek transliteration of the Hebrew name *Yohanan* (יוֹחָנָן *yôḥānān* or יְהוֹחָנָן *yĕhôḥānān*), a theophoric name meaning "Yahweh is [or 'has been'] gracious" (2 Kgs 25:3; 1 Chr 26:3; Ezra 10:6; Neh 6:18; 12:22; Jer 40:8).

The Greek name Ἰωάννης is not a hypocoristic form of יוֹחָנָן *yôḥānān* or יְהוֹחָנָן *yĕhôḥānān* but simply a transliteration of the Hebrew form of the name into Greek with the addition of the Greek masculine ending -ης; see G. Mussies, "Jewish Personal Names in Some Non-Literary Sources," in *Studies in Early Jewish Epigraphy*, ed. J. W. van Henten and P. W. van der Horst (Leiden: Brill, 1994) 242–76. How frequently does the name Ἰωάννης occur in the Hellenistic and Roman period? The answer to this question has a bearing on the question of whether Revelation is a pseudepigraphon. If the name "John" was uncommon, the possibility of pseudepigraphy is made more plausible, providing there is a famous person by that name whom the recipients of Revelation would assume was its author. In the later first century Asia Minor, there are two such possibilities, John the Apostle and John the Elder. A survey of the evidence suggests that it is not correct to claim that the name Ἰωάννης seldom occurs in the pre-Christian period (*EWNT* 2:518). Rather, "John" appears to have been a relatively common Jewish name in the Hellenistic period. Seventeen different men named Ἰωάννης are mentioned in Josephus (A. Schalit, *Namenwörterbuch zu Flavius Josephus* [Leiden: Brill, 1968]; A. Schlatter, "Die hebräischen Namen bei Josephus," in *Kleiner Schriften zu Flavius Josephus*, ed. K. H. Rengstorf [Darmstadt: Wissenschaftliche Buchgesellschaft, 1970] 168), five different people named Ἰωάννης are mentioned in the Jewish papyri (*CPJ* 3:182), three different individuals in 1 Maccabees, and six different individuals in the NT (Odelain-Séguineau, *Lexicon*, 186–87). However, just one person named "John" appears in the major corpus of Jewish inscriptions, *CIJ* 1:517 (no. 717, lines 17, 47). The name "John" does not occur in the Aphrodisias inscription (Reynolds, *Aphrodisias*) or in Philo of Alexandria.

This repetition of the author's name, together with the frequent use of first-person singular verb forms that regularly punctuate the vision narratives, serves to emphasize his role as a witness to the revelatory visions he narrates, a phenomenon with parallels in other Jewish apocalypses (Dan 7:2, 15; 8:1; 9:2; 10:2; 4 Ezra 2:33, 42; 3:1; *3 Apoc. Bar.* 1:1, 7; 4:1, 9; 5:1 [the name "Baruch" occurs even more frequently in the Slavonic version, doubtless revealing a literary tendency]). The repetition of the name of the ostensible author was doubtless part of a legitimization strategy in pseudonymous compositions, particularly apocalypses. Since Revelation is an apocalypse, it would be natural for a modern interpreter to assume that the name "John" is a pseudonym (Becker, *BZ* 13 [1969] 101–2; Vanni, "L'Apocalypse," 28 n. 6; Strecker, *KD* 38 [1992] 33; P. Vielhauer and G. Strecker in Schneemelcher, *NTA* 2:529 [German ed.]). It is striking that the name "John" only appears in the framework of Revelation (1:1–3:21; 22:6–21) and not in the main part of the composition (4:1–22:5).

**2a** ὃς ἐμαρτύρησεν τὸν λόγον τοῦ θεοῦ καὶ τὴν μαρτυρίαν Ἰησοῦ Χριστοῦ ὅσα εἶδεν, "who now bears witness to all the visions he saw which is the message from God, that is, the witness borne by Jesus." The verb μαρτυρεῖν, "to witness," occurs only here and in 22:16, 18, 20, and therefore probably belongs to the latest version of Revelation (see *Introduction,* Section 5: Source Criticism). In other early Christian texts, cognates of μαρτ- are used for the proclamation of the Gospel (Acts 10:42–43; 18:5; 20:21; Eph 4:17). The phrase ὁ λόγος τοῦ θεοῦ, "the word/ message of God," occurs seven times in Revelation (1:2, 9; 6:9; 17:17 [plural: οἱ λόγοι τοῦ θεοῦ]; 19:9 [plural: οὗτοι οἱ λόγοι ἀληθινοὶ τοῦ θεοῦ]; 19:13; 20:4). Four times the phrases "the word of God" and "the testimony by Jesus" are closely associated or virtually equated (1:2, 9; 6:9; 20:4). John's use of this phrase suggests that he considers himself a prophet in the tradition of the OT prophets who received the word of God (Hos 1:1; Joel 1:1; Jer 1:2, 4, 11). In the LXX the phrase λόγος κυρίου, "word of the Lord," is a stereotypical formula used to categorize a sequence of revelatory experiences (Zech 1:1; Jonah 1:1; Mic 1:1; Zeph 1:1). It is possible that the καί joining "the word of God" and "the witness of Jesus Christ" is epexegetical; i.e., "the word of God" is further defined by the phrase "the witness of Jesus Christ." It is possible to understand the phrase "the witness of Jesus Christ" in two ways; i.e., "of Jesus" is either a subjective genitive, "the witness borne by Jesus," or an objective genitive, "the witness about Jesus Christ." The first alternative seems more likely, because in Revelation the witness is given by the subject of the phrase (6:9; 11:7; 12:11; 20:4; see Strathman, *TDNT* 4:500; Trites, *Witness,* 156–58). This further suggests that the phrase τὴν μαρτυρίαν Ἰησοῦ Χριστοῦ, "the testimony borne by Jesus," i.e., "what Jesus testifies," means "the contents of the book" (Dehandschutter, "Witness," 285), because it is followed by "whatever he saw."

ὅσα, a neuter plural accusative correlative adjective from ὅσος, is used here to denote size or quantity and emphasizes the completeness of the revelation transmitted by John. Since this clause is in apposition to the accusative noun cluster "the message from God, namely, the testimony by Jesus," John claims to have *seen* a message, a striking idiom probably based on the usage of OT prophetic books (see Amos 1:1: "the words of Amos which he *saw*"; Hab 1:1: "the oracle of God which Habakkuk *saw*").

**3** μακάριος ὁ ἀναγινώσκων καὶ οἱ ἀκούοντες τοὺς λόγους τῆς προφητείας καὶ τηροῦντες τὰ ἐν αὐτῇ γεγραμμένα ὁ γὰρ καιρὸς ἐγγύς, "How fortunate is the one who reads aloud and those who both hear these prophetic words and obey what is written herein, for the time is near." This is the first of seven beatitudes or makarisms in Revelation (14:13; 16:15; 19:9; 20:6; 22:7, 14). It is very similar to the beatitude found in Rev 22:7, and both beatitudes may be derived from Luke 11:28 (cf. John 12:47) or the tradition underlying that saying: "Blessed rather are those who hear the word of God and keep it!" The saying in John 12:47a is a negative parallel: "If anyone hears my sayings and does not keep them, I do not judge him." The emphasis on *hearing* and *doing* the word of God is also found in

Luke 8:21; 12:47; Matt 7:24–27 = Luke 6:47–49; Rom 2:13; Jas 1:22; see Ezek 33:31–32. This use of a saying of Jesus is unusual because, unlike other sayings in Revelation with close parallels in the Synoptic tradition, this one is not attributed to Jesus. Both Rev 1:3 (and 22:7) and Luke 11:28 are expressed in the form of a beatitude. The content of the beatitude in both texts uses substantival participial constructions referring to οἱ ἀκούοντες, "those who hear," and τηροῦντες, "those who keep." The object of ἀκούοντες in Rev 1:3 is "the words of prophecy," while in Luke 11:28 it is "the word of God." There is an interesting parallel in an inscription from the synagogue in Sardis (which may refer to the opening of a Torah scroll) where verbs for reading and obeying also occur together: Εὑρὼν κλάσας ἀναγνῶθι φύλαξον, "Having found and having broken open, read and observe" (Trebilco, *Jewish Communities*, 51). Since John has just referred to himself as ὁ ἐμαρτύρησεν τὸ λόγον τοῦ θεοῦ, "who now bears witness to the word of God" (1:2), he clearly equates "the words of prophecy" with "the word of God." There can be little doubt that John refers here to a traditional saying of Jesus preserved in Luke 11:28: "But he [Jesus] said: Blessed rather are those who hear the word of God and obey it!" There are four possible ways of understanding his use of this saying. First, it could have been adapted by John directly from Luke 11:28 (unlikely). Second, it could have been drawn from oral tradition and used independently in Luke 11:28 and Rev 1:3 (Boismard, "Rapprochements," 53–63; Vos, *Synoptic Traditions*, 54–60). Third (more specifically than the previous possibility), as a saying of Jesus drawn from oral tradition, it could have entered Christian discourse as a saying suitable for use in certain settings such as Luke 11:28; Rev 1:3; 22:7. Fourth, the beatitude could have been a pronouncement used orally in connection with the reading of Scripture in Christian services of worship and from there entered Luke 11:28; Rev 1:3; 22:7 by different routes.

The third possibility is probably correct, for Luke 11:28 is a Lukan formulation. A parallel in an apocalyptic setting is found in the Greek text of *1 Enoch* 99:10, "And then blessed are all who hear [οἱ ἀκούσαντες] the words of the wise and learn them that they might obey the commands of the Most High [ποιῆσαι τὰς ἐντολὰς τοῦ ὑψίστου]." A close parallel is the acclamation of the people of Rome to Nero when he returned from Greece, as reported by Dio Cassius 62.20.5, Μακάριοι οἵ σου ἀκούοντες, "Blessed are those who hear you!" In the context, Nero is greeted as a god.

The reference to "the one who reads aloud," i.e., the lector, is so translated because ancient texts were nearly always read aloud (Balogh, *Philologus* 82 [1927] 213; Balogh's exaggerations are corrected by Knox, *GRBS* 9 [1968] 421–35). Terms for reading and hearing (ἀναγνῶναι—ἀκούειν; *legere—audire*) were often used synonymously (Herodotus 1.48), or together as an idiomatic expression referring to two aspects of a single activity. Ancients who read silently (with lips moving but with no audible sound) were rare; they include Alexander the Great (Plutarch *De fortuna Alex.* 340A), Julius Caesar (Plutarch *Brut.* 5.3), Ambrose (Augustine *Conf.* 6.3), and Augustine (Augustine *Conf.* 8.12). The ability to read silently is also assumed in Attic drama (Euripides *Hippolytus* 856–74; Aristophanes *Knights* 116–27), while it is entertained as a possibility for rhetoricians memorizing speeches (Quintilian 11.32–34) and for female catechumens who were forbidden to speak in church (Cyril of Jerusalem *Procatechesis* 14); see Slusser, *JBL* 111 (1992) 499, and especially Gilliard, *JBL* 112 [1993] 689–94, in which most of the extant evidence is carefully discussed. In many ancient texts terms for "read" and "hear" are used synonymously (as in Rev 1:3), since reading was always audible because it was always done aloud (Herodotus 1.48; Augustine *Ep.* 147; *Conf.* 10.3; Cassiodorus *Inst. div. lec.* 1.29; Balogh, *Philologus* 82 [1927] 206–10; Henrikson, *CJ* 25 [1929–30] 182–90). This insight has important interpretive significance, for ancient authors not only chose words to convey the meanings they intended but also chose words whose *sounds* effectively communicated those meanings (Stanford, *Sound of Greek,* 77–78). Since most Jewish apocalypses are pseudepigraphic (i.e., written in the name of a famous ancient Israelite), they were not designed to be read to a group (two possible exceptions are *Apoc. Elijah* 1:13 and *Apoc. Zeph.* 8:5) but were intended for private rather than public reading (Lebram, "The Piety of the Jewish Apocalypses," in *Apocalypticism,* ed. D. Hellholm, 173). A feature unique to Revelation and the *Shepherd of Hermas* is that they were explicitly intended for oral performance (Rev 1:3; 22:18; cf. Hermas *Vis.* 2.4.3; 1.3.3–4). References to the reading of letters in congregations is found in 1 Thess 5:27; Col 4:16; since Revelation has an epistolary framework, the author may be capitalizing on this practice. In the phrases οἱ ἀκούοντες ... καὶ τηροῦντες, "those who hear ... and keep," the blessing pronounced applies only to those who *both* hear and keep the words of John's book, since the article goes with both substantival participles.

The term προφητεία refers to the *written composition,* as the phrase "the things written in *it*" (i.e., in the prophecy) suggests. The closest term in Hebrew is נְבוּאָה *nĕbû'â,* which is translated προφητεία three times in the LXX (2 Chr 15:8; 2 Esdr 6:14; Neh 6:12). For examples of προφητεία meaning "written prophecy," see 2 Chr 32:32, ἰδοὺ γέγραπται ἐν τῇ προφητείᾳ Ησαιου, "Behold it is written in the prophecy [i.e., 'prophetic book'] of Isaiah"; cf. 2 Esdr 6:14; Matt 13:14. προφητεία can also refer to the oral *proclamation* itself (LXX 2 Chr 15:8; 2 Esdr 5:1; 6:14; Jer 23:31). The term λόγοι, particularly since it occurs in the plural, could be taken to mean "oracles."

The phrase ὁ γὰρ καιρὸς ἐγγύς, "for the time is near," provides reason for listening to and obeying John's revelatory book. The identical phrase occurs at the conclusion of the book in Rev 22:10, but nowhere else in Revelation does ὁ καιρός occur with a similar meaning, with the possible exception of 11:18, where ὁ καιρός is the time for judging the dead and rewarding the righteous. Here ὁ καιρός refers to ἃ δεῖ γενέσθαι ἐν τάχει, "events which must quickly come to pass," mentioned in v 1 and certainly includes the imminent return of Jesus mentioned in 22:7, 20 (ἔρχομαι ταχύ). ὁ καιρός (which can mean a point in time or a period of time, like χρόνος) is an important technical eschatological term (indicated by the presence of the definite article), which refers to the impending crisis that will overtake the world and that involves a traditional program of eschatological events. The phrase ὁ καιρὸς ἤγγικεν, "the time is near" (Luke 21:8), the claim of false prophets, is virtually synonymous with ὁ καιρὸς ἐγγύς (Rev 1:3), and both may be dependent on the phrase "and the time arrived" (Aram. וְזִמְנָא מְטָה *wĕzimnā' mĕṭâ*) in Dan 7:22, translated ὁ καιρὸς ἔφθασεν, "the time has come," in Theodotion and ὁ καιρὸς ἐδόθη, "the time is appointed," in the LXX, referring to the time when the holy ones receive the kingdom. The connection between the arrival of ὁ καιρός and the kingdom of God is also found in Mark 1:15, where it is said that πεπλήρωται ὁ καιρὸς καὶ ἤγγικεν ἡ βασιλεία τοῦ θεοῦ, "the time is fulfilled, the kingdom of God is near." The phrase πρὸ καιροῦ, "before the time" (Matt 8:29; 1 Cor 4:5), also appears to refer to the final judgment. The time of judgment is also described with the phrase ἐν τῷ ἐσχάτῳ καιρῷ, "in the last time," in *Did.* 16:2 and ὑστατίῳ καιρῷ, "in the last time," in *Sib. Or.* 5.74, 348, 361, but most other uses of καιρός and χρόνος (and related temporal terms) in the singular or plural refer to events that will characterize the period immediately preceding the end but not the end itself, e.g., ἔσχατοι καιροί, "the last times" (Ign. *Eph.* 11:1), ἔσχατος καιρός, "the last time" (1 Pet 1:5), ἔσχατος χρόνος, "last time" (Jude 18), ἐσχάτη ὥρα, "last hour" (1 John 2:18[2x]), ἔσχατοι χρόνοι, "last times" (1 Pet 1:20), ἐσχάτη ἡμέρα, "last day" (John 6:39, 40, 44, 54; 11:24; 12:48), ἔσχατοι ἡμέραι, "last days" (Jas 5:3; 2 Pet 3:3; 2 Tim 3:1; see Heb 1:2).

### Explanation

The first sentence in Revelation functions as the author's own descriptive title of his composition, like the initial sentences in many Greco-Roman and early Jewish works. Revelation was originally written on a papyrus roll. According to ancient literary conventions, the shortest possible title of a composition (i.e., the name of the work in one word and the author's name in the genitive), often abstracted from the first sentence, was inserted at the end of a composition and called a subscription. With the development of the codex or page format, titles were moved to the beginning of works. The earliest form of the subscription of Revelation is "Apocalypse of John." It is remotely possible that the author himself formulated this subscription. When the codex form was widely adopted by Christians in the second century, the subscription was moved to the beginning of Revelation, analogous to the same change in other works, where it became a *superscription*. Although the NRSV construes the genitive as an objective genitive by translating the title "Revelation to John" (a meaning that fits the sense of 1:2), the many analogies in ancient titles suggest that the appropriate translation is "Revelation *of* [i.e. 'by'] John." The term "revelation" in 1:1 refers not to the literary form of Revelation but rather to the revelatory experience of the author on the basis of which the book was written.

The title provides divine authority for the entire book by giving the stages by which the revelation was mediated to John: God gave it to Jesus Christ, who transmitted it through his angel to his servant John for the benefit of the servants of God, i.e., the Christians associated with the seven churches to which the work is addressed. Jewish and Greco-Roman apocalypses often use a single otherworldly figure to mediate revelatory visions and auditions. However, the notion of a principal angelic mediator, mentioned only in the prologue and epilogue, is in tension with the main part of the book, where such an *angelus interpres,* "interpreting angel," appears only in Rev 17:1–18; 21:9–22:6. This apparent discrepancy is one indication that the composition of Revelation took place in stages and that the many discrete vision reports incorporated into the book have been welded into a new (though by no means consistent) unity by the author. John, the recipient of this revelation, reports in the third person that he has faithfully borne witness to the word of God and to the testimony of Jesus.

The first of seven beatitudes is placed here (cf. 14:13; 16:15; 19:9; 20:6; 22:7, 14). John's preference for the number seven both as a symbolic number and an organizational principle suggests that the inclusion of precisely *seven* beatitudes, though unnumbered, is hardly accidental. This pronouncement of blessing upon reader and upon those who both hear and obey (repeated in 22:7) is very likely based on the practice of beginning or concluding readings or presentations of the words of God (whether Scripture or other types of revelatory messages) with various "read and keep" or "hear and obey" formulas often connected with a beatitude (Matt 7:24, 26; cf. Luke 6:47, 49; Luke 11:20; John 12:47; Hermas *Vis.* 5.5; *2 Clem.* 19:1–3). This verse also makes it evident that the author intended, even designed, his composition to be read aloud before Christian congregations assembled for worship. Since he calls his book "the words of this prophecy" (NIV) and the prophetic books of the Hebrew Bible had been included in synagogue services as readings complementary to readings from the Pentateuch, John places his book on an equal footing with OT Scripture.

# C. Epistolary Prescript (1:4–5c)

*Bibliography*

**Berger, K.** "Apostelbrief und apostolische Rede: Zum Formular frühchristlicher Briefe." *ZNW* 65 (1974) 191–207. ———. "'Gnade' im frühen Christentum." *NedTTs* 27 (1973) 1–25. **Bickerman, E.** "Altars of Gentiles: A Note on the Jewish 'Ius Sacrum.'" In *Studies in Jewish and Christian History.* Part 2. Leiden: Brill, 1980. 324–46. **Bruce, F. F.** "Holy Spirit in the Qumran Texts." ALUOS 6 (1966–68) 49–55. ———. "The Spirit in the Apocalypse." In *Christ and Spirit in the New Testament.* FS C. F. D. Moule, ed. B. Lindars and S. Smalley. Cambridge: Cambridge UP, 1973. 333–44. **Burney, C. F.** "A Hebraic Construction in Rev." *JTS* 22 (1920–21) 371–76. **Dix, G. H.** "The Seven Archangels and the Seven Spirits." *JTS* 28 (1927) 233–50. **Doty, W. G.** *Letters in Primitive Christianity.* Philadelphia: Fortress, 1973. **Exler, F. X. J.** *The Form of the Ancient Greek Letter of the Epistolary Papyri (3rd c. B.C.–3rd c. A.D.): A Study in Greek Epistolography.* Washington, DC: The Catholic University of America, 1923. **Ford, J. M.** "'He that Cometh' and the Divine Name (Apocalypse 1:4, 8; 4:8)." *JSJ* 1 (1970) 144–47. **Friedrich, G.** "Lohmeyer's These über 'Das paulinische Briefpräscript' kritisch beleuchtet." *ZNW* 46 (1955) 272–74. **Helyer, L. R.** "The Prototokos Title in Hebrews." *SBT* 6 (1976) 3–28. **Hockel, A.** *Christus der Erstgeborene: Zur Geschichte der Exegese von Kol. 15.* Düsseldorf, 1965. **Joüon, P.** "Apocalypse 1:4." *RSR* 21 (1931) 486–87. **Kavanagh, M. A.** *Apocalypse 22:6–21 as Concluding Liturgical Dialogue.* Rome: Pontifical Gregorian University, 1984. **Lieu, J. M.** "'Grace to You and Peace': The Apostolic Greeting." *BJRL* 68 (1985) 161–78. **Lohmeyer, E.** "Probleme paulinischer Theologie I: Briefliche Grussüberschriften." *ZNW* 26 (1927) 158–73. **Michaelis, W.** "Die biblische Vorstellung von Christus als dem Erstgeborenen." *ZST* 23 (1954) 137–67. **Nilsson, M. P.** "Zwei Altäre aus Pergamon." *Eranos* 54 (1956) 167–73. **Osten-Sacken, P. von der.** "Christologie, Taufe, Homologie: Ein Beitrag zu Apc. 1:5f." *ZNW* 58 (1967) 255–66. **Robb, J. D.** "Ho erchomenos ('Who is to Come'—NEB)." *ExpTim* 73 (1961–62) 338–39. **Roller, O.** *Das Formular der paulinischen Briefe.* Stuttgart: Kohlhammer, 1933. **Schlütz, K.** *Isaias 11:2 (die sieben Gaben des hl. Geistes) in den ersten vier Jahrhunderten.* Münster: Aschendorff, 1932. **Schneider, J.** "Brief." *RAC* (1954) 2, cols. 563–85. **Schnider, F.,** and **Stenger, W.** *Studien zum neutestamentlichen Briefformular.* Leiden: Brill, 1987. **Schüssler Fiorenza, E.** "Redemption as Liberation: Apoc 1:5f. and 5:9f." *CBQ* 36 (1974)

220–32. **Schweizer, E.** "Die sieben Geister in der Apokalypse." *EvT* 11 (1951–52) 502–12. **Sekki, A. E.** *The Meaning of RUAH at Qumran.* SBLDS 110. Atlanta: Scholars, 1989. **Stowers, S.** *Letter Writing in Greco-Roman Antiquity.* Philadelphia: Westminster, 1986. **Strugnell, J.** "The Angelic Liturgy at Qumran." In *Congress Volume.* VTSup 7. Leiden: Brill, 1960. 318–45. **Sukutris, I.** "Epistolographie." RESup 5 (1931) 210–11. **Swete, H. B.** *The Holy Spirit in the New Testament.* London: Macmillan, 1910. **Vanni, U.** "Liturgical Dialogue as a Literary Form in the Book of Revelation." *NTS* 37 (1991) 348–72. ———. "Un esempio di dialogo liturgico in Ap 1,4–8." *Bib* 57 (1976) 453–67. **White, J. L.** *The Body of the Greek Letter.* 2nd ed. Missoula, MT: Scholars, 1972. ———. *Light from Ancient Letters.* Philadelphia: Fortress, 1986. ———. "New Testament Epistolary Literature in the Framework of Ancient Epistolography." *ANRW* II, 25/2:1730–56. ———. "Saint Paul and the Apostolic Letter Tradition." *CBQ* 145 (1983) 433–44. **Yarbro Collins, A.** "Numerical Symbolism in Jewish and Early Christian Apocalyptic Literature." *ANRW* II, 21/1:1221–87.

## Translation

[4]*John to the*[a] *seven churches in Asia. Grace and peace to you from*[b] [c]*the One who is and who was and who is coming*[d] *and from the seven spirits* [e]*which are*[e] *before his throne* [5]*and from Jesus Christ,* [a]*the faithful witness,*[a] *the firstborn from*[b] *the dead, and the ruler of the kings*[c] *of the earth.*

## Notes

4.a. The presence of the definite article in Eng. conveys the erroneous impression that there were but seven churches in the Roman province of Asia. There were more than just the seven named in v 1, but these seven form a group with special significance for the author.

4.b. Variants: (1) ἀπὸ ὁ ὤν] 𝔓[18] (? illegible, yet no space for τοῦ or θεοῦ) א A C 025 Andreas. (2) ἀπὸ τοῦ ὁ ὤν] Byzantine. (3) ἀπὸ κυρίου ὁ ὤν] Byz 19[2016]. (4) ἀπὸ θεοῦ ὁ ὤν] 046 Oecumenius[2053]. Since the prep. ἀπό is always followed by the gen. case, style-conscious copyists corrected John's grammar by inserting a definite article in the gen., τοῦ, or the gen. form θεοῦ, "God," or κυρίου, "Lord," so that the stereotyped phrase that follows could be construed as a nom. of apposition. It appears, however, that John regarded the entire threefold predication ὁ ὤν καὶ ὁ ἦν καὶ ὁ ἐρχόμενος as an *indeclinable* divine name (Schmid, *Studien* 2:248).

4.c. Variant: (1) omit θεοῦ] 𝔓[18] א A C 025 94 598 fam 1611[2050] lat syr cop Andr e[2026] f[2031 2056 2073corr] g i[1685 2042] n[-2429] Apringius Andreas. (2) insert θεοῦ] 046 Oecumenius[2053] fam 1006[1006 1841] fam 1611[1611 1854 2329] 2351 Andr e[2026] f[2031 2056 2073corr] g i[1685 2042] n[-2429] 94 598 Byzantine Victorinus (*a deo*); Primasius (*a deo;* D G); Tyconius[2] (*a deo patre et a filio hominis*); Beatus (*a deo*). (3) omit τοῦ] 𝔓[18] א A C 025 fam 1611[2050]. (4) insert τοῦ] TR Primasius (*ab eo;* R); Fulgentius; it[gig h] (*ab eo*); vg (*ab eo*) Andr n[2429]. Readings (2) and (4) are obvious attempts to correct the difficult phrase ἀπὸ ὁ ὤν. Further, the interchange of θυ (the way θεοῦ was commonly abbreviated) and τοῦ would be facilitated by their orthographical similarity.

4.d. The entire phrase ὁ ὤν καὶ ὁ ἦν καὶ ὁ ἐρχόμενος consists of three nominative clauses, each with a definite article and linked to the others with the copula καί. Syntactically, three distinct entities could be represented here, yet semantically it is clear that all three noun clauses represent one person, God. The phrases could be correctly translated "he who is and he who was and he who is coming," a rendering as ambiguous as the Gk. The clauses are translated with a single "He" at the beginning to make it clear that one entity is being referred to. Three separate definite articles were probably used by John because of the anomalous ἦν, "was," which he used (ungrammatically) because Gk. has no imperfect ptcp., and the verb εἰμί has no aor. form. John was then compelled to use the article with the final ptcp. ἐρχόμενος.

4.e-e. Variants: (1) ἅ] (𝔓[18]) (though the letters before εν[ω]πιον are not legible, there is space only for ἅ, not τῶν); C fam 1611 Andr i[2042] 94 Byzantine; Tischendorf, *NTGraece;* WHort; B. Weiss, *Johannes-Apokalypse,* 101; Merk, *NT;* Nestle-Aland[27] ; UBSGNT[4]. (2) ἅ ἐστιν] Oecumenius[2053] Andreas. (3) ἅ εἰσιν] Andr e[2029] n[2429] 2019. (4) τῶν] א A 2681 Andr i[-2042] Andr m; Byz 17[241] Andr/Byz 3[1733]; WHort[marg]; Charles (1:11–13, though he rejects the phrase καὶ ἀπὸ τῶν πνευμάτων τῶν ἐνώπιον τοῦ θρόνου αὐτοῦ as an interpolation). Variant (1), the neut. pl. nom. relative pronoun ἅ, translated "which are" (supplying the understood verb ἐστί), is syntactically peculiar in that the pronoun has not been attracted to the case of the noun cluster it modifies (τῶν ἑπτὰ πνευμάτων), in which case it would be ὧν (though no MS exhibits this reading; see Hoskier, *Text* 2:32). This lack of attraction, however, is a phenomenon not uncommon in Revelation (Mayser, *Satzlehre*, 101; Turner, *Syntax*, 324; BDR § 294). Variant (2), ἅ ἐστιν, "which is," supplies the linking verb εἶναι, a natural embellishment since in Revelation the relative pronoun is usually connected with a finite verb, so that the origin of the variant can be explained as an expansion of ἅ, and is supported chiefly by the Andreas commentary tradition. Reading (3) uses the third-person pl. form of εἶναι with a neut. pl. subject. In classical Gk., pl. neut. subjects are usually used with third-person sing. verb forms; in Hellenistic Gk., personal subjects tend to be used with third-person pl. verb forms, while impersonal subjects and pronouns (e.g., ταῦτα, ἅ) tend to be used with third-person sing. verb forms (BDR § 133). Revelation is inconsistent; sing. verbs are used with neut. pl. subjects (e.g., 1:19; 2:27; 4:8; 13:14; 18:14; 19:14; see Charles, 1:cvli), and pl. verbs are also used with neut. pl. subjects (e.g., 1:19; 3:2, 4; 5:14; 9:20; 11:18; 15:4; see Charles, 1:cvli). Reading (4) very probably originated through attraction to the preceding ἀπὸ τῶν ἑπτὰ πνευμάτων (B. Weiss, *Johannes-Apokalypse*, 90; Schmid, *Studien* 2:98).

5.a-a. The noun cluster ὁ μάρτυς ὁ πιστός, "the faithful witness," is a nom. of apposition modifying "Jesus Christ" in the gen. (see Schmid, *Studien* 2:239); this irregular use of the nom. also occurs in 2:13; 20:2 (ptcps. in the appositional nom. are found in 2:20; 3:12; *7:9; 8:9; 9:13; 14:12, *14; *21:12[2x]; asterisked passages have anarthrous ptcps.). Some MS witnesses attempted to correct this solecism by substituting a relative clause: ὃ μάρτυς πιστός ἐστιν] Andr/Byz 4a 4b. While Nestle-Aland[27] and UBSGNT[4] place a comma between ὁ μάρτυς and ὁ πιστός, indicating that these are two separate predications of Jesus rather than a single restrictive attributive noun cluster, it is more natural to take the adjective πιστός as standing in an attributive relation to ὁ μαρτύς. If ὁ μάρτυς ὁ πιστός is regarded as a single predicate, then a total of *three* predications are found in v 5, and groups of *three* are favored by John; see Norden, *Agnostos Theos*, 351: "The Apocalyptist really indulges in triadic formulas" (he then lists the following examples: 1:4, 8, 9, 17; 2:2, 3, 5; 4:9, 11; 8:7; 10:6; 17:8). ὁ πρωτότοκος and ὁ ἄρχων are then the other two predicates.

5.b. Variant: (1) omit ἐκ] *lectio originalis;* Andr f g i l n 94 1773 2019. (2) insert ἐκ] Andreas; Victorinus[ΑΤΦ] (Haussleiter, *Victorinus,* 19). Reading (2) is based on assimilation to Col 1:18 (πρωτότοκος ἐκ τῶν νεκρῶν).

5.c. Variants: (1) βασιλέων] *lectio originalis.* (2) βασιλείων] ℵ* (βασειλείων); 2351. Either an itacism (as apparently in ℵ) or an assimilation to βασιλεία in v 6a.

## Form / Structure/ Setting

### I. OUTLINE

C. Epistolary prescript (1:4–5c)
 1. *Superscriptio:* John (v 4a)
 2. *Adscriptio:* to the seven churches in Asia (v 4b)
 3. *Salutatio* (v 4c–5c)
  a. Well-wishes (v 4c)
   (1) Grace wish
   (2) Peace wish
  b. Ultimate source of well-wishes (v 4d)
   (1) From God
    (a) The one who is
    (b) The one who was
    (c) The one who is to come
   (2) From the seven spirits before the throne
   (3) From Jesus Christ (v 5a–c)
    (a) The faithful witness (5a)

(b) The firstborn of the dead (5b)
(c) The ruler of kings on earth (5c)

## II. LITERARY ANALYSIS

Like ancient Greek letters generally (Aune, *New Testament,* 162–64), and most NT letters as well, Rev 1:4–5a opens with a formal *praescriptio,* or "prescript," which contains three formal features, (1) the *superscriptio* (the name of the sender, in the nominative), (2) the *adscriptio* (the name of the receiver, in the dative of indirect object), and (3) the *salutatio* or "salutation." Like the salutations introducing Pauline and Deutero-Pauline letters in the NT, the salutation in Rev 1:4c–5a consists of two elements (Aune, *New Testament,* 184–86). The first element is a grace and peace wish, while the second element consists of a closer specification of the ultimate source of grace and peace, namely, God, the seven spirits, and Jesus Christ. This salutation differs strikingly both from the salutations in ordinary Greek letters and from the salutations in early Christian letters. In Greek private letters the salutation typically consists of the single term χαίρειν, "greetings," sometimes amplified in forms such as πλεῖστα χαίρειν, "warmest greetings." In the NT the χαίρειν salutation is found only in Jas 1:1 and in the two embedded letters in Acts 15:23; 23:26, while in the Apostolic Fathers χαίρειν is used in the *praescriptiones* of six of the seven letters of Ignatius of Antioch (Aune, *New Testament,* 215–16). In early Christian letters, the grace and peace wish is present, but the ultimate divine source(s) of grace and peace exhibit significant differences, as the following synoptic comparison indicates:

*Group 1: Well-wishes alone*

| | |
|---|---|
| 1 Thess 1:1b | Grace to you and peace |
| 1 Pet 1:2b | May grace and peace be multiplied to you |
| Jude 2 | May mercy, peace, and love be multiplied to you |

*Group 2: Well-wishes with single divine source*

| | |
|---|---|
| Col 1:2b | Grace to you and peace<br>from God our Father |

*Group 3: Well-wishes with two divine sources*

| | |
|---|---|
| Rom 1:7b | Grace to you and peace<br>from God our Father and the Lord Jesus Christ |
| 1 Cor 1:3 | Grace to you and peace<br>from God our Father and the Lord Jesus Christ |
| 2 Cor 1:2 | Grace to you and peace<br>from God our Father and the Lord Jesus Christ |
| Gal 1:3 | Grace to you and peace<br>from God the Father and our Lord Jesus Christ |

| Eph 1:2 | Grace to you and peace<br>from God our Father and the Lord Jesus Christ |
|---|---|
| Phil 1:2 | Grace to you and peace<br>from God our Father and the Lord Jesus Christ |
| 2 Thess 1:2 | Grace to you and peace<br>from God the Father and the Lord Jesus Christ |
| 1 Tim 1:2b | Grace, mercy, and peace<br>from God the Father and Christ Jesus our Lord |
| 2 Tim 1:2b | Grace, mercy, and peace<br>from God the Father and Christ Jesus our Lord |
| Titus 1:4b | Grace and peace<br>from God the Father and Christ Jesus our Savior |
| Philem 3 | Grace to you and peace<br>from God our Father and the Lord Jesus Christ |
| 2 Pet 1:2 | May grace and peace be multiplied to you<br>in the knowledge of God and of Jesus our Lord |
| 2 John 3 | Grace, mercy and peace will be with us<br>from God the Father and from Jesus Christ the<br>Father's Son, in truth and love |
| Polycarp<br>*Phil. inscr.* | Mercy and Peace be multiplied to you<br>from God almighty and Jesus Christ our savior |

This synoptic comparison of salutations in early Christian letters reveals that the phrase "grace to you and peace" in the first part of the salutation in Rev 1:4–5a is typical of Pauline and some Deutero-Pauline letters (Ephesians, Colossians, 2 Thessalonians, Titus). However, Rev 1:4–5c is distinctive because it mentions no fewer than *three* divine sources of grace and peace:

> from the one who is and who was and who is coming
> and from the seven spirits which are before his throne
> and from Jesus Christ,
> > the faithful witness,
> > the firstborn from the dead,
> > and the ruler of the kings of the earth.

It seems clear that the author has elaborated the basic pattern of Christian epistolary salutations in three ways. First, rather than explicitly mentioning the name "God" or "God the Father," he has substituted a title consisting of three elements, which he himself formulated (see *Comment* on 1:4). Second, he has qualified the name "Jesus Christ" (omitting the typical designation "Lord") with three titles in the nominative of apposition that focus on three of the central moments in the story of Jesus, his earthly life, his resurrection, and his

eschatological triumph. Third, the author has inserted a third source of grace
and peace, "the seven spirits before the throne" (see *Comment* on 1:4). The result
is a highly formal arrangement of three ultimate sources for the grace and peace
wish, emphasized by the threefold repetition of the preposition ἀπό, "from," with
the entire structure framed by three titles of God and three titles of Jesus Christ.

### III. THE HYPOTHESIS OF A LITURGICAL SETTING

Some scholars have proposed that the salutations with which many NT letters
begin, following the general pattern "Grace to you and peace from God our Father
and the Lord Jesus Christ" (e.g., Rom 1:7; 1 Cor 1:3; 2 Cor 1:2; Gal 1:3; Eph 1:2;
Phil 1:2; 2 Thess 1:2; cf. Col 1:2; 1 Thess 1:1; 1 Tim 1:2) are derived from the
introductory greeting that began Christian services of worship, a "formula of
introduction" to the service (Delling, *Worship,* 48–50; Cullmann, *Worship,* 23;
Schlier, *Galater,* 30). Vanni goes further by proposing that Rev 1:4–8 reflects a
liturgical dialogue (*Bib* 57 [1976] 453–67; id., *L'Apocalisse,* 101–13; see Kavanagh,
*Liturgical Dialogue,* 117–21). The schema that Vanni finds is the following (*Bib* 57
[1976] 460–61; id., *L'Apocalisse,* 107–8):

*Lector* (ὁ ἀναγινώσκων):
[4b]Grace to you and peace
from him who is and who was and who is to come,
and from the seven spirits who are before his throne,
[5]and from Jesus Christ the faithful witness,
     the firstborn from the dead, and the ruler of kings on earth.

*Assembly* (οἱ ἀκούοντες):
To him who loves us
and has freed us by his blood,
[6]and made us a kingdom, priests to his God and Father.
To him be glory and dominion for ever and ever. Amen.

*Lector:*
[7]Behold, he is coming with the clouds
and every eye will see him,
every one who pierced him;
and all tribes of the earth will wail on account of him.

*Assembly:*
Even so. Amen.

*Lector:*
[8]I am the Alpha and the Omega,
—says the Lord God—
who is and who was and who is to come,
the Almighty.

Vanni argues that recognizing this passage as a liturgical dialogue solves the
problem of the apparent lack of unity in this section. Rev 1:3 has revealed the
existence of a reader or lector and a group of listeners, the assembly. The two

amens (vv 6, 7) lend a clear liturgical flavor to the passage. An abrupt change of person occurs in the passage between 1:4–5a (χάρις ὑμῖν, "grace to you," a second-person plural pronoun) and 1:5b–6 (τῷ ἀγαπῶντι ἡμᾶς καὶ λύσαντι ἡμᾶς ... καὶ ἐποίησεν ἡμᾶς, "to the one who loved *us*, and washed *us* ... and made *us*," three first-person plural pronouns).

## Comment

**4a** Ἰωάννης ταῖς ἑπτὰ ἐκκλησίαις ταῖς ἐν τῇ Ἀσίᾳ, "John to the seven churches in Asia." This *superscriptio*, which contains the name of the sender, is striking for its brevity and lack of any title or claim to authority (for an example of an elaborately expanded epistolary *superscriptio*, see Rom 1:1–6). In the phrase ταῖς ἑπτὰ ἐκκλησίαις, "to the seven churches," the definite article anticipates v 1, where the churches are specifically named. ταῖς ἐκκλησίαις is a dative of indirect object in this elliptical epistolary formula, which omits a verb and object (such as ἔγραψε ταῦτα, "wrote these things"). This is the *adscriptio*, or address of the letter, and is remarkable for the fact that, like the *superscriptio*, it is unadorned and unexpanded (for an example of an amplified *adscriptio*, see Ign. *Eph. praef.; Rom. praef.*). In view of the prominence and symbolic significance of the number seven in Revelation (it occurs fifty-four times), the fact that *seven* churches are addressed is significant. The number is not chosen to symbolize the universal Church, a notion found in the Canon Muratori 171–72, where the seven churches addressed by Paul are thought to symbolize *all* the churches (since "seven" does not symbolize "completeness," a view justly criticized by A. Yarbro Collins, "Numerical Symbolism," 1276–78). Rather, the number seven emphasizes the divine origin and authority of the message of John, since seven is primarily a number with cosmic significance and is therefore associated with heavenly realities. In the phrase ἐν τῇ Ἀσίᾳ, "in Asia," the definite article is used anaphorically, i.e., "referring back" to Asia as one of the two parts of the world generally known (the other is ἡ Εὐρώπη, "Europe"), both of which are normally used with the definite article; this articular use of Asia occurs even when it refers to the Roman province (see Acts 2:9). In *Iliad* 2.416, "Asia" is limited to a small part of Lydia on the Aegean coast of Asia Minor, though the Greeks later (ca. 750–500 B.C.) understood the term to apply to the land masses outside Europe now designated as Africa and Asia. Cicero (*Pro Flacc.* 27) observed that Asia consists of the regions of Phrygia, Mysia, Caria, and Lydia. Judaism had a strong presence in Asia Minor; there were more that fifty Jewish communities here with perhaps a total Jewish population of one million (P. W. van der Horst, "Jews and Christians in Aphrodisias in the Light of Their Relations in Other Cities of Asia Minor," *NedTTs* 143 [1989] 106–7).

**4b** χάρις ὑμῖν καὶ εἰρήνη, "Grace to you and peace." This distinctively Christian salutation is a combination of the Hebrew and Aramaic peace wish, שָׁלוֹם *šālôm*, and the common Greek epistolary salutation χαίρειν, though the use of χάρις, "grace," is a distinctively Christian term with an entirely different meaning from χαίρειν, with which it is nevertheless etymologically related. It is possible that the epistolary formula "grace and peace" was originated by Paul (O. Kuss, *Der Römerbrief* [Regensburg, 1957] 12). Yet this appears doubtful since the formula already appears in the superscription of Paul's first letter (1 Thess 1:1), and it has parallels (if not verbally identical parallels) in *2 Apoc. Bar.* 78:2 and LXX Esth 9:30.

**4c** ἀπὸ ὁ ὢν καὶ ὁ ἦν καὶ ὁ ἐρχόμενος, "from the One who is and who was and who is coming." Following the Pauline style, the source of grace and peace is emphasized, though Paul usually mentions only "God our/the Father" and "our/the Lord Jesus Christ" in his epistolary salutations. In Revelation, John refers to God only as "my/his [Jesus'] Father" (1:6; 2:27; 3:5, 21; 14:1), but here, perhaps intentionally, he omits the designation "Father" from the greeting. In fact, he transforms this part of the traditional Christian salutation by referring to God using this very elaborate set of three clauses, each of which functions as a divine title. Though unattested elsewhere in early Christian literature, this distinctive phrase occurs three times in Revelation (here; 1:8; 4:8). There is some variation in word order. In 1:4; 1:8, the phrase is ὁ ὢν καὶ ὁ ἦν καὶ ὁ ἐρχόμενος, while in 4:8, ὁ ἦν and ὁ ὢν are transposed. A shorter, bipartite formula, perhaps a more traditional form that John expanded, is ὁ ὢν καὶ ὁ ἦν, "who is and who was," which occurs twice (11:17; 16:5). This bipartite formula is expanded to a tripartite formula in 16:5 through the addition of the predicate ὁ ὅσιος, "the holy one." ὁ ὢν, "the one who is" (a substantival participle from the verb εἰμί, "to be"), was, among Greek-speaking Jews, a popular name for God ultimately derived from the phrase ἐγώ εἰμι ὁ ὤν, "I am the one who is," in the LXX translation of the Hebrew phrase אהיה אשר אהיה 'ehyeh 'ăšer 'ehyeh, "I am who I am," in Exod 3:14. Josephus places the phrase ὁ ὤν on the lips of Elijah in 1 Kgs 19:10 (*Ant.* 8.350) but omits it from his version of Exod 3:14 (*Ant.* 2.276). Philo often uses the phrase ὁ ὤν of God, sometimes in combination with θεός, "God" (e.g., ὁ ὢν θεός, "the God who is"; ὁ ὄντως ὢν θεός, "the God who truly is"). The phrase ὁ ὤν is used at least eight times as a divine name, with the asterisks marking passages that allude to Exod 3:14 (*Mos.* 1.75; *Som.* 1.231; *Mut.* 11; *Det.* 160; *Quod Deus* 110; *Op.* 172; *Leg.* 3.181; *Abr.* 121); see J. Krämer, *Der Ursprung der Geistmetaphysic* [Amsterdam, 1964] 83 n. 213). Presumably the popularity of ὁ ὤν as the name for God among Greek-speaking Jews influenced the later insertion of the phrase in the LXX text of Jeremiah, where the phrase ὁ ὤν occurs four times, always in the context of prayer (1:6; 4:10; 14:13; 39:17). The title was familiar to Jews in Asia Minor as attested by an inscription on an altar from Pergamon that reads θεὸς κύριος ὁ ὢν εἰς ἀεί, "God, the Lord who exists forever." Despite the objection of Delling (*Worship,* 78–79), this is very probably an allusion to the LXX version of Exod 3:14 (Nilsson, *Eranos* 54 [1956] 169–70; Bickerman, "Altars of Gentiles," 341–42), for even though the expression εἰς ἀεί, "forever," is not found in direct connection with ὁ ὤν, Exod 3:15 does describe the name of God as a ὄνομα αἰώνιον, "an eternal name," a feature emphasized by Philo (*Mut.* 12; cf. *Mos.* 1.74f–75). Numenius, a second-century A.D. Middle Platonic philosopher, refers to the supreme being as ὁ ὤν (frag. 12, in É. des Places, *Numenius: Fragments* [Paris: Société d' Édition "Les Belles Lettres," 1973] 55–56; see brief commentary on p. 108). Normally, Numenius uses the term τὸ ὄν, "Being, Existence" (frags. 2.23; 3.1, 8, 9; 4a.7, 9, 12; 5.5, 6, 14, 18 [bis]; 6.7, 8, 15; 7.2, 13, 14; 8.2). The Greek magical papyri, many of which exhibit clear Jewish influence (*ISBE,* rev. ed., 3:219, s.v. "magic"), reflect the popularity of divine names borrowed from Judaism and also use ὁ ὤν as a divine name, often in connection with Ἰάω, "Iao," a divine name with close associations with the Hebrew divine name YHWH (often vocalized as Yahweh and shortened in ancient texts as Yahu). *PGM* LXXI.3–4, for example, has several points of contact with Rev 1:8 (the divine names ὁ ὤν, κύριος, and παντοκράτωρ): "The God who is, Iao, Lord Almighty [ὁ θεὸς ὢν ὁ Ἰάω, κύριος παντοκράτωρ]." For other magical texts containing the divine predicate ὁ ὤν, see *PGM* XII.111; XIII.1020, 1048. The title ὁ ὤν also occurs on several amulets. A bloodstone amulet in the British Museum depicts Helios and Selene, with the inscription "Iaô, Sabaôth, Abrasax, the Existent One [ὁ ὤν]" on the reverse (Goodenough, *Jewish Symbols* 2:259; vol. 3 fig. 1116). One amulet, apparently of Jewish origin, has the inscription "One God in the heavens [ἐν οὐρανοῖς] who exists [ὁ ὤν] and who existed before [προών], the one greater than all, who dominates all beings in midheaven" (Delatte-Derchain, *Les intailles magiques*, 266, no. 381; cf. Peterson, *Εἷς Θεός*, 260–61); the plural form οὐρανοῖς is either a Semitism or reflects an elevated hymnic style, and ὁ προών is a more literary grammatical choice than ὁ ἦν in Rev 1:4. On another amulet (Bonner, *Magical Amulets*, 108–9, no. 151), the words ἐγώ and ὁ ὤν, "I am the one who is," are found on either side of a mummy, an allusion to LXX Exod 3:14. A Christian amulet (British Museum, 56473), of uncertain date, has the divine names Iaôth Sabath Adônaei on the obverse with ὁ ὤν on the reverse (Bonner, *Magical Amulets*, 225). A Christian amulet of uncertain date has ὁ ὤν on the reverse, with one *crux potens* at the top and another at the bottom, while the obverse reads "Iaoth Sabath Adonaei," with one *crux potens* above and three below (C. Bonner, "Amulets Chiefly in the British Museum," *Hesperia* 120 [1951] 333–34, no. 46).

John uses the phrase ὁ ὤν four times (1:4, 8; 11:17; 16:5), twice in the context of prayer (11:17; 16:5), like the LXX variants in Jeremiah. He is the first Christian author to use this divine name; it rarely occurs among later Christian authors (see *PGL*, 418). Why does John use this divine name twice in the opening sections of his book (vv 4, 8)? Just as Moses was told by God to accredit his message by telling the people that ὁ ὤν had sent him, so John appears to be authenticating his prophetic book by claiming that its actual source is none other than ὁ ὤν. ὁ ὤν is understood by Philo as the divine name that Moses, as a prophet, used to authenticate his message (*Mos.* 1.75; *Mut.* 11).

A similar threefold temporal description of divinity is widespread in Greco-Roman literature beginning with Homer (F. Büchsel, *TDNT* 2:399). In a reference to a hymn to Zeus that has perished, Menander Rhetor (1.342) mentions that "Zeus was before all things [Ζεὺς πρὸ πάντων ἐγένετο]" but that this statement contradicted other elements in the hymn. Plato *Timaeus* 37E preserves the traditional formula λέγομεν γὰρ δὴ ὡς ἦν ἔστιν τε καὶ ἔσται, "For we say that it [Eternal Being] was and is and will be" (see Plato *Leges* 4.715e). Empedocles (frag. 14, line 9 in M. R. Wright, *Empedocles: The Extant Fragments* [New Haven: Yale UP, 1981] 100–101 [text], 177–79 [translation and commentary]): ἐκ τῶν πάνθ' ὅσα τ' ἦν ὅσα τ' ἔστι καὶ ἔσται ὀπίσσω, "From them [fire, air, water] comes all that was and is and will be hereafter." Here, however, this *time formula* is used not of divinity but of aspects of the material world. Plutarch preserves an inscription from the base of a statue of Athena, whom the Egyptians identified with Isis: "I am all that has been, and is, and shall be [ἐγώ εἰμι πᾶν τὸ γεγονὸς καὶ ὂν καὶ ἐσόμενον], and my robe no mortal has yet uncovered" (*De Iside et Osiride* 354C [tr. LCL]; cf. 352a; 372f–373ah). A similar passage is found in Pausanias 10.12.10: "Zeus was, Zeus is, Zeus shall be; O mighty Zeus [Ζεὺς ἦν, Ζεὺς ἔστιν, Ζεὺς ἔσσεται· ὦ μεγάλε Ζεῦ]." The setting of this hexameter line is important, for Pausanias attributes it to the Peliades ("Doves"), the female priestesses of Zeus who were cult officials at the oracle of Zeus at Dodona; the setting therefore connects Zeus with prophecy since the *tripartite prophecy formula* is also based on the three moments of past, present, and future. In *Asclepius* 14.17–18 (Nock-Festugière, *Hermès Trismégiste* 2:313): *deus aeternus . . . hoc est, hoc fuit, hoc erit semper,* "The eternal God . . . is the one who is, the one who was, and the one who will always be." In *Asclepius* 29.5–7 (Nock-Festugière, *Hermès Trismégiste* 2:337): *si enim animal mundus uiuensque semper et fuit et est et erit, nihil in mundo mortale est,* "if the world itself is a living being and was and is and will be, nothing in the world is mortal." Finally in *Asclepius* 134.25–26 (Nock-Festugière, *Hermès Trismégiste* 2:344): *et sine hoc nec fuit aliquid nec est nec erit,* "and without whom nothing was, nothing is, nothing will be" (see John 1:3). The last two passages from *Asclepius,* however, concern not divinity but the world and material reality.

Instead of the phrase ὁ ἐρχόμενος, "the one who will come," one fully expects the temporal expression ὁ ἐσόμενος, "the one who will be" (Kraft, 31). This expression is found in Clement of Alexandria (*Strom.* 5.6), who claims that the name of God is pronounced Ἰαουέ, which he interprets as "the one who is and who will be [ὁ ὢν καὶ ὁ ἐσόμενος]."

*Excursus 1A: The Tripartitate Divine Name in the Targumim*

**Bibliography**

**Chester, A.** *Divine Revelation and Divine Titles in the Pentateuchal Targumim.* Tübingen: Mohr-Siebeck, 1986. **Fitzmyer, J. A.** *A Wandering Aramean: Collected Aramaic Essays.* Missoula, MT: Scholars, 1979. **Grossfeld, B.** *A Bibliography of Targum Literature.* 2 vols. Cincinnati: Hebrew Union College; New York: Ktav, 1972–77. **Hayward, R.** *Divine Name and Presence: The Memra.* Totowa, NJ: Allanheld, Osmun, 1981. **Kaufman, S. A.** "On Methodology in the Study of the Targums and Their Chronology." *JSNT* 23 (1985) 117–24. **McNamara, M.** *The New Testament and the Palestinian Targum to the Pentateuch.* Rome: Pontifical Biblical Institute, 1966. ———. *Palestinian Judaism and the New Testament.* Wilmington, MD: Glazier, 1983. ———. *Targum and Testament.* Grand Rapids, MI: Eerdmans, 1972. **Schürer, E.** *The History of the Jewish People in the Age of Jesus Christ.* Rev. and ed. G. Vermes and F. Millar. Edinburgh: T. & T. Clark, 1973. 1:99–114. **Trudinger, P.** "The Apocalypse and the Palestinian Targum." *BTB* 16 (1986) 78–79. **Unnik, W. C. van.** "A Formula Describing Prophecy." *NTS* 19 (1962–63) 86–94. **York, A. D.** "The Dating of Targumic Literature." *JSJ* 5 (1974) 49–62.

According to McNamara (*New Testament,* 103), the tripartite divine name in Rev 1:4, 8; 4:8 is a paraphrase of the divine name Yahweh revealed to Moses in Exod 3:14. There Moses was told to tell his people that "אהיה [*'ehyeh,* 'I will be'] sent me to you" (LXX: ὁ ὢν ἀπέσταλκέν μοι πρὸς ὑμᾶς). Through the influence of this passage, ὁ ὢν became a name for God in Hellenistic Judaism. John, however, was not influenced by this LXX tradition. Turning to rabbinic tradition, McNamara shows that the rabbis were interested in the threefold occurrence of אהיה *'ehyeh* in Exod 3:14. In *Exod. Rab.* 3:14 (McNamara, *New Testament,* 105): "R. Isaac [ca. A.D. 300] said: The Holy One Blessed be He said to Moses: Say to them: 'I am he who was [שהייתי *šhyyty*] and I am he (who is) now [עכשיו *'kšyw*], and I am he (who will be) for ever.' Wherefore is it said thrice, 'I am [אהיה *'ehyeh*].'" According to McNamara, the closest parallel to the tripartite divine name in Revelation is *Tg. Ps.-J.* Deut 32:39 (*New Testament,* 111): "When the Memra of the Lord will be revealed to redeem his people he will say to all the nations: 'See now that *I am He who is and who was and I am He who will be* [אנא הוא דהוי *'n' hw' dhwy whwyt w'n' hw' d'tyd lmhwy*] והוית ואנא הוא דעתיד למהוי] and there is no other God beside me.'" רהוי *dhwh* consists of the relative particle ד *d* prefixed to the participle הוי *hwy*, the equivalent of ὁ ὤν. הוית *hwyt* is the qal perfect presupposing ד *d*, the equivalent of ὁ ἦν. עתיד למהוי *'tyd lmhwy* corresponds to ἐσόμενος rather than to ἐρχόχμενος. While McNamara prefers the view that the author of Revelation was dependent on *Tg. Ps.-J.* Deut 32:39, he concedes that both might be dependent on a common liturgical tradition (*New Testament*, 112). McNamara's proposal that the tripartite title for God in Rev 1:4, 8; 4:8 draws *directly* (or even indirectly) on *Tg. Ps.-J.* is not convincing because his early dating of that targumic text is not persuasive (see the problem of early dating according to Fitzmyer, *Aramean*, 17–18; York, *JSJ* 5 [1974] 49–62; Kaufman, *JSNT* 23 [1985] 117–24). It is more probable to assume that both Revelation and the *Tg. Ps.-J.* make use of a formula that goes back to a liturgical tradition of the first century A.D. (Chester, *Divine Revelation*, 208). McNamara thinks that John is not dependent on the Greek versions of the tripartite divine name found in Plato, Plutarch, Pausanias, and the *Asclepius* (*New Testament*, 102: "The author of the Apocalypse draws his imagery and language from the OT and from Judaism and it is to be presumed that he is also dependent on these same sources for his designation of God as 'He who is and who was and who is to come'").

**4d** καὶ ἀπὸ τῶν ἑπτὰ πνευμάτων ἃ ἐνώπιον τοῦ θρόνου αὐτοῦ, "from the seven spirits which are before his throne." The phrase "the seven spirits of God" is found in Rev 3:1; 4:5 (where it is probably an explanatory gloss); 5:6. The fact that τῶν ἑπτὰ πνευμάτων is articular suggests that the phrase is familiar to the readers (on the basis of the evidence from Qumran discussed below, this is probably the correct way to understand this use of the definite article). The phrase "spirits of God" is not found in the OT (though the singular form "Spirit of God" occurs ninety-four times). The plural term רוחות *rûḥôt*, "spirits," is never used of *angels* in the OT.

There are several major ways of interpreting the significance of "the seven spirits." (1) A widespread and ancient Christian view that this is a way of representing the Holy Spirit in its fullness (Cowley, *Apocalypse*, 186: "He said '*seven*,' referring to the completeness of his gift.") appears to have originated in the LXX version of Isa 11:2–3, which describes seven benefits of the Spirit of God to be enjoyed by the future Davidic king: "The Spirit of God will rest upon him, a spirit of [1] wisdom and [2] understanding, a spirit of [3] counsel and [4] might, a spirit of [5] knowledge and [6] godliness; the Spirit will fill him with [7] the fear of the Lord" (only six benefits are found in the MT; six are mentioned in 4Q*161* = 4QIsaiah Pesher[a] 8–10 iii 11–13; and six are mentioned in rabbinic literature: cf. *b. Sanh.* 93ab; *Num. Rab.* 13.11; *Gen. Rab.* 2.4.97; *Ruth Rab.* 7.2). This view was taken up into both early Judaism (*1 Enoch* 61:11) and early Christianity (Justin *Dial.* 39.2; 87.2; *Cohort. ad Graec.* 32; Irenaeus *Adv. haer.* 3.18.2; Victorinus *Comm. in Apoc.* 1.1 [Haussleiter, *Victorinus*, 16–19]), though it was probably unknown to John; see Schlütz, *Isaias 11:2*. Many modern commentators, for various reasons (but often implicitly from the perspective of later trinitarianism), understand the seven spirits as representing the Holy Spirit (Beckwith, 424–27; Bruce, "Spirit," 336–37; Sweet, 98; Metzger, *Code*, 23–24; Smalley, *Thunder*, 130; Talbert, 14; Bauckham, *Theology*, 25, 110–15): (a) The seven spirits are sometimes identified with the Holy Spirit because they are mentioned here in an epistolary salutation between God and Christ (Bruce, "Spirit," 336–37). Bousset ([1906] 184–85) called attention to the Trinitarian formula in Justin, *1 Apol.* 6, which mentions "the true

God," "the Son who came from him," "the army of the other good angels," and "the prophetic Spirit," i.e., *four* supernatural beings: God, the Son of God, the angels, the prophetic Spirit. Also 1 Tim 5:21 contains an oath formula, "In the presence of God and of Christ Jesus and of the elect angels," a passage quoted in connection with Rev 1:4 by Andreas of Caesarea (Schmid, *Studien* 1/1:14). (b) One Holy Spirit is seven because he is manifest in each of the seven churches (Swete, *Holy Spirit*, 274; Allo, 9). (c) The author inserts the salutation after writing out the visions of Rev 4–5 where the seven spirits are mentioned (Beckwith, 426–27). (d) Based on a reading of Zech 4 where the seven lamps (4:2), said to represent "the eyes of the Lord, which range through the whole earth" (4:10), are somehow connected with the Spirit of God (4:6; Caird, 15). All of these explanations, however, are artificial and unconvincing. In part this is because of the later conceptualization of God in terms of three interrelated persons, Father, Son, and Holy Spirit.

(2) A second important view, in my opinion certainly the correct one, understands the seven spirits as the seven principal angels of God. In early Jewish literature the term "spirits" was used only rarely as a synonym for "angels" (*Jub.* 1:25; 2:2; 15:31–32; *1 Enoch* 61:12, "spirit of light"), or of various types of heavenly beings (*1 Enoch* 75:5, "the spirit of the dew"; see *2 Enoch* 12:2 [J], "flying spirits"; 16:7, "the heavenly winds, and spirits and elements and flying angels"); see *TDNT* 6:375–76. More commonly, the term "spirits" is used in early Judaism for demonic spirits; see *Comment* under Rev 16:13–14; 18:2. *T. Reub.* 2:1–9 speaks of seven spirits of deceit given to man by Beliar (the functions of the seven spirits of error are discussed in 3:1–8), and seven other (good) spirits given to man at creation by which every human deed is done (by listing "sleep" as the eighth spirit in 3:1, the redactor brings this teaching in line with the Stoic view of the eight divisions of the soul; see J. von Arnim, *Stoicorum Veterum Fragmenta*, vol. 2, nos. 823–33). However, angels are designated "spirits" in the Qumran literature (Sekki, *RUAH*, 145–71). In 1QM 12:8–9 the phrase צבא מלאכים *ṣbʾ mlʾkym*, "host of angels," is used as a parallel to צבא רוחיו *ṣbʾ rwḥyw*, "host of his spirits." For a list of references to such expressions in 4QShirShabb, see Newsom, *Songs*, 25. The unique phrase "Lord of Spirits" occurs *104 times* in the Parables of Enoch, i.e., *1 Enoch* 37–71, and only there in *1 Enoch* (see Black, *Enoch*, 189–92). Elsewhere the phrase is rare and occurs in 2 Macc 3:24; LXX Num 16:22; 27:16; *1 Clem.* 64:1 (δεσπότης τῶν πνευμάτων); two Jewish grave inscriptions from Delos, dating from the second or first century B.C. (Deissmann, *Light*, 423–35). The phrase may have an exegetical origin in the phrase "God of the spirits of all flesh," which occurs in Num 16:22; 27:16. The closest parallel is 2 Macc 3:24, "the Sovereign of spirits and of all authority" (NRSV). Ps 104:4 reads "who makest the winds [Heb. רוחות *rûḥot*] thy messengers, fire and flame thy ministers," an important passage in view of the association with the seven spirits of God with seven torches of fire in 4:5. In an explanatory gloss in 4:5, the seven torches of fire burning before the throne are interpreted by John as the seven spirits of God. Again in 5:6 the seven eyes of the Lamb are interpreted as "the seven spirits of God sent out into all the earth." Though commentators formerly noted the absence of the phrase from the OT and early Jewish literature (Beckwith, 424), that situation has changed with the publication of the Dead Sea Scrolls, for "spirits" (רוחותם *rwḥwtm* or the construct form רוחי *rwḥy*) is a common designation for angels at Qumran. 1QH 3:22 refers to "spirits of knowledge"

(4Q*405* 19ABCD 4, "[sp]irits of the knowledge of truth and righteousness;" 4Q*405* 17:3, "spirits of knowledge and understanding"). Specifically the phrase רוחות אלוהים *rûḥôt ʾĕlôhîm*, "spirits of God," is found in 4Q*403* 1 i 43; 1 ii 8,9; 4Q*404* 5:5; 4Q*405* 6:7; 4Q*405* 20 ii 21–22 11; 4Q*405* 23 i 9–10; 4QShirShabb 3–4:4; see Newsom, *Songs,* 25, passim). 4Q*403* 1 ii 9 reads "spirits of God, shapes of flaming fire" (Newsom, *Songs,* 229). Again, 4Q*405* 23 i 8–9 indicates that "holy angels" and "spirits of God" are synonymous: "Whenever the elim of knowledge enter by the portals of glory, and whenever the holy angels [מלאכי קודש *mlʾky qwdš*] go out to their dominion, the portals of entrance and the gates of exit make known the glory of the King, blessing and praising all the spirits of God [רוחות אלוהים *rwḥwt ʾlwhym*] at (their) going out and at (their) coming in by the ga[t]es of holiness" (Newsom, *Songs,* 324). In the NT, only in Heb 1:14 are angels called spirits. The "seven spirits" of Rev 1:4 are equivalent to "the seven spirits of God" of 3:1, 4:5; 5:6 and must be identified with "the seven angels who stand before God" in 8:2. Thus the view that the seven spirits are the seven archangels (*TWNT* 6:450) seems correct.

For groups of seven, see the seven princes of Persia and Media "who saw the king's face and sat first in the kingdom" (Esth 1:14), elsewhere described as the "seven counselors" of the king (Ezra 7:14). For groups of seven *angels,* see *T. Levi* 18:2, where "seven men in white clothing," obviously angels, participate in Levi's consecration as priest. Enoch saw seven stars (= angels) bound together in punishment for ten thousand ages because of their rebellion against God (*1 Enoch* 21:3–6). 4QShirShabb refers to seven hierachically ordered angelic priesthoods, each presiding in one of the seven sanctuaries of the heavenly temple and each ruled over by seven chief angelic princes and their deputies (see Newsom, *Songs,* 31–35; Strugnell, "Angelic Liturgy," 318–45). These seven angelic princes are probably identical with the "seven holy angels who present the prayers of the saints and enter into the presence of the glory of the Holy One" (Tob 12:15). In Luke 1:19, Gabriel identifies himself as one of those "who stand in the presence of God." The Ethiopic text and one Greek MS (designated G by M. Black and Gr[Pan] by M. A. Knibb) of *1 Enoch* 20:2–8 list a group of *six* angels who watch: Uriel, Raphael, Raguel, Michael, Saraqael, and Gabriel. Yet the Greek text G adds to 20:7, "seven names of archangels." A duplicate Greek text (Black's G2; Knibb's GR[Pana]) lists a seventh angel named Remiel, and the text concludes "names of seven archangels" (see Black, *Apocalypsis,* 32). The seven archangels are also mentioned occasionally in Coptic-Gnostic texts (*Orig. World* 104.19; 105.10).

A grouping of *four* angels is attested in 1QM 9:12–15, each name written on a shield on one of the towers: Michael, Gabriel, Sariel, and Raphel. A slightly different group of four is found in *1 Enoch* 19:1, where the paraphrastic Greek text of Syncellus reads "And when the four great archangels, Michael and Uriel and Raphael and Gabriel, heard, they looked down upon the earth from the sanctuary of heaven" (Black, *Apocalypsis,* 23). This division of heavenly and earthly hosts is found in the OT (Num 2:3–31). The belief in four archangels is also found in biblical and postbiblical tradition. Prior to the Dead Sea Scrolls, Sariel is never numbered among the four archangels.

(3) A third major interpretation understands the seven spirits in terms of ancient Near Eastern groups of seven astral deities.

*Excursus 1B: The Spirit in Revelation*

**Bibliography**

**Bruce F. F.** "The Spirit in the Apocalypse." In *Christ and Spirit in the New Testament*. FS C. F. D. Moule, ed. B. Lindars and S. Smalley. Cambridge: Cambridge UP, 1973. 333–44. **Jeske, R. L.** "Spirit and Community in the Johannine Apocalypse." *NTS* 31 (1985) 452–66. **Smidt, J. C. de.** "The Holy Spirit in the Book of Revelation—Nomenclature." *Neot* 28 (1994) 229–44.

Discussions of the Spirit in Revelation have frequently been flawed by the tendency to read the evidence from the perspective of conceptions of the Spirit extraneous to the book itself (e.g., de Smidt, *Neot* 28 [1994] 229–44). At the outset, it is important to note that the phrases "the Spirit of God" and "the Holy Spirit" never occur in Revelation. The analysis of the Spirit in Revelation is complex because of the composition history of Revelation, which exhibits changing conceptions of the Spirit.

In the final stage of composition, the Second Edition, the Spirit is frequently the subject of the verb λέγει, which indicates that the Spirit is conceived in personal terms, and as the means of prophetic inspiration. The role and function of the Spirit at this final stage of composition is primarily *prophetic;* i.e., the Spirit is considered to be the divine agent through which divine revelation is mediated to human beings. In the proclamations to the seven churches in Rev 2–3, the refrain "Let the one with ears hear what the Spirit says to the churches" is repeated seven times (2:7, 11, 17, 29; 3:6, 13, 22). Since each of the proclamations is presented as the word of the exalted Christ, a close relationship between Christ and Spirit is presupposed, one that is theologically similar to the Fourth Gospel, though not expressed in the same language (John 14:25–26; 15:26; 16:13–14). Outside of Rev 2–3, the Spirit is the subject of λέγει in 14:13, which has the features of a prophetic oracle: "'Certainly,' says the Spirit, 'that they might rest from their labors, for their works follow after them.'" In my view, this verse is an interpolation inserted by the author-editor during the final stages of composition and so belongs to the same compositional level as the aforementioned sayings in Rev 2–3 (see *Comment* on 14:13). The only other occurrence of "Spirit" (along with "the Bride") as the subject of λέγειν is in 22:17, the conclusion of the book, which also belongs to the final stage of composition: "The Spirit and the Bride say, 'Come!'" One further related passage is Rev 19:10, where it is said that "the testimony concerning Jesus is the Spirit of prophecy." This passage, too, appears to be an expansion connected with the final edition of Revelation (see *Comment* on 19:10). This association of witnessing to Jesus and the Spirit of prophecy is analogous to that found in the proclamations to the seven churches.

In earlier layers of Revelation, the role and function of the Spirit is primarily associated with an *apocalyptic* understanding of inspiration. The phrase ἐν πνεύματι, "in the Spirit," i.e., "in ecstasy" or "in a trance," occurs four times in the earlier form of the text (1:10; 4:2; 17:3; 21:10). While it is obvious that the Spirit is here connected with revelatory experience, that experience has a markedly apocalyptic character; i.e., the seer does not mediate the word of God through the inspiration of the Spirit, but the Spirit is the divine agent who mediates apocalyptic visions.

The other significant occurrences of the term πνεῦμα are found in the phrase "the seven spirits [of God]" (1:4; 3:1; 4:5; 5:6). While many scholars have maintained that the seven spirits of God, particularly those mentioned in 1:4, refer to the Holy Spirit (Beckwith, 426–27; Bruce, "Spirit," 333–37) or to the fullness of the one Spirit of God (de Smidt, *Neot* 28 [1994] 241), that equation does not hold up to scrutiny (see *Comment* on 1:4).

**5a** καὶ ἀπὸ Ἰησοῦ Χριστοῦ, ὁ μάρτυς ὁ πιστός, "and from Jesus Christ the faithful witness." The three christological titles found in vv 5a–c may be derived from Ps 89:38, 28(LXX 88:38, 28): (1) LXX Ps 89:38b, καὶ ὁ μάρτυς ἐν οὐρανῷ πιστός, "the faithful witness in heaven [i.e., 'the moon']" = ὁ μάρτυς ὁ πιστός, "the faithful witness"; (2) LXX Ps 89:28a, κἀγὼ πρωτότοκον θήσομαι αὐτόν, "and I will make him the firstborn" = ὁ πρωτότοκος τῶν νεκρῶν, "the firstborn of the dead"; (3) LXX Ps 89:28b, ὑψηλὸν παρὰ τοῖς βασιλεῦσιν τῆς γῆς, "the most exalted among the kings of the earth" = καὶ ὁ ἄρχων τῶν βασιλέων τῆς γῆς, "the ruler of the kings of the earth" (see also Prov 14:5; Jer 42:5; Isa 8:2; 43:10; 55:4). Though the title κύριος, "Lord," is usually associated with the name "Jesus Christ" in the Pauline epistolary prescripts, in this prescript that title is replaced with the distinctive phrase "the faithful witness." The title "Lord" is used of Jesus five or six times in Revelation (11:8; 14:13[?]; 17:14; 19:16; 22:20, 21), though the phrase "Lord Jesus" occurs only in 22:20, 21, "Lord Jesus Christ" never occurs, and the title "Lord" is more typically applied to God (fourteen times). An expanded version of the christological designation "faithful witness" is found in Rev 3:14 in the form ὁ μάρτυς ὁ πιστὸς καὶ ἀληθινός, "the faithful and true witness." The phrase ὁ μάρτυς μου ὁ πιστός μου, "my faithful witness," is applied to Antipas in Rev 2:13. The term μάρτυς, "witness," is a christological title only here and in 3:14, though the substantival participle based on the cognate verb μαρτυρεῖν occurs in 22:20, where Jesus is referred to as ὁ μαρτυρῶν ταῦτα, "the one who attests to this message." The term occurs just three times elsewhere in Revelation, always in connection with those who die for their faith (2:13; 11:3; 17:6), suggesting the possibility that μάρτυς here connotes the faithful witness who has sealed his testimony through *death* in v 5a (Holtz, *Christologie*, 143; Rusam, "Formeln," 94), just as the second, "firstborn from the dead," emphasizes his *resurrection* (v 5b) and the third, "the ruler of the kings of the earth," underlines his *exaltation* (v 5c). The NT, of course, contains traditions of the testimony or witness that Jesus maintained before Pilate (1 Tim 6:13 states that Christ Jesus "testified" [τοῦ μαρτυρήσαντος] before Pontius Pilate; cf. Matt 27:11–14 = Mark 15:1–5 = Luke 23:1–5; John 18:33–38). However, there are weighty reasons why the title μάρτυς is *not* a reference to the historical Jesus but a reference to the exalted Jesus who guarantees the truth of the revelation transmitted through John: (1) Though Jesus is rarely referred to as a μάρτυς, Ignatius does refer to Jesus Christ as the μάρτυς "in whom I am bound"; i.e., the exalted Christ is his witness in an oath (*Phld.* 7:2; see 5:1; *Rom.* 1:1). (2) The ultimate derivation of the title "Amen" in Rev 3:14 from Isa 65:16 indicates that Jesus as "the faithful and true witness" is in grammatical apposition to ὁ ἀμήν and functions as a translation and interpretation of it (Rissi, *Future*, 21; Satake, *Gemeindeordnung*, 115 n. 1). (3) It is the exalted Jesus who testifies in Rev 22:20, not the historical Jesus. It is of course true that in the Fourth Gospel, it is the historical Jesus, or perhaps more appropriately the Johannine Jesus, who is often the subject of the verb μαρτυρεῖν; i.e., he testifies to the truth that he has received from God (John 3:32; 4:44; 5:31; 7:7; 8:14, 18; 13:21; 18:37). The term πιστός occurs eight times in Revelation (1:5; 2:10, 13; 3:14; 17:14; 19:11; 21:5; 22:6), always with the meaning "faithful, trustworthy"; similarly the term πίστις in Revelation always means "faithfulness, trustworthiness" and never has the connotation of Christian belief in God or Christ (Karrer, *Johannesoffenbarung*, 204 n. 283). Here the phrase "faithful witness" is particularly applicable to Jesus Christ as the source of the revelation that

John transmits to his audience, for it underlies its truth and reliability *Ep. Lugd.* 2:3 (Musurillo, *Acts*, 82–83) has an allusion to Rev 1:5 that was used in a martyrological context: "For it was their joy to yield the title of martyr to Christ alone, who was the true and faithful witness [τῷ πιστῷ καὶ ἀληθινῷ μάρτυρι], the firstborn [πρωτοτόκῳ] of the dead, and the prince [ἀρχηγῷ] of God's life."

**5b** ὁ πρωτότοκος τῶν νεκρῶν, "the firstborn from the dead." This striking title is an instance of paradox, for the notions of birth and death are obviously antithetical. In all probability, the writer did not formulate this title, for the title ἀρχή, πρωτότοκος ἐκ τῶν νεκρῶν, "the beginning, the firstborn from the dead," occurs earlier in Col 1:18 (in the context of a hymn incorporated into that letter). Since Colossians was circulated in the Roman province of Asia, including Laodicea (Col 4:16), one of the seven churches to whom Revelation was addressed, the title may have become part of the christological tradition of the region. The term πρωτότοκος occurs only here in Revelation, though it is a *varia lectio* for πρῶτος in the phrase "the first and the last" in 1:17; 2:8 (see *Notes* on both passages), an absolute titular use with a parallel only in Heb 1:6. Here the phrase implies that while Jesus is the first to have conquered death, he is also not the last but provides the precedent for the subsequent resurrection of believers who have died. πρωτότοκος, an important and debated christological term in early Christianity, was used in both literal and figurative senses. (1) In its literal sense, πρωτότοκος (which first appears in the LXX) was frequently used to refer to a firstborn son (Luke 2:7 [Jesus]; Philo *Leg. All.* 2.48; *Sac.* 19; *Sob.* 21), though the term can be applied as well to an only son (*CIJ* 2:1510 = *CPJ* 3:157). (2) The figurative extensions of meaning are based primarily on the great prestige and status enjoyed by the firstborn son in a family and involves the notions of primacy in time and rank and privilege in inheritance and succession (Deut 21:15–17; see *TDOT* 2:121–27). There are several theologically significant figurative uses of πρωτότοκος: (a) Israel is called the πρωτότοκος or "firstborn" of God in the LXX (Exod 4:22 [see 4QDibHam 3:6]; LXX Jer 38:9[MT: 31:9; echoes Exod 4:22]; Sir 36:11 [*var. lect.*]; 4 Ezra 6:58 [*primogenitum*]; *Jub.* 2:20), and God's people are disciplined as a parent would discipline the πρωτότοκος (*Pss. Sol.* 13:9; 18:4). This use of the term is based on the metaphor of *adoption* (Michaelis, *TDNT* 6:874) but also emphasizes the notion of a special, privileged status. (b) In one coronation psalm, the king of Israel is called God's firstborn (LXX Ps 88:28[MT 89:28]), a passage interpreted messianically in early Judaism (*Exod. Rab.* 19.7[81d]; Str-B 3:258). Again, the metaphor of *adoption* rather than that of birth is in view (Michaelis, *TDNT* 6:874), and the point of the metaphor is the exalted status of the king by virtue of his special relationship to God. (c) Levi, in view of his special status, is called the πρωτότοκος, though Reuben is literally the firstborn (Philo *Sac.* 119). (d) In Jewish literature, terms for the "firstborn" (בְּכִיר, רֵאשִׁית *rēʾšît, bĕkîr*) were used of the Torah, Adam, Jacob (*Prayer of Joseph* in Origen *In Joh.* 12.31), Israel, and the Messiah (Str-B 3:257–58).

In the NT and early Christian literature, πρωτότοκος was used figuratively of Jesus in two distinct and perhaps related ways. (1) *In a Protological Context.* In Col 1:15, in the context of a hymn, Christ is called the πρωτότοκος πάσης κτίσεως, "the firstborn of all creation." While some early Christians, particularly Arians, read this text as affirming that Christ was a created being, the term πρωτότοκος is actually used to emphasize the special status enjoyed by Christ (Lohse, *Colossians*,

48–49). A functionally equivalent phrase about Christ is found in Rev 3:14: ἡ ἀρχὴ τῆς κτίσεως τοῦ θεοῦ, "the beginning of God's creation." It is unnecessary to invent a special category for the meaning of πρωτότοκος in Col 1:15, such as "existing first, existing before" (Louw-Nida, § 13.79). The use of πρωτότοκος in Col 1:15 appears to have been borrowed from, or at least influenced by, Jewish Wisdom speculation, which used the language of primacy and priority to speak of Wisdom as the first of God's creation and even as preexistent (Prov 8:22; Wis 24:9; Philo Leg. All. 1.43; W. Michaelis, TDNT 6:871–81; id., ZST 23 [1954] 137–67). In early Christianity, the term πρωτότοκος continued to be used as a way of characterizing the Λόγος, or "Word" (Justin 1 Apol. 33.3; Tatian Orat. 5), understood to be identical with the preincarnate Jesus. It was an important way of describing the status of Jesus (Justin 1 Apol. 46.2; see 1 Apol. 53.2; Origen Contra Cels. 6.17), sometimes in a titular sense (Heb 1:6; 1 Apol. 23.2; see 1 Apol. 63.15).

(2) In a Resurrection Context. A phrase almost identical to that found in Rev 1:5 occurs in Col 1:18: ἀρχή, πρωτότοκος ἐκ τῶν νεκρῶν, "the beginning, firstborn from the dead" (ἐκ is missing in 𝔓⁴⁶ ℵ* 2495 Irenaeus^Lat [primogenitus mortuorum]), where it is parallel to the phrase πρωτότοκος πάσης κτίσεως, "firstborn of [i.e., 'superior to'] all creation" (Col 1:15). It appears likely that the term πρωτότοκος in v 18 was chosen precisely because of the neat parallelism to πρωτότοκος in v 15 (using the same term in two different ways in the same context is an instance of paronomasia). There is evidence, however, that words belonging to the semantic field of high status or rank (πρῶτος, πρωτότοκος) or temporal priority (ἀρχή, ἀπαρχή) were used for the resurrection of Jesus outside Col 1:15–20 and Rev 1:5: (1) Rom 8:29 is the earliest text in which the term πρωτότοκος (which is probably derived from pre-Pauline Christian tradition; see Deichgräber, Gotteshymnus, 153) is used of Jesus as the first of a new group of people when the author refers to Jesus as the πρωτότοκον ἐν πολλοῖς ἀδελφοῖς, "firstborn among many brothers" (see also Heb 12:23, which refers to Christians as "the assembly of the firstborn," i.e., those who share the inheritance of Christ the Firstborn; see Attridge, Hebrews, 375). Though the term πρωτότοκος is not explicitly linked with the resurrection, many commentators assume that connection in light of Col 1:18 and Rev 1:5 (Sanday-Headlam, Romans, 218; Dunn, Romans 1:484–85). (2) A similar phrase appears in Acts 26:23: "the first to rise from the dead [πρῶτος ἐξ ἀναστάσεως νεκρῶν]." (3) Acts 3:15 says that "You killed the ruler of life [ὁ ἀρχηγὸς τῆς ζωῆς], whom God raised from the dead." Here ἀρχηγός refers to the status of Jesus before he was executed. (4) In 1 Cor 15:20–23, Paul speaks of Christ as the "firstfruits" (ἀπαρχή) of the resurrection from the dead, i.e., as the first to be resurrected to be followed by a general resurrection (1 Cor 15:20–23). The association of the term πρωτότοκος with the resurrection of Jesus in Col 1:18 and Rev 1:5, and perhaps also in Rom 8:29, indicates the presence of a traditional conception.

That in Rev 1:5 the "firstborn of the dead" is also "the ruler of the kings of the earth" suggests that John is alluding specifically to LXX Ps 88:28 (see Comment on 1:5a). This possibility is enhanced by the fact that two other terms also found in 1:5, ὁ μάρτυς, "witness," and πιστός, "faithful," also occur together in LXX Ps 88:38, of the moon: καὶ ὁ μάρτυς ἐν οὐρανῷ πιστός, whose "testimony in heaven is trustworthy" (Charles, 1:14; Deichgräber, Gotteshymnus, 183 n. 4). In this allusion to Ps 89:28, John has modified the royal/messianic term πρωτότοκος by qualifying it with the phrase "of the dead."

**5c**   καὶ ὁ ἄρχων τῶν βασιλέων τῆς γῆς, "and the ruler of the kings of the earth." Though this title occurs only here in Revelation, it is a functional equivalent to "king of kings," which is applied to Jesus in Rev 17:14 and 19:16 (see *Comment* on 17:14). The phrase "kings of the earth" occurs seven times elsewhere in Revelation (6:15; 17:2, 18; 18:3, 9; 19:19; 21:24), while the parallel phrase "the kings of the whole world" occurs in 16:14; these phrases are consistently used in a *negative* sense in Revelation. A relatively close though antithetical parallel to Rev 1:5 is 17:18, where the Harlot is identified as ἡ πόλις ἡ μεγάλη ἡ ἔχουσα βασιλείαν ἐπὶ τῶν βασιλέων τῆς γῆς, "the great city which has dominion over the kings of the earth." Another relatively close parallel occurs in *T. Moses* 8:1: "a king of the kings of the earth [*rex regum terrae*]." The Latin Vulgate translates the phrase "ruler of the kings of the earth" with *princeps regnum terrae*, a title with significant political ramifications since it could designate the Roman emperor. ὁ ἄρχων (found only here in Revelation), the substantival participle of the verb ἄρχω, was one of several terms used to translate *princeps* from Latin into Greek (Mason, *Greek Terms*, 27, 198; it does *not* however occur in official imperial titulature, 113); others relevant to the political imagery of Revelation include βασιλεύς (15:3; 17:14; 19:16), δεσπότης (Rev 6:10), and κύριος (17:14; 19:16). In addition to inscriptional evidence, many Greek authors used ἄρχων of the Roman *princeps* (Aelius Aristides 19.5; 20.15; 25.56; 26.23, 107; Dio Chrysostom 32.60; 37.34; Marcus Aurelius 3.5.1; Philostratus *Vita Apoll.* 7.1). Latin Christian authors frequently referred to Christ as *imperator* (Tertullian *De exhort. cast.* 12; *De fuga in pers.* 10; Cyprian *Ep.* 15.1; 3.5; Ps.-Cyprian *De mont. Sina et Sion* 8; *Acts Scill.* 2).

### Explanation

Revelation is the only Jewish or Christian apocalypse that is framed as a *letter*, with the epistolary prescript in 1:4–5a and a concluding postscript in 22:21. The main part of the work, however, contains no explicitly epistolary features. Hellenistic epistolary prescriptions typically consisted of three elements, the superscription (sender), the adscription (addressee), and the salutation. "Grace to you and peace" is a distinctively Christian salutation that first appears in Paul's letters (see 1 Thess 1:1). It is often expanded to make the divine source of grace and peace explicit: "Grace to you and peace from God our/the Father and our/the Lord Jesus Christ" (e.g., 1 Cor. 1:3; 2 Cor. 1:2). The elaborate salutation in Rev 1:4–5a is a distinctively Johannine expansion of the traditional Pauline salutation. The addressees are the seven Christian congregations of western Anatolia (they are mentioned by name in 1:11; 2:1–3:22), all of which were within approximately a hundred miles of Ephesus. The phrase "from him who is and who was and who is to come" (v 4) alludes to the LXX version of Exod 3:14, where the divine name "the one who is" (used three more times in 1:8; 11:17; 16:5) occurs. This name was familiar in Hellenistic Judaism in both Egypt and Anatolia, though in early Christian texts it is found only in Revelation. Just as Moses is told by God to tell the people that "the one who is" had sent him, so John legitimates his prophetic book by claiming that it was inspired by "the one who is."

The "seven spirits who are before his throne" is not a phrase referring to the Holy Spirit, as so many commentators have claimed, but rather a reference to the seven archangels who stand continually in the presence of God (4:5; 5:6; 8:2).

This reference emphasizes the heavenly origin of the revelatory visions that the author is about to narrate. Three titles of Jesus in v 5 correspond to three important aspects of his role: (1) As *faithful witness* (1:2, 9; 2:13; 3:14; 6:9; 12:11; 17:6; 22:20), he faithfully proclaimed the message of God, which led to his crucifixion. (2) As *firstborn from the dead* (found only in Rev 1:5 and in Col 1:18 in the NT), the *theologia gloriae*, "theology of glory," referring to the resurrection triumph of Christ, is deftly combined with the *theologia crucis*, "theology of the cross," for the term "firstborn" has royal/messianic associations, while the phrase "of those who are dead" refers to Jesus' triumph over death. (3) As *ruler of the kings of the earth*, his future role as universal sovereign is emphasized (17:14; 19:16).

# D. Doxology (1:5d–6)

## Bibliography

**Arndt, W.** "A Royal Priesthood." *CTM* 19 (1948) 241–49. **Best, E.** "Spiritual Sacrifice: General Priesthood in the New Testament." *Int* 14 (1960) 273–99. **Brown, S.** "The Priestly Character of the Church in the Apocalypse." *NTS* 5 (1958–59) 224–31. **Campion, L. G.** *Benedictions and Doxologies in the Epistles of Paul.* Oxford: Kemp Hall Press, 1934. **Caspari, W.** "Das priestliche Königreich." *TBl* 8 (1929) 105–10. **Coune, M.** "Un royaume de prêtres. Ap. 1,5–8." *AsSeign* 20 (1973) 9–16. **Eastwood, C.** *The Priesthood of All Believers: An Examination of the Doctrine from the Reformation to the Present Day.* Minneapolis: Augsburg, 1962. **Elliott, J. K.** "The Language and Style of the Concluding Doxology to the Epistle to the Romans." *ZNW* 72 (1981) 124–30. **Feuillet, A.** "Les chrétiens prêtres et rois d'après l'Apocalypse: Contribution à l'étude de la conception chrétienne du sacerdoce." *RevThom* 75 (1975) 40–66. ———. *The Priesthood of Christ and His Ministers.* Garden City: Doubleday, 1975. **Fohrer, G.** "'Priesterliches Königtum,' Ex. 19,6." *TZ* 19 (1963) 359–62. **Moran, W. L.** "A Kingdom of Priests." In *The Bible in Current Catholic Thought,* ed. J. L. McKenzie. New York: Herder & Herder, 1962. 7–20. **Schelkle, K. H.** *Discipleship and Priesthood.* New York: Herder and Herder, 1965. **Schüssler Fiorenza, E.** "Redemption as Liberation: Apoc 1:5f. and 5:9f." *CBQ* 36 (1974) 220–32. **Scott, R. B. Y.** "A Kingdom of Priests (Exodus xix 6)." *OTS* 8 (1950) 213–19. **Trudinger, P.** "The Apocalypse and the Palestinian Targum." *BTB* 16 (1986) 78–79. **Werner, E.** "The Doxology in Synagogue and Church: A Liturgico-Musical Study." *HUCA* 19 (1945–46) 275–351.

## Translation

[5d][a]*To* [b]*him who loves* [b] [c]*us and freed* [d] *us* [e] *from* [f] *our* [g] *sins by his blood,* [6][a]*and made* [b] *us* [c] *a kingdom,* [d] *priests* [e] *to his* [f]*God* [ga] *and Father. To him is* [h]*the glory and the power* [h] [ij]*for ever.* [i] *Amen.* [j]

## Notes

5d.a. Variant: omit τῷ] א*.

5d.b-b. Variant: (1) ἀγαπῶντι] 𝔓[18] א A C 046 fam 1006[1006 1841] fam 1611[1611 1854] (fam 1611[2050 2329]: ἀγαπόντι); Andr f[2023 2073] i[2042] Byzantine. (2) ἀγαπήσαντι] Oecumenius[2053 2062] Andreas; it[gig h] Beatus vg (*dilexit*). Reading (1) is a present ptcp. that has been corrected in reading (2) to an aor. ptcp. to make it consistent with the aor. ptcp. λύσαντι that immediately follows.

5d.c. Variant: insert φησιν] Andr a c.

5d.d. Variant: (1) λύσαντι] 𝔓[18] ℵ A C fam 1611[1611 2050 2329] 2351 Andreas it[h] syr[ph h] arm Primasius; Tischendorf, *NT Graece;* B. Weiss, *Johannes-Apokalypse,* 4; WHort; von Soden; Nestle-Aland[27]; *TCGNT,* 729; *TCGNT[2],* 662; Holtz, *Christologie,* 63. (2) λούσαντι] 025 046 fam 1006 Oecumenius[2053 2062] Andr d e[2057] f[2023 2073] g h[2060] i[2042] l n[-2429] 94 598 Byzantine it[gig] vg cop[bo] eth. Reading (1), an aor. ptcp. from λύειν, "to release, set free," is the *lectio difficilior* that was corrected to reading (2), an aor. ptcp. from λούειν, "to wash," in accord with OT imagery, e.g., LXX Isa 40:2.

5d.e. Variant: (1) ἡμᾶς] *lectio originalis.* (2) omit ἡμᾶς] ℵ*.

5d.f. Variant: (1) ἐκ] 𝔓[18] ℵ A C 046 fam 1611 1778 Oecumenius[2053 2062] Andreas Tischendorf, *NT Graece.* (2) ἀπό] 025 fam 1006 2351 Andr f[2023 2073] g i[2042] n[-2429] 94 Byzantine.

5d.g. Variant: (1) ἡμῶν] *lectio originalis.* (2) omit ἡμῶν] A Andr a[1].

6.a-a. The clause that begins καὶ ἐποίησεν and concludes with αὐτοῦ is impossible Gk. It should be a subordinate clause introduced with the pronoun ὅς, which would refer to τῷ ἀγαπῶντι. However, the author has chosen to make it into an independent clause, contrary to normal Gk. usage (see Bousset [1906] 188–89), for the logical, though certainly not the grammatical, subject of ἐποίησεν is τῷ ἀγαπῶντι. The author has simply chosen to drop out the necessary ὅς in order to place great emphasis on this statement; see Norden, *Agnostos Theos,* 387.

6.b. Variants: (1) ἐποίησεν] Oecumenius[2053 2062] Andreas; (2) ποιησαντι] 046 fam 1611[1854] 2019 Andr n[2429] Byz 14[325 456 517] Byz 15[42 3367 468] Byz 16[61 69]. Nestle-Aland[26] incorrectly lists 2053 and 2062 in support of this reading; they belong to the Oecumenius group supporting ἐποίησεν. In the phrase καὶ ἐποίησεν, the καί coordinates the finite verb ἐποίησεν to the two substantival ptpcs. in v 5d, τῷ ἀγαπῶντι . . . καὶ λύσαντι, which is grammatically problematic. Copyists therefore changed the verb into the dat. ptcp. ποιήσαντι in agreement with the two ptcps. in v 5d (Hoskier, *Text* 2:34; Schmid, *Studien* 2:242). As it stands, ἐποίησεν represents a Semitic construction in that the last verbal form in a series of coordinated ptcps. may be replaced with a finite verb (Charles, 1:cxlv; Mussies *Morphology,* 326).

6.c. Variants: (1) ἡμᾶς] ℵ it[gig] Andreas Byzantine; Tertullian Victorinus Primasius. (2) ἡμῖν] 𝔓[18] (though only υμ is visible, according to the editors of POxy 1079 = 𝔓[18], a stroke over the space following μ indicates that the MS must have read ὑμῖν; A Oecumenius[2053 2062] fam 1611[1854 2344] 2016 Andr l Byz 13[2058] Byz 14[325 456 517] Byz 15[42 367 468]. (3) ἡμῶν] C 1611 2048 2329. The original reading was certainly ὑμᾶς βασιλείαν, "us a kingdom," and is one of a group of original readings preserved by the agreement of ℵ and the Koine group (Schmid, *Studien* 2:130–35).

6.d. Variants: (1) βασιλείαν] 𝔓[18] ℵ A C 94 Andr f[2023 2073] g i[2042] l Byzantine. (2) βασιλεῖς καί] Andreas. (3) βασίλειον] 046 fam 1611[1854 2050] 2351.

6.e. In the phrase βασιλείαν, ἱερεῖς, "a kingdom, priests," ἱερεῖς is probably pl. nom. (though the pl. nom. and acc. are identical in form) and used in apposition to βασιλείαν in the acc. For examples of the nom. used in apposition to an oblique case in Revelation, see 1:5; 2:13; 3:12, 21; 6:8; 8:9; 9:13; 14:12; 20:2 (Turner, *Style,* 157–58; BDF § 136–37; Mussies, *Morphology,* 92–94). The reading βασίλειον ἱεράτευμα, "royal priesthood," is attested by twelve minuscules: fam 1611[1854*] 2351; Byz 14[325 456 517] Byz 15[42 367 468] Byz 16[61 69] Andr e[2026 comm] Andr/Byz 4c[2070 comm]. This reading appears to be based on a correction of the LXX reading βασιλείαν, ἱερεῖς, "kingdom, priests," in Exod 19:6, made to conform with Symmachus and Theodotion, which nevertheless varies from the MT, since מלכת כהנים *mmlkt khnym,* "a kingdom *of* priests," is pointed as a construct noun (literally translated in Aquila and the vg). However, the unpointed Heb. text could be construed to mean "a kingdom, priests," and this is how two fragmentary targums on Exod 19:6 read: "And you will be before Me kings and priests [מלכין וסהנין *mlkyn wshnyn*] and a holy nation" (Klein, *Fragment-Targums* 1:82; 2:50); "And you will be unto My name, kings and priests [מלכין וסהנין *mlkyn wshnyn*] and a holy nation" (Klein, *Fragment-Targums* 1:174; 2:132).

6.f. The scribe of 𝔓[18] first wrote τοῦ θυ (the latter a common abbreviation for θεοῦ) but then corrected it to θω, i.e., θεῷ, but simply wrote a superlinear ω over τοῦ without erasing the ου. Andr/ Byz 3[2196] also has this reading, which is certainly an error.

6.g. Variant: insert ἡμῶν] 2351.

6.h-h. Variant: τὸ κράτος καὶ ἡ δόξα] 𝔓[18]; singular reading.

6.i-i. Variants: (1) omit τῶν αἰώνων] 𝔓[18] A 046 792 fam 1611[2050]; Andr c[2052] g[2071] i[-2042] m[2037 2046]; Byz 13[498 1704 2058] Byz 14[325 456 468 517]; Byz 15[42 367] 1773; Andr/Byz 2b[582] Andr/Byz 4[2070 2305]; WHort. (2) τῶν αἰώνων] ℵ C 046 fam 1006[1006] fam 1611[1611 1854] Oecumenius [2053] it[gig.h,ar] vg syr[ph,h]; Tischendorf, *NT Graece;* B. Weiss, *Johannes-Apokalypse,* 135; von Soden, *Text* [*TCGNT[2]*, 663]. The strength of the MSS attesting to the omission of τῶν αἰώνων and the fact that it is easy to account for its insertion but more difficult to account for its omission suggest that it was an early addition to the text. Yet the formula εἰς τοὺς αἰῶνας τῶν αἰώνων occurs twelve more times in Revelation in passages where the phrase is relatively undisputed (1:18; 4:9, 10; 5:13; 7:12; 10:6; 11:15; 14:11 [εἰς αἰῶνας αἰώνων]; 15:7; 19:13; 20:10; 22:5), suggesting that those passages influenced the addition of τῶν αἰώνων in 1:6, which must be considered a harmonistic interpolation.

6.j-j. Variant: omit εἰς τοὺς αἰῶνας ἀμήν] fam 1611²³⁴⁴.

## *Form/Structure/Setting*

### I. OUTLINE

D. Doxology (1:5d–6)
   1. The recipient of praise (v 5d)
      a. The one who loves us
      b. The one who has freed us
         (1) From our sins
         (2) Means of freedom: by his blood
      c. The one who has made us
         (1) A Kingdom to his God and Father
         (2) Priests to his God and Father
   2. The particular attributes used in praise (v 6a)
      a. Glory
      b. Power
   3. Temporal extent of attributes: for ever (v 6b)
   4. Concluding amen (v 6c)

### II. LITERARY ANALYSIS

By virtue of its position immediately following the epistolary prescript, the doxology (with close parallels in 5:13; 7:12) exhibits the character of an epistolary convention with its closest parallel in Gal 1:1–5 (see Schüssler Fiorenza, *Priester für Gott*, 172).

### III. LITERARY FORM

A doxology is a short liturgical formula that usually ascribes to God the attribute of glory (δόξα), which may be amplified through the inclusion of a number of other attributes as well. A doxology is formally distinct from a benediction, or *berakah*, which is typically introduced by the term ברוך or εὐλογητός, "blessed" (see Pss 41:13; 72:18–19; 89:52; 106:48; Tob 13:18; *1 Enoch* 84:1–4). Yet there are instances in which the forms are mixed; see *1 Enoch* 90:40, "I woke up and blessed the Lord of righteousness and ascribed glory to him." Doxologies are rare in Judaism but occur frequently in early Christian texts; on the other hand, benedictions occur frequently in early Judaism but are rare in early Christian texts (Deichgräber, *Gotteshymnus,* 40–43). If a doxology is strictly defined as a formula that includes the term δόξα or כבוד *kābôd* (both meaning "glory"), there are no synagogue prayers that can be properly designated doxologies (A. Baumstark, *Comparative Liturgy* [London, 1958] 67). However, the term doxology can be understood in a broader sense that includes Jewish *berakah,* "blessing," formulas as well as Christian doxologies (Heiler, *Prayer,* 333). Werner (*HUCA* 19 [1945–46] 276–77; id., *Sacred Bridge,* 273–74), however, does not think that the formal presence or absence of the terms *gloria,* δόξα, or כבוד *kābôd* can be used as an essential criterion for defining a doxology (2 Cor 1:20, which contains the term δόξα, is *not* a doxology, while 1 Tim 6:16 *is* a doxology though the term δόξα is missing). According to Wieder (*HUCA* 19 [1945–46] 276–81), only two features are characteristic of the doxology: (1) it must contain a proclamation of God's praise; (2) it must affirm the eternity of God. There are no benedictions in Revelation.

Doxologies generally consist of four stereotypical elements: (1) Mention is first made of the one to whom some attribute is ascribed (usually in the dative case, less frequently in the genitive). (2) Mention is then made of the specific attribute(s), of which δόξα, "glory," is the most common (usually in the nominative). (3) A formula is used describing the unending extent of time during which the one praised will possess this attribute or these attributes, usually "forever" or "for ever and ever," or "to all generations" (Eph 3:21) or "from generation to generation" (*Mart. Pol.* 21), followed by (4) a concluding "amen." Including 1:6, five doxologies are found in Revelation (4:9 [a peculiar text since it refers to the reiterated recitation of a doxology]; 5:13–14; 7:12; 19:1).

Doxologies have several functions when they occur in written texts. (1) *They can be used to conclude a religious text,* with the text functioning as a surrogate for a service of worship (4 Macc 18:24; cf. Tobit 14:15 [*var. lect.* MS S]; 3 Macc 7:23; *1 Clem.* 64:2; *2 Clem.* 20:5; *Acts Carpus* [Greek rec.] 47; *Acts Carpus* [Latin rec.] 7; *Acts Justin* [rec. A, B, and C] 6; *Mart. Apollonius* 47; *Mart. Perpetua* 11; *Mart. Pionius* 23; *Mart. Fruct.* 7.2; *Mart. Conon* 6; *Mart. Marian* 13.5; *Mart. Julius* 4.5; *Mart. Dasius* 12.2; *Mart. Agape* 7.2; *Mart. Irenaeus* 6; *Mart. Crispina* 4.2; *Test. Forty Martyrs* 3). Similarly, doxologies can be used to conclude a *section* of a religious text (Rom 11:36; 1 Tim 1:17; 1 Pet 4:11; *1 Clem.* 20:12; 32:4; 38:4; 43:6; 45:7; 50:7; 58:2; 61:3; *Mart. Perpetua* 1).

(2) Doxologies may have a special *epistolary function* either in the opening (Gal 1:5; Rev 1:6) or concluding (Rom 16:25–27; Phil 4:20; 1 Tim 6:16; 2 Tim 4:18; Heb 13:21; 1 Pet 5:11) portions of letters.

(3) Doxologies can be used in direct discourse to introduce a prayer (1 Chr 29:11) or, more frequently, to conclude a liturgy narrated within a text (Rev 4:9; 5:13–14; 7:12; 19:1; Tob 14:15 [*var. lect.* MS S]; *1 Enoch* 39:10, 13; *Did.* 8:2; 9:2, 3, 4; 10:2; 10:4, 5).

(4) Doxologies can be referred to in indirect discourse (Rev 4:9). The benedictions in *1 Enoch* are frequently referred to in this way (25:7; 27:5; 36:4; 39:9; 81:3; 83:11).

Doxologies can be addressed to God in either the third person singular or the second person singular. Doxologies in the third person singular frequently use the relative pronoun ᾧ or the intensive pronoun αὐτῷ, both in the dative of indirect object or the dative of advantage (*dativus commodi*) or the dative of possession. Doxologies in the second person singular are comparatively rare (none occur in the NT, and only seven in the Apostolic Fathers). Some are introduced with σου, a pronoun in the genitive of possession, e.g., *Did.* 8:2: "Yours is the power and the glory for ever" (see also *Did.* 9:4; 10:5), while more commonly they are introduced with σοί, a pronoun in the dative of advantage, e.g., *Did.* 9:2: "To you is the glory for ever" (see also *Did.* 9:3; 10:2, 4; *1 Clem.* 61:3).

Each of the four elements (with the exception of the concluding "amen") can be expanded in a variety of ways: (a) by adding and qualifying attributes (1 Tim 1:17: "to the King of ages, immortal, invisible, the only God"); (b) by adding attributes (two attributes: 1 Tim 1:17; 1 Pet 4:11; *Did.* 8:2; 9:4; 10:5; *1 Clem.* 20:12; 61:3; 64:1; four attributes: Jude 24–25; *Mart. Pol.* 21; five attributes: *1 Clem.* 65:2), or by adding qualifying phrases (Eph 3:21); and (c) by the addition of various expressions for unending time (Eph 3:21: "to all generations, for ever and ever"). Rom 16:25–27 is an even more extensive doxology in which (a) has been subject to elaborate expansion, but the other sections are left undeveloped.

There are a number of features of the doxology in Rev 1:5d–6 that are unusual. The doxology is striking with regard to both form and content. In *form* it is a compound doxology, made up of two main clauses introduced by constructions using the dative of advantage:

τῷ ἀγαπῶντι ἡμᾶς καὶ λύσαντι ἡμᾶς . . .
αὐτῷ ἡ δόξα καὶ τὸ κράτος . . .

"To the one who loves us and washed us . . .
to him be the glory and the might . . . ."

This type of doxology occurs just three other times in the NT: Rom 16:25–27, τῷ δὲ δυναμένῳ . . . μόνῳ σοφῷ θεῷ . . . ᾧ ἡ δόξα . . . ; Eph 3:20–21, τῷ δὲ δυναμένῳ . . . αὐτῷ ἡ δόξα . . . ; Jude 24–25, τῷ δὲ δυναμένῳ . . . μόνῳ θεῷ σωτῆρι ἡμῶν . . . δόξα μεγαλωσύνη κράτος καὶ ἐξουσία . . . .

In *content*, the doxology in Rev 1:5d–6 contains a brief narrative that focuses on the central salvific events of the Christian dispensation: "To the one who loves us and freed us from our sins through his blood and made us a kingdom and priests to his God and Father." No other doxology incorporates such a brief narrative into its structure. Further, this doxology is addressed to Christ, while Christian doxologies are almost exclusively addressed to God. Rom 9:5 has been interpreted by some as a doxology to Christ, though it is likely that the underlying Greek should be read "God who is over all be blessed for ever, amen," rather than " Christ who is God over all be blessed for ever, amen" (Dunn, *Romans* 2:535–36; for a more detailed discussion see Cranfield, *Romans* 2:464–70).

There is a general structural relationship between Rev 1:5d and Titus 2:14 consisting of two parts: the first refers to the sacrifice of Jesus, while the second refers to the formation of a people (Rev 1:6 is based on Exod 19:6, while Titus 2:14b is based on Exod 19:5):

| *Rev 1:5d–6* | *Titus 2:14* |
|---|---|
| τῷ ἀγαπῶντι ὑμᾶς | ὃς ἔδωκεν ἑαυτὸν ὑπὲρ ἡμῶν |
| [5d] To him who loved us | Who gave himself for us |
| | |
| καὶ λύσαντι ἡμᾶς ἐκ τῶν ἁμαρτιῶν | ἵνα λυτρώσηται ἡμᾶς ἀπὸ πάσης |
| and freed us from our sins | to redeem us from all |

ἐν τῷ αἵματι αὐτοῦ
by his blood,

καὶ ἐποίησεν ἡμᾶς βασιλείαν
6 and made us a kingdom,

ἱερεῖς τῷ θεῷ καὶ πατρὶ αὐτοῦ
priests to his God and Father.

ἀνομίας
iniquity

καὶ καθαρίσῃ ἑαυτῷ
and to purify for himself

λαὸν περιούσιον
a people of his own

ζηλωτὴν καλῶν ἔργων.
who are zealous for good deeds.

## Comment

**5d**  τῷ ἀγαπῶντι ἡμᾶς καὶ λύσαντι ἡμᾶς ἐκ τῶν ἁμαρτιῶν ἡμῶν ἐν τῷ αἵματι αὐτοῦ, "To him who loves us and freed us from our sins by his blood." Vv 5d–6 contain a compound doxology consisting of *two* phrases in the *dativus commodi*, a liturgical form that is comparatively rare in the NT (see Rom 16:25–27; Jude 24–25). The doxology introduced in v 5d is further distinguished by virtue of the fact that no other doxology is introduced with the substantival participle τῷ ἀγαπῶντι, "to the one who loves," or the two substantival participles τῷ ἀγαπῶντι καὶ λύσαντι, "to the one who loves and freed." Further, it is the earliest doxology directed to *Christ* alone rather than to God (in 5:13, however, a doxology is directed to both God and the Lamb). It is syntactically possible that the doxology in Rom 9:5 is directed to Christ, but exegetically doubtful (Cranfield, *Romans* 2:464–70). A relatively early doxology to the "Lord Messiah" occurs in *Odes Sol.* 17:17 (ca. A.D. 125), but later doxologies are often trinitarian and directed to God and Christ and the Holy Spirit (*Apost. Const.* 8.15.9; 8.40.4; 8.41.5). The two motifs joined in this passage are those of the *love* of Jesus for humanity and the expression of that love through voluntary death that *frees* certain beneficiaries. This combination of *motive* plus *action* has a traditional ring, for there are a number of formulaic statements that contain the motif of the voluntary self-sacrifice of Christ (Deichgräber, *Gotteshymnus*, 112–13). In Gal 2:20, Paul speaks of "the son of God who *loved* me and *gave* himself for me [τοῦ ἀγαπήσαντός με καὶ παραδόντος ἑαυτὸν ὑπὲρ ἐμοῦ]," just as in Eph 5:2 "Christ *loved* us and *gave* himself up for us [ἠγάπησεν ἡμᾶς καὶ παρέδωκεν ἑαυτὸν ὑπὲρ ἡμῶν]" (see Eph 5:25, "Christ *loved* the church and *gave* himself up for her"). These formulaic passages all coordinate the two motifs of love and death, though death is referred to under the metaphors of "giving" and "freeing." The voluntary, sacrificial nature of the death of Christ and the salvific benefits of that death are central features of early Christian catechesis: Mark 10:45 = Matt 20:28 ("The Son of Man came . . . to *give* his life as a ransom for many"), John 10:11 ("the good shepherd *lays down* his life for the sheep"; cf. John 10:15, 17), Gal 1:4 ("Who *gave* himself for our sins"), Titus 2:14 ("Who *gave* himself for us"), 1 Tim 2:6 ("Who *gave* himself as a ransom for all"), 1 John 3:16 ("he *laid down* his life for us"). The *willingness* of Christ to die, however, is not invariably mentioned: 1 Cor 15:3 ("Christ died for our sins"), 1 Pet 3:18 ("Christ also died for sins once for all"); see also Rom 5:8; 14:15; 1 Cor 8:11; 1 Thess 5:9–10. The love of *God* for his people is mentioned frequently in early Christian literature (John 3:16; Rom 9:13; 2 Cor 9:7; Eph 2:4; 1 Thess 1:4; 2 Thess

2:13, 16; Heb 12:6; 1 John 4:10; *1 Clem.* 56:4; *Barn.* 1:1; Ign. *Trall.* inscr.; *Rom.* inscr.). "Jesus," however, is only occasionally the subject of the verb ἀγαπᾶν, and then in passages that are predominantly Johannine (John 11:5; 13:1, 23, 34; 14:21; 15:9, 12; 19:26; 21:7; Eph 5:2, 25; Rev 3:9).

The phrase λύειν τινὰ ἐκ/ἀπὸ τῶν ἁμαρτιῶν, "to free someone from sin," occurs only here in the NT and in the Apostolic Fathers. λύειν means "to release, rescue" in the literal sense of setting free from being tied up, chained, or imprisoned (Louw-Nida, § 18.18) and, in figurative extensions, to set free from political domination, sickness, as in Luke 13:16, or sin, as in Rev 1:5 (Louw-Nida, § 37.127). Thus, "to free someone from sin" is a metaphor that implies that individuals are held captive by their sins and that release from this captivity has been secured by Christ. In effect, λύειν ἐκ τῶν ἁμαρτιῶν means "to forgive sins," and this meaning (though not using this idiom) occurs in later Christian literature (Ps.-Clement *Ep. James* 2, 6; Ps.-Clement *Hom.* 54.2; cf. *PGL*, 817). In the final edition of Revelation, since people are "ransomed for God by the blood" (ἠγόρασας τῷ θεῷ ἐν τῷ αἵματι) of the Lamb (5:9), i.e., God is the new owner, λύειν and ἀγοράζειν are virtually synonymous (see Holtz, *Christologie*, 65–68). The language of new ownership of those ransomed is also found in Rev 14:4, which refers to the 144,000 who have been "redeemed [ἠγοράσθησαν] from humanity as the firstfruits for God and the Lamb." The redemption metaphor occurs in Paul (Gal 3:13; 4:5; 1 Cor 6:20; 7:23; cf. 1 Pet 1:18; 2 Pet 2:1), and it is possible that the metaphor originated with him (Holtz, *Christologie*, 67). According to Rev 7:14, those who came through the great tribulation "washed their robes and made them white by the blood [ἐν τῷ αἵματι] of the Lamb" (on the verb "wash," see the variant λούσαντι in *Note* 1:5d.d.). There are parallels in pagan literature, as in Ps.-Hippocrates *Morb. sacr.* 4, where it said (speaking of the ritual procedures of Greek public cults) that "the Divine cleanses, sanctifies, and purifies [καθαῖρον καὶ ἁγνίζον καὶ ῥύμμα] us from the greatest and most wicked of our sins [ἁμαρτημάτων]."

**6a** καὶ ἐποίησεν ἡμᾶς βασιλείαν, ἱερεῖς τῷ θεῷ καὶ πατρὶ αὐτοῦ, "and he made us a kingdom, priests to his God and Father." John alludes here to Exod 19:6, where the Hebrew phrase ממלכת כהנים *mamleket kōhănîm,* "kingdom of priests," is ambiguous and can be understood as "a royalty of priests" (Fohrer, *TZ* 19 [1963] 359–62) or "kings [who are] priests," i.e., "priestlike kings," to mention just two options (see Durham, *Exodus,* 263). The phrase is rendered idiomatically by the LXX version: βασίλειον ἱεράτευμα, "royal priesthood," which is cited in 1 Pet 2:9 and Ign. *Eph.* 9:2 (long recension). The literal Greek version of the OT by Aquila reads βασιλεία ἱερέων, "kingdom of priests," which is how Mussies thinks the phrase in Rev 1:6 should be understood (*Morphology,* 94); cf. 4Q504 = 4QDibHamᵃ frag. 4, line 10: "[a kingdom of] priests and a holy people." Yet it is clear that, when Rev 1:6 is compared with 5:10 (where the phrase βασιλείαν καὶ ἱερεῖς, "kingdom and priests," is found, also alluding to Exod 19:6), John is thinking in terms of two privileges of the people of God rather than just one (as in the MT, LXX, and Aquila). The second-century A.D. Greek translations of Symmachus and Theodotion render the phrase as βασιλεία ἱερεῖς, "a kingdom, priests," thus reflecting the same understanding of Exod 19:6 found in Rev 1:6; 5:10. The Ethiopic text of *Jub.* 16:18 has "a kingdom and priests" (the translation "a kingdom of priests" in Charlesworth, *OTP* 2:88 is therefore incorrect), though the Latin text reads *regnum sacerdotale,* "a kingdom of priests," or "a priestly kingdom." The Ethiopic text seems to be confirmed by *Jub.* 33:20, which has "a nation of priests, and a royal nation" (Charlesworth, *OTP* 2:120), or "a priestly and royal nation" (Sparks, *AOT,* 104). In allusions to Daniel, John seems to reflect a Greek version similar to Theodotion rather than to the LXX (Swete, *Old Testament in Greek,* 48). McNamara (*Targum,* 227–30) has shown that all the texts of the targums understand ממלכת כהנים *mamleket kōhănîm,* "kingdom of priests," as two distinct substantives, though the targums use the paraphrase "kings and priests" rather than John's "a kingdom, (and) priests." The same understanding is reflected in allusions to Exod 19:6 in Philo (*Abr.* 56; *Sob.* 66), 2 Macc 2:17; and the Peshitta Syriac *mlkwt' wksn,* "a kingdom and priests," a reading so close to Rev 1:6; 5:10, however, that it may have been influenced by the NT. Similarly, 4Q*504* 4 line 10 alludes to Exod 19:6 with the phrase כוהנים וגוי קדוש [ממלכת] [*mmlkt*] *kwhnym wgwy qdwš,* "a kingdom of priests and a holy people" (M. Baillet, *Qumran Grotte 4,* vol. 3, DJD 7 [Oxford: Clarendon, 1982] 154–56). John, then, appears to be drawing on a very early Jewish understanding of Exod 19:6 in terms of two distinct privileges rather than the single one reflected in the MT and LXX. Isa 61:6 addresses the people of Israel with these words: "You shall be called the priests of the Lord."

The term ἱερεύς occurs just three times in Revelation (1:6; 5:10; 20:6; the first two allude to Exod 19:6) and in each instance is used in the plural to describe the status of Christians. The related term ἱεράτευμα, "priesthood," is applied to Christians in 1 Pet 2:5, 9 (the latter also alludes to Exod 19:6). Using an extended metaphor in Rom 15:16, Paul speaks of himself as "a minister [λειτουργόν] of Christ Jesus to the Gentiles in the priestly service [ἱερουργοῦντα] of the gospel of God." Here ἱερουργεῖν means "to serve as a priest" (Dunn, *Romans* 2:859–60), though Paul himself rather than ordinary Christians is in view. ἱερουργεῖν is specifically used by Philo in referring to something that the whole people can do (*Spec. Leg.* 2.145; *Mos.* 2.229); the verb ἱεράσθαι is used the same way in Philo *Mos.* 2.24. In two references in Josephus, however, ἱερουργεῖν apparently means "to offer sacrifice" (*J.W.* 5.14, 16) without implying the priestly status of those doing so. These metaphors are only rarely applied to ordinary Christians in early Christian literature (Irenaeus *Adv. haer.* 4.8.3 ["all the righteous have the priestly rank"]; Clement Alex. *Strom.* 7.7; Tertullian *De oratore* 28.1–2 [*sacerdotes*]; *De exhort. cast.* 7 [quotes Rev 1:6]; *De monogamia* 7 [quotes Rev 1:6]; Esaias Abbas *Or.* 5.3; *Apost. Const.* 2.25). Cyprian later refers to the "priesthod of martyrdom" (*Ep.* 20.3), a conception close to that found in Rev 20:6. Oecumenius thought Christians were appropriately designated priests because they are enjoined in Rom 12:2 to offer themselves as living sacrifices to God (*Comm. in Apoc.* 5:10; Hoskier, *Oecumenius,* 81–82). The Stoics reportedly held, in an aphorism with wide variations, that "the wise are the only priests" (Diogenes Laertius 7.119; Origen *Comm. in Joh.* 2.10 [on 1:4]; Stobaeus *Ecl.* 2.67.20; see *SVF* 3:604–10), while for Marcus Aurelius (3.4.3), the good man is "a priest and minister of the gods." A priest may normally be defined as a religious specialist who performs religious rites, usually sacrificial rituals at a fixed location (e.g., an altar), and in so doing functions as an intermediary acting for or on behalf of a community (W. G. Oxtoby, "Priesthood: An Overview," *EncRel* 11:528–29). Here (as in 5:10; 20:6) there can be no sacrifice involved and no community to represent, nor are these priests specialists since all who have been freed or ransomed by Christ's death (1:6; 5:10), who have participated in the first resurrection (20:6), have this status. It is possible that the universal application of "priesthood" is the result of the spiritualization of the notion of "sacrifice" that characterized early Christianity, for everyone can offer the sacrifice of prayer. The notion of the "priesthood of believers," or "general priesthood" (meaning that every Christian has direct access to God), particularly emphasized in a polemical way by Martin Luther, is distinguished from the ministerial priesthood in Roman Catholicism, which regards the latter as superior to the "priesthood of the laity" (cf. Schelkle, *Discipleship*, 108–37, and his insistence that πρεσβύτερος, "elder," should be translated "priest" [the English term "priest" is in fact etymologically derived from πρεσβύτερος]), while most branches of Protestantism do not (Eastwood, *Priesthood;* see the instructive excursus by N. Brox, *Der erste Petrusbrief,* 2nd ed. [Neukirchen: Benziger/Neukirchener, 1986] 108–10).

**6b** αὐτῷ ἡ δόξα καὶ τὸ κράτος εἰς τοὺς αἰῶνας, "To him is the glory and the power for ever." The context of this second doxology reveals that it too is directed to Christ just like the first one in v 5d. However, this doxology is phrased in a more conventional way and therefore has many close parallels in early Christian literature (Rom 11:36; 16:27; Gal 1:5; 2 Tim 4:18; 1 Pet 4:11; 2 Pet 3:18; Heb 3:21; *1 Clem.* 20:12; 32:4; 38:4; 43:6; 45:7; 50:7 58:2; 64:1; 65:2; *2 Clem.* 20:5; *T. Abr.* [Rec. A] 20:15; *T. Abr.* [Rec. B] 14:9), particularly 1 Pet 4:11, ᾧ ἐστιν ἡ δόξα καὶ τὸ κράτος εἰς τοὺς αἰῶνας τῶν αἰώνων, ἀμήν, "To whom is the glory and the might for ever, amen." Another close parallel occurs in *Apoc. Sedr.* 16:10, ᾧ ἡ δόξα καὶ τὸ κράτος εἰς τοὺς αἰῶνας τῶν αἰώνων. ἀμήν, "To whom [is] the glory and the might for ever, amen." The same doxological form occurs with some frequency in early Judaism, whence it was derived (1 Chr 29:11[LXX]; 4 Macc 18:24; *Grk. Apoc. Ezra* 7:16; *T. Job* 53:10).

*Explanation*

The doxology of vv 5d–6 immediately follows the epistolary prescript of vv 4–5a. While nearly all of Paul's letters have a thanksgiving section directly following the epistolary prescription, only Galatians (like Rev 1:4–6) omits the thanksgiving entirely and substitutes a doxology, while 2 Corinthians omits the thanksgiving and includes a benediction. Doxologies normally consist of four elements: (1) address to God in the dative ("to whom"), (2) the ascription of glory (δόξα), (3) the unending validity of the ascription of glory ("forever"), and (4) the concluding "amen" (cf. Phil 4:20; 2 Tim 4:18). This doxology is unusual in that it is addressed to Christ rather than to God. Each element can be expanded in various ways. Here "him" (= Christ) is modified by several verbal forms describing in temporal sequence the redemptive action of God through Christ: he has *loved* us, *freed* us from our sins, and *made* us a kingdom, priests. In Jewish and Christian texts, doxologies often function to conclude a section of text (4 Macc 18:24; 1 Esdr 4:40, 59). They are used in Christian letters to close the main section (Phil 4:20; 2 Tim 2:18; Heb 13:21), or in a few cases to close the entire letter (Rom 16:25–27; 2 Pet 3:18; Jude 24–25; *1 Clem.* 65:2).

# E. Two Prophetic Oracles (1:7–8)

## Bibliography

**Bickerman, E.** "Altars of Gentiles: A Note on the Jewish 'Ius Sacrum.'" In *Studies in Jewish and Christian History.* Part 2. Leiden: Brill, 1980. 324–46. **Boyd, W. J. P.** "'I am Alpha and Omega' (Rev. 1:8; 21:6; 22:13)." *SE* 2 [= TU 87] (1964) 526–31. **Delling, G.** "Die Altarinscrift eines Gottesfürchtigen in Pergamon." *NovT* 7 (1964–65) 73–80. **Hayward, R.** *Divine Name and Presence in the Memra.* Totowa, NJ: Allanheld, Osmun, 1981. **Lindars, B.** *New Testament Apologetic.* London: SCM, 1961. **Nestle, E.** "Alpha und Omega, San und Sigma." *Philologus* 70 (1911) 155–57. **Nilsson, M. P.** "Zwei Altäre aus Pergamon." *Eranos* 54 (1956) 167–73. **Perrin, N.** "Mark XIV.62: The End Product of a Christian Pesher Tradition?" *NTS* 12 (1965–66) 150–55. ———. *Rediscovering the Teaching of Jesus.* New York/Evanston, IL: Harper & Row, 1967. **Scott, R. B. Y.** "'Behold, He Cometh with Clouds.'" *NTS* 5 (1958–59) 127–32. **Stanford, W. B.** "The Significance of the Alpha and Omega in Revelation I.8." *Hermathena* 98 (1964) 43–44. **Stendahl, K.** *The School of St. Matthew.* Philadelphia: Fortress, 1968. **Vanni, U.** "Un esempio di dialogo liturgico in Ap 1:4–8." *Bib* 57 (1976) 453–67. **Vos, L. A.** *The Synoptic Traditions in the Apocalypse.* Kampen: Kok, 1965. 60–71. **Yarbro Collins, A.** "The 'Son of Man' Tradition and the Book of Revelation." In *The Messiah: Developments in Earliest Judaism and Christianity,* ed. J. H. Charlesworth. Minneapolis: Fortress, 1992. 536–68.

## Translation

> [7] Indeed, he is coming[a] with[b] the clouds,
> and every eye will see[c] him, including those who pierced[d] him.
> Then all the societies[e] of the world will mourn[f] for him.
> Assuredly! Amen!
>
> [8] "I am[a] the Alpha and the Omega,"[a][b] says the Lord God,
> "The one who is and who was and the coming one,
> the Almighty."

## Notes

7.a. The verb ἔρχεται, "comes," is in the present tense, yet it is parallel to the verb ὄψεται, "will see," in the next line and therefore must be construed as a futuristic use of the present, a usage typically found in oracles (see Herodotus 7.140, 141; BDR § 323). There are several instances in Revelation of this use of ἔρχεται as *futurum instans* (1:4, 7, 8; 2:5, 16; 3:11; 4:8; 9:12; 11:14; 16:15; 22:7, 12, 20; the same usage occurs twenty-six times in the Fourth Gospel). Burney (*Aramaic Origin,* 150–52) considered this use of ἔρχεται to be a Semitism, though in this he is wrong. A similar juxtaposition of ἔρχεται with a verb in future tense is found in Matt 17:11; Luke 12:54–55; John 14:3 (BDR § 323.1).

7.b. Variant: ἐπί] C Oecumenius[2053 2062] (text and commentary). This substitution is in agreement with the Septuagint version of the OG Bible (see Rev 14:14), while the phrase μετὰ τῶν νεφελῶν is based on Theodotion (P. Grelot, "Les versions grecques de Daniel," *Bib* 47 [1966] 386–87).

7.c. Variants: (1) ὄψεται] A C 025 Andr c e f g i l n[-2065] 94 1773 2019. (2) ὄψονται] ℵ fam 1611[1611] 2351 sa bo syr[ph h] arm[4] Victorinus Andreas (Andr a b d h n[2065] 598). The original reading is certainly ὄψεται (fut. third-person sing., "he/she/it will see"), which was replaced by ὄψονται, through assimilation to the form of κόψονται that follows (see Schmid, *Studien* 2:122).

7.d. Variant: (1) insert ἐπί before αὐτόν] Andreas. (2) omit ἐπί] ℵ* 792 fam 1611[2050 2344] 2351 Andr/Byz 2b[582] Primasius. (3) omit ἐπ' αὐτόν] Andr a c.

7.e. The term φυλή, "tribe" (RSV, NRSV), is a general term for various forms of social organization, usually a constituent element of a πόλις, "city-state," or ἔθνος, "nation," though the term can also be used in the broader sense of "people" (NIV, NEB) or "nation" (BAGD, 869 [though the references there to Xenophon *Cyropaedia* 2.5 and Dionysius of Halicarnassus 2.7 are inappropriate]). The term "society" has been chosen because it is as elastic in English as φυλή is in Gk., referring to organized human communities of varying sizes and constituencies. Elsewhere in Revelation the author strings together a quasi-formulaic set of four terms for human societies in an attempt to be inclusive (5:9; 7:9; 11:9; 13:7; 14:6): φυλή, "tribe," γλῶσσα, "tongue," λάος, "people," and ἔθνος, "nation." Probably he does not include such synonyms in Rev 1:7 because he is reproducing a traditional formulation.

7.f. ἐπί + acc. can indicate the object of mourning after verbs of mourning such as κόπτειν, κλαίειν, and πενθεῖν (see Helbing, *Kasussyntax*, 73): (1) κόπτειν (2 Kgdms 1:12; 11:26 [*var. lect.*]; LXX Zech12:10); (2) κλαίειν (2 Kgdms 1:12; *T. Job* 43:11; 53:4; Luke 23:28[2x]; Rev 18:11); (3) πενθεῖν (LXX 1 Kgdms 16:1; 2 Kgdms 13:37; 14:2; 19:1; 2 Chr 35:24; 1 Esdr 9:2; 2 Esdr 10:6; Hos 10:5; Isa 66:10; *T. Reub.* 1:10; 3:15; Rev 18:11); (4) θρηνεῖν (LXX 2 Kgdms 3:33; 2 Chr 35:25; Lam 1:1; Ezek 32:16, 18); (5) στενάζειν (Ezek 26:16; 28:19). Though this is frequently judged a Hebraism, this is doubtful in view of POxy 1.115, lines 3ff.: ἔκλαυσα ἐπὶ τῶι εὐμοίρωι, "I mourned for the blessed one" (MM, 345). BAGD, 289, construes ἐπί in the phrase κόψονται ἐπ᾽ αὐτον in terms of feelings or actions directed toward a person or thing.

8.a-a. There is a certain unevenness here since the Gk. letter A is spelled ἄλφα, while the letter Ω is written but not spelled out (the Latin MSS usually give the Gk. letters A and Ω). The reason is simply that Gk. grammarians did not coin the word ὦμεγα until the seventh century A.D., and thereafter it began to be inserted into MSS of Revelation here and in 21:6; 22:13. See Nestle, *Philologus* 70 [1911] 155–57; Metzger, *Manuscripts*, 6–7 n. 13 (where Nestle's references are substantially supplemented).

8.b. Variants: (1) omit ἀρχὴ καὶ τέλος] A C ℵ³ 025 046 fam 1006[1006 1841] fam 1611[1611] Oecumenius[2053] [2062] Andr i[2042] 1 94 Primasius Ambrose Byzantine; Tischendorf, *NT Graece;* WHort; von Soden, *Text;* Nestle-Aland[27]; *TCGNT[1]*, 732; *TCGNT[2]*, 663. (2) insert ἀρχὴ καὶ τέλος] ℵ* fam1611[1854 2050 2329] 2351 Andreas it[gig h] vg cop[bo] Beatus. (3) ἡ ἀρχὴ καὶ τὸ τέλος] fam 1611[2329] cop[bo]. Readings (2) and (3) are scribal insertions influenced by the use of the phrase in similar contexts in 21:6; 22:13, in which, however, both words are articular, as in reading (3).

## *Form/Structure/Setting*

### I. OUTLINE

E. Two prophetic oracles (vv 7–8)
  1. Prophecy of the coming of Jesus (v 7)
    a. First couplet: The Parousia as salvation (v 7ab)
      (1) He comes with the clouds (v 7a)
      (2) Every one will witness his coming (v 7b)
    b. Second couplet: The Parousia as judgment (v 7cd)
      (1) Those who pierced him will see him (v 7c)
      (2) All the tribes of the earth will mourn because of him (v 7d)
  2. Three self-predications of the Lord God (v 8)
    a. I am the Alpha and the Omega (v 8a)
    b. [I am] the One who is, was, and is to come (v 8b)
    c. [I am] the Almighty (v 8c)

### II. LITERARY ANALYSIS

Rev 1:7–8 consists of two discrete units with no intrinsic literary connections, which are linked together only by virtue of the fact that they are sandwiched between two carefully defined textual units, the doxology in 1:5b–6 and John's vision and commission in 1:9–3:22. The author regularly places two oracles together at various points in his narrative, with the second often amplifying the first (e.g., 13:9; 14:13; 16:15; 19:9; 21:5–8; 22:12–15, 18–20; see Aune, *Prophecy,* 327). These and other prophetic oracles that the author has inserted in various contexts throughout his work provide evidence for the author's prophetic activity, which must have been exercised for many years previously. Revelation itself is a kind of *magnum opus* in which the author's previous work (some of which was formulated as much as twenty to thirty years earlier, i.e., in the 60s and 70s of the first century A.D.) was incorporated into a new and more comprehensive context.

The first oracle (v 7), which is unattributed, is introduced by the particle ἰδού, "behold," and concludes with ναί, ἀμήν, "yes, amen," both characteristic of early Christian prophetic speech. The oracle in v 7 is formed by the conflation of two allusions to the OT, Dan 7:13 and Zech 12:10–14, a combination also found in Matt 24:30 (see Stendahl, *School,* 212–15; Yarbro Collins, "'Son of Man,'" 536–47). The similarities between Matt 24:30 and Rev 1:7 make it highly probable that there is some kind of traditional link between the two, while the differences indicate that neither text is directly dependent upon the other (Vos, *Synoptic Traditions,* 60–71). In the Aramaic text of Dan 7:13, the verbal clause אתה הוה 'ātēh hăwâ consists of the participle אָתֵה 'ātēh (from אֲתָה 'ătâ, "come"), together with the perfect verb הֲוָה hăwâ, "to be, become," in a periphrastic construction meaning "came." The LXX version translated this periphrasis with the imperfect ἤρχετο, "came" (J. Ziegler, ed., *Daniel,* 169–70), while in Theodotion it is rendered with the present participle ἐρχόμενος, "coming." The text of Rev 1:7a is also similar to Theodotion in that the preposition μετά is used in both. In Rev 1:7, on the other hand, the verb is changed from the past to the present (i.e., futuristic present) verb ἔρχεται, changing the allusion to Dan 7:13 to an oracle referring to a future rather than a past event (Yarbro Collins, "'Son of Man,'" 541). The striking feature of the first oracle is that it does not explicitly mention "the one like a son of man" found in Dan 7:13.

Dan 7:13 and Zech 12:10–12 are also combined (for a discussion of the allusion to Zech 12:10–12, see below) in Matt 24:30 (though there the allusions to Dan 7:13 and Zech 12:10–12 occur in reverse order):

> καὶ τότε κόψονται πᾶσαι αἱ φυλαὶ τῆς γῆς,
> Then all the tribes of the earth will mourn,

> καὶ ὄψονται τὸν υἱὸν τοῦ ἀνθρώπου ἐρχόμενον
> and they will see the Son of Man coming

> ἐπὶ τῶν νεφελῶν τοῦ οὐρανοῦ μετὰ δυνάμεως καὶ δόξης πολλῆς
> on the clouds of heaven with power and great glory.

A relatively apocopated version, which combines allusions to Dan 7:13 and Zech 12:10–12, is still recognizable in *Did.* 16:8:

> τότε ὄψεται ὁ κόσμος τὸν κύριον
> Then the world will see the Lord

> ἐρχόμενον ἐπάνω τῶν νεφελῶν τοῦ οὐρανοῦ
> coming on the clouds of heaven

A similar combination appears in Justin *Dial.* 14.8:

> οἱ δὲ εἰς τὴν δευτέραν αὐτοῦ παρουσίαν
> But others [prophets] refer to his second coming

> ὅτε ἐν δόξῃ καὶ ἐπάνω τῶν νεφελῶν παρέσται
> when in glory and upon the clouds he will appear

> καὶ ὄψεται ὁ λαὸς ὑμῶν
> and your people will see

> καὶ γνωριεῖ εἰς ὃν ἐξεκέντησαν,
> and recognize the one whom they pierced,

> ὡς Ὡσηέ [sic! Zechariah] εἷς τῶν δώδεκα προφητῶν,
> as Hosea [i.e., Zechariah] one of the twelve prophets,

> καὶ Δανιὴλ προεῖπον, εἰρημένοι εἰσί.
> and Daniel have predicted.

The second oracle, found in v 8, is unusual in that it, as well as the oracle in 21:5–8, is attributed to *God*. Since the three phrases that constitute the oracle in v 8 belong to the author, this oracle must have arisen within his prophetic ministry upon a previous occasion.

### Comment

**7a** Ἰδοὺ ἔρχεται μετὰ τῶν νεφελῶν, "Indeed, he is coming with the clouds." The demonstrative particle ἰδού, derived from the verb ὁρᾶν, "to see," occurs twenty-six times in Revelation. ἰδού, frequently translated "behold," has two different related meanings (Louw-Nida, § 91.10, 13; the discussion in *EDNT* 2:173 is overly subtle): (1) It functions as a marker of strong emphasis indicating the validation of the statement it introduces and can be translated "indeed, certainly," and in Revelation is always used with this meaning in *speech* (thirteen times: 1:7, 18; 2:10, 22; 3:8, 9[2x], 20; 5:5; 9:12; 11:14; 21:3, 5). (2) It functions as a marker to draw attention to that which it introduces and can be translated "look, listen, pay attention." In Revelation it is always used with this meaning in *narrative* (thirteen times: 4:1, 2; 5:6; 6:2, 5, 8, 12; 7:9; 12:3; 14:1, 14; 15:5; 19:11). In Revelation, as in the LXX, when a substantive follows καὶ ἰδού, it is always in the nominative case. In the LXX, καὶ ἰδού is a common way of translating the Hebrew phrase וְהִנֵּה *wĕhinēh*, though as Fitzmyer observes (*Luke* 1:121), it represents the Aramaic וְהָא *wĕhā'* equally well. Here it functions to affirm the truth of the prediction of the coming of Jesus that immediately follows (Fiedler, *Formel*, 42), and as such functions in very much the same way as the concluding responses ναί, ἀμήν, "assuredly, amen." This particular saying is in the third person but clearly functions very similarly to three (or four) related first-person sayings (ἰδού in the first is a *varia lectio* with poor attestation):

Rev 3:11    [ἰδοὺ] ἔρχομαι ταχύ·
             [Indeed] I am coming soon.

Rev 16:15     Ἰδοὺ ἔρχομαι ὡς κλέπτης.
                Indeed, I am coming like a thief.

Rev 22:7      καὶ ἰδοὺ ἔρχομαι ταχύ.
                Indeed, I am coming soon.

Rev 22:12     Ἰδοὺ ἔρχομαι ταχύ.
                Indeed, I am coming soon.

Variations on this same phrase occur twice more with the different, though functionally analogous, introductory particles ναί and ἀμήν:

Rev 22:20a    ναί, ἔρχομαι ταχύ.
                Surely, I am coming soon.

Rev 22:20b    Ἀμήν, ἔρχου κύριε Ἰησοῦ.
                Amen, come Lord Jesus.

This phrase is a clear allusion to Dan 7:13 (elsewhere alluded to in Revelation only in 1:13; 14:14), where it is similarly phrased as a third-person statement, though within the context of a narrative, not a speech. The allusion is particularly striking, however, because of the unexpected absence of a reference to the phrase "like a son of man," a comparison that is found in 1:13 and 14:14 (see *Comments* there). However, this is not the only clear allusion to Dan 7:13 in early Christian literature that omits or avoids the "like a son of man" comparison. Other passages that omit this phrase include *Did.* 16:8; Justin *1 Apol.* 52.3; *Dial.* 14.8; 120.4 (see Borsch, *Son of Man*, 48). The demonstrative particle ἰδού has also been taken over from Dan 7:13 (as a way of rendering the Aramaic verb וַאֲרוּ *waʾărû*, "and I saw"), but there it functions as a marker to draw attention to something described in a narrative, while in Rev 1:7a it functions to underscore the reliability of the statement that follows.

Dan^MT 7:13     וַאֲרוּ עִם־עֲנָנֵי שְׁמַיָּא *wasʾărû ʿim-ʿănānê šĕmayyāʾ*
                And I saw with the clouds of heaven,

                כְּבַר אֱנָשׁ אָתֵה הֲוָא *kĕbar ʾĕnaš ʾātēh hăwāʾ*
                one like a son of man came

Dan^LXX 7:13    καὶ ἰδοὺ ἐπὶ τῶν νεφελῶν τοῦ οὐρανοῦ
                And behold on the clouds of heaven

                ὡς υἱὸς ἀνθρώπου ἤρχετο
                one like a son of man came

Dan^Theo 7:13    καὶ ἰδοὺ μετὰ τῶν νεφελῶν τοῦ οὐρανοῦ
                And behold with the clouds of heaven

                ὡς υἱὸς ἀνθρώπου ἐρχόμενος
                one like a son of man coming

The preposition μετά, "with," is found in Theodotion (reflecting the Aramaic preposition עִם *ʿim*), while the LXX version (only extant in MSS 88 and 967, but reflected in the Syro-Hexapla as well) has ἐπί, "on, upon"; see Ziegler, *Daniel*, 169–70. There are several texts that refer to the coming of Christ with clouds (Matt 24:30 = Mark 13:26 = Luke 21:27; Matt 26:64 = Mark 14:62; *Did.* 16:8; *Apoc. Pet.* 1; Justin *1 Apol.* 51.9; *Dial.* 14.8; 31.1; 120.4; see 4 Ezra 13:3).

**7b** καὶ ὄψεται αὐτὸν πᾶς ὀφθαλμός, "and every eye will see him." This part of v 7 contains an allusion to Zech 12:10b in the phrase καὶ ὄψεται, "and [every eye] will see," though the LXX text of Zech 12:10 has the synonymous phrase καὶ ἐπιβλέψονται, "and they will see." When quoted in Matt 24:30 and John 19:37, however, the verb used in both cases is ὄψονται, "they will see." It is quite possible that Dan 7:13 and Zech 12:10 are also conflated in Mark 13:26 and Luke 21:27, both of which read καὶ τότε ὄψονται τὸν υἱὸν τοῦ ἀνθρώπου ἐρχόμενον ἐν νεφέλαις [Luke: νεφέλῃ], "and then they will see the son of man coming with clouds [Luke: a cloud]" (Perrin, *Jesus*, 182–83). In these two passages, however, the presence of Zech 12:10 is betrayed *only* by the phrase καὶ τότε ὄψονται, "and then they will see," a phrase that Matthew amplifies into an explicit reference to Zech 12:10 in Matt 24:30. Yet Dan 7:13 in the MT is introduced with a verb of seeing (Aramaic חזה *ḥzh;* Greek ἐθεώρουν), though in a past tense since it was used to describe a vision that occurred in the past: "I saw in the night visions." The future tense of the verb ὁρᾶν, "to see," is frequently used in introducing allusions to Dan 7:13 (Mark 13:26 = Matt 24:30 = Luke 21:27; Mark 14:62 = Matt 26:64; John 1:51; cf. Acts 7:56 [where the verb is θεωρῶ]; *Did.* 16:8; *Apoc. Peter* 6; Justin *1 Apoc.* 51). The phrase "every eye" turns the event into one of universal significance. In this connection, *Did.* 16:8 is of particular interest: τότε ὄψεται ὁ κόσμος τὸν κύριον ἐρχόμενον ἐπάνω τῶν νεφελῶν τοῦ οὐρανοῦ, "then the world will see the Lord coming upon the clouds of heaven." Here the universal perspective is clearly expressed through the use of the term κόσμος; cf. the use of κόσμος as the subject of a verb of cognition in John (1:10; 14:19). Behind Matt 24:30; Rev 1:7; John 19:37, Lindars (*Apologetic*, 124) reconstructs a common original text:

καὶ ὄψονται εἰς ὃν ἐξεκέντησαν
And they will look at the one whom they pierced

καὶ κόψονται ἐπ᾽ αὐτὸν πᾶσαι αἱ φυλαὶ τῆς γῆς.
and all the tribes of the earth will mourn because of him.

Here it is quite possible that ὄψονται was used to replace the ἐπιβλέψονται of Zech 12:10 because it differs from κόψονται only in the initial κ of the latter; i.e., it represents a wordplay in the early Christian OT interpretation (Perrin, *Jesus*, 182). The phrase "every eye," however, is not found in Zech 12:10–14 and constitutes a universalistic emphasis that is repeated in the phrase πᾶσαι αἱ φυλαὶ τῆς γῆς, "all the tribes of the earth." Zech 12:10, 12 are also combined with Dan 7:13 in Ps.-Epiphanius *Testimonia* 100.1 (R. V. Hotchkiss, *A Pseudo-Epiphanius Testimony Book* [Missoula, MT: Scholars, 1974] 76): Ζαχαρίας λέγει· Ὄψονται τὸν υἱον τοῦ ἀνθρώπου ἐρχόμενον ἐπὶ τῶν νεφελῶν· καὶ κόψονται φυλαὶ κατὰ φυλάς, "Zechariah says: 'They will see the son of man coming on the clouds and the tribes will mourn in turn.'" The antiquity of this passage is suggested in part by the fact that the preposition ἐπί, "on, upon," is found in the LXX versions, while μετά is found in Theodotion (see Ziegler, *Daniel*, 169–70).

**7c** καὶ οἵτινες αὐτὸν ἐξεκέντησαν, "including those who pierced him." This is an allusion to Zech 12:10b, where a literal translation of the MT reads "And they shall look upon me whom they have pierced [אלי את אשר־דקרו *'ēlay 'ēt 'ăšer-dāqārû*]." The MT is problematic here, and אלי *'ēlay*, "unto me," has frequently been emended to אליו *'ēlayw*, "unto him." S. R. Driver claims that more than fifty MSS support the reading אליו *'ēlayw* (*The Minor Prophets* [Edinburgh: T. C. and E. J. Jack, 1906] 266), which also fits the context since עליו *'ālāyw*, "upon him," occurs twice, once in each of the following two clauses in Zech 12:10b. Yet אלי *'ēlay* is certainly the *lectio difficilior,* for if the "me" in the pronominal affix in אלי *'ēlay* refers to Yahweh, who is the speaker, then the passage is very difficult to interpret satisfactorily. R. L. Smith suggests that Yahweh is claiming that the people had metaphorically pierced him by their evil ways (*Micah-Malachi,* WBC 32 [Waco: Word, 1984] 276). The RSV favors the emendation אליו *'ēlayw:* "when they look on him whom they have pierced," while the REB tries to combine אלי *'ēlay* with אליו *'ēlayw:* "Then they will look on me, on him whom they have pierced." Most LXX MSS read καὶ ἐπιβλέψονται πρὸς με ἀνθ' ὧν κατωρχήσαντο, "they will look upon me whom they treated despitefully." Here the verb κατορχεῖσθαι, "to dance in triumph over, treat despitefully" (LSJ 930), apparently reflects a form based on the root דקר *dqr*, "to pierce," but mistakenly read as based on the root רקד *rqd,* "to dance, leap about." The verb ἐξεκέντησαν is used together with the pronoun αὐτόν in Rev 1:7, as well as in John 19:37, where αὐτόν is omitted, though understood (as well as Aquila [σὺν ᾧ ἐξεκέντησαν], Theodotion [ὃν ἐξεκέντησαν] and Lucian [εἰς ὃν ἐξεκέντησαν]; Symmachus has ἔμπροσθεν ἐπεξεκέντησαν), and is therefore closer to the Hebrew text. Jellicoe (*Septuagint,* 87) claims that the citation from Zech 12:10 in Rev 1:7 reflects a Theodotionic reading, perhaps more accurately described as a proto-Theodotionic reading. Justin reads "and your people will see [ὄψεται] and will recognize whom they have pierced [εἰς ὃν ἐξεκέντησαν]" (*Dial.* 14.8); cf. *1 Apol.* 52.12: "and then they will see the one whom they pierced [εἰς ὃν ἐξεκέντησαν]" (see *Dial.* 32.2); this is identical with the Lucianic text. In *Dial.* 64.7, the allusion to Zech 12:10 is phrased differently: "those who pierced him will see him and shall mourn him [ὃν ὁρᾶν μέλλουσι καὶ κόπτεσθαι οἱ ἐκκεντήσαντες αὐτόν]" (see *Dial.* 118.1).

**7d** καὶ κόψονται ἐπ' αὐτὸν πᾶσαι αἱ φυλαὶ τῆς γῆς, "then all the tribes of the earth shall wail on account of him." This alludes to Zech 12:12, which begins "The land shall mourn, each family by itself" (NRSV). While הארץ *hā'āreṣ* in Zech 12:12 can mean either "land (of Israel)" or "earth," it probably means the former. Yet in Rev 1:7d, the universalizing tendency noted above is again emphasized in the phrase "all the tribes of the earth." Matt 24:30 has a closely similar version: καὶ τότε κόψονται πᾶσαι αἱ φυλαὶ τῆς γῆς, "and then all the tribes of the earth will mourn."

**7e** ναί, ἀμήν, "Assuredly! Amen!" ναί, "yes," is used to mark an emphatic affirmation of a statement (Louw-Nida, § 69. 1) and is used in this way three times in Revelation (1:7; 16:7; 22:20; cf. 14:13 *var. lect.*). ναί, "yes," is used as a functional equivalent to ἀμήν, "amen" (both terms are used interchangeably in the following texts: Matt 23:26 = Luke 11:51; 2 Cor 1:20; Rev 1:7; 22:20; *Acts Thom.* 121; see Berger, *Amen-Worte,* 6–9); see *Notes* on 14:13. Further, the relatively rare introductory formula ναὶ λέγω ὑμῖν (Matt 11:9 = Luke 7:26; 12:5) is obviously equivalent to ἀμὴν λέγω ὑμῖν. It therefore makes little sense for ναί and ἀμήν to be separated into two semantic domains in Louw-Nida, §§ 69.1, 72.6.

**8a** ἐγώ εἰμι τὸ ἄλφα καὶ τὸ ὦ, λέγει κύριος ὁ θεός, "'I am the Alpha and the Omega,' says the Lord God." The divine predicate "Alpha and Omega" occurs twice more in Revelation, once of God in 21:6 (as here), and once of Christ in 22:13 (see Clement of Alex. *Strom.* 4.25; Tertullian *De monog.* 5). Since alpha and omega are the first and last letters in the Greek alphabet, this divine title emphasizes the sovereignty of God in a way similar to the titles "the beginning and the end" (21:6; 22:13; see 3:14) and "the first and the last" (1:17; 2:8; 22:13). In Jewish alphabet symbolism, the Hebrew word אמת *'emet*, "truth," was understood as a way of designating God as beginning, middle, and end, because א was the first letter of the Hebrew alphabet, מ the middle letter, and ת the last letter. The vowels A and Ω occur together in the magical papyri as a permutation and abbreviation of the seven vowels (*PGM* IV.411, 528, 992, 993, 1224, 2351; V.363, 367; VII.476, 720; XIII.849–59[twice], 931; XLIV [illustrated with a figure holding a staff with the letters A and Ω on either side]; see Stanford, *Hermathena* 98 [1964] 43–44). Further, in the magical papyri, the seven vowels often function explicitly as a divine name (*PGM* XIII.39; XXI.11–14). This seven-vowel divine name can be used in self-predications (perhaps under the influence of Egyptian magic, where the magician pretends to be the deity): "I am ΑΕΗΙΟΥ[Ω ΑΕΗΙΟΥΩ]" (*PGM* III.661), or in *PGM* XIII.207: "Lord, I imitate [you by saying] the seven vowels . . . A EE HHH" etc. Occasionally AΩ is found in conjunction with another divine name, as in "Abrasax AΩ" (*PGM* V.363, 367; cf. IV.528), or as a divine name (under the supposition that the seven vowels, individually, in various combinations, and collectively symbolize the divine name), e.g., "I call upon you with your name AΩ ΕΥ ΗΟΙ" etc. (*PGM* IV.1182–83; cf. IV.992–93, 3238–39). Further, the letter aleph was understandably associated with the concept of beginning or ἀρχή: "First origin of my origin, ΑΕΗΙΟΥΩ, first beginning [ἀρχή . . . πρώτη] of my beginning" (*PGM* IV.487–88). The divine name most frequently used in the magical papyri is Iao, a name also used in conjunction with AΩ in sequences of vowel permutations functioning as *voces magicae*, "magic words," often juxtaposed with series of other divine names (see Aune, "Iao," *RAC*, 17:1–12). Farrer (*Images*, 263–68) argued in a forced manner that IAΩ, the Greek form of the Tetragrammaton *yhwh*, means "I am the Alpha and the Omega." In *Gos. Eg.* 3.43.8–44.9, the unpronounceable name is made up of the seven Greek vowels (in a Coptic text), each written twenty-two times (the number of letters in the Hebrew alphabet), in the order IHOΥΕΑΩ, which Böhlig et al. speculate might mean Ἰήου ἐ(στὶν) A (καὶ) Ω, i.e., "Jesus is the Alpha and the Omega" (*Gos. Eg.*, 173). For an instance in which the single letter א is used for the name of God in a magical context, see Isbel, *Incantation*, 60–63 (text 19.2): "In the name of the LORD and 'I-am-who-I am' [ואהיא א ב‹ו›שב *bš<w>m ' w'hy' 'šr 'hy*]"; here the waw can be understood epexegetically to mean *id est*. In a similar text, the phrase "in the name of """" [אאאאאא בשום *bšwm """"*]" occurs (27.2; Isbel, *Incantation*, 79).

The combination "Lord and God" occurs eleven times in Revelation (1:8; 4:8, 11; 11:17; 15:3; 16:7; 18:8; 19:6; 21:22; 22:5, 6), but relatively infrequently in the rest of the NT (usually in the phrase "my/your Lord and my/your God": Matt 4:7, 10; 22:37; Mark 12:29; Luke 1:16; John 20:28).

**8b** ὁ ὤν καὶ ὁ ἦν καὶ ὁ ἐρχόμενος, ὁ παντοκράτωρ, "'The one who is and who was and the one who comes, the Almighty.'" On the first three divine predicates, see *Comment* on 1:4. The term παντοκράτωρ, referring to God's supremacy over all creation (from the terms πᾶν, "all," and κρατεῖν, "to rule"), occurs nine times in Revelation (1:8; 4:8; 11:17; 15:3; 16:7, 14; 19:6, 15; 21:22) and is a favorite designation for God found frequently in early Jewish sources, and occasionally in pagan sources (for discussions of this title, see Höfer in Roscher, *Lex.* 3:1558–59; Michaelis, *TDNT* 3:914–15; MM, 478; Beskow, *Rex Gloriae*, 295–307; Horsley, ed., *New Docs* 3:118). In Revelation the term is *always* used of God (as is ὁ ὢν καὶ ὁ ἦν, etc. in 1:4, 8; 4:8; 11:17) and occurs nine times (1:8; 4:8; 11:17; 15:3; 16:7, 14; 19:6, 15; 21:22), though never in the secondary frame of Revelation, i.e., in 1:1–3, 12–20; 2:1–3:22; 22:6–21. The title occurs six times in the fixed invocation κύριε/κύριος ὁ θεὸς ὁ παντοκράτωρ (4:8; 11:17; 15:3; 16:7; 19:6; 21:22). Elsewhere in the NT the title occurs only in a quotation from Amos 3:13 in 2 Cor 6:18. The term occurs nearly 170 times in the LXX, most frequently as a translation of the divine titles צְבָאוֹת *sĕbā'ôt* (KB³, 3:934–35; in the transliterated form σαβαωθ [and related spellings], the name occurs frequently in the magical papyri and on magical gems) and שַׁדַּי *šadday* (often translated *omnipotens* in the Latin Vulgate; see KB, 4:1319–21). παντοκράτωρ occasionally occurs in other Jewish Greek literature also (*T. Abr.* [Rec. A] 8:3; 15:12; *Par. Jer.* 1:5; 9:6; *3 Apoc. Bar.* 1:3; *Ep. Arist.* 185.2; *Pr. Man.* 2.22.12 [Denis, *Fragmenta*, 115]; *Sib. Or.* 1.66; 2.330; *T. Sol.* 3:5; 6:8). It also occurs in four Jewish inscriptions from Gorgippia (Trebilco, *Jewish Communities*, 136) and in a dedicatory inscription from the Sardis synagogue (Robert, *Sardes*, 48–49; Lifschitz, *Donateurs*, no. 20). παντοκράτωρ occurs with some frequency in the magical papyri, sometimes as the result of Jewish influence (*PGM* III.218; XIII.761–62), but often clearly not (*PGM* IV.272, 1375; VII.668; XII.71, 238, 250; XIV.17). In the magical papyri, παντοκράτωρ is used of Agathos Daimon (*PGM* XII.238; XIVa.9; LXXI.1–5), Typhon-Seth (*PGM* IV.272; VII.962; XIVc.17), Albalal (*PGM* IV.968), Adonai (*PGM* IV.1552), Helios (*PGM* XXIIa.19), and Hermes (*PGM* VII.668); cf. Nock, *Essays* 1:383. The title is applied to Helios in an invocation in Macrobius *Sat.* 1.23.21. A relatively close parallel to Rev 1:8 (which includes the title ὁ ὢν) is found in *PGM* LXXII.3: ὁ ὢν θεὸς ὁ Ἰάω, κύριος παντοκράτωρ, "The God who is, Iao, Lord Almighty." The title also occurs with some frequency in early Christian texts (*PGL*, 1005) such as the Apostolic Fathers (*Did.* 10:3; *1 Clem.* inscr.; 2:3; 32:4; 56:6; 60:4; 62:2; Pol. *Phil.* inscr.; Hermas *Vis.* 3.3.5; *Sim.* 5.7.4 [*var. lect.*]; *Diogn.* 7.2; *Mart. Pol.* 14.1; 19.2). In Christian magical papyri, the title is most frequently used in connection with other divine titles in invocations (*PGM* 1.1; 8.1; 9.1; 13a.1; 21.1, 43–45; 24.1; Kropp, *Koptische Zaubertexte* 2:176, 178, 180; Delatte, *Anecdota Atheniensia*, 15.1, 11, 14; 26.7; 55.13; 409.23; 410.11, 13; 413.25; 477.9–10), where it is frequently applied to Christ. The Greek and Hebrew forms of the title are occasionally juxtaposed as if they represented different titles (Kropp, *Koptische Zaubertexte* 2:181, "Pantokrator Sa[baoth]," and 2:182, "Jao Sabaoth Adonai Eloi, Pantokrator"; cf. 2:188).

### Explanation

This is the first occurrence in Revelation of the phenomenon of the "amplified oracle"; i.e., a prophetic saying is appended to another one for the purpose of expanding or interpreting it (for seven other examples of the same phenomenon in Revelation, cf. 13:9; 14:13; 16:15; 19:9; 21:5–8; 22:12–15; 22:18–20). These prophetic oracles (which may be the products of the author himself or of others in the prophetic circle to which he belonged) are identifiable on formal grounds, underscore the prophetic character of the author's ministry, and constitute sources that have been inserted at various points in Revelation. In early Christianity, prophetic pronouncements could receive a responsory "amen" (1 Cor 14:6) and could also be subject to evaluation and interpretation (1 Cor 14:29). In this instance, the first oracle is uttered by a heavenly voice, while the second oracle begins with an affirmatory response, "Even so. Amen" (v 7b). The first oracle uses a traditional combination of allusions to Dan 7:13 and Zech 12:10 to predict the Parousia ("coming") of Christ as a cosmic event that will be witnessed by all and anticipates the distress and fear of unbelievers about to experience judgment (and so anticipates 19:11–16). Predictions in Revelation of the imminent return of Christ occur primarily in the framework of the book and are formulated as first-person sayings of the exalted Jesus (3:11; 16:15 [an interpolation]; 22:7, 12, 20[2x]). Though the explicit title "Son of Man" does not occur here (see 1:13; 14:14), the phrase "he is coming with clouds" is a clear allusion in v 7 to Dan 7:13, the source of the title. The imminence of the Parousia and of the end of the world is a central emphasis of Revelation (1:3; 16:15; 22:7, 12, 20). The second oracle is attributed to the "Lord God" (who speaks just twice in Revelation, here and in the climactic scene in 21:5–8) and contains three self-predications introduced with the phrase "I am": (1) the Alpha and the Omega (drawn from Hellenism), (2) the one who is and who was and who is to come (a combination of Jewish and Hellenistic divine names), and (3) the Almighty (borrowed from Judaism). In the highly stratified society of John's day, deities and rulers were accorded strings of extravagant titles. One of John's strategies for underlining the majesty and power of God and Christ in contrast to Satan and the earthly rulers in league with him is the use of titles of dignity drawn from various sources. The divine name "Alpha and Omega" (synonymous with "Beginning and End," 21:6; 22:13, and "First and Last," 1:17) was drawn from Hellenistic revelatory magic, where it is an abbreviation of the seven vowels widely believed to constitute a name of the highest God. John's developing Christology is evident when the same divine names that he earlier ascribed to God are applied to Christ.

# II.  John's Vision and Commission    (1:9–3:22)
## A.  Vision of "One like a Son of Man"    (1:9–20)

*Bibliography*

**Aune, D. E.** "The Apocalypse of John and Graeco-Roman Revelatory Magic." *NTS* 33 (1987) 481–501. **Bacchiocci, S.** *From Sabbath to Sunday: A Historical Investigation of the Rise of Sunday Observance in Early Christianity.* Rome: Pontifical Gregorian University, 1977. **Bartina, S.** "En su mano derecha siete asteres." *Estudios Eclesiásticos* 26 (1952) 71–78. **Bauckham, R.** "The Lord's Day." In *From Sabbath to Lord's Day,* ed. D. A. Carson. Grand Rapids, MI: Zondervan, 1982. 221–50. ———. "The Role of the Spirit in the Apocalypse." *EvQ* 52 (1980) 66–83. ———. "The Worship of Jesus in Apocalyptic Christianity." *NTS* 27 (1980–81) 322–41. **Beckwith, R. T.,** and **Stott, W.** *This Is the Day: The Biblical Doctrine of the Christian Sunday in Its Jewish and Early Church Setting.* London: Marshall, Morgan and Scott, 1978. **Beyerlin, W.** *Origins and History of the Oldest Sinaitic Traditions.* Oxford: Blackwell, 1965. **Black, M.** "The Throne-Theophany Prophetic Commission and the 'Son of Man': A Study in Tradition-History." In *Jews, Greeks and Christians: Religious Cultures in Late Antiquity,* ed. R. Hamerton-Kelly and R. Scroggs. Leiden: Brill, 1976. 57–73. **Boismard, M. E.** "'L'Apocalypse' ou 'les Apocalypses' de St Jean." *RB* 56 (1949) 507–41. **Bourguignon, E.** *Religion, Altered States of Consciousness, and Social Change.* Columbus: Ohio State UP, 1973. **Brown, R. E.** *The Semitic Background of the Term "Mystery" in the New Testament.* Philadelphia: Fortress, 1968. **Bruce, F. F.** "The Oldest Greek Version of Daniel." *OTS* 20 (1977) 23–40. ———. "The Spirit in the Apocalypse." In *Christ and the Spirit in the New Testament,* ed. B. Lindars and S. S. Smalley. Cambridge: Cambridge UP, 1973. 333–44. **Casey, M.** *Son of Man.* London: SPCK, 1979. **Charlesworth, J. H.** "The Jewish Roots of Christology: The Discovery of the Hypostatic Voice." *SJT* 39 (1986) 19–41. ———. *The Old Testament Pseudepigrapha and the New Testament.* SNTSMS 54. Cambridge: Cambridge UP, 1985. **Chernus, I.** *Mysticism in Rabbinic Judaism.* Berlin/New York: de Gruyter, 1982. **Collins, J. J.** *Daniel with an Introduction to Apocalyptic Literature.* FOTL 20. Grand Rapids, MI: Eerdmans, 1984. **Dahl, N. A.** "Formgeschichtliche Beobachtungen zur Christusverkündigung in der Gemeindepredigt." In *Neutestamentliche Studien.* FS R. Bultmann, ed. W. Eltester. BZNW 21. Berlin: de Gruyter, 1954. 1–9. **Dalman, G.** *Die Worte Jesu.* Vol. 3. Darmstadt: Wissenschaftliche Buchgesellschaft, 1960. **Dean-Otting, M.** *Heavenly Journeys: A Study of the Motif in Hellenistic Jewish Literature.* Frankfurt am Main: Lang, 1984. **Deissmann, A.** "Lord's Day." *Encyclopedia Biblica* 3:2813–16. **Dugmore, C. W.** "The Lord's Day and Easter." In *Neotestamentica et Patristica.* FS O. Cullmann. Leiden: Brill, 1962. 272–81. **Eltester, W.** "Die siebenarmige Leuchter und der Titusbogen." In *Judentum, Urchristentum, Kirche.* FS J. Jeremias. Berlin: de Gruyter, 1960. 62–76. **Fenasse, J.-M.** "Le Jour du Seigneur: Apocalypse 1:10." *BVC* 61 (1965) 29–43. **Feuillet, A.** "Le fils de l'homme de Daniel et la tradition biblique." *RB* 60 (1953) 170–202, 321–46. **Finkel, A.** "The Pesher of Dreams and Scripture." *RevQ* 4 (1960) 357–70. **Frings, J.** "Das Patmosexil des Apostels Johannes nach Apk. 1:9." *TQ* 104 (1923) 20–31. **Gagé, J.** *Les classes sociales dans l'empire Romain.* Paris: Payot, 1964. **Ganschinietz, R.** "Iao." *RE* 9 (1914) 699–700. **Garnsey, P.** *Social Status and Legal Privilege in the Roman Empire.* Oxford: Clarendon, 1970. **Giblet, J.** "De revelatione Christi gloriosi in Apoc. 1:9–20." *Collectanea Mechliniensia* 43 (1958) 495–97. **Goodenough, E. R.** "The Menorah among Jews of the Roman World." *HUCA* 23 (1950–51) 449–92. **Güttgemanns, E.** "Die Semiotik des Traums in apokalyptischen Texten am Beispiel von Apokalypse Johannis 1." *LB* 59 (1987) 7–54. **Hanson, J. S.** "Dreams and Visions in the Graeco-Roman World and Early Christianity." *ANRW* II, 23/2:1395–1427. **Heckenbach, J.** "Hekate." *RE* 7 (1912) 2769–82. **Himmelfarb, M.** "Apocalyptic Ascent and the Heavenly Temple." In *Society of Biblical Literature: 1987 Seminar Papers*, ed. K. H. Richards. Atlanta: Scholars, 1987. 210–17. ———. "From Prophecy to Apocalypse: The *Book of Watchers* and Tours of Heaven." In *Jewish Spirituality: From the Bible to the Middle Ages*, ed. A. Green. New York: Crossroad, 1986. 149–53. **Horgan, M. P.** *Pesharim: Qumran Interpretations of Biblical Books.* Washington, DC: Catholic Biblical Association, 1979. **Jeansonne, S. P.** *The Old Greek Translation of Daniel 7–12.* CBQMS 19. Washington, DC: Catholic Biblical Association, 1988. **Jeremias, J.** "κλείς." *TDNT* 3:744–53. **Jeske, R. L.** "Spirit and Community in the Johannine Apocalypse." *NTS* 31 (1985) 452–66. **Johannessohn, M.** "Das biblische καὶ ἰδού in der Erzählung samt seiner hebräischen und griechischen Bibel." *Zeitschrift für vergleichende Sprachforschung* 66 (1939) 145–95; 67 (1942) 30–84. **Joüon, P.** "Apocalypse I:13: *periezosmenon pros tois mastois.*" *RSR* 24 (1934) 365–66. **Kohl, H.** "Kleiduchos." *RE* 11 (1921) 593–600. **Kraus, T.** *Hekate: Studien zu Wesen und Bild der Göttin in Kleinasien und Griechenland.* Heidelberg: Winter, 1960. **Kroll, J.** *Gott und Hölle: Der Mythos vom Descensus kampfe.* Leipzig/ Berlin: Teubner, 1932. **Lewis, I. M.** *Ecstatic Religion: An Anthropological Study of Spirit Possession and Shamanism.* Baltimore: Penguin, 1971. **Lietzmann, H.** *Der Menschensohn: Ein Beitrag zur Neutestamentlichen Theologie.* Freiburg i. B.; Leipzig: Mohr-Siebeck, 1896. **Lindblom, J.** "Theophanies in Holy Places in Hebrew Religion." *HUCA* 32 (1961) 91–106. **Lloyd, G. E. R.** *Magic, Reason and Experience: Studies in the Origins and Development of Greek Science.* Cambridge: Cambridge UP, 1979. **Lohse, E.** "Der Menschensohn in der Johannes-apokalypse." In *Jesus und der Menschensohn*, ed. R. Pesch and R. Schnackenburg. Freiburg: Herder, 1975. 415–20. **Lührmann, D.** "Epiphaneia." In *Tradition und Glaube: Das frühe Christentum in seiner Umwelt.* FS K. G. Kuhn, ed. G. Jeremias, H.-W. Kuhn, and H. Stegemann. Göttingen: Vandenhoeck & Ruprecht, 1971. 185–99. ———. "φαίνω." *TDNT* 9:1–10. ———. *Die Offenbarungsverständnis bei Paulus und in den paulinischen Gemeinden.* Neukirchen: Neukirchener, 1965. **Lust, J.** "Daniel 7:13 and the Septuagint." *ETL* 54 (1978) 62–69. **Meyers, C. L.** *The Tabernacle Menorah: A Synthetic Study of a Symbol from the Biblical Cult.* Missoula, MI: Scholars, 1976. **Michael, J. H.** "A Slight Misplacement in Revelation 1:13–14." *ExpTim* 42 (1930–31) 380–81. **Moering, E.** "Ἐγενόμην ἐν πνεύματι." *TSK* 92 (1919) 148–54. **Mommsen, T.** *Römisches Strafrecht.* 1899. Repr. Darmstadt: Wissenschaftliche Buchgesellschaft, 1955. **Moule, C. F. D.** "'The Son of Man': Some of the Facts." *NTS* 41 (1995) 277–79. **Müller, U. B.** *Messias und Menschensohn in jüdischen Apokalypsen und in der Offenbarung des Johannes.* Gütersloh: Mohn, 1972. **Newman, B.** "The Fallacy of the Domitian Hypothesis: Critique of the Irenaeus Source as a Witness for the Contemporary-Historical Approach to the Interpretation of Revelation." *NTS* 10 (1963) 13–39. **Oke, C. C.** "The Misplacement in Revelation 1, 13–14." *ExpTim* 43 (1931) 237. **Oppenheim, A. L.** *The Interpretation of Dreams in the Ancient Near East.* Transactions of the American Philosophical Society n.s. 46/3. Philadelphia: The American Philosophical Society, 1956. **Pax, E.** "Epiphanie." *RAC* 5:832–909. **Pearcy, L. T.** "Theme, Dream, and Narrative: Reading the *Sacred Tales* of Aelius Aristides." *TAPA* 118 (1988) 377–91. **Peek, W.** "Die Hydrophore Vera von Patmos." *RMP* 107 (1964) 315–25. **Pfister, F.** "Epiphanie." *RESup* 4:278ff. **Pleket, H. W.** "Religious History." In *Syngrammata: Studies in Graeco-Roman History*, ed. W. den Boer. Leiden: Brill, 1979. **Quispel, G.** "Ezekiel 1:26 in Jewish Mysticism and Gnosis." *VC* 34 (1980) 1–13. **Ramirez, J. M. C.** "El tema del 'Misterio' divino en la 'Regla de la Communidad' de Qumran." *ScrT* 7 (1975) 481–97. ———. "El 'Misterio' divino en los escritos posteriores de Qumran." *ScrT* 8 (1976) 445–75. **Ramlot, L.** "Apparition du Ressuscité au deporte de Patmos (Apoc. 1:9–20)." *BVC* 36 (1960) 16–25. **Rehkopf, F.** "Grammatisches zum Griechischen des Neuen Testaments." In *Der Ruf Jesu und die Antwort der Gemeinde.* FS J. Jeremias, ed. E. Lohse. Göttingen: Vandenhoeck & Ruprecht, 1970. 213–25. **Rordorf, W.** *Sunday: The History of the Day of Rest and Worship in the Earliest Centuries of the Christian Church.* Philadelphia: Westminster, 1968. **Rowland, C.** "The Vision of the Risen Christ in Rev. i. 13ff.: The Debt of an Early Christology to an Aspect of Jewish Angelology." *JTS* 31 (1980) 1–11. **Russell, D. A.,** and **Wilson, N. G.** *Menander Rhetor: Edited with Translation and Commentary.* Oxford: Clarendon, 1981. **Saffrey, H. D.** "Relire l'Apocalypse à Patmos." *RB*

82 (1975) 385–417. **Salter, T. B.** *"Homoion huion anthrôpou* in Rev 1.13 and 14.14." *BT* 44 (1993) 345–50. **Sanders, J. N.** "St. John on Patmos." *NTS* 9 (1963) 75–85. **Schmidt, J.** "Patmos." *RE* 18 (1949) 2174–91. **Segal, A. F.** *Two Powers in Heaven: Early Rabbinic Reports about Christianity and Gnosticism.* Leiden: Brill, 1977. **Sharpe, E. F.** "'I Was in the Spirit on the Lord's Day': Reflections on Ecstatic Religion in the New Testament." *Prudentia* Supplement (1985) 119–31. **Sickenberger, J.** "Die Deutung der Engel der sieben apokalyptischen Gemeinden." *RQ* 35 (1927) 135–49. **Skinjar, A.** "Fui mortus, et ecce sum vivens in saecula saeculorum." *VD* 17 (1937) 97–106. **Slater, T. B.** *"Homoios huion anthropou* in Rev 1.13 and 14.14." *BT* 44 (1993) 349–50. **Sperber, D.** "The History of the Menorah." *JJS* 16 (1965) 135–59. **Stanford, W. B.** "The Significance of the Alpha and Omega in Revelation I.8." *Hermathena* 98 (1964) 43–44. **Stearns, J. B.** *Studies of the Dream as a Technical Device in Latin Epic and Drama.* Lancaster: Lancaster, 1927. **Stott, W.** "A Note on the Word KYPIAKH in Rev. 1.10." *NTS* 12 (1965–66) 70–75. **Strand, K. A.** "Another Look at 'Lord's Day' in the Early Church and in Rev. i.10." *NTS* 13 (1966–67) 174–81. **Strobel, A.** "Die Passah-Erwartung in Lk. 17.20f." *ZNW* 49 (1958) 157–96. **Unnik, W. C. van.** *Het godspredikaat "Het begin en het einde" bij Flavius Josephus en in de openbaring van Johannes.* Mededelingen der Koninklijke Nederslandse Akademie van Wetenschappen, Afd. Letterkunde, Nieuwe Reeks 39/1. Amsterdam: Noord-Hollansche Uitgevers Maatschappij, 1976. **Vanni, U.** "Il 'Giorno del Signore' in Apoc.1.10, giorno di purificazione e di discernimento." *RevistB* 26 (1978) 187–99. **Vassiliadis, P.** "The Translation of Martyria Iesou in Revelation." *BT* 36 (1985) 129–34. **Vermeule, E.** *Aspects of Death in Early Greek Art and Poetry.* Berkeley: University of California, 1979. **Voss, J.** *Die Menorah: Gestalt und Funktion des Leuchters im Temple zu Jerusalem.* OBO 128. Freiburg, Schweiz: Universitätsverlag; Göttingen: Vandenhoeck & Ruprecht, 1993. **Weiser, Z.** "Zur Frage nach den Beziehungen der Psalmen zum Kult: Die Darstellung der Theophanie in den Psalmen und im Festkult." In *Festschrift Alfred Bertholet.* Tübingen: Mohr-Siebeck, 1950. 513–49. **Wilson, R. R.** "Prophecy and Ecstasy: A Reexamination." *JBL* 98 (1979) 321–37. ———. *Prophecy and Society in Ancient Israel.* Philadelphia: Fortress, 1980. **Wolff, C.** "Die Gemeinde des Christus in der Apokalypse des Johannes." *NTS* 27 (1980–81) 186–97. **Wortmann, D.** "Neue magische Gemmen." *Bonner Jahrbücher* 175 (1975) 63–82. **Yarbro Collins, A.** Review of *The Use of Daniel in Jewish Apocalyptic Literature and in the Revelation of St. John,* by G. K. Beale. *JBL* 105 (1986) 734–35. **Yarden, L.** *Tree of Light: A Study of the Menorah, The Seven-Branched Lampstand.* Ithaca: Cornell UP, 1971.

## *Translation*

⁹ᵃ*I, John,*[b] *your brother and companion*[c] *in the tribulation and* [d]*kingdom and endurance* [e] *in Jesus,*[e] *was on the island called Patmos because of the word of God and* [f]*my witness* [g]*to* [h]*Jesus.*[ga] ¹⁰*I fell into a prophetic trance*[a] *on the Lord's day and heard a* [b]*loud sound behind* [c]*me*[b] *(like that of a trumpet),* ¹¹ᵃ*saying:*[b] [c]*"Write*[d] [e]*what*[f] *you see*[e] *in a roll and*[g] *send it to the seven churches, to Ephesus, and to Smyrna, and to Pergamon, and to Thyatira,*[h] [i]*and to Sardis,*[i] *and to Philadelphia, and to Laodicea."*[j]

¹²*Then*[a]*I turned to see the voice*[b]*speaking*[c] *to me.*[b] *Upon turning around I saw seven golden menorahs,*[d] ¹³*and in the midst of the*[a]*menorahs*[b] *one*[c]*like a*[d]*son*[c] *of man wearing a long robe and with a golden sash encircling his chest.*[e] ¹⁴*His head,*[a]*that is,*[a] *his white*[b] *hair,*[c]*was like*[d] *white wool,*[c] *like snow, and his eyes were like a flame of fire,* ¹⁵*and his feet were like bronze when smelted*[a] *in a furnace, and his voice was like the sound of cascading water.* ¹⁶*In*[a]*his right hand*[a] *he had seven stars, and a sharp double-edged sword projected from his mouth, and his face was like the sun shining in full strength.*

¹⁷*And when I saw him, I fell at his feet as though dead, and he placed his right hand upon me, saying:*[a]

*"Stop being afraid.*[b]
*I am the First* [c] *and the Last,* [18]*even* [a] *the Living One,*
*And I was dead, but* [b] *behold* [c]*I now live* [c] *for ever and ever,*[d]
*And I have the keys* [e] *to* [f] *Death and Hades.*
[19]*Therefore* [a] *write down what you will see,*[b] *that is,*[c] *the events which are now happening and the events which* [d]*will* [e]*happen* [d] *hereafter.* [20]*As for the secret meaning* [a] *of the seven stars which* [b] *you saw* [c]*in my right hand* [c] *and the seven golden menorahs, the seven stars are the* [d] *angels of the seven churches, and the seven menorahs are the* [e] *seven churches.*"

## Notes

9.a-a. This sentence has been punctuated in a very different way by B. Newman (*NTS* 10 [1963] 135 n. 3): "I John . . . was on the Island of Patmos. Because of the word of God and the testimony of Jesus, I fell into a trance . . . ." The problem here, however, is that it is not obvious how "the word of God and the testimony of Jesus" could have caused John to fall into a trance.

9.b. The name John is anarthrous because the phrase ὁ ἀδελφὸς ὑμῶν καὶ συγκοινωνός, "your brother and companion," is in apposition to it, and in such cases proper names are anarthrous (e.g., 1:1; 2:20; 9:14; 16:12; 22:16, 21; cf. Mussies, *Morphology*, 191).

9.c. Variant: κοινωνός] fam 1006[1006 1841] Andr i[2042] Byzantine.

9.d. Variants: (1) insert ἐν] Oecumenius[2053 2062] it[h.]. (2) insert ἐν τῇ] Andreas. Reading (2) is a correction based on the author's tendency to repeat both the prep. and the article in a series of substantives (Schmid, *Studien* 2:193, 217), and also because when several attributives are connected with καί and apply to a single person or thing, only one article is used (Robertson, *Grammar*, 785–86), and here θλίψις cannot be understood as ἐν Ἰησοῦ.

9.e-e. Variants: (1) ἐν Ἰησοῦ] ℵ* C 025 fam 1611[1611 2050] Oecumenius[2053comm] Andr l; it[gig] vg syr[ph] cop[bo] Primasius[f]. (2) ἐν Χριστῷ] A. (3) ἐν Χριστῷ Ἰησοῦ] ℵ[2] fam 1006[1006 1841] 2351 Andr f[2031 -2036] i[2042] n 94 2019 Byzantine Beatus it[h]. (4) *en iesu christo*] Primasius. (5) Ἰησοῦ Χριστοῦ] fam 1611[2329] Andreas syr[h]. (5) omit] Oecumenius[2053]. It is strange that the variant ἐν Ἰησοῦ Χριστῷ is attested only in Latin; see reading (4). The difficulty of understanding ἐν Ἰησου has led to the correction in reading (5).

9.f. Variants: (1) Omit διά before τὴν μαρτυρίαν] A C Oecumenius[2053 2062] fam 1006 fam 1611[1611] [2344] 1678 2014. (2) Insert διά before τὴν μαρτυρίαν] ℵ Andreas Byzantine; von Soden, *Text*. In the original text of Revelation, διά was almost certainly absent; its presence can be accounted for by the fact that in the MS tradition of Revelation, if two or more substantives follow a prep., there is a tendency to repeat the prep. as well as the article (Schmid, *Studien* 2:217). Further, the phrase διὰ τὴν μαρτυρίαν is a stereotypical phrase in Revelation found in 6:9; 20:4.

9.g-g. The translation "to Jesus" indicates that the ambiguous Ἰησοῦ is construed here as an obj. gen.; see *Comment* on 1:9.

9.h. Variants: (1) omit Χριστοῦ] ℵ* A C 025 fam 1611[1611 2050 2329] Oecumenius[2053 2062] Andreas it[h gig] vg eth. (2) insert Χριστοῦ] ℵ[2] fam 1006 2351 Andr a c d f[2023 2073] g i[-2036] n[-2429] 94 1773 Byzantine it[a] syr cop Primasius.

10.a. In the phrase ἐν πνεύματι (lit. "in a/the spirit," but here translated "into a prophetic trance"; see *Comment* for a discussion), πνεύματι is anarthrous, making the meaning of the phrase ambiguous. John uses the prep. ἐν, "in," followed by an articular noun in the dat. case seventy times in Revelation, so he exhibits no hesitancy in using this common Gk. construction. Yet the article can be optionally or incidentally omitted from such prep. phrases, a phenomenon occurring in classical Gk. that became even more prevalent in Koine Gk. (Mayser, *Satzlehre*, 35–40). This is an exegetically significant point, for here the anarthrous πνεύματι *could* refer to the Spirit of God (see *Comment* under v 10).

10.b-b. Variants: (1) ὀπίσω μου φωνὴν μεγάλην] ℵ C fam 1611[1611 1854 2329] 1678 1778 Andreas; the Latin witnesses consistently have *post me vocem magnam* (it[gig] vg Primasius Beatus h); syr TR Tischendorf, *NT Graece;* WHort; Bousset (1906) 192; Merk, *NT;* Nestle-Aland[27] ; UBSGNT[4]. (2) φωνὴν ὀπίσω μου μεγάλην] 046 94 fam 1006 2351 Andr i[2042] n[2065] Byzantine. (3) φωνὴν μεγάλην ὀπισθέν μου] A; WHort[marg]; Charles, 2:239. (4) φωνὴν μεγάλην ὀπίσω μου] Andr n[2432]; B. Weiss, *Johannes-Apokalypse*, 127, 159. (5) φωνῆς μεγάλης] Oecumenius[2053 2062]. (6) φωνῆς μεγάλης ὀπίσω μου] Andr d. (7) φωνῆς ὀπίσω] fam 1611[2050]. This selection of variants reflects only part of the confusion in the MS tradition. Readings

(5), (6), and (7) are obviously attempts to make λεγούσης congruent with its antecedent by changing the gender of the antecedent. The strongest external attestation is reading (1). Readings (2) through (7) place the obj. of ἤκουσα (which can be either in the gen. or the acc.) immediately after the verb, which is a stylistic tendency of the author, particularly when he uses ἤκουσα (twenty-eight instances of verb + obj.).

10.c.   In the phrase ὀπίσω μου, "behind me," μου (like μοι and με) is an enclitic personal pronoun declined from ἐγώ and used unemphatically. Though emphatic personal pronouns (ἐμοῦ, ἐμοί, ἐμέ) tend to be used with preps. (Mussies, *Morphology*, 161), this is the only instance in Revelation in which an unemphatic personal pronoun is used with a prep. (here an improper prep.). ὀπίσω + gen. occurs 3 times in Revelation (1:10; 12:15; 13:3); while it is an adv. in profane Gk., there are only a few instances in which it functions as a prep. with the gen. case (M. Johannessohn, *Gebrauch der Kasus*, 215–16; Hilhorst, *Sémitismes*, 1–4, lists 6 examples), while it occurs 312 times in the LXX, 27 times in the NT, and 2 times in the Apostolic Fathers (Hermas *Vis.* 3.7.8; *Sim.* 9.2.7). ὀπίσω + gen., which in the LXX nearly always translates the Heb. אַחֲרֵי *'aḥărê* or אַחַר *'aḥar*, is therefore an instance of a *stylistic* Hebraism.

11.a.   The present ptcp. λεγούσης, "saying," is in the gen. case because it has been attracted to the case of σάλπιγγος, "trumpet," which immediately precedes it; it should, however, be an acc. modifying φωνὴν μεγάλην, "a loud voice," and just such a scribal correction to λεγούσαν is found in א² only. An almost identical solecism occurs in *Mart. Pol.* alternate ending 5 (Musurillo, *Acts*, 20–21): "Irenaeus who was in Rome heard a voice like a trumpet-call saying [ἤκουσεν φωνὴν . . . ὡς σάλπιγγος λεγούσης]: 'Polycarp has suffered martyrdom.'" Here λεγούσης has been attracted to the case of σάλπιγγος. It is not impossible, however, that this wording has been influenced by Rev 1:11.

11.b.   Variant: (1) Insert μοι] fam 1611¹⁶¹¹ ¹⁸⁵⁴ it^h cop^bo eth arm Primasius. (2) Insert μοι Ἰωάννη] Oecumenius²⁰⁵³ ²⁰⁶².

11.c.   Variant: (1) insert ἐγώ εἰμι τὸ α καὶ τὸ ω, ὁ πρῶτος καὶ ὁ ἔσχατος, καί] Andreas. (2) omit] A C א fam 1006¹⁰⁰⁶ ¹⁸⁴¹ fam 1611²⁰⁵⁰ ²³²⁹ 2351 Andr f²⁰²³corr g i²⁰³⁶ l 94 1773 Byzantine lat syr cop^sa. (3) Ἰωάννη] Oecumenius²⁰⁵³.

11.d.   The aor. imper. γράψον is used here because the author has in mind the specific complete action of writing a revelatory book.

11.e-e.   Variant: omit ἃ βλέπεις] א*.

11.f.   Variant: (1) ὅ] A Oecumenius²⁰⁵³ Primasius (*quae*); Beatus (*quod*); it^gig and it^h (*quod*); all modern editions. (2) ἅ] fam 1611¹⁸⁵⁴ Andr c d f²⁰⁷³ l syr^ph cop.

11.g.   Variant: omit καί] א.

11.h.   Variant: (1) εἰς Θυάτειρα (neut. acc.)] א Oecumenius²⁰⁵³ Andreas Byzantine; WHort. (2) εἰς Θυάτειραν (fem. acc.)] A C (both Θυάτιραν); 046 fam 1611¹⁶¹¹ ¹⁸⁵⁴ ²⁰⁵⁰ 2351 it^gig (*tyathiram*); h (*tyatyram*); Andr l 598 1773. (3) ἐν Θυατείροις] 025. On the declension of the neut. pl. τὰ Θυάτειρα, see BDF § 57; Moulton-Howard, *Accidence*, 128; the minuscules have a wide range of spelling variations (Hoskier, *Text* 2:41–42). While it is easy to understand how Θυάτειρα could be changed to Θυάτειραν, a reverse change would be more difficult to account for, except that the final -ν in acc. endings was often represented by a supralinear stroke in the space following the preceding letter. Reading (1) is therefore the *lectio difficilior,* while reading (2) has misconstrued Θυάτειρα as a fem. sing. acc. (Schmid, *Studien* 2:189).

11.i-i.   Variant: omit καὶ εἰς Σάρδεις] א* Byz 13⁴⁹⁸.

11.j.   With the exception of Nestle-Aland²⁷ and UBSGNT⁴, most Gk. texts and commentators have preferred the spelling Λαοδίκιαν, both here and in 3:14, a reading supported by A C א. On the other hand, the spelling Λαοδίκειαν is widely attested in inscriptions, in Strabo, and elsewhere. The otherwise important agreement between A and C is weakened in this case because of the many itacistic errors found in those MSS (Schmid, *Studien* 2:189).

12.a.   Variant: insert ἐκεῖ] 046 fam 1006 2351 Andreas.

12.b-b.   The peculiar phrase λαλεῖν μετ' + gen. occurs six times in Revelation (1:12; 4:1; 10:8; 17:1; 21:9, 15). It occurs only four times elsewhere in the NT (Mark 6:50; John 4:27; 9:37; 14:30), and eight times in Hermas (*Vis.* 1.4.3; 3.10.1; *Mand.* 11.2; *Sim.* 5.3.2; 5.4.5; 6.3.2; 9.1.1; 9.11.1). However, the phrase does occur occasionally in the LXX, sometimes as a way of translating the phrase עִם דִּבֶּר *dibbēr 'im,* "to speak with" (Dan 8:18; 9:22; 10:11, 15, 19), or אֶל דִּבֶּר *dibbēr 'ēl,* "to speak to, with" (Ezek 3:10), or אֵת דִּבֶּר *dibbēr 'ēt,* "to speak with" (Gen 35:13, 14, 15).

12.c.   Variants: (1) ἐλάλει] א C 046 fam 1006¹⁰⁰⁶ ¹⁸⁴¹ fam 1611¹⁸⁵⁴ ²³²⁹ Oecumenius²⁰⁵³ ²⁰⁶² Andr c e²⁰²⁶ f²⁰²³ g i¹⁶⁸⁵ ²⁰⁷⁴ l n²⁴²⁹ 94 598 1773 2019. (2) ἐλάλησεν] fam 1611¹⁶¹¹ Andreas. (3) λάλει] A. The verb ἐλάλει is a progressive impf., suggesting that John turned while the voice was still speaking to him. The impf. has overwhelming attestation (Hoskier, *Text* 2:43), compared with the weak evidence for the aor. (2) and the present (3).

12.d. The Gk. term translated "menorahs" is λυχνίας, from λυχνία, commonly rendered "lampstand" (RSV, NRSV, NIV, REB), "standing lamp" (NEB), or (inappropriately) "candlestick" (AV), here an anarthrous noun, suggesting that the readers were not familiar with it. Since "menorah" (even though it is simply a transliteration of the Heb. term מנרה *měnōrâ* or מנורה *měnōrâ*, "lampstand") is a technical term for the sacral lampstand or lampstands that stood first in the wilderness tabernacle and later in the first and second temples, the main question for the interpreter is whether the author intends these seven lampstands to be understood in that tradition. There is no indication that John conceived of these as branched lampstands with seven oil lamps like the traditional Jewish menorah used as a religious symbol. Neither is there evidence that precisely *seven* such lampstands ever stood in the tabernacle or temples of Judaism. Nevertheless, it appears that John, who regards seven as a heavenly number expressing the will and sovereignty of God, conceives of this scene in 1:9–20 as a heavenly revelation reflecting the archaic patterns of temple imagery characteristic of such revelations in the Jewish apocalyptic tradition.

13.a. Variant: (1) omit ἑπτά] A C P fam 1611[1611 2050] it[h] syr cop Irenaeus[Lat] (Sanday-Turner, *Nouum Testamentum*, 193); Cyprian Victorinus Primasius. (2) insert ἑπτά] ℵ Andreas Byzantine 2351; bracketed by Bousset ([1906] 193), who apparently considers the presence of ἑπτά part of the original text (*Textkritische Studien*, 8 n. 7). For another similar insertion of ἑπτά, see *Notes* on 5:6. A tendency to omit ἑπτά in Andreas is evident in 6:1 (also fam 1611[2344] cop); 15:8 (also 051 it[gig]); 16:1 (also 051 fam 1611[1854] it[h] cop Beatus). Other omissions of ἑπτά occur in 1:20 (2329 it[a h] Primasius); 3:1 (181 2015); 5:6 (A); 10:3 (𝔓[47]); 10:4 (first ἑπτά: 𝔓[47]; second ἑπτά: 𝔓[47*] C it[gig]); 15:7 (first ἑπτά: 2329; second ἑπτά: ℵ 94).

13.b. See *Note* 12.b.

13.c-c. Variant: (1) υἱόν] ℵ fam 1006[1841] fam 1611[1611 2050 2329] Byzantine; Tischendorf, *NT Graece*. (2) υἱῷ] A C fam 1006[1006] fam 1611[1611 1854] Oecumenius[2053 2062] 2351 2681 Andreas; B. Weiss, *Johannes-Apokalypse*, 118. See *Notes* under 14:14 for the MS evidence for υἱόν there. The phrase translated "like a son of man" is ὅμοιον υἱὸν ἀνθρώπου in Gk. Normally the comparative adj. ὅμοιος is used with the dat. of the person or thing to which something is compared, i.e., υἱῷ, or even with the gen. (BAGD, 566–67). ὅμοιος is used twenty-one times in Revelation, and nineteen times it is correctly used with a dat. (the two exceptions are 1:13; 14:14). Here and in 14:14 the phrase ὅμοιον υἱὸν ἀνθρώπου is a solecism in which υἱόν is incorrectly attracted to the case of ὅμοιον (BDR § 182.4); B. Weiss regards it as a "senseless" attraction (*Johannes-Apokalypse*, 118). Nevertheless, υἱόν is clearly the *lectio difficilior* and is certainly correct both here and in 14:14 (Schmid, *Studien* 2:249). ὅμοιος (a comparative adj.) and ὡς (a comparative particle) belong to the same semantic field; the difference is that ὡς does not affect the case of the noun with which it is used, while ὅμοιος requires that the substantive it modifies be either the dat. or the gen. (cf. Charles, 2:35–37). In Rev 1:13; 14:14, therefore, the author uses ὅμοιος as if it were ὡς, though he obviously knows the correct construction.

13.d. The translation "*a son of man*" (RSV, NIV; Bratcher-Hatton, *Revelation*, 30; Salter, *BT* 44 [1993] 349–50) is more appropriate than "*the son of man*" (NRSV).

13.e. Variants: (1) μαστοῖς] C Andreas Byzantine Nestle-Aland[27], UBSGNT[4]. (2) μαζοῖς] A fam 1006 Andr e[2057] f[2023] i[2036]. (3) μασθοῖς] Andr g[-2045*] h i[2042 2074] 1773. Readings (2) and (3) are collateral forms of μαστοῖς in reading (1).

14.a-a. καί here functions in an epexegetical or explanatory way.

14.b. Variant: omit λευκαί] Oecumenius[2053 2062].

14.c-c. Variant: omit ὡς ἔριον λευκόν] 1611.

14.d. Variant: ὡσεί for ὡς] C Andreas. Weak attestation is combined with the fact that this is contrary to the usual style of Revelation; ὡσεί also appears as a correction of ὡς in 1:17; 16:3 in ℵ, in 16:13 in 𝔓[47] and ℵ, and in 13:3 in Byzantine (Schmid, *Studien* 2:98).

15.a. Variant: (1) πεπυρωμένης] A C Primasius; B. Weiss, *Johannes-Apokalypse*, 160; WHort; UBSGNT[4]; Nestle-Aland[27]; *TCGNT*[1], 732; *TCGNT*[2], 663–64. (2) πεπυρωμένῳ] ℵ fam 1611[2050] Andr g[-2045] Oecumenius[2053 2062] Tischendorf, *NT Graece*. (3) πεπυρωμένοι] 025 2351 Andreas Byzantine syr[h] WHort[mg]; von Soden, *Text*. Reading (1), the pf. pass. fem. ptcp. πεπυρωμένης, "burned, refined," is problematic, since it has no obvious syntactic relationship with any other word or phrase in this sentence and is probably a peculiar form of the gen. abs., and despite its lack of widespread support is the *lectio difficilior* and probably original. Further, πεπυρωμένης is probably the original reading because it best explains the origin of the other, more syntactically correct readings (*TCGNT*[1], 732; *TCGNT*[2], 663–64) and is best understood as a shortened and unusual form of the gen. abs. (Rehkopf, "Grammatisches," 214–19; BDR § 424.10; Beckwith, 439). In Revelation the gen. abs. occurs only here and perhaps in 17:8; 19:20 (cf. BDR § 424.10). The presence of the gen. abs. in Revelation is often denied altogether

(Charles, 1:cxxxviii). Even though the gen. abs. as a ptcp. is normally linked to a noun or pronoun that is not the subject of the sentence, it is possible to omit either the noun or (more frequently) the pronoun with which the ptcp. agrees (examples: Matt 17:14, ἐλθόντων; Acts 21:10, ἐπιμενόντων; Acts 21:31, ζητούντων; Smyth, *Greek Grammar*, § 2072; Moulton, *Prolegomena*, 74, 236; BDR § 423; Mayser, *Satzlehre*, § 157g). There are also examples of the gen. abs. that are not "absolute" in the sense that they have no syntactical connection with the rest of the sentence (cf. Luke 17:12). In this case the fem. pronoun αὐτῆς has been omitted. Yet to which noun in the sentence does πεπυρωμένης refer? Possibly to the fem. noun καμίνῳ, "oven, furnace," in which case the relevant clauses should be translated "like gleaming bronze in a smelter when it is burning." Yet this is semantically doubtful. On the other hand, if the difficult term χαλκολιβάνῳ is understood as a *fem.* noun, ἡ χαλκολίβανος (see *Comment* on 1:15), then the clauses make sense both syntactically and semantically: "like brass when smelted in a furnace." Reading (2), including א (with a small group of related minuscules containing the text of Revelation in the Andreas commentary), reads πεπυρωμένῳ, correcting it to agree in gender and number with χαλκολιβάνῳ, since καμίνῳ is a fem. noun. In reading (3), πεπυρωμένοι is in agreement with οἱ πόδες, "the feet."

16.a-a.  Variant: (1) χειρὶ αὐτοῦ] א A C 025 fam 1611^1611 1854 2329 1678 1778. (2) αὐτοῦ χειρί] fam 1006^1006 1841 2351 TR. (3) αὐτοῦ (omit χειρί)] fam 1611^2050 Oecumenius^2053 2062 it^gig it^h Victorinus Primasius. Reading (3) omits χείρ because ὁ δεξιός means "right hand" and is used with that meaning without χείρ in Rev 1:17, 20; 2:1; 5:1, 7; the restrictive attributive form ἡ χείρ + pronoun + ἡ δεξία occurs in 10:5; 13:16.

17.a.  The present ptcp. λέγων, "saying," occurs nearly 800 times in the LXX as a translation of the Heb. inf. construct לאמר *lēʾmôr*, "saying," often following the finite verb form וידבר *wayĕdabbēr*, "and he said"; the idiom is also found in Aram. (Ezra 5:11; A. Cowley, *Aramaic Papyri*, 16:8; 20:6; 30:7). In the NT this pleonastic use of the ptcp. λέγων is often considered a Hebraism (Moulton-Howard, *Accidence*, 454). While the inf. construct occasionally is used in place of a finite verb meaning "to say" (2 Sam 2:22; Isa 49:9; Zech 7:3), more frequently it is used to supplement another verb for speaking with the meaning "as he said," "with these words," or simply "thus," i.e., as a counterpart to the use of the ὅτι *recitativum* in Gk. (S. Thompson, *Apocalypse*, 69–70). The present ptcp. λέγων used in various cases occurs as an introduction to direct discourse fifty-three times in Revelation, fourteen times following another verb of speaking (4:1; 5:9; 6:10; 7:3, 10, 13; 10:8; 14:18; 15:3; 17:1; 18:2, 18; 19:17; 21:9 [ἐλάλησεν μετ' ἐμοῦ λέγων]). Yet because there are many examples in Gk., this construction should be regarded as a Gk. idiom enhanced by the influence of the LXX in the NT (Porter, *Verbal Aspect*, 105).

17.b.  The prohibition μὴ φοβοῦ, "stop being afraid," uses the present imper. because of its durative significance, i.e., in order to prohibit what is taking place at the time of speaking (as the context makes clear). Prohibitions using μή + the present imper. or the aor. subjunctive relate to the *fut.*, since only then can the speaker's prohibition be acted upon. However, prohibitions with the present imper. or aor. subjunctive can prohibit (1) an action taking place when the prohibition is expressed, (2) an action likely to occur in the fut., or (3) a type of conduct—only the context can determine which (J. P. Louw, *AcCl* 2 [1959] 43–57). The only prohibition in Revelation using μή + the present imper. occurs in 5:5, while prohibition using μή + the aor. subjunctive occurs five times (6:6; 7:3; 10:4; 11:2; 22:10).

17.c.  πρωτότοκος, "first born," is found in place of πρῶτος, "first," only in A. The same substitution also occurs in 2:8, which is supported only by A and Andr i^2034. Both alterations are probably influenced by the occurrence of πρωτότοκος in 1:5 (see *Comment* on 1:5).

18.a.  The καί, here translated "even," is epexegetical.

18.b.  καί is translated "but," since it functions here as a καί *adversativum* (cf. Aejmelaeus, *Parataxis*, 14–15; Denniston, *Particles*, 292–93).

18.c-c.  ζῶν εἰμι is probably a present periphrastic, a relatively rare construction (Fanning, *Verbal Aspect*, 312–13), though ζῶν may be an independent adjectival predicate ptcp.

18.d.  Variant: insert ἀμήν] א^1 fam 1611^2329 2351 Beatus syr Andreas Byzantine. This reading is certainly secondary and has also been inserted by various MSS at other points in Revelation (cf. *Notes* on 4:9, 10; 5:13; 11:15). The insertion has probably been triggered by the phrase "for ever and ever."

18.e.  Variant: κλεῖδας (fem. acc. pl.)] 025 046 fam 1006^1841 2351. The acc. pl. of κλείς has two forms, κλεῖς and κλεῖδας (Moulton-Howard, *Accidence*, 131–32; Mussies, *Morphology*, 108). It is somewhat peculiar that the Atticistic forms of κλείς occur in Revelation (1:18; 3:7; 9:1; 20:1; with the exception of this *var. lect.*), while the normal Hellenistic forms occur in Matt 16:19; Luke 11:52; *1 Clem.* 43:3; cf. *Par. Jer.* 4:3 (2x).

18.f.  The translation reflects the view that τοῦ θανάτου καὶ τοῦ ᾅδου, "Death and Hades," are obj. gens. rather than possessive gens. (see under *Comment*).

19.a. The particle οὖν occurs just six times in Revelation, always in the later parts of the text: 1:19; 2:5, 16; 3:3(2x), 19. The οὖν *narrativum*, however, occurs frequently in the Fourth Gospel but *never* in Revelation (Ruckstuhl-Dschulnigg, *Stilkritik,* 63–67). Abbott (*Johannine Grammar,* 479 n. 4) regards the absence of οὖν *narrativum* as important because "like Acts, it [Revelation] is largely made up of narrative, so that we might have expected narrative οὖν in abundance if it had been written by the hand that wrote the Fourth Gospel."

19.b. The second person sing. aor. verb εἶδες is translated "will see" (cf. RSV, "see"), rather than with a past tense (NEB, NIV, "have seen"; AV, "hast seen"), because it functions very much like an epistolary aor. (Allo, 15); i.e., while the visions that John was about to record were yet to be seen by him, from the standpoint of the reader they belong to the *past.* εἶδες can therefore be taken as a general statement that includes the two specific aspects ἅ εἰσίν, "what is" (i.e., "the present," or "the events that are now happening"), and ἅ μέλλει γενέσθαι, "what will be" (i.e., "the future," or "the events that will happen hereafter"). For a more detailed discussion, see *Comment* on 1:19.

19.c. καί, "and," is understood here as epexegetical and so translated "that is," since two aspects included in the verb εἶδες are included in the two following relative clauses (see *Note* 19.a).

19.d-d. The periphrastic construction μέλλει γενέσθαι presents both textual and exegetical problems. In the NT, μέλλειν is frequently used periphrastically with infs., eighty times with the present inf. (in Revelation there are nine occurrences: 2:10[2x], 3:10; 6:11; 8:13; 10:4, 7; 12:5; 17:8), eight times with the aor. inf. (Luke 21:36; Acts 12:6; Rom 8:18; Gal 3:23; Rev 1:19; 3:2, 16; 12:4), and three times with the fut. inf. (Acts 11:28; 24:15; 27:10). In Rev 1:19, the aor. inf. γενέσθαι (the reading preferred by Tischendorf, *NT Graece;* Nestle-Aland[27]; and UBSGNT[4]) is supported by C ℵ* and the Byzantine minuscules. The present inf. γινέσθαι (preferred by WHort; Bousset [1906], 169; Charles, 2:243), is supported by ℵ[2] A (which actually reads γείνεσθαι) Oecumenius[2053 2062] fam 1006 fam 1611[2050·2344] 2351 2681 Andreas. In addition to having strong textual support, this reading initially appears more likely in view of the fact that in periphrastic constructions with μέλλειν and the inf., the present inf. occurs far more frequently than either the fut. or aor. inf. (Schmid, *Studien* 2:98). On the other hand, it must be observed that while μέλλειν with the present inf. occurs nine times in Revelation, μέλλειν with the aor. inf. occurs three times (not counting Rev 1:19); this fact makes it difficult to choose between γινέσθαι and γενέσθαι (Schmid, *Studien* 2:208). One reason for expressing future actions by means of the periphrastic construction using μέλλειν and a present, fut., or aor. inf. rather than a simple fut. ind. is that the former permits the user to make semantic, though not temporal, distinctions (Rijksbaron, *Syntax and Semantics of the Verb,* 33). Exegetically, it is possible to construe ἅ μέλλει with the aor. inf. γενέσθαι as summarizing the entire action represented by the verb (i.e., "the events about to happen"), while ἅ μέλλει with the present inf. γινέσθαι can be understood in an inceptive sense, i.e., "the events that will soon begin to unfold." Since these future events have not yet begun to happen, but rather John is commanded to write down what he sees, from a semantic perspective the aor. inf. appears most appropriate in this context.

19.e. Variant: (1) γενέσθαι (aor. inf.)] ℵ** C 025 046 fam 1611[2050] ; Tischendorf, *NTGraece;* B. Weiss, *Johannes-Apokalypse,* 52; Merk, *NT;* Nestle-Aland[27]; UBSGNT[4]. (2) γίνεσθαι (present inf.)] ℵ[2] A fam 1006 fam 1611[1611 1854 2329] Oecumenius[2053 2062] 2351 2681 Andreas; WHort; Bousset (1906) 198; Charles, 2:243. While μέλλειν was used with the fut. inf. in classical Gk., in the NT, μέλλειν usually occurs with the present inf. (eighty-four times in the NT, according to MM, 395); examples in Revelation: 2:10; 3:10; 6:11; 8:13; 10:4, 7; 12:5; 17:8. This perhaps gives reading (2) a certain probability (Bousset [1906] 169; Schmid, *Studien* 2:208), though it makes reading (2) the *lectio difficilior,* and it is easier to account for replacing the aor. inf. with the present inf. than the reverse. Yet μέλλειν + aor. inf. occurs with relative frequency in Koine Gk., with NT examples in Acts 12:6; Rom 8:18; Gal 3:23 (MM, 395–96; BDR § 338; Horsley, *New Docs* 3:148). For instances of μέλλειν + aor. inf. in Revelation, see 3:2, 16; 12:4.

20.a. This verse begins with two noun groups connected by καί, (1) τὸ μυστήριον τῶν ἑπτὰ ἀστέρων, "the secret meaning of the seven stars," and (2) τὰς ἑπτὰ λυχνίας τὰς χρυσᾶς, "the seven golden menorahs." The neut. noun τὸ μυστήριον (which can either be nom. or acc. in form) *could* be an acc. since (a) it could be the obj. of γράψον, "write," in v 19 (very unlikely), in which case repunctuation would be required to link vv 19–20 (Tischendorf, *NT Graece,* concludes v 19 with a comma, while Zahn, 1:207–8 n. 60, argues, I think correctly, for a period), (b) it could ultimately depend on εἶδον in v 12 (Mussies, *Morphology,* 100), a view that is also unlikely since τὸ μυστήριον is not what John saw but the *meaning* of what he saw (yet cf. *Par. Jer.* 9:29: τὰ μυστήρια ἅ εἶδε, "the mysteries that he saw"), (c) it could be an *acc. abs.* (Charles, 1:33–34), a rare construction that has no syntactical relationship to the rest of the sentence, or (d) it could be an adv. acc. of respect (Zerwick-Grosvenor, *Grammatical*

*Analysis* 2:744), a dubious proposal since the parallels are not convincing. One indication that τὸ μυστήριον might be an acc. is the fact that the pl. noun τὰς λυχνίας in the second noun group is in the acc. and is roughly parallel to the noun group introduced by τὸ μυστήριον. Yet it is also possible that τὰς λυχνίας is an acc. through attraction to the acc. pl. relative pronoun οὕς, "which"; i.e., the second noun group would then function as the obj. of εἶδες. If this accounts for the acc. case of the second noun group, then it is possible (even probable) that τὸ μυστήριον is a *nom.* rather than an acc. A further problem lies in the fact that the second noun group, headed by τὰς ἑπτὰ λυχνίας, *should* be in the gen. case since it is parallel to τῶν ἑπτὰ ἀστέρων in the first noun group (dependent on τὸ μυστήριον) and should therefore also be dependent on τὸ μυστήριον. Whether nom. or acc., it is clear that τὸ μυστήριον functions very much like a gloss abruptly introducing the theme or problem of interpretation and therefore functions much like the title of a book or the topic of a paragraph. There is a similar syntactical problem with the phrase τὸ γὰρ ἀδύνατον τοῦ νόμου, i. Rom 8:3, which (if it is in the nom. case) has been regarded as "a sort of nominative absolute" (Sanday-Headlam, *Romans,* 191–92), or more recently as an acc. in apposition to a noun cluster in the acc. at the end of v 3 (Cranfield, *Romans* 1:378). It must be translated something like "With regard to the mystery of," or "As for the symbolic meaning of." The best solution to the problem here is to regard τὸ μυστήριον as a *nom. abs.* or *pendent nom.* (Zerwick, *Greek* §§ 25–31), even though a pronoun in an oblique case is missing from the following clauses. This solution has the advantage that a similar construction is found several times elsewhere in Revelation and thus coheres with the author's peculiar style (2:26; 3:12, 21). When they occur, pendent noms. are consistently used at the conclusion of a unit of text in Revelation.

20.b. The relative pronoun οὕς, "which," should be ὧν but has unaccountably resisted attraction to the case and number of the immediately preceding pl. gen. ἀστέρων, which it modifies (οὕς does agree with ἀστέρων in gender and number, though not case). Variants: (1) οὕς] ℵ A C 025 fam 1611[1611] [1854 2050 2329] 1678 1778 Oecumenius[2053 2062]. (2) ὧν] fam 1006 2351 Andr f[2023 2073] j[2036 2042] n 94 2019 TR.

20.c-c. Variants: (1) ἐπὶ τῆς δεξιᾶς] *lectio originalis.* (2) ἐπὶ τὴν δεξιάν μου] Oecumenius[2053 2062] Andr h[2302]. (3) ἐν τῇ δεξιᾷ μου] A fam 1611[1611] 598 2038 Andr d[2055] syr cop[sa] arab. (4) ἐπὶ τῆς λυχνίας] fam 1611[2329]. Variant (2) is significant as one of the few parallels to the phrase ἐπὶ τὴν δεξιάν in Rev 5:1, which is probably the basis for this scribal alteration. Variant (3) was derived from Rev 2:1. Note that while variant (1) means "in my right hand," the parallel phrase in 13:16, ἐπὶ τῆς χειρὸς αὐτῶν τῆς δεξιᾶς means "on/upon their right hand."

20.d. Schmid (*Studien* 2:198) incorrectly claims that ἄγγελοι should have a definite article. Since ἄγγελοι lacks the article, it is clearly the predicate, though the author *could* have made ἄγγελοι articular; it would still function clearly as the predicate since it would be an articular noun or noun cluster in the second or predicate position. When εἶναι, "to be," is used as a linking verb, the word or word cluster determined by the definite article is the subject, while the noun or noun cluster that constitutes the predicate is anarthrous; if both noun or noun clusters are articular, then the *first* one is the subject (cf. L. C. McGaughy, *Toward a Descriptive Analysis of EINAI as a Linking Verb in New Testament Greek* [Missoula, MT: Scholars, 1972] 49–54, rules 3c and 3d). Some of the exceptions to these rules are disputed by D. A. Carson, "The Purpose of the Fourth Gospel: John 20:31 Reconsidered," *JBL* 106 (1987) 639–51.

20.e. Variants: (1) αἱ λυχνίαι αἱ ἑπτὰ ἑπτά] A 046 fam 1006[1006 1841] fam 1611[1611] latt Andr f[2073] i[2042] 94 Byzantine; B. Weiss, *Johannes-Apokalypse,* 161; WHort; (2) αἱ λυχνίαι αἱ ἑπτά] fam 1611[2329] it[a] it[h] Primasius; Charles, 1:35; Nestle-Aland[27]. (3) ἑπτὰ λυχνίαι ἑπτά] ℵ*. (4) αἱ ἑπτὰ λυχνίαι ἑπτά] Oecumenius[2053] 2351. (5) αἱ ἑπτὰ λυχνίαι ἃς εἶδες ἑπτά] Andreas. (6) αἱ λυχνίαι αἱ ἑπτὰ αἱ χρυσαῖ ἃς εἶδες, ἑπτά] syr[ph]. In the phrase αἱ ἑπτὰ ἑπτά, the articular ἑπτά is part of the noun cluster αἱ λυχνίαι αἱ ἑπτά, "the seven menorahs," which forms the subject of the sentence, while the anarthrous ἑπτά is part of the anarthrous noun cluster ἑπτὰ ἐκκλησίαι, "the seven churches," which forms the predicate of the sentence, suggested by the fact that the noun cluster is anarthrous (cf. the rule summarized in *Note* 20.c.).

## *Form/Structure/Setting*

### I. OUTLINE

II. John's vision of Christ and his commission (1:9–3:22)
   A. Vision of "one like a son of man" (1:9–20)

1. Setting of the vision (v 9)
    a. The identity of John the seer (v 9)
        (1) He is the recipients' brother (v 9a)
        (2) What he shares with them in Jesus (v 9b)
            (a) Tribulation
            (b) Kingdom
            (c) Endurance
    b. Circumstances of the vision (v 9cd)
        (1) Location: island of Patmos (v 9c)
        (2) Reasons for being on Patmos (v 9d)
            (a) For the word of God
            (b) For the testimony of Jesus
2. Initial revelatory experiences (vv 10–11)
    a. John fell into a trance (v 10a)
    b. He heard a voice loud like a trumpet behind him (v 10b)
    c. The two commands of the voice (v 11)
        (1) Write down this vision (v 11a)
        (2) Send it to the seven churches (v 11b)
            (a) To Ephesus
            (b) To Smyrna
            (c) To Pergamon
            (d) To Thyatira
            (e) To Sardis
            (f) To Philadelphia
            (g) To Laodicea
3. The vision of the one like a son of man (vv 12–20)
    a. Introduction: John turned to see the voice (v 12a)
    b. The vision (vv 12b–16)
        (1) Seven golden menorahs (v 12b)
        (2) Description of the one like a son of man (vv 13–16)
            (a) His location: in the midst of the menorahs (v 13a)
            (b) His appearance (vv 13b–16)
                [1] His clothing (v 13b)
                    [a] Long robe
                    [b] Golden sash around him
                [2] His head (v 14)
                    [a] His hair (v 14a)
                        {1} Like white wool
                        {2} Like snow
                    [b] His eyes like a flame (v 14b)
                [3] His feet: like molten bronze (v 15a)
                [4] His voice: like the sound of cascading water (v 15b)
                [5] Associated symbols (v 16)
                    [a] Seven stars in his right hand (v 16a)
                    [b] Sword (v 16b)
                        {1} Sharp
                        {2} Double-edged
                        {3} Projecting from his mouth

           [6] His face: like the sun shining in full strength (v 16c)
     c. John's reaction: he fell down as dead (v 17a)
     d. The message of the exalted Christ (vv 17b–20)
        (1) He placed his right hand on John (v 17b)
        (2) His message of assurance (vv 17c–20)
           (a) Command: Do not be afraid (v 17c)
           (b) Reasons (vv 17d–18)
              [1] I am the first and the last (v 17d)
              [2] I am the living one (v 18a)
              [3] I was dead, but I now live for ever (v 18b)
              [4] I have the keys of Death and of Hades (v 18c)
           (c) Renewed command to write and initial interpretation of
              Christophany (vv 19–20)
              [1] Command to write what he will see (v 19)
                 [a] The events now happening (v 19a)
                 [b] The events that will happen (v 19b)
              [2] Interpretation of the seven stars and the seven
                 menorahs (v 20a)
                 [a] The seven stars are the angels of the seven
                    churches (v 20b)
                 [b] The seven menorahs are the seven churches
                    (v 20c)

## II. LITERARY ANALYSIS

### A. Introduction

The literary form of 1:9–20 is complex because it is closely related to 2:1–3:20, and it shows unmistakable signs of editorial revision (see below *Introduction,* Section 5: Source Criticism). Rev 1:9–20 is often categorized as a prophetic call narrative. Yet that traditional literary form is hardly applicable since there is no evidence that this commission is intended to be understood as John's *inaugural* vision. In fact, Rev 10:8–11 may be considered a separate call narrative, modeled after Ezek 2:8–3:7 (see *Form/Structure/Setting* under 10:1–11). Yet it is important to consider the extent to which 1:9–20 conforms in any particular formal way to ancient commission visions.

### B. Types of Commission Visions

Zimmerli (*Ezekiel* 1:97–100) has distinguished two types of prophetic call narratives in the OT: (1) A *visionary dialogue with Yahweh* (often lacking a visionary element) in which the prophet's reluctance is overcome, as in the calls of Moses, Gideon, Saul, and Jeremiah (Exod 3:1–22; 4:1–17; 6:2–12; 7:1–7; Judg 6:15–16; 1 Sam 9:21; Jer 1:4–10). (2) A *throne-room vision* (lacking the dialogical element) in which prophetic commission is given following a vision of the throne of Yahweh, as in the visions of Micaiah ben Imlah, Isaiah, and Ezekiel (1 Kgs 22:19–22 [though Micaiah *himself* is not called]; Isa 6:1–8; Ezek 1:1–3:15; 10:1–22). Black ("Throne-Theophany," 67–69) suggests that the same type of theophanic prophetic call is found in Dan

7:9–13 (which is dependent on Ezek 1; cf. A. Feuillet, *RB* 60 [1953] 170–202, 321–46) and in *1 Enoch* 14:18–22; 46:1–3; 60:1–3; 70–71; 89:52; 90:20–23, 31–33, 37–38. Yet these texts exhibit much more variety than Black suggests: (1) While Dan 7:9–13 is certainly a throne theophany, it lacks a prophetic commission and hardly fits Zimmerli's typology. (2) *1 Enoch* 14:18–22 represents the culmination of a heavenly journey. (3) Enoch's celestial journey, his vision of God upon his throne, and the divine commission are found in 14:8–16:3; 70:1–71:17. (4) *1 Enoch* 46:1–8; 60:1–6 are indeed throne visions, but they lack the element of prophetic commission. (5) *1 Enoch* 90:20–39 is a throne vision, though the throne is upon earth, and the entire scene is one that focuses on eschatological judgment.

## C. The Setting of the Vision

One of the characteristic features of Jewish ascent traditions is the conception of heaven as a temple that provides the examplar for both the earthly tabernacle and the temple in Jerusalem. *1 Enoch* 1–36 contains the earliest ascent in Jewish literature; the heavenly edifices through which Enoch passes to reach the divine throne are part of one enormous heavenly temple (Himmelfarb, *Ascent to Heaven*, 14–16).

When John, in 4:1, is invited to "Come up hither," he recognizes the voice as the one that he previously heard speaking to him like a trumpet (1:10). If this voice, which is that of the exalted Jesus, is spoken from heaven, it is probable that the vision of Rev 1:9–20 should be understood as set in the heavenly throne room. When John says "at once I was in the spirit" (4:2a), being "in the spirit" clearly constitutes a necessary precondition for his vision of the heavenly throne room. The phrase "in the spirit" occurs four times in Revelation (1:10; 4:2; 17:3; 21:10); in three of these passages it is preceded by an invitation to "come," on a journey for the purpose of experiencing a revelatory vision, once to heaven (4:2), once to "the wilderness" (17:3), and once to "a high mountain" (21:10).

## D. The Analysis of the Vision

In the ancient world, literary accounts of dreams and visions characteristically consisted of two main elements, (1) the setting and (2) the dream or vision proper (on the literary structure of ancient Near Eastern dreams, see Oppenheim, *Interpretation*, 186–97; on the literary structure of Greco-Roman and early Christian dreams and visions, see Hanson, "Dreams and Visions," 1400–14). In the vision of 1:9–20, vv 9–10a provide the setting of the vision, while vv 10b–20 constitute the vision proper. The vision in vv 10b–20 consists of five elements: (1) a commission to write (v 11), followed by (2) the epiphany of a divine figure, presumably the one who gave the commission to write (vv 12–16), followed by (3) the terrified reaction of the seer coupled with the self-identification of the divine figure (vv 17–18), then (4) a reiterated command to write a vision narrative (v 19), and finally, (5) an extraordinarily brief interpretation of just two aspects of the epiphany, the seven menorahs and the seven stars (v 20).

Rev 1:9–20 contains an *epiphany* of a divine figure coupled with a *commission to write*. In broad terms the genre of this passage is closest to that of the *symbolic vision* (Collins, *Daniel*, 118–19), consisting of two parts, the vision (1:9–19) and the interpretation (1:20). There are only two other symbolic visions in Revelation, one in 7:1–17 (the vision, vv 1–12; the interpretation, vv 13–17) and the other in 17:1–18 (the vision, vv 1–6; the interpretation, vv 7–18). The presence of allusions to Dan 7:9–14; 10:2–9, 15–17 suggests that the genre of 1:9–20 might have been derived from these OT models, or at least influenced by them. There are also some striking similarities to *Apoc. Zeph.* 6:11–13 (Charlesworth, *OTP* 1:513; in Sparks, ed., *AOT*, 922–23, this passage is enumerated as 2:10–12).

| *Rev 1:13–1* | *Dan 10:5–9* | *Apoc. Zeph. 6:11–15* |
|---|---|---|
| 13b one like a son of man | 5b a man | 11b a great angel |
| 13c clothed with a long robe | 5c clothed in linen | |
| 13d a golden girdle round his breast | 5d loins girded with gold | |
| | 6a body like beryl | |
| | 6b face like lightning | 11b face shining like the rays of the sun |
| 14a head and hair white as wool (Dan 7:9) | | |
| 14b eyes like a flame of fire | 6c eyes like flaming torches | |
| 15a feet like burnished bronze | 6d arms and legs like gleam of burnished bronze | 12b his feet like bronze melted in a fire |
| | 6e sound of words like noise of multitude | |
| 16a seven stars in his right hand | | |
| 16b two-edged sword issued from his mouth | | |
| 16c face like sun shining in full strength | [cf. v 6b] | [cf. v 11b] |

The description of Joseph in *Jos. As.* 5:5 (cf. Esth 8:15) is also relevant (Charlesworth, *OTP* 2:208):

And Joseph was dressed in an exquisite white tunic, and the robe which he had thrown around him was purple, made of linen interwoven with gold, and a golden crown (was) on his head, and around the crown were twelve chosen stones, and on top of the twelve stones were twelve golden rays. And a royal staff was in his left hand, and in his right hand he held outstretched an olive branch.

Later in the same document Aseneth sees an angel who resembles Joseph with respect to his robe, crown, and royal staff, "except that his face was like lightning, and his eyes like sunshine, and the hairs of his head like a flame of fire of a burning torch, and hands and feet like iron shining forth from a fire, and sparks shot forth from his hands and feet" (*Jos. As.* 14:9).

In the so-called Mithras Liturgy (*PGM* IV.475–834), an appearance of Mithras, who comes to the magical practitioner, is described (*PGM* IV.634–37, 692–704; tr. Betz, *Greek Magical Papyri*, 50–52):

> When you have seen this, the rays will turn toward you; look at the center of them. For when you have done this, you will see a youthful god, beautiful in appearance, with fiery hair, and in a white tunic and a scarlet cloak, and wearing a fiery crown. . . . Now when they [seven additional gods] take their place, here and there, in order, look in the air and you will see lightning bolts going down, and lights flashing, and the earth shaking, and a god descending, a god immensely great, having a bright appearance, youthful, golden-haired, with a white tunic and a golden crown and heaven around, moving upward and downward in accordance with the hour. Then you will see lightning bolts leaping from his eyes and stars from his body.

In this *symbolic description*, the lemma ὅς ἐστιν, "which is," introduces a gloss that interprets the meaning of the golden shoulder of the young bull in Mithras' right hand, just as Rev 1:20 uses the lemma τὸ μυστήριον to introduce the meaning of the seven stars in the right hand of the exalted Christ and the seven golden lampstands.

Another description of an angelic vision is found in the description of the angel Iaoel in *Apoc. Abr.* 11:2–3, which has several similarities to Rev 1:9–12 (Charlesworth, *OTP* 1:694):

> The appearance of his body was like sapphire, and the aspect of his face was like chrysolite, and the hair of his head like snow. And a kidaris (was) on his head, its look that of a rainbow, and the clothing of his garments (was) purple; and a golden staff (was) in his right hand.

## IV. THE INFLUENCE OF DAN 7 ON REV 1

G. F. Beale (*Daniel*, 154–77) has argued that Dan 7 provided the author with an exegetical pattern that determined the structure and composition for Rev 1 (as well as for Rev 4–5; 13; 17; cf. *Daniel*, 178–267). From his analysis of these chapters, Beale argues that Daniel provided the primary model for the Revelation as a whole. He provides a list that summarizes the parallels between Rev 1 and Dan 7 (*Daniel*, 172):

1. God enthroned (Rev 1:4; Dan 7:9a).
2. Numerous heavenly beings surround the throne (Rev 1:4; Dan 7:10b).
3. Son of man's universal rule (Rev 1:4; Dan 7:13–14).
4. Saints and the kingdom (Rev 1:6, 9; Dan 7:18, 22, 27a).
5. The coming of a son of man on clouds with authority (Rev 1:7a; Dan 7:13).
6. Image of a book associated with judgment (Rev 1:11; Dan 7:10).
7. Detailed description of a heavenly figure and his environment (Rev 1:12–16; Dan 7:9–10).

8. The seer expresses emotional distress because of the vision (Rev 1:17a; Dan 7:15).
9. The seer receives heavenly counsel consisting of an interpretation of part of the vision (Rev 1:17–20; Dan 7:16–17ff.).

Beale argues that the density of references to Dan 7 (and parallel material in Dan 10) indicates that Rev 1:8–20 is a "midrash" on Dan 7 and 10 and that allusions to other OT literature (Ezek 1–3; 8–11; 43) have been attracted to the infrastructure that Dan 7 and 10 have provided for Rev 1:8–20. In part this stems from Beale's conviction that the author of Revelation does not allude to OT texts in an atomistic manner but is aware of the literary setting and context of those texts. This conclusion is unlikely, however, for the term "midrash" should be reserved for oral or written expositions of biblical texts, while the focus in Rev 1 (as in Rev 4–5; 13; 17) is not on *interpreting* Dan 7 but on the use of allusions to Dan 7 (and other OT passages) to legitimate the features of John's vision. That is, Dan 7 and 10 appear to be not the *object* of interpretation in Rev 1:8–20 but rather a *means* of interpretation (cf. A. Yarbro Collins, *JBL* 105 [1986] 734–35). A second weakness of Beale's proposal lies in the fact that the sequence of motifs in the vision report of Rev 1:9–20 is largely traditional and that even Dan 7 and 10 (perhaps also Ezek 1–3) were very probably structured in conformity with an existing visionary schema. Another problem lies in the fact that Beale does not address those scholars who have argued that Ezekiel provided the major structural model for Revelation (e.g., Boismard, *RB* 56 [1949] 507–41; Vanhoye, *Bib* 43 [1962] 436–76); both hypotheses cannot be true.

## V. SOURCE CRITICISM OF 1:9–20

That there are *two* commands to write and both are differently phrased, one by the "voice like a trumpet" (v 11a: ὃ βλέπεις γράψον) and the other by the exalted Jesus (v 19: γράψον οὖν ἃ εἶδες), suggests the possibility that a literary seam is present here, and that the material in between these commands has been interpolated. The repetition of the command to write in v 19 appears to be an instance of the redactional technique that has been called a "repetitive resumption," the purpose of which is to pick up the strand of the narrative where it was left in v 11. The original command to write in v 11 ("write what you see") does not necessarily include the kind of oral dictation by the risen Christ that follows in Rev 2–3. However, when the author inserted the epiphany of the risen Christ in vv 12–18, he rephrased the command to write so that it would include the dictation of the seven proclamations as well as the visionary material that followed (v 19): "Therefore write down what you will see, that is, the events which are now happening and the events which will happen hereafter."

The first-person narrative of Rev 1:9–11 looks very much like the original beginning of Revelation (which probably immediately followed the title in 1:1–3), which was very probably followed by Rev 4:1–6:17 (for details, see *Introduction*, Section 5: Source Criticism). Rev 1:12–20, the vision of the exalted Christ, was later inserted, and the command to write was reiterated along with a brief explanation of the meaning of the seven stars and the seven golden lampstands. Rev 1:12–20, then, was inserted in order to introduce the proclamations to the seven churches, which the author secondarily wanted to include at the beginning of his composition. There are close verbal links between the epiphany in 1:12–20 and the self-predications of the exalted Christ found in most of the proclamations to the seven churches in 2:1–3:21, suggesting that both sections were inserted into the earlier composition together. The reader is apparently meant to identify the "voice like a trumpet" in v 10b with the exalted Christ, for when John turns around to see who is speaking to him (v 12), he sees "one like a son of man." This epiphany apparently takes place on earth; yet when John is summoned to ascend to heaven in 4:1, the invitation comes from "the first voice which I had heard speaking to me like a trumpet," i.e., the voice of 1:11. Yet how can the exalted Christ now suddenly be in heaven? And if the "voice like a trumpet" is not the exalted Christ, how can the one with a "voice like a trumpet" now suddenly be speaking from heaven? These problems are quickly resolved if 4:1 originally followed 1:9–11, for then John heard a "voice like a trumpet" commanding him to write what he saw, and was immediately summoned to ascend to heaven by that same voice in 4:1.

*Comment*

**9a** Ἐγὼ Ἰωάννης, "I, John." The phrase "I, John" also occurs in 1:1, 4, 9; 22:8 (and 21:2 as a variant reading); cf. the analogous phrase "I, Jesus" (22:16). Both here and in 22:8 the phrase "I, John" immediately follows a brief oracle attributed to God (1:8) and speech of Christ (22:5–6) and therefore serves primarily to indicate a change in speakers and not an emphasis on John's authority. The analogous phrase "I, Daniel" occurs seven times in the apocalyptic sections of Daniel (7:15; 8:15, 27; 9:2; 10:2, 7; 12:5); no similar phrase occurs in any of the OT prophetic books. The phrase "I, Baruch" occurs frequently in *2 Apoc. Bar.* (8:3; 9:1; 10:5; 11:1; 13:1; 32:8; 44:1). For similar phrases identifying the speaker, cf. "I, Enoch" (*1 Enoch* 12:3), "I, Artaxerxes" (Ezra 7:21), "I, Simon Peter" (*Gos. Pet.* 14.60), "I, Salathiel [= Ezra]" (4 Ezra 3:1), and "I, Paul" (2 Cor 10:1; Gal 5:2; Eph 3:1). In all of these contexts the phrase has a formal, authoritative force; yet at the same time the phrase is used pseudonymously in apocalypses.

**9b** ὁ ἀδελφὸς ὑμῶν καὶ συγκοινωνός, "your brother and fellow participant." The Greek phrase is a nominative of apposition modifying the name "John," and since it contains a single definite article governing two substantives connected with καί, "and," the substantives refer to the same thing (Robertson, *Grammar*, 785–86). Kraft (39) incorrectly calls this construction a hendiadys (i.e., one idea expressed through two nouns connected with "and"). By using the terms "brother" and "fellow participant," the author is using the language of social equality, a rhetorical device intended to foster compliance (cf. the use of the same device in Philem 8–9 and *Barn.* 1:8; 4:9; see N. Petersen, *Rediscovering Paul* [Philadelphia: Fortress, 1985] 131–51; J. Schütz, *Paul and the Anatomy of Apostolic Authority* [Cambridge: Cambridge UP, 1975] 221).

**9c** ἐν τῇ θλίψει καὶ βασιλείᾳ καὶ ὑπομονῇ ἐν Ἰησοῦ, "in the tribulation and kingship and endurance in Jesus." Here the three substantives θλίψει, βασιλείᾳ, and ὑπομονῇ are probably all governed by the single definite article before θλίψει, and thus all refer to the same person or thing (Robertson, *Grammar,* 784–85; Zerwick, *Greek* § 184); the substantives θλῖψις and ὑπομονή are occasionally found paired (Rom 5:3–4; 2 Cor 6:4). However, the prepositional phrase ἐν Ἰησοῦ, "in

76 REVELATION 1:9–20

Jesus," indicates that this cannot be so since it is certainly problematic to speak of the "tribulation in Jesus," so that "in Jesus" must be taken either with ὑπομονῇ alone, or possibly with βασιλείᾳ καὶ ὑπομονῇ (a variant reading has the definite article with βασιλεία; see *Notes*). This suggests that "in Jesus" is a later gloss. It is possible that "tribulation" here refers to "*the* Great Tribulation" (7:14), just as "the hour of testing coming upon the whole world" (3:10) may also refer to the Great Tribulation (Charles, 1:21), though it is striking that the author refers to it in three very different ways. The endurance exhibited by Jesus (i.e., the verbal portrait of his way of responding to suffering in gospel traditions) is emphasized by several early Christian authors (2 Thess 3:5; Heb 12:2; 1 Pet 2:21–24 [cf. 4 Macc 1:11; 17:19–23; 18:24, where the martyr who endures until death, thereby "conquering" his adversaries, is an expiation for the Jewish community]; Ign. *Rom.* 10:3; the verb ὑπομονεῖν occurs in Ign. *Poly.* 3:2: "who endured in every way for our sakes"). In Ign. *Rom.* 10:3 the genitives in the phrase ἐν ὑπομονῇ Ἰησοῦ Χριστοῦ, "in the endurance of Jesus Christ," may be construed as objective genitives with the meaning "the patient waiting for Christ" (Lightfoot, *Apostolic Fathers*, 2/2, 234) or as subjective genitives (which is more likely, since Ignatius shows little interest in eschatology) with the meaning "with the endurance which Jesus Christ exhibited." This emphasis may also be reflected in Rev 3:10: "the command concerning the endurance I practiced" (see *Notes* on 3:10). In *Poly.* 3:2, Ignatius refers to the exemplary endurance of Jesus "who for our sakes accepted suffering, who in every way endured [ὑπομείναντα] for our sakes" (LCL tr.). The noun ὑπομονή, "endurance," occurs seven times in Revelation, either in the introductory sections in Rev 1–3, which are part of the Second Edition (1:9; 2:2, 3, 19; 3:10), or in redactional glosses added to the central section in Rev 4:1–22:5 (13:10; 14:12). ὑπομονή, "endurance" or "perseverance" (cf. the closely related terms καρτερεῖν/καρτερία), was a term designating a type of virtue practiced by Cynics (Diogenes *Ep.* 27, 47) and by Stoics (Seneca *Ep. Mor.* 67.10; Epictetus 2.2.13; Musonius Rufus 25.8–9; Arnim, *SVF* 3:64.18 [ὑπομονή is subordinate to courage]; 65.2; 67.40), and Stoic influence is evident in the frequent use of ὑπομονή in 4 Macc (1:11; 7:9; 9:8, 30; 15:30; 17:4, 12, 17, 23; see Hadas, *Maccabees*, 178 n. 13; B. A. G. M. Dehand-schutter, "Martyrium und Agon: Über die Wurzeln der Vorstellung vom ΑΓΩΝ im vierten Makkabäerbuch," in *Die Entstehung der jüdischen Martyrologie*, ed. J. W. van Henten [Leiden: Brill, 1989] 215–19). The Stoic use of ὑπομονή was part of the *agon* motif, i.e., the struggle of the sage against the emotions in his quest for virtue (Philo *Agr.* 111–20; *Praem.* 52); yet this *agon* motif was adopted by Jewish and Christian writers and applied to the suffering and death of the righteous person (Philo *Prov.* 106, 120). 4 Macc 1:11 reflects a view coherent with that expressed in Revelation: "By their endurance [τῇ ὑπομονῇ] they conquered [ἐνικήσαντες] the tyrant." It is through the endurance of suffering that the Jewish martyrs conquer (νικᾶν) their adversaries (4 Macc 9:30; cf. Seneca *Ep. Mor.* 67.10–11). The quality of "endurance" is important to Ignatius (*Eph.* 3:1; *Trall.* 1:1; *Rom.* 10:3; *Smyrn.* 12:2), but only in *Rom.* 10:3 is the noun ὑπομονή closely linked to Jesus. Ignatius uses the verb ὑπομονεῖν six times, once with Christ as subject: "who endured in every way for us" (*Poly.* 3:2). In Rom 5:3, Paul claims that "tribulation produces endurance [θλῖψις ὑπομονὴν κατεργάζεται]" (cf. 2 Cor 6:4; Jas 1:3).

**9d** ἐγενόμην ἐν τῇ νήσῳ τῇ καλουμένῃ Πάτμῳ, "I was on the island called Patmos." Patmos (now Patino), one of the Sporades islands, is thirty miles or forty-five kilometers in circumference and is located thirty-seven miles west-southwest from Miletus, fifty miles from ancient Ephesus. During the Hellenistic period, Patmos, along with the islands of Lipsos and Leros, were part of the territory of Miletus. The territory of Miletus consisted of the city of Miletus, the surrounding countryside, and the islands (Saffrey, *RB* 82 [1975] 388–91, with inscriptional evidence). These three islands were also designated as the φρούρια, "fortresses," of Miletus, since the city was a major maritime power and these islands protected her Aegean side by guarding the entrance to the Latmique Gulf where Miletus was located. Beginning with the second century B.C., Patmos and the other two islands were populated by a garrison of reliable Milesians, called φρούροι, whose leader was designated a φρούραρχος, or "commandant," who functioned as a resident governor for Miletus. Patmos was certainly not a deserted island. In an inscription from Patmos dating to the second century B.C. (*SEG* 1068.2), a certain Hegemandros was honored by the Association of Torch Runners on Patmos. The inscription mentions the presence of a gymnasium on the island and mentions that Hegemandros was gymnasiarch seven times and that he had funded the erection of a stone statue of Hermes as well as performed other benefits for his fellow citizens and athletes. An inscription from the second century A.D. (G. Kaibel, *Epigrammatica Graeca ex lapidibus conlecta* [Berlin: Reimer, 1878] no. 872) honors Bera, a hydrophore, "priestess," of Artemis (ὑδροφόρος was the Milesian term for such priestesses), and reveals the presence of a cult and temple of Artemis on Patmos, complete with a public feast, a procession, and the recitation of hymns in honor of the goddess (Saffrey, *RB* 82 [1975] 399–407; cf. Peek, *RMP* 107 [1964] 315–25). It is also likely that the inhabitants of Patmos had their own tradition of the birth of Artemis on that island (Saffrey, *RB* 82 [1975] 407–10), which may have influenced the version of the Apollo-Leto myth used in Rev 12. Miletus, of course, is not one of the seven cities addressed by John, either because he himself was from Miletus and is addressing only other cities, or (more likely) because there was not yet a Christian community at Miletus. In Acts 20:17–38, which narrates Paul's meeting with the Ephesian elders at Miletus, there is no hint that a local Christian community existed. A Christian presence there during the first part of the second century, perhaps suggested by 2 Tim 4:20, was certainly in existence by the middle of the second century as reflected in *Acts of John* 18–19; 37.

The use of the aorist verb ἐγενόμην, "I was," has suggested to some interpreters that John's presence on Patmos was temporary and that at the time of writing he was no longer on Patmos. This use of the aorist in itself (the basic narrative tense), however, neither confirms nor denies that view, though it appears likely that the author was in fact no longer on Patmos (Lohmeyer, 13; Eckhardt, *Johannes,* 73). The aorist and imperfect are primarily used in narrative contexts (the aorist in past contexts as a *background* narrative tense, while the imperfect is used in past contexts as the *foreground* narrative tense; cf. Porter, *Verbal Aspect,* 151), and the author of Revelation exhibits a marked preference for the use of aorist (451 times) rather than the imperfect (20 times). Even though the aorist often functions to indicate complete past action, and the imperfect incomplete past action, the use of the aorist itself does not prove that John is no longer on Patmos.

It is true that those banished by a particular emperor could be recalled or given amnesty upon that emperor's death. Eusebius specifically claims that this happened to John and that, following the death of Domitian, the Roman senate recalled all those who had been banished, and John, he claims, went from Patmos to Ephesus (*Hist. eccl.* 3.20.8–9). This agrees with the fact that Nerva, the successor of Domitian, proclaimed a recall of his predecessor's exiles in A.D. 96 (Pliny *Ep.* 1.5.10; 9.13.5). In Christian tradition John was recalled from banishment to Patmos upon the death of "the tyrant" (Clement Alex. *Quis dives salv.* 42, also quoted in Eusebius *Hist. eccl.* 3.23.5–19), and similarly, Origen (*Comm. in Matt.* 16.6 on Matt 20:22–23), relates that "the emperor [βασιλεύς] of the Romans, as tradition teaches, condemned John . . . to Patmos island." Though Clement did not specifically identify "the tyrant," nor Origen "the emperor of the Romans" with Domitian, Eusebius states quite clearly that the emperor was in fact Domitian (*Hist. eccl.* 3.20.8–9; cf. Eusebius *Chronicle*). Victorinus of Petau (d. ca. A.D. 304), who wrote in Latin but was dependent on the Greek works of Origen, says that "[John] was on the island of Patmos, condemned to the mines by Caesar Domitian, where he saw the apocalypse, which he published after being released on the death of the emperor" (*Comm. in Apoc.* 10.3; Haussleiter, ed., *Victorinus,* 92). In *Hist. eccl.* 3.23.1, Eusebius mentions the tradition that John returned from banishment after the death of Domitian and in 3.23.2–3 quotes Irenaeus *Hist. eccl.* 2.22.5; 3.3.4 to the effect that John survived until the reign of Trajan. According to the confused tradition in Epiphanius (*Pan.* 51.12.1–2), John left Patmos when he was over ninety years old during the reign of Claudius Caesar (A.D. 41–54). Some confusion results from the fact that Claudius was one of the names of Nero, who is referred to both as Nero Claudius and as Nero Claudius Caesar. There is therefore general agreement that John was banished to the island of Patmos by a Roman emperor, and some agreement that this emperor was Domitian. Some notices are ambiguous (e.g., Clement of Alexandria and Origen) and make it possible to argue that the emperor who banished John was Nero rather than Domitian (Hort, xvii). According to the Syriac apocryphal "History of John the Son of Zebedee" (W. Wright, *Apocryphal Acts of the Apostles* [London and Edinburgh: Williams and Norgate, 1871] 2:55):

> After these things, when the Gospel was increasing by the hands of the Apostles, Nero, the unclean and impure and wicked king, heard all that had happened at Ephesus. And he sent (and) took all that the procurator had, and imprisoned him; and laid hold of S. John and drove him into exile; and passed sentence on the city that it should be laid waste.

The angel of the Lord then appeared to Nero and frightened him into releasing John, and Nero thereafter did not dare to interfere with the affairs of the province of Asia (Wright, *Apocryphal Acts* 2:56–57). In one place Eusebius mentions that "Peter was crucified head downwards at Rome, Paul beheaded, and John exiled to an island" (*Demonstr. evang.* 3.5 [116c]; W. J. Ferrar, tr., *Eusebius*), giving the impression that these events occurred in close temporal proximity and that they occurred in Rome.

First of all it must be emphasized that Pliny *Hist. nat.* 4.12.69 does *not* refer to Patmos as a Roman penal colony or as a place of banishment as many scholars have erroneously claimed (Bousset [1906] 192; Swete, 12; Charles, 1:21; Lohmeyer, 15; Lohse, 19; Kraft, 40). Further, there is no historical evidence that any other individual was banished to Patmos (contra Metzger, *Code,* 25). Roman legal practice exhibited a dual penalty system (described at length by Garnsey, *Social Status,* 103–80), in that the *dignitas,* "status," of the defendant was more important than the crime committed. Members of the upper-class orders (*honestiores*) were usually given more lenient punishments in the courts than were those from the lower orders (*humiliores*). In cases where *humiliores* were given the death penalty, *honestiores* were punished with banishment (A. Berger, *Roman Law*, 633). First of all, the term *exilium* or *exsul*, "exile," could refer to voluntary or involuntary departures from a region or country. Voluntary exile was permitted those of higher status who had been condemned to death, but they were usually subsequently deprived of both citizenship and property. There were two primary forms of compulsory expulsion, *relegatio*, "banishment," and *deportatio*, perpetual "deportation," the former more lenient than the latter. *Relegatio* might be temporary (cf. the three-year term mentioned in Pliny *Ep.* 10.56) or permanent. Further, it could be *relegatio ad* or *in*, "banishment to," a place or *relegatio ab* or *extra*, "banishment from," a place. (1) Suetonius (*Titus* 8.5) speaks of banishment *in asperrimas insularum*, "to the harshest of islands." Juvenal alludes to banishment to the island of Gyara in the Aegean sea (*Satires* 1.73). The Stoic philosopher Musonius Rufus was confined to this barren island and worked on a forced labor battalion building Nero's canal through the isthmus of Corinth. (On *relegatio ad* or *in*, see K. von Fritz, *RE* 16 [1933] 893–94.) In referring to John's exile to Patmos, Jerome uses the phrase *in Patmos insulam relegatus*, "banished to the island of Patmos." (2) On *relegatio ab* or *relegatio extra*, "banishment from," a person's home territory, see *Digest* 47.14.3.3; 48.22.7.10–22. In *De exilo* 604B, Plutarch addresses an exile from Sardis. Dio Chrysostom was exiled from his native Italy by Domitian and was recalled after Domitian's death, but was free to travel wherever he wanted (Dio Chrysostom *Or.* 13; C. P. Jones, *Dio Chrysostom*, 45–55). Exile was a subject frequently treated in the writings of such Greek and Roman philosophers as Teles, Musonius, Plutarch, Favorinus, and Seneca. For a list of known places of exile, see Balsdon, *Romans*, 113–15.

There are then four possible ways of explaining how John was present on Patmos as an exile: (1) He may have been condemned to death and gone into voluntary exile to a place of his own choosing. (2) He may have been condemned to *deportatio*, involving permanent banishment to a particular place and loss of all rights (including Roman citizenship) and property (*Digest* 48.22.6; 48.22.14.3; 48.22.15). (3) He may have been temporarily or permanently banished to a particular place, i.e., *relegatio in insulam* or *relegatio ad insulam*, "banishment to an island," a punishment that did *not* normally involve forfeiture of Roman citizenship or property (*Digest* 48.22.7.2: *Haec est differentia inter deportatos et relegatos, quod in insulam relegari et ad tempus et in perpetuum quis potest*, "There is this difference between those deported and those relegated to an island, that a person can be relegated to an island both for a period and permanently"; cf. *Digest* 48.14.1). Yet a decurion who has been relegated ceases to be a decurion (*Digest* 50.2). (4) Finally, he may have been temporarily or permanently banished from his home territory, i.e., *relegatio ab*. In such cases the governor would customarily make this pronouncement (*Digest* 48.22.7.17): *illum prouincia illa insulisque eis relego excedereque debebit intra illum diem*, "I relegate him from this province and its islands; and he must leave by such and such a date." These last three are specifically enumerated by Marcian in the *Digest* 48.22.5 (Watson, tr., *Justinian*): *Exilium triplex est: aut certorum locorum interdictio, aut lata fuga, ut omnium locorum interdicatur praeter certum locum, aut insulae vinculum, id est relegatio in insulam*, "Exile is of three kinds:

prohibition from certain determined places, imposed banishment so that [the exile] is forbidden all places except for one determined place, or a tie to an island, that is, relegation to an island." Ulpian, on the other hand, enumerates just *two* categories of *relegati*, i.e., "relegated persons" (*Digest* 48.22.7; Watson, tr., *Justinian*): *Relegatorum duo genera: sunt quidam, qui in insulam relegantur, sunt, qui simpliciter, ut prouiuciis eis interdicatur, no etiam insula adsignetur*, "There are two classes of relegated persons: There are certain persons who are relegated to an island, and there are those who are simply barred from a province, but are not assigned an island." Callistratus, referring to an edict of Hadrian, lays down degrees of punishment for exiles: (1) those who are relegated for a limited period of time, (2) those who are relegated permanently, (3) those who are relegated to an island, and (4) those who are deported to an island (*Digest* 48.19.28.13). Of the four possibilities for explaining John's situation enumerated above, the third was held by Tertullian, *De praescr.* 36 ("*Ioannes . . . in insulam relegatur*"), though the terminology was fluid in the second century and he may have simply inferred John's situation from Rev 1:9. The first two possibilities presuppose that John belonged to a higher social level, i.e., the *honestiores*, a possibility that both Ramsay (*Letters*, 84) and Caird have rejected too quickly. According to Ulpian, provincial governors have no right to deport an individual to an island, though urban prefects do (*Digest* 48.22.6), that is, unless the island is geographically part of the province they govern (*Digest* 48.22.7.1). Provincial governors must seek written approval for their proposal from the emperor (*Digest* 48.22.6). The fact that some Christians in Asia Minor had apparently been *beheaded* suggests that they belonged to the upper classes or were soldiers (see *Comment* on 20:4). Yet even the second and third possibilities involve penalties applied to criminals with some social standing, i.e., those who could support themselves in exile (Garnsey, *Social Status*, 120; Mommsen, *Römisches Strafrecht*, 968ff.). It appears that provincial governors made frequent use of *relegatio* (Garnsey, *Social Status*, 119; Pliny *Ep.* 10.56; *Digest* 47.9.4.1). Letters or speeches in which consolation was offered to an exile was a *topos*, "commonplace," among ancient moral philosophers (Cicero *Tusculan Disputations* 3.34); for an example, see Plutarch's *De exilo*. In *De consolatione at Helviam*, Seneca wrote from exile to comfort his mother.

**9e** διὰ τὸν λόγον τοῦ θεοῦ καὶ τὴν μαρτυρίαν Ἰησοῦ, "because of the word of God and my witness to Jesus." Variations on the two phrases (usually combined) "the word of God and the witness to Jesus" occur several times in Revelation:

| | |
|---|---|
| 1:2 | ὃ ἐμαρτύρησεν τὸν λόγον τοῦ θεοῦ<br>who bore witness to the message from God |
| | καὶ τὴν μαρτυρίαν Ἰησοῦ Χριστοῦ ὅσα εἶδεν<br>that is, the witness borne by Jesus, as much as he saw |
| 1:9 | διὰ τὸν λόγον τοῦ θεοῦ<br>because of the word of God |
| | καὶ τὴν μαρτυρίαν Ἰησοῦ<br>and my witness to Jesus |
| 6:9 | διὰ τὸν λόγον τοῦ θεοῦ<br>because of the word of God |

καὶ διὰ τὴν μαρτυρίαν ἣν εἶχον
and because of the witness which they bore

20:4      διὰ τὴν μαρτυρίαν Ἰησοῦ
because of their witness to Jesus

καὶ διὰ τὸν λόγον τοῦ θεοῦ
and because of the word of God

Two related phrases are combined in two further instances:

12:17      τῶν τηρούντων τὰς ἐντολὰς τοῦ θεοῦ
who keep the commandments of God

καὶ ἐχόντων τὴν μαρτυρίαν Ἰησοῦ
and maintain their witness to Jesus

14:12      οἱ τηροῦντες τὰς ἐντολὰς τοῦ θεοῦ
those who keep the commandments of God

καὶ τὴν πίστιν Ἰησοῦ
and maintain faithfulness to Jesus

Finally, the phrase λόγος [or λόγοι] τοῦ θεοῦ, "word [or 'words'] of God," occurs a total of seven times in Revelation, three times in addition to those already cited above (17:17; 19:9, 13), yet in very different contexts. Finally, variations on the phrase "the witness of/to Jesus" occur twice in 19:10:

τῶν ἐχόντων τὴν μαρτυρίαν Ἰησοῦ
who maintain the witness to Jesus

ἡ γὰρ μαρτυρία Ἰησοῦ ἐστιν τὸ πνεῦμα τῆς προφητείας
for the witness to Jesus is the spirit of prophecy

The second phrase, τὴν μαρτυρίαν Ἰησοῦ, "my witness to Jesus," could be understood as either an *objective* genitive, and so be translated "the testimony *about* [or 'the witness to'] Jesus" or "witness (unto death) to Jesus" (Vassiliadis, *BT* 36 [1985] 133), or a *subjective* genitive, "the witness borne *by* Jesus." The phrase μαρτυρία Ἰησοῦ occurs five times in Revelation (1:2, 9; 12:17; 19:10; 20:4). In several instances in Revelation, a genitive is dependent on μαρτυρία and should be construed as subjective (1:2; 11:7; 12:11; cf. 6:9), but there are other instances in which it seems contextually appropriate to construe the genitive as objective (12:17; 14:12; 17:6; 19:10[2x]; 20:4).

John's presence on Patmos has been explained in several ways: (1) He had been exiled to Patmos by the Roman authorities. (2) He traveled to Patmos for the purpose of proclaiming the gospel. (3) He went to Patmos in order to receive a revelation. The first explanation, held by many church fathers (Clement Alex. *Quis dives* 42; Origen *Hom. in Mt.* 7.51; 16.6; Eusebius *Hist. eccl.* 3.18; Jerome *De vir. illustr.* 10), appears most probable, even though it requires certain qualifications (see below). Tertullian preserves the view that John was exiled from

Rome (*De praescr.* 36), a view possibly confirmed by Eusebius (*Demonstr. evang.* 3.5 [116c]). John states that he was on Patmos διά, "because of," the word of God and the testimony of Jesus. Yet since διά with the accusative can express both cause ("because of," "on account of") and purpose ("for"; cf. BDF § 222), there is no grammatical basis for excluding any of the three explanations. On the other hand, the use of similar phrases in 6:9; 20:4 in explicit connection with martyrdom suggests that John's presence on Patmos was the result of a capital penalty inflicted on him by Roman authorities. In Roman law *poena capitalis,* "capital punishment," denoted not only the death penalty but also loss of *caput,* i.e., citizenship or liberty (A. Berger, *Roman Law,* 634).

**10a** ἐγενόμην ἐν πνεύματι ἐν τῇ κυριακῇ ἡμέρᾳ, "I fell into a prophetic trance on the Lord's day." This phrase occurs twice in Revelation (here and 4:2), while a similar phrase, ἀπήνεγκέν με ἐν πνεύματι, "he carried me away in the Spirit" or "in a spirit" or (preferably) "in a trance," occurs twice (17:3; 21:10). The closest verbal parallel in the OT is the LXX version of Mic 3:8, which has the phrase ἐν πνεύματι κυρίου, "by the Spirit of the Lord," referring to the authority behind Micah's prophetic message. Yet this is an *instrumental* dative, while in Rev 1:10 it is a locative of place or sphere. The phrase ἐν πνεύματι, "in the Spirit," occurs several times in the Apostolic Fathers (*Did.* 11:7, 8, 9, 12; *Barn.* 9:7; 10:2, 9; 14:2) but is always connected with inspired speaking; i.e., πνεύματι is an instrumental dative of means. Paul and the Pauline tradition used the phrase ἐν πνεύματι in the general sense of the participation of Christians in the Christian community, which is coextensive with the Spirit (Rom 8:9; 14:17; Eph 2:18, 22; 3:3–5; 4:3; 5:18; 6:18; Col 1:8). Jeske (*NTS* 31 [1985] 460–64) incorrectly finds this view in Rev 1:10. The problem in this passage is whether ἐν πνεύματι (1) indicates an ecstatic state (and is thus analogous to phrases such as ἐν ἐκστάσει, "in a trance," Acts 11:5; 22:17, or ἐγένετο ἐπ᾽ αὐτὸ ἔκστασις, "he fell into a trance," Acts 10:10; cf. Bousset [1906] 192; Müller, *Prophetie und Predigt,* 49; Sharpe, "Reflections," 119–31), (2) refers to an actual experience of divine inspiration in general apart from ecstatic behavior (Hill, *New Testament Prophecy,* 73; Jeske, *NTS* 31 [1985] 452–64), or (3) is strictly a literary appropriation of conventional apocalyptic language used to authenticate fabricated vision reports. The last proposal is weakest, since the matter of the authenticity of revelatory experiences narrated in apocalypses is an insoluble problem simply because the phenomenology of revelatory experience conforms to stereotypical behavioral and literary conventions and expectations (Lewis, *Ecstatic Religion*). Lindblom unsuccessfully tried to distinguish between actual revelatory experience and literary artifice in Revelation (*Gesichte und Offenbarungen,* 206–39). One must take refuge in the comparative study of altered states of consciousness, for all inspired speech or narrations of visionary experiences are based on revelatory trance experiences, usually exhibiting behavior modifications. Contemporary anthropologists distinguish *possession trance,* involving possession by spirits, and *vision trance,* typically involving visions, hallucinations, and out-of-body experiences (Bourguignon, *Religion, Altered States;* Lewis, *Ecstatic Religion;* Wilson, *Prophecy and Society,* 21–88; id., *JBL* 98 [1979] 321–37). By using the phrase ἐν πνεύματι, John claims to have experienced a *vision trance,* for nowhere in Revelation does he claim to speak through divine inspiration. The fact that John does not mention ritual preparations for a revelatory experience (e.g., prayer [cf. Dan 9:3; 10:2–3; 4 Ezra 3:1–36; Hermas *Vis.* 2.1.1] or fasting [cf.

4 Ezra 5:20–30; 6:31–59; 9:23–37; 13:50–51; Hermas *Vis.* 2.2.1; 3.1.1–2]) or the behavioral modifications that may have accompanied such experiences does not mean that they did not occur.

The phrase ἐν πνεύματι, "in the spirit," occurs four times in Revelation (1:10; 4:2; 17:3; 21:10). Three of these involve responses to an invitation by an angelic being to come (1) *to the heavenly world* (4:1: ἀνάβα ὧδε, καὶ δείξω σοι, "Come up here and I will show you . . ."), (2) *to the wilderness* (17:1: δεῦρο, δείξω σοι, "Come, I will show you . . ."), and (3) *to a high mountain* (21:9: δεῦρο, δείξω σοι, "Come, I will show you . . ."). The term πνεῦμα, "spirit," in these passages is commonly taken to refer to the Spirit of God and so is capitalized in modern English translations (AV [1:10 only]; RSV; NEB; NIV), and is so understood by many commentators (Beckwith, 435; Beasley-Murray, 112; Sweet, 114; Mounce, 133; Lohse, 19, 37; Lohmeyer, 44–45). Yet in all four occurrences of the phrase ἐν πνεύματι, "in [the] spirit," the noun is anarthrous, though that reveals little, since the article can be omitted optionally from nouns following a preposition. Of the seven uses of the term πνεῦμα in the singular in Revelation, ten use the articular form τὸ πνεῦμα, and all but 19:10 (see *Comment*) clearly refer to the Spirit of God (2:8, 11, 17, 29; 3:6, 13, 22; 14:13; 22:17). Strangely, the phrase ἐν τῷ πνεύματι in the sense of "inspired by the Spirit" occurs just once in the NT, in Luke 2:27, of Simeon (the phrase is twice used in the instrumental sense of "by the Spirit" in Luke 4:1; Acts 19:21; cf. *Barn.* 11:11). The phrase ἐν πνεύματι, however, does occur several times in very different senses in the NT (Luke 1:17; John 4:23, 24; Acts 1:5; Rom 2:29; 8:9; 1 Cor 14:6; Eph 2:22; 3:5; 5:18; 6:18; Col 1:8; 1 Tim 3:16), often in an instrumental sense (Matt 22:43; Acts 1:5; 1 Cor 14:16). There is, then, no reason for understanding any of these four passages as references to the Spirit of God. The phrase ἐν πνεύματι is an idiom that refers to the fact that John's revelatory experiences took place not "in the body" but rather "in the spirit," i.e., in a vision trance (Charles, 1:22; Swete, 13; Kraft, 95). In 1 Cor 14:15, Paul contrasts two states in which Christians can pray, τῷ πνεύματι, "with/in the spirit," and τῷ νοΐ, "with/in the mind." Caird (59) correctly and idiomatically translates ἐγένομην ἐν πνεύματι with the phrase "I fell into a trance."

The adjective κυριακός, "of the Lord," occurs in early Christian literature, not in Greek literature, though it does occur in inscriptions and papyri, where it is usually connected with imperial administration, particularly finance, and means "imperial" (Deissmann, *Light,* 361–64; id., *Bible Studies,* 217–18). After surveying the uses of the adjective κυριακός in early Christian literature, Bauckham concludes that κυριακός is virtually synonymous with (τοῦ) κυρίου where the latter is used adjectivally with a noun, except when it functions as an objective genitive (Bauckham, "Lord's Day," 224–25; against W. Foerster, *TDNT* 3:1096). Further, κυριακὴ ἡμέρα is not synonymous with ἡμέρα (τοῦ) κυρίου, since the latter phrase traditionally referred to the eschatological Day of the Lord (Rordorf, *Sunday,* 208); probably for this reason the former phrase became the common Christian term for Sunday (Bauckham, "Lord's Day," 225). Some have argued that this expression (which later referred to Sunday as the distinctive Christian day of worship commemorating the day of Jesus' resurrection) may have been derived from the phrase κυριακὸν δεῖπνον, "the Lord's supper," in 1 Cor 11:20 (Rordorf, *Sunday,* 221), but this view is both unlikely and undemonstrable (cf. the arguments in Bauckham, "Lord's Day," 226–27). The earliest occurrence in the papyri of the term κυριακή (used absolutely) for Sunday is found in a fourth-century document (POxy 3407.15–16; Horsley, *New Docs* 2:207). This conforms to other expressions such as ἡ Σεβαστή [ἡμέρα], "the Emperor's day," and ἡ κρονική [ἡμέρα], "Cronus' day," i.e., Saturday, yet it is highly unlikely that the Christian designation κυριακὴ ἡμέρα was formulated in conscious opposition to the imperial cult as Deissmann contended (*Light*, 363–66; id., *Bible Studies*, 218–19). The first day of the week has special significance in early Christianity (1 Cor 16:2; Acts 20:7); this day is called the "eighth day" in *Barn.* 15:9. The term κυριακή is later used absolutely to refer to Sunday: *Did.* 14:1; Ign. *Magn.* 9:1 (κυριακή is contrasted with σαββατίζοντες, apparently contrasting the tendency of some Judaizing Christians to observe the weekly Sabbath, in contrast with Christians who hold a weekly celebration on Sunday); *Gos. Pet.* 12.50 (ἡ κυριακή replaces μία [τῶν] σαββάτων, "the first [day] of the week," found in the Synoptic parallels); Clement Alex. *Strom.* 17.12. Melito of Sardis, in Eusebius *Hist. eccl.* 4.26.2, wrote a treatise entitled Περὶ κυριακῆς, but since only the title survives, the content of the work cannot be known. The expression κυριακὴ ἡμέρα, "the Lord's day,") is found in Dionysius of Corinth in Eusebius *Hist. eccl.* 4.23.8; Origen *Contra Celsum* 8.22. In *Did.* 14:1 we find the pleonastic expression κατὰ κυριακὴν δὲ κυρίου συναχθέντες, "and when you gather on the Lord's (day) of the Lord," rejected as impossible by Audet (*La Didachè*, 460) and therefore emended by him in agreement with the Georgian version to read καθ' ἡμέραν δὲ κυρίου, "on the day of the Lord"; he considered κυριακήν to be a marginal gloss that first interpreted ἡμέραν and later displaced it.

While the meaning of κυριακὴ ἡμέρα in Rev 1:10 is widely understood to be a new Christian designation for Sunday, some even argue that it refers specifically to Easter Sunday (Strobel, *ZNW* 49 [1958] 185; Dugmore, "Lord's Day," 274–78; Strand, *NTS* 13 [1966–67] 174–81; arguments against this view are found in Rordorf, *Sunday*, 209–15, and Bauckham, "Lord's Day," 230–31). According to this view, Sunday, the weekly Christian day of worship, developed out of the annual commemoration of the resurrection of Jesus on Easter Sunday. This is problematic, however, since κυριακή never unambiguously means Easter Sunday, and Asia Minor (the region where many crucial texts originated: Rev 1:10; *Did.* 14:1; Ign. *Magn.* 9:1; *Gos. Pet.* 35, 50) was a region in which Easter was celebrated on 14 Nisan from the early second century A.D. on. Though many of the early Christian references to ἡ κυριακὴ (ἡμέρα) *could* refer either to Sunday or Easter (*Did.* 14:1; Ign. *Magn.* 9:1; *Gos. Pet.* 35, 50), some clearly refer to Sunday (*Acts Pet.* 29; *Acts Paul* 7: "And Paul cried out to God on the Sabbath as the Lord's day drew near" [Schneemelcher, *NTA* 2:371]). Further, the Gnostic association of the Ogdoad ("the eighth") with the Lord's day assumes the Christian association of κυριακή, Sunday, with the "eighth" day (*Barn.* 15:2; *2 Enoch* 33:7; *Ep. Apost.* 18 (Coptic); Clement *Excerpta ex Theodoto* 63; cf. Bauckham, "Lord's Day," 230). A less common view is that κυριακὴ ἡμέρα in Rev 1:10 refers to the eschatological Day of the Lord, i.e., that John was transported in his vision to the eschaton (Bacchiocchi, *From Sabbath*, 123–31). Why then did John not use the more common expression ἡμέρα (τοῦ) κυρίου, which occurs frequently in the LXX and the NT?

**10b** καὶ ἤκουσα ὀπίσω μου φωνὴν μεγάλην ὡς σάλπιγγος, "I heard a loud sound behind me (like that of a trumpet)." Even though this phrase may be an allusion to Ezek 3:12 (LXX: καὶ ἤκουσα κατόπισθεν μου φωνὴν σεισμοῦ μεγάλου, "and I heard behind me the sound of a great earthquake"), that does not mean that the phrase "behind me" lacks all special significance. In rabbinic Judaism the *Bath Kol* was regarded as a word or voice heard without seeing the one speaking. *T. Meg.* 32a says "Whence do we know that we may consult a *Bath Kol*? Because it is said (Isa 30:21): 'And thine ears shall hear a word behind thee saying' . . ." (Lieberman, *Hellenism*, 195). This suggests the essentially revelatory character of the voice.

A number of different metaphors are used in Revelation to capture the loudness of the voices heard by John. The sound of these voices is compared to the blast of a trumpet (as here; cf. *Apoc. Sedr.* 11:19; Charlesworth, *OTP* 1:612: 11:13), to the sound of thunder, and to the sound of roaring water. The sound of a trumpet or *shofar* was part of the Sinai theophany according to Exod 19:16; 20:18 (in both passages the phrase שׁוֹפָר קוֹל *qôl šôpār*, "sound of a trumpet," occurs). The motif of the sound of the trumpet continued to be used in theophanic contexts (Isa 18:3; Joel 2:1; Zech 9:14; Ps 47:5); it was also used in the Israelite cult (2 Sam 6:15; Isa 27:13; Joel 2:15; Ps 81:3). The use of the *shofar* in cultic settings could therefore be considered an imitation of the voice of Yahweh (Weiser, "Frage," 523–24), or the imagery of the Sinai theophany could have been influenced by the use of the *shofar* in the cult (Beyerlin, *Origins*, 135–36). The voice of Athena is compared to a trumpet in the introductory theophanic scene in Sophocles *Ajax* 17, where the uncommon term used is κώδων, "trumpet or bell of a trumpet" (Greek tragedies frequently begin with a divine theophany; cf. *Comment* on 22:20). Thunder is called the trumpet (σάλπιγξ) of Zeus (Nonnos *Dionysiaca* 2.558–59; 6.230–31). The noun phrase φωνὴ μεγάλη, "a loud sound," occurs twenty times in Revelation (1:10; 5:2, 12; 6:10; 7:2, 10; 8:13; 10:3; 11:12, 15 [n.b. that the plural form φωναὶ μεγάλαι occurs only here]; 12:10; 14:7, 9, 15, 18; 16:1 [here the unusual order μεγάλης φωνῆς occurs]; 16:17; 19:1, 17; 21:3). The same phrase occurs nearly fifty times in the LXX, usually in the dative form φωνῇ μεγάλῃ, three times in the accusative (LXX Gen 27:34; 1 Esdr 3:11; Sir 50:16), and once in the nominative (LXX Esth 1:1). The regular use of the adjective following the noun reflects Hebrew and Aramaic usage. For the idiomatic use of the dative phrase φωνῇ μεγάλῃ, "with a loud voice," see *Comment* on 5:2. However, in four additional instances in the LXX, the adjective is placed *before* the noun (1 Esdr 5:64; 9:10; Prov 2:3; 26:25; cf. Rev 16:1). The phrase also occurs in the Greek texts of the Pseudepigrapha (*Adam and Eve* 5:2; 29:11; *T. Abr.* 5:9; *Par. Jer.* 2:2; *2 Apoc. Bar.* 11:3; *Sib. Or.* 3.669; 5.63).

**11a** λεγούσης· ὃ βλέπεις γράψον εἰς βιβλίον, "saying, 'Write what you see in a book.'" The command to write (γράψον, an aorist imperative) occurs twelve times in Revelation, once in each of the seven proclamations (2:1, 8, 12, 18; 3:1, 7, 14), and five times more generally, very likely referring to the entire book (here; 1:19; 14:13; 19:9; 21:5). These reiterated commands are important for the book as a whole, for John presents himself not as the author or originator of his message but rather as a mediator of the message revealed to him. Perhaps the closest verbal parallel is LXX Isa 30:8, γράψον . . . ταῦτα . . . εἰς βιβλίον, "write . . . these things . . . in a book," yet in Isaiah the reason is so that written prophecy can be a witness against the people at a *later* time (Lohmeyer, 16, and Kraft, 43, regard 1:11 as consciously modeled after Isa 30:8). Moses is commanded by God to write, a command probably referring to the ten commandments (Exod 34:27–28). In Deut 31:19, 21 (a passage similar to Isa 30:8), God commands Moses to write down a song (recorded in Deut 32:1–43) so that it will function as a witness against Israel. Again in Deut 31:24–27, the book of the law that Moses wrote was placed in the ark as witness against Israel. In *Jub.* 1:5–7, after the Lord revealed "what (was) in the beginning and what will occur (in the future)" (*Jub.* 1:4b; tr. Charlesworth, *OTP* 2:52), Moses is commanded to write so that Israel will know how faithful God has been to them. At the conclusion of Tobit (12:20), the angel Raphael commands Tobias and Tobit "to write down everything which has happened in a book" (γράψατε πάντα τὰ συντελεσθέντα εἰς βιβλίον), thus providing supernatural motivation for the composition of Tobit.

Supernatural commands to write the substance of a divine revelation, occasionally found in Judaism (see Isa 30:8; 4 Ezra 14), are much more common in Greco-Roman texts, in which the gods often command people to write books while asleep: Plato *Phaedo* 4.60E–61B; Callimachus *Aetia* 1.1.21–22; Propertius 3.3; Cicero *Academica priora* 2.16.51 (quoting Ennius *Annales* 5); Pausanias 1.21.2 (Dionysius appeared in a dream to Aeschylus while he was gathering grapes and urged him to write tragedy); Pliny *Ep.* 3.5.4 (Nero Claudius Drusus, who had died in 9 B.C., appeared to Pliny the Elder in a dream urging him to write the history of Germany); Aelius Aristides *Or.* 48.2 (Asclepius had ordered Aristides to write down his dreams; the present account is a summary of his original diary of some 300,000 lines; cf. *Or.* 48.3, 8); Dio Cassius 73.23.2 (the author claims that καί μοι καθεύδοντι προσέταξε τὸ δαιμόνιον ἱστορίαν γράφειν, "and while I was sleeping the god commanded me to write history"; the present narrative, he claims, is the result); in 79.10.1–2, Dio claims that the deceased Severus appeared to him and ordered him to write about the life of Caracalla; POxy 1381.8.160–70 tells how Imouthes, an Egyptian god associated with Sarapis and identified with Asclepius, orders a devotee to write in praise of the god. These examples (for others, see Stearns, *Studies*, 9–11) suggest that the claim of receiving a divine commission in a dream to write a literary composition had become a stock literary device in which the dream functions as a prelude to the literary work itself (Stearns, *Studies*, 1–7), thus providing divine legitimation for the composition. In Menander Rhetor II.17 (Russell-Wilson, *Menander Rhetor*, 207–9), the author recommends that a hymn to Apollo begin with a claim to divine inspiration, another clear indication of the stereotypical literary character of this motif. The earliest full example of this phenomenon in Greek literature (cf. *Iliad* 1.1–7) is found in Hesiod *Theogony* 22–34; cf. West, *Theogony*, 158–61). Though the mechanics are never specified, Apollonius of Tyana is said to have emerged from the oracular cave of Trophonius with a volume [i.e., 'roll'] filled with the sayings of Pythagoras (Philostratus *Vita Apoll.* 18.19–20). Lines 1–2 of the Sarapis aretalogy from Delos read ὁ ἱερεὺς Ἀπολλώνιος ἀνέγραψεν κατὰ πρόσταγμα τοῦ θεοῦ, "The priest Apollonius wrote by the command of the god" (Engelmann, *Aretalogy*, 7; English translation and commentary in Danker, *Benefactor*, 186–91). Often in magical procedures for procuring divine revelations, the author advises the practitioner to keep a small tablet handy to record whatever the supernatural revealer says (*PGM* VIII.89–91; XIII.90, 646). In *PGM* XIII.211, for example, it says "when the god comes in, look down and write the things [he] says and whatever name he may give you for himself." It is odd that John does not say that he wrote κατ' ἐπιγαγήν or καταπρόσταγμα or κέλευσιν, all meaning "by command" and all used in such contexts (Nock, *Essays* 1:47; H. W. Pleket, "Religious History," 158–59). These and other similar expressions (e.g., ἐξ ἐπιταγῆς, "by command") do not occur in the classical era but are first met in the Hellenistic and Roman period, probably influenced by Near Eastern conventions (Bömer, *Sklaven* 3:207–8). The Lord's command to Moses to write in Exod 17:14 (καταγράψον) is understood in *Barn.* 12:9 as a command of Moses to Joshua/Jesus to write a prophecy of future events. Hermas is commanded by the Ancient Lady to write two revelatory books and send one each to Clement and Grapte (*Vis.* 2.4.3). The Shepherd also commands Hermas to write the *Parables* and *Mandates* (*Vis.* 5.5).

**11b** καὶ πέμψον ταῖς ἑπτὰ ἐκκλησίαις, εἰς Ἔφεσον καὶ εἰς Σμύρναν καὶ εἰς Πέργαμον καὶ εἰς Θυάτειρα καὶ εἰς Σάρδεις καὶ εἰς Φιλαδέλφειαν καὶ εἰς Λαοδίκειαν, "'and send it to the seven churches, to Ephesus, and to Smyrna, and to Pergamon, and to Thyatira, and to Sardis, and to Philadelpia, and to Laodicea.'" The commands to "write and send" constitute a commission form functionally equivalent to the OT prophetic commission "go and tell" (cf. Isa 6:1–13; Jer 1:1–10; Ezek 1:1–3:27; Amos 7:14–17). This means that John's recording of the commission to "write and send" his revelatory narrative to the seven churches functions as a divine legitimation functionally equivalent to the narration of divine commissions in OT prophetic books. The command to the author to write down his visions and to send them to seven Christian communities refers back to 1:4, where the epistolary *adscriptio* mentions the seven churches in Asia as the destination of the entire composition. Rev 1:11 then refers to the composition as a whole, not to the seven proclamations in 2:1–3:22 (Ramsay, *Letters*, 36–37).

**12a** καὶ ἐπέστρεψα βλέπειν τὴν φωνὴν ἥτις ἐλάλει μετ' ἐμοῦ, "Then I turned to see the voice speaking to me." The article with φωνή is anaphoric, referring back to the noun φωνή first mentioned in 1:10. The same voice is again referred to in 4:1, where the phrase ἡ φωνὴ ἡ πρώτη, "the first voice," is articular, referring back to 1:10, 12, and even contains clear verbal allusions to both 1:10 (ἤκουσα ὡς σάλπιγγος, "I heard as a trumpet") and 1:12 (λαλούσης μετ' ἐμοῦ, "speaking with me"). The motif of a sudden turning around in connection with a visionary experience also occurs in John 20:24, *Ep. Hippocrates* 15 (ἐγὼ δὲ ἐπιστραφεὶς ὁρέω . . . , "Then I, when I turned around, saw . . ." [Hercher, *Epistolographi graeci*, 296]), and Plutarch *Lycurgus* 23.2–4 (Lycurgus thought he heard the voice of a man behind him, but on turning around found no one there and therefore regarded the voice as a divine message). How is it possible to "see" a voice? The MT of Exod 20:18 reads: וכל העם ראים את הקולת *wĕkol hāʿām rōʾîm ʾet haqqôlot,* "and all the people saw the voice." There are two passages in the LXX in which φωνή is used as the object of a verb of seeing; the first is LXX Exod 20:18, a literal translation of the MT: καὶ πᾶς ὁ λαὸς ἑώρα τὴν φωνήν, "And all the people saw the sound." The second is LXX Dan 7:11: ἐθεώρουν τότε τὴν φωνήν, "then I beheld the voice" (this nonliteral translation of the Aramaic of Dan 7:11 is corrected in Theodotion to ἐθεώρουν τότε ἀπὸ φωνῆς, "then I looked because of the voice"). The peculiarity of the LXX Exod 20:18 is commented on by Philo (*Mos.* 2.213), who refers to commands οὓς ἐθέσπισεν ἄνευ προφήτου ὁ θεὸς διὰ φωνῆς—τὸ παραδοξότατον—ὁρατῆς, "which God, without a prophet, proclaimed through a voice which, paradoxically, was visible." In *Decal.* 46–47 and *Mig.* 47–48, Philo further discusses the meaning of the paradoxical expression in Exod 20:18. In *Mig.* 47–48 he quotes two other related passages, LXX Exod 20:22, ὑμεῖς ἑωράκατε, ὅτι ἐκ τοῦ οὐρανοῦ λελάληκα πρὸς ὑμᾶς, "You have seen that I spoke to you from

heaven," and LXX Deut 4:12, καὶ ὁμοίωμα οὐκ εἴδετε, ἀλλ' ἢ φωνήν, "and you did not see an image, but a voice." For Philo the voice of God is visible because of the power of sight that resides in the soul (*Mig.* 49–50). Traces of rabbinic speculation on Exod 20:18 are also found in the *Mechilta d'Rabbi Simon b. Jochai* (ed. J. N. Epstein and E. Z. Melamed [Jerusalem, 1955] 154): בנוהג שבעולם אי אפשר לראות ...
את הקל אבל כן . . . ראו את הקולות bnwhg šbʿwlm ʾy ʾpšr lrʾwt ʾt hql ʾbl kn . . . rʾw ʾt hqwlwt, "Normally it is impossible to see sound, but here the people did" (tr. Jacobson, *Exagoge*, 100). Several OT prophets refer to "words" that they "saw" (Isa 2:1; 13:1; Jer 23:18; Amos 1:1; Mic 1:1; Hab 1:1; cf. Nah 1:1), though here it is clear that the voice is the figure of speech called synecdoche (the part for the whole). Charlesworth (*SJT* 39 [1986] 19–41; id., *OT Pseudepigrapha and the NT*, 128–31) has suggested that in Rev 1:12 "the Voice" should be capitalized since it represents, he claims, a hypostatic heavenly creature. Since a sound or voice cannot be seen, Charlesworth argues that "the Voice" was a hypostatic heavenly creature that could be seen. Since the voice John heard is associated with "one like a son of man" (1:13), Charlesworth argues that the earlier tradition of the hypostatic voice has been both linked with and subordinated to the son-of-man figure in the Johannine redaction. He adduces four texts in which he finds evidence for such a hypostatic Voice (*SJT* 39 [1986] 29–37): *Apoc. Sedr.* 2:3; *Mart. Isa.* 9:2; Cologne Mani Codex 56–57; *Apoc. Abr.* 9:1–10). According to Cologne Mani Codex 57.12–16 (R. Cameron and A. J. Dewey, eds. and trs., *The Cologne Mani Codex* [Missoula, MT: Scholars, 1979] 44–45), "A voice stole in at me, calling from the throne room. It came over to me, took hold of my right hand and picked me up." In *Apoc. Sedr.* 2:1, Sedrach "invisibly received a voice in his hearing" (καὶ φωνὴν ἀοράτως ἐδέξατο ἐν ταῖς ἀκοαῖς), which claimed that it had been sent by God to carry him to heaven (2:2). However, with the exception of the *Apocalypse of Abraham* (ca. late first century A.D.), all of these texts are late (late second century A.D. and following). Further, in none of these texts is a voice the object of a verb of seeing, nor does the term "voice" appear in any of them as anything more than a figure of speech, i.e., personification. In short, Charlesworth assumes rather than demonstrates that a belief in a hypostatic Voice existed in early Judaism, and there is nothing in Rev 1:10, 12; 4:1 to lend any support to his hypothesis of a hypostatic voice. There was a tendency in early Judaism to substitute "voice" for "voice of God" or as a surrogate for the name of God to avoid the anthropomorphic conception of God speaking; see Josephus' use of the term φωνή in this way: *Ant.* 1.85 (Gen 15:13); *Ant.* 2.267–69 (Exod 3:2–4:23); *Ant.* 3.88–90 (Exod 19:16–20:1); *Ant.* 8.352 (1 Kgs 19:9); cf. O. Betz, *TDNT* 9:290–92. In some Coptic-Gnostic texts there is a clear tendency to hypostatize the Voice, such as the "I am the Voice" sayings in *Thund.* 14.12 and *Trim. Prot.* 42.4 (see also *Trim. Prot.* 40.8–9; 42.9–16).

**12b** καὶ ἐπιστρέψας εἶδον ἑπτὰ λυχνίας χρυσᾶς, "Upon turning around I saw seven golden menorahs." This imagery suggests that a "temple" is the ambiance for John's vision, and it is likely that "the seven torches of fire burning before the throne" (4:5) are heavenly menorahs (at the very least they should be understood as *models* for the menorahs used in the temple), which, like the one or ones in the temple, were positioned to burn "before the Lord" (Exod 27:21; Lev 24:2–4; cf. 1 Kgs 11:36). Since "menorah," even though it is simply a transliteration of the Hebrew מנרה *mĕnōrâ* or מנורה *mĕnōrâ*, "lampstand," is a technical term for the sacral lampstand or lampstands that stood first in the wilderness tabernacle and later in the first and second temples, the main question for the interpreter is whether the author intended these seven lampstands to be understood in that tradition. There is no explicit indication that John conceived of these as *branched* lampstands with seven oil lamps like the traditional Jewish menorah used as a religious symbol. The idea of a group of precisely *seven* menorahs is unknown from Jewish literature. These seven lampstands are understood as arranged in a circle around the exalted Christ (1:13a; 2:1). In part this vision is based on the vision in Zech 4:1–14 (written shortly before the completion of the second temple in 516 B.C.). There a *single* lampstand is mentioned, with seven separate lamps (Zech 4:2), allegorically interpreted to represent "the eyes of the Lord, which range through the whole earth" (Zech 4:10), perhaps even here an astronomical reference to the seven "planets" of antiquity. The allusion to Zech 4:1–14, together with the redolent Jewish imagery in this passage, suggests that the term λυχνία should be translated "menorah" (K. Gamber, *Das Geheimnis der sieben Sterne* [Regensburg: Pustet, 1987] 24–26). Zech 4 is also picked up in Rev 11:4, where *two* lampstands are mentioned as well as two olive trees (mentioned in Zech 4:3, 11–14). Ancient representations of the menorah often show *two* menorahs flanking the Torah shrine (Yarden, *Tree of Light*, plates 93, 94, 95, 101, 109, 110, 114, 119, 130, 193, 194, 206). The lampstand of Zech 14:2 was in turn inspired by the lampstand that was one of the furnishings of the Jerusalem temple. The Mosaic golden lampstand is described in Exod 25:31–40 and Num 8:1–4 as an important piece of sacred furniture in the tabernacle (cf. Josephus *Ant.* 3.144–46), and is variously described as lit every evening (Exod 30:8), or as extinguished at night (1 Sam 3:3), or as burning continually (Lev 24:1–4). This became a popular view reflected in the magical papyri; cf. *PGM* IV.3069–70: "I conjure [you] by the one in holy Jerusalem before whom the unquenchable fire burns for all time." Cf. *PGM* IV.1219–22 (Betz, *Greek Magical Papyri*, 61), "before whom the unquenchable lamp continually burns, the great God . . . who is radiant at Jerusalem." Josephus claims that three lights burned throughout the day, while the rest were lit in the evening (*Ant.* 3.199). The vessels of the Solomonic temple were reportedly looted by the Babylonians (2 Chr 36:7, 10, 18; Ezra 1:7; Dan 1:2), but only Jer 52:19 explicitly states that lampstands (note the plural) were taken from the temple immediately prior to its destruction in 586 B.C. The lampstand was stolen in 170 B.C. by Antiochus IV (1 Macc 1:21; Josephus *Ant.* 12.250 refers to lampstands in the plural), and when the sanctuary was purified and rededicated, it was replaced with another one (1 Macc 4:49–50). According to Josephus this one was seen by Pompey (*Ant.* 14.72). The author of 4 Ezra, referring to the plundering and destruction of the second temple by the Romans, says "the light of our lampstand has been put out" (10:22), using the removal of the lampstand as a symbol of the worship life of the temple. A bas-relief depicting Roman soldiers carrying the lampstand from the second temple is found on the Arch of Titus, erected in A.D. 81 (Yarden, *Tree of Light*, plate 4), an event described by Josephus (*J.W.* 7.148; the problematic history of that stolen menorah is traced as far as possible in Yarden, *Tree of Light*, 3–8). Several passages in the OT indicate that Solomon's temple had *ten* separate lampstands, arranged in two groups of five, though they are not explicitly described as branched (1 Kgs 7:49; cf. 2 Chr 4:7, 20–21; 1 Chr 28:15); historically these are the earliest forms of the menorah (Voss, *Menora*, 17–20). The rabbis tried to harmonize these discordant traditions by proposing that the Mosaic menorah was flanked in the temple by five lampstands on either side (*b. Menaḥ.* 98b). 1 Chr 28:15 mentions "the golden lampstands [מנרת *měnôrot*] and their lamps" and a silver "lampstand [מנורה *měnôrâ*] and its lamps." Josephus transmits the strange tradition that Solomon had 10,000 lampstands made but set only one of them up in the temple to burn all day (*Ant.* 8.90). The temple lampstands seen by Zechariah are accorded cosmic significance in Zech 4:10b, "These seven are the eyes of the Lord, which range through the whole earth." Philo regards the golden menorah as a symbol of heaven (*Quaest. in Ex.* 2.73, 81, 95), and the lamps themselves symbolize the stars (*Quaest. in Ex.* 2.73, 104), or the planets (Philo *Quaest. in Ex.* 2.78; Josephus *J. W.* 5.217; Clement Alex. *Strom.* 5.6). According to Philo, the reason is that the seven planets, including the sun, are light-bringers like the lamps on the menorah (Philo *Quis Her.* 216–25). Eupolemus *Fragmenta* 2.7–8 observes that Solomon had ten golden lampstands constructed (following 1 Kgs 7:49) but adds the detail that seventy lamps were also made, seven for each lampstand (cf. B. Z. Wachholder, *Eupolemus: A Study of Judaeo-Greek Literature* [Cincinnati: Hebrew Union College; Jewish Institute of Religion, 1974] 186–87). On the history of the menorah, see Sperber, *JJS* 16 (1965) 135–59, and Voss, *Menorah*.

**13a** καὶ ἐν μέσῳ τῶν λυχνιῶν ὅμοιον υἱὸν ἀνθρώπου, "and in the midst of the menorahs there was one like a son of man." The placement of the seven lampstands may be significant, for in Jewish tradition the temple menorah was oriented so that it would burn "before the Lord" (Exod 27:21; Lev 24:2–4), and these lampstands are obviously situated to burn before the exalted Christ. The heavenly character of this vision is made clearer if the "seven torches of fire" that burn before the throne (4:5) are construed as the heavenly counterparts of earthly menorahs.

The phrase "one like a son of man" (like 14:14) is an apparent allusion to the phrase כבר אנש *kěbar ʾěnāš*, "like a son of man," in Dan 7:13 (Lietzmann, *Menschensohn*, 56–57; Slater, *BT* 44 [1993] 349–50). However, the synonymous phrase כדמות בני אדם, "like a son of man," occurs in Dan 10:16, continuing an earlier angelophany described in Dan 10:5–6 in a way very similar to Rev 1:13–15. Dalman (*Die Worte Jesu*, 206, followed by Casey, *Son of Man*, 144–45) thought this more likely to be an allusion to Dan 10:5–6, 16, 18. Somewhat surprisingly, there is nothing in the way that the appellation "son of man" is used in Rev 1:13 or 14:14 to suggest any influence from or even any awareness of the extensive use of the title in the Gospels, for the anarthrous phrase υἱὸς ἀνθρώπου is an allusion to Dan 7:13 (Lietzmann, *Menschensohn*, 56–57). When Justin refers to the son of man mentioned in Dan 7:13, he uses the anarthrous phrase ὡς υἱὸς ἀνθρώπου (*1 Apol.* 51.9; *Dial.* 31.1, 3; 32.1; 76.1[2x]; 79.2; 100.3 [ὡς lacking]; 126.1), though when he refers to the title in the synoptic Gospels, he uses the arthrous phrase ὁ υἱὸς τοῦ ἀνθρώπου (*Dial.* 76.7; 100.3); see Borsch, *Son of Man*, 43; Moule, *NTS* 41 (1995) 277; Skarsaune, *Prophecy*, 88–90. The phrase in the Gospels and Acts regularly occurs with the definite article: ὁ υἱὸς τοῦ ἀνθρώπου; the anarthrous phrase υἱὸς ἀνθρώπου occurs in John 5:27 (the only anarthrous occurrence of the phrase in the sayings traditions); Heb 2:6; Rev 1:13; 14:14. Hare (*Son of Man*, 90–96) argues that the anarthrous phrase in John 5:27 expresses a quality or status, i.e., the incarnate status of the Son.

While in the MT of Dan 7:13 the "one like a son of man" is presented to the Ancient of Days (thus clearly distinguishing the two figures), here the "one like a son of man" is described as if he is identical with the Ancient of Days. This identification was not necessarily original with John, but may already be presupposed by the LXX version of Dan 7:13 found in MS 967 (Giessen, *Daniel*, 108): ἤρχετο ὡς υἱὸς ἀνθρώπου καὶ ὡς παλαιὸς ἡμερῶ(ν) παρῆν καὶ οἱ παρεστηκότες προσήγαγον αὐτῷ, "he came like a son of man and like the Ancient of Days was present, and those who were near approached him." In MS 88 the reading is similar (Giessen, *Daniel*, 39–40): ὡς υἱὸς ἀνθρώπου ἤρχετο, καὶ ὡς παλαιὸς ἡμερῶν παρῆν, καὶ οἱ παρεστηκότες παρῆσαν αὐτῷ, "he came like a son of man, and like the Ancient of Days was present, and those who were near were present with him." The verb παρῆσαν in MS 88 has obviously been influenced by the preceding παρῆν; the superior reading is προσήγαγον as found in MS 967. This reading is found in the only two extant LXX MSS of Daniel, the Codex Chisianus (MS 88, dependent on the Syro-Hexapla) and the incomplete Chester Beatty papyrus codex 967 (late second or early third century A.D.). A third witness is the Syrian translation by Paul of Tella (A.D. 616–17), the fifth column (the LXX) of Origen's Hexapla, the so-called Syro-Hexapla. MS 88, however, is also dependent on the recension of the LXX found in Origen's Hexapla. MS 967 is one of the earliest extant copies of parts of the LXX and constitutes the only extant pre-Hexaplaric text of the LXX (Giessen, *Daniel*, 17). It identifies the one like a son of man with the Ancient of Days, though it is unclear whether this was intentional or the result of scribal error, or whether this was pre-Christian or reflects Christian exegesis (Bodenmann, *Naissance*, 73–74 n. 192). A. Yarbro Collins (in J. J. Collins, *Comm. Daniel*, 103) supposes (plausibly) that ἕως παλαιοῦ ἡμερῶν, "to the Ancient of Days," was erroneously transcribed as ὡς παλαιὸς ἡμερῶν, "as the Ancient of Days." If the change was intentional, the precedent for this exegetical step may have been based on Ezek 1:26, in which Ezekiel saw something like a throne, "and upon the image of the throne was an image like a human form." The *Tg. Ezek.* 1:26 reads (Levey, *Tg. Ezek.*, 22) "and above the throne was the likeness of the appearance of Adam." *1 Enoch* 46:1 (composed late in the first century A.D.), however, understands Dan 7:13 to refer to two distinct figures: "And there I saw one who had a head of days, and his head (was) white like wool; and with him (there was) another, whose face had the appearance of a man, and his face (was) full of grace, like one of the holy angels" (tr. M. A. Knibb, *Enoch* 2:131). This passage alludes both to Ezek 1:26 (which contains the phrase אדם כמראה דמות *děmût kěmarʾēh ʾādām*, "the likeness as the appearance of a man") and to Dan 7:9, with Dan 7:13 providing the connecting link (Feuillet, *RB* 60 [1953] 180ff.; Quispel, *VC* 34 [1980] 1–2).

A critical reading is ὡς παλαιὸς ἡμερῶν, "as the Ancient of Days," in Rahlfs (*Septuaginta*) instead of ἕως παλαιὸς ἡμερῶν, "unto the Ancient of Days." Montgomery (*Daniel*, 304) regarded the ὡς as simply a pre-Christian error for ἕως, citing Rev 1:14 as evidence (see also A. Yarbro Collins in J. J. Collins, *Comm. Daniel*, 103). In agreement, Ziegler has reconstructed the LXX text of Dan 7:13 to read καὶ ἕως παλαιοῦ ἡμερῶν παρῆν, "and he came to the Ancient of Days" (Montgomery, *Daniel*, 304). Ziegler regards the reading ὡς παλαιὸς ἡμερῶν, "as an Ancient of Days," as a secondary corruption of ἕως παλαιὸς ἡμερῶν, "unto the Ancient of Days," as the phrase in the LXX presupposed by Tertullian and Cyprian, a view shared by Jeansonne (*OG Translation*, 96–99), followed by Yarbro Collins ("'Son of Man,'" 554), but disputed by Stuckenbruck (*Angel*, 213–18). Jeansonne (98–99) points out that in Dan 2:43 MS 967 reads καὶ ἕως, but MS 88 has καὶ ὡς, and in Dan 4:30 (LXX: v 33) MS 967 has ὡς while MS 88 has ἕως. Yet Jeansonne's conclusion that the LXX version of Dan 7:13 does *not* present the Son of Man as a divine figure is somewhat problematic: (1) On balance, the use of the preposition ἐπί in the phrase "on the clouds" (MSS 88 and 967), compared with the use of the preposition μετά in the phrase "with the clouds" (Theod.), very likely underscores the divinity of the Son of Man figure (see *Comment* on 14:14). (2) Her argument that "nowhere else does the OG [Old Greek = LXX] translation hint of a divine Son of Man" (113) is without force since the Son of Man figure is mentioned only in Dan 7:13. (3) She does not consider the probable dependence of Dan 7:13 upon Ezek 1:26; in the latter passage God is hesitantly described in human form seated on a throne. (4) She also neglects to consider the understanding of Dan 7:13 found in Rev 1:13, which apparently reflects an exegetical tradition that Dan 7:13 refers to one rather than two figures. Yet whether or not the identification of the Son of Man with the Ancient of Days reflected in MSS 88 and 967 was intentional, it is clear that it *could* be understood that way, and Rev 1:13 provides clear evidence that it was understood as referring to the Son of Man as identical with the Ancient of Days.

Rev 1:13–14 may reflect an early stage of the later rabbinical polemic against the "two powers" heresy. Proponents of this heresy, often identified with Christians and/or Gnostics, interpreted certain biblical texts in such a way that angelic beings or divine hypostases in heaven were understood as equivalent to God (cf. Segal, *Two Powers*, x). This heresy was traced back to Elisha b. Abuya, nicknamed Aher, "Other" (ca. A.D. 110–35). This heresy had an earlier phase, reaching into the first century A.D., in which the two powers were complementary, and a second phase in which the two powers were understood as antagonistic (Segal, *Two Powers*, 17). Dan 7:9–10 appears to have been as important exegetically for the "heretical" view as it was to the rabbinic defense against it. One passage that may reflect the time of Akiba (early second century A.D.) is *b. Ḥag.* 14a (I. Epstein, tr., *Babylonian Talmud*):

> One passage says: "His throne was fiery flames" (Dan. 7:9) and another passage says: "Until thrones were placed; and One that was ancient of days did sit"—there is no contradiction; One (throne) for Him, and one for David: this is the view of R. Akiba.

If authentic, this suggests that early second century A.D. rabbinical authorities identified the "son of man" figure in Dan 7:13 with the Davidic Messiah (cf. *Midr. Ps.* 21:5). In the continuation of the passage quoted from *b. Ḥag.* 14a, the two figures of Dan 7:9–13 are understood as God's two aspects of mercy and justice. This identification is also reflected in the formulation of a new messianic name ענני *'nny*, "Cloud-Man," and בר ניפלי *br nyply*, "Son of the Cloud" (G. Vermes in Black, *Aramaic*, 327–28). If the rabbis were antagonistic to any tradition of a man-like figure in heaven beside God (Segal, *Two Powers*, 52), it is striking that Rev 1:13–14 also avoids interpreting Dan 7:9–13 in terms of *two* figures. This polemic based on Dan 7:9–10 is correlated in rabbinic sources with references to God as first and last (Isa 44:6; 41:4); cf. Rev 1:17b, with the elaborate interpretation of the divine name (Segal, *Two Powers*, 33–34):

> I was in Egypt.
> I was at the Sea.

> I was in the past,
> I will be in the future to come.
> I am in this world,
> I am in the world to come.

This is comparable to the divine name in Rev 1:8: "who is and who was and who is to come," and with an emphasis on God as one who raises people from the dead based on Deut 32:39: "See now that I, even I, am He. I kill and I revive" (Segal, *Two Powers*, 84). These texts are all based on speculation on the significance of the divine name and, when combined with allusions to Dan 7:9–13, suggest that John is preserving a Jewish polemic *against* understanding Daniel as referring to the two powers.

The "son of man" is mentioned in Revelation only twice: here in 1:13 and in 14:14. Both uses of the term appear to be based directly on Dan 7:13 rather than on Christian tradition. Lohse observes that the phrase "he is coming with clouds" in 1:7a is an allusion to Dan 7:13, though the designation "Son of Man" is lacking ("Der Menschensohn," 415–16). The mention of "one like a son of man" in v 13 is within the context of John's commission in 1:9–20; the scene depicted in Dan 7:13 is not relegated to the future but is experienced as present.

**13b** ἐνδεδυμένον ποδήρη καὶ περιεζωσμένον πρὸς τοῖς μαστοῖς ζώνην χρυσᾶν, "wearing a long robe with a golden sash encircling his chest." The phrase "wearing a long robe" may be an allusion to the vision of Dan 10:5, in which the revelatory angel is described as "clothed in linen" (LXX: ἐνδεδυμένος βύσσινα), or to the vision of Ezek 9:2, which also describes an angelic being as "clothed in linen" (LXX: ἐνδεδυκὼς ποδήρη). Similarly, the reference to "a golden sash encircling his chest" may be an allusion to Dan 10:5, where it is said of the angelic revealer "whose loins were girded with gold of Uphaz" (note that the LXX reads "whose loins were girded with linen" [περιεζωσμένος βυσσίνῳ]). This is similar to Rev 15:6, which describes the seven bowl angels as having "their breasts girded with golden girdles." One of the problems in interpreting vv 13–16 is determining the significance of the imagery used to depict the exalted Christ. One common, but unfounded, view is that Christ is presented in priestly garments (cf. Wolff, *NTS* 27 [1980–81] 189). The term ποδήρης occurs twelve times in the LXX and always refers to a garment worn by the high priest, though the term is used to translate *five different* Hebrew words, so that the Greek term ποδήρης can hardly be understood as a technical term: (1) חֹשֶׁן *ḥōšen*, "breastplate," found only in the Priestly writer and most often translated λογεῖον, "oracular breastplate" (e.g., Exod 28:15, 22), but translated ποδήρης in Exod 25:7; 35:9; (2) מְעִיל *mě'îl* in Exod 28:4; 29:5; (3) אֵפוֹד *'ēpôd*, "ephod," in Exod 28:31; (4) בַּד *bad* in Ezek 9:2, 3, 11; and (5) מַחֲלָצוֹת *maḥălāṣôt* in Zech 3:4. Actually, the most common Hebrew term for the robes of the high priests and priests in the OT is כֻּתֹּנֶת *kětōnet*, which is usually translated χιτών (e.g., Exod 28:4, 39, 40; 29:5, 8; 35:19; 39:27; 40:14; Lev 6:3). ποδήρης is also used of the high priest's robe in Wis 18:24; Sir 27:8; 45:81; *Ep. Arist.* 96 (the vestments of the high priest are described in 96–98); Josephus *Ant.* 3.153; and Philo *Leg. All.* 2.56. In *T. Levi* 8:2–10, which contains a list of priestly vestments intended for the heavenly consecration of Levi, his robe is called ἡ στολὴ τῆς ἱερατείας, "the robe of the priesthood." Philo *Mos.* 2.109–10 uses the term ὑποδύτης, which he distinguishes from the ἐρωμίς, "ephod." Philo describes the purple robe, using the alternate term ποδήρης, in some detail (*Mos.* 118–21). Robes and belts (which gathered the robes at the waist) were basic articles of clothing in the ancient Mediterranean world used by both men and women (cf. *Odyssey* 6.38). Since the "one like a son of man" is wearing only a long robe and a golden sash, these two garments by themselves cannot be claimed to be priestly vestments. Nothing is said about the rest of the vestments (the ephod, the trousers, the turban, the crown, and so forth), nor are the material and color of the robe specified. There is therefore no clear intention on the part of the author to conceptualize the appearance of the exalted Christ in priestly terms. With regard to the term ζώνη, "sash," the Hebrew term אבנט *'abnēṭ* is often translated ζώνη in the LXX (Exod 28:4, 39, 40; 29:9; 36:36; Lev 8:7, 13; 16:4). With regard to the placement of the belt or sash around the *chest* (οἱ μαστοί), which would seem more appropriate around the *waist,* it is interesting to note that in the fresco depicting Mithras killing the bull in the Mithraeum at Marino, Mithras is wearing a golden belt that encircles his chest (Vermaseren, *Mithriaca III,* plate 4); the same location of the belt is found in two other bas-reliefs of the Mithraic *tauroctone,* "bull-slaying scene," found in Vermaseren, *Mithraica III,* plates XX (a relief from Nersae) and XXI (a relief from Neuenheim). However, the *cingulum,* "belt," like the *balteus,* "shoulder band (used for a dagger-sheath)," were often used for securing a short sword and were therefore appropriate for warriors (Vergil *Aeneid* 12.940–44).

The epiphanic language of Greek poetry often emphasizes the *golden* appearance of the garments and accoutrements of the gods (cf. Williams, *Callimachus,* 39). The epiphanies of Zeus in *Iliad* 8.41–46 and of Poseidon in *Iliad* 13.20–27 (both passages nearly identical verbally) became the model for the use of gold in divine epiphanies. Callimachus *Hymn to Apollo* 32–35 is representative: "Golden is the tunic of Apollo and golden his mantle, his lyre and his Lyctian bow and his quiver; golden too are his sandals; for rich in gold is Apollo" (tr. G. R. Mair, LCL). This epiphanic language could also be applied to the description of heroes, as in Vergil *Aeneid* 1.589–94, where Aeneas is described as "splendid in bright light, grand as a god," for Venus had "made his eyes shine out with power and joy-like ivory carved to beauty, like some work of silver or Parian marble chased with gold" (tr. Copely, *Vergil,* 19–20). In *Odyssey* 9.544–45, Circe is depicted as wearing a golden girdle (ζώνην . . . χρυσείην).

**14a** ἡ δὲ κεφαλὴ αὐτοῦ καὶ αἱ τρίχες λευκαὶ ὡς ἔριον λευκὸν ὡς χιών, "His head and his white hair were like white wool, or snow." This is an allusion to Dan 7:9, where God is depicted as an old man, called the Ancient of Days, and his hair is compared to pure wool. The same metaphor in which the hair of God is mentioned and its whiteness compared with wool is mentioned in the theophany described in *1 Enoch* 46:1; 71:10 (the so-called Parables of Enoch in *1 Enoch* 37–71, probably no earlier than the late first century A.D.) and is certainly dependent on Daniel as well: "his head was white like wool." In *Apoc. Abr.* 11:2, it is said of the angel Iaoel that "the hair of his head [was] like snow." The son of Lamech was born with hair white like wool (*1 Enoch* 106:2, 10), which is understood as characteristic of angels (*1 Enoch* 106:5–6). The metaphor of comparing the head of an old man to snow also occurs in *Jos. As.* 22:7 (a description of the aged Jacob). In keeping with the ancient Near Eastern attitude toward the elderly, this metaphor conveyed such notions as respect, honor, wisdom, and high social status.

The mention of *both* the head and the hair is at first sight problematic, for only the hair could be white. The καί is therefore epexegetical or explanatory, i.e., "his head, that is, his white hair, was like white wool," using the order of the general and the specific. The repetition of the adjective λευκός is awkward. The detailed description of "one like a son of man" in vv 14–15 begins with the head and eyes and then turns to the feet, a stereotyped pattern of description often found in ancient sources (e.g., Philostratus *Vitae soph.* 552).

**14b** καὶ οἱ ὀφθαλμοὶ αὐτοῦ ὡς φλὸξ πυρός, "and his eyes were like a flame of fire." This clause may be an allusion to Dan 10:6, where the angelic revealer is described as having "eyes like flaming torches." In *1 Enoch* 106:5–6, the newborn son of Lamech has "eyes like the rays of the sun," understood to be a characteristic of angels. It is said of Jacob the patriarch that "his eyes (were) flashing and darting (flashes of) lightning" (*Jos. As.* 22:7). In Greek tradition the eyes of the gods were thought to have a special quality, which was usually described as bright and shining (*Iliad* 3.397; *Hymn to Aphrodite* 1.181; cf. Mussies, "Identification," 4). According to Apollodorus 2.4.9, Herakles "flashed a gleam of fire from his eyes [πυρὸς δ' ἐξ ὀμμάτων ἔλαμπεν αἴγλην]," an indication that he was a son of Zeus. The comparison of eyes with fire is a frequent metaphor in Greek and Latin literature (*Iliad* 13.474; 19.366; *Odyssey* 19.446; Ps.-Hesiod *Scut.* 72; Euripides frag. 689 [Nauck, *Tragicorum graecorum*]; Herodian 1.7.5; Apollodorus 2.4.9; Vergil *Aeneid* 6.300; 12.102; cf. *Neuer Wettstein,* ad Rev 1:14), used in contexts where humans are described in ways that are characteristic of the gods (Statius *Silv.* 1.1.103 [the eyes of Domitian's equestrian statue]; Suetonius *Augustus* 79.2 [the eyes of Augustus]).

**15a** καὶ οἱ πόδες αὐτοῦ ὅμοιοι χαλκολιβάνῳ ὡς ἐν καμίνῳ πεπυρωμένης, "and his feet were like bronze when smelted in a furnace." The reference to "feet like bronze" alludes to the phrase "arms and legs like the gleam of burnished bronze" in Dan 10:6. The "one like a son of man" described here is apparently *barefoot,* and it is worth noting that Israelite priests apparently wore no special footgear when officiating in the tabernacle or temple. In *Acts of John* 90, in the context of a retelling of the transfiguration of Jesus, his feet are described as being whiter than snow. The famous Prima Porta statue of Augustus portrays the emperor, rather atypically, as *barefoot.* According to Hannestad (*Roman Art,* 51), this is generally understood as an indication that the individual depicted is in the sphere of the divine, and that the statue of Augustus portrays the deceased and deified emperor. Similarly, one panel of the Ravenna reliefs depicts four deceased members of the imperial family including Augustus, and perhaps Antonia (Claudius' mother), Germanicus, and Drusus, all barefoot (Hannestad, *Roman Art,* 100–101 fig. 63). The Vatican statue of Claudius as Jupiter also portrays the emperor as barefoot (Hannestad, *Roman Art,* 104 fig. 65). According to Fraenkel (*Horace,* 204 n. 4), in the literary presentation of divine epiphanies in Horace and in Greek poetry, the appearance of the god, anticipated in prayer, is frequently described in detail, and "special attention was paid to the god's gait, and sometimes also to the manner in which he was to set his feet on the ground and to his footwear" (e.g., Sophocles *Antigone* 1144; Aristophanes *Frogs* 330–31; *Persians* 659–60; Catullus 61.9–10; Vergil *Georgics* 2.7–8). In the brief description of the Great King of Persia in Aeschylus, *Persians* 660–62, only his sandals and royal tiara are mentioned (i.e., he is described "from head to foot"). In Callimachus *Hymn* 2.3, the feet of Apollo are described in epiphanic language as καλῷ ποδί, "with beautiful foot." In *PGM* XIII.705, the magical practitioner is advised to look at the *feet* of the god when he appears, not his face. Bare feet were also required in certain ritual situations, such as the procession that bore the ashes of Augustus (Suetonius *Aug.* 100.4), and for Pythagoreans, who sacrificed and entered temples (Iamblichus *De vita Pyth.* 85, 105). In the brief theophanic description in Exod 24:9–11, only the feet of God are seen on a pavement of sapphire.

The difficult compound word χαλκολιβάνῳ, "bronze," is found just twice in Revelation (here and 2:18) and nowhere else in ancient Greek literature. The word is variously translated "burnished bronze" (RSV, NRSV), "fine brass" (AV), "bronze" (NIV), "burnished brass." The most informed discussion of this word is found in C. Hemer, *Letters*, 111–17. The first element in the compound is the noun χαλκός, which was applied to copper and to brass (the alloy of copper with zinc) but most commonly to bronze (the alloy of copper with tin), which was also called ὀρείχαλκος, a metal used for manufacturing Roman imperial coins (Caley, *Orichalcum*, 1). The second element in this compound noun is λίβανος, "frankincense," which is masculine when the tree from which the incense is derived is meant and either masculine or feminine when the incense itself is meant (it is synonymous with λιβανωτός, "frankincense," which is also found in both masculine and feminine genders). The morphology of the compound stem formation of nouns exhibits great variety (Palmer, *Greek*, 258–60; Moulton-Howard, *Accidence*, 268–92). In determinative compounds, the second member is determined by the first; i.e., χαλκολίβανος could mean "brass-like λίβανος," i.e., "yellow frankincense" (LSJ, 1974), i.e., "amber," or "the glowing metal named from amber by this name" (Hort, 17; cf. Moulton-Howard, *Accidence*, 280). The masculine noun λίβανος is also a designation for "Lebanon," so that the term χαλκολίβανος could conceivably be understood as "Lebanese brass" or "brass from Lebanon" (LSJ, 1974). Yet it is philologically doubtful that the second element in such a compound would be used to describe the first element. The Suida construes the term as neuter, χαλκολίβανον, and provides a short and incorrect definition (A. Adler, *Suidae Lexicon* [Leipzig: Teubner, 1928–35] 4:783): χαλκολίβανον: εἶδος ἠλέκρου τιμιώτερον χρυσοῦ, "*Chalkolibanon:* a kind of electrum more valuable than gold." Ausonius regards it as masculine, ὁ χαλκολίβανος. Rehkopf ("Grammatisches," 215–16) has made a good case for construing it as feminine, ἡ χαλκολίβανος. Attempting to counter the view that the ancients could never have produced zinc commercially (R. J. Forbes, *Metallurgy in Antiquity* [Leiden: Brill, 1950] 275–76), Hemer argues that an alloy of copper with metallic zinc was made in Thyatira (cf. Rev 2:18), a purer brass than that normally used in coinage (*Letters*, 116). More speculative, however, is Hemer's view that χαλκολίβανος is therefore a "copulative compound" (i.e., a coordinative compound; cf. Moulton-Howard, *Accidence*, 269–70) meaning "copper-zinc," with the unique term λίβανος (derived from the verb λείβειν, "to pour forth"), perhaps a specialized local metallurgical term for zinc isolated through a process of distillation.

**15b** καὶ ἡ φωνὴ αὐτοῦ ὡς φωνὴ ὑδάτων πολλῶν, "and his voice was like the sound of cascading water." This verse may combine allusions to Ezek 43:2 and Dan 10:6. In the first passage the arrival of the glory of God sounded like the sound of mighty waters, and in the second passage it is said of the angelic revealer that "the sound of his words was like the noise of a great multitude." This is one of three instances in which the Hebrew text of Ezekiel is quoted exactly in Greek translation (Vanhoye, *Bib* 43 [1962] 437). The other two passages are Rev 10:10, which quotes Ezek 3:3, and Rev 18:1, which quotes another phrase from Ezek 43:2. This phrase was derived either from Ezek 1:24 or 43:2; the phrase "the sound of many waters" occurs in both passages, though in neither passage is the phrase used for the sound of a voice. Ezek 43:2 reads "And behold the glory of the God of Israel came from the east; and the sound of his coming was like the sound of many waters [MT: וקולו כקול מים רבים *wĕqôlô kĕqôl mayim rabbîm;* LXX: καὶ φωνὴ τῆς παρεμβολῆς ὡς φωνὴ διπλασιαζόντων πολλῶν]." The simile ὡς φωνὴ ὑδάτων πόλλων, "like the sound of many waters," occurs twice more in Revelation (14:2; 19:6) and also occurs in 1QH 2:27: "the bellowing of their voice was like the noise of many waters [וכהמון מים רבים שאון קולם *wkhmwn mym rbym š'wn qwlm*]." According to *Sepher ha-Razim* 4.10, the voice of the angels of water is like the voice of waters or the voice of many waters (כקול מים רבים *kĕqôl mayim rabbîm;* see Morgan, *Sepher ha-Razim,* 68 n. 6). The phrases "a voice of many waters" and "a voice like the roaring of the sea" are used as metaphors for the voice of God in *Apoc. Abr.* 17:1 and for the singing of the living creatures in *Apoc. Abr.* 18:1.

**16a** καὶ ἔχων ἐν τῇ δεξιᾷ χειρὶ αὐτοῦ ἀστέρας ἑπτά, "In his right hand he had seven stars." Charles (1:29–30) regarded ἔχων as a participle functioning as a finite verb and thus reflecting a Semitic idiom, a view supported by S. Thompson (*Apocalypse,* 107–8) but rightly rejected by Beyer (*Semitische Syntax,* 208–9). Attributive participles from ἔχειν, "to have," occur 60 times in Revelation and 107 times in Hermas (the latter indicating idiomatic popular Greek usage). According to ancient sidereal lore, seven stars could represent (1) the seven planets, (2) Ursus Major (a constellation with seven stars), or (3) the Pleiades (another constellation of seven stars); each of these possibilities requires a short discussion.

(1) In antiquity, the "seven stars" are often used to represent the seven "planets" (Sun, Moon, Jupiter, Mercury, Mars, Venus, and Saturn). Though these seven planets were almost universally accepted in the Hellenistic and Roman world, there were three different planetary orders (Beck, *Planetary Gods,* 1–11): (a) The order based on distance from the earth has two variants (because the positions of Venus, Mercury, and the Sun cannot be determined relative to each other): (i) the older "Egyptian" order: Saturn, Jupiter, Mars, Venus, Mercury, Sun, and Moon, and (ii) the later "Chaldean" order, which came to dominate late Hellenistic astronomy (note the position of the Sun in the center): Saturn, Jupiter, Mars, Sun, Venus, Mercury, and Moon. (b) The astrological, horoscopic order (probably originally based on distance, though priority was given to the Sun and Moon for other reasons): Sun, Moon, Saturn, Jupiter, Mars, Venus, and Mercury. (c) The Mithraic "grade" order: Saturn, Sun, Moon, Jupiter, Mars, Venus, and Mercury. In some of the depictions of Mithras slaying the bull, the presence of seven stars in the field symbolizes the seven planets (Vermaseren, *Mithraica III,* 9 [plate IV], 12 [plate XII], 37; Vermaseren, *CIMRM,* 1127B, 1206, 1216, 1727, 2244, 2354, 2359). Clement Alex. (*Strom.* 5.6) compares the menorah in the Jewish temple with the planets (see *Comment* on 1:12) and compares the light in the middle and in the highest position with the sun, following the "Chaldaean" order.

(2) Seven stars can also represent the stars that form the constellation Ursa Major, known as ἡ Ἄρκτος, "the Great Bear"; the *Septentriones,* the seven plowing

oxen; ἡ Ἅμαξα, "the Wain"; or (in the United States) the Big Dipper (Aratus *Phaen.* 26–27; *Corp. Herm.* frag. 6.13 [Scott, *Hermetica* 1:412–13; A. J. Festugière, *Hermès Trismégiste* 3:37]; Vettius Valens 13.27; see Job 9:9; 38:32, where the Hebrew term עַיִשׁ *'ayiš* is translated "Bear" in the RSV and NRSV and "Great Bear" in KB³, 778).

(3) In addition, since there are seven stars in the constellation Pleiades, this sidereal group could be alluded to (Malina, *Revelation,* 70). This constellation was apparently known to the author of Job 38:31, where the Hebrew term כִּימָה *kîmâ* refers to "das Siebengestirn," i.e., Pleiades (KB³, 450).

**16b** καὶ ἐκ τοῦ στόματος αὐτοῦ ῥομφαία δίστομος ὀξεῖα ἐκπορευομένη, "and a sharp double-edged sword projected from his mouth." This bizarre image is found only in Revelation, where variations of the phrase "the sword of his mouth" (always referring to Christ) occur four times (1:16; 2:16; 19:15, 21), while the accompanying phrase "the one who has the sharp, two-edged sword" occurs only in 2:12. The distribution of the anaphoric article with ῥομφαία, "sword," in Revelation is somewhat perplexing. ῥομφαία is anarthrous in 1:16 but appropriately articular in 2:12, 16. Again, as though referring to a different sword, ῥομφαία is anarthrous in 19:15 but expectedly articular in 19:21. This suggests that the two units of text in which these terms are clustered were not composed at the same time or were not included in the final composition at the same time. It appears that 19:11–21 was composed *before* all or part of 1:9–3:22, and that the motif of the "sharp two-edged" sword that issues from the mouth of the exalted Christ is derived from 19:15, 21 (see *Comment* on those verses; cf. Fekkes, *Isaiah,* 117).

The specific function of the sword is mentioned in 2:16 (the exalted Christ will fight those who do not repent in the Christian congregation at Sardis) and in 19:15 (to smite the nations) and 19:21 (to slay the armies of the kings of the earth). The function in 2:16 appears to be a secondary application of the metaphor, which tends to confirm our view that 19:11–21 was composed first. The term ῥομφαία was normally used to refer to a large sword used both for cutting and piercing, while μάχαιρα was used for a short sword or a dagger (the somewhat arbitrary rule of thumb for archaeologists is that the latter is sixteen inches or shorter). The Roman legionary carried a *gladius,* a straight sword. The Hebrew term חרב *ḥereb* is used in the OT for *both* the two-edged short sword or dagger (LXX Judg 3:16: μάχαιρα δίστομος) and the single-edged long sword (Josh 6:21; cf. Snodgrass, *Arms and Armor,* 97–98; O. Kaiser, *TDOT* 5:155). The phrase "sharp as a two-edged sword" occurs in Prov 5:4, and the two-edged sword is also mentioned in Ps 146:6; Sir 21:3.

That the sword issues from the *mouth* of Christ suggests that the sword is a metaphor for the tongue, i.e., for the words he speaks. Speech is frequently compared to a sword or dagger, and the emphasis on sharpness suggests the effectiveness or power of the words (4Q*436* = 4QBarĕki Napši⁰ [tr. García Martínez, *Dead Sea Scrolls,* 437]: "You will place my mouth like a sharpened sword"). This is the case in Ahiqar 100b (2.18) = tr. Porten-Yardeni, *Textbook,* 2:37: "Soft is the speech of a king (yet) it is sharper and mightier than a [double-]edged knife" (cf. Charlesworth, *OTP* 2:500). Reason, effective speech, and the word of God are often compared with a sword or dagger (Pss 52:2; 57:4; Wis 18:15–16; Eph 6:17; Heb 4:12; the term μάχαιρα is used in the last two references). It is possible that v 16a is based on an allusion to Isa 49:2, where in the context of the second Servant

Song, the speaker says "He [God] made my mouth like a sharp sword," perhaps in combination with Isa 11:4, "he shall smite the earth with the rod [MT: שֵׁבֶט; LXX: τῷ λόγῳ] of his mouth, and with the breath of his lips he shall slay the wicked" (see *Comments* on 19:15, 21). In Heb 4:12, the word of God is said to be "sharper than any two-edged sword." In all these passages, the "sword" is clearly a metaphor for judgment (A. T. Hanson, *Wrath*, 166–67). In the Jewish magical text entitled "The Sword of Moses," the term "sword" is apparently a metaphor for the Ineffable Name of God (see M. Gaster, "The Sword of Moses," in *Studies and Texts* [New York: Ktav, 1971] 1:288–337). Note that the phrase בְּפִי חֶרֶב *běpî ḥereb* or ἐν στόματι ῥομφαίας, literally "with the mouth of the sword," is an idiom for "with the edge of the sword" (e.g., LXX Josh 6:20; 8:20; Judg 1:8, 25; 4:15, 16; 20:37; 21:10; 1 Kgs 15:8; 22:19; *T. Levi* 6:5; *Jos. As.* 26:5), so that the phrase ἐκ τοῦ στόματος αὐτοῦ ῥομφαία, "the sword from his mouth," could be construed as a play on words. The swords (כִּידֹנִים *kydnym*) described at some length in 1QM 5:11–14, for use in the eschatological struggle by the sons of light, are scimitars (i.e., curved swords) with a single edge. In Cleanthes' famous hymn to Zeus, the thunderbolt wielded by Zeus is called two-edged in line 10 (ἀμφήκη . . . κεραυνόν), suggesting the analogy with a two-edged sword.

**16c** καὶ ἡ ὄψις αὐτοῦ ὡς ὁ ἥλιος φαίνει ἐν τῇ δυνάμει αὐτοῦ, "and his face was like the sun shining in full strength." This may be an allusion to Dan 10:6, where it is said of the angelic revealer that "his face [was] like the appearance of lightning." In the description of the angel in Rev 10:1, it is said that "his face was like the sun." The face could be compared with the sun as a metaphor for beauty (Wis 7:29; *Jos. As.* 14:9; 18:9), but more frequently as a metaphor for sanctity, divinity, or transcendence, often in theophanies or angelophanies (e.g., the transfiguration in Matt 17:2, "his face shone like the sun," a phrase not found in Mark or Luke; see also Rev 10:1; *2 Enoch* [rec. J and A] 1:5; 19:2; 4 Ezra 7:97, 125; *Apoc. Zeph.* 6:11; cf. *1 Enoch* 14:21; 106:2). There is also a widespread Judeo-Christian tradition that emphasizes the brightness of the faces of the righteous, often comparing their faces with the radiance of the sun or the stars (Matt 13:43; 4 Ezra 7:97, 125; *T. Job* 31:5; *b. Ber.* 17a; cf. Exod 34:29; Dan 12:3; *1 Enoch* 38:4; *2 Apoc. Bar.* 51:3; for references to rabbinic literature, see Str-B 1:752; 3:790; Stone, *4 Ezra*, 245 n. 46). In *Jos. As.* 14:9 (tr. Charlesworth, *OTP* 2:225), "his face was like lightning, and his eyes like sunshine, and the hairs of his head like a flame of fire of a burning torch." The phrase "in full strength" (literally "in its might") refers to the brightness of the sun unimpeded by clouds (cf. Judg 5:31).

**17a** καὶ ὅτε εἶδον αὐτόν, ἔπεσα πρὸς τοὺς πόδας αὐτοῦ ὡς νεκρός, "And when I saw him, I fell down at his feet as though dead." The stereotypical responses of recipients of visions upon the appearance of supernatural revealers constitute recurring literary themes in revelatory literature and are of two main types, both involving fear and prostration (Bauckham, *NTS* 27 [1980–81] 323–24). In one type the visionary is extremely frightened and involuntarily prostrates himself or herself (Rev 1:17; Isa 6:5; Ezek 1:28; Dan 8:17; 10:9–11; Luke 24:5; *1 Enoch* 14:14, 24; *2 Enoch* 1:7; *Apoc. Abr.* 10:2; *Jos. As.* 14:10), while in the other type the prostration is the result of reverential awe (Josh 5:14; Rev 19:10; 22:8; see *Comment* on 19:10; 4 Ezra 4:11; cf. the voluntary kneeling for prayer in Hermas *Vis.* 1.1.2; 1.2.1). In the first type the simile of death as a response to a divine epiphany, as in Rev 1:17, is less common. The reference to death can simply be a way of saying that the visionary fainted, or it can allude to the cataleptic state associated with trance experiences. According to Matt 28:4, those guarding the tomb of Jesus became ὡς νεκροί, "as dead men," a consequence of the terror caused by an angelic appearance. In *T. Abr.* [A] 9:1 (tr. Charlesworth, *OTP* 1:886), when Michael appeared to Abraham, the latter "fell upon his face on the ground as one dead." When Uriel appeared to Ezra, the seer "lay there like a corpse" (4 Ezra 10:30). That this death simile plays a literary function greater than simply a stereotypical response to a divine epiphany is suggested by the reassuring words of the risen Lord in Rev 1:18, where he says "I was dead, and behold I am living forever." Further, there is a traditional connection in ancient Judaism between revelation and death; see Exod 20:19: "Let not God speak with us lest we die." A similar perspective is reflected in Deut 5:22–27 and was taken up in the later Midrashim (*Exod. Rab.* 29:4; 34:1; *Cant. Rab.* 5.16.3; *Num. Rab.* 10:1; *b. Šabb.* 88b; see Chernus, *Mysticism,* 33–57). Further, in admittedly late rabbinic traditions, "the mystic who accepts this self-annihilation will be resurrected by the dew of life which God will pour upon him" (Chernus, *Mysticism,* 40). Thus the lethal dangers that must be faced in the quest for divine revelation, particularly in Jewish Merkavah mysticism, can be overcome by divine intervention. It is possible that the terror experienced in connection with a theophany was eventually transformed into the theme of danger in revelatory ascents (see Gruenwald, *Apocalyptic,* 37; J. Maier, "Das Gefärdungsmotiv bei der Himmelsreise in der Jüdischen Apokalyptik und 'Gnosis,'" *Kairos* 5 [1963] 18–40). The close association between death and trance is found in a number of different cultures; see J. Bremmer, *The Early Greek Concept of the Soul* (Princeton: Princeton UP, 1983) 29–32.

It is striking that the stereotypical motif of inadequacy or insufficiency, frequently included in OT prophetic call narratives (Hafemann, *Suffering,* 90–98; id., *Paul,* 39–62), is conspicuous by its absence both here in Rev 1:9–20 and in 10:1–11.

**17b** καὶ ἔθηκεν τὴν δεξιὰν αὐτοῦ ἐπ' ἐμὲ λέγων, "he then placed his right hand on me, saying." This can be construed as an act of investiture (see Dan 10:10, 18) as well as an act of comfort and assurance.

**17c** μὴ φοβοῦ· ἐγώ εἰμι ὁ πρῶτος καὶ ὁ ἔσχατος **18a** καὶ ὁ ζῶν, "'Stop being afraid. I am the First and the Last, even the Living One.'" This response of the exalted Christ has the form of an *oracle of assurance,* which typically begins with an admonition to "fear not," followed by a supportive promise intended to comfort and alleviate the anxiety of an individual who has addressed a lament to God (Aune, *Prophecy,* 94–95, 117–18, 266–68, 281, 304–6). Here, however, the oracle of assurance functions rather to comfort the seer who has reacted in fear to this christophany.

The *ego-eimi* or "I am" self-predication formula occurs five times in Rev (1:8, 17; 2:23; 21:6 [textual problem]; 22:16), always with a predicate in the nominative case. The *ego-eimi* formula occurs a total of forty-eight times in the NT, almost always attributed to Christ or God and therefore of christological or theological interest. It occurs five times in Matthew (14:27; 22:32; 24:5; 26:22, 25), three times in Mark (6:50; 13:6; 14:62), four times in Luke (1:19; 21:8; 22:70; 24:39), twenty-four times in John, six times in Acts (9:5; 10:21; 18:10; 22:3, 8; 26:29), and five times in Revelation. The "I am" formula is particularly important for Johannine studies (see Brown, *John* 1:533–38; Schnackenburg, *John* 2:79–89). The "I am" formula in Revelation is uttered exclusively by God (1:8; 21:6) and Christ (1:17; 2:23; 22:16) and is used to make divine predications of the speaker:

1:8     "I am [ἐγώ εἰμι] the Alpha and the Omega, says the Lord God, the one who is and was and is coming, the Almighty."

1:17    "I am [ἐγώ εἰμι] the First and the Last and the Living One."

2:23    "I am [ἐγώ εἰμι] the one who searches mind and heart."

21:6    "I am [ἐγώ εἰμι] the Alpha and the Omega, the Beginning and the End."

22:16   "I am [ἐγώ εἰμι] the root and offspring of David, the bright morning star."

The striking absolute use of the "I am" formula (i.e., *without* a predicate) occurs eight times in John (6:20; 8:24, 28, 58; 13:19; 18:5, 6, 8) and three times in the synoptic Gospels (Matt 14:27; Mark 6:50; cf. 13:6). In these passages it is probably an allusion to the OT formula "I am He," meaning "I am Yahweh" (Dodd, *Fourth Gospel*, 93–96; Brown, *John* 1:535–37), and has no counterpart in Revelation. The Johannine Jesus predicates seven metaphors of himself using the "I am" formula: (1) "I am the bread of life" (6:35, 48) and the closely related "I am the living bread descended from heaven" (6:51), (2) "I am the light of the world" (8:12), (3) "I am the door" (10:7, 9), (4) "I am the good shepherd" (10:11, 14), (5) "I am the resurrection and the life" (11:25), (6) "I am the way, the truth, and the life" (14:6), and (7) "I am the true vine" (15:1, 5). The only connection between these predications and those in Revelation is the predication of Christ that he is "the living one" in 1:17 and the emphasis on life in John 14:6, its connection with resurrection in John 11:25, and the attributive participle "living" used with the bread metaphor in John 6:51.

The formula ὁ πρῶτος καὶ ὁ ἔσχατος, "the first and the last," was probably derived from Deutero-Isaiah: (1) Isa 44:6, ἐγὼ πρῶτος καὶ ἐγὼ μετὰ ταῦτα, literally "I am first and I am after these things"; (2) Isa 41:4, ἐγὼ θεὸς πρῶτος, καὶ εἰς τὰ ἐπερχόμενα ἐγώ εἰμι, "I, God, am first, and with regard to what is to come, I am He"; and (3) Isa 48:12, ἐγώ εἰμι πρῶτος, καὶ ἐγώ εἰμι εἰς τὸν αἰῶνα, "I am first, and I am forever." The fact that the divine predicate "the first and the last" occurs three times in Deutero-Isaiah suggests its importance in that composition, though the attempt of R. P. Merendino to organize Isa 40–48 around the theme of "the first and the last" is overdone (*Der Erste und der Letzte: Eine Untersuchung von Jes 40–48*, VTSup 31 [Leiden: Brill, 1981]). This formula also occurs in 2:8 and at the conclusion of Revelation in 22:13, where it is also applied to Christ and associated with (and mutually interpreted by) two other divine predicates: "I am the Alpha and the Omega, the First and the Last, the Beginning and the End." The version of the formula in 22:13 suggests that John has expanded this traditional wording through the addition of ὁ ζῶν in 1:18, a predicate that functions as a double entendre referring both to a traditional Jewish designation for God and to the triumph of Jesus over death through his resurrection. One of the closest parallels is the phrase "I am the first and the last" in a series of eighteen "I am" predications in the Coptic-Gnostic tractate *Thund.* 13.16. Though the two adjectives πρῶτος and ἔσχατος, and the present substantival participle ζῶν, are each predicates of the exalted Christ, they each have separate articles because the author wishes both to emphasize and to differentiate sharply each of these predicates as three distinctive aspects of Christ (Robertson, *Grammar,* 785). Yet this formula is also found in Greek literature (van Unnik, *Het godspredikaat,* 74–76): Hesiod *Theog.* 34, σφᾶς δ᾽ αὐτὰς πρῶτον τε καὶ ὕστατον αἰὲν ἀείδειν, "But always to sing of themselves [i.e., the Muses] both first and last" (the same is said of Zeus in *Theog.* 48). In *Theog.* 1.3, the elegist addresses Apollo: ἀλλ᾽ αἰεὶ πρῶτόν τε καὶ ὕστατον ἔν τε μέσοισιν ἀείσω, "but always will I hymn [you] first and last and in the middle." It is also found in *Hymni Homerici* 21, where it is said that to Apollo the odist "always sings first and last" (πρῶτόν τε καὶ ὕστατον αἰὲν ἀείδει); cf. 1.18. Yet these three references refer not to "First and Last" as a divine predicate but to the honor paid to the Muses or Apollo by singing hymns to them at the beginning and end of their poems.

The verb ζᾶν, meaning "to live (again)," is used of Jesus only here and in 2:8, a statement that refers back to this predicate. In Jewish tradition, God is often designated אלהים חיים *ʾĕlōhîm ḥayyîm;* LXX: θεὸς ζῶν, "the living God" (Deut 5:26; 1 Sam 17:26, 36; Jer 10:10; 23:36; Dan 6:27 [Aram.: אלהא חיא *ʾĕlōhāʾ ḥayyāʾ;* LXX: θεὸς ζῶν). A parallel phrase, first found in Hosea, is אל חי *ʾēl ḥāy,* "living God" (Hos 2:1[Eng. 1:10]; Pss 42:3; 84:3; Josh 3:10). The phrase "the living God" also occurs in early Jewish literature (Bel 14:5, 25; 3 Macc 6:28; *Jub.* 1:25; 21:4) and is frequently found in the NT (Matt 16:16; 26:63; John 6:57 [ὁ ζῶν πατήρ, "the living Father," occurs only here in the NT]; Acts 14:15; Rom 9:26; 2 Cor 3:3; 1 Thess 1:9; 1 Tim 4:10; Heb 3:12; 9:14; 10:31; 12:22; Rev 7:2; *2 Clem.* 20:2; Hermas *Vis.* 2.3.2; 3.7.2; *Sim.* 6.2.2). The related phrase "the living Lord" is comparatively rare and occurs only in LXX Esth 16:16; 2 Macc 7:33; 15:4. The predicate "the Living One," however, is not found in the OT, though it does begin to appear in early Judaism (Sir 18:1: ὁ ζῶν εἰς τὸν αἰῶνα, "the One who lives forever"; *2 Apoc. Bar.* 21:9, 10; *Sib. Or.* 3.763); a frequent OT oath formula is "as the Lord lives" (Judg 8:19; Ruth 3:13; 1 Sam. 14:39; 2 Sam 15:21; 2 Kgs 2:2). In pagan religious literature, particularly the Greek magical papyri, the phrase "the living god" occurs several times in various combinations: ὁ θεὸς ὁ ζῶν, "the living god" (*PGM* IV.959; cf. the Christian magical papyri *PGM* 5a.11; 5b.25; 5c.5); ὁ μέγας ζῶν θεός, ὁ εἰς τοὺς αἰῶνας τῶν αἰώνων, "the great living god who is eternal" (*PGM* IV.1039); ὁ ζῶν θεός, "the living god" (*PGM* XII.79); θεὸς ζῶν, "the living god" (*PGM* IV.559; VII.823); ὁρκίζω σε κατὰ τοῦ παντοκράτορος θεοῦ ζῶντος ἀεί, "I adjure you by the almighty god who lives forever" (*PGM* IV.1550–52). At the same time, Christ lives because he has been raised from the dead, a fact that is spelled out in the next clause in v 18.

**18b** καὶ ἐγενόμην νεκρὸς καὶ ἰδοὺ ζῶν εἰμι εἰς τοὺς αἰῶνας τῶν αἰώνων, "'And I was dead, but behold I now live for ever and ever.'" In this phrase ζῶν εἰμι, "I now live," is a periphrastic present, a rare construction in Revelation (the only other instance is the periphrastic present imperative γίνου γρηγορῶν, "be watchful," in Rev 3:2). While it might at first appear that ζῶν is an adjectival participle in the predicate nominative, the periphrastic interpretation is preferable since the participle lacks an article, is intransitive, and serves to describe a situation (P. F. Regard, *La phrase nominale dans la langue du Nouveau Testament* [Paris, 1918] 118;

W. J. Aerts, *Periphrastica* [Amsterdam: Hakkert, 1965] 69–70). The author probably chooses this construction because it is antithetical to the immediately preceding phrase ἐγενόμην νεκρός, "I was dead" (temporal); "I am now in a state of being alive" (eternal). The two motifs of death and eternal life are juxtaposed in *Tg. Ps.-J.* 1 Sam 2:6 (tr. Harrington-Saldarini, *Targum Jonathan*, with additions to MT in italics): "He puts to death *and speaks so as to make alive;* he brings down to Sheol, *and he is also ready* to bring up *in eternal life.*" The phrase "I am alive forever" has close parallels in the phrase "to the one who lives for ever" (which occurs four times, 4:9, 10; 10:6; 15:7), a formula applied to *God,* though in 1:18 it is applied to *Christ* (this is another distinction between the first and second editions of Revelation). There are parallels to this phrase in the OT (Theod Dan 4:34, τῷ ζῶντι εἰς τὸν αἰῶνα, "to the One who lives forever"; LXX Dan 6:27, θεὸς μένων καὶ ζῶν εἰς γενεὰς γενεῶν ἕως τοῦ αἰῶνος, "God who abides and lives from generation to generation, even for ever"; Theod Dan 6:27, θεὸς ζῶν καὶ μένων εἰς τοὺς αἰῶνας, "God who lives and abides for ever"; LXX Dan 12:7, ὤμοσε τὸν ζῶντα εἰς τὸν αἰῶνα θεόν, "he swore by the God who lives for ever") and in early Judaism (*1 Enoch* 5:1, "He who lives for ever" [here the Greek text, expanded by a doublet (Knibb, *Enoch* 2:65), reads θεὸς ζῶν ἐποίησεν αὐτὰ οὕτως, καὶ ζῇ εἰς πάντας τοὺς αἰῶνας, "the living God made them thus and he lives for ever"]).

The phrase καὶ ἰδού, "and behold," is a Septuagintism that occurs twelve times in Revelation (1:18; 4:1, 2; 6:2, 5, 8; 7:9; 12:3; 14:1, 14; 19:11; 22:7); on ἰδού, which occurs twenty-nine times, see *Comment* on 1:7a. Here it functions as a marker emphasizing the truth of the statement that immediately follows (Fjedler, *Formel,* 42). There is a significant parallel in 2 Cor 6:9:

> ὡς ἀποθνῃσκοντες καὶ ἰδοὺ ζῶμεν
> as dying, but indeed we live

**18c** καὶ ἔχω τὰς κλεῖς τοῦ θανάτου καὶ τοῦ ᾅδου, "'I hold the keys to Death and Hades.'" The reference to the exalted Jesus as the possessor of *keys* calls to mind the reference to his possession of the "key of David" in Rev 3:7b, though there is no apparent relationship between the metaphors. The genitives τοῦ θάνατου καὶ τοῦ ᾅδου, "of Death and of Hades," could be either objective or possessive genitives (i.e., "the keys *to* Death and Hades" [as above] or "the keys *belonging* to Death and Hades"). If construed as objective genitives, Death and Hades must be understood spatially, as in Rev 20:13. But if understood as possessive genitives, they must be understood as personifications, as in Rev. 6:8. They must be objective genitives since Death is never described in ancient texts as possessing keys, and very few attribute keys to Hades (cf. Pausanias 5.20.3, where, in a brief *ekphrasis* ["description of a work of art"; cf. *Form/Structure/Setting* in Rev 17], Pausanias describes how Ploutos, often an alias of Hades, is shown holding the key that he has just used to lock up Hades [in *Orphic Hymns* 18.4, Ploutos is described as possessing "the keys of the entire earth"]). Later rabbinic sources mention keys that belong to God alone and are not entrusted to angels (Ginzberg, *Legends* 6:318–19; only a few of the references are mentioned in Bousset [1906] 197; Charles, 1:33). According to some sources, God retains three keys for himself that he does not entrust to an angel: the keys of rain, of childbirth, and of the revival of the dead (*b. Taʿan.* 2a; *Gen. Rab.* 73.3; *Deut. Rab.* 7.6; *Midr. Ps.* 78.5). *Tg.*

*Neof.* Gen 30:22 refers to four keys that God alone possesses: the key of rain, the key of provision, the key of graves (מפתח דקבריה *mptḥ dqbryh;* cf. Sokoloff, *DJPA,* 473), and the key of barrenness (a similar list is found in *Tg. Yer.* Deut 28:12). However, *b. Sanh.* 113a reports that the key of rain was given to Elisha, and *Midr. Ps.* 78.5 reports that the key of barrenness was given to Elisha and the key of resurrection to Elijah. The possessive genitive is often understood as implying the tradition of the *descensus ad inferos,* "(Christ's) descent to Hell," for if the keys formerly belonged to the personified Death and Hades, they must have been forcibly taken from them (Kroll, *Gott und Hölle,* 10–11; Bousset [1906] 198; for references to this conception in Coptic-Gnostic documents, see *Teach. Silv.* 104.1–14; 110.19–30; *Trim. Prot.* 36.4; *Testim. Truth* 32.24–33.8 [here the language of the harrowing of "Hades" is a metaphor for the world]). For a discussion of Death and Hades as personifications, see *Comment* on 6:8.

In early Jewish underworld mythology, the netherworld was not thought of as having doors or gates. In the dramatization of Christ's descent to hell in *Odes Sol.* 42.17, the notion that hell has a door is presupposed when the dead cry out asking for him to open the door to let them come out. The image of Jesus as keybearer in Rev 1:18 appears to be derived from the popular Hellenistic conception of the goddess Hekate as keybearer. Hekate both originated in Asia Minor and was very popular there during the Hellenistic and Roman periods. She is the primary mythological figure associated with the possession of the keys to the gates of Hades. Hekate *trimorphos,* "having three forms or shapes," was given a cosmic significance connected with her threefold identity as Juno Licina, Trivia, and Luna (Catullus 34.9) or Selene/Luna (= moon) in heaven, Artemis/Diana on earth, and Persephone/Proserpina in Hades (cf. Hesiod *Theog.* 412–17, 427; Orph. *Hymni* 1.2; Servius *Comm. in Verg. Aen.* 4.511; *Scholia in Aristophanem Plutum* 594). In *PGM* IV.2836–37, after Hekate is explicitly identified with Mene, Artemis, Persephone, and Selene, we read, "Beginning and end [ἀρχὴ καὶ τέλος] are you, and you alone rule all. For all things are from you, and in you do all things, Eternal one, come to their end." The tendency to elevate important regional divinities like Hekate to the role of cosmic queen can be seen in the similar claim that Aphrodite controls the three cosmic zones of heaven, earth, and sea (*Orphic Hymns* 55.5; the *du-Stil,* "thou style": καὶ κρατέεις τρισσῶν μοιρῶν). The *Orphic Hymns* (probably written in Asia Minor during the second century A.D.) describe Hekate as "the keybearing mistress of the entire cosmos" (1.7). Hekate is frequently given the epithet κλειδοῦχος, "keybearer" (Orph. *frag.* 316; *Orphic Hymns* 1.7; cf. Kohl, *RE* 11 [1921] 593–600). Persephone, with whom Hekate is often identified, is said to command the gates of Hades in the bowels of the earth (*Orphic Hymns* 29.4). Other divine beings are also thought to have custody of various keys. Pindar (*Pyth.* 8.1–4; cf. C. M. Bowra, *Pindar* [Oxford: Clarendon, 1964] 85) claims that the goddess Ἡσυχία, Quiet, "holds the last keys of counsel and war." Proteus holds the keys of the sea (*Orphic Hymns* 25.2), and Zeus holds the keys to joy and sorrow (*Orphic Hymns* 73.6). Parmenides describes the goddess Dike ("Justice") as holding κληῖδας ἀμοιβούς, "rewarding keys," because the keys that open and close both reward and punish (L. Taran, *Parmenides* [Princeton: Princeton UP, 1965] 15). The Egyptian deity Anubis is frequently associated with keys; in *PGM* IV.1466, Anubis is called "key-bearer and guardian," and in *PGM* IV.341–42 is called "the one who has the keys to Hades" (cf. S. Morenz, "Anubis mit dem Schlüssel," in *Religion und*

*Geschichte des Alten Ägypten* [Cologne; Vienna: Böhlau, 1975] 510–20). The leontocephaline god of Mithraism (sometimes identified with Saturn or Aios) is sometimes depicted holding keys, but no text explains what this symbol means (*CIMRM*, 78, 103, 125, 168; cf. indices s.v. "Aion," 1:333; 2:403); a brief discussion of this symbol is found in L. A. Campbell, *Mithraic Iconography and Ideology*, EPRO 8 (Leiden: Brill, 1968) 352–53. It is likely that the keys were thought to control access to the astrological or planetary gates through which souls descend to embodiment and ascend to salvation (H. M. Jackson, "The Meaning and Function of the Leontocephaline in Roman Mithraism," *Numen* 32 [1985] 17–45; Beck, *Planetary Gods*, 63). Another Mithraic figure, Cautes, is sometimes depicted holding up a key (*CIMRM*, 1110, 1163), perhaps symbolizing his ability to unlock the gates of heaven for rain. In both texts and iconography, keys symbolize the power held by the respective deities over various aspects of life. The angel Michael is described in *3 Apoc. Bar.* 11:2 as the holder of the keys of the kingdom of heaven. Aeacus is also described as the keeper of the keys of Hades (Apollodorus, 3.12.6; *CIG* 3:933, no. 6298; G. Kaibel, *Epigrammatica Graeca* [Berlin, 1878] 262–63, no. 646; cf. Isocrates *Euagoras* 15). Elsewhere he is described as keeping the gate of Hades (Lucian *Dial. mort.* 6[20].1).

**19** γράψον οὖν ἃ εἶδες καὶ ἃ εἰσὶν καὶ ἃ μέλλει γενέσθαι μετὰ ταῦτα, "'Therefore write down what you will see, that is, the events which are now happening and the events which will happen later.'" For the phrase γράψον οὖν, "therefore write," see *Comment* on 1:11. In the main clause, John refers to just two subjects, i.e., "what y᾽ u see, namely," (1) "the present" and (2) "the imminent future." It has often been supposed that this passage, translated differently, provides the reader with an outline of Revelation. "What you saw" supposedly deals with the vision he has just received (1:9–20), "what is" covers the situation as it exists in each of the seven churches (chaps. 2–3), and "what is about to happen after these things" deals with future, i.e., the eschatological events in Rev 4:1–22:5 (Swete, 21; Bousset [1906] 198; Charles, 1:33; Lohse, 22; Vielhauer, *Geschichte*, 496–97). Aside from the fact that this division reveals nothing of the structure of the extensive section in chaps. 4–22, it does not appreciate the fact that some of the ensuing visions in chaps. 4–22 deal with the past (e.g., Rev 12), just as sections of chaps. 2–3 focus on the future (Beasley-Murray, 68; Roloff, 45; Sweet, 19; Caird, 26: "a grotesque over-simplification"). Therefore it is best to take this verse as a modification by John of the widespread Hellenistic tripartite prophecy formula in which he appears to refer to the past, present, and future, but in actuality means to emphasize only the present and future (see below on ἃ εἶδες). The phrase ἃ εἶδες, "what you see," could refer to the vision that John saw in vv 12–20, yet since he is still "within" this vision when he writes v 19, this seems both artificial and unlikely. ἃ εἶδες seems to refer to the first commission to write in v 11: ὃ βλέπεις, γράψον, "write what you see." In v 19, John uses the aorist verb εἶδες primarily because he is adapting the tripartite prophecy formula (see below) and needs to refer to past time. Further, the neuter plural relative pronoun ἃ refers to the substance of his vision no less than the neuter singular relative pronoun ὅ; John uses ἃ instead of ὅ in v 19 because it conforms to the neuter plural definite article, which tends to be used in the tripartite prophecy formula. V 19, therefore, seems to constitute a kind of double entendre; the tenses conform to the necessity of referring to the past, present, and future in the tripartite prophecy formula, but the author is using εἶδες as an epistolary aorist; i.e., while the visions he was about to record were yet to be seen by him, from the standpoint of the reader they belong to the past. This sentence can therefore be understood "Write what you see, namely [taking καί as epexegetical], the events of the present and of the future." The phrase μετὰ ταῦτα, "after this," usually begins clauses, sentences, or units of text in Revelation; only here and in 4:1; 9:12 (see *Notes* there) is it used at the end of a sentence. The entire phrase ἃ μέλλει γενέσθαι μετὰ ταῦτα in 1:19 is in fact closely paralleled to the recurring phrase ἃ δεῖ γενέσθαι [μετὰ ταῦτα/ἐν τάχει] (1:1; 4:1; 22:6). There is a relatively close linguistic parallel in LXX Isa 48:6, ἃ μέλλει γίνεσθαι (Swete, cxlii; Kraft, 49), where the MT reads simply וּנְצֻרוֹת *ûneṣurôt*, "and hidden things," though the context certainly involves divine revelation. This indicates the redactional character of 4:1 (see *Comment* there).

**20a** τὸ μυστήριον τῶν ἑπτὰ ἀστέρων οὓς εἶδες ἐπὶ τῆς δεξιᾶς μου καὶ τὰς ἑπτὰ λυχνίας τὰς χρυσᾶς, "'As for the secret meaning of the seven stars which you saw in my right hand and the seven golden menorahs.'" The peculiar grammatical character of this verse clearly indicates that it is a gloss (Kraft, 49), though one that the author himself has inserted in order to link the commission vision of 1:9–20 to the proclamations to the seven churches in Rev 2–3. Malina argues that, since allegorical interpretation is essentially foreign to Revelation, v 20 is a later interpolation (*Revelation,* 75). This verse contains the first (hence anarthrous) mention of the angels of the seven churches to whom each of the proclamations is addressed. The term μυστήριον (the Aramaic term רז *rāz,* "mystery," is a Persian loanword found in biblical Aramaic, not biblical Hebrew), literally "mystery," was a quasi-technical term in both prophetic and apocalyptic texts in early Judaism and early Christianity. The term occurs four times in Revelation (1:20; 10:7; 17:5, 7). In the OT, a dream was sometimes a revelatory medium whose message was a רז, "mystery," requiring interpretation (Dan 2:18, 19, 27, 28, 29, 30, 47[2x]; 4:9[MT: 4:6]). The biblical commentaries from Qumran indicate that the members of that community regarded OT prophecies (like dreams) as mysteries requiring interpretation (the transference of the techniques of dream interpretation to the exegesis of biblical texts is discussed by Finkel, *RevQ* 4 [1960] 357–70). 1QpHab 7:4–5 (tr. M. Horgan, *Pesharim,* 16): "the interpretation [פשרו *pšrw*] of it concerns the Teacher of Righteousness, to whom God made known all the mysteries of the words of his servants the prophets [רזי דברי עבדיו הנבאים *rzy dbry ʿbdyw hnbʾym*]." In the Qumran Pesharim the Hebrew term רז *raz* occurs just three times (1QpHab 7:5, 8, 14). In Qumran, then, the term רז *raz,* "mystery," concerns things about the community and the situation in which they found themselves that were hidden in the prophetic writings and not fully known to the prophet. The פשר *pešer,* "interpretation," which corresponded to the רז *raz,* "mystery," could not be understood by unaided human wisdom but was revealed by God to specially chosen human interpreters. The term μυστήριον is used as a mystery formula to introduce eschatological scenarios (Aune, *Prophecy,* 250–52, 333). μυστήριον occurs twice in the Greek text of *1 Enoch* 103:1; 104:12 (the term also occurs in the Ethiopic text of 104:10, where there is a lacuna in the Greek text). In all three contexts the term is used to introduce an eschatological scenario: 103:1, "I understand this mystery [ἐπίσταμαι τὸ μυστήριον τοῦτο]"; 104:12, "And again I know a second mystery [καὶ πάλιν γινώσκω μυστήριον δεύτερον]"; 104:10 (tr. Knibb, *Enoch*), "And now I know this mystery." In *Par. Jer.*

9:29, Jeremiah's prophetic visions are called "mysteries," i.e., the secret plans of God (Wis 2:22), on analogy with earthly kings who keep their counsels and intentions secret (Tob 12:7, 11; Jdt 2:2; 2 Macc 13:21): "Now Jeremiah transmitted all the mysteries which he saw [τὰ μυστήρια ἃ εἶδε] to Baruch." Paul uses μυστήριον (which refers both to the secret as well as its disclosure) to introduce an eschatological scenario in 1 Cor 15:51–52: "Behold! I tell you a mystery [μυστήριον]." The mystery formula also occurs in Rom 11:25–26: "I want you to understand this mystery [μυστήριον] brethren." A close parallel is found in the eclectic pagan document *Corpus Hermeticum* 1.16 (called *Poimandres*): τοῦτό ἐστι τὸ κεκρυμμένον μυστήριον μέχρι τῆσδε τῆς ἡμέρας, "This is the mystery concealed until this day." In the NT, "the mystery of God hidden for ages but now revealed" and close variations occur with some frequency (cf. 1 Cor 2:7; Rom 16:25–26; Eph 3:5, 9–10; Col 1:26–27; 2 Tim 1:9–10; Titus 1:2–3; 1 Pet 1:20; cf. Lührmann, *Paulus,* 113–17; N. A. Dahl, "Formgeschichtliche Beobachtungen," 3–9). Hatch (*Essays,* 59–62) points out that in the Christian apologists the term μυστήριον is used with such synonyms as σύμβαλον, τύπος, and παραβολή, all meaning "symbol" or "symbolic representation." Examples: (1) Justin *1 Apol.* 27, the serpent in false religions is understood as a σύμβολον μέγα καὶ μυστήριον, "a great symbol and mystery." (2) Justin *Dial.* 40.1, τὸ μυστήριον τοῦ προβάτου . . . τύπός ἦν τοῦ Χριστοῦ, "the mystery [i.e., 'symbol'] of the lamb . . . was a type of Christ." (3) Justin *Dial.* 68.6, τὸ εἰρημένον πρὸς Δαυεὶδ ὑπὸ θεοῦ ἐν μωστηρίῳ διὰ Ἡσαίου . . . ἐξηγήθη, "What was spoken to David by God *symbolically* was explained through Isaiah" (cf. Justin *Dial.* 44.2; 78.9).

**20b** οἱ ἑπτὰ ἀστέρες ἄγγελοι τῶν ἑπτὰ ἐκκλησιῶν εἰσιν, "'the seven stars are the angels of the seven churches.'" The angels of the seven churches are mentioned collectively only here in Revelation and individually in the introductions to each of the seven proclamations (2:1, 8, 12, 18; 3:1, 7, 14). The association of stars with angels is found in *PGM* I.72 (tr. Betz, *Greek Magical Papyri,* 5): "At once there will be a sign for you like this: "(A blazing star) will descend and come to a stop in the middle of the housetop, and when the star (has dissolved) before your eyes, you will behold the angel [ἄγγελος] whom you have summoned and who has been sent." In this section of *PGM* I, the terms θεός and ἄγγελος are used interchangeably. In *PGM* VII.796–801 (tr. Betz, *Greek Magical Papyri,* 140), "The entering angel [ἄγγελος] is subordinate to the sun, and as subordinate to the sun he enters—so he enters in the form of your friend whom you recognize, with a shining star [ἀστέρα] upon his head, and sometimes he enters like a fiery star [πύρινον ἀστέρα]." This text is interesting not only because of the star = angel imagery but also for the fact that the angel is said to appear in the guise of the practitioner's friend; i.e., he "represents" someone else. *PGM* XIII.144–47 mentions "the stars of glittering forms," which is then followed by a lemma introducing an interpretive gloss very similar to Rev 1:20: "these are the angels who first appeared [οὗτοί εἰσιν οἱ πρῶτοι φανέντες ἄγγελοι]" (an almost identical text is found in *PGM* XIII.449–453). In *1 Enoch* 21:3–6, a group of seven stars represents angels who are being punished, and other references also suggest that stars = evil angels (18:13–16; 86:1–3; 88:3: large fallen stars with private parts like horses). The cuneiform sign for "god" can be vocalized either as *ilu,* "god," or *kakkabu,* "star"; Kokabel also happens to be the name of one of the Watchers in *1 Enoch* 8:2. Isa 14:12 reads "How you are fallen from heaven, O Day Star, son of Dawn." The Hebrew phrase הֵילֵל בֶּן־שָׁחַר *hêlēl ben-šāḥar* is translated in the LXX as ὁ ἑωσφόρος ὁ πρωὶ ἀνατέλλων, "the Morning Star who rises early." Here Morning Star is to be understood as the planet Venus, twelve times brighter than the fixed star Sirius (cf. Hesiod *Theog.* 381; *Iliad* 23.226).

The seven ἄγγελοι, literally "angels," are those to whom the seven proclamations in Rev 2–3 are addressed. Determining the identity of these ἄγγελοι continues to be a major problem in the interpretation of Revelation (see *Excursus 1C*). The term ἄγγελος, like the Hebrew מַלְאָךְ *malʾāk*, means "messenger" and may refer to a supernatural being or a human being. The term ἄγγελος occurs seventy-seven times in Revelation, and only in 1:20–3:22 is the term used for the angels of the seven churches (eight times). Elsewhere in Revelation ἄγγελος is used of supernatural beings serving as messengers or agents of God (within 1:20–3:22, this meaning is clearly intended in 3:5).

**20c** καὶ αἱ λυχνίαι αἱ ἑπτὰ ἑπτὰ ἐκκλησίαι εἰσίν, "'and the seven menorahs are the seven churches.'" The seven menorahs were mentioned in the earlier part of this vision report in vv 12, 13. The equation of these menorahs with the churches is also carried through only in 2:5, where Christ, addressing the church at Ephesus, threatens to remove their menorah from its place, i.e., to blot out the Christian community at Ephesus. Elsewhere in Revelation the two witnesses of Rev 11:4 are described as "two menorahs standing before the Lord."

*Excursus 1C: The "Angels" of the Seven Churches*

**Bibliography**

**Brownlee, W.** "The Priestly Character of the Church in the Apocalypse." *NTS* 5 (1958–59) 224–25. **Daniélou, J.** *The Angels and Their Mission.* Westminster: Newman, 1953. **Culianu, I. P.** "The Angels of the Nations and the Origins of Gnostic Dualism." In *Studies in Gnosticism and Hellenistic Religions.* FS G. Quispel, ed. R. van den Broek and M. J. Vermaseren. EPRO 91. Leiden: Brill, 1981. 78–91. **Davies, W. D.** "A Note on Josephus, Antiquities 15.136." *HTR* 47 (1954) 135–40. **Enroth, A.-M.** "The Hearing Formula in the Book of Revelation." *NTS* 36 (1990) 598–608. **Golden, J.** *The Fathers according to Rabbi Nathan.* New York: Schocken, 1974. **Hughes, P. E.** *The Book of Revelation.* Leicester: Inter-Varsity, 1990. **Lülsdorff, R.** "ΕΚΛΕΚΤΟΙ ΑΓΓΕΛΟΙ: Anmerkungen zu einer untergegangnen Amtsbezeichnung." *BZ* 36 (1992) 104–8. **Michl, J.** *Die Engelvorstellung in der Apokalypse.* Munich: Hueber, 1937. **Sickenberger, J.** "Die Deutung der Engel der sieben apokalyptischen Gemeinden." *RevQ* 35 (1927) 135–49. **Söderblom, N.** "Lev Fravashis: Étude sur le traces dans le mazdéisme d'une ancienne conception sur la survivance des morts." *RHR* 39 (1899) 229–60, 373–418. **Walton, F. R.** "The Messenger of God in Hecataeus of Abdera." *HTR* 48 (1955) 255–57. **Wink, W.** *Unmasking the Powers.* Philadelphia: Fortress, 1986. **Wojciechowski, M.** "Seven Churches and Seven Celestial Bodies." *BN* 45 (1988) 48–50.

The term ἄγγελος, "angel, messenger," occurs seventy-seven times in Revelation in both singular and plural forms. Only eight of these references are problematic, those that refer to "the angels of the seven churches" (1:20) and the seven occurrences of the singular term ἄγγελος as the particular addressee of each of the seven proclamations to the churches (2:1, 8, 12, 18; 3:1, 7, 14). Since most of the sixty-nine occurrences of the term ἄγγελος or ἄγγελοι refer to benevolent supernatural beings who serve as mediators and messengers between God and his creation (Satan is called an ἄγγελος in 9:11, and his followers are called ἄγγελοι in 12:7, 9), most scholars presume that the eight problematic references must also refer to beneficent supernatural beings (e.g., Prigent, 34). This argument is flawed, however, since it is a form of *petitio principii*, i.e., assuming in the premise of an argument the conclusion that is still to be proved.

Before reviewing the various interpretations that scholars have proposed, let us first consider some specific implications of relevant portions of the text of Revelation that must be taken into account in any solution to the identity and function of these seven ἄγγελοι. (1) Each of the seven proclamations addresses the "angel" of each church directly as an individual entity complete with second person singular pronouns and verb forms. A close reading of the seven proclamations in Rev 2–3 clearly suggests that this is a literary fiction, which the author is simply not able to maintain consistently. Sometimes the address shifts to the second person *plural,* a shift that occurs when a particular group within the church is addressed. Three examples will suffice: (a) "Do not fear what *you* will suffer [μέλλεις πάσχειν; second person singular finite verb]; behold the devil will caste *some of you* [ἐξ ὑμῶν; plural pronoun] into jail" (2:10). (b) "But I have against *you* [σου; singular pronoun] that you have [ἔχεις; second person singular verb] there *those who hold* [κρατοῦντας; plural substantival participle] the teaching of Balaam" (2:14; same construction in v 15). (c) "I know where *you* dwell [κατοικεῖς; second person singular verb] where the throne of Satan is . . . Antipas my witness, my faithful one, who was killed among *you* [παρ' ὑμῖν; plural pronoun]. (2) The ἄγγελος of each church is addressed as if he *is* the church; i.e., each one functions as the alter ego of each congregation. The angel-church can be commended for acceptable behavior (2:2–3, 6) but rebuked for unacceptable behavior (2:4–5). While the first command given to the author to write a revelatory book specifies that he sent it *to the seven churches,* with no mention of the fictive angelic recipients (1:11), and the message of each proclamation is clearly said to be spoken by the Spirit ταῖς ἐκκλησίαις, "to the churches" (2:7, 11, 17, 29; 3:6, 13, 22), the addressee of each of the proclamations is the ἄγγελος to which that message is directed (2:1, 7, 12, 18; 3:1, 7, 14), suggesting the equivalency of churches and angels. (3) Several important characteristics of these ἄγγελοι are evident in Rev 1:20: (a) The fact that the first occurrence of ἄγγελοι in 1:20 is anarthrous indicates that the author did not assume that his audience was familiar with these figures (e.g., they cannot be identical with the seven archangels of 8:2 or the seven bowl angels of 15:6). That these ἄγγελοι were created by the author is in part confirmed by the fact that there are no parallels in the literature of early Judaism or early Christianity that provide insight into how these figures should be interpreted. (b) Since the seven stars are interpreted as the angels of the seven churches, and the seven menorahs as the seven churches, it appears that the angels and the churches are not identical. (c) The seven angels appear to constitute a particular group, alongside other groups of seven angels in Revelation, i.e., the seven archangels who function as trumpet angels (8:2) and the seven bowl angels (15:6). The first mention of these last two groups is articular, suggesting that the author assumed that they were known to his audience. (4) The seven ἄγγελοι, either individually or collectively, are not mentioned elsewhere in Revelation (though note other groups of seven angels in 8:2; 15:6). (5) All references to these ἄγγελοι τῶν ἑπτὰ ἐκκλησιῶν occur in the final edition or version of Revelation. (6) There is no indication that these ἄγγελοι are present in heaven. (7) The phenomenon of addressing a group as if it were an individual and using second person singular verb forms and pronouns is a widespread literary phenomenon (address to the daughter of Zion in Zeph 3:14–20; speech to Tyre in Ezek 27), though in Hos 9:1–6; 14:1–3, Israel is initially addressed in singular pronouns and verb forms, which then switch to plural forms. In early Christian epistolary literature, which is usually addressed to particular churches, the verbs and pronouns are always second person plural in form (this also occurs in prophetic speeches, e.g., Zeph 2:1–5). (8) Early Christian letters are characteristically addressed to churches of a particular geographical location, and only exceptionally to individuals or to groups who were part of those communities.

There has been a great deal of scholarly debate regarding how these ἄγγελοι should be identified. It is safe to say that no single solution is without problems. The major views on the identity of the ἄγγελοι of Rev 1:20; Rev 2–3 can be placed in three major categories: (1) supernatural beings, 2) human beings, (3) heavenly bodies (for surveys of the options, see Kraft, 50–52; Satake, *Gemeindeordnung*, 150–55; Hemer, *Letters*, 32–34; Müller, 87–89; Karrer, *Brief*, 169–86).

(1) The first category, *supernatural beings*, can be subdivided into three further possibilities: (a) guardian angels who guide and protect each congregation, (b) personified heavenly counterparts to the earthly Christian communities, (c) visionary counterparts of the community prophets.

(a) The term ἄγγελος is used in various texts (primarily Jewish apocalypses) to refer to heavenly representatives of earthly nations, and by extension this has suggested to many scholars that the ἄγγελοι in question refer to the angelic guardians or representatives of the earthly churches (W. J. Harrington, *Apocalypse*, 80–81; Beasley-Murray, 68–70; Karrer, *Brief*, 185–86). One of the earliest traces of this conception is found in LXX Deut 32:8: "he [God] established the boundaries of the nations according to the number of the angels of God [ἀγγέλων θεοῦ]." The same view may also be reflected in Sir 17:17: "He appointed a ruler for every nation, but Israel is the Lord's own portion." Michael is the champion or the prince of the nation of Israel (Dan 10:13, 21; 12:1; cf. *1 Enoch* 20:5). This conception appears to be transferred to the Christian church in Hermas, *Sim.* 8.3.3, where Michael is referred to as "the one who has power over this people and governs them." Daniel also refers to angelic patrons, or "princes," of Persia (Dan 10:13, 20) and the prince of Greece (Dan 10:20). This conception of guardian angels, which can guide and protect *nations* (Bousset-Gressmann, *Religion des Judentums*, 324–25; Wink, *Unmasking the Powers*, 87–107), may be related to the notion of heavenly guardians or guides for individuals; i.e., individuals can also have angelic patrons (Str-B 1:781–83; 2:707–8; 3:437–40). The earliest references to guardian angels who protect individuals are found in *Jubilees* and *Tobit*. *Jub.* 35:17 refers to "the guardian of Jacob" as being stronger than "the guardian of Esau." Raphael, one of the seven archangels (Tob 12:14), was sent from heaven to protect Tobias and heal Tobit (Tob 2:16–17; 5:4–5a). Gabriel, the angel who appeared to Daniel, was the guardian angel of Darius the Mede (Dan 11:1). Guardian angels are mentioned just twice in the NT (Matt 18:10; Acts 12:15; two other passages sometimes cited, 1 Cor 11:10; Heb 1:14, are irrelevant). The various means and occasions whereby good angels protect people from destruction are discussed in *Pirqe R. El.* 15 (for another reference to angels who protect individuals see *Acts of Paul* 7). Many early Christian thinkers regarded the angels of the seven churches as the heavenly guardians of the churches (Gregory Naz. *Or.* 42; Origen *Hom. on Luke* 23; Basil *Comm. on Isa.* 1.46; Hippolytus *De ant.* 59; Eusebius *Comm. on Ps.* 47, 50; Wink, *Unmasking the Powers*, 192 n. 6). In what may be a Christian development of the Jewish conception of the angels of the nations, *Asc. Isa.* 3.15 refers to the descent of "the angel of the church which is in the heavens." Wink thinks that the angels of the churches represent the corporate character or *Gestalt* of each Christian community but is reluctant to speak of the possible metaphysical reality of such figures (*Unmasking the Powers*, 70–78), and so his view merges with those who see the angels of the communities as heavenly counterparts to the earthly congregations.

(b) The term could also refer to heavenly or spiritual counterparts of earthly communities (Ramsay, *Letters*, 69–70; Bousset [1906] 201; Charles, 1:34–35; Lohmeyer, 20; Holtz, *Christologie*, 113–16; Satake, *Gemeindeordnung*, 150–55; Ford, 386–87; Beasley-Murray, 69–70; Sweet, 73). The suggestion that the Persian *fravashis* are a parallel phenomenon (first suggested in Hastings, *Dictionary of the Bible* 4:991, and picked up by Swete, 22, has been elaborated by Beasley-Murray [69] into the "heavenly counterparts of earthly individuals and communities") is a phenomenological parallel providing little enlightenment (see G. Gnoli, "Fravashis," *EncRel* 5:413–14). The *fravashis*, "spirits of the just," originated as spirits of the dead (Söderblom, *RHR* 39 [1899] 229–60, 373–418) who were a combination of ancestral spirits, guardian spirits, and transcendental doubles of the soul. A different, more proximate background for the conception of heavenly counterparts to earthly communities is *Asc. Isa.* 3:15, which contains an enigmatic reference to "the angel of the church which is in heaven," by which is meant the angelic representative of the celestial Church, the heavenly counterpart to the earthly Church. The origins of this conception are problematic.

(c) The term has also been construed to mean the visionary counterpart of such a community prophet (Schüssler Fiorenza, *Revelation*, 145–46; Enroth, *NTS* 36 [1990] 604).

(2) The ἄγγελοι as *human beings*. This category can be further subdivided into three different possibilities: (a) Human messengers or emissaries, (b) Christian prophets, perhaps members of a prophetic guild represented in each of the seven communities, perhaps prophetic messengers sent by John from Patmos to each of the churches (Spitta, 38–39; Kraft, 50–52; Talbert, 17), or (c) the bishops or leaders of each of the seven communities (Grotius, *Annotationes* 8:251; Zahn, 1:209–17; Str-B 3:790–92; Müller, 101; Hughes, *Revelation* 30–31; for a survey of this view, see Satake, *Gemeindeordnung*, 151–55). It is of course also possible to maintain that the ἄγγελοι of the seven churches represent the local leadership of the communities without specifying a specific type of leader (H. W. Günther, *Der Nah- und Enderwartungshorizont in der Apokalypse des heiligen Johannes* [Würzburg: Echter, 1980] 151–52).

(a) ἄγγελος can be a designation for a human messenger or emissary. In the LXX, ἄγγελος is occasionally used of human emissaries of God. According to Mal 2:7, the Jewish priest is regarded as a מַלְאַךְ יְהֹוָה־צְבָאוֹת *maPak YHWH şĕbāʾôt* (LXX: ἄγγελος κυρίου παντοκράτορος), "a messenger of the Lord Sabaoth." Hecataeus of Abdera (late fourth century A.D.), quoted in Diodorus Siculus 40.3.5–6, speaks of the Israelite high priest "as a messenger [ἄγγελος] to them of God's commandments; at their assemblies and other gatherings, they say, he proclaims the commandments of God" (Walton, *HTR* 48 [1955] 255–57).

(b) Since the term ἄγγελος is used of human messengers of God (see above), then it is arguable that the ἄγγελοι of Rev 2–3 are Christian prophets, perhaps even members of a prophetic guild. The term ἄγγελος means "messenger," whether human or divine. Josephus observed that the Jews had received the holiest of their laws "through messengers [δι' ἀγγέλων] from God" (*Ant.* 15.136); here he could be referring to angels (see *Jub.* 1:27–29; 2:1; 5:6, 13; Acts 7:38, 53; Gal 3:19; Heb 2:2; Hermas *Sim.* 8.3.3), though W. D. Davies has argued that prophets are intended (*HTR* 47 [1954] 135–40). Hag 1:13 refers to "Haggai the messenger of the Lord [MT: מַלְאַךְ יְהֹוָה *maPak YHWH;* LXX: ὁ ἄγγελος κυρίου]." The term is also used of a prophetic messenger in LXX Mal 1:1; 3:1. The term ἄγγελος is frequently used to translate the Hebrew מַלְאָךְ *maPāk,* "messenger" (see Isa 42:26; Hag 1:12–13 ['Αγγαῖος ὁ ἄγγελος κυρίου, "Haggai the messenger of the Lord"]; 2 Chr 36:15–16. In the Midrash *Wayyiqra Rabba* (ed. M. Margolies [Jerusalem, 1953] 3], R. Yohanan states that "the prophets were called מלאכים [*mPkym*, i.e., ἄγγελοι]." Josephus regarded himself as a prophet (Aune, *Prophecy*, 139–44, 153) but speaks of himself as a "messenger" (*J.W.* 3.392, ἐγὼ δ' ἄγγελος ἥκω σοι, "I, a messenger, have come to you"). In a disputed passage (*Ant.* 15.136), Josephus says, "we have learned the noblest of our doctrines and the holiest of our laws from the messengers sent by God [δι' ἀγγέλων παρὰ τοῦ θεοῦ]." Epictetus stated that "the true Cynic must know that he is a messenger [ἄγγελος] sent from Zeus to people" (*Discourses* 3.22.23). Several scholars have argued that the ἄγγελοι mentioned here are prophets, not angels (Hill, *New Testament Prophecy*, 30). The *'Abot R. Nat.* 34 contains a list of synonyms for "prophet" (Golden, *Fathers*, 34): "By ten names were prophets called, to wit: ambassador, trusted, servant [עֶבֶד *ʿbd*], messenger [שָׁלִיחַ *šlîḥ*], visionary, watchman, seer, dreamer, prophet, man of God" (מלאך *ml'k* is noteworthy for its absence). Lülsdorff (*BZ* 36 [1992] 104–8) argues convincingly that the ἄγγελοι of 1 Tim 3:16 (cf. 5:21) is used for *human* messengers of God, the apostles who witnessed the resurrection of Jesus.

(c) Some commentators assert that each ἄγγελος to which a proclamation is directed is a human being, either a bishop or presiding officer of the church addressed. According to Billerbeck (Str-B 3:790–91; cf. Lülsdorff, *BZ* 36 [1992] 106; Ysebaert, *Amtsterminologie*, 22), since the ἄγγελοι of the seven churches are the recipients of letters, it is presupposed that they are on earth, and that they should be understood as humans rather than angels. Some have found a parallel in the שליח צבור *šlîḥ ṣbûr*, "synagogue messenger" (Lightfoot, *Horae Hebraicae* 2:90–95; Str-B 3:790–92), though such a subordinate position cannot seriously be proposed for the role of the ἄγγελος in each of the seven churches. This view founders on the identification of the seven stars with the angels of the seven churches in 1:20, for it is highly unlikely that such emissaries could represent each community so exclusively (Hemer, *Letters,* 33), so those who hold this view must deny that the ἄγγελοι of 1:20 are *the* angels of the seven churches (Zahn, *Introduction* 3:413, appeals to the absence of the article with ἄγγελοι; but see *Note* 1:20.b.). Since the ἄγγελος of each church receives blame and condemnation as well as praise, proponents of this view argue that it is ludicrous to suppose that these are *good* angels sent by God (Zahn, 1:211).

Each of the seven proclamations concludes with the stereotypical proclamation formula "Let the one with ears hear what the Spirit announces to the churches." This formula means that each of the seven proclamations is intended to be read by all the congregations. It also indicates that the Spirit is addressing the *churches;* i.e., even though each proclamation is addressed to the angel of that congregation, it is clearly addressed to each church, so that the angels must be understood as surrogates for the churches.

(3) *Heavenly bodies.* Some scholars have proposed that the seven stars (= angels) represent the (seven) stars of Ursa Minor or the Pleiades (Bousset [1906] 196; Kraft, 46). *1 Enoch* 18:13–16; 21:1–6 mention seven fallen stars, which represent angels (on the star = angel equation, see *Comment* on 9:1). *2 Enoch* 30:2–3 (cf. 27:3, MS J) mentions seven stars created by God: the sun, moon, and five planets, i.e., the most important and influential of the heavenly bodies, a view held by Wojciechowski (*BN* 45 [1988] 48–50), who proposes a correlation between each of the seven proclamations and the symbolism or properties attributed by the ancients to the sun, moon, and five planets.


### *Excursus 1D: The Tripartite Prophecy Formula*

#### *Bibliography*

Unnik, W. C. van. "A Formula Describing Prophecy." *NTS* 9 (1962–63) 86–94 (repr. W. C. van Unnik, *Sparsa Collecta: The Collected Essays of W. C. van Unnik.* Leiden: Brill, 1980. Part 2). Windisch, H. *Der Barnabasbrief.* Tübingen: Mohr (Siebeck), 1920.

The threefold emphasis on the past, present, and future is a formula closely associated with prophecy throughout the Greco-Roman world, though it is rarely found in Jewish texts. Though the wording of the formula and the order in which past, present, and future are mentioned varies, nevertheless the formula emphasizes the vast knowledge and wisdom at the disposal of the poet, diviner, or prophet (with regard to Revelation, it is particularly significant that the author implicitly correlated the prophecy formula with the formula John uses to describe God as "the one who is, and who was, and the coming one" [1:4, 8; 4:8; cf. 11:17; 16:5]). While the tripartite prophecy formula that mentions the past, present, and future is the focus of our interest, the bipartite prophecy formula that mentions just two of the three motifs also occurs. The tripartite prophecy formula is of Hellenistic origin, though later it was widely adopted by Christian authors of the second century A.D. to describe OT prophecy. Many parallels to the tripartite prophecy formula have been collected by Windisch (*Barnabasbrief,* 307) and van Unnik (*NTS* 9 [1962–63] 86–94). In the Greek world, parallels to the tripartite prophecy formula begin with the description of Chalcas' oracular skill in *Iliad* 1.70: ὃς ᾔδη τά τ' ἐόντα τά τ' ἐσσόμενα πρό τ' ἐόντα, "who knew what is and what will be and what was before." Similarly in Hesiod *Theog.* 38, the author claims that the Muses inspired him to tell τά τ' ἐόντα τά τ' ἐσσόμενα πρό τ' ἐόντα, "what is and what will be and what was before" (cf. *Theog.* 31–32; Hesiod frag. 204, line 113, restored in M. L. West, *Hesiod: Theogony* [Oxford: Clarendon, 1966] 166: [ὅσσά τ' ἔην ὅσα τ' ἔ]στι καὶ ὁππόσα μέλλει ἔσεσθαι, "what was and what is and what will be"). According to *Certamen Homeri et Hesiodi* 97, Hesiod asks, Μοῦσα ἄγε μοι τά ἐόντα τά τ' ἐσσόμενα πρό τ' ἐόντα, τῶν μὲν μηδὲν ἄειδε, "Come now, Muse, do not sing to me of what is and what will be and what was before." Diodorus 9.3.2 preserves a Delphic oracle (probably not historical) that says that a golden tripod should be sent to the person ὃς σοφίᾳ τά τ' ἐόντα τά ἐσσόμενα προδέδορκεν, "who in wisdom has foreseen what is and what will be" (a similar version of this oracle is found in Diogenes Laertius 1.33); see Fontenrose, *Oracle,* 293. Two versions that lack the tripartite prophecy formula, Plutarch *Solon* 4.2 and Diogenes Laertius 1.28, simply indicate that the tripod should be given to the wisest man; this very important text suggests that the formula is one way of describing wisdom. The tripartite prophecy formula is also applied to the mythical Proteus in *Orphic Hymns* 25.4–5 (written ca. first century A.D.): ἐπιστάμενος τά τ' ἐόντα ὅσσα τε πρόσθεν ἔην ὅσα τ' ἔσσεται ὕστερον αὖτις, "knowing what is and what was and what will be hereafter." Similarly, in Ovid *Metamorphoses* 1.517–18, Apollo speaks as the oracular divinity *par excellence: per me, quod eritque fuitque estque, patet,* "by me what will be and what was and what is are revealed." Apollo was associated with the tripod, according to a late allegorical interpretation, because "the sun has had knowledge of the past, sees the present, and will see the future" (Fulgentius *Mythologies* 17, in L. G. Whitbread, *Fulgentius the Mythographer* [Ohio State UP, 1971] 58). In Vergil *Eclogues* 4.392–93 (LCL tr. with modifications), the oracular powers of Proteus are emphasized through the use of the tripartite prophecy formula: *novit namque omnia vates, quae sint, quae fuerint, quae mox ventura trahantur,* "for the seer has knowledge of all things—what is, what has been, what is about to happen shortly." In *PGM* V.256–60 (tr. Betz, *Greek Magical Papyri,* 105), the magical practitioner demands special knowledge from the gods that clearly falls into the categories of present, past, and future: "Unless I know what is in the minds of everyone [ἐὰν μὴ γνῶ τὰ ἐν ταῖς ψυχαῖς ἁπάντων] . . . and unless I know what has been and what shall be [ἐὰν μὴ γνῶ τὰ γεγονότα καὶ τὰ μέλλοντα ἔσεσθαι] . . . I will [threats follow]." The prophetic character of the practitioner's intentions becomes clear in *PGM* V.285–97 (tr. Betz, *Greek Magical Papyri,* 106): "I will not let god or goddess give oracles until I, NN, know through and through what is in the minds of all men . . . so that I can tell them whatever has happened and is happening and is going to happen to them [τὰ προγεγονότα αὐτοῖς καὶ ἐνεστῶτα καὶ τὰ μέλλοντα αὐτοῖς ἔσεσθαι]." These examples of the formula throughout Greco-Roman antiquity clearly indicate that the tripartite prophecy formula referred to the prophetic or oracular powers of various poets and diviners. Prognoses made by physicians must have appeared similar to divination or prophecy in character (G. E. R. Lloyd, *Magic, Reason and Experience: Studies in the Origins and Development of Greek Science* [Cambridge: Cambridge UP, 1979] 45), and therefore the tripartite prophecy formula was also used of physicians who practiced "forecasting" (πρόνοια): "For if he discover and declare unaided by the side of his patients the present, the past, and the future [τά τε παρεόντα καὶ τὰ προγεγονότα καὶ τὰ μέλλοντα ἔσεσθαι] . . . he will have more credibility" (Ps.-Hippocrates *Progn.* 1). In Ps.-Hippocrates *Epidemics* 1.11, the physician is advised λέγειν τὰ προγενόμενα, γινώσκειν τὰ παρεόντα, προλέγειν τὰ ἐσόμενα, "Declare the past, diagnose the present, foretell the future" (LCL tr.).

Early Christian authors use the formula to characterize OT prophecy (*Barn*. 1:7; 5:3; cf. 17:2, "I write to you concerning things present or things to come" [περὶ τῶν ἐνεστώτων ἢ μελλόντων γράφω ὑμῖν], a bipartite formula; Theophilus *Apol*. 1.14; 2.9 [Theophilus includes the Sibyl as a prophet]; 2.33; Irenaeus 4.33.1; Hippolytus *De Anticristo* 2). In Ps.-Clementine *Hom*. 2.6.1, the formula is understood to characterize the true prophet: "The true prophet is one who at all times knows all things, the past as it happened, the present as it actually is, and the future as it actually will be" (cf. *Hom*. 2.10.1; *Rec*. 1.21.7).

The formula occurs a few times in early Jewish literature. The bipartite prophecy formula occurs in the *T. Job* 47:9: "Job" says, "And the Lord spoke to me in power, revealing to me things present and things to come [τὰ γενόμενα καὶ τὰ μέλλοντα]." A different version of the bipartite prophecy formula is found in *Jub*. 1:4 (Charlesworth, *OTP* 2:52): "And the Lord revealed to him [Moses] both what (was) in the beginning and what will occur (in the future)." In *Jub*. 1:26, where the bipartite formula is repeated, the parallel is very close to Rev 1:19 (Charlesworth, *OTP* 2:54): "And you write down for yourself all of the matters which I shall make known to you on this mountain: what (was) in the beginning and what (will be) at the end." In the Hellenistic Jewish tragedian Ezekiel *Exagoge* 89, Raguel interprets that part of the dream Moses had that suggested he would become a prophet: ὄψει τά τ' ὄντα τά τε πρὸ τοῦ τά θ' ὕστερον, "You will see the present, the past, and the future." Philo uses the formula of the human νοῦς, "mind," representing the divine in man (*Spec. Leg*. 1.334; *Leg. All*. 2.42). The same formula occurs in a position structurally similar to Revelation at the beginning of the revelation of the Savior to John in *Ap. John* 2.16: *tenou aiei etamok ebol é ou petšoop auô ou petaf šôpe auô ou petše e*, "Now I have come to teach you what is, and what was, and what will be" (based on the Coptic text of Codex II in Krause and Labib, *Drei Verisonen*, 112). Similarly, in *Tri. Trac*. 95.17–19 (tr. J. M. Robinson, *Nag Hammadi*, 83), it is said that "the Logos received the vision of all things, those which pre-exist and those which are now, and those which will be."

### Excursus 1E: The Number Seven

**Bibliography**

**Abramowitz, C.** "The Number Seven." *Dor le Dor* 15 (1986–87) 56–57. **Aletti, J. N.** "Essai sur la symbolique céleste de l'Apocalypse de Jean." *Christus* 28 (1981) 40–53. **Boll, F.** "Hebdomas." PW 14.2, 2547–78. **D'Ooge, M. L.** *Nicomachus Gerasenus: Introduction to Arithmetic*. New York, 1926. **Endres, F. C.,** and **Schimmel, A.** *Das Mysterium der Zahl: Zahlensymbolik im Kulturvergleich*. 2nd ed. Cologne: Diederichs, 1985. **Forstner, D.** *Die Welt der Symbole*. 2nd ed. Innsbruck; Vienna; Munich: Tyrolia, 1967. **Gamber, K.** *Das Geheimnis der sieben Sterne: Zur Symbolik der Apokalypse*. Regensburg: Pustet, 1987. **Giesen, H.** "'Das Buch mit den sieben Siegeln': Bilder und Symbole in der Offenbarung des Johannes." *BK* 39 (1984) 59–65. ———. "Symbole und mythische Aussagen in der Johannesapokalypse und ihre theologische Bedeutung." In *Metaphorik und Mythos im Neuen Testament*, ed. K. Kertelge. Freiburg; Basel; Vienna: Herder, 1990. 255–77. **Robbins, F. E.** "The Tradition of Greek Arithmology." *CP* 16 (1921) 97–123. **Roscher, W. H.** "Die Sieben- und Neunzahl in Kult und Mythologie der Griechen." In *Abhandlungen der Sächsischen Gesellschaft der Wissenschaften*. Phil.-hist. kl. 21 no. 4, 1903. ———. *Hebdomadenlehren der griechischen Philosophie und Ärzte*. Leipzig, 1906. ———. *Die hippokratische Schrift der Siebenzahl und ihr Verhältnis zum Alt Pythagorismus*. Paderborn, 1913. **Varley, D.** *Seven: The Number of Creation*. London: G. Bell & Sons, 1976. **Yarbro Collins, A.** "Numerical Symbolism in Jewish and Early Christian Apocalyptic Literature." *ANRW* II, 21/1:1221–87.

In language the use of number presupposes the ideas of order and structure. Numerical arrangements in time constitute rhythm (e.g., the seven-day week), while numerical arrangements in space constitute geometrical figures. Traditions about the significance of particular numbers originated in Babylonia and Egypt and became incorporated into later traditions of the meaning of various numbers (Hippolytus *Ref.* 4.43). In the Greek world, numerical symbolism was particularly important in Pythagoreanism (Hippolytus *Ref.* 1.2; 4.51), and aspects of Pythagorean number symbolism were adopted by Plato. While the seven-day week is a cultural convention (found originally unconnected in both Greco-Roman antiquity and in Judaism), the number seven may have a lunar origin (each phase of the moon takes seven days), and the menstrual cycle of the human female follows the lunar cycle of twenty-eight days. In antiquity, the Greeks and Romans knew seven "planets," each of which bore the name of a Roman deity (sun, moon, Mercury, Venus, Mars, Jupiter, Saturn). Ancient alchemy connected each of these planets with an earthly metal (sun = gold; moon = silver; Mercury = mercury; Venus = copper; Mars = iron; Jupiter = tin; Saturn = lead).

The most significant symbolic number in Revelation is the number seven. According to D. Varley (*Seven*, 1), "of all the numbers, [seven] has had the greatest symbolic significance for humanity in all ages and in all parts of the world." The author was preoccupied with the symbolic significance of the number seven (commonly understood to signify completeness), which he used fifty-four times. In fact, the number seven is a symbol for the divine or providential design or pattern evident both in the cosmos and in history. He also favored groupings of seven (heptads) as a structural device. He explicitly arranged four extensive sections of his work in heptads: *seven* proclamations (chaps. 2–3), *seven* seals (6:1–8:5), *seven* trumpets (8:8–11:19), and *seven* bowls (15:1–16:21).

M. Terentius Varro (116–27 B.C.) wrote a work called *Hebdomades* (now lost), in which he speculated on the various significances of the number seven and the ways in which seven served as a structural principle throughout the universe and in human life (Aulus Gellius *Noctes Atticae*, 3.10.1–17). It was probably Varro who invented the canon of the seven hills of Rome (R. Gelsomino, *Varrone e i sette colle di Roma* [Rome: Universita degli Studi de Siena, 1975]). One frequent literary form is the arithmology, a list in which the pervasive character of the number seven in the cosmos and human life is cataloged (Clement Alex. *Strom.* 6.16; Macrobius *Comm. in Somnis Scipionis* 6.5–82).

## Explanation

John's divine commission narrated in 1:9–20 introduces not only the proclamations to the seven churches dictated to him by the exalted Christ (2:1–3:22) but the main part of Revelation as well (4:1–22:5). This is a commission for a *particular task* (i.e., to write what he will see and hear), not a report of the inaugural vision calling him to a prophetic vocation (like those of many OT leaders and prophets; cf. Exod 3:1–12; Judg 6:11–17; Isa 6:1–13; Ezek 1:1–3:11). Part of John's inaugural vision may be preserved in 10:8–11, itself modeled after part of Ezekiel's inaugural vision in Ezek 2:8–3:4 (much as the commission of Ezra in 4 Ezra 14 is modeled after that of Moses in Exod 3:1–12). The purpose of this visionary commission to write is to provide divine legitimation for a controversial message. By referring to himself as the "brother" and "fellow participant" (v 9), the author emphasizes the social equality that exists between himself and his audience, a rhetorical device he uses to foster the acceptance of his revelatory authority and to encourage compliance to the message he brings. That which the author shares with his audience includes the persecution they have experienced, the knowledge that despite their marginal situation they are really part of a kingdom ruled over by God and Christ (1:6; 5:10), and the kind of unflagging endurance in suffering even to the point of death as exhibited by the historical Jesus.

The circumstances surrounding John's visionary experience are briefly recounted in vv 9–10a. He received the vision on the tiny island of Patmos. The most likely reason for his presence there was because of a Roman juridical decision involving the capital penalty of exile "on account of the word of God and the testimony of Jesus," i.e., because he was a Christian, though we cannot be sure just which type of exile was involved and whether it was voluntary or involuntary. The notion that John suffered exile is first found in Clement of Alexandria, ca. A.D. 190 (*Quis div.* 42). Contrary to a view perpetuated by many commentaries on Revelation, there is no evidence that Patmos was ever a Roman penal colony. Actually, exile (which had several voluntary and involuntary forms) was a relatively lenient form of punishment in Roman jurisprudence, usually reserved for people of wealth and position (part of a pervasive legal double standard). People who were exiled under a particular emperor were usually granted amnesty upon that emperor's death. At any rate, John's use of the past tense suggests that he was no longer on Patmos when he narrated his revelatory experiences there. The vision occurred on the "Lord's day" (probably Sunday, as the Christian day of worship commemorating the Lord's resurrection) when John was suddenly "in the spirit," i.e., in a trance. This experience may have been intentionally correlated to occur when other Christians were at worship, for prophesying was an activity exercised in early Christian worship.

The vision itself (vv 11–20) was experienced in a state of trance, i.e., "in the spirit" (1:10; 4:2; 17:3; 21:10), perceived to be a normal vehicle for receiving prophetic and apocalyptic revelations. The vision consisted of an epiphany of the heavenly Christ, framed by the command that John write what he will *see* (and hear) in a scroll to be sent to the seven churches (vv 11, 19), a functional equivalent of the OT messenger formula "go and tell." On turning around, John first saw seven golden menorahs (interpreted in v 20 as symbolizing the seven churches), and in their midst stood "one like a son of man" (an allusion to Dan 7:13 with no hint of influence from the Son of Man traditions in the Gospels), with white hair, eyes like fire, feet like polished bronze, and a voice like the roar of "rushing waters" (NIV). Using this combination of imagery, which originally referred to *two* figures in Dan 7:9–14, one "like a son of man" (Dan 7:13) and the Ancient of Days (Dan 7:9), the author has virtually equated the two figures. He held seven stars in his right hand (interpreted in v 20 as the angels of the seven churches), a sharp sword issued from his mouth, and his face shown like the sun. John responds in a manner typical for characters in such vision reports: he falls down paralyzed with fear. The awesome figure utters an oracle of assurance urging John not to be afraid and identifies himself with a series of descriptive phrases that leave the reader no doubt that this is none other than the exalted Jesus. In vv 17b–18, he not only describes himself with the divine titles "the First and the Last," also used in 2:8; 22:13 (a divine title drawn from Isa 41:4; 44:6; 48:12), and "the Living One" (titles that were appropriate only for God), but he also refers to his death and resurrection and to the fact that he possesses the keys to Death and to Hades. According to the ancient mythical view, both heaven and the underworld were linked to this world by doors or gates. In Hellenistic Anatolia, the ancient goddess

Hekate was accorded universal sovereignty as mistress of the cosmos and was popularly thought to hold the keys to Hades. John therefore portrays Christ as usurping the authority of Hekate as well as that of every other natural or supernatural authority. The command to write in v 19 involves just two subjects: "what you see, namely" (1) "the present" and (2) "the imminent future," a modification of the widespread Hellenistic tripartite prophecy formula that emphasized the past, present, and future.

The entire vision is a pastiche of allusions to Jewish epiphany language. The main source of imagery for his epiphany is Dan 10:5–14 (probably a description of the angel Gabriel), with features drawn from the description of God in Dan 7:9 (hair white like wool) and of the mysterious figure in Dan 7:13 ("one like a son of man"). The description of Christ also owes something to ancient grandiose depictions of the appearance of great kings (cf. *Jos. As.* 5:6; Dio Chrysostom *Or.* 3.73–85) and Israelite high priests (Josephus *Ant.* 4.154, 171). In Jewish literature, similar epiphanic language is found in *Jos. As.* 14:8–11; *Apoc. Zeph.* 9:12–10:9. Significantly, the exalted Christ is described using imagery drawn from descriptions of God (cf. Ezek 1:26–28, upon which Dan 7 is probably dependent) and prominent angelic figures. Similar descriptions of divine beings seen in epiphanies are found in the Greek magical papyri and in descriptions of divine epiphanies in Greek literary texts. The author uses various visual attributes and verbal attributes from the visions in the descriptions of Christ that form the introductions to the seven letters, thereby linking 2:1–3:22 to the introductory commission vision. The entire scene has enough similarities to various OT epiphanies to make it entirely plausible to the reader familiar with that background. The metaphorical character of what John sees is made obvious in v 20, where the seven stars are interpreted as the seven angels of the churches and the seven menorahs as the seven churches themselves (one of the few passages in Revelation in which allegorical interpretations are presented). The seven menorahs are primarily reminiscent of the seven-branched golden menorah of the tabernacle and temple (Exod 25:31–41), also seen in Zechariah's vision (Zech 4:1–2), which today is the religious symbol of Judaism.

# B. Proclamations to the Seven Churches (2:1–3:22)

## Bibliography

**Balcer, J. M.** *Sparda by the Bitter Sea: Imperial Interaction in Western Anatolia.* BJS 52. Chico: Scholars, 1984. **Benner, M.** *The Emperor Says: Studies in the Rhetorical Style in Edicts of the Early Empire.* Göteborg: Acta Universitatis Gothoburgensis, 1975. **Berger, K.** "Apostelbrief und apostolische Rede: Zum Formular frühchristlicher Briefe." *ZNW* 65 (1974) 190–231. **Clabeaux, J. J.** *A Lost Edition of the Letters of Paul: A Reassessment of the Text of the Pauline Corpus Attested by Marcion.* CBQMS 21. Washington, DC: Catholic Biblical Association, 1989. **Dahl, N. A.** "The Origins of the Earliest Prologues to the Pauline Letters." *Semeia* 12 (1978) 233–

**77. Dibelius, M.** "Wer Ohren hat zu hören, der höre." *TSK* 83 (1910) 461–71. **Dieterich, A.** "Himmelsbriefe." In *Kleine Schriften.* Leipzig; Berlin: Teubner, 1911. 234–42. ————. "Weitere Beobachtungen zu den Himmelsbriefen." In *Kleine Schriften.* Leipzig; Berlin: Teubner, 1911. 243–51. **Dijkstra, M.** "Prophecy by Letter (Jeremiah XXIX 24–32)." *VT* 33 (1983) 319–22. **Enroth, A.-M.** "The Hearing Formula in the Book of Revelation." *NTS* 36 (1990) 598–608. **Exler, F. J.** *The Form of the Ancient Greek Letter of the Epistolary Papyri.* Washington, DC: Catholic University of America, 1923. **Fehling, D.** "Zur Funktion und Formgeschichte des Proömiums in der älteren griechischen Prosa." In *ΔΩΡΗΜΑ.* FS H. Diller. Athens: Griechische Humanistische Gesellschaft, 1975. 61–75. **French, D. H.** *Roman Roads and Milestones of Asia Minor.* Oxford: BAR, 1981. ————. "The Roman Road-System of Asia Minor." *ANRW* II, 7/2:698–729. **Fridh, Å. J.** *Terminologie et Formules dans les variae de Cassiodore.* Stockholm: Almqvist & Wiksell, 1956. **Gamble, H.** "The Redaction of the Pauline Letters and the Formation of the Pauline Corpus." *JBL* 94 (1975) 403–18. **Gerhardsson, B.** "De kristologiska utsagorna i sändebreven i Uppenbarelseboken (kap.2–3)." *SEÅ* 30 (1965) 70–90. **Goodspeed, E. J.** *New Solutions of New Testament Problems.* Chicago: University of Chicago, 1927. **Hahn, F.** "Die Sendschreiben der Johannesapokalypse: Ein Beitrag zur Bestimmung prophetischer Redeformen." In *Tradition und Glaube: Das frühe Christentum in seiner Umwelt.* FS K. G. Kuhn, ed. G. Jeremias, H.-W. Kuhn, and H. Stegemann. Göttingen: Vandenhoeck & Ruprecht, 1971. 372–94. **Hartman, L.** "Form and Message: A Preliminary Discussion of 'Partial Texts' in Rev 1–3 and 22,6ff." In *L'Apocalypse,* ed. J. Lambrecht. 129–49. **Hubert, M.** "L'Architecture des lettres aux sept eglises." *RB* 67 (1960) 349–53. **Johnson, A. C., Coleman-Norton, P. R., and Bourne, F. C.** *Ancient Roman Statutes: A Translation with Introduction, Commentary, Glossary and Index.* Austin: University of Texas, 1961. **Karrer, M.** *Die Johannesoffenbarung als Brief: Studien zu ihrem literarischen, historischen und theologischen Ort.* Göttingen: Vandenhoeck & Ruprecht, 1986. **Kern, O.** *Die Inschriften von Magnesia am Maeander.* Berlin: W. Spemann, 1900. **Kipp, T.** "Edictum." *RE* 5:1940–48. **Kirby, J. T.** "The Rhetorical Situations of Revelation 1–3." *NTS* 34 (1988) 197–207. **Lähnemann, J.** "Die sieben Sendschreiben der Johannes-Apokalypse: Dokumente für die Konfrontation des frühen Christentums mit hellenistisch/römischer Kultur und Religion in Kleinasien." In *Studien zur Religion und Kultur Kleinasiens.* 2 vols. Ed. S. Sahin, E. Schwertheim, and J. Wagner. Leiden: Brill, 1978. **Meinardus, O. F. A.** "The Christian Remains of the Seven Churches of the Apocalypse." *BA* 37 (1974) 69–82. ————. *St. John of Patmos and the Seven Churches of the Apocalypse.* Athens: Lycabettus, 1974. **Mellink, M. J.** "Archaeology in Asia Minor." *AJA* 78 (1974) 105–30; 79 (1975) 201–22; 80 (1976) 261–90; 81 (1977) 289–322; 82 (1978) 315–28. **Merkelbach, R.** "Zwei Texte aus dem Sarapeum zu Thessalonike." *ZPE* 10 (1973) 45–54, esp. 49–54. **Millar, F.** *The Emperor in the Roman World.* 252–59. **Mitton, C. L.** *The Formation of the Pauline Corpus of Letters.* London: Epworth, 1955. **Müller, U. B.** "Literarische und formgeschichtliche Bestimmung der Apokalypse des Johannes als einem Zeugnis frühchristlicher Apokalyptik." In *Apocalypticism,* ed. D. Hellholm. 599–619. ————. *Prophetie und Predigt im Neuen Testament.* Gütersloh: Mohn, 1975. **Muse, R. L.** "Revelation 2–3: A Critical Analysis of Seven Prophetic Messages." *JETS* 29 (1986) 147–61. **Pax, E.** "Jüdische und christliche Funde im Bereich der Sieben Kirchen der Apokalypse." *BibLeb* 8 (1967) 264–78. **Ramsay, W. M.** *The Cities and Bishoprics of Phrygia.* 2 vols. Oxford: Clarendon, 1895–97. **Rife, J. M.** "The Literary Background of Rev. II–III." *JBL* 60 (1941) 179–82. **Rudberg, G.** "Zu den Sendschreiben der Johannes-Apokalypse." *Eranos* 11 (1911) 170–79. **Schmithals, W.** "On the Composition and Earliest Collection of the Major Epistles of Paul." In *Paul and the Gnostics.* Nashville: Abingdon, 1972. 239–74. **Scobie, C. H. H.** "Local References in the Letters to the Seven Churches." *NTS* 39 (1993) 606–24. **Shea, W. H.** "The Covenantal Form of the Letters to the Seven Churches." *AUSS* 21 (1983) 71–84. **Sherk, R. K.** *Roman Documents from the Greek East: Senatus Consulta and Epistulae to the Age of Augustus.* Baltimore: Johns Hopkins, 1969. **Sokolowski, F.** "Propagation of the Cult of Sarapis and Isis in Greece." *GRBS* 15 (1974) 441–48. **Speyer, W.** *Bücherfunde in der Glaubenswerbung der Antike.* Göttingen: Vandenhoeck &

Ruprecht, 1970. **Stauffer, E.** *Christus und die Caesaren: Historische Skizzen.* 5th ed. Hamburg: Wittig, 1960. **Stübe, R.** *Der Himmelsbrief.* Tübingen: Mohr-Siebeck, 1918. **Sykutris, J.** "Epistolographie." PWSup 5 (1931) 185–220. **Tengbom, L. C.** *Studies in the Interpretation of Revelation Two and Three.* Ann Arbor: University Microfilms International, 1977. **Woude, A. S. van der.** "The Book of Nahum: A Letter Written in Exile." *OTS* 20 (1977) 108–26. **Yamauchi, E.** *The Archaeology of New Testament Cities in Western Asia Minor.* Grand Rapids, MI: Baker, 1980. **Zalewski, W.** *Untersuchungen über die literarische Gattung der Apokalypse 1–3.* Rome: Pontificia Universitate Gregoriana, 1973. **Weinreich, O.** "Antike Himmelsbriefe." *ARW* 10 (1907) 566–67. **Zimmermann, H.** "Christus und die Kirche in den Sendschreiben der Apokalypse." In *Unio Sanctorum.* FS L. Jaeger. Paderborn: Bonifacius, 1962.

*Form / Structure / Setting*

## I. LITERARY FORM

### A. Introduction

The form or genre of the proclamations to the seven churches has been a subject of extensive scholarly discussion. The analysis of their form has two closely related aspects, the determination of their *internal* literary structure and the determination of the *external* literary form or genre to which they have the closest generic relationship. In recent years a number of literary forms have been proposed as genres to which the seven proclamations have the closest phenomenological relationship: (1) the revelatory letter (Berger, *ZNW* 65 [1974] 212–19; Müller, "Apokalyptik," 601 n. 6a), (2) prophetic speech forms (Müller, *Prophetie und Predigt,* 47–107), (3) the covenant suzerainty treaty (Shea, *AUSS* 21 [1983] 71–84), or (4) one of the types of Greek oratory (Kirby, *NTS* 34 [1988] 197–207). The view preferred in this commentary, however, is that *the seven proclamations constitute a mixed genre created by the author.* The primary literary genre to which the seven proclamations belong is that of the *royal* or *imperial edict,* while the secondary literary genre or mode (a term proposed by A. Fowler, *Kinds of Literature: An Introduction to the Theory of Genres and Modes* [Cambridge: Harvard UP, 1982] 106–11) is that of a prophetic speech form that may be designated the *parenetic salvation-judgment oracle* (Aune, *Prophecy,* 326).

The seven proclamations never existed independently of Revelation but were designed specifically for their present literary setting by the author (Ramsay, *Letters,* 38–39). Though each is addressed to an individual Christian congregation in southwestern Asia Minor, they were intended to be read together and heeded by each of the congregations. This is clear from the stereotyped formula found at the end of each proclamation, "Let the one who has an ear hear what the Spirit declares to the churches," and by the statement in 2:23, "And all the churches shall know that I am the one who searches both mind and heart."

### B. Literary Structure

An analysis of the internal structure of the seven proclamations indicates that they share seven stereotypical features, each of which must be discussed in some detail:

1. *The Adscriptio,* or destination, and the command to write are part of the literary setting of each proclamation, since the messages themselves only begin

following the τάδε λέγει, "thus says," formula. The *adscriptiones* exhibit several important features: (a) The *adscriptio,* "destination," occurs in the dative before the *superscriptio,* "sender," in each proclamation, e.g., τῷ ἀγγέλῳ τῆς ἐν τῷ δεῖνι ἐκκλησίας, "to the angel of the church at such-and-such." The *adscriptio* cannot therefore be understood as an epistolary feature, since that form (name of recipient in the dative followed by name of sender in the nominative) is limited to epistolary petitions, complaints, and applications sent from an inferior to a superior (Exler, *Form,* 65–67; more recently, J. L. White, *The Form and Structure of the Offical Petition* [Missoula, MT: Scholars, 1972]). (b) The author does not consistently maintain his unique literary device of addressing each proclamation to an ἄγγελος who functions as the *alter ego* of each congregation. The author occasionally shifts from second-person singular pronouns and verbs to second- and third-person plural forms, such as when he addresses a particular group within a congregation (those about to be arrested in Smyrna, 2:10; those who have succumbed to Balaam's teaching at Pergamon, 2:14; those who have accepted the teaching of the Nicolaitans, 2:15; those in Thyatira who have not accepted Jezebel's teaching, 2:20–22 [those who follow Jezebel are explicitly addressed in 2:24: ὑμῖν δὲ λέγω, "but to you (plural) I say"]). Several times the author forgets (or temporarily abandons) the literary device he has adopted in addressing each of the proclamations to the angel of a particular church and addresses a congregation directly in second-person plural forms (2:13, 20). (c) With the exception of 2:1, all the proclamations begin with the conjunction καί, "and," which superficially coheres well with the paratactic Hebraistic style used by the author. Yet there are several stylistic features that clearly set Rev 2–3 apart from the literary framework within which it is set. While 245 (or 73.79 percent) of the 337 sentences in Revelation begin with καί (following the punctuation of Nestle-Aland[27]), only 9 (20.5 percent) of the 44 sentences in Rev 2–3 begin with καί. This stylistic difference between Rev 2–3 and the rest of the book is quite remarkable. Similarly, three of the seven occurrences of δέ, "and, but," in Revelation occur in Rev 2–3 (2:5, 16, 24), and of the thirteen occurrences of ἀλλά, "but," in Revelation, eight occur in Rev 2–3 (2:4, 6, 9[2x], 14, 20; 3:4, 9). The concentration of these stylistic features in Rev 2–3 suggests that the author is intentionally trying to write in an elevated style when composing the speeches of the exalted Christ. Admittedly, the occasional use of δέ or ἀλλά does not at first sight appear to be elevated style when compared with the style of other NT authors, and there is a complete absence in Revelation of the usual contrastive particles μέν and δέ, which characterize most classical and Hellenistic authors. But when taken on their own, these subtle variations suggest that John considered them to be a more elevated style of diction. Another possibility is that the stylistic differences between Rev 2–3 and the rest of the book may indicate the presence of a later addition to the work, perhaps by one who is not the author of the rest of Revelation.

2. *The Command to Write.* The command to write, expressed by the aorist imperative γράψον is located at the beginning of each proclamation between the *adscriptio* and the τάδε λέγει formula. The command to write is part of the "write and send" formula (a variation of the OT "go and tell" formulas; cf. Aune, *Prophecy,* 90, 330), though the second part has been suppressed, since the complete formula γράψον . . . καὶ πέμψον, "write . . . and send," has already been applied to all seven proclamations in 1:11. Since the object of the verb λέγει, found in each proclama-

tion, is τάδε, the entire message introduced by τάδε also functions as the object of the aorist imperative γράψον. Though literary accounts of supernatural revealers commanding that people write the substance of their revelations are found in Judaism (see *Comment* on 1:11), such divine commands are even more frequent in Greco-Roman texts (see *Comment* on 1:11). The many occurrences of this phenomenon indicate that it is a stock literary device used to legitimate the resultant compositions (J. B. Stearns, *Studies of the Dream as a Technical Device in Latin Epic and Drama* [Lancaster: Lancaster, 1927] 1–7; cf. Menander Rhetor 2.17, where the author recommends that in composing a hymn to Apollo, one should begin with a claim to divine inspiration).

3. *The* τάδε λέγει *Formula.* τάδε was an obsolete form in Hellenistic Greek that had archaic associations similar to the obsolete English phrase "thus saith." This intentional archaism had two associations for the readers of Revelation: (1) as a (prophetic) messenger formula occurring more than 250 times in the LXX (used to translate the Hebrew phrase יהוה אמר כה *kōh 'āmar YHWH,* "thus says Yahweh"; see *Comment* on 2:1) and (2) as a proclamation formula characteristic of Persian royal diplomatic letters and edicts (see *Comment* on 2:1). In either case, D. Fehling ("Funktion," 61–75) has demonstrated that this third-person formula introduces and provides justification for the use of the first person in the text that follows.

4. *The Christological Predications.* The speaker, i.e., the subject of the verb λέγει, is the exalted Christ identified by a series of descriptive titles that are (with the exception of 3:14) connected with the vision in 1:9–20 (2:1, cf. 1:16; 2:8, cf. 1:17–18; 2:12, cf. 1:16; 2:18, cf. 1:14; 3:1, cf. 1:4, 16; 3:7, cf. 1:18; 3:14, cf. 1:5). Four times the attributes of Christ are introduced with the substantival participle ὁ ἔχων, "the one having," twice belonging to the semantic subdomain of "have, possess" (2:18; 3:1b; cf. Louw-Nida, § 57.1) and twice belonging to the subdomain of "grasp, hold" (2:12b; 3:7b), a meaning shared by the substantival participle ὁ κρατῶν in 2:1 (cf. Louw-Nida, § 18.2). Since each proclamation ends with a proclamation formula (see below) introduced by ὁ ἔχων, this has the effect of framing and therefore introducing a greater degree of symmetry into the structure of the proclamations. Unlike the usual order of royal and imperial edicts, however, the actual *name* of the exalted Christ is never given. The cumulative effect of these titles is to unify the seven proclamations as pronouncement of the exalted Christ who commissioned John to write in 1:9–20.

5. *The Narratio.* The so-called οἶδα clause, "I know" clause, introduces the *narratio,* "narrative," section of each of the seven proclamations. Like the *dispositio,* "arrangement," that follows, each *narratio* is extremely varied, using a number of optional elements. This clause is not identical with the central message of each proclamation (contra Hahn, "Sendschreiben," 370–77) but provides a brief narrative of the situation of each congregation (including the past and present), a sort of diagnosis of the positive and negative behavior of each congregation, which then serves as a basis for the *dispositio,* "arrangement," that immediately follows. The finite verbs in the *narrationes* are limited to past and present tenses in the indicative, since the content is governed by the semantic significance of οἶδα, "I know." In Greek literary letters, verbs of perception such as οἶδα, "I know," ἀκούω, "I hear," and πυνθάνομαι, "I learn about," all belonging to the semantic domain of "learn and know" (Louw-Nida, §§ 27.1–26; 28.1–16), are sometimes used to introduce the opening section of a letter (see *Comment* on 2:2).

There are two stereotypical phrases that occur in the *narrationes* of some of the proclamations. (1) The phrase σου τὰ ἔργα, "your works," occurs four times after οἶδα, "I know," in Rev 2:19; 3:1, 8, 15 (cf. 2:2, where the variation τὰ ἔργα σου occurs) and once within a proclamation in 3:2. The οἶδα clause makes it clear that the exalted Christ is fully aware of the conduct of all members and factions of each of the seven congregations. (2) The second phrase, ἀλλὰ ἔχω κατὰ σοῦ [ὀλίγα] ὅτι, is found three times (2:4, 14, 20). The general approval implied in various statements following οἶδα in five of the proclamations (2:2–3, 9, 13, 19; 3:8) is contrasted with criticism introduced with the contrasting adversative particle ἀλλά. An alternate device is the use of paradox in 3:1b, so that the καί that links the two antithetical clauses functions as καί *adversativum*: "I know your works; you have the name of being alive, but [καί] you are dead." Two positive formulations of this phrase (ἀλλὰ τοῦτο ἔχεις ὅτι, in 2:6, and ἀλλὰ ἔχεις ὀλίγα ὀνόματα, in 3:4) break the pattern in that they *follow* the *dispositio* in 2:5 and 3:4, respectively, but refer to past or present situations using verbs in the present tense.

6. *The Dispositio* functions as the central section of each of the seven proclamations. The term *dispositio* (meaning "arrangement") was used by Quintilian for the effective and unified arrangement of the various parts of a speech (*Institutio oratoria* 3.3.1) but has been derived from its later application to parts of official documents in medieval diplomatics (cf. Fridh, *Terminologie*, 9–10). The *dispositio* is closely connected to the *narratio*, for the *narratio* serves as the basis for assertions made in the *dispositio*. The *dispositio* differs from the other structural elements in the seven proclamations in that it is not formally marked with a stereotypical phrase used consistently throughout. Yet the *dispositio* is marked by the use of verbs in the imperative and future indicative (futuristic presents also occur, such as ἔρχομαι, "I come," βάλλω, "I throw," and μέλλω, "I am about to"). The following sections of the seven proclamations function as *dispositiones:* (a) 2:5–6; (b) 2:10; (c) 2:16; (d) 2:22–25; (e) 3:2–4; (f) 3:9–11; and (g) 3:16–20. Four are introduced with imperatives: 2:5, μνημόνευε, "remember"; 2:10, μηδὲν φοβοῦ, "do not fear"; 2:16, μετανόησον, "repent"; and 3:2, γίνου γρηγορῶν καὶ στήρισον, "be watchful and strengthen," while three are introduced with future indicatives or present indicatives functioning as future indicatives: 2:22, ἰδοὺ βάλλω, "behold I will cast" (the future character of βάλλω is demonstrated by the fact that it is parallel to ἀποκτενῶ, "I will kill," in 2:23); 3:9, ἰδοὺ διδῶ ... [digression] ... ἰδοὺ ποιήσω, "Behold I will give ... behold I will make"; and 3:16, μέλλω σε ἐμέσαι, "I will vomit you."

The term μνημόνευε, "remember," occurs twice with μετανόησον, "repent" (2:5; 3:3). This emphasis on remembering the past serves to idealize it, and this nostalgic perspective supports a late first century A.D. date for Revelation. The demand for *repentance* (μετανοεῖν) is a motif occurring frequently in the *dispositiones*, often found within a conditional context in which the threat of eschatological judgment is introduced as the only alternative: 2:5a, μετανόησον ... εἰ δὲ μή, "repent ... but if not"; 2:5b, ἐὰν μὴ μετανοήσῃς, "if you do not repent"; 2:16, μετανόησον οὖν· εἰ δὲ μή, "therefore repent; but if not"; 2:22, ἐὰν μὴ μετανοήσωσιν, "if they do not repent"; and 3:3, καὶ μετανόησον. ἐάν οὖν μὴ γρηγορήσῃς, "and repent. Therefore if you are not watchful." The conditional threat of judgment introduced in these ways is identified with negative aspects of the Parousia in the such phrases as ἔρχομαι σοι, "I will come to you" (2:5, 16; 3:3), and ἥξω ὡς κλέπτης, "I will come as a thief" (3:3).

7. *The Proclamation Formula.* This third-person formula is found at the end of each of the seven proclamations, either in the penultimate position (2:7, 11, 17) or in the final position (2:29; 3:6, 13, 22): Ὁ ἔχων οὖς ἀκουσάτω τί τὸ πνεῦμα λέγει ταῖς ἐκκλησίαις, "Let the one with an ear hear what the Spirit says to the churches" (it also occurs in a variant form in 13:9, Εἴ τις ἔχει οὖς ἀκουσάτω, "If anyone has an ear, let him hear," where the formula *introduces* rather than concludes an oracle). A similar injunction occurs in 13:18: ὁ ἔχων νοῦν ψηφισάτω, "Let the one with understanding consider." Placed at the conclusion of each of the seven proclamations, this formula functions as a *proclamation* formula, i.e., as an injunction to an audience to pay very close attention to the message that it accompanies. Dibelius coined the term *Weckformel,* "alertness formula," for the parallels found in the synoptic Gospels (*Die Formgeschichte des Evangeliums,* 6th ed., ed. G. Bornkamm [Tübingen: Mohr-Siebeck, 1971] 248). This formula has no close verbal parallels in ancient literature with the exception of the parable tradition found in the synoptic Gospels and in some apocryphal gospels. There is, however, a partial model for its use in Ezek 3:27, which contains parallels to the opening and closing sections of each of the proclamations:

> But when I speak with you, I will open your mouth, and you shall say to them, "Thus says the Lord God"; *let those who will hear, hear* [ὁ ἀκούων ἀκουέτω] and let those who refuse to hear refuse.

When the proclamation formula concludes an oracle, it functions as a *prophetic signature* (in early Christian literature, other examples of a prophetic signature are found only in 1 Cor 14:37–38 and *Odes Sol.* 3:10–11; cf. D. E. Aune, "The Odes of Solomon and Early Christian Prophecy," *NTS* 28 [1982] 438–39). Proclamation formulas (variously phrased) often introduce OT prophetic oracles with such expressions as "Hear the word of Yahweh" (1 Kgs 22:19; Amos 7:16; Jer 29:20). Originally derived from public announcements in assemblies and courts of law (cf. Mic 6:2; Jer 2:4), proclamation formulas were used to introduce legal instruction (Prov 4:1; Job 13:6; 33:1, 31; 34:2, 16; Isa 49:1; 51:4) and instruction in wisdom (Deut 32:1; Prov 7:24; Ps 49:1; Isa 28:23). The aorist imperative ἀκούσατω, "let him/her/it hear," is used *transitively* with the clause beginning with the interrogative pronoun τί, "what," functioning as the object: "let him hear *what the Spirit says to the churches*" (in parallel expressions in the synoptic Gospels, ἀκούσατω is always used *intransitively*). The formula "He who has ears, let him hear" (and variants) is an aphorism rooted in the Jesus tradition (see *Comment* on 2:7), and these intentional allusions to a reiterated saying of Jesus suggest that the formula was firmly rooted in the liturgy of the early Christian communities in the Roman province of Asia so that their use could authenticate the author's revelatory encounter with the exalted Christ. The proclamation formula is formulated in the third person (as is the introductory τάδε λέγει, "thus says," formula) and appears to introduce a new speaker, the Spirit, since the first promise-to-the-victor formula, which follows it in 2:7b, is formulated in the first person: "To the one who conquers I will give . . ." (as they all are with the exception of 2:11b). Yet it is doubtful whether that is the author's intention, since the promise-of-victory formula is placed before the proclamation formula in the last four proclamations. Consequently, the author is emphasizing the close association of the Spirit with the exalted Christ, perhaps as the prophetic Spirit who mediates the latter's message. The proclamation formulas all use λέγει, "says," as the verb of declaration, just as in the τάδε λέγει formula, thus bracketing each proclamation.

8. *The Promise-to-the-Victor Formula.* This formula exhibits variety in form and structure and placement. It is placed *after* the proclamation formula in the first three proclamations (2:7b, 11b, 17b), but *before* it in the last four (2:26–27; 3:5, 12, 21), suggesting that the two formulas are closely related. John was intent on including a present substantival participle from the verb νικᾶν, "to conquer," at the beginning of the promise-of-victory formula, though he used three very different syntactical constructions to do so: (a) In the phrase τῷ νικῶντι δώσω αὐτῷ, literally, "to the one who conquers I will give to him," in 2:7, 17, the substantival participle τῷ νικῶντι, "to the one who conquers," is a dative of respect, while αὐτῷ, "to him," is the indirect object of δώσω. (b) In 2:11; 3:5, ὁ νικῶν, "the one who conquers," is the subject of a verb. (c) In 2:26; 3:12, 21, ὁ νικῶν, "the one who conquers," is a pendent nominative, a construction functionally parallel to (a).

### III. THE PROBLEM OF GENRE

#### A. *The "Heavenly Letter"*

In general the "heavenly letter" is a didactic letter ostensibly written by God himself and contains instructions, admonitions, threats, warnings, and exhortations of a moral or religious nature. Heavenly letters usually consist of three parts: (1) an introduction detailing the circumstances surrounding the discovery and its deciphering, (2) moral or religious promises and threats, and (3) a conclusion of magical protections against all sorts of perils (Sykutris, PWSup 5 [1931] 206; Stübe, *Himmelsbrief,* 5–7).

Heavenly letters are mentioned several times in ancient literature (see Koep, *Das himmlische Buch*). Aelius Aristides, a famous orator and resident of Smyrna writing during the second half of the second century A.D. in *Or.* 47.78 (B. Keil, *P. Aelii Aristidis Smyrnaei Quae Supersunt Omnia* [Berlin, 1989] 2:394; tr. C. A. Behr, *P. Aelii Aristidis Opera Quae Exstant Omnia* [Leiden: Brill, 1976] 2:291), refers to such a letter:

> Once when she [his aged nurse] was in bed, he [Asclepius] restored her by sending me from Pergamum and foretelling that I would make my nurse easier. And at the same time, I found a letter [ἐπιστολήν] lying before my feet in the Temple of Zeus Asclepius, and made it an omen. I discovered every particular written in it, all but explicitly.

Though the contents of the letter are not mentioned, it appears that it contained a prescription for the cure of his nurse (Sokolowski, *GRBS* 15 [1974] 443). The letter was probably part of the dream in which Asclepius predicted to Aristides that he could help his nurse (C. A. Behr, *Aelius Aristides and the Sacred Tales* [Amsterdam: Hakkert, 1969] 194).

#### B. *The Prophetic Letter*

Whatever genre or genres the seven proclamations represent, they exhibit few features derived from the Hellenistic epistolary tradition (contra Deissmann, *Bible*

*Studies,* 54; Ramsay, *Letters,* 38–39; Kirby, *NTS* 34 [1988] 200). Unlike the Pauline-like epistolary framework of Revelation (1:4–5; 22:21), the seven proclamations exhibit not a single characteristic feature of the early Christian epistolary tradition, a fact that must have been the result of deliberate choice. The seven proclamations do use the τάδε λέγει formula, which can be understood as an ancient Near Eastern epistolary prescript. In general, however, the seven proclamations do not rigidly replicate the generic features of *any* known ancient literary form (Hartmann, "Form," 142; Karrer, *Brief,* 159–60). Though John was certainly not without literary models, he chose not to follow them rigidly.

Since letters were often used in the ancient world to communicate divine revelation (Aune, *Prophecy,* 72–73; Dijkstra, *VT* 33 [1983] 319–22), there is some justification in speaking of "oracular letters" or "prophetic letters." The royal archives of the kingdom of Mari contain cuneiform letters containing advice to king Zimri-Lin from the gods of Mari sent to him by "prophets" (for a bibliography and some translations see Beyerlin, *Texts,* 122–28). An interesting collection of five texts written on potsherds has survived from Hellenistic Egypt, ca. 168 B.C. (T. C. Skeat and E. G. Turner, "An Oracle of Hermes Trismegistos at Saqqara," *Journal of Egyptian Archaeology* 54 [1968] 199–208; cf. *Sammelbuch griechischer Urkunden aus Ägypten* 10 [1969] 159–60, no. 10574). The texts include rough and final drafts of a letter to the king of Egypt. One copy of the rough draft (text B) reads as follows:

> Regarding the matters disclosed to me by the thrice-great god Hermes concerning oracles for the sovereign, I wish to announce that [the insurgent] Egyptians will quickly be defeated and that the king is to advance immediately to the Thebaid.

The final draft (text E) is framed as a letter:

> To King Ptolemy and to King Ptolemy the Brother and to Queen Cleopatra the Sister, greetings. Horus the priest of Isis at the sanctuary of Sebenutos in the city of Isis wishes to make an announcement about certain oracles to the sovereigns, that [the insurgent] Egyptians will be defeated quickly and that the king is to advance immediately to the Thebaid.

The texts from both Mari and Egypt prove only that prophetic or oracular revelations could be communicated in epistolary as well as oral form without the epistolary format influencing the form and content of the message itself.

Prophetic letters are found embedded in the OT and early Jewish literature as well (Berger, *ZNW* 65 [1974] 221–19). 2 Chr 21:12–15 (cf. the parallel in Jos. *Ant.* 9.99–101) is a letter attributed to Elijah the prophet with an announcement of judgment introduced with the customary prophetic messenger formula "thus says Yahweh." Most of these prophetic letters are connected with Jeremiah and his scribe Baruch (Jer 29:4–23[LXX 36:4–23], 24–28[LXX 36:4–28], 30–32[LXX 36:30–32]; Dijkstra considers Jer 29:24–32 a single letter; *2 Apoc. Bar.* 77:17–19; 78–87; Epistle of Jeremiah; *Par. Jer.* 6:15–7:4; 7:24–35). The letters in Jer 29, like that in 2 Chr 21:12–15, are introduced with prophetic rather than epistolary formulas (D. Pardee, *Handbook of Ancient Hebrew Letters* [Chico, CA: Scholars, 1982] 175–78, 181). The prophetic book of Nahum may originally have been a prophetic letter (van der Woude, *OTS* 20 [1977] 108–26). *1 Enoch* 91–108, the so-called Epistle of Enoch, is also a prophetic letter (the Greek text of *1 Enoch* 100:6 refers to the entire composition as Ἐπιστολὴ Ἐνώχ, "The Letter of Enoch" (Milik, *Enoch*, 47–57, though see M. Black, *Enoch*, 283, for qualifications).

After discussing the prophetic letter as a form embedded in longer compositions, K. Berger (*ZNW* 65 [1974] 214) observes that "The letters of Revelation are therefore primarily to be regarded as exemplars of the genre of the prophetic letter which never died out completely." However, the diversity in form and content found in prophetic letters ascribed to Elijah, Jeremiah, Baruch, and *1 Enoch* argues against the notion of a unified prophet letter tradition in early Judaism (Karrer, *Brief*, 49–59).

## C. *The Prophetic Oracle*

Several scholars have argued that the seven proclamations are examples of a type of early Christian prophetic speech and that the τάδε λέγει formula is equivalent to the OT prophetic messenger formula (Hahn, "Sendschreiben"; Müller, *Prophetie und Predigt*). Hahn regards the "letters" of Rev 2–3 as a particular type of prophetic speech with a relatively fixed sequence of elements exhibiting limited variation. Müller has identified each "letter" as a type of prophetic sermon exhibiting one of two basic elements of prophetic speech, the parenetic sermon of repentance (*Bussparaklese*) or the sermon of salvation (*Heilspredigt; Prophetie*, 47–104). Rev 2:1–7 exhibits the basic form of the first, and most common, type: (1) accusation (2:4), (2) admonition (2:5a), (3) conditional threat of judgment (2:5b). With variations, this form occurs in 2:12–17, 18–29; 3:1–6, 14–22. The sermon of salvation is found in pure form in 2:8–11, and in combination with the parenetic sermon of repentance in 3:1–6.

A more satisfactory approach is to identify the seven proclamations with the "paraenetic salvation-judgment oracle" (Aune, *Prophecy*, 326). This type of prophetic speech was rooted in early Judaism, but when taken over by early Christians it developed some distinctive features. Such oracles were directed primarily to members of the Christian community and therefore reflect a strong emphasis on moral exhortation. Improper behavior is discouraged by threats of judgment and exclusion, while proper behavior is encouraged by promises of salvation and reward. Since this prophetic speech form was used in a variety of situations, it incorporates a variety of subordinate features. Most of the constituent elements are optional rather than mandatory.

## D. *The Imperial Edict*

While several scholars have observed that the τάδε λέγει formula resembles the style of royal and imperial decrees promulgated by Persian kings and Roman magistrates and emperors (Stauffer, *Christus*, 198; Lähnemann, "Sendschreiben," 200), G. Rudberg is the only scholar to argue that the seven proclamations reflect the form and content of royal and imperial edicts (*Eranos* 11 [1911] 170–79). He observed that the same juxtaposition of praise and censure found in the seven proclamations (with the exception of the proclamations to Smyrna in 2:8–11 and Philadelphia in 3:7–13) occurs in an inscribed decree or letter of Darius I found in Magnesia (Rudberg, *Eranos* 11 [1911] 172–73). He noted that while the formula τάδε λέγει κύριος, "thus says the Lord" (like the synonymous phrases οὕτως λέγει κύριος and εἶπε κύριος), was used in the LXX for divine pronouncements, τάδε λέγει was also used to introduce the rescripts and letters of Persian kings and corresponded to the simple λέγει, "he says," formula in edicts of Roman magistrates and emperors (Rudberg, *Eranos* 11 [1911] 173–76). Rudberg concluded that John used this form to present the exalted Christ as a king addressing his subjects.

The primary distinction between edicts and letters is that the prescript of edicts used the form ὁ δεῖνα λέγει, "so-and-so says," or ὁ δεῖνα κελεύει, "so-and-so commands," *imperator dicit,* "the emperor says," while epistolary prescripts used the formula ὁ δεῖνα τῷ δεῖνι χαίρειν, "so-and-so to so-and-so, greetings" (W. Larfeld, *Griechische Epigraphik,* 3rd ed. [Munich: Beck, 1914] 427–32). *Edicta,* "edicts" (the usual Greek equivalent to *edictum* was διάταγμα; cf. Plutarch *Marcellus* 14.7), were public announcements by an emperor or magistrate setting forth orders or policies (T. Kipp, "Edictum," *RE* 5:1940–48). The *edictum* was one of four types of *constitutiones,* i.e., judicial decisions; the other three were *mandata,* "mandates" (internal directives to officials in the imperial service), *decreta,* "decrees" (actual judicial decisions pronounced by the emperor in court), and *rescripta,* "rescripts" (imperial correspondence); cf. Berger, *Roman Law,* s.v. *"constitutiones principum."* *Edicta,* the form used for communications directed toward the general public, were heterogeneous (W. Kunkel, *An Introduction to Roman Legal and Constitutional History,* 2nd ed. [Oxford: Clarendon, 1973] 127–28). *Rescripta* consisted of two types, the imperial letter or *epistula* (Sherk, *Roman Documents,* 189–97) and the *subscriptio* or "marginal" decision of the emperor, written at the bottom of the actual petition or *libellus.* Edicts were formal and public, while letters were informal and private. Imperial edicts did not have universal application but were valid only for the region and people for whom they were originally intended (Sherwin-White, *Letters,* 651).

M. Benner (*The Emperor Says,* basing her work on the research of Fridh on the rhetoric of the sixth-century decretal forms preserved in Cassiodorus *Variae* [*Terminologie et Formules dans les Variae de Cassiodore* (Göteborg: Acta Universitatis Gothoburgensis, 1956)]) rhetorically analyzed thirty-seven imperial edicts and about a hundred allusions to edicts primarily of the first century A.D. (see the brief critique by M. Winterbottom, *Gnomon* 49 [1977] 419–20). The advice given to emperor Marcus Aurelius by the Stoic philosopher M. Cornelius Fronto suggests the propriety of such a rhetorical analysis of edicts (*Ep. ad Verum imp.* 2.1; C. P. Haines, *Marcus Cornelius Fronto,* LCL [Cambridge: Harvard UP, 1929] 2:138–39):

> Which of them [previous emperors between Tiberius and Vespasian] could address people or Senate in a speech of his own? Which draw up an edict [*edictum*] or a rescript [*epistulam*] in his own words . . . ? Now *imperium* is a term that not only connotes power but also speech, since the exercise of *imperium* consists essentially of ordering and prohibiting. If he did not praise good actions, if he did not blame evil actions, if he did not exhort to virtue, if he did not warn off from vice, a ruler would belie his name and be called imperator for no purpose.

Though the primary rhetorical genre of edicts was that of the deliberative speech (Benner, *The Emperor Says,* 22), the author of the ruler or magistrate was such that the inclusion of the persuasive element was voluntary rather than necessary. The presence of praise and censure (characteristic of epideictic speech, the *genus demonstrativum*) together with exhortations to pursue the good and avoid the bad (characteristic of deliberative speech, the *genus deliberativum*) indicates that edicts are inevitably a mixed genre.

The first formal element of the edict is the *praescriptio*, "introduction," which gives the title(s) and name(s) of the issuing magistrate or emperor. This is followed by a verb of declaration in Latin (*dicit* or *dicunt*, "he says" or "they say") and in Greek (λέγει or λέγουσι, "he says" or "they say"); cf. Mason, *Greek Terms*, 127; Millar, *Emperor*, 221–22. The primary function of the *praescriptio* is to state the authority behind the edict. The text of the edict then follows with the magistrate or emperor speaking in the first person and addressing the recipients in the second person plural. Unlike the recipients of letters, those who receive an edict are not formally addressed by their proper names either in the *praescriptio* or in the body of the decree.

The central section of the edict exhibits great variety but can optionally consist of the following elements (Benner, *The Emperor Says*, 33–175, examines thirty-seven decrees using the following schema): (1) the *proemium*, "preface," intended to produce benevolence and interest on the part of the addressees; (2) the *promulgatio*, "proclamation," a "publishing" phrase such as "I make known that"; (3) the *narratio*, "narration," a clear, concise account of the state of the matter, the facts leading up to the enactment, etc.; (4) the *dispositio*, or "arrangement," the central part of the document expressing the decisions; and (5) the *sanctio*, "sanction," or *corroboratio*, "corroboration," i.e., final clauses intended to bring about obedience to the enactment.

The *praescriptio*, with the verb of declaration, is the only formal characteristic consistently recurring in imperial edicts (Benner, *The Emperor Says*, 26). Each of the seven proclamations begins with a *praescriptio* similar to those found in imperial edicts, except that in them the verb of declaration *precedes* the christological predications, while in imperial edicts it *follows* the name(s) and title(s) of the issuing magistrate(s) or emperor. Yet there are exceptions such as Xerxes' letter to Pausanias in Thucydides 1.129.3: ὧδε λέγει βασιλεὺς Ξέρξης Παυσανίᾳ, "Thus says King Xerxes to Pausanias." Another example is the parody of a proclamation of sacral law by Cronus in the guise of a priest in Lucian, *Saturnalia* 10: Τάδε λέγει Κρονοσόλων, "Thus says Cronosolon" (combining the names of Cronus, the divine father of Zeus, and Solon, the famous Athenian lawgiver). Along with names and titles in the *praescriptio*, Roman edicts could incorporate participial phrases that further described the authority of the author(s), such as we read in Appian *Bella civilia* 4.2.8: "Marcus Lepidus, Marcus Antonius, and Octavius Caesar, chosen by the people [οἱ χειροτονηθέντες] to set in order and regulate the republic."

While no counterpart to the *prooemium* is found in the seven proclamations, its absence is appropriate in eastern provinces where the traditions of absolute sovereignty, first of the Persian monarchs and then of the Hellenistic kings, were predominant.

The *narratio*, which occurs with some frequency in Roman edicts, often has the character of reported information (*renuntiatum est nobis*). The *narratio* has a functional counterpart in the οἶδα clauses in each of the proclamations. Like the epistolary parallels to οἶδα, "I know," terms from closely related semantic subdomains such as ακούειν, "to hear," γινώσκειν, "to come to know," ἐπιγινώσκειν, "to learn about," and πυνθάνεσθαι, "to learn," are used to introduce the *narrationes* of royal and imperial edicts. A particularly relevant example is the edict of Claudius quoted in Jos. *Ant.* 19.280–84:

Tiberius Claudius Caesar Augustus Germanicus, of tribunician power, declares [λέγει]: "Since I have known [ἐπιγνούς] from the beginning that the Jews in Alexandria called 'Alexandrians' were joint-colonizers with the Alexandrians. . . ."

Another relevant document is a letter of Darius I, originally inscribed during his lifetime, 521–486 B.C., but subsequently recopied in the second century A.D. (Kern, *Inschriften*, no. 115; reprinted with informative notes in *SIG* 1, no. 22, and conveniently reprinted with bibliography and notes in Meiggs-Lewis, *Inscr.* no. 12): Βασιλεῦ [Βα]σιλέων Δαρεῖος ὁ Ὑστάσπεω Γαδάται δούλῳ τάδε λέγ[ι], πυνθάνομαί σε τῶν ἐμῶν ἐπιταγμάτων οὐ κατὰ πάντα πειθαρχεῖν, "The king of kings Darius Hystaspes to his servant Gadatas says the following: 'I have learned that you did not obey my commands in every respect.'" Here πυνθάνομαι, "I have learned" (a historical present), with the infinitive introducing indirect discourse, functions much like the οἶδα of the seven proclamations. Similarly, in an inscription of Hadrian, A.D. 117–38 (E. M. Smallwood, *Documents Illustrating the Principates of Nerva, Trajan and Hadrian* [Cambridge: Cambridge UP, 1966] no. 462, analyzed in Benner, *The Emperor Says*, 161–62), the *narratio* is introduced with a participial construction using πυθόμενος.

The *dispositio* occurs in each proclamation, except that it is not introduced with the usual ordaining verb meaning "I command" but is influenced by the conditional style of prophetic speech consisting of ethical exhortations usually matched by conditional threats. In the inscribed letter of Darius to Gadatas discussed above, Darius goes on to praise Gadatas for cultivating Syrian fruit trees in Ionia (ἐπαίνω σὴν πρόθεσιν), lines 8–17, but threatens to punish him for attempting to tax Apollo's sacred gardeners (ὅτι δὲ τὴν ὑπὲρ θεῶν μου διάθεσιν ἀφανίζεις . . .), lines 17–29. Thus the *narratio* has both a positive and negative element just as the *narrationes* in the seven proclamations do.

Finally, statements with a function similar to the *sanctio* or *corroboratio* of Roman edicts are regularly found at the close of each proclamation in the conditional promise of victory.

The author's use of the royal/imperial edict form is part of his strategy to polarize God/Jesus and the Roman emperor, who is but a pale and diabolical imitation of God. In his role as the eternal sovereign and king of kings, Jesus is presented as issuing solemn and authoritative edicts befitting his status. One oracular deity, Zeus at Heliopolis, replied in the form of *rescripta,* "written replies," to written consultations transmitted in sealed *diplomata,* folded tablets with written instructions, or *codicilii,* written responses (Macrobius *Sat.* 1.23.14–16, referring to a consultation of Trajan). The seven proclamations share a similar structure, which consists of (1) an introduction, (2) a central section (introduced by οἶδα, "I know"), and (3) a double conclusion, containing (a) a call for vigilance and (b) a victory saying. This structure is adapted from that of the royal or imperial edict discussed above. Yet, into this relatively rigid formal structure, the author introduces a great deal of variation. The reason for including seven separate proclamations (making it possible for each community to read the divine edict of each of the other communities) is that imperial edicts did not have universal application but were valid only for the region and people for whom they were promulgated (Sherwin-White, *Letters,* 651).

*E. The Seven Proclamations as a Corpus*

While the form of each of the seven proclamations is that of the royal or imperial edict, as a *collection,* they have no close analogies. However, since each proclamation was intended for a specific congregation, the fact that they were all distributed to all the congregations is analogous to the publication of imperial edicts.

Early Christianity knew several collections of seven, (1) an early collection of ten Pauline letters addressed to seven churches (even Jerome *Ep.* 53, could state: "The Apostle Paul wrote to seven churches"), (2) the seven genuine letters of Ignatius of Antioch, and (3) the canonical collection of seven catholic letters. E. J. Goodspeed proposed that a collection of seven Pauline letters (Romans, 1–2 Corinthians, Galatians, Philippians, Colossians, 1–2 Thessalonians, and Philemon), with Ephesians as a pseudonymous "cover letter" provided a model for John's collection of seven letters introducted by the "cover letter" of Rev 1:4–20 (*New Solutions,* 21–28). Goodspeed thought that the salutation in Rev 1:4 showed Pauline influence (*New Solutions,* 24), and that the composition of Revelation ca. A.D. 90 established the *terminus ad quem,* i.e., the latest date, for the formation for the Pauline corpus of seven letters (*New Solutions,* 87). Similarly, Mitton (*Formation,* 33) argues that the seven-letter Pauline corpus served as a model for both Rev 2–3 and Ignatius.

Recently it has been persuasively argued that a pre-Marcionite corpus of ten Pauline letters (in the order Galatians, 1–2 Corinthians, Romans, etc.), directed to *seven* churches, existed before the larger corpora of fourteen letters, introduced by the so-called Marcionite Prologues, which also preserve the "Marcionite" order (Clabeaux, *Lost Edition,* 1–2, 147). As evidence for the existence of a seven-letter corpus, the so-called Marcionite Prologues (which are not Marcionite at all) in their original form introduced a corpus of Pauline letters to seven communities (Dahl, *Semeia* 12 [1978] 233–77), and the Syriac order of the Pauline letters is supported in Codex Sinaiticus and Ephrem (Clabeaux, *Lost Edition,* 2). Schmithals ("Collection," 239–74) has proposed that the earliest corpus of Pauline letters consisted of seven letters in a fixed order: 1 Corinthians, 2 Corinthians, Galatians, Philippians, 1 Thessalonians, 2 Thessalonians, and Romans (for a thorough critique of this proposal, see Gamble, *JBL* 94 [1975] 403–18).

*IV. Why These Seven Churches?*

There is no obvious reason for John to have addressed these particular seven churches, though there has been a great deal of speculation. The choice of just these seven Christian congregations is problematic in view of the fact that there were many other important Christian congregations in Asia Minor, e.g., Colossae (Col 1:2), Hierapolis (Col 4:13), Troas (Acts 20:5; 2 Cor 2:12), and perhaps Magnesia and Tralles, to which Ignatius of Antioch addressed letters, ca. A.D. 115.

In the ancient church, *seven* churches addressed by John were widely regarded as a symbol of the universal church. According to the Muratorian Canon (ca. A.D. 180), "John also, though he wrote in the Apocalypse to seven churches, neverthe-less speaks to them all." Similarly, Victorinus (*Comm. in Apoc.* 1.7 [Haussleiter, *Victorinus,* 28–29]) observes, *sed quia quod uni dicit, omnibus dicit,* "but what he says to one, he says to all." Victorinus also claims that Paul taught that the churches are structured by the number seven and that he wrote to seven churches (Romans,

Corinthians, Galatians, Ephesians, Thessalonians, Philippians, and Colossians). In addition, he claims that Paul wrote to some individuals in order not to exceed the total number of seven churches (*Comm. in Apoc.* 1.7 [Haussleiter, *Victorinus,* 28]). That may reflect the author's original intention. Lohmeyer (42) says, "As a whole [the seven letters] form parts of a book intended for the entire early Christian community." Ezek 25–32 is addressed to seven nations (Ammon, Moab, Edom, Philistia, Tyre, Sidon, and Egypt), perhaps representing all Gentiles.

Yet all seven were within one hundred miles of Ephesus in the Roman proconsular province of Asia and might have formed an established circular route for itinerant Christian prophets and teachers, perhaps since Paul's day. Ramsay proposed that the seven churches were all located on a circular road that functioned as a postal route (Ramsay, *Letters,* 185–96; see the map facing p. 1). However, Ramsay's proposals concerning Roman roads have turned out to be based on a minimum of archeological fact combined with a healthy dose of conjecture, as recent research on the Via Tauri (the road connecting Constantinople, Ancyra, and the Cilician Gates) has shown (French, *Roman Roads,* 33). Ramsay's hypothesis of a circular post road has no firm basis in archeological fact but is rather an inference based on the location of cities. According to F. Starr (quoted in French, *ANRW* II, 7/2:700),

> Ramsay, for instance, wrote many pages on the routes of Roman highways, but his work actually centred about his search for cities. . . . Only by searching first for the roads can the ancient itineraries be profitably used for the identification of a city. Obviously, until the course of a road is positively known, it is impossible to speculate on the possible location of cities along it.

During the period when the Roman Republic controlled the province of Asia (133–31 B.C.), Ephesus was the administrative center of the province. Paved roads began at Ephesus, the *caput viae,* and radiated outwards, as evidence from the seven known Republican milestones suggests (French, *ANRW* II, 7/2:707 and Map 1). Though the roads themselves have not been discovered, the milestones indicate that one road went north from Ephesus to Pergamon, for which there is evidence during the early imperial period from Augustus to Nero (French, *ANRW* II, 7/2:707 and Map 2), and another east from Ephesus to Apameia.

Based on the evidence found in the historical allusions in the seven proclamations, John was familiar with the situations of each church and may have exercised an itinerant prophetic ministry himself. In the aftermath of the fall of Jerusalem following the first Jewish revolt of A.D. 66–73, Anatolia had become perhaps the most important geographical center of Christianity in the ancient world. By A.D. 100 there may have been as many as eighty thousand Christians living in proconsular Asia (Reicke, *New Testament Era,* 303, though Reicke does not provide any evidence for this conjecture). Each of the seven proclamations is addressed to the "angel" of that particular church. Since John consistently uses the Greek term ἄγγελος, "angel, messenger," of supernatural beings subordinate to God, it is likely that the term has that meaning in each of the proclamations. Various scholars have tried to argue that the term "angel" actually refers to a local leader such as bishop, or that translated "messenger" it refers to a representative of John sent to each church with a copy of his circular apocalypse. Yet the idea that each church is represented in the heavenly world by an angelic figure who somehow personifies that church, though without parallel, seems to be John's meaning.

# 1. The Proclamation to Ephesus (2:1–7)

*Bibliography*

**Agnew, F. H.** "On the Origin of the Term *Apostolos*." *CBQ* 38 (1976) 49–53. ———. "The Origin of the NT Apostle-Concept: A Review of Research." *JBL* 105 (1986) 75–96. **Bammer, A.** "Wo einst ein Weltwunder stand: Letzte Ergebnisse österreichischer Forschungen im antiken Ephesos." *Altertum* 21 (1975) 27–35. **Barrett, C. K.** "Gnosis and the Apocalypse of John." In *The New Testament and Gnosis*. FS R. McL. Wilson, ed. A. H. B. Logan and A. J. M. Wedderburn. Edinburgh: T. & T. Clark, 1983. 125–37. **Bauer, W.** *Orthodoxy and Heresy in Earliest Christianity*. 2nd ed. Ed. G. Strecker. Tr. R. A. Kraft and G. Krodel et al. Philadelphia: Fortress, 1971. **Bean, G. E.** *Aegean Turkey*. 2nd ed. London: Ernest Benn; New York: W. W. Norton, 1979. **Beloch, K. J.** *Die Bevölkverung der griechisch-römischen Welt*. 1886. Repr. New York: Arno, 1979. **Bielmeier, P. A.** "Der Angelos der sieben Gemeinden in Apo. 2 und 3." *TGl* 25 (1933) 207–8. **Borger, R.** "NT²⁶ und die neutestamentliche Textkritik." *TRu* 52 (1987) 1–58. **Brox, N.** "Nikolaos und Nikolaiten." *VC* 19 (1965) 23–30. **Burchner, H.** "Ephesos." PW 5/2:2772–2822. **Clark, A. C.** "Apostleship: Evidence from the New Testament and Early Christian Literature." *VoxEv* 19 (1989) 49–82. **Crossan, J. D.** *In Fragments: The Aphorisms of Jesus*. San Francisco: Harper & Row, 1983. **Duncan-Jones, R. P.** *The Economy of the Roman Empire: Quantitative Studies*. Cambridge: Cambridge UP, 1974. **Elliger, W.** *Ephesos: Geschichte einer antiken Weltstadt*. Stuttgart, 1985. **Engelmann, H.** "Zum Kaiserkult in Ephesos." *ZPE* 97 (1993) 279–89. **Filson, F. V.** "Ephesus and the New Testament." *BA* 8 (1945) 73–80. **Gangemi, A.** "L'albero della vita (Ap. 2:7)." *RevistB* 25 (1977) 337–56. **Haacker, K.** "Verwendung und Vermeidung des Apostelbegriffs im lukanischen Werk." *NovT* 30 (1988) 9–38. **Hahn, F.** "Der Apostolat im Urchristentum." *KD* 20 (1974) 54–77. **Heiligenthal, R.** "Wer waren die 'Nikolaiten'? Ein Beitrag zur Theologiegeschichte des frühen Christentums." *ZNW* 82 (1991) 133–37. **Hemer, C. J.** "Unto the Angels of the Churches: 1. Introduction and Ephesians; 2. Smyrna and Pergamum." *BurH* 11 (1975) 4–27. **Hilgenfeld, A.** "Die Christus-Leute in Korinth und die Nikolaiten in Asien." *ZWT* 15 (1872) 158–60. **Hölbl, G.** *Zeugnisse ägyptischer Religionsvorstellungen für Ephesus*. EPRO 73. Leiden: Brill, 1978. **Hogarth, D. G.** *The Archaic Artemision*. London: British Museum, 1908. **Holtz, T.** "Die 'Werke' in der Johannesapokalypse." In *Geschichte und Theologie der Urchristentums: Gesammelte Aufsätze*, ed. E. Reinmuth and C. Wolff. WUNT 57. Tübingen: Mohr-Siebeck, 1991. 347–61. **Horsley, G. H. R.** "The Inscriptions of Ephesos and the New Testament." *NovT* 34 (1992) 105–68. **Janzon, P.** "Nikolaiterna i Nya Testamentet och i fornkyrkan." *SEÅ* 21 (1956) 82–108. **Karwiese, S.** *Die Marienkirche in Ephesos*. Vienna: Verlag der Österreichischen Akademie der Wissenschaften, 1989. **Keil, J.** *Ephesos: Ein Führer durch die Ruinenstätte und ihre Geschichte*. 5th ed. Vienna: Österreichisches Archäologisches Institut, 1964. ———. "Die erste Kaiserneokorie von Ephesos." *NumZ* n.s. 12 (1919) 115–20. **Knibbe, D.,** and **Alzinger, W.** "Ephesos vom Beginn der römischen Herrschaft in Kleinasien bis zum Ende der Principatszeit." *ANRW* II, 7/2:748–830. **Koester, H.** "GNOMAI DIAPHOROI: The Origin and Nature of Diversification in the History of Early Christianity." In *Trajectories through Early Christianity*. Philadelphia: Fortress Press, 1971. 114–57. **Lethaby, W. R.** "The Earlier Temple of Artemis at Ephesus." *JHS* 37 (1917) 1–16. **Marcus, R.** "The Tree of Life in Proverbs." *JBL* 62 (1943) 117–

20. **May, H. G.** "The Sacred Tree on Palestine Painted Pottery." *JAOS* 59 (1939) 251–59.
**Meinardus, O. F. A.** *St. Paul in Ephesus and the Cities of Galatian and Cyprus.* New Rochelle:
Caratzas Brothers, 1978. **Miltner, F.** *Ephesos: Stadt der Artemis und des Johannes.* Vienna:
Deuticke, 1958. **Mussies, G.** "Pagans, Jews and Christians at Ephesus." In P. W. van der Horst
and G. Mussies. *Studies on the Hellenistic Background of the New Testament.* Utrecht: Rijksuniversiteit
te Utrecht, 1990. 177–94. **Oster, R.** *A Bibliography of Ancient Ephesus.* Metuchen, NJ:
Scarecrow, 1987. **Perrot, A.** "Les représentations de l'arbre sacré sur les monuments de
Mésopotamie et d'Élam." *Babyloniaca* 17 (1937) 1–144. **Pick, B.** "Die Neokorien von
Ephesos." In *Corolla Numismatica.* London: Oxford UP, 1906. 234–44. **Prigent, P.** "L'Hérésie
asiatique et l'église confessante de l'Apocalypse à Ignace." *VC* 31 (1977) 1–22. **Rogers, G. M.**
*The Sacred Identity of Ephesos: Foundation Myths of a Roman City.* New York: Routledge, 1991.
**Rougé, J.** *Recherches sur l'organisation du commerce maritime en Méditerranée sous l'Empire romain.*
Paris: S.E.V.P.E.N., 1966. **Rudberg, G.** "Zu den Sendschreiben der Johannes-Apokalypse."
*Eranos* 11 (1911) 170–79. **Schille, G.** *Die urchristliche Kollegialmission.* ATANT 48. Zürich:
Zwingli, 1967. **Schnackenburg, R.** "Apostles before and during Paul's Time." In *Apostolic
History and the Gospel.* FS F. F. Bruce, ed. W. W. Gasque and R. P. Martin. Grand Rapids, MI:
Eerdmans, 1970. 278–303. ————. "Ephesus: Entwicklung einer Gemeinde von Paulus zu
Johannes." *BZ* 35 (1991) 41–64. **Schüssler Fiorenza, E.** "Apocalyptic and Gnosis in the Book
of Revelation." *JBL* 92 (1973) 565–81. **Sickenberger, J.** "Die Deutung der Engel der sieben
apokalyptischen Gemeinden." *RQ* 35 (1927) 135–49. **Tonneau, R.** "Ephèse au temps de saint
Paul." *RB* 38 (1929) 5–34, 210–50. **Vögtle, A.** "Τῷ ἀγγέλῳ τῆς . . . Ἐκκλησίας." *ORPB* 67
(1966) 323–37. **Wankel, H., Börker, C.,** and **Merkelbach, R.** *Die Inschriften von Ephesus.* 8 vols.
Bonn, 1979–84. **Warden, P. D.,** and **Bagnall, R. S.** "The Forty Thousand Citizens of Ephesus."
*CP* 83 (1988) 220–23.

### Translation

$^1$*To the angel $^a$of the church in Ephesus $^a$ write: "Thus says the one who holds the
seven stars in his $^b$right hand,$^b$ who walks in the midst of the seven golden $^c$ lampstands:
$^2$I know $^a$ your deeds, namely,$^b$ your $^c$ effort and endurance. $^d$Because $^e$ you cannot bear $^f$
wicked people, and so have tested those $^g$ who call themselves 'apostles,' $^h$but $^i$ who really
are not, for $^j$ you found them liars. $^3$And you have endurance and have borne patiently
because of my name, and you have not $^a$become weary.$^a$ $^4$But I hold this against you that
$^a$you have lost $^a$ $^b$your first love.$^b$ $^5$Remember therefore how far $^a$you have fallen $^a$ and
repent and do the deeds you did formerly. If not, $^b$I will come to you,$^b$ $^c$and I will remove
your menorah from its place, unless you repent. $^6$But you have this in your favor, you
despise the deeds of the Nicolaitans, which I also $^a$ despise. $^7$Let the person with an ear
hear $^a$ what the Spirit announces $^b$ to the churches. I will allow the one who conquers $^c$ to
eat from $^d$ the tree of life which is found in the Paradise of God. "$^e$*

### Notes

1.a-a. Variants: (1) τῆς ἐν Ἐφέσῳ] ℵ fam 1611$^{2344}$ Andreas Byzantine. (2) τῷ ἐν Ἐφέσῳ] A C fam
1611$^{1854}$ syr$^s$ WHort; Charles, 1:cxx. (3) τῷ τῆς Ἐφέσῳ] 2019 Andr n$^{2429}$. (4) τῆς Ἐφεσίων] Andr a c f$^{2031}$
$^{2056}$ i$^{1685\ 2074}$ 1773. τῆς, the grammatically appropriate definite article of reading (1), which goes with the
genitive noun ἐκκλησίας, "church," has the strongest supporting textual evidence and is preferred by
Nestle-Aland$^{27}$ and UBSGNT$^4$. Yet τῷ, reading (2), with the definite article in the dative, is found in both
A and C (their agreement is normally regarded as indicative of a superior text). Charles preferred τῷ
based on the rule that in Revelation a prep. phrase (such as ἐν Ἐφέσῳ) can precede an anarthrous noun
(e.g., ἐκκλησίας) but cannot stand between the article and its noun, as would be the case with the reading
τῆς ἐν Ἐφέσῳ ἐκκλησίας (Charles, 1:clvii; Charles is followed by Swete, 23; Lohmeyer, 21). Bousset,

however, phrased this rule in a more nuanced manner: "A prepositional phrase is rarely placed between an article and its substantive" ([1906] 176), and cites Rev 2:1 as an exception. This view is shared by Schmid (*Studien* 2:197–98) and by Delobel, in an important discussion of this passage ("Le texte de L'Apocalypse," 158–61). In spite of the stereotyped introduction to the proclamations to each of the seven churches, the variants differ widely. τῷ instead of τῆς is supported in 2:1 by A C fam 1611[1854]; in 2:8 by A; in 2:18 by A; in 3:1 by 046, though in 2:12; 3:7, 14, τῆς is attested by all important witnesses (a relatively full survey of the textual witnesses is provided by Charles, 2:244, by Delobel, "Le text de L'Apocalypse," 159 n. 34, and by Borger, *TRu* 52 [1987] 42–45). Charles, noting that the evidence for an original τῷ becomes weaker and almost nonexistent for 3:1, 7, 14, suggests that the self-confidence of the copyists increased as they wrote (2:244). Schmid observes that the article before ἐκκλησίας is more difficult to dispense with than the repetition of the article modifying τῷ ἀγγέλῳ; since he could have written τῷ ἀγγέλῳ τῷ τῆς ἐν Ἐφέσῳ ἐκκλησίας, he probably found it easier to eliminate τῷ than τῆς (*Studien* 2:198). This in fact is close to variant (3), where the scribe may have had a defective exemplar at this point (since he omits ἐν) and simply corrected the reading.

1.b-b.   Variants: (1) δεξιᾷ αὐτοῦ] *lectio originalis*. (2) δεξιᾷ αὐτοῦ χειρί] ℵ*. (3) δεξιᾷ χειρί] Andr l. (4) δεξιᾷ χειρὶ αὐτοῦ] Andr/Byz 4a; Andr/Byz 4b. (5) χειρὶ αὐτοῦ] 792 syr[ph] Tyconius[2].

1.c.   Variants: (1) χρυσέων (uncontracted form of χρυσῶν, from χρύσεος, the uncontracted form of χρυσοῦς)] A C. (2) χρυσίων (from χρυσίον)] fam 1611[2050].

2.a.   The verb οἶδα, "I know," is often described as perfect in form but present in meaning (Bauer-Aland, 1127; Louw-Nida, § 172; Mussies, *Morphology*, 347, does *not* regard οἶδα as the perfect tense corresponding to εἶδον). Yet K. L. McKay, "On the Perfect and Other Aspects in New Testament Greek," *NovT* 23 (1981) 298–303, argues that "there appears to have been no doubt in the minds of Greeks from the time of Homer to well beyond the time of the New Testament that οἶδα was in every respect a perfect" (298–99). In contrast to the perfect ἔγνωκα (from γινώσκειν), οἶδα rarely, if ever, suggests an action whereby a state of knowledge occurred. This coheres with the stative perfective meaning of οἶδα as expressing a state of knowledge with little or no reference to how that knowledge was acquired (McKay, *NovT* 23 [1981] 302–3).

2.b.   Since the phrase καὶ τὸν κόπον καὶ τὴν ὑπομονήν σου is probably to be understood as including the two major aspects of the ἔργα of the Ephesians, the καί that introduces the two nouns should be understood to function in an explanatory or epexegetical way.

2.c.   Variant: (1) omit σου after κόπον]A C 025 fam 1611[1854] Oecumenius[2053] Andr f g i n 94 598 1773 2019 lat syr[ph] Victorinus (Haussleiter, *Victorinus*, 32–33); Tischendorf, *NT Graece*, WHort; B. Weiss, *Johannes-Apokalypse*, 161; Nestle-Aland[27]; *TCGNT*[1], 731. (2) σου after κόπον] ℵ 2351 Andreas Byzantine vg[ms] syr[ph] (Nestle-Aland[26] incorrectly cites Victorinus, where *opera tua* is only a marginal reading in MS Am2; corrected in Nestle-Aland[27]); von Soden, *Text*; Merk, *NT*. Since κόπος and ὑπομονή are the two types of ἔργα referred to, the insertion of σου is an attempt to coordinate ἔργα with κόπος and ὑπομονή, both of which are followed by σου (Bousset [1906] 203–4; Schmid, *Studien* 2:86).

2.d.   Variants: (1) insert καί] majority of MSS. (2) omit καί] A Andr/Byz[1328] bo it[1]. Since A is the only MS of any significance to omit καί, the omission was either the result of an error (B. Weiss, *Johannes-Apokalypse*, 74) or an attempt to indicate that the ὅτι clause that follows was not dependent on οἶδα.

2.e.   καὶ ὅτι can introduce an object clause dependent on the verb οἶδα ("I know . . . that"), or ὅτι can mean "because," and the entire clause can be construed as subordinate to the main clause that follows, καὶ ἐπείρασας . . . ἀποστόλους, which is the way in which this clause has been understood and translated here (Bousset [1906] 203f–4). The use of a comma after κακούς in Nestle-Aland[26] indicates that the editors understand ὅτι as introducing an object clause.

2.f.   Variants: (1) βαστάσαι] fam 1611[2344] Andr d f g h i[1685 2074] n[2429] 94 2019. (2) βαστάξαι] fam 1611[1611] Andreas.

2.g.   The construction here consists of a present substantival ptcp. from λέγω coordinated with a finite verb: τοὺς λέγοντας . . . εἰσίν; similar constructions occur in 2:9, 20; 3:9.

2.h.   Variants: (1) omit εἶναι] ℵ* A C 025 fam 1611[1854 2329] Oecumenius[2053] syr[h] vg. (2) εἶναι before καί] ℵ[2] 2351 Andreas Byzantine it vg[cl] Victorinus Primasius. Reading (2) is the obj. of the substantival ptcp. τοὺς λέγοντας and is placed after ἀποστόλους by most minuscules, and probably arose as a correction.

2.i.   καί is used here to link two clauses, the second of which is antithetical to the first, functioning as a καί *adversativum*, which can be translated "but" (see Blomqvist, *SGU* 13 [1979] 47, who is otherwise skeptical about the occurrence of καί *adversativum* in sources written by native speakers of Gk.); see 2:9.

2.j.   Since the clause introduced by καί provides the reason for the statement in the preceding clause, it may be translated "for."

3.a-a.   Variants: (1) καὶ οὐ κεκοπίακες] A C; κεκοπίακας: Andr a b[2059] c d. (2) καὶ οὐκ ἐκοπίασας] ℵ

2351 Andreas Byzantine. (3) omit] Andr l. Since the regular form for the second person sing. pf. active ind. is -κας, reading (1) is the *lectio difficilior;* B. Weiss (*Johannes-Apokalypse,* 161–62) regards κεκοπίακες as a scribal error.

4.a-a. Variants: (1) ἀφῆκες] א* C fam 1006[1841]. (2) ἀφῆκας] A 2351.

4.b-b. The noun cluster τὴν ἀγάπην σου τὴν πρώτην, "my first love," with a poss. pronoun between the articular noun and its articular adj., is an unusual construction in Greek but common in Hebrew and found eight times in Revelation (2:4, 13, 19; 3:12; 10:2, 5; 11:17; 13:16; see *Introduction,* Section 7: Syntax). A different word order, including the omission of the article before ἀγάπην, is attested only in A: τὴν πρώτην σου ἀγάπην.

5.a-a. Variants: (1) πέπτωκας] A C 046 fam 1006 fam 1611 Oecumenius[2053] Andr f[2073] i[2042] 94 Primasius and Beatus (*cecideris*). (2) πέπτωκες] א WHort. (3) ἐκπέπτωκας] Andreas syr[ph] it[gig] vg (*excideris*).

5.b-b. The dative of disadvantage is used in the phrase ἔρχομαί σοι (the same phrase also occurs in v 16), where ἔρχομαι πρός σε is expected (Moulton, *Prolegomena,* 75).

5.c. Variants: (1) omit ταχύ] א A C 025 fam 1611[1854 2050 2329 2344] Oecumenius[2053] vg syr[ph]. (2) insert ταχύ after ἔρχομαί σοι] Andreas Byzantine it[t] vg[mss] syr[h] Primasius 2351. The phrase ἔρχομαί σοι ταχύ also occurs in 2:16, and the phrase ἔρχομαι ταχύ occurs five times (3:11; 11:14; 22:7, 12, 20). In view of the strong agreement of the important uncial MSS and the strong support of the version, it appears that ταχύ was added to v 5 on analogy with its occurrence in 2:16, as well as in 3:11; 11:14; 22:7, 12, 20.

6.a. κἀγώ, formed by crasis from the conjunction καί and the pronoun ἐγώ, occurs five times in Revelation (2:6, 28; 3:10, 21; 22:8) and each time places emphasis on the personal pronoun.

7.a. The aor. imper. ἀκουσάτω, "let him/her hear," is in the aor. because a specific message is being presented for those who ought to have the ability to understand it; the implications of the message are not the issue here. Cf. K. L. McKay, "Aspect in Imperatival Constructions in New Testament Greek," *NovT* 27 (1985) 215–16.

7.b. The verb λέγει is probably a progressive present (Burton, *Syntax,* 7–8) or a durative present (BDF § 318[2]); i.e., the message of the Spirit does not belong to the past but continues to be valid for the churches.

7.c. τῷ νικῶντι appears to be the obj. of the verb δώσω, in which case the pronoun αὐτῷ is redundant (an identical construction is found in 2:17; cf. 6:4; 21:6). Yet in the light of parallel constructions in which ὁ νικῶν is a pendent nom. or nom. abs. (see *Notes* under 2:26; 3:12, 21), it is more consistent to regard τῷ νικῶντι as a dat. of respect, and to consider αὐτῷ not as redundant but as the obj. of the verb δώσω.

7.d. Here the prep. ἐκ, "from," introduces a partitive gen. in an elliptical expression that could be translated "eat fruit from" or "eat the fruit of."

7.e. Variants: (1) omit μου after θεοῦ] א A C fam 1611[1854 2329] Andreas syr[ph]. (2) μου after θεοῦ] fam 1006[1006 1841] fam 1611[1611 2050] Oecumenius[2053] 2351 Byzantine latt syr[h] cop; WHort[mg]. Insertion of μου is influenced by its use in 3:2 (*TCGNT*[2], 664).

## *Form/Structure/Setting*

### I. OUTLINE

1. The Proclamation to Ephesus (12:1–7)
   a. The *adscriptio:* to the angel of the church in Ephesus (v 1a)
   b. Command to write (v 1b)
   c. The τάδε λέγει formula (v 1c)
   d. Christological predications (v 1c)
      (1) The One with the seven stars in his right hand
      (2) The One who walks in the midst of the seven golden menorahs
   e. The *narratio:* "I know your conduct" (vv 2–4)
      (1) Your deeds (v 2a)
         (a) Your effort

    (b) Your endurance
  (2) You do not tolerate the wicked (v 2b)
    (a) You tested the so-called apostles
    (b) You found them to be liars
  (3) You have endurance (v 3)
    (a) You have borne patiently because of my name (v 3b)
    (b) You have not become weary (v 3c)
f. The *dispositio* (vv 4–6)
  (1) Accusation: you have abandoned your first love (v 4)
  (2) Remedy: remember your original state (v 5)
    (a) Repent (v 5b)
    (b) Do the deeds you did before (v 5c)
  (3) Threat: if you do not do so (v 5d)
    (a) I will come to you
    (b) I will remove your menorah from its place
  (4) Concluding positive feature (v 6)
    (a) You hate the Nicolaitans (v 6b)
    (b) I also hate them (v 6c)
g. The proclamation formula (v 7a)
h. The promise-to-the-victor formula: access to the tree of life in the paradise of God (v 7b)

## II. HISTORICAL-GEOGRAPHICAL SETTING

Under the Roman empire, Ephesus, Smyrna, and Pergamon were the three greatest cities in the Roman province of Asia. Two of the three, Ephesus and Smyrna, were bitter rivals (Dio Chrysostom *Or.* 34.48). Though Ephesus was a great harbor city, she was of much greater importance administratively than commercially (Rougé, *Recherches*, 85–93, 126–33). Strabo describes Ephesus as the largest ἐμπόριον, "commercial center," in Asia (14.1.24). The narrowing of the entrance to the harbor by Attalos III (ca. 159–38 B.C.) apparently unwittingly facilitated the silting up of the harbor (Strabo 14.1.24).

The determination of the populations of ancient cities is problematic. First, ancient cities consisted not only of those who lived within the city walls but also those who lived within the territory controlled by the city. Second, there are very few explicit indications of the population of ancient cities, and even these are problematic (Duncan-Jones, *Economy*, 260–61). Third, there is no reliable way of determining population density, or the population that a water supply or agricultural produce will support. Most modern estimates of the population of Ephesus during the Roman empire are based on the notion that the city had at least 40,000 male citizens, apart from minors, women, and slaves, which if included would make an estimated total population of ca. 225,000. This was the conclusion of Beloch (*Bevölkerung*, 230–31), accepted by Broughton ("Roman Asia Minor," in *An Economic Survey*, ed. T. Frank, 4:812–16), but slightly reduced (to 200,000) by Magie (*Roman Rule* 1:585; 2:1446 n. 50). This view has also been maintained by Duncan-Jones (*Economy*, 260–61 n. 4). Warden and Bagnall (*CP* 83 [1988] 220–23), however, have shown that Broughton confirmed Beloch's estimate by incorrectly reading an inscription (*I. Eph.* 951). The inscription states that Aurelius Barenus entertained, in addition to magistrates, πολείτας χειλίους τεσσαράκοντα, a figure that means not 40,000 citizens but 1,040 citizens (though the editors of *I. Eph.* 951 erroneously understand the phrase to refer to "40,000 Bürger"). In a relevant passage in *Ep.* 10.116 (LCL tr.), Pliny writes to Trajan about the practice of people celebrating various occasions by throwing a party for magistrates and common people. "My own feeling," writes Pliny, "is that invitations of this kind may sometimes be permissible, especially on ceremonial occasions, but the practice of issuing a thousand or even more seems to go beyond all reasonable limits, and could be regarded as a form of corrupt practice." This indicates the impossibility of reading 40,000 rather than 1,040. This means that the figures of 225,000 or 200,000, while not impossibly large, are speculative and not based on any kind of objective estimate from antiquity.

Ephesus, an early Greek colony in the central portion of southwestern Asia Minor known as Ionia, is named after the mythical son of the river Cayster. The city is located on the south side of the Cayster river (now called Küçük Menderes). Because of silting over the centuries, the city is now located six miles inland. According to legend, the Ionian colonization was led by Androclus, the son of Codrus, king of Athens, who also founded Ephesus (Strabo 14.1.3; Pausanias 7.2.7; the most complete form of Ephesus' foundation myth is found in Athenaeus *Deipn.* 8.361), one of twelve cities in the Ionian league (Strabo 8.7.1). The other eleven included Miletus, Myus, Lebedus, Colophon, Priene, Teos, Erythrae, Phocaea, Clazomenae, Chios, and Samos. The earliest Greek loanword in Hebrew is *Yâwân* (Gen 10:2; 1 Chr 1:5), the mythical ancestor of coastland peoples including the Kittim (Gen 10:4; 1 Chr 1:7), which in turn is based on the Greek name *Iôn*, the eponymous ancestor of the Ionian Greeks (Euripides *Ion* 1575–88; Apollodorus 1.7.3), called *Iaones* or *Iônes* by Greeks (*Iliad* 13.685; *Hom. Hymn to Apollo* 147). Elsewhere in the OT *Yâwân* is used as the generic term for Greeks (Isa 66:19; Ezek 27:13; Joel 3:6[MT 4:6]; Zech 9:13; Dan 8:21; 10:20; 11:2) and referred to Greek settlements in Greece, Asia Minor, Cyprus, and Rhodes. Daniel mentions the king of Javan (8:21), the prince of Javan (10:20), and the kingdom of Javan (11:2), which refer to the Greek and Macedonian empire founded by Alexander and the Hellenistic kingdoms instituted by his successors.

Throughout its long and complex history, Ephesus was subject to a series of kingdoms and empires. The history of Ephesus can be divided into three periods (Keil, *Ephesos*, 12–30).

1. *Ephesus the Old Ionian City* (foundation to capture by Croesus, ca. 900 to 555 B.C.). Croesus, king of Lydia, captured the city ca. 555 B.C. (Herodotus 1.26).

2. *Ephesus the Greek City* (ca. 555 to 290 B.C.). The city was soon taken, along with Lydia itself, by Cyrus the Persian in ca. 546 B.C.. Ephesus was the only Ionian city that avoided participating in the abortive Ionian revolt against Persia (499–494 B.C.). After the Persian wars, Ephesus was part of the Delian League (an Athenian maritime confederacy), but revolted ca. 412 and thereafter sided with Sparta during the Peloponnesian war (431–404 B.C.); in 386, as a result of "the King's Peace," Ephesus was again under subjection to the Persians. When Ionia was liberated by Alexander in 334 B.C., Ephesus came under the control of a series of Hellenistic rulers.

3. *Ephesus the Hellenistic and Roman City* (ca. 290 B.C. to A.D. 1000). Lysimachus controlled the region around Ephesus after the death of Alexander (323 B.C.), and

pacified the region ca. 302 B.C. (Pausanias 1.9.7). He built a wall six miles in circumference around the city about 287 B.C. (Strabo 14.1.21). In 197, Antiochus III of Syria conquered the southern coast of Asia Minor and made Ephesus his second capital. Ephesus was subject to Eumenes of Pergamon in 190 and was under the Pergamene rulers until 133, when Attalos III of Pergamon died and willed his empire to Rome. Thereafter it became the official residence of the governor of the Roman province of Asia. Ephesus was originally located on Mount Pion but was moved by the Lydian king Croesus to a level region east of Pion. The worship of Ephesian Artemis predates the Greek colonization of Ionia (Pausanias 7.2.6; see Burkert, *Greek Religion,* 149–52). Ephesian Artemis was originally an Anatolian goddess of hunting and fertility called Cybele (i.e., Κυβέλη, or in transliterated Lydian Κυβήβη) in Phrygia and Ma in Cappadocia, and in Ephesus and Sparta, Opis (Macrobius *Sat.* 5.22.4–6) or Oupis (Callimachus *Hymn to Artemis* 204.240; Athenaeus 14.619b). The Ephesians later claimed that Apollo and Artemis had been born not in Delos but in Ephesus (Tacitus *Annals* 3.60–63; see Strabo 14.1.20). The earliest temple to Artemis was destroyed by the Cimmerians, ca. 660 B.C. This was rebuilt twice, followed by a major reconstruction by Croesus, ca. 550 B.C. (his name is incised on column bases now found in the British Museum), unfinished until ca. 430 B.C., and destroyed by arson in 356 B.C. According to Herodotus, the archaic temple was one of the more remarkable temples of his day (1.148). In 356 B.C. the earlier temple was burned and shortly thereafter was rebuilt under the supervision of the Macedonian architect Deinocrates (Vitruvius 1.1.4). The resultant edifice was considered one of the seven wonders of the ancient world (Pausanias 4.31.8; 7.5.4; see D. Knibbe, "Ephesus," PWSup 12 [1970] 254–56). The platform on which the temple was built measured more than 100,000 square feet. This rebuilt temple of Artemis, or Artemision (referred to in Acts 19:23–41), was located northeast of the city (in Asia Minor several important temples were located in places often remote from the center of town, such as the Didymeion of Miletus and the Asclepieion of Pergamon). The temple was a famous place of sanctuary (ἀσυλία) in the ancient world (Pausanias 7.2.8; Strabo 14.1.23; Jos. *Ant.* 15.89; Ps.-Apollonius *Ep.* 65; Dio Cassius 48.24.2). The inviolate character of the Artemision also made it one of the most important ancient financial centers in the ancient world, since huge monetary deposits were placed there from all over the Levant (Dio Chrysostom *Or.* 31.54–55; Caesar *Bell. civ.* 3.33; Plautus *Bacchides* 312; Aristides *Or.* 42.522; *CIG* 2:2953b; Nicolaus of Damascus frag. 65; Diogenes Laertius 2.51). Though few traces of the temple itself remain (it was destroyed by the Ostrogoths in A.D. 262 and thereafter served as a quarry for building materials), the great altar, which stood near the western façade of the temple precinct has been located. The central role of Artemis was reflected in the name of one of the months, Artemision (March/ April), during which the Artemisia, a festival including games was held (*I. Eph.* Ia.24; Xenophon Eph. *Ephesian Tale* 1.1–3). Octavian arranged for a cult to Rome and Julius Caesar to be established in Ephesus and Nicaea in the provinces of Asia and Bithynia, respectively, specifically intended for Romans living in those provinces (Dio Cassius 51.20.6–7), since Romans were accustomed to give divine honors only to deceased emperors. During the Roman imperial period, cities honored by being chosen as sites for the erection of temples to patron deities (e.g., Artemis) and the imperial cult assumed the title νεωκόρος, "temple-keeper" (see Acts 19:35 and *CIG* 2:2972, where Ephesus is described as a νεωκόρος τῆς Ἀρτέμιδος, "temple-keeper of Artemis"). The term νεωκόρος, earlier used of a "temple-keeper" (and which today is the designation for custodians of Greek Orthodox churches), was by the mid-first century A.D. applied to cities in Roman Asia that had been granted the right to build temples in honor of important deities (Friesen, *Twice Neokoros*, 56–59). Ephesus was a *civitas neocora* (an official title in the second century, which appears on local coins) no less than *four* times, i.e., first to Ephesian Artemis, and thereafter to three emperors including Domitian, ca. A.D. 90 (later transferred to Vespasian), and one for Hadrian, ca. A.D. 130 (Keil, *NumZ* n.s. 12 [1919] 115–20; Friesen, *Twice Neokoros*, 56–59). Coins from Ephesus depict the four "neocorate" temples (see Bean, *Aegean Turkey*, pl. 64; Dittenberger, *OGIS*, 481; B. V. Head, *Historia Nummorum: A Manual of Greek Numismatics*, rev. ed. [London: Spink, 1963] 498; *Brit. Mus. Inscr.* 481.4).The buildings excavated by archeologists include a library built in honor of the Roman governor of Asia, C. Julius Celsus Polemeanus (A.D. 106–7), a temple in honor of Hadrian (A.D. 117–38), erected toward the beginning of his reign (see Keil, *NumZ* n.s. 12 [1919] 118–20), a fountain in honor of Trajan, and traces of a temple in honor of Domitian (identified in 1960 by the discovery of the head and one forearm of a colossal statue of Domitian), perhaps originally dedicated to Vespasian (Keil, *NumZ* n.s. 12 [1919] 124–26; Magie, *Roman Rule* 2:1432–34; Bammer, *Altertum* 21 [1975] 33–34), and a temple of Serapis (second century A.D.), notable for its massive façade of eight stone columns forty-six feet high and nearly five feet in diameter. The dedication of a temple to Domitian, which also included a terrace, indicates the gratitude of the Ephesians, who prospered under Domitian (Knibbe-Alzinger, *ANRW* II, 7/2:816–21). In 29 B.C. the Romans in the province of Asia received permission to dedicate a temple in Ephesus to Roma and Divus Julius jointly. The theater (see Acts 19:23–41), which could accommodate about 24,000 people, has been excavated.

There is very little actual evidence for the presence of Judaism in Ephesus during the Hellenistic and Roman periods. Alexander the Great had granted civil rights to the Jews of Ionia, and they actually received *isonomia* (i.e., their own laws and customs were respected equally with those of the Greeks) from Antiochus II (Jos. *Ag. Ap.* 1.22). The presence of a synagogue in Ephesus is mentioned in Acts 18:26; 19:8; *I. Eph.* 4.1251 mentions ἀρχισυνάγωγοι and πρεσβύτεροι (presumably Jewish synagogue officials), though no archeological remains and comparatively few Jewish inscriptions have been found (Horsley, *NovT* 34 [1992] 121–27). Josephus indicates that there was a large Jewish community in Ephesus by the mid-third century B.C. (*Ant.* 12.125–126, 166–68, 172–73).

Ephesus, which reached its heyday in the Hellenistic and Roman period, was an important center for early Christianity and is frequently mentioned in the NT (Acts 18:19–28; 19:1; 20:16–17; 1 Cor 15:32; 16:8; 1 Tim 1:3; 2 Tim 1:18; 4:12). Paul wrote 1 Corinthians from Ephesus, where he had experienced an "open door," i.e., a ready acceptance of the gospel (1 Cor 16:8–9), and he also mentions that he had "fought with beasts at Ephesus" (1 Cor 15:32), though he probably is speaking metaphorically, borrowing a phrase from Hellenistic moral philosophy's description of a wise man's struggle with hedonism (A. J. Malherbe, "The Beasts at Ephesus," *JBL* 87 [1968] 71–80). Paul's first visit to Ephesus was rather brief, and he left Priscilla and Aquila there when he pressed on to Syria (Acts 18:19–21). They were instrumental in harnessing the abilities of Apollos of Alexandria, who had experienced only the baptism of John (Acts 18:24–26), like a number of others in

Ephesus (Acts 19:1–7). The length of Paul's second visit, narrated in Acts 19:1–40, is somewhat problematic, for Acts 19:8 states that he spent *three months* teaching in a synagogue, Acts 19:10 relates that he spent *two years* teaching and preaching in a rented hall, and, finally, Acts 20:31 states that he spent *three years* in Ephesus. Since the number "three" is probably redactional, while "two" may well reflect old tradition, Paul probably spent eighteen to twenty-two months in Ephesus (see G. Luedemann, *Paul, Apostle to the Gentiles: Studies in Chronology* [Philadelphia: John Knox, 1984] 178–79). While Acts 19 contains a number of exciting episodes (the baptism of disciples of John, vv 1–7; the seven sons of Scaeva, vv 11–20; Demetrius the silversmith, vv 23–41), there is very little about the Christian community at Ephesus. Irenaeus, however, claims that Paul did found a Christian community at Ephesus (*Adv. haer.* 3.3.4), which is implicitly confirmed in Acts 20:17, 28. Acts 20:17–38 narrates a meeting between Paul and the "elders" (πρεσβύτεροι, v 17, also described as "bishops," ἐπίσκοποι, v 28) of the church at Ephesus at Miletus, where he predicts that after he leaves (dies?) "fierce wolves will come in among you, not sparing the flock; and from among your own selves will arise men speaking perverse things, to draw away the disciples after them" (20:29–30). Since the deutero-Pauline letter Ephesians was probably not originally written to Ephesus but is a circular letter of very general character, it reveals nothing about Christianity there during the late first century A.D., when it was probably written (Kümmel, *Introduction*, 352–56). The brief proclamation to the church at Ephesus in Rev 2:1–7 shows no trace of Pauline influence (Schnackenburg, *BZ* 35 [1991] 56–58).

At the beginning of the second century, several varieties of Christianity appear to have co-existed in Ephesus (Koester, "GNOMAI DIAPHOROI," 154–55): (1) the church established by Paul, (2) a Jewish-Christian "school" (e.g., Cerinthus, Irenaeus *Adv. haer.* 1.21; 3.3.4), (3) a heretical sect called the Nicolaitans (Rev 2:6), and (4) a Jewish-Christian group led by John of Patmos.

Ignatius of Antioch wrote a letter to the church at Ephesus while he was on a forced march through the province of Asia on his way to Rome, ca. A.D. 110. Onesimus was the bishop of Ephesus (Ign. *Eph.* 1:3; 6:2), whom John Knox rather speculatively identified with the runaway slave of the same name in Philem 10, and who became an associate of Paul (Col 4:9). However, the name is a relatively common one, particularly for slaves, since it means "useful." Onesimus was accompanied by Burrhus, a deacon, and several other Ephesian Christians, including Crocus, Euplous, and Fronto (*Eph.* 2.1). Ignatius warns the Ephesians about false teachers who call themselves Christians and who are itinerants (*Eph.* 7:1; cf. *Did.* 11–13; Schoedel, *Ignatius*, 59).

By the late second century, it was believed that the apostle John spent his declining years in Ephesus and survived to the reign of Trajan, A.D. 98–117 (Irenaeus 3.3.4; Eusebius *Hist. eccl.* 3.1). At Ephesus he reportedly wrote the Gospel bearing his name (Eusebius *Hist. eccl.* 5.8.4) and was eventually buried there (Eusebius *Hist. eccl.* 3.39.5–6; 5.24.3). The Basilica of St. John was erected on the traditional site of his tomb during the reign of Justinian (A.D. 527–65). Later tradition also placed Mary, the mother of Jesus, in Ephesus, which is the location of the traditional site of her grave, though the place where she reportedly died is now a sixth- or seventh-century Byzantine chapel (Elliger, *Ephesos*, 200). Since archeological evidence makes it clear that the Church of Mary was not constructed under after A.D. 431, the Council of Ephesus, which convened on 22 June 431, could not have met there (Karwiese, *Marienkirche*, 27–28, contra M. Simonetti, "Ephesus," *EEC* 1:275). Nevertheless, the tradition that the Council met there may be an anachronistic statement based on the fact that the Council met in the Roman stoa south of the Olympeion, constructed by Hadrian but destroyed ca. A.D. 400; the Roman stoa was the basis for the earliest construction of the Church of Mary, ca. A.D. 511 (Karwiese, *Marienkirche*, 42–44). The presence of Mary at Ephesus, however, was opposed by Epiphanius (*Pan.* 11.24), who claimed that "we do not know if she died and if she was buried" (*Pan.* 78.11). Ephesus was the traditional residence, in later life, of John the Apostle (Eusebius *Hist. eccl.* 3.1). Timothy is remembered as the first bishop of Ephesus (Eusebius *Hist. eccl.* 3.4.5, a tradition based on 1 Tim 1:3; Titus 1:5). Ephesus is also the site for Justin's dialogue with Trypho the Jew (*Dial.* 2–8; Eusebius *Hist. eccl.* 4.18.6).

## Comment

**1a** τάδε λέγει ὁ κρατῶν τοὺς ἑπτὰ ἀστέρας ἐν τῇ δεξιᾷ αὐτοῦ, "Thus says the one who holds the seven stars in his right hand." τάδε, a neuter plural accusative form from the demonstrative pronoun ὅδε, was obsolete in Koine Greek even though it is found seven times in Revelation (2:8, 12, 18; 3:1, 7, 14). The form is found, however, over 250 times in the LXX (a translation of the Hebrew phrase כה אמר יהוה *kōh ʾāmar YHWH*, "thus says the Lord"). The unusual word order (object, verb, subject) follows the LXX (Rudberg, *Eranos* 11 [1911] 178). The phrase οὕτως εἶπε κύριος, "thus says the Lord," is essentially synonymous. In LXX Jeremiah, τάδε λέγει + *nomen sacrum* occurs only through the end of Jer 29, while οὕτως εἶπε + *nomen sacrum* occurs for the first time in Jer 30:1 and thereafter through the rest of the book. H. St. J. Thackeray argued that this reflected the work of two translators ("The Greek Translators of Jeremiah," *JTS* 4 [1902–3] 245–66; cf. id., "The Bisection of Books in Primitive Septuagint MSS," *JTS* 9 [1906–7] 88–98; for a careful assessment of this translational feature, see E. Tov, *The Septuagint Translation of Jeremiah and Baruch*, HSM 8 [Missoula, MT: Scholars, 1976] 56–58; for a different assessment, see S. Soderlund, *The Greek Text of Jeremiah*, JSOTSup 47 [Sheffield: JSOT, 1985] 212–14). In spite of its obsolescence, ὅδε continued to be used in official formulas to refer to something following (G. Thieme, *Die Inschriften von Magnesia am Maeander und das Neue Testament* [Borna-Leipzig: Noske, 1905] 23; Mayser, *Satzlehre*, 73–74). The phrase thus has an antique ring, not unlike the English expression "thus saith" (but see Rydbeck, *Fachprosa*, 88–97). As the Greek translation of the Hebrew messenger formula כה אמר יהוה, "thus says the Lord," τάδε λέγει is a prophetic speech form (see Acts 21:11; Ign. *Phld.* 7:3). In Hellenistic literature, the phrase τάδε λέγει Ζεύς, "thus says Zeus," is attributed to the priestess of Zeus at Dodona as an introduction to oracular speech; see A. Adler, ed., *Suidae Lexicon* (Leipzig: Teubner, 1928–38) vol. 2, s.v. "Δωδώνη." Similarly, the προφήτης, "prophet," of Zeus-Ammon introduces an oracle with the formula τάδε λέγει Ἄμμων, "thus says Ammon" (Plato, *Alc.* 2.149b). A saying of Bacchus is introduced by Βάκχος ἔλεξε τάδε, "Bacchus spoke thus" (Palatine Anthology, Garland of Philip 36.2; Gow-Page, *Greek Anthology*, 34–35). Frequently τάδε λέγει is used to introduce a Persian decree. Yet the form ὁ δεῖνα τῷ δεῖνι τάδε or ὧδε λέγει, "thus says so-and-so to so-and-so," which occurs in Herodotus 3.40, is *not* an adaptation of the style of Persian kings (as maintained by G. A. Gerhard, "Untersuchung zur Geschichte des griechischen Briefes I," *Philologus* 64 [1905] 53) but is an indigenous fifth-century Greek formula (M. van den Hout, "Studies in Early Greek Letter-Writing," *Mnemosyne* 4 [1949] 25ff.; H. Koskenniemi, *Studien zur Idee und Phraseologie des griechischen Briefes bis 400 n. Chr.* [Helsinki: Akateeminen Kirjakauppa, 1956] 156). The so-called oriental or Persian *epistolary* style is actually the style of Persian royal *decrees*. The style is occasionally imitated in fictional letters, e.g., "The king of kings, great Artaxerxes says to the Coans thus [τάδε λέγει]," Ps.-Hippocrates *Ep.* 8 (R. Hercher, *Epistolographi Graeci* [Paris: Editore Ambrosio Firmin Didot, 1873] 290). Several Persian edicts are quoted in the OT with τάδε λέγει as the introductory formula in the LXX (2 Chr 36:23; 1 Esdr 2:3; Jdt 2:5; Esth 3:13). The term λέγει (or κελεύει) is the characteristic form of an edict (Mason, *Greek Terms*, 127; Millar, *Emperor*, 221–22). A selection of Roman edicts (translated into Greek from Latin) includes Appian, *Bell. civ.* 4.2.8–11, in which the introductory formula is ὅτως λέγει, "thus says." Five edicts of Augustus from 7–6 and 4 B.C. are all introduced with λέγει (Ehrenberg-Jones, *Documents,* no. 311).

**1b** ὁ περιπατῶν ἐν μέσῳ τῶν ἑπτὰ λυχνιῶν τῶν χρυσῶν, "who walks in the midst of the seven golden lampstands." This participial phrase refers back to the description of the vision of the exalted Christ in 1:12–13, where the seven golden lampstands are interpreted as the seven churches in 1:20. The only added feature here is the fact that Christ is said to *walk* in the midst of the lampstands, which can only be an allegory for the unseen presence of Christ among the Christians of the seven congregations. This is a reference to the presence of Christ in *all* the congregations, a fact reiterated at the close of each of the seven proclamations by the refrain "Let the person with an ear hear what the Spirit announces to the *churches*." Bousset is correct in seeing a reference here to vv 4–5, in which Christ threatens to remove the lampstand of the Ephesians from its place unless they repent ([1906] 203), but the detailed prophetic knowledge that the risen Christ, speaking through John, possesses regarding each of the congregations is reflected in the "I know" clauses in each of the proclamations (2:2–3, 9, 13, 19; 3:1b, 8, 15; see *Comment* on 2:2a).

**2a** οἶδα τὰ ἔργα σου καὶ τὸν κόπον καὶ τὴν ὑπομονήν σου, "I know your deeds, namely, your effort and endurance." The term οἶδα, "I know," occurs immediately following the christological predications in each of the seven proclamations (2:2, 9, 13, 19; 3:1, 8, 15), five times within the stereotypical phrase οἶδα τὰ ἔργά σου (2:2) or οἶδα σου τὰ ἔργα (2:19; 3:1, 8, 15). There is a close parallel between the triad of virtues here and those in 1 Thess 1:3: "remembering before our God and Father your work of faith [τοῦ ἔργου τῆς πίστεως] and labor of love [τοῦ κόπου τῆς ἀγάπης] and steadfastness of hope [τῆς ὑπομονῆς τῆς ἐλπίδος] in our Lord Jesus Christ." This close association of the three nouns ἔργα, κόπος, and ὑπομονή in two different literary contexts suggests a traditional formulation, despite the fact that in 1 Thess 1:3 these nouns are linked with πίστις, ἐλπίς, and ἀγάπη in the genitive. The term ἔργον occurs twenty times in Revelation but has a relatively heavy concentration in Rev 2–3, where it occurs twelve times. The term οἶδα (and synonyms) is also occasionally found introducing the body of letters, e.g., Dionysius Antiochenus *Ep.* 39 (Hercher, *Epistolographi graeci,* 266), Isocrates *Ep.* 2 (Hercher, *Epistolographi graeci,* 320), and Ps.-Hippocrates *Ep.* 14 (Hercher, *Epistolographi graeci,* 295). In providing models for letters of repentance and mixed letters, Ps.-Libanius *Epistolary Styles* 63, 92 (= Ps.-Proclus 12, 41 in Hercher, *Epistolographi graeci,*

9, 13) begins with οἶδα. In Greek letters, the use of a verb for "to know" or "to learn," indicating the reception of information, often marks the transition to the main part of the letter (Ign. *Magn.* 1:1; *Trall.* 1:1). Yet the same expression is often found in edicts, e.g., the edict of Claudius, which has the typical verb of declaration (λέγει, "says") followed by ἐπιγνούς ἀνέκαθεν, "having known from the first" (Jos. *Ant.* 19.281). Yet in spite of the conventional formulaic use of οἶδα, something much deeper is being referred to, namely, the knowledge that the exalted Jesus has of all human affairs upon the earth.

The translation "your deeds, namely, your effort and endurance," reflects the view that the first καί is epexegetical and that the two nouns that follow, τὸν κόπον, "effort," and τὴν ὑπομονήν, "endurance," are both qualified by the possessive pronoun σου, "your," and therefore are two aspects of the ἔργα, "deeds," of the Ephesian Christians (Bousset [1906] 203; Lohmeyer, 21–22). The noun κόπος, "effort," is a cognate of the verb κοπιᾶν, "to give up" (see Louw-Nida, § 25.289) in v 3; this is an example of deliberate paronomasia (Charles, 1:49; BDF § 481.1; Turner, *Syntax,* 148), i.e., the use of the same word or word-stem with different meanings in close proximity. For other examples of paronomasia, see Rev 2:2b, 22; 3:10; 11:18; 14:8; 18:6[3x], 20, 21; 22:18, 19 (see BDF § 488.1; Turner, *Syntax,* 148).

**2b** καὶ ὅτι οὐ δύνῃ βαστάσαι κακούς, "Because you cannot bear wicked people." The author again uses paronomasia or a pun, for the two aorist verbs βαστάσαι and ἐβάστασας (v 3) occur in close proximity (L. L. Thompson, *Revelation,* 49); in both instances the verb has the same meaning, but the first occurrence is used negatively, the second positively: that the Ephesians cannot "endure" wicked people, while they are "enduring" for the sake of Christ. The term κακοί, "wicked people," refers to the self-styled apostles mentioned in v 2c. The κακοί represent a generic type of which the false ἀπόστολοι are specific types.

**2c** καὶ ἐπείρασας τὰς λέγοντας ἑαυτοὺς ἀποστόλους καὶ οὐκ εἰσίν καὶ εὗρες αὐτοὺς ψευδεῖς, "and so have tested those who call themselves 'apostles,' but who really are not, for you found them liars." This is one of several instances reflected in the seven proclamations that reveal conflict between competing authorities within Christian congregations (see 2:6, 14–15, 20–23). Some have suggested that the κακοί of v 2b, clearly identical with the false ἀπόστολοι of v 2c, are also identical with the Nicolaitans mentioned in v 6 (Bousset [1906] 204; Kraft, 56; Müller, 102), or (more likely) that the Nicolaitans are a specific type of the generic group of κακοί. However, the verbs in v 2 are in the aorist tense: ἐπείρασας, "endured," εὗρες, "found," indicating that the episode involving the testing and unmasking of the false apostles was an event of the *past* (just *how* long ago, of course, cannot be determined), while the verbs in v 6 describing the Nicolaitans are in the *present* tense, indicating that they are a continuing threat. For this reason it is doubtful that the "so-called apostles" of 2:2 are identical with the Nicolaitans of 2:6, who are also mentioned as opponents in Pergamon (2:15), where no mention is made of any claim to be apostles. Even though the term "Nicolaitan" is absent from the proclamation to Thyatira, the opponents there may belong to this same group as well (Müller, 96–99; Karrer, *Brief,* 195–203). Conflict within Christian communities was endemic in the early church (see Matt 7:15–23), though in each document in which such conflict is evident, only the viewpoint of one side is represented. Since opponents are usually castigated with an arsenal of stereotypical insults, it is difficult if not impossible to discover the *real* issues in the conflict.

The Ephesian Christians have apparently "tested" (ἐπείρασας) the so-called apostles and found them to be charlatans. The notion that it is necessary to test or examine various types of Christian leaders to determine whether they are legitimate is probably based ultimately on the motif of testing prophets in the OT (Aune, *Prophecy*, 87–88). In the NT and early Christian literature, it is primarily *prophets* who are tested (1 Cor 14:29; 1 John 4:1–3; *Did.* 11:7–12; see Aune, *Prophecy*, 217–29), and perhaps by analogy or extension the notion of testing was applied to other early Christian leaders such as apostles (1 Thess 5:21; Rev 2:2; *Did.* 11:3–6), teachers (*Did.* 11:1–2), or just ordinary Christians (*Did.* 12:1–5).

The term ἀπόστολος occurs three times in Revelation (2:2; 18:20; 21:14) and is used with three different meanings (see *Comments* on 18:20; 21:14).

> Brief summary of the three different meanings: (1) In anticipation of the discussion below, in 2:2 "apostle" is a term for a special messenger, an itinerant missionary, whose legitimacy could be confirmed or disconfirmed by certain unstated criteria (as in *Did.* 11). (2) In 18:20 "saints and apostles and prophets" are explicitly victims of "Babylon" who (at least metaphorically) witness her destruction from heaven, so "apostles" refers to a restricted group of special messengers, including but not necessarily limited to the Twelve. (3) In 21:14, in the phrase "the Twelve Apostles," the technical term "the Twelve" is used to qualify the vaguer expression "apostles" (as in 18:20), and therefore implicitly excludes Paul.

In the earliest extant Christian literature, the Pauline letters, while the term ἀπόστολος is used in a variety of ways (Georgi, *Gegner*, 39–49; Hahn, *KD* 20 [1974] 56–61; Schille, *Kollegialmission*, 13–18; Ysebaert, *Amtsterminologie*, 5–7), οἱ ἀπόστολοι is *never* clearly used in the sense of "the [Twelve] apostles" (except in the Deutero-Pauline letters), a meaning that is consciously emphasized, though not invented, by the author of Luke-Acts. Of the eighty occurrences of ἀπόστολος in the NT, sixty-nine occur in these two constituent bodies of literature, the *Corpus Paulinum* (including nine occurrences in the Deutero-Pauline letters) and Luke-Acts. ἀπόστολος occurs thirty-five times in the Pauline letters and thirty-four times in Luke-Acts. The term occurs with surprising rarity in the other Gospels (Matt 10:2; Mark 3:14, 30; John 13:16), suggesting that "apostleship" is a post-Easter development that has been grafted onto the undoubtedly earlier conception of "the Twelve" (Agnew, *JBL* 105 [1986] 78). Paul's opponents apparently called themselves "apostles" (2 Cor 11:5; 12:11; Georgi, *Gegner*, 39). This is confirmed by the fact that Paul thought it necessary to coin the term ψευδαπόστολος, "false apostle" (used in the plural in 2 Cor 11:13), a term that occurs very few times subsequently in early Christian literature (Justin *Dial.* 35.3 [Justin inserts this term in an allusion to Matt 24:11]; Hegesippus in Eusebius *Hist. eccl.* 4.22.6; Ps.-Clement *Hom.* 16.21; *Apost. Const.* 6.9.6). In Rev 2:2 the term ἀπόστολος (meaning "messenger" or "emissary") probably refers to itinerant missionaries (Müller, 101–2), but it is not possible to deduce anything more specific about their character or origin (Ysebaert, *Amtsterminologie*, 17). The Tübingen school thought that the "false apostles" of Rev 2:2 were supporters of Paul or even Paul himself, though there is no evidence to support this proposal. It is striking that Paul's speech to the Ephesian elders in Acts 20:17–38 includes predictions of heretical outsiders (analogous to the self-proclaimed but false apostles of Rev 2:2) and heretical insiders (analogous to the Nicolaitans of Rev 2:6). In Acts 20:29 Luke's Paul refers to "savage wolves who will come in among you, not sparing the flock" (v 29), i.e., itinerant heretics, while a future internal threat is mentioned in v 30: "Some even from your own group will come distorting the truth in order to entice the disciples to follow them." Ignatius of Antioch also warned the Ephesian Christians, ca. A.D. 110, about the dangers of itinerant teachers (*Eph.* 7:1; 9:1). There are numerous references in the NT and early Christian literature to a broader, less technical Christian use of the term ἀπόστολος (examples of this usage are found in Acts 14:4, 14; Rom 16:7; 1 Cor 12:28; 15:7; 2 Cor 8:23; Phil 2:25; *Did.* 11:3–6; Hermas *Sim.* 9.15.4; 9.15.5; 9.25.2; Irenaeus *Adv. haer.* 2.21.1; Tertullian *Adv. Marc.* 4.24.1). Agnew (*CBQ* 38 [1976] 49–53) cites examples from the nonliterary papyri where ἀπόστολος means "courier" or "official courier," a usage very close to John 13:6. For John ἀπόστολος is not simply a descriptive term but a title of honor (21:14), since he thinks that those who have arrogated this title to themselves have done so improperly; v 2a indicates that the author regards these self-proclaimed apostles as κακοί, "wicked people." The term ἀπόστολος during the time of Paul was used in a variety of ways (Georgi, *Gegner*, 39–49; Schnackenburg, "Apostles," 296, 301). While Luke was the first author to consistently use the term οἱ ἀπόστολοι in the technical sense of "the [Twelve] apostles" (Ysebaert, *Amtsterminologie*, 7–8), this usage did not originate with him (Mark 6:7, 30; Matt 10:2; Rev 21:14; Holtz, *EDNT* 1:363). The term "apostle" also means "itinerant missionary" (Acts 14:4, 14; 1 Cor 9:5). There may also have been wandering missionaries who were broadly designated "apostles," both by themselves and by others (1 Cor 12:29; 2 Cor 11:3; Eph 4:11; *Did.* 11; see Hahn, "Apostolat," 58–61). The phrase "who call themselves apostles" implies that they are not legitimate apostles (just as in 2:20, Jezebel "calls herself a prophetess" but is considered a *false* prophetess). Other pejorative labels that reflect conflict *within* Christian congregations are "false brother" (Gal 2:4), "false teacher" (2 Pet 2:1; *Did.* 11:1–2; Justin *Dial.* 82.1), and "false prophet" (Matt 7:15; 24:11 [= Mark 13:22]; 1 John 4:1; Hermas *Mand.* 11.1–2, 4, 7; *Did.* 11:5–10; 16:3); it is likely that these designations, together with that of "false apostle," overlap in meaning (1 Tim 4:1–5; 2 Pet 2:1 [false prophet = false teacher]; *Did.* 11:3–6 [(false) apostle = false prophet]) and are simply used for those who deviate markedly from the beliefs and behavior of those who affix the labels. The situation reflected here is that itinerant Christian teachers, called "apostles," have sought entry into the Ephesian church but have been rejected. Speaking through the *persona* of the exalted Christ, John is fully aware of the identity of these "apostles" but thinks of them as charlatans. Since Ephesus may have been the center of his activity, he may actually have had personal experience in the testing and rejection of these "apostles." These apostles may be identical with the Nicolaitans named in v 6. Neither these itinerant "apostles" nor the Nicolaitans were able to gain a foothold in the Ephesian church. The problem of itinerant apostles and prophets, and how to determine whether or not they are legitimate, is specifically discussed in *Did.* 11–13. Several features of Rev 2:2 appear in *Did.* 12:1: "Let everyone who comes in the name of the Lord be received, but when you have tested [δοκιμάσαντες] him you shall know him and you will have understanding of the right [true] and the left [false]."

This sentence contains a distinctive rhetorical pattern found elsewhere in 2:1–3:22. It consists of three polysyndetic clauses (i.e., each clause is introduced with καί, "and"): (1) "and so [καί] have tested those who call themselves 'apostles,'" (2) "but [καί] who really are not," (3) "for [καί] you found them liars." In 2:9 the author again uses three similar polysyndetic clauses: (1) "and [καί] the slander of those who call themselves Jews," (2) "but [καί] are not," (3) "but [καί] are in fact a synagogue of Satan." A variation in the same pattern recurs in 3:9: (1) "Behold, I will cause those of the synagogue of Satan who call themselves Jews," (2) "but [καί] are not," (3) "for [καί] they are lying." The same structure might be expected in 2:20, where (1) "that woman Jezebel, who calls herself a prophetess [but is not]," (2) "and who teaches and misleads my servants."

**3** καὶ ὑπομονὴν ἔχεις καὶ ἐβάστασας διὰ τὸ ὄνομά μου καὶ οὐ κεκοπίακες, "And you have endurance and have borne patiently because of my name, and you have not become weary." Rhetorically, this polysyndetic sentence consists of three short parallel clauses, each with a finite verb, the first in the present tense indicating their current situation, the second in the aorist indicating their past behavior, and the third in the perfect indicating that they have been faithful up to the present time. The word "name" in the phrase "because of my name" is an example of metonymy in which "name" refers to the person of the exalted Jesus, so that the whole phrase really means "because of me." In the Gospels, Jesus anticipates that his followers will be hated "because of my name" (Matt 10:22; Mark 13:13 = Matt 22:49 = Luke 21:17). Suffering "because of the name" is also found in Hermas *Vis.* 3.2.1; *Sim.* 9.28.3, suggesting that this phrase becomes a *topos* used in contexts of early Christian suffering and martyrdom. A close parallel to Rev 2:3 occurs in Pol. *Phil.* 8:2, where the two motifs of endurance and suffering because of his name are juxtaposed: "Therefore let us be imitators of his endurance [ὑπομονῆς αὐτοῦ], and if we suffer because of his name [ἐὰν πάσχωμεν διὰ τὸ ὄνομα αὐτοῦ], let us glorify him."

**4** ἀλλὰ ἔχω κατὰ σοῦ ὅτι τὴν ἀγάπην σου τὴν πρώτην ἀφῆκες, "But I hold this against you that you have lost your first love." The adversative particle ἀλλά occurs frequently in Hellenistic Greek literature but just thirteen times in Revelation, and eight of these instances occur in Rev 2–3 (2:4, 6, 9[2x], 14, 20; 3:4, 9). The common connective particle δέ also occurs more frequently in Rev 2–3 than in the rest of Revelation (see *Comment* on 2:5). These two stylistic features suggest that the author is providing the words of the exalted Christ with what he regarded as a dignified style; see J. A. L. Lee, "Some Features of the Speech of Jesus in Mark's Gospel," *NovT* 27 (1985) 1–26. It is worth observing that 73.89 percent of the 337 sentences in Revelation begin with καί. In Rev 2–3, however, which contains 44 sentences, only 9 begin with καί, i.e., 20.5 percent. Not a single sentence begins with καί in the proclamation to the Ephesians, and the other occurrences of καί occur only at the beginning of each proclamation (2:8, 12, 18; 3:1, 7, 14), with the exception of the proclamation to Thyatira, where καί is used at the beginning of three of the eight sentences in the proclamation (2:21, 23, 26). The stereotyped phrase ἔχω κατὰ σοῦ [ὀλίγα] ὅτι occurs as part of the *narratio* here and in 2:14, 20. The phrase ἔχειν τι κατὰ τινός, "to have something against someone," occurs in Matt 5:23; Mark 11:25 (see Acts 24:19, where the synonymous phrase τι ἔχειν πρὸς τινά occurs; see also Acts 19:38; 25:19; 1 Cor 6:1), while ἔχειν κατὰ τινος, "to have [something] against someone," i.e., without the object, occurs in Hermas *Mand.* 2.2; *Sim.* 9.23.2. In Rev 2:4, ὅτι introduces a clause that is the object of the ἔχω but that must be translated in English as an object clause in apposition to an unexpressed object of ἔχω (such as τι or τοῦτο), i.e., "I have [something] against you, [namely,] that."

**5a** μνημόνευε οὖν πόθεν πέπτωκας καὶ μετανόησον καὶ τὰ πρῶτα ἔργα ποίησον, "Remember therefore how far you have fallen and repent and do the deeds you did formerly." The verb μνημονεύειν is used twice in Rev 2–3 (here and 3:3), both located in the *dispositiones* of their respective proclamations, and both refer to the moral and spiritual state that each congregation previously enjoyed but from which it has since departed. The emphasis on "remembering" is a recurring topos in moral parenesis that emphasizes that parenesis supposedly contains nothing new or original (A. J. Malherbe, *Paul and the Thessalonians: The Philosophic Tradition of Pastoral Care* [Philadelphia: Fortress, 1987] 7). The theme of "remembering" occurs in parenetic contexts in both the NT and other early Christian literature (Eph 2:11; 1 Thess 2:9; 2 Pet 3:1; Jude 5; *1 Clem.* 53:1), as well as in Greco-Roman literature (Dio Chrysostom *Or.* 17.2; 77/78.39; Plutarch *Quomodo adul.* 70d; Seneca *Ep.* 94.21). Reminding an audience of the teaching they received in the past (whether or not a verb meaning "to remember" is present) was a device frequently used in early Christian texts to encourage those addressed to live up to or to recapture earlier moral and spiritual standards (see Rom 15:15; 1 Cor 15:1; Gal 1:6–9; 3:2–3; 5:7; 1 Thess 1:5–10; 2:13–14; 4:1–2, 9; 2 Pet 1:12–13; 3:1–2). In the OT and early Judaism, the motif of "remembering" was sometimes used in contexts where people were summoned to repentance (Isa 44:21; 46:8–9; Mic 6:5; Sir 7:28; 23:14; 28:6–7; 38:22). This statement appears to imply that the author had a lengthy acquaintance with the history of each of these congregations. A stylistic peculiarity of this passage is the pattern οὖν . . . καί + finite verb . . . καί + finite verb (Ruckstuhl-Dschulnigg, *Stilkritik*, 74), found only here and in 2:5 in Revelation, but found ten times in the Fourth Gospel (1:39; 4:28; 9:7; 18:10, 12–13, 16, 33; 20:2, 6, 8).

**5b** εἰ δὲ μή, ἔρχομαι σοι καὶ κινήσω τὴν λυχνίαν σου ἐκ τοῦ τόπου αὐτῆς, ἐὰν μὴ μετανοήσῃς, "If not, I will come to you, and I will remove your menorah from its place, unless you repent." Verbs meaning "come" (ἔρχεσθαι and ἥκειν) are used five times in Rev 2–3 (2:5, 16, 25; 3:3, 11). Three times they are used in the negative sense of Christ's coming to judge a community (2:5, 16; 3:3) and twice in the very different and positive sense of the Parousia of Christ (2:25; 3:11). This is nothing less than a threat to obliterate the Ephesian congregation as an empirical Christian community. 1 Kgs 11:36 uses the term "lamp" (נר) as a metaphor for the tribe of Benjamin, which will always belong to Judah: "Yet to his son [Rehoboam] I will give one tribe [Benjamin], that David my servant may always have a lamp before me in Jerusalem." The phrase "before me" suggests that this is a cultic image drawn from the placement of menorahs (n.b. that there are ten mentioned in 1 Kgs 7:49) before the *paroket*, "curtain," that concealed the *Debir* or Holy of Holies. This may be the source of the imagery that John employs here. The presence of the connective particle δέ in this verse is one of seven occurrences in Revelation, three of which occur in Rev 2–3 (2:5, 16, 24); this is a subtle indication (along with the more concentrated presence of ἀλλά) that the words of the exalted Christ are presented in a slightly elevated style, at least as far as our author is concerned (see *Comment* on v 4).

**6** ἀλλὰ τοῦτο ἔχεις, ὅτι μισεῖς τὰ ἔργα τῶν Νικολαϊτῶν ἃ κἀγὼ μισῶ, "But you have this in your favor, you despise the deeds of the Nicolaitans, which I also despise." The adversative ἀλλά, "but," marks the beginning of a new thought, suggesting that the false apostles of v 2 are not to be identified with the Nicolaitans, a distinction made clear by the aorist tense of the verbs in v 2, while the present tense is used here. The Nicolaitans appear to be a minority group of Christians trying to gain a hearing and a more extensive following in the Ephesian church and are also mentioned in connection with the church in Pergamon (2:15); see *Excursus 2A: The Nicolaitans*. Some have regarded the Nicolaitans as a symbolic rather than a historical designation, primarily because apocalyptic literature rather consistently avoids the actual names of protagonists and antagonists. While this is generally true, Rev 2–3 is only apocalyptic because it is linked to Rev 4:1–22:5, which clearly belongs to the apocalyptic genre. It is worth noting in this connection that the name "Antipas," doubtless a historical figure, is mentioned in 2:13.

### *Excursus 2A: The Nicolaitans*

*Bibliography*

**Barrett, C. K.** "Gnosis and the Apocalypse of John." In *The New Testament and Gnosis*. FS R. McL. Wilson. Edinburgh: T. & T. Clark, 1983. 125–37. **Brox, N.** "Nikolaus und die Nikolaiten." *VC* 19 (1965) 23–30. **Fox, K. A.** "The Nicolaitans, Nicolaus and the Early Church." *SR* 24 (1994) 485–96. **Goguel, M.** "Les Nicolaites." *RHR* 115 (1937) 5–36. **Harnack, A.** "The Sect of the Nicolaitans and Nicolaus, the Deacon in Jerusalem." *JR* 3 (1923) 413–22. **Heiligenthal, R.** "Wer waren die 'Nikolaiten'? Ein Beitrag zur Theologiegeschichte des frühen Christentums." *ZNW* 82 (1991) 133–37. **Hilgenfeld, A.** "Die Christus-Leute in Korinth und die Nikolaiten in Asien." *ZWT* 15 (1872) 200–226. ———. *Die Ketzergeschichte des Urchristentums*. Hildesheim: Olms, 1963. **Janzon, P.** "Nikolaiterna i Nya Testamentet och i fornkyrkan." *SEÅ* 21 (1956) 82–108. **Kraft, H.** "Nikolaos und die Nikolaiten." In *Offenbarung*. 72–74. **MacKay, W. M.** "Another Look at the Nicolaitans." *EvQ* 45 (1973) 565–81. **Räisänen, H.** "The Nicolaitans: Apoc. 2; Acts 6." *ANRW* II, 26/2:1602–44. **Seesemann, L.** "Nikolaos und die Nikolaiten: Ein Beitrag zur ältesten Häresiologie." *TSK* 66 (1893) 47–82. **Sieffert, A. E. F.** "Nikolaiten." *RE* 14 (1904) 63–68. **Simon, M.** "De l'observance rituelle à l'ascèse: recherches sur le décret apostolique." *RHR* 193 (1978) 27–104. **Topham, M.** "Hanniqola'ites." *ExpTim* 98 (1986) 44–45.

The Nicolaitans are mentioned explicitly only in 2:6 (in the proclamation to Ephesus) and 2:15 (in the proclamation to Pergamon). In 2:6, it is simply said that the Ephesian Christians hate the works (i.e., the behavior) of the Nicolaitans. In 2:14–15, the "teaching of Balaam" is apparently identical with the "teaching of the Nicolaitans" and consists of eating meat previously sacrificed to pagan deities and the practice of fornication (Bousset [1906] 213; Caird, 38–39; Räisänen, *ANRW* II, 26/2:1606). It is likely that "Jezebel" and her followers, who are devotees of "the deep things of Satan" (2:20–24), constitute a group of Nicolaitans in Thyatira, since they also are said to practice fornication and eat meat previously sacrificed to pagan deities. The view that "those who say that they are Jews" (2:9; 3:9) should be linked with the Nicolaitans (as is done by Koester, *Introduction* 2:253) appears extremely doubtful (Janzon, *SEÅ* 21 [1956] 83–84). In connection with the charge of eating meat devoted to idols, it is not clear whether participation in cultic meals in pagan temples is involved or it is simply a matter of buying meat in temple meat markets. There is disagreement among scholars on whether the charge of sexual immorality should be taken literally. It is likely that the charge of sexual immorality refers to various forms of idolatry, such as eating meat previously sacrificed to pagan gods (Lohmeyer, 29; Kraft, 69–71; Caird, 44; L. L. Thompson, *Revelation*, 122, 227 n. 23; Räisänen, *ANRW* II, 26/2:1616–17). Earlier, scholars argued that the Nicolaitans were Paulinists since they, like Paul, ignored the Apostolic Decree of Acts 15 (Hilgenfeld, *Ketzergeschichte*, 220–26; Simon, *RHR* 193 [1978] 74–75). The Nicolaitans are considered by many modern scholars to have been Gnostics (Harnack, *JR* 3 [1923] 413–22). However, it is striking that in surviving Gnostic sources, the name "Nicolaitans" does not occur, nor does sexual libertarianism play a significant role. Further, in the Nag Hammadi texts, which represent a spectrum of ancient Gnostic sects and trends, the issue of eating meat sacrificed to pagan deities is not mentioned (Heiligenthal, *ZNW* 82 [1991] 135–36).

The Nicolaitans are also discussed by a number of church fathers (see Hilgenfeld, *Ketzergeschichte,* 408–11), though most (if not all) of these references seem to be based on Rev 2:6, 14–15 coupled with the name "Nicolaus," one of the seven deacons according to Acts 6:5, and a heavy admixture of legend and imagination. Irenaeus (*Adv. haer.* 1.26.3) and Hippolytus, who is dependent on him (*Ref.* 7.36.3; ed. Marcovich, *Hippolytus*), trace the Nicolaitans back to Nicolaus of Antioch, one of the seven mentioned in Acts 6:1–6; both authors clearly allude to Rev 2:6; 2:14–15. While little is known of this Nicolaus, Acts 6:5 indicates or suggests the following: (1) Nicolaus was a Gentile. (2) He was a native of Antioch. (3) He was a convert to Judaism. (4) As the last of the seven to be listed, his status may have been relatively low. (5) He may have shared a critical attitude toward the temple and the Law similar to Stephen, another member of the seven (Acts 6:14–15). (6) He may have fled Jerusalem when the persecution mentioned in Acts 8:1 began (Fox, *SR* 24 [1994] 489). In *Adv. haer.* 3.11.1, Irenaeus claims that the Gospel of John was written as a response to the errors taught by Cerinthus and the Nicolaitans. Clement of Alexandria (*Strom.* 2.20; 3.4) attributed the heretical movement of the Nicolaitans to the misunderstanding of the followers of Nicolaus of Antioch. Clement of Alexandria (*Strom.* 3.25.5– 26.3 = Eusebius *Hist. eccl.* 3.29.2–4) defends Nicolaus against charges of immorality and sexual indulgence and instead considers him motivated by chastity. Other patristic testimonia regarding the Nicolaitans are found in Tertullian *Praescr.* 33; *Adv. Marc.* 1.29.2; Epiphanius *Pan.* 25.1.1–7.3 (entitled "Against Nicolaitans" and containing novelistic elements about Nicolaus' relationship with his wife); Ps.-Tertullian *Adv. haer.* 1.6; Theodoret *Haer.* 3.1; Philastrius 33.1; Augustine *Haer.* 5. Brox (*VC* 19 [1965] 23–30) argues that like other Gnostic sects the Nicolaitans were concerned to demonstrate their apostolic origin and called themselves Nicolaitans after the deacon mentioned in Acts 6:5. Outside of Revelation, the earliest mention of the Nicolaitans is found in Irenaeus *Adv. haer.* 1.26.3, and it is not clear there whether he considers the Nicolaitans to be a second-century Gnostic sect or he has simply compiled a catalog of heretical sects and knows of the Nicolaitans from Rev 2:6, 15. Harnack thought that the second-century Nicolaitans were connected with the late first-century group in Ephesus and Pergamon mentioned in Revelation (*JR* 3 [1923] 413–22). The teaching of the Nicolaitans can safely be inferred *only* from Rev 2:14 (see *Comment* on how 2:15 should be construed grammatically), where eating sacrificial food offered to pagan gods and sexual immorality are mentioned. Since "Jezebel" is charged with beguiling the servants of God to practice immorality and eat food sacrificed to idols (2:20), it is probable that she and her followers in Thyatira are Nicolaitans (Barrett, "Gnosis," 128). Further, this group in Thyatira has learned "the deep things of Satan" (2:24), which may have meant to them "the deep things of God," a knowledge claimed by some Gnostics (Irenaeus *Adv. haer.* 2.28.9; Hippolytus *Rev.* 5.6). Lightfoot (*Horae Hebraicae* 4:204–5) speculated that the term "Nicolaitans" came not from Nicolaus, their supposed founder, but from the Aramaic word ניכולה, which means "let us eat" (the verb אכל has the identical triliteral stem in Hebrew and Aramaic); see *Tg. Isa.* 22:13: ניכול בסר אמרין, "saying, 'Let us eat flesh.'" In another etymological attempt to identify Balaam with the Nicolaitans, the name Νικολαΐτης is constructed from νικά + λαόν, "he conquers" + "the people," just as Βαλαάμ, i.e., בִּלְעָם, is constructed from בָּלַם *bĕlam* + עָם *'ām*, "he destroyed, devoured" + "(the) people." The difference, however, is decisive: "Balaam" is a pejorative name, while "Nicolaus" is a name of honor like "Alexander," meaning "king of men" (Seesemann, *TSK* 66 [1893] 49). The extremely speculative nature of these proposals leads to the conclusion that "Nicolaus" is an actual rather than a symbolic name (Räisänen, *ANRW* II, 26/2:1608).

**7a** ὁ ἔχων οὖς ἀκουσάτω τί τὸ πνεῦμα λέγει ταῖς ἐκκλησίαις, "Let the person with an ear hear what the Spirit announces to the churches." This formula occurs at the conclusion of each of the seven proclamations (2:11, 17, 29; 3:6, 13, 22) and occurs in a variant form in Rev 13:9. Placed at the conclusion of the seven letters, this expression functions as a *proclamation* formula, i.e., as an injunction to the audience to pay attention to the message that has (or will be) delivered. This proclamation formula (in German often labeled the *Weckruf* or *Weckformel*), or hearing formula (Enroth, *NTS* 36 [1990] 598), can function in at least two ways (Enroth, *NTS* 36 [1990] 598–99): (1) *esoteric function*, i.e., as an indication that what has (or will) be said has a deeper, hidden meaning (Dibelius, *TSK* 83 [1910] 471; Hahn, "Sendschreiben," 390); (2) *parenetic function*, i.e., the hearer or reader is enjoined to hear and obey what has (or will) be proclaimed (H. Räisänen, *Die Parabeltheorie im Markusevangelium* [Helsinki: Finnische Exegetische Gesellschaft, 1973] 85–86). The use of an imperative verb is characteristic. When the proclamation formula concludes an oracle, it functions as a *prophetic signature* and appeals to the hearers to hear and understand divine revelation; cf. 4Q267 = 4QDamascus Document[b] frag. 2, lines 5–6 (tr. García Martínez, *Dead Sea Scrolls,* 49): "open their ears and hear profound things and understand [everything that happens when it comes upon them]." In early Christian literature, other examples of the prophetic signature are found only in 1 Cor 14:37–38 and *Odes Sol.* 3:10–11 (Aune, *NTS* 28 [1982] 438–39). The phrase "open your ears" functions as an introductory proclamation formula in *Odes Sol.* 9:1. Proclamation formulas often introduce OT prophetic oracles, such as "Hear the word of Yahweh" (1 Kgs 22:19; 1 Chr 18:18; Amos 7:16; Jer 29:20; 42:15), often with the name of the recipient in the vocative (Jer 2:4; 7:2; 19:3; 22:11; Ezek 6:3; 13:2; 21:3). The proclamation formula, probably derived from usage in public assemblies and in courts of law (see Mic 6:2; Jer 2:4), was used to introduce instruction in the law (Prov 4:1; Job 13:6; 33:1, 31; 34:2, 16; Isa 49:1; 51:4) and instruction in wisdom (Deut 32:1; Prov 7:24; Ps 49:1; Isa 28:23).

The formula "Let the person with an ear hear" (and variants), an aphorism rooted in the Jesus tradition (see *Excursus 3A: The Sayings of Jesus in Revelation*), is found in six independent variant versions (Crossan, *Fragments,* 68–73). It occurs seven times in the synoptic Gospels (Mark 4:9, 23; Matt 11:15; 13:9, 43; Luke 8:8; 14:35) and six additional times as variant readings (Mark 7:16; Matt 25:29; Luke 8:15; 12:21; 13:9; 21:4). In noncanonical literature, the formula occurs six times in *Gos. Thom.* 8, 21, 24, 63, 65, 96 (once as an introductory formula, *Gos. Thom.* 24, with the other five occurrences as conclusions to parables); once in *Acts Thom.* 82; twice in the *Gospel of Mary* (BG 8502, 7:9; 8:10–11), four times in the *Soph. Jes. Chr.* (CG III, 97:21–23; 98:21–22; 105:10–12; BG 8502, 107:18–108:1); and ten times in the *Pistis Sophia* ([ed. Schmidt-Till] 1.17 [p. 16, line 4], 1.18 [2x: p. 16, lines 27–28; p. 17, line 17], 1.33 [p. 32, lines 9–10], 42 [p. 44, line 15], 1.43 [2x: p. 45, lines 5, 11]; 2.68 [p. 128, line 16], 2.86 [p. 128, line 16]; 2.87 [p. 128, lines 31–32]; 3.124 [p. 204, line 28]; 3.125 [p. 206, lines 29–30]). Closely related formulas include Matt 19:12, ὁ χωρῶν χωρείτω, "let the one who understands understand"; Rev 13:18, ὁ ἔχων νοῦν ψηφισάτω, "let the one who has understanding reckon"; and Ignatius, *Smyrn.* 6:1, ὁ χωρῶν χωρείτω, "let the one who understands understand" (perhaps an allusion to Matt 19:12; Lightfoot, *Apostolic Fathers* 2/2, 304).

The six versions of the sayings are the result of the variation of three separate elements: (1) opening variations that include constructions using a relative clause

(Mark 4:9: ὃς ἔχει ὦτα ἀκούειν ἀκουέτω, "who has ears to hear, let him hear"), a conditional clause (Mark 4:23: εἴ τις ἔχει ὦτα ἀκούειν ἀκουέτω, "if anyone has ears, let him hear"; cf. Rev 13:9), and, the most common form, the participial clause (Matt 11:15: ὁ ἔχων ὦτα ἀκουέτω, "the one who has ears, let [him] hear"; cf. 13:9, 43; Luke 8:8; 14:35; Rev 2:7, 11, 17, 29; 3:6, 13, 22), (2) reference to the *ear* (singular or plural), and (3) the verb "hear" (occurring once or twice: Mark 4:9, 23; Luke 8:8; 14:35; *Gos. Thom.* 8, 21; *Sophia of Jesus Christ*). The formula in Rev 2–3 has no verbally exact counterpart in any of the other texts cited above. Further, the verb ἀκουσάτω, is used *transitively* in Rev 2–3 but *intransitively* in the other texts listed above. Does the *singular* οὖς have any significance in contrast with the plural? In folklore, each ear can be thought of as communicating with a different internal faculty (S. Thompson, *Motif-Index of Folk-Literature*, D1721.3; J1289.8). Thus, the saying in Matt 10:27, "And what you hear in your ear, proclaim on the housetops," can be reformulated in *Gos. Thom.* 33a (and POxy 1.20–21) to read "What you shall hear in your ear [and] in the other ear, that preach fro·n your housetops." According to M. Marcovich (*Studies in Graeco-Roman Religions and Gnosticism* [Leiden: Brill, 1988] 57–58), disciples of the gnostic Jesus are expected to hear canonical sayings in one ear and their gnostic interpretations in the other.

Third-person imperatives occur sixteen times in Revelation in eleven different passages, and with the exception of 13:9, the clauses in which they are found all exhibit a strikingly similar structure: (1) definite article, (2) substantival participle or substantival adjective, (3) third-person imperative verb, (4) adverb or object clause (Mussies, *Morphology*, 323). Further, those that occur in the body of Revelation have often been considered to be interpolations or redactional additions.

(a) Seven of these third-person imperatives occur at the conclusion of each of the seven proclamations (2:7, 11, 17, 29; 3:6, 13, 22): (1) ὁ (2) ἔχων οὖς (3) ἀκουσάτω (4) τί τὸ πνεῦμα λέγει ταῖς ἐκκλησίαις.

(b) Rev 13:9: (1) x (2) εἴ τις ἔχει οὖς (3) ἀκουσάτω.

(c) Rev 13:18: (1) ὁ (2) ἔχων νοῦν (3) ψηφισάτω (4) τὸν ἀριθμὸν τοῦ θηρίου.

(d) Four third-person imperatives are clustered in Rev 22:11: v 11a: (1) ὁ (2) ἀδικῶν (3) ἀδικησάτω (4) ἔτι; v 11b: (1) ὁ (2) ῥυπαρὸς (3) ῥυπανθήτω (4) ἔτι; v 11c: (1) ὁ (2) δίκαιος (3) δικαιοσύνην ποιησάτω (4) ἔτι; v 11d: (1) ὁ (2) ἅγιος (3) ἁγιασθήτω (4) ἔτι.

(e) Two third-person imperatives occur in Rev 22:17: v 17b: (1) ὁ (2) ἀκούων (3) εἰπάτω (4) ἔρχου; v 17c: (1) ὁ (2) θέλων (3) λαβέτω (4) ὕδωρ.

The phrase "what the Spirit says to the churches" may imply that the Spirit is identical with Christ (E. Schweizer, *TDNT* 6:449) or that the exalted Christ speaks to each of the seven churches through the Spirit, i.e., the Spirit of prophecy (F. F. Bruce, "The Spirit in the Apocalypse," 340).

**7b** τῷ νικῶντι δώσω αὐτῷ φαγεῖν ἐκ τοῦ ξύλου τῆς ζωῆς, "I will allow the one who conquers to eat [the fruit] of the tree of life." Each of the seven proclamations concludes with a promise to the one who conquers (2:7, 11, 17, 26–28; 3:5, 12, 21). The use of the term νικᾶν, "to conquer, be victorious," can be either a military or an athletic metaphor, though in Revelation it is probably drawn from military language since it often involves the possibility of death. Athletic imagery is used in 4 Ezra 7:127–28, where life is compared to a contest "which every man who is born on earth shall wage, that if he is defeated he shall suffer what you have said, but if he is victorious [*vicerit*] he shall receive what I have said" (see Wis 4:2). The tree of life is mentioned four times in Revelation (2:7; 22:2, 14, 19). The reward for the victorious Christian is the privilege of eating (the fruit) of the tree of life in the paradise of God (22:2, 14, 19). This is a traditional Jewish eschatological conception reflected in the later *3 Enoch* 23:18 (tr. P. Alexander, in Charlesworth, *OTP* 1:308), which refers to the "the righteous and godly who shall inherit the garden of Eden and the tree of life in the time to come." This must be understood as a restoration of God's original intention for humankind that was frustrated by sin, for Adam and Eve were expelled from the Garden of Eden to prevent them from eating of the tree of life (Gen 3:24). A number of other Jewish texts use the *eating* of the fruit of the tree of life as a metaphor for salvation (*1 Enoch* 25:5; *3 Enoch* 23:18; *T. Levi* 18:11; *Apoc. Mos.* 28:4; *Apoc. Elijah* 5:6), and this metaphor continues ιο be used by Christian authors (*T. Jacob* 7:24). The tree of life is frequently associated with paradise, its traditional location. The tree of life is first mentioned in the OT in Gen 2:9; 3:23–24 (where the phrase is articular and refers to a well-known concept, and where the Yahwist writer uses it to frame the story of the tree of the knowledge of good and evil; see Westermann, *Genesis* 1:211–14). A more mythological poetic description of the primal garden of God is found in Ezek 31:2–9, in which v 8 specifically refers to trees in the Garden of God. The tree of life is not simply a symbol for eternal life alone but also represents the *cosmic center of reality* where eternal life is present and available, and where God dwells. The cosmic tree or tree of life represents the sacrality of the world in terms of its creation, fertility, and continuation and, therefore, is a tree of immortality. In ancient Egypt the "tree of life" provided the gods and the dead with wisdom and eternal youth. In Babylonian mythology, two trees are found at the entrance to heaven, the tree of life and the tree of truth. In M. Eliade's sevenfold classification of tree symbolism (*Patterns in Comparative Religion* [Cleveland; New York: World, 1963] 266–67, 283–90), two major categories are (1) the tree as a *symbol of life* and (2) the tree as the *center of the world*. There is evidence that the menorah, or seven-branched lampstand, represented the tree of life (Goodenough, *HUCA* 23 [1950–51] 451–52). In *Par. Jer.* 9:1, for example, "Jeremiah" refers in prayer to the "fragrant aroma of living trees, true light which enlightens me [τὸ θυμίαμα τῶν δένδρων τῶν ζώντων, τὸ φῶς τὸ ἀληθινὸν τὸ φωτίζον με]." For this reason the motif of "light" or "flame" is often associated with the tree of life (1QH 6:17–18; *Odes Sol.* 11:19). The tree or plant of life was a theme familiar in ancient Near Eastern mythology (see *Gilgamesh Epic* 9.266–95). Gen 3:22–24 indicates that eating the fruit of the tree of life gives eternal life, yet in ancient Near Eastern folklore, the tree, like immortality itself, was ultimately inaccessible (according to Gen 3:24, cherubim and the flaming sword guarded the tree).

There were two primary tree-of-life traditions in Judaism that eventually merged with one another. (1) One tradition often used in apocalyptic literature originated in Gen 2:9; 3:23–24 and involved *eschatological access to the tree of life in the heavenly paradise,* clearly a metaphor for the enjoyment of eternal life. In early Judaism Paradise was located in a heavenly region (e.g., Paul in 2 Cor 12:2–3, and the author of *2 Enoch* 8:1, where paradise is located in the third heaven). In Jewish tradition the tree of life is mentioned in a very similar context in *T. Levi* 18:11: "And he will permit the saints to eat from the tree of life" (καὶ δώσει τοῖς ἁγίοις φαγεῖν ἐκ τοῦ ξύλου τῆς ζωῆς); here the verbal similarity to Rev 2:7 is so close that *T. Levi* 18:11 must be a gloss dependent on Rev 2:7. Another passage dependent on Rev 2:7 is

*Apoc. Elijah* 5 (Charlesworth, *OTP* 1:750): "It will be granted to them [saints] to eat from the tree of life." *1 Enoch* 24:4–25:5 contains a tradition about the trees in the primal garden that is related to Ezek 31:2–9; 28:1–19; 47:6–12; see *1 Enoch* 32:2–6 (where Enoch is shown the tree of knowledge from which Adam and Eve ate). *2 Enoch* 8:1–3 describes Enoch's visit to the third heaven, where the tree of life stands among the other fruitful and fragrant trees. 4 Ezra 7:123 mentions the revelation of Paradise and the incorruptible, abundant, and healing-promoting fruit it contains, but the tree of life itself is not mentioned. And in 4 Ezra 8:52 we read "it is for you that paradise is opened, the tree of life is planted, the age to come is prepared, a city is built, rest is appointed."

(2) The other Jewish tradition uses the symbol of the tree(s) of life as a *metaphor for the elect community*. This tradition makes its appearance in Proverbs (in passages that appear independent of the Genesis tradition; the phrase is anarthrous), where the "tree of life" (i.e., the "living tree") is used as a metaphor for life itself (3:18 [quoted in 4 Macc 18:16]; 11:30; 13:12; 15:4). It probably also owes its origin to passages like Isa 60:21 ("Your people shall all be . . . the shoot of my planting") and Ps 1:3 ("He will be like a tree"). The cosmic tree motif, that is, a tree that unites a multilayered cosmos (underworld, earth, heavens) by its growth at the center of the *axis mundi,* "center of the world" (*EncRel* 15:27–28) is clearly found in 1QH 6:14–18, in which a tree planted by God overshadows the whole earth, its top reaches heaven and its roots go down to the Abyss, and all the rivers of Eden water it (see Ps.-Philo *Bib. Ant.* 12:8). This tree is clearly a metaphor for the *community.* In 1QH 8:5–6, the "trees of life" again represent the elect community, a metaphor partially drawn from Isa 60:21 (see 1QS 8:5; 11:8). This same notion is found in *Pss. Sol.* 14:3 (Charlesworth, *OTP* 2:663): "the Lord's paradise, the trees of life, are his devout ones." Similarly in *Odes Sol.* 11:16–21 the seer sees fruitful trees in Paradise, which are metaphors for believers. In *Apoc. Adam* 6:1, "fruit-bearing trees" is a metaphor for fertile descendants. *Gos. Truth* 36:35–37 (Robinson, *Nag Hammadi,* 46): "He [the Father] knows his plantings because it is he who planted them in his paradise."

The motif of ointment derived from the tree of life is found in an Ophite ritual (Origen *Contra Cels.* 6.27), and in quite a different context is also connected with the baptism of Jesus (Ps.-Clement *Recog.* 1.45). The oil of life that is derived from the tree of life is also found in early Judaism. *Adam and Eve* 36:2 (Charlesworth, *OTP* 2:272) refers to "the tree of his mercy, from which flows the oil of life," while in the parallel text in the *Apoc. Mos.* 9:3 (Charlesworth, *OTP* 2:273), Adam asks Eve and Seth to pray that God will "send his angel into Paradise and give me from the tree out of which the oil flows." They go to Paradise in search of the oil of life (*Adam and Eve* 40:1–3; *Apoc. Mos.* 13) but are told that this oil will only be available in the last times (*Adam and Eve* 42; *Apoc. Mos.* 13:2–3). This tree is specifically identified as the "tree of life" only in *Apoc. Mos.* 28:2. In the Gnostic *Ap. John* 21:16–22:9, "the tree of their life" (21:24) is depicted as deadly, rather than life-giving. In Epiphanius *Pan.* 1.26.5.1 (tr. F. Williams, *The Panarion of Epiphanius of Salamis [Book 1.1–46]* [Leiden: Brill, 1987]), an unknown Gnostic group is described: "And thus, when they read, 'I saw a tree bearing twelve manner of fruits every year, and he said unto me, This is the tree of life,' in apocryphal writings [this appears to be based on Rev 22:1–2, perhaps simply incorrectly attributed by Epiphanius to a noncanonical document], they interpret this allegorically of the menses." For this group menstrual blood, from twelve cycles each year, is the blood of Christ.

In later Judaism the centrality of the Torah led to the view that the tree of life symbolized the Torah. This view finds clear expression in *Tg. Neof.* Gen 3:24 (tr. McNamara, *Targum and Testament,* 121): "For the Law is the tree of life for all who study it, and everyone who observes its precepts lives and endures as the tree of life in the world to come. The Law is good for those who serve it in this world, like the fruits of the tree of life." In modern Judaism, the decorative wooden dowels on which the Torah scroll is rolled are called "trees of life."

**7c** ὅ ἐστιν ἐν τῷ παραδείσῳ τοῦ θεοῦ, "which is found in the Paradise of God." The term παραδείσος, "paradise," is an Iranian loanword (Old Persian: *paridaida;* Avestan: *pairidaêza*) meaning "park, garden," used in Greek from the fourth century B.C. with the same meaning (Xenophon *Anab.* 1.2.7; 1.3.14; 2.4.14; Jos. *J.W.* 4.467; 6.6; *Ant.* 7.347; 8.186; 9.225; 10.46, 226; 12.233; *Ag. Ap.* 1.141). Philo defines it as a dense place full of all kinds of trees (*Quaest. in Gn.* 1.6). The term is transliterated into Hebrew as פרדס *pardēs* three times in the later parts of the OT (Neh 2:8; Eccl 2:5; Cant 4:13) and occurs forty-six times in the LXX, most frequently as a translation for the Hebrew גַּן *gān,* "garden" (Gen 2:8, 9, 10, 15, 16; cf. Philo *Op.* 153–54; Jos. *Ant.* 1.37). The specific phrase παράδεισος τοῦ θεοῦ, "Paradise of God," occurs four times in the LXX (Gen 13:10 [Hebrew גַּן יהוה *gan YHWH*]; Ezek 28:13; 31:8, 9; cf. Isa 51:3 where the phrase παράδεισος κυρίου [Hebrew גַּן יהוה *gan YHWH*] is parallel to Eden) and rarely in Greco-Jewish literature (*Jos. As.* 16.14; 18.9; cf. *Pss. Sol.* 14:3, παράδεισος τοῦ κυρίου). In Gen 2–3, the Garden of Eden is located somewhere in Mesopotamia, and several other texts suggest more vaguely that Paradise was located somewhere on the earth (*PGM* III.541; *1 Enoch* 24:3–4; 32:3; Philo *Quaest. in Gn.* 4.51; *Adam and Eve* 40:1–2; Theophilus, *Ad Autolycum* 2.24). In Luke 23:43 it is used to designate the dwelling place for the righteous dead (see *1 Enoch* 60:8; 70:3; 77:3 ["Garden of Justice"]; *Adam and Eve* 25:1–3; 4 Ezra 7:36; *T. Abr.* [rec. B] 10:2; *Apoc. Sedr.* 9:1; 12:1; 16:6). In some texts it is nearly equivalent to "heaven" (*PGM* IV.3027–28). In early Judaism, Paradise was used as the heavenly region from which Adam was expelled and was specifically associated with the third heaven (2 Cor 12:2–3; *2 Enoch* 8:1). The new Jerusalem that descends to earth out of heaven from God (21:10) has within it the tree of life (22:2). Therefore Paradise, though considered in many strands of thought to be a heavenly region, will henceforth permanently be relocated upon the new earth. For the various early Christian uses of παράδεισος, see *PGL,* 1010–12. There is an important parallel in *1 Enoch* 24–25, where Enoch is escorted to a distant place on the earth where he sees seven mountains that form a throne upon which God will sit when he visits the earth, and where the tree of life may be found, the fruit of which will be given to the chosen (*1 Enoch* 25:4–6).

## Explanation

Ephesus was arguably the most illustrious city of Asia Minor. As a great seaport, it was a center of travel, trade, and commerce and the seat of the Roman governor of the province of Asia (central western Asia Minor). Ephesus was also the center of the imperial cult, boasting six imperial temples, one honoring Roma and Julius Caesar, two honoring Augustus, one honoring Domitian, and two honoring Hadrian (S. R. F. Price, *Rituals and Power: The Roman Imperial Cult in Asia Minor* [Cambridge: Cambridge UP, 1984] 254–56). During the reign of Domitian, Ephesus became the *neokoros,* or warden, of the imperial temple in the province of Asia (Acts 19:35; *I. Eph.* VI.2040). Since the mid-first century, Ephesus had also been an important Christian center (Acts 18–20; 1 Cor 15:32; 16:8). The Ephesian church receives a generally positive evaluation (vv 2–3). They have worked hard and have patiently endured persecution and ostracism at the hands of pagan fellow citizens and perhaps even relatives. In Christian literature of the late first and early second centuries, the importance of living exemplary lives and of enduring opposition and suffering patiently is emphasized (see Jas 1:2–4; 1 Pet 1:6–7; 2:11–18; 3:13–4:6). They are a pure church that has not been corrupted by false apostles whom they have tested and unmasked. The term "apostle" means "emissary" and was widely used in early Christianity for itinerant missionaries. Like other religious movements, Christianity had its share of charlatans. It was also a diverse movement, and beliefs and practices thought perfectly appropriate in one region might be regarded as deviant in another. Christian communities were scattered throughout the ancient world and were connected by providing hospitality to traveling Christians including apostles, prophets, and teachers (3 John 5–8). Some of these were primarily interested in fleecing the flock (Hermas *Mand.* 11.12; *Did.* 11:6) and in bed and breakfast (*Did.* 11:9; 12:1–4). The second-century pagan author Lucian of Samosata depicts Peregrinus (a Cynic philosopher who converted to Christianity and then back again) as just such a Christian confidence man and parasite (*De morte Per.* 11–13, 16). In *Did.* 11–13, an early second-century Christian document, elaborate "tests" for itinerant apostles and prophets are recommended. The Ephesians are particularly commended for opposing the Nicolaitans (a group also mentioned in 2:15). These apostles are probably not to be identified with the Nicolaitans named in v 6. John, of course, is an outsider no less than these false apostles and Nicolaitans; for him they are competitors for the loyalty of the community. The Nicolaitans are mentioned by several early Christian writers (Irenaeus *Adv. haer.* 1.26.3; 3.11.1; Hippolytus *Haer.* 7.24); they regard Nicolaus of Antioch, one of the first deacons mentioned in Acts 6:5, as their founder. This is probably speculation based on inferences from Rev 2:6, 15. For more on the Nicolaitans, see below under 2:12–17. Nevertheless, the church is faulted for "abandoning the love you had at first" (v 5). They are exhorted to remember their previous condition and with that in mind to repent and behave as they once did. If they fail to do so, Christ threatens to "come" to them (not in the Parousia but in an act of temporal judgment; see 2:16) and blot their community out of existence. These are enigmatic remarks, but they may point to the fact that second-generation Christians had developed a comfortable accommodation with the pagan world. John himself appears to be a separatist and intolerant of any other stance.

One part of the two-part conclusion of each of the proclamations is the formula "He who has ears, let him hear / what the Spirit says to the churches" (v 7a). In OT prophetic oracles, the recipients are frequently enjoined to "Hear the word of Yahweh!" (1 Kgs 22:19; Amos 7:16; Jer 42:15). The first part of this saying is found in various formulations seven times in the sayings of Jesus in the synoptic Gospels (e.g., Mark 4:9, 23; Matt 11:15; 13:9, 43; Luke 8:8; 14:35) and five additional times in variant readings. In other words, the motto "he who has an ear, let him hear" was closely associated with the traditions of the sayings of the earthly Jesus and probably originated with him. John uses the phrase as an appropriate concluding refrain for these prophetic proclamations of the heavenly Jesus.

# 2. The Proclamation to Smyrna     (2:8–11)

### Bibliography

**Bean, G.** *Aegean Turkey.* 2nd ed. London: Benn; New York: Norton, 1979. **Bogaert, P.-M.** "La 'seconde mort' à l'époque des *tannim.*" In *Vie et survie dans les civilisations orientales,* ed. A. Théodorides et al. AOB 3. Leuven: Leuven UP, 1983. **Borgen, P.** "Polemic in the Book of Revelation." In *Anti-Semitism and Early Christianity: Issues of Polemic and Faith,* ed. C. A. Evans and D. A. Hagner. Minneapolis: Fortress, 1993. 199–211. **Brongers, H. A.** "Die Zehnzahl in der Bible und in ihrer Umwelt." In *Studia Biblica et Semitica,* ed. W. C. van Unnik and A. S. van der Woude. Wageningen: H. Veenman en Zonen, 1966. 30–45. **Buschmann, G.** *Martyrium Polycarpi: Eine formkritische Studie.* BZNW 70. Berlin; New York: de Gruyter, 1994. **Cadoux, C. J.** *Ancient Smyrna.* Oxford: Oxford UP, 1938. **Dehandschutter, B.** *Martyrium Polycarpi: Ein literar-kritische studie.* BETL 52. Leuven: Leuven UP, 1979. **Eisenhut, W.** "Die römische Gefängnisstrafe." *ANRW* II, 1/2:268–82. **Fraser, P. M.** *Rhodian Funerary Monuments.* Oxford: Clarendon, 1977. **Hanfmann, G. M. A.** *Sardis from Prehistoric to Roman Times.* Cambridge: Harvard UP, 1983. **Hare, D. R. A.** *The Theme of Jewish Persecution of Christians in the Gospel according to St. Matthew.* SNTSMS 6. Cambridge: Cambridge UP, 1967. **Hemer, C. J.** "Unto the Angels of the Churches: 1. Introduction and Ephesians; 2. Smyrna and Pergamum." *BurH* 11 (1975) 4–27, 56–83, 110–35, 164–90. **Hengel, M.** *Eigentum und Reichtum in der frühen Kirche: Aspekte einer frühchristlichen Sozialgeschichte.* Stuttgart: Calwer, 1973. **Johnson, S. E.** "Early Christianity in Asia Minor." *JBL* 77 (1958) 1–17. **Jones, A. H. M.** *The Criminal Courts of the Roman Republic and Principate,* ed. J. A. Crook. Oxford: Blackwell, 1972. **Keil, J.** *Die Inschriften der Agora von Smyrna.* Istanbul: Istanbuler Forschungen, 1950. **Kimelman, R.** "*Birkat Ha-Minim* and the Lack of Evidence for an Anti-Christian Prayer in Late Antiquity." In *Jewish and Christian Self-Definition:* Vol. 2. *Aspects of Judaism in the Graeco-Roman Period,* ed. E. P. Sanders et al. Philadelphia: Fortress, 1981. 226–44. **Kraemer, R. S.** "On the Meaning of the Term *Jew* in Greco-Roman Inscriptions." *HTR* 82 (1989) 35–53. **Lohse, E.** *Synagogue des Satans und Gemeinde Gottes: Zum Verhältnis von Juden und Christen nach der Offenbarung des Johannes.* Münster: Institutum Judaicum Delitzschianum, 1992 (= "Synagogue of Satan and Church of God: Jews and Christians in the Book of Revelation." *SEÅ* 58 (1993) 105–23). **Mayer-Maly, T.** "Carcer." *Der Kleine Pauly* 1 (1964) 1054. **Mealand, D. L.** "Philo of Alexandria's Attitude to Riches." *ZNW* 69 (1978) 258–64. **Mommsen, T.** *Römisches Strafrecht.* Leipzig, 1899. **Pedley, J. G.** *Ancient Literary Sources on Sardis.* Cambridge: Harvard UP, 1972. **Peri, I.** "*Ecclesia* und *synagoga* in der lateinischen Übersetzung des Alten Testaments." *BZ* 33 (1989) 245–51. **Scholer, D. M.** "Tertullian on Jewish Persecution of Christians." *StudP* 17/2 (1982) 821–28. **Schrage, W.** "Meditation zu Offenbarung 2,8–11." *EvT* 48 (1988) 388–403. **Sevenster, J. N.** *The Roots of Pagan Anti-Semitism in the Ancient World.* Leiden: Brill, 1975. **Tomson, P. J.** "The Names Israel and Jew in Ancient Judaism and in the New Testament." *Bijdragen* 47 (1986) 120–40, 266–89. **Yarbro Collins, A.** "Vilification and Self-Definition in the Book of Revelation." *HTR* 79 (1986) 308–20. **Zeitlin, S.** "The Edict of Augustus Caesar in Relation to the Judaeans of Asia." *JQR* 55 (1964–65) 160–63.

### Translation

[8]*And to the angel of the church in Smyrna write: "Thus says the First* [a] *and the Last, the one who died* [b] *and came to life.* [c] [9]*I know* [a] *your* [b] *tribulation and poverty (yet you are actually rich!) and* [c] *the slander* [d] *of* [e] *those who* [f] *call* [c] *themselves Jews,* [g] *but* [h] *are not, but* [i] *are* [j] *a synagogue of Satan.* [k] [10]*Fear nothing* [a] *you will suffer.* [b] *Behold, Satan will shortly throw* [c] *some* [d] *of you into prison so that you might be tested,* [e] *and you will have* [f] *tribulation* [e] *for ten days.* [g] *Be faithful to the point of death, and I will give you the garland* [h]

*of life.* [11]*Let the person with an ear hear what the Spirit announces to the churches. The one who conquers will absolutely not* [a] *be harmed* [b] *by the second death."* [c]

## Notes

8.a. Variant: πρῶτος is replaced with πρωτότοκος, "first born," in A and Andr i[2034]. This, along with a similar replacement in 1:17, attested only in A, is theologically motivated and influenced by the single occurrence of πρωτότοκος in 1:5.

8.b. The phrase γίνεσθαι νεκρός, "to die," is also used in Rev 1:18.

8.c. ἔζησεν, "lived," is translated here as an inceptive aor. (with verbs denoting a state or condition), hence "came to life."

9.a. Variants: (1) σου τὴν θλῖψιν] A C P fam 1611[1611 1854 2329] Oecumenius[2053] syr[ph] cop. (2) σου τὰ ἔργα καὶ τὴν θλῖψιν] ℵ Andreas Byzantine. Since the phrase τὰ ἔργα σου καὶ (2:2) or σου τὰ ἔργα [καί] (2:19; 3:1, 8, 15) occurs four times in the seven proclamations, it is not difficult to see how it could be inserted at this point. τὰ ἔργα σου is also inserted before ποῦ κατοικεῖς in 2:13 (see *Notes* there), where it is supported only by Andreas Byzantine.

9.b. Variants: (1) omit τὰ ἔργα καί] A C 025 fam 1611[1611 1854 2329] Oecumenius[2053] 2344 it[gig] vg syr[ph] cop eth Primasius Apringius. (2) insert τὰ ἔργα καί] ℵ 2351 Andreas Byzantine syr[h]. Reading (2) was mechanically inserted on the basis of 2:2.

9.c-c. τὴν βλασφημίαν/ἐκ τῶν λεγόντων, "the slander of those who say." The prep. ἐκ + the gen. functions as a subjective gen. For this reason scribal improvement occasionally omitted the ἐκ (fam 1611[1854 2329] Oecumenius[2053] 2351 Andreas), though the presence of ἐκ in a subjective gen. is the *lectio difficilior* and therefore probably original (cf. the Pauline use of the subjective gen. in the phrase τὸ ἐξ ὑμῶν ζῆλος, "your zeal," 2 Cor 9:2). Further, the author of Revelation shows a marked preference for ἐκ (BDR § 212).

9.d. Variant: τήν inserted before ἐκ τῶν λεγόντων] ℵ syr. Bousset ([1906] 174) suggests that this reading is correct, since ℵ tends to omit the article.

9.e. Variant: omit ἐκ] 2351.

9.f. The inf. εἶναι (part of the construction ἐκ τῶν λεγόντων . . . εἶναι, lit. "of those who say that") serves to introduce indirect discourse (Votaw, *Infinitive,* 8–9).

9.g. Variant: Ἰουδαίων for Ἰουδαίους] C ℵ* fam 1611[2050 2329 2344] eth arm. This is probably the result of a mechanical assimilation of the case of Ἰουδαίους to that of the preceding substantival ptcp. τῶν λεγόντων (Schmid, *Studien* 2:98).

9.h. καί here links two clauses, the second of which is antithetical to the first and is therefore an instance of καί *adversativum,* which can be translated "but" (cf. Blomqvist, *KAI adversitivum,* 47, who is otherwise skeptical of this use of καί in texts written by native Gk. speakers).

9.i. The conjunction ἀλλά belongs to the same semantic field as the previous καί, which functions as a καί *adversativum* (cf. *Note* 9.h.).

9.j. The verb εἰσίν has been elided for stylistic reasons.

9.k. In the phrase συναγωγὴ τοῦ σατανᾶ, the gen. τοῦ σατανᾶ, "of Satan," can be construed as a descriptive gen., i.e., "a Satanic synagogue," or (more likely) a possessive gen., i.e., "a synagogue belonging to Satan." A close (antithetical) parallel is the phrase συναγωγὴ τοῦ κυρίου (Num 16:3; 20:4; 26:9; 31:16), which is also a possessive gen., "the assembly belonging to the Lord." There are other instances in which συναγωγή is followed by a proper noun in the gen., such as "the synagogue of the Freedman, of the Cyrenians, of the Alexandrians" (Acts 6:9), or "the synagogue of the Jews" (Acts 13:5; 14:1; 17:1), or "an assembly of righteous men" (Hermas, *Mand.* 11.9, 13, 14), a gen. of content or apposition, i.e., "a synagogue consisting of Jews" (BDF § 167; BDR § 167). For parallel expressions in Hellenistic Jewish literature, see *T. Benj.* 11:2–3, where the phrases συναγωγὴ τῶν ἐθνῶν, "assembly of the Gentiles," and συναγωγαὶ ἐθνῶν, "assemblies of the Gentiles," are part of a Christian interpolation referring to Christian gatherings consisting of Gentiles (Hollander–de Jonge, *Testaments,* 82, 443–44). See also *Pss. Sol.* 17:16, συναγωγαὶ ὁσιων, "the synagogues of the pious"; *CIJ* 1.718 συν]αγωγὴ Ἑβρ[αίων], "synagogue of the Hebrews."

10.a. Variants: (1) μηδέν] ℵ Andreas Byzantine; Tischendorf, *NT Graece;* WHort[marg], Bousset (1906) 209; von Soden, *Text.* (2) μή instead of μηδέν] A C 046 fam 1611[2050] Andr d l Ø[254]; Byz 1[911] Byz 4[141] Byz 12[627 2048] eth bo arm; WHort; B. Weiss, *Johannes-Apokalypse;* Merk, *NT;* Charles, 2:247. Variant (1) is the *lectio difficilior* and therefore probably original, since μηδέν (acc. sing. neut.) does not agree with the following pronoun ἅ (nom. or acc. pl. neut.), thus explaining the correction of μηδέν to μή (Schmid,

*Studien* 2:86–87). The substitution of μή for μηδέν, on the other hand, can be explained by the formulaic character of the phrase μὴ φοβοῦ/μὴ φοβεῖσθε (Rev 1:17; Matt 10:28, 31; 14:27; 17:7; 28:10; Mark 5:36; 6:50; Luke 1:13, 30; 2:10; 5:10; 8:50; 12:7, 32; John 6:20; 12:15; Acts 18:9; 27:24; *Adam and Eve* 16:5; 18:3; 21:4; *1 Enoch* 104:6; *Jos. As.* 26:2; 28:7). Variant (1) is probably original because it is the *lectio difficilior* despite the usually significant agreement between A and C.

10.b. Variants: (1) πάσχειν] ℵ A C fam 1611¹⁶¹¹ Oecumenius²⁰⁵³ Andreas. (2) πάθειν] fam 1006 fam 1611¹⁸⁵⁴ ²⁰⁵⁰ ²³²⁹ 2351 Andr d i²⁰⁴² n⁻²⁴²⁹ 94 Byzantine.

10.c. Variants: (1) βάλλειν] *lectio originalis*. (2) βάλειν] fam 1006 fam 1611¹⁶¹¹ ²⁰⁵⁰ Byzantine. (3) λάβειν] 2351. Reading (3) is the result of metathesis.

10.d. The prep. phrase ἐξ ὑμῶν, "from/of you," is a partitive gen. (intensified by the prep. ἐκ), which functions as the *obj.* of the periphrasis μέλλει βάλλειν, "will throw"; cf. BDR § 164. The partitive gen. can be used as the obj. of a verb when the entire obj. is not affected by the action of the verb. Therefore an indefinite pl. obj., such as τινας, "some," is understood. For other examples of the partitive gen. functioning as the obj. of the verb, cf. 2:7; 2:17 (simple partitive gen.); 5:9. See *Introduction*, Section 7: Syntax, V. Cases, under "partitive genitive." Since the entire congregation will not be affected, John cannot continue the literary device of addressing the congregation through the angel using second-person sing. pronouns and verb forms. He could hardly express the idea "some of you" with the phrase ἐξ σου, so he had to drop the device and address the congregation with the pl. pronoun ὑμῶν, "of you [plural]."

10.e-e. Variant: omit καὶ ἕξετε θλῖψιν] it^gig Tertullian (*Scorp.* 12).

10.f. ἕξετε, "you will have," is a fut. ind., which can be taken as the second coordinated verb in the preceding ἵνα clause, ἵνα πειρασθῆτε καὶ ἕξετε, "with the result that you will be tempted and you will have," or it can be taken as a separate clause introduced with καί (Bousset [1906] 209 n. 6). Because of a tendency to understand both verbs as part of the same subordinate ἵνα clause, some scribes corrected ἕξετε to read ἔχητε, a present subj., in conformity with πειρασθῆτε. Variants: (1) ἕξετε] ℵ Byzantine; Tischendorf, *NT Graece;* B. Weiss, *Johannes-Apokalypse;* Merk, *NT;* Nestle-Aland²⁷; UBSGNT⁴; Schmid, *Studien* 2:98–99. (2) ἔχητε] A 025 fam 1611¹⁸⁵⁴ ²³⁴⁴ 254 598 2019 2038 Andr e²⁰⁵⁷ Andr n²⁰⁶⁵ Primasius WHort; Charles, 2:247). Yet is it possible that the author intended both the aor. subj. pass. πειρασθῆτε *and* the fut. ind. ἕξετε to be coordinated within a single ἵνα clause? *First,* the author of Revelation uses the rare construction ἵνα + fut. ind. in ten other passages (3:9 [two fut. inds.]; 6:4, 11; 8:3; 9:4, 5, 20; 13:12; 14:13; 22:14; only seven other instances occur in the rest of the NT: Luke 14:10; 20:10; John 7:3; Acts 21:24; 1 Cor 9:18; Gal 2:4; Eph 6:3). MS A has a propensity to use the fut. ind. in ἵνα clauses, where it occurs sixteen times (2:22, 25; 3:9[2x]; 6:4, 11; 8:3; 9:4, 5, 20; 13:12; 14:13; 15:4; 17:17; 18:14; 22:14; cf. Mussies, *Morphology*, 322). ἵνα + fut. ind. is occasionally found in late Gk.; cf. POxy 6.939, line 19: ἵνα σε εὐθυμότερον καταστήσω, "that I may make you more cheerful"; cf. POxy 7.1068, lines 5, 19 (MM, 304). In later Christian authors, cf. *PGL*, 673.1. *Second,* Eph 6:3, which alludes to two OT passages, Exod 20:12; Deut 5:16, includes both an aor. subjunctive and a fut. ind. within a single ἵνα clause: ἵνα εὖ σοι γένηται [aor. subjunctive] καὶ ἔσῃ [fut. ind.] μακροχρόνιος ἐπὶ τῆς γῆς, "that it might be good for you and you might live long upon the earth." Although this saying is probably dependent on two LXX passages, Exod 20:12; Deut 5:16, in neither passage is ἵνα used with the fut. ind. That means that the author of Ephesians, writing ca. A.D. 90, like the author of Revelation, uses two verbs dependent on ἵνα, an aor. subjunctive and a fut. ind. *Third,* since it is not always easy to draw a hard and fast line dividing intention, anticipation, and will, there is inevitable overlap in the use of the fut. ind. and the subjunctive and the imper. (McKay, *Grammar*, 148). Nevertheless, it is likely that ἵνα πειρασθῆτε and καὶ ἕξετε form the basis of two separate clauses.

10.g. Variants: (1) ἡμερῶν] Andreas. (2) ἡμέρας] fam 1006 fam 1611¹⁶¹¹ 2351 Andr i²⁰⁴² ²⁰⁷⁴ n⁻²⁴²⁹ 94 Byzantine.

10.h. στέφανος, "wreath, garland, crown," is here rendered "garland." The term διάδεμα, more appropriately translated "diadem, crown" is found three times in Revelation (12:3; 13:1; 19:12).

11.a. The emphatic use of the double negative οὐ μή is the strongest way of negating a fut. event or condition (Moulton, *Prolegomena*, 187–92; BDF § 365). While οὐ μή occurs ninety-six times in the NT, it is concentrated in quotations or allusions to the LXX (thirteen times) and frequently in the Gospels in the words of Jesus. οὐ μή occurs sixteen times in Revelation, thirteen times with the aor. subjunctive (2:11; 3:3, 12; 15:4; 18:7, 21, 22[3x], 23[2x]); 21:25, 27) and three times with the fut. ind. (3:5; 9:6; 18:14). In several instances οὐ μή occurs in passages alluding to the LXX (15:4). It occurs four times in Rev 2–3, providing (together with other stylistic features) a somewhat dignified level of discourse (2:11; 3:3, 5, 12), and eight times in Rev 18 (vv 7, 14, 21, 22[3x], 23[2x]), where it appears to function in a similar way.

11.b. ἀδικηθῇ is a prohibitory subjunctive used here with the emphatic negative οὐ μή (Burton, *Syntax* § 76).

11.c. In the phrase ἐκ τοῦ θανάτου τοῦ δευτέρου, "by the second death," ἐκ with the gen. is used in an instrumental sense (cf. MM, 190), or as the cause or agent of a pass. verb. Since this prep. phrase functions as the subject of the aor. pass. verb ἀδικηθῇ, the deep structure (following transformational grammar) of this sentence has this pattern: ὁ θάνατος ὁ δεύτερος [subject] οὐ μὴ ἀδικήσει [verb] τὸν νικῶντα [object], "The second death will not harm the one who conquers." In Heb. the "efficient cause" or "personal agent" is connected to the pass. verb by the prefix ל (*l*, equivalent to the Gk. dat.), or less commonly מִן *min*, "from," indicating origin (GKC § 121f).

## *Form/Structure/Setting*

### I. OUTLINE

2. Proclamation to Smyrna (2:8–11)
   a. The *adscriptio:* to the angel of the church in Smyrna (v 8a)
   b. The command to write (v 8b)
   c. The τάδε λέγει formula (v 8c)
   d. Christological predications (v 8d)
      (1) The First and the Last
      (2) The One who died and came back to life
   e. The *narratio:* "I know your conduct" (v 9)
      (1) Your tribulation (v 9a)
      (2) Your poverty (though you are rich) (v 9b)
      (3) The slander you endured (v 9c)
         (a) From those who claim to be Jews but are not
         (b) From those who are a synagogue of Satan
   f. The *dispositio* (v 10)
      (1) Do not fear what you will suffer (v 10a)
         (a) Satan will throw some of you into prison (v 10b)
            [1] Purpose: God is testing you
            [2] Length of time: you will suffer for "ten" days
      (2) Admonition and promise (v 10c)
         (a) Admonition: Be faithful to death
         (b) Promise: I will give you the crown of life
   g. The proclamation formula (v 11a)
   h. The promise-to-the-victor formula: the one who conquers will not be harmed by the second death (v 11b)

### II. HISTORICAL-GEOGRAPHICAL SETTING

Smyrna (modern Izmir) was a large port city located forty miles north of Ephesus (320 stadia according to Strabo 14.1.2; 14.2.29) on the gulf into which the Hermus river flowed, with a population estimated at 100,000. According to legend, Smyrna was founded by an Amazon (Strabo 11.5.4; 12.3.21) and named after her (Strabo 14.1.4). According to Aristides, Smyrna was actually founded *three* times, once by Tantalus or Pelops, again by Thesus, and finally by Alexander the Great (Aelius Aristides *Or.* 17.3–5; 18.2; 21.3–4, 10h; Pausanias 7.5.1–3). Smyrna was originally settled by Aeolian Greeks (ca. 1000 B.C.), constituting one of twelve Aeolian cities

(Pausanias 7.5.1), but soon became part of the Ionian league (Strabo 14.1.4; Pausanias 7.5.1). A number of great literary figures came from Smyrna. According to tradition, Homer was associated with Smyrna (Strabo 12.3.27; 14.1.37; Pausanias 7.5.12). Other famous poets associated with Smyrna include Mimnermus, Bion, and Quintus Smyrnaeus. Smyrna was destroyed by Alyattes, king of Lydia early in the sixth century B.C. (Herodotus 1.14), and existed only as a village for ca. 400 years (Strabo 14.1.37). The city was reportedly refounded by Alexander the Great (Pausanias 7.5.2), but more likely by Antigonus and Lysimachus ca. 290 B.C. at its present site on the slopes of Mount Pagus (Strabo 14.37 [646]). In 193 B.C., Smyrna became the first city in Asia Minor to erect a temple in honor of *dea Roma* (Tacitus *Annals* 4.56). In A.D. 23, Tiberius permitted the construction of a temple in honor of the emperor Augustus and his mother Livia and the Senate, though without specifying its location (Tacitus *Annals* 4.37–38). In A.D. 26, emperor Tiberius chose Smyrna (one of eleven applicants) to be a νεωκόρος, "temple warden," for the cult of Tiberius, Livy, and the Senate (Tacitus *Annals* 4.55–56; see Friesen, *Twice Neokoros*, 15–21). The *conuentus* (i.e., a district based in a particular city for juridical purposes) of Smyrna included Magnesia by Sipylus, the Macedonian Hyrcanians, a large part of Aeolis, Clazomenae, Erythrae, Chios, Phocaea, Cyme, and Myrina (A. H. M. Jones, *Cities*, 79). During the Roman period, Smyrna was a center for science and medicine (Strabo 12.8.20) and renowned for its fine wine, its beautiful buildings, and its wealth (Strabo 14.1.15). Smyrna had a number of temples, including the temple of Asclepius (Pausanias 2.36.9; 7.5.9; Tacitus *Annals* 3.63). The city suffered a devastating earthquake in A.D. 177 or 178 (Aristides *Or.* 18, 19) and another in 180 but was rebuilt under the patronage of the emperor Marcus Aurelius. The best description of ancient Smyrna is found in Aelius Aristides *Or.* 17, who devoted five orations to the city (*Or.* 17, 18, 19, 20, 21).

Though Smyrna is mentioned only twice in the NT (Rev 1:11; 2:8), it became an important Christian center in the second century A.D. Ignatius of Antioch, on a forced march to Rome where he would be martyred, stopped at Smyrna and there wrote letters to four other churches in the region. When he arrived at Troas, he wrote a letter to the Smyrnaean church and a personal letter to Polycarp, the bishop of Smyrna. The *Acts of Paul* apparently contained an account of a visit to Smyrna by Paul before coming to Ephesus (7; cf. *NTA* 2:387), and a visit to Smyrna by the apostle John and his disciples is mentioned in the *Acts of John* 37, 45, as a response to an invitation by the people of Smyrna (55). There was also a Jewish presence in Smyrna as Rev 2:9 suggests, and as a number of inscriptions confirm (Hemer, *BurH* 11 [1975] 62). A famous inscription from A.D. 123–24 (*IGRom* 4:1431.29; *CIJ* 2:742.29), during the reign of Hadrian, refers to a contribution of 10,000 drachmae for some unknown public works project by οἱ ποτὲ Ἰουδαῖοι, "former Jews," or "people formerly of Judaea" (A. T. Kraabel, "The Roman Diaspora," *JJS* 33 [1982] 455).

### Comment

**8a** καὶ τῷ ἀγγέλῳ τῆς ἐν Σμύρνῃ ἐκκλησίας γράψον, "And to the angel of the church in Smyrna write." See *Comment* on 2:1.

**8b** τάδε λέγει ὁ πρῶτος καὶ ὁ ἔσχατος, ὃς ἐγένετο νεκρὸς καὶ ἔζησεν, "Thus says the First and the Last, the one who died and came to life." The phrase "the First and the Last" occurs three times in Revelation (1:17; 2:8; 22:13), always of Christ, and is an allusion to the divine title found in Isa 41:4; 44:6; 48:12. Ramsay (*Letters,* 269–70), followed more cautiously by Hemer (*Letters,* 61–64), speculated that the Smyrnaeans would recognize a striking analogy between the physical renewal of their city and the phrase "the one who died and came to life," because of the destruction of Smyrna by the Lydians in 600 B.C., followed by three centuries of relative desolation concluded by the refounding of Smyrna as a polis two miles south of the ancient site in 290 B.C. (at the modern site of Izmir) by Antigonus and Lysimachus (cf. Strabo 14.1.37; Pausanias 7.5.1–3). Aelius Aristides (*Or.* 21) celebrated the second restoration of Smyrna by Marcus Aurelius and Commodus after the earthquate of A.D. 178 and compares Smyrna with the legendary phoenix. It is striking that the usual verbs used in connection with statements about the resurrection of Jesus (ἐγείρειν, ἀνίστημι) never occur in Revelation. The verb ζᾶν, "to live (again)," is used of Jesus elsewhere in Revelation only in 1:18 (to which this passage alludes) and in the rest of the NT in Mark 16:11; Luke 24:5, 23; Acts 1:3; Rom 14:9a; 2 Cor 13:4a. For the use of ζᾶν in connection with the resurrections of others, see *Comment* on Rev 20:4.

**9a** οἶδα σου τὴν θλῖψιν καὶ τὴν πτωχείαν, ἀλλὰ πλούσιος εἶ, "I know your tribulation and your poverty (yet you are actually rich!)." This is an obvious example of paradox. The situation of this community and their eventual triumph (v 10) is paralleled in 4QpPs[a] 1–10 ii 10–11: "the congregation of the poor ones, who will accept the appointed time of affliction, and they will be delivered from all the traps of Belial" (tr. Horgan, *Pesharim,* 196). The "poverty" of the Smyrnaean Christians is apparently literal poverty (*TDNT* 6:911; *EDNT* 3:195), but it is used in opposition to πλούσιος, "rich," understood figuratively, probably in terms of eschatological wealth (Luke 6:20 = Matt 5:3; Matt 6:19–21 = Luke 12:33–34; Luke 12:21; 2 Cor 6:10; Jas 2:5). The Stoics also used the Greek and Latin terms for "wealth" figuratively (Seneca *Ep.* 62.3). Philo was dependent on the Stoic paradox that only the wise and virtuous person was really "rich" (Philo *Praem.* 104; *Som.* 1.179; *Plant.* 69 [here he uses παραδοξολογεῖν, "paradox"]; *Sob.* 56; *Fug.* 17; *Quod Omn. Prob.* 8, "You call those rich [πλουσίους] who are utterly destitute"; Arnim, *SVF* 1, § 220; 3, § 589–603). The term πτωχοί, "poor," is used literally in 13:16 (in opposition to πλούσιοι, "rich") but figuratively in 3:17. The fact that no mention is made of the economic poverty of the other six Christian communities suggests that the situation of this congregation is unusual. Their "poverty" can be construed in several ways (Hemer, *Letters,* 68): (1) They represent the lowest classes of society (1 Cor 1:26; Jas 2:5). (2) They had their property confiscated or stolen by their hostile pagan neighbors. (3) They had been reduced to penury through the liberality of their giving (2 Cor 2:8). (4) Uncompromising Christians found it difficult to make a living in a pagan environment (Bousset [1906] 242–43; Charles, 1:56; Caird, 35; Roloff, *Revelation,* 48). The first suggestion is problematic since it is now recognized that early Christianity was not a movement restricted to the lower classes; it encompassed the social spectrum (Grant, *Society,* 79–95; Malherbe, *Social,* 29–59; Holmberg, *Sociology,* 21–76), though no generalization can reveal the social and economic status of the Christians in Smyrna. The second and third suggestions are improbable, while the last is regarded by many commentators as the basis for Smyrnaean poverty.

**9b** καὶ τὴν βλασφημίαν ἐκ τῶν λεγόντων Ἰουδαίους εἶναι ἑαυτούς, "and the slander of those who call themselves Jews." The term βλασφημία, "slander," a term particularly appropriate for those who belong to a συναγωγὴ τοῦ σατανᾶ, "synagogue of *Satan*," since the name שָׂטָן *śāṭān*, "Satan," means "opponent" or "adversary," as does the Greek term διάβολος, "devil." Here it is important to realize that the term "Jews" is used positively (i.e., of those who are committed to do the will of God) but that, according to John, those who call themselves Ἰουσαῖοι do not live up to the standard implied in that designation (see Gutbrod, *TDNT* 3:382); i.e., here and in 3:9 (where a close parallel occurs) the author is not condemning Jews generally but only those associated with synagogues in Smyrna and Philadelphia. This is analogous to Paul's claim that to be a Jew means to be circumcised in heart, which can even apply to those who are not physically circumcised, i.e., non-Jews (Rom 2:28–3:1; cf. his figurative use of "Israel" in Gal 6:16; cf. 1 Cor 10:18). It is even possible that the author is implying that none but his own community are true Jews (Tomson, *Bijdragen* 47 [1986] 286). βλασφημία, "blasphemy," is frequently used in Revelation for reviling or speaking irreverently of God (13:6; 16:9, 11, 21), but is used here in the more general sense of "slander" (Mark 15:29; Rom 3:8; 1 Cor 10:30; 1 Pet 4:4). The specific form of βλασφημία, "slander," was apparently a by-product of Jewish-Christian hostility in Sardis and involved either *verbal slander* (in Acts 13:45; 18:6, the verb βλασφημέω is used to describe Jews who reviled Paul, and in Acts 14:2 it is said that the Jews "poisoned the minds" of the Gentiles against Paul and Barnabas) or the *denunciation of Christians before Roman or civic authorities*. Jewish Christians in the late first century A.D. were still able to maintain connections with Jewish communities and so avoid the possible obligations of emperor worship. In certain situations, therefore, Jews had the option of denouncing such Christians to the authorities, and it may be this practice to which the term βλασφημία refers (Hemer, *Letters*, 7–9). An example of such denunciation occurs in Acts 18:12–17, in which Jews brought charges against Paul before Gallio, who considered the case to be an intramural Jewish problem. Verbal slander is a less specific understanding of βλασφημία and could involve the spreading of false rumors about Christians by Jews (Justin *Dial.* 17.1; 108.2; 117.3; Tertullian *Ad nat.* 1.14; Origen *Contra Celsum* 6.27). Christians were accused of various types of criminal or antisocial behavior (Justin *1 Apol.* 26.7; *2 Apol.* 12; Athenagoras *Leg.* 3.31; Theophilus *Ad Autolycum* 3.4; Tertullian *Apol.* 4.11). Some Jews were also vulnerable to denunciation, for some apparently avoided the head tax of two drachmas imposed by Titus (Jos. *J.W.* 7.218; Dio Cassius 65.2) by practicing Judaism privately or by concealing their nationality (Suetonius *Dom.* 12.2). According to a tradition stemming from the last days of Jesus in Jerusalem, the Jews urged Pilate to execute Jesus (Mark 15:12–14; Matt 27:22–23; Luke 23:20–23; John 19:6–7, 14–15). This tradition has influenced the depiction of Jews in *The Martyrdom of Polycarp* (ca. A.D. 155), in which they angrily denounce Polycarp publicly (12:2–3), actively call for his execution (13:1), and try to prevent Christians from retrieving his body (17:2; 18:1). This account, however, is historically tendentious as well as strikingly anti-Jewish, consciously formulated in an attempt to replicate the Gospel narratives of the passion of Jesus (Abrahams, *Studies*, 67–68; Musurillo, *Acts*, xiv; Dehandschutter, *Martyrium*, 251 n. 646). Buschmann (*Martyrium*, 156–57) argues that the anti-Judaism in *The Martyrdom of Polycarp* functioned as a weapon against Judaizing Christians. Justin Martyr, who moved from Asia Minor to Rome, mentioned that Jews persecuted Christians (*Dial.*

16.4; 95.4; 110.5; 131.2; 133.6; *1 Apol.* 31.5) and also that they cursed Christians in their synagogues (*Dial.* 16.4; 47.4; 93.4; 95.4; 96.2; 108.3; 133.6; 137.2; cf. Epiphanius *Haer.* 29.2; see W. Schrage, *TDNT* 7:838–39), perhaps referring to the so-called Birkat ha-Minim, or curse against the heretics, which was primarily directed against Jewish Christians (see Kimelman, "*Birkat Ha-Minim*," 226–44). Justin is also of the opinion that Jews have spread false rumors about Christians (*Dial.* 17.1; 108.2; 117.3). According to Acts 26:11, when Paul persecuted Jewish Christians, he attempted to force them to βλασφημεῖν, i.e., probably to curse Christ (see Justin *1 Apol.* 31). Eusebius (*Hist. eccl.* 5.16.12) quotes Apollinarius (latter half of second century A.D.), who affirms the Jewish persecution of Christians in Asia Minor. There are many passages in both the Pauline letters and Acts that describe Jewish persecution of Christians in various ways (1 Thess 2:14–16; Gal 1:13–14, 23; 1 Cor 15:9; Phil 3:6; Acts 7:1–8:3; 9:1–9; 13:44–52; 14:1–7, 19; 17:5–9, 13; 21:27–36). Here it is important to recognize that the emphasis on Jewish hostility and persecution as a major cause of the suffering of Christians was in part a theological convention in Christian apologetics requiring little or no evidence (Hare, *Jewish Persecution*). One frequently occurring theme is that of the violent death of the prophets; i.e., Israel is guilty for rejecting the word of God by persecuting and killing the prophets who brought that word (Neh 9:26; 1 Kgs 19:14; Ezra 9:11; Jub 1:12; Jos. *Ant.* 9.13.2; 10.3.1; Matt 5:11–12 = Luke 6:23, 26; Matt 23:29–36 = Luke 11:47–51; Acts 7:51–52; Justin, *Dial.* 17.1). The Gospel of John may reflect historical experience in the expulsion from the synagogue of followers of Jesus (John 9:22; 12:42; 16:2). Tertullian referred to Jewish synagogues as *fontes persecutionum,* "fonts of persecution" (*Scorp.* 10.10; cf. 15; *Praescr. haer.* 26.6), though here he is referring to the historical experiences of the apostles as he understood them from the NT (see Scholer, *StudP* 17/2 [1982] 821–28). In v 10, the Smyrnaeans are told that the Devil is about to throw them into prison; John has just called the Jews a synagogue of Satan (v 9). Further, Antipas has already been killed (v 13), and John expects that more Christians will be executed (v 10b). If Christians had suffered legal penalties at the hands of Roman authorities in Smyrna, such actions were probably initiated by local citizens, and this passage strongly suggests that the Jews actively participated in the process.

The Roman legal system had two major institutions for indicting those who violated the laws. The *quaestiones,* "sitting juries," never used in Asia Minor, and the *cognitio,* "judicial inquiry," procedure. A *cognitio* placed the examination and decision of a judicial case squarely into the hands of a Roman magistrate. Charges against defendants had to be made by a private prosecutor, an *accusator,* who could be either an injured party or a personal enemy, or by a *delator,* often motivated by financial reward; an *index,* "informer," was one who denounced a crime without being a formal accuser in a trial (A. Berger, *Roman Law,* s.v. "*accusatio,*" "*delator,*" "*index*"; Sherwin-White, *Letters,* 778–79; A. H. M. Jones, *Criminal Courts*). The accusation was normally submitted in written form (the *libellus accusatorius*) to a magistrate willing to accept it and place it on an official list of those awaiting criminal trial. The magistrate had to decide whether the accused should be imprisoned, be placed under house arrest (supervised by a military guard), or be charged bail. It could also be signed by additional witnesses in a *subscriptio,* "subscription." In Pliny *Ep.* 96, which describes Pliny's legal proceedings against Christians at the beginning of the second century A.D., the initiative in accusing Christians came from the provincials, as in other second-century A.D. cases where the evidence is clear (Sherwin-White, *Letters,* 697).

The meaning of Ἰουδαῖος is problematic; it could have at least four meanings in Jewish inscriptions (Kraemer, *HTR* 82 [1989] 35–53; see also the corrective discussion in van der Horst, *Epitaphs*, 68–72): (1) a person born a Jew (*CIJ* 296, 678, 680, 697); Josephus qualifies the term "Jew" with the phrase Ἰουδαῖοι μὲν γένος ὄντες, "Jews by birth" (*J.W.* 2.119); (2) a pagan adherent to Judaism, not a proselyte (cf. Dio Cassius 37.17.1); (3) someone from Judea, not necessarily a Jew (perhaps *CIJ* 742); (4) a name (*CIJ* 710, 711); and (5) a person who obeys the will of God, i.e., is "circumcised in heart" if not in body (Rom 2:28–3:1; cf. Rev 2:9). It should be noted in connection with (3) that, according to Solin, Ἰουδαῖος and *Iudaeus* almost always denote membership in a Jewish religious community and hardly ever denote ethnic or geographic origin; see H. Solin, "Juden und Syrer im westlichen Teil der römischen Welt," *ANRW* II, 29/2:587–89. During the late first cent. A.D., Judaism was a major diaspora ethnic group in the Roman empire. Of an estimated total population of sixty million, between four and five million were Jews (i.e., ca. 7 percent of the total population), while Christians constituted a minuscule minority group that probably numbered no more than fifty thousand by the end of the first century A.D. (Wilken, *Christians*, 31).

**9c** καὶ οὐκ εἰσὶν, ἀλλὰ συναγωγὴ τοῦ σατανᾶ, "but are not, but are a synagogue of Satan." This statement, taken with that which immediately precedes in v 9b, constitutes an antithetical statement (in which the infinitive εἶναι introduces indirect discourse). John could be referring to Jews who had forsworn their faith and maintained only an ethnic tie to Judaism (see the discussion in Sevenster, *Anti-Semitism*, 89–144). A second-century A.D. inscription from Smyrna (*IGRom* 4:1431.29; *CIJ* 2:742.29) lists a group of people designated as οἱ ποτὲ Ἰουδαῖοι, which some have understood to mean "former Jews," who had donated the sum of 10,000 drachmas to the city and received citizenship by abandoning their ancestral religion. Yet A. T. Kraabel has convincingly argued that the phrase should be translated "people formerly of Judaea," i.e., immigrants from Palestine, since a record of public works, he argues, would be an inappropriate place to record one's apostasy ("The Roman Diaspora: Six Questionable Assumptions," *JJS* 33 [1982] 455). Understood in this way, the inscription provides important evidence that Jewish immigration from Palestine continued into the second century A.D. Similarly, an inscription from Miletus (*CIJ* 2:748) reveals that Jews had their own reserved seats in the theater in spite of the pagan religious character of the setting. In an inscription from Hypaepa south of Sardis, the phrase Ἰουδαίων νεωτέρων, "junior Jews," occurs, i.e., a group of young Jewish boys belonging to the ephebic system of athletic education (*CIJ* 2:755). It is perhaps more likely, however, that the author of Revelation is referring not to apostate Jews but rather to Jews who are opposed to Christianity; see A. Yarbro Collins, "Vilification and Self-Definition in the Book of Revelation," *HTR* 79 (1986) 308–20.

This is the first of two occurrences of the phrase "synagogue of Satan" in Revelation (the other occurrence is in 3:9). This phrase may reflect the beginnings of the separation of the church from the synagogue, for the phrase "church of Satan" seems impossible to imagine (Peri, *BZ* 33 [1989] 245). There is a related parallel in John 8:44, where Jesus claims that the "father" of the Jews with whom he speaks is the Devil. Rev 3:9 is a very close parallel: ἰδοὺ διδῶ ἐκ τῆς συναγωγῆς τοῦ σατανᾶ τῶν λεγόντων ἑαυτοὺς Ἰουδαίους εἶναι, καὶ οὐκ εἰσὶν ἀλλὰ ψεύδονται, "Behold, I will cause those of the synagogue of Satan who call themselves Jews but are not but lie." The phrase "synagogue of Satan" has a very close parallel in the expression עדת בליעל *ʿdt blyʿl*, "congregation of Belial," in 1QH 2:22 and 1QM 4:9 ("Belial" is an alternate name for Satan in 2 Cor 6:15; *T. Reub.* 2:4 [for fifteen other references in *T. 12 Patr.*, see Hollander-de Jonge, *Testaments*, 93]; *Jub.* 15:33; CD 6:9), and in the LXX συναγωγή is used to translate עדה *ʿēdâ* over 100 times (T. Gaster, *IDB* 3:227). 1QS 5:1–2 has the parallel expression עדת אנשי העול *ʿdt ʾnšy hʿwl*, "congregation of the perverse men"; cf. 1QM 15:9, עדת רשעה *ʿdt ršʿh*, "congregation of wickedness." *Barn.* 5:13 and 6:6 have the phrase πονηρευομένων συναγωγαί, "groups/synagogues of evil people." This may reflect a cosmological dualism that divides the world of humanity into two separate and hostile camps, with Christians by implication belonging to the "synagogue of the Lord" (Yarbro Collins, *Combat Myth*, 159). On the other hand, the opposite conception of the people of God is reflected in the phrases קהל יהוה *qĕhal YHWH* (Num 16:3; 20:4) and עדת יהוה *ʿădat YHWH* (Num 31:16), translated συναγωγή [τοῦ] κυρίου in the LXX (Num 16:3; 20:4; 26:9; 31:16), a possessive genitive meaning "the assembly belonging to the Lord." The term συναγωγή, "synagogue," refers to an empirical community, i.e., members of a Jewish community who meet for worship (cf. Louw-Nida, §§ 11.44; 11.45), to be distinguished from the *place* where such groups meet (cf. Louw-Nida, § 7.20; cf. Luke 7:5; possibly Jas 2:2). See the excursus on "The Term συναγωγή" in Dibelius-Greeven, *James*, 132–34; Zahn, *Introduction* 1:94–95. It is also important to note that the term συναγωγή, "synagogue," was not an exclusively Jewish term (Schürer, *History* 2:429–31). There are a number of other terms in addition to συναγωγή, "synagogue," that Jews in Asia Minor used for their places of worship; these include προσευχή, "place of prayer" (Jos. *Ant.* 14.112–13), σαββατεῖον (*Ant.* 16.162–65), perhaps a term for a private home in which Sabbath services were held (Zeitlin, *JQR* 55 [1964–65] 161–63), and τόπος, "place" (Jos. *Ant.* 259–61; see Krauss, *Synagogale Altertümer* [Berlin; Vienna: Harz, 1922] 24–25; Hanfmann, *Sardis*, 110–13).

One of the striking features of Revelation is the virtual absence of the typical features of the polemic between Jews and Christians, or the inner Christian concern with the threat of Judaizing. The two references to Ἰουδαῖοι in Revelation (2:9; 3:9) are similar in that the claim to be Jews is rejected; they are instead labeled a "synagogue of Satan." In 2:9, the issue of their "blasphemy" is mentioned, which may be the denunciation of Christians to local authorities by Jews. All of this is extramural. The only two references to "Israel" occur in 7:4; 21:12. It is striking that, apart from the controversy of eating meat previously sacrificed to a pagan deity (2:15, 20), certainly an intramural issue in Acts 15, there is a complete absence of controversial issues and terms such as νόμος, "Law," διαθήκη, "covenant," περιτομή, "circumcision," Sabbath and festival observance, fasting, and the legitimacy of sacrifices. This all may suggest that the author, while certainly of Jewish origin, espoused a "Pauline" type of inclusivism, with the major exception of the issue of the propriety of eating meat sacrificed to pagan deities.

**10a** μηδὲν φοβοῦ ἃ μέλλεις πάσχειν, "Fear nothing you will suffer." This is an awkward expression since μηδέν, "nothing," is the object of φοβοῦ, "fear," but it is a neuter accusative singular and does not agree with the neuter accusative plural pronoun ἅ, "which," which is the object of the infinitive πάσχειν, "suffer." The second-person *singular* imperative φοβοῦ is probably used to maintain the literary fiction of referring to the angel of the community addressed in v 8a. Unlike the more common formulaic expression μὴ φοβοῦ, "do not be afraid," which occurs in Rev 1:17 and frequently in the NT (cf. *Notes* on 2:10), in which the general attitude of fear is prohibited, the phrase μηδὲν φοβοῦ ἃ μέλλεις πάσχειν commands the Smyrnaeans specifically to be afraid of none of the sufferings that they will shortly experience.

**10b** ἰδοὺ μέλλει βάλλειν ὁ διάβολος ἐξ ὑμῶν εἰς φυλακήν, "Behold, the Devil is about to cast some of you into prison." In John's view, local authorities who oppose the people of God are simply agents of Satan, as this statement makes clear. There is no explicit connection between the βλασφημία of the Jews mentioned in v 9 and impending imprisonment, though the work of Satan or the Devil is seen behind both (Schrage, *EvT* 48 [1988] 391). Under the Roman legal system, imprisonment was usually not a punishment in itself; rather it was used either as a means of coercion to compel obedience to an order issued by a magistrate or else as a place to temporarily restrain the prisoner before execution (Berger, *Roman Law,* 381, 633; Mommsen, *Strafrecht,* 960–80; for some exceptions, see Jos. *J.W.* 6.434; Eisenhut, *ANRW* II, 1/2:268–82). Here it appears that imprisonment, viewed as a period of testing, is primarily for the purpose of coercion. According to Gaius (*Digest* 48.19.29; tr. Watson, *Justinian*), "Those condemned to the extreme penalty immediately lose their citizenship and their freedom. This fate therefore anticipates their death, sometimes by a long period, as happens in the case of those who are condemned to the beasts. Again, it is often the custom for them to be kept [alive] after their condemnation, so that they may be interrogated under torture against others." According to Callistratus (*Digest* 48.19.35; tr. Watson, *Justinian*), "In the mandates given by the emperors to provincial governors, it is provided that no one is to be condemned to permanent imprisonment; and the deified Hadrian also wrote a rescript to this effect." There were, of course, exceptions (*Digest* 48.19.8.9; tr. Watson, *Justinian*): "Governors are in the habit of condemning men to be kept in prison or in chains, but they ought not to do this; for punishments of this type are forbidden. Prison indeed ought to be employed for confining men, not for punishing them."

**10c** ἵνα πειρασθῆτε καὶ ἕξετε θλῖψιν ἡμερῶν δέκα, "that you might be tested, and you will experience tribulation for ten days." The juxtaposition of aorist and future verbs here is significant. The aorist subjunctive πειρασθῆτε is used because the aorist summarizes the meaning that the Smyrnaean Christians will derive from the whole persecution experience, i.e., *testing,* while in the future indicative ἕξετε, the future tense focuses simply on the element of anticipation: it will be limited to "ten" days. The subject of the second-person *plural* aorist passive subjunctive πειρασθῆτε and the future active indicative ἕξετε is the implied indefinite plural of the partitive genitive [τινές] ἐξ ὑμῶν, "[some] of you," i.e., the group that will experience imprisonment. The phrase "ten days" is used for an undefined but relatively short period of time, perhaps because it is the sum of the fingers of both hands (Gen 24:55; Num 11:19; Neh 5:18; Jer 42:7; Dan 1:12–15); *m. 'Abot* 5:1–6 contains a list of ten things of various kinds. Ten can also function as a number signifying completeness; see Brongers, "Zehnzahl," 30–45.

**10d** γίνου πιστὸς ἄχρι θανάτου, καὶ δώσω σοι τὸν στέφανον τῆς ζωῆς, "Be faithful unto death, and I will give you the wreath of life," is an example of paradox. The implied subject of the second-singular aorist imperative γίνου apparently refers to the angel of the community and indicates that this sentence is addressed to the entire community, not simply to those referred to in v 10bc. The phrase τῆς ζωῆς, "of life," is an appositive or epexegetical genitive, so that the whole phrase means "the wreath consisting of life" (M. Zerwick, *Greek* § 45). The term στέφανος is used three times in Revelation referring to a wreath presumably made of some kind of leaves (2:10; 3:11; 6:2; see *Excursus 2C: Ancient Wreath and Crown Imagery*). The exalted Christ himself promises to bestow the wreath of life on faithful Christians (see Philo *Leg. All.* 1.80, where God crowns the person who strives after virtue). The context makes it clear that the wreath is a metaphor for a posthumous reward. Even though such wreaths were never awarded posthumously either to victorious athletes or for military achievements, it appears that this must in fact be a victory wreath expressing the agon motif. The metaphor of the award of a posthumous wreath benefactor is reflected not only here in Rev 2:10 but also in Heb 2:9, where it is claimed that Jesus was crowned with glory and honor for the suffering of death, and in *Mart. Pol.* 17:1 where it is said that Polycarp the martyr "was wreathed with the wreath of immortality." In *Mart. Pol.* 17:1, however, the presence of the term βραβεῖον, "reward, prize," indicates that athletic imagery is in view. According to Stewart, it is not until ca. A.D. 150 that the imagery of the athletic contest (including the prize of the wreath presented to the victor) is applied to martyrdom in *Mart. Pol.* 17–19; *Sib. Or.* 2.39–55; *Mart. Carpus* [Greek Rec.] 35; [Lat. Rec.] 3.5 (Stewart, "Greek Crowns," 122). However, this passage in Revelation antedates those references by more than fifty years. Suffering and dying for one's beliefs is frequently described using metaphors drawn from athletic contexts (2 Macc 6:10; 9:8; 11:20; 14:4; 17:11–16; *T. Job* 4:10; 27:3–5; Phil 2:16; 3:14; 2 Tim 2:5; 4:7–8; Heb 12:1–2; *1 Clem.* 5:1–7 [note the use of the metaphors ἀθληταί, ἀθλεῖν, βραβεῖον, ὑπομονή]; 6:2; Ign. *Pol.* 2:3; 3:1; Pol. *Phil.* 9:2; *Mart. Pol.* 17:1; 18:3; 19:2; Hermas *Mand.* 12.5.2; *Sim.* 8.3.6). Similarly, the metaphor of the victory wreath is often used as a metaphor for the heavenly reward awaiting the Christian who suffers and perhaps even dies for his or her faith (*Pass. Mont.* 14:5; *Mart. Lyons* 42). The exact phrase "crown of life" occurs only in Jas 1:12, though analogous expressions occur elsewhere in the NT, where "crown" or "wreath" is a metaphor for the eschatological reward of eternal life: "imperishable wreath" (1 Cor 9:25), "crown of righteousness" (2 Tim 4:8), an "unfading crown of glory" (1 Pet 5:4; *Asc. Isa.* 9:10–11; *T. Benj.* 4:1; derived from Judaism, see LXX Jer 13:18; LXX Lam 2:15; 1QH 9:25; 1QS 4:7), the "crown of immortality" (*Mart. Pol.* 17:1; *Mart. Lyons* 36, 38, 42), or simply "crown" (Rev 3:11; *2 Clem.* 7:3; *Gk. Apoc. Ezra* 6.17; *Apoc. Elijah* 1:8; 5 Ezra 2:4; *Asc. Isa.* 9:25). In all these passages, the wreath or crown is a metaphor for the future reward of the righteous, which occurs in early Judaism (see Wis 5:16; *2 Apoc. Bar.* 15:8; a "crown of glory" is mentioned in 1QH 9:25 and 1QS 4:7). Aelius Aristides (*Or.* 27.36; see P. W. van der Horst, *Aelius Aristides and the New Testament*, SCHNT 6 [Leiden: Brill, 1980] 82) has a relatively close parallel: "These are adorned with the wreath of the immortals [τῷ τῶν ἀθανάτων στεφάνῳ]," i.e., they share the immortality of the gods. The "wreath" image appears to be derived from athletic language (2 Tim 2:5) and is closely associated with martyrdom. Yet in 4 Maccabees (composed ca. A.D. 50), the imagery of victorious athletes is used of Jewish martyrs (6:10; 11:20; 13:15; 15:29; 16:16; 17:11–16).

There are, it should be noted, several examples of citizens awarded the honor of a wreath posthumously by the *demos* or a city, frequently with a representation of the wreath on the sepulchral monument encircling the name of the awarding body, usually δῆμος (see *MAMA* 8 [1962] 408.13–14, from Aphrodisias; Horsley, *New Docs* 2:50), or, particularly in Rhodes, by the particular secular or cult society (a κοινόν or θίασος) to which the deceased had belonged (Fraser, *Funerary Monuments,* 68). One example is found in the following honorific inscription in honor of Dionysodoros (*IG* 155; Fraser, *Funerary Monuments,* 62 n. 357): "To the account of Dionysodoros, the Benefactor, who was crowned with a golden crown for ever [στεφανωθέντος χρυσέωι στεφάνωι εἰς τὸν ἀεὶ χρόνον] (the cost of) the crown that was bought," meaning that Dionysodoros would remain a permanent benefactor and would be honored annually with the coronation of the funerary monument. Ramsay (*Letters,* 256–59) and Hemer (*Letters,* 59–60) have suggested that the phrase "crown of life" is an allusion to the "crown" metaphor that was frequently applied to Smyrna on coins and inscriptions and by rhetoricians (Philostratus *Vita Apoll.* 4.7), though this is not at all persuasive given the ubiquitous nature of the crown metaphor.

**11a** ὁ ἔχων οὖς ἀκουσάτω τί τὸ πνεῦμα λέγει ταῖς ἐκκλησίαις, "Let the person with an ear hear what the Spirit announces to the churches." See *Comment* on 2:7. *Tg. Isa.* 22:14 juxtaposes the motif of hearing with the threat of the second death mentioned in v 11b (tr. Chilton, *Isaiah Targum;* words added to MT in italics): "*The prophet said,* With my ears *I was hearing when this was decreed before* the Lord God of hosts: 'Surely this *sin* will not be forgiven you until you die *the second death,*' says the Lord God of hosts."

**11b** ὁ νικῶν οὐ μὴ ἀδικηθῇ ἐκ τοῦ θανάτου τοῦ δευτέρου, "The one who conquers will absolutely not be harmed by the second death." The unusual phrase "the second death" is also found in 20:6 (ὁ δεύτερος θάνατος) and in 20:14; 21:8 (ὁ θάνατος ὁ δεύτερος), and its incorporation into this context was certainly based on these references, which were present in the first edition of Revelation (see *Comment* on 20:6). Here it is worth noting that the promise of a new name mentioned in 2:17 is found in combination with the threat of the "second death" in *Tg. Isa.* 65:15 (tr. Chilton, *Isaiah Targum*): "You shall leave your name to my chosen for an oath, and the Lord God will slay you with the second death; but his servants, the righteous, he will call by a different name" (see Bogaert, "La 'seconde mort,'" 205–6). In *Tg. Onq.* Deut 33:6 (tr. Grossfeld, *Targum Onqelos*): "May Reuben live an everlasting life and not die a second death." Cf. Fragmentary Targums P and V on Deut 33:6 (M. L. Klein, *Fragment-Targums* 2:88, 188): "May Reuben live in this world; and may he not die a second death, by which (death) the wicked die in the world to come." Cf. *Tg. Neof.* Deut 33:6; *Tg. Onq.* 33:6; *Tg. Isa.* 22:14; *Tg. Jer.* 51:39, 57; *Pirqe R. El.* 34.

*Excursus 2B: Anatolian Jewish Communities and Synagogues*

### Bibliography

**Applebaum, S.** "The Legal Status of the Jewish Communities in the Diaspora." In *CRINT,* ed. M. de Jonge and S. Safrai. Philadelphia: Fortress, 1974. I/1, 420–63. ———. "The Organization of the Jewish Communities in the Diaspora." In *CRINT,* ed. M. de Jonge and S. Safrai. Philadelphia: Fortress, 1974. I/1, 464–503. **Barrett, C. K.** "Jews and Judaizers in the Epistles of Ignatius." In *Jews, Greeks and Christians: Religious Cultures in Late Antiquity.* FS W. D. Davies, ed. R. Hamerton-Kelly and R. Scroggs. SJLA 21. Leiden: Brill, 1976. 220–44. **Blanchetière, F.** "Le juif et l'autre: la diaspora Asiate." In *Etudes sur le judaïsme* *hellénistique,* ed. R. Kuntzmann and J. Schlosser. Paris: Cerf, 1984. 41–59. ———. "Juifs et non juifs: Essai sur la diaspora en Asie Mineure." *RHPR* 54 (1974) 367–82. **Brooten, B. J.** *Women Leaders in the Ancient Synagogue.* Chico, CA: Scholars, 1982. **Chiat, M. J. S.** *Handbook of Synagogue Architecture.* Chicago: Scholars, 1982. **Goodman, M.** "Nerva, the *fiscus Judaicus* and Jewish Identity." *JRS* 79 (1989) 40–44. **Graetz, H.** "Die Stellung der kleinasiatischen Juden unter der Römerherrschaft." *MGWJ* 30 (1886) 329–46. **Grant, M.** *The Jews in the Roman World.* London: Dorset, 1973. **Harris, H. A.** *Greek Athletics and the Jews.* Cardiff: University of Wales, 1976. **Horst, P. W. van der.** "Jews and Christians in Aphrodisias in the Light of Their Relations in Other Cities of Asia Minor." *NedTTs* 43 (1989) 106–21. **Juster, J.** *Les Juifs dans l'empire romain.* 2 vols. Paris: Geuthner, 1914. **Kittel, G.** "Das kleinasiatische Judentum in der hellenistisch-römischen Zeit: Ein Bericht zur Epigraphik Kleinasiens." *TLZ* 69 (1944) 9–20. **Kraabel, A. T.** "The Diaspora Synagogue: Archaeological and Epigraphic Evidence since Sukenik." *ANRW* II, 19/1:477–510. ———. "Impact of the Discovery of the Sardis Synagogue." In *Sardis from Prehistoric to Roman Times: Results of the Archaeological Exploration of Sardis 1958–75,* ed. G. M. A. Hanfmann. Cambridge: Harvard UP, 1983. 178–90, 284–85. ———. "Paganism and Judaism—the Sardis Evidence." In *Paganisme, Judaisme, Christianisme.* FS M. Simon, ed. A. Benoit, M. Philonenko, and C. Vogel. Paris: Boccard, 1978. 13–33. ———. "The Roman Diaspora: Six Questionable Assumptions." *JJS* 33 (1982) 445–64. ———. "Synagoga Caeca: Systematic Distortion in Gentile Interpretations of Evidence for Judaism in the Early Christian Period." In *"To See Ourselves as Others See Us": Christians, Jews and "Others" in Late Antiquity,* ed. J. Neusner and E. S. Frerichs. Chico, CA: Scholars, 1985. 219–46. ———. "Unity and Diversity among Diaspora Synagogues." In *The Synagogue in Late Antiquity,* ed. L. I. Levine. Philadelphia: American Schools of Oriental Research, 1987. 51–61. **Levine, L. I.** *Ancient Synagogues Revealed.* Detroit: Wayne State UP, 1982. **Lifschitz, B.** *Donateurs et fondateurs dans les synagogues juives.* Paris: Gabalda, 1967. **Moehring, H.** "The *Acta pro Judaeis* in the *Antiquities* of Flavius Josephus." In *Christianity, Judaism and Other Greco-Roman Cults,* ed. J. Neusner. Leiden: Brill, 1975. 3:124–58. **Rajak, T.** "Jewish Rights in the Greek Cities under Roman Rule: A New Approach." In *Approaches to Ancient Judaism: 5. Studies in Judaism and Its Greco-Roman Context,* ed. W. S. Green. Atlanta: Scholars, 1985. 19–35. ———. "Was there a Roman Charter for the Jews?" *JRS* 74 (1984) 107–23. **Sevenster, J. N.** *The Roots of Pagan Anti-Semitism in the Ancient World.* Leiden: Brill, 1975. **Silberschlag, E.** "The Earliest Record of Jews in Asia Minor." *JBL* 52 (1933) 66–77. **Smallwood, E. M.** "Domitian's Attitude toward the Jews and Judaism." *CP* 51 (1956) 1–13. ———. *The Jews under Roman Rule: From Pompey to Diocletian.* Leiden: Brill, 1976. **Sukenik, E. L.** *Ancient Synagogues in Palestine and Greece.* London: Oxford UP, 1934. **Tarn, W. W.,** and **Griffith, G. T.** *Hellenistic Civilisation.* Cleveland; New York: World Books, 1961. **Tcherikover, V.** *Hellenistic Civilization and the Jews.* New York: Jewish Publication Society of America, 1961. **Trebilco, P.** *Jewish Communities in Asia Minor.* SNTSMS 69. Cambridge: Cambridge UP, 1991.

Among the first Jewish expatriates to Asia Minor were those who fled to Sardis after the Babylonian capture of Jerusalem in 586 B.C., for Obad 20 mentions exiles from Jerusalem in Sepharad, an Aramaic name for Sardis, as a bilingual Lydian-Aramaic inscription indicates (S. A. Cook, "A Lydian-Aramaic Bilingual," *JHS* 37 [1917] 77–87). Josephus has preserved a letter from Antiochus III to Zeuxis, governor of Lydia, containing instructions concerning the settlement of two thousand Jewish families who had been moved from Mesopotamia and resettled in Phrygia (Jos. *Ant.* 12.148–53). Philo observed that the Jews were numerous in both Asia Minor and Syria (*Leg.* 245). By the first century A.D., the Jewish communities in Asia Minor had become large and influential (Jos. *Ant.* 14.259–61; 16.171, 235), and there is evidence for several dozen flourishing synagogues in the Roman province of Asia. There is inscriptional evidence for organized Jewish communities in Caria, at Myndus (*CIJ* 756), Hyllarima (A. Laumonier, *BCH* 58 [1934] 379, 516–17), and Aphrodisias; in Phrygia at Acmonia (*MAMA* 6:264 = *CIJ* 766; this Julia Severa inscription dates to the late first century A.D., so this location is the earliest synagogue in Asia Minor attested by an inscription), Apamea (*CIJ* 774), Synnada (*MAMA* 4:90), and Hierapolis (*CIJ* 775 = *IGRom* 4:834), in Lydia at Hypaepa (*CIJ* 755), Philadelphia (*CIJ* 754), and Sardis (Robert, *Sardes,* passim), and on the coast at Smyrna (*CIJ* 741), Miletus (*CIJ* 748; Jos. *Ant.* 14.244–46), Teos (*CIJ* 744), Phocaea (*CIJ* 738), and Ephesus (*IBM* 3:676–677; Acts 18:19, 26; 19:8). Acts refers to four specific synagogues in Pisidian Antioch (13:14), Iconium (14:1), Philippi (16:13), and Ephesus (18:19, 26; 19:8). John refers to "synagogues of Satan" at Smyrna (Rev 2:9) and Philadelphia (Rev 3:9). The discovery and excavation of the synagogue at Sardis—the largest ancient synagogue yet discovered—indicates the presence in Sardis of a very large, wealthy, and influential Jewish synagogue (Kraabel, "Impact," 178–90). Though it is difficult to give an accurate estimate of the number of Jews who resided in the cities of Asia Minor, P. W. van der Horst has suggested that it may have been as high as one million by the first century A.D. (*NedTTs* 43 [1989] 106–7).

According to Josephus, the Roman government repeatedly granted the Jews the right to live in accordance with their own ancestral laws and customs. In two extensive digressions, Josephus quotes thirty documents that deal with various phases of the relationship of Anatolian Jews to their Greek neighbors. All but the most ancient *collegia* had been dissolved in Rome by Julius Caesar (Suetonius *Divus Iulius* 42.3; Jos. *Ant.* 14.213–16), though Jewish synagogues were explicitly exempted. The *collegia* were dissolved again later by Augustus (Suetonius *Divus Augustus* 32.1). Occasionally *collegia* were declared *collegia illicita,* "illegal associations," when their purposes were judged to be subversive. Some have argued that Judaism was formally considered a *religio licita,* "approved cult," though the phrase *religio licita* did not originate in Roman legal terminology but is first found in Tertullian (*Apol.* 21.1). The term that did have legal significance was *collegia licita,* "legal associations." The Jewish synagogues were apparently exempt from these dissolutions because of their antiquity. These special privileges accorded to Jewish communities were a constant source of irritation since the assumption underlying citizenship in a Greek polis was that everyone had to participate in the religious cult upon which it was founded (Sevenster, *Roots,* 164). Hostility between Jews and pagans in the diaspora took many forms. The conflict between the Alexandrian Jews and Greeks was one that lasted a very long time (Jos. *J.W.* 2.487; Philo *Leg.* 120; *Flacc.* 25ff.; *CPJ* 1:65ff.). The tensions between the Greeks and the Jews frequently flared up into confrontations, sometimes resulting in Jewish massacres (Jos. *J.W.* 2.266–70; 2.461–65; 2.466–76; 2.477–79; 7.46–53; *Ant.* 18.374–79).

The extent to which individual Jews enjoyed citizenship in the Greek cities of the Roman province of Asia is an exceedingly problematic issue (for a review of this issue, see Trebilco, *Jewish Communities,* 167–85). Citizenship in the Roman province of Asia had two levels: residents of the Greek cities could be citizens of their own cities as well as citizens of the Roman empire. However, since citizenship in the local Greek cities of Asia involved participation in city cults, it was problematic for observant Jews. The failure of enfranchised Jews to worship the gods of the cities in which they lived caused friction with local Gentiles (see Jos. *Ant.* 12.125–25, where the Ionians complained to Marcus Agrippa in 14 B.C. that, if the Jews were to be their equals [συγγενεῖς], they should worship the gods of the Ionians). Though Josephus claims that the Hellenistic kings granted citizenship (πολιτεία) to the Jews in certain cities in Asia Minor, Lower Syria, and Antioch (*Ant.* 12.119; 16.160; *Ag. Ap.* 2.39), there are weighty arguments against accepting this claim (Tcherikover, *Hellenistic Civilization,* 329–30; Trebilco, *Jewish Communities,* 167–72). Jews could be citizens of the Greek cities within which they lived as well as Roman citizens. In Acts 21:39, the author has Paul claim that he is a citizen of Tarsus (full citizenship for Jews in Greek cities, however, is denied by Tarn-Griffith, *Hellenistic Civilisation,* 221–23, who claim that Paul has only "potential citizenship"), while several other passages in Acts indicate that Paul was also a Roman citizen (16:37; 22:25; 23:27). In A.D. 212, the emperor Caracalla granted Roman citizenship to all free inhabitants of the Roman empire in the *Constitutio Antoniniana.*

Like Jews throughout the Roman empire, those in the Roman province of Asia were required to pay a poll tax of two denarii for each Jewish male from three to sixty years of age, deposited in the *fiscus Iudaicus* in Rome, a central treasury for these revenues (see the documents in *CPJ*, nos. 160–229, and the essays in *CPJ* 1:80–82; 3:111–16; Goodman, *JRS* 79 [1989] 40–44). The poll tax applied not only to professing Jews but also to Jews who tried to keep their origins secret, apostate Jews, and Jews who converted to other religions, including Christianity (Suetonius *Dom.* 12.2; cf. Smallwood, *Jews,* 371–76; sixty-nine ostraca from Edfu, Egypt, contain receipts for Jews who paid this tax during the principates of Vespasian to Domitian [*CPJ* 2:119–36]). This tax was strictly imposed under Domitian (Pliny *Pan.* 42; Suetonius *Dom.* 12.2; Dio Cassius 67.4.6), so that two types of sestertius minted in A.D. 96 under Nerva had the inscription *FISCI IVDAICI CALVMNIA SUBLATA,* "The malicious proceedings with regard to the *fiscus Iudaicus* are abolished" (*CAH* 11:191; Cayón, *CMIR* 1:299). A self-imposed temple tax in the amount of a half-shekel, then two denarii, was collected from every male Jew (including freedmen and proselytes) between the ages of twenty and fifty and transported to Jerusalem where it defrayed the expense of public sacrifices and municipal needs (Exod 20:11–16; Jos. *Ant.* 14.110–13; 18.312–13; *J.W.* 7.218; Philo *Spec. Leg.* 1.77–78; *Leg.* 156; Matt 17:24; see Trebilco, *Jewish Communities,* 13–16). During the reign of Augustus, a number of Jewish communities in Asia Minor (including Ephesus, Sardis, and the Roman province of Asia) petitioned the emperor and other high officials for permission from Rome to send the temple tax to Jerusalem (Philo *Leg.* 315–15; Jos. *Ant.* 16.162–68, 171–73; Trebilco, *Jewish Communities,* 15–16).

The social and legal status of Jews in the western Diaspora is a very complex historical issue with no easy solutions. It is readily apparent that the rights and privileges enjoyed by Jews and Jewish communities varied from region to region and from period to period. Many earlier studies, however, including that of Juster, are flawed because they exhibit a marked tendency to fill the gaps in the evidence with speculations based on later assumptions of what Jews would or would not do in a variety of situations. Many Jews were Roman citizens, partly because Jewish slaves owned by Roman citizens automatically became enfranchised when manumitted by their owners (Juster, *Les Juifs* 2:15). Generally, the formally manumitted slaves of Roman citizens became freedmen whose descendants would be full-fledged citizens (see A. N. Sherwin-White, *The Roman Citizenship* [Oxford: Clarendon, 1973] 322–31). The Roman citizenship of Paul (Acts 16:37–38; 22:25–29; 23:27) may have been inherited from an ancestor who was a slave who had become enfranchised. During the first century A.D., the primary social distinction was between Roman citizens (*cives Romani*) and aliens or provincials (*peregrini*). By the late first century A.D., the extent of enfranchisement led to a further distinction between the upper-class *honestiores* (including senators, equestrians, and decurions) and the lower-class *humiliores.* Some scholars have estimated that up to a million Jews lived in Asia Minor by the first century A.D. While that figure appears exaggerated, it is likely that most Anatolian Jews lived in or near the major urban centers. B. Reicke estimates that about eighty thousand Christians lived in Asia Minor after A.D. 100 (*The New Testament Era,* 303; the source for this number, however, is unclear), and J. H. Elliott has claimed that a majority of these lived in rural areas, a claim for which he offers no substantial proof (*A Home for the Homeless: A Sociological Exegesis of 1 Peter, Its Situation and Strategy* [Philadelphia: Fortress, 1981] 63–64). Pliny (given to rhetorical exaggeration) reports that Christianity had spread through the villages and rural areas (*Ep.* 10.96.9–10). Several of the nearly one hundred inscriptions (three in Hebrew, the rest in Greek) discovered in connection with the excavation of the Sardis synagogue reveal that eight Jewish members of that synagogue were also members of the municipal council (G. M. A. Hanfmann, *Sardis from Prehistoric to Roman Times: Results from the Archaeological Exploration of Sardis 1958–1975* [Cambridge: Harvard UP, 1983] 171). Such provincial councilors (*decuriones*) were hereditary positions held by people of wealth. Other upper-class members of Sardis included Aurelius Basileides, a former procurator, and Paulus, a *comes* (i.e., a "count"). Other wealthy donors were citizens of Sardis, like Hippasios the Second.

   H. A. Harris has argued that diaspora Judaism was far more diverse than generally recognized and provides some evidence that Jews took part in Greek athletics and were spectators at Greek athletic events. He explores the implications of the menorah incised on the wall of the gymnasium at Priene, a Greek city on the Maeander southeast of Ephesus and a few miles downstream from Tralles (*Greek Athletics*, 93–94, esp. plate 1). Literary evidence suggests that many young Jewish men participated in Greek athletics in Jerusalem when it was under the control of Antiochus Epiphanes, 175–163 B.C. (2 Macc 4:7–20; Jos. *Ant.* 12.241; 19.335–37). For Palestine, Harris shows that Greek games, held in specially constructed amphitheaters, hippodromes, and stadiums, are attested in Caesarea Maritima (Jos. *J.W.* 1.415; *Ant.* 15.341) and Jerusalem (Jos. *Ant.* 15.268–73). Athletic buildings are also attested for Tiberias (Jos. *J.W.* 2.618–19; 3.539; *Life* 92) and Tarichaeae, also on the shore of the sea of Galilee (Jos. *J.W.* 2.599; *Life* 132). Stadiums (which had to be 200 yards long) were surrounded by a banking that typically accommodated ten thousand spectators. Since the population of Sepphoris and Tiberias was predominantly Jewish (cf. A. H. M. Jones, *The Herods of Judaea* [Oxford: Clarendon, 1938] 178), the spectators at such events must have been predominantly Jewish. Harris goes on to demonstrate convincingly that Philo of Alexandria was familiar with the intimate details of athletic events and must frequently have been a spectator himself (*Greek Athletics*, 51–93; cf. Philo *Agr.* 111–17). Further, Jewish parents probably allowed their children to participate (*Spec. Leg.* 2.229–30). Harris (*Greek Athletics*, 91–93) understands lines 82–93 of the famous "Letter of Claudius to the Alexandrians" (*CPJ* 2, no. 153) to forbid Jewish *participation* at games, not Jewish attendance. All this suggests that diaspora Judaism was far more enmeshed in Hellenistic culture than had been previously thought possible.

*Excursus 2C: Ancient Wreath and Crown Imagery*

### Bibliography

**Baus, K.** *Der Kranz in Antike und Christentum.* Theophaneia 2. Bonn: Hanstein, 1940. **Blech, M.** *Studien zum Kranz bei den Griechen.* Berlin; New York: de Gruyter, 1982. **Brekelmans, A. J.** *Martyrerkranz: Eine symbolgeschichtliche Untersuchung im frühchristlichen Schriftum.* Rome: Libreria Editrice dell' Università Gregoriana, 1965. **Broneer, O.** "The Isthmian Victory Crown." *AJA* 66 (1962) 259–63. **Dehandschutter, B.** "Martyrium und Agon: Über die Würzeln der Vorstellung vom ΑΓΩΝ im Vierten Makkabäerbuch." In *Die Entstehung der jüdischen Martyrologie,* ed. J. W. van Henten. Leiden: Brill, 1989. 215–19. **Deubner, L.** "Die Bedeutung des Kranzes im klassischen Altertum." *ARW* 30 (1933) 70–104. **Frend, W. H. C.** *Martyrdom and Persecution in the Early Church.* Oxford: Clarendon, 1965. **Goodenough, E. R.** "The Crown of Victory in Judaism." *Art Bulletin* 28 (1946) 139–59. **Grundmann, W.** "στέφανος, κτλ." *TDNT* 7:615–36. **Hesseling, D. C.** *De usu coronarum apud Graecos.* Leiden: Brill, 1886. **Higgins, R.** *Greek and Roman Jewellery.* 2nd ed. Berkeley; Los Angeles: University of California, 1980. **Hoffmann, H.,** and **Davidson, P. F.** *Greek Gold: Jewelry from the Age of Alexander.* Mainz am Rhein: von Zabern, 1965. **Hussey, G. B.** "Greek Sculptured Crowns and Crown Inscriptions." In *Papers of the American School of Classical Studies at Athens.* Vol. 5, Archaeological Institute of America. Boston: Damrell and Upham, 1892. **Klauser, T.** "Aurum Coronarium." In *Gesammelte Arbeiten zur Liturgiegeschichte, Kirchengeschichte und* *christlichen Archaeologie,* ed. E. Dassman. JAR 3. Münster Westfalen: Aschendorff, 1974. 292–309. **Klein J.** *Der Kranz bei den alten Griechen: eine religionsgeschichtliche Studie auf Grund der Denkmäler.* Günzberg, 1912. **Köchling, J.** *De coronarum apud antiquos vi atque usu.* Giessen, 1914. **Maxfield, V. A.** *The Military Decorations of the Roman Army.* Berkeley; Los Angeles: University of California, 1981. **Pfitzner, V. C.** *Paul and the Agon Motif.* Leiden: Brill, 1967. **Rush, A. C.** *Death and Burial in Christian Antiquity.* Washington, 1941. **Stevenson, G. M.** "The Conceptual Background to Golden Crown Imagery in the Apocalypse of John (4:4, 10; 14:14)." *JBL* 114 (1995) 257–72. **Stewart, Z.** "Greek Crowns and Christian Martyrs." In *Mémorial André-Jean Festugière: Antiquité païenne et chrétienne,* ed. E. Lucchesi and H. D. Saffrey. Geneva: Cramer, 1984. 119–24.

In the ancient world, wreaths were used in a variety of settings with a spectrum of connotations, including victory, peace, honor, and immortality.

(1) *Glory, honor, and status.* This meaning is made explicit in the phrase "crown of glory," which occurs frequently in Jewish and Christian sources (Isa 28:5, עֲטֶרֶת צְבִי *'ăteret ṣĕbî;* LXX Jer 13:18; LXX Lam 2:15; 1QS 4:7 [כליל כבוד *klyl kbwd*]; 1QH 9:25 [לכליל כבוד *lklyl kbwd*]; 1 Pet 5:4; *Asc. Isa.* 9:10–11; *T. Benj.* 4:1). (a) A symbol of honor and emblem of office representing kingship, often associated with a special robe, often purple, and a signet ring (2 Kgs 11:12; 2 Chr 23:11; Esth 2:17; 1 Macc 1:8–9; 6:14–15; Sir 40:4; *Jos. As.* 5:5; 18:6; Jos. *J.W.* 1.671; *Ant.* 17.197; John 19:1–2; Artemidorus *Oneir.* 1.77). The phrase στέφανος δικαιοσύνης, "wreath of righteousness," is used of the king in *Ep. Arist.* 280, but it also has other applications in *T. Levi* 18.2 and 2 Tim 4:8. (b) Awards for benefactors of cities and κοινά, or voluntary associations (Aeschines *Against Ctesiphon* 45; Jos. *Ant.* 14.153). Numerous examples of inscriptions on gravestones depict a wreath encircling the word ὁ δῆμος, "the people," indicating that the deceased had received such an award during his or her lifetime (see Petzl, *Smyrna* 1/23, nos. 1–117; Lucian *De luctu* 19); see Epictetus 1.19.29. Occasionally wreaths were awarded posthumously, generally by the *demos* or city, but occasionally by the society to which the deceased had belonged (see Fraser, *Funerary Monuments,* 68); sometimes these wreaths were of gold (Aeschines *Against Ctesiphon* 10, 46, 147, 258; Demosthenes *De corona* 54–55, 84, 116; *OGIS* 339.96; *IGRom* 3:739, col. 4, chap. 15, line 94; col. 5, chap. 17, line 47; col. 11, chap. 30, line 12; J. Benedum, *ZPE* 25 (1977) 272–74, 274–75). (c) Gold wreaths or crowns were the typical form in which gifts were presented to kings, emperors, and generals by individuals and cities seeking to honor them (Jos. *Ant.* 14.35, 304; 16.296; Jos. *J.W.* 7.105 [Vologeses, the Parthian king, presented Titus with a gold crown after he had conquered the Jews]).

(2) *Victory or achievement.* (a) Wreaths or crowns as prizes in competitions, particularly athletic contests (Aeschines *Against Ctesiphon* 179; Philo *Quod Omn. Prob.* 26; *T. Job* 4:10), especially the Olympic Games (Klein, *Kranz,* 64). The tombstones of famous athletes could depict prizes they had won, such as the unknown athlete from the Rhamnous deme in Attica whose tomb depicts a pine crown encircling the term "Isthmia" and a wild celery crown encircling the term "Nemea" (B. F. Cook, *Greek Inscriptions* [Berkeley: University of California, 1987] 20). (b) Wreaths or crowns as military awards. The Greeks awarded gold crowns to soldiers who had distinguished themselves for conspicuous bravery (Arrian *Anab.* 7.5.4–6). The Romans had a more organized system and awarded six different crowns as military decorations, i.e., *coronae militares* (Aulus Gelius *Noctes Atticae* 5.6.1–27; Pliny *Hist. nat.* 22.4.6–8; Maxfield, *Military Decorations,* 67–81): (i) The *corona obsidionalis,* "siege crown," was the award for rescuing a besieged army or town. (ii) The *corona civica,* "civic crown," was awarded for saving a person's life in battle and then holding on to the conquered area (Pliny *Hist. nat.* 16.3.7; 16.5.14; Livy 6.20.7). (iii) The *corona navalis* or *corona rostrata,* "naval crown," was for conspicuous bravery in naval battles. (iv) The *corona muralis,* "city wall crown" (actually made in the shape of a wall), was awarded to the first soldier to scale a wall (Pliny *Hist. nat.* 16.3.7; Livy 6.20.7). (v) The *corona vallaris,* "rampart crown" (actually made in the form of camp ramparts), was

awarded to the first soldier to breech the perimeter of an enemy army camp (Pliny *Hist. nat.* 16.3.7). (vi) The *corona aurea,* "gold crown," was for various other forms of military achievements. (vii) The *corona ovalis,* "ovation crown," made of myrtle, was worn by generals who entered the city in an ovation (Plutarch *Marcellus* 22.1–2; Jos. *J.W.* 7.124). (c) The *aurum coronarium,* "gold for crowns," was a form of tribute or taxation in which wreaths of gold were contributed by a conquered country and sometimes worn by the victorious general in his Roman triumph (Livy 37.46.4; 38.37.4; 39.7.1; Cicero *Leges* 24). Over four hundred gold crowns were carried in the triumph of Aemilius Paulus (Plutarch *Aem.* 34.5). Augustus claims that he returned 35,000 pounds of *aurum coronarium* during his fifth consulship (*Res Gestae Divi Augusti* 21). This practice was derived from the Hellenistic kings, who were presented with gold crowns on their accession and after victories. (d) Wreaths or crowns as ceremonial objects buried with the dead, perhaps symbolizing their victories in life (see Higgins, *Jewellery,* 123–24).

(3) *An expression of joy and celebration.* (a) The στέφανος νυμφικός, "wedding crown," was worn by brides (Euripides *Iph. Aul.* 905–6; Chariton 3.2.16; *Jos. As.* 21:5). (b) Vegetation crowns were worn by participants at symposia, banquets, or wedding feasts (Plutarch *Quaest. conv.* 3.1–2; *Acts Thom.* 5).

(4) Roman captives were sold as slaves *sub corona,* "under the crown," apparently referring to the fact that their heads were garlanded (Aulus Gellius *Noctes Atticae* 6.4), apparently signifying subjection and subservience.

(5) *Cultic and religious uses.* (a) Gold crowns were thought particularly appropriate for deities to symbolize their sovereignty, exalted status, and divinity (*Hymni Hom.* 6.1, 7; 32.6; Philo *Leg.* 103; Pausanias 1.17.3; Ep Jer 9; *PGM* IV.698, 1027), though crowns of various types of vegetation were also used (Tertullian *De corona* 7; *Hymni Hom.* 6.18), and statues of the gods were frequently crowned (Aristophanes *Pl.* 39; Dio Chrysostom 12.60; Athenaeus *Deipn.* 10.437b; Ep Jer 8; Pausanias 2.17.4; Clement of Alex. *Paed.* 2.8), or gold crowns were dedicated to them (Jos. *J.W.* 1.357 = *Ant.* 14.488; Pausanias 2.17.6). Isis appears with a *corona multiformis* in Apuleius *Metam.* 11.3. The Sun, a Greek deity without a cult, was regularly depicted as crowned (*3 Apoc. Bar.* 6:2), a conception reflected in Jewish synagogue mosaics such as the one at Beth Alpha and Hammath Tiberias (Hachlili, *Jewish Art,* 304–5; *NEAEHL* 1:191; 2:576). The angel Sandalphon, according to *b. Ḥag.* 13b, ties crowns to the head of God (see Gruenwald, *Apocalyptic,* 65–66 n. 135). A crown consisting of the prayers of Israel is placed on the head of God according to *3 Enoch* 15B.2; see *3 Enoch* 48B.1. (b) Wreaths or crowns were worn by priests and worshipers when praying and sacrificing (Thucydides 4.80.4; Xenophon *Anab.* 7.1.40; *Cyr.* 3.3.34; Plato *Rep.* 328C; Vergil *Aeneid* 7.135; Heliodorus 7.8; Lucian *Tim.* 4; Apuleius *Metam.* 11.24; *Mart. Pionius* 18.4). A coin of Agrippa I (A.D. 37–44) depicts him sacrificing with a patera and crowned with a wreath by two diminutive female figures (Meshorer, *Jewish Coins,* 140, no. 93). Israelite high priests wore a miter or turban (Exod 29:6; 39:30; Lev 8:9; 1 Macc 10:20; Jos. *Ant.* 3.157) with a gold "frontlet" (Exod 28:36–37), later referred to as a στέφανος χρύσεος, "gold wreath" (Sir 45:12; 1 Macc 10:20; Philo *Mos.* 2.114; Jos. *Ant.* 3.172; 12.45; *J.W.* 5.235), or a כתר כהונה *keter kĕhunnâ,* "crown of the priesthood" (*m. ʾAbot* 4:17), or simply a στέφανος (*T. Levi* 8.2, 9; Jos. *Ant.* 20.12; Eusebius *Hist. eccl.* 10.4.2). (c) Sacrificial animals were wreathed with a garland, and the verb στεφανοῦν is sometimes used in this connection, as in Lucian *De sacr.* 12 (see Aeschines *Against Ctesiphon* 164; Lucian *De Syr. dea* 58; *De luct.* 19; Acts 14:13; see Betz, *Lukian,* 68 n. 1). (d) Wreaths were worn by priests and worshipers while marching in religious processions (Livy 27.37.13; 40.37.3; 43.13.8; Pliny *Hist. nat.* 18.2.6; Athenaeus *Deipn.* 5.195a, 197f, 198a) or attending cultic feasts (*OGIS* 383.138–40; *SIG* 372.27; 398.36). (e) Crowns were dedicated to various divinities and were permanently placed in their sanctuaries (Aeschylus *Eum.* 39). (f) Wreaths or crowns were used as metaphors for the eschatological reward of the righteous (*T. Job* 40:3; *T. Abr.* [B] 10:9 [Enoch the scribe

wears three "crowns of witness"]; *Gk. Apoc. Ezra* 6:17; *Asc. Isa.* 7:22; 9:24; Wis 5:16; 5 Ezra 2:42–45; *Apoc. Elijah* 1:8; 1 Cor 9:25; 2 Tim 4:7–8; 1 Pet 5:4; Rev 3:11; Hermas *Sim.* 8.2.1– 4; 8.3.6; see Mach, *Engelglaubens*, 191–208).

(6) The victory wreath as a metaphor for the reward of the martyr (4 Macc 17:15; Rev 2:10; see Jas 1:12).

(7) The wreath as a symbol of immortality and peace in funerary art. Clement of Alexandria observed that the crown was the symbol of untroubled tranquility and for that reason the dead were crowned (*Paed.* 2.8). The wreath was an extremely common motif in Jewish funerary art (Hachlili, *Jewish Art*, 318). A typical form of this motif was a pair of winged Victories (perhaps understood as angels in Judaism; Avigad, *Beth She'arim* 3:285), holding a single crown or wreath between them (Goodenough, *Art Bulletin* 28 [1946] 143; Hachlili, *Jewish Art*, 206–7, 318 fig. 1, 340). See, for example, the lid of the eagle sarcophagus from Beth She'arim, which is decorated with two wreaths (*NEAEHL* 1:247).

In the Hellenistic world, wreaths were made of sprigs of laurel, myrtle, ivy, olive, oak, pine, wild celery, vines, and various flowers or of metallic representations of these leaves in gold, silver, or bronze (the significance of various kinds of crowns made of organic material is discussed in Artemidorus *Oneir.* 1.77). After 200 B.C. some wreaths consisted of stylized leaves in groups of three sewn on a band (Higgins, *Jewellery*, 176). Funeral wreaths were often very flimsy, since they were never actually worn (Higgins, *Jewellery*, 157). The "crown of life" is not drawn from martial imagery, for the simple reason that there is no evidence that Romans ever gave posthumous awards (Maxfield, *Military Decorations*, 138). Golden wreaths were frequently awarded to civic benefactors (Danker, *Benefactor*, 61, no. 3, line 9; 62, no. 4, line 11; 78, no. 12, line 47; 90, no. 16, line 27, Petzl, *Smyrna* 1/23, no. 215, lines 7–8). A similar honor, paid by members of a voluntary association, is mentioned in an inscription from Cyme or Phocaea (*CIJ* 2:738): "The synagogue of the Jews honored Tation the daughter of Straton, son of Empedon, with a gold crown and seat of honor."

From the third century on, the Christian martyr was often described as a victorious soldier or athlete (Frend, *Martyrdom*). In a number of early Christian authors, beginning with Paul, athletic imagery is used of the Christian life and of the victory represented by the attainment of immortality, but not specifically in connection with martyrdom (Ign. *Pol.* 1:2; 2:3; *2 Clem.* 7:1–5). Ignatius of Antioch, who used sacrificial imagery of his own impending death (*Rom.* 2, 4), never used the image of "crown" or the conception of "victory" when describing or anticipating his impending martyrdom (Stewart, "Greek Crowns," 121). Crown and prize imagery first appears in connection with martyrdom ca. A.D. 150, in *Mart. Pol.* 17–19, *Sib. Or.* 2.39–55, and *Mart. Carpus* (Greek Rec.) 35; (Lat. Rec.) 3.5 (Stewart, "Greek Crowns," 122). The equation of the martyr with the athletic champion pervades *Martyrs of Lyons* (1.11, 17, 36, 48, 41; 2.7).

## Explanation

Smyrna, a city with excellent harbor facilities that was prosperous in both Hellenistic and Roman times, lay forty miles north of Ephesus, its major rival. Smyrna became a center for the imperial cult when, in competition with eleven other cities, she was granted the right to have a temple to Tiberius, Livia, and the Senate in A.D. 29 (Tacitus *Annals* 4.55–56). This community, which apparently had few if any wealthy members (v 9), had experienced severe persecution as the apparent result of Jewish "slander." They are not *real* Jews, claims John, but a synagogue of Satan. This implies that Christians are the *true* Israel (a widespread Christian view; cf. John 4:23–24; Gal 6:16; Phil 3:3; 1 Pet 2:9–10; *Barn.* 4:6–7; Justin

*Dial.* 11.5) and that unconverted Jews are outside the people of God. The term "slander" here in all likelihood refers to the Jewish role in denouncing Christians to Roman authorities. Since Jews had a special status, exempting them from certain cultic obligations, Jewish Christians had the option of taking advantage of those benefits by claiming to be Jews. In Bithynia, ca. A.D. 110, there is evidence that pagan *delatores* ("accusers" in criminal proceedings) denounced Christians to the authorities (Pliny *Ep.* 10.96). According to Roman legal practice, such accusers had to prosecute the case in court! The prediction that some Christians will be shortly imprisoned (v 10) indicates the seriousness of the situation. Roman prisons were used for just three reasons, none of which was a form of punishment: to compel obedience to the order of a magistrate, to confine the accused until trial, or to detain until execution. That actual executions are implied is probable based on the fate of Antipas (mentioned in 2:13) and the occasional mention of Christian martyrs (6:9–11; 11:7; 20:4). The reward for faithfulness is the "crown [or, more accurately, 'wreath'] of life," a metaphor for eternal life (v 10b). In the Greek world, wreaths were used as prizes in athletic contests and have also been found among objects buried with the dead, perhaps symbolizing their victories in life. The "wreath of life" is not drawn from military imagery, however, for neither the Greeks nor the Romans ever gave posthumous awards. In v 11 the victorious Christian is promised exemption from the second death (see under 20:14).

# 3. The Proclamation to Pergamon (2:12–17)

*Bibliography*

**Birt, I.** "Der Thron des Satans." *Philologische Wochenschrift* 52 (1932) 1203–10. **Bockmuehl, M.** "The Noachide Commandments and New Testament Ethics." *RB* 102 (1995) 72–101. **Borger, R.** "NA²⁶ und die neutestamentliche Textkritik." *TRu* 52 (1987) 1–58. **Braverman, J.** "Balaam in Rabbinic and Early Christian Traditions." In *Joshua Finkel Festschrift,* ed. S. B. Hoenig and L. D. Stitskin. New York: Jewish Publication Society, 1974. 41–50. **Callan, T.** "The Background on the Apostolic Decree (Acts 15:20, 29; 21:25)." *CBQ* 55 (1993) 284–97. **Deer, D. S.** "Whose faith/loyalty in Revelation 2.13 and 14.12?" *BT* 38 (1987) 328–30. **Dietrich, E. L.** "Die 'Religion Noahs,' ihre Herkunft und ihre Bedeutung." *ZRGG* 1 (1948) 301–15. **Duncan-Jones, R. P.** *The Economy of the Roman Empire: Quantitative Studies.* Cambridge: Cambridge UP, 1974. **Feldman, L. H.** "Josephus' Portrait of Balaam." *SPA* 5 (1993) 48–83. **Greene, J. T.** "Balaam: Prophet, Diviner, and Priest in Selected Ancient Israelite and Hellenistic Jewish Sources." In *Society of Biblical Liberature 1989 Seminar Papers,* ed. D. J. Lull. Atlanta: Scholars, 1989. 57–106. **Hackett, J. A.** *The Balaam Text from Deir 'Alla.* Chico, CA: Scholars, 1980. **Hemer, C. J.** "Unto the Angels of the Churches: 1. Introduction and Ephesians; 2. Smyrna and Pergamum." *BurH* 11 (1975) 4–27. **Hansen, E. V.** *The Attalids of Pergamon.* Ithaca, NY: Cornell UP, 1947. **Hoftijzer, J.,** and **Koiij, G. van der.** *Aramaic Texts from Deir 'Alla.* Leiden: Brill, 1976. **Isenberg, M.** "The Sale of Sacrificial Meat." *CP* 70 (1975) 271–73. **Klauck, H.-J.** "Das Sendschreiben nach Pergamon und der Kaiserkult in der Johannesoffenbarung." *Bib* 73 (1992) 153–82. **Levine, L.** *Caesarea under Roman Rule.* Leiden: Brill, 1975. **MacKay, W. M.** "Another Look at the Nicolaitans." *EvQ* 45 (1973) 111–15.

**Malina, B. J.** *The Palestinian Manna Tradition.* Leiden: Brill, 1968. **Moore, M. S.** *The Balaam Traditions: Their Character and Development.* SBLDS 113. Atlanta: Scholars, 1990. **Müller, K.** *Torah für die Völker: Die noachidischen Gebote und Ansätze zu ihrer Rezeption im Christentum.* SKI 15. Berlin: Institute Kirche und Judentum, 1994. **Mussies, G.** "Antipas." *NovT* 7 (1964–65) 242–44. **North, R.** "Thronus Satanae Pergamenus." *VD* 28 (1950) 65–76. **Ohlemutz, E.** *Die Kulte und Heiligtümer der Götter in Pergamon.* 2nd ed. Darmstadt: Wissenschaftliche Buchgesellschaft, 1968. **Pick, B.** "Die Neokorie-Temple von Pergamon und der Askleipos des Phyromachos." In *Festschrift Walther Judeich zum 70. Geburtstag.* Weimar: Boehlaus, 1929. 28–44. **Radt, W.** *Pergamon: Geschichte und Bauten, Funde und Erforschung einer antiken Metropole.* Cologne, 1988. **Rohde, E.** *Pergamon: Burgberg und Altar.* Berlin: Henschelverlag, 1982. **Simon, M.** "The Apostolic Decree and Its Setting in the Ancient Church." *BJRL* 52 (1970) 437–60. **Stouannos, B.** "'Horou ho thronos tou Satana' (Apok 2:13)." *Deltion Biblikon Meleton* 4 (1976) 133–40. **Sweet, J. P. M.** "Maintaining the Testimony of Jesus: The Suffering of Christians in the Revelation of John." In *Suffering and Martyrdom in the New Testament,* ed. W. Horbury and B. McNeil. Cambridge: Cambridge UP, 1981. 101–17. **Trites, A.** "Μάρτυς and Martyrdom in the Apocalypse." *NovT* 15 (1973) 73–80. **Vermes, G.** "The Story of Balaam." In *Scripture and Tradition in Judaism: Haggadic Studies.* 2nd ed. Leiden: Brill, 1973. 127–77. **Wood, P.** "Local Knowledge in the Letters of the Apocalypse." *ExpTim* 73 (1961–62) 263–64. **Ziegenaus, O.,** and **Luca, G. de.** *Altertümer von Pergamon: Das Asklepieion.* 2 vols. Berlin: de Gruyter, 1968–75.

## Translation

[12] *Then write to the angel of* [a] *the church in Pergamon, "Thus says the one with the sharp two-edged sword:* [13] *'I know* [a] *where you live, where the throne of Satan is located. You hold my* [b] *name, and you did not renounce your faith in me* [c] *even* [d] *in the days of* [e] *Antipas,* [f] [g] *my* [h] *faithful witness,* [g] *who* [i] *was publicly* [j] *executed,* [k] *where Satan dwells.* [14] *But I have* [a] *against you* [a] [b] *the fact that* [b] *you have there those who hold the teaching of Balaam who taught* [c] *Balak* [d] [e] *to put* [e] *a stumbling block before the sons of Israel,* [f] *to eat sacrificial meat and to commit fornication.* [15] *Thus you too include those who hold the teaching of the* [a] *Nicolaitans* [b] *as well.* [b] [16] *Therefore* [a] *repent. If you do not, I will come* [b] *to you quickly, and I will fight with them* [c] *with the sword of my mouth.* [17] *Let the person with an ear hear what the Spirit announces to the churches. To the one who conquers,* [a] *I will give him* [b] *a share of the hidden manna,* [a] *and I will give him a white stone, and upon the stone a new name is inscribed which no one knows except the recipient.'"*

## Notes

12.a. Variant: τῷ] fam 1611[2050].

13.a. Variants: (1) omit τὰ ἔργά σου καί] 𝔓[43] ℵ A C 025 fam 1611[1854 2050 2329] Oecumenius[2053] Andr l it vg syr[ph] cop. (2) insert τὰ ἔργά σου καί] Andreas Byzantine 2351 syr[h] [von Soden, *Text*]. The fact that the stereotypical expression οἶδά σου τὰ ἔργα (2:19; 3:1, 8, 15) or οἶδα τὰ ἔργά σου (2:2) occurs four times has resulted in the scribal insertion of τὰ ἔργά σου here following οἶδα.

13.b. Variant: σου] ℵ*.

13.c. In the phrase τὴν πίστιν μου, the poss. pronoun is probably an obj. gen. so that the entire phrase refers to the faith or loyalty of the Pergamene community to Christ, "(your) faith in me" (Bousset, [1906] 212; Charles, 1:61; Deer, *BT* 38 [1987] 328–30); see 14:12.

13.d. Variants: (1) καί] A C fam 1611[2050 2329 2344] Oecumenius[2053]; B. Weiss, *Johannes-Apokalypse,* 107, 163; [von Soden, *Text*]. (2) omit καί] ℵ Andreas Byzantine; Tischendorf, *NT Graece*; WHort[mg]; Andreas Byzantine it[gig] it[t] vg[mss] Primasius Beatus. The omission of καί appears to be a correction (Schmid, *Studien* 2:87).

13.e. Variants: (1) omit ἐν αἷς before ᾽Αντείπας] (𝔓[43]; in this fragmentary papyrus segment there is not room for καί before ἐν and ἐν αἷς after ἡμέραις, according to W. E. Crum and H. I. Bell, *Wadi Sarga: Coptic and Greek Texts* [Hauniae: Gyldendal,1922] 44; however, it is equally possible that καί was missing from 𝔓⁴³ and αἷς present); A C Oecumenius²⁰⁵³ fam 1611²³²⁹ Andr l n²⁰⁶⁵. (2) Omit ἐν before αἷς] 046 fam 1006¹⁰⁰⁶ ¹⁸⁴¹ 2351 Andr i²⁰⁴² 94 Byzantine. (3) ἐν αἷς] Andreas TR.

13.f. Since the name Ἀντιπᾶς (nom.) should be in the gen. case (Ἀντιπᾶ, like σατανᾶ in v 13a), Lachmann conjectured that Ἀντιπᾶ must have been the original reading, though unsupported in the MS tradition. Yet Mussies (*NovT* 7 [1964–65] 242–44) has provided several examples in which proper names are treated as indeclinable on analogy with Semitic names not adapted to Gk. paradigms: *CIJ* 944: Παρηγορης υιος Ανανιας [instead of Ανανιου], "Paregores son of Ananias" (see also *CIJ* 1007, 1085, 1086). R. Borger (*TRu* 52 [1987] 45–47) has proposed an ingenious solution to the problem based on the itacized variant ἀντείπας (א^c A together with nearly thirty minuscules; see Hoskier, *Text* 2:68; several similar variants are attested by a very small number of minuscules), which is a second-person sing. aor. verb from ἀντιλέγειν, "to speak against," meaning "you [sing.] spoke against." Tischendorf (*NT Graece* 2:915) printed the name Ἀντείπας, observing that the Coptic and Syriac versions had mistakenly read Ἀντείπας as a verb from ἀντιλέγειν (*NTGraece* 2:916). Borger (45–47) has assembled the evidence from the Philoxenian and Harclean Syriac versions, which reflect this way of construing the text.

13.g-g. The noun cluster ὁ μάρτυς μου ὁ πιστός μου is in the nom. of apposition modifying the personal name Antipas, which, though indeclinable, nevertheless is in the gen. case (Mussies, *Morphology*, 191); see 1:5; 2:20; 3:12; 8:9; 9:13; 14:12; 20:2.

13.h. Variants: (1) μου] A C fam 1611²⁰⁵⁰ Oecumenius²⁰⁵³ 2351 syrʰ [von Soden]. (2) omit μου] א Andreas Byzantine vg syrᵖʰ.

13.i. Variant: omit ὅς] Byz 17²⁰⁷⁸ ²⁴³⁶ Byz 19 Andr/Byz 4a 4b⁻¹⁸²⁸ 4c²⁰⁷⁰ itᵈᵉᵐ.

13.j. The phrase παρ᾽ ὑμῖν, usually translated "among you" (so RSV), can be construed to mean "in some-one's house, city, company" (BAGD, 610), yet παρά with the dat. can also mean "in your sight," i.e., "in public."

13.k. The verb ἀποκτείνειν, normally translated "to kill," "to put to death," when pertaining to judicial proceedings, can be rendered "condemn to death" (LSJ, 205), hence "execute."

14.a-a. Variant: omit κατά σου] א*.

14.b-b. Variants: (1) omit ὅτι] C fam 1611¹⁶¹¹ ¹⁸⁵⁴ Oecumenius²⁰⁵³ Andr l; itᵃ vgʷʷ Primasius. (2) εἰ instead of ὅτι] fam 1611²³²⁹.

14.c. Variants: (1) τῷ Βαλάκ] A C syrˢ. (2) omit τῷ Βαλάκ] א*. (3) τόν Βαλάκ] א¹ fam 1006¹⁰⁰⁶ ¹⁸⁴¹ fam 1611¹⁶¹¹ ²⁰⁵⁰ ²³²⁹ Oecumenius²⁰⁵³ 2351 Andr e²⁰²⁶ f²⁰²³ g i l n 1773 2019 Byzantine. (4) ἐν τῷ Βαλααμ τόν Βαλάκ] Andreas TR.

14.d. The name Balak is articular. In general, proper names in Revelation are anarthrous, but τῷ Βαλάκ is articular because the name itself is indeclinable and the article is required to indicate syntactical function (Charles,1:cxxi). Indeclinable names are always articular when they function as the direct or indirect obj. of a verb (B. Weiss, "Der Gebrauch des Artikels bei den Eigennamen," *TSK* 86 [1913] 349ff.; BDR § 260.3).

14.e-e. Variant: βασιλεῖν] A.

14.f. Variant: καί before φαγεῖν] 2351.

15.a. Variants: (1) τῶν before Νικολαϊτῶν] א fam 1006 fam 1611²⁰⁵⁰ ²³²⁹ Oecumenius²⁰⁵³ 2351 Andreas. (2) omit τῶν] A C fam 1611¹⁶¹¹ ¹⁸⁵⁴ Byzantine. The term "Nicolaitans" occurs twice in Revelation, in 2:6 (where the word has the definite article; see *Notes* on 2:6) and in 2:15 (where the article is bracketed in Bousset [1906] 213; Nestle-Aland²⁷; UBSGNT⁴). Some think that the presence of the article in 2:6 guarantees the presence of the article in 2:15. Errors of omission are rarely common to A C Byzantine (or A Byzantine when C has a lacunae), though this may be one of those instances (Schmid, *Studien* 2:138). Charles attributes the presence of the article in 2:6 to the fact that there "Nicolaitans" is a "description of a certain class" (the term "ethnic substantive" is better; see Mussies, *Morphology*, 151–52), but it is absent in 2:15 where "Nicolaitans" is a proper name (1:cxxi), in accordance with the general rule that proper names are anarthrous in Revelation. The absence of the article, however, is the *lectio difficilior*, since it is easy to account for the addition of the article in א and Andreas but difficult to account for its omission. It is likely that "Nicolaitans" in 2:15 was originally anarthrous on analogy with the preceding phrase τήν διδαχήν Βαλαάμ, "the teaching of Balaam," where the indeclinable proper name Balaam lacks the article (Mussies, *Morphology*, 195). This is facilitated by the fact that the author probably regards the teachings of Balaam as identical with that of the Nicolaitans (see *Comments* on 2:14–15).

15.b-b. Variants: (1) omit ὁμοίως] 1. (2) ὁ μίσω] Andreas.

16.a. Variant: (1) οὖν] A C 046 fam 1006¹⁰⁰⁶ fam 1611¹⁶¹¹ ¹⁸⁵⁴ syrᵖʰ copᵇᵒˢᵃ. (2) omit οὖν] א 025 fam 1611²³²⁹ Oecumenius²⁰⁵³ 2351 Andreas latt syrʰ; Tischendorf, *NT Graece*. οὖν may have been omitted because of similarity with the preceding -σον by taking μετανόησον with ὁμοίως (*TCGNT*², 664).

16.b. The dat. of disadvantage is probably used consciously in the phrase ἔρχομαί σοι, "I will come to you," rather than the expected (and more neutral) ἔρχομαι πρός σε (see Moulton, *Prolegomena*, 75; *Note* on 2:5, where the same phrase occurs).

16.c. Variant: μετά σου] fam 1611²⁰⁵⁰ Primasius.

17.a-a. In the phrase δώσω αὐτῷ τοῦ μάννα τοῦ κεκρυμμένου, "I will give him [some] of the hidden manna," the partitive gen. functions as the obj. of the verb. This is one of the few examples in the NT of this idiom (see Acts 21:36). For instances in Revelation in which ἐκ or ἀπό + the partitive gen. functions as the subject or obj. of the verb, see 2:7, 10, 17; 5:9; 11:9; 21:6; 22:19; see BDR § 164.

17.b. Variants: (1) φαγεῖν before τοῦ μάννα] fam 1611¹⁶¹¹ ¹⁸⁵⁴ ²³⁴⁴ 2351 Andreas itᵃ ᵍⁱᵍ copˢᵃ syrʰ Beatus. (2) φαγεῖν ἐκ inserted before τοῦ μάννα] ℵ 367 468 469 1828 1957 2019 2050 2056 2073 2254. Reading (2) is based on Rev 2:7, coupled with the general Hellenistic tendency to intensify the partitive gen. with the preps. ἐκ and ἀπό. Some MSS insert ἀπό before τοῦ μάννα.

## *Form/Structure/Setting*

### I. OUTLINE

3. The proclamation to Pergamon (2:12–17)
   a. The *adscriptio:* to the angel of the church in Pergamon (v 12a)
   b. The command to write (v 12a)
   c. The τάδε λέγει formula (v 12b)
   d. Christological predication: the One who has the sharp two-edged sword (v 12b)
   e. The *narratio:* "I know your conduct" (vv 13–15)
      (1) Difficult circumstances suggested: you live where Satan's throne is located (v 13a)
      (2) Affirmation (v 13b)
         (a) You hold my name fast
         (b) You did not renounce your faith in me
      (3) Difficult circumstances amplified: the instance of Antipas (v 13c–d)
         (a) He was my faithful witness
         (b) He was killed among you
         (c) He was killed where Satan dwells
      (4) Accusations (vv 14–15)
         (a) Some hold the teaching of Balaam (who taught Balak to lead Israel astray) (v 14)
            [1] Eat meat sacrificed to idols
            [2] Practice fornication
         (b) You have some who hold the teaching of the Nicolaitans (v 15)
   f. The *dispositio* (v 16)
      (1) Command: repent (v 16a)
      (2) Threat: if you do not repent (v 16b)
         (a) I will come to *you* soon
         (b) I will make war against *them* with the sword of my mouth
   g. The proclamation formula (v 17a)
   h. The promise-to-the-victor formula (v 17b)
      (1) I will give them hidden manna
      (2) I will give them a white stone with a new name known only to the recipient

## II. HISTORICAL-GEOGRAPHICAL SETTING

Pergamon (modern Bergama), reportedly named after the founder Pergamus, is located in Mysia, sixteen miles from the sea in the fertile Caicus valley. The official divine protectress of Pergamon was Athena Nicephorus ("who brings victory"). Pergamon was a city of little importance before the Hellenistic period, when it was subjected to Greco-Macedonian rule under Alexander. Lysimachus, one of Alexander's successors, controlled western Asia Minor, and Philetaerus held the fortress of Pergamon for him. After a series of events beginning with the killing of Lysimachus by Seleucus in 281 B.C., Pergamon became independent under Philetaerus, who came into possession of the treasury of Lysimachus, which consisted of nine thousand talents. Philetaerus founded what became known as the Attalid dynasty, which made the kingdom of Pergamon one of the great powers of western Asia Minor. Philetaerus passed the rule on to his nephew Eumenes in 263 B.C. (he was never called "king"), and he in turn to his cousin's son Attalus I Soter (241–197 B.C.), who assumed the title "king" after decisively defeating the Celts in 230 B.C. Eumenes II, the eldest son of Attalus I, succeeded his father in 197 B.C. and began a Hellenizing policy continued by his brother Attalus II Philadelphia (159–138 B.C.). Finally, Attalus III Philometor Euergetes (138–133 B.C.), the son of Eumenes II, wrote the "Testament of Attalus," in which he bequeathed his kingdom to Rome (*OGIS*, 338).

Though the original Greek population was probably small, the Attalids relied on a Greek bureaucracy and a largely Greek standing army. Pergamon became a Roman ally late in the third century B.C., and in 133 B.C. the Attalids left their kingdom to the Romans, which became the Roman province of Asia (the first Roman province in Asia Minor; Bithynia became a province in 74 B.C.). One of the important events in the history of Pergamon was the defeat of the Celtic tribes in 230 B.C., and it was in commemoration of this event that the great altar of Zeus was constructed. Sacrificial victims were burned twenty-four hours a day, seven days each week by a rotating group of priests (Metzger, *Code*, 34).

One of the great libraries of the ancient world, rivaling the one in Alexandria, was located in Pergamon, and the city was so famous for book production that the modern term "parchment" (the thin skins of certain animals, usually sheep, used for writing) was derived from "Pergamon." One of its most famous citizens was the physician Galen (ca. A.D. 129–99), who began caring for gladiators in Pergamon and eventually became a court physician of emperor Marcus Aurelius in Rome.

The Roman governor, a man of consular rank who governed as proconsul, arrived in Ephesus (where the imperial procurators had their headquarters), but it is possible that the seat of government remained at Pergamon and that the proconsul had a permanent residence there (*CAH* 11:581; *Kleine Pauly* 1:636). After 27 B.C., Asia was a senatorial province of Rome. The Roman senate selected an ex-consul annually by lot and sent him to Asia as a proconsul, accompanied by three legates (*legati pro praetore*) and a *quaestor*. Procurators were occupied with the interests of the emperor. After Vespasian, the primary procurator had procurators in different regions of the province as subordinates. For judicial purposes, the province was divided into nine provinces. On fixed days the governor would stop in larger cities for the purpose of administering justice and there convene the *conventus juridicus*, "juridical gathering"; see Kornemann, *RE* 4:1173. In 29 B.C. the

Provincial League of Asia asked permission to establish a cult in honor of Octavian and (perhaps) Dea Roma (Dio Cassius 51.20.6; Tacitus *Annals* 4.37; see Friesen, *Twice Neokoros,* 7–15); this temple was depicted on the reverse of Augustan coins issued between 20 and 18 B.C. (see C. H. V. Sutherland, *The Cistophori of Augustus* [London: Royal Numismatic Society, 1970] 36, 103). Other coins depict a statue of Augustus and some of Augustus and Dea Roma in the temple (see Pick, "Die Neokorie-Tempel," 28–44).

Though Jews are not mentioned in the proclamation to Pergamon, there is evidence suggesting that there was a Jewish presence in Pergamon as early as the late second century B.C. Josephus records a decree of the people of Pergamon that can be dated either to the reign of Antiochus VII Sidetes, 138–29 B.C., or to Antiochus IX Cyzicenus, 113–95 B.C. (*Ant.* 14.247–55). This decree mentions that Jewish envoys had arrived in Pergamon after the Roman senate had ruled favorably on the affairs of Hyrcanus I and records the agreement of the Pergamenes to see that the senatorial decree was obeyed and to do everything possible on behalf of the Jews (see Schürer, *History* 1:204–5; 3/1, 18). In the first century B.C., Cicero mentions that in 62 B.C. Flaccus confiscated some gold in Pergamon that the Jewish communities in Roman Asia had intended to send to Jerusalem, including one hundred pounds of gold from the Jewish community in Apamea (*Pro Flacco* 28.68).

*Comment*

**12a** καὶ τῷ ἀγγέλῳ τῆς ἐν Περγάμῳ ἐκκλησίας γράψον, "Then write to the angel of the church in Pergamon." The population of Roman Pergamon has been estimated at 200,000 (Magie, *Roman Rule* 1:585; Frank, *Economic Survey* 4:812–16). A different, and perhaps more realistic, estimate is provided by the second-century A.D. physician Galen, who put the population of Pergamon, including women and slaves, at 120,000 (*De cognoscendis* 9). In *De propriorum anim.* 9, Galen says that Pergamon had 40,000 citizens and equal numbers of women and slaves, i.e., ca. 22 percent to 25 percent of the total population. Based on this evidence, Duncan-Jones (*Economy,* 260–61 n. 4) claims that Pergamon in the second century A.D. had a free adult population of ca. 80,000 together with 40,000 slaves, suggesting a total population of about 180,000. Duncan-Jones assumes that the free adult male population is 28.6 percent of the free population (*Economy,* 264 n. 4).

**12b** τάδε λέγει ὁ ἔχων τὴν ῥομφαίαν τὴν δίστομον τὴν ὀξεῖαν, "Thus says the one with the sharp two-edged sword." This repeats the mention of sword in 1:16, which is sharp and two-edged, and which also issues from the mouth of the exalted Christ (1:16; 2:16). The author has chosen to place the first motif ("sharp, two-edged") here and delays mentioning the second motif ("of my mouth") until 2:16. Thus the statement that the exalted Christ "has" the sword in v 12 means not that he holds it in his hand but that it issues from his mouth (W. Michaelis, *TDNT* 6:667). The sword proceeding from the mouth of Christ is further mentioned in 19:15, 21. The term ῥομφαία was normally used to refer to a large sword used both for cutting and piercing, while μάχαιρα was used for a short sword or a dagger (the somewhat arbitrary rule of thumb for archeologists is that the latter is sixteen inches or shorter). The Hebrew term חרב *ḥereb* is used in the OT for *both* the two-edged short

sword or dagger (Judg 3:16; LXX: μάχαιρα δίστομος) and the single-edged long
sword (Josh 6:21; see A. M. Snodgrass, *Arms and Armour of the Greeks* [Ithaca: Cornell
UP, 1967] 97–98; see O. Kaiser, *TDOT* 5:155). The phrase "sharp as a two-edged
sword" occurs in Prov 5:4, and the two-edged sword is also mentioned in Ps 146:6;
Sir 21:3. This is similar to the proverb found in Ahiqar 2.18 (tr. Charlesworth, *OTP*
2:500): "A king's word is gentle, but keener and more cutting than a double-edged
dagger." Reason, effective speech, or God's word is often compared with a sword
or dagger (Pss 52:2; 57:4; Wis 18:15–16; Eph 6:17; Heb 4:12; the term μάχαιρα is
used in the last two references). In Isa 49:2, in the context of the second Servant
Song, the speaker says "He [God] made my mouth like a sharp sword."

**13a** οἶδα ποῦ κατοικεῖς, ὅπου ὁ θρόνος τοῦ σατανᾶ, "I know where you live,
where the throne of Satan is located." The fact that θρόνος is articular suggests that
the author is alluding to a specific throne (either literally or figuratively), which he
expects the readers to recognize. The throne of Satan (i.e., of the Dragon) is
mentioned again in 13:2, where the Dragon (previously identified by such aliases
as the Devil and Satan in 12:9) gives it to the Beast from the Sea, which clearly
suggests the association of the throne with the imperial cult. The throne of the
Beast is again mentioned in 16:10, when the fifth bowl angel plunges his kingdom
in darkness by pouring out the bowl of plagues on his throne. In neither 13:2 nor
16:10, however, is this throne localized, while in 2:13 it is placed in Pergamon. In
view of our reconstruction of the composition history of Revelation, it is likely that
the "throne of Satan" of 2:13 (part of the Second Edition) has been derived from
13:2 and/or 16:10 (*Introduction*, Section 5: Source Criticism). The central problem
in this verse is the difficulty of determining what the author specifically meant by
the "throne of Satan."

There are a number of possibilities that have been suggested for identifying the
"throne of Satan," some very specific and others very general: (1) *The temple of
Augustus and Roma* (Zahn, 1:249; H. Schlier, *Principalities and Powers in the New
Testament* [New York: Herder and Herder, 1961] 29; Hemer, *Letters*, 87), also known
as the "Sebastion." This temple was built, perhaps at the foot of the acropolis of
Pergamon, by permission of Augustus in 29 B.C. (its site has never been located).
It was the first imperial temple in the Roman province of Asia and was one of the
more important centers of the imperial cult (Mellor, ΘΕΑ ῬΩΜΗ, 140–41; J. C.
Fayer, *Il culto della dea Roma: Origine e diffusione nell'Impero* [Trimestre Pescara, 1976]
109–11). In the second century A.D., Telephus of Pergamon wrote a two-volume
book about this sanctuary, now lost (*FrGrHist* 505 T 1). This view coheres well with
the view expressed in *T. Job* 3:5b; 4:4c, where a pagan temple is called ὁ τόπος τοῦ
Σατανᾶ, "the place of Satan."

(2) *The Great Altar of Zeus Soter* (Deissmann, *Light*, 280 n. 2; Lohmeyer, 25; Rohde,
*Pergamon*, 60–62; cf. L. L. Thompson, *Revelation*, 173). This elaborate columned
structure was constructed during the reign of Eumenes II (197–59 B.C.) to
commemorate a Pergamene victory of the Gauls in 190 B.C. It was decorated with
elaborate bas-reliefs depicting the Gigantomachy (battle between the Olympian
gods and the giants) and, like the Temple of Augustus and Roma, was located on
the acropolis (Pausanias 5.13.8). Reportedly, this acropolis could be seen from all
sides at a great distance (Aristides *Or.* 23.13). Further, the equation altar = throne
is an ancient one.

(3) *The judge's bench or tribunal* (βῆμα) where the proconsul sat to judge could be

referred to here as the throne of Satan. The term θρόνος is occasionally used for a judges bench (Plutarch *Praec. ger. reipub.* 807b). The Roman proconsul resided in Pergamon, and it was to Pergamon that Christians in the surrounding area were brought after being denounced by informers even at a later date (*Mart. Carpus* 1–23). The Province of Asia was divided into first nine, then eleven, regions; in the main city of each area (one of which was Pergamon), the *conventus juridicus,* "judicial assembly," was convened by the proconsul or the legates and a court of provincial judges called the *centumviri.* In a trial, the first stage involved a hearing *in iure,* i.e., before the jurisdictional magistrate (the praetor), while the second stage of the trial was the *iudicium centumvirale,* i.e., an appearance before a court selected from the *centumviri* (Philostratus *Vitae soph.* 1.22; Berger, *Roman Law,* 386, 521).

(4) *The temple of Asklepios* (Bousset [1906] 211; Swete, 34; Zahn, 253–63; Hadorn, 48; Schmitz, *TDNT* 3:166; Kraft, 64). Pergamon was one of the major centers for the cult of Asklepios (Lucian *Icar.* 24; Pausanias 2.26.8; Polybius 32.15.1; Galen *De anat. admin.* 1.2; Aristides *Or.* 42.4; Statius *Silvae* 3.4.21–25; Philostratus *Vita Apoll.* 4.34), though Epidaurus (on the eastern part of the Peloponnesus) remained the primary center. The cult was founded in Pergamon by Archias, who purportedly brought it from Epidaurus (Pausanias 2.26.8; Aristides *Or.* 39.5; E. J. Edelstein and L. Edelstein, *Asclepius: A Collection and Interpretation of the Testimonies* [Baltimore: Johns Hopkins, 1945] 2:249). This temple was located about one mile from the acropolis and included a number of temples, including a large temple of Asklepios and three smaller ones for Asklepios, Hygeia, and Apollo, a theater that could accommodate ca. 3,500. Aristides called Pergamon "the hearth of Asklepios" (*Or.* 23.15). The temple of Asklepios was dedicated to Asklepios Soter ("savior") and his mythical daughter Hygieia (Aristides *Or.* 23.15; 39.6); later he was called Zeus Asklepios. A new temple of Zeus Asklepios was built as part of the Asklepieion by L. Cuspius Pactumenius Rufinus in A.D. 142 (Aristides *Or.* 42.6; Galen *De anat. admin.* 1.2; see Behr, *Aelius Aristides,* 27–28). Asklepios was linked in special ways with the symbol of the serpent, which Christians associated with Satan (Rev 12:9, 14, 15; 20:2; 1 Cor 11:3).

(5) *Pergamon as a center of Christian persecution,* exemplified by the execution of Antipas (2:13b). Eichhorn (1:93) construes "the throne of Satan" as *Satanae imperium,* "the dominion of Satan," which caused the oppression of Christians in Pergamon.

(6) *Pergamon as a major center of the imperial cult* (Bousset, [1906] 211–12; Charles,1:61; Kraft, 63–64; Hemer, *Letters,* 82–87). While Pergamon did function as one among many important centers for the imperial cult, there is no explicit evidence in 2:12–17 (or in Rev 2–3) to suggest that the imperial cult was a major problem for the Christians of Asia or for the author of the final edition of Revelation.

(7) *Pergamon as an important center for Greco-Roman religion generally* (Andreas *Comm. in Apoc.* 2.13 [Schmid, *Studien* 1/1, 29], describes the city as κατείδωλος, "full of idols"; Ramsay, *Letters,* 291–98; Roloff, 54; Metzger, *Code,* 34–35).

(8) *The shape of hill on which the city was built.* Wood (*ExpTim* 73 [1961–62] 264) has suggested that this is an allusion to the shape of the major hill within the city, particularly when approached from the south.

To conclude, it appears that the "throne of Satan" should be identified not with a specific architectural feature of Roman Pergamon (in part because so little is actually known about first-century Pergamon) but rather with the *Roman opposition* to early Christianity, which the author of Rev 2–3 perceived as particularly malevolent in that city. The view of Eichhorn (1:93) mentioned above under (5) is the view open to least objection, and perhaps view (3) may have provided the necessary link between the perception of persecution and the legal authorities in Pergamon.

**13b** καὶ κρατεῖς τὸ ὄνομά μου καὶ οὐκ ἠρνήσω τὴν πίστιν μου, "You hold my name, and you did not renounce faith in me." This clause is in the rhetorical form of an antithesis in which the initial positive statement ("hold my name") is reiterated and reinforced through a negative statement ("you did not renounce faith in me"). In form it is similar to Cant 3:4, "I held him, and would not let him go." A similarly formulated clause occurs in Rev 3:8, "you have kept [ἐτήρησας] my word and have not denied [ἠρνήσω] my name." What is involved in the public and open declaration of the Christian's relationship to Christ contrasted with the public refusal to admit that one is a Christian? Frequently the terms "confess"/ "deny" are used antithetically in early Christian literature (Matt 10:32–33; Luke 12:8–9; John 1:20; Titus 1:16; 1 John 2:23; Ign. *Smyrn.* 5:1–2; *Mart. Pol.* 9:2; Hermas *Sim.* 9.28.4, 7). The fact that κρατεῖν and ἀρνεῖν are the antonyms used here, together with the fact that κρατεῖν is not used elsewhere in early Christian literature with "the name" of Jesus as its object, indicates that this cannot be considered a traditional formulation. In Heb 4:14 the verb κρατεῖν is used in the phrase "hold fast our confession," referring to the confession that Jesus is the Son of God, and the synonym κατέχειν occurs in Heb 10:23 in the synonymous phrase "hold fast the confession." The motif of denying πίστις, "faith," in Christ (note the wordplay in the adjective πιστός, "faithful," used in v 13c) has a verbal parallel in 1 Tim 5:8, in which failure to provide for one's family is considered a denial of faith (τὴν πίστιν ἤρνηται). It is theologically significant that the verb πιστεῖν does not appear in Revelation (see Boring, 95), though it occurs ninety-eight times in the Fourth Gospel.

**13c** καὶ ἐν ταῖς ἡμέραις Ἀντιπᾶς ὁ μάρτυς μου ὁ πιστός μου, "even in the days of Antipas, my faithful witness." The name Antipas is a diminutive form of the common Greek name Antipatros (see Reynolds-Tannenbaum, *Godfearers*, 97–98; Petzl, *Smyrna* 2/2:353–54). The shortened form is not widely attested (it is used of an Idumean and his son in Jos. *Ant.* 14.1.3–4, and of a son of Herod the Great by Malthace in Jos. *Ant.* 17.1.3 (see M. Fränkel, ed., *Römische Zeit*, vol. 2 of *Altertümer von Pergamon* [Berlin: de Gruyter, 1895] 524, line 2). Antipatros was a Greek name without any Hebrew equivalent. It was popular in Greece and Macedonia in Hellenistic and Roman times (*CPJ* 1:29; Petzl, *Smyrna* 2/2:102, 429.6) and is used of five different Jewish men in the Jewish papyri: *CPJ* 1:28.20; 29.10; 125.2; 2:201.1–2 (the same person is mentioned again in 207.1–2); 3:407.3. There is not a single occurrence of the diminutive form of the name Antipas in documentary evidence from the Aegean islands, Cyprus and Cyrenaica, and the full form of the name Antipatros occurs 168 times in those regions in inscriptions and other evidence (Fraser-Matthews, *Names* 1:47). The noun phrase ὁ μάρτυς μου ὁ πιστός μου, "my faithful witness," is a nominative of apposition modifying "Antipas," which is an indeclinable noun but syntactically must be in the genitive case (for other examples see 1:5; 20:2). The name "Antipas" is anarthrous because names followed by nominatives of apposition are regularly anarthrous in Revelation (Mussies, *Morphology*, 191). The verb μαρτυρεῖν used in the sense of "to die as a martyr" and the noun μαρτυρία in the sense of "martyrdom" first occurs in *Mart. Pol.* 1:1, while the term μάρτυς meaning "martyr" is first found in *Mart. Pol.* 14:2 (Polycarp died ca. A.D. 155/56, though the exact date is disputed); see *TWNT* 4:505. According to Trites (*NovT* 15 [1973] 73–80), there was a five-stage process whereby μάρτυς was transformed from "witness" to "witness through death," i.e., "martyr": (1) first, it has the original forensic sense of witness in a court of law; (2) then, it is applied to someone who testified in faith in court and is killed as a consequence; (3) death comes to be regarded as part of the witness; (4) μάρτυς comes to mean "martyr"; (5) the notion of "witness" disappears and the terms μάρτυς, μαρτύριον, μαρτυρία, and μαρτυρεῖν are used to refer to martyrdom. However, while this development seems logical enough, semantic development is rarely so neat.

**13d** ὃς ἀπεκτάνθη παρ' ὑμῖν, ὅπου σατανᾶς κατοικεῖ, "who was publicly executed where Satan dwells." The plural form of the pronoun ὑμῖν, "you," indicates that the address has shifted from the angel of the church to the members of the church who are now addressed directly (see the same phenomenon in 2:10, 19–20, 23–24). The phrase "where Satan dwells" means either that someone representing Satan lives in Pergamon or that evil is present in a particularly potent way in Pergamon. It is presumably an alternate way of saying "where the throne of Satan is located" (v 13a). Kraft (65) suggests that the ὅπου, "where," indicates that Antipas was executed because he refused to sacrifice to the statue of the emperor, but this is too speculative. The verb κατοικεῖν, "dwell" (and οἰκεῖν, "live, dwell," which belongs to the same semantic domain), is used in a variety of ways of supernatural beings who inhabit temples or individuals; it is used of God dwelling in his temple (Matt 23:21; Acts 7:48; 17:24; see 1 Cor 3:16, where Christians constitute a metaphorical temple in which the Spirit of God dwells), of the fullness of God dwelling in Christ (Col 1:19), of Christ dwelling in the heart of the believer (Eph 3:17), of God dwelling in the person who keeps his commandments (*T. Benj.* 6:4; *T. Jos.* 10:2–3; *T. Zeb.* 8:2; *T. Dan.* 5:1; Hermas *Mand.* 3.1; 10.1.6; *Barn.* 16:8), of the Holy Spirit dwelling in believers (Hermas *Mand.* 5.1.2; 10.2.5), of demons dwelling in an individual (Luke 11:26; Hermas *Mand.* 5.2.4–8), and of Satan dwelling in a person's heart (*Mart. Isa.* 1:9 [Denis, *Fragmenta*, 107]; see Luke 22:3; John 13:27; Acts 5:3).

**14a** ἀλλ' ἔχω κατὰ σοῦ ὀλίγα, "But I hold a minor matter against you." Variations on this phrase (without ὀλίγα) occur in 2:4, 20, as part of the *narratio* of the proclamations to the seven churches. On the infrequent occurrence of ἀλλά in Revelation and on the phrase ἔχειν τι κατά τινος, "to have something against someone," see *Comment* on 2:4.

**14b** ὅτι ἔχεις ἐκεῖ κρατοῦντας τὴν διδαχὴν Βαλαάμ, "that you have there those who hold the teaching of Balaam." The association of opponents with disreputable characters from the past (guilt by association) is one technique used to vilify them (du Toit, *Bib* 75 [1994] 410). The mention here of Balaam (cf. Jude 11; 2 Pet 2:15) and later of Jezebel (2:20) are examples of that technique, as are references to such paradigmatically disreputable characters elsewhere in Jewish literature as *Jannes and Jambres* (4Q267= 4QDᵃ 3 ii 14; 4Q269= 4QDᵈ frag. 2, line 2; 6Q15= 6QDamascus Document frag. 3, line 2; 2 Tim 3:8; *b. Menaḥ.* 85a; cf. Pliny *Hist. nat.* 30.2.11; Apuleius *Apol.* 90; Str-B 3:660–64; McNamara, *Targum*, 90–93); *Nadab and Abihu* (1QM 17:2); *Korah* (Ps.-Philo *Bib. Ant.* 16:1–7; 57:2). The error of Balaam is also mentioned in Jude 11 and 2 Pet 2:15 and appears to be connected with the teaching of the Nicolaitans (Rev 2:15). In rabbinic literature, Balaam and Abraham are seen as opposites, and the followers of Balaam are contrasted with those of Abraham (see *m. 'Abot* 5:19). Actually, the earliest evidence for regarding accomplished sinners as disciples of Balaam is found in Rev 2:14; Jude 11; 2 Pet 2:15–16 (Vermes, "Balaam," 135, 172). The figure of Balaam, mentioned in Num 22–24, is very complex in the history of biblical tradition (Greene, "Balaam," 57–106). In 1967 at Deir 'Alla, fragments of a book of Balaam inscribed on a plaster wall dating from the mid-eighth century B.C. (though the exemplar from which the text was copied was perhaps centuries older) were discovered (A. Lemaire, "Fragments from the Book of Balaam Found at Deir 'Alla," *BARev* 11 [1985] 26–39). The reconstructed title of at least part of this text is "Inscription/text/book of [Ba]laam [son of Beo]r, the man who was a seer of the gods" (Lemaire, *BARev* 11 [1985] 35).

**14c** ὃς ἐδίδασκεν τῷ Βαλὰκ βαλεῖν σκάνδαλον ἐνώπιον τῶν υἱῶν Ἰσραὴλ φαγεῖν εἰδωλόθυτα καὶ πορνεῦσαι, "who taught Balak to put a stumbling block before the sons of Israel, to eat sacrificial meat and to commit fornication." The term εἰδωλόθυτος is a pejorative term meaning "animals sacrificed to idols." The pejorative denotation of the term suggests that it was probably coined in Hellenistic Judaism as a polemical counterpart to the neutral denotation of the Greek word ἱερόθυτος (1 Cor 10:28; Plutarch *Quaest. conv.* 729c; see Conzelmann, *1 Corinthians*, 139); a related term is θεόθυτος, "sacrificial victim." There is slim evidence for the Jewish origin of εἰδωλόθυτος, however, for it occurs outside of early Christian literature only in two first-century A.D. Jewish sources, 4 Macc 5:2 and Ps.-Phocylides *Sententiae* 31 (reproduced in *Sib. Or.* 2.96). Part of the flesh of victims sacrificed in Greek temples was consumed by priests and worshipers on the premises, while the rest was sold to the public in the market place. Therefore, φαγεῖν εἰδωλόθυτα, "to eat meat sacrificed to idols" could refer to four possible situations: (1) participation in the sacral meal in a temple, (2) accepting sacrificial meat distributed during a public religious festival, (3) the practice of eating meat purchased at the market-place that had originally been part of a pagan sacrifice (the possibilities are formulated too narrowly by Fee, *1 Cor.*, 357–63), or (4) the sacral meals shared by members of a club or association, i.e., an ἔρανος, θίασος, or *collegium*, a context in which Christians mingled with non-Christians, though scholars who imagine that such *collegia* had the character of trade guilds (e.g., Beasley-Murray, 86, 89–90; Yarbro Collins, *Crisis*, 132), are mistaken, for there was no ancient equivalent to the medieval trade guild or modern labor union, since *collegia* had no regulatory or protective functions (Finley, *Economy*, 138; R. MacMullen, *Roman Social Relations 50 B.C. to A.D. 284* [New Haven; London: Yale UP, 1974] 18–19). Opposition to this practice is also articulated in v 20. The phrase ἐδίδασκεν . . . φαγεῖν εἰδωλόθυτα is similar to the phrase in v 20b, with "Jezebel" as the subject: διδάσκει . . . φαγεῖν εἰδωλόθυτα, "she is teaching . . . to eat food sacrificed to idols." Though it is not completely clear precisely what is involved, it would appear that actual participation in sacrificing and eating victims in Greek temples is less likely than participating in the ritual banquets associated with public holy days and festivals or buying sacrificial meat from the market and eating it at home. The practice of eating meat sacrificed to pagan gods is mentioned several times elsewhere in the NT (Acts 15:20, 29; 21:25; 1 Cor 8:1, 4, 7, 10; 10:19). For details, see *Excursus 2D: Eating Food Sacrificed to Idols.*

The imperfect verb ἐδίδασκεν does not function in a way that fits neatly into typical grammatical discussions of the use of the imperfect in the NT or nonbiblical Koine Greek. This is an example of the *consequential* use of the imperfect, in which the action of the verb is a completed action, but the imperfect is used because the consequences of Balaam's teaching, i.e., the actions or response of those taught, are closely connected with the action of teaching (see Rijksbaron, *Syntax*, 17–19). This is expressed syntactically by the three objects of ἐδίδασκεν in the aorist infinitive, βαλεῖν, "to cast," φαγεῖν, "to eat," and πορνεῦσαι, "to fornicate." Just nineteen imperfects occur in Revelation (discounting the twenty imperfects that have no contrasting aorist forms; see *Introduction*, Section 7: Syntax).

There appears to be a close connection between the two prohibitions mentioned in this verse (and Rev 2:20) and the apostolic decree in Acts 15, for only in Acts 15:20 [here the phrase τῶν ἀλισγημάτων τῶν εἰδώλων = εἰδωλόθυτος], 29; 21:25; Rev 2:14, 20 are the notions of πορνεία and εἰδωλόθυτος closely connected (Simon, *BJRL* 52 [1970] 442, 450). The list of prohibitions promulgated by the Jerusalem council in Acts 15 itself reflects the tradition of the Noachide Laws (Bockmuehl, *RB* 102 [1995] 93–95). The Noachide Laws reflect the early Jewish view that God gave pre-Sinaitic law to all people, Gentiles as well as Jews (Dietrich, *ZRGG* 1 [1948] 301–15; Callan, *CBQ* 55 [1993] 284–97; Bockmuehl, *RB* 102 [1995] 72–101). These Laws, from a Jewish perspective, provided a common ethical and ritual basis for both Jews and Gentiles. This conception was based primarily on Gen 9:3–6, where Noah prohibits the consumption of the blood of slaughtered animals and murder. The earliest extant text in which Gen 9:3–6 is expanded into a body of Noachic law is *Jub.* 7:20 (tr. Vanderkam, *Jubilees* 2:46–47):

> Noah began to prescribe for his grandsons the ordinances and the commandments—
> every statute which he knew. He testified to his sons that they should do what is right,
> cover the shame of their bodies, bless the one who had created them, honor father and
> mother, love one another, and keep themselves from fornication, uncleanness, and
> from all injustice.

While there is some ambiguity, it appears that the tradition of the Noachide Laws has influenced Ps.-Phocylides *Sent.* 3–8 (first century B.C. to first century A.D.); see Wilson, *Mysteries*, 69. In *b. Sanh.* 56b and *t. 'Abod. Zar.* 8.4, the two laws of Gen 9:3–6 are expanded to seven, though other rabbinic sources vary in the number of Noachide Laws (Bockmuehl, *RB* 102 [1995] 87–91): the prohibition of idolatry, blasphemy, murder, adultery, robbery, and eating meat torn from a living animal and the positive command to have recourse to established courts of justice. In Acts 15 the issue appears to have been the halakhic status of gentile Christians, not simply the issue of table fellowship (Bockmuehl, *RB* 102 [1995] 93). The list of prohibitions in the apostolic decree in Acts 15:20, 29 includes abstention from meat sacrificed to idols, from blood, from what is strangled, and from fornication, all similar to prohibitions associated with the Noachide Laws (Bockmuehl, *RB* 102 [1995] 94–95).

This verse refers not simply to the biblical tradition about Balaam but rather to the haggadic traditions of Balaam that circulated widely in early Judaism (see Vermes, "Balaam," 162–64). The only point of contact with the biblical narrative is the statement of Balaam in Num 24:14: "Come, I will let you know what this people will do to your people in the latter days" (in the JE narrative Balaam is blameless), combined with the statement of Moses in Num 31:16 (NRSV): "These women here, on Balaam's advice, made the Israelites act treacherously against the Lord in the affair of Peor" (the Priestly writer, who blames the disobedience of Israel on Balaam's counsel, is chiefly responsible for his subsequent bad press). Inferences from Num 31:16 were read into 24:14, which was expanded by suggesting that Balaam advised Balak to induce the Israelites to sin against their God through enticing them into the sin of fornication (Ps.-Philo *Bib. Ant.* 18:13). Parallel traditions are preserved in Philo *Mos.* 1.294–99, Jos. *Ant.* 4.126–30, *y. Sanh.* 28cd. In all three texts, Balaam counsels Balak to beguile the Israelites with prostitutes who will persuade them to abandon their religion and then to demonstrate this abandonment by participating in the worship of pagan gods. According to Jewish tradition, Balak followed Balaam's advice, leading to debauchery and idolatry, thereby using Num 31:16 to establish a link between Num 25:1–2, which states that Israel consorted with Moabite women, who, according to v 2, "invited the people to the sacrifices of their gods, and the people ate, and bowed down to their gods." In 1 Cor 10:6–8, Paul alludes to both Exod 32:1–6 and Num 25:1–18, in the context of dealing with the problem of eating sacrificial meat.

A close association is assumed by Judaism to exist between idolatry and sexual immorality (Exod 32:15–16; Wis 14:12–31; *T. Reub.* 4:6; *T. Benj.* 10:10 [in the phrase διὰ τῆς πορνείας καὶ εἰδωλολατρείας, "through immorality and idolatry," the nouns are linked with a single article, indicating that they describe aspects of the same thing]; *3 Apoc. Bar.* 8:5; *Sipre Deut.* 171; *b. Sanh.* 82a; *b. Šabb.* 17b; *b. Meg.* 25a; *b. Ketub.* 13b; see Simon, *BJRL* 52 [1970] 446–47). In the OT, the idolatry of Israel is frequently condemned through the use of the metaphor of prostitution and sexual immorality (Jer 3:2; 13:27; Ezek 16:15–58; 23:1–49; 43:7; Hos 5:4; 6:10). Idolatry is often regarded as the root of all other forms of vice; according to Wis 14:12, "the invention of idols is the beginning of fornication," and Wis 14:27 says "for the worship of the unspeakable idols is the beginning, cause, and end of every evil." Sexual immorality (πορνεία) can also be considered "the mother of all evil" (*T. Sim.* 5:3). The connection between idolatry and sexual misdeeds in Judaism is taken over by Christianity (Acts 15:20, 29; 21:25; Rom 1:23–25; Gal 5:19f–21; 1 Cor 6:9–11; 1 Thess 1:9 together with 4:3; Rev 22:15).

**15** οὕτως ἔχεις καὶ σὺ κρατοῦντας τὴν διδαχὴν τῶν Νικολαϊτῶν ὁμοίως, "Thus you too include those who hold the teaching of the Nicolaitans as well." The οὕτως, "so, thus, in this way," coordinates the phrase that it introduces with the statement that immediately precedes in v 15, by way of interpretation or explanation. Thus, "the teaching of Balaam" is the same as "the teaching of the Nicolaitans" (against MacKay, *EvQ* 45 [1973] 111–15). The καὶ σύ, "you too," refers to the presence of this influence in Ephesus previously mentioned in 2:6; the concluding ὁμοίως, "as well, likewise, similarly," also compares the situation in Pergamon with that in Ephesus. This close coordination between the Nicolaitans (for more details, see *Comment* on 2:6) and Balaam may suggest the reason that John has chosen "Balaam" as a symbol.

**16a** μετανόησον οὖν, εἰ δὲ μή, ἔρχομαί σοι ταχύ, "Therefore repent. If you do not, I will come to you quickly." Though the phrase ἔρχομαι ταχύ, "I will come soon," occurs five times in Revelation (3:11; 22:7, 12, 20; cf. 16:15), two different kinds of "coming" are meant. In Rev 22:7, 12, 20 (cf. 16:15), the verb ἔρχεσθαι, "to come," clearly refers to the Parousia, while Rev 2:16; 3:11 must be interpreted as "comings" in judgment preceding the final and decisive coming of Jesus (G. R. Beasley-Murray, "The Eschatology of the Fourth Gospel," *EvQ* 18 [1946] 97–108;

id., "The Relation of the Fourth Gospel to the Apocalypse," *EvQ* [1946] 173–86).

**16b** καὶ πολεμήσω μετ᾽ αὐτῶν ἐν τῇ ῥομφαίᾳ τοῦ στόματός μου, "and I will fight with them with the sword of my mouth." This, together with v 12, is an allusion to 1:16 (see *Comment* there). Since τοῦ στόματος is an epexegetical genitive, the metaphorical character of the expression "the sword, that is, my mouth" becomes evident. Here the sword is an implicit metaphor for the tongue, and so for the word or law pronounced by the risen Christ.

**17a** ὁ ἔχων οὖς ἀκοουσάτω τί τὸ πνεῦμα λέγει ταῖς ἐκκλησίαις, "Let the person with an ear hear what the Spirit announces to the churches." See *Comment* on 2:7.

**17b** τῷ νικῶντι δώσω αὐτῷ τοῦ μάννα τοῦ κεκρυμμένου, "To the one who conquers, I will give him a share of the hidden manna." The term "manna" (from the Hebrew term מָן הוּא *mān hû'*, "what is it?" in Exod 16:15; see Jos. *Ant.* 3.32: τί τοῦτ᾽ ἔστιν, "what is it?") refers to the miraculous feeding narrated in Exod 16:4–36 (retellings of the story are found in Jos. *Ant.* 3.26–32; Ps.-Philo *Bib. Ant.* 10:7). Manna is often called "bread from heaven" (Neh 9:15; Ps 105:40; John 6:31–33, 50–51; *Apost. Const.* 8.12.26), the "food of angels" (LXX Ps 77:25[MT 78:25]; Wis 16:20; *b. Yoma* 75b; 4 Ezra 1:19; *Adam and Eve* 4:2; see *Jos. As.* 16:14), and occasionally "bread of life" (*Jos. As.* 8:5; John 6:35, 48). According to one tradition, manna is produced in the third heaven (*b. Ḥag.* 12b). One of the eschatological expectations of early Judaism was that the future time of salvation would correspond to the period of wilderness wandering in which God would again supply manna miraculously (Volz, *Eschatologie*, 388). According to *2 Apoc. Bar.* 29:8 (tr. Charlesworth, *OTP* 1:631), "And it will happen at that time that the treasury of manna will come down again from on high, and they will eat of it in those years because these are they who have arrived at the consummation of time" (see also *Sib. Or.* 7.149; *Hist. Rech.* 13:2; *Num. Rab.* 11.2 on Num 6:22; *Qoh. Rab.* 1:9). Manna is called לחמו של עולם הבא *lḥmw šl 'wlm hb'*, "the bread of the age to come" (*Gen. Rab.* 82.8 on Gen 35:17). According to *Jos. As.* 16:14 (tr. Burchard in Charlesworth, *OTP* 2:229), "And all the angels of God eat of it [i.e., 'honeycomb' in the context, but note the proverbial sweetness of manna] and all the chosen of God and all the sons of the Most High, because this is a comb of life, and everyone who eats of it will not die for ever (and) ever."

The adjectival participle τοῦ κεκρυμμένου, "hidden," is problematic and has three possible explanations. (1) Manna is "hidden" in the sense that it is reserved only for those who enter into the age to come (Malina, *Manna Tradition*, 101; Bietenhard, *Der Tosefta-Traktat Sota*, 73–74 n. 42). (2) Manna is "hidden" because it was placed in a jar that was set before the Lord (Exod 16:32–36) and will one day again be made available to the righteous by the Messiah (a view also found in Samaritan eschatology). There was a legend in Judaism that Jeremiah hid the ark to keep it from being carried off to Babylon (2 Macc 2:4–6; Eupolemus frag. 4 [Eusebius *Praep. evang.* 9.39.5; Holladay, *FHJA* 1:134]; Alexander Polyhistor [*FrGrHist*, 723, F 5]; Ginzberg, *Legends* 6:19 nn. 111–12), and the manna was hidden along with it. (3) The heavenly manna referred to in the OT will be restored in heaven through eternal life. The meaning of this metaphor, however, is clear; victorious Christians will be rewarded with eternal life in which intimate fellowship with God will be enjoyed.

**17c** καὶ δώσω αὐτῷ ψῆφον λευκήν, "and I will give him a white stone." Beryl is called "a well-known white stone, very valuable" in *Cyranides* 1.2.6; on beryl in Revelation, see *Comment* on 21:20. ψῆφος means "pebble," "stone," and so "gem" (Philostratus *Vita Apoll.* 3.27; Artemidorus *Oneir.* 2.5: "the stone in a ring we call a ψῆφος"); it can even be used in the more specific sense of "magical gem" or "magical amulet" (*PGM* XII.209, 280; cf. IV.937, 1048, 1057). Most frequently, however, since ψῆφοι were used for voting, ψῆφος came to mean "vote." The adjective λευκοί, "white," is used of *favorable* votes (*SEG* 26:1817.80; see Horsley, *New Docs* 1:39; Horsley, *New Docs* 4:209). The precise meaning of this "white stone" remains uncertain; the most likely explanation is that it represents an amulet (see *Comment* on v 17d). The most extensive survey of proposed solutions to the problem is found in Hemer, *Letters,* 96–104: (1) a "jewel" in Israelite-Jewish tradition; (2) white stones indicating a vote of acquittal, black a vote of condemnation (Ovid *Metamorphoses* 15.41–42; Plutarch *Alc.* 202D; *Mor.* 186F; Aelian *De nat. anim.* 13.38; Lucian *Dial. meretr.* 9; the ψῆφος is found in association with νικᾶν, i.e., "victory" in the sense of "acquittal" [Theophrastus *Characters* 17.8; Aeschylus *Eum.* 741], and the "prevailing vote" can be called a νικητήριος ψῆφος [Heliodorus *Aethiopica* 3.3]. This is close to the view of Andreas [*Comm. in Apoc. ad loc.*], who interprets the phrase "they shall receive a white stone" with τουτέστι νικῶσαν, "that is, they will be victorious"); (3) a token of membership or recognition; (4) an amulet on which a divine name is inscribed (Artemidorus *Oneirocritica* 5.26); (5) a token of gladiatorial discharge; (6) an allusion to initiation into the cult of Asklepios; and (7) a writing material with a significant form or color. In Hermas *Sim.* 9.4.6, the stones (= Christians) used in building the tower (= the church) all turned white when they became part of the building.

**17d** καὶ ἐπὶ τὴν ψῆφον ὄνομα καινὸν γεγραμμένον ὃ οὐδεὶς οἶδεν εἰ μὴ ὁ λαμβάνων, "and upon the stone a new name is inscribed which no one but the recipient knows." The white stone mentioned in v 17c must be interpreted in connection with the inscription of a secret name. A major problem is that of determining whether a divine name (i.e., the name of God and/or Jesus) is written on the stone, or the name of the conquering Christian who receives the stone. Hemer argues that the "new name" refers to a name given the conquering Christian (*Letters,* 102–3). The phrase "new name" occurs in Isa 62:2, while the related term "different name" is found only in Isa 65:15. In *Tg. Isa* 65:15b this notion of a "different name" is connected with another concept found in Revelation, the second death: "and the Lord YHWH will slay you with the second death [cf. Rev 2:11], but his servants, the righteous, he will call by a different name [שמא אוחרנא *šmʾ ʾwhrnʾ*]." There is an obvious parallel with Rev 3:12, where the exalted Christ says that the name of God, the name of the city of God, and "my own new name [τὸ ὄνομά μου τὸ καινόν]" will be written on the conquering Christian (see 19:12, where the exalted Christ appears under the imagery of a conquering warrior who "has a name inscribed which no one knows but he himself"). The likelihood that this passage refers to the secret name(s) of God and/or Jesus together with the fact that this "new name" is inscribed on a white stone inevitably suggests that the imagery of the magical amulet is in view (W. Heitmüller, *"Im Namen Jesu": Eine sprache- und religionsgeschichtliche Untersuchung zum Neuen Testament* [Göttingen: Vandenhoeck & Ruprecht, 1903] 174–75; 234–35; Bousset [1906] 215; Beckwith, 461–63; Clemen, *Erklärung,* 373–74; Charles, 1:66–67; Lohmeyer, 27; Lohse, 29; Metzger, *Code,* 36). According to ancient Egyptian tradition, the sun god Re had a true name that remained a secret until revealed to Isis (Morenz, *Egyptian Religion,* 21). Magical amulets normally have an image on the obverse and a magical text on the reverse; when worn, the image would be easily seen while the text (often containing secret magical names) would be concealed.

While the precise function of the amulet is left unspecified, it appears that it is a reward for perseverance and that it therefore guarantees the permament protection of the possessor (see *T. Job* 46:7–47:11). A close parallel to Rev 2:17 is found in a magical procedure in *PDM* xii.6–20 (Betz, *Greek Magical Papyri*, 152): "You bring a ring of iron and you bring a white stone which is in the shape of a grape . . . Write this name on it [etc.]." Magical procedures that give instruction for making amulets (and other *materia magica*) occasionally mention the importance of inscribing secret names on amulets (*PGM* I.146: ὑπὸ δὲ τὸ ἔδραμος τοῦ λίθου τὸ ὄνομα τοῦτο (κρύβε), "below the design on the stone is this name (conceal it!)." Names that cannot be spoken are occasionally mentioned in the magical papyri (*PGM* XIII.763–64, 845). If the inscribed white stone is an amulet, the "new name" is perhaps that of God or (more probably) Christ (see Phil 2:9, where God bestows on the exalted Jesus "the name which is above every name," i.e., *kyrios;* see v 11). The *new* name is probably in contrast to the great variety of *old* pagan names for various supernatural beings found on amulets and magical gems. Origen argued for the magical efficacy of such Hebrew names for God as "Sabaoth" and "Adonai" (*Contra Celsum* 1.24). The magical use of the formula "the God of Abraham, the God of Isaac, and the God of Jacob" is particularly powerful (*Contra Celsum* 4.33; 5.45; cf. Justin *Dial.* 85, 135), as are the names "the God of Israel," "the God of the Hebrews," and "the God who drowned the king of Egypt and the Egyptians in the Red Sea" (*Contra Celsum* 4.34). Jewish exorcists reportedly had many ἰσχυρὰ ὀνόματα, "powerful names," at their disposal (see Matt 12:27 = Luke 11:19; Acts 19:11–20; Jos. *Ant.* 8.45–49; Justin *Dial.* 85; Irenaeus *Adv. haer.* 2.6.2). Christians, too, used the name Jesus Christ to perform healings and exorcisms (Acts 3:6; 4:10; 9:34; 16:18; Justin *2 Apol.* 6.6; *Dial.* 30.3; 76.6; 85.2; Irenaeus *Adv. haer.* 2.32.4; 2.49.3; *Epideixis* 97; Origen *Contra Celsum* 1.6, 25, 67; 3.24; *Acts of John* 41; Eusebius *Demonstr. evang.* 3.6; Arnobius *Adv. nat.* 1.46; Lactantius *Div. inst.* 2.16; 4.27). Mark 9:38–41 (= Luke 9:49–50) is an anecdote about the disciples forbidding an unauthorized person from casting out demons in the name of Jesus; this pericope reflects the fact that, in early Christian tradition, the purely magical effect of the name of Jesus was accepted (Eitrem, *Demonology*, 31). A surprisingly large number of early Christian magical amulets have been recovered, though none dates as early as the second century A.D.: H. Leclercq, "Amulettes," *DACL* 1:1795–1822; Bonner, *Magical Amulets*, 208–28; F. Eckstein and J. H. Waszink, "Amulett," *RAC* 1 (1950) 407–10; Daniel-Maltomini, *Supplementum Magicum* 1, nos. 20–36; Delatte-Derchain, *Les intailles magiques*, 283–87. On the magical use of the name of Jesus in early Christianity, see D. Aune, "Magic in Early Christianity," *ANRW* II, 23/2:1545–49; id., "Jesus II (im Zauber)," *RAC* 17:821–37.

## Excursus 2D: Eating Food Sacrificed to Idols

### Bibliography

**Barrett, C. K.** "Things Sacrificed to Idols." *NTS* 11 (1964–65) 138–53 (= *Essays on Paul.* Philadelphia: Westminster, 1982. 40–59). **Böckenhoff, K.** *Das apostolische Speisegesetz in den ersten fünf Jahrhunderten.* Paderborn, 1909. **Brunt, J.** "Rejected, Ignored, or Misunderstood? The Fate of Paul's Approach to the Problem of Food Offered to Idols in Early

Christianity." *NTS* 31 (1985) 113–24. **Cadbury, H. J.** "The Macellum of Corinth." *JBL* 53 (1934) 134–41. **Dow, S.,** and **Gill, D. H.** "The Greek Cult Table." *AJA* 69 (1965) 103–14. **Farnell, L. R.** "Sacrificial Communion in Greek Religion." *HibJ* 2 (1904) 306–23. **Fee, G. D.** "Εἰδωλόθυτα Once Again: An Interpretation of 1 Corinthians 8–10." *Bib* 61 (1980) 172–97. ———. "II Cor vi.14–vii.1 and Food Offered to Idols." *NTS* 23 (1977) 140–61. **Gill, D. W. J.** "The Meat-Market at Corinth (1 Corinthians 10:25)." *TynBul* 43 (1992) 389–93. ———. "*Trapezomata:* A Neglected Aspect of Greek Sacrifice." *HTR* 67 (1974) 117–37. **Gilliam, J. F.** "Invitations to the Kline of Sarapis." In *Collectanea Papyrologica.* FS H. C. Youtie, ed. A. E. Hanson. Part 1. Bonn: Habelt, 1976. **Lietzmann, H.** *An die Korinther I/II.* 5th ed. HNT 9. Tübingen: Mohr-Siebeck, 1969. 49–51 (excursus on *Kultmahle*). **Mischkowski, H.** *Die heiligen Tische im Götterkultus der Griechen und Römer.* Köningsberg, 1917. **Nabers, N.** "The Architectural Variations of the Macellum." *Opuscula Romana* 9 (1973) 173–76. **Ruyt, C. du.** *Macellum, marché alimentaire des Romains.* Louvain-la-Neuve, 1983. **Tomson, P. J.** *Paul and the Jewish Law: Halakha in the Letters of the Apostle to the Gentiles.* CRINT 3/1. Assen; Maastricht: Van Gorcum; Minneapolis: Fortress, 1990. **Waele, F. J. de.** "A Roman Market at Corinth." *AJA* 34 (1930) 453–54. **Will, E.** "Banquets et salles de banquet dans les cultes de la Grece et de l'Empire romain." In *Mélanges d'histoire et d'archéologie offerts à Paul Collart.* Lausanne: Bibliotheque historique vaudoise, 1976. 353–62. **Willis, W. L.** *Idol Meat in Corinth: The Pauline Argument in 1 Corinthians 8 and 10.* Chico, CA: Scholars, 1985. **Yerkes, R. K.** *Sacrifice in Greek and Roman Religions and Early Judaism.* New York: Scribner's, 1952.

In the ancient Mediterranean world, sharing food was perhaps the most common way of establishing a sacred bond between individuals and between individuals and their deities. According to Greek sacrificial protocol, holocaust offerings (animal carcasses wholly consumed by fire) were rare; normally only the useless parts were burned (the bones, fat, and gall bladders), while the meat and organs were eaten by the sacrificers (see Hesiod *Theog.* 536–41, 553–57; Burkert, *Greek Religion*, 55–59). When the number and size of the victims made immediate consumption by the participants impossible, the edible portions were sold to the public in the *macellum* or meat market (Pliny *Ep.* 10.96.10: "flesh of sacrificial victims is on sale everywhere," a translation reflecting the emendation of Koerte, accepted by Sherwin-White, *Letters,* 709–10) or were publicly distributed on special occasions such as festivals (Jos. *J.W.* 7.16; Ammianus Marcellinus 22.12.6; Augustine *Ep.* 29.9). The architectural remains of several *macella* from the Roman period have been discovered (Nabers, *Opuscula Romana* 9 [1973] 173–76). Of special interest is the *macellum* at Corinth. Though this *macellum* has not yet been definitively identified, two inscriptions connected with it that record the names of donors have been found (Cadbury, *JBL* 53 [1934] 134–41; Gill, *TynBul* 43 [1992] 389–93; de Waele, *AJA* 34 [1930] 453–54). Sacrificial meat was also consumed at socio-religious occasions at temples and at the private homes of the wealthy through invitation. Such occasions at temples are reflected in the papyrus invitations to the κλίνη, "couch," of Sarapis; hence, κλίνη connotes "a dinner at which one reclines to eat." Thirteen such invitations have now been discovered (the thirteenth invitation is POxy 3693, where references to the other twelve are given; a helpful summary discussion of these texts is found in Horsley, *New Docs* 1:5–9). Surviving terra-cotta statuettes and numismatic depictions of a reclining Sarapis confirm the notion that the deity was thought to be present on such ocasions (Gilliam, "Invitations," 317). Judging by the size of the banquet rooms in excavated sanctuaries, between seven and ten persons could be present (Will, "Banquets," 353–62). A striking illustration of religious life in imperial Pergamon came to light in 1976 during the excavations sponsored by the German Archaeological Institute, when what appears to have been a cultic dining room was uncovered (Radt, *Pergamon,* 307–13). An altar was found, and traces of vine branches and leaves and grape clusters on the walls suggest that Dionysos was the deity honored at sacral meals held there. A surviving painting of a human figure (from the waist down) clad in oriental dress suggests the syncretistic character of the cult, which may have provided the kind of setting in which Christians were tempted to compromise with paganism and eat food sacrificed to idols.

Meat was not a regular part of the diet of most people, except when distributed publicly (Macmullen, *Paganism,* 41). Most people in Greece and Italy lived primarily on a diet of flour, in earlier times made into porridge (*puls*) and later baked into bread (H. Bolkestein, *Wohltätigkeit und Armenpflege im vorchristlichen Altertum: Ein Beitrag zum Problem "Moral und Gesellschaft"* [Groningen: Bouma's Boekhuis, 1967] 365). Meat was eaten primarily in connection with religious rituals of various types. Christians, like Jews, often refused to eat sacrificial meat, and the issue is occasionally mentioned in the NT and early Christian literature (1 Cor 8:1, 4, 7, 10; 10:19; Acts 15:20, 29; 21:25; *Did.* 6:3; Aristides *Apol.* 15.5; Justin *Dial.* 35; Tertullian *Apol.* 9; Clement Alex. *Strom.* 4.16; *Paed.* 2.1; Origen *Contra Cels.* 8.28–30; *Comm. in Mt.* 11.12; Clem. *Hom.* 7.8; Clem. *Recog.* 4.36), a fact known to Lucian (*De morte Per.* 16). In *Did.* 6:3 (as part of the two-ways tradition that may well be derived from a Jewish source), we find the injunction ἀπὸ δὲ εἰδωλοθύτου λίαν πρόσεχε, "But be particularly wary of meat offered to idols." 1 Cor 8:1–13 probably refers to eating sacrificial meat in temples, while 10:23–11:1 refers to sacrificial meat sold in the marketplace (Fee, *Bib* 61 [1980] 178), indicated by the phrase πᾶν τὸ ἐν μακέλλῳ πωλούμενον ἐσθίετε, "eat everything sold in the meat market."

Making sacrifices to pagan gods and partaking of the edible portions of such sacrificial victims was forbidden in Exod 34:15, though occasionally Jews were forced to do precisely that (2 Macc 6:7, 12; 7:42). Since sacrificial meat was taboo for Jews (4 Macc 5:2; *m. 'Abod. Zar.* 2.3), authorities sometimes made special arrangements for Jewish communities to secure nonsacrificial meat (Jos. *Ant.* 14.261). Yet eating sacrificial meat was occasionally practiced by Jews, as *T. Hullin* 2.13 indicates, reflecting the experiences of the second-century Jewish community at Caesarea (Levine, *Caesarea,* 45, where the text is quoted). A warning against εἰδωλόθυτα is found in Ps.-Phocylides *Sententiae* 631, a first-century A.D. poem of Jewish origin: αἷμα δὲ μὴ φαγέειν, εἰδωλοθύτων ἀπέχεσθαι, "Do not eat blood; abstain from meat sacrificed to idols" (yet this line is found in only one MS and is probably an early interpolation; see D. Young, *Theognis,* 2nd ed. [Leipzig: Teubner, 1971] 100). The most probable source is Acts 15:29; see P. van der Horst, *The Sentences of Pseudo-Phocylides* (Leiden: Brill, 1978) 135–36. Although 1 Cor 10:23–11:1 appears to assume that a Christian entering a butcher shop could not tell which cuts were sacrificial and which not, it probably refers to meat eaten in homes when the difference was no longer apparent. Other references indicate that sacrificial meat in the marketplace was somehow readily distinguishable (Pliny *Ep.* 10.96.10; Isenberg, *CP* 70 [1975] 272). Trypho the Jew is made to claim that he knows of Christians who eat sacrificial meat (Justin, *Dial.* 34). Justin claims that they are heretics, i.e., Marcionites, Valentinians, Basilidians, and Saturnilians (*Dial.* 35.6). Irenaeus claims that heretics (Valentinians, Basilidians, Saturnilians) both eat sacrificial meat and attend pagan festivals (*Adv. haer.* 1.6.3; 1.24.5; 1.28.2), and Eusebius claims the same for the Basilidians (*Hist. eccl.* 4.7.7). Yet no surviving Gnostic text (including those from Nag Hammadi) refers to eating sacrificial meat, though there are some references to libertine indulgence in sexual promiscuity (e.g., Marcus the Gnostic). In the NT, eating sacrificial meat is often associated with sexual promiscuity (Acts 15:29; 21:25; Rev 2:14, 20); these two motifs are also connected in Num 25:1–2, to which Rev 2:14, 20 alludes. There are two possibilities at both Pergamon and Thyatira: the liberal elements eating sacrificial meat are either the wealthier members of their communities or the ordinary people who are tempted to participate in the civic and private festivities associated with Hellenistic religion. Participation in cultic meals united the participants; those who avoided such occasions erected barriers between themselves and their neighbors. Christians of high social status were more integrated into society than those from the lower class.

The controversial issue of eating food sacrificed to idols must be understood within the broader context of the problems attendant on table fellowship between Jews and Gentiles in early Christianity (Gal 2:11–14; Mark 7:1–23; Acts 10:9–16, 28; 11:3–10). Apart from a Christian context, there is very little evidence from antiquity to suggest that Jews had table fellowship with Gentiles (this view is exaggerated in the review of the evidence by P. F. Esler, *Community and Gospel in Luke-Acts* [Cambridge: Cambridge UP, 1987] 76–86). In ancient diaspora Judaism there were certainly degrees of scrupulosity, so that table fellowship certainly took place at least occasionally between Jews and Gentiles; see J. D. G. Dunn, "The Incident at Antioch (Gal. 2:11–18)," *JSNT* 18 (1983) 3–75, who cites *m. Ber.* 7:1 and *b. ʿAbod. Zar.* 8a-b. The primary reason for avoiding taking meals with Gentiles was the problem of ritual impurity; see G. Alon, "The Levitical Uncleanness of Gentiles," in *Jews, Judaism and the Classical World* (Jerusalem: Magnes, 1977) 146–89.

A variety of sacrifices mandated in the OT are eaten at least in part by the priests and Levites (Num 18:8–24; Lev 6:26; Deut 18:1–4; see Jos. *Ant.* 4.75; 1 Cor 9:13) or by the sacrificer and his family (Lev 7:6; Deut 12:7; 14:22–28; Philo *Spec. Leg.* 1.221–22; 1 Cor 10:18; Heb 13:10). The Jewish counterpart of food sacrificed to idols was called the זבח שלמים *zbḥ šlmym*, "sacrifice of communion," in which the sacrificial victim offered to God was also shared by the priest and the person making the sacrifice, who ate it at home with his family (de Vaux, *Ancient Israel*, 426–29). The offering and particularly the eating of this sacrifice of communion were not permitted to Gentiles (Jos. *Ant.* 3.318–19). Similarly, Passover lambs could not be eaten by Jews who were ritually unclean or by Gentiles (Jos. *J.W.* 6.426–27).

### Explanation

Pergamon, "the most famous place of Asia" (Pliny *Hist. nat.* 5.126), was located sixty-eight miles north of Smyrna and had an estimated population of 120,000. Occupying a high rocky elevation, Pergamon was the site of an enormous altar of Zeus now displayed in reconstructed form in the Pergamon Museum in Berlin. Pergamon was an important center for the imperial cult. It was the site of the first and most important temple to the deified Augustus. "Satan's throne" (v 13) may refer to this center of imperial worship or, less likely, to the great altar of Zeus (the equation altar = throne is very old and widespread). It is also possible that "Satan's throne" refers to the βῆμα or seat of judgment used by Roman magistrates in Pergamon. The Pergamene Christians are commended for their steadfastness even in the face of persecution. Antipas, mentioned only here in early Christian literature, may have been executed for failing to sacrifice to the cult of deified emperors, though there is no explicit evidence that supports such a view. Antipas is called "my faithful witness" (NIV); the Greek term for "witness" is μάρτυς, a term that shortly came to include the idea of dying for the faith present in our word "martyr." Nevertheless, the church is censured for tolerating some who hold the teaching of Balaam and eat food sacrificed to idols and practice immorality. In early Judaism and early Christianity, heresy was not so much *heterodoxy* (deviant opinions or doctrines) as *heteropraxy* (deviant practices); some Jews and Christians assumed that idolatry and immorality went hand in hand. Balaam was a non-Israelite diviner whose contact with Israel is narrated in Num 22–24 and who was regarded as instrumental in leading Israel into idolatrous and immoral practices (Num 25:1–5; 31:16). In later Jewish tradition, Balaam is regarded as a paradigmatic false prophet (Philo *Mos.* 1.263–304; Jos. *Ant.* 4.126–30).

The practice of eating food sacrificed to idols was problematic for both Jews and Christians. Ancients rarely ate meat, and when they did it was typically in connection with public or private religious celebrations in which the edible parts of sacrificial animals were eaten. Such meat was taboo for Jews (4 Macc. 5:2–3; *m. ʿAbod. Zar.* 2:3), a prohibition sometimes taken over by early Christians, particularly Jewish Christians (Acts 15:29). Paul, however, was equivocal on the subject (1 Cor 8:4–13; 10:14–11:1). The Nicolaitans (v 15) are accused of teaching sexual immorality and eating meat offered to idols, both libertine practices. This poses a certain difficulty for identifying them with Gnostics, for in the Gnostic texts from the Coptic library from Nag Hammadi, there is not a trace of libertine indulgence in sexual promiscuity or of eating sacrificial meat.

The Pergamene Christians are urged to repent; otherwise Christ threatens to *come* to them in judgment. This "coming" does not refer to the Parousia (though that event is presented from a juridical rather than a salvific perspective; see 19:11–16). Those who conquer are promised hidden manna and a white stone with a new name inscribed on it. "Manna" (a Hebrew term meaning "what is it?") was the name for miraculous "bread" supplied to the Israelites by God (Exod 16:1–36). Jews expected God to repeat that miracle in the last days (John 6:31–34; *2 Apoc. Bar.* 29:8). Manna is therefore another metaphor for eternal life (as in John 6:49–51). The white stone may be a reference to an amulet inscribed with a secret divine name (see *PGM* I.146; XII.6–20).

# 4. The Proclamation to Thyatira    (2:18–29)

## Bibliography

**Black, M.** "Some Greek Words with Hebrew Meanings in the Epistles and Apocalypse." In *Biblical Studies in Honor of William Barclay,* ed. J. R. McKay and J. F. Miller. London: Collins, 1976. 135–46. **Bockmuehl, M.** "The Noachide Commandments and New Testament Ethics: With Special Reference to Acts 15 and Pauline Halakhah." *RB* 102 (1995) 72–101. **Böckenhoff, K.** *Das apostolische Speisegesetz in den ersten fünf Jahrhunderten.* Paderborn, 1903. **Borgen, P.** *Paul Preaches Circumcision and Pleases Men.* Trondheim: TAPIR, 1983. ———. *Philo, John and Paul: New Perspectives on Judaism and Early Christianity.* Atlanta: Scholars, 1987. **Brooten, B. J.** *Women Leaders in the Ancient Synagogue.* Chico, CA: Scholars, 1982. **Cohen, S.** "Women in the Synagogues of Antiquity." *Conservative Judaism* 34 (1980) 25–26. **Collins, J. N.** *Diakonia: Reinterpreting the Ancient Sources.* New York: Oxford UP, 1990. **Gangemi, A.** "La stella del mattino (Apoc. 2,26–28)." *RivB* 26 (1978) 241–74. **Hemer, C. J.** "Unto the Angels of the Churches: 3. Thyatira and Sardis." *BurH* 11 (1975) 110–35. **Johnson, L. T.** "The New Testament's Anti-Jewish Slander and the Conventions of Ancient Polemic." *JBL* 108 (1989) 419–41. **Lähnemann, J.** "Die sieben Sendschreiben der Johannes-Apokalypse: Dokumente für die Konfrontation des frühen Christentums mit hellenistisch/römischer Kultur und Religion in Kleinasien." In *Studien zur Religion und Kultur Kleinasiens.* 2 vols. Ed. S. Sahin, E. Schwertheim, and J. Wagner. Leiden: Brill, 1978. **Ljung, I.** "Om 'Isebel' i Samaria, Tyatira och frankerrit." *SEÅ* 54 (1989) 127–34. **Ozanne, C. G.** "The Language of the Apocaypse." *TynBul* 16 (1965) 3–9. **Schiffman, L. H.** "Laws Concerning Idolatry in the Temple Scroll." In *Uncovering Ancient*

*Stones.* FS H. N. Richardson, ed. L. M. Hopfe. Winona Lake, IN: Eisenbrauns, 1994. 159–75. **Seland, T.** *Jewish Vigilantism in the First Century c.e.* Trondheim: Doctor Artium Dissertation, 1990. **Soggin, A.** "Zum zweiten Psalm." In *Wort-Gebot-Glaube.* FS W. Eichrodt. Zürich: Zwingli, 1970. **Tatton, C.** "Some Studies of New Testament *Diakonia.*" *SJT* 25 (1972) 423–34. **Thiel, W.** "Der Weltherrschaftsanspruch des judäischen Königs nach Psalm 2." In *Theologische Versuche.* Berlin: de Gruyter, 1971. **Unnik, W. C. van.** "A Greek Characteristic of Prophecy in the Fourth Gospel." In *Text and Interpretation.* FS M. Black, ed. E. Best and R. McL. Wilson. Cambridge: Cambridge UP, 1979. 211–29. **Wilhelmi, G.** "Der Hirt mit dem eisernen Szepter: Überlegungen zu Psalm II 9." *VT* 27 (1977) 196–204.

## Translation

[18] *Then to the angel of the* [a] *church* [b] *in Thyatira, write, "Thus says the son of God, whose* [c] *eyes are like a flame* [d] *of fire and his feet as burnished bronze.* [19] *I know your works, namely, your love and faithfulness and* [a] *service* [b] *and* [a] *your* [c] *endurance. Your recent behavior is better* [d] *than before.* [20] *But I have this* [a] *against you, that* [b] *you have tolerated* [b] *that woman* [c] *'Jezebel,'* [d] [e] *who calls* [e] *herself a prophetess and who teaches* [f] *and misleads* [g] *my* [h] *servants, to fornicate and to eat meat sacrificed to idols.* [21] *And I have given her time* [a] *to repent,* [a] *but* [b] *she did not want* [c] *to repent of* [c] *her fornication.* [22] *Behold* [a] *I will throw* [a] *her into a sickbed,* [b] *and* [c] *I will cause* [c] *those who commit fornication with her great tribulation. If they will not reject* [d] *her* [e] *behavior,* [23] *then* [a] *I will kill her children with the plague.* [b] *Then* [c] *all the churches will know that I am the one who searches mind and heart, and I will give to each of you in accordance with your deeds.* [24] *I say to the rest of you in Thyatira, as many as do not hold this teaching, who do not know what* [a] *people call* [a] *'the secrets* [b] *of Satan,' I will not put* [c] *any other burden upon you.* [25] *Only* [a] *maintain what you have until* [b] *I come.* [26] *And* [a] *as for the one who conquers* [a] *and* [b] *who keeps* [b] *my works until the end, I will give him authority over the nations,* [27] *and he will drive them* [a] *with an iron scepter,* [a] *as when ceramic jars* [b] *are shattered.* [b] [28] *Just as I received it from my father, so* [a] *I will give the morning star to him.* [29] *Let the person with an ear hear what the Spirit announces to the churches."*

## Notes

18.a. Variants: (1) τῷ] A Andr/Byz 4c²³⁰⁵. (2) omit τῆς] C. (3) τοῖς] Oecumenius²⁰⁵³ Andr c²⁰⁵² Andr i²⁰¹⁵ Byz 4¹⁷¹⁹ Byz 19⁶⁶⁴ ²⁰¹⁶ Andr/Byz 3¹⁶¹⁷ Andr/Byz 4a⁶¹⁶.

18.b. Variant: omit ἐκκλησίας] A.

18.c. Variant: omit αὐτοῦ] A Andr b²⁰⁵⁹ d 1 n²⁴²⁹ 2019 syrᵖʰ.

18.d. Variant: φλόξ] ℵ Andr e h n²⁴²⁹ 181 2019. Originated in a scribal assimilation to the phrase φλὸξ πυρός in 1:14.

19.a-a. Variant: omit τὴν διακονίαν καί] ℵ* 598.

19.b. Variant: omit τήν] A 2019.

19.c. Variant: omit σου] ℵ fam 1611²³²⁹ 598 792 Byz 17²⁴¹ itᵈᵉᵐ,ᵍⁱᵍ,ᵗ vgᶜ,ᴰ,ᴼ,ᵀ Origen Beatus Primasius; Tischendorf, *NT Graece.*

19.d. The comparative adj. πλείονα, a neut. acc. pl., based on πολύς, "much, many," is the only comparative adj. in Revelation. Since there are also two superlatives in Revelation, τιμιωτάτου (18:12) and τιμιωτάτῳ (21:11), Mussies suggests the reason for the absence of comparative forms lies in the absence of comparison categories in the Heb. and Aram. adj. systems (*Morphology,* 138).

20.a. ἀλλὰ ἔχω κατὰ σου ὅτι ἀφεῖς τὴν γυναῖκα Ἰεζάβελ, "But I have this against you that you have allowed that woman 'Jezebel.'" The word "this" in the translation has been supplied in the interests of English usage; the ὅτι clause functions as the obj. of ἔχω (see *Comment* on 2:4). Ancient scribes also supplied a variety of objs. of ἔχω, including: (1) πολύ] ℵ fam 1611²⁰⁵⁰ 598 2019 Andreas syrᵖʰ arm⁴ itᵍⁱᵍ.

(2) πολλά] 1773 Andr b[2081] i[-2042] Primasius Cyprian Ambrose. (3) ὀλιγά] Byzantine TR. (4) ὀλιγὰ πολύ] Andr e[2026].

20.b-b. Variants: (1) ἀφεῖς] ℵ* A 025 046 fam 1611[1854] Oecumenius[2053] 2351 Andreas. (2) ἀφήκας] ℵ¹ fam 1611[1611 2050] Andr d e[2057] h[2280*] 2019 vg[ms] syr cop. (3) ἀφίης] fam 1006[1006 1841 2626] 2681.

20.c. Variant: (1) τὴν γυναῖκα] ℵ C 025 fam 1611[1611 2344] Oecumenius[2053] it vg cop[bo,sa] arm eth Tertullian; Tischendorf, *NT Graece;* WHort; von Soden, *Text.* (2) σοῦ after τὴν γυναῖκα] A 046 fam 1006[1006] fam 1611[1854] 2351 Andr f[2073] Andr i[2042] Andr n[2065] Andr/Byz 4b[1828] Byzantine syr[ph] syr[h] Cyprian Primasius; WHort[mg]. The reading τὴν γυναῖκα σοῦ means "your wife" and presupposes either that the ἄγγελος, "angel," of 2:18 is actually the bishop of Thyatira, the view argued by Zahn, 1:286ff. (see *Comment* on 1:20), or that it is a metaphor that means a prominent woman in the community (Ramsay, *Letters,* 341; he argues that copyists tended to drop σοῦ to avoid calling Jezebel the wife of the Church). σου is probably inserted because of the frequency with which σου occurs in the preceding verses (B. Weiss, *Johannes-Apokalypse,* 162; *TCGNT* ¹, 734–35; *TCGNT* ², 664).

20.d. "Jezebel" lacks the definite article (except in A) because it is followed by a nom. ptcp. clause in apposition (Mussies, *Morphology,* 191).

20.e-e. Variants: (1) ἡ λέγουσα] ℵ* A C Oecumenius[2053] fam 1611[2329]. (2) τὴν λέγουσαν] ℵ¹, fam 1611[1854 2050] Andreas. (3) ἡ λέγει] fam 1006 fam 1611[1611] 2351 Andr f[2023] i 94 Byzantine. Reading (1), ἡ λέγουσα, "who calls," is the *lectio difficilior* because it is a solecism since it is a nom. of apposition that must be linked *semantically* with the acc. clause τὴν γυναῖκα Ἰεζάβελ, "that woman 'Jezebel,'" though *syntactically* it should have been in the acc. (Mussies, *Morphology,* 63). Some copyists substituted the syntactically appropriate acc. form found in readings (2) and (3).

20.f. Here the ind. διδάσκει, "she teaches," is problematic, with three possible solutions: (1) The phrase καὶ διδάσκει may function like the inf. διδάσκειν, which is dependent on ἀφεῖς, i.e., "you allowed (her) to teach" (Lancellotti, *Sintassi Ebraica,* 109). (2) The ind. διδάσκει may be an equivalent to the subjunctive ἵνα διδάσκῃ, "that she teaches," a clause dependent on ἀφεῖς, "you allow," i.e., "you have allowed that she teach" (Mussies, *Morphology,* 336). This construction is understood this way by the Latin Vulgate: *quia permittis mulierem Hiezabel . . . docere, et seducere,* "because you permit the woman Jezebel . . . to teach and to lead astray." A verbal parallel is found in John 12:7: ἄφες αὐτὴν ἵνα εἰς τὴν ἡμέραν τοῦ ἐνταφιασμοῦ μου τηρήσῃ αὐτό, "Permit her to keep it for the day of my burial." This translation is at odds with most modern versions and commentators, who prefer to render the first two words independently from the rest of the sentence: "Leave her alone." (3) Another possibility is the Semitism in which a ptcp. is coordinated with a finite verb (Moulton-Howard, *Accidence* 2:428–29; Charles, 1:cxliv–vi; Mussies, *Morphology,* 326–27; S. Thompson, *Apocalypse,* 66–67), so that the phrase could be translated "who calls herself a prophetess and teaches."

20.g. Here the verb πλανάω, "to lead astray," may be used transitively with the complimentary infs. πορνεῦσαι, "to fornicate," and φαγεῖν, "to eat," in which case it should be translated "to induce to" or "to deceive into." However, since there are few if any examples of πλανάω used with a complementary inf., this proposal is speculative.

20.h. In the noun cluster τοὺς ἐμοὺς δούλους, the poss. adj. ἐμός occurs only here in Revelation; elsewhere poss. pronouns in the gen. of poss. are used. Poss. adjs., however, occur fifty-one times in the Gospel and Letters of John.

21.a-a. Here ἵνα with the subjunctive μετανοήσῃ is a final or purpose clause.

21.b. καί here functions in an adversative sense and has been translated "but."

21.c-c. The phrase μετανοεῖν ἐκ, "to repent of," occurs five times in Revelation (2:21, 22; 9:20, 21; 16:11), though not once in the rest of the NT, the LXX, or the Apostolic Fathers. It does occur once in *T. Abr.* 12:13: μετανοήσωσιν ἐκ τῶν ἁμαρτιῶν αὐτῶν, "they might repent of their sins." The equivalent phrase μετανοεῖν ἀπο is found in LXX Jer 8:6 ("No man repents of [Gk. μετανοῶν ἀπό; Heb. עַל נֹחָם *niḥām 'al*] his wickedness") and Acts 8:22 ("Repent, therefore, of this wickedness of yours [μετανόησον οὖν ἀπὸ τῆς κακίας σου ταύτης]"). The idiom μετανοεῖν ἀπό is also found in *1 Clem.* 8:3 in a "quotation" from LXX Ezek 33:11: μετανοήσατε, οἶκος Ἰσραήλ, ἀπὸ τῆς ἀνομίας ὑμῶν, "repent, house of Israel, of your iniquity" (at this point LXX Ezek 33:11 reads ἀποστροφῇ ἀποστρέψατε ἀπὸ τῆς ὁδοῦ ὑμῶν, "turn away from your ways"). This quotation has been attributed to the *Apoc. Ezek.* frag. c (A.-M. Denis, *Fragmenta,* 122–23) or frag. 2 (see Charlesworth, *OTP* 1:494). Heb 6:1 has the related phrase μετάνοια ἀπὸ νεκρῶν ἔργων, "repentance from dead works." *Jos. As.* 9:2 has "[Aseneth] wept . . . and repented of [μετανόει ἀπό] her gods." Justin, *Dial.* 109.1 uses μετανοεῖν ἀπό: "But that the Gentiles would repent of the evil in which they lived in error" (also 121.3). Charles (1:71) suggests that μετανοεῖν ἐκ reflects the Heb. מִן שׁוּב *šûb min,* "turn from," and K. G. C. Newport proposed that in Revelation μετανοεῖν ἐκ should be translated "turn away from" ("The Use of ἐκ in Revelation: Evidence of Semitic Influence," *AUSS* 24 [1986] 225–26).

Similarly, according to Behm (*TDNT* 4:1006), μετανοεῖν in the post-apostolic period means "to turn away," and can be a synonym of ἐπιστρέφειν (see Justin *Dial.* 30.1; Clement of Alex. *Quis div. salv.* 39).

22.a-a.  Variants: (1) βαλῶ (fut. ind.)] ℵ² 0025 fam 1006 fam 1611^{1611 2050 2329} 2351 it^{gig t} vg^{cl} cop^{sa} Tertullian. (2) καλῶ (present ind. from καλεῖν)] ℵ*. The verb βάλλω, "to throw, cast," is a futuristic present, a judgment confirmed by the fact that the *fut.* ind. verb ἀποκτενῶ, "I will kill," is used in v 23.

22.b.  Variant: (1) κλίνην] ℵ C 025 046 fam 1006^{1006} fam 1611^{1611 1854 2344} Oecumenius^{2053} it^{gig,ar} vg syr^{ph,h} cop^{bo}; *TCGNT*¹, 735; *TCGNT*², 665. (2) φυλακήν] A.

22.c-c.  The verb βάλλω must be supplied a second time with the obj. clause "those who commit fornication," though with the meaning "to cause, bring about" (Louw-Nida, § 13.14). Since the first use of βάλλω is literal and the second use metaphorical, this is a subtle use of paronomasia (for other occurrences of paronomasia in Revelation, see 2:2[2x]; 3:10; 18:6[3x], 20, 21; 22:18, 19; cf. BDF § 488.1; Turner, *Syntax*, 148).

22.d.  On the phrase μετανοεῖν ἐκ, see *Note* 2:21.d. Here the phrase appears to mean "turn away from," "reject," for how can someone repent of what someone else is doing? Cf. REB: "unless they renounce what she is doing." The RSV at this point is overly literal: "Unless they repent of her doings." NIV: "unless they repent of her ways."

22.e.  Variants: (1) αὐτῆς] ℵ C 025 046 fam 1006^{1006 1841} fam 1611^{1611 2050 2329} Oecumenius^{2053txt} Andr c f^{2023corr} j^{2042} l 94; it^{gig} vg syr^h cop^{bo,sa} Tertullian Cassiodorus Tyconius; *TCGNT*¹, 735; *TCGNT*², 665. (2) αὐτῶν] A fam 1611^{1854 2344} Oecumenius^{2062} Andreas it syr arm eth Cyprian Primasius Ps-Ambrose.

23.a.  καί is used here to introduce the apodosis of the fourth type of conditional clause (BDR § 371): ἐάν + subjunctive in the protasis (suggesting that the protasis has the possibility of becoming a reality), usually with a tense in the ind. in the apodosis (here a fut. ind.).

23.b.  ἀποκτενῶ ἐν θανάτῳ, lit. "I will kill with death," can be interpreted in two ways leading to two quite different translations: (1) as a Hebraism or Aramaism in which the noun in the dat. intensifies the verb, i.e., "I will surely kill," or (2) as a noun in the dat. meaning "plague," i.e., "I will kill with the plague."

(1) The phrase does resemble a Hebraism or Aramaism (evidence for the latter is now found in 1QapGen 20:10–11) in which the verb is intensified by the dat. of an abstract cognitive (i.e., the dat. of *manner*), e.g., θανάτῳ θανατούσθω, "let him be put to death" (Lev 20:15; see Exod 21:12; 31:15; Lev 20:2; Ezek 3:18; see Thackeray, *Grammar*, 48–49; Zerwick, *Greek* § 60; BDF § 198.6; BDR § 198.8, 9). Another example is Luke 22:15, ἐπιθυμίᾳ ἐπεθύμησα, lit. "with desire I desired," i.e., "I have greatly desired" (the identical expression occurs in Gen 31:30). The same idiom can be expressed in Gk. without the use of cognates, e.g., θανάτῳ ἀποθανεῖσθε, "you will certainly die" (Gen 2:17; cf. Gen 3:4; Num 26:65; Judg 13:22; 1 Kgs 14:39; Sir 14:17); θανάτῳ ἀποκτενεῖτε αὐτούς, "you will surely kill them" (Exod 22:19). In Hermas *Sim.* 8.7.3, the following phrase occurs: θανάτῳ ἀποθανοῦνται, "they will surely die." In this instance Hermas reproduces an idiom with exact parallels in the LXX. In Luke 22:15, the phrase ἐπιθυμίᾳ ἐπεθύμησα is exactly paralleled in LXX Gen 31:30. There are other instances in which this idiom is without close parallel (e.g., Acts 5:28: παραγγελίᾳ παρηγγείλαμεν; Jas 5:17: προσευχῇ προσηύξατο), which indicates that the style of the LXX is being imitated. A similar construction is found in classical Gk. (see C. A. Lobeck; *Paralipomena Grammaticae Graecae* [Leipzig, 1837] 523–27); see Sophocles *Philoctetes* 79: φύσει . . . πεφυκότα; Plato *Phaedrus* 265c: παιδιᾷ πεπαῖσθαι; Hippocrates *Art.* 10: ὁμιλίη ὁμιλεῖν; Aelian *Hist. nat.* 8.15: νίκη ἐνίκησε (A. Hilhorst, *Sémitismes et Latinismes dans le Pasteur d'Hermas* [Nijmegen: Dekker & Van de Vegt, 1976] 150–53). In spite of these Gk. parallels, the construction remains relatively rare in pagan Gk. literature and relatively common in the LXX (where it occurs about 200 times), which means that it is a *stylistic* Hebraism.

(2) In favor of the second view are passages in the LXX such as Ezek 33:27, θανάτῳ ἀποκτενῶ, "I will kill with pestilence," since the Heb. term דבר *deber*, meaning "plague, pestilence," is regularly translated in the LXX with the Gk. term θάνατος, so that some scholars consider this to be one of the clearest lexical Hebraisms in Revelation (Ozanne, *TynBul* 16 [1965] 5). However, as Black observes ("Some Greek Words," 136), the Gk. word θάνατος, like the Aram. מחא *mētā'*, could mean "death" or "plague," a suggestion supported by the fact that the modern Gk. term θανατικό means "disease." The phrase ἐν θανάτῳ in Rev 6:8 means "with pestilence" (see 18:8; Ezek 6:12: ἐν θανάτῳ τελευτήσει, "he will die by pestilence"). The use of the prep. ἐν indicates that θανάτῳ is used as a dat. of means and must therefore mean "by pestilence." This interpretation is reinforced by the threat in v 22 that Jezebel will become ill and her followers experience tribulation (illness?).

23.c.  Here καί functions as a consecutive particle introducing a clause that describes the result of the verbal action in the previous conditional sentence (Zerwick, *Greek* § 455; Ljungvik, *Syntax*, 62–63; Mussies, *Morphology*, 342); see *Notes* on 3:10; 11:3; 14:10; 20:10.

24.a-a.  The verb λέγουσιν is an impersonal pl. that can be translated with the indefinite "one" or "people"; see 12:6; 18:14; 20:4 (Mussies, *Morphology*, 231; S. Thompson, *Apocalypse*, 18–22; Rydbeck, *Fachprosa*, 27–45; BDF § 130; BDR § 130).

24.b. Variants: (1) τὰ βαθέα] A C fam 1006[1006 1841] fam 1611[1611 1854] 2351 Byzantine Andr d f[2023] i[2042] 194. (2) τὰ βάθη] ℵ fam 1611[1611 2050 2329 2344] Oecumenius[2053] 2349 Andreas lat. The neut. acc. pl. βαθέα (with an acute accent on the penult) is based on the adj. βαθύς, while the very similar form βάθεα (with an acute accent on the antipenult) is an uncontracted acc. pl. from the substantive τὸ βάθος (Moulton-Howard, *Accidence*, 60). Robertson (*Grammar*, 232) is confident that only the adj. βαθέα can be correct in Rev 2:24. Since βάθη is the contracted form of the acc. pl. of βάθος, it is impossible to decide whether βαθέα without an accent is based on the adj. βαθύς or the substantive βάθος. Variant (1) has the strongest attestation. βαθέα means literally "depths," i.e., "the content of knowledge which is very difficult to know—'deep secrets, secrets difficult to find out about'" (Louw-Nida, § 28.76), i.e., secret things that can be known only by initiates.

24.c. Variants: (1) βάλλω] A C 025 fam 1005[1006 1841] fam 1611[1854] Oecumenius[2053] it[gig] syr[ph,h]. (2) βαλῶ] ℵ 046 fam 1611[1611 2050 2329] Oecumenius[2062] 2351 Tyconius Primasius it[a] vg.

25.a. πλήν, "only," is a particle or conjunction, used here (its only occurrence in Revelation) with limitative force meaning "however," "nevertheless," "only," a classical usage (Thucydides 8.70) that also appears in Hellenistic literature (Plutarch *Romulus* 18; *Lycurgus* 16; Polybius 3.49.7; Epictetus 1.28.17), including the LXX (Deut 2:34–35; Josh 6:24) and the NT (1 Cor 11:11; Eph 5:33; Phil 3:16; 4:14); see M. E. Thrall, *Greek Particles in the New Testament* (Grand Rapids, MI: Eerdmans, 1962) 20. In classical Gk. πλήν usually introduces an exception and is then translated "except" or "except that" (J. Blomqvist, *Greek Particles in Hellenistic Prose* [Lund: Gleerup, 1969] 77), while in Aristotle and Theophrastus it is used to modify a previous statement, where it can be translated either as an exception or adversatively (Blomqvist, *Greek Particles*, 80). πλήν is also used in a progressive sense to introduce a new subject or new element in the description (Blomqvist, 88). Blomqvist (92–97) also focuses on the distinctive features of the use of πλήν in the LXX. In Rev 2:25, as in Paul, πλήν is used to conclude a discussion by emphasizing what is important (BDR § 449.2). For an extensive discussion of πλήν in Hellenistic literature, see Blomqvist, *Greek Particles*, 75–100.

25.b Variants: (1) ἄχρι οὗ] ℵ C fam 1611[1611 2329] Oecumenius[2053]. (2) ἄχρις οὗ] Andreas Byzantine 2351. (3) ἕως οὗ] A Byz 17[241].

26.a-a. ὁ νικῶν, "as for the one who conquers," is a substantival ptcp. that is a pendent nom. or nom. abs. referring to the logical though not grammatical subject that is mentioned again with the sing. acc. resumptive pronoun αὐτῷ in the proper case syntactically (BDF § 466.4). The ptcp. standing before the main clause in a *casus pendens* is a construction found in Gk. (Moulton-Howard, *Accidence*, 425) as well as Heb. (GKC § 143; Lancellotti, *Sintassi Ebraica*, 83) and Aram. (Black, *Aramaic*, 51–55), though here the construction appears to follow a Semitic model (Beyer, *Semitische Syntax*, 217). The same construction occurs in 3:12, 21; 21:7(*var. lect.*); cf. 2:7, 17, where the dat. case is used as a functional equivalent to the pendent nom.

26.b-b. ὁ τηρῶν is a pendent nom. coordinated with ὁ νικῶν (see *Note* 26.a-a.; the *casus pendens* also occurs in 3:12, 21; 6:8).

27.a-a. The Gk. phrase ἐν ῥάβδῳ σιδηρᾷ, "with an iron rod," in LXX Ps 2:9 is an ambiguous rendering of the Heb. phrase בשבט ברזל *bĕšebeṭ barzel*, for שבט *šebeṭ* can refer to a shepherd's crook or staff (which doubled as an instrument for herding animals and a weapon) or a royal scepter. Understood as a shepherd's crook or staff, the phrase "iron crook" can be understood as an oxymoron, i.e., the linking of opposite notions in one expression, since a shepherd's crook is used for the benefit and guidance of the flock, whereas an *iron* crook emphasizes its use as a weapon (Wilhelmi, *VT* 27 [1977] 202).

27.b-b. Variants: (1) συντρίβεται (present ind. pass.)] ℵ A C fam 1611[1854 2050] it[gig] cop. (2) συντριβήσεται (fut. ind. pass.)] Andreas Byzantine 2351.

28.a The protasis of the comparative clauses in this verse is introduced with the particle ὡς, "as," while the καί that introduces the apodosis functions like οὕτως and should therefore be translated "so." The protases and apodoses of comparative clauses can be introduced with a variety of comparative particles (with the apodosis frequently occurring before the protasis): ὡς / ὥσπερ / καθώς / καθάπερ ... οὕτως / οὕτως καί / καί / κατὰ τὰ αὐτά (BDR § 453.1; Turner, *Syntax*, 320). Examples: (1) ὡς ... οὕτως (Matt 24:38); (2) ὡς ... οὕτως καί (1 Cor 7:14); (3) ὥσπερ ... οὕτως (Matt 12:40; 13:40; 24:27 = Luke 17:24; Matt 24:37); (4) καθώς ... οὕτως (Luke 11:30; 17:27); (5) καθώς ... κατὰ τὰ αὐτά (Luke 17:28, 30); (6) ὡς ... καί (Matt 6:10 [= *Did.* 8:2]: ὡς ἐν οὐρανῷ καὶ ἐπὶ γῆς, "as in heaven, so upon earth"); Acts 7:5: ὡς οἱ πατέρες ὑμῶν καὶ ὑμεῖς, "as your fathers did, so you do"; Gal 1:9; Phil 1:20; that this is not a Semitism but is common in Hellenistic Gk. is evident from the parallel in Plutarch *De recta rat. aud.* 38E (BDR § 453.1), and the parallels listed in E. Lohmeyer, *Das Vater-Unser*, 3rd ed. (Zürich: Zwingli, 1952) 77; Lohmeyer also claims that "This καί is therefore not possible in Aram., but is pure Greek"; (7) καθώς ... καί (John 7:57; 1 John 2:18).

*Form/Structure/Setting*

## I. OUTLINE

4. The proclamation to Thyatira (2:18–29)
    a. The *adscriptio:* to the angel of the church in Thyatira (v 18a)
    b. The command to write (v 18a)
    c. The τάδε λέγει formula (v 18a)
    d. Christological predications: Christ is (v 18a–c)
        (1) The Son of God (v 18a)
        (2) The One with eyes like fire (v 18b)
        (3) The One with feet like burnished bronze (v 18c)
    e. The *narratio:* "I know your conduct" (vv 19–21)
        (1) Your behavior (v 19a)
            (a) Love
            (b) Faithfulness
            (c) Service
            (d) Endurance
        (2) Your recent behavior is better than before (v 19b)
        (3) Accusation: "I have this against you" (vv 20–21)
            (a) You have tolerated "Jezebel" (v 20)
                [1] She calls herself a prophetess (v 20a)
                [2] She teaches and misleads my servants (v 20b)
                    [a] To fornicate
                    [b] To eat meat sacrificed to idols
            (b) Previous warnings to "Jezebel" (v 21)
                [1] I gave her time to repent (v 21a)
                [2] She refuses to repent of her fornication (v 21b)
    f. The *dispositio* (vv 22–25)
        (1) Threat of imminent retribution (vv 22–23a)
            (a) I will throw "Jezebel" into a sickbed (v 22a)
            (b) I will afflict those who fornicate with her with great
                tribulation, if they do not repent (v 22b)
            (c) I will kill her "children" with the plague (v 23a)
        (2) Christological axiom: The revelation of Christ through
            judgment to the churches (v 23bc)
            (a) Christ searches mind and heart (v 23b)
            (b) Christ gives to each in accordance with their deeds (v 23c)
        (3) To those uninfluenced by "Jezebel's" teachings (called the
            deep things of Satan (v 24–25)
            (a) I give you no other burden (v 24c)
            (b) Hold what you have until I come (v 25)
    g. The promise-to-the-victor formula (vv 26–28)
        (1) Recipients (v 26a)
            (a) Those who conquer
            (b) Those who keep my word until the end
        (2) The reward (vv 26b–28)

(a) I will give them the kind of authority I received from my
Father (vv 26b, 28a)
[1] I will give them authority over the nations (v 26b)
[2] They will rule the nations with an iron scepter as
when ceramic pots are smashed (v 27)
(b) I will give them the morning star (v 28b)
h. The proclamation formula (v 29)

## II. HISTORICAL-GEOGRAPHICAL SETTING

Thyatira (modern Ahisar) was located about thirty-five miles inland, between Pergamon and Sardis in northern Lydia, or Mysia (Strabo 13.4). According to legend, Thyatira was first established as a shrine to the sun god Tyrimnus and named Pelopia. The city was considered a Macedonian settlement (Strabo 13.4), and was reconstructed by Seleucus Nicator (301–281 B.C.) as a frontier garrison. It was subject to Pergamon after 190 B.C. (Livy 37.44.4; L. Robert, *Villes d'Asie Mineure: Études de geographie ancienne* [Paris: de Boccard, 1962] 252–60) and to Rome after 133 B.C. In 155 B.C. Prusias marched to Pergamon and in his retreat went to Thyatira (Polybius 32.15). In 132 B.C. the city was captured by Aristonicus, the son of Eumenes II (Strabo 14.38; on the early history of Thyatira, see Magie, *Roman Rule* 2:977–78). Within the Roman *provincia Asia,* Thyatira belonged to the *conventus* of Pergamon until the time of Caracalla (A.D. 211–17), when Thyatira became the leading city in a separate *conventus* (A. H. M. Jones, *Cities,* 83). Lydia of Thyatira, who lived in Philippi, was Paul's first Christian convert in Europe (Acts 16:14–15, 40) and sold purple goods as a trade she had probably learned in Thyatira, which was particularly known for its dyeing process and had a strong guild of dyers (Magie, *Roman Rule* 1:48; 2:812 n. 80). According to a writing attributed to the Alogoi (a Christian sect in Asia Minor that was opposed to Montanism), a Christian church did not exist in Thyatira in the late first century when John wrote (Epiphanius *Pan.* 51.33.1), though Epiphanius claims that the entire city became Montanist (ca. A.D. 200) and that thereafter a true Christian church could be found in Thyatira (Epiphanius, *Pan.* 51.33.3–4). One of the significant characteristics of Thyatira was the prominence of various trade guilds, including associations of clothiers, bakers, tanners, potters, linen workers, wool merchants, slave traders, shoemakers, dyers, and copper smiths (Magie, *Roman Rule* 1:48; 2:812 n. 78; A. H. M. Jones, *Cities,* 83; Hemer, *BurH* 11 [1975] 110).

*Comment*

**18a** καὶ τῷ ἀγγέλῳ τῆς ἐν Θυατείροις ἐκκλησίας γράψον, τάδε λέγει ὁ υἱὸς τοῦ θεοῦ, "Then to the angel of the church in Thyatira, write, 'Thus says the Son of God.'" The phrase ὁ υἱὸς τοῦ θεοῦ, "the Son of God," occurs forty-six times in the NT (and only here in Revelation), but this is the only instance in the NT in which "the Son of God" is the subject of a transitive verb of speaking. In the NT the title is used of the exalted Jesus (as here) in just a few passages: Acts 13:33; Rom 1:3; Col 1:13; 1 Thess 1:9–10; Heb 1:5; 5:5. Roman emperors characteristically claimed in their titulature introducing official letters and decrees that they were "sons of god" in the special sense that they were sons or adopted sons of their deified predecessors. A letter from Augustus to Ephesus begins this way: Αὐτοκράτωρ Καῖσαρ θεοῦ Ἰουλίου υἱός, "Emperor Caesar, son of the god Julius" (J. Reynolds, *Aphrodisias and Rome* [London: Society for the Promotion of Roman Studies, 1982] document 12, line 1, p. 101).

**18b** ὁ ἔχων τοὺς ὀφθαλμοὺς αὐτοῦ ὡς φλόγα πυρός, "whose eyes are like a flame of fire." This phrase is a repetition with variations of that in 1:14b: καὶ οἱ ὀφθαλμοὶ αὐτοῦ ὡς φλὸξ πυρός, "and his eyes were like a flame of fire." This repetition is part of the author's program of atomizing the constituent descriptive features of the vision of 1:9–20 and utilizing them in Rev 2–3 to link these sections together. The phrase φλόγα πυρός is a possible allusion to LXX Ps 103:4, quoted in Heb 1:7; *1 Clem.* 36:3 (see D. A. Hagner, *The Use of the Old and New Testaments in Clement of Rome*, NovTSup 34 [Leiden: Brill, 1973] 46, 180).

**18c** καὶ οἱ πόδες αὐτοῦ ὅμοιοι χαλκολιβάνῳ, "and his feet as burnished bronze." This same phrase occurs in 1:15a, whence it was derived to serve as a thematic link between the christophany of 1:9–20 and the proclamations to the seven churches in 2:1–3:22.

**19a** οἶδά σου τὰ ἔργα καὶ τὴν ἀγάπην καὶ τὴν πίστιν καὶ τὴν διακονίαν καὶ τὴν ὑπομονήν σου, "I know your works, namely, your love and faithfulness and service and your endurance." In 2:2, the concepts κόπος, "labor, toil," and ὑπομονή, "endurance," are subordinated to τὰ ἔργα, and here too it appears that ἔργα, "works," is a general term more closely defined by the four nouns in the polysyndetic list that follows. This indicates that the four terms "love and faith and service and endurance" are all terms that emphasize various aspects of the behavior of Christians. It is also striking that each of these terms occurs in the Second Edition of Revelation, with one possible exception: (1) ἀγάπη (2x: 2:4, 19), (2) πίστις (4x: 2:13, 19; 13:10; 14:12 [the last two are almost certainly expansions]), (3) διακονία (1x: 2:19), and (4) ὑπομονή (7x: 1:9 [First Edition]; 2:2, 3, 19; 3:10; 13:10; 14:12 [the last two are almost certainly later additions]). ἀγάπη occurs just twice in Revelation, here and in 2:4 (see *Comment* there). Here πίστις (which occurs four times in Revelation; see *Comment* on 2:13) means "dependability, faithfulness" (Karrer, *Brief*, 204 n. 283). The term διακονία, "service, ministry" (which occurs only here in Revelation), occurs a total of thirty-three times in the NT and is found in two very different lists of spiritual gifts in 1 Cor 12:4–6 (which speaks of "varieties of gifts . . . varieties of service [διακονιῶν] . . . varieties of working") and Rom 12:6–8; however, there is no similarity between other items on these lists and Rev 2:19. διακονία has the basic meaning of speaking or acting on behalf of others or attending someone for the purpose of performing a range of tasks (Collins, *Diakonia*, 77–95). The genitive (here σου) after the abstract noun διακονία usually designates the person or agent carrying out a task. Cognates of διακονία were used for servants, waiters, priests, statesmen, tradesmen, messengers, and so forth, i.e., a spectrum of roles from menial to privileged (the menial aspect of διακονία is emphasized by H. W. Beyer, *TDNT* 2:82–87). However, when Collins (*Diakonia*, 339) refers to this usage of διακον- as "churchmen," he is wide of the mark, for the σου refers to the angel of the church at Thyatira, who exercises the ministry of service as a surrogate for the *entire community*.

**19b** καὶ τὰ ἔργα σου τὰ ἔσχατα πλείονα τῶν πρώτων, "Your recent behavior is better than before." Again the term ἔργα is used as a general term for the behavior of the Christians in Thyatira, but this time in a diachronic sense of the progress in Christian behavior, certainly implying an earlier knowledge of the character of this Christian community.

**20a** ἀλλὰ ἔχω κατὰ σου ὅτι ἀφεῖς τὴν γυναῖκα Ἰεζάβελ, ἡ λέγουσα ἑαυτὴν προφῆτιν, "But I have this against you, that you have tolerated that woman 'Jezebel,' who calls herself a prophetess." "Jezebel," according to John, claims to be a prophetess and has corrupted some of the servants of Jesus in Thyatira. The author has derived the name "Jezebel" from the name of the wife of Ahab king of Israel (869–850 B.C.), the daughter of Ethbaal king of Tyre and Sidon, famous for influencing Ahab to worship Canaanite gods (1 Kgs 16:31; Jos. *Ant.* 8.317). The story of Jezebel is narrated in 1 Kgs 18–21; 2 Kgs 9 (and in a rewriting of the biblical account with some additional material in Jos. *Ant.* 8.316–59; 9.47, 108, 122–23) and includes her campaign to kill the prophets of Yahweh (1 Kgs 18:4, 13; Jos. *Ant.* 8.330, 334; 9.108), her support of 450 prophets of Baal and 400 prophets of Asherah (1 Kgs 18:19; Jos. *Ant.* 8.330, 334), her attempt to kill Elijah (1 Kgs 19:1–3; Jos. *Ant.* 8.347), how she framed Naboth, who was consequently stoned to death (1 Kgs 21:1–16; Jos. *Ant.* 8.355–59), and how, in fulfillment of the prophecy of Elijah (1 Kgs 21:23), Jehu had Jezebel killed by defenestration, after which she was eaten by dogs on the street (2 Kgs 9:30–37; Jos., *Ant.* 9.122–24). Though Jezebel is accused of "harlotries and sorceries" (2 Kgs 9:22), there is nothing in the preceding narrative to support such charges, which suggests that they are metaphors for abandoning the worship of Yahweh (note that the *Tg. Ps.-J.* 2 Kgs 9:22 reads "*idols* and sorceries" in place of "harlotries and sorceries"). Jezebel was also remembered as a "painted woman" (2 Kgs 9:30; Hippolytus *Comm. in Dan.* on 13:31 [*Susanna*]). Since "Jezebel" apparently occupied a very influential position in the Christian community of Thyatira, it is important to consider the role of women in leadership positions in both Anatolian Judaism and Christianity.

There are some nineteen inscriptions from ca. 27 B.C. through the sixth century A.D. in which women bear such titles as ἀρχισυνάγωγος and ἀρχισυναγωγίσσα, "head of the synagogue," ἱέρισσα, "priestess," μήτηρ συναγωγῆς, "mother of the synagogue," πρεσβυτέρα, "elder," and προστάτης and ἀρχήγισσα, "leader." Cohen (*Conservative Judaism* 34 [1980] 25–26) and Brooten (*Women Leaders*) argue convincingly that these are functional rather than honorific titles. One of the more relevant evidential inscriptions is from Sardis (*CIJ* 741). In the Greco-Roman world, inscriptional evidence suggests that women frequently played the role of patronesses; see R. MacMullen, "Women in Public in the Roman Empire," *Historia* 29 (1980) 211; E. L. Will, "Women's Roles in Antiquity: New Archeological Views," *Science Digest* (March 1980) 35–39. In early Christianity, several women of probable Jewish origin held important offices. Junia was an apostle (Rom 16:7); Phoebe was a deacon and a προστάτις, "patroness" (Rom 16:1–2; on her role a patroness, see P. Jewett, "Paul, Phoebe, and the Spanish Mission," in *The Social World of Formative Christianity and Judaism*, ed. J. Neusner et al. [Philadelphia: Fortress, 1988] 142–61); Prisca was a teacher and missionary (Acts 18:2, 18, 26; Rom 16:3–4; 1 Cor 16:19; 2 Tim 4:19).

It is possible that "Jezebel" was a patroness or hostess of one of the house churches that made up the Christian community at Thyatira who found herself in conflict with other Christian patrons, probably over an attempt to accommodate Christian practices to the surrounding culture by justifying the eating of meat offered to idols (see *Excursus 2D: Eating Food Sacrificed to Idols*).

**20b** καὶ διδάσκει καὶ πλανᾷ τοὺς ἐμοὺς δούλους πορνεῦσαι καὶ φαγεῖν εἰδωλόθυτα, "and who teaches and misleads my servants, to fornicate and to eat meat sacrificed to idols." While the syntax of this sentence is problematic (see *Note* 2:20.d.), the essential meaning is clear. The Christian community at Thyatira bears a collective responsibility for tolerating "Jezebel" by allowing her to teach heretical opinions that cause them to wander from the truth and in consequence to indulge in sexual immorality and to eat meat from animals sacrificed to idols. The charge of teaching fornication or sexual immorality (πορνεύειν) links this female figure with that of the Great Whore of Babylon, with whom the nations of the world have fornicated (14:8; 17:2; 18:3; 19:2). The charge that "Jezebel" teaches Christians to practice sexual immorality is probably groundless and reflects the stock slander (unaffected by the facts) typically leveled at opponents by ancient writers (Johnson, *JBL* 108 [1989] 419–41). Nearly all the uses of the πορν- cognates in Revelation are figurative rather than literal; the only exceptions are found in three vice lists in 9:21; 21:8; 22:18. The term "fornication" is probably used here in the sense of "apostasy," a usage found frequently in the OT. The historical Jezebel was charged with sexual immorality and the practice of witchcraft (2 Kgs 9:22), and that has probably influenced the present context. The accusation of illicit sexual behavior is leveled against the female followers of Dionysos (Euripides *Bacchae* 223–23, 237–38, 260–61, 353–54, 487, 957–58, though the charge is shown groundless by eyewitnesses, 686–87). On the close association between idolatry and immorality, see *Comment* on 2:14.

On the eating of sacrificial meat, see *Comment* on 2:14. The historical Jezebel was a worshiper of Baal (1 Kgs 16:31), perhaps specifically Melqart of Tyre. The connection here between prophecy and eating sacrificial meat has a significant parallel in Philo *Spec. Leg.* 1.315–17 (Borgen, *Paul*, 73; Borgen, *Philo*, 226), a passage discussed in detail by Seland (*Jewish Vigilantism*, 73–80, 98–107, 123–25, 136–37, 147–53). There Philo, alluding to Deut 13:1–11, deals with what appears to be a contemporary problem (LCL tr.):

Further if anyone cloaking himself under the name and guise of a prophet [σχῆμα προφητείας] and claiming to be possessed by inspiration lead us on to the worship of the gods recognized in the different cities, we ought not to listen to him and be deceived [ἀπατωμένους] by the name of prophet. For such a one is no prophet, but an imposter, since his oracles and pronouncements are falsehoods invented by himself.

Philo goes on to suggest that even if such things are done by friends or relatives, they must be considered enemies and should by lynched. 11QTemple 44:18–20 also paraphrases the law of the prophet who advocates idolatrous worship (see Schiffmann, "Idolatry," 163–66).

**21a** καὶ ἔδωκα αὐτῇ χρόνον ἵνα μετανοήσῃ, "And I have given her time to repent." This suggests that the exalted Christ has already denounced "Jezebel's" behavior in the past, either through the prophetic ministry of John or possibly through one of his prophetic associates, but that she has chosen not to respond. 4Q*175* = 4QTestim 5–8, based on Deut 18:18–19, speaks of a prophet whom God will raise up and who will speak all the words that he is commanded (tr. García Martínez, *Dead Sea Scrolls*, 137): "And it will happen that the man who does not listen to my words, that the prophet will speak in my name, I shall require a reckoning from him."

**21b**  καὶ οὐ θέλει μετανοῆσαι ἐκ τῆς πορνείας αὐτῆς, "but she did not want to repent of her immorality." Just as "Jezebel" does not repent of sexual immorality, so the rest of humanity that was not killed by the plagues following the sounding of the sixth trumpet also refused to repent (οὐ μετανόησαν) of their murders, sorceries, sexual immorality (πορνεία), or thefts (9:21). It is important to determine whether πορνεία, "sexual immorality," here is literal or metaphorical. In Revelation the πορν- terms are usually used in a metaphorical sense: πορνεία (14:8; 17:2, 4; 18:3; 19:2); πορνή (17:1, 5, 15, 16; 19:2); πορνεύειν (17:2; 18:3, 9). When πορν- cognates are used literally, they are part of vice lists (πορνεία in 9:21; πόρνος in 21:8; 22:15). The verb μετανοεῖν, "to repent," is used five times in Revelation in the negative sense of that from which one turns away, expressed with the preposition ἐκ + the genitive of separation, or the so-called ablatival genitive (2:21, 22; 9:21, 22; 16:11). Elsewhere, that from which one turns is expressed with the preposition ἀπό + the genitive of separation (LXX Jer 8:6; Acts 8:22; *1 Clem.* 8:3). Heb 6:1 has μετάνοια ἀπὸ νεκρῶν ἔργων, "repentance from dead works" (see the phrase μετάνοιαν ἁμαρτιῶν, "repentance from sins," in Hermas *Mand.* 3.3; *Sim.* 8.6.6, in which the notion of separation is intensified by the prepositions ἐκ or ἀπό). Cf. *Ep. Arist.* 188: μετατιθεὶς ἐκ τῆς κακίας καὶ εἰς μετάνοιαν ἄξεις, "you [God] turn some from wickedness and will lead them toward repentance."

**22a**  ἰδοὺ βάλλω αὐτὴν εἰς κλίνην καὶ τοὺς μοιχεύοντας μετ᾽ αὐτῆς εἰς θλῖψιν μεγάλην, "Behold I will throw her into a sickbed, and I will cause those who commit fornication with her great tribulation." The expression βάλλω αὐτὴν εἰς κλίνην, "I will throw her into a sickbed," is a Hebrew idiom that means "to cast upon a bed of illness," i.e., to punish someone with various forms of sickness (Charles, 1:71–72; see Exod 21:18; 1 Macc 1:5; Jdt 8:3). In one part of a complex curse on a Jewish amulet from the Cairo Geniza (TS K1.42, lines 31–33), we read: "may they fall into bed with sickness [יפול במטה בחדירה *yippôl bammitâ baḥadîrâ*] as long as he dwells in the place that they stole" (Schiffman-Swartz, *Incantation*, 85, 88). In the ancient tradition first found in Deut 13:5–11, false prophets are to be executed (cf. 4Q*375* =Apocryphon of Moses 1.4–5; 11QTemple 54.10–15; 61:1–2; 4Q*158*=4QReworked Pentateuch<sup>a</sup> frag. 6, line 8; Philo *Spec. Leg.* 1.315–17 ), it is surprising that "Jezebel" is not threatened with death, though her "children" are (v 23). That the two clauses in this verse are parallel is indicated by the fact that the verb βάλλω is not repeated, though it is understood as the verb whose object is τοὺς μοιχεύοντας, "those who fornicate." "Those who commit fornication" with Jezebel do not seem to be confined exclusively to her followers or disciples; rather they include those who have been drawn into the circle of the prophetess and her school and have been negatively influenced by her teachings, i.e., have practiced both the eating of meat sacrificed to idols and illicit forms of sexual behavior.

**22b**  ἐὰν μὴ μετανοήσωσιν ἐκ τῶν ἔργων αὐτῆς, "If they do not repent of her behavior." Those who fornicate with "Jezebel" are urged to repent, although repentance does not appear to be a live possibility for "Jezebel" herself (she has previously been given an opportunity to repent but had not done so; see *Comment* on v 21). This clause strongly suggests that the "fornication" mentioned in v 22a is metaphorical, for why should those who commit fornication with "Jezebel" repent of *her* behavior? It is true, however, that in biblical tradition those who lead others astray in a calculating and insidious way bear a greater responsibility.

**23a**  καὶ τὰ τέκνα αὐτῆς ἀποκτενῶ ἐν θανάτῳ, "then I will kill her children with
the plague." The phrase τὰ τέκνα αὐτῆς, "her children," refers to the group that
should probably be identified with the disciples of "Jezebel" or members of her
prophetic circle; see Isa 8:18; Amos 7:14 (Lähnemann, "Die sieben Sendschreiben,"
532 n. 30). Like "Jezebel" herself, this group of her hardened followers may have
been given an opportunity to repent previously but, like "Jezebel" herself, had not
done so. Some understand these "children" to refer to this woman's literal children
(Beckwith, 467), but this is unlikely. A sixth-century A.D. curse appeals to the Holy
God, Gabriel, and Michael to "strike down Philadelphe; and her children, lord lord
lord God God, strike them down with her" (Daniel-Maltomini, *Supplementum
Magicum* 2:61, lines 1–3), presumably referring to the woman's actual children.
According to the *Mart. Carpus* 24–34 (ed. Musurillo, 24–27), when the Roman
proconsul was in residence at Pergamon, Papylus from Thyatira was one of the
Christians brought before him. When the proconsul asked him if he had any
children (τέκνα ἔχεις), he said that he did. Further questioning revealed that these
were *spiritual* children: "I have children in the Lord in every province and city."

**23b**  καὶ γνώσονται πᾶσαι αἱ ἐκκλησίαι ὅτι ἐγώ εἰμι ὁ ἐραυνῶν νεφροὺς καὶ
καρδίας, "Then all the churches will know that I am the one who searches mind and
heart." This is an allusion to Jer 17:10a, "I the Lord search the mind and try the
heart," which is confirmed by the allusion to the second part of Jer 17:10 in v 23c:
"to give to every man according to his ways, according to the fruit of his doings."
This allusion has important christological significance, since the original speaker
in Jer 17:10 was Yahweh, but now it is the exalted Christ who possesses the same
omniscience. There are several passages in the Gospels in which the supernatural
knowledge and insight of Jesus is emphasized (Matt 9:4; John 2:25; 4:29, 39; 16:30;
18:4; 21:17). In Judaism and early Christianity it is frequently affirmed that God
knows the mind and heart of each person (1 Sam 16:7; 2 Sam 14:20; 1 Kgs 8:39; 1
Chr 28:9; 2 Chr 6:30; Pss 44:21; 139:1–6, 23; Wis 7:1; Sir 1:30; 15:18; 42:18–19; Sus
42; Bar 3:32; 2 Macc 9:5; *2 Apoc. Bar.* 83:2–3; Jos. *J.W.* 5.413; Philo *Op.* 69; *Som.* 1.87;
*PGM* IV.3046–47 [a magical procedure possibly of Jewish origin]; Matt 6:4, 6, 18;
Acts 1:24; 15:8; Rom 2:16; 1 Cor 4:5; 14:25; Heb 4:12–13; Ign. *Phld.* 7:1; *Teach. Silv.*
116.3). Just as God knows everything about individuals, so prophets have insight
into the secrets of a person's heart (Sir 44:3; Jos. *Ant.* 15.375; 18.198; John 4:19
[compared with vv 29, 39]; 1 Cor 13:2; 14:24–25; Ps.-Clement *Hom.* 2.6.1; see
Sandnes, *Paul,* 96–98). In 4QMess ar 1:8, it is claimed "he [possibly Enoch] will
know the secrets of man [אנשא רזי וידע *wydʿ rzy ʾnšʿ*]," and "he will know the secrets
of all living things [חייא כול רזי וידע *wydʿ rzy kwl ḥyyʾ*]" (see the brief commentary in
García Martínez, *Qumran,* 21–22). Many secrets were revealed to Enoch, the secrets
of the holy ones (*1 Enoch* 106:19), the secrets of sinners (*1 Enoch* 104:10; cf. 83:7),
and even the secrets of God (*1 Enoch* 103:2; 104:12).

**23c**  καὶ δώσω ὑμῖν ἑκάστῳ κατὰ τὰ ἔργα ὑμῶν, "and I will give to each of you in
accordance with your deeds." This is probably an allusion to Jer 17:10b (since v 10a
is alluded to in v 23b), even though the LXX version of Jer 17:10b differs somewhat
from the proverb found here in v 23c: τοῦ δοῦναι ἑκάστῳ κατὰ τὰς ὁδοὺς αὐτοῦ, "to
give to each in accordance with his ways." This is one version (see also Rev 18:6;
20:12, 13; 22:12) of a widespread saying dealing with retributive justice found in the
OT, in which the phrase κατὰ τὰ ἔργα is used with such verbs as διδόναι, ἀποδίδοναι,
and κρίνειν in a context of judgment (often eschatological) in early Judaism and

early Christianity (Pss 27:4[2x]; 61:13; 86:2; Prov 24:12; Sir 16:12, 14; *Pss. Sol.* 2:16, 34; 17:8; Jer 27:9; Lam 3:64; Rom 2:6; 2 Cor 11:15; 2 Tim 4:14; Ign. [long rec.] *Magn.* 11:3; *2 Clem.* 17:4). While the OT frequently mentions that God tries the heart and the kidneys, and though the notion of recompense for one's works is also found frequently outside Jeremiah (Pss 28:4; 62:13; Prov 24:12), only in Jer 17:10 (and Rev 2:23) are the two conceptions found together (Wolff, *Jeremia*, 171). This is a proverbial saying that also occurs in Ps 62:12(LXX 61:13) and Prov 24:12: God ἀποδίδωσιν ἑκάστῳ κατὰ τὰ ἔργα αὐτοῦ, "will repay each in accordance with his works," and has close parallels in Rev 20:13 (the dead will be judged κατὰ τὰ ἔργα αὐτῶν, "in accordance with their works") and 22:12 (ἀποδοῦναι ἑκάστῳ ὡς τὸ ἔργον ἐστὶν αὐτοῦ, "to repay to each in accordance to his work"). This particular proverbial formulation of the principle of *lex talionis* (i.e., "the law of retaliation") circulated in ancient Israel (Pss 28:4[LXX 27:4]; 62:12[LXX 61:13]; Prov 24:12), in early Judaism (Sir 35:19a[LXX 35:22]; *Jos. As.* 28:3; *Pss. Sol.* 2:16, 34–35; 17:8–9), and in early Christianity (Matt 16:27; Rom 2:6; 2 Tim 4:14; 1 Pet 1:17; *1 Clem.* 34:3; *2 Clem.* 11:6; 17:4; cf. 2 Cor 11:15). Many of these sayings occur in an eschatological context in which God rewards and judges the deeds of people (Matt 16:27; Rom 2:6; 1 Pet 1:17; *1 Clem.* 34:3; *2 Clem.* 17:4). According to Conzelmann (*Theology*, 147), judgment by works is the standard of the entire NT, including Paul. Here it is noteworthy that the author switches to plural pronouns. The problem is whether these pronouns refer to *all* the members of the congregation or simply to those who have been supporters of "Jezebel." Since in v 24 the author expressly addresses those who have resisted the influence of "Jezebel" with plural pronouns and verb forms, the ὑμῖν of v 23 probably should be restricted to the followers of "Jezebel."

**24a** ὑμῖν δὲ λέγω τοῖς λοιποῖς τοῖς ἐν Θυατείροις, "I say to the rest of you in Thyatira." Although the plural pronoun ὑμῖν, "you," occurs here, it is apparent that this saying is not addressed to the same group addressed in v 23 but includes vv 24–25 and is directed to those other members of the church at Thyatira who have not been involved with "Jezebel." This is one of the places in Rev 2–3 in which the literary device of addressing the proclamations to the angels of the churches is abandoned and a specific group of people within a church is addressed clearly and directly (see 2:13, 20, 24, 25[2x]).

**24b** ὅσοι οὐκ ἔχουσιν τὴν διδαχὴν ταύτην, οἵτινες οὐκ ἔγνωσαν τὰ βαθέα τοῦ σατανᾶ ὡς λέγουσιν, "as many as do not hold this teaching, who do not know what people call 'the deep things of Satan.'" Here ὡς λέγουσιν, literally "as they say," is a citation formula that suggests that the phrase "the deep things of Satan" is a central concern of the Nicolaitans. There are two ways of understanding this phrase: (1) The quotation can be taken at face value: the Nicolaitans were involved in a kind of Satanism that has parallels in several second-century Gnostic groups. (2) John has sarcastically substituted "Satan" for "God," or has added "Satan" to the term "depths," in order to convey his view of the real focus of their theology, just as he labeled Jews "a synagogue of Satan" (2:9; 3:9), rather than a synagogue of God.

The "deep things of Satan" may have originated as a Gnostic motto, though the Gnostics did not have a monopoly on the term "depth." 1 Cor 2:10 refers to the Spirit as searching τὰ βάθη τοῦ θεοῦ, "the depths of God." The phrase "the depths" is used in prophetic contexts, such as LXX and Theod Dan 2:22, where it is said that God knows τὰ βαθέα (cf. Rom 11:33). In a possibly Gnostic context God himself can be defined as βάθος or Depth (*Acts Thom.* 143; Hippolytus *Ref.* 6.30.7), though *1*

*Clem.* 40:1 can refer to "the depths of divine knowledge [τὰ βάθη τῆς θείας γνώσεως]." Irenaeus *Adv. haer.* 2.22.1: "they claim [*dicunt*] that they have found out the mysteries of Bythus [*profunda Bythi*]." Hippolytus, *Ref.* 5.6.4: "They call themselves Gnostics, claiming that they alone know the depths [τὰ βάθη]." The Valentinian first principle is called τὸ βάθος (Clement Alex. *Exc. ex Theod.* 29). Similarly, according to Hippolytus (*Ref.* 6.30.7), the Valentinians called the Father ῥίζα καὶ βάθος καὶ βυθός, "Root and Deep and Depth." Clement of Alexandria speaks of "the depths of knowledge" (*Strom.* 5.88.5; τὰ μὲν τῆς γνώσεως βάθη). See also *Acts Thom.* 143; H. Schlier, *TDNT* 1:517–18. In *PGM* IV.978 (tr. Betz, *Greek Magical Papyri*), "I conjure you, holy light, holy brightness, breadth, depth [βάθος]" (see IV.970). In a spell for a divine revelation in *PGM* XII.155–58, "I call upon you [several lines of *voces magicae*, i.e., magical gobbledygook] let there be depth [βάθος], breadth, length, brightness."

**24c**   οὐ βάλλω ἐφ᾽ ὑμᾶς ἄλλο βάρος, "I will not put any other burden upon you." There is a relatively close parallel to this statement in Acts 15:28: μηδὲν πλέον ἐπιτίθεσθαι ὑμῖν βάρος πλὴν τούτων τῶν ἐπάναγκες, "not to lay any greater burden on you except these necessary matters." Here βάλλω ἐπί, "put upon," corresponds to ἐπιτίθεσθαι in Acts 15:28, and βάρος πλήν in Acts 15:28 corresponds to βάρος πλήν here in Rev 2:24c–25. The context of Acts 15:28 is the Apostolic Decree, in which abstention from meat sacrificed to idols is enjoined, just as immorality and the consumption of meat offered to idols is condemned in Rev 2:20. Many scholars think that the Apostolic Decree is clearly in the mind of the author (Zahn, 1:292–93; Bousset [1906] 221; Charles, 1:74). The problem with this conclusion is that the letter in Acts 15:23–29 is part of Luke's editorial work, and it is extremely doubtful that John of Patmos knew and used the Acts of the Apostles (Räisänen, *ANRW* II, 26/2:1611), though it is possible that both Revelation and Acts were dependent on a popular catchword (Müller, *Theologiegeschichte*, 18). The prohibitions listed in the Apostolic Decree include abstention from meat sacrificed to idols, from fornication, from what has been strangled, and from blood. Only the first two prohibitions are mentioned in the immediate context (2:20; cf. 2:14). The prohibitions in the Apostolic Decree in Acts 15 reflect the Jewish conception of the Noachide Laws, i.e., the pre-Sinaitic laws incumbent on all people, which also regulate the relations between Jews and non-Jews.

**25**   πλὴν ὃ ἔχετε κρατήσατε ἄχρις οὗ ἂν ἥξω, "Only maintain what you have until I come." Here the verbs ἔχετε and κρατήσατε are in the second person plural, indicating that the author has temporarily abandoned the literary device of addressing this proclamation to the angel representing the church in Thyatira (see also 2:13, 20, 24, 25[2x]). This statement has a close parallel in 3:11, where the motif of the coming of Christ (i.e., the Parousia) is combined with that of "maintaining what you have" (κράτει ὃ ἔχεις), though there the verbs are in the second person *singular*.

**26a**   καὶ ὁ νικῶν καὶ ὁ τηρῶν ἄχρι τέλους τὰ ἔργα μου, "And as for the one who conquers and keeps my works until the end." This promise-to-the-victor formula differs from the parallel formulas in Rev 2–3 in that the substantival participle ὁ νικῶν (τῷ νικῶντι in 2:7, 17) is coordinated with an additional substantival participle, ὁ τηρῶν, "who keeps," which serves to further delineate the specific meaning of ὁ νικῶν. Though both substantival participles are masculine singular, they clearly imply that *all* Christians (whether men or women) who conquer and keep the works of Christ will receive the promised reward. The phrase "my works" (i.e., the works of the exalted Christ) occurs only here in Revelation (though the phrase τὰ ἔργα σου, "your works," refers to the deeds of God in 15:3). The expression "keep my works" is extremely problematic, for one "keeps" or "obeys" not *works* but instructions or commands. Here "keeping my works" may refer to the works that have been commanded by Jesus. In Johannine parlance, one τηρεῖν, "keeps," the λόγος, "word," of Jesus (John 8:51, 52, 55; 14:23, 24; 15:20; 17:6; 1 John 2:5) or the ἐντολαί, "commands," of Jesus (John 14:15, 21; 15:10; 1 John 2:3, 4; 3:22, 24; 5:3); see *Comment* on 3:8. In 1 John 3:18 the author exhorts the readers (NRSV), "let us love, not in word of speech, but in truth and action [ἐν ἔργῳ]." Jesus performs τὰ ἔργα in the Fourth Gospel, but there the term primarily means "miracles" (5:36; 7:3, 21 [singular]; 10:25, 32, 37; 14:11, 12; 15:24; see Brown, *John* 1:525–32; Schnackenburg, *John* 1:518–21), although it can also refer to the entire ministry of Jesus (17:4). The term is twice used in the synoptic Gospels for the miracles of Jesus (Matt 11:2; Luke 24:19).

**26b** δώσω αὐτῷ ἐξουσίαν ἐπὶ τῶν ἐθνῶν, "I will give him authority over the nations." Again the αὐτῷ, literally "him," refers to *all* who conquer (whether men or women), underlining the figurative character of the reward, since taking it literally would mean that the entire group of conquering Christians would rule the nations as a body, which clearly is inappropriate for the kingship model presupposed here. Vv 26b–27 are closely modeled after Ps 2:8–9, as the following synopsis indicates:

| *Rev 2:26b–27* | *LXX Ps 2:8–9* |
|---|---|
| | ⁸αἴτησαι παρ' ἐμοῦ, <br> Ask of me, |
| ²⁶ᵇδώσω αὐτῷ <br> I will give to him | καὶ δώσω σοι <br> and I will give to you |
| ἐξουσίαν ἐπὶ τῶν ἐθνῶν <br> authority over the nations | ἔθνη τὴν κληρονομίαν σου <br> nations as your inheritance |
| | καὶ τὴν κατάσχεσίν σου <br> and as your possession |
| | τὰ πέρατα τῆς γῆς <br> the ends of the earth. |
| ²⁷καὶ ποιμανεῖ αὐτοὺς <br> and he will rule them | ⁹ποιμανεῖς αὐτοὺς <br> You will rule them |
| ἐν ῥάβδῳ σιδηρᾷ <br> with an iron rod | ἐν ῥάβδῳ σιδηρᾷ <br> with an iron rod |
| ὡς τὰ σκεύη τὰ κεραμικὰ <br> as ceramic pot | ὡς σκεῦος κεραμέως <br> as a clay pot |
| συντρίβει <br> is shattered. | συντρίψεις αὐτούς. <br> you will shatter them. |

Various quotations or allusions to Ps 2 are found in some parts of the NT (Acts 2:26–27; 4:25–26; 13:33; 19:15; Heb 1:5; 5:5), and Ps 2:7 in particular was understood in early Christianity as a messianic psalm (Acts 13:33; Heb 1:5; 5:5; Justin *Dial.* 61.6; 88.8; 122.6; see Lindars, *Apologetic*, 139–44). The motif of the Christian sharing sovereignty with Christ is also found in *Odes Sol.* 29:8 (tr. Charlesworth, *OTP*): "And He gave me the sceptre of His power, that I might subdue the devices of the Gentiles, And humble the power of the mighty." The Messiah is spoken of in 12:10 as possessing ἐξουσία, "authority," and similarly ἐξουσία over every "tribe and people and language and nation" is given to the Beast in Rev 13:7, presumably by God (passive of divine activity). The "scepter" and the shepherd's "crook" are closely related (the Assyrian term *ḫaṭṭu* can mean both "scepter" and "staff of a shepherd," though the latter is always used in a figurative sense; *AD* 6:153–55). The crook is a symbol of royalty in Mesopotamian art and literature and is included in the relief at the top of the basalt Code of Hammurabi. God is referred to twice under the metaphor of shepherd in the OT (Pss 23:1; 80:2), and his possession of a comforting shepherd's staff is part of the shepherd metaphor in Ps 23:4b; Mic 7:14. The scepter is primarily associated with the royal role of meting out justice (Isa 11:4; Ps 45:7) and is frequently used in a context of punishment (Isa 10:5, 26; 30:31; Ps 110:2; Job 9:34; 21:9; Lam 3:1)

**27** καὶ ποιμανεῖ αυτοὺς ἐν ῥάβδῳ σιδηρᾷ ὡς τὰ σκεύη τὰ κεραμικὰ συντρίβεται, "and he will drive them with an iron scepter, as when ceramic jars are shattered." This continues the allusion to Ps 2:9, which is elsewhere understood as a description of the Messiah (Rev 12:5; 19:15; *Pss. Sol.* 17:23–24) but here is applied to the conquering Christian with whom Christ will share his messianic rule (see the bestowal of the morning star, another messianic symbol in v 28). ποιμαίνειν can mean "to herd, tend, guide or govern," but this meaning is problematic, since the context strongly suggests that it has a *negative* meaning. This verse alludes to LXX Ps 2:9, where the verb form תרעם *trʿm* is ambiguous:

> You shall break them [תרעם *trʿm*] with a rod of iron [בשבט ברזל *bšbṭ brzl*], and dash them in pieces [תנפצם *tĕnappĕṣēm*] like a potter's vessel.

Though the pointing of תְּרֹעֵם *tĕrōʿēm* in the MT means that the Masoretes thought the verb form was derived from רעע *rʿ*, "to devastate, break in pieces" (an Aramaic loanword corresponding to the Hebrew stem רצץ *rṣṣ*), the unpointed consonantal text is itself ambiguous and can be pointed תְּרְעֵם *tirʿēm*, based on the triliteral stem רעה *rʿh*, "to shepherd" (Str-B 4:794). Allusions to Ps 2:9 are also found in Rev 12:5; 19:15 (though nowhere else in the NT), where the identical phrase found in 2:27 occurs: ἐν ῥάβδῳ σιδηρᾷ. The phrase in 2:27 was probably derived by the author from 12:5; 19:15. Rev 12:5 alludes only to the first stichos: "who will drive [ὃς μέλλει ποιμαίνειν] all the nations with an iron crook" (see *Notes* on 12:5). Again in Rev 19:15, only the first stichos of Ps 2:9 is alluded to: "he will rule [ποιμανεῖ] them with a rod of iron." Since the LXX version of Ps 2:9 translates תרעם *trʿm* as ποιμανεῖ, "he will herd" or "he will govern," it appears that the Hebrew term רעע *rʿ*, "to devastate, break in pieces," was confused with רעה *rʿh*, "to shepherd, rule" (Black, "Some Greek Words," 137). It also appears that the author of Revelation (in this instance) was dependent on the LXX rather than the Hebrew text, particularly in light of the following evidence. Ps 2:9 is also alluded to in *Pss. Sol.* 17:23b–24a, a composition originally written in Hebrew ca.

50 B.C., though surviving primarily in Greek and Syriac translations (though the Syriac was probably dependent on the Greek):

> May he smash the sinner's arrogance like a potter's vessel.
> With a rod of iron [ἐν ῥάβδῳ σιδηρᾷ] may he break in pieces [συντρίψαι] all their
> substance.

Although the couplet in Ps 2:9 is found here in reverse order and the second person singular verbs are changed to third person singular, dependence on Ps 2:9 is clear. Here it is noteworthy that תרעם *trʿm* in Ps 2:9 is rendered by the optative or infinitive form συντρίψαι, suggesting that the translator understood the Hebrew verb form underlying συντρίψαι to be based on the Aramaic stem רעע *rʿ*. A similar allusion is possible in Dan 2:40b, written in Aramaic ca. 164 B.C.: "and like iron [כפרזלא *kēparzēlāʾ*] which crushes [די מרעע *dî mĕrāʿaʿ*], it shall break and crush all these." Though this passage does not demonstrably allude to Ps 2:9, it nevertheless associates "iron" (פרזל *parzel*) with the verb "crush" (רעע *rʿ*), as in Ps 2:9, and provides evidence *against* the vocalization preserved in the MT (Wilhelmi, *VT* 27 [1977] 198). Soggin ("Zum zweiten Psalm," 195) regards the MT vocalization of תרעם *trʿm* as the *lectio difficilior*. Yet Wilhelmi (*VT* 27 [1977] 199) points to an important parallel in Mic 5:6: "they shall rule [MT 5:5: ורעו *wĕrāʿû*; LXX 5:5: ποιμανοῦσιν] the land of Assyria with the sword [LXX: ἐν ῥομφαίᾳ]." This indicates that the verb רעה *rʿh* can be used in a negative context (see Jer 6:3), for Köhler–Baumgartner (KB³) erroneously regards the Aramaic verb רעע *rʿ* as the stem behind ורעו *wĕrāʿ* (Wilhelmi, *VT* 27 [1977] 199). However, it is important to observe that in Mic 5:6 *subjugation* rather than *destruction* is in view, as an Egyptian text that exhibits parallels to Ps 2:9 suggests (Thiel, "Weltherrschaftanspruch," 53ff.). Wilhelmi argues convincingly for the propriety of construing תרעם *trʿm* of Ps 2:9 as derived from רעה *rʿh*, on the basis of the antithetical character of the two lines, the parallel in Mic 5:6, and the interpretation of the verb in the LXX (*VT* 27 [1977] 201–4). Like the translator of *Pss. Sol.* 17:24a, Symmachus renders the Hebrew verb תרעם *trʿm* in Ps 2:9 with the Greek verb συντρίψεις, "you will shatter, crush," while Aquila used προσρήξεις, "you will dash, beat against," a verb with a similar meaning. This evidence combines to suggest that the author of Revelation was dependent on the mistranslated LXX version, rather than on the Hebrew original. However, Charles (1:75–76) argues that ποιμαίνειν both in Rev 2:27 and in 19:15, where it is parallel to πατάξῃ, "he will smite," has a secondary meaning "to lay waste, destroy." Yet רעה *rʿh* in Hebrew and ποιμαίνειν in Greek can *both* mean "to shepherd" as well as "to rule," and the latter can certainly be given a contextually negative meaning in both MT and LXX Ps 2:9 as well as in Rev 2:27; 12:5; 19:15 without resorting to the hypothesis of dependence on a mistaken LXX translation (Black, "Some Greek Words") or on an unattested meaning for ποιμαίνειν (Charles).

*Pss. Sol.* 17:23b–24a; Rev 2:27; 12:5; 19:19 all interpret Ps 2:9 in a messianic sense, though the interpretations found in the *Psalms of Solomon* and Revelation appear to be independent interpretations of that OT passage and not dependent on a particular exegetical tradition. And yet it is evident that Ps 2:9 was probably construed in a messianic sense because of its proximity to Ps 2:7, which is alluded to or quoted several times in the NT (Matt 3:16–17 = Mark 1:10–11; Luke 3:21–22; Matt 4:3; John 1:49; Acts 13:33; Heb 1:5; 5:5; 7:28) and widely construed as a messianic text in early Christianity (Lindars, *Apologetic,* 139–44), and is perhaps interpreted messianically in an allusion found in 1QSa 2:11–12.

The term "the nations" occurs some twenty-three times in Revelation (2:26; 11:2, 18; 15:3; 16:19; 18:23; 19:15; 20:3, 8; 21:24, 26; 22:2), including five times in the phrase "all the nations" (12:5; 14:8; 15:4; 18:3, 23), and seven times in the varied lists, which include "every tribe, language, people, and nation" (5:9; 7:9; 10:11; 11:9; 13:7; 14:6; 17:15). All but four of these references are negative (15:4; 21:24, 26; 22:2).

**28a** ὡς κἀγὼ εἴληφα παρὰ τοῦ πατρός μου, "as I received it from my Father." This phrase is somewhat ambiguous since the object of εἴληφα, "I received," is left unstated. Either it could be understood to refer to the ἐξουσία, "authority," which the exalted Christ has received from his Father (and for that reason he is able to confer authority over the nations to those who conquer), or it could refer to the morning star (cf. v 28b) that Christ has received from his Father and can therefore bestow on the victors. It is more probable that the phrase refers to the authority mentioned in v 26b, since the OT allusions in v 27 appear almost parenthetical, and when v 27 is ignored, v 28a is most naturally construed as referring to the ἐξουσία, "authority," that will be granted to the victorious Christian, analogous to the victory that Christ received from his Father. The phrase "my Father" in the mouth of the exalted Jesus occurs three times in Revelation (2:28; 3:5, 21) but thirty-seven times in all the Gospels but Mark, i.e., thirteen times in Matthew, three times in Luke, twenty-one times in John, and two times in the *Gospel of Thomas* (e.g., Matt 7:21; 10:32, 33; 11:27; 12:50; 16:17; Luke 10:32; 22:29; 24:49; John 5:17; 6:32; 8:38, 49, 54; 10:10; *Gos. Thom.* 99[2x]; see J. Jeremias, *Prayers,* 29–54).

**28b** καὶ δώσω αὐτῷ τὸν ἀστέρα τὸν πρωϊνόν, "and I will give the morning star to him." Again, the αὐτῷ, literally "him," refers to *all* conquering Christians (whether men or women), and the metaphorical character of the reward is even more evident than in v 26b, for there is but one morning star, and to take this promise literally would somehow involve the *corporate* possession of the morning star by all conquering Christians, which would be meaningless. The "morning star," "day star," and "evening star" are three modern ways of referring to the planet Venus (known in ancient Babylonia as the star of Ishtar), which appears at dawn before the sun and so was understood in ancient times as the herald of a new day. Though Venus is a planet and not a star, the ancients often referred to Venus as the largest star (Pliny, *Hist. nat.* 2.37). According to Cicero (*De nat. deor.* 2.53; LCL tr.), "Lowest of the five planets and nearest to the earth is the star of Venus [*stella Veneris*], called in Greek Φωσφόρος [see 1 Pet 1:19] and in Latin "*Lucifer* when it precedes the sun, but when it follows it *Hesperos*" (Pliny *Hist. nat.* 2.36–38; Manilius *Astron.* 1.177–78). After the sun and the moon, it is the brightest object in the sky. The "morning star," used as a christological predicate in an "I am" formulation, is also mentioned in Rev 22:16. *Receiving* the morning star, however, is quite different from *being* the morning star (see *Comment* on 22:16). The gift of the morning star must refer to the fact that the exalted Christ shares his messianic status with the believer who conquers. The "morning star," referred to more technically as φωσφόρος, literally "light-bearer," is also mentioned in 2 Pet 1:19. φωσφόρος is also personified in *Sib. Or.* 5.516 as fighting with the stars and is listed third after the sun and the moon (see Judg 5:20). In Isa 14:12 the fall of a tyrant is celebrated with the words "How you are fallen from heaven, O Day Star [MT: חילל *hyll,* "shining one";

LXX: ἑωσφόρος, "morning star"], son of Dawn [or as a proper name, Helel ben Shachar]." This metaphor is used of the Eschatological Antagonist in 4 Ezra 4:29 (tr. Stone in Charlesworth, *OTP* 1:575): "His right eye is like a star rising at dawn [ὡς ἀστὴρ τῷ πρωὶ ἀνατέλλων] and the other is unmoving." This usage is almost certainly based on the Lucifer tradition, which is derived from Isa 14:12. In a magical prayer, arguably of Jewish origin (Deissmann, *Light,* 261–62), an adjuration is made "by god, light-bearer [φωσφόρος]" (*PGM* IV.3045; cf. 3068). In *PGM* V.209–10, a magical prayer is addressed to "Master, Iao, Light-bearer [δέσποτα Ἰάω, φωσφόρε]" (see *PGM* LXXVIII.12), perhaps in the sense of Gen 1:3. In all four instances φωσφόρος functions as a divine name and could also be translated "morning star" or, less probably, "torch-bearer." The parallelism in Job 38:7 suggests that "the morning stars [כּוֹכְבֵי בֹקֶר *kôkbê bōqer*]" are identical with "the sons of God [בְּנֵי אֱלֹהִים *běně 'ělōhîm*]" (i.e., angels). The meaning of the MT is completely changed in the LXX version of Job 38:7: "When the stars [ἄστρα] were begotten, all my angels [ἄγγελοι] praised me with a loud voice." In *Jos. As.* 14:1, the ἑωσφόρος, "morning star," arose in the east at the conclusion of the prayer of Aseneth, who takes it as a good omen (tr. Charlesworth, *OTP* 2:224): "So the Lord God listened to my prayer, because this star rose as a messenger and herald of the light of the great day." In a later passage, the face of Aseneth is compared to the sun, and her eyes are compared to a rising morning star (18:9). See R. Staats ("Die Sonntagnachgottesdienste der christlichen Frühzeit," *ZNW* 66 [1975] 242–63), who argues that early Christian worship took place in darkness before Sunday morning. The star metaphor is used in Judaism with messianic associations, originating in Num 24:17 (*T. Levi* 18:3; *T. Judah* 24:1; Justin *Dial.* 106.4; Hippolytus, *Comm. in Dan.* 1.9; Origen, *Contra Cels.* 1.59–60). The messianic symbolism of the star may be used in association with the Matthaean version of the birth of Jesus (Matt 2:2, 10), a motif greatly expanded in *Prot. Jas.* 21.2 and Clement of Alex. *Exerpt. ex Theod.* 74, and mythologized even further in an account of the initial appearance of Christ in the world in Ign. *Eph.* 19:2 (see Matt 24:30).

**29** ὁ ἔχων οὖς ἀκουσάτω τί τὸ πνεῦμα λέγει ταῖς ἐκκλησίαις, "Let the person with an ear hear what the Spirit announces to the churches." See *Comment* on 2:7. Though this proclamation formula appeals to the hearer with the masculine singular substantival participle ὁ ἔχων, "the one who has," it clearly refers to all those who are able to understand the message conveyed by the Spirit to the churches, whether men or women.

## Explanation

Thyatira, situated at the most important junction of roads between Lydia and Mysia, was located forty-five miles southeast of Pergamon. The church is commended for its faith and service and patient endurance, like the Ephesian church (2:2–3). Unlike the Ephesian Christians, however, their present spiritual condition is judged healthier than formerly (v 19). Like the Pergamenes, they are denounced for tolerating heretics (vv 20–23). An unnamed woman prophetess whom the author nicknames "Jezebel" is charged with teaching Christians to indulge in sexual promiscuity and eat sacrificial meat (see under 2:12–17), though these charges may reflect stereotypical rhetorical slander and need not be taken literally. The similarity between "Jezebel's" program and that of the Nicolaitans (see 2:14–

15) suggests that she is a local leader of that sect. The fact that a woman exercised such an influential leadership role in late first-century Christianity is not unique. Ancient Jewish inscriptions from Anatolia and elsewhere testify to many important leadership roles held by women in synagogues. Later the Christian prophetess Ammia was active in Philadelphia (Eusebius *Hist. eccl.* 5.17.3–4). When Christ says "I gave her time to repent" (v 21), the statement likely refers to an earlier prophetic judgment speech delivered by John or a member of his prophetic circle. The threat that "Jezebel" and her circle will become sick and suffer tribulation and even death (v 22–23) is perhaps the kind of judgment implied in earlier references to the "coming" of Christ (2:5, 16). Physical illness among Christians was something understood as divine punishment for sin (1 Cor 11:29–30). "Jezebel" is the name of the infamous foreign wife of Ahab king of Israel, whose checkered career is recounted in 1 Kgs 16:28–19:3; 2 Kgs 9:22, 30–37. She had a corps of 900 prophets of Baal (1 Kgs 18:19), fought against the true prophets of Yahweh (1 Kgs 18:4), and was known for introducing "harlotries and sorceries" to Israel. Thyatiran "Jezebel" may have used her prophetic gift to legitimate the kind of deviant practices of which she is accused in v 20, though this is far from certain. Philo, in a paraphrastic and apparently updated version of Deut 13:1–11, warned his readers against would-be prophets who might lead people to adopt pagan practices (*Spec. Leg.* 1.315–16; LCL tr., a passage pointed out to me by Peder Borgen):

> Further if anyone cloaking himself under the name and guise of a prophet and claiming to be possessed by inspiration lead us on to the worship of the gods recognized in the different cities, we ought not to listen to him and be deceived by the name of prophet. For such a one is no prophet, but an imposter, since his oracles and pronouncements are falsehoods invented by himself.

Vv 24–25 specifically address those members of the church who are not followers of "Jezebel" and who have not learned "the deep things of Satan," a possible reference to the "profound" teachings of "Jezebel." John may be parodying a motto of "Jezebel" by substituting the word "Satan" for "God" (see 1 Cor 2:10). In vv 26–27, the one who conquers is promised a delegated share of Christ's sovereign rule (see 5:10; 20:4; 22:5; cf. 2 Tim 2:12).

# 5. The Proclamation to Sardis   (3:1–6)

### Bibliography

**Bauckham, R.** "The Delay of the Parousia." *TynBul* 31 (1980) 3–36. ———. "Synoptic Parousia Parables and the Apocalypse." *NTS* 23 (176–77) 162–76. **Buckler, W. H.,** and **Robinson, D. M.** *Greek and Latin Inscriptions.* Part 1. Leiden: Brill, 1932. **Calder, W.** "Philadelphia and Montanism." *BJRL* 7 (1922) 309–54. **Cook, S. A.** "A Lydian-Aramaic Bilingual." *JHS* 37 (1917) 77–87. **Crossan, J. D.** *The Historical Jesus: The Life of a Mediterranean Jewish Peasant.* San Francisco: Harper, 1991. **Donfried, K. P.** *The Setting of Second Clement in Early Christianity.* NovTSup 38. Leiden: Brill, 1974. **Frey, J.** "Erwägungen zum Verhältnis der Johannesapokalypse zu den übrigen Schriften des Corpus Johanneum." In *Die johanneische Frage: Ein Lösungsversuch,* ed. M. Hengel. Tübingen: Mohr-Siebeck, 1993. 326–49. **García Martínez, F.** "Las Tablas celestes en el Libro de los Jubileos." In *Palabra y Vida.* FS J. A. Díaz, ed. A. Vargas-Machuca and G. Ruiz. Madrid, 1984. 333–50. **Gusmani, R.** *Neue epichorische Schriftzeugnisse aus Sardis (1958–1971).* Cambridge: Harvard UP, 1975. **Hanfmann, G. M. A.** *Letters from Sardis.* Cambridge: Harvard UP, 1972. ———. *Sardis from Prehistoric to Roman Times: Results of the Archaeological Exploration of Sardis, 1958–75.* Cambridge: Harvard UP, 1983. **Hemer, C. J.** "The Sardis Letter and the Croesus Tradition." *NTS* 19 (1972–73) 94–97. ———. "Unto the Angels of the Churches: 3. Thyatira and Sardis." *BurH* 11 (1975) 110–35. **Koep, L.** *Das himmlische Buch in Antike und Christentum: Eine religionsgeschichtliche Untersuchung zur altchristlichen Bildersprache.* Bonn: Hanstein, 1952. **Koester, H.** *Ancient Christian Gospels: Their History and Development.* London: SCM; Philadelphia: Trinity, 1990. **Kraabel, A. T.** "Melito the Bishop and the Synagogue at Sardis: Text and Context." In *Studies Presented to George M. A. Hanfmann.* Mainz: von Zabern, 1971. 77–85. ———. "Paganism and Judaism: The Sardis Evidence." In *Paganisme, Judaïsme, Christianisme.* Paris: de Boccard, 1978. 13–33. **Krauss, S.** *Talmudische Archäologie.* Leipzig: Fock, 1910–12. **Mitten, D. G.** "A New Look at Ancient Sardis." *BA* 29 (1966) 38–68. **Paul, S. M.** "Heavenly Tablets and the Book of Life." *JANESCU* 5 (1973) 345–53. **Pedley, J. G.** *Ancient Literary Sources on Sardis.* Cambridge: Harvard UP, 1972. **Petzl, G.** *Die Inschriften von Smyrna.* Bonn: Habelt, 1982–87. **Ratté, C. T., Howe, N.,** and **Foss, C.** "An Early Imperial Pseudodipteral Temple at Sardis." *AJA* 90 (1986) 45–68. **Smitmans, A.** "Das Gleichnis vom Dieb." In *Wort Gottes in der Zeit.* FS K. H. Schelke, ed. H. Feld and J. Nolte. Düsseldorf: Patmos, 1973. 43–68. **Wilken, R. L.** "Melito, the Jewish Community at Sardis, and the Sacrifice of Isaac." *TS* 37 (1976) 53–69. **Yarbro Collins, A.** "The Son of Man Tradition and the Book of Revelation." In *The Messiah: Developments in Earliest Judaism and Christianity,* ed. J. H. Charlesworth. Minneapolis: Fortress, 1992. 536–68.

*Translation*

¹ *To the angel of the church in Sardis write: "Thus says the one who has the seven spirits of God, namely* [a] *the seven stars: 'I know your conduct that you have a reputation* [b] *for* [c] *being alive, but* [d] *you are actually dead!* ²ᵃ*Be vigilant* [a] *and* [b]*strengthen* [c] *those who remain* [d] *but are on the point of death, for I have found your conduct* [e] *far from perfect in the sight of my God.* ³*Remember, therefore, what you have received* [a]*and heard,*[b] *obey* [a] *that and repent. If, therefore, you do not watch, I will come* [c] *like a thief, and you will not know* [d] *at what moment* [e] *I will come to you.* ⁴*But you have a few individuals* [a] *in Sardis who have not soiled their garments. They* [b] *will walk with me in white, because they are worthy.*[c] ⁵*The one who conquers thus* [a] *will be clothed with a white garment, and* [b]*I will certainly not* [b] *erase his name from the Book of Life, and I will acknowledge his name before my father and before the holy angels.* ⁶*The one who has ear, let him hear what the Spirit declares to the churches.'"*

*Notes*

1.a. The term καί, "and," can be construed as either epexegetical (as here), which understands the seven spirits of God as identical with the seven stars, or as a copulative, which assumes that they are distinct. See under *Comment* below.

1.b. Here ὄνομα, lit. "name," means "reputation" (Louw-Nida, § 3.265).

1.c. ὅτι is used to introduce an explanatory or epexegetical clause (Louw-Nida, § 91.15).

1.d. The καί here is a καί *adversativum* and should be translated "but," since it connects two statements that are antithetical in meaning. This phenomenon is found in classical and Hellenistic Gk. (Deniston, *Particles,* 292–93), and particularly in the LXX (Aejmelaeus, *Parataxis,* 14–15).

2.a-a. In the periphrastic present imper. γίνου γρηγορῶν, "be vigilant," γίνου (a present mid. imper. from γίνομαι) occasionally replaces forms derived from εἶναι, "to be" (BDR § 98.1; 354.1; Conybeare-Stock, *Septuagint*, § 72.b; see Rev 2:10); in this case ἴσθι (second-person sing. present imper.); see Sir 18:33: μὴ γίνου . . . συμβολοκοπῶν. Many consider periphrastic constructions using the present ptcp. to be Semitisms, since they occur so frequently in Heb. and Aram. (the verb "to be" in Heb. [היה *hyh*] and Aram. [הוא *hwʾ*] was often used in periphrastic constructions with a ptcp. expressing a durative value (Mussies, *Morphology*, 331). However, the periphrastic present can hardly be a statistical Semitism in Revelation since it occurs just twice, here and in 1:18: ἰδοὺ ζῶν εἰμι, "behold I am living." There are numerous parallels in Gk. literature (Kühner-Gerth, *Satzlehre* 1:38–39; Mayser, *Satzlehre* 2/1, 223–24; Conybeare-Stock, *Septuagint*, § 72), though these are to some extent discounted in BDR § 353. A periphrastic construction may have been chosen here because it forms an expression antithetical to the preceding νεκρὸς εἶ, "you are dead" (Mussies, *Morphology*, 331).

2.b. Variants: (1) στήρισον] A C 025 Oecumenius²⁰⁵³ fam 1006¹⁰⁰⁶ ¹⁸⁴¹ Andr f ²⁰²³ ²⁰⁷³txt i²⁰⁴² l⁻¹⁷⁷⁸. (2) τήρησον] fam 1611¹⁶¹¹ ²⁵⁴⁴ Andr f²⁰²³ i⁻²⁰⁴² 2019 Byzantine syrʰ. (3) στήριξον] Andreas TR. (4) στήρηξον] Erasmus¹. Reading (3) is the Attic form, while readings (1) and (2) are both Hellenistic forms. On the tendency to introduce Atticisms into the NT textual tradition, see G. D. Kilpatrick, "Atticism and the Text of the Greek New Testament," in *Neutestamentliche Aufsätze*, ed. J. Blinzler, O. Kuss, and F. Mussner [Regensburg: Pustet, 1963] 125–37).

2.c. Here the periphrastic present ptcp. γινου γρηγορων is coordinated with the aor. imper B στήρισον, though another durative verb could be expected; this same pattern is also found in 2:5; 3:3, 19; 10:8; 11:1, 6 (Mussies, *Morphology*, 340–41). Mussies suggests that the author may have found a second durative value superfluous and instead used the unmarked aor.

2.d. The neut. pl. phrase τὰ λοιπά refers here to people rather than things (i.e., the assumption that neut. adjs. indicate only non-living things is incorrect; cf. 1 Cor1:27–28; Heb 7:7; Demosthenes, *Or.* 8.41); see 2:24, where τοῖς λοιποῖς can be masc. or neut. and is similarly following by a defining relative clause (BDR § 138.1; Mussies, *Morphology*, 124; Delebecque, 172).

2.e. In the phrase σου τὰ ἔργα, τά is omitted by A and C and, following this strong combination of A and C, WHort; B. Weiss, *Johannes-Apokalypse*, 165; and Charles, 2:254, have omitted it. While the addition of the definite article could have occurred through assimilation to the phrase σου τὰ ἔργα in 3:1 (B. Weiss, *Johannes-Apocalypse*, 108, 165), the omission of the article is clearly an error (Schmid, *Studien* 2:87).

3.a-a. Variant: Omit καὶ ἤκουσας καὶ τήρει] fam 1006 Andr f²⁰²³ g i²⁰⁴² Byzantine.

3.b. Since ἤκουσας is coordinated with the preceding pf. ind. active εἴληφας, it is explained by some as an example of an aor. verb with the value of a pf. (Mussies, *Morphology*, 338), though others suggest that εἴληφας is perhaps a pf. with aoristic value (Burton, *Moods and Tenses* § 88; Moulton, *Prolegomena*, 144–45). Bousset, who tried to make a temporal distinction between the pf. and the aor. in this verse ([1906] 223), proposed that the pf. εἴληφας refers to action up to and including the present, while ἤκουσας refers to a specific point of time in the past. This appears to be an instance in which a more heavily marked verbal form (the pf.) forms a syntagmatic unit with a less heavily marked verbal form (the aor.), used in a progression in which the pf. provides a basis for the aor. (Porter, *Verbal Aspect*, 191). Yet since the aor. has an unmarked temporal value, the author may have decided that a second pf. would be superfluous; i.e., the aor. functions in a way parallel to the pf. (see Porter, *Verbal Aspect*, 192); cf. Rev 5:7; 8:5.

3.c. The phrase ἐπὶ σέ is inserted here by ℵ Byzantine, probably under the influence of the phrase ἥξω ἐπί σέ in the second half of the verse (Schmid, *Studien* 2:131). The phrase is omitted by A C 025 and about fifty minuscules (Hoskier, *Text* 2:94) but is regarded as original by Bousset (1906) 156 n. 1 (but cf. 223).

3.d. Variants: (1) γνῷς] A C fam 1611¹⁶¹¹ ¹⁸⁵⁴ Oecumenius²⁰⁵³ Andreas. (2) γνώσῃ] ℵ fam 1006 fam 1611²³²⁹ ²³⁴⁴ 2351 Byzantine; Tischendorf, *NT Graece;* WHortᵐᵍ. Reading (2) is probably a correction of (1), since in Revelation the aor. subjunctive occurs fourteen times following οὐ μή (Schmid, *Studien* 2:31).

3.e. The acc. phrase ποίαν ὥραν is an acc. indicating extent of time (BDR § 161.6); since the term ὥρα lit. means "hour" but is frequently used figuratively as a generic expression for a point of time (Louw-Nida, § 67.1), it is appropriate to translate it here simply as "moment," or simply "when."

4.a. The term ὀνόματα, lit. "names," is used here in a figurative sense for "people, persons," very likely with an emphasis on their *individuality* (Louw-Nida, § 9.19). The same idiom also occurs in Rev 11:13; Acts 1:15 (possible 18:15), occasionally in the LXX, but in genealogical contexts in which people are represented by their names (Num 1:2, 18, 20; 3:40, 43; 26:53, 55), and twice in the Apostolic Fathers (see Ign., *Smyrn.* 13:1; *Pol.* 8:3). Numerous examples from the Gk. papyri contain this idiom (Deissmann,

*Bible Studies,* 196–97; MM, 451). For inscriptions, see Horsley, *New Docs* 2, § 113; Horsley, *New Docs* 4, § 58 (Wankel, *I. Eph.* 2.555, line 1).

4.b. The καί that introduces this sentence is not translated since it lacks semantic content and functions simply as a marker indicating the beginning of a new sentence.

4.c. The pl. masc. nom. adj. ἄξιοι is a predicate nom. modifying the pl. neut. nom. ὀνόματα because the latter refers to a group of important people (Mussies, *Morphology,* 138).

5.a. Variant: (1) οὕτως] A C ℵ fam 1006[1006] fam 1611[2344] Andr f[2023,2031] g l n 94 1773 it[gig.ar] vg syr[ph.h] cop[bo,sa] arm eth. (2) οὗτος] ℵ[3] 025 046 Andreas Byzantine. οὕτως possibily omitted because it seemed superfluous (*TCGNT,* 736; *TCGNT*[2], 665).

5.b-b. οὐ μή with the fut. ind. is relatively rare in the NT (Moulton, *Prolegomena,* 190; Robertson, *Grammar,* 873–74), but it occurs twice in Revelation (3:5; 18:14; cf. 9:6, *var. lect.*). οὐ μή + fut. ind. occurs with relative frequency in the LXX (Gen 21:10, *var. lect.* A; Lev 19:13; Num 5:3; 35:33; Deut 6:14, *var. lect.* A; 7:16, *var. lect.* A; 21:23, *var. lect.* A; 28:30–31[2x], *var. lect.* A; 29:19; 1 Kgdms 29:7; 2 Kgdms 14:10, *var. lect.* A L; Mic 4:3[2x], *var. lect.* 8ḤevXIIgr 11:34–35, Ziegler, *Duodecim prophetae,* 214–15; Hab 2:19, *var. lect.* 8 ḤevXIIgr 18:38–39).

## *Form/Structure/Setting*

### I. OUTLINE

5. The proclamation to Sardis (3:1–6)
   a. The *adscriptio:* to the angel of the church in Sardis (v 1a)
   b. The command to write (v 1a)
   c. The τάδε λέγει formula (v 1b)
   d. Christological predications (v 1b)
      (1) The One who has the seven spirits of God
      (2) The One who has the seven stars
   e. The *narratio:* "I know your conduct" (v 1c)
      (1) You have a reputation for being alive
      (2) You are actually dead
   f. The *dispositio* (vv 2–4)
      (1) Exhortation (v 2a)
         (a) Be vigilant
         (b) Strengthen what remains and is on the point of death
      (2) Accusation: I have found your conduct far from perfect in the sight of my God (v 2b)
      (3) Exhortation: Remember (v 3a)
         (a) What you received and heard
         (b) Obey that and repent
      (4) Threat: What will happen if you do not watch (v 3b)
         (a) I will come like a thief
         (b) You will not know at which hour I will come to you
      (5) A few in Sardis have not soiled their garments (v 4a)
         (a) Reward: They will walk with me in white (v 4b)
         (b) Reason: They are worthy (v 4b)
   g. The promise-to-the-victor formula (v 5)
      (1) They will be clothed in white (v 5a)
      (2) I will not erase their names from the book of life (v 5b)
      (3) I will acknowledge them (v 5c)

(a) Before my Father
(b) Before the holy angels
h.  The proclamation formula (v 6)

## II. HISTORICAL-GEOGRAPHICAL SETTING

Sardis, one of the more illustrious cities of ancient Anatolia and a major rival of such cities as Smyrna and Ephesus, was located forty miles southeast of Thyatira and forty-five miles east of Smyrna. It was the capital of the kingdom of Lydia and seat of the famous and wealthy Croesus. This wealth was based on the gold found in the river Pactolus, which flowed through the middle of the city, and on its famous woven textiles (Sophocles *Phil.* 391–95; Dio Chrysostom *Or.* 78.31; Juvenal *Satire* 14.298–300; Lucan *Pharsalia* 3.209–10; Philostratus *Vita Apoll.* 6.37; Pliny *Hist. nat.* 33.66).The prosperity of Sardis resulted in part from its location on a number of important trade routes and its position as the terminus of the Royal Road. Sardis was ruled by the Persians from 547 B.C. until liberated by Alexander (Arrian *Anabasis* 1.17.3–6), who built a temple to Zeus there. The Hellenistic period in Sardis extended from 334 B.C. to A.D. 17, from Alexander's entry into the city to the earthquake of A.D. 17, which destroyed most of the Hellenistic city (Tacitus *Annals* 2.47; Pliny *Hist. nat.* 2.86.200; Suetonius *Tib.* 48.2; Seneca *Nat. quaest.* 6.1.13; Strabo 12.8.18). Sardis was rebuilt with aid from the emperors Tiberius and Claudius (Strabo 13.4.8). Between 281 and 190 B.C., Sardis was the capital of the Seleucid kingdom. The city was refounded by Antiochus III in 213 B.C. During this period the temple of Artemis was erected, the fourth largest Ionic temple known to have been constructed in the ancient world (Hanfmann, *Sardis* [1983], 129 fig. 178). While there were many temples located in Sardis, the remains of only two have been found, the famous temple of Artemis (just mentioned) and an architecturally conservative pseudodipteral temple, possibly dedicated to Vespasian (Ratté et al., *AJA* 90 [1986] 45–68). Sardis was ruled by the kings of Pergamon from 190 to 133 B.C. and came under Roman hegemony thereafter. The ancient citadel, which benefited from Roman reconstruction, was proverbially inviolable (Strabo 13.4.5; Lucian *De merc. cond.* 13; Polyaenus 4.9.4) and boasted a temple dedicated to Augustus. Sardis was under Roman rule from 133 B.C. until ca. A.D. 395, when control over the city passed to eastern Roman or Byzantine authority where it remained until A.D. 616 when it was destroyed by the Sassanian king Chosroes II. While earlier over-generous estimates put the population of Sardis at ca. 200,000 (D. Magie, *Roman Rule* 1:585), a more realistic estimate is probably somewhere between 60,000 and 100,000. Sardis was excavated by the Harvard-Cornell Expedition from 1958 to 1975, and the results have been reported in numerous annual reports and many summary volumes (for a bibliography, see Hanfmann, *Sardis* [1983], xvii–xxxv).

One of the more significant discoveries was the Sardis synagogue (called Beth Alpha), the largest known ancient synagogue, built in several phases from the third through the seventh century. The main hall of the structure was astonishingly large: twenty meters wide and fifty-four meters long, large enough to hold a thousand people. In the synagogue were discovered about eighty inscriptions (mostly regarding donations), which reveal that many members of the synagogue were wealthy citizens and officeholders (eight men are identified as members of the city council, a hereditary function open only to wealthy families). The discovery of the Sardis synagogue reveals a Jewish community far larger, wealthier, and more powerful than had previously been imagined. The first Jewish settlers in Sardis may have arrived shortly after the fall of Jerusalem in 586 B.C., since Obad 20 mentions "Sepharad" ("Sfard" in Lydian and Persian), an Aramaic designation for Sardis, as a Lydian-Aramaic bilingual inscription attests (Cook, *JHS* 37 [1917] 80). A large group of Jews from Mesopotamia were settled by Antiochus III in west-central Anatolia in the late third century B.C. (Josephus *Ant.* 12.147–53; see Robert, *Sardes,* 9–21). By the first century A.D. they had become a wealthy and influential group with a place of worship (Josephus *Ant.* 14.235, 259–61; 16.171), with the right to send the temple tax to Jerusalem (Josephus *Ant.* 16.171), and were assured the provision of ritually clean food (Josephus *Ant.* 14.261). The influence of the Jewish community in Sardis is revealed in a letter from the proconsul of Asia toward the end of the first century B.C. to the magistrates and council of Sardis conveying the decision of Caesar that the Jewish practice of collecting money and sending it to Jerusalem should not be hindered (Josephus *Ant.* 16.171; Pedley, *Sardis,* no. 212). Plutarch wrote *De exilo* (late first to early second century A.D.) to an exile from Sardis, identified with some probability with Menemachus of Sardis.

## Comment

**1a** καὶ τῷ ἀγγέλῳ τῆς ἐν Σάρδεσιν ἐκκλησίας γράψον, "To the angel of the church in Sardis write." See *Comment* on 2:1a.

**1b** τάδε λέγει ὁ ἔχων τὰ ἑπτὰ πνεύματα τοῦ θεοῦ καὶ τοὺς ἑπτὰ ἀστέρας, "Thus says the one who has the seven spirits of God, namely the seven stars." Here καί, "namely," can be understood epexegetically, since the seven spirits of God constitute a heavenly reality, while the seven stars are a symbol of a heavenly reality. Thus the seven stars are angels, just as the seven spirits are angels (see *Comment* on 1:4). The "seven spirits which are before the throne" were mentioned in the epistolary prescript in 1:4. These seven angels are probably understood by John as identical with the seven archangels who stand in the presence of God (see 8:2). The seven stars have already been mentioned in 1:16, where they are seen by John in the right hand of the exalted Jesus, and in 1:20, where they are identified as "the angels of the seven churches." Thus the seven spirits of God are indirectly identified by John as the angels of the seven churches (a possibility mentioned by Andreas of Caesarea on Rev 3:1; Schmid, *Studien* 1/1, 36). The mention of the seven stars is an intentional allusion to 1:16.

**1c** οἶδά σου τὰ ἔργα ὅτι ὄνομα ἔχεις ὅτι ζῇς, καὶ νεκρὸς εἶ, "I know your conduct that you have a reputation for being alive, but you are actually dead!" The author uses the antithetical device of paradox, indicating that the καί linking the two parts of the statement is adversative. The contrasting metaphors are "life" and "death," which represent moral and spiritual vitality and morbidity.

**2a** γίνου γρηγορῶν καὶ στήρισον τὰ λοιπὰ ἃ ἔμελλον ἀποθανεῖν, "Be vigilant and strengthen those who remain but are on the point of death." Here the author shifts the metaphor from characterizing the congregation as a whole as being "dead," to describing some members of the congregation who are not "dead" but rather weak and "on the point of death" (on τὰ λοιπά as people rather than non-living things, see *Note* 3:2.d.). Understood in this way, the congregation is charged with caring for other members, perhaps alluding to Ezek 34:4: "You have not strengthened the weak." Some have speculated that this injunction to be vigilant, together with the threat of an unexpected day of reckoning in v 3b, reflects the Croesus tradition (Ramsay, *Letters,* 357–59; Hemer, *Letters,* 131–33). After an initial battle with Cyrus, Croesus withdrew to the supposedly impregnable citadel at Sardis, not suspecting that Cyrus would march against Sardis (Herodotus 1.76–77). Cyrus, however, marched to Sardis quickly and unobserved (1.79). Sardis was captured after a two-week siege (Herodotus 1.76–84). The moral lessons derived from this series of events (one must avoid pride, arrogance, and over-confidence and be prepared for unexpected reversals of fortune) became a *topos* for later historians and moralists (Hemer, *NTS* 19 [1972–73] 94–97).

**2b** οὐ γὰρ εὕρηκά σου τὰ ἔργα πεπληρωμένα ἐνώπιον τοῦ θεοῦ μου, "for I have not found your conduct perfect in the sight of my God." It is difficult not to understand the phrase "I have not found your conduct perfect" as *ironical* in view of v 2a. Certainly the language of this phrase is based on the juridical metaphor of standing in the presence of God and having one's works finally evaluated (cf. a similar metaphor in 3:5). Here εὑρίσκειν is based on juridical language, i.e., "finding" someone guilty or innocent, frequently in the passive voice (Sir 44:17, 20; Theod Dan 5:27; Acts 5:39; 23:9; 1 Cor 15:15; 2 Cor 5:3; 1 Pet 1:7; 2 Pet 3:14; cf. Rev 2:2: "you found them [i.e., the so-called apostles] false," and Theod Dan 5:27: θεκελ, ἐστάθη ἐν ζυγῷ καὶ εὑρέθη ὑστεροῦσα, "Thekel, it was weighed in a scale and was found wanting"). The verb πληροῦν is used here with the meaning "to make complete or perfect" (2 Thess 1:11; Phil 2:2), a meaning found six times in Johannine literature in the fixed expression "your/our joy might be perfect," i.e., the perfect passive of πληροῦν with ἡ χαρά (John 3:29; 15:11; 16:24; 17:13; 1 John 1:4; 2 John 12). Closer parallels, however, are found in the Matthaean redactional use of τέλειος, "perfect, complete," as in Matt 5:48, where disciples are told to be perfect (τέλειοι) as God is perfect (τέλειος), and Matt 19:21 where Jesus tells the rich young ruler what to do if he wants to be perfect (τέλειος), both passages dealing with ethical perfection, as in Rev 3:2b. The perfection of complete obedience to the Torah in 1QS is made clear by the repeated use of the adjective תָּמִים *tāmîm,* "complete, perfect" (1:8; 2:2 ["the men of God's lot who walk perfectly [הֹהולכים תמים *hahôlkîm tāmîm*] in all his ways"]; 3:3 [= 4QSC 1 ii 5], 9 [= 4QSA frag. 2, line 5]; 4.22; 8.20, 21; 9:2, 6, 8, 9 [= 4QSD frag. 3, line 8], 19 [= 4QSB frag. 8, line 2 = 4QSD 3 ii 3]). The performance evaluation reflected in 3:2 has an analogy in 1QS 9:2 (cf. 4QSD frag. 3, line 3): "For two years as to the perfection of his way and as to his counsel he shall be tested." The phrase ἐνώπιον τοῦ θεοῦ, "before God," is a formula found frequently in the OT either as ἐνώπιον τοῦ θεοῦ or as ἐνώπιον τοῦ κυρίου, "before the Lord," and is used in a variety of ways in the NT (see *EDNT* 1:462). The phrase occurs eleven times in Revelation (3:2, 5 [ἐνώπιον τοῦ πατρός]; 7:15 [ἐκνώπιον τοῦ θρόνου τοῦ θεοῦ]; 8:2, 4; 9:13; 11:4 [ἐνώπιον τοῦ κυρίου], 16; 12:10; 15:4; 16:19). In Revelation the phrase is usually used in a *local* sense, meaning "in the sight of," i.e., before the heavenly presence of God (3:5; 7:15; 8:2, 4; 9:13; 11:16; 12:10), or before God in the cultic sense of worshiping in his earthly temple (15:4). The phrase is used once figuratively meaning "in the opinion of God" or "with the full knowledge of God" (3:2). The phrase "my God" (which occurs here and four additional times, all in 3:12) is a distinctive expression attributed to Jesus found elsewhere in the NT only in John 21:17 ("I am ascended to my Father and your Father, and my God and your God") and in the cry from the cross (Mark 15:34 = Matt 27:46; the Markan version reproduces the LXX version of Ps 21:2[MT 22:2]:

ὁ θεός μου, ὁ θεός μου, "my God, my God," while Matthew uses vocatives: θέε μου, θέε μου, "my God, my God").

**3a** μνημόνευε οὖν πῶς εἴληφας καὶ ἤκουσας καὶ τήρει καὶ μετανόησον, "Remember, therefore, what you have received and heard; obey that and repent." The contrast between the past and present, although there is no way of determining the intervening period of time, is an indication that the Christian community in Sardis had been in existence for some years, perhaps as long as a generation. This is one of several indications that the final edition of Revelation was written toward the end of the first or beginning of the second centuries A.D. The verb μνημονεύειν, "remember," also used in 2:5 of the previous moral and spiritual standards of the community from which they have lapsed, is a recurring *topos* in moral parenesis (see *Comment* on 2:5). The first pair of verbs, εἴληφας καὶ ἤκουσας, "you received and heard" (on the tenses, see *Note* 3:3.b.), probably refers to the Christian traditions transmitted to the Sardinians when their congregation was founded. The verb λαμβάνειν, "to receive," is used here in the sense of the beginning point of Christian faith, a usage characteristic of the Fourth Gospel (1:12; 3:11, 32–33; 5:43; 12:48; 13:20; 17:8; see Frey, "Verhältnis," 356). The second pair of verbs, τήρει καὶ μετανόησον, "obey that and repent," are both in the imperative and are an example of the literary device *hysteron-proteron*, "last-first" (i.e., placing two events in reverse order, a phenomenon that occurs frequently in Revelation: 3:17; 5:5; 6:4; 10:4, 9; 20:4–5, 12–13; 22:14), since one would normally expect the mention of "repentance" before "obey." On the stylistic peculiarity οὖν + καί + finite verb + καί + finite verb, see *Comment* on 2:5.

**3b** ἐὰν οὖν μὴ γρηγορήσῃς ἤξω ὡς κλέπης, καὶ οὐ μὴ γνῷς ποίαν ὥραν ἤξω ἐπὶ σέ, "If, therefore, you do not watch, I will come like a thief, and you will not know at what moment I will come to you." The motif of the coming of Christ occurs several times in the proclamations to the seven churches (2:5, 16, 25; 3:3, 11), using two synonymous verbs for coming, ἔρχεσθαι and ἤκειν. However, there appear to be two types of "coming" involved, a coming in judgment, which has negative connotations (2:5, 16; 3:3), which is apparently distinct from the return of Christ, which has positive connotations (2:25; 3:11). This saying has a close parallel in Rev 16:15: Ἰδοὺ ἔρχομαι ὡς κλέπης, "Behold I come as a thief," and indicates that the metaphor of an unexpected nocturnal break-in by a robber, used of the Parousia or second coming of Christ, could be applied to Christ's "coming" in other ways. In 1 Thess 5:2, the unexpectedness of the coming of the Day of the Lord is compared to the unexpected arrival of a thief: ἡμέρα κυρίου ὡς κλέπης ἐν νυκτὶ οὕτως ἔρχεται, "the Day of the Lord comes as a thief in the night." The same phrase occurs in 2 Pet 3:10: ἤξει δὲ ἡμέρα κυρίου ὡς κλέπης, "But the Day of the Lord will come as a thief." In both these passages, which share a common tradition (i.e., the latter is presumably dependent on the former), the Day of the Lord, not Christ, is compared to the unexpected coming of a burglar. In the parable of the Watchful Householder from Q (Matt 24:42–44 = Luke 12:39–40; see Stroker, *Extracanonical,* 111–12), the necessity of the householder to be watchful in case a thief comes unexpectedly is interpreted as an exhortation to watchfulness for the unexpected coming of the Son of Man. The reference to the Son of Man is widely (and correctly) regarded as a secondary addition to the tradition (Lindars, *Son of Man,* 97–98; Jeremias, *Parables,* 48–49; Fitzmyer, *Luke* 2:985; Kloppenborg, *Formation of Q,* 149; Koester, *Gospels,* 153; Crossan, *Historical Jesus,* 250–51); i.e., it is probable that an earlier version of Q lacked the application of the unexpected coming of the thief with the unexpected Parousia of the Son of Man. In *Gos. Thom.* 21, no christological application is found (Jeremias, *Parables,* 49): "Therefore I say: If the lord of the house knows that the thief is coming, he will stay awake before he comes and will not let him dig through into his house of his kingdom to carry away his goods." A parallel saying occurs in *Gos. Thom.* 103: "Blessed is the man who knows in which part of the night the robbers will come, so that he will rise and collect his [  ] and gird up his loins before they come in." A comparison of these texts indicates the hermeneutical interest in interpreting the metaphors used in the sayings of Jesus and makes it probable that the identification of the thief with the Son of Man (Matt 18:44; Luke 12:40) is a later development of the Q tradition, which has in turn influenced the formulation of the "I" sayings in Rev 3:3 and 16:15, though the insertion of the Son of Man saying was unknown to our author.

**4a** ἀλλὰ ἔχεις ὀλίγα ὀνόματα ἐν Σάρδεσιν ἃ οὐκ ἐμόλυναν τὰ ἱμάτια αὐτῶν, "But you have a few individuals in Sardis who have not soiled their clothes." The verb ἔχεις, "you have," is a second person singular referring to the "angel" to whom this proclamation is addressed, while the ὀνόματα, "names, individuals," refers collectively to a group within the congregation of Sardis. Here "clothes" is a metaphor for an individual's moral and spiritual condition (see also 7:13–14; 22:14). In Zech 3:1–5, Zechariah is depicted as wearing dirty clothes while standing before the angel of the Lord, a metaphor for the sins of both the priest and the people (the removal of these dirty clothes explicitly represents the removal of guilt; cf. Zech 3:4). In *1 Apoc. Jas.* 28.16–17, James says to Jesus, referring to his teflon-like clothing (tr. J. M. Robinson, *Nag Hammadi,* 263): "You walked in mud, and your garments were not soiled." Again in *Great Pow.* 44.25–26, which is part of an apocalyptic scenario, it is said of the archon of the west that "the defilement of his garments is great"; i.e., he is a wicked person. Similarly, *Teach. Silv.* 105.13–16 (tr. J. M. Robinson, *Nag Hammadi,* 389) exhorts the reader to "strip off the old garment of fornication."

**4b** καὶ περιπατήσουσιν μετ᾽ ἐμοῦ ἐν λευκοῖς, ὅτι ἄξιοί εἰσιν, "They will walk with me in white, because they are worthy." The notion of "walking" with the exalted Christ while wearing white garments means to enjoy a close relationship to him. The specific manner and place in which the author thought that this promise would be fulfilled is difficult to imagine. There is a parallel in Rev 14:4 that refers to the 144,000 following the Lamb wherever he goes, utilizing the language of discipleship. The verb περιπατεῖν is frequently used in the NT with the meaning "behave," and occasionally one finds the parallel expression περιπατεῖν ἀξίως, "to behave worthily," e.g., 1 Thess 2:12: περιπατεῖν ὑμᾶς ἀξίως τοῦ θεοῦ, "to behave in a manner worthy of God" (see Col 1:10; Eph 4:1; Pol. *Phil.* 5:1). Elsewhere in Revelation the notion of "worthiness" is attributed only to God or Christ. Normally the adjective ἄξιος is used in Revelation only of God or Christ, but in other early Christian literature ἄξιος and cognates occur more frequently, particularly in Ignatius (e.g., *Eph.* 4:1; *Magn.* 2:1; 12:1). Further, περιπατεῖν can be used as a synonym for "discipleship," as in John 8:12: "the one who follows [ἀκολουθῶν] me will not walk [περιπατήσῃ] in darkness but will have the light of life" (see John 12:35; 1 John 1:6–7; 2:6, 11). The language of Rev 3:4 is very possibly influenced by Gen 5:22 and 6:9 (both P Document) where it is said of both Enoch and Noah that they "walked with God" (which the LXX renders weakly by "pleased God," using the verb εὐαρεστέω), which similarly appears to mean that they enjoyed an unmediated relationship to God. Similarly, Abraham is commanded to "walk before" God (Gen 17:1). On white garments, see *Comment* on v 5a.

**5a** ὁ νικῶν οὕτως περιβαλεῖται ἐν ἱματίοις λευκοῖς, "The one who conquers thus will be clothed with a white garment." The οὕτως, "thus, so," refers to the reward of white garments mentioned in v 4b (cf. John 3:8). White garments symbolize a range of positive meanings that center on the concept of ritual and moral purity (see Hermas *Vis.* 4.3.5). Heavenly messengers are frequently described as wearing white garments (2 Macc 11:8; Matt 28:3 = Mark 16:5; John 20:12; Acts 1:10; Rev 4:4; 19:14; Hermas *Vis.* 4.2.1; *T. Levi* 8:2; Lucian *Philops.* 25), and in Dan 7:9; *1 Enoch* 14:20, God is described as wearing white (just as deities in the Greco-Roman world were thought to wear white). Priests in the ancient world often wore white (Exod 28:4; Lev 16:4; Jos. *Ant.* 11.327, 331; 20.216–18; *J.W.* 2.123, 137 [Essenes habitually wore white; see Hippolytus *Ref.* 9.19]; Lucian *Alex.* 11; Ps.-Lucian *De dea Syria* 42), as did worshipers who participated in sacrifices and processions (*Acts John* 38). By the first century A.D., the dead were buried in white in Judaism (see Krauss, *Talmudische Archäologie* 1:550 n. 212; Ps.-Philo*Bib. Ant.* 64.6), a practice found in the Greco-Roman world (Plutarch *Quaest. Rom.* 26.270D–F), and perhaps based on this custom the notion developed that white garments will be awarded to the righteous after judgment as a heavenly reward (*b. Šabb.* 114a; Rev 6:11; 7:9, 13; Hermas *Sim.* 8.2.3; see Lucian *Peregr.* 40 [Peregrinus is seen wearing white garments after his suicide]). The term "garment" was used as a metaphor for the physical body (2 Cor 5:2–4; *Asc. Isa.* 10.35), often implied with the use of "put off" and "put on" language (Col 2:11; 2 Pet 1:14; 4 Ezra 2:45) and perhaps by extension as a metaphor for a heavenly reward (Rev 3:4, 18; 6:11; 7:9, 13; *Asc. Isa.* 8.14–15; 9.24–26; 10.40) and a symbol of salvation or immortality (*Acts of Paul* 38; *Apoc. Thom.* [*NTA* 2:802], which speaks of the garment of eternal life, i.e., the garment that is eternal life; 5 Ezra 2:39; *Dial. Sav.* 143.11–15). In the story of the Transfiguration, Jesus' garments suddenly become bright white (Mark 9:2 = Matt 17:2 = Luke 9:29).

**5b** καὶ οὐ μὴ ἐξαλείψω τὸ ὄνομα αὐτοῦ ἐκ τῆς βίβλου τῆς ζωῆς, "and I will not erase his name from the Book of Life." This may be an allusion to Exod 32:32 (where Moses intercedes for Israel): "But now if you will forgive their sin—and if not, blot me out of the book which you have written." The motif of a Book of Life in which the names of the saved are written and the motif of the erasure of a person's name from such a Book are extremely widespread in the OT and early Judaism, sometimes used together and sometimes separately. The possibility of having one's name erased from the Book of Life suggests that fidelity to God rather than any type of predestinarian system is the reason for having one's name inscribed in the Book of Life in the first place (see Rev 17:8). The traditional character of this pronouncement in Rev 3:5 is evident in the close parallel to vv 5a and 5b in *Odes Sol.* 9:11, where the two motifs of *conquering* and of *having one's name inscribed in a heavenly book* are combined in a positive formulation (tr. Charlesworth, *OTP*): "Put on the crown in the true covenant of the Lord, And all those who have conquered will be inscribed in His book." In Judaism and early Christianity, the primary setting of the Book of Life motif was the judgment scene in which God is seated upon his throne surrounded by heavenly courtiers (Dan 7:9–10; Rev 20:12–15; *1 Enoch* 47:3; 90:20). The origin of this metaphor is certainly that of the ancient Near Eastern royal court, where records were made available to the king for dispensing justice (Ezra 4:15; Esth 6:1), though the idea itself goes back to Sumerian and Akkadian literature (Paul, *JANESCU* 5 [1973] 345–53).

There is a small "library" of at least three types of heavenly books referred to in the OT and in early Jewish and early Christian literature:

(1) The *Book of Life* functioned as a heavenly record of those who were considered righteous or worthy (*1 Enoch* 108:3; *Jub.* 30:22; *T. Jacob* 7:27–28; Luke 10:20; Phil 4:3; Rev 3:5; 13:8; 17:8; 21:27; *1 Clem.* 53:4 [quotation of Exod 32:32]; Hermas *Vis.* 1.3.2; *Mand.* 8.6; *Sim.* 2.9; *Apoc. Pet.* 17 [Hennecke-Schneemelcher, *NTA* 2:683]; Clementine *Hom.* 9.22; *Gos. Truth* 21.3–5; Koep, *Himmlische Buch*, 68–89; H. Balz, "βιβλίον," *EWNT* 1:512–24).

(2) The *Book of Deeds* serves as a record of the good and bad deeds a person had performed (*1 Enoch* 89:61–64; 90:17; 104:7; 108:7; *2 Enoch* 19:3–5 [Rec. J and A]; 53:2 [Rec. J and A]; *Jub.* 5:12–13; 23:30–32; 30:20–23; 32:21–22; *Asc. Isa.* 9.21–23; see Koep, *Himmlische Buch*, 46–68). In Judaism this is often conceived of as *two* books, one for the deeds of the righteous and the other for the deeds of the wicked (*Jub.* 30:22; 36:10; *b. Ta'an.* 11a; *Lev. Rab.* 26 [on 21:1]; *Gen. Rab.* 81 [on 35:1]).

(3) The *Book of Destiny*, or the "heavenly tablets," records the history of the world (4Q*180* = 4QAges of Creation frag. 1, line 3) and/or the destinies of people before they are born (Ps 56:8; 139:16; *Jub.* 5:12–19; 16:9; 23:32; *1 Enoch* 81:2; 93:1–3; 106:19; 107:1; *2 Enoch* 22:12 [Rec J and A]; 53:2 [Rec. J]; *T. Asher* 2:10; 7:5; *T. Levi* 5:4; see the *Prayer of Joseph* [Origen *Comm in Gen.*; *PG* XII.73B]: "I have read in the heavenly tablets everything that will come to pass upon you and your sons"; 4Q*537* = 4QApocryphon of Jacob frag. 1, lines 3–4 [tr. García Martínez, *Dead Sea Scrolls*, 265]: "[And I took the tablets and read. There were written all my privations] and all my troubles and all that was to happen to me."). Access to this book signifies a knowledge of hidden teaching or future events (Hermas *Vis.* 1.3.3–4; Eusebius *Hist. eccl.* 6.38).

The Books of Deeds and the Book of Life are distinguished in Rev 20:12 (for the redactional character of 20:12c, see *Comment* there). The motif of having one's name *erased* from, or *blotted out* of, the Book of Life is a metaphor for judgment (Exod 32:32–33; Ps 69:27–28; *1 Enoch* 108:3; *Jub.* 30:22), based on the notion of expulsion or disenfranchisement from the record of citizenship. Originally, however, to be *blotted out* of the Book of Life meant "to die" (Exod 32:32–33; Ps 69:27–28; Isa 4:3). The phrase "Book of Life" occurs six times in Revelation in two forms: (1) ἡ βίβλος τῆς ζωῆς, "the book of life," occurs twice in Revelation (3:5; 20:15 [*var. lect.* τὸ βιβλίον Byzantine]), and (2) a synonymous phrase, τὸ βιβλίον τῆς ζωῆς, "the book of life," using the faded diminutive τὸ βιβλίον, is found four times in Revelation (13:8 [*var. lect.* ἡ βίβλος; see *Notes* on 13:8]; 17:8; 20:12; 21:27 [*var. lect.* ἡ βίβλος fam 1611²⁰⁵⁰ Andreas h⁻²³⁰² Andreas 1]). The textual evidence suggests that the author used *both* forms interchangeably (for the special problems in Rev 10, see *Notes* on 10:2, 8, 9, 10). The idea of a Book of Life as a kind of heavenly citizen registry is frequently referred to in ancient Israelite and Jewish literature (Exod 32:32–33 [an old tradition belonging to JE]; Ps 69:28; Dan 12:1; *Jub.* 30:22; 1QM 12:1–2) and occurs also in the NT and early Christian literature (Luke 10:20; Phil 4:3; Heb 12:23; Hermas *Sim.* 2.9; *1 Clem.* 53:4 [quoting Exod 32:32]; cf. Isa 4:3; Ezek 13:9). Ezek 13:9 refers to "the book of the house of Israel," perhaps a tribal roll of all the people, perhaps originating in David's census mentioned in 2 Sam 24:2, 9 (cf. Jer 22:30; Ezra 2:62). This tribal roll becomes a metaphor for being enrolled in the book of Yahweh (Exod 32:32–33; cf. Ps 87:6: "The Lord . . . registers the peoples"). In Ps 69:28 this book is called סֵפֶר הַיִּים *sēper ḥayyîm*, "the Book of Life" or "the Book of the Living." *Jub.* 30:22 refers to two books, the Book of Life and the Book of those who will be destroyed. According to *Jos. As.* 15:4 (Charlesworth, *OTP* 2:226), the heavenly man addresses Aseneth with the following message: "For behold, your name was written [ἐγράφη] in the book of the living [τῇ βίβλῳ τῶν ζώντων] in heaven; in the beginning of the book, as the very first of all, your name was written by my finger, and it will not be erased [ἐξαλειφθήσεται] forever." The same motif is found in *T. Levi* 18:59–60 (MS *e* only, which contains a lengthy insertion between 18:2 and 18:3; Gk. text in de Jonge, *Testaments*, 46–48): "Your offspring will be recorded in the book of the remembrance of life [ἐν βιβλίῳ μνημοσύνου ζωῆς] , and your name will not be erased [ἐξαλειφθήσεται], nor the name of your offspring for ever." A "Book of Remembrance" (MT: ספר זכרון *sēper zikkārôn;* LXX: βιβλίον μνημοσύνου), which "was written before him of those who feared the Lord," is mentioned in Mal 3:16.

The motif of the Book of Life can be used in an entirely negative way, as in *Pistis Sophia* 1.33 (ed. Schmidt-Till, *Schriften* 1:34, lines 5–6 = ed. Schmidt-MacDermot, *Pistis Sophia*, 55): "Let them be effaced from the book of the living, and let them not be written with the righteous." This negative usage is also found in rabbinic literature (Str-B 2:169–70). The twelfth benediction of the *Shemoneh Esreh*, Eighteen Benedictions or *Berakhoth*, reads as follows (J. J. Petuchowski, "Jewish Prayer Texts of the Rabbinic Period," in *The Lord's Prayer and Jewish Liturgy*, ed. J. J. Petuchowski and M. Brocke [New York: Seabury, 1978] 29):

> For the apostates let there be no hope, and uproot the kingdom of arrogance, speedily and in our days. May the Nazarenes and the sectarians [מנים *minîm*] perish as in a moment. Let them be blotted out of the book of life, and not be written together with the righteous. You are praised, O Lord, who subdues the arrogant.

In Athens, whenever any citizen was sentenced to be executed for a crime, his name was first erased [ἐξαλείφεται] from the roll of citizens (Dio Chrysostom *Or.* 31.84). An example of this procedure is found in Xenophon *Hellenica* 2.3.51, when Critias strikes the name of Theramenes from the roll of citizens (ἐξαλείφω ἐκ τοῦ καταλόγου) so that he could be condemned to death. The frequency with which the term ἐξαλείφω occurs in precisely this context indicates that it is a technical term for erasing the names of citizens from the registry. The roll of citizens liable for service was called a καταλόγος (Xenophon *Hellenica* 2.3.20; Aristophanes *Equites* 1369), but some were able through influence to have their names removed from this list (Aristophanes *Pax* 1180–81).

**5c** καὶ ὁμολογήσω τὸ ὄνομα αὐτοῦ ἐνώπιον τοῦ πατρός μου καὶ ἐνώπιον τῶν ἀγγέλων αὐτοῦ, "and I will acknowledge his name before my father and before the holy angels." The term ὁμολογεῖν, "to confess," is used only here in Revelation and in a context that contains a number of traditional elements. This is very probably an allusion to an "I saying" of Jesus found in other versions in Q (Luke 12:8; Matt 10:32) and *2 Clem.* 3:2 (see Donfried, *Setting of Second Clement*, 60–61):

| Rev 3:5 | Luke 12:8 | Matt 10:32 | 2 Clem. 3:2 |
|---|---|---|---|
| πᾶς ὃ ἂν<br>Every one who | πᾶς οὖν ὅστις<br>Therefore every-<br>one who | τὸν<br>The one who | |
| ὁμολογήσῃ ἐν<br>confesses | ὁμολογήσῃ ἐν<br>confesses | ὁμολογήσαντά<br>confesses | |

| | | | |
|---|---|---|---|
| | ἐμοὶ ἔμπροσθεν<br>me before | ἐμοὶ ἔμπροσθεν<br>me before | με ἐνώπιον<br>me before |
| | τῶν ἀνθρώπων<br>people | τῶν ἀνθρώπων<br>people | τῶν ἀνθρώπων<br>people |
| | καὶ ὁ υἱὸς τοῦ<br>Also the son of | | |
| | ἀνθρώπου<br>man | | |
| ὁμολογήσω<br>I will confess | ὁμολογήσει<br>will confess | ὁμολογήσω<br>I will confess | ὁμολογήσω<br>I will confess |
| τὸ ὄνομα<br>the name | | κἀγὼ<br>and I | |
| αὐτοῦ<br>his | ἐν αὐτῷ<br>him | ἐν αὐτῷ<br>him | αὐτὸν<br>him |
| ἐνώπιον<br>before | | ἔμπροσθεν<br>before | ἐνώπιον<br>before |
| τοῦ πατρός<br>the Father | | τοῦ πατρός<br>the Father | τοῦ πατρός<br>the Father |
| μου<br>my | | μου<br>my | μου<br>my |
| | | τοῦ ἐν τοῖς<br>in the | |
| | | οὐρανοῖς<br>heavens | |
| καὶ ἐνώπιον<br>and before | ἔμπροσθεν<br>before | | |
| τῶν ἀγγέλων<br>the angels | τῶν ἀγγέλων<br>the angels | | |
| αὐτοῦ<br>his | τοῦ θεοῦ<br>of God | | |

The dissimilarity in wording argues against the literary interdependence of v 5c and Matt 10:32 or Luke 12:8, or the Q document (Yarbro Collins, "Son of Man," 560). This allusion is verbally closest to *2 Clem.* 3:2, which, together with Rev 3:5, reflects a parallel tradition similar to but not dependent upon the versions of the saying in Luke 12:8; Matt 10:32, or in Q (Donfried, *Second Clement,* 61). The verb ὁμολογεῖν occurs only here in Revelation and is therefore not part of the author's normal vocabulary (in contrast with ten occurrences in the Johannine literature

(John 1:20[2x]; 9:22; 12:42; 1 John 1:9; 2:23; 4:2, 3, 15; 2 John 7) but reflects the usage of the author's oral or written source. ὁμολογεῖν here is used with the accusative of the person or thing, as in *2 Clem.* 3:2, though in Luke 12:8; Matt 10:32 the Aramaism ἐν + dative occurs (BDF § 220.2; BDR § 220.3), though this construction does not occur in the LXX. The author has substituted τὸ ὄνομα αὐτοῦ, "his name," for αὐτόν, "him," to be consistent with the metaphor of not erasing "his name" from the Book of Life mentioned in v 5a. The use of the more idiomatic accusative with the verb ὁμολογεῖν suggests that the author, like the author of *2 Clem.* 3:2, is dependent on a less Semitizing version of this saying of Jesus, probably from oral tradition. In Luke 12:8, the phrase "the Son of Man" (and the alteration of the verb from first person singular to third person singular) is a secondary addition by Luke (Fitzmyer, *Luke* 1:958).

*Explanation*

Christ is described as he "who has the seven spirits of God, namely the seven stars," an allusion to 1:16–20, in which the seven spirits should be understood as the seven archangels (see 4:5; 5:6; 8:2; a metaphor probably originating from Zech 4:2, 6, 10). This church receives primarily censure; only a minority of Christians "have not soiled their garments" (v 4). Christ knows the real state of their works: though they may appear hale and hearty to others, they are in reality on the point of spiritual death (v 1b). They are encouraged to wake up and change their ways before it is too late (v 2). In the NT, watchfulness is an indispensable characteristic of the people of God in view of the imminence of the end (Mark 13:33–37; Matt 25:13). For those who fail to awake and repent, Christ threatens to come unexpectedly, like a thief (v 3). This is a relatively clear allusion to a saying of Jesus also preserved in Matt 24:42–44; Luke 12:39–40 (see Rev 16:15). The saying has three distinctive motifs, the exhortation to watch, the metaphor of the thief (first occurring in 1 Thess 5:2, and later in 2 Pet 3:10), and the unexpected time of arrival. However, only in Rev 3:5 and 16:15 is the thief identified with Christ.

Those who conquer will be rewarded with white garments (vv 4b–5a), probably not so much an allusion to the flourishing garment industry as a metaphor of ritual, moral, and spiritual purity. White garments were worn at religious festivals and when performing cultic acts such as sacrifice. Victorious Roman generals wore white togas when celebrating triumphs in Rome.

Further, their names will not be blotted out of the Book of Life, another metaphor for eternal life. Ancient Israel had some kind of roll of citizens (Ps 69:28; Isa 4:3), and Athens and some other Greek cities had the custom of erasing from the rolls the names of citizens executed by the state (Dio Chrysostom *Or.* 31.84–85; Xenophon *Hellenica* 2.3.51). Having one's name written in the Book of Life thus suggests heavenly citizenship (Heb 12:23; 1 Pet 1:17). The idea of a "book of life" (frequently mentioned; see 13:8; 17:8; 20:15; 21:7) from which one's name could be erased is common in Judaism (Exod 32:32–33; *Jub.* 30:20–22; *Jos. As.* 15:3). Christ's promise to confess the victorious Christian's name before the Father and his angels alludes to a saying of Jesus found in the Q tradition (Matt 10:32 = Luke 12:8) and in Mark 8:38 = Luke 9:26, though John was probably dependent on oral rather than written tradition.

# 6. The Proclamation to Philadelphia    (3:7–13)

## Bibliography

**Bakker, W. F.** *Pronomen Abundans and Pronomen Coniunctum: A Contribution to the History of the Resumptive Pronoun with the Relative Clause in Greek.* Amsterdam: North-Holland, 1974. **Black, M.** "Some Greek Words with Hebrew Meaning in the Epistles and Apocalypse." In *Biblical Studies in Honour of William Barclay,* ed. J. R. McKay and J. F. Miller. London: Collins, 1976. 135–46. **Brown, S.** "Deliverance from the Crucible: Some Further Reflexions on 1QH iii.1–18." *NTS* 14 (1968) 247–59. ⸻. "The Hour of Trial (Rev 3:10)." *JBL* 85 (1966) 308–14. **Edgar, T. R.** "R. H. Gundry and Revelation 3:10." *GTJ* 3 (1982) 19–49. **Gundry, R. H.** *The Church and the Tribulation.* Grand Rapids, MI: Zondervan, 1973. **Hemer, C. J.** "Unto the Angels of the Churches: 4. Philadelphia and Laodicea." *BurH* 11 (1975) 164–90. **Hirschfeld, O.** "Zur Geschichte des römischen Kaiserkultus." In *Kleine Schriften.* Berlin: Weidmann, 1913. **Korn, J. H.** *PEIRASMOS: Die Versuchung des Gläubigen in der griechischen Bibel.* BWANT 4/20. Stuttgart: Kohlhammer, 1937. **Kuhn, K. G.** "New Light on Temptation, Sin, and Flesh in the New Testament." In *The Scrolls and the New Testament,* ed. K. Stendahl. New York: Harper & Brothers, 1957. 94–113. **Lövestam, E.** "Apokalypsen 3:8b." *SEÅ* 30 (1965) 91–101. **Mueller, T.** "The Word of My Patience in Revelation 3:10." *CTQ* 46 (1982) 231–34. **Thompson, L.** "A Sociological Analysis of Tribulation in the Apocalypse of John." *Semeia* 36 (1986) 147–74. **Townsend, J. L.** "The Rapture in Revelation 3:10." *BSac* 137 (1980) 252–66. **Wilkinson, R. H.** "The στῦλος of Revelation 3:12 and Ancient Coronation Rites." *JBL* 107 (1988) 498–501. **Winfrey, D. G.** "The Great Tribulation: Kept 'Out of' or 'Through'?" *GTJ* 3 (1982) 3–18.

## Translation

[7]*And to the angel of the church in Philadelphia, write: "Thus says* [a]*the Holy One, the True One,*[a] *the One who has the* [b] *key of* [c]*David, who opens so that* [d] *no one can shut,*[e] *and who shuts so that* [f] *no one can* [g]*open.*[h] [8] *I know your conduct. Behold, I have placed* [a] *before you an open* [b] *door, which no one is able to shut,* [c]*because you have limited strength. Yet* [d] *you have obeyed my command and did not deny my name.* [9]*Behold, I will cause* [a] *those* [b] *of the synagogue of Satan* [c]*who call themselves Jews* [c] *(but* [d] *are not,* [e]*but are lying)—behold, I will force them* [f]*to come* [g] *and grovel* [h] *at your feet so that* [i] [j]*they will know* [j] *that I have loved* [k] *you.* [10a]*Because you have obeyed* [b] [c]*my command to endure,*[d] *so I* [d] *will preserve* you[e] [f]*from the time of affliction* [g] *which will come upon the whole earth to afflict* [h] *the inhabitants of the earth.* [11a]*I am coming soon. Keep what you have that no one takes away your wreath.* [12]*As for the one who conquers,*[a] *I will make him* [b] *a pillar in the temple of my* [c] *God, and he will never ever* [d] *leave it. Moreover, I will inscribe upon him* [e] *the name of my God and the name of the city of my God, the* [f] *New Jerusalem,* [g] [h]*which descends* [h] *from* [i] *heaven from my God and my* [j] *new name.* [13]*The one with an ear, let him hear what the Spirit declares to the churches.'"*

## Notes

7.a-a. Variants: (1) ὁ ἅγιος, ὁ ἀληθινός] C Andreas Byzantine latt syr cop Epiphanius. (2) ὁ ἀληθινὸς, ὁ ἅγιος] ℵ A. (3) ὁ ἅγιος] fam 1611²⁰⁵⁰ Oecumenius²⁰⁵³. (4) ὁ ἄγγελος ἀληθινός] 2351.

7.b. Variant: omit τήν] ℵ*.

7.c. Variants: (1) omit τοῦ before Δαυίδ] A C fam 1611¹⁶¹¹ ¹⁸⁵⁴; WHort; Bousset (1906) 173, 226; Charles, 2:256; Nestle-Aland²⁷ ; UBSGNT⁴. (2) τοῦ before Δαυίδ] 2351. Reading (1) is almost certainly the original reading (Schmid, *Studien* 2:87).

7.d. Here καί is used as a καιconsecutivum; i.e., it introduces a coordinate clause that gives the consequence or result of the action expressed in the previous clause (see Zerwick, *Greek* § 455; Ljungvik, *Syntax*, 62–63; Aejmelaeus, *Parataxis*, 15–18). Mussies (*Morphology*, 342) proposes that the fut. ind. here has a potential aspect ("so that nobody will be able to shut") but ignores the syntactic role of καί as a consecutive particle. For other examples of καίconsecutivum, see 11:3; 14:10; 20:10; possible instances occur in 2:23; 3:10

7.e. Variants: (1) κλείσει] ℵ A C 025 fam 1611²⁰⁵⁰ ²³²⁹ cop Irenaeusᴸᵃᵗ (Sanday-Turner, *Nouum Testamentum*, 194); Tyconius. (2) κλείει] fam 1611¹⁶¹¹ ¹⁸⁵⁴ Oecumenius²⁰⁵³ Andreas latt Primasius Hippolytus (*Comm. in Dan.* 4.34). κλείσει is a third-person sing. fut. ind. that is parallel to the third-person sing. present ind. ἀνοίγει.

7.f. See *Note* 7.d.

7.g. ἀνοίγει is a conative present representing action attempted but not accomplished. Some copyists changed ἀνοίγει into the fut. ind. form ἀνοίξει (ℵ fam 1006¹⁰⁰⁶¹⁸⁴¹ fam 1611²⁰⁵⁰²³²⁹²³⁴⁴ Byzantine), in agreement with κλείσει (Schmid, *Studien* 2:131).

7.h. Variant: insert εἰ μὴ ὁ ἀνοίγων καὶ οὐδεὶς ἀνοίξει] 2351.

8.a. In the LXX, διδόναι is often used as a synonym of τιθέναι, since Heb. נתן *nātan* can mean both "to give" and "to place, set" (Thackeray, *Grammar*, 39; Robertson, *Grammar*, 95; Black, *Aramaic Approach*, 132–33; id., "Some Greek Words," 145–46). According to Louw-Nida, § 85.32 (τίθημι) and 85.33 (δίδωμι) belong to the same semantic subdomain.

8.b. Variant: ἀνεῳγμένην (fem. pf. pass. ptcp.)] 2351 Andreas.

8.c. The relative clause ἥν οὐδεὶς δύναται κλεῖσαι αὐτήν, lit. "which no one is able to shut it," uses the redundant personal pronoun αὐτήν which is usually considered pleonastic and so has been frequently regarded as a Hebraism (*BDR* § 297; Turner, *Syntax*, 325). In Heb. the indeclinable relative pronoun אֲשֶׁר, "which" (like the indeclinable relative pronoun דִי in Aram.) must, for the sake of clarity, be accompanied by pronouns and adverbs that more closely identify the person or thing in question. The same construction, however, is found in Coptic, Hellenistic Gk. (POxy 117, line 15; 1070, line 22), and modern Gk. (J. Vergote, "Grec Biblique," *DBSup* 3:1356). On this construction, see Bakker, *Pronomen Abundans*, 9–46, and Moulton-Howard, *Accidence*, 434–35. Black exaggerates when he argues that the construction "may be possible in Greek, but it is not native to it, as it is in Hebrew and Aramaic" (*Aramaic*, 100). In Revelation the *pronomen abundans*, i.e., the pleonastic or resumptive personal pronoun occurs nine times (here; 7:2, 9; 12:6, 14; 13:8, 12; 17:9; 20:8). The pleonastic personal pronoun in a relative clause is an idiom that occurs frequently in the LXX (Gen 10:14; 20:13; 28:13; 41:19; Exod 4:17; Lev 16:32; Deut 11:25; Josh 22:19; Judg 18:6; Ruth 3:2; 1 Kgs 11:34; Neh 8:12; Joel 3:7; Amos 9:12; see Thackeray, *Grammar*, 46); it sometimes occurs, however, when the corresponding idiom is not found in the Heb. text (e.g., Isa 1:21; see Moulton-Howard, *Accidence*, 435), and it also occurs in Hellenistic Gk. of a relatively high register (Luke 3:16, 17; *1 Clem.* 21:9). It also occurs ten times in the NT outside Revelation (Matt 3:11–12 = Luke 13:17; [Matt 10:11; 18:20, *var. lect.* MS B]; Mark 1:7 = Luke 3:16; Mark 7:25; 9:3; 13:19 [Luke 8:12; 12:43, *var. lect.* MS B]; John 1:27; Gal 2:10). The resumptive adv. occurs twice in 12:6, 14; see *Note* 12:6.a. Relative clauses with the *pronomen abundans* are Gk. if they are independent or parenthetical clauses (i.e., *nonessential*) but show Semitic influence if they are dependent clauses (i.e., *essential*). Here in Rev 3:8, the relative clause is *essential;* see *Introduction*, Section 7: Syntax, III. Pronouns.

8.d. If the phrase μικρὰ δύναμις means "little spiritual power" (Louw-Nida, § 12.44), then the conjunction καί is used here in an adversative sense and should be translated "but"; i.e., in spite of the spiritually weak condition of the Philadelphian community, they have nevertheless obeyed the word of Christ. Lövestam (*SEÅ* 3 [1965] 91–101), however, argues that this καί does not have an adversative force, since μικρὰ δύναμις refers not to "spiritual power" but rather to "limited strength"; i.e., δύναμις here means the ability to exert force in the performance of some action (Louw-Nida, § 76.1). While that is probably correct, καί here seems to function as a marker of emphasis (Louw-Nida, § 91.12), indicating unexpectedly that despite their weakness they nevertheless have proven obedient.

9.a. Variants: (1) διδῶ] A C syrᵖʰ; all modern editions except von Soden, *Text.* (2) δίδωμι] 025 046 Oecumenius²⁰⁵³ 2351 Andreas Byzantine; von Soden, *Text.* (3) δέδωκα] ℵ sa. (4) δώσω] bo eth. Reading (1), because of the rarity of the form, is the *lectio difficilior* and certainly the original reading. Reading (2) is a correction of (1) (Schmid, *Studien* 2:88), as is reading (3). The verb διδῶ (for the form, a contraction of διδόω, which would normally be δίδωμι, because of the replacement of -μι- with -ω-; see BDF § 94; BDR § 94; Mussies, *Morphology*, 284–85), lit. "I give," is a Hebraism, since the verb נתן *nātan* can mean both "to give" and "to make," and, though it is usually translated in the LXX with διδόναι, "to give," it is occasionally translated with ποιεῖν, "to make" (Exod 18:25; Lev 19:28; Deut 16:18; Josh 17:13; Isa 43:3; see Helbing, *Kasussyntax*, 52–53). More frequently, however, the LXX translators tended to use διδόναι for נָתַן *nātan* even when the latter was used in the sense of "to make" (e.g., Gen 17:20; 48:4; Exod 23:27; Num 5:21; Isa 42:24; Jer 24:9). This same Hebraism also occurs occasionally in the NT (see Luke 1:77; Acts 2:27 [quoting Ps 16:10]; 10:40; 13:35 [quoting Ps 15:10]; 14:3). Without discussing the use of διδόναι as a Hebraism, Louw-Nida (§ 90.51) identify one function of διδόναι, glossed as "cause," as a marker of causative relations, nearly empty of semantic content, meaning "to cause, to bring about, to produce." The object of διδῶ is the partitive gen. [τινὰς] ἐκ τῆς συναγωγῆς, "[some] from the synagogue."

9.b. The prep. phrase ἐκ τῆς συναγωγῆς..., "from the synagogue...," is a partitive gen. (intensified by the prep. ἐκ, "of/from"), which functions as the obj. of the verb διδῶ; see BDR § 164. John frequently uses the partitive gen. (usually with ἐκ, sometimes with ἀπό) as the subject or obj. of various verbs. In this particular instance, the idiom is used atypically, since it is apparently not just *some* of those who are part of the synagogue of Satan (the partitive gen. as obj. usually presupposed an indefinite pl.), but *all*.

9.c-c. Variant: omit εἶναι from phrase τῶν λεγόντων ἑαυτοὺς Ἰουδαίους εἶναι] Oecumenius²⁰⁵³ 256 (a bilingual MS in which both Gk. and Armenian agree in this omission). Omission of εἶναι a correction; see 2:9, where εἶναι is omitted only by syrᵖʰ.

9.d. The καί here is a καί *adversativum*, which must be translated as "but," since it functions here as a conjunction linking two antithetical statements.

9.e. In Revelation, ἀλλά functions as a relatively strong adversative particle, which is of interest here because it follows a καί *adversativum* with which it is essentially synonymous.

9.f. The ἵνα clause here is a substitute for an inf. and introduces either a final clause (BDF § 369.2; BDR § 369.5) or a consecutive clause (i.e., ἵνα + a finite verb functions like an inf. that indicates the result of an action; see BAGD, 681), either of which can be understood by the ambiguous translation "so that they will come and worship." Further, ποιεῖν ἵνα can mean "to cause, effect," with the ἵνα + finite verb functioning in a manner similar to a complementary inf. (BDF §§ 392.1e; 408; 476.1).

9.g. Variants: (1) ἥξουσιν (fut. ind.)] ℵ A C 025 792 fam 1006¹⁰⁰⁶ fam 1611²⁰⁵⁰ ²³²⁹. (2) ἥξωσι (aor. subjunctive)] 046 fam 1611¹⁶¹¹ fam 1006 fam 1611¹⁸⁵⁴ ²³⁴⁴ 2351. Reading (2) is probably a correction (Schmid, *Studien* 2:73); see *Notes* on 6:4, 11; 8:3; 9:4, 5, 20; 13:12; 14:13; 22:14.

9.h. Variants: (1) προσκυνήσουσιν] ℵ A C 025 fam 1006¹⁰⁰⁶ fam 1611²⁰⁵⁰ ²³²⁹. (2) προσκυνήσωσιν] 046 fam 1611¹⁶¹¹ ¹⁸⁵⁴ ²³⁴⁴ fam 1006¹⁸⁴¹ 2351. The verb προσκυνεῖν occurs 24 times in Revelation, sometimes with the dat. (or ἐνώπιον, or ἔμπροσθεν), sometimes with the acc., and twice is used intransitively (5:14; 11:1). προσκυνεῖν + dat. occurs rarely, if ever, in Gk. prior to the first century A.D., with the striking exception of the LXX (Helbing, *Kasussyntax*, 296–98), where προσκυνεῖν + dat. occurs 123 times and προσκυνεῖν + acc. 6 times (Horst, *Proskynein*, 38). προσκυνεῖν + dat. occurs frequently in the NT and is also found in Josephus, Lucian, and Cassius Dio. Usually προσκυνεῖν + dat. is thought to be used in the sense of "to worship," i.e., God or the Dragon (4:10; 7:11; 11:16; 19:4, 10; 22:9), while προσκυνεῖν + acc. is thought to mean "to bow, prostrate oneself" or "to do homage to," i.e., before the Beast and his image (13:4, 12; 14:9, 11; 20:4); see Lohmeyer, 124 (dependent on Bousset [1906] 163); Charles, 1:cxli, 211–12 (G. B. Winer, *Grammatik des neutestamentlichen Sprachidioms*, 2nd ed. [Leipzig, 1825] § 24, has the reverse opinion: προσκυνεῖν + dat. is used for "to bow before someone," while προσκυνεῖν + acc. means "to worship.") However, J. Horst has rejected this distinction as untenable (*Proskynein*, 33–43, esp. 39). The dat. is used with terms for God (4:10; 7:11; 11:16; 14:7; 19:4, 10; 22:9), an angel (19:10), the Dragon (13:4), the Beast (13:4), and the image of the Beast, τῇ εἰκόνι τοῦ θηρίου (13:15; τὴν εἰκόνα] A 1) or τῇ εἰκόνι αὐτοῦ (16:2; 19:20; Lohmeyer, 124, regards these as exceptions), while the acc. is used with reference to the Beast (13:8: αὐτόν] A C 𝔓⁴⁷ Byzantine; αὐτῷ] ℵ Andreas), with τὸ θηρίον (13:12), with τὸ θηρίον καὶ τὴν εἰκόνα αὐτοῦ (14:9, 11; 20:4), and with τὰ δαιμόνια καὶ τὰ εἴδωλα (9:20). προσκυνεῖν is also used with the preps. ἐνώπιον (3:9; 15:4) and ἔμπροσθεν (22:8), followed by gens. of place. In summary: (1) προσκυνεῖν + dat. is consistently used of God and the Dragon. (2) προσκυνεῖν + dat. is used with εἰκών when used alone. (3) προσκυνεῖν + dat. is used once with θηρίον; usually the acc. is used with θηρίον. (4) προσκυνεῖν + acc. is used with τὴν εἰκόνα when linked with θηρίον by καί. Conclusion: in every instance but Rev 3:9, cultic worship is in view, and the supposed contrast between the attitude of worship and adoration and that of external physical bowing or prostration is untenable. The evidence adduced by Helbing, *Kasussyntax*, 296–98, points clearly in this direction, and Buttmann (*Grammar*, 147) observes: "in the Apocalypse it [προσκυνεῖν] is construed with both the dat. and acc. (as in the Septuagint) without the slightest difference." For further discussion of προσκυνεῖν, see *Comment* on 4:10.

9.i. The καί here functions as a καί *consecutivum*, introducing the consequence of the action in the previous clause (see Aejmelaeus, *Parataxis*, 15–18).

9.j-j. Variants: (1) γνῶσιν] Andreas. (2) γνώσει] 2351. (3) γνώσῃ] ℵ 69 cop^sa Primasius. (4) γνώσονται] fam 1611^2050 Andr f 2019. (5) γνώσωσιν] fam 1006^1006.

9.k. The aor. ind. ἠγάπησα has the force of a pf. (see 4:11: ἔκτισας; 11:17: εἴληφας; 14:18: ἤκμασαν; 18:3: ἐπόρνευσαν; ἐπλούτησαν).

10.a. The ὅτι clause that begins this sentence is in an unusual position, since in the vast majority of instances dependent clauses follow the main clause (other examples of ὅτι clauses in the pre-position are found in Rev 3:16; 18:7; see Turner, *Syntax*, 345).

10.b. The aor. circumstantial participle ἐτήρησας here does not have a present meaning reflecting the Semitic pf. as S. Thompson claims (*Apocalypse*, 40; he contradicts this view on p. 55 by erroneously interpreting this sentence as reflecting a Heb. waw consecutive).

10.c-c. The phrase τὸν λόγον τῆς ὑπομονῆς μου is problematic. Though the position of μου after τῆς ὑπομονῆς might suggest that it modifies only that substantive (Buttmann, *Grammar*, 155), it is more probable that μου should be taken with the idea expressed by the entire noun cluster (e.g., Heb 1:3; Col 1:13; Winer, *Grammar*, 297); see Rev 13:3: ἡ πληγὴ τοῦ θανάτου αὐτοῦ, "his mortal wound." This is made virtually certain by v 8, where ὁ λόγός μου, "my word," is identical with the phrase ὁ λόγος τῆς ὑπομνῆς μου in this verse. If the substantive in the gen. is construed as an *obj.* gen., then the phrase can be rendered "my word [i.e., 'command'] concerning endurance" (this understanding is reflected in the translation above). Charles takes μου with τῆς ὑπομονῆς and understands the entire clause τὸν λόγον τῆς ὑπομονῆς μου to mean "the Gospel of the endurance practised by Christ" (1:89). The RSV and NRSV take μου with the entire noun cluster: "my word of patient endurance." The REB and NIV also take μου with the entire noun cluster but understand τῆς ὑπομονῆς as an obj. gen.; REB: "my command to stand firm" (see NEB: "you have kept my command and stood fast"); NIV: "my command to endure patiently."

10.d. The crasis κἀγώ functions as an emphatic use of the pronoun ἐγώ, a meaning conveyed in the translation by an italicized *I*. κἀγώ here may also introduce a consecutive clause indicating the result of the verbal action in the preceding clause (see *Note* 7.d.).

10.e. The phrase σε τηρήσω, "you I will keep," with the acc. sing. pronoun functioning as the obj. of the verb before which it is placed (personal pronouns in oblique cases follow the verb 139 times and precede the verb just 14 times; see Mussies, *Morphology*, 329) probably emphasizes the pronoun (conveyed in the translation by not italicizing the pronoun "you") and at the same time conforms to a chiastic pattern a b b′a′ (ἐτήρησας . . . μου/σε τηρήσω), frequently found in Revelation.

10.f-f. In the phrase τηρήσω ἐκ τῆς ὥρας τοῦ πειρασμοῦ, the prep. ἐκ should be understood as a marker of dissociation meaning "independent from (someone or something)," "from," "independent of" (Louw-Nida, § 89.121). The phrase τηρεῖν ἐκ occurs in the NT only here in Rev 3:10 and in John 17:15. Many scholars have insisted that ἐκ is a prep. of motion meaning "out from within," "out of," "forth from," and cannot mean a stationary position outside its obj. but is used only of "situations and circumstances *out of which* one is brought; it presupposes that the person in question was previously in the situation or circumstance" (Brown, *JBL* 85 [1966] 310; see Robertson, *Grammar*, 598; Gundry, *Tribulation*, 55–56). However, there are numerous examples of ἐκ used of a position "outside," "beyond" (LSJ, 498–99), used to denote a position outside an object, with no prior existence within the object or any thought of emergence from the object (Townsend, *BSac* 137 [1980] 254; Winfrey, *GTJ* 3 [1982] 6); see *Iliad* 14.130; *Odyssey* 19.7; Herodotus 2.142; 3.83; 5.24; Josh 2:13; Pss 33:19[LXX 32:19]; 56:13[LXX 55:13]; Prov 21:23 (διατηρεῖν ἐκ); 23:14; Josephus *Ant.* 12.407 (ῥύεσθαι ἐκ); 13.200 (ῥύεσθαι ἐκ); Acts 15:29; John 12:27; Heb 5:7; Jas 5:20.

10.g. πειρασμός, meaning "testing" (Louw-Nida, § 27.46) or "temptation" (Louw-Nida, § 88.308), is used here to connote the "affliction" or "disaster" that is the means by which God is understood to test or try people. In early Jewish literature, πειρασμός has the meaning "chastisement, tribulation, persecution" (Wis 3:5; 11:10; Sir 2:1; Jdt 8:24–27; Luke 8:13 [here ἐν καιρῷ πειρασμοῦ, "in time of trial," means "in time of tribulation"]; Acts 20:19; 2 Cor 11:26; Heb 2:18; 1 Pet 1:6 [Hatch, *Essays*, 71–73]). In Rev 3:10, the author is probably referring to the tribulations that are described in the remainder of his book.

10.h. πειράζειν is usually translated "to try," "to make trial of," "to test," and in the NT usually applies only to believers (Bousset [1906] 228). Yet since the trial referred to is an eschatological event experienced by all people, from which Christians will be delivered (LXX Dan 12:1, 10; LXX Zeph 1:7–18; Brown, *JBL* 85 [1966] 311–13), it can appropriately be translated "afflict."

11.a. Variant: insert ἰδού] Andr i^-2042 94 it^a vg^cl Tyconius^1 Beatus^var. lect. (Romero-Pose, *Sancti Beati* 1:403); Apringius.

12.a. ὁ νικῶν, "as for the one who conquers," is a substantival ptcp., which is a pendent nom. or nom. abs. (i.e., it is does not enter into the syntax of the sentence). It is the antecedent referred to with the pronoun αὐτόν, which is placed in the syntactically appropriate acc. case. See the relevant discussion in *Notes* under 2:26.

**12.b.** Variant: αὐτῷ] ℵ fam 1611¹⁶¹¹ ¹⁸⁵⁴ 2351 Andr c e g h i⁻²⁰⁴² 2019; Byz 1¹⁸⁵⁹ ²⁰²⁷ Byz 13⁴⁹⁸ Byz 17²⁴¹.

**12.c.** Variant: omit μου] Byz 3³⁸⁵ 2019 Andr i²⁰⁸² syrᵖʰ 2351 Victorinus (*Comm. in Apoc.* 3.3; ed. Haussleiter, *Victorinus,* 42–43). The phrase θεοῦ μου occurs four times in this verse, which may account for the omission of μου.

**12.d.** Variant: omit ἔτι] ℵ 792 arm².

**12.e.** The phrase ἐπ᾽ αὐτόν can be translated "on it" (referring to the pillar) or "on *him*" (referring to the previous αὐτόν, "him," i.e., ὁ νικῶν, "the one who conquers"), though the latter is preferable since the author elsewhere refers to names written on the foreheads of the faithful (14:1; 22:4; see 7:3; 17:5; 19:12). However, for an example of a divine name written on a pillar in a temple, see *PGM* VIII.40–41: "Your true name is inscribed on the sacred pillar [τῇ ἱερᾷ στήλῃ] in the innermost sanctuary at Hermopolis." Bousset ([1906] 19, 230) suggests a possible allusion to this verse in Ignatius *Phld.* 6.1 ("[Those who do not speak of Jesus Christ] for me are tombstones and graves of the dead [στῆλαι εἰσιν καὶ τάφοι], on whom are inscribed only the names of people"), yet this is probably incorrect, since στήλη here clearly means "gravestone," a meaning well attested in Gk. literature

**12.f.** The definite article τῆς is used here with Ἰερουσαλήμ because it is familiar to the audience (see 21:10); the article is only rarely used with the geographical name Ἰεροσόλυμα/Ἰερουσαλήμ (BDR § 261.3).

**12.g.** Ἰερουσαλήμ, "Jerusalem," occurs 3 times in Revelation (3:12; 21:2, 10), always with this spelling (sometimes referred to as the Jewish form). The same form is also followed by Hebrews (a single occurrence in 12:22) and in *1 Clement* (a single occurrence in 41:2). The spelling Ἰεροσόλυμα, on the other hand, is consistently used in Mark (10 times) and John (12 times), while Paul and Matthew apparently prefer Ἰερουσαλήμ, though both forms in fact occur in those authors. Paul uses Ἰερουσαλήμ in Rom 15:19, 25, 26, 31; 1 Cor 16:3; Gal 4:25, 26, while the form Ἰεροσόλυμα is used only in Gal 1:17, 18; 2:1). Matthew uses Ἰεροσόλυμα 11 times, while Ἰερουσαλήμ occurs just twice, both in Matt 23:37. In Luke-Acts, Ἰεροσόλυμα occurs 27 times (4 times in Luke; 23 times in Acts), while Ἰερουσαλήμ occurs 63 times (27 times in Luke; 36 times in Acts). D. D. Sylva argues that Ἰεροσόλυμα (the sacral name "holy Salem") is juxtaposed with Ἰερουσαλήμ in Luke-Acts as an implicit etymology of the latter ("Ierousalem and Hierosoluma in Luke-Acts," *ZNW* 74 [1983] 207–21). Altogether, Ἰεροσόλυμα occurs 63 times in the NT, while Ἰερουσαλήμ occurs 76 times. In the LXX, the form Ἰερουσαλήμ is the only form used in books translated from the Heb. canon and occurs 660 times; the form Ἰεροσόλυμα is found only in the apocryphal or deuterocanonical books of the LXX. In the MT, the name is normally spelled יְרוּשָׁלַ͏ִם *yĕrûšālaim,* with the regular *qere* יְרוּשָׁלַיִם *yĕrûšālayim,* while the *kethib* is probably יְרוּשָׁלֵם *yĕrûšālēm* (Joüon, *Grammar* 1:72–73; *TDOT* 6:348). Four times the name is spelled יְרוּשָׁלַיִם *yrušlym* (*yĕrûšālayim;* 1 Chr 3:5; 2 Chr 25:1; Esth 2:6; Jer 26:18). The Gk. form Ἰεροσόλυμα may reflect the spelling of the name with the *he* locale, as in 2 Chr 32:9: יְרוּשָׁלַ͏ְיְמָה *yĕrûšālaymâ.* Josephus only uses the form Ἰεροσόλυμα. In the Jewish pseudepigrapha extant in Gk., Ἰεροσόλυμα occurs just 13 times (6 in the fragments of Eupolemus), while Ἰερουσαλήμ occurs 77 times; both forms occur in *Fragmenta anonyma* and in the fragments of Eupolemus. Elliott and Kilpatrick have argued that in the Gospels and Acts Ἰερουσαλήμ is used in Jewish contexts, while Ἰεροσόλυμα is used in gentile contexts; see J. K. Elliott, "Jerusalem in Acts and the Gospels," *NTS* 23 (1976–77) 462–69; G. D. Kilpatrick, *NovT* 25 (1983) 318–19. However, the presence of textual variants makes this argument problematic, and for this reason Elliott's view is disputed by J. M. Ross, "The Spelling of Jerusalem in Acts," *NTS* 38 (1992) 474–76. The most that can be said is that Ἰεροσόλυμα appears to be the Hellenistic name favored by non-Jewish authors or Jewish authors who are addressing non-Jews; Ἰερουσαλήμ, on the other hand, is a faithful transcription of the Heb. spelling, has a sacral ring, and is used primarily by Jews (J. Jeremias, "ΙΕΡΟΥΣΑΛΗΜ/ΙΕΡΟΥΣΟΛΥΜΑ," *ZNW* 65 [1974] 273–76). Ἰερουσαλήμ is used in Revelation and Hebrews because they are referring to the eschatological or heavenly city. The use of Ἰεροσόλυμα exclusively in John and Ἰερουσαλήμ exclusively in Revelation is one of many arguments for a difference in authorship (see E. Zellweger, *Das Neue Testament im Lichte der Papyrusfunde* [Frankfurt am Main: Lang, 1985] 154). However, the fact that several authors use *both* forms interchangeably suggests that this is not a reliable index for distinguishing authorship or editorial strands. On the problem of orthography, see BDR § 56; Moulton-Howard, *Accidence,* 147–48; R. Schütz, "Ἰερουσαλημ and Ιεροσολυμα im NT," *ZNW* 11 (1910) 169–87.

**12.h-h.** Variants: (1) ἡ καταβαίνει] fam 1006¹⁰⁰⁶ ¹⁸⁴¹ Andr d f²⁰²³ ²⁰⁷³ g i²⁰⁴² 94 2019; Byzantine. (2) τῆς καταβαίνουσης] ℵ² Andr b²⁰⁸¹ 1773 Tyconius. (3) τῇ καταβαινούσῃ] Andr b²⁰⁸¹*. The fact that ἡ καταβαίνουσα is in the nom. is problematic, since it is in apposition with the gen. noun cluster τῆς καινῆς Ἰερουσαλήμ, and therefore should be in the gen.

12.i. Variants: (1) ἐκ] (2) ἀπό] fam 1006$^{1006\,1841}$ Andr i$^{2042}$ 94 Byzantine.
12.j. Variant: omit μου] fam 1006$^{1006\,1841}$ fam 1611$^{1854}$ Oecumenius$^{2053}$; Andr h i$^{2042}$ l; Byzantine cop$^{bo\,mss}$.

*Form/Structure/Setting*

### I. OUTLINE

6. The proclamation to Philadelphia (3:7–13)
   a. The *adscriptio:* to the angel of the church in Philadelphia (v 7a)
   b. The command to write (v 7a)
   c. The τάδε λέγει formula (v 7b)
   d. Christological predications (v 7b)
      (1) The holy one
      (2) The true one
      (3) The One who has the key of David
         (a) The One who opens so that no one can shut
         (b) The One who shuts so that no one can open
   e. The *narratio:* "I know your conduct" (v 8)
      (1) Because you have limited strength (v 8c)
         (a) I have placed before you an open door (v 8b)
         (b) No one can shut this door (v 8b)
      (2) You have kept my word (v 8d)
   f. The *dispositio* (3:9–11)
      (1) Your "Jewish" adversaries (v 9)
         (a) Their description (v 9a)
            [1] They are a synagogue of Satan
            [2] They claim to be Jews but are lying
         (b) Their fate (v 9bc)
            [1] They will come and grovel at your feet
            [2] They will learn that I have loved you
      (2) The coming time of affliction (v 10)
         (a) You have obeyed my command to endure (v 10a)
         (b) I will keep you from the time of affliction (v 10bc)
            [1] It will come on the whole world
            [2] It will afflict the inhabitants of the earth
      (3) Promise: I am coming soon (v 11)
         (a) Exhortation: Keep what you have (v 11b)
         (b) Reason: So that no one takes away your wreath (v 11b)
   g. The promise-to-the-victor formula (v 12)
      (1) I will make them pillars in the temple of my God (v 12a)
      (2) They will never leave the temple of my God (v 12b)
      (3) I will inscribe names upon them (v 12c)
         (a) The name of my God
         (b) The name of the city of my God (v 12d)
            [1] Called the New Jerusalem
            [2] It descends from heaven from my God
         (c) My new name (v 12e)
   h. The proclamation formula (v 13)

## II. HISTORICAL-GEOGRAPHICAL SETTING

The city of Philadelphia is located about twenty-eight miles southeast of Sardis and sixty miles east of Smyrna at the foot of the Tmolus mountains (Pliny *Hist. nat.* 5.30). It was founded between 189 (when the Attalid dynasty of Pergamon annexed the region) and 138 B.C., possibly by Attalus II Philadelphus of Pergamon (159–138 B.C.), though some doubt whether this view is correct (J. B. Lightfoot, *Apostolic Fathers*, 1/1, 237; Hemer, *Letters*, 153–54), since it is based exclusively on a statement of Stephanus of Byzantium (s.v. Φιλαδέλφια, where he states that Philadelphia was the ’Αττάλου κτίσμα τοῦ Φιλαδέλφου, "a foundation of Attalus Philadelphus"). This statement is contradicted by Joannes Lydus (*De mensibus* 3.32), who claims that the Egyptians founded Philadelphia, which suggests that the founder was Ptolemy Philadelphus (308–246 B.C.), who conquered extensive territories in Asia Minor. According to A. H. M. Jones (*Greek City*, 17), this foundation was the reorganization of a native Lydian town, since it was organized by trades rather than by tribes (A. H. M. Jones, *Cities*, 54, 70, 73, 83–84), though the guilds were actually called tribes (*Greek City*, 162). Strabo reported that the city, which was located in a region of Phrygia called Κατακαυμένη, "burnt over" (i.e., a volcanic region), was subject to earthquakes so frequently that new cracks in the city wall appeared daily and few citizens actually lived in the city (12.8.18; 13.4.10). After the devastating earthquake of A.D. 17, in which Philadelphia was one of twelve cities leveled, the emperor Tiberius exempted Philadelphia from tribute for five years and sent a senatorial commission to inspect the damage and administer aid (Tacitus *Annals* 2.47). The rebuilt city responded to these benefactions by adding "Neocaesareia" to its name. Similarly, the city became "Philadelphia Flavia" under the Flavian emperor Vespasian (A.D. 69–79), and it was honored with the title *Neokoros*, "temple warden [for the imperial cult]," in A.D. 214 under Caracalla. The land surrounding Philadelphia was fertile, and the vintage of the area was famous (Virgil *Georgics* 2.98; Pliny *Hist. nat.* 5.30; 14.9). Evidence for a Jewish community in Philadelphia is apparently reflected in Rev 3:9, where they are called a "synagogue of Satan," and is confirmed by an inscription in neighboring Deliler, dating from the third century A.D. (*CIJ* II.754 = Lifschitz, *Donateurs*, no. 28). One inscription from Philadelphia (first century B.C.) contains the regulations of a private religious association that have an extremely high moral tone (Dittenberger, *SIG*, no. 985; tr. Grant, *Hellenistic Religions*, 28–30), presented as commands of Zeus to the owner of the house, while the house itself was dedicated to the goddess Agdistis (closely associated with the Anatolian goddess Cybele). The site of ancient Philadelphia has never been excavated, and few statues and inscriptions have been found there. Among the festivals celebrated in Philadelphia was the *Jovialia Solaria* (*CIG*, 3427, 3428, 3416), the *Communia Asiae* (*CIG*, 1068, 3428), and the *Agustalia Anaitea* (*CIG*, 3424).

The earliest reference to the presence of a Christian community in Philadelphia is in Rev 1:11; 3:7. About A.D. 110, Ignatius of Antioch, who was under arrest and being escorted to Rome, stayed briefly in Philadelphia (Ign. *Phld.* 6:3) and later wrote a letter to the church there. That letter indicates that the Philadelphian church was organized along the lines of a monarchical episcopate, with presbyters and deacons subordinate to a bishop (Ign. *Phld.* inscr.), and suggests the presence of a Judaizing influence on the Christian community there (*Phld.* 6:1). Eusebius briefly mentions Ammia of Philadelphia, a prophetess active probably during the first half of the second century A.D., whom the female Montanist prophetesses claimed as a predecessor (*Hist. eccl.* 5.17.3–4). During the middle of the second century, *Mart. Pol.* 19:1 mentions that eleven Philadelphian Christians died as martyrs with Polycarp of Smyrna.

## Comment

**7a** καὶ τῷ ἀγγέλῳ τῇ ἐν Φιλαδελφείᾳ ἐκκλησίας γράψον, "And to the angel of the church in Philadelphia, write." See *Comment* on 2:1.

**7b** τάδε λέγει ὁ ἅγιος, ὁ ἀληθινός, ὁ ἔχων τὴν κλεῖν Δαυίδ ὁ ἀνοίγων καὶ οὐδεὶς κλείσει καὶ κλείων καὶ οὐδεὶς ἀνοίγει, "Thus says the Holy One, the True One, the One with the key of David, who opens so that no one can shut and shuts so that no one can open." The phrase "holy and true" is used elsewhere in Revelation only once in an imprecatory prayer addressed to God in 6:10 in an asyndetic form ὁ ἅγιος, ὁ ἀληθινός, "the holy, the true," though the two terms are not used together elsewhere in early Jewish or early Christian literature as titles or attributes of God (on the separate occurrence of these two titles as attributes of God, see *Comment* on 6:10). The substantivized adjective ἅγιος, "holy," is only used occasionally of Jesus (Mark 1:24 = Luke 4:34; John 6:69; Acts 3:14; 4:27, 30; *1 Clem.* 23:5 [allusions to LXX Isa 13:22 and Mal 3:1 in which ἅγιος is substituted for ἄγγελος]; *Diogn.* 9.2; Justin *Dial.* 116.1; Clement of Alex. *Paed.* 1.7; cf. Luke 1:35; 1 John 2:20). The term "holy" was an epithet used in the cult of the Roman emperor (Sauter, *Kaiserkult*, 105–16). The adjectives ἀληθινός and ἀληθής are only occasionally used of Jesus (Mark 12:14 = Matt 22:16; John 7:18), and in Rev 19:11 ἀληθινός is used as the name of the rider on the white horse. The reference to the key of David is a clear allusion to Isa 22:22: "And I will place on his shoulder the key of the house of David; he shall open, and none shall shut; and he shall shut and none shall open." In the context of Isa 22:22, the key, the robe, and the sash (v 21) are symbols of the authority and power of the royal vizier or steward, in this case of Eliashib, who will take the place of the disgraced and exiled Shebna (vv 15–20; see 2 Kgs 18:18 = Isa 36:3). *Tg. Isa.* 22:22 (Chilton, *Isaiah Targum* 44–45) expands on the promise to Eliakim: "And I will place the key *of the sanctuary and the authority* of the house of David *in his hand;* and he will open, and none shall shut; and he will shut, and none shall open." However, this promise is reversed in *Tg. Isa.* 22:25. Chilton argues that the promise to Eliakim was understood as permanent in an earlier form of the targumic tradition, much like the formulation in Rev 3:7; Matt 16:19 (B. Chilton, "Shebna, Eliakim, and the Promise to Peter," in *The Social World of Formative Christianity and Judaism,* ed. J. Neusner et al. [Philadelphia: Fortress, 1988] 322–24). This does not mean the key to the *heavenly* kingdom, as in Matt 16:19 (contra Hadorn, 60; Bousset [1906] 226). Matt 16:19 also alludes to Isa 22:22 (J. A. Emerton, "Binding and Loosing— Forgiving and Retaining," *JTS* 13 [1962] 325–31). The indeclinable Δαυίδ is an objective genitive, and the phrase refers to the key *to* the Davidic or messianic kingdom, i.e., to the true Israel (Horst, *Proskynein,* 254). A relatively close parallel is found in a Coptic magical exorcism (Kropp, *Koptische Zaubertexte* 2:151–52): "Davithe with the golden hair, whose eyes are lightning, you are the one in whose hand is the key of deity; when you shut, no one can open again, and when you open, no man can shut again." The fact that this papyrus very probably dates from the fifth century A.D. (see V. Stegemann, *Die Gestalt Christi in den koptischen Zaubertexten*

[Heidelberg: Bilabel, 1934] 19–20) suggests that the author is dependent on Revelation.

**8a** οἶδά σου τὰ ἔργα, "I know your conduct." The supernatural knowledge of the exalted Christ is emphasized in the οἶδα clauses found in the proclamations to the seven churches (2:2, 3, 9, 13, 19; 3:1, 15). The supernatural knowledge of Christ is frequently mentioned in the Fourth Gospel (1:47–48; 2:25; 4:16–19; 6:61, 64; 18:4; 21:17).

**8b** ἰδοὺ δέδωκα ἐνώπιόν σου θύραν ἠγεῳμένην, ἣν οὐδεὶς δύναται κλεῖσαι αὐτήν, "Behold, I have placed before you an open door, which no one is able to shut." This statement, which describes how the exalted Christ has used his power of opening and shutting on behalf of the Philadelphian community, may be an allusion to the introduction to the oracle about Cyrus in Isa 45:1, supplemented by the phrase "open door," found in the allusion to Isa 22:22 in v 7. The proverbial character of this saying has prompted Kraft to consider it an originally independent prophetic saying (81). But what is the meaning of this "open door" metaphor? There are essentially two possible meanings: (1) opportunities for effective evangelization (1 Cor 16:9; 2 Cor 2:12; Col 4:3; see Ramsay, *Letters,* 404; Charles, 1:87), especially the conversion of the Jews; see v 9 (Caird, 51); (2) guaranteed access to eschatological salvation (see Luke 13:24), i.e., entrance into the messianic kingdom, i.e., the New Jerusalem; see Isa 26:2 interpreted eschatologically (Beckwith, 480; Bousset [1906] 227; Lohmeyer, 35; Kraft, 81; Lohse, 33; Roloff, 61). The metaphor of the "open door" is found twice in the undisputed letters of Paul (1 Cor 16:9; 2 Cor 2:12) and also occurs in Col 4:3; Acts 14:27 (on the metaphorical use of θύρα in early Christian literature, see *PGL,* 658). In all these contexts (except Acts 14:27), it means that opportunities to proclaim the gospel have been made possible, and for this reason Louw-Nida (§ 71.9) understand ἀνοίγω θύραν as an idiom meaning "to make it possible." It is therefore probable that the metaphor has a fixed meaning among Christians and refers to opportunities for evangelization (Ramsay, *Letters,* 404); however, the fact that missionary activity is never mentioned elsewhere in Revelation and also that such an emphasis does not fit the context makes this meaning doubtful. In Acts 14:27 the door is open to the hearers, not the proclaimers. In *Barn.* 16:9, a person "opens the door" by repenting, a usage with a parallel in John 10:7–9, and with an even closer parallel in *Midr. Cant.* 5:2. In Isa 45:1, the Lord promises to "open doors" before Cyrus, i.e., to allow him victories in his campaigns of conquest; i.e., he will be able to break down the gates of besieged cities. There are no parallels in early Jewish literature outside the NT within the first century or earlier, which suggests the Hellenistic origin of this figure of speech (Deissmann, *Light,* 303), though the metaphor is used in various ways in later rabbinic literature (Str-B 3:484–85). Epictetus frequently uses the phrase ἡ θύρα ἤνοικται with the meaning "I am free to go anywhere" (e.g., 1.9.20; 3.8.6), but it can also refer to the ultimate freedom to commit suicide (3.13.14; see 3.22.34).

**8c** ὅτι μικρὰν ἔχεις δύναμιν, "because you have limited strength." This ὅτι clause concludes the sentence begun in v 8ab and provides the reason that the exalted Christ has placed an open door before the Philadelphian Christians. They have limited strength and are not able to open such metaphorical doors with their own resources. This statement suggests that the Christian community was relatively small, and indeed we know from the report of Strabo that the population of Philadelphia itself was relatively small since many chose to live outside the city on farms (12.8.18; 13.4.10).

**8d** καὶ ἐτήρησάς μου τὸν λόγον καὶ οὐκ ἠρνήσω τὸ ὄνομά μου, "Yet you have obeyed my command and have not denied my name." The phrase τηρεῖν τὸν λόγον, "to keep the word," is repeated in v 10, and is found with a plural object in 22:7, 9: τηρεῖν τοὺς λόγους (see John 8:51, 52, 55; 14:23, 24; 15:20; 17:6; 1 John 2:5; cf. Luke 11:28: φυλάσσειν τὸν λόγον τοῦ θεοῦ; 1 Kgdms 15:11). In 1 John 2:3–5, the phrases τηρεῖν τὰς ἐντολάς and τηρεῖν τὸν λόγον have the same meaning (Spicq, *Lexicographie* 1:252). In Hebrew the term דבר *dābār* can mean "word" as well as "commandment" (1QS 1:13, where the phrase דברי אל *dibrê ʾēl* means "commands of God"), and the Decalogue is called "the ten words" (see *Excursus 12B: The Commandments of God and the Torah*). The parallel phrase τηρεῖν τὰς ἐντολάς, "to keep the commandments," occurs in Rev 12:17; 14:12 (see Matt 19:17; John 14:15, 21; 15:10; 1 Tim 6:14; 1 John 2:3, 4; 3:22, 24; 5:3). In John and 1 John, the phrases are therefore used interchangeably, just as they are in Revelation. The two clauses "you have obeyed my commands" and "you have not denied my name" express the same notion using an antithetical style; i.e., the first statement is *positive* followed by a second formulated in a *negative* way (cf. 2:13: "you keep my name and you have not denied my faith"), so that obeying the commands of Christ involves not denying his name. Denying the name of Christ is a motif that involves the rejection of the Christian faith (Luke 12:9–10 = Matt 10:33; 2 Tim 2:12; *Mart. Pol.* 9:2–3; Justin *1 Apol.* 31.6), though such a "denial" can be achieved by behavior as well as verbally (1 Tim 5:8; Titus 1:16; 2 Pet 2:1; Jude 4; *1 Clem.* 2–3; see Schlier, *TDNT* 1:470). Failure to hold the correct doctrine about Christ can also be construed as denying Christ (1 John 2:22).

**9a** ἰδοὺ διδῶ ἐκ τῆς συναγωγῆς τοῦ σατανᾶ τῶν λεγόντων ἑαυτοὺς Ἰουδαίους εἶναι, καὶ οὐκ εἰσὶν ἀλλὰ ψεύδονται, "Behold, I will cause those of the synagogue of Satan who call themselves Jews (but are not; they are lying)—." This statement, with the exception of the last word, is verbally identical with the statement made in 2:9 (see *Comment* there). This is not a complete sentence since διδῶ has the partitive genitive as an object but lacks an infinitive. In this use of διδόναι with the meaning "to cause," the result of the action of the verb would normally be indicated by an accusative (here the partitive genitive is equivalent to the accusative αὐτούς) and an infinitive (or, in the style of Revelation, a ἵνα clause). In the next clause, the author resumes the thought begun in v 9a by switching to a verb with nearly the same meaning, ποιήσω, "to cause" (Louw-Nida, § 13.9, mistakenly separate the causal meaning of ποιεῖν from the causal meaning of διδόναι, Louw-Nida, § 90.51), and then provides a more explicit object than that found in v 9a, αὐτούς, "them," followed by a ἵνα clause, which indicates the result of the action. This is an instance of a participle followed *not* by two more participles, as one might expect, but by two finite verbs; here εἶναι in ordinary Greek would be expressed through the present participle ὄντων, while ψεύδονται would be written as ψευδόμενων. For other examples of this Semitic syntactical phenomenon see 1:5–6, 17–18; 2:2, 9, 20, 23; 7:14; 12:2; 13:11; 14:2–3; 15:2–3; 20:4 (Schmid, *Studien* 2:242–43; Mussies, *Morphology*, 326–28).

**9b** ἰδοὺ ποιήσω αὐτοὺς ἵνα ἥξουσιν καὶ προσκυνήσουσιν ἐνώπιον τῶν ποδῶν σου, "behold, I will force them to come and grovel at your feet." This is an allusion to Isa 60:14, "all who despised you shall bow down at your feet," and perhaps also to Isa 49:23, "They shall bow down before you and lick the dust of your feet" (see Fekkes, *Isaiah*, 133–35). This same motif occurs in 1QM 19:6 with a doublet in 12:14–15 (tr. García Martínez, *Dead Sea Scrolls*, 115): "Their kings shall wait on you, [all your oppressors] lie prone before you, and they shall lick the dust of your feet]." The ironical use of this motif is clear: in all these passages the Gentiles are expected to grovel before Israel, while in Rev 3:9 it is the Jews who are expected to grovel before the feet of this (largely gentile) Christian community. The verb προσκυνεῖν occurs twenty-four times in Revelation (for a discussion of the syntax of this verb see *Note* 3:9.h.). The occurrences of προσκυνεῖν in Revelation can be grouped into three overlapping meanings (see J. Horst, *Proskynein*, 253–91): προσκυνεῖν is used (1) in connection with the cult of the Beast (13:4, 8, 12, 15; 14:9, 11; 16:2; 19:20; 20:4; cf. 9:20), (2) in connection with hymns of praise directed toward God or the Lamb (4:10; 5:14; 7:12; 11:16; 15:4; 19:4), and (3) in connection with a variety of other situations: (a) the prostration of Jews before the Philadelphian community (3:9); (b) those who worship in the temple (11:1); (c) the prohibition of worshiping an angel (19:10; 22:8–9); and (d) the summons of the angels to worship the Creator as an aspect of the content of the gospel (14:7). The prostration of Jews before the Philadelphian Christians has been explained by commentators either as referring to the success of the Christian mission or as the fulfillment of eschatological prophecy (Bousset [1906] 227). This verse cannot refer to the final conversion of Israel mentioned in Rom 11:25–32 (contra Hadorn, 60; Weiss-Heitmüller, 50), since it concerns only the Philadelphian community. Further, not *all* Jews will prostrate themselves before the Philadelphian Christians since the phrase διδῶ ἐκ τῆς συναγωγῆς, "I will compel *some* from the synagogue . . . to grovel at your feet," includes a partitive genitive used as the object of the verb διδόναι. This prostration has no religious significance but is simply the traditional (oriental) expression of homage and honor, which we have chosen to translate "grovel." Yet there is irony in this statement since in some strands of Jewish eschatology the *Gentiles* were expected to become ultimately subject to Israel (Isa 45:14; 49:23; 60:14; Zech 8:20–23; *1 Enoch* 10:21; *Sib. Or.* 3.716–20, 725–31), whereas here it is the *Jews* who will prostrate themselves before gentile Christians. This verse therefore concerns the eschatological exaltation of the people of God, i.e., Christians (Lohmeyer, 36). This eschatological expectation, which John has reversed, is expressed in Isa 60:14: "The sons of those who oppressed you shall come bending low to you; and all who despised you shall bow down at your feet; they shall call you the City of the Lord, the Zion of the Holy One of Israel." Note that the possible allusion to this verse in Rev 3:9 is made more probable by the clearer allusion in 3:12 to the fact that victorious Christians will have (among others) the name of "the city of my God, the new Jerusalem" written on them. A similar reversal is expressed in Isa 49:23: "Kings shall be your foster fathers, and their queens your nursing mothers. With their faces to the ground they shall bow down to you [προσκυνήσουσιν σοι] and lick the dust of your feet."

**9c** καὶ γνῶσιν ὅτι ἐγὼ ἠγάπησά σε, "so that they will know that I have loved you." This is a doubtful allusion to Isa 43:4: κἀγώ σε ἠγάγησα, "I loved you" (Fekkes, *Isaiah*, 136–37). The notion of "love" conveyed here is not primarily that of affection but rather that of election. The verb ἀγαπᾶν occurs just three times in Revelation, once referring to self-preservation (12:11) and twice to the self-sacrificing love that Christ had for his people (1:5; 3:9; cf. John 13:1; Gal 2:20; Eph 5:2).

**10a** ὅτι ἐτήρησας τὸν λόγον γῆς ὑπομονῆς μου, "Because you have obeyed my command to endure." This is an extremely difficult phrase grammatically (see *Note* 3:10.c-c.). On the phrase "obey my command," see *Comment* on 3:8d. The two uses of the verb τηρεῖν in vv 10a and 10b are examples of paronomasia, in which each usage has a different meaning; τηρεῖν in v 10a means "obey" (Louw-Nida, § 36.19), while in v 10b it means "keep, preserve, cause to continue" (Louw-Nida, § 13.32);

for other examples of paronomasia in Revelation, see 2:2[2x], 22; 11:18; 14:8; 18:6[3x], 20, 21; 22:18, 19; cf. BDF § 488.1; Turner, *Syntax*, 148. The term ὁ λόγος occurs eighteen times in Revelation, often meaning "gospel," i.e., "the divine revelation through Christ and his messengers" (BAGD, 478 [1.b.β]; Bauer-Aland, 970–71). The phrase ὁ λόγος τοῦ θεοῦ, meaning "the message from God," occurs four times in Revelation (1:2, 9; 6:9; 20:4), while the phrase ὁ λόγος [τῆς ὑπομονῆς] μου, i.e., the command of the exalted Christ, occurs twice (3:8, 10). Frequently this use of ὁ λόγος for the gospel message is linked to the suffering and death of Jesus (Thompson, *Semeia* 36 [1986] 150–53). An interesting plural use occurs in the phrase οἱ λόγοι τοῦ θεοῦ; see the OT phrase דברי אלוהים *dibrê ʾĕlôhîm* (17:17; 19:9; 21:5; cf. 22:6). In 17:17 it means "the promises of God," while in the other three references it refers to the message embodied in Revelation. V 10 in its entirety is regarded as a redactional addition by Charles (1:89), partly because he mistakenly regarded the seven proclamations as antedating most of Revelation (Charles, 1:46–47).

**10b** κἀγώ σε τηρήσω ἐκ τῆς ὥρας τοῦ πειρασμοῦ τῆς μελλούσης ἔρχεσθαι ἐπὶ τῆς οἰκουμένης ὅλης, "so I will preserve you from the time of affliction which will come upon the whole earth." This clause also presents grammatical difficulties for the interpreter (see *Note* 3:10.f-f.). The preservation motif is also found in *Odes Sol.* 9:6 (tr. Charlesworth, *OTP*): "So that none of those who hear shall fall in the war." A relevant parallel occurs in the eschatological scenario found in *Did.* 16:5: "Then the fiery test [τὴν πύρωσιν τῆς δοκιμασίας] of the human world will come, and many shall be offended and be lost, but those who endure [οἱ ὑπομείναντες] by means of their faith shall be saved by the 'curse' [i.e., Jesus?] itself." However the last phrase may be interpreted (Wengst, *Schriften*, 99 n. 137; Rordorf, *Doctrine*, 197–98 n. 6), the eschatological tribulation affects all humanity, and "endurance" means to remain faithful in an adverse situation. The phrase "the whole earth" (which also occurs in 12:9; 16:14; cf. 13:3: ὅλη ἡ γῆ, "the whole earth") is synonymous with "the inhabitants of the earth" in v 10c.

The three main problems in Rev 3:10 are (1) the meaning of τηρήσω ἐκ, "preserve from," (2) the meaning of τῆς ὥρας (τοῦ πειρασμοῦ), "the hour (of testing)," and (3) the meaning of πειρασμός, "temptation, testing."

(1) Here τηρεῖν means "to cause a state to continue" (Louw-Nida, § 13.32); i.e., the exalted Christ seems to promise that the situation of the Philadelphian Christians will not be adversely affected by the hour of tribulation that is approaching (see *Note* 3:10.f-f.). Apart from Rev 3:10, the only other occurrence of τηρήσω ἐκ, "I will keep from," in Greek literature is found in John 17:15: ἐρωτῶ . . . ἵνα τηρήσῃς αὐτοὺς ἐκ τοῦ πονηροῦ, "I ask . . . that you will protect them from the evil one." Brown (*JBL* 85 [1966] 310) argues that here the ἐκ refers to a situation out of which people are taken (presupposing that they had actually been in such a situation), not their separation from that situation, i.e., a genitive of source not separation.

(2) The fact that τῆς ὥρας τοῦ πειρασμοῦ is articular indicates that it refers to an event with which the author assumed his audience was familiar, i.e., a period of great distress and suffering that early Judaism (Dan 12:1; *T. Mos.* 8:1; *Jub.* 23:11–21; *2 Apoc. Bar.* 27:1–15; see Volz, *Eschatologie*, 147–63) and early Christianity (Matt 24:15–31; Mark 13:7–20; Rev 7:14) expected would immediately precede the eschatological victory of God. Rev 7:14 designates this period as ἡ θλίψις ἡ μεγάλη, "the Great Tribulation." A special designation for this period is "the woes of the

Messiah" (Hos 13:13; Isa 26:16–19; Mic 4:9–10; Hag 2:6; Mark 13:8; Matt 24:8; Volz, *Eschatologie*, 147). However, if it refers to the "tribulation" in Rev 6–19 (6:2–17; 8:6–9:21 12:13–17; 13:7; 16:1–21; 17:6), then Christians do not appear to be "kept out" (τηρεῖν ἐκ) of it. Further, "the hour of trial" refers generically to all the trials that precede the return of Christ; it should not be identified with the plagues narrated in 9:3–21 (for the exclusive punishment of the wicked), from which the Christian remnant of Israel is protectively sealed in 7:1–8.

(3) The substantive πειρασμός occurs only here in Revelation (the verb πειράζειν occurs three times: 2:2, 10; 3:10); the presence of these cognates in Rev 2–3 is one indication of the distinctive literary character of this section of the book. πειρασμός has two primary meanings: (a) "testing," in the sense of trying to learn the nature or character of someone or something by subjecting them or it to extensive examination (Louw–Nida, § 27.46), or (b) "temptation," in the sense of attempting to cause someone to sin (Louw-Nida, § 88.308). Since this "hour of trial" will come "upon the whole earth to afflict those who dwell on the earth" (v 10c), i.e., the wicked, this is perhaps the only instance in which πειρασμός and πειράζειν are used not of the "proving" or "testing" of the people of God but rather of the ungodly. Here temptation refers not only to the testing of the the faith of believers but to an eschatological event as well (Korn, *PEIRASMOS*, 86; Kuhn, "New Light," 202; Brown, *JBL* 85 [1966] 310), yet it must be considered a "trial" since it is the means whereby the faith of Christians will be demonstrated.

This verse has been a *crux* for the modern argument between the Pretribulation and Posttribulation views on when Christ will return (see Gundry, *Tribulation*, and the responses by Townsend, *BSac* 137 [1980] 252–66; Edgar, *GTJ* 3 [1982] 19–49; and Winfrey, *GTJ* 3 [1982] 3–18). Unfortunately, both sides of the debate have ignored the fact that the promise made here pertains to Philadelphian Christians *only* and cannot be generalized to include Christians in the other churches of Asia, much less all Christians in all places and times. Furthermore, to be "preserved from the hour of tribulation" means not that they will be physically absent but rather that they will not be touched by that which touches others.

**10c** πειράσαι τοὺς κατοικοῦντας ἐπὶ τῆς γῆς, "to afflict the inhabitants of the earth." This clause is parallel to the clause immediately preceding, resulting in an awkward attempt at poetic parallelism (perhaps a redactional addition to the text). The phrase οἱ κατοικοῦντες ἐπὶ τῆς γῆς, "those who dwell on the earth," is a favorite of the author's and occurs eight more times in Revelation (6:10; 8:13; 11:10[2x]; 13:8; 14[2x]; 17:8) and three additional times with varied phraseology (13:12; 14:6; 17:2), always in the negative sense of non-Christian persecutors of Christians. The phrase "inhabitants of the earth" (יושב הארץ *yōšēb hā'āreṣ* or יושבי הארץ *yōšbê hā'āreṣ*) occurs with some frequency in the OT, though in the Pentateuch it usually means "native Palestinians" (Lam 4:12; Isa 24:6, 17; 26:9, 18, 21; Jer 1:14; 25:29, 30; 38:11; Ezek 7:7; Dan 4:35[2x]; Zeph 1:18). The phrase also occurs frequently in early Jewish literature reflecting an awareness of the nations of the world, often in a universalistic eschatology in early Jewish apocalyptic, where it also has a predominantly negative connotation (*1 Enoch* 37:2, 5; 40:6, 7; 48:5; 53:1; 54:6; 55:1, 2; 60:5; 62:1; 65:6, 10, 12; 66:1; 67:7, 8; 70:1; 4 Ezra 3:12, 34, 35; 4:21, 39; 5:1, 6; 6:18, 24, 26; 7:72, 74; 10:59; 11:5, 32, 34; 12:24; 13:29, 30; *2 Apoc. Bar.* 25:1; 48:32, 40; 54:1; 55:2; 70:2, 10; *T. Abr.* [Rec. A] 3:12; [Rec. B] 6:6; Ps.-Philo, *Bib. Ant.* 3.3, 9, 12; 4.16; CD^a 10:9).

**11a** ἔρχομαι ταχύ, "I am coming soon." The emphasis on the imminent coming of the exalted Jesus occurs frequently in Rev (2:5, 16; 22:7, 12, 20), though often the simple fact of his coming is mentioned without the element of imminence (1:7; 2:25; 16:15; 22:20). These references are restricted to Rev 1–3; 22 (with the exception of the intrusive 16:15), which suggests that this emphasis is part of the theological perspective of the final edition.

**11b** κράτει ὃ ἔχεις, ἵνα μηδεὶς λάβῃ τὸν στέφανόν σου, "Keep what you have that no one takes away your wreath." The notion of λαμβάνειν τὸν στέφανον τινός, "to take away someone's wreath," is a metaphor for being disqualified in a contest. The way this exhortation is phrased suggests that the Philadelphians already have their crowns but must take care that no one take them away.

**12a** ὁ νικῶν ποιήσω αὐτὸν στῦλον ἐν τῷ ναῷ τοῦ θεοῦ μου, "As for the one who conquers, I will make him a pillar in the temple of my God." The reference here is neither to the actual temple nor to the Christian community, but rather to the *heavenly* temple, and is a metaphor for eschatological salvation (G. Klinzing, *Die Umdeutung des Kultus in der Qumrangemeinde und im Neuen Testament* [Göttingen: Vandenhoeck & Ruprecht, 1971] 201). For the emphasis on the "pillars" in a description of the eschatological Jerusalem, see *1 Enoch* 90:28–29, where the phrases "old house" and "new house" symbolize the earthly and the eschatological Jerusalem, respectively, which includes the temple though it is not specifically mentioned (Black, *Enoch,* 278). The term στῦλοι, "pillars," is used by Paul as a metaphor for leaders in the Jerusalem church (Gal 2:9), and Peter and Paul are referred to as στῦλοι, "pillars," in *1 Clem.* 5:2 (cf. *Ep. Lugd.* 1.6, 17); in 1 Tim 3:15, the church is described as στῦλος καὶ ἑδραίωμα τῆς ἀληθείας, "the pillar and foundation of the truth." The metaphor of an individual as a pillar, i.e., a person of central importance for a particular community, is found often in the Greco-Roman world (Euripides *Iph. Taur.* 57; Pindar *Olymp.* 2.81–82; Lycophron *Alex.* 281; *Vita Aesopi* G 106 [B. E. Perry, *Aesopica: Studies in Text History of Life and Fables of Aesop:* Vol. 1. *Greek and Latin Texts* [Urbana: University of Illinois, 1952] 1:68]). This notion also appears in Philo; cf. *Quaest. in Ex.* 1.21 (tr. LCL; this sentence survives in a Greek fragment as well as in an Armenian translation): "For good men are the pillars of whole communities [κίονές ἐστιν δήμων ὅλων], and they support cities and city-governments as if they were great houses" (cf. Philo *Mig.* 124). The metaphor of the temple is occasionally used in early Christian literature for the church (1 Cor 3:16–17; 2 Cor 6:16; Eph 2:19–22; 1 Pet 2:4–10). Nevertheless, despite the claim of U. Wilckens (*TDNT* 7:734–35), there is no apparent connection between the reference in Gal 2:9 and the notion of the church as a spiritual temple (Betz, *Galatians,* 99 n. 404). "Pillar" is used in a metaphorical sense in Prov 9:1, though the imagery is probably drawn not from temple architecture but from that of a banqueting hall; the "house" of wisdom is the world, and the "pillars" are the "pillars of heaven" (see Job 26:11). Here in v 12, the phrase ἐν τῷ ναῷ, "in the temple," excludes any allusion to the external freestanding pillars of the Solomonic temple, Jachin and Boaz (1 Kgs 7:15–21; 2 Chr 3:15–15; Josephus *Ant.* 8.77–78), or to pillars in the peristyle of other ancient temples. Yet there is evidence of freestanding pillars *within* ancient temples, such as the pair of pillars, one of gold and the other of emerald, that Herodotus saw in the temple of Melkart-Herakles (Herodotus 2.44). A relatively close parallel to Rev 3:12 is found in *Jos. As.* 17:6, a scene following Aseneth's request that the heavenly man bless the seven virgins that are her handmaids (tr. Charlesworth, *OTP* 2:231):

And Aseneth called the seven virgins and stood them before the man. And the man blessed them and said, "May the Lord God the Most High bless you. And you shall be seven pillars in the City of Refuge, and all the fellow inhabitants of the chosen of that city will rest upon you for ever (and) ever."

This is similar to Hermas *Vis.* 3.8.2, which mentions seven women who support the tower of Hermas vision, each woman representing a virtue. Bousset ([1906] 230, following Hirschfeld, "Kaiserkultus," 501–2), followed in turn by several other scholars (Charles, 1:91; Kiddle-Ross, 53–54 [who embellish the parallel by adding that the priest hoped "to achieve prolonged communion with the power of the god"]; Lohmeyer, 37; Mounce, 121), calls attention to the supposed practice of the retiring priest of the imperial cult involved in the installatic n of a statue of himself within the imperial temple with an inscription containing his name, his father's name, his home town, and his years in office. However, Hemer (*Letters*, 166, who cites Bousset incorrectly and wrongly claims that the latter did not specify the specific source of this idea) finds no evidence for such a practice and observes that since Philadelphia did not receive the neocorate until A.D. 213, the relevance of this practice, even if historical, is dubious. Hemer's instincts were correct. Hirschfeld was referring to a practice documented in the *Lex Narbonensis* (*CIL* XII.6038) for the regulation of the imperial cult at Gallia Narbonensis (Spain) founded in honor of the *Numen Augusti* in A.D. 11. Though no such statues have been found at Narbo, inscribed statue bases have been found at Tarraco and Lugudunum (Hirschfeld, "Kaiserkultus," 502). However, the parallel is so farfetched (Prigent, 72, is skeptical of its relevance) that Bousset should never have cited it.

Wilkinson (*JBL* 107 [1988] 498–501) has suggested that the pillar metaphor is based on an aspect of Israelite and Near Eastern coronation ritual; i.e., it is a reference to the "king's pillar" in the temple of Solomon. He refers to 2 Kgs 11:14, which refers to Joash "standing near the pillar, as the custom was," and 2 Kgs 23:3, where Josiah is also described as "standing near the pillar" (see 2 Chr 34:31, which speaks only of Josiah "in his place"). Yet these obscure references probably refer to the traditional practice of the king to stand by one of the freestanding pillars Jachin or Boaz (see 1 Kgs 7:15–20) during ceremonial occasions, certainly not coronations exclusively (contra the implication in de Vaux, *Ancient Israel*, 102–3). Wilkinson's claim that the pillar metaphor identified the believer "with a functional symbol of royal stability and hence the institution of kingship" (*JBL* 107 [1988] 500) is as speculative as it is dubious.

**12b** καὶ ἔξω οὐ μὴ ἐξέλθῃ ἔτι, "and he will never ever leave it." The emphasis here follows the image of the victorious Christian as a pillar in the temple of God, i.e., as a permanent part of the temple of God and hence a continual participant in the divine worship that takes place there. *Pss. Sol.* 3:14 speaks of the lot of the righteous as "a place of great delight in the temple of the Lord."

**12c** καὶ γράψω ἐπ' αὐτὸν τὸ ὄνομα τοῦ θεοῦ μου, "Moreover, I will inscribe upon him the name of my God." This is a metaphor for both divine ownership and the dedication of the one so inscribed to God. This is perhaps an allusion to Exod 28:36–38, where instructions are given for writing the inscription "Holy to the Lord" on a gold plate to be mounted on the front of Aaron's high priestly headdress, on his forehead. In Philo, *Mos.* 2.114–15 reflects the apparently traditional idea (not supported by the Hebrew Bible or the LXX) that the Tetragrammaton יהוה *YHWH* was inscribed on this gold plate (the same idea is found in Jos. *J.W.* 5.235; *Ant.* 3.178; *Ep. Arist.* 98; Origen *Frag. in Ps.* 2.2). However, in *Mig.* 103, Philo gets it right, observing that the gold plate has ἁγίασμα κυρίῳ, "holy to the Lord," inscribed on it. Isa 43:7 refers to "everyone who is called by my name." According to *b. B. Bat.* 75b: "Three are called by the name of the Holy One blessed be He, and they are the following: the righteous, the Messiah, and Jerusalem" (Str-B 3:795–96). It is significant that the motifs of the inscription of a divine name and a pillar in the sanctuary are combined in *PGM* VIII.40–41: "Your true name is inscribed on the sacred pillar [τῇ ἱερᾷ στήλῃ] in the innermost sanctuary at Hermopolis."

**12d** καὶ τὸ ὄνομα τῆς πόλεως τοῦ θεοῦ μου, τῆς καινῆς Ἰερουσαλὴμ ἡ καταβαίνουσα ἐκ τοῦ οὐρανοῦ ἀπὸ τοῦ θεοῦ μου, "and the name of the city of my God, the New Jerusalem, which descends from heaven from my God." The inscribing of the name of the new Jerusalem signifies citizenship in the heavenly city. The new name of Jerusalem is a matter of rabbinic speculation; according to *Gen. Rab.* 49 (31a), Abraham knew that Jerusalem would be called "throne of Yahweh" (Jer 3:17). The heavenly Jerusalem is mentioned three times in Revelation (3:12; 21:2, 10; though the adjective "new" occurs only in 3:12 and 21:2) within the context of very similar formulaic clauses:

| *Rev 3:12* | *Rev 21:2* | *Rev 21:10* |
|---|---|---|
| τῆς καινῆς<br>the new | τὴν πόλιν<br>the city | τὴν πόλιν<br>the city |
| | τὴν ἁγίαν<br>the holy | τὴν ἁγίαν<br>the holy |
| Ἰερουσαλὴν<br>Jerusalem | Ἰερουσαλὴν<br>Jerusalem | Ἰερουσαλὴν<br>Jerusalem |
| | καινὴν<br>new | |
| ἡ καταβαίνουσα<br>descending | καταβαίνουσαν<br>descending | καταβαίνουσαν<br>descending |
| ἐκ τοῦ οὐρανοῦ<br>from heaven | ἐκ τοῦ οὐρανοῦ<br>from heaven | ἐκ τοῦ οὐρανοῦ<br>from heaven |
| ἀπὸ τοῦ θεοῦ<br>from God | ἀπὸ τοῦ θεοῦ<br>from God | ἀπὸ τοῦ θεοῦ<br>from God |
| μου<br>my | | |

It is likely that the saying of the exalted Jesus in 3:12 has been derived from 21:2, 10, which is from an earlier edition of Revelation. The adjectival participle ἡ καταβαίνουσα is a nominative in apposition to the indeclinable τῆς Ἰερουσαλήμ, a genitive of content that has the definite article because it is well known to the readers. The phrase "from God" is redundant, but it does make it clear that "heaven" is a circumlocution for the name of God (see 1 Macc 3:18–19, 50, 60; 4:10; Dan 4:23; Mark 11:30–31 = Matt 21:25 = Luke 20:4–5; Luke 15:18, 21; John 3:27; Hecataeus of Abdera *apud* Diodorus 40.3.4 [where he misunderstands the Jewish use of οὐρανός as divine]; see Bietenhard, *Die himmlische Welt*, 80–82; on "heaven" as a circumlocution for God, see Houtman, *Himmel*, 107–10). Nowhere in Revelation, however, is the term "heaven" alone used as a circumlocution for God.

**12e** καὶ τὸ ὄνομά μου τὸ καινόν, "and my new name." The bestowal of a "new name" (mentioned in 2:17) in biblical tradition ordinarily means a change of status or function for a city or nation (Isa 1:26; Isa 60:14; 65:15; Jer 3:17; 23:6; 33:16; Ezek 48:35; Zech 8:3) or a change in the character, conduct, or status of an *individual* (Gen 17:5, 17; 32:27–28; 41:45; Dan 1:7; Mark 3:17; John 1:42). Speaking of the future glory of restored Israel, Isa 62:2 reads "you shall be called by a new name [LXX τὸ ὄνομα σου τὰ καινόν], which the mouth of the Lord will give," while 65:15 speaks of the righteous: "but his servants he will call by a different name [LXX ὄνομα καινόν]." In early Christianity, the "new name" of Isa 62:2; 65:15 was thought to be the name "Christian" (Cyprian *Ad Quirinum* 1.22; Eusebius *Demonstr. evang.* 2.3.80; *Hist. eccl.* 1.4.3–4; Ignatius *Magn.* 10 [longer version; Lightfoot, *Apostolic Fathers* 2/3, 175]; see Ignatius *Magn.* 10:1; Clement Alex. *Paed.* 1.5; *Apost. Const.* 3.15). In *T. Levi* 8:14 (in what is very probably an interpolation, though probably not of Christian origin; see Ulrichsen, *Grundschrift*, 194–95), it is said of the offspring of Levi, "he will be called with a new name [ὄνομα καινόν]." Ramsay suggested that the theme of the new name would have been meaningful to the Philadelphian Christians since the name of their city had been renamed twice. The first new name was "Neokaisareia" (after Tiberius or Germanicus), given to the city after the earthquake of A.D. 17, while the second, "Flavia," the family name of the emperor Vespasian, was given during his reign, i.e., A.D. 70–79 (Ramsay, *Letters*, 397–98, 409–12).

*Explanation*

Philadelphia, located twenty-eight miles southeast of Sardis, suffered extensive damage in the great earthquake of A.D. 17 (Tacitus *Annals* 2.47.3–4) and had repeatedly experienced devastating quakes of lesser magnitude (Strabo 12.8.18). Heavily dependent on viticulture because of a rich volcanic soil (Strabo 13.4.11), the city would have been radically affected had Domitian's edict of ca. A.D. 92 ordering that half the vineyards in the provinces be cut down and planted anew been put into effect (see *Comment* on 6:6). In a clear allusion to Isa 22:22, Christ designates himself as the one "who has the key of David, who opens and no one shall shut, who shuts and no one opens" (v 7), probably referring to his power to admit or bar people from his heavenly kingdom (see Matt 16:19). The exalted Christ has set an "open door" before the Philadelphian Christians (v 8), a metaphor that may refer to opportunities for missionary activity (see 1 Cor 16:9; 2 Cor 2:12), but more probably to their "reserved seats" in the eschatological kingdom. The Christian community appears to be relatively small and poor, but they have nevertheless remained steadfast in their faith (v 8). There was apparently a Jewish synagogue there (v 9), and Philadelphian Christians had apparently suffered from accusations by Jews before Roman authorities as in Smyrna (v 9). Because they have kept the testimony of Jesus by patiently enduring persecution, they will be kept from "the hour of trial which is coming on the whole world" (v 10). This refers to the coming eschatological period of tribulation (9:3–21) from which they will be protected (7:1–8). Similarly, in the final petition of the Lord's Prayer (Matt. 6:13 = Luke 11:4), the "temptation" refers to the attacks of Satan in the eschatological conflict. "Those who dwell upon the earth" (v 10) are unbelievers (see 6:19; 11:10; 13:8, 14; 17:8) who repeatedly refuse to repent in spite of the eschatological plagues unleashed by God (e.g., Rev 6:1–17; 8:6–21). Christ's promise to come soon (v 11) should be understood not as a coming in judgment (as in 2:5, 16; 3:3) but as the Parousia in which he comes to rescue and save his people (22:7, 20). Those who conquer will be made pillars in the temple of God (v 12), a feature that suggests that the new Jerusalem should be understood as a metaphor for the Christian community rather than an enormous material building. Revelation is a book containing numerous graffiti; conquering Christians will have inscribed on them the names of God, the city of God, and the new Jerusalem (v 12), varied metaphors indicating eschatological salvation. Reference to the new Jerusalem that descends from heaven anticipates the more detailed description in 21:2–22:5. Philadelphia was near the region where Montanism or the "new prophecy" arose after the middle of the second century emphasizing the imminent great tribulation (v 10) and the descent of the new Jerusalem (which was expected to alight at Pepuza, seventy miles east of Philadelphia). Montanism drew its inspiration from Revelation and possibly emphasized this prophetic proclamation to the Philadelphian church.

# 7. The Proclamation to Laodicea    (3:14–22)

## Bibliography

**Abt, A.** *Die Apologie des Apuleius von Madaura und die antike Zauberei.* Giessen: Töpelmann, 1908. **Anderson, C. P.** "Who Wrote 'The Epistle from Laodicea'?" *JBL* 85 (1966) 436–40. **Bauckham, R.** "Synoptic Parousia Parables and the Apocalypse." *NTS* 23 (1976–77) 162–76. ———. "Synoptic Parousia Parables Again." *NTS* 29 (1983) 129–34. **Berger, P. R.** "Kollyrium für die blinden Augen, Apk. 3:18." *NovT* 27 (1985) 174–95. **Cortes, E.** "Una interpretacion judia de Cant 5,2 en Ap 3,19b–20." *RCT* 4 (1979) 239–58. **Feuillet, A.** "Le Cantique des Cantiques et l'Apocalypse." *RSR* 49 (1961) 321–53. **Gagniers, J. des** et al. *Laodicée du Lycos: Le Nymphée.* Quebec: Les Presses de l'Université Laval; Paris: Éditions E. de Boccard, 1969. **Gill, D.** "*Trapezomata:* A Neglected Aspect of Greek Sacrifice." *HTR* 67 (1974) 117–37. **Gillet, L.** "Amen." *ExpTim* 56 (1944–45) 134–36. **Gilliam, J. F.** "51–52: Invitations to the Kline of Sarapis." In *Collectanea Papyrologica.* FS H. C. Youtie, ed. A. E. Hanson. Part 1. Bonn: Habelt, 1976. 315–24. **Hemer, C. J.** "Unto the Angels of the Churches: 4. Philadelphia and Laodicea." *BurH* 11 (1975) 164–90. **Horst, P. W. van der.** "Moses' Throne Vision in Ezechiel the Dramatist." *JJS* 34 (1983) 21–29. **Hunter, L. W.** "Cicero's Journey to the Province of Cilicia." *JRS* 3 (1913) 73–97. **Johnson, S. E.** "Laodicea and Its Neighbors." *BA* 13 (1950) 1–18. **Lightfoot, J. B.** *St. Paul's Epistles to the Colossians and to Philemon.* London: Macmillan, 1875. **Lloyd, G. E. R.** "Hot and Cold, Dry and Wet in Early Greek Thought." *JHS* 84 (1964) 92–106. **Markschies, C.** "'Sessio ad Dexteram': Bemerkungen zu einem altchristlichen Bekenntnismotiv in der christologischen Diskussion der altkirchlichen Theologen." In *Le*

*Trône de Dieu,* ed. M. Philonenko. Tübingen: Mohr-Siebeck, 1993. 252–317. **Peterson, E.** "Beiträge zur Interpretation der Visionen im Pastor Hermae." In *Frühkirche, Judentum und Gnosis.* Rome; Freiburg; Vienna: Herder, 1959. 254–70. ———. "Kritische Analyse der fünften Vision." In *Frühkirche, Judentum und Gnosis.* Rome; Freiburg; Vienna: Herder, 1959. 271–84. **Porter, S. E.** "Why the Laodiceans Received Lukewarm Water (Revelation 3:15–18)." *TynBul* 38 (1987) 143–49. **Roloff, J.** "'Siehe, ich stehe vor der Tür und klopfe an': Beobachtungen zur Überlieferungsgeschichte von Offb. 3,20." In *Vom Urchristentum zu Jesus.* FS J. Gnilka, ed. H. Frankenmölle and K. Kertelge. Freiburg; Basel; Vienna: Herder, 1989. 452–66. **Rudwick, M. J. S.,** and **Green, E. M. B.** "The Laodicean Lukewarmness." *ExpTim* 69 (1957–58) 176–78. **Silberman, L. H.** "Farewell to ὁ ἀμήν: A Note on Rev 3:14." *JBL* 82 (1963) 213–15. **Trudinger, P.** "Ho Amen (Rev III:14), and the Case for a Semitic Original of the Apocalypse." *NovT* 14 (1972) 277–79. **Will, E.** "Banquets et salles de banquet dans le cultes de la Grece et de l'Empire romain." In *Mélanges d'histoire et d'archeologie offerts à Paul Collart,* ed. P. Ducrey. Lausanne: Bibliotheque Historique Vaudoise, 1976. 353–62. **Wood, P.** "Local Knowledge in the Letters of the Apocalypse." *ExpTim* 73 (1961–62) 263–64.

### Translation

[14] *And to the angel of the church in Laodicea, write: "Thus says the Master Workman,[a]* [b] *the faithful* [c] *and true Witness, the* [d] *Origin* [e] *of the* [f] *creation of God.* [15] *'I know your conduct, that you are neither cold nor hot.* [a] *I wish* [a] *you were either cold or hot!* [16] *So, because you are tepid and neither* [a] [b] *cold nor hot,* [b] *I will vomit you from my mouth.* [17] *Because you say* [a] *"I am wealthy and I have become rich and need nothing,"* [b] *but* [c] *you do not know that you are the one who is miserable and* [d] *pitiful and poor and blind and naked,* [18] *I advise you to buy from me gold purified by fire that you might be rich, then white garments that you might be clothed that* [a] *the shame of your nakedness might not be manifest,* [b] *and then medication* [c] [d] *to apply* [d] *to your eyes that you might regain your sight.* [19] *Those whom I love I chastise and discipline; therefore be earnest* [a] *and repent.* [20] *Behold, I stand before the door* [a] *and knock. If any one hears my voice and opens* [a] *the door,* [b] *then I will come in to visit him and I will share a meal with him and he with me.* [21] *As for the one who conquers,* [a] *I will allow* [b] *him to sit with me on my throne, just as I also conquered* [c] *and sat with my Father on his throne.* [22] *Let the one who has an ear hear what the Spirit declares to the churches.'"*

### Notes

14.a. Silberman thinks that the Gk. term ὁ ἀμήν is a mistranslation of אָמוֹן *'āmôn* in Prov 8:30, which should be rendered "Master Workman" (see *Comment* on 3:14).

14.b. Variant: καί] ℵ*.

14.c. Variants: (1) ὁ instead of καί] fam 1611[2050] Oecumenius[2053text] 2351 Andr i[2042] syr[h]. (2) καί ὁ] ℵ C (ἀληθεινός) Andr i[2042].

14.d. Variant: καί before ἡ ἀρχή] ℵ syr[ph] arm[1].

14.e. For ἀρχή in the sense of "first cause, origin," see Louw-Nida, § 89.16. Here ἀρχή could also mean "ruler," sharing the same semantic subdomain with ἄρχων (Louw-Nida, § 37.48–95).

14.f. Variant: ἐκκλησίας for κτίσεως] ℵ*.

15.a-a. Variant: omit ὄφελον ψυχρὸς ἦς ἢ ζεστός] A fam 1006[1006]. This is clearly an example of homoioteleuton, for the eye of an early scribe obviously jumped from the ζεστός of v 15a to the ζεστός of v 15b, omitting an entire clause.

16.a. Variants: (1) οὔτε] ℵ A C 046 fam 1611[1611 2329] Andreas. (2) οὐ] fam 1006 fam 1611[1854] Oecumenius[2053] 2351 Andr c d f[2023] g[2045] i[2042] 94 Byzantine Beatus.

16.b-b. Variants: (1) ψυχρὸς οὔτε ζεστός] A 025 itᵃ vg syrᵖʰ copˢᵃ. (2) ψυχρὸς εἶ οὔτε ζεστός] fam 1611²⁰⁵⁰. (3) ζεστὸς εἶ οὔτε ψυχρός] ℵ¹. (4) ζεστὸς οὔτε ψυχρὸς εἶ] ℵ*. (5) ζεστός] Andr d⁻⁷⁴³.

17.a. Variants: (1) ὅτι] A C fam 1611¹⁶¹¹ ²⁰⁵⁰ ²³²⁹ Andr a¹ f²⁰²³ g i²⁰³⁶ l lat syr TR. (2) omit ὅτι before πλούσιος] ℵ 025 046 fam 1006 fam 1611¹⁸⁵⁴ Oecumenius²⁰⁵³ 2351 Andreas Byzantine vgᵐˢˢ.

17.b. Variant: οὐδενός] ℵ Andreas Byzantine 2351.

17.c. The conjunction καί is used here in an adversative sense, καί *adversativum*, and must be translated "but."

17.d. Variant: ὁ before ἐλεεινός] A fam 1006 fam 1611¹⁶¹¹ ²³²⁹ 2351 Byzantine.

18.a. καί is used here to introduce a result clause.

18.b. Variant: φανῇ] 2351 Andr e.

18.c. Variant spelling: (1) κολλύριον] ℵ C fam 1006 fam 1611¹⁶¹¹ ²³²⁹ ²³⁴⁴. (2) κολλούριον] A 025 fam 1611¹⁸⁵⁴ ²⁰⁵⁰ Oecumenius²⁰⁵³ 2351 Andreas.

18.d-d. Variants: (1) ἐγχρῖσαι] ℵ A C fam 1611²⁰⁵⁰ ²³²⁹ Oecumenius²⁰⁵³ 94 2019. (2) ἵνα ἐγχρίσῃ] fam 1006 fam 1611¹⁶¹¹ 2351 Andr i²⁰⁴² Byzantine. (3) ἔγχρισον] fam 1611¹⁸⁵⁴ Andreas syr.

19.a. Variants: (1) ζήλευε] A C 046 fam 1611⁻²³⁴⁴ fam 1006¹⁸⁴¹ Andr i²⁰⁴² 94. (2) ζήλωσον] ℵ 0169* (the first scribe wrote ζήλευε [present active imper. second person sing.], the first reading, but then corrected it to read ζήλωσον [aor. active imper. second person sing.] with a superlinear ωσον); Oecumenius²⁰⁵³ Andreas. The original reading was ζήλευε, which was corrected to agree with the following aor. form μετανόησαν. ζηλοῦν here means "to set one's heart on," i.e., "to be deeply committed to something, with the implication of accompanying desire" (Louw-Nida, § 25.76).

20.a-a. Uncial fragment 0169* has accidentally omitted the following twelve words by jumping from the first to the second occurrence of θύραν, "door": καὶ κρούω· ἐὰν τις ἀκούσῃ τῆς φωνῆς μου καὶ ἀνοίξῃ τὴν θύραν, "and knock; if anyone hears my voice and opens the door." Yet the original scribe caught this omission and placed a siglum after the first θύραν καί, and at the foot of the page has written κρούω ἐ[ά]ν τ[ις] ἀκού[σῃ τῆς] [φων]ῆς μ[ου] καὶ ἀνοίξη τὴν θύραν καί.

20.b. Variants: (1) καί] ℵ 0169 fam 1006¹⁰⁰⁶¹⁸⁴¹ fam 1611¹⁸⁵⁴ ²³²⁹ ²³⁴⁴ 2351; Byzantine; syrᵖʰ; Tischendorf, *NT Graece;* Bousset ([1906] 233 n. 2); and Charles (1:101; 2:261); bracketed by Nestle-Aland²⁷ and UBSGNT⁴. (2) Omit καί] A fam 1611¹⁶¹¹ ²⁰⁵⁰ Oecumenius²⁰⁵³ Andreas; latt syrʰ cop; WHortᵐᵃʳᵍ; B. Weiss (*Johannes-Apokalypse*, 116); von Soden, *Text;* Merk, *NT.* Here καί introduces the apodosis of a conditional sentence in such a way that it must be construed as a Hebraism corresponding to the waw consecutive in Heb. (Beyer, *Semitische Syntax*, 69). For this reason καί is very probably the original reading (Schmid, *Studien* 2:131, 243). Two other examples of this Hebraism are found in 10:7; 14:10. Since it is more difficult to account for the addition of καί to the text than to explain its deletion, it is the *lectio difficilior* and must be considered the preferred reading.

21.a. ὁ νικῶν, "as for the one who conquers," is a conditional substantival ptcp. that is a pendent nominative or nominative absolute, i.e., a substantive in the nominative placed at the beginning of a clause without regard to the syntax (for a more detailed discussion, see *Note* 2:26.a.).

21.b. The phrase δώσω αὐτῷ καθίσαι, lit., "I will give him to sit," reflects the Heb. idiom נתן ל *nātan lĕ*, "to allow, permit" (BDR § 392.6); see Rev 11:3.

21.c. Variant: νενείκηκα καὶ κεκάθικα] 0169* (both pf. active ind. first-person sing.); singular reading; corrected in 0169ᶜᵒʳʳ to read ἐνείκησα καὶ ἐκάθισα (both aor. active ind. first-person sing.).

## *Form/Structure/Setting*

### I. OUTLINE

        (3) The origin of God's creation
    e. The *narratio:* "I know your conduct" (vv 15–17)
        (1) The "cold" and "hot" metaphors (vv 15–16)
            (a) You are neither "cold" nor "hot" (v 15a)
            (b) I wish you were either "cold" or "hot" (v 15b)
            (c) I will vomit you from my mouth (v 16)
                [1] Because you are "tepid"
                [2] Because you are neither "cold" nor "hot"
        (2) Your imagined condition: a hybris soliloquy (v 17)
            (a) I am wealthy (v 17a)
            (b) I have become rich (v 17a)
            (c) I need nothing (v 17a)
        (3) Your true condition: a denunciation (v 17b)
            (a) You are wretched
            (b) You are pitiable
            (c) You are poor
            (d) You are blind
            (e) You are naked
   f. The *dispositio* (vv 18–20)
        (1) Admonition using shopping metaphors (v 18)
            (a) Buy purified gold from me that you might be rich
            (b) Buy white garments from me
                [1] That you might be clothed
                [2] That the shame of your nakedness might not be public
            (c) Buy medication from me
                [1] to apply to your eyes
                [2] to regain your sight
        (2) Christological axiom (v 19)
            (a) Those whom I love (v 19a)
                [1] I chastise
                [2] I discipline
            (b) Because of this love (v 19b)
                [1] Be earnest
                [2] Repent
        (3) Christ as outsider: the visitor metaphor (v 20)
            (a) The visitor calls: I stand before the door knocking (v 20a)
            (b) Will the visitor be acknowledged? (v 20b)
                [1] If any one hears my voice
                [2] If any one opens the door
            (c) The visitor is admitted (v 20b)
                [1] I will come in to visit him (v 20c)
                [2] I will share a meal with him
                [3] He will share a meal with me (v 20c)
   g. The promise-to-the-victor formula (v 21)
        (1) They will sit with me on my throne (v 21a)
        (2) Just as I sat down with my Father on his throne (v 21b)
   h. The proclamation formula (v 22)

## II. HISTORICAL-GEOGRAPHICAL SETTING

Antiochus II (261–246 B.C.) fortified the earlier city of Diospolis as a Seleucid outpost between 261 and 253 B.C., naming it after his wife or sister, Laodice (Λαοδίκη). The city was called "Laodicea on the Lycus" (Λαοδίκεια ἐπὶ Λύκῳ or *Laodicea ad Lycum*) and "Laodicea of Asia" (Λαοδίκεια τῆς ᾿Ασίας) to distinguish it from at least four other cities of the same name founded by the Seleucids (*Kleine Pauly* 3:482–84). It was situated on a plateau in the fertile valley of the Lycus river on a prominent trade route. It was six miles south of Hierapolis (Col 4:13), important for its wool industry, eleven miles west of Colossae, and a hundred miles east of Ephesus on a major road (Strabo 14.2.29). After 188 B.C., the city came under the rule of the Pergamenes. Laodicea came under the control of the Romans in 133 B.C. The annual contribution of ca. twenty pounds in gold of the Jewish community of Laodicea to Jerusalem, along with the contributions of Jewish communities from three other cities, was seized in 62 B.C. (Cicero *Pro Flacco* 28–68; Schürer, *History* 3:27; Mitchell, *Anatolia* 2:33). This reflects the presence of a large Jewish community (Jos. *Ant.* 14.241–43). Laodicea became prosperous during the last part of the first century B.C. and, despite experiencing damaging earthquakes during the reigns of Tiberius and Nero, became a major urban center by the second century A.D. Located in a region prone to earthquakes, Laodicea was damaged by an earthquake during the reign of Tiberius (A.D. 17), who aided the city in rebuilding (Strabo 12.8.18). When destroyed by an earthquake in A.D. 60, the city was so wealthy that it was able to refuse imperial financial assistance in rebuilding (Tacitus *Annals* 14.27). Expensive garments made of black wool were one of its most important exports (Strabo 12.8.16). The water in Laodicea was extremely hard, though potable (Strabo 13.4.14) Laodicea was the capital of the Cibyratic *conventus* (i.e., the juridical center; see Cicero *Ad Atticum* 5.15), comprising twenty-five communities, including Hydrela, Themisonium, Hierapolis, Colossae, Eriza, Ceretapa Diocaesarea, and Cibyra (Jones, *Cities*, 73–75). In letters of Cicero written between 51 and 50 B.C. from Cilicia (e.g., *Ad Atticum* 5.15), he reveals that he held judicial assizes in the major cities of Cilicia, including Laodicea (Hunter, *JRS* 3 [1913] 73–97). Under the emperor Diocletian, Laodicea became the metropolis of the province of Phrygia.

The Christian community at Laodicea was closely connected with that of Colossae and is mentioned five times in Colossians (2:1; 4:13, 15, 16[2x]); the two cities were located only a short distance apart in the Lycus valley. The name of at least one early Laodicean Christian is known to us: in secondary greetings to the Christians at Laodicea (Col 4:15), Paul mentions Nympha or Nymphas (the accusative form Νύμφαν can be either masculine or femine) and the church at her/ his house; Paul also encourages Archippus to fulfill his ministry faithfully, and it is possible that he too was from Laodicea. The dating of Colossians depends in part on whether it is considered an authentic Pauline letter. If Colossians is Pauline, it could have been written either during Paul's Ephesian imprisonment (ca. A.D. 52–54) or (more probably) during his Roman imprisonment (ca. A.D. 56–58). Though Paul apparently wrote a letter to Laodicea (Col 4:16), it has not survived (though see below). Tertullian claimed that what the Great Church called "the Letter to the Ephesians," the heretics (i.e., Marcionites) called "the Letter to the Laodiceans," and that they had changed the title (*Adv. Marc.* 5.11.12; Epiphanius *Pan.* 42.9.4; 42.12.3; Filastrius *Haer.* 89; see A. Harnack, *Marcion* [Darmstadt: Wissenschaftliche Buschgesellschaft, 1960] 134*–49*). A number of modern scholars have agreed (on slim evidence) that canonical Ephesians is the "lost" letter to the Laodiceans (Lightfoot, *Colossians*, 274–81). The Muratorian Canon (lines 63–66) mentions a letter to the Laodiceans (*ad Laudicenses*) forged by Marcionites (*NTA* 1:36). The apocryphal Epistle to the Laodiceans, an obvious forgery employing typical Pauline phrases (particularly drawn from Philippians), was circulated as the missing Pauline letter (translation and bibliography *NTA* 2:42–46). Neither Colossae nor Laodicea was evangelized by Paul personally (Col 2:1), but these cities, as well as Hierapolis, may have been evangelized by Epaphras (Col 1:6–7; 4:12–13) during Paul's Ephesian ministry (Acts 19:10). It is possible that the lost letter to Laodicea was written by Epaphras, not Paul (see Anderson, *JBL* 85 [1966] 436–40).

## III. THE PROBLEM OF REV 3:20

The origins of Rev 3:20, which contains the metaphor of Christ knocking at the door (the subject of the famous painting *The Light of the World* by Holman Hunt) are explained in three different ways: (1) as an allusion to Cant 5:2 (Cortes, *RCT* 4 [1979] 239–58; Feuillet, *SRS* 49 [1961] 321–53; Kraft, 86; Sweet, 109), (2) as an originally independent prophetic oracle pronounced by a Christian prophet in the name of the exalted Jesus (Bultmann, *History,* 134–35; Müller, *Prophetie und Predigt,* 75), or (3) as an adaptation by John of a saying of Jesus from the Synoptic tradition, specifically the parable of the doorkeeper, which exists in two relatively independent versions (Mark 13:33–37; Luke 12:35–38).

Since Rev 3:20 has the form of an "I saying" and is not in narrative form, if it is based on a parable of Jesus, that parable has been radically rewritten. The motifs of "knocking" and "opening" are present in Luke 12:36b, while the motif of the common meal is found in Luke 12:37b (Roloff, "Siehe," 460–61), though it must be observed that the returning κύριος does not eat with his servants but rather serves them a meal. Nevertheless, a plurality of servants is mentioned in Luke 12:35–38, while only a single individual who might hear and open the door is mentioned in Rev 3:20. The version of the parable in Mark 13:33–37, however, does have a single individual appointed as doorkeeper for the house. Three features common to both versions of the parable, however, are absent from Rev 3:20: (1) the central character is the *owner of the house,* (2) *he is returning to his own house,* and (3) the servants or doorkeeper are charged with *watching for his unexpected return.* Though Roloff argues that these motifs are all presupposed in Rev 3:20, that is pure conjecture. Bauckham (*NTS* 23 [1976–77] 162–76; id., *NTS* 29 [1983] 129–34; see Joachim Jeremias *Parables,* 54–55) argues that this parable has been "deparabolized" in Rev 3:20.

A survey of the interpretations of Rev 3:20 proposed by major commentators suggests the polyvalent character of the imagery of the saying. Most commentators understand the passage in connection with the eschatological coming of Christ (Bousset [1906] 233; Swete, 63–64; Sweet, 109). A few commentators understand the saying (in connection with v 19b) to refer to a *present* "coming" of Christ to summon people to repentance or conversion (Charles, 1:100–101; Beasley-Murray, 106–7). Yet neither view necessarily excludes the other (Lohmeyer, 39).

The motif of dining together found in the saying can be understood in several ways:

(1) as a metaphor for intimate fellowship (Mounce, 128ff.), (2) as an allusion to the eschatological messianic banquet (Beckwith, 491; Kiddle-Ross, 20; Lohmeyer, 39; Lohse, 35; Müller, *Prophetie und Predigt*, 75; Bauckham, *NTS* 23 [1976–77] 172), or (3) as a reference to the celebration of the Lord's Supper (Caird, 58; Roloff, "Siehe," 464–65). Again, these interpretations can hardly be considered mutually exclusive.

The eschatological interpretation of Rev 3:20, based primarily on the supposition that it is a modified version or "deparabolization" of the parable of the doorkeeper in Luke 12:35–38, has no real justification in the saying itself. Rather, this view supposes that the recipients of Revelation were familiar with this parable tradition and that the author consciously intended the audience to catch the allusion to the Parousia parable of Jesus (Roloff, "Siehe," 462). Charles is quite right in insisting that the meaning of the possible sources of Rev 3:20 is a question quite different from that of the meaning of the saying in its present context. If Rev 3:20 is understood as alluding to Luke 12:35–38, Jesus may be understood as the returning master of the house, while the one who opens the door is a servant functioning as the doorkeeper. However, if the saying is understood in its own terms, the imagery is unique. The speaker is a deity who begs admission to the home of the worshiper. The meal they share (provided by the worshiper) either inaugurates or celebrates the relationship between the worshiper and the deity. In a Christian context, it is natural to think of the meal as the Lord's Supper, at which the risen Jesus was thought spiritually present (see Luke 24:30–31).

Two types of sacral meals from Greco-Roman religious practice suggest themselves as possible parallels to Rev 3:20. The first type is reflected in the numerous papyrus invitations to the κλίνη of Sarapis (κλίνη means literally, "couch," but with the connotation "dinner at which one reclines to eat"). The invitations to attend a dinner with the god Sarapis, of which thirteen have now been discovered (the thirteenth invitation is POxy 3693, where the editor provides references to the other twelve; a helpful discussion of these texts is found in Horsley, *New Docs* 1:5–9 [at that point only eleven such invitations were known]). Almost all the invitations were issued under the name of a particular host. PKöln 57 (tr. Horsley, *New Docs* 1:5), however, is an exception: "The god calls you to a banquet being held in the Thoereion tomorrow from the 9th hour." This invitation implies that the god is understood as *present* at the banquet, an implication confirmed by both terra-cotta statuettes and numismatic depictions of a reclining Sarapis (Gilliam, "Invitations," 317; Gill, *HTR* 67 [1974] 117–37; the latter discusses τραπεζώματα, i.e., offerings to a deity placed on a sacrificial table for a meal at which the god was somehow regarded as present in the midst of the worshipers). Judging by the size of the banquet rooms in excavated sanctuaries, between seven and ten persons could be present (Will, "Banquets," 353–62). Though such banquets apparently had little to do with revelatory divination, they do reveal an ancient conception of one type of relationship between worshipers and deities that provides a possible background for understanding early Christian problems regarding eating sacrificial meat (a taboo of particular concern to John; see Rev 2:14, 20 and *Excursus 2D: Eating Meat Offered to Idols*). A different type of invitation is represented by those preserved in connection with the cult of Zeus Panamaros, attested from the second century B.C. to the fourth century A.D., though most of the inscriptions date from the second century A.D. (the inscriptions are collected in J. Hatzfeld, "Inscriptions de Panamara," *BCH* 51 (1927) 57–122, and also in *SEG* 4:247–61). The god himself is depicted as the host of the meals (e.g., *SEG* 4:247.2; 250.2). A similar type of sacrificial meal is the *lectisternia,* a funerary meal eaten in the presence of the deified dead (Servius on Vergil *Aeneid* 10.76; Livy 5.13.6).

A second type of sacral meal is that prepared by Greco-Roman magicians either to attract and establish a permanent bond with a πάρεδρος δαίμων, "assistant god," or as part of the ritual procedure for summoning a god or *daimon* for (among other things) purposes of divination. These meals provided the setting for an appearance of a supernatural revealer and are potentially helpful for understanding the significance of Rev 3:20. A πάρεδρος δαίμων is a deity, usually minor, which a magician secured as a lifelong companion and servant who could provide him with a variety of services. *PGM* I.96–131 contains a lengthy list of such services:

> If you give him a command, straightway he performs the task: he sends dreams, he brings women, men without the use of magical material, he kills, he destroys, he stirs up winds from the earth, he carries gold, silver, bronze, and gives them to you whenever the need arises. And he frees from bonds a person chained in prison, he opens doors, he causes invisibility so that no one can see you at all, he is a bringer of fire, he brings water, wine, bread and [whatever] you wish in the way of foods.

An important feature of the πάρεδρος δαίμων is his role as a prophetic or oracular medium, attested in PGM I.173–77:

> He will tell you what things will happen both when and at what time of the night or day. And if anyone asks you "What do I have in mind?" or "What has happened to me?" or even "What is going to happen?", question the messenger [ἄγγελος] and he will tell you in silence. But you speak to the one who questions you as if from yourself.

A πάρεδρος δαίμων is a divine being, for the Greeks used the terms δαίμων and θεός interchangeably (Abt, *Zauberei,* 253–57), and the terms δαίμων, θεός, and ἄγγελος are used interchangeably in the magical papyri (*PGM* I, which contains several spells for acquiring a *paredros daimon,* equates the term with θεός, "god" [lines 40, 77, 86, 88, 89, 90, 92, 93], with ἄγγελος, "angel" [lines 76, 78, 87, 172, 176], and with πνεῦμα ἀέριον, "aerial spirit" [line 97]). The spells for enlisting the services of such a *daimon* have a relatively consistent morphology (spells for acquiring a *paredros daimon* include *PGM* I.1–42, 42–95, 96–195; IV.1840–70; XIa.1–40; XII.14–95). *PGM* I.1–42 is an example of this type of ritual procedure whose purpose is summarized in the introductory sequence (I.1–3): "A [*daimon* comes] as an assistant who will reveal everything to you clearly and will be your [companion and] will eat and sleep with you." Procedures to recruit a personal *paredros daimon* consist of the following elements: (1) Preliminary preparations (purification, e.g., abstention from sexual intercourse, I.41–42) are required. (2) Sacrificial ritual (πρᾶξις) is peformed. (3) Invocation or epiklesis (ἐπῳδή) is spoken. (4) The god or *daimon* "enters in." (5) The god or *daimon* is greeted. (6) The adept asks the name of the god or *daimon,* knowledge of which is necessary for future invocations (*PGM* I.160–61, 167; XIII.210–11; *PDM* xiv.60ff.). (7) The adept reclines and dines with the god or *daimon* (*PGM* I.37–38, 84–87, 168–70; IV.1859–60; XII.20–23). (8) The god or *daimon* is asked questions by the adept and answers them. (9) The god or *daimon* (or the adept) is dismissed. A *paredros daimon* has immediate tenure (*PGM* I.165–66: "Be inseparable from me from this day forth through all the time of my life"), and since he is not, in fact, inseparable, he can be recalled easily whenever the practitioner so desires (*PGM* I.88–90, 181–88). Spells for the purpose of invoking a supernatural revealer are very similar in structure and may involve sharing a ritual meal with the god or *daimon* (*PDM* xiv.55ff., 550ff.) or the use of a ritual throne or tripod (the traditional throne of Apollo) for his epiphany (throne: *PGM* I.332–33; V.31–35; tripod: *PGM* III.192–93, 291–95; IV.3197ff.; XIII.104ff.). The significance of the throne as a place for a revelatory epiphany has been discussed by E. Peterson ("Beiträge," 254–70), who finds the conceptual world of Hellenistic magical revelation reflected in Hermas *Vis.* 1.2.2; 3.1.4. Like the throne or tripod, the table prepared for the deity functioned as the place of epiphany. Sometimes an image of the expected deity was placed on the table along with the meal (*PGM* IV.1859–60; XII.18–20). The sacral meal tended to focus on bread and wine, but could also include incense, spices, fruits, and flowers. The function of the meal, never explicitly discussed, appears to be the establishment of a permanent bonding between the worshiper and the god or *daimon* by sharing food (the most common way of establishing a sacred bond in the ancient Near East to the present day). These various procedures for recruiting a *paredros daimon* or summoning a revealer commonly took place in the privacy of the magician's home (a priest or temple servant could use a temple, or part of a temple, from which the public was excluded; a poor man could use lonely places outside the city); all that was necessary was a solitary place where a meal could be set out (*PGM* I.84; III.334; IV.59, 2041, 2374; VII.541; XIII.6, 8; XXXVIII.5; LXXVIII.1; XCIII.15; *PDM* xii.70, 90; xiv.340, 780). *PGM* IV.1851–67 contains a procedure in which a *paredros daimon* is used in love magic, with some features similar to Rev 3:20:

> Go late at night to the house [of the woman] you want, knock on her door with the Eros and say: "Lo, she NN resides here; wherefore stand beside her and, after assuming the likeness of the god or *daimon* whom she worships, say what I propose." And go to your home, set the table, spread a pure linen cloth, and seasonal flowers, and set the figure upon it. Then make a burnt offering to it and continuously say the spell of invocation. And send him, and he will act without fail.

Here the smitten practitioner carries a magical image of the god Eros (his *paredros daimon*) to the house of his beloved, where he knocks on the door. The god is to assume the identity of the deity to whom the woman is devoted, stand beside her as she sleeps, and speak to her either through a vision or a dream.

Rev 3:20 may be compared to another passage in early Christian apocalyptic literature with stronger ties to the conceptual world of magical revelation, Hermas *Vis.* 5.1:

> While I was praying at home and sitting on my dining couch [καθίσαντος εἰς τὴν κλίνην], there entered [εἰσῆλθεν] a man glorious to look on, in the dress of a shepherd, covered with a white goatskin, with a bag on his shoulders and a staff in his hand. And he greeted me, and I greeted him back. And at once he sat down by me, and said to me, "I have been sent by the most revered angel to dwell with you the rest of the days of your life."

E. Peterson ("Kritische Analyse," 271–76) has shown the numerous links between this passage and Hellenistic magical revelation, including sitting as the posture for receiving revelation, the use of the verb εἰσέρχεσθαι, "to enter in," and the greeting of the revealer (*PGM*I.327; IV.1002, 1007, 1015, 1019, 1023, 1030, 1045, 1121, 3220; VII.1014; XIII.12, 210, 608; LXII.34). Peterson does not mention the correspondence between the permanent relationship established between Hermas and the Shepherd and that between the magician and the *paredros daimon*. Further, there are no philological obstacles against translating the phrase καθίσαντος εἰς τὴν κλίνην as "sitting on the dining couch"; i.e., Hermas was eating when the Shepherd appeared to him. This and other passages in Hermas reveal that Hellenistic magical divination has had a positive impact on the author's conception of revelatory phenomena. The currency of associating *paredroi daimones* as revelatory mediators in Greco-Roman revelatory divination meant that early Christian leaders tended to categorize deviant forms of Christian prophecy in terms of the possession of a personal prophetic spirit or *daimon* (early Christian authors commonly equated magic and Greco-Roman religion and always used the term δαίμων of evil supernatural beings).

Against this background, Rev 3:20 needs be interpreted neither eschatologically (i.e, the appearance of Christ at the door understood as a metaphor for the Parousia) nor individualistically (Christ knocks at the door of the heart). As a Christian text, however, it reveals some features not totally compatible with its present setting. The door upon which the risen Jesus knocks must be that of the worshiper's home. Christian homes were commonly used as gathering places for worship, yet in this passage it appears that only an *individual* Christian is involved, not a congregation. In that respect the saying still shows its connections with private ritual practices. The verb John uses for the entry of the risen Jesus, εἰσέρχεσθαι, "to enter in," is a commonplace term for entry, yet can also be a *terminus technicus* for the entry of a summoned god or *daimon* in the language of Greco-Roman magical revelation (Peterson, "Kritische Analyse," 271–76). The meal to be shared by Jesus and the worshiper may be construed as the Lord's Supper, but it probably is a meal intended to be shared only by two, Jesus and the worshiper. Taken together, these parallels suggest that the imagery of Rev 3:20 is compatible with the conceptual world of Hellenistic magical divination. In this difficult passage, however, it is not possible to argue that Rev 3:20 reflects only the conceptual imagery of magical divination. Rather, it appears that the metaphorical character of the saying exhibits a polyvalent ambiguity produced by the author's combination of imagery from Jewish, Christian, and Greco-Roman traditions. If Rev 3:20 can be construed as reflecting imagery from Hellenistic magical divination, this is one more piece of evidence suggesting that John has turned the tables by placing the initiative completely in the hands of the risen Jesus and relegating the worshiper to the role of respondent.

### Comment

**14a** καὶ τῷ ἀγγέλῳ τῆς ἐν Λαοδικείᾳ ἐκκλησίας γράψον, "And to the angel of the church in Laodicea, write." See *Comment* on 2:1a.

**14b** τάδε λέγει ὁ ἀμήν, ὁ μάρτυς ὁ πιστὸς καὶ ἀληθινός, ἡ ἀρχὴ τῆς κτίσεως τοῦ θεοῦ, "'Thus says the Amen, the faithful and true Witness, the Origin of the creation of God.'" Three important and related christological titles occur in this introductory clause: (1) the Amen, (2) the faithful and true Witness, and (3) the Origin of the creation of God.

(1) The unusual titular use of the term ὁ ἀμήν, "Amen" (only here in the NT), is probably an allusion to the Hebrew text of Isa 65:16 (cf. 25:1), where the name of God is mentioned in connection with the use of both blessings and oaths in the phrases יִתְבָּרֵךְ בֵּאלֹהֵי אָמֵן *yitbārēk bē'lōhê 'āmēn*, literally, "he shall bless by the God of Amen," and יִשָּׁבַע בֵּאלֹהֵי אָמֵן *yiššābaʿ bē'lōhê'āmēn*, literally, "he shall swear by the God of Amen." In both cases *BHS* suggests that אָמֵן *'āmēn* could be vocalized either אָמוּן *'ēmûn*, "faithfulness," or אֹמֶן *'ōmen*, "faithfulness," because both phrases are rendered τὸν θεὸν τὸν ἀληθινόν, "the true God," in the LXX. Both phrases are changed in the *Tg. Isa.* to "the living God." It appears, however, that אָמֵן *'āmēn* stood in the Hebrew text of Isa 65:16 used by Aquila, who translated it πεπιστωμένως (his usual way of translating אָמֵן *'āmēn;* see Num 5:22; Deut 27:15; Pss 41:13; 72:19; 89:53[MT 52]; Jer 11:5), as well as in the Hebrew text used by Symmachus, who simply transliterated it τὸν θεὸν ἀμήν (Charles, 1:94; Schlier, *TDNT* 1:337; Jepsen, *TDOT* 1:322). The translators of the Latin Vulgate also read אָמֵן *'āmēn,* which they transliterated as *amen.* This title for God is found only in Isa 65:16, but its connection with blessing and taking oaths probably indicates that both must be confirmed by God himself in order to be valid, or perhaps that God, who is sometimes depicted in the OT as swearing oaths, need not swear by another since he is his own witness (Heb 6:13–17, alluding to Gen 22:1b; see Attridge, *Hebrews,* 178–82). This notion is treated briefly by Philo (*De sacr.* 91–92; LCL tr.):

> For our conception of an oath is an appeal to God as a witness on some disputed matter. But nothing is uncertain or open to dispute with God.... Truly He needs no witness, for there is no other god to be His peer.

Christologically this title is significant since it attributes to Christ a title associated only with God (Rissi, *Future,* 92 n. 17; Holtz, *Christologie,* 142). Oecumenius (*Comm. in Apoc.* 3:14; Hoskier, *Oecumenius,* 64) explains that ὁ ἀμήν means that what is said is the truth (ὁ ἀληθινός) and that the term ἀμήν means ναί, "yes," a view repeated by Arethas (*Comm. in Apoc.* 9; Migne, *PG* CVI.560D); see Berger, *Amen-Worte,* 6–9. According to *Mek. de-Rabbi Ishmael, Kaspa* 2 (Lauterbach, *Mekilta* 3:160), oaths that are not responded to with "Amen" are invalid. "Amen" is a strong affirmative expression meaning "truly," and this is reflected in the LXX, where ἀμήν is regularly translated γένοιτο, "may it be so."

(2) The phrase ὁ μάρτυς ὁ πιστὸς καὶ ἀληθινός, "the faithful and true witness," has a close parallel in Rev 1:5, where Jesus Christ is called ὁ μάρτυς ὁ πιστός, "the faithful witness"; only here and in Rev 1:5 is Jesus Christ called a μάρτυς. The Hebrew term אָמֵן *'mn* can mean *both* πιστός and ἀληθινός as the translations in the LXX attest. This compound title serves to define the essential meaning of "Amen" (Berger, *Amen-Worte,* 109). Similarly, the exalted Jesus refers to himself as ὁ μαρτυρῶν ταῦτα, "the one who testifies these things" (Rev 22:20). There is perhaps an allusion here to Ps 89:38(LXX 88:38), in which the moon is described as ὁ μάρτυς ἐν οὐρανῷ πιστός, "a faithful witness in heaven" (cf. Job 16:19). A major interpretive problem in both 3:14 and 1:5 is whether Jesus Christ as μάρτυς refers to the historical Jesus, i.e., his faithfulness in completing his earthly ministry through his death (Holtz, *Christologie,* 143), or to the exalted Jesus who guarantees the truth of the revelation transmitted through John. This second view is more probable for several reasons (see *Comment* on 1:5). On the other hand, in the

Gospel of John, it is the historical Jesus who is the subject of the verb μαρτυρεῖν; i.e., he testifies to the truth that he has received from God (John 3:32; 4:44; 5:31; 7:7; 8:14, 18; 13:21; 18:37). In Rev 2:13, the martyr Antipas is also called ὁ μάρτυς μου ὁ πιστός μου, "my faithful witness." The phrase "faithful and true" is the name of the rider on the white horse in Rev 19:11, who is clearly the Messiah. Elsewhere the adjectives are reserved for the prophetic message that John has received and transmits: οἱ λόγοι πιστοὶ καὶ ἀληθινοί, "the message is trustworthy and true" (21:5; 22:6). In 3 Macc 2:11, in the context of prayer, God is called "trustworthy and true" (πιστὸς εἶ καὶ ἀληθινός).

(3) The phrase ἡ ἀρχὴ τῆς κτίσεως τοῦ θεοῦ, "the beginning of the creation of God," may reflect dependence on Col 1:15 (cf. 1:18), a possibility supported by the likelihood that the churches of Colossae and Laodicea exchanged letters (Col 4:16), which may account for the apparent dependence of Rev 3:14 on Col 1:15 (see Lightfoot, *Colossians*, 41–44): Rev 3:14 refers to ἡ ἀρχὴ τῆς κτίσεως τοῦ θεοῦ, "the beginning of the creation of God," while Col 1:15 has the phrase πρωτότοκος πάσης κτίσεως, "firstborn of all creation" (n.b. that ἀρχή = πρωτότοκος in Col 1:18). The term ἀρχή can have several meanings: (1) beginning (temporal or aspectual), (2) ruler, authority, office, (3) cause. The emphasis on the *temporal* priority of Christ to all creation is found frequently in early Christian literature and was perhaps the product of the identification of Christ with the wisdom of God. According to John 1:2–3, "He was in the beginning [ἐν ἀρχῇ] with God; all things were made through him." LXX Prov 8:22, referring to Wisdom, says "The Lord created me in the beginning [LXX, ἀρχή; MT, ראשׁית *rēʾšît*] of his ways." In early Christianity the term ἀρχή was used with some frequency as a title for Christ (Justin *Dial.* 61.1; 62.4 [alluding to Prov 8:22]; Theophilus *Ad Autol.* 2.10 [tr. R. M. Grant, *Theophilus of Antioch Ad Autolycum* (Oxford: Clarendon, 1970)], "He is called Beginning [ἀρχή] because he leads and dominates [ἄρχει καὶ κυριεύει] everything fashioned through him"; 2.13; Tatian *Oratio ad Graec.* 5.1; Clement Alex. *Eclogae proph.* 4.1; *Strom.* 6.58.1; 7.1; Origen *Hom. in Gen.* 1.1; *Comm. in Joh.* 1.19, "He is called the Beginning [ἀρχή] to the extent that he is Wisdom"; see Lampe, *PGL*, 235a; Daniélou, *Jewish Christianity*, 166–68). ἀρχή was also regarded as a hypostasis among the Gnostics (Irenaeus *Adv. haer.* 1.18.1) and was the name of one of the Valentinian aeons (Hippolytus *Ref.* 6.38.4). See C. F. Burney, "Christ as the ᾽ΑΡΧΗ of the Creation," *JTS* 17 (1926) 160–77. The formula ἀρχὴ καὶ τέλος, "beginning and end," was a widespread ancient title for God (see *Comment* on Rev 21:6), which is applied to Christ in 22:13.

Silberman has ingeniously argued that the three titles of the exalted Christ in this passage reflect Jewish speculation on Prov 8:22, 30 and Gen 1:1 (the term ראשׁית *rēʾšît* in Prov 8:22 was used in rabbinic Judaism as a key to the ראשׁית *rēʾšît* in Gen 1:1). Silberman maintains that these titles are three well-known OT epithets of wisdom: (1) ὁ ἀμήν, "the Amen," in this context is obviously understood as a title of Christ. Silberman (followed by Trudinger, *NovT* 14 [1972] 277–79) maintains that ὁ ἀμήν in this verse is a mistranslation of the Hebrew term אָמוֹן *ʾāmôn*, a term describing wisdom in Prov 8:30 and applied to the Torah in *Gen. Rab.* 1.1, where the unusual word אָמוֹן *ʾāmôn* is explained by listing various possible meanings attested in the OT: "pedagogue" (Num 11:12), "covered" or "clad" (Lam 4:5), "hidden" (Esth 2:7), "great" (Nah 3:8). Another way of understanding the word אמון *ʾmwn* of Prov 8:30 is then achieved by revocalizing it to אוּמָן *ʾûmān* (a rabbinic form of the Hebrew word אָמָּן *ʾammān* found in Cant 7:2), meaning "master workman." (2) ὁ μάρτυς ὁ πιστὸς καὶ ἀληθινός, "the faithful and true witness," Silberman understands as a literal rendering of two phrases from Prov 14: (a) Prov 14:5, עד אמונים ʿēd ʾĕmûnîm = ὁ μάρτυς ὁ πιστός, and (b) Prov 14:25, עד אמת ʿēd ʾĕmet = ὁ μάρτυς ὁ ἀληθινός; both of these epithets are chosen because אמון ʾmwn in Prov 8:30 was used as the starting point for wordplay with the root אמן ʾmn. (c) ἡ ἀρχὴ τῆς κτίσεως τοῦ θεοῦ, "the origin of the creation of God," according to Silberman, is an interpretive rendering of ראשית דרכו rēʾšît darkô (see W. D. Davies, Paul, 152). In summary, Silberman has proposed that Rev 3:14 would have read in Hebrew כה אמר האמון עד אמונים עד אמת ראשית דרכו [Prov 14:5] kōh ʾāmar hāʾāmôn ʿēd ʾĕmûnîm ʿēd ʾĕmet rēʾšît darkô. This phrase is also reminiscent of several passages in the NT in which the preincarnate Jesus is linked with creation, perhaps in connection with an early Jewish exegetical tradition connected with בראשית bĕrēšît, "in the beginning," of Gen 1:1 (see Hilary Ps. 2: "Breshith . . . tres significantias in se habet, id est 'in principio' et 'in capite' et 'in filio'").

**15a** οἶδά σου τὰ ἔργα ὅτι οὔτε ψυχρὸς εἶ οὔτε ζεστός, "I know your conduct, that you are neither cold nor hot." "Cold" and "hot" are figures of speech meaning "against me" and "for me" or "hostile towards me" and "friendly towards me." In OT wisdom literature, the images of the "hot" (negative) and "cold" (positive) person relate to the motif of self-control, for "hot" is a pejorative metaphor for a lack of control (Prov 15:18), while "cold" is a positive metaphor for restraint (Prov 17:27; m. ʾAbot 1:17); see J. G. Williams, Those Who Ponder Proverbs: Aphoristic Thinking and Biblical Literature (Sheffield: Almond, 1981) 29–30. Thus the phrase איש חמה ʾîš ḥēmâ, literally "man of heat," means "an angry man" (Prov 16:4; 19:19; 27:4; Isa 51:13; Ezek 23:25; cf. Prov 22:24 (איש חמות ʾîš ḥēmôt). Some have suggested that the terms "cold," "hot," and "lukewarm" are metaphors drawn from the water supply of the city of Laodicea, which was lukewarm, which, in contrast to the hot medicinal springs of Hierapolis and the pure cold water of Colossae, is a metaphor for barrenness or ineffectiveness (Rudwick-Green, ExpTim 69 [1957–58] 176–78; Hemer, Letters, 186–91). According to Tyconius, the phrase "neither cold nor hot" means that "it is useless" (F. LoBue and G. C. Willis, The Turin Fragments: Commentary on Revelation [Cambridge: Cambridge UP, 1963] 74–75). At Laodicea there are remains of an aqueduct that probably carried water from hot mineral springs five miles south; this would have cooled slowly and become tepid and emetic when it finally arrived at Laodicea (Rudwick-Green, ExpTim 69 [1957–58] 177). Strabo observed that the water at Laodicaea was extremely hard, though drinkable (13.4.14). Porter (TynBul 38 [1987] 143–49) cites Herodotus 4.181.3–4 as evidence that the imagery of Rev 3:15–16 was drawn from the city's water supply. Herodotus describes the radical temperature changes in the hot spring at the Oasis of Siwah in Libya, which is reportedly hot during the night and cold during the day (LCL tr.):

> They have another spring of water besides, which is warm [χλιαρόν] at dawn, and colder [ψυχρότερον] at market-time, and very cold [ψυχρόν] at noon; and it is then that they water their gardens; as the day declines the coldness [ψυχροῦ] abates, till at sunset the water grows warm [χλιαρόν]. It becomes ever hotter and hotter till midnight, and then it boils [ζέει; the verbal cognate of ζεστός] and bubbles; after midnight it becomes ever cooler till dawn.

This text is paraphrased in Arrian Anab. 3.4.2 (though the rare term χλιαρός is avoided) and rationally explained by Lucretius De rerum natura 6.848–78. Porter also cites Xenophon *Memorabilia* 3.13.3, which refers to a conversation with a person who complained that the drinking water at home was warm (θερμόν), though his servants used it for both washing and drinking.

**15b** ὄφελον ψυχρὸς ἦς ἢ ζεστός, "I wish you were either cold or hot!" Cold or hot water is desirable for various purposes, but from this ethical perspective lukewarm water is not. The phrase "neither cold nor hot" can be taken to indicate vacillation, or being pulled one way and another. Epictetus criticizes the person who cannot decide on a particular way of living (2.2.12; 4.2.4–10), and Matthew also preserves sayings that emphasize the necessity of choice (Matt 6:24, "No one can serve two masters"; 12:30, "Whoever is not with me is against me"); cf. A. Bonhöffer, *Epiktet und das Neue Testament* (Giessen: Töpelmann, 1911) 307–8. ὄφελον is an introductory particle used with indicative, imperfect, and aorist verbs to express an unattainable wish (BDR § 359.1), which can be translated "oh that," "would that" (Bauer-Aland, 1211). For similar uses of ὄφελον, see 1 Cor 4:8; 2 Cor 11:1; Gal 5:12; Ignatius *Smyrn.* 12:1 (J. B. Lightfoot, *Apostolic Fathers* 2/3, 321). It is *not* an unaugmented form of ὤφελον but a participle with ἐστίν expressed or understood (BDR § 67.2). Here it is used with the imperfect ἦς to express present time (Bauer-Aland, 1211).

**16** οὕτως ὅτι χλιαρὸς εἶ καὶ οὔτε ζεστὸς οὔτε ψυχρός, μέλλω σε ἐμέσαι ἐκ τοῦ στόματός μου, "So, because you are tepid and neither hot nor cold, I will vomit you from my mouth." The term χλιαρός, "warm, tepid, lukewarm," refers to the mean temperature between cold and hot. Here the verb ἐμεῖν, "vomit" (see Durling, *Medical*, 152), is a coarse figure of speech meaning "utterly reject." In Lev 18:25, 28; 20:22, the expression "to vomit" out of the land is used of the fate of the Canaanites upon Israel's entry into Palestine, and the potential fate of the Israelites themselves.

**17a** ὅτι λέγεις ὅτι πλούσιός εἰμι καὶ πεπλούτηκα καὶ οὐδὲν χρείαν ἔχω, "Because you say 'I am wealthy and I have become rich and need nothing.'" A close parallel is found in a diatribe of Epictetus in which he attributes the following statement to his discussion partner, an imperial bailiff: ἀλλ' ἐγώ πλούσιός εἰμι καὶ οὐδενὸς χρεία μοί ἐστιν, "But I am rich and need nothing" (Arrian *Epict. Diss.* 3.7.29; cf. R. M. Royalty, Jr., "The Streets of Heaven: The Imagery and Ideology of Wealth in the Apocalypse of John," Diss., Yale, 1995, 209). In form, the statement in Rev 3:17, as in Epictetus, is a *hybris soliloquy*, a short form with close parallels in other speeches of denunciation; for analogies, see *Comment* on 18:7. The similarity between the statement here and that in Epictetus suggests a conventional excuse. A similar soliloquy is found in Hos 12:9 (cf. Zech 11:5):

> Ephraim has said, "Ah, I am rich,
> > I have gained wealth for myself;
> in all of my gain
> > no offense has been found in me that would be sin."

An analogous soliloquy is found in *1 Enoch* 97:8–9:

> Woe to you, who have wrongfully acquired silver and gold, while saying: "We have become rich, have treasure and have everything that we want; now we want to expand what we own, because we have gathered silver and our storage bins are full."

Rhetorically, essentially the same claim is repeated three times for emphasis. The statement "I am wealthy" preceding "I have become rich" is an instance of *hysteron-*

*proteron,* i.e., the reversal of the logical order of events, a figure of speech found several times in Revelation (3:3; 5:5; 6:4; 10:4, 9; 20:4–5, 12–13; 22:14). The emphasis on the literal wealth of the Laodiceans is in tension with the view that Revelation was written in the late 60s during the reign of Nero, for Laodicea was destroyed by an earthquake in A.D. 60, though the city did reject the offer of an imperial subsidy to help in rebuilding. In this context, it seems appropriate to understand the "wealth" of the Laodiceans figuratively. In 1 Cor 1:5 Paul says of the Corinthians, ἐπλουτίσθητε ἐν αὐτῷ, "you have been made rich by him [Christ]." God is rich and grants riches to those who have a proper relationship to him (Rom 2:4; 10:12; 11:33; 2 Cor 6:10; 9:11; Eph 2:4; Phil 4:19; Jas 2:5 [the poor of the world are rich in faith]; *Barn.* 1:3; 19:2 [speaks of being πλούσιος τῷ πνεύματι, "rich in spirit"]; Hermas *Sim.* 1.9–11; *Ep. Diog.* 5.13; Philo *Leg. alleg.* 1.34; 3.163; *Rer. div. her.* 27). The claim that they are rich indicates pride in the possession of salvation, similar to 1 Cor 4:8, where Paul shames the Corinthians with a series of ironical statements including "Already you have become rich!" (Bousset [1906] 270–71; Müller, 136; Roloff [ET] 64–65).

**17b** καὶ οὐκ οἶδας, ὅτι σὺ εἶ ὁ ταλαίπωρος καὶ ἐλεεινὸς καὶ πτωχὸς καὶ τυφλὸς καὶ γυμνός, "but you do not recognize that you are the one who is miserable and pitiful and poor and blind and naked." The ignorance of the Laodicean church is in explicit contrast with the knowledge of the risen Christ emphasized in v 15a. The repetition of the conjunction καί, "and," connecting these five adjectives in the predicate nominative is an instance of the use of polysyndeton, which is a rhetorical way of underlining the truly desperate condition of the Laodicean congregation. Unlike the first two adjectives, the last three are used in a figurative sense, which the author will develop in positive exhortations in v 18. "Blind" refers to the inability of the Laodiceans to understand or comprehend their true condition, and the metaphor of blindness is sometimes used of the wicked (4Q266 = 4QDamascus Document^a frag. 1, line 16). The term πτωχός, "poor," is obviously used here figuratively in contrast to "wealthy," which is understood literally in v 17a. Philo accepted the Stoic paradox that only the wise man is really "rich" (cf. Arnim, *SVF* 3:589–603), and this is expressed in *Quod Omn. Prob.* 9: "You call those poor who are surrounded with silver and gold and a huge amount of landed possessions."

**18a** συμβουλεύω σοι ἀγοράσαι παρ᾽ ἐμοῦ χρυσίον πεπυρωμένον ἐκ πυρὸς ἵνα πλουτήσῃς, "I advise you to buy from me gold purified by fire that you might be rich." Paradox is involved here, for how are the "poor" able to "purchase" a commodity as expensive as gold? There is perhaps an allusion to Isa 55:1–2, where the hungry person with no money is encouraged to "come, buy, and eat." Obviously poverty, purchasing, and gold are used as metaphors. Laodicea was a financial center and the home of a number of extremely wealthy people (Hemer, *Letters,* 191–92).

**18b** καὶ ἱμάτια λευκὰ ἵνα περιβάλῃ καὶ μὴ φανερωθῇ ἡ αἰσχύνη τῆς γυμνότητός σου, "then white garments that you might be clothed that the shame of nakedness might not be manifest." White garments are frequently referred to in Revelation (3:4–5; 4:4; 6:11; 7:9, 13, 14; 19:8, 14; see *Comment* on 3:5a). Such garments have several kinds of association. They are the color used on festal or sacral occasions and can also symbolize purity (see Eccl 9:8; Ps 104:2).

**18c** καὶ κολλούριον ἐγχρῖσαι τοὺς ὀφθαλμούς σου ἵνα βλέπῃς, "then medication to apply to your eyes that you might regain your sight." This reference to eye medication (on κολλύριον, see Durling, *Medical*, 207) is often thought to reflect the historical situation of Laodicea. During the first century A.D. there was a medical school at Laodicea (Strabo 12.8.20), where a famous ophthalmologist, Demosthenes Philalethes, practiced. The so-called Phrygian powder used as an ingredient in eye medications cannot be specifically linked with Laodicea, though the city lies within the boundaries of ancient Phrygia (Hemer, *Letters*, 196–99).

The negative aspects of the last three adjectives in v 17b ("poor," "blind," "naked") are transformed into positive exhortations in v 18 (in the order 1, 3, 2), where the Laodiceans are advised to buy three commodities from the exalted Christ, (1) gold, (2) white garments, and (3) medication. The reason for each commodity is explained in a purpose clause (ἵνα + subjunctive): (1) that you might be rich, (2) that you might be clothed and that the shame of your nakedness might not be manifest, and (3) that you might regain your sight.

**19** ἐγὼ ὅσους ἐὰν φιλῶ ἐλέγχω καὶ παιδεύω· ζήλευε οὖν καὶ μετανόησον, "Those whom I love I chastise and discipline; therefore be earnest and repent." The first clause is a proverbial statement that alludes loosely to Prov 3:12 (quoted verbatim from the LXX in Heb 12:6, *1 Clem.* 56:4, and Philo *Congr.* 177):

> ὃν γὰρ ἀγαπᾷ κύριος παιδεύει,
> For whom the Lord loves he disciplines,

> μαστιγοῖ δὲ πάντα υἱὸν ὃν παραδέχεται.
> and he chastens every son whom he accepts.

In Rev 3:19 the "Lord" of Prov 3:12 is implicitly understood to mean the exalted Christ, and the proverb is attributed to him in the first person. This proverbial saying involves the application of the common theme in wisdom literature of *educative discipline,* in which the necessity of disciplining or chastening one's children, motivated by love and concern for their ultimate well-being (Prov 13:24; 23:12–14; 29:17; Philo *Det.* 145), is applied to the relationship between God and his people (Deut 8:5; Job 5:17–18; Ps 94:12–15; Prov 3:11–12; Jer 2:30; 5:3; Jdt 8:27; Sir 22:6; 30:1; 2 Macc 6:12–17; *Pss. Sol.* 10:1–3; 14:1; Philo *Det.* 146; 4Q504 = 4QDibHamᵃ 3:5–7 [tr. García Martínez, *DSS*, 414]: "For you called Israel 'my son, my first-born' and have corrected us as one corrects a son"; 1 Cor 11:32; Heb 12:7–11). Occasionally, the positive function of discipline is applied to the relationship between God and the king (2 Sam 7:14–15), and to the self-discipline of the wise man (Philo *Leg. All.* 2.90). Here it is extended to the relationship between the exalted Christ and Christians. The theme of educative discipline was applied to the relationship between God and his people, at least in part, to explain the deeper significance of the experience of suffering and deprivation

**20a** Ἰδοὺ ἔστηκα ἐπὶ τὴν θύραν καὶ κρούω, "Behold, I stand before the door and knock." This is an epiphany motif in which both the door and the knocking are metaphorical. This epiphany motif has a parallel in Callimachus *Hymn to Apollo* 3: καί δή που τὰ θύρετρα καλῷ ποδὶ Φοῖβος ἀράσσει, "It must be that Phoebus, with beautiful foot, kicks at the door."

**20b** ἐάν τις ἀκούσῃ τῆς φωνῆς μου καὶ ἀνοίξῃ τὴν θύραν, καὶ εἰσελεύσομαι πρὸς αὐτόν, "If any one hears my voice and opens the door, then I will come in to visit him." In this conditional clause, ἐάν + subjunctive in the protasis indicates that the condition is assumed as possible (the subjunctive indicating a future action with some uncertainty).

**20c** καὶ δειπνήσω μετ᾽ αὐτοῦ καὶ αὐτὸς μετ᾽ ἐμοῦ, "and I will share a meal with him and he with me." δειπνεῖν means "to eat a meal" with no reference to the time of day or the type of food (though the noun δεῖπνον can refer specifically to the main meal of the day usually eaten in the evening, "supper," "dinner"). The verb δειπνεῖν *can* refer to the Passover meal in Jewish (Jos. *Ant.* 2.312) and Christian contexts (Luke 22:20), as well as to pagan sacral meals (POxy 110, 523). Does this mean that the exalted Jesus will *host* the meal? If this verse is a reformulated version of the parable of the doorkeeper in Mark 13:33–37; Luke 12:35–37, then it can be argued that Jesus is not a guest but the returning householder, and therefore the one who hosts the meal (Roloff, "Siehe," 463). However, since the verb δειπνεῖν simply means "to eat a meal," or "to have a dinner" (Louw-Nida, § 23.30), there is no semantic basis for suggesting that Jesus is in fact the host. It is more likely, particularly since the conditional clause in this verse does not assume the reality but rather the possibility of the condition, that the exalted Jesus is the *guest* rather than the host (see Karrer, *Brief,* 215 n. 331).

**21a** ὁ νικῶν δώσω αὐτῷ καθίσαι μετ᾽ ἐμοῦ ἐν τῷ θρόνῳ μου, "As for the one who conquers, I will allow him to sit with me on my throne." While the promise that Christians will reign with Christ occurs occasionally in the NT (2 Tim 2:12), it occurs with striking frequency in Revelation (1:6; 5:10; 20:4, 6; 22:5) and is a conception partially modeled after Dan 7:18, 27. The enthronement of the twelve apostles as judges of the twelve tribes of Israel is mentioned in Q (Luke 22:30 = Matt 19:28). The promise that the victorious Christian will sit with Christ on his throne is based on ancient Near Eastern and Israelite kingship and enthronement imagery. A similar promise is found in 4Q*521* = 4Q Messianic Apocalypse 2 ii 7: "For he will honour the devout [חסידים *ḥsîdîm*] upon the throne of eternal royalty" (tr. García Martínez, *DSS,* 394). A vision report centered on the motif of enthronement is found in the second century B.C. Hellenistic Jewish dramatist Ezekiel, *Exagoge* 68–82 (tr. H. Jacobson, *The Exagoge of Ezekiel* [Cambridge: Cambridge UP, 1983] 55):

> I had a vision of a great throne on the top of mount Sinai
> and it reached till the folds of heaven.
> A noble man was sitting on it,
> with a crown and a large sceptre in his
> left hand. He beckoned to me with his right hand,
> so I approached and stood before the throne.
> He gave me the sceptre and instructed me to sit
> on the great throne. Then he gave me the royal crown
> and got up from the throne.
> I beheld the whole earth all around and saw
> beneath the earth and above the heavens.
> A multitude of stars fell before my knees
> and I counted them all.
> They paraded past me like a battalion of men.
> Then I awoke from my sleep in fear.

This throne vision, the earliest extant example of a postbiblical Merkavah vision (van der Horst, *JJS* 34 [1983] 21–29), reflects the influence of Ezek 1, Exod 24, and

Dan 7 and is striking because, in lines 74–76, Moses actually *replaces* God on the throne, an action that implies the deification of Moses (van der Horst, *JJS* 34 [1983] 25). The notion of a σύνθρονος θεοῦ, "one enthroned with God," may apply equally well to one seated *with* God on his throne or to one who has a throne *beside* the throne of God, such as Metatron in *3 Enoch*, whose name could be derived from the Greek term μετάθρονος, "enthroned with," though the term is unattested in Greek (S. Liebermann, "Metatron, the Meaning of His Name and His Functions," in Gruenwald, *Apocalyptic;* 235–41; but see Stuckenbruck, *Angel,* 71 n. 69). According to *T. Levi* 13:9, "Whoever teaches good things and practices them shall be enthroned [σύνθρονος] with kings, as was Joseph my brother" (reflecting the Stoic notion of the virtuous man as king; see Hollander-de Jonge, *Testaments,* 167); yet in Job 36:7 it is claimed that God sets the righteous with kings upon the throne. The Chronicler makes it clear in several passages that the throne of Israel is in reality the throne of God: 1 Chr 28:5 (Solomon will sit on the throne of the kingdom of Yahweh over Israel), 1 Chr 29:23 ("Solomon sat on the throne of the Lord"), and 2 Chr 9:8 (God has set Solomon on "his [i.e., 'God's'] throne"). For the Chronicler the kingdom of Israel is actually the kingdom of God (2 Chr 13:8). References to Christ *seated* on a throne in Revelation are rare. In the interim, the Lamb is apparently depicted as *standing* before the throne of God (5:13; 6:16; 7:9–10, 15, 17). In 7:17, however, the phrase τὸ ἀρνίον τὸ ἀνὰ μέσον τοῦ θρόνου, "the Lamb who is in the midst of the throne," is difficult to understand. Does it mean that the Lamb is *seated* on the throne, or does it simply mean that the Lamb stands in the vicinity of the throne? In *T. Job* 33:1–9, Job tells the kings from the east who have come to visit him that his real throne is an everlasting one in heaven.

How many can occupy a single throne at one time? The ancient world was familiar with the image of a *bisellium,* a "double-throne." In Rev 12:5 the Child is caught up to God and his throne (which may imply enthronement), and 22:1, 3 mentions "the throne of God and the Lamb" (i.e., apparently a single throne on which both sit). In *Orphic Hymns* 62.2, Dike (the personification of Justice) is described as one "who sits upon the sacred throne of Zeus" (i.e., *with* Zeus?). This tradition occurs earlier in Sophocles *Oedipus Coloneus* 1382, where Dike is explicitly described as "sitting with" (ξύνεδρος) Zeus (ἣ καὶ Ζηνὸς ἄνακτος ἐπὶ θρόνον ἱερὸν ἵζει), though his throne is not specifically mentioned. Lucian (*Peregrinus* 29) quotes a Sibylline verse to the effect that Proteus will be "co-enthroned [σύνθρονον] with Hephaestus and Herakles." One of the most famous of the Roman imperial cameos, the Gemma Augustea (Hannestad, *Roman Art,* 78–82, with fig. 51) shows Augustus and Dea Roma seated side by side on a single throne. The double-throne, called a *bisellium* (Varro *De lingua Latina* 5.128; Neumann, "Bisellium," PW 3:502), was a well-known image in the ancient world. Markschies ("'Sessio ad Dexteram,'" 260–65) has collected references to some of the many instances of two deities enthroned on a *bisellium,* including Zeus and Hera (*LIMC,* IV.1, 684; IV.2, 415 [plate 206], 416 [plate 208], Hades and Persephone (*LIMC,* IV.1, 378 = IV.2, 213 [plate 58]; IV.2, 220 [plate 126]), Despoina and Demeter (Pausanias 8.37.4), and Demeter and Kore (*LIMC,* IV.1, 866–67; IV.2, 578 [plates 253, 256, 259]; IV.1, 865; IV.2, 581 [plates 287–90]). The theological significance of this use of a *bisellium* in 3:21 is the equality that it presumes between those who share such a throne.

**21b**   ὡς κἀγὼ ἐνίκησα καὶ ἐκάθισα μετὰ τοῦ πατρός μου ἐν τῷ θρόνῳ αὐτοῦ, "just as I also conquered and sat with my Father on his throne." This is an allusion to Ps

110:1, one of the most important OT messianic texts in the early Church (see Hay, *Psalm 110;* M. Hengel, "'Setze dich zu meiner Rechten!' Die Inthronisation Christi zur Rechten Gottes und Psalm 110,1,'" in *Le Trône de Dieu,* ed. M. Philonenko [Tübingen: Mohr-Siebeck, 1993] 108–94). Allusions to Ps 110:1 may also be present, though less obviously so, in Rev 12:5 (where the male child is "caught to God and to his throne") and 22:1, 3 (where the phrase "the throne of God and of the Lamb" occurs twice). A distinctive feature of this allusion to Ps 110:1 is that it is placed in the mouth of the exalted Jesus (for similar first-person accounts of the *sessio ad dextram dei* [i.e., "the session at the right hand of God"], see *Apoc. Pet.* 6 and *Ap. Jas.* 14.30–31). It is striking that the theologoumenon of Christ's exaltation to the right hand of God, so common in early Christianity, is hardly mentioned in Revelation, and so few possible allusions to Ps 110:1 occur in the book. One group of MSS of Ethiopic Enoch (Eth I) reads "And the Elect One shall in those days sit on my throne" (*1 Enoch* 51:3); the other major family (Eth II) reads "on his·[i.e., 'the Elect One's'] throne" (see Black, *Enoch,* 214; Knibb, *Enoch* 2:135). *1 Enoch* 55:4, however, states that powerful kings will see "my Chosen One sit down on the throne of my glory and judge in the name of the Lord of Spirits" (see 61:8). Other passages in *1 Enoch* simply state that "the Chosen One will sit on the throne of glory" (45:3) or "the Chosen One will sit on his throne" (51:3). Wis 9:4 reads "Give me the wisdom that sits by your throne [τὴν τῶν θρόνων πάρεδρον σοφίαν]" (here θρόνων is probably a plural of majesty; see Winston, *Wisdom,* 202).

**22** ὁ ἔχων οὖς ἀκουσάτω τί τὸ πνεῦμα λέγει ταῖς ἐκκλησίαις, "Let the one who has an ear hear what the Spirit declares to the churches." See *Comment* on 2:7.

### Explanation

Laodicea was located forty miles southeast of Philadelphia, was destroyed in an earthquake in A.D. 60 (*Sib. Or.* 5.290–91), and was subsequently rebuilt (*Sib. Or.* 4.107–8). An imperial temple was constructed after the quake. It was the most important city in the Lycus valley, where two other cities also contained Christian communities, Hierapolis and Colossae (Col 4:13). Probably the city and certainly the surrounding area had a large Jewish population (Cicero *Pro Flac.* 28.68; Jos. *Ant.* 12.147–53). Unlike the other letters, the attributes of Christ enumerated in the introduction, Amen, the faithful and true witness, and the beginning of God's creation (an allusion to Col 1:15?), are not drawn from the Patmos vision in 1:9–20. The community is condemned for being neither cold nor hot but lukewarm (vv 15–16). This metaphor for ineffectiveness may be drawn from the region's water supply. While the "hot" springs of Hierapolis were famous for their medicinal properties, the "cold" water of Colossae was prized for its purity. The tepid waters of Laodicea, however, were both abundant and bad.

Though the church thinks herself rich and lacking nothing, it is actually "wretched, pitiable, poor, blind, and naked" (v 17). To remedy this deplorable spiritual state, they require "gold" refined by the fires of testing and patient endurance, "white garments" of purity, and "eye salve" to restore their sight (v 18). Laodicea was in fact the site of a medical school, which apparently had a secret recipe for an effective and widely known eye salve (Galen *De san. tuend.* 6.12).

The famous metaphor of Christ standing at the door and knocking (v 20) has been explained as an allusion to Cant 5:2 or to a modified saying of Jesus found in

Luke 12:35–38 (see Mark 13:33–37). Greco-Roman revelatory magic had a special procedure for enlisting the services of a *paredros daimon,* or "assisting divinity," which involved preparing a meal and sharing it with the god (e.g., *PGM* I.1–42, 42–95, 96–195; IV.1840–70). This procedure is parodied here, for it is the risen Jesus who is in control of the situation, not the practitioner. The victorious Christians will be able to sit with Christ upon his throne (using the metaphor of the *bisellium,* or "double-throne"), just as Christ sat upon the throne of his Father (v 21), another reference to sharing Christ's reign (see 2:26–27).

*Excursus 3A: The Sayings of Jesus in Revelation*

### Bibliography

**Aune, D. E.** "Christian Prophets and the Sayings of Jesus." In *Prophecy in Early Christianity and the Ancient Mediterranean World.* Grand Rapids, MI: Eerdmans, 1983. 233–45. **Bauckham, R.** "Synoptic Parousia Parables and the Apocalypse." *NTS* 23 (1977) 162–76. **Boring, M. E.** "The Apocalypse as Christian Prophecy." In *Society of Biblical Literature 1974 Seminar Papers,* ed. G. MacRae. Missoula, MT: Scholars, 1974. 2:43–62. ———. *The Continuing Voice of Jesus: Christian Prophecy and the Gospel Tradition.* Louisville: Westminster/John Knox, 1991. ———. *Sayings of the Risen Jesus: Christian Prophecy in the Synoptic Tradition.* Cambridge: Cambridge UP, 1982. **Bultmann, R.** *History.* **Dunn, J. D. G.** "Prophetic 'I'-Sayings and the Jesus Tradition: The Importance of Testing Prophetic Utterances within Early Christianity." *NTS* 24 (1978) 175–98. **Hill, D.** "On the Evidence for the Creative Role of Christian Prophets." *NTS* 20 (1974) 262–74. **Neugebauer, F.** "Geistsprüche und Jesuslogien." *ZNW* 53 (1962) 218–28. **Vos, L. A.** *Synoptic Traditions.*

Statements attributed to the exalted Jesus are frequently quoted in Revelation. Some of these resemble sayings of Jesus found in the synoptic Gospels. Did John know one or more of the written Gospels or oral Jesus traditions that were eventually incorporated into the Synoptic tradition and re-present them as sayings of the exalted Jesus? Or, does the fact that John is a prophet who mediates words of the exalted Jesus suggest one way that some sayings of Jesus entered into the Synoptic tradition, i.e., not as sayings preserved from the historical Jesus but as prophetic sayings of the risen Lord mediated by early Christian prophets?

The most detailed study of the subject is that of L. A. Vos. While all the possible sayings of Jesus in Revelation must be classified as allusions rather than quotations, Vos contends that some uses of the sayings of Jesus in Revelation are more direct than others. He argues that the more direct allusions are located primarily in the first three chapters. He finds eight sayings of Jesus reflected in direct allusions, some used more than once: 1:3a (Luke 11:28); 1:7 (Matt 24:30); 2:7, etc. (7x; Matt 11:15; 13:9; etc.); 3:2–3; 16:15 (Matt 24:42–43 = Luke 12:39–40); 3:5c (Matt 10:32 = Luke 12:8); 3:20 (Mark 13:29; Matt 24:33; cf. Luke 12:35ff.); 3:21 (Luke 22:28–30; Matt 19:28); 13:10b (Matt 26:52b). Vos does not think that John was familiar with a written Gospel or Gospels. Regarding early Christian prophetic activity and the Jesus traditions, Vos does not believe that utterances of the risen Jesus through prophets were assimilated to the sayings tradition. Quite the reverse. John adapted "the current sayings of Jesus as a mediatory means for the expression of his prophecy" (Vos, *Synoptic Traditions,* 224).

Vos occupies a mediating position in comparison with R. H. Charles and H. B. Swete. Charles, who thinks that John was familiar with the Gospels of Matthew and Luke, has perhaps the longest list of possible allusions (twenty-six; see 1:lxxxii–lxxxvi). A more conservative list is proposed by H. B. Swete (clvi–clvii), who lists just four certain allusions:

3:3 (Matt 24:43); 3:5 (Matt 10:32); 13:10 (Matt 26:52); 21:6 and 22:17 (John 4:10; 7:37), in addition to the phrase "the one who has an ear, let him hear," found eight times.

The sayings of the exalted Jesus in Revelation that have the strongest claim for being derived from the tradition of the sayings of Jesus are four in number, found in eleven texts: (1) Rev 1:3; cf. 22:7 (Luke 11:28), (2) the "He who has an ear let him hear" saying, found eight times (2:7, 11, 17, 29; 3:6, 13, 22; 13:9), (3) Rev 3:3; 16:15 (Matt 24:43–44), (4) Rev 3:5 (Matt 10:32 = Luke 12:28; Mark 8:28 = Luke 9:26). A comparison of these texts with the Synoptic texts they resemble does not indicate that John was personally familiar with written texts of any of the canonical Gospels. Yet that possibility cannot be absolutely excluded, particularly in view of the loose and fluid way in which early Christian authors quoted and alluded to both OT and NT texts during the late first and early second centuries A.D. Drawing together the discussions of each of these texts (see *Comment* under each text), it appears that John's intentional allusions to the tradition of the sayings of Jesus presuppose that such traditions had a firm place in the liturgy of the early Christian communities in Anatolia. The authority of these texts was so well established that John was able to use allusions to them to authenticate the written presentation of his own revelatory encounter with the exalted Jesus. However, it is not necessary to suppose that these allusions were primarily the result of a fully conscious literary artifice. Rather, they appear to have been drawn from the distinctive modes of speech that entered into Christian discourse from both the Gospel texts themselves and the oral traditions within which such texts were transmitted.

# III. The Disclosure of God's Eschatological Plan  (4:1–22:9)

## A. John's Heavenly Ascent  (4:1–2a)

## B. The Sovereignty of God, the Investiture of the Lamb, and the First Six Seals  (4:2b–7:17)

### 1. Vision of the Heavenly Throne Room  (4:2b–5:14)

#### a. The Heavenly Worship of God  (4:2b–11)

*Bibliography*

**Baird, W.** "Visions, Revelations and Ministry." *JBL* 104 (1985) 651–62. **Bauckham, R.** "The Eschatological Earthquake." In Bauckham, *Climax.* 199–209. **Baumgarten, J. M.** "The Duodecimal Courts of Qumran, Revelation, and the Sanhedrin." *JBL* 95 (1976) 59–78. **Baumstark, A.** "Trishagion und Queduscha." *Jahrbücher für Liturgiewissenschaft* 3 (1923) 18–32. **Beal, G. K.** "The Problem of the Man from the Sea in IV Ezra 13 and Its Relation to the Messianic Concept in John's Apocalypse." *NovT* 25 (1983) 182–88. **Bietenhard, H.** *Die himmlische Welt im Urchristentum und Spätjudentum.* Tübingen: Mohr-Siebeck, 1951. **Bousset, W.** "Die Himmelsreise der Seele." *ARW* 4 (1901) 136–69, 229–73. **Brewer, R. R.** "The Influence of Greek Drama on the Apocalypse of John." *ATR* 18 (1936) 74–92. ———. "Rev 4:6 and Translations Thereof." *JBL* 71 (1952) 227–32. **Brown, J. P.** "Archery in the Ancient World: 'Its Name Is Life, Its Work Is Death.'" *BZ* 37 (1993) 26–42. **Cabaniss, A.** "A Note on the Liturgy of the Apocalypse." *Int* 7 (1953) 78–86. **Cross, F. M.** "The Council of Yahweh in Second Isaiah." *JNES* 12 (1953) 274–77. **Culianu, I. P.** *Psychanodia: Vol 1. A Survey of the Evidence concerning the Ascension of the Soul and Its Relevance.* EPRO 99. Leiden: Brill, 1983. **Dean-Otting, M.** *Heavenly Journeys: A Study of the Motif in Hellenistic Jewish Literature.* Frankfurt: Lang, 1984. **Delling, G.** "Zum gottesdienstlichen Stil der Johannesapokalypse." *NovT* 3 (1959) 107–37. **Dieterich, A.** *Eine Mithrasliturgie.* 3rd ed. Leipzig: Teubner, 1923. **Engnell, I.** *The Call of Isaiah.* Uppsala: Almqvist & Wiksel, 1949. **Feuillet, A.** "Les vingt-quatre vieillards de l'Apocalypse." *RB* 65 (1958) 5–32. **Fiensy, D. A.** *Prayers Alleged to Be Jewish: An Examination of the Constitutiones Apostolorum.* BJS 65. Chico, CA: Scholars, 1985. **Flowers, H. J.** "The Vision of Revelation IV–V." *ATR* 12 (1930) 525–30. **Flusser, D.** "Jewish Roots of the Liturgical Trisagion." *Immanuel* 3 (1973–74) 37–43. ———. "Sanktus und Gloria." In *Abraham unser Vater.* FS O. Michel, ed. O. Betz, M. Hengel, and P. Schmidt. Leiden: Brill, 1963. 129–52. **Gangemi, A.** "La struttura liturgica dei capitoli 4 e 5 dell'Apocalisse di S. Giovanni." *Ecclesia Orans* 4 (1987) 301–58. **Giblet, J.** "De visione templi coelestis in Apoc. IV,1–11." *Collectanea Mechliniensia* 43 (1958) 593–97. **Goodenough, E. R.** "Greek Garments on Jewish Heroes." In *Biblical Motifs,* ed. A. Altmann. Cambridge: Harvard UP, 1966. 221–37. **Grosjean, P.** "Les vingt-quatre vieillards de l'Apocalypse: A propos d'une liste galloise."

*AnBoll* 72 (1954) 192–212. **Gruenwald, I.** *Apocalyptic and Merkavah Mysticism.* Leiden: Brill, 1980. **Hagg, E.** "Die Himmelfahrt des Elias nach 2 Kg, 1–15." *TTZ* 78 (1969) 18–32. **Hall, R. G.** "Living Creatures in the Midst of the Throne: Another Look at Revelation 4.6." *NTS* 36 (1990) 609–13. **Halperin, D. L.** "Ascension or Invasion: Implications of the Heavenly Journey in Ancient Judaism." *Religion* 18 (1988) 47–67. ———. *The Faces of the Chariot: Early Jewish Responses to Ezekiel's Vision.* Tübingen: Mohr-Siebeck, 1987. ———. "Heavenly Ascension in Ancient Judaism: The Nature of the Experience." In *Society of Biblical Literature 1987 Seminar Papers,* ed. K. H. Richards. Atlanta: Scholars, 1987. 218–32. ———. *The Merkavah in Rabbinic Literature.* New Haven: American Oriental Society, 1980. **Heinemann, J.** *Prayer in the Talmud.* Berlin; New York: de Gruyter, 1977. **Himmelfarb, M.** "Apocalyptic Ascent and the Heavenly Temple." In *Society of Biblical Literature 1987 Seminar Papers,* ed. K. H. Richards. Atlanta: Scholars, 1987. 210–17. **Hommel, P.** "Giebel und Himmel." *IM* 5 (1955) 11–55. ———. *Studien zu den römischen Figurengiebeln der Kaiserzeit.* Berlin, 1954. **Hubbell, C. G.** "The Preparation of the Heavens for Judgment (Rev 4)." *New Church Review* 7 (1900) 446–53. **Hurtado, L. W.** "Revelation 4–5 in the Light of Jewish Apocalyptic Analogies." *JSNT* 25 (1985) 105–24. **Keel, O.** *Yahweh-Visionen und Siegelkunst: Eine neue Deutung der Majestätsschilderungen in Jes 6, Ez 1 und 10 und Sach 4.* Stuttgart: Katholisches Bibelwerk, 1977. **Kilpatrick, G. D.** "Style and Text in the Greek New Testament." In *Studies in the History and Text of the New Testament in Honor of Kenneth Willis Clark,* ed. B. L. Daniels and M. J. Suggs. Salt Lake City: University of Utah, 1967. 153–60. **Leiser, B. M.** "The Trisagion of Isaiah's Vision." *NTS* 6 (1960–61) 261–63. **Lentzen-Deis, F.** "Das Motiv der 'Himmelsöffnung' in verschiedenen Gattungen der Umweltliteratur des Neuen Testaments." *Bib* 50 (1969) 301–27. ———. *Die Taufe Jesu nach den Synoptikern: Literarische und gattungsgeschichtliche Untersuchungen.* Frankfurt am Main: Knecht, 1970. **MacCormack, S.** *Art and Ceremony in Late Antiquity.* Berkeley: University of California, 1981. **Maier, J.** "Das Gefährdungsmotiv bei der Himmelsreise in der jüdischen Apokalyptik und 'Gnosis.'" *Kairos* 5 (1963) 18–40. **Martin, A.** *La titulature épigraphique de Domitien.* Beiträge zur klassichen Philologie 181. Frankfurt am Main: Athenäum, 1987. **McCurdy, G. H.** "Traces of the Influence of Plato's Eschatological Myths in Parts of the Book of Revelation and the Book of Enoch." *TAPA* 41 (1910) 65–70. **McKay, K. J.** "Door Magic and the Epiphany Hymn." *CQ* 17 (1967) 184–94. **McKenzie, J. L.** "The Elders in the OT." *Bib* 40 (1959) 522–40. **Metzger, M.** *Königsthron und Gottesthron: Thronformen und Throndarstellungen in Ägypten und im Vorderen Orient.* Neukirchen: Neukirchener, 1985. **Michael, J. H.** "Ten Thousand Times Ten Thousand." *ExpTim* 46 (1934–35) 567. **Michl, J.** *Die Engelvorstellung in der Apokalypse.* Munich: Heuber, 1937. ———. *Die 24 Ältesten in der apokalypse des hl. Johannes.* Munich: Heuber, 1938. **Morray-Jones, C. R. A.** "Paradise Revisited (2 Cor 12:1–12): The Jewish Mystical Background of Paul's Apostolate." *HTR* 86 (1993) 177–217. **Mourelatos, A. P. D.** *The Route of Parmenides.* New Haven: Yale UP, 1970. **Mowry, L.** "Revelation 4–5 and Early Christian Liturgical Usage." *JBL* 71 (1952) 75–84. **Mullen, E. T.** *The Divine Council in Canaanite and Early Hebrew Literature.* HSM 24. Chico, CA: Scholars, 1980. **Müller, C. D. G.** *Die Engellehre der koptischen Kirche.* Wiesbaden: Harrassowitz, 1959. **Neef, H.-D.** *Gottes himmlischer Thronrat: Hintergrund und Bedeutung von sôd JHWH im Alten Testament.* Stuttgart: Calwer, 1994. **Neuenzeit, P.** "'Ich will dir zeigen, was geschen muss' (Apok 4,1): Zum Problem der Tragik im neutestamentlichen Existenzverständnis." *BibLeb* 1 (1960) 223–36. **Nickelsburg, G. W. E.** "Enoch, Levi and Peter: Recipients of Revelation in Upper Galilee." *JBL* 100 (1981) 575–600. **Niditch, S.** "The Visionary." In *Ideal Figures in Ancient Judaism,* ed. G. W. E. Nickelsburg and J. J. Collins. Missoula, MT: Scholars, 1980. **Oster, R.** "The Ephesian Artemis as an Opponent of Early Christianity." *JAC* 19 (1976) 24–44. ———. "Numismatic Windows in the Social World of Early Christianity: A Methodological Inquiry." *JBL* 101 (1982) 195–223. **Peterson, E.** *Das Buch von den Engeln: Stellung und Bedeutung der heiligen Engel im Kultus.* Leipzig: Hegner, 1935. ———. "Der himmlische Lobgesang in Kap. 4 und 5 der Geheimen Offenbarung." *Liturgisches Leben* 7 (1934) 297–306. **Pietersma, A.,** et al., eds. and trs. *The Apocalypse of Elijah: Based on P. Chester Beatty 2018.* Atlanta: Scholars, 1981. **Price, M. J.,** and **Trell, B. L.** *Coins and Their Cities: Architecture on the Ancient Coins of Greece, Rome and Palestine.* London, 1977. **Rinaldi, G.** "La Porta Aperta nel Cielo (Ap 4:11)." *CBQ* 25 (1963) 336–47. **Robinson, H. W.** "The Council of Yahweh." *JTS* 45 (1944) 151–57. **Ross, J. M.** "Some Unnoticed Points in the Text of the New Testament." *NovT* 25 (1983) 59–72. **Rowland, C.** "The Visions of God in Apocalyptic Literature." *JSS* 10 (1980) 137–54. **Sauter, F.** *Der römische Kaiserkult bei Martial und Statius.* Stuttgart; Berlin: Kohlhammer, 1934. **Schäfer, P.** "New Testament and Hekhalot Literature: The Journey into Heaven in Paul and in Merkabah Mysticism." *JJS* 35 (1984) 19–35. **Schmitt, A.** *Entrückung-Aufnahme-Himmelfahrt.* Stuttgart: Katholisches Bibelwerk, 1973. **Scholem, G. G.** *Jewish Gnosticism, Merkabah Mysticism, and Talmudic Tradition.* 2nd ed. New York: Jewish Theological Seminary of America, 1965. ———. *Major Trends in Jewish Mysticism.* 2nd ed. New York: Schocken, 1954. **Schweizer, E.** "Die sieben Geister in der Apokalypse." *EvT* 11 (1951–52) 502–12. **Scoralick, R.** *Trishagion und Gottesherschaft: Psalm 99 als Neuinterpretation von Tora und Propheten.* Stuttgart: KBW, 1989. **Segal, A. F.** "Heavenly Ascent in Hellenistic Judaism, Early Christianity and Their Environment." *ANRW* II, 23:1333–94. ———. *Paul the Convert.* New Haven; London: Yale UP, 1990. 34–71. **Seitz, C. R.** "The Divine Council: Temporal Transition and New Prophecy in the Book of Isaiah." *JBL* 109 (1990) 229–47. **Skinjar, A.** "Vigintiquattuor seniores." *VD* 16 (1936) 333–38, 361–68. **Spinks, B. D.** "The Jewish Sources for the Sanctus." *HeyJ* 21 (1980) 168–79. ———. *The Sanctus in the Eucharistic Prayer.* Cambridge: Cambridge UP, 1991. **Tabor, J. D.** *Things Unutterable: Paul's Ascent to Paradise in Its Greco-Roman, Judaic, and Early Christian Contexts.* Lanham: University Press of America, 1986. **Taran, L.** *Parmenides: A Text with Translation, Commentary, and Critical Essays.* Princeton: Princeton UP, 1965. **Trell, B. L.** "A Further Study in Architectura Numismatica." In *Essays in Memory of Karl Lehman,* ed. L. F. Sandler. New York, 1964. ———. *The Temple of Artemis at Ephesos.* New York, 1945. **Unnik, W. C. van.** "Die 'Geöffneten Himmel' in der Offenbarungsvision des Apokryphons des Johannes." In *Apophoreta.* FS E. Haenchen, ed. W. Eltester. Berlin: Töpelmann, 1964. ———. "1 Clement 34 and the Sanctus." *VC* 5 (1951) 204–48. **VanderKam, J. C.,** and **Milik, J. T.** "The First *Jubilees* Manuscript from Qumran Cave 4: A Preliminary Publication." *JBL* 110 (1991) 243–70. **Walker, N.** "The Origin of the 'Thrice-Holy.'" *NTS* 5 (1959–60) 132–33. **Weinreich, O.** "Türöffnung im Wunder- Prodogien- und Zauberglauben der Antike, des Judentums und Christentums." *TBA* 5 (1929) 200–464. **Werner, E.** "The Doxology in Synagogue and Church: A Liturgico-Musical Study." *HUCA* 19 (1945–46) 276–328. ———. *The Sacred Bridge: Liturgical Parallels in Synagogue and Early Church.* New York: Schocken, 1970. **Yarbro Collins, A.** "The Seven Heavens in Jewish and Christian Apocalypses." In *Cosmology and Eschatology in Jewish and Christian Apocalypticism.* Leiden: Brill, 1996. 21–54. **Zahn, T.** "Die Tiersymbole der Evangelisten." In *Forschungen zur Geschichte des neutestamentlichen Kanons.* Leipzig: Erlangen, 1888–1929. 2:257–75.

## Translation

[1]*After this I saw, and behold,* [a]*a door was opened* [a] *in heaven, and* [b]*the first voice which I heard like a trumpet* [c]*spoke to me:*[dc] [e]*"Come up* [e] *here, and I will reveal to you what must happen after this."* [2a]*Immediately* [b] *I was in* [c] *a prophetic trance,*[c] *and behold a throne was situated* [d] *in heaven, and someone* [e] *was seated* [f] *upon* [g]*the throne.*[g] [3a]*The one seated* [ab] *there was like jasper* [c]*and carnelian* [d] [e]*in appearance,*[e] *and a rainbow* [f] *encircled the throne* [g]*like emerald* [e]*in appearance.*[eg] [4ab]*Twenty-four thrones* [b] *encircled that throne, and on the thrones sat* [c]*twenty-four elders dressed in* [d] *white* [e] *robes with gold crowns on their heads.* [5]*From* [a] *the throne came lightning and rumbling and thunder, and seven blazing torches (* [b]*which are* [b] *the* [c] *seven spirits of God) were burning before the throne.*[d] [6]*There was also before the throne* [a]*something like* [a] *a glassy* [b] *sea like crystal.*

<sup>cd</sup>*In the midst of the throne* <sup>c</sup> *and around the throne* <sup>d</sup> *were four cherubim* <sup>e</sup> *covered with eyes on the front and on the back.*

7
> *And the first cherub was like a lion,*
> *and the second cherub was like an ox,*
> *and the third cherub had* <sup>a</sup> *a* <sup>b</sup> <sup>c</sup>*face like a human,*<sup>c</sup>
> *and the fourth cherub* <sup>d</sup> *was like a flying eagle.*

<sup>8</sup>*And the* <sup>a</sup> *four cherubim, each of whom* <sup>b</sup> *had* <sup>c</sup> *six wings, were covered with eyes on the outside* <sup>d</sup>*and on the inside,*<sup>d</sup> *and day and night they did not cease chanting,* <sup>e</sup>

> <sup>f</sup>*"Holy, holy, holy, Lord* <sup>g</sup> *God Almighty,*<sup>f</sup>
> *Who was and Who is and is the One who comes."*

<sup>9</sup>*And when* <sup>a</sup> *the cherubim give* <sup>b</sup> *glory and honor and thanksgiving to the One seated upon* <sup>c</sup>*the throne* <sup>c</sup> *who lives for ever and ever,* <sup>d</sup> <sup>10</sup> *the twenty-four elders* <sup>a</sup>*prostrate themselves before the One sitting on the throne and they worship* <sup>b</sup> *the One who lives for ever and ever,* <sup>c</sup> *and* <sup>d</sup>*they cast* <sup>d</sup> *their garlands before the throne, chanting,*

11
> *"Worthy are you, our Lord* <sup>a</sup> *and* <sup>b</sup> *God,*<sup>ac</sup>
> *To receive* <sup>d</sup>*glory and honor and power,*<sup>d</sup>
> *Because you created* <sup>e</sup> <sup>f</sup>*all things*
> *And by your will they* <sup>gh</sup>*existed,* <sup>i</sup>*yes* <sup>h</sup> *were created."* <sup>i</sup>

### Notes

1.a-a. Variants: (1) θύρα ἠνεῳγμένη] ℵ A (lacuna in C) 025 Andr a b d g l¹⁷⁷⁸ n⁻²⁴²⁹ 598 Byzantine. (2) θύρα ἀνεῳγμένη] 046 0169ᶜᵒʳʳ fam 1006¹⁰⁰⁶ ¹⁸⁴¹ fam 1611¹⁸⁵⁴ Andr c e f h i l¹⁶⁷⁸ ⁻²⁰⁸⁰ n²⁴²⁹ 94 1773 2019 2351. (3) θύραν ἀνεῳγμένην] 0169* (corrected to θύρα ἀνεῳγμένη). (4) θύρα ἐν τῷ οὐρανῷ ἠνεῳγμένη] Oecumenius²⁰⁵³.

1.b. Variant: insert ἰδού] ℵ fam 1611²³⁴⁴ 94 itᵖ Primasius (omits *et*); Cassiodorus.

1.c-c. Variants: (1) λαλούσης μετ' ἐμοῦ] *lectio originalis*. (2) λεγούσης μετ' ἐμοῦ] Andr e²⁰²⁶ h. (3) μετ' ἐμοῦ λέγουσα] cop ˢᵃ ᵐˢˢ. (4) μετ' ἐμοῦ λαλοῦσα] fam 1611²³²⁹. (5) λαλοῦσα μετ' ἐμοῦ] Oecumenius²⁰⁵³ Byz 3⁵²² Andr l. (6) λαλοῦσαν μετ' ἐμοῦ] ℵ Byz 17⁴⁶⁹ itᵍⁱᵍ Primasius Ambrose. On the idiom λαλεῖν μετ' ἐμοῦ, see *Notes* on 1:12. In reading (1), the *lectio difficilior* and the reading with the best MS attestation, λαλούσης (present fem. gen. sing. ptcp.), "speaking, spoke," is a solecism since it has been attracted to the case of σάλπιγγος, "trumpet," though it should modify ἡ φωνή, "the voice," and should have the form λαλοῦσα (a nom. sing. fem. present ptcp.), either reading (4) or (5). This has a grammatical parallel in LXX Ezek 43:6: "And behold a voice from the house speaking to me" (καὶ ἰδοὺ φωνὴ ἐκ τοῦ οἴκου λαλοῦντος πρός με); here λαλοῦντος, which should modify φωνή, has been attracted to the case and gender of οἴκου. Similarly, in *T. Abr.* (Rec. B) 3:3, "And they heard a voice speaking from its branches" (ἤκουον δὲ φωνὴν ἐκ τῶν κλάδων αὐτῆς λεγούσης), λεγούσης has been attracted to the case of αὐτῆς, though it should have the form λέγουσαν. For other examples of the *constructio ad sensum*, see *Notes* on 9:13; 11:15.

The peculiar phrase λαλούσης μετ' ἐμοῦ λέγων, involving two different verbs of speaking (on λαλεῖν μετ' + gen., see *Notes* on 1:12), has close parallels in 10:8; 17:1; 21:9.

1.d. Variants: (1) λέγων] A (lacuna in C) ℵ* 0169 Andr i²⁰⁴² l⁻¹⁷⁷⁸ Byzantine. (2) λέγουσα] ℵ¹ Andreas. (3) καί λέγουσαν μοι] Andr n²⁴²⁹ 2019. (4) omit] fam 1611¹⁸⁵⁴ ²³²⁹. Reading (1), the masc. form of the ptcp., is an *ad sensum* construction also found in 9:13; 11:15 (see *Notes* on both passages); see Schmid, *Studien* 2:236. The ptcp. λαλῶν, "saying," is omitted in the translation as redundant, since it is a Hebraism that functions like ὅτι *recitative* to introduce direct speech. The ptcp. λέγων, "saying," is frequently used redundantly in Revelation following other verbs of saying, and not in congruence with the case of the noun it should modify; i.e., syntactically it is an anacolouthon or solecism (see Rev 4:8; 5:12; 11:15). Since λέγων modifies ἡ φωνή, "the voice," it should be expressed as the fem. nom. form λέγουσα, "saying." These two features indicate that this is an intentional Hebraism on the part of the author in which the term לֵאמֹר *lē'mōr*, "so as to say," is used to introduce direct speech corresponding to the more conventional Gk. use of ὅτι, "that" (D. Tabachovitz, *Die Septuaginta und das Neue Testament* [Lund: Gleerup, 1956] 12–13, 18). The following examples of λέγων/λέγοντες in the LXX illustrate this incongruity: Gen 15:1, 4; 22:20; 38:13, 24; Exod 18:6; 45:16; Lev 8:31; 2 Kgdms 15:31; 3 Kgdms 1:51;

20:9 (MT: 21:9). A close parallel is found in *T. Abr.* (Rec. A) 10:12: "and immediately a voice [φωνή] came from heaven to the Archistrategos saying [λέγων] thus" (here λέγων, a solecism, should have the form λεγοῦσα). λέγων here may be construed as a nom. of apposition, separated by six words from the noun it modifies, just as in Rev 4:1 φωνή and λέγων are separated by nine words.

1.e-e. Variant: ἀνάβητι] A. Scribal correction; in the second-person sing. aor. imper., the endings -βα and -βητι are the apocopated and unapocopated forms, respectively, and alternate in usage (Moulton-Howard, *Accidence*, 210).

2.a. Variants: (1) omit καί before εὐθέως] ℵ A 0169* fam 1006¹⁰⁰⁶ ¹⁸⁴¹ fam 1611¹⁶¹¹ ²⁰⁵⁰ ²³²⁹ Oecumenius²⁰⁵³ Andr i²⁰⁴² Andr n²⁰⁶⁵ Byzantine. (2) καί before εὐθέως] 0169ᶜᵒʳʳ fam 1611¹⁸⁵⁴ ²³⁴⁴ Andreas itᵍⁱᵍ vgᶜˡ syrᵖʰ Primasius Victorinus Apringius. (3) εὐθέως δέ] ℵ* Byz 1²⁰²⁷. The insertion of καί in reading (2) has very weak MS support and is certainly secondary. Since 245 of the 337 sentences in Revelation (73.79 percent) begin with καί, there would be a strong harmonizing tendency to insert καί at the beginning of sentences where it was lacking. εὐθέως occurs only here in Revelation. Of the thirty-six times where εὐθέως occurs elsewhere in the NT, in most instances it is used at the beginning of sentences or clauses; the phrase καὶ εὐθέως occurs eighteen times, and εὐθέως is used with δέ seven times in the NT.

2.b. εὐθέως, "immediately," is one of only three adjectival adverbs ending with -ως in Revelation (the others include ὁμοίως, "similarly," 2:15; 8:12; πνευματικῶς, "spiritually, prophetically," 11:8 (Mussies, *Morphology*, 137, 350).

2.c-c. Variant: τῷ before πνεύματι] (0169; sufficient space before abbreviation πνι for the definite article) arm.

2.d. The impf. verb ἔκειτο, "situated," has no contrasting aor. form and so cannot be distinguished either semantically or temporally from the aor. tense; it therefore functions as a neutral past tense.

2.e. Variant: ὁ before ἐπί] ℵ* Andr/Byz 2b*. 

2.f. Variant: καθήμενον] 0169 fam 1611²³²⁹ Andr/Byz 4a⁶¹⁶ Primasius. The present ptcp. καθήμενος, "sitting," is used here as a finite verb (see 4:4; 14:14; for other examples in Revelation, see Mussies, *Morphology*, 325).

2.g-g. Variant: τοῦ θρόνου] Andreas.

3.a-a. Variants: (1) καὶ ὁ καθήμενος] ℵ A (lacuna in C) 025 046 0169 fam 1611¹⁶¹¹ ²⁰⁵⁰ ²³²⁹ 2351 latt syr cop. (2) omit καὶ ὁ καθήμενος] Andreas Byzantine. Reading (2) is an error of haplography; the previous word is καθήμενος (Schmid, *Studien* 2:73).

3.b. Variant: after καθήμενος add ἐπὶ τὸν θρόνον: 0169ᶜᵒʳʳ (inserted by a later hand in small letters above the line); copˢᵃ ᵇᵒ.

3.c. Variant: καὶ σμαράγδῳ] 0462; Byz 15.

3.d. Variant: σαρδίνῳ] fam 1611¹⁶¹¹ ¹⁸⁵⁴.

3.e-e. The term ὁράσει (which occurs twice in this verse) is a dat. of respect (BDR § 197).

3.f. Variants: ἱερεῖς] ℵ* A (hiatus in C) fam 1611²³²⁹ Andr i arm⁴ eth. Here ἱερεῖς, "priests," makes no sense and may have arisen by misunderstanding κυκλόθεν on analogy with the use of κυκλόθεν in v 4, where it is used of twenty-four thrones and twenty-four elders (Zahn, 1:319 n. 4), or simply as an itacistic scribal error (Schmid, *Studien* 2:73).

3.g-g. Variants: (1) ὅμοιος ὁράσει σμαραγδίνῳ] ℵ² A Oecumenius²⁰⁵³ fam 1611²³⁴⁴ Andreas lat copˢᵃ ᵇᵒ. (2) ὁμοίως ὅρασις σμαραγδίνων] fam 1006 2351 Byzantine. (3) ὁμοίως ὡς ὅρασις σμαράγδου] Andr l¹⁶⁷⁸ ¹⁷⁷⁸. Since the antecedent of ὅμοιος is ἶρις (a fem. sing. noun), the appropriate form should be ὅμοια (fem. sing. adj.). Since the adverb ὁμοίως, like ὡς, does not reflect the gender and case of its antecedent, ὅμοιος was corrected to ὁμοίως in readings (2) and (3).

4.a. Variant: omit καί] 046 fam 1006¹⁰⁰⁶ ¹⁸⁴¹ Andr i²⁰⁴² Andr l¹⁶⁷⁸ ¹⁷⁷⁸ Byzantine syrʰ.

4.b-b. Variants: (1) θρόνοι εἴκοσι τέσσαρες] 2351 Andreas Byzantine; WHort; von Soden, *Text*; Bousset (1906) 245; Merk, *NT*. (2) θρόνους εἴκοσι τέσσαρες] ℵ A (lacuna in C) Oecumenius²⁰⁵³ (θρόνους κδ); Andr l; Andr/Byz 4a²⁵⁰; Tischendorf, *NT Graece*; B. Weiss, *Johannes-Apokalypse*, 168; Charles, 1:115; UBSGNT⁴; Nestle-Aland²⁷. (3) θρόνους εἴκοσι τέσσαρας] Andr f²⁰⁷³ n²⁴²⁹. (4) εἴκοσι τέσσαρας θρόνους] conjecture by Charles, 2:262 (elsewhere in Revelation εἴκοσι τέσσαρες is placed before its noun, e.g., 4:4b, 10; 5:8; 11:16, with the exception of 19:4). The pl. masc. acc. θρόνους in reading (1) signals a break in the syntax, since καὶ ἰδού in v 2 is always followed by substantives in the nom. case (if θρόνους is original, the author probably sees it as the obj. of εἶδον in v 1). θρόνους, however, is just the first of a string of accs., εἴκοσι τέσσαρας πρεσβυτέρους καθημένους περιβεβλημένους, so that there is incongruence in this sentence regarding whether θρόνους or θρόνοι is the original reading. Some scholars have suggested that this verse is an addition, either by a later hand (J. Weiss, *Offenbarung*, 54) or by that of the author himself in a revision of a vision composed earlier (Charles, 1:115–16). Yet this assumption is problematic since then the twenty-four elders would suddenly appear in v 10 (n.b. that οἱ εἴκοσι τέσσαρες πρεσβύτεροι in v 10 is articular, referring back to the first anarthrous occurrence of πρεσβύτεροι in v 4). Even though the text traditions in Andreas and Byzantine contain the correction θρόνοι (which is congruent with εἴκοσι τέσσαρες), the remaining pl. accs. are left uncorrected. In the phrase εἴκοσι τέσσαρες, εἴκοσι, "twenty," is indeclinable, while τέσσαρες, "four," is normally the nom. pl. (masc. and fem.) but is used interchangeably with the normal acc. pl. (masc. and fem.) τέσσαρας (Westcott-Hort, *Introduction*, Appendix, 138; Moulton, *Prolegomena*, 36; Mussies, *Morphology*, 219; BDR § 46.2b). Nevertheless, since τέσσαρες is textually secure, and the author also uses the acc. form τέσσαρας in the next clause, which is also textually secure, it is probable that reading (1) is the *lectio originalis* (Schmid, *Studien* 2:74). Elsewhere in Revelation εἴκοσι τέσσαρες is used to modify pl. noms. (4:10; 5:8; 11:16; 19:4). However, the sudden switch to the acc. suggests that the author might be intending the string of accs., including θρόνους in readings (2) and (3), to be objects of εἶδον in v 1, even though this is exceedingly awkward (Schmid, *Studien* 2:245).

4.c. Variant: τούς before εἴκοσι] 2351.

4.d. Variant: omit ἐν] A (lacuna in C) 025 fam 1611[1854]; Andr f[2023] i[2042] n[2429] lat; WHort; Charles, 2:263. Ten of twelve occurrences of περιβαλέσθαι take the acc. in Revelation (3:18; 7:9, 13; 10:1; 11:3; 12:1; 17:4; 18:16; 19:8, 13); the two exceptions take the dat. (3:5; 4:4). Probably a scribal omission, like that in 3:5, has occurred since A also omits instrumental ἐν elsewhere (B. Weiss, *Johannes-Apokalypse*, 134; Schmid, *Studien*, 2:88, 108).

4.e. Variant: Omit ἱματίοις] ℵ fam 1611[1854 2050 2329] Andr l. The elliptical phrase ἐν λεύκοις (which may have influenced this passage) occurs only in 3:4 (see John 20:12), while ἐν ἱματίοις λεύκοις occurs elsewhere only in 3:5.

5.a. The καί that begins this sentence is left untranslated because it is a discourse marker indicating the beginning of a new sentence or clause and lacks independent semantic significance.

5.b-b. Variants: (1) ἅ εἰσιν] ℵ[1] 024 fam 1611[2050] Andreas 792 Byz 1[2256] Byz 11[1597] Byz 19[1094]; Tischendorf, *NT Graece;* WHort; von Soden, *Text;* Merk, *NT;* Nestle-Aland[27]; UBSGNT[4]. (2) ἅ ἐστιν] A (lacunae in C and ℵ*) eth; B. Weiss, *Johannes-Apokalypse*, 8. (3) αἵ εἰσιν] fam 1006[1006 1841] Andr c d e[2057] f[2023 -2073] g i l 94 1773 Byzantine; Bousset (1906) 248. (4) καί] 2351. (5) εἰς] fam 1611[2329]. The original reading is probably (1). ἅ εἰσιν, lit. "which is," has not been attracted to the fem. case of its logical antecedent ἑπτὰ λαμπάδες (in Revelation the only example of a relative pronoun attracted to the gender and case of a substantive that it modifies is in 18:6, ἐν τῷ ποτηρίῳ ᾧ) but is congruent with τὰ ἑπτὰ πνεύματα. The third-person pl. verb with a neut. pl. subject (BDR § 133) is a normal Gk. idiom; however, third-person pl. forms occur frequently in the NT and Revelation with neut. pl. subjects, but usually when the subject is a living being, e.g., ζῷα, "cherubim" (4:8, 9; 5:14; 19:4), ὄρνεα, "birds" (19:21); see Mussies, *Morphology*, 231. When a predicate nom. is used in a relative clause in Revelation, the relative pronoun is sometimes attracted to the gender of the predicate nom., as here in reading (1) and in 5:8, but at other times to the gender of the substantive that the relative clause modifies (e.g., 5:6).

5.c. Variant: omit τά] fam 1006[1006 1841] Andr c f g i[2042] 94 1773 Byzantine. The presence of the article is original (Schmid, *Studien* 2:198), in conformity with the general rule that a predicate nom. is articular if the author wishes to emphasize a particular quality or function of the substantive (e.g., 1:8, 17; 2:23; 3:17; 7:14; 11:4; 18:23; 20:5, 14; 21:6; 22:13, 16). The Byzantine text has a tendency to omit such articles (see *Notes* on 5:8; 21:12, 22).

5.d. Variant: αὐτοῦ after θρόνου] fam 1006 fam 1611[1611cor 1854] 2351 Byzantine syr[h] cop[sa mss].

6.a-a. Variants: (1) ὡς] *lectio originalis*. (2) omit ὡς] Oecumenius[2053] Andr a b c d syr[ph] cop[sa] Primasius. The comparative particle ὡς, "as, like," is used here and elsewhere in Revelation in a way probably reflecting Semitic influence; i.e., it is a Septuagintism. See T. Muraoka, "The Use of ὡς in the Greek Bible," *NovT* 7 (1964–65) 51–72; A. Hilhorst, *Sémitismes*, 134–36, who observes, "From all the evidence, ὡς is one of several means serving to indicate that the prophet has access to a different reality (see Acts 11:5: εἶδον ἐν ἐκστάσει ὅραμα), which the language of this world can only describe by approximation" (136).

6.b. In the phrase ὡς θάλασσα, the noun is anarthrous, which is unusual in Revelation; θάλασσα occurs twenty-six times, and only three occurrences are anarthrous (4:6; 14:7; 15:2); see BDR § 253.2 and *Notes* on 15:2. ὡς occurs seventy times in Revelation, and fifty-nine times it is followed by a noun, which is usually anarthrous. In five instances only is the noun articular: ὡς ὁ ἥλιος (1:16; 10:1), ὡς τὰ σκεύη (2:27), ὡς ἡ ἄμμος (20:8), and ὡς τὸ ἔργον (22:12).

6.c-c. The phrase ἐν μέσῳ τοῦ θρόνου, lit. "in the midst of the throne," is problematic because it is followed by the phrase καὶ κύκλῳ τοῦ θρόνου, "and around the throne." The two phrases are apparently in tension, for it is not at all clear how the four cherubim can be both "in the midst" and "around" the throne at the same time. The RSV translates both phrases as "and round the throne, on each side of the throne," suggesting that the καί linking the two phrases is epexegetical, with the second phrase more closely defining the first. The same interpretation is reflected in the REB, "In the centre, round the throne itself," and the NIV, "In the center, around the throne." The NRSV abandons this view: "Around the throne, and on each side of the throne." The phrase ἐν μέσῳ τοῦ θρόνου is therefore understood by Bousset ([1906] 249) and Charles (1:118–19) as a gloss. According to Ezek 1:26, the four cherubim are situated *below* the throne, i.e., underneath God (Ezek 10:20). This conception is based on the traditional notion that God was "enthroned on the cherubim" (1 Sam 4:4; 2 Sam 6:2; 2 Kgs 19:15; 1 Chr 13:6; Pss 80:1; 99:1; Isa 37:16; Pr Azar 1:32; *Ladder of Jacob* 2:7) and riding on the cherubim (2 Sam 22:11; 1 Chr 28:18; Ps 18:10; Sir 49:8). Kraft (98) interprets "throne" here to mean "heaven" (possible in some contexts; cf. Matt 6:34), but this is impossibly abrupt and conflicts with the obvious meaning of θρόνος in the phrase immediately following. Elsewhere in Revelation, the cherubim are described as "around the throne," but never "in the midst of the throne." Hall (*NTS* 36 [1990] 610) argues that the four cherubim are part of the throne, for like the carved legs of a chair they both surround the throne and support it. While this accords with the tradition of the cherubim as constituting God's throne-chariot, such a conception is found nowhere else in Revelation and conflicts with the notion of the four cherubim prostrating themselves before the throne (5:8; 19:4; see Lohmeyer, 48). The best solution is probably to understand the phrase ἐν μέσῳ to mean "around," i.e., "on every side of," the throne (BAGD, 507), i.e., between the throne and a more remote point (Behm, 32; Brewer, *JBL* 71 [1952] 227–32), i.e., "in the immediate vicinity of" (Mounce, 137).

6.d-d. Variant: omit καὶ ἐν μέσῳ τοῦ θρόνου] Oecumenius²⁰⁵³ it^gig Cassiodorus.

6.e. The term ζῷα, "creatures," is translated "cherubim" here and in all subsequent uses of the term (pl.: 4:8, 9; 5:6, 8, 11, 14; 6:1, 3, 5, 6, 7; 7:11; 14:3; 15:7; 19:4; sing.: 4:7[4x]; 6:7), because John is clearly referring to Ezek 1:5–25, where the חיות *ḥyywt*, "creatures," are identified as cherubim in Ezek 10:20; see *Comment* on 4:6. Irenaeus, referring to the four creatures of Rev 4:7, refers to them as Χερουβίμ, "cherubim" (*Adv. haer.* 3.11.8).

7.a. Here the masc. sing. nom. ptcp. ἔχων, a predicate adj. (translated "has"), is a solecism since it should modify the neut. sing. nom. noun τὸ τρίτον ζῷον, "the third cherub." Yet the difference between the correct form of the ptcp., ἔχον, and the form used here, ἔχων, perhaps arose because of the phonetic similarity between o and ω (BDR § 28; Mussies, *Morphology*, 138). Further, ἔχων here functions like the finite verb ἔχει (GKC § 116f-i), perhaps reflecting the Heb. nominal construction לֹו יֵשׁ *yēš lô*, lit. "there is to him," or the Aram. equivalent, אִית לֵהּ *'yt lēh* (see Mussies, *Morphology*, 325). ἔχων is attested by A (C has a lacuna) 046 fam 1006¹⁰⁰⁶ ²³²⁹ fam 1611²³⁴⁴ 2351 and is considered the more original reading by Tischendorf, *NT Graece;* WHort; Nestle-Aland²⁷; UBSGNT⁴; Merk, *NT.* ἔχον is supported by א and a number of MSS from the Andreas and Byzantine texts and is considered original by Schmid, *Studien* 2:233–34.

7.b. τὸ πρόσωπον is articular because something that belongs to an individual (here the face) is described as possessing a certain quality (Winer, *Grammar*, 134).

7.c-c. Variants: (1) τὸ πρόσωπον ὡς ἀνθρώπου] A (lacuna in C) fam 1611²³⁴⁴ Andr n²⁴²⁹ 2019 it^a vg syr^ph. (2) τὸ πρόσωπον ὡς ἀνθρώπος] Oecumenius²⁰⁵³ fam 1611²³⁴⁴ Andreas syr^h. (3) τὸ πρόσωπον ὡς ὅμοιον ἀνθρώπῳ] א it^gig ᵗ. (4) πρόσωπον ἀνθρώπου] fam 1006¹⁰⁰⁶ ¹⁸⁴¹ fam 1611¹⁶¹¹ Andr d i²⁰⁴² n⁻²⁴²⁹ 94 Irenaeus^Lat Byzantine. When ὡς is used in a peculiar way, there is a tendency to omit it in the MS tradition (for references, see Schmid, *Studien* 2:225).

7.d. Variant: omit ζῷον] fam 1006¹⁰⁰⁶ ¹⁸⁴¹ Andr g i²⁰⁴² 94 Byzantine.

8.a. Variant: omit τά before τέσσαρα] Andreas Byzantine.

8.b. Variant: omit αὐτῶν after ἕν καθ᾽ ἕν] fam 1006 2351 Byzantine it^t.

8.c. Variants: (1) ἔχων] A 046 fam 1006¹⁰⁰⁶ fam 1611¹⁸⁵⁴ ²³²⁹ ²³⁴⁴ 2351; Andr a¹ b e²⁰²⁶ f²⁰³¹ ²⁰⁷³ h n⁻²⁰⁶⁵; 598 1773 2019. (2) ἔχον] fam 1006¹⁸⁴¹ Oecumenius²⁰⁵³ Andreas Byzantine. (3) ἔχοντα] 025 fam 1611¹⁶¹¹ ²⁰⁵⁰ 2351; Andr l; Victorinus (*habentes*). (4) εἶχον] א lat. Reading (1) is probably original, and here the present masc. nom. ptcp. ἔχων, translated as a simple past, "had," modifies ἕν καθ᾽ ἕν, "each one," and so should have the form ἔχον (neut. present nom. sing. ptcp.); see *Note* 7.a.

8.d-d. Variants: (1) καὶ ἔσωθεν] *lectio originalis*. (2) ἔσωθεν καὶ ἔξωθεν] 2351 (εσωθεν ϛ εξοθεν). (3) καὶ ἔξωθεν καὶ ἔσωθεν] 046. (4) omit] fam 1611²⁰⁵⁰ Andr e l.

8.e. λέγοντες, "saying, chanting" (a masc. nom. pl. ptcp.), is incongruent with the noun cluster it should modify, τὰ τέσσερα ζῷα, "the four cherubim" (a neut. nom. pl. noun); it should be λέγοντα (neut. nom. pl. ptcp.).

8.f-f. Variants: (1) ἅγιος κύριος ὁ παντοκράτωρ] 2351. (2) ἅγιος repeated seven times] Andr l¹⁶⁷⁸. (3) ἅγιος repeated eight times] א*. (4) ἅγιος repeated nine times] Byzantine.

8.g. κύριος ὁ θεὸς ὁ παντοκράτωρ is in the vocative, though normally in this phrase the usual form of the vocative, κύριε, is used (11:17 [*var. lect.* κύριος] 𝔓⁴⁷); 15:3; 16:7); see *Notes* on 15:3.

9.a. The temporal adverb ὅταν, "when, whenever," refers not to a *repeated* action but to a unique action (see *Comment* on 4:9).

9.b. Variants: (1) ὅταν δώσουσιν (fut. ind.)] A 025 fam 1611[1611 2050] Andr a d f[2073] i[2036] l[-1678] n[2429] 94 1773 2019. (2) ὅταν δώσωσιν (aor. subjunctive)] ℵ 046 fam 1611[1854] 2351 Andreas; Bousset (1906) 252. (3) ὅταν δῶσι (aor. subjunctive)] fam 1006 Andr c f[2023] i[2042] Byzantine. (4) ὅταν δώσει (fut. ind.)] Oecumenius[2053]. In Revelation, ὅταν is used five times with the aor. subjunctive (9:5; 10:7; 11:7; 17:10; 20:7), twice with the present subjunctive (10:7; 18:9), once with aor. ind. (8:1), and once with the fut. ind. (4:9); see Schmid, *Studien* 2:219; BDF § 382.4; BDR §§ 382.3, 4.

9.c-c. Variants: (1) τὸν θρόνον] ℵ A (lacunae in C) fam 1611[1854 2050]. (2) τοῦ θρόνου] 2351 Andreas Byzantine. Reading (2) is probably the result of assimilation to v 10 but violates the normal usage of Revelation (Schmid, *Studien* 2:74).

9.d. Variant: insert ἀμήν] ℵ 2351 Andr e[2057] Byz 1[911] Byz 17[2017] syr[ph] arm. A reflexive scribal insertion after doxological expressions.

10.a. Variant: καί] ℵ.

10.b. The verb προσκυνεῖν, "to worship," occurs nineteen times in Revelation with an obj. either in the dat. or the acc. It is true that when προσκυνεῖν means "worship," that which is worshiped is usually in the dat.; see Rev 4:10; 11:16; 13:4(2x); 14:7; 16:2; 19:4, 10(2x), 20; 22:9 (Charles, 1:211–12, exaggerates the consistency of this usage), but it is also true that προσκυνεῖν can mean "worship" when followed by an acc. of the person or thing worshiped (see Rev 9:20; 13:8 [13:4 reads προσεκύνησαν τῷ θηρίῳ, "they worshiped the beast," while 13:8 reads πρισκυνήσουσιν αὐτόν, sc. τὸ θηρίον, though a relatively strong variant reading of αὐτόν is αὐτῷ; see *Notes* on 13:8]). G. D. Kilpatrick ("Style," 154–55) argued that since Atticistic grammarians condemned the dat. construction and recommended the acc. construction, we should expect scribes to have changed the dat. objs. into acc. objs. However, G. D. Fee ("Rigorous or Reasoned Eclecticism—Which?" in *Studies in New Testament Language and Text,* FS G. D. Kilpatrick, ed. J. K. Elliott, NovTSup 44 [Leiden: Brill, 1976] 182–83) objects to this view and observes that προσκυνεῖν + dat. occurs six times without MS variation (4:10; 7:11; 11:16; 19:4, 10; 22:9), seven times as a majority reading with only one or several MSS with the acc. (13:4[2x]; 14:7; 19:10; 13:15; 16:2; 19:20), five times with acc. in all but a few late MSS (9:20; 13:12; 14:9, 11; 20:4), and once where the evidence is evenly divided between dat. and acc. (13:8). ὁ θεός (or pronouns representing ὁ θεός) always uses the dat., while neut. nouns (particularly τὸ θηρίον) usually take the acc.

10.c. Variant: ἀμήν] ℵ fam 1611[2329] Andr e[2026] g; it[t] syr[ph].

10.d-d. Variants: (1) βαλοῦσιν] *lectio originalis;* Andr c[2060] d e[2057] f[2023corr] g h i[2042] l[-2080] 94. (2) βάλλουσι(ν)] ℵ* 046 fam 1611[1854 2050 2329] Oecumenius[2053] Andreas vg[ms]. (3) βαλλοῦσι(ν)] Andr c[-2069] Andr g[2071] Andr Ø[254] Andr/Byz 2b[620 1918]. (4) βάλοντες] fam 1611[1611] vg[mss].

11.a. ὁ κύριος and ὁ θεός are articular noms. used as vocatives (Schmid, *Studien* 2:205); there are eighteen other occurrences of this construction in Revelation (6:10; 12:12[2x]; 15:3[3x]; 18:4, 10[2x], 16, 19, 20[3x]; 19:5[4x]). The regular vocative form κύριε is found in 7:14; 15:3, 4; 16:7; 22:20. The reading ὁ κύριος καὶ ὁ θεὸς ἡμῶν is attested by A (C has a lacuna at this point) and Byzantine. The variant κύριε ὁ θεὸς ἡμῶν (which apparently has been assimilated to the phrase κύριε ὁ θεός, which occurs in 11:17; 15:3; 16:7) is supported by the Andreas texts.

11.b. Variant: omit ὁ before θεός] 2351.

11.c. Variant: add ὁ ἅγιος after ἡμῶν] 2351.

11.d-d. The attributes of glory, honor, and might (τὴν δόξαν καὶ τὴν τιμὴν καὶ τὴν δύναμιν) are all arthrous because they denote that which is due or requisite (Winer, *Grammar,* 134–35).

11.e. According to Mussies (*Morphology,* 338), ἔκτισας is an aor. with a perfective value; yet since creation can be regarded as an event of the past, the aor. is a fully appropriate tense (see the use of the aor. ind. of κτίζειν to describe creation (Mark 13:19; 1 Cor 11:9; Eph 2:15; Col 1:16; Rev 10:6; *Did.* 10:3; *1 Clem.* 60:1; Hermas *Mand.* 12.4.2).

11.f. Variant: τά before πάντα] 2351.

11.g. Variants: (1) omit οὐκ] *lectio originalis.* (2) insert οὐκ] 046 Andr f[2073 2254] Andr l; Byz 2[18] Byz 16[61 69] Andr/Byz 4b[1828]. J. M. Ross regards reading (2) as original, translating the entire phrase "by thy will they were non-existent and then were created" ("Some Unnoticed Points in the Text of the New Testament," *NovT* 25 [1983] 72). The external evidence for reading (2), however, is so weak that it must be regarded as a scribal correction.

11.h-h. Variants: (1) ἦσαν καί] A ℵ fam 1006[1006 1841] fam 1611[1611] Oecumenius[2053] 2351 Byzantine it[gig ar t] vg Beatus; *TCGNT* [2], 665. (2) εἰσὶ καί] 025 fam 1611[1854 2050 2344] Andreas cop[sa]. (3) ἐγένοντο καί] fam 1611[2329]. (4) omit ἦσαν καί] Andr n[2429] 2019 Primasius Fulgentius. Here the expected reading, ἐκτίσθησαν καὶ ἦσαν (as *TCGNT* [2], 665, points out), was resolved by inserting οὐκ (see *Note* 11.g.) or the omission of ἦσαν καί, as in reading (4). Reading (2) is an attempt to resolve the reading by juxtaposing a present tense with the aor. pass. ἐκτίσθησαν.

11.i-i. The last part of this line is difficult to translate and has given rise to a number of variants. Nestle-Aland²⁷ and UBSGNT⁴ read ἦσαν καὶ ἐκτίσθησαν, lit. "they were and were created." The καί can be construed as epexegetical so that the second verb can be understood as a more specific reference to the same verbal action, i.e., "they existed, that is, were created" (Beckwith, 504). A omits καὶ ἐκτίσθησαν (C has a lacuna here), and it is possible that the ambiguous ἦσαν was glossed by a copyist with καὶ ἐκτίσθησαν in an attempt to clarify its meaning (Charles, 1:134). It is more likely, however, that the omission of καὶ ἐκτίσθησαν was intentional since it could seem redundant after ἦσαν.

## *Form/Structure/Setting*

### I. OUTLINE

III. The disclosure of God's eschatological plan (4:1–22:9)
  A. John's heavenly ascent (vv 1–2a)
    1. He sees an open door in heaven (v 1a)
    2. He is invited to ascend (v 1b–c)
      a. Speaker: the voice like a trumpet of 1:10
      b. Purpose: to be shown future events
    3. He instantly experiences a vision trance (v 2a)
  B. The sovereignty of God, the investiture of the Lamb, and the first six seals (4:2b–6:17)
    1. Vision of the heavenly throne room (4:2b–5:14)
      a. The heavenly worship of God (4:2b–11)
        (1) The One enthroned (vv 2b–3)
          (a) Appearance (v 3a)
            [1] Like jasper
            [2] Like carnelian
          (b) A rainbow like an emerald surrounds the throne (v 3b)
        (2) Those around the throne (vv 4–7)
          (a) The twenty-four elders (v 4)
            [1] Seated on twenty-four thrones (v 4b)
            [2] Dressed in white robes (v 4c)
            [3] Wearing gold wreaths (v 4d)
        (3) Manifestations of God's holy presence (v 5a)
          (a) Lightning
          (b) Rumblings
          (c) Thunderclaps
        (4) Objects before throne (v 5b–6a)
          (a) Seven blazing torches (= the seven spirits of God)
          (b) A sea of glass like crystal
        (5) The four living creatures around the throne (v 6b–8b)
          (a) Location: in the midst of the throne and around it (v 6b)
          (b) First general description: covered with eyes (v 6b)
          (c) Individual descriptions (v 7)
            [1] The first: like a lion (v 7a)
            [2] The second: like an ox (v 7b)
            [3] The third: face like a human (v 7c)

[4] The fourth: like a flying eagle (v 7d)
    (d) Second general description (v 8a–b)
        [1] Each had six wings (v 8a)
        [2] Each was covered with eyes (v 8b)
(6) The heavenly liturgy (vv 8c–11)
    (a) The worship of the four creatures (vv 8c–9)
        [1] Their unceasing chant of the trisagion (v 8c–e)
            [a] Ascription: holy, holy, holy
            [b] Object of worship: the Lord God the Almighty
            [c] Divine predicates: Who was and is and is to come
        [2] The hymn in *oratio obliqua* (v 9)
            [a] Ascriptions:
                {1} Glory
                {2} Honor
                {3} Thanks
            [b] Object of praise (God)
                {1} The One seated on the throne
                {2} Who lives forever
    (b) The response of the twenty-four elders (vv 10–11)
        [1] They bow down before the One enthroned (v 10a)
        [2] They worship the eternal One (v 10b)
        [3] They cast their wreaths before the throne, chanting
            (v 10c)
        [4] Their hymn (v 11)
            [a] Major predicate: You are worthy (v 11a)
            [b] Address: our Lord and God (v 11a)
            [c] Divine attributes (v 11b)
                {1} Glory
                {2} Honor
                {3} Power
            [d] Reasons for praise (v 11c)
                {1} God created everything
                {2} Everything was created by God's will

## II. LITERARY ANALYSIS

A new stage of John's revelatory vision begins in 4:1, where the scene shifts from earth to heaven. That the visionary's perspective oscillates between earth and heaven in the following chapters is one indication that various sources have been placed within a redactional framework. The first compositional question that arises is whether 4:1–2a serves as an introduction to the entire central section of the book (4:2b–22:9) or merely as an introduction to the seal narrative in 4:2b–6:17. In my view, it functions in both ways, a position supported by the fact that the seal narrative does not conclude neatly but serves as an anticipation of much of what follows. Most of the material that follows (4:1–19:10) focuses on the terrible eschatological tribulations that will occur before the Parousia of Christ. This extended emphasis on the time of trouble before the end (often called the "messianic woes") also characterizes the longer eschatological scenarios found in early Christian literature (Mark 13 and par.; 2 Thess 2:1–12; *Did.* 16).

Even though this is the first major section of the main part of Revelation, it cannot be strictly limited to 4:1–8:1 since the book or roll with seven seals can be understood as containing the entire scenario of eschatological events through 22:5. The seven seals encompass the seven trumpets, while the seventh trumpet encompasses the seven bowls. Irenaeus considers this section to be John's *second* vision, for he cites Rev 5:6 and observes: *et post haec in secunda visione deundem dominum videns,* "And after these things seeing the same Lord in a second vision" (*Adv. haer.* 4.20.11).

Structurally, Rev 4–6 is a single text unit. The scene clearly shifts in 7:1 to a new text unit introduced with the phrase μετὰ τοῦτο, "after this," which is used in Revelation only for major breaks in sequence. Rev 4:1 is introduced with the phrase μετὰ ταῦτα, "after this," so that the entire unit 4:1–6:17 is framed by these two narrative formulas.

The sequence of tenses exhibits the author's characteristic shift from past tenses in the first part of the vision narrative, to present and future tenses in the middle, and then back to past tenses toward the conclusion of the vision episode. In this chapter, John begins with two aorists, εἶδον, "I saw" (v 1), and ἤκουσα, "I heard" (v 1), followed by a brief invitation uttered by a voice from heaven in direct discourse introduced by the present participle λέγων,"saying" (v 1). This is followed by two more past tenses in v 2, an aorist, ἐγενόμην, "I was," and an imperfect, ἔκειτο, "situated." Thereafter follows a series of three generic presents emphasizing habitual or characteristic actions (excluding the verb εἰσίν, which is also a generic present with a timeless significance): ἐκπορεύονται, "was emitting" (v 5), γέμουσιν, "they are covered" (v 8), and ἔχουσιν, "they have" (v 8).

More remarkably, these are followed by four verbs in the future tense: δώσουσιν, "they will give" (v 9), πεσοῦνται, "they will fall" (v 10), προσκυνήσουσιν, "they will worship" (v 10), and βάλουσιν, "they will throw" (v 10). These future tenses present a formidable interpretive problem. One solution is to regard them as representing Semitic past tenses (on this problem see Mussies, *Morphology,* 343–47). Lancellotti (*Sintassi Ebraica,* 65) regards these futures as Semitisms representing imperfects. These cannot simply be ascribed to vividness; they must be attributed to the seer's awareness that these events have not yet occurred.

The vision report concludes with a hymn in direct discourse, which concludes the text unit when a new unit is introduced with an aorist verb in the narrative formula καὶ εἶδον, "then I saw" (5:1).

### III. LITERARY FORM OF REV 4: THE THRONE-VISION REPORT

The vision in Rev 4:1–6:17 is set in the heavenly throne room, and when it begins John is apparently on earth, or more specifically on Patmos. He sees an open door in heaven and hears an invitation to ascend to heaven (4:1): "Come up here, and I will reveal to you what must happen after this." This vision, then, begins explicitly with the heavenly ascent of the seer, though this feature is neither a necessary nor invariable feature of such visions. Throne-vision reports, often involving heavenly ascents, occur frequently in both prophetic and apocalyptic literary contexts in early

Judaism as well as in the later rabbinic hekalot literature. Throne-vision *reports* (a narrated revelatory experience associated with prophets) must be distinguished from heavenly throne-room *descriptions* (though both types share the same imagery); both occur within a variety of literary and liturgical settings (e.g., *T. Levi* 3:4–9; *Ladder of Jacob* 2:7–22; *Questions of Ezra* 21; *3 Enoch* 28:7–10; 32:1–2; 35:1–6; the Christian liturgy of St. Mark from Alexandria [F. E. Brightman, *Eastern Liturgies* (Oxford: Clarendon, 1896) 1:131]; *Orig. World* 104.35–106.11). The focus of the throne vision is God enthroned in his heavenly court surrounded by a variety of angelic beings or lesser deities (angels, archangels, seraphim, cherubim) who function as courtiers. All such descriptions of God enthroned in the midst of his heavenly court are based on the ancient conception of the divine council or assembly found in Mesopotamia, Ugarit, and Phoenicia as well as in Israel. The Hebrew terms used for such assemblies include עדה *'ēdâ* (Ps 82:1), קהל *qāhāl* (Ps 89:6), and סוד *sôd* (Ps 89:8; Jer 23:18, 22; Job 15:8; see Gen 1:26; 11:7; Exod 15:11). The members of this heavenly assembly are called "gods" (Exod 15:11; Pss 8:6; 29:1; 82:6[MT 5]), "sons of God" (Pss 29:1; 89:7[MT 8]), "sons of the gods" (Job 1:6; 2:1), "sons of the Most High" (Ps 97:7), or "holy ones" (Deut 33:2–3; Ps 89:6, 7; Zech 14:5). The motif of the divine council is frequently associated with prophecy in the OT, for prophets were thought able to join the assembly, to hear the deliberations of the council, and then to announce God's will upon the earth; according to Jer 23:18, "For who has stood in the council of the Lord so as to see and to hear his word?" (see Jer 23:22; Amos 3:7; 1 Kgs 22:19–22 = 2 Chr 18:18–22; Job 15:8; on Amos 7:15, "Yahweh took me [to the divine assembly] from following the flock," see Andersen-Freedman, *Amos,* 399–400). Most throne visions, for obvious reasons, are set in heaven, though in some the earthly temple and heavenly throne room merge (e.g., Isa 6:1–13). J. N. Oswalt argues that attempts to prove that the vision of Isa 6 took place in *either* the earthly or heavenly temple are overly literal ways of interpreting a text with theological concerns (*The Book of Isaiah, Chapters 1–39* [Grand Rapids, MI: Eerdmans, 1986] 176). One particular type of throne vision, the judgment scene, is frequently conceptualized as occurring on the earth (Matt 19:28–30; 25:31–46; Rev 20:4–6, 11–15; Dan 7:9–12; *1 Enoch* 90:20–38; *T. Abr.* [Rec. A] 12:3–18).

Particular throne visions characteristically function in one of six ways: (1) *Enthronement Scenes,* i.e., someone is rewarded by God by coronation, enthronement, or investiture (Dan 7:13–14; 4 Ezra 2:42–48; Ezekiel Trag. *Exagoge* 68–82; *Odes Sol.* 36; Rev 3:21 [see *Comment* on 3:21]). (2) *Judgment Scenes,* i.e., God or the Messiah judges (i.e., rules) and rewards the righteous and punishes transgressors (Ps 82:1–8; Zech 3:1–7; Dan 7:9–12; *1 Enoch* 25:3; 45:3; 47:3–4; 62:1–6; 69:26–29; *Apoc. Mos.* 22:1–29:6; Matt 19:28–30 [= Luke 22:28–30]; 25:31–46; Rev 20:4–6; 20:11–15). (3) *Commission Scenes,* i.e., God commissions an emissary to perform a particular task (1 Kgs 22:19–22 = 2 Chr 18:18–22; Job 1:6–12; 2:1–6; Isa 6:1–13; Ezek 1:4–3:11; Amos 7:14–15 [see Andersen-Freedman, *Amos,* 399–400]; *1 Enoch* 14:8–16:3; 71:5–17 [Enoch is carried by the spirit to the presence of God in the highest heaven, where he is installed as the Son of Man; an elaboration of Gen 5:24]; *Asc. Isa.* 10:1–16; *Jub.* 17:15–16). (4) *Eschatological Heavenly Festal Gathering Scenes,* i.e., scenes based on the real or imagined cultic practices of the second temple or of the Sinai theophany are used to depict an eschatological gathering of heavenly and earthly beings to praise and worship God before his throne (Rev 7:9–12 [see *Form/Structure/Setting* on Rev 7; Rev 14:1–5]; Heb 12:22–24; 4 Ezra 2:42–45; 13:5–50; *Odes*

*Sol.* 36). (5) *Vision of God as the Goal of Merkavah Mysticism* (*3 Enoch* 1:6–12; 7.1; *Sepher ha-Razim* 7 [ed. M. Morgan, 81–86]; cf. *T. Levi* 5:1). (6) *Literary Throne Scenes*, i.e., the primarily literary use of the throne vision is as a vehicle for commenting on earthly events in the narrative (2 Kgs 22:19–20; Job 1:6–12; 2:1–6; Rev 4:1–6:17; 11:15–18; 14:1–5; 19:1–8; *Jub.* 17:15–16).

One important though optional introductory motif to the throne vision of Rev 4:1–6:17 is the heavenly ascent motif found in vv 1–2a. D. Halperin ("Heavenly Ascension," 218–20) divides Jewish heavenly ascent literature and references to heavenly ascents into five groups: (1) Rabbinic sources contain several third-person accounts of individuals who made heavenly journeys: Alexander the Great (*t. Tamid* 32b; *y. ʿAbod. Zar.* 3.1, 42c), R. Joshua b. Levi (*b. Ketub.* 77b), and Moses (*Pesiq. R.* 20). (2) Some Jewish apocalypses contain first-person accounts narrating the heavenly ascensions of famous biblical characters such as Adam, Enoch, Abraham, Levi, and Baruch. One problem with this literature is the extent to which the "I" of the narrator may be identified with the "I" of the implied author. (3) The hekalot literature (see Schäfer, *Synopse zur Hekhalot-Literature*) contains *descriptions* of heavenly ascents (some in the first person, some in the third), as well as *prescriptions* for such ascents (often in second person). An example of the latter is the discourse of R. Nehuniah b. ha-Qanah in *Hekalot Rabbati* (summarized in G. Scholem, *Jewish Gnosticism*, 9–13). (4) There are supposed experiences of "ecstatic mysticism" associated with Talmudic references to "the four who entered *pardes*," *merkabah*, and *maʿasah merkabah*. (5) Paul gives an account of his heavenly ascent in 2 Cor 12:1–10, and John describes his heavenly ascent and what he saw in the heavenly court in Rev 4:1–22:9.

I. P. Culianu bases his typology of apocalyptic writings on the character who experiences revelation (*Psychanodia* 1:6–7): (1) "call" apocalypses, unknown in the Greco-Roman world (*1 Enoch, 2 Enoch, Testament of Moses, Testament of Abraham, Ascension of Isaiah, 4 Apocalypse Baruch*), (2) apocalypses by accident (Er in Plato *Republic* 613e–621d; Aridaios-Thespesios of Soli in Plutarch *De sera numinis* 563b–568–69), and (3) "quest" apocalypses, involving incubation or use of hallucinogens or various psycho-physical techniques, e.g., fasting, breath control, etc. (Timarchus of Chaeronea in Plutarch *De genio Socratis*).

There are six scenes in Revelation that center on the heavenly throne room: (1) 4:2–6:17, (2) 7:9–17, (3) 11:15–19, (4) 14:1–5 (here the scene of the Lamb on Mount Zion with the 144,000 in v 1, 3b–5 is juxtaposed with the author's audition of a heavenly liturgy in vv 2–3a, with an explicit mention of the throne), (5) 15:2–8, and (6) 19:1–8.

## IV. REV 4 AND MERKAVAH MYSTICISM

2 Cor 12:1–10 and Rev 4 are the only first-person autobiographical reports of a heavenly ascent found in early Christianity or, for that matter, early Judaism. In an attempt to isolate and analyze the earliest postbiblical evidence for Jewish Merkavah ("chariot") mysticism, which appears in fully developed form in the hekalot literature, I. Gruenwald focuses on several throne visions in early Jewish apocalyptic literature that he regards as part of the extensive Merkavah tradition (*1 Enoch* 14; 71; *2 Enoch; Apoc. Abr.* 9–19; *Asc. Isa.* 6–9; see Gruenwald, *Apocalyptic*, 29–62). One of the texts that Gruenwald discusses is the "Merkavah vision" in Rev 4 (*Apocalyptic*,

62–72). Gruenwald cautiously suggests that, because the Merkavah vision in Rev 4 has a number of "discrepancies," i.e., features that depart from other, more typical Merkavah visions, the author is conveying not a true visionary ecstatic experience so much as a pastiche of literary features and conventions derived from various sources, including the Merkavah tradition (e.g., the technical terms "a door opened in heaven" and "I was in the spirit"). The distinctive features of Rev 4 that Gruenwald singles out are the following: (1) The author knows only one heaven, not the plurality of as many as seven heavens found in Jewish apocalypses and Merkavah literature. (2) The twenty-four elders, while they have some parallels in Jewish literature, are not part of the Merkavah tradition and betray the eclecticism of the author. (3) The throne of God has two peculiar features: (a) that the four living creatures are "in the midst of the throne and round about the throne" may reflect the Jewish tradition that the four living creatures bear the firmament over their heads and that the throne is located on the firmament (so they cannot see God), and (b) the four living creatures are listed in a different order from that found in Ezek 1, and they have six wings rather than the four wings of the creatures in Ezek 1; these peculiarities further indicate the eclectic character of the vision in Rev 4. (4) Gruenwald then turns to the *Apocalypse of Paul* (a composition dependent in part on Revelation) and points out that the throne of God appears to be located in the heavenly temple, though apart from Isa 6 the temple is never mentioned in Merkavah visions; this suggests that the author of the *Apocalypse of Paul*, like the author of Revelation, has produced a blend of literary motifs.

While Gruenwald is quite correct in suggesting that the vision in Rev 4 has a literary and eclectic character (though he is suitably cautious about distinguishing between "genuine" and "literary" accounts of ecstatic experiences), his assessment of Rev 4 (and other apocalyptic vision narratives) is nevertheless not without a number of difficulties: (1) By "Merkavah mysticism," Gruenwald has in mind the fully developed mystical tradition found in the hekalot texts (see Schäfer, *Synopse zur Hekhalot-Literatur*), which focus on heavenly ascensions and earthly appearances of angels who reveal secrets, providing detailed instructions for obtaining the desired revelatory experiences. He assumes rather than demonstrates that biblical texts in which vision narratives are presented (primarily 1 Kgs 22; Job 1; Isa 6; Ezek 1) in fact represent early forms of the Merkavah experience (though a visionary *ascent* is narrated only in 1 Kgs 22). By labeling nearly all vision narratives that focus on the heavenly throne of God as "Merkavah mysticism," Gruenwald assumes a unity of tradition where none can be demonstrated. He also assumes that such texts reflect actual experience, though again in the absence of demonstration. (2) Though the three-level cosmology of Revelation is striking for its antiquity (Paul knows of at least three heavens in 2 Cor 12:2–3), the idea of the cosmos of seven heavens that appears in early Jewish apocalyptic cannot be confirmed earlier than the first century A.D. Like Revelation, several Jewish apocalypses, including the five apocalypses that constitute *1 Enoch*, the *Testament of Abraham*, and the *Apocalypse of Ezra*, know only the three-tiered universe (heaven, earth, underworld).

## Comment

**1a** μετὰ ταῦτα εἶδον, καὶ ἰδοὺ θύρα ἠνεῳγμένη ἐν τῷ οὐρανῷ, "After this I saw, and behold, a door was opened in heaven." There are several characteristic ways in which vision reports are introduced in Revelation. The phrase μετὰ ταῦτα εἶδον, καὶ ἰδού, "after this I saw, and behold," occurs only here and in 7:9, while the shorter phrase μετὰ ταῦτα εἶδον, "after this I saw," occurs in 7:1 (in the form μετὰ τοῦτο εἶδον, "after this I saw"); 15:5; 18:1; in the LXX this phrase occurs only in Dan 8:4. The expression (καὶ) εἶδον, καὶ ἰδού, "(then) I saw, and behold," occurs more frequently (6:2, 5, 8; 14:1, 14; 19:11; see LXX Ezek 1:4, 15; 2:9; 8:2; 10:1, 9; 37:8; Dan 10:5; 12:5; Zech 2:1, 5; 5:1, 9; 6:1). The particle ἰδού, "behold," is also used to introduce visions in 4:2; 12:3, but it is used more frequently elsewhere in the NT (Matt 1:20; 2:13, 19; Acts 1:10; 10:30; 12:7). The Aramaic particle אָה *hā'* is similarly used to introduce vision narratives in 1QapGen 19:14; 22:27. Just as the keys to Death and Hades (1:18) presuppose a door to the underworld, so here the entrance to the heavenly world is also conceptualized in terms of a door. The passive perfect participle ἠνεῳγμένη, "was opened," is used as a circumlocution for divine activity; i.e., it is *God* who opens the heavenly door for John. Parallels in ancient literature suggest that the image of the open door in heaven is appropriate for introducing a divine revelation, particularly in the form of an epiphany. Three important motifs are closely interwoven in vv 1–2: the door to the heavenly world opened by God, the voice from heaven that summons John, and the ensuing vision of God upon his heavenly throne.

The most thorough examination of the motif of the "opening door" in ancient religious traditions is that of Weinreich (*TBA* 5 [1929] 200–464), who discusses the motif in connection with epiphanies (including divine appearances and voices), prodigies, miraculous releases (usually from prisons), magic, and prayer. Though Weinreich discusses some important passages in John and Acts, he mentions neither Rev 4:1 nor 3:20. Further, his discussion exhibits several problematic features, the most significant of which is the separation of epiphanic traditions from magical traditions (on the problem of facile distinctions between magic and religion, see Aune, "Magic," *ANRW* II, 23/2:1510–16). In the OT, the conception of a "door of heaven" occurs just twice (Gen 28:17; Ps 78:23), and only Gen 28:17 concerns an epiphanic revelation (on the motif of the "open heavens," which occurs just once in the OT, see *Comment* on 19:11). In *1 Enoch* 14:14b–15, there is an exceptionally close verbal and conceptual parallel, "I saw in my vision, and behold another door was opened before me," and in vv 18ff., Enoch sees a throne upon which God is seated. The conception of a "door of heaven" is much more common in Greek tradition; see *Iliad* 5.749–50, where the Horai are designated as the gatekeepers of the gates of heaven and Olympus. Another close parallel to Rev 4:1 is in a fragmentary hexameter poem in the epic tradition entitled "On Nature," by Parmenides, written toward the beginning of the fifth century B.C. (Diels-Kranz, *FVS* 1:227–31 [Parmenides, frag. B1]; English translation in K. Freeman, *Ancilla to the Pre-Socratic Philosophers* [Cambridge: Harvard UP, 1948] 41–46; the interpretation of this fragment varies widely, see Taran, *Parmenides*, 17–30). In the introduction, Parmenides depicts himself as drawn along in a chariot escorted by maidens (line 5) also called Heliades, i.e., daughters of the sun (line 8), upward to the gate dividing night from day. The goddess Dike, who possesses the appropriate keys, is persuaded by the Heliades to open the large door. Once inside, an unnamed goddess takes his right hand and expounds various philosophical doctrines to him. In the remaining fragments of the composition, the goddess provides cosmological information on the nature of the heavens and the origins of the sun, moon, stars, fire, and other aspects of the cosmos. That this kind of revelatory journey experience has numerous parallels in ancient literary remains suggests that the revelatory vision report of

Parmenides is in fact a literary device serving as a formal proem, which expresses his attainment of truth as divine revelation (Taran, *Parmenides,* 30–31). Since the imagery blurs the traditional distinctions between a celestial journey and an underworld journey, it is clear that the motif of the journey itself (understood as a quest for knowledge) is of central significance (Mourelatos, *Route,* 14–16). Though the journey motif is certainly dependent on the prototypical epic journey in the *Odyssey* (Mourelatos, *Route,* 16–25), the motif of a divinely guided tour and the use of revelatory discourses attributed to a divine revealer (an unnamed goddess in Parmenides) are independent of the epic tradition (frag. B2). The similarities between these widely separated conceptions cannot be based on historical connections but belong rather to a widespread ancient revelatory *topos* based on common cosmological conceptions. The common function of each "open door" passage (Rev 4:1; *1 Enoch* 14:14b–15a; Parmenides frag. B1) is to introduce a revelatory scene. A close parallel occurs in the Coptic-Gnostic tractate *Apoc. Paul* 21.24–28 (tr. Robinson, *Nag Hammadi,* 258–59): "[Then I gazed] upward and [saw the] Spirit saying [to me], 'Paul, come! [Proceed toward] me!' Then as I [went], the gate opened, [and] I went up to the fifth [heaven]." *T. Levi* 2:6 contains a close parallel to Rev 4:1 (and *1 Enoch* 14:14b–15a), though a door is not explicitly mentioned: "And behold the heavens were opened and an angel of God said to me, 'Come in, Levi'" (M. de Jonge in Sparks, *AOT,* 526). Yet the *Testaments of the Twelve Patriarchs* are late, and it is possible that this and other passages (see *T. Judah* 24:2) are dependent on the NT. Similarly, in *T. Levi* 5:1 we read, "And thereupon the angel opened to me the gates of heaven, and I saw the holy temple, and upon a throne of glory the Most High" (M. de Jonge in Sparks, *AOT,* 528). Gnostic cosmologies often conceive of seven or more heavens, each of which has a door that must be opened before ascent through the various levels is possible (*Apoc. Paul* 21.22–24.1; *Great Pow.* 41.7–8).

The motif connecting divine epiphanies with a heavenly door is particularly important in southwest Asia Minor in the Hellenistic and Roman periods. The world-famous Temple of Artemis at Ephesus, according to numismatic and literary evidence (Hommel, *IM* 5 [1955] 29–55), had a door in the front pediment that was apparently used for a ritual epiphany of the goddess (Trell, "Further Study," 346–49; Oster, *JBL* 101 [1982] 217). Pliny (*Hist. nat.* 14.2.9) refers to a stairway to the roof of the temple, and a coin in the Berlin collection shows a figure in the central opening of the temple (Price-Trell, *Coins,* 129, fig. 229). In addition to the inscriptional and literary evidence for epiphanies at the Ephesian Artemision in the second century A.D. (*SIG* 867.35; Pliny *Hist. nat.* 36.97), there is numismatic evidence suggesting that Greek and Roman temple pediments (in a tradition originating in the Near East; see Hommel, *IM* 5 [1955] 33–38) often depicted the heavenly world, with the presence of such figures as the Horai who possessed the keys to the door of heaven (Pausanias 5.11.7; Lucian *Trag.* 33; *Sac.* 8; Eusebius *Praep. evang.* 3.11.38; Quintus Smyrnaeus 2.598; Nonnus *Dion.* 2.175; see Hommel, *IM* 5 [1955] 47). The pediment as a symbolic representation of the heavenly world is also found on Roman temples (Hommel, *Studien*). This suggests that even though the association of divine epiphany with heavenly doors is found in one form or another throughout the ancient world, the associated motifs are not only literary but cultic and a familiar phenomenon in Asia Minor. Since the motifs of the open door or open gate of heaven and the conception of the "open heavens" are used occasionally in the same documents (see Rev 4:1; 19:11; *T. Levi* 2:6; 5:1), it is probably as incorrect to regard the door image as limiting the vision only to the seer as it is to regard the "open heavens" as a more inclusive image (against Swete, 66; Charles, 1:107). A passage from the so-called Mithras Liturgy contains both the motif of the open doors and that of the trance (*PGM*IV.625–28): "Then open your eyes, and you will see the doors open and the world of the gods which is within the doors, so that from the pleasure and joy of the sight your spirit runs ahead and ascends."

**1b** καὶ ἡ φωνὴ ἡ πρώτη ἣν ἤκουσα ὡς σάλπιγγος λαλούσης μετ᾽ ἐμοῦ λέγων, "and the first voice which I heard like a trumpet speaking to me, saying." This is a redactional gloss intended to link this section with 1:9–20. The "first voice" must be the voice in 1:10–11, which commanded John to write a book and send it to the seven churches. However, the author apparently wishes to distinguish the "first voice" of 1:10–11 from the "second voice" of 1:17–20; i.e., the "first voice" is not the exalted Christ that summons John to the heavenly world in 4:1 but an *angelus interpres,* or "interpreting angel." Though a distinction between two speakers cannot be found in 1:9–20 (Beckwith, 436), Zahn (1:317–18) and Roloff (44–45) nevertheless think that the speaker in 1:11 is an angel, while the speaker in 1:19 is Christ. For Bousset ([1906] 243) and Beasley-Murray (111–12), the "first voice" was that of Christ in 1:10–20, and so is the voice of 4:1. This is clearly a redactional attempt to unify the textual units of the final edition of Revelation (see *Introduction*, Section 5: Source Criticism).

The participle λέγων, "saying," is frequently used redundantly in Revelation following other verbs of saying, and not in congruence with the case of the noun it should modify, i.e., an anacolouthon (see Rev 4:8; 5:12; 11:15). Since λέγων modifies ἡ φωνή, "the voice," it should be expressed as the feminine nominative form λέγουσα, "saying." These two features indicate that this is an intentional Hebraism on the part of the author in which the term לֵאמֹר *lē᾽mōr,* "so as to say," is used to introduce direct speech corresponding to the more conventional Greek use of ὅτι, "that" (D. Tabachovitz, *Die Septuaginta, und das Neue Testament* [Lund: Gleerup, 1956] 12–13, 18). The following examples of λέγων/λέγοντες in the LXX illustrate this lack of concord: Gen 15:1, 4; 22:20; 38:13, 24; Exod 18:6; 45:16; Lev 8:31; 2 Kgdms 15:31; 3 Kgdms 1:51; 20:9(MT 21:9). The peculiar phrase λαλούσης μετ᾽ ἐμοῦ λέγων (parallels occur in 10:8; 17:1; 21:9), or λαλεῖν μετά + genitive, is apparently linked to the verb δεικνύναι in Christian apocalyptic contexts (see 4:1; 17:1; 21:9; Hermas *Sim.* 5.3.2–3; 5.4.5; 9.1.1). I have not found any other parallels of these two expressions occurring in the same context.

**1c** ἀνάβα ὧδε, καὶ δείξω σοι ἃ δεῖ γενέσθαι μετὰ ταῦτα, "'Come up here, and I will reveal to you what must happen after this.'" This invitation is designed to introduce the reader to the extended vision sequence found in 4:1–22:9 and not simply to the textual unit consisting of 4:1–8:1. However, the reference to "what must happen after this" may also refer specifically to the revelation contained in the sealed scroll that is the focus of the second part of the throne scene found in 5:1–14, which is opened by the Lamb in stages (6:1–17; 8:1). This statement by the angel alludes to Theod Dan 2:29, where Daniel tells Nebuchadnezzar that his dream involved τί δεῖ γενέσθαι μετὰ ταῦτα, "what must happen after this" (cf. 2:45). Allusions to LXX Dan 2:29 are also found in Rev 1:1; 22:6 (see *Comments*). The adverb of place, ὧδε, which indicates a position relatively near the speaker, indicates that the speaker is located in heaven. This makes the redactional identification of the speaker with the exalted Christ in 1:10 problematic, for the vision in 1:9–20 is presented as though it occurred on earth, whereas now the exalted Christ would suddenly and unexpectedly be speaking from heaven. The verb δείκνυναι occurs eight times in Revelation (1:1; 4:1; 17:1; 21:9, 10; 22:1, 6, 8); in six instances the subject is an *angelus interpres*, "interpreting angel" (17:1; 21:9, 10; 22:1, 6, 8). That the speaker takes no further part in John's ascent to the heavenly court (i.e., does not in fact "reveal," "make known," or "explain" anything—the meanings of δείκνυναι) strongly suggests that 4:1 is a redactional passage that the author has inserted to unify a complex sequence of visions he has blended together to form a continuous narrative. This is in part confirmed by the phrase ἃ δεῖ γενέσθαι μετὰ ταῦτα, which imitates 1:19: ἃ μέλλει γενέσθαι μετὰ ταῦτα. These, together with 9:12 (see *Notes* there), are the only instances in Revelation in which the phrase μετὰ ταῦτα *concludes* a sentence or clause. The invitation to "come up here" is paralleled in two angelic invitations for the author to "come, I will show you" (17:1; 21:9), where a revelatory vision is in view.

**2a** εὐθέως ἐγενόμην ἐν πνεύματι, "Immediately I was in a prophetic trance." The phrase ἐν πνεύματι, literally "in the spirit," occurs four times in Revelation (1:10; 4:2; 17:3; 21:10). Three of these involve responses to an invitation by an angelic being to come: 4:1, ἀνάβα ὧδε, καὶ δείξω σοι; 17:1, δεῦρο, δείξω σοι; 21:9, δεῦρο, δείξω σοι. The term πνεῦμα, "spirit," in these passages is commonly taken to refer to the Spirit of God, and therefore capitalized in modern English translations (AV [1:10 only]; RSV; NEB; NIV), and is so understood by many commentators (Beckwith, 435; Beasley-Murray, 112; Sweet, 114; Mounce, 133; Lohse, 19, 37; Lohmeyer, 44–45). Yet in all four occurrences of the phrase ἐν πνεύματι, "in [the] spirit," the noun is anarthrous. Of the seven uses of the term πνεῦμα in the singular in Revelation, ten use the articular form τὸ πνεῦμα, and all but 19:10 (see *Comment*) clearly refer to the Spirit of God (2:8, 11, 17, 29; 3:6, 13, 22; 14:13; 22:17). John uses the preposition ἐν, "in," followed by an articular noun in the dative case seventy times in Revelation, so he exhibits no hesitancy in using such a common Greek construction. Strangely, the phrase ἐν τῷ πνεύματι in the sense of "inspired by the Spirit" occurs just once in the NT in Luke 2:27, of Simeon (the phrase is twice used in the instrumental sense of "by the Spirit" in Luke 4:1; Acts 19:21). The phrase ἐν πνεύματι, however, does occur several times in very different senses in the NT (Luke 1:17; John 4:23, 24; Acts 1:5; Rom 2:29; 8:9; 1 Cor 14:6; Eph 2:22; 3:5; 5:18; 6:18; Col 1:8; 1 Tim 3:16), often in an instrumental sense (Matt 22:43; Acts 1:5; 1 Cor 14:16). There is, then, no compelling reason for understanding any of these four passages as references to the Spirit of God. The phrase ἐν πνεύματι is an idiom indicating that John's revelatory experiences took place not "in the body" but rather "in the spirit," i.e., in a vision trance (Charles, 1:22; Swete, 13; Kraft, 95). In 1 Cor 14:15, Paul contrasts two states in which Christians can pray, τῷ πνεύματι, "with/in the Spirit," and τῷ νοΐ, "with/in the mind." Caird (59) correctly and idiomatically translates ἐγένομην ἐν πνεύματι with the phrase "I fell into a trance."

Another problem with the phrase ἐγενόμην ἐν πνεύματι is its narrative relationship to the first occurrence of the phrase in 1:10, since both phrases are identical. Several solutions have been suggested: (1) It is possible that the author simply intends to remind the reader of the continuation of his vision trance, as in Ezek 11:1, 5 (Bousset [1906] 244). Yet in Ezek 11:1, the prophet is (apparently) physically transported by the Spirit to the east gate of the temple (11:1), where the Spirit falls upon him and inspires him to prophesy (11:5). (2) Rev 4:1 marks the beginning of the main vision narrative of the book, and the narrator wants to emphasize the divine inspiration of the vision narrative that follows (Lohmeyer,

45). (3) Some commentators have argued that a higher form of ecstasy was necessary for the heavenly ascent narrated in 4:1ff. (Swete, 67; Roloff, 66) and that it is a response to the invitation ἀνάβα (Lohmeyer, 45 ). (4) The hearing of the voice, which brought on the first ecstatic experience (1:10), now causes the narrator to fall into a trance for the second time. (5) The author has combined the narratives of visions received on different occasions, and therefore either 4:2a was added as a gloss (J. Weiss, *Offenbarung*, 54 n. 1) or 4:1–2a was added to connect Rev 1–3 with Rev 4–9 (Charles, 1:110–11).

**2b** καὶ ἰδοὺ θρόνος ἔκειτο ἐν τῷ οὐρανῷ, "and behold a throne was situated in heaven." The throne of God, a symbol of sovereignty, is the central feature of OT, Jewish, and early Christian conceptions of heaven, and is modeled after the throne rooms of earthly kings. The term θρόνος occurs forty-seven times in Revelation, and all but seven instances refer to the heavenly throne of God (or Christ, in 3:21). Here κεῖμαι appears to function as a verbal copula, similar to εἰμί and γίνομαι, so that the prepositional phrase "in heaven" is used as predicate with κεῖμαι (see 21:6). There is a verbal parallel in Cebes *Tabula* 5.1, θρόνον τινὰ κείμενον κατὰ τὸν τόπον, "a throne situated in the place."

**2c** καὶ ἐπὶ τὸν θρόνον καθήμενος, "and someone was seated upon the throne." This is the first occurrence of the formula καθήμεν- ἐπί, "seated upon," which occurs twenty-seven times in Revelation (here καθήμενος is the anarthrous subject of a clause). As a circumlocution for the name of God, the formula occurs twelve times in five different grammatical forms: (1) [ὁ] καθήμενος ἐπὶ τὸν θρόνον (4:2; 20:11), (2) τῷ καθημένῳ ἐπὶ τῷ θρόνῳ (4:9; 5:13; 7:10; 19:4), (3) τοῦ καθημένου ἐπὶ τοῦ θρόνου (4:10; 5:1, 7; 6:16), (4) *ὁ καθήμενος ἐπὶ τῷ θρόνῳ (21:5), and (5) *ὁ καθήμενος ἐπὶ τοῦ θρόνου (7:15). Aside from the two asterisked exceptions, the case of ὁ θρόνος after ἐπί is determined by the case of ὁ καθήμενος. These occurrences of the formula all function as circumlocutions for the name of God since no other names for God are placed in syntactical connection with any of these passages, with the exception of 7:10; 19:4. There are at least two instances in which the term "throne" itself appears to function as a circumlocution for the name of God (4:10; 8:3). The phrase "throne of God," in which the divine name is specifically mentioned, is relatively uncommon in Revelation (7:15; 22:1, 3; cf. 12:5). A figure like a son of man is also described as seated on a cloud (14:14, 15, 16), and a messianic figure is described as seated on a (white) horse (19:11, 19, 21). In Greco-Jewish literature, God is rarely referred to as "the one seated upon the throne," and rarely is the phrase used as a circumlocution for the divine name (Sir 1:8, but cf. *Adam and Eve* 37:4, where the phrase "the Father of all who sits upon his throne" occurs). In the LXX the phrase ὁ καθήμενος ἐπὶ τῶν χερουβίν, "the one seated upon [or 'over'] the cherubim," is found in Pss 79:2; 98:1; cf. LXX Dan 3:55, "Blessed is the one who sees the abyss seated on the cherubim" (the source of a phrase used in magical formulas; see A. M. H. Audollent, *Defixionum tabellae* [1904, repr. Frankfurt am Main: Minerva, 1967] no. 241, lines 25–26; *PGM* VII.264, 633; *PGM* 21.5). However, the formula ὁ καθήμενος ἐπὶ τοῦ θρόνου is used to refer to Adam or Abel several times in *T. Abr.* [Rec. A] 11:4, 6; 12:11; 13:2; [Rec. B] 8:7. In contrast, the formula ὁ καθήμενος ἐπί as a divine epithet occurs with great frequency in Greco-Roman magical formulas in the magical papyri and inscribed on magical gems, lamellae, and defixiones (see L. Robert, "Amulettes grecques," *Journal des Savants* [1981] 10–12); e.g., *PGM* IV.1012–13, 1110, 2768–69; VII.633; XII.87–88;

XXIIb.10–13; XXXV.1–12; XXXVI.4, 77; Delatte-Derchain, *Les intailles magique,* no. 460. On a silver lamella from Beirut now in the Louvre, each of seven daimones ῖs invoked with the formula ἐπικαλοῦμαι, "I invoke," followed by the substantival ᾳccusative participle τὸν καθέμενον followed by ἐπί, with the case governed by ἐπί being variously the genitive (the first five invocations), the accusative (the sixth invocation), and the dative (the seventh invocation), without any apparent distinction in meaning (Robert, *Journal des Savants* [1981] 10–11; Bonner, *Magical Amulets,* 101–2; cf. Preisendanz 2:160, notes on *PGM* XXXV).

**3a**    καὶ ὁ καθήμενος ὅμοιος ὁράσει λίθῳ ἰάσπιδι καὶ σαρδίῳ, "The one seated there was like jasper and carnelian in appearance." Here the phrase ὁ καθήμενος, "the seated one," corresponds to the Hebrew appellative יושׁב *yōšēb,* "the enthroned one," as a designation for God (Ps 22:4). These semiprecious stones suggest colors, and it is interesting to note that, of the OT prophets, only Ezekiel had visions in which colors are evident. Jasper is an opaque stone that tends to be red but is also found in yellow, green, and grayish blue. Since jasper is used as a simile for the appearance of God, it is used later in Revelation as an image for the overall appearance of the New Jerusalem, which manifests the glory of God (21:11), and is the material from which its walls are constructed (21:18), as well as the first of its twelve foundations (21:19). Throne scenes in Jewish apocalyptic literature do not usually use precious stones as metaphors for describing the throne of God (L. L. Thompson, *Revelation,* 86). However, the throne vision in Ezek 1 mentions several precious stones and metals (v 16, chrysolite; v 26, sapphire; v 27, gleaming bronze), and *T. Abr.* (Rec. A) 12:4–6 (tr. Sanders in Charlesworth, *OTP* 1:889) says:

> And between the two gates there stood a terrifying throne with the appearance of terrifying crystal, flashing like fire. And upon it sat a wondrous man, bright as the sun, like unto a son of God. Before him stood a table like crystal, all of gold and byssus.

In some angelic epiphanies, precious stones can be used in the description (e.g., Dan 10:5–6, where gold, beryl, and burnished bronze are used to describe the girdle, body, and legs of the angel). To a certain extent John uses the precious stones drawn from the description of the heavenly Jerusalem in describing God and his throne. Three precious stones are used in the throne scene and in the description of the New Jerusalem: jasper (4:3; 21:11, 18, 19), carnelian (4:3; 21:10), and crystal (4:6; 22:1; cf. Ezek 1:22). Sapphire, mentioned in the description of the throne in Ezek 1:26, occurs in Revelation only in 21:19.

**3b**    καὶ ἶρις κυκλόθεν τοῦ θρόνου ὅμοιος ὁράσει σμαραγδίνῳ, "and a rainbow encircled the throne like emerald in appearance." The rainbow is based oι an allusion to the throne vision in Ezek 1:27–28, just as the description of the heavenly throne in 4Q405 20–22 i 10–11, also dependent on Ezek 1, speaks of "a radiant substance with glorious colors, wondrously hued" (Newsom, *Songs,* 306; see Rowland, *JSS* 10 [1980] 143 n. 14). However, the Hebrew term קשׁת *qešet,* literally the "bow" of the warrior, is also used of the "rainbow" in Gen 9:13; Ezek 1:28. When accompanied by the phrase בענן *be'ānān,* "in the cloud" (the widespread view suggested by Gunkel that Yahweh hung up his warrior's "bow" on the clouds, causing the "arrows" of rain to cease, is problematic; see Westermann, *Genesis* 1:473), קשׁת was consistently translated τόξον in the LXX (including Ezek 1:28) and *arcus* in the Vulgate (which means both bow as weapon and bow as rainbow, and so occurs in some Latin MSS as an alternate to the Greek loanword *iris*). Vergil speaks of the *nubibus arcus,* the "bow of the clouds" (*Aeneid* 5.88). By using ἶρις in 4:3, the author has chosen a pagan term for "rainbow" (Brown, *BZ* 37 [1993] 35; K. H. Rengstorf, *TDNT* 3:341), presumably for the sake of clarity, for Josephus must explain to his readers that the terms τοξεία and τόξον mean ἶρις (*Ant.* 1.103). The choliambic poet Aeschrio compared the rainbow to the warrior's bow: ἶρις δ᾽ἔλαμψε, καλὸν οὐρανοῦ τόξον, "The rainbow gleamed, the beautiful bow of the sky" (E. Diehl, *Anthologia Lyrica Graeca,* 3rd ed. [Leipzig: Teubner, 1954] fasc. 3, p. 121). From the Greek side, the famous prayer of Sappho to Aphrodite (Dionysius of Hal. *De comp. verb.* 24) addresses the goddess as ποικιλόθρον᾽ ἀθάνατ᾽, "many-color-throned immortal one." The author emphasizes that the throne of God is the focus of a series of concentric circles made up of first a rainbow, then a circle of the four cherubim (v 6b, καὶ κύκλῳ τοῦ θρόνου), then a circle of the twenty-four thrones upon which the twenty-four elders sit (v 4, καὶ κυκλόθεν τοῦ θρόνου θρόνους εἴκοσι τέσσαρες). According to 5:11 (and again in 7:11), a great host of angels also encircled the throne (κύκλῳ τοῦ θρόνου). The adverb κυκλόθεν occurs three times in Revelation (4:3, 4, 8), and the form κύκλῳ occurs three times (4:6; 5:11; 7:11). The notion that heaven is arranged in concentric circles around the throne of God is found in *1 Enoch* 71:6–8 and in a more elaborate way in *3 Enoch* 33:1–34:2 (for other parallels in Merkavah texts, see P. Alexander in Charlesworth, *OTP* 1:287 n. 34c). In biblical tradition, the rainbow is primarily associated with the flood narrative, in which it is a divine sign that guarantees that a flood of this magnitude will never again occur (Gen 9:13–16).

**4a** καὶ κυκλόθεν τοῦ θρόνου θρόνους εἴκοσι τέσσαρες, "Twenty-four thrones encircled that throne." A more conventional conception of the arrangement of heavenly beings who surround God on his heavenly throne is for them to flank the throne on the right and on the left, as in 1 Kgs 22:19, "I saw the Lord sitting on his throne, with all the host of heaven standing beside him to the right and to the left of him." The same arrangement is found in the *Apostolic Church Order* 18, εἴκοσι γὰρ καὶ τέσσαρές εἰσι πρεσβύτεροι, δώδεκα ἐκ δεξιῶν καὶ δώδεκα ἐξ εὐωνύμων, "for there are twenty-four elders, twelve on the right and twelve on the left." There can be no doubt, however, that the author understands the twenty-four elders as encircling the throne (for κεκλόθεν as "encircle," see 3 Kgdms 5:4; Sir 50:13; Zach 2:5; 4 Macc 5:1; Michl, *Ältesten,* 5). For the location of many thrones near the throne of God, see Dan 7:9 (apparently set up for the purpose of judgment; cf. Dan 7:10b). For the conception of one or more thrones in each of a series of heavens, apparently occupied by an angelic leader (this is made explicit through scribal additions in several MSS; see Knibb in Charlesworth, *OTP* 2:166 n. m), see *Asc. Isa.* 7:14, 19, 24, 29, 31, 33, 35; 8:9; 9:10, 24; 11:40. According to the conception found in the *Sepher ha-Razim* 1.8, seven overseers sit on seven thrones. Part of the third firmament is described in 3.3–4 (tr. Morgan, 61):

> Within, three princes sit on their thrones; they and their raiment have an appearance like fire and the appearance of their thrones is like fire, fire that gleams like gold, for they rule over all the angels of fire.

In the fifth firmament "are twelve princes of glory seated upon magnificent thrones, the appearance of their thrones is like that of fire" (*Sepher ha-Razim* 5.3–4; tr. Morgan, 73). According to *3 Enoch,* the angelic being named Metatron is given "a throne like the throne of glory." The term "thrones" is also used as a metaphor for members of the angelic host (Col 1:16; *T. Levi* 3:8; *Asc. Isa.* 7:27; *T. Adam* 4:8; *Apoc. Elijah* 1:10; 4:10; *2 Apoc. Enoch* [Rec. J] 20:1; *Apost. Const.* 8.12.8, 27), suggesting some form of dominion subordinate to that of God. Thrones are also metaphors for the heavenly reward of the righteous (*1 Enoch* 108:12; *Apoc. Elijah* 1:8).

**4b** καὶ ἐπὶ τοὺς θρόνους εἴκοσι τέσσαρας πρεσβυτέρους καθημένους, "and on the thrones sat twenty-four elders." Since the noun πρεσβύτεροι is anarthrous, it appears that the author assumes that these figures are unknown to his readers, though there are no close extant parallels in apocalyptic literature to such a heavenly group. The term elder is found frequently in the OT where the Hebrew term זָקֵן *zāqēn* is often translated by the Greek term πρεσβύτερος (G. Bornkamm, *TDNT* 6:654). There are two OT passages in which a group of "elders" is depicted as present before Yahweh: (1) Isa 24:23, which describes an eschatological event ("For the Lord of hosts will reign on Mount Zion and in Jerusalem, and before his elders he will manifest his glory"), and (2) Exod 24:9–10, the narrative of the seventy elders who accompanied Moses up to Mount Sinai where they had a vision of God. The author may have derived his conception of twenty-four elders surrounding the heavenly throne of God from these two passages, or may at least be alluding to them (see Feuillet, *RB* 65 [1958] 13–14; Fekkers, *Isaiah*, 141–43). In ancient Israel, as in the rest of the Near East (with the exception of Egypt), the term "elder" was used as a designation for authority and leadership in various social groupings, including families, clans, tribes (Judg 11:5–11), and cities (Judg 8:14; 11:3; Ruth 4:1–4); see McKenzie, *Bib* 40 [1959] 522–40; Conrad, *TDOT* 4:122–31. The term is also used of a leadership position with national importance as in the phrases "the elders of Israel" or the "elders of the people" (Exod 3:16, 18; 4:29; 12:21; 18:12; Num 11:14–17; Josh 7:6; 8:10). In some instances there were assemblies of the "elders of Israel" for particular purposes (1 Kgs 8:1–3; 2 Kgs 23:1–2). In the Qumran Community, elders were accorded a place of honor after the priests (1QS 6:8; CD 9:4). The term was retained in early Judaism for various types of religious and political authorities (1 Macc 1:26; 7:33; 11:23; 12:35; 2 Macc 13:13; 14:37; 1 Esdr 6:5, 8, 11, 27; 7:2; 3 Macc 1:8; Bar 1:4; Jdt 6:16; Mark 7:3, 5 [= Matt 15:2]; 8:31 [= Matt 16:21; Luke 9:22]; 11:27 [= Matt 21:23; Luke 20:1]; 14:43 [= Matt 26:47]; 53 [= Matt 26:57]; 15:1 [= Matt 27:1]; Matt 26:3; 27:3, 12, 20, 41; 28:12; Luke 7:3; 22:52; Acts 4:5, 8, 23; 6:12). In early Jewish synagogue organization, the πρεσβύτεροι were members of the γερουσία, "council," of local Jewish communities (*CIJ* 378, 650c, 650d, 653b, 663, 731, 732, 800, 803, 829, 931, 1277, 1404), though the earliest dated evidence for the use of πρεσβύτερος as a title is found in the mid-third century A.D. (Schürer, *History* 3:1, 102 n. 56). In early Christianity the term πρεσβύτερος is frequently used for a leadership role (Acts 11:30; 14:23; 20:17; 1 Tim 5:1, 17, 19; 1 Pet 5:1, 5; Jas 5:14; *2 Clem.* 17:3, 5; Ign. *Magn.* 2:1; 3:1; 6:1; 7:1; *Trall.* 3:1; 7:1; Hermas *Vis.* 2.4.2, 3). In Ignatius, the college of elders is often called a πρεσβυτήριον, "presbytery" (e.g., *Eph.* 2:2; 4:1; 20:2; *Magn.* 2:2), a term that was also used for the Jewish Sanhedrin (Luke 22:66; Acts 22:5).

*Excursus 4A: The Twenty-Four Elders*

**Bibliography**

**Avi-Yonah, M.** "A List of Priestly Courses from Caesarea." *IEJ* 12 (1962) 137–42.
**Baumgarten, J. M.** "The Duodecimal Courts of Qumran, Revelation, and the Sanhedrin."

*JBL* 95 (1976) 59–78. **Feuillet, A.** "Les vingt-quatre vieillards del'Apocalypse." *RB* 65 (1958) 5–32. **Grosjean, P.** "Les vingt-quatre vieillards del'Apocalypse: A propos d'une liste galloise." *AnBoll* 72 (1954) 192–212. **McKenzie, J. L.** "The Elders in the OT." *Bib* 40 (1959) 522–40. **Michl, J.** *Die Engelvorstellung in der Apokalypse.* Munich: Heuber, 1937. ———. *Die 24 Ältesten in der apokalypse des hl. Johannes.* Munich: Hueber, 1938. **Müller, C. D. G.** *Die Engellehre der koptischen Kirche.* Wiesbaden: Harrassowitz, 1959. **Petraglio, R.** "Des influences de l'Apocalypse dans la 'Passio Perpetuae' 11–13." In *L'Apocalypse de Jean: Traditions exégétiques et iconographiques,* ed. Y. Christe. Geneva: Librairie Droz, 1979. **Skinjar, A.** "Vigintiquattuor seniores." *VD* 16 (1936) 333–38, 361–68. **Stegemann, V.** *Die Gestalt Christi in den koptischen Zaubertexten.* Heidelberg: Bilabel, 1934. **Winter, P.** "Twenty-Six Priestly Courses." *VT* 6 (1956) 215–17.

There have been many attempts to identify the twenty-four elders of Revelation 4–5, though no solution has found universal acceptance. Since no other early Jewish or early Christian composition depicts God in his heavenly court surrounded by twenty-four elders, it is probable that John himself has created the twenty-four elders for this scene (Gunkel, *Schöpfung und Chaos,* 306), though many of the other constituent features of this throne-room scene have been drawn from various OT passages as well as from apocalyptic tradition. Angelic councils, for example, are frequently mentioned in the OT (Ps 89:7; Job 1:6; 2:1; Dan 7:9–10; *1 Enoch* 47:2–3; 60:2; see Bornkamm, *TDNT* 6:668). According to Exod 24:9–11, seventy elders (זְקֵנִים *zĕqānîm*) of Israel ascended Mount Sinai with Moses, Aaron, Nadab, and Abihu, where they saw the God of Israel and ate and drank before him (see also Num 11:16–17, 24–25). The *Mart. Perpetua* 12 is part of a vision narrated by Saturus in which he and his companions are carried by four angels up a hill and into the heavenly throne room where they hear the *sanctus* chanted continually by angels wearing white robes and see an aged man with white hair with four elders (*seniores*) on his right and left and others behind him, though the total number is not specified. Since *The Martyrdom of Perpetua and Felicitas* was probably written ca. A.D. 200 in North Africa, the conception of heaven has almost certainly been influenced by the imagery of Revelation (Petraglio, "Passio Perpetuae," 11–13, 15–29, esp. 27). Actually, the literary *function* of the twenty-four elders within Revelation is far more important than any speculation regarding their supposed identity (an identity that the author was simply not concerned to specify more closely). The twenty-four elders play an important role in the heavenly worship of God and are described in the following ways: (1) They wear white robes and gold crowns (4:4b). (2) They prostrate themselves before God in worship (4:10a; 5:14b; 11:16; 19:4) and offer him their golden crowns (4:10b) as part of a heavenly liturgy (4:8–11; 5:11–14; 7:11–12; 19:1–8) to which they may respond with "Hallelujah" and "Amen" (19:4b). (3) They sing hymns of praise to God (4:11; 5:9–10; 11:17–18). (4) They have harps and censers full of incense that are said to represent the prayers of Christians (5:8). (5) Individual elders make comments to John (5:5; 7:13), and on one occasion an elder acts as a *senior interpres,* i.e., an "interpreting elder" (7:14–17), a functional equivalent to the stock apocalyptic figure of the *angelus interpres,* "interpreting angel" (found in Revelation only in 17:1–18). (6) If the enigmatic statement in 20:4 ("Then I saw thrones, and seated on them were those to whom judgment was committed") refers to the twenty-four elders (and this is far from certain), then they also have an explicitly judicial function. (7) While the twenty-four elders play a central role in Rev 4–5 (where they are mentioned seven times), they are peripheral in the throne scenes in the rest of the book (7:11, 13; 11:16; 14:3; 19:4), perhaps suggesting that they have been exported to these other text units from Rev 4.

Attempts to identify the twenty-four elders have given rise to many different proposals (for a detailed survey to 1920, see Charles, 1:128–33), some of which can be combined. (1) The heavenly counterparts of the leaders of the twenty-four priestly courses of the second temple period described in 1 Chr 23:6; 24:7–18 (Völter, 5–6; Charles, 1:131–32; Beasley-Murray, 114; Mounce, 135–36). This is perhaps the most cogent explanation, though it must be admitted that with the exception of carrying harps and censers containing the prayers of the saints (5:8), the twenty-four elders do not exhibit priestly functions. The author has inserted these figures into a heavenly throne scene containing more traditional features. While the Chronicler traced the twenty-four priestly divisions to the time of David, they probably originated in the late fourth century B.C. In the organization of the priesthood that prevailed throughout the second temple period, and continued to the third or fourth century A.D. (see the third- or fourth-century A.D. inscription from Caesarea described by M. Avi-Yonah, *IEJ* [1962] 137–42; id., "Caesarea," *NEAEHL* 1:279), the priesthood was divided into twenty-four "courses" (Hebrew מִשְׁמָרוֹת *mišmĕrôt;* Greek ἐφημερίδες), each of which served twice in the temple in Jerusalem for one week at a time, from sabbath to sabbath (Jos. *Ant.* 7.365–66; *Life* 2; in *Ag. Ap.* 2.108 [extant only in Latin], Josephus mentions four priestly "families" [*tribus*], probably referring to the four מִשְׁמָרוֹת *mišmĕrôt* that returned from exile; Ezra 2:36; Neh 7:39; *y. Ta'an.* 68a; *t. Ta'an.* 2.1–2; *b. 'Arak.* 12b; *m. Ta'an.* 4:2; Luke 1:5, 8; see Jeremias, *Jerusalem,* 198–207; CRINT 1/2, 587–96; Schürer, *History* 2:245–50; Str-B 2:55–68). The priesthood of the Qumran community was divided into twenty-six courses (probably the result of their special calendar); according to 1QM 2:2, "the twenty-six chiefs of the classes [רָאשֵׁי הַמִּשְׁמָרוֹת *r'wy hmšmrwt*] shall serve together with their classes" (though 4QMishmarot is not yet published, it is discussed briefly in Schürer, *History* 2:248); see Winter, *VT* 6 (1956) 215–17. In 2 Kgs 19:2; Jer 19:1, a group of people called the "elder priests" or "senior priests" (Hebrew זִקְנֵי הַכֹּהֲנִים *zqny hkhn'ym;* Greek οἱ πρεσβύτεροι τῶν ἱερέων) are mentioned but with no further explanation (*TDOT* 4:128). The leaders of each of the twenty-four courses of priests could be called שָׂרִים *śrym,* "princes" (Ezra 8:24, 29; 20:5; 2 Chr 36:14), רָאשִׁים *r'šym,* "heads" (1 Chr 24:4; 1QM 2:2), or זְקֵנִים *zqnym,* "elders" (perhaps 2 Kgs 19:2; Jer 19:1). In the Mishna the phrases זִקְנֵי כֹהֲנִים *zqny khnym,* "elders of the priests" (*m. Yoma* 1:5), and זִקְנֵי בֵית אָב *zqny byt 'b,* "elders of the father's house" (*m. Tamid.* 1:1; *m. Mid.* 1:8) occur (the latter constitute divisions within each of the מִשְׁמָרוֹת *mišmĕrôt* or "courses"; see *y. Ta'an.* 68a, quoted in Schürer, *History* 2:245).

(2) The twenty-four divisions of musicians, descendants of Levi, who prophesied with lyres, harps, and cymbals (1 Chr 25:1–31; cf. 35:15; Ezra 2:41; 3:10; Neh 7:44; Jos. *Ant.* 7.367; see Schürer, *History* 2:250–56). However, this is not really a serious possibility in view of the relatively minor status of the twenty-four courses of Levites, each of which was structured to correspond to one of the courses of priests. Further, the Levites had declined in status during the Hellenistic period, yielding ground to the priests (CRINT, 1/2, 597).

(3) Heavenly representatives of Israel and the Church, i.e., twenty-four as the sum of the twelve sons of Israel and the Twelve Apostles, an old view found in Victorinus *Comm. in Apoc.* IV.3 (ed. Haussleiter, *Victorinus,* 50); cf. Charles, 1:132–33. Swete interpreted the twenty-four elders as representing the church in its totality (68–69), while analogously Hurtado understands the elders to be "the heavenly representatives of the elect" (*JSNT* 25 [1985] 113). Ignatius speaks of a σύνδεσμον ἀποστόλων, "band of apostles" (presumably twelve in number), and a συνέδριον θεοῦ, "council of God," reflected in the college of presbyters (*Trall.* 3:1), called the συνέδριον τοῦ ἐπισκόπου, "council of the bishop" (*Phld.* 8:1). The presbyters in fact represent the συνέδριον τῶν ἀποστόλων, "council of the apostles" (*Magn.* 6:1), which is possibly considered a heavenly council (see *Trall.* 3:1; 12:2) rather than simply a historical grouping (Lightfoot, *Apostolic Fathers,* 2/2, 158; however, see Schoedel, *Ignatius,* 113, who argues against this view). The conception of a συνέδριον τῶν πρεσβυτέρων is a known form of civic association for which there is some evidence from Asia Minor, particularly from Philadelphia (*CIG* 3417) and Ephesus (C. Curtius, "Inschriften aus Ephesos," *Hermes* 4 [1870] 199, 203, 224).

(4) Individual Christians who had sealed their faith through martyrdom, now glorified and participating in an exalted heavenly life (Eichhorn, 1:160–61 [who thinks that the *number* is based on the twenty-four priestly courses]; Stuart, 2:110; Feuillet, *RB* 65 [1958] 5–32; Kraft, 97). The transformation of the righteous into angelic form is mentioned in Luke 20:36. Thrones are sometimes used as a metaphor for the heavenly reward of the righteous (*1 Enoch* 108:12). In *T. Job* 33:3, 5, 7, 9, Job speaks of an eternal throne that he has in heaven, and the garments, thrones, and crowns reserved for the righteous in the seventh heaven are frequently mentioned in *Asc. Isa.* (7:22; 8:26; 9:12; 11:40); when Isaiah ascends, he is gradually transformed into an angel (*Asc. Isa.* 9:30). *Apoc. Elijah* (P. Chester Beatty 2018) 2:4–5 (tr. Pietersma, *Elijah*): "For everyone who will obey his voice will receive thrones and crowns" (= 1:8 in Charlesworth, *OTP* 1:736). Sometimes crowns alone are used as metaphors for the heavenly reward of the righteous (5 Ezra 2:42–45). In this instance, the number twenty-four must also be accounted for, perhaps as the sum of the twelve tribes of Israel and the Twelve Apostles, or as a symbol for continuous, twenty-four-hour worship, day and night.

(5) The saints of the OT (Michl, *Ältesten*, 92–116; Swete, 118; Harrington, *Apocalypse*, 109). Michl argues that the elders are in reality transformed figures from the old covenant. Exemplary ancient Israelites are called πρεσβύτεροι in Heb 11:2, an honorific term for men of wisdom and experience who often functioned as judges (Josh 24:31; Judg 2:7; Ruth 4:2; Philo *Sobr.* 16; *Mos.* 1.4; Jos. *Ant.* 13.292). According to *b. Ber.* 17a, the eschatological reward of the righteous is to sit before God with crowns on their heads. *Qoh. Rab.* 1.11 (tr. Freedman and Simon, *Midrash Rabbah* 8:36):

> In the Hereafter, however, the Holy One, blessed be He, will number for Himself a band of righteous men of His own and seat them by Him in the Great Academy; as it is said, "Then the moon shall be confounded and the sun ashamed for the Lord of hosts will reign in mount Zion and in Jerusalem, and before His elders shall be glory" (Isa XXIV, 23). It is not written here "Before His angels, His troops, or His priests" but "before His elders shall be glory."

A parallel text is found in *Tanhuma, Shemot* 29 (cf. *Qoh. Rab.* 1.11):

> The Holy One, blessed be He, will in the future cause the elders of Israel to stand as in a threshing floor, and He will sit at the head of them all as president [אב בית דין *'ab bêt dîn*], and they will judge the nations of the world.

(6) Angelic members of the heavenly court (סוד אלהים *sôd 'ĕlōhîm*), or an angelic order, which surround the throne of God (Beckwith, 498–99; Kiddle, 76–84; Roloff, 67–68). One weakness of this view, however, is that angels are rarely called elders in Jewish texts (see Isa 24:23 below). In the OT, God is frequently conceptualized as surrounded by angelic courtiers (1 Kgs 22:19; Job 1:6; 2:1). In later rabbinic literature, this heavenly court, the בית דין של שמים *bêt dîn šel šāmayyim* (*Mek. de-Rabbi Ishmael, Nezikin* 10; Lauterbach, *Mekilta* 3:81), corresponded to the earthly בית דין *bêt dîn*, "house of judgment." In the OT, such beings are variously called "Seraphim" (Isa 6:2), "spirits" (1 Kgs 22:21), "sons of God" (Job 1:6), and "elders" (Isa 24:23: "Then . . . the Lord of hosts will reign on Mount Zion and in Jerusalem, and before his elders [Hebrew זקנים *zĕqānîm;* Greek πρεσβύτεροι] he will manifest his glory"). The *Apoc. Zeph.* A (fragment quoted in Clement *Strom.* 5.11.77) depicts the heavenly world in a way similar to Rev 4 and presents angels as seated on thrones (tr. Wintermute in Charlesworth, *OTP* 1:508):

> And a spirit took me and brought me up into the fifth heaven. And I saw angels who are called "lords," and the diadem was set upon them in the Holy Spirit, and the throne

of each of them was sevenfold more (brilliant) than the light of the rising sun. (And they were) dwelling in the temples of salvation and singing hymns to the ineffable most high God.

There is a contrary Jewish tradition that angels had no knees and so were unable to sit (*y. Ber.* 2c; *Bereshit R.* [ed. Theodor-Albeck], 738; see Gruenwald, *Apocalyptic*, 66–67), a tradition apparently based on the phrase ורגליהם רגל ישרה *wĕraglêhem regel yĕšārâ*, "and their legs were straight," in Ezek 1:7. There was a widespread Jewish tradition that no one is permitted to sit in the presence of God (4Q405 20 ii 2 [see Newsom, *Songs*, 303–9]; *b. Ḥag.* 15a; *3 Enoch* 16). In the mythic cosmology of Justin the Gnostic, Elohim and Edem produced twenty-four angels, twelve males and twelve females (Hippolytus *Ref.* 5.26.1–6; ed. Marcovich, *Hippolytus*). The twenty-four elders frequently appear in Coptic magical texts (Kropp, *Koptische Zaubertexte* 3:83–85; Müller, *Engellehre*, 85–87), where they are understood as angels (as they are throughout eastern Christianity). Since the number twenty-four corresponds to the number of letters in the Greek alphabet, each is given a name beginning with one of the twenty-four letters (Kropp, *Koptische Zaubertexte* 2:114, 203; 3:130–32). The twenty-four elders transmit the prayers of the saints to the Lamb (Rev 5:8), corresponding to a widespread Jewish apocalyptic tradition that angels and archangels present the prayers of the saints to God (Tob 12:12, 15; *3 Apoc. Bar.* 11:4; Clement Alex. *Exc. ex Theod.* 27.2; Origen *De princ.* 1.8.1; Rev 8:3–5; see Charles, 1:143–44).

(7) Figures from astral mythology, such as the twenty-four Babylonian star-gods of the zodiac, grouped around the polar star and divided over the north and south as judges of the living and the dead (Gunkel, *Schöpfung und Chaos*, 302–8; Boll, *Offenbarung*, 36). According to Diodorus Siculus 2.31.4 (LCL tr.):

Beyond the circle of the zodiac they designate twenty-four other stars, of which one half, they say, are situated in the northern parts and one half in the southern, and of these those which are visible they assign to the world of the living, while those which are invisible they regard as being adjacent to the dead, and so they call them "Judges of the Universe" [δικαστὰς τῶν ὅλων].

Another term for these figures is "Decans" since they were often thought to consist of thirty-six figures, each of which dominates ten degrees of the Zodiac. Malina argues that the twenty-four elders are decans, moving from celestial figures who dominate each ten degrees of the Zodiacal circle to figures who dominate each of the twelve hours of the day and the twelve hours of the night (*Revelation*, 93–97). In both the shorter and longer recensions of *2 Enoch* 4:1, angelic leaders are called "elders" (tr. Andersen in Charlesworth, *OTP* 1:110–11): "They led before my face the elders, the rulers of the stellar orders." Andersen suggests that the missing link between Revelation and *2 Apoc. Enoch* might be supplied by the Beth Alpha mosaic, which depicts a zodiac, symbols for the four seasons, and in the center the sun-god surrounded by twenty-three stars and the moon, i.e., twenty-four heavenly bodies (in Charlesworth, *OTP* 1:110–11 n. 4.a; on the Beth Alpha mosaic, see Hachlili, *Jewish Art*, 308–9 and plate 73).

What kinds of associations did the number twenty-four have? (1) The twenty-four hours of the day. This is the most common use of the number and suggests the fullness of time, for the elders are said to worship God continually, day and night (4:10). In the *T. Adam* 1:1–2:12, the particular type of praise or prayer for each of the twenty-four hours of the night and the day is listed. (2) The traditional twenty-four authors of the books of the OT (Victorinus *Comm. in Apoc.* IV.3 [ed. Haussleiter, *Victorinus*, 50]; Ps.-Tertullian *Carmen adv. Marc.* 4.198–210; Swete, 212–13; Beckwith, 262–63, 271 n. 70). This conjecture is based on the ancient view (the dominant rabbinical view) that the Hebrew OT contains twenty-four canonical books (Beckwith, 240–41). A baraita in *b. B. Bat.* 14b–15a lists twenty-four authors of the various OT books, and there is a parallel in the *Gos. Thom.* 52, "His disciples said to him, 'Twenty-four prophets spoke in Israel and all of them spoke about you.'" Similarly, the anonymous *Vitae Prophetarum* is a collection of thumbnail sketches of the lives of twenty-four Israelite prophets. (3) Symbols of the cosmos (Boll, *Offenbarung*, 26–27; Dornseiff, *Alphabet*, 75, 122–25; Stegemann, *Zaubertexten*, 27). (4) The twenty-four lictors of Domitian. Roman magistrates were accompanied by the number of *lictores* (bodyguards) carrying *fasces* (an axe protruding from a bundle of rods, signifying authority) corresponding to the degree of *imperium* to which they were entitled (Mommsen, *Römisches Staatsrecht* 1:355–56). During the monarchy, kings had twelve lictors, and under the Republic consuls also had twelve, while dictators had twenty-four (A. Berger, *Roman Law*, 565). Augustus also seems to have had twelve lictors from 31 to 23 B.C., though it is possible that he had twenty-four lictors until 27 B.C. (Mommsen, *Römisches Staatsrecht* 1:385 n. 5). The maximum number of lictors was raised by Domitian from twelve to twenty-four (Dio 67.4.3; Suetonius *Dom.* 4; Mommsen, *Römisches Staatsrecht* 1:388; Alföldi, *Repräsentation*, 102). Domitian presided at games flanked by various priests wearing gold crowns (Suetonius *Dom.* 4.4; LCL tr.):

> He presided at the competitions in half-boots, clad in a purple toga in the Greek fashion, and wearing upon his head a golden crown with figures of Jupiter, Juno, and Minerva, while by his side sat the priest of Jupiter and the collece of the Flaviales, similarly dressed, except that their crowns bore his image as well.

The Q saying in Matt 19:28 (and par. Luke 22:30) predicts that in the new world the Twelve Apostles will sit on twelve thrones and judge the twelve tribes of Israel (12 + 12). Hippolytus held the view that the twelve disciples were chosen from the twelve tribes (*Ref.* 5.8.12; ed. Marcovich, *Hippolytus*). Perhaps the Q saying was influenced by Ps 122:3–5, which refers to Jerusalem as the destination to which the tribes go up and as the place where thrones for judgment are set. In the *T. Abr.* (Rec. A) 13:6, judgment is exercised by "the twelve tribes of Israel," a text later modified to "the twelve apostles" (M. R. James, *The Testament of Abraham* [Cambridge: Cambridge UP, 1892] 92). In early Judaism, deliberative bodies of thirty-six (not twenty-four) members are common and represent 12 + 12 + 12. The earliest attestation of such a special body is found in the king's council mentioned in the 11QTemple, the *Temple Scroll* (57:11–13; tr. Yadin, 2:257): "And the twelve leaders of his people (shall be) with him [i.e., the king], and of the priests twelve, and of the Levites twelve. They shall sit together with him for judgment . . . ." For later references to a thirty-six-member body, see *m. Sanh.; b. Sanh.* 97b; *b. Sukk.* 45b; see E. E. Urbach, *Sages*, 439ff. Deliberative bodies of *twelve* members are mentioned several times in literature from Qumran (Baumgarten, *JBL* 95 [1976] 59): (1) twelve men and three priests (1QS 8:1); (2) a court of twelve (4QOrd 2 iv 3–4); (3) twelve priests (1QM 2:1); (4) twelve chiefs of the people, twelve priests, and twelve Levites (11QTemple 57:11–13). On the basis of 4QpIsa[d], Baumgarten proposes that two groups consisting of twelve priests and twelve laymen constituted an eschatological judicial council of twenty-four (Baumgarten, *JBL* 95 [1976] 64; but see Horgan, *Pesharim*, 125–31).

**4c** περιβεβλημένους ἐν ἱματίοις λευκοῖς, "dressed in white robes." The author exhibits a consistent interest in what various figures in his visions wear (he uses the term περιβάλλειν, "to wear," twelve times, while ἐνδύειν, "to wear," occurs three times). Clothing is often clearly metaphorical (3:5, 18). Whenever a vision segment features a new major figure, the clothing of the figure is routinely mentioned, often with the term περιβάλλειν: the 144,000 (7:9), the mighty angel (10:1), the two witnesses (11:3), the cosmic woman (12:1), the Great Whore (17:4), the personified city of Rome (18:16), and the Bride of the Lamb (19:8). The term ἐνδύειν, "to wear," is used to describe the apparel of the exalted Christ (1:13), the seven bowl angels (15:6), and the armies of heaven (19:14). John makes clothing an essential part of an individual's characteristics. He regards nudity as shameful (3:18), very probably reflecting the typically Eastern disapprobation of Greco-Roman nudity. When describing garments, the colors "white" and "black" in Greek often simply mean "light" and "dark." In Judaism, white or light garments connoted joy, purity, and social dignity, while dark or colored garments were worn by women and lower-class men (Krauss, *Talmudische Archäologie* 1:144–45). According to Exod 28:4; Lev 16:4, the high priest wore only a white linen ephod on the Day of Atonement when he entered the Holy of Holies. Dan 7:9 reports that God himself wore garments white as snow. Josephus reports that the Levites urged Agrippa to convene the Sanhedrin to ask permission to have Levitical singers (ὑμνῳδοί) wear linen robes (λινῆν στολήν), like the priests, and have them memorize the hymns they sang in the temple (*Ant.* 20.216–18); n.b. that there were originally twenty-four divisions of these temple musicians (1 Chr 25:1–31; cf. 35:15; Ezra 2:41; 3:10; Neh 7:44); see H. Gese, "Zur Geschichte der Kultsänger am zweiten Tempel," in *Abraham unser Vater*, FS O. Michel, ed. O. Betz, M. Hengel, and P. Schmidt (Leiden: Brill, 1963) 222–34. It is generally thought that these robes were white (Goodenough, "Greek Garments," 231). Josephus also reports that the Essenes gave initiants a white robe, which they continued to wear as members of the community (*J.W.* 2.123, 137). According to Plutarch, women in mourning wore white robes (ἱμάτια), and corpses were dressed in white to symbolize the purity of the soul (*Quaest. Rom.* 26 [270D–F]; cf. Ps.-Philo *Bib. Ant.* 64:6, where the deceased Samuel is seen in a séance wearing a white garment, probably a burial garment). The Jewish tradition that angels wore white is reflected in the NT (Mark 16:5; Matt 28:3; Luke 24:4; John 20:12; Acts 1:10; cf. Krauss, *Talmudische Archäologie* 1:550 n. 212) and in early Jewish literature (2 Macc 11:8; *T. Levi* 8:2). Garments used in Greek and Roman religious rituals are usually described as white (Aeschines *Against Ctesiphon* 77; Vergil *Aeneid* 10.539; Apuleius *Metamorphoses* 11.9, 10; *Acts of John* 38).

**4d** καὶ ἐπὶ τὰς κεφαλὰς αὐτῶν στεφάνους χρυσοῦς, "with golden crowns on their heads." Wreaths and white garments (see v 4c) were appropriate cultic attire for praying, sacrificing, and marching in religious processions (Aeschines *Against Ctesiphon* 77; Apuleius *Metamorphoses* 11.9). Suetonius *Dom.* 4.4 depicts Domitian wearing a gold crown (*corona aurea*) with images of Jupiter, Juno, and Minerva on it and surrounded by the priest of Jupiter and members of the college of Flaviales (established by Domitian for the cult of the deified Flavian emperors), each wearing a gold crown with an image of Domitian on it. Priests of the imperial cult in Asia Minor customarily wore gold crowns displaying busts of the emperor(s) and family members, a custom largely limited to Asia Minor (this phenomenon is discussed in J. Inan and E. Alföldi-Rosenbaum, *Römische und frühbyzantinische Porträtplastik aus der Türkei: Neue Funde*, 2 vols. [Mainz am Rhein: von Zabern, 1979] 38–47; for examples, see nos. 135, 137, 186, 225, 230, 264, 311, 326 with discussions and plates; further examples are found in J. Inan and E. Rosenbaum, *Roman and Early Byzantine Portrait Sculpture in Asia Minor* [London: Oxford UP, 1966] nos. 111, 143, 151, 169, 174, 190, etc.).

**5a** καὶ ἐκ τοῦ θρόνου ἐκπορεύονται ἀστραπαὶ καὶ φωναὶ καὶ βρονταί, "From the throne came lightning and rumbling and thunder." To this point John has used past tenses as the background tense for describing this vision. With ἐκπορεύονται, "come from," he changes to the present indicative in order to place in the foreground heavenly phenomena that occur continually; therefore, he uses the generic present to refer to this continual activity. In the OT the Hebrew word קול *qôl*, "sound, voice," is often used in the plural form קולות *qôlôt* to mean "thunder" and is frequently translated in the LXX with the Greek term φωναί, as in the following passages: Exod 9:23, 28, 29, 33, 34; 19:16; 1 Sam 12:17, 18. In the context of storm phenomena associated primarily with the Sinai theophany (Exod 19:16–19; Jeremias, *Theophanie*, 100–111), which served as the model for later theophanic scenes (Isa 29:6; Pss 18:6–16[LXX 17]; 77:18[LXX 76:19]), it is clear that φωναί should be translated not "voices" (AV, RSV) but rather "rumblings" (NIV, NRSV), a term synonymous with βρονταί; the NEB avoids the problem by including just two atmospheric elements, "flashes of lightning and peals of thunder." There are four lists of atmospheric and seismic phenomena that are used in theophanic contexts in Revelation (4:5; 8:5; 11:19; 16:18; see *Comment* on 4:5), and each of them differs slightly from the others as the following comparison reveals:

Rev 4:5a:      καὶ ἐκ τοῦ θρόνου ἐκπορεύονται ἀστραπαὶ καὶ φωναὶ καὶ βρονταί
               "From the throne came lightning and rumbling and thunder"

Rev 8:5c:      καὶ ἐγένοντο βρονταὶ καὶ φωναὶ καὶ ἀστραπαὶ καὶ σεισμός
               "and there was thunder and rumbling and lightning and an earthquake"

Rev 11:19c:    καὶ ἐγένετο ἀστραπαὶ καὶ φωναὶ καὶ βρονταὶ καὶ σεισμοῖς καὶ χάλαζα
               μεγάλη
               "and there was lightning and rumbling and thunder and an earthquake
               and great hail"

Rev 16:18–21:  καὶ ἐγένοντο ἀστραπαὶ καὶ φωναὶ καὶ βρονταὶ καὶ σεισμὸς ἐγένετο μέγας
               . . . καὶ χάλαζα μεγάλη
               "Then there were lightning and rumbling and thunder and there was a
               great earthquake . . . and great hail"

Several observations can be made about these lists (on the earthquake, see *Comment* on 8:5; on the large hail, see *Comment* on 11:19c): (1) The most frequently occurring pattern is ἀστραπαὶ καὶ φωναὶ καὶ βρονταί (4:5; 11:19; 16:18), with a slight reordering in the remaining passage (8:5, βρονταὶ καὶ φωναὶ καὶ ἀστραπαί). This list of storm phenomena clearly forms the core of all four lists. A very similar list occurs in *Jub.* 2:2, which refers to the creation of ἄγγελοι φωνῶν, βροντῶν, ἀστραπῶν, "angels of the sounds, thunders, and lightnings" (Greek text of Epiphanius in Denis, *Fragmenta*, 71; on the corruption of the Ethiopic text, see VanderKam, *Jubilees* 2:8; Hebrew text of 4Q*216*= 4QJub<sup>a</sup> has only הקולות *haqqôlôt*, "voices" or "thunders"; see VanderKam and Milik, *JBL* 110 [1911] 257–60). Very similar also is *Apoc. Abr.* 30:8, where the last in a series of ten plagues is described as "thunder, voices, and destroying earthquakes" (tr. Charlesworth, *OTP* 1:704). (2) The two lists in 11:19 and 16:18–21 are virtually identical, though the σεισμός in 11:19 is qualified as μέγας, and the lengthy description of the magnitude and extent of the earthquake in 16:19–20 interrupts the mention of χάλαζα μεγάλη, the effects of which are also described at some length. (3) The theophanic use of storm phenomena, such as lightning, rumblings, and thunder, grew out of the narrative of the Sinai theophany in Exod 19:16–18, where five phenomena are mentioned, thunder, lightning, a thick cloud, a loud trumpet blast, and an earthquake (essentially repeated in *Tg. Onq.* Exod 19:16 and *Tg. Ps.-J.* Exod 19:16), initially repeated in Ps.-Philo *Bib. Ant.* 11:4, and then enormously expanded primarily through the use of seismic disturbances in Ps.-Philo *Bib. Ant.* 11:5 (tr. Charlesworth, *OTP* 2:318):

> And behold the mountains burned with fire, and the earth quaked, and the hills were disturbed, and the mountains were rolled about, and the abysses boiled, and every habitable place was shaken, and the heavens were folded up, and the clouds drew up water, and flames of fire burned, and thunderings and lightnings were many, and winds and storms roared, the stars gathered together.

(4) While Bauckham ("Earthquake," 199–209) is the only one who has discussed these lists in some detail, he exaggerates the conscious influence of the Sinai tradition. A similar list of four atmospheric and seismic disturbances is found in LXX Esth 1:1d–e, where they are part of a dream in which violence against the Jews is anticipated:

> And this was his dream: Behold, there were sounds and tumult, thunderings and an earthquake [φωναὶ καὶ θόρυβος, βρονταὶ καὶ σεισμός], confusion on earth. And behold two great dragons [δράκοντες] came forth, both ready for battle, and their cry was great.

The thunderbolt was closely associated with the Greek god Zeus, as it was with his Roman counterpart Jupiter, and was consequently used as a symbol suggesting the divinity of several Roman emperors including Domitian (*BMC* 2:381, no. 381; 389, no. 410; 399, no. 443; R. Fears, "The Cult of Jupiter and Roman Imperial Ideology," *ANRW* II, 17/1:79) and Trajan (*BMC* 3:174, no. 825; 190, no. 899; Schowalter, *Emperor,* 112, suggests incorrectly that Pliny would have objected to this symbolism in the light of such passages as *Pan.* 1.3).

**5b** καὶ ἑπτὰ λαμπάδες πυρὸς καιόμεναι ἐνώπιον τοῦ θρόνου, "and seven blazing torches burned before the throne." This may be an allusion to Zech 4:2 (see *Comment* on 5:6). Since the view is frequently found in early Judaism that angels are made of fire, it is possible that seven angelic beings are referred to here (as the allegorical interpretation in v 5c makes clear), or that the seven blazing torches represent the menorah. *2 Apoc. Bar.* 21:6 mentions countless beings constituted of flame and fire who stand around the throne of God, and 4 Ezra 8:21–22 speaks of the hosts of angels who stand before God's throne and at his command are changed to wind and fire. The seven burning torches would most naturally appear to represent the seven-branched menorah before the ark in the tabernacle (Exod 25:31–40; 27:20–21; Lev 24:1–4; Zech 4:2; cf. 2 Chr 4:7). The custom of carrying sacred fire (πῦρ) before emperors was an integral feature of imperial ceremonial by the mid-third century A.D. when Herodian wrote his history of Rome (1.8.4; 1.16.4; 2.3.2; 2.8.6; 7.9.1; 7.6.2), and probably much earlier (it is mentioned by Cassius Dio 72.35.5, where the term φῶς is used). Taylor (*Roman Emperor,* 195–96) suggested that the custom of carrying sacred fire before the emperor began when Augustus entered Alexandria on 1 August 30 B.C. Cumont suggests that the custom of carrying sacred fire before the Roman emperors symbolized the perpetuity of their power and can be traced back through Alexander and his successors to Persian traditions (*Oriental Religions,* 137). The possible historical relationship between the supposed custom of torch bearers preceding the triumphator in the Roman triumphal processions is tenuous because torches are mentioned in connection with triumphs in only a very few problematic texts (e.g., Suetonius *Div. Iul.* 37.2), and Versnel (*Triumphus,* 118–19) casts doubt on the correctness of this reconstruction. The history and significance of this imperial symbol are discussed in detail by Alföldi (*MDAIRA* 49 [1934] 111–18), who observes that "in the first century of the imperial period accompanying the emperor with torches in the daytime had already come into use" (116). See also Ps 50:3, "Our God comes, he does not keep silence, before him is a devouring fire [LXX 49:3, πῦρ ἐναντίον αὐτοῦ καυθήσεται]."

**5c** ἅ εἰσιν τὰ ἑπτὰ πνεύματα τοῦ θεοῦ, "which are the seven spirits of God." The "seven spirits which are before his [i.e., 'God's'] throne" were mentioned in 1:4 as part of the epistolary prescript (for a discussion of these seven spirits, see *Comment* on 1:4) and again in 3:1, where the exalted Christ is described as "having the seven spirits of God and the seven stars." The seven spirits of God are again mentioned in 5:6 in an allegorical interpretation of the seven eyes of the Lamb (this is also an interpretive gloss; see *Comment* on 5:6). Since the seven spirits of God are described as "before his throne" in 1:4, and the seven torches are similarly situated "before the throne" in 4:5, 4:5 has been turned into an allusion to 1:4 by the explanatory phrase "which are the seven spirits of God." This is probably an interpretive gloss introduced by the lemma ἅ εἰσιν (perhaps inspired by 3:1), which was added by the author to help the reader understand the meaning of the vision (cf. the gloss in 4:1). The present indicative εἰσιν, "is," is the gnomic present or present of general truth, describing something that will always be true. (For other interpretive glosses see 5:6, 8.)

**6a** καὶ ἐνώπιον τοῦ θρόνου ὡς θάλασσα ὑαλίνη ὁμοία κρυστάλλῳ, "There was also before the throne something like a glassy sea like crystal." This is probably based on an allusion to Ezek 1:22, where the prophet sees "the likeness of a firmament, shining like crystal," spread out over the heads of the living creatures (*Tg. Ezek.* 1:22 compares the firmament to a great ice field). One of the features of the temple of Solomon was an enormous bronze basin of water mounted on twelve bronze oxen, three facing each of the cardinal directions (1 Kgs 7:23–26; Jos. *Ant.* 8.79–80; according to 2 Kgs 16:17, Ahaz later removed the base and substituted one made of stone). This basin was called הים *hayyām,* "the sea" (1 Kgs 7:24; 2 Kgs 16:17), הים מוצק *hayyām mûṣāq,* "the molten sea" (1 Kgs 7:23; 2 Chr 4:2), or ים הנחשת *yām hannĕḥōšet,* "the bronze sea" (2 Kgs 25:13; Jer 52:17; 1 Chr 18:8). W. F. Albright and others have emphasized the cosmic significance of this basin and its relationship to smaller portable lavers (*Archaeology and the Religion of Israel,* 4th ed. [Baltimore: Johns Hopkins, 1956] 148–50), though de Vaux is more cautious (*Ancient Israel,* 328–29). The Babylonian term *apsû* referred both to the subterranean freshwater ocean upon which all life is based and to the basin of holy water in the temple (Albright, *Archaeology,* 148–49). Gen 1:7 (cf. *Jub.* 2:4) speaks of the waters above the firmament and the waters below the firmament; i.e., the primeval world ocean is divided into two halves. There are several references in the OT and early Jewish literature to a heavenly ocean above the solid vault of heaven (Pss 29:10 ["Yahweh sits enthroned on the heavenly ocean (מבול *mabbûl*)"]; 104:3; 148:4; *1 Enoch* 54:7; *2 Enoch* [Rec. J] 3:3; [Rec. A] 4:2; *T. Abr.* [Rec. B] 8:3; *T. Adam* 1:5; *T. Levi* 2:7; *Gen. Rab.* 1:6; *Apoc. Paul* 21), which is the source of rain (Gen 7:11; 8:2; Ps 104:13; Amos 9:6). In ancient Egyptian mythology, Nun, "the father of the gods," is the personified primeval ocean, identical with the Lake of Dawn, from which the sun rises and which is the primary obstacle separating the dead person from the sun (Morenz, *Egyptian Religion*, 167–69). Exod 24:10 contains an old tradition of the pavement of sapphire (the firmament) under the feet of God (*Tg. Onq.* Exod 24:10 avoids this anthropomorphism by substituting "the throne of his glory"), which was clear like the heaven. In 15:2 a "sea of glass mingled with fire" combines the motifs of a celestial sea above which the throne of God is set and the river (or rivers) of fire that flows from his throne (see *Comment* on 15:2). According to *b. Ḥag.* 14b, the pure alabaster pavement before the throne of God had the appearance of water. Several texts mention a celestial river (*T. Abr.* [Rec. B] 8:3; *2 Apoc. Bar.* [Gk.] 2:1; *Apoc. Paul* 22).

**6b** καὶ ἐν μέσῳ τοῦ θρόνου καὶ κύκλῳ τοῦ θρόνου τέσσαρα ζῷα γέμοντα ὀφθαλμῶν ἔμπροσθεν καὶ ὄπισθεν, "In the midst of the throne and around the throne were four cherubim covered with eyes in front and in back." In Isa 6:2, the Hebrew phrase מִמַּעַל לוֹ *mimmaʿal lô*, "from above him," is translated κύκλῳ αὐτοῦ, "around him," in the LXX, which indicates that John follows the way in which the LXX conceived of the location of the cherubim and seraphim (on the problematic phrase ἐν μέσῳ τοῦ θρόνου, see *Note* 4:6.c-c.). Beckwith (501–2) suggested that the arrangement reflects that of the Greek amphitheater, a view amplified by Brewer (*ATR* 18 [1936] 74–92) and accepted by Ford (74). The use of ζῷα, "cherubim," is the result of the author's dependence on Ezek 1:5–25, where the term חַיּוֹת *ḥayyôt*, "living creatures," is used, which is translated ζῷα in the LXX (see Oecumenius *Comm. in Apoc.* ad 4:6–8; Hoskier, *Oecumenius*, 72). When חיה *ḥayyâ*, "living creature," is used in the OT, it refers to "a dangerous animal, untamed, living free, and usually large" (KB³, 297), and the plural form of the term with this meaning occurs only rarely (see Isa 35:9; Ps 104:25; Dan 8:4). In Ezek 1–3 the term חַיּוֹת *ḥayyôt* is a vague, general term for living creatures, defined more fully in terms of their human form (Zimmerli, *Ezekiel* 1:120). In Ezekiel the living creatures are implicitly understood to bear up the moveable throne of God (see *2 Apoc. Bar.* 51:11), though the notion that God rode on the cherubim is made explicit only outside Ezekiel (2 Sam 22:11; Ps 18:11; see Metzger, *Königsthron und Gottesthron*, 309–51). The divine attribute "who is enthroned above the cherubim" occurs in hymns (Pss 80:1; 99:1) and prayers (Isa 37:16). In Ezek 10:20, the חַיּוֹת *ḥayyôt*, "living creatures," are explicitly identified as כְּרוּבִים *kĕrûbîm*, "cherubim," an equation that Zimmerli considers a later editorial development (*Ezekiel* 1:232–33) and an identification also made in *Apoc. Abr.* 10:9. In later hekalot literature, however, the cherubim are regularly distinguished from the ḥayyot (Schäfer, *Synopse*, §§ 100N, 103N, 119N; see Olyan, *Thousand*, 33–34). In 4QShirShabb, the cherubim but not the hayyot are mentioned, perhaps implying their identification and a preference for the term cherubim. The phrase "covered with eyes in front and in back" alludes to Ezek 1:18; 10:12, where it said that the wheels (אוֹפַנִּים *ʾôpannîm*) beside the living creatures were "full of eyes round about [MT מְלֵאֹת עֵינַיִם סָבִיב *mĕlēʾît ʿêynayim sabîb;* LXX πλήρεις ὀφθαλμῶν κυκλόθεν]." The Hebrew word for "wheels," אוֹפַנִּים *ʾôpannîm*, was used to mean a type of angelic being in later Jewish literature (*1 Enoch* 71:7; 4QShirShabb lines 4–5; *3 Enoch* 1:8; 2:1; 6:2; 7:1; 25:5–7; 33:3; 39:2; 48A:1; *b. Ḥag.* 12b; see G. F. Moore, *Judaism* 1:368, 409). The so-called *Ladder of Jacob* 2:8 speaks of "the four-faced cherubim [i.e., the 'living creatures' of Ezek 1], bearing also the many-eyed seraphim [i.e., the 'wheels' of Ezek 1]." The term "eyes" can be a metaphor for "stars" (Manilius *Astronomica* 1.132–43; Plutarch *Sept. sap. conv.* 161F; *De facie* 928B; Boll, *Offenbarung*, 36). There are several frescoes of Mithras showing him covered with stars (see Vermaseren, *Mithraica III,* plates III, IV, XI, XII). There are pictures of pantheistic, composite divinities on both papyri and amulets, which depict them covered with eyes (Hopfner, *Offenbarungszauber* 2:213, 215; see Eitrem, *Papyri Osloenses,* 41). One such deity is depicted with four wings, one frontal face with eight animal heads of lesser size, and covered with eyes (Keel, *Yahweh-Visionen,* 270, plate 194). In Middle Egyptian hieroglyphics, the ideogram of the eye functions as a generic determinative with the sense "eye, see, action of the eye" (see A. Gardiner, *Egyptian Grammar,* 2nd ed. [London: Oxford UP, 1950] 32, 450–51). Osiris was portrayed by means of an eye and a scepter, and some ancients claimed that the name Osiris meant πολυόφθαλμον, "many-eyed" (Plutarch *De Is. et Os.* 354F–355A; Diodorus Siculus 1.11.2), a symbol for omniscience. Argos was a monster of Greek mythology with the epithet Panoptes (Πανόπτης) because he was usually depicted as having "many eyes" (Aeschylus *Prom. Vinct.* 569, 978; Apollodorus *Bib.* 2.1.3; Pherecydes in scholion to Euripides *Phoen.* 116; Ovid gives the number as one hundred in *Metam.* 1.625–27).

**7a** καὶ τὸ ζῷον τὸ πρῶτον ὅμοιον λέοντι, **7b** καὶ τὸ δεύτερον ζῷον ὅμοιον μόσχῳ, **7c** καὶ τὸ τρίτον ζῷον ἔχων τὸ πρόσωπον ὡς ἀνθρώπου, **7d** καὶ τὸ τέταρτον ζῷον ὅμοιον ἀετῷ πετομένῳ, "And the first cherub was like a lion, and the second cherub was like an ox, and the third cherub had a face like a human, and the fourth cherub was like a flying eagle." In two passages in Ezekiel, the author describes the חיות *ḥayyôt,* "cherubim" or "living creatures," which are associated with the throne of God in the prophet's vision. In Ezek 1:5–14 (a problematic text subject to much redaction; see Zimmerli, *Ezekiel* 1:81–106), four such creatures are described, each shaped like a human being and each with four wings (each of the seraphim in Isa 6:2 has six wings), but each of the four has a different face (a man, a lion, an ox, and an eagle), and each face looked in a different direction. In 4Q385–389, a rewritten form of portions of Ezekiel, each creature has four faces, though the order of the faces differs from that of Ezekiel: lion, eagle, calf, man (4Q385–386 = 4QPseudo-Ezekiel[a] frag. 4, lines 8–9). In Rev 4:7, on the other hand, there are four cherubim, one resembling a lion, the second an ox, the third a man, and the fourth an eagle. Nothing is said that restricts these likenesses to the *face* of the creature only. In Ezek 10:14 (omitted in the LXX, suggesting that it was a late gloss; v 14 occurs only in Origen's Hexapla, see Ziegler, *Ezechiel,* 126), the faces of the cherubim are again described: the first has the face of a cherub (replacing that of the ox in Ezek 1:10), the second that of a man, the third that of a lion, and the fourth that of an eagle (note the difference in order from Ezek 1). In *b. Ḥag.* 13b the order is man, ox, lion, eagle, while in *Apoc. Abr.* 18 the order is lion, man, ox, eagle. H. Zimmern argued that the four faces of the living creatures in Ezekiel resembled the principal constellations in the four quarters of the zodiac, perhaps corresponding to the four seasons of the year: man = fall, lion = winter, ox = spring, eagle = summer (KAT[3], 631ff.). In Ezek 1:5–14 it is implied, though never explicitly stated, that the four creatures bear the throne of God (see 2 Sam 22:11; Ps 18:11; *T. Adam* 4:8; *3 Enoch* 33:3; Appendix to *3 Enoch* 24:15 [Charlesworth, *OTP* 1:309]; *Sepher ha-Razim* 7.1–2 [tr. Morgan, 81]). In the *Tg. Ezek* 1:6, it is said that each of the faces had four faces, sixteen to each creature, with sixty-four faces in all (Levey, *Tg. Ezek,* 20). This kind of elaboration is also found in *3 Enoch* 21:1–3 (tr. Alexander in Charlesworth, *OTP* 1:277):

There are four creatures [חיות *ḥayyôt*] facing the four winds. Each single creature would fill the whole world. Each of them has four faces and every single face looks like the sunrise. Each creature has four wings and every single wing would cover the world. Each one of them has faces within faces and wings within wings. The size of a face is 248 faces, and the size of a wing is 365 wings.

The clause in v 7c, ἔχων τὸ πρόσωπον ὡς ἀνθρώπου, "has the face of a human," disturbs the careful symmetry and stereotypical phraseology of the descriptions of the first, second, and fourth creatures. Instead, we would have expected the phrase to read ὅμοιον προσώπῳ ἀνθρώπου, "like a human face." Since ἔχων is a solecism (it is masculine in gender, though it modifies the neuter noun ζῷον) and, further, is used as a finite verb (a characteristic usage; see 1:16; 4:7, 8; 6:2, 5; 9:17, 19; 10:2; 11:2; 19:12; 21:12), it appears that John is consciously altering a source. One possible motivation for the alteration is the similarity between the reconstructed phrase and the phrase ὅμοιον υἱὸν ἀνθρώπου, "like a son of man," in 1:13; 14:14, which is also a solecism and therefore stems from John. Cf. the parallel phrase καὶ τὰ πρόσωπα αὐτῶν ὡς πρόσωπα ἀνθρώπων, "and their faces are like human faces" (Rev 9:7). In connection with v 7d, it is worth noting that the phrase in 4:7, ἀετῷ πετομένῳ, "flying eagle," has a verbal parallel in 8:13, ἀετοῦ πετομένου, "flying eagle."

A magic square for healing that was popular in the ancient world was based on Rev 4:7; see LXX Ezek 1:10 (M. Marcovich, *Studies in Graeco-Roman Religions and Gnosticism* [Leiden: Brill, 1988] 38–39):

| Rev 4:7<br>(Ezek 1:10) | P. Mag. Copt. Lond.<br>Ms. Or. 1013 A<br>(= V.24–25 Kropp) |
|---|---|

| | | |
|---|---|---|
| Α Λ Φ Α | Μόσχος | the face of Bull |
| Λ Ε Ω Ν | Λέων | the face of Lion |
| Φ Ω Ν Η | Ἀετός | the face of Eagle |
| Α Ν Η Ρ | Ἄνθρωπος | the face of Man |

The magic square is made up of the names of the four cherubs that surround the heavenly throne, with which they are identified by the author of Kropp V.24. Ἄλφα refers to Hebrew aleph = "ox," and Λέων and Ἄνθρωπος obviously refer to the "lion" and the "man." Φωνή refers to the "eagle," according to Marcovich, because in Revelation the eagle plays a special role as the voice of God (Rev 8:13).

In the ancient world there are a number of different representations of a leontocephaline, snake-encircled god with a human body found in association with Mithraic sanctuaries (J. R. Hinnells, "Reflections on the Lion-headed Figure in Mithraism," *Acta Iranica* 5 [1975] 333–69; H. M. Jackson, "The Meaning and Function of the Leontocephaline in Roman Mithraism," *Numen* 32 [1985] 17–45). One such lion-headed figure (often designated Saturn or Aion, but who may be Arimanius [see R. L. Gordon, "Franz Cumont and the Doctrines of Mithraism," in *Mithraic Studies*, ed. J. Hinnels, 2 vols. (Manchester: Manchester UP, 1975) 1:221–29]), discovered in the Sidon mithraeum, has two pairs of wings and a snake curling around his body and holds a set of keys (*CIMRM* 1:78). Another figure of the lion-headed, winged god was discovered at Castel Gandolfo, with four arms, lion masks on his stomach and knees, and an eye on his chest (*CIMRM* 1:326). For other leontocephaline statues, see indices, s.v. "Aion," in *CIMRM* 1:333; 2:403; M. Le Glay, "Aion," *Lexicon Iconographicum Mythologiae Classicae* (Zürich; Munich, 1981)

1/1, 399–411. In the Ophite astrological scheme of seven planetary archons who guard the way to the celestial world (Origen *Contra Cels.* 6.30), each archon has either an animal shape (the first four have the shapes of a lion, a bull, a snake, and an eagle, respectively) or an animal face (the last three have the faces of a bear, a dog, and an ass, respectively). In the so-called Mithras Liturgy (*PGM* IV.475–834), the seven Τυχαί are depicted as seven virgins with the faces of asps (662–63), and then seven other gods, called πολοκράτορες, "pole-rulers," are said to have the faces of black bulls (673–74).

Irenaeus identifies the four Evangelists with the four living creatures of Rev 4:6–7 (*Adv. haer.* 3.11.8), though he does not explicitly identify Revelation as the source: lion (John), ox (Luke), human face (Matthew), flying eagle (Mark). This order for the Gospels is extremely unusual but is also found in Victorinus *Comm. in Apoc.* 4.3–4 (Haussleiter, *Victorinus*, 48–51), which suggests that the order of the symbols and the Evangelists has nothing to do with the order of a collection of the Gospels (the various orders of the four Gospels are listed and discussed in Metzger, *The Canon of the New Testament* [Oxford: Clarendon, 1987] 296–97). The normal order of the gospels elsewhere in Irenaeus is Matthew, John, Luke, Mark. Though it has often been called the "Western" order of the gospels, this designation is problematic since evidence is found for this order in the East as well as the West. The present canonical order of the gospels (Matthew, Mark, Luke, John) is associated with Eusebius and Jerome and is not earlier than the late fourth century A.D. Skeat has argued convincingly that Irenaeus (who writes ca. A.D. 185) drew on an earlier source that suggests the existence of a codex with all four gospels ca. A.D. 170 (T. C. Skeat, "Irenaeus and the Four-Gospel Canon," *NovT* 34 [1992] 194–99); this agrees with Zahn's judgment that this tradition originated with an exegete or homilist of the second century A.D. not known by name ("Die Tiersymbole," 2:265). Jerome's recension of Victorinus *Comm. in Apoc.* 4.4 (Haussleiter, *Victorinus,* 51) has a different order: lion (Mark), man (Matthew), ox (Luke), and eagle (John); inexplicably, F. C. Grant has read Irenaeus as if this order were present there (*The Gospels: Their Origin and Growth* [New York: Harper & Row, 1957] 5, 65–66) and makes it one of several arguments for the priority of Mark. On this problem, see T. Zahn, "Die Tiersymbole," 2:257–75; H. Leclercq, "Évangelistes (Symboles des)," *DACL* 5/1 (1922) 845–52; J. Michl, *Engelvorstellungen* 1:88–103.

The author's reference to a *flying* eagle suggests the ancient visual convention of depicting the eagle with its wings spread. The eagle with spread wings is a symbol used in pagan and Jewish religious art (Delatte-Derchain, *Les intailles magiques*, no. 396; Hachlili, *Jewish Art*, 332–34).

A golden eagle was reportedly mounted over the portal of the Herodian temple (Jos. *J.W.* 1.650–51; *Ant.* 17.151–55; see Y. Meshorer, *Ancient Jewish Coinage* [Dix Hills, NY: Amphora, 1982] 2:129). The gable or pediment of a temple was called ἀετός, "eagle," or ἀετώμα (Jos. *Ant.* 3.131, of the tabernacle) in Greek, presumably because of the resemblance to outspread wings. Examples of eagles with spread wings include the carved eagle with garlands on the underside of the lintel from the Gush Ḥalav synagogue (ca. A.D. 250–550) in Upper Galilee (E. M. Meyers, C. L. Meyers, and J. F. Strange, *Excavations at the Ancient Synagogue of Gush Ḥalav* [Winona Lake, IN: Eisenbrauns, 1990] 89–90), carved eagles with spread wings on a lintel of a Jewish building in Dabura in the Golan (*NEAEHL* 2:545), two eagles with spread wings on lintels from Safed, Japhiʻa, and the Golan (*NEAEHL* 2:545; Hachlili, *Jewish Art*, 208, 212–13, 221 [plates 23, 26, 94]), and a single eagle with spread wings on a capital and a gable on the synagogue lintel of Umm el-Qanatir (Hachlili, *Jewish Art,* plate 23; *NEAEHL* 2:542–43). A graffito of a flying eagle is also found in the catacombs of Beth She'arim (Avigad, *Beth She'arim* 3:22).

**8a** καὶ τὰ τέσσαρα ζῷα, ἓν καθ' ἓν αὐτῶν ἔχων ἀνὰ πτέρυγας ἕξ, "And the four cherubim, each of whom had six wings." While the living creatures described in Ezek 1:6 have *four* wings each, the seraphim in Isa 6:2 are described as having *six* wings (two for covering their faces; two for covering their genitalia; two for flying). In *Apoc. Abr.* 18, as in Isa 6:2, the living creatures have six wings. In *b. Ḥag.* 13b there is an attempt to harmonize the four wings in Ezekiel with the six wings in Isaiah (see Gruenwald, *Apocalyptic,* 56). John's conception of the ζῷα is clearly composite, for while they are described as having *four* wings in Ezek 1:6, they are described as having *six* wings in Rev 4:8, in dependence on the description of the seraphim in Isa 6:2 (the only OT passage mentioning these six-winged beings). According to the *Sepher ha-Razim* 7.13–14 (tr. Morgan, 82), the ḥayyot and the opanim, who bear the throne of God, have six wings each, the same number of wings as the cherubim of Isa 6:2 and Rev 4:8. Philo of Byblos mentions a depiction of Kronos with four eyes in front and four in the rear (two of which were awake, while two slept), a way of depicting an all-seeing god, and six wings, four on his shoulders and two on his head (Attridge-Oden, *Philo,* 56–59, from Eusebius *Praep. evang.* 1.10.10.36–37). Though nothing further is said about the function of the wings in Revelation, according to Ezekiel, the wings of the creatures made an extremely loud noise (1:24; 3:12–13; 10:5) and were later understood to be the means whereby they produced their song (*b. Ḥag.* 13b). This view is found in *Tg. Ezek.* 1:24 (Levey, *Ezekiel,* 22), "And I heard the sound of their wings, like the sound of many waters, like a sound from before Shaddai; as they went, the sound of their words were as though they were thanking and blessing their Master, the ever living King of the worlds." See also *Tg. Ezek.* 3:12 (Levey, *Ezekiel,* 25), "Then the spirit lifted me up, and I heard behind me a great quaking sound, for they were offering praise and saying, 'Blessed by the glory of the Lord from the place of the abode of His Shekinah.'"

There are many representations of four-winged gods and genii from the ancient Near East, particularly on cylinder seals (Keel, *Yahweh-Visionen,* 194–216), some of which have from two to four human faces (Keel, 216–43). A six-winged deity with a winged cap is depicted on a late sixth-century B.C. chalcedony scarab from Cyprus pictured and discussed in J. Boardman, *Archaic Greek Gems* (London, 1968), no. 40, plate 3 with discussion on p. 32; see J. Boardman, *Greek Gems and Finger Rings* (New York: Abrams, n.d.) 143 and no. 286. An engraved jasper amulet depicts a deity with three pairs of wings (i.e., six wings) and holding an *ankh* symbol in each hand, like Egyptian gods (Delatte-Derchain, *Les intailles magiques,* no. 39).

**8b** κυκλόθεν καὶ ἔσωθεν γέμουσιν ὀφθαλμῶν, "were covered with eyes on the outside and on the inside." This phrase is parallel to that in v 6b, and both frame the description of the cherubim, though the former is arranged with the two adverbs at the beginning rather than the end of the clause and uses κυλόθεν instead of ἔμπροσθεν, and ἔσωθεν in place of ὄπισθεν. However, it is not clear whether these eyes cover the cherubim all over or they cover the *wings* of the cherubim. See *3 Enoch* 25:6 (tr. Alexander in Charlesworth, *OTP* 1:280), "All the ophanim ['wheels'] are full of eyes and full of wings, eyes corresponding to wings and wings corresponding to eyes." Some have suggested that these many-eyed creatures represent the category of angels called ἐγρήγοροι, "watchers" (*Jub.* 4:15; 8:3; 10:5; *1 Enoch* 1:5; 10:7; Spitta, 279).

**8c** καὶ ἀνάπαυσιν οὐκ ἔχουσιν ἡμέρας καὶ νυκτός, "and they do not cease day and night." E. Peterson (*Von den Engeln,* 385–86 n. 8) maintains that the notion of *ceaseless* praise is not found in early Judaism and argues against the various examples cited by Charles (1:125–26), contending that many of them are from Christianized texts. Peterson is quite correct, for while many of the texts cited by Charles refer to the heavenly praise accorded God by angelic beings (*1 Enoch* 40:4–7; 61:9–13; 69:25; 71:11; *2 Enoch* 17:9; 19:6; 20:4), none clearly emphasizes *ceaseless* praise. *1 Enoch* 39:12 is a passage in which "those who do not slumber" recite the *Qěduššah* (though here the fact that praise is offered by the עירים *'îrîm* or ἐγρήγοροι, "the wakeful ones" or "watchers," implies nothing about the unceasing nature of their praise; see the helpful note in Black, *1 Enoch,* 106–7). Among early Jewish texts there appears to be a single exception, *T. Levi* 3:8: "there praises to God are offered eternally [ἐν ᾧ ὕμνοι ἀεὶ τῷ θεῷ προσφέρονται]." A second text occurs in *2 Enoch* 17:1 (Rec. J and A), which speaks of "unceasing voices"; yet it is extremely late (medieval) and heavily Christianized. According to *Tg. Ps.-J.* Gen 32:26, the angels offer praise to God in accordance with the Jewish ritual plan of hours. See also *Mart. Perpetua* 12.2 (Krüger-Ruhbach, *Märtyrerakten,* 40): *et audiuimus uocem unitam dicentem,* Ἅγιος, ἅγιος, ἅγιος, *sine cessatione,* "and we heard voices chanting in unison, 'Holy, holy, holy,' without ceasing."

The terms "day and night" form a hendiadys meaning a twenty-four-hour day, which by extension means "without ceasing" or "without interruption" (Josh 24:8; Neh 4:9; Pss 1:2; 32:4; 88:1; Isa 62:6; Jer 9:1; 16:13; Luke 18:7; *1 Clem.* 20:2; 24:4; Jos. *J.W.* 6.301). It is, of course, obvious that this description is not given from the perspective of what John sees in the heavenly court but is based rather on his knowledge of the character of the heavenly liturgy and may be based on a traditional interpretation of Isa 6:3 (Jörns, *Evangelium,* 25). This is clear in the redundant phrase διὰ παντὸς νυκτὸς καὶ ἡμέρας, "continually, night and day" (Mark 5:5; cf. Jos. *Ant.* 13.217), similar to the phrase here ἀνάπαυσιν οὐκ ἔχουσιν ἡμέρας καὶ νυκτός, "they have no rest day and night." The hendiadys "day and night" occurs several times elsewhere in Revelation (7:15; 12:10; 14:11; 20:10) and frequently in the OT and early Jewish and early Christian literature (Gen 8:22; Lev 8:35; 1 Sam 25:16; 28:20; 1 Kgs 8:59; 1 Chr 9:33; 2 Chr 6:20; 42:3; 55:10; Isa 28:19; Lam 2:18; Acts 9:24; *1 Clem.* 24:4; Jos. *J.W.* 3.174; 5.31; 6.274; *Ant.* 5.60; 6.223). The reverse hendiadys "night and day," identical in meaning, also occurs frequently (Deut 28:66; 1 Sam 9:24; 1 Kgs 8:29; Esth 4:16; Isa 27:3; Jer 14:17; Mark 5:5; Luke 2:37; Acts 20:31; 26:7; 1 Thess 2:9; 3:10; 2 Thess 3:8; 1 Tim 5:5; 2 Tim 1:3; Ign. *Rom.* 5:2; *Barn.* 19:37; Jos. *Ant.* 2.274; 7.367; 16.260; *Ag. Ap.* 1.164, 199). There are a number of Jewish and Christian texts in which the hendiadys "day and night" is used hyperbolically for lengthy or continuous prayer or divine service (Neh 1:6; Ps 88:1; Luke 18:7; 1 Thess 3:10; 1 Tim 5:5; 2 Tim 1:3; Jos. *Ant.* 7.367).

**8d** λέγοντες· ἅγιος ἅγιος ἅγιος κύριος ὁ θεὸς ὁ παντοκράτωρ, "chanting, 'Holy, holy, holy, Lord God Almighty.'" Vv 8d and 8e constitute a short hymn of two lines (Deichgräber, *Gotteshymnus,* 49–50), the first line derived from a traditional reading of Isa 6:3 and the second line perhaps based on traditional Jewish exegesis of Exod 3:14 and Deut 32:39 (Jörns, *Evangelium,* 26–27). The threefold repetition of "holy" is called the *Qĕduššah* in Hebrew, the *sanctus* or the *tersanctus,* "thrice holy," in Latin, and the *trisagion,* "thrice holy," in Greek. The *Qĕduššah* first appears in Isa 6:3, where it is chanted by the seraphim in the context of Isaiah's inaugural vision, and may have been part of a hymn regularly chanted in the temple liturgy or at least a cultic liturgical formula (Engnell, *Call of Isaiah,* 35–36), in which the threefold repetition functions to emphasize the transcendence of God (Spinks, *Sanctus,* 18):

> Holy, holy, holy is the Lord of hosts;
> the whole earth is full of his glory.

The context in Isa 6 is Isaiah's vision of the divine council, i.e., a heavenly throne-room scene in which God presides over a council of angelic beings (1 Kgs 22:19–23; Jer 23:18; Job 1–2; 15:8; Pss 82:1, 6; 89:7), a conception found in Mesopotamian and Canaanite mythology (see Robinson, *JTS* 45 [1944] 151–57; Cross, *JNES* 12 [1953] 274–77; Mullen, *Divine Council;* Seitz, *JBL* 109 [1990] 229–47). In Qumran this notion was developed to the extent that the community regarded itself as standing in the midst of God and his angels (1QS 11:7–9; 1QH 3:19–22; 11:13–14; 1QM 12:1–5; see Mach, *Engelglaubens,* 209–16). The *Qĕduššah* does not occur in the rest of the OT, though the term "holy" occurs three times in Ps 99, in a way that suggests dependence on Isa 6 (see Scoralick, *Trishagion*). The *Qĕduššah* became part of both Jewish liturgy (Heinemann, *Prayer,* 230–33) and Christian liturgy (Spinks, *Sanctus*), and after the fourth century A.D., it was found in virtually all versions of the eucharistic prayer in Christianity. In the traditional liturgy of the synagogue, with three services daily together with an additional service on Sabbaths and festivals, the combination of Isa 6:3 and Ezek 3:12 ("Blessed be the glory of the Lord from his place") occurs in three different places, the *Qĕduššah dĕ 'Amida,* the *Qĕduššah dĕ Yoṣer,* and the *Qĕduššah dĕ Sidra* (P. Birnbaum, *Daily Prayer Book* [New York: Hebrew Publishing Company, 1977] 74, 84, 131). Though the earliest explicit mention of the *Qĕduššah* occurs in *t. Ber.* 1.9 (late Tannaitic period), the core of which consists of Isa 6:3 together with Ezek 3:12, it is likely that it had already been incorporated into synagogue liturgy by the Mishnaic period (Heinemann, *Prayer,* 24, 230–32). While forms of the *Qĕduššah* occur in early Jewish apocalyptic literature as well as in the later hekalot literature, the relationship between those occurrences and synagogue liturgy is problematic. Scholem (*Major Trends,* 40–79), Gruenwald (*Apocalyptic,* 183–84 and passim), and Morray-Jones (*HTR* 86 [1993] 177–217) argue that the latter developed out of the former. Allusions to Isa 6:3 and Ezek 3:12 are also found in *Apost. Const.* 7.35.3, in a section that very probably represents a Christian redaction of Hellenistic Jewish synagogal prayers (Fiensy, *Prayers,* 134, 178, 199 [reconstructed Jewish text]; tr. Fiensy, 69):

> And the holy Seraphim together with the six-winged Cherubim singing the victory ode to you cry out with never-ceasing voices, "Holy, holy, holy Lord Sabaoth, heaven and earth are full of your glory." And the other multitudes of the orders: angels, archangels, thrones, dominions, rulers, authorities, powers, cry out and say, "Blessed is the glory of the Lord from his place."

The first occurrence of the *Qĕduššah* in early Christian literature is Rev 4:8, and one of the major issues from the standpoint of the history of liturgy is whether it was adapted from Jewish worship as many scholars have contended (Mowry, *JBL* 71 [1952] 84; Cabaniss, *Int* 7 [1953] 76–87; Rowland, *JSS* 10 [1980] 145; Prigent, 87–89). It is also quoted in *1 Clem.* 34:6 (nearly contemporaneous with Revelation), in which Isa 6:3 is conflated with Dan 7:10 (the latter passage is alluded to in Rev 5:11): "For the Scripture says, 'Ten thousand times ten thousand stood by him, and a thousand thousands ministered to him, and they cried, "Holy, holy, holy Lord Sabaoth, the entire creation is filled with his glory."'" Here it is noteworthy that the phrase κύριος σαβαώθ found in LXX Isa 6:3 is used (see *Comment* on 4:8e), but Clement substitutes κτίσις for γῆ. Van Unnik has argued that *1 Clem.* 34:6 was drawn not from Jewish or Christian liturgy but from a written source, indicated by the explicit use of the quotation formula "for the Scripture says" (*VC* 5 [1951] 225), though the combination of Dan 7:10 with Isa 6:3 suggests dependence on a florilegium. Tertullian appears to be the first Christian author who provides evidence for the use of the trisagion in Christian liturgy (*De oratione* 3):

> He [God the Father] to whom that surrounding circle of angels cease not to say, "Holy, holy, holy." In like wise, therefore, we too, candidates for angelhood, if we succeed in deserving it, begin even here on earth to learn by heart that strain hereafter to be raised unto God, and the function of future glory.

An allusion to Isa 6:3 is found also in *Apost. Const.* 8.12.27, the latter of which (like *1 Clem.* 34:6) alludes to Dan 7:10 (tr. Darnell in Charlesworth, *OTP* 2:694):

> the cherubim and the six-winged seraphim, with two covering up their feet, and with two their heads, and with two flying; and saying together with thousands on thousands of archangels, and ten thousand times ten thousand angels, incessantly [ἀκαταπαύστως] and loudly crying out—and all the people together, let them say—"Holy, holy, holy is Lord Sabaoth, the heaven and earth are full of his glory!"

Here the last phrase, "heaven and earth are full of his glory," reflects a slight expansion of the phrase "the whole earth is full of his glory" in Isa 6:3. This expansion became the canonical form of the trisagion in the eucharistic liturgies of Chrysostom, James, Mark, Adai and Mari, and Serapion (Werner, *HUCA* 19 [1945–46] 298; Spinks, *Sanctus*, 116–21), though the phrase "heaven and earth" was also used in early Judaism (Flusser, "Sanktus," 131–47; see 1QH 16:3; *Tg. Isa.* 6:3). The Qĕduššah is also part of the heavenly liturgy according to *Mart. Perpetua* 12, where a vision is recounted that was purportedly experienced by Saturus and Perpetua, in which they found themselves in heaven before God (tr. Musurillo, *Acts*): "We also entered and we heard the sound of voices in unison chanting endlessly [*sine cessatione*], 'Holy, holy holy!' In the same place we seemed to see an aged man with white hair and a youthful face, though we did not see his feet."

The Qĕduššah also occurs in early Jewish literature. Isa 6:3 is quoted, for example, in *1 Enoch* 39:12–13 (tr. Knibb, *Enoch*):

> Those who do not sleep bless you, and they stand before your glory and bless and praise and exalt, saying: "Holy, holy, holy, Lord of Spirits; he fills the earth with spirits." And there my eyes saw all those who do not sleep standing before him and blessing and saying: "Blessed are you, and blessed is the name of the Lord for ever and ever!"

Here it is evident that the author understands δόξα or כָּבוֹד *kābôd*, "glory," as "spirits"; i.e., "Lord of Hosts" is understood as identical with the equally biblical phrase "God of spirits" (Num 16:22; 27:16; see Flusser, "Sanktus," 138–39). The *Qĕduššah* also occurs in the longer recension of *2 Enoch* [J] 21:1 [MS M22] (tr. Andersen in Charlesworth, *OTP* 1:134), as a song of praise sung by cherubim and seraphim before God and clearly alluding to that version of Isa 6:3 in which the phrase "heaven and earth" replaces "the whole earth":

> Holy, Holy, Holy, Lord Lord Sabaoth,
> Heaven and earth are full of his glory.

The *Qĕduššah* is also frequently included in the prayers of hekalot literature, such as the *Ma'aseh Merkavah* (Swartz, *Mystical Prayer*, §§ 549.9 [MS M22 only]; 550.4b; 555[3x]; 556; 592.10; 595.4), and in *Hekalot Rabbati* and parallels (see Schäfer, *Synopse*, §§ 94, 95, 97, 99, 101, 102, 104, 105, 126, 146). Sometimes the *Qĕduššah* is quoted not as part of the heavenly liturgy but rather as a text from Isa 6:3 with the introductory formula כַּדָּבָר שֶׁנֶּאֱמַר *kaddābār šenne'ĕmar*, "as it is said" (Schäfer, *Synopse*, §§ 152, 153, 154, 155, 156, 157, 158, 159, 160, 164, 165, 166, 168, 169, 273, 274, 306[2x], 322, 334). The liturgical use of the *Qĕduššah* may perhaps be presupposed by the introductory formula שִׁישׁר אוּם לפנין *šeyyisrā'ēl 'ômēr lĕpānāyw*, "when Israel spoke before him" (Schäfer, *Synopse*, § 161; cf. § 179). *Par. Jer.* 9:3–6 contains a short and distinctive prayer of Jeremiah, which begins with "Holy, holy, holy" and concludes by addressing God as "Almighty Lord of all creation, unbegotten and incomprehensible [κύριε παντοκράτωρ πάσης κτίσεως, ὁ ἀγέννητος καὶ ἀπερινόητος]." The *Qĕduššah* is also found in *3 Enoch*, in a form reflecting the combination of Isa 6:3 with Ezek 3:12, the form that characterizes the *Qĕduššah* in modern synagogue prayers but is not attested prior to the second century A.D. In *3 Enoch* 1:12, Enoch sings praises to God in heaven, and angelic beings respond with "'Holy, holy, holy' [Isa 6:3], and 'Blessed be the glory of the Lord in his dwelling place' [Ezek 3:12]" (see also *3 Enoch* 20:2; 40:2; Appendix to *3 Enoch* 22B:7). The *Qĕduššah* also occurs in the *Sepher ha-Razim* 7.16–17 (tr. Morgan, 83), an early Jewish magical text influenced by hekalot literature (Gruenwald, *Apocalyptic*, 233), in the first line of an angelic hymn sung in the seventh firmament: "Holy, holy, holy is the Lord of Hosts, / The whole world is full of his glory."

The *Qĕduššah* is also used in magical texts either produced by Jews or Christians or influenced by Jewish or Christian *nomina sacra*. In an apotropaic copper amulet from Smyrna of uncertain date, the obverse contains the inscription "Seal of the living God, guard him who wears this. Holy, holy, holy, Lord Sabaoth, heaven and earth are full of thy glory" (Goodenough, *Jewish Symbols* 2:231; vol. 3, fig. 1054). Note that the phrase "the whole earth" of Isa 6:3 is often rendered "heaven and earth" in Christian versions of the *Qĕduššah*, though the same change is sometimes found in Hellenistic Jewish sources (E. R. Goodenough, *By Light, Light: The Mystic Gospel of Hellenistic Judaism* [New Haven: Yale UP, 1935] 307, 324). Similarly, in a lengthy Coptic exorcism, which appears to be a Jewish magical text lightly Christianized, the Christian form of the *Qĕduššah* appears in Greek: "Holy, holy, holy, Lord Sabaoth, / Heaven and earth are [fu]ll of thy glory" (Kropp, *Koptische Zaubertexte* 2:178; a verbally similar text in Greek is also found in a Coptic curse text in Kropp, *Koptische Zaubertexte* 2:235). *Ladder of Jacob* 2:6–22 has what resembles a magical hymn in which the *Qĕduššah* in 2:18–19 is followed by seven divine names followed by a string of transliterated Hebrew words resembling *voces magicae* (tr. H. G. Lunt in Charlesworth, *OTP* 2:408):

> Holy, Holy, Holy, Yao, Yaova, Yaoil, Yao,
> Kados, Chavod, Savaoth,
> Omlemlech il avir amismi varich,
> eternal king, mighty, powerful, most great,
> patient, blessed one!

Some amulets begin with the *Qĕduššah;* see M. Naldini, "Due papiri cristiani della collezione fiorentina," *Studi Italiani di Filologia Classica* 33 (1961) 216–18 (see van Haelst, *Catalogue,* no. 754); M. Naldini, "Testimonianze cristiane negli amuleti greco-egizi," *Augustinianum* 21 (1981) 179–88.

The divine epithet κύριος ὁ θεὸς ὁ παντοκράτωρ, "Lord God Almighty," has been substituted for the phrase κύριος σαβαώθ (יהוה צבאות *YHWH ṣĕbāʾôt*) found in LXX Isa 6:3, probably because it is a divine title preferred by the author. It occurs five times in Revelation (4:8; 11:17; 15:3; 16:7; 21:22); all but the last occurrence is found in a context of praise or prayer. According to Delling (*NovT* 3 [1959] 127–34), this title was taken over from Hellenistic Judaism. In *Mart. Pol.* 14, the aged Polycarp begins his prayer the same way: "O Lord, God almighty [κύριε ὁ θεὸς ὁ παντοκράτωρ]." A similar but shorter address in prayer to God in the vocative is κύριε παντοκράτωρ (*T. Abr.* 15:12; *Par. Jer.* 1:5; 9:6); see also *Par. Jer.* 1:6; 9:6. The same title is of course also used in nonprayer contexts, as in *3 Apoc. Bar.* 1:3, where an angel appears to Baruch and says, "thus says the Lord God Almighty." It is clear that in Rev 4:8, as in Isa 6:3, the function of the *Qĕduššah* is to provide a solemn introduction for uttering the divine name. According to the *Tg. Deut.* 32:3, it is impossible for one of the angels of the heights to invoke the name of God without having said "holy, holy, holy" three times (M. L. Klein, *Fragment-Targums* 1:113, 225; 2:85, 182). In the LXX the Hebrew phrase יהוה צבאות *YHWH ṣĕbāʾôt* is often translated as κύριος σαβαώθ (fifty-four times in Isaiah; three times elsewhere), transliterating rather than translating צבאות *ṣĕbāʾôt*. κύριος appears to be a distinctive Christian translation of יהוה *YHWH* not found in Jewish MSS of the Greek OT, but rather represented by the tetragrammaton written in archaic letters or the transliterated Greek form Ἰάω (Jellicoe, *Septuagint,* 271–72; Skehan, DJD 9:167–86, on pap4QLXXLeviticus[b], which has Ἰάω in frag. 20.4, but never κύριος). But σαβαώθ is also translated παντοκράτωρ, "almighty," elsewhere in the LXX no less than a hundred times, though never in Isaiah. The phrase κύριος ὁ θεὸς ὁ παντωκράτωρ occurs seven times in the LXX as a translation of יהוה אלהי הצבאות *YHWH ʾĕlōhê haṣṣĕbāʾôt* (Hos 12:6; Amos 3:13; 4:13; 5:8 [MT has only יהוה *YHWH,* while a few MSS add צבאות *ṣĕbāʾôt*], 14, 15, 16; 9:5; Nah 3:5 [MT has only יהוה צבאות *YHWH ṣĕbāʾôt*]). In *Orat. Man.* frag. 22.11 (A.-M. Denis, *Fragmenta,* 115), Manasseh addresses a prayer to God: "Lord Almighty, God of our fathers [κύριε παντωκράτορ, ὁ θεὸς τῶν πατέρων ἡμῶν]." The title "Lord of hosts" (יהוה צבאות *YHWH ṣĕbāʾôt*) occurs on three Aramaic ostraca (Porten, *Elephantine,* 109).

**8e** ὁ ἦν καὶ ὁ ὢν καὶ ὁ ἐρχόμενος, "'Who was and who is and is the One who comes.'" On this divine title, see *Comment* on 1:4. The *Qĕduššah* in v 8d is linked with a threefold exposition of the divine name, a phenomenon that occurs elsewhere in early Jewish texts. An example is the expanded version of the *Qĕduššah* found in *Tg. Isa.* 6:3 (tr. Chilton, *Isaiah Targum*):

> Holy in the heavens of the height, his sanctuary, holy upon the earth, the work of his might, holy in eternity is the Lord of hosts; the whole earth is filled with the brilliance of his glory.

In this targumic interpretation, each "holy" is given a specific meaning, and in this sense may be analogous to Rev 4:8e, where the threefold repetition of "holy" is connected, perhaps by design, to three characteristics of God. Another possible example is found in the hekalot literature (Schäfer, *Synopse*, § 126, p. 62):

והארץ אומרת יהוה מלך יהוה מלך (יהוה) ימלוך לעולם ועד.

*wĕhāʾāreṣ ʾômeret YHWH melek YHWH mālak*
*(YHWH) yimlo(w)k lĕʿôlām wāʿed*

And the earth says, "The Lord was king, the Lord is king,
the Lord will be king for ever and ever."

This acclamation is preceded by the *Qĕduššah* by several lines and bears a certain similarity to the divine title "who was, is, and is to come."

**9** καὶ ὅταν δώσουσιν τὰ ζῷα δόξαν καὶ τιμὴν καὶ εὐχαριστίαν τῷ καθημένῳ ἐπὶ τῷ θρόνῳ τῷ ζῶντι εἰς τοὺς αἰῶνας τῶν αἰώνων, "And when the cherubim give glory and honor and thanksgiving to the One seated upon the throne who lives for ever and ever." This hymnic summary exhibits the features of a doxology: (1) the divinity to whom some attribute is ascribed, usually in the dative case (τῷ καθημένῳ ἐπὶ τῷ θρόνῳ), (2) specific attributes listed, of which δόξα, "glory," is the most common, usually in the nominative (δόξαν καὶ τιμὴν καὶ εὐχαριστίαν), and (3) a formula describing the unending extent of time during which the one praised will possess these attributes (εἰς τοὺς αἰῶνας τῶν αἰώνων). Only the concluding "amen" is lacking. The temporal adverb ὅταν, "when, whenever," does not suggest repeated action here but refers to a unique event as it does in 8:1; 10:7; 11:7; 12:4; 17:10; 20:7 (Lohmeyer, 49; Mussies, *Morphology*, 345). *When* the cherubim give glory and honor and thanksgiving to God, *then* the twenty-four elders will worship God, cast their wreaths before the throne, and sing the ἄξιος song (v 10). This occurs just once in this text unit, namely in 5:13–14, when all creation ascribes blessing and honor and glory and might to God; it is precisely then that the elders fall down to worship God (Mussies, *Morphology*, 345). The problem here is that, since the action of giving glory and honor and praise to God cannot refer to the chanting of the trisagion, the ascription of glory and honor and praise to God is mentioned, *but the hymn itself is omitted*. This is the only place in Revelation where a hymn is summarized but not reproduced except in *oratio obliqua*, or "indirect discourse" (cf. 14:3–4, where the new song sung in heaven is mentioned though not included in the narrative). Some scholars have been tempted to reconstruct the hymn (Jörns, *Evangelium*, 67–70, 73), but such an exercise is pointless. The phrase "the one who sits on the throne" is a circumlocution for the name of God; see *Comment* on 4:2. On the synonymous pair "glory and honor," see *Comment* on 21:26. The phrase "who lives for ever and ever" is an epithet of God repeated three or four more times in Revelation (4:10; 5:14 [*var. lect.*]; 10:6; 15:7) but used of Christ in 1:18. References to God as "living forever" are occasionally found in the OT, though "living forever and ever" is never found: Isa 57:15 (κατοικῶν τὸν αἰῶνα); Theod Dan 4:34 (ὁ ζῶν εἰς τὸν αἰῶνα); 12:7 (ὁ ζῶν εἰς τὸν αἰῶνα θεός). The notion of the righteous "living forever" occurs in John 6:51, 58; *Barn.* 6:3; 8:5; 9:2; 11:10, 11 (2x). The ascription of "glory and honor" to God can be construed as based on the widespread use of benefactor language in the Greco-Roman world (Danker, *Benefactor,* 470; J. H. Elliott, "Patronage and Clientism in Early Christian Society," *Forum* 3/4 [1987] 399–48).

**10a** πεσοῦνται οἱ εἴκοσι τέσσαρες πρεσβύτεροι ἐνώπιον τοῦ καθημένου ἐπὶ τοῦ θρόνου, "the twenty-four elders prostrate themselves before the One sitting on the throne." For the phrase "the one sitting on the throne" as a periphrasis for the name of God, see *Comment* on 4:2. There are a few texts that depict heavenly beings bowing down before God (Brettler, *King,* 104); one such text is 4QDeut^a 32:43, "Rejoice, O heavens with him; bow down before him," and another is Ps 29:1–2, "Ascribe to the Lord, O divine beings . . . bow down to the Lord, majestic in holiness." No analogous court ceremonial for Israelite kings is known from the extant sources. This is the first occurrence in Revelation of the paired verbs πίπτειν, "to fall down," and προσκυνεῖν, "to worship," which are used to describe two stages of a single act of adoration and thus are very nearly synonymous (they are also paired in 5:14; 7:11; 11:16; 19:10; 22:8). This combination is widely attested: Ps 72:11; Dan 3:5, 6, 10, 11, 15; Matt 2:11; 4:9; 18:26; Acts 10:25; 1 Cor 14:25; *Apoc. Moses* 27:5; *Jos. As.* 28:9; *T. Job* 40:6; Jos. *Ant.* 7.95; 9.11; 10.213.

**10b** καὶ προσκυνήσουσιν τῷ ζῶντι εἰς τοὺς αἰῶνας τῶν αἰώνων, "and they worship the One who lives for ever and ever." Vv 10a and 10b constitute a couplet consisting of two cola in synonymous parallelism (cf. the very similar couplet in 19:4, which exhibits progressive or climactic parallelism). The verb προσκυνεῖν, "to worship," occurs nineteen times in Revelation with an object either in the dative or the accusative. Kilpatrick ("Style," 154–55) argued that since Atticistic grammarians condemned the dative construction and recommended the accusative construction, we should expect scribes to have changed the dative objects into accusative objects. On the divine epithet "the one who lives for ever and ever," see *Comment* on 4:9. Philo (*Leg.* 116) describes prostration (προσκύνησις) before the emperor as a barbarian practice (cf. Aristotle *Rhet.* 1361a.36).

**10c** καὶ βαλοῦσιν τοῦ στεφάνους αὐτῶν ἐνώπιον τοῦ θρόνου λέγοντες, "and they cast their wreaths before the throne, chanting." This action signifies both subordination and homage and has parallels in historical accounts of conquered rulers presenting their crowns to the conqueror (Tacitus *Annals* 15.29) and in rulers who take crowns from conquered kings (2 Sam 1:10; 12:30; 1 Chr 20:2; cf. Ezek 21:26) or rulers who voluntarily put aside their crowns (Plutarch *De frat. amore* 488D). The Magi reportedly fell down and worshiped the infant Jesus and then presented him with rich gifts (Matt 2:11). Tertullian reports that followers of Mithras, after receiving a crown and putting it on their heads, take it off and proclaim that Mithras is their crown (*De corona* 15). Gold crowns were frequently presented to Roman emperors for a variety of reasons; this practice was inherited from Hellenistic kingship tradition (see *Excursus 2A: Ancient Wreath and Crown Imagery*). The Roman emperor was presented with gold crowns by the senate and delegates from provincial cities on such varied occasions as accessions, consulships, victories, and anniversaries (S. MacCormack, *Art and Ceremony,* 58; F. Millar, *Emperor,* 140–43). Arrian (*Anabasis Alexandri* 7.23.2) reports that on one occasion embassies (πρεσβεῖαι) arrived from Greece; the envoys (πρέσβεις), who were themselves wearing wreaths, came forward and presented golden wreaths (στεφάνοι χρύσοι) to Alexander as if honoring a god. Herodian (8.7.2), describing an episode during the reign of the emperor Maximus (early third century A.D.), says that Italian cities sent delegations (πρεσβείας) of their prominent citizens dressed in white and wearing laurel wreaths and bearing statues of the gods and golden wreaths to pay homage to Maximus. The term "throne" (which can be used, by figurative extension, to mean a "ruling power" or a "supernatural force or power"; see Louw-Nida, §§ 12.44; 37.70) is used here as a circumlocution for the name of God, as it is also in 7:3; 8:9. The "throne of glory" (Heb 4:16) and the "throne of majesty" (Heb 8:1) are also circumlocutions for the name of God (O. Michel, *Der Brief an die Hebräer*, 12 ed., MeyerK 13 [Göttingen: Vandenhoeck & Ruprecht, 1966] 209); see also Jer 14:21, where "thy name" and "thy glorious throne" are parallel; 4 Macc 17:18; Wis 9:10. On the motif of casting crowns before the throne of God, see *3 Enoch* 18. There are only a very few texts that suggest that God himself wears a crown. According to Ezekiel Trag. (*Exagoge* 71), God wears a diadem and holds a scepter. A crown consisting of the prayers of Israel is placed on the head of God according to *3 Enoch* 15B.2; see *3 Enoch* 48B.1. Without comment, Josephus mentions that Sossius (the Roman governor of Syria) dedicated a gold crown to God at the temple in Jerusalem (Jos. *J.W.* 1.357 = *Ant.* 14.488).

11 ἄξιος εἶ ὁ κύριος καὶ ὁ θεὸς ἡμῶν, "'Worthy are you, our Lord and God.'" This colon introduces a four-line hymn to God, with the final two cola, introduced by ὅτι, in synonymous parallelism (Charles, 1:133; Mowry, *JBL* 71 [1952] 77; Lohse, 37; Deichgräber, *Gotteshymnus*, 50; Jörns, *Evangelium*, 74; Roloff [ET] 68):

ἄξιος εἶ ὁ κύριος καὶ ὁ θεὸς ἡμῶν,
λαβεῖν τὴν δόξαν καὶ τὴν τιμὴν καὶ τὴν δύναμιν,
ὅτι σὺ ἔκτισας τὰ πάντα
καὶ διὰ τὸ θέλημά σου ἦσαν καὶ ἐκτίσθησαν.

Lohmeyer (49–50), on the other hand, arranges the hymn in five lines by considering καὶ ἐκτίσθησαν as the fifth line, though this is probably not correct because the parallelism of the last two cola would then be ignored. Delling, on the other hand (*NovT* 3 [1959] 114), following Horst (*Proskynein*, 276), proposes three cola, each consisting of three emphases: (1) the ἄξιος predication followed by two divine names, (2) three substantives dependent on λαβεῖν, and (3) three creation sayings. This colon begins with an ascription of worthiness to God based on the fact that he has created all things (v 11c); note that in 5:9 the phrase ἄξιος εἶ introduces a hymn addressed to the Lamb. Here ἄξιος means "what is fitting or proper" (Louw-Nida, § 66.6), which means that the ascription of glory, honor, and power to God on the part of his worshipers is fully appropriate, because God is creator (v 11c). This short hymn is couched in the *du-Stil*, "thou style," a style that has antecedents in Hebrew (1 Chr 29:10; 1QS 11:15), as well as in Greco-Jewish and early Christian literature (LXX Dan 3:26; *Did.* 8:2; 9:3–4; 10:2, 4, 5). The term ἄξιος is used as an epithet appropriate for benefactors in the Greco-Roman world (Luke 7:4; F. F. H. von Gaertringen, *Inschriften von Priene* [Berlin: Reimer, 1906] 6, lines 26–27; 114, lines 33–34), either in the third person (Rev 5:12, ἄξιόν ἐστιν, "he is worthy"; Luke 7:4, ἄξιός ἐστιν, "he is worthy") or in the first person (ἄξιος εἶ, "you are worthy," Rev 4:11; 5:9; see the letter from a soldier to his father in which he says ἄξιος [ε]ἶ, "you are worthy," in Llewelyn, *New Docs* 6:156–57). The attribute of ἄξιος, used of God (and Christ), has few parallels outside Revelation and apparently none that occur earlier (Deichgräber, *Gotteshymnus,* 50–51; see the excursus on ἄξιος in Jörns, *Evangelium,* 56–73). See Jos. *Ant.* 8.53, τὸν μὲν θεὸν εὐλογεῖν ἄξιον, "it is appropriate to praise God." The hymn does have some of the formal features of an acclamation (Peterson, *Εἷς Θεος,* 176–80; Lohmeyer, 50). The term ἄξιος is used at the beginning of two more hymns, both directed to the Lamb (5:9, 12), where worthiness is based on his death (see *Comments* there).

There is reason to suppose that in Revelation the application of the titles κύριος, "Lord," and θεός, "God," to the God of the Christians was in part an antithetical reflection of the application of those titles to Roman emperors. Rome never had a ceremony to deify a living emperor (Liebeschuetz, *Religion,* 74), but the posthumous deification of emperors began with a *senatus consultum,* or senatorial decree, introduced by the Triumvirs and passed by the senate. The ritual of postmortem deification, or apotheosis, was ritualized in the ceremony of *consecratio* (Liebeschuetz, *Religion,* 77; for a discussion of this ritual in the later empire, see MacCormack, *Art and Ceremony,* 93–158). The effect of the new status of Julius Caesar as *divus Iulius* was the legitimation of his adopted heir Octavian as *divi filius,* "son of the god." Before 42 B.C., the terms *divus* and *deus* were virtually synonymous; after 42 B.C., *divus* was used almost excusively of a god who had once been a mortal. Though the notion of the divinity of the Roman emperor lies behind Rev 4:11, there is an important difference to be made between emperors who were deified posthumously by an act of the senate and emperors who claimed divinity or to whom divinity was ascribed while yet living. During the first century A.D. two living emperors appear to have claimed to be gods, Gaius and Domitian (such a claim was thought to violate the *gravitas* and *dignitas* of a Roman emperor; i.e., it was considered tacky). According to Philo, Gaius was indelicate enough to claim divinity for himself (Philo *Leg.* 353), and Suetonius claims that Gaius assumed the title *optimus maximus Caesar,* "Caesar best and greatest" (*Cal.* 22.1), a traditional title for the chief deity of the Roman pantheon, *Jupiter Optimus Maximus,* and also that he was greeted as *Jupiter Latiaris* (Suetonius *Cal.* 22.2; Dio Cassius 59.28.5). Pliny claims that Domitian also regarded himself as the equal of the gods (*Pan.* 33.4, *cumque se idem quod deos*). According to Suetonius, Domitian had procurators send out letters in the name of *dominus et deus noster,* "our Lord and God," and he also required that he be addressed in the same way (*Dom.* 13.2). Dio Cassius (67.5.7) reports that Domitian insisted on being called δεσπότης καὶ θεός, "master and god" (δεσπότης is used to translate both *dominus* and *princeps;* see Mason, *Greek Terms,* 34), and he also relates an incident in which Juventius Celsus, about to be condemned, bowed before Domitian and addressed him as δεσπότης τε καὶ θεός, "master and god" (67.13.4). Elsewhere Dio Chrysostom claims that Greeks and barbarians (i.e., not Romans) called Domitian δεσπότης καὶ θεός, "master and god" (*Or.* 45.1). The recognition of the divinity of living emperors becomes more frequent in the second century A.D. Lucian calls Marcus Aurelius θεὸς Μάρκος, "god(like) Marcus" (*Alex.* 48), and the tutor of the two sons of the emperor Septimus Severus (ca. A.D. 145–211) θεῶν διδάσκαλος, "teacher of the gods" (Philostratus *Vitae Sophistae* 2.23). A second-century A.D. inscription from the Chersonesus refers to Antoninus Pius (A.D. 137–61) as θεὸς ἡμῶν καὶ δεσπότης, "our god and master" (*IGRom* 1:861). *Deus,* "god," was a title given to emperors before the time of Martial and Statius (Vergil *Georgics* 1.6; Calpurnius *Eclogues* 1.84). Statius used the *deus* predication of the emperor just once (1.1.62, referring to the large equestrian statue of Domitian erected ca. A.D. 91, "the present beauty of the god [*dei*] makes labor sweet"), while Martial has it more than a dozen times (5.5.1, 4; 6.64.5–6; 7.5; 7.8.1, 2; 7.40.2; 7.99.5–8; 8.82.1–4; 9.28.5; 9.65.1–2; 9.101.23–24; 10.34.1; 10.93.2; 14.74; see Sauter, *Kaiserkult*, 47–51). The title *deus* as a form of address to the emperor was rejected by Pliny *Panegyricus* 2.3, who says "Nowhere should we flatter him as a god and a divinity [*nusquam ut deo, nusquam ut numini blandiamur*]" (*Pan.* 1.6.3), though he frequently addresses Trajan as *dominus*. In Latin, *dominus*, "Lord," was an imperial title used of the emperor, frequently by Martial (2.924; 4.67.4; 5.2.6; 5.5.3; 6.64.14; 7.12.1; 8.1.1; 8.31.3; 8.82.2; 9.16.3; 9.20.2; 9.23.3; 9.24.6; 9.28.7; 79.8; 84.2) and occasionally by Statius (3.3.103, 110; 4.2.6; 5.1.42, 112, 261), but it was not used by any poets before them (Sauter, *Kaiserkult,* 34). The title also frequently occurs in Pliny the Younger, who regularly addresses Trajan in his letters as *domine* (*Ep.* 10.2.1; 10.3A.1; 10.5.1; 10.6.1; 10.8.1; see Sherwin-White, *Letters,* 557–58). The two titles used in tandem of Domitian, *dominus et deus,* "Lord and God," are predicates that Sauter claims had an oriental flavor (*Kaiserkult,* 32, 36–39); this double title occurs several times in Martial (5.8.1; 7.34.8; 9.66.3), but in only one passage in Suetonius (*Dom.* 13.2) and two in Dio Cassius (67.4.7; 67.13.4). After Domitian's death, the double title was rejected by Martial (10.72.3, 8): *Dicturus dominum deumque non sum,* "I think not to address any man as Lord and God," and *Non est hic dominus, sed imperator,* "Not a Lord is here, but an emperor" (see Sauter, *Kaiserkult,* 31). While Pliny also rejects Domitian's acceptance of divine titles, he does not hesitate to apply the traditional epithets of Capitoline Jupiter, i.e., Optimus Maximus, "Best and Greatest," to Trajan (*Pan.* 2.7; 88.4, 8–9; *Ep.* 2.13.8; 3.13.1).

L. L. Thompson (*Revelation,* 104–7) has critically examined the literary sources that claim Domitian demanded to be called "our Lord and our God" and concludes that they are historically inaccurate. However, the fact that emperors before and after Domitian were called *deus* and *dominus* undercuts his argument, as do the presence of the two titles in tandem in Martial and the separate use of *deus* (1.1.62) and *dominus* (3.3.103, 110; 4.2.6; 5.1.42, 112, 261) in Statius. Further, Thompson does not deal with the two very different settings in which Dio Cassius claims that the title was used of Domitian (67.4.7; 67.13.4), nor does he adequately evaluate the independent testimony of Dio Chrysostom (*Or.* 45.1). Thompson is correct, however, in observing that the title *dominus et deus* never occurs in inscriptions, coins, or medallions (though the reason is simply that only official titulature was used in such contexts) and in arguing that Domitian did not demand greater divine honors than his imperial predecessors or successors (*Revelation,* 105–7).

Earlier emperors had rejected the title *dominus,* e.g., Augustus (Suetonius *Aug.* 53.1), Tiberius (Suetonius *Tib.* 27), and Claudius (Tacitus *Annals* 2.87.12.11), yet it was apparently used of Nero with his tacit approval (Martial 7.45.7; Suetonius *Vit.* 11.2; see Sauter, *Kaiserkult,* 32). In an exhaustive survey of the epigraphical evidence of the imperial titles of Domitian in Martin, the title *dominus,* "Lord," never occurs, suggesting that it was not part of that emperor's *official* titulature. However, in some inscriptions from Egypt, the title ὁ κύριος, "Lord," does occasionally crop up (A. Martin, *La titulature,* 150–60, nos. 12, 15, 48). The formula *divi Vesp. f* [*ilius*], "son of the god Vespasian," does occurs frequently in inscriptions (Martin,

*La titulature,* 187–89). Another title of Domitian attested some seventy-one times is *cens. perp.,* "censor for life"; in Greek this is translated in a variety of ways, τιμητὴς διὰ βίου, or διηνεκής, or αἰώνιος (Martin, *La titulature,* 192–93). This last translation is particularly interesting, since αἰών is used to describe the length of time that the titles ascribed to God in Revelation will be valid (5:13; 7:12).

**11b** λαβεῖν τὴν δόξαν καὶ τὴν τιμὴν καὶ τὴν δύναμιν, "'To receive glory and honor and power.'" This colon is closely parallel to the second colon in the hymn of thanksgiving in 11:17–18, ὅτι εἴληφας τὴν δύναμίν σου τὴν μεγάλην, "for you have received your great power." Since the synonymous word pair "glory and honor" (see *Comment* on 21:26) has just been used in the doxology in 4:9 with εὐχαριστία as the third substantive, by switching to δύναμις as the third substantive here, the author has emphasized it (Jörns, *Evangelium,* 37). Like ἄξιος, "worthy," in v 11a, these predications are all appropriate for one of high status. In *De cor.* 108, Demosthenes claims ἄξιος εἰμ᾽ ἐπαίνου τυχεῖν, "I am worthy to get credit," because through his public service δόξαι καὶ τιμαὶ καὶ δυνάμεις, "reknown, distinction, and strength," accrued to Athens. The phrase τιμῆς ἄξιος, "worthy of honor," closely parallel to the phrase ἄξιος λαβεῖν τὴν τιμήν, "worthy to receive honor," here in 4:11, is found in benefactor contexts; see 1 Tim 6:1 and the phrase ἀξίαι τιμαί, "worthy honors," in Inscription 86 in Roueché, *Aphrodisias,* 137.

**11c** ὅτι σὺ ἔκτισας τὰ πάντα καὶ διὰ τὸ θέλημά σου ἦσαν καὶ ἐκτίσθησαν, "'Because you created everything / And by your will they existed, yes were created.'" One of the major difficulties of this clause, reflected in the variety of textual variants extant, is the apparently illogical order of the verbs ἦσαν, "they were," i.e., "they existed," and ἐκτίσθησαν, "they were created" (see *Notes* on 4:11); i.e., the "existence" of everything seems to precede creation. This can perhaps be explained as an instance of *hysteron-proteron,* i.e., the inversion of events, which sometimes occurs in Revelation (see *Comments* on 3:17; 5:2, 5; 6:4; 10:4, 9; 19:13; Beckwith, 504). While an emphasis on God as *creator* is not a central way of characterizing God in Revelation, the theme, important in Hellenistic Jewish apologetic literature, appears in a variety of ways. The verb κτίζειν, "create," is used only here and in Rev 10:6, where (in the context of an oath), in contrast to the more generic expression "everything," God is referred to elaborately as "the one who created the heaven and what is in them, the earth and what is on it, and the sea and what is in it." The verb ποιεῖν is also used in a similar context in Rev 14:7, where an angel orders all people to worship "the One who made [τῷ ποιήσαντι] the heaven and the earth and the sea and the springs." Christ is referred to as ἡ ἀρχὴ τῆς κτίσεως, "the beginning of creation," in Rev 3:14 (κτίσις), and the term κτίσμα, "creature," implying the creative activity of God, is used in 5:13; 8:13. Finally, the renewal of creation is announced by God in 21:5, "Behold I make all things new." The generic way of referring to what God created as "everything" is typically expressed with participles or finite verbs based on κτίζειν and ποιεῖν together with τὰ πάντα in the accusative in Judaism (Wis 9:1; Sir 18:1; Gk. *1 Enoch* 9:5; *Jos. As.* 12:1; *Sib. Or.* 3.20), in early Christianity (Acts 7:50; Eph 3:9; Col 1:16; *Did.* 10:3; Hermas *Mand.* 1.1; *Sim.* 5.5.2; Justin *Dial.* 55.2), and occasionally in Greco-Roman literature, where the verb ποιεῖν is regularly used, with the exception of the magical papyri (Epictetus 4.7.6 [ὁ θεὸς πάντα πεποίηκεν τὰ ἐν τῷ κόσμῳ, "God made everything in the cosmos"]; Aelius Aristides *Or.* 43.7 [Ζεὺς τὰ πάντα ἐποίησεν, "Zeus made everything"]; *PGM* IV.1709–10 [τὸν πάντα κτίσαντα θεὸν μέγαν, "by the great god who created everything"]; XIII.62–63, 571 [τὸν πάντα κτίσαντα, "(by) the one who created everything"]; see IV.3077). Ignatius refers obliquely to God as ὁ θελήσας τὰ πάντα, "the one who willed all things" (*Eph. inscr.; Rom. inscr.*).

The celebration of God as creator of all things occurs here in v 11 within the context of a hymn of praise. Similarly, an emphasis on God as creator is found frequently in hymns of praise (Pss 8:3; 33:6–9; 95:5; 102:25; 136:5–9; see H.-J. Kraus, *Psalms*, 36–37), as part of the invocation in prayers (Wis 9:1; *Jos. As.* 12:1; *PGM* IV.1709–10, 3077; XIII.62–63, 571), and in oaths (Rev 10:6).

*Explanation*

The open door in heaven that John is invited to enter uses conventional apocalyptic imagery to signal the beginning of the otherworldly journey of the author. Just as a heavenly throne-room scene introduces the narratives of the seven trumpets (8:2–5) and the seven libation bowls (15:1–8), so the longest throne-room scene in 4:1–5:14 serves not only to introduce the narrative of the seven seals (6:1–8:1) but also to introduce the entire series of visions that constitute the body of Revelation. Beginning each major vision segment in the heavenly throne room serves to anchor each series of events in the sovereignty of God, who controls events that transpire upon earth. The first introductory scene in 4:1–5:14 is the longest and most detailed, since the author must acquaint the readers with both the conventional and unconventional imagery he uses to depict the divine court with its sights and sounds, which will reappear and be amplified in later scenes.

When John saw the open door in heaven and was invited to enter by the same voice he had heard earlier (1:10), he again was "in the spirit"; i.e., he fell into a prophetic trance necessary for a visionary ascent to heaven. Further, the phrase suggests that the otherworldly journey that followed was an out-of-body experience. Just as ancient cosmology conceptualized a door or gates connecting earth with the underworld (see 1:18), the notion of a door separating earth from heaven was common in Greek tradition, though rare in the OT (cf. Gen 28:17; Ps 78:23). The three motifs of the heavenly door, the invitation to enter, and a vision of the throne room of God found in Rev 4 are literary conventions characteristic of ancient apocalyptic and revelatory literature (see *1 Enoch* 14:14–15; *T. Levi* 2:6; 5:1). Immediately, John found himself present as an observer in the heavenly throne room. Throughout the ancient world, high gods (such as the Greek Zeus, the Roman Jupiter, the Babylonian Marduk, and the Israelite Yahweh) were conceptualized as great kings dwelling in magnificent heavenly palaces with innumerable subservient supernatural courtiers. Occasionally, OT prophets are depicted as making visionary ascents to the heavenly court where, by eavesdropping on the proceedings, they learn what will transpire on earth in the future (1 Kgs 22:17–23; Isa 6:1–7; 40:1–2; Zech 3:1–5). In fact, Jeremiah defines a true prophet as one who has been present in the council of heaven (Jer 23:18).

John describes what he sees in some detail, and, though the description has some unique features (e.g., the twenty-four elders), it generally tallies with conventional OT and Jewish traditions of epiphanies of God and visions of the heavenly throne room (John, for example, is dependent on Ezekiel's vision of the glory of God, Ezek 1:4–28). The very first thing John sees is the magnificent throne of God (symbolizing his univeral sovereignty), but, unlike Ezekiel, he carefully avoids any description of God himself (v 3). The throne was surrounded by a rainbow that looked like an emerald, and the One seated on it had the appearance of jasper and carnelian. Twenty-four "elders" encircle the throne, seated on thrones with gold wreaths on their heads and wearing white garments (v 4). The number twenty-four (only used of this group of "elders" in Revelation) symbolizes both cosmic kingship and the sum of the twelve tribes of Israel plus the Twelve Apostles, together constituting the new people of God. The cosmic symbolism of the circle is reflected in the encircling rainbow "round" the throne (v 3), then the four living creatures or cherubim encircling the throne (v 6), then the circle of twenty-four elders (v 4), all encircled by an innumerable multitude of angels (5:11). God, at the center of all, represents the *axis mundi*, the center of the cosmos. The thunder and lightning emanating from the throne (v 5) are reminiscent of the Sinai theophany in the OT (Exod 19:16–18; 20:18–20), which became part of OT theophanic imagery generally (see Isa 29:6). The four living creatures described in vv 6–8 (from Ezek 1:5, 10) are based on OT conceptions of the angelic seraphim and cherubim, depicted as located both above (Isa 6:2) and beneath (Ezek 1:5–25) the throne of God. After the time of Irenaeus (ca. A.D. 180), the four creatures came to symbolize the four Gospels (Matthew = the lion; Luke = the ox; Mark = the man; John = the eagle) and have suggested to some the relative chronological order of each of the Gospels. The seven torches of fire (v 5) are based on the menorah of the tabernacle and temple (see Zech 4:1–10), while "sea of glass" (v 6) may represent the transcendence of God, his separation from the created order.

The scene is one of divine worship, for the four living creatures sing the trisagion, "thrice holy," and are joined in song by the twenty-four elders who worship God and cast their crowns at his feet (vv 8–11). The heavenly liturgy depicted in vv 8–11 has been the subject of some speculation. Is it a reflection of Christian liturgy familiar to John? In spite of some traditional elements that certainly had a place in Jewish as well as Christian liturgy, the throne-room liturgy appears to be a Johannine creation based on his knowledge of Roman imperial court ceremonial, as well as aspects of Jewish and Christian liturgical traditions.

*Excursus 4B: Hymns in Revelation*

*Bibliography*

**Baillet, M.** "Psaumes, hymnes, cantiques et prières dans les manuscrits de Qumran." In *Le Psautier: Ses origines ses problemes littéraires, son influence*, ed. R. De Langhe. Louvain: Institut Orientaliste, 1962. 339–405. **Berger, K.** "Hellenistische Gattungen im Neuen Testament." *ANRW* II, 25/2:1031–1432, 1831–85. **Bremer, J. M.** "Greek Hymns." In *Faith, Hope and Worship: Aspects of Religious Mentality in the Ancient World*, ed. H. S. Versnel. Leiden: Brill, 1981. 193–215. **Charlesworth, J. H.** "Jewish Hymns, Odes and Prayers (ca. 167 B.C.E.–135 C.E.)." In *Early Judaism and Its Modern Interpreters*, ed. R. A. Kraft. and G. W. E. Nickelsburg. Atlanta: Scholars, 1986. 411–36. ———. "Prolegomenon to a New Study of the Jewish Background of the Hymns and Prayers in the New Testament." *JJS* 33 (1982) 265–85. **Deichgräber, R.** *Gotteshymnus und Christushymnus in der frühen Christenheit: Untersuchungen zu Form, Sprache und Stil der frühchristlichen Hymnen*. Göttingen: Vandenhoeck & Ruprecht, 1967. **Delling, G.** "Zum gottesdienstlichen Stil der Johannesapokalypse." *NovT* 3 (1959) 107–37. **Dormeyer, D.** *Das Neue Testament im Rahmen der antiken Literaturgeschichte: Eine Einführung*. Darmstadt: Wissenschaftliche, 1993. **Farris, S.** *The Hymns of Luke's Infancy*

*Narratives: Their Origin, Meaning and Significance.* Sheffield: JSOT, 1985. **Flusser, D.** "Psalms, Hymns and Prayers." In *Jewish Writings of the Second Temple Period,* ed. M. E. Stone. CRINT 2/2. Philadelphia: Fortress; Assen: Van Gorcum, 1984. 551–77. **Furley, W. D.** "Praise and Persuasion in Greek Hymns." *JHS* 115 (1995) 25–46. **Grözinger, K.-E.** "Singen und ekstatische Sprache in der frühen jüdischen Mystik." *JSJ* 11 (1980) 66–77. **Harris, M. A.** *The Literary Function of Hymns in the Apocalypse of John.* Ann Arbor, MI: University Microfilms, 1989. **Hengel, M.** "Hymns and Christology." In *Between Jesus and Paul.* Philadelphia: Fortress, 1983. 78–96. **Holm-Nielsen, S.** "The Importance of Late Jewish Psalmody for the Understanding of Old Testament Psalmodic Tradition." *ST* 13 (1960) 1–53. ———. "Religiöse Poesie des Spätjudentums." *ANRW* II, 19/1:152–86. **Janko, R.** "The Structure of the Homeric Hymns: A Study in Genre." *Hermes* 109 (1981) 9–24. **Jörns, K.-P.** *Das hymnische Evangelium: Untersuchungen zu Aufbau, Funktion und Herkunft der hymnischen Stücke in der Johannesoffenbarung.* Gütersloh: Mohn, 1971. **Kittel, B.** *The Hymns of Qumran: Translation and Commentary.* Chico, CA: Scholars, 1981. **Krenz, E.** "Epideiktik and Hymnody: The New Testament and Its World." *BR* 40 (1995) 50–97. **Kroll, J.** *Die christliche Hymnodik bis zu Klemens von Alexandreia.* 2nd ed. Darmstadt: Wissenschaftliche Buchgesellschaft, 1968. **Kuhn, H.-W.** *Enderwartung und gegenwärtiges Heil: Untersuchungen zu den Gemeindeliedern von Qumran.* Göttingen: Vandenhoeck & Ruprecht, 1966. **Lattke, M.** *Hymnus: Materialien zu einer Geschichte der antiken Hymnologie.* Freiburg: Universitätsverlag; Göttingen: Vandenhoeck & Ruprecht, 1991. **Martin, R. P.** *Carmen Christi: Philippians 2:5–11 in Recent Interpretation and in the Setting of Early Christian Worship.* Rev. ed. Grand Rapids, MI: Eerdmans, 1983. ———. *Worship in the Early Church.* Grand Rapids, MI: Eerdmans, 1964. **Miller, A. M.** *From Delos to Delphi: A Literary Study of the Homeric Hymn to Apollo.* Mnesosyne 93. Leiden: Brill, 1986. **Newsom, C. A.** *The Songs of the Sabbath Sacrifice.* Atlanta: Scholars, 1985. **Norden, E.** *Agnostos Theos: Untersuchungen zur Formengeschichte religiöser Rede.* 4th ed. Darmstadt: Wissenschaftliche Buchgesellschaft, 1956. **O'Rourke, J.** "The Hymns of the Apocalypse." *CBQ* 30 (1968) 399–409. **Race, W. H.** "Aspects of Rhetoric and Form in Greek Hymns." *GRBS* 23 (1982) 5–14. **Reif, S. C.** *Judaism and Hebrew Prayer: New Perspectives on Jewish Liturgical History.* Cambridge: Cambridge UP, 1993. **Russell, D. A.** "Aristides and the Prose Hymn." In *Antonine Literature,* ed. D. A. Russell. Oxford: Clarendon, 1990. 19–219. **Sanders, J. T.** *The New Testament Christological Hymns: Their Historical Religious Background.* Cambridge: Cambridge UP, 1971. **Sauter, F.** *Der römische Kaiserkult bei Martial und Statius.* Stuttgart; Berlin: Kohlhammer, 1934. **Schattenmann, J.** *Studien zum neutestamentlichen Prosahymnus.* Munich: Beck, 1965. **Schille, G.** *Frühchristliche Hymnen.* Berlin: Evangelische Verlaganstalt, 1965. **Schuller, E. M.** *Non-Canonical Psalms from Qumran: A Pseudepigraphic Collection.* Atlanta: Scholars, 1986. **Seidel, H.** "Lobgesänge im Himmel und auf Erden." In *Gottesvolk: Beiträge zu einem Thema biblischer Theologie.* FS S. Wagner, ed. A. Meinhold and R. Lux. Berlin: Evangelische Verlagsanstalt, 1991. 114–24. **Strecker, G.** *Literaturgeschichte des Neuen Testaments.* Göttingen: Vandenhoeck & Ruprecht, 1992. **Thompson, L. L.** "Cult and Eschatology in the Apocalypse of John." *JR* 49 (1969) 330–50. **Thraede, K.** "Hymnus I." *RAC* 16:915–46. **Touilleux, P.** *L'Apocalypse et les cultes de Domitien et de Cybele.* Paris: Librairie Orientaliste Paul Geuthner, 1935. **Wengst, K.** *Christologische Formeln und Lieder des Urchristentums.* Gütersloh: Mohn, 1972. **Wünsch, R.** "Hymnos." PW, 1st series, 9:140–83.

An important feature of the heavenly throne-room ceremonial in Revelation is the presence of sixteen hymns or hymnlike compositions at various points in the narrative (4:8c, 11; 5:9b–10, 12b, 13b; 7:10b, 12; 11:15b, 17–18; 12:10b–12; 15:3b–4; 16:5b–7b; 19:1b–2, 3, 5b, 6b–8). With the exception of the single independent hymn in 15:3b–4, they are arranged in seven antiphonal units (4:8–11; 5:9–14; 7:9–12; 11:15–18; 16:5–7; 19:1–4, 5–8). It now appears that John did not quote or modify traditional Jewish or Christian hymns with which he was familiar; rather he wrote new hymns for their present context making use of some traditional Jewish and Christian liturgical traditions and forms, including the hallelujah, the amen, the *sanctus* (4:8), doxologies (5:13; 7:10, 12; 19:1), and acclamations (4:11; 5:9, 12). Though the OT contains very little information about the liturgy of the temple, it is possible that the post-exilic indications of the important role that music and singing purportedly played in the temple reflect pre-exilic practice (1 Chr 15:16–22; 23:1–6, 24–32; 25:1–8; Sir 47:8–10; 1 Macc 4:54–55; see Reif, *Hebrew Prayer,* 29–30, 45–46, 50), though even these texts must be viewed critically. The OT occasionally suggests that angels and other heavenly beings sing praise to God (Isa 6:3; Pss 103:20; 148:2). The conception that angels are the chief participants in a perpetual heavenly liturgy was carried over in an expanded and embellished form into Jewish apocalypses and testaments (*2 Enoch* 18:8–9; 19:3; 42:4; *Apoc. Zeph.*, frag. A; *T. Job* 51:1–4; 52:12; *3 Enoch* 24–40; *Apoc. Abr.* 18:3; *T. Abr.* 20:12; *T. Isaac* 6:1–6, 24; *T. Adam* 1:4). Yet, apart from the *sanctus,* such songs are rarely reproduced (*3 Enoch* 20:2; 39:2; see *Apoc. Abr.* 17:6–21). The Romans (borrowing from Hellenistic kingship traditions) developed an elaborate imperial court ceremonial that included the singing of hymns and the shouting of acclamations to the emperor by those present in court (Dio Cassius 59.24.5; Tacitus *Annals* 14.15; Suetonius *Nero* 20.3). Unlike other apocalyptic writers, John, dependent on both Jewish traditions about the heavenly liturgy and Hellenistic and Roman court ceremonial, used hymns as a narrative device to interpret the significance of eschatological events. The temporal perspective of the hymns ranges from the complete realization of eschatological events (16:5–7; 19:1–2), to the partial realization of eschatological events (11:15–18; 12:10–12), to totally future expectation (15:3–4; 19:5–8).

Prose as well as poetic hymnic texts were widely used in liturgical contexts in the Greco-Roman world (for an excellent preliminary survey of the subject, see Krenz, *BR* 40 [1995] 50–97). There were two main types of hymns in Greek literary tradition, the *cult* or *subjective* hymn and the *rhapsodic* or *objective* hymn (Miller, *From Delos to Delphi,* 1–9). The *cult* hymn was intended to persuade a god to act on behalf of the speaker (and so is framed in the *du-Stil,* i.e., the "you [sing.] style") and consists of three parts: (1) The invocation contains honorific epithets of the god addressed. (2) The *hypomnesis,* "reminder," recounts how the god has responded to the speaker's devotion in the past. (3) The cult hymn concludes with the actual request to which the first two parts have been leading. The *rhapsodic* hymn presupposes a human audience, is framed in the third person *er-Stil,* "he/she style," and consists of three parts: (1) The *exordium* announces the speaker's intent to praise the god and includes honorific epithets of the god. (2) The *midsection* (attached to the *exordium* by a relative pronoun, called the "hymnic relative") consists of either a general description of the god's nature (*descriptio*) or a narrative of a specific episode or sequence of episodes from the god's mythic experiences (*narratio*), though some hymns can combine both elements. (3) The *epilogue* is the final element and contains a salutation and perhaps a request or the speaker's intention to compose another hymn in the future.

The similarity between the hymns in Revelation and imperial hymns composed in honor of the emperor provides evidence that attributes used of the emperors were also used by John of God in the hymns of Revelation (Touilleux, *L'Apocalypse,* 100–103, with additional references): (1) "Holy One" (ἅγιος, Rev 6:10; ὅσιος, 15:4; 16:5); cf. *sacer,* "holy one," "sacred one" (Martial 5.1.190; 5.2.177; Statius *Silvae* 4.2.5; 5.1.187; 5.2.177; Ovid *Fasti* 6.810); cf. *sanctus,* "holy" (Ovid *Fasti* 2.63, 127; Valerius Flaccus 1.11; for references in Martial and Statius, see Sauter, *Kaiserkult,* 105–16, "Sanctus als Kaiserepitheton"); (2) "Glory" (δόξα, 4:11; 5:12, 13; 7:12; 19:1, 7); cf. *terrarum gloria,* "glory of the earth" (Martial 2.91.1); (3) "Salvation" (σωτηρία, 13:10; 19:1); cf. *salus,* "salvation" (Martial 2.91.1; 5.1.7); (4) "Authority" (ἐξουσία, 12:10); cf. *potestas, potens,* "power, authority" (Martial 9.79.7; Dio Cassius 4.1); (5) "Worthy to receive power" (5:12); cf. *quo non dignior has subit habenas* (Statius *Silvae* 1.103); (6) "Righteous are your judgments" (19:1); cf. *honorem judiciorum celestium* (Statius *Silvae* 3.4.53); (7) "Our God, the Almighty" (19:6); cf. *dominus et deus noster, dominus terrarum, dominus mundi,* "our Lord and God, Lord of the earth, Lord of the world" (Martial 1.4.2; 7.55; 8.32.6).

A prayer ascribed to Enoch in *1 Enoch* 84:2–3 has similarities to the hymns of Revelation (tr. Knibb, *Enoch*):

> Blessed (are) you, O Lord King, and great and powerful in your majesty, Lord of the whole creation of heaven, King of Kings, and God of the whole world! And your kingly authority, and your sovereignty and majesty will last for ever, and for ever, and your power for all generations. And all the heavens (are) your throne for ever, and the whole earth your footstool for ever, and for ever and ever. For you made, and you rule, everything, and nothing is too hard for you, and no wisdom escapes you; it does not turn away from your throne, nor from your presence. [Petition follows.]

The singing or chanting of hymns was an integral part of the worship of early Christians (1 Cor 14:26; Col 3:16; Jas 5:13; Pliny *Ep.* 10.96 [who refers to *carmen Christo*]; *Odes of Solomon*). Col 3:16 and Eph 5:19 refer to ψαλμοί, "psalms," ὕμνοι, "hymns," and ᾠδαὶ πνευματικαί, "spiritual songs," but these terms do not seem to represent sharp distinctions among different types or genres of hymns (Kroll, *Hymnodik,* 5–6). In Greek usage, ὕμνος refers to a hymn or ode sung in praise of gods or heroes (LSJ, 1849). Scholars have identified and analyzed a number of hymns or hymnic fragments that are embedded in early Christian writings (Schille, *Hymnen;* Martin, *Worship,* 39–52; Deichgräber, *Gotteshymnus;* Berger, *Formgeschichte,* 239–47; id., "Hymnische Gattungen," 1149–71; Dormeyer, *Literaturgeschichte,* 133–34). One of the first to identify hymns and hymn fragments in the NT was the classical scholar Eduard Norden, who distinguished several forms of hymnic rhetoric found in prose hymns in classical literature and the NT, including the *du-Stil,* addressed directly to the god (*Agnostos Theos,* 143–63), the *er-Stil,* a predication about a god not addressed to the god (163–66), and the participial predication or relative-clause predication (168–76); see Krenz, *BR* 40 (1995) 72–73. Several hymns based on OT models are embedded in the Lukan infancy narrative, including the *Magnificat* (Luke 1:46–55), the *Benedictus* (Luke 1:68–79), the *Gloria in excelsis* (Luke 2:14), and the *Nunc Dimittis* (Luke 2:29–32); see Farris, *Hymns.* Some of these hymns were directed to God (Rom 11:33–36; 2 Cor 1:3–4; Eph 1:3–14; 1 Tim 1:17; 1 Pet 1:3–5; Col 1:12–14), while others narrate the mission of Christ, frequently including pre-incarnation and post-resurrection themes, particularly the *abasement* and *exaltation* motifs (John 1:1–14; Phil 2:6–11; Eph 2:14–16; 5:14; Col 1:15–20; 1 Tim 3:16; Heb 1:3; 1 Pet 2:21–25; Ignatius *Eph.* 7:2; 19:1–3). While Greek hymns were written in both poetic and prose forms, early Christian hymns lack meter (they are also not written in "metrical prose" as Bichsel claims in *ADB* 3:351) but do exhibit various forms of Semitic poetic parallelism.

## *Excursus 4C: The Cosmology of Ancient Ascent Narratives*

### Bibliography

**Dean-Otting, M.** *Heavenly Journeys: A Study of the Motif in Hellenistic Jewish Literature.* Frankfurt am Main: Lang, 1984. **Furley, D. J.** "The Cosmological Crisis in Classical Antiquity." In *Cosmic Problems.* Cambridge: Cambridge UP, 1989. 223–35. ———. *The Formation of the Atomic Theory and Its Earliest Critics.* Vol. 1 of *The Greek Cosmologists.* Cambridge: Cambridge UP, 1987. **Gaster, T. H.** "Cosmogony." *IDB* 1:702–9. **Lloyd, G. E. R.** "Greek Cosmologies." In *Ancient Cosmologies,* ed. C. Blacker and M. Loewe. London: Allen and Unwin, 1975. 198–224. **Malina, B. J.** *On the Genre and Message of Revelation: Star*

*Visions and Sky Journeys.* Peabody: Hendrickson, 1995. **Nilsson, M. P.** *Greek Piety.* Tr. H. J. Rose. New York: Norton, 1969. 96–103. **Scott, A.** *Origen and the Life of the Stars: A History of an Idea.* Oxford: Clarendon, 1991. **Tabor, J. D.** *Things Unutterable: Paul's Ascent to Paradise in Its Greco-Roman, Judaic, and Early Christian Contexts.* Lanham, MD: University Press of America, 1986. **Wright, M. R.** *Cosmology in Antiquity.* London; New York: Routledge, 1995. **Yarbro Collins, A.** "The Seven Heavens in Jewish and Christian Apocalypses." In *Cosmology and Eschatology in Jewish and Christian Apocalypticism.* Leiden: Brill, 1996. 21–54.

It is striking that Revelation does not reflect more specifically the cosmology typical of the Hellenistic and Roman period, in which the cosmos was thought to consist of seven heavens. Paul's account of his own ascent to the third heaven reflects a cosmology of at least three heavens (2 Cor 12:1–5). John knows only a single heaven as the dwelling place of God and his angels. This older cosmology consisted of a three-tiered universe consisting of heaven above, earth in the middle, and the underworld beneath (the three-tiered universe is also reflected in several apocalypses, including the five apocalypses that constitute *1 Enoch,* the *Testament of Abraham,* and the *Apocalypse of Ezra;* cf. *Testament of Solomon;* Rev 18:3). That cosmology is reflected in Rev 5:3, where the entire cosmos is comprehended by the categories heaven, earth, and under the earth; in 5:13 the sea is added, making four regions (see 14:7, where God is celebrated as the creator of heaven, earth, and sea). The author of Revelation also speaks simply of heaven and earth as comprehending all creation (20:11; 21:1). The abyss (9:1, 2, 11; 11:7; 17:8; 20:1, 3) appears to be located in the underworld, and it is likely that the lake of fire is also located in the underworld (19:20; 20:10, 14, 15; 21:8). It should be noted, however, that those who worship the Beast and receive its mark "will be tormented with fire and sulphur in the presence of the holy angels and in the presence of the Lamb" (14:10). The earth itself was thought to be a flat disk surrounded on all sides by water. Below the earth was the underworld, which was the realm of the dead, called Sheol by the Israelites but Hades by the Greeks. Above the earth was the vault of heaven containing the heavenly bodies and, in the highest place, God and his angelic entourage.

The new cosmology that developed during the Hellenistic period, and quickly displaced older cosmologies, regarded the earth as a sphere (Cleomedes 1.8–9; Ptolemy *Math. synt.* 1.3). The earth was thought to be a stationary center surrounded by seven planets (including the sun and moon), each of which moved in its own sphere (Aristotle *De caelo* 2.13 [292ab]; Theon Smyrn. 148.6–7; Philo *Conf.* 5; see Scott, *Stars,* 55). The earth was at the same time the "innermost" as well as the "lowest" part of the cosmos. The seven planets were enclosed by an eighth sphere consisting of the fixed stars (Alcinous *Did.* 14; Philo *Cher.* 22). God was thought to dwell in the highest heaven or sphere, usually the seventh or eighth heaven (*Corp. Herm.* 1.26), with various supernatural beings located at various levels below him.

Many Jewish apocalypses narrate a heavenly journey by an ancient worthy, the goal of which is typically the seventh or highest heaven, where God himself is seated resplendent on his throne of glory. The apocalypses that have a cosmology consisting of the earth with seven heavens above include the *3 Apoc. Bar.* and the *Mart. Isa.* (6:1–11:43). Though the notion of a universe consisting of seven heavens did not originate within Judaism, the conception of the seventh heaven as the place where God sits upon his throne of glory is probably of Jewish origin. Since God was thought to be enthroned upon the cherubim over the ark in the *Debir* or Holy of Holies, it is possible that the structure of the temple in Jerusalem was seen as a symbol of the structure of the cosmos. Since the holiness of the temple itself was commonly held to extend to the boundaries of the Holy City, it is possible to see a sevenfold progression through a series of concentric boundaries to the innermost Holy of Holies: (1) Jerusalem, (2) Court of the Gentiles, (3) Court of Women,

(4) Court of Israelites, (5) Court of Priests, (6) Holy Place, (7) Holy of Holies. The cosmic interpretation of the temple is implicitly coordinated with the heavenly spheres by Josephus, who states that the third portion of the tabernacle is reserved for God alone, because heaven is inaccessible to people (*Ant.* 3.123, 181), possibly reflecting a cosmology of three heavens (see 2 Cor 12:2–4), reflected in the basic structure of the tabernacle or temple with its outer court, holy place, and most holy place. It is perhaps significant that many heavenly journeys are connected in various ways with the Jerusalem temple and conceptualize the heavenly world as a temple. In *3 Apoc. Bar. praef.* 2, the setting is the place where the most holy place once stood. Though Baruch's heavenly journey goes only to the fifth heaven, Origen (*De principiis* 2.3.6) refers to a work of Baruch's that mentions seven heavens. Origen may thus have been familiar with a more complete version of this apocalypse. The site of the most holy place is also the setting for a vision in *2 Apoc. Bar.* 34:1; 35:1.

The magical handbook *Sepher ha-Razim* contains descriptions of each of the seven heavens together with the names of the angelic hosts that inhabit each one and which particular magical procedures they can help the magical practitioner to perform. At the apex of this cosmic structure is "The seventh firmament, all of it is sevenfold light, and from its light all the (seven) heavens shine. Within it is the throne of glory, set on the four glorious *Hayot*" (Morgan, *Sepher ha-Razim*, 81).

# b. The Investiture of the Lamb (5:1–14)

## Bibliography

**Achtemeier, P. J.** "Revelation 5:1–14." *Int* 40 (1986) 283–88. **Augrain, C.** "Le Christ vainquer dans l'Apocalypse." *AsSeign* 24 (1970) 29–35. ―――. "La grande doxologie (Ap 5:11–14)." *AsSeign* 24 (1970) 29–35. **Aulén, G.** *Christus Victor: An Historical Study of the Three Main Types of the Idea of the Atonement.* Tr. A. G. Hebert. New York: Macmillan, 1969. **Bauckham, R.** "The Conversion of the Nations." In *Climax.* 238–337. ―――. "The Worship of Jesus." In *Climax.* 118–49. **Benoit, P.** "Ἅγιοι en Colossiens 1.12: Hommes ou Anges?" In *Paul and Paulinism,* ed. M. D. Hooker and S. G. Wilson. London: SPCK, 1982. 83–99. **Bergmeier, R.** "Die Buchrolle und das Lamm (Apk 5 und 10)." *ZNW* 76 (1985) 225–42. **Bilabel, F.** "Zur Doppelausfertigung ägyptischer Urkunden." *Aegyptus* 6 (1925) 93–113. **Birt, T.** *Die Buchrolle in der Kunst, archäologisch-antiquarische Untersuchungen zum antiken Buchwesen.* Leipzig: Teubner, 1907. **Brückner, W.** *Die grosse und die kleine Buchrolle in der Offenbarung Johannes 5 und 10.* Giessen: Töpelmann, 1923. **Bundy, E. L.** "The Quarrel between Kallimachos and Apollonios: Part I. The Epilogue of Kallimachos' *Hymn to Apollo*." *CSCA* 5 (1972) 39–94. **Burney, C. F.** *The Aramaic Origin of the Fourth Gospel.* Oxford: Clarendon, 1922. **Casel, O.** "Die λογικὴ θυσία der antiken Mystik in christlich-liturgischer Umdeutung." *Jahrbuch für Liturgiewissenschaft* 4 (1924) 37ff. **Charles, J. D.** "An Apocalyptic Tribute to the Lamb (Rev 5:1–14)." *JETS* 34 (1991) 461–73. ―――. "Imperial Pretensions and the Throne-Vision of the Lamb: Observations on the Function of Revelation 5." *CTR* 7 (1993) 85–97. **Daly, R. J.** *Christian Sacrifice: The Judaeo-Christian Background before Origen.* Washington, DC: The Catholic University of America, 1978. ―――. *The Origins of the Christian Doctrine of Sacrifice.* Philadelphia: Fortress, 1978. **Davis, R. D.** *The Heavenly Court Judgment of Revelation 4–5.* Lanham, MD: University Press of America, 1992. **Delebecque, É.** "'Je vis' dans l'Apocalypse." *RevThom* 88 (1988) 460–66. **Dequeker, L.** "The Saints of the Most High." *OTS* 18 (1973) 108–87. **Fairman, H. W.** "The

Kingship Rituals of Egypt." In *Myth, Ritual, and Kingship: Essays on the Theory and Practice of Kingship in the Ancient Near East and in Israel*, ed. S. H. Hooke. Oxford: Clarendon, 1958. 74–104. **Fischer, L.** "Die Urkunden in Jer 32:11–14 nach den Ausgrabungen und dem Talmud." *ZAW* 30 (1910) 137–42. **Ford, J. M.** "The Divorce Bill of the Lamb and the Scroll of the Suspected Adulteress: A Note on Apoc. 5,1 and 10,8–11." *JSJ* 2 (1971) 136–43. **Frankfort, H.** *Kingship and the Gods: A Study of Ancient Near Eastern Religion as the Integration of Society and Nature.* Chicago: University of Chicago, 1948. **Gornatowski, A.** "Rechts und Links im antiken Aberglauben." Diss., Breslau, 1936. **Goodspeed, E. J.** "The Book with Seven Seals." *JBL* 22 (1903) 70–74. **Gressmann, H.** *Musik und Musikinstrumente im Alten Testament.* Giessen: Töpelmann, 1903. **Groningen, B. A. van.** *La composition littéraire archaique grecque.* Amsterdam: Noord-Hollandsche Uitg. Mij., 1958. **Halpern, B.** *The Constitution of the Monarchy in Israel.* HSM 25. Chico, CA: Scholars, 1981. **Haran, M.** *Temples and Temple-Service in Ancient Israel: An Inquiry into the Character of Cult Phenomena and the Historical Setting of the Priestly School.* Oxford: Clarendon, 1978. **Houtman, C.** *Der Himmel im Alten Testament: Israels Weltbild und Weltanschauung.* OTS 30. Leiden: Brill, 1993. **Jeremias, Joachim.** " Ἀμνὸς τοῦ θεοῦ—παῖς θεοῦ." *ZNW* 34 (1935) 115–23. **Kaligula, L.** *The Wise King: Studies in Royal Wisdom as Divine Revelation in the Old Testament and Its Environment.* ConBOT 15. Lund: Gleerup, 1980. **Kelso, J. L.** *The Ceramic Vocabulary of the Old Testament.* BASORSup 5–6. New Haven: American Schools of Oriental Research, 1948. **Koep, L.** *Das himmlische Buch in Antike und Christentum.* Bonn: Hanstein, 1952. **Koffmahn, E.** *Die Doppelurkunden aus der Wüste Juda.* STDJ 5. Leiden: Brill, 1968. **Maas, M.,** and **Snyder, J. M.** *Stringed Instruments of Ancient Greece.* New Haven; London: Yale UP, 1989. **McKinnon, J.** *Music in Early Christian Literature.* Cambridge: Cambridge UP, 1987. **Médebielle, P. A.** *L'Expiation dans l'Ancient et le Nouveau Testament.* Rome: Pontifical Biblical Institute, 1923. **Mowry, L.** "Revelation 4–5 and Early Christian Liturgical Usage." *JBL* 71 (1952) 75–84. **Müller, H.-P.** "Die himmlische Ratsversammlung: Motivgeschichtliches zu Apc 5:1–5." *ZNW* 54 (1963) 254–67. **Münchow, C.** "Das Buch mit sieben Siegeln." *ZZ* 31 (1977) 376–83. **Nielsen, J.** *Incense in Ancient Israel.* Leiden: Brill, 1986. **Peterson, E.** *Das Buch von den Engeln: Stellung und Bedeutung der heiligen Engel im Kultus.* Leipzig: Hegner, 1935. **Piper, O.** "The Apocalypse of John and the Liturgy of the Ancient Church." *CH* 20 (1951) 10–22. **Preuschen, E.** *Origenes Werke.* GCS 10/4. Leipzig: Hinrichs, 1903. **Quasten, J.** *Musik und Gesang in den Kulten der heidnischen Antike und christlichen Frühzeit.* 2nd ed. Münster: Aschendorff, 1973. **Roberts, C. H.,** and **Skeat, T. C.** *The Birth of the Codex.* London: British Academy, 1983. **Roller, O.** "Das Buch mit den sieben Siegeln." *ZNW* 36 (1937) 98–113. **Russell, E.** "A Roman Law Parallel to Revelation Five." *BSac* 115 (1958) 258–64. **Sattler, W.** "Das Buch mit sieben Siegeln: Studien zum literarischen Aufbau der Offenbarung Johannis." *ZNW* 21 (1922) 43–53. **Schüssler Fiorenza, E.** "Redemption as Liberation: Apoc 1:5f. and 5:9f." *CBQ* 36 (1974) 220–32. **Scott, R. B. Y.** *The Original Language of the Apocalypse.* Toronto: University of Toronto, 1928. **Stadelmann, L. I.** *The Hebrew Conception of the World.* AnBib 39. Rome: Biblical Institute, 1970. **Staritz, K.** "Zur Offenbarung Johannis 5:1." *ZNW* 30 (1931) 157–70. **Stefanović, R.** "The Background and Meaning of the Sealed Book of Revelation 5." Diss., Andrews University, 1995. **Süring, M. L.** *Horn Motifs in the Hebrew Bible and Related Ancient Near Eastern Literature and Iconography.* Berrien Springs: Andrews University, 1982. **Swanson, D. C.** "Diminutives in the Greek New Testament." *JBL* 77 (1958) 134–51. **Unnik, W. C. van.** "'Worthy is the Lamb': The Background of Apoc. 5." In *Mélanges Bibliques en hommage au R. P. Béda Rigaux*, ed. A. Descamps et al. Gembloux: Duculot, 1970. 445–61.

### Translation

[1] Then [a] I saw [b] in the right hand [b c] of the One seated on [d] the throne [d] a scroll written both [e] inside and on the back [e] and sealed with [f] seven seals. [f] [2] Then I saw a mighty [a] angel proclaiming with a loud voice, "Who is worthy to open the scroll by [b] breaking its seals?" [3] No one was able, [a] either in heaven [b] or [c] on earth [d] or [e] under the earth, [d] to open the scroll

or^f *to look into it.* ^4*Then*^a *I*^b *wept* ^c*a great deal,*^c *because no one was found worthy to open the scroll or to look into it.* ^5*Then* ^a *one of the elders said* ^b *to me, "Stop weeping,*^c *behold the lion of the tribe of Judah, the descendant* ^d ^c*of David, he* ^f*has conquered* ^f ^g*so that he is able to open* ^g *the book and* ^h*its seven seals."*

^6*Then I saw,*^a *between the throne and* ^b*the four cherubim* ^c *and the elders, a lamb* ^d *standing*^e *as though slain, with* ^f *seven horns and seven eyes (which* ^g *are the* ^h*spirits of God* ^i*sent out* ^i *to the entire earth).* ^7*He* ^a ^b*came and* ^c*took* ^b *the scroll* ^d ^e*from the right hand of the One seated on the throne.*^e

^8*And when he took the scroll, the four cherubim and the twenty-four elders fell*^a *before the* ^b *Lamb, each* ^c *with a kithara* ^d *and a golden pan filled with incense (which* ^e *represents the* ^f *prayers* ^g *of* ^h*God's people* ^h*).* ^9*Then they chanted*^a *a new song:*

*"You are worthy to receive the book / and open its seals,*
*Because you were slain and you redeemed for* ^b *God / by your death* ^c
*People* ^d *from every tribe and tongue / and people and nation,*
10      *and made them*^a *for our God / a kingdom* ^b *and priests.*
                *And* ^c*they will reign* ^c *upon the earth."*

^11*Then I saw and I heard* ^a*the sound of many angels encircling the throne, and the cherubim* ^b *and the elders (their number was myriads and myriads and thousands of thousands),* ^12*chanting*^a *with a loud voice:*

*"Worthy* ^b *is the Lamb who was slain to receive*
*power and wealth and wisdom*
*and might and honor and glory and praise."* ^c

^13*Then I heard every created being*^a *in heaven and on earth* ^b*and under the earth* ^b *and upon the sea* ^c*and everything* ^d *in them responding,*^e

*"To the One who sits on* ^f*the throne* ^f *and to the Lamb*
^g*be praise*^h *and honor and glory and power* ^g *for ever."*^i

^14*And the four cherubim*^a *responded,*^b *"Amen," and the elders prostrated themselves and worshiped.*^c

## Notes

1.a. καί is translated "then" here because it is a coordinating conjunction frequently functioning as a link between main clauses that indicates a temporal sequence in a narrative sequence (like the Hebrew waw consecutive).

1.b-b. Variant: ἐν τῇ δεξιᾷ] 792; Latin witnesses that read *in dextera:* it^gig vg Cyprian Victorinus (Haussleiter, *Victorinus,* 61); Tyconius³ Primasius Cassiodorus. This variant arose as a correction of the unusual expression ἐπὶ τὴν δεξιάν, "in the right hand." The use of ἐπί in Revelation is problematic (see Schmid, *Studien* 2:209–13). The phrase ἐπὶ τὴν δεξιάν could mean "in the right hand," "on/upon the right hand" (Bousset [1906] 254), or "at the right side" (cf. LXX Ps 120:5, ἐπὶ χεῖρα δεξιάν, "at your right hand"; BAGD, 288); evidence for these possibilities is surveyed in Stefanovič, "Background," 145–57). In the phrase ἐπὶ τὴν δεξιάν (a *lectio originalis* found only there in Revelation), ἐπί probably means "in," just as the phrase ἐπὶ τῆς δεξιᾶς μου in 1:20 (also found only there in Revelation) means "in my right hand," as the parallel ἐν τῇ δεξιᾷ χειρὶ αὐτοῦ, "in his right hand," in 1:16 indicates. The author is dependent on the imagery of Ezek 2:9–10, where the phrase ἐν αὐτῇ, "in it [i.e., 'the hand']," is used for the location of the unrolled scroll handed to the prophet. It must also be observed that the phrase ἐπὶ τὴν δεξιάν is a variant for ἐπὶ τῆς δεξιᾶς in Rev 1:20 attested by Oecumenius^2053 2062 Andr h^2302. However, the phrase ἐν τῇ χειρί, "in the right hand," is used to describe the location of the little scroll held by the angel in Rev 10:2, 8.

1.c. Variant: insert καὶ ἐν μέσῳ] 2351.

1.d-d. Variant: τὸν θρόνον] Hippolytus (*Comm. in Dan.* 4.34) Andr g^2071 andr i^2015. Harmonistic correction since acc. used with first ἐπί.

1.e-e. Variants: (1) ἔσωθεν καὶ ὄπισθεν] A (lacuna in C) fam 1611²³²⁹ ²³⁴⁴ Oecumenius²⁰⁶²Andr a b e²⁰⁵⁷ f syrʰ Origen (*Comm. in Jo.* 5.6; ed. Preuschen, *Origenes Werke,* 103, 28) Cyprian Epiphanius TR; Tischendorf, *NT Graece;* WHort; von Soden, *Text;* Merk, *NT;* Nestle-Aland²⁷; UBSGNT⁴; *TCGNT* ¹; Charles, 2:267; G. Reichelt, *Buch,* 80–91. (2) ἔμπροσθεν καὶ ὄπισθεν] ℵ Andr f²⁰³¹ copˢᵃ Origen. (3) ἔσωθεν καὶ ἔξωθεν] 025 046 fam 1006 fam 1611¹⁶¹¹ ¹⁸⁵⁴ ²⁰⁵⁰ Oecumenius²⁰⁵³ 2351 Andreas Byzantine itᵍⁱᵍ vg syrᵖʰ arm copᵇᵒ Hippolytus (*Comm. in Dan.* 4.34); Bousset (1906) 254; Roller, *ZNW* 36 (1937) 98–99; Staritz, *ZNW* 30 (1931) 158–59; Holtz, *Christologie,* 32. (4) ἔξωθεν καὶ ἔσωθεν] 94. Extensive discussion of these variants occurs in Zahn, 1:328–31; G. Reichelt, *Buch,* 80–91. Reading (1) is awkward because of the juxtaposition of ἔσωθεν and ὄπισθεν, which are not opposites, for the first adv. means "within, on the inside" (Louw-Nida, § 83.16), while the second means "the back of," "[from] behind," or "on the back" (Louw-Nida, § 83.41). Variants (2), (3), and (4) are all attempts to correct the awkward juxtaposition of these two adverbs. Variant (2) has "in front and behind" (influenced by the identical phrase in 4:6) and also reverses the advs. found in LXX Ezek 2:10, which may have influenced the wording of this variant. Variant (3) has "inside and outside" (this pair of antonyms occurs in Luke 11:40; 2 Cor 7:5), and variant (4) has "outside and inside." Zahn favors reading (1), because he takes ὄπισθεν not with ἔσωθεν but with the following phrase, which results in this translation: "a book written within and sealed on the back side with seven seals" (Zahn, 1:327–34). For Zahn, the βιβλίον is therefore a *codex* (i.e., a book with pages), not a scroll. Birt regards Zahn's view as impossible (*Buchrolle,* 86 n. 2). The main problem with this way of construing the sentence is the clear allusion to Ezek 2:9–10, where the scroll is filled with writing on both sides. LXX Ezek 2:10 has the phrase καὶ ἐν αὐτῇ γεγραμμένα ἦν τὰ ὄπισθεν καὶ τὰ ἔμπροσθεν, "and in it were written things outside and inside." Reading (1) is the *lectio difficilior* with relatively strong attestation, and it is therefore probably the *lectio originalis.*

1.f-f. σφραγῖσιν ἑπτά, "seven seals," is anarthrous because the seals are mentioned for the first time here and are unknown to the readers; the second and repeated mentions of these seven seals all have the anaphoric definite article (5:2, 5, 9; 6:1, 3, 5, 7, 9, 12; 8:1).

2.a. Variant: omit ἰσχυρόν] fam 1611¹⁸⁵⁴ Andreas Hippolytus (*Comm. in Dan.* 4.34).

2.b. Since the term ἀνοῖξαι is a technical term for breaking the seal or seals of a papyrus roll (Xenophon *Resp. Lacedaem.* 6.4; Plutarch *Caes.* 68; Birt, *Buchrolle,* 86 n. 2), the two phrases ἀνοῖξαι τὸ βιβλίον and λῦσαι τὰς σφραγῖδας are virtually synonymous, indicating that the καί that connects them is epexegetical, or explanatory, and should therefore be translated "by" or "that is."

3.a. Variant: ἠδύνατο (impf.)] Hippolytus (*Comm. in Dan.* 4.34). Spelling variant.

3.b. Variant: add ἄνω after οὐρανῷ] 046 fam 1006 Andr c i¹⁶⁸⁵ ²⁰⁴² 94 Byzantine 2351.

3.c. Variant: οὔτε] ℵ fam 1611²⁰⁵⁰ ²³²⁹ Andr c d i²⁰⁴² n·²⁴²⁹ 94 2019 Byzantine Hippolytus (*Comm. in Dan.* 4.34).

3.d-d. Variant: omit οὐδὲ ὑποκάτω τῆς γῆς] ℵ fam 1611¹⁸⁵⁴ ²³⁴⁴. Explicable as an omission through homoioteleuton; i.e., the copyist strayed from the first τῆς γῆς to the second, omitting everything in between.

3.e. Variant: οὔτε] fam 1611²⁰⁵⁰ ²³²⁹ Andr c d g i²⁰⁴² n·²⁴²⁹ 94 2019 Byzantine Hippolytus (*Comm. in Dan.* 4.34).

3.f. Variant: οὐδέ] fam 1611¹⁶¹¹ Oecumenius²⁰⁵³ Andreas Hippolytus (*Comm. in Dan.* 4.34).

4.a. Variant: omit καί] A fam 1611¹⁸⁵⁴ ²⁰⁵⁰ ²³²⁹.

4.b. Variant: insert ἐγώ before ἔκλαιον]2351.

4.c-c. Variant: πολλοί] Andr a¹ ²¹⁸⁶ b²⁰⁵⁹ h¹⁷⁷⁸ Hippolytus (*Comm. in Dan.* 4.34).

5.a. καί functions here as a marker indicating the beginning of a new sentence.

5.b. The past tense "said" is used to translate λέγει, found here in the historical present.

5.c. The prohibition μὴ κλαῖε, "stop weeping," uses the present tense because of its *durative* significance; the prohibition involves stopping an action in progress, as the impf. verb and adv. ἔκλαιον πολύ, "I wept profusely," indicate. The only other occurrence of a prohibition in Revelation expressed by μή + the present imper. is found in 1:17; see *Note* 1:17.b.

5.d. The term ῥίζα, lit. "root," means "shoot" (Fekkes, *Isaiah,* 152) or, less metaphorically, "descendant" (Louw-Nida, § 10.33), similar to the use of שֹׁרֶשׁ *šōreš* (KB³, 1530–32).

5.e. Variant: add καὶ τὸ γένος before Δαυίδ] Hippolytus (*Comm. in Dan.* 4.34). Imported from 22:16.

5.f-f. The aor. verb ἐνίκησεν is unusual because the inf. ἀνοῖξαι is dependent upon it. Scott (*Apocalypse,* 20) proposed that νικᾶν was a translation of the Aram. verb זְכָא *zĕkā',* "to be worthy, able," so that the phrase ἐνίκησεν … ἀνοῖξαι should be translated "he was able … to open." Torrey (*Apocalypse,* 107–8), though not referring to Scott, also suggests that since the Aram. verb זְכָא *zĕkā',* means "to conquer," but also "to succeed in, attain to, be worthy of," with an inf. following (e.g., *Tg. Ps.* 118:22; *Tg. Job* 20:17), it also has that meaning here. Scott and Torrey are correct that זְכָא *zĕkā'* can mean both "to conquer" and "to be worthy" (Levy, *Wörterbuch* 1:534–35; Dalman, *Handwörterbuch,* 128).

5.g-g. Variants: (1) ἀνοῖξαι] A 025 Oecumenius[2053] (omits τὸ βιβλίον καί) Andreas. (2) ὁ ἀνοίγων] 046 2351 Byzantine. (3) λῦσαι] ℵ fam 1611[2344] vg[cl]. The inf. ἀνοῖξαι completes the meaning of ἐνίκησεν and may be construed as an inf. of *purpose* (Charles, 1:140) or (more likely) as an inf. of *result* (BDR § 391.8; Holtz, *Christologie,* 37 n. 1; Delebecque, 182).

5.h. Variant: insert λῦσαι] ℵ Oecumenius[2062] Andr d Hippolytus (*Comm. in Dan.* 4.34).

6.a. Variants: (1) εἶδον] 𝔓[24] Oecumenius[2053 Comm] fam 1611[2050]; all modern editions. (2) εἶδον καί] fam 1611[1611] 1678 1778 Oecumenius[2053 Text] syr[h]. (3) ἰδοὺ καί] A. (4) ἰδού] Andr e[2026 2057]. (5) εἶδον καὶ ἰδού] fam 1006 lat Andr f[2073] TR. Variant (5) is a conflation of variants (1) and (2) with variants (3) and (4). Variants (3) and (4) are attested primarily by A. The phrase [καὶ] εἶδον καὶ ἰδού, "[and] I saw, and behold," occurs several times in secure readings in Revelation (4:1; 6:2, 5, 8; 7:9; 14:1, 14; 19:11) and might have encouraged the harmonistic combination of εἶδον and ἰδού found in reading (5). Visual confusion between εἶδον and ἰδού is possible, since εἶδον is frequently spelled ἴδον, with only the final ν distinguishing it from ἰδού, a factor accounting for the origins of readings (3) and (4). Several examples of this confusion are documented in the LXX MS tradition: in LXX Ezek 10:8, B reads ἴδον, while A reads ἰδού; and in LXX 2 Chr 21:23, B reads ἴδε, while A reads ἰδού; in Tobit 2:2, ℵ[1] reads ἴδε, while ℵ[2] has ἰδού. The phrase [καὶ] εἶδον [= ἴδον] καὶ ἰδού does occur in the LXX (where it translates the Heb. phrases וארא והנה *wāʾēreʾ wěhinnēh* or ראיתי והנה *rāʾîtî wěhinnēh*), particularly in Ezekiel (1:4, 15; 2:9; 8:7, 10; 10:1, 9; 37:8; 44:4; cf. Jer 4:2), though it is relatively rare in other Jewish-Greek literature (see *Jos. As.* 10:16; 14:9). This is particularly the case in 5:6, where the neut. noun and ptcps. could be construed either as noms. or as accs. (see below under *Note* 5:6.d.).

6.b. Variant: insert ἐν μέσῳ] Hippolytus (*Comm. in Dan.* 4.34).

6.c. See *Comment* on 4:6.

6.d. Here it is possible that the term ἀρνίον, "lamb," a diminutive form of ἀρήν, "sheep," should actually be translated "ram" (see *Excursus 5A: Christ as the Lamb;* see Charles, 1:141; Ford, 86; Böcher, 47). While the ἀρνίον in v 6 has *seven horns,* and rams, not lambs, have horns, the translation "ram" might seem more appropriate (like the rendering of ἀρνίον as "ram" in 13:11; see *Notes* there). The primary reason that most scholars prefer "lamb" for the twenty-eight references to ἀρνίον used of Christ in Revelation is because of the associations of the lamb with OT sacrificial imagery, particularly Passover (even though goats and oxen were also used as Passover victims). Rams were of course used in a variety of OT sacrificial rituals (see *Excursus 5A*), and there is no reason that the sacrificial associations cannot be retained while using the translation "ram." There are parallels with the apocalyptic rams of Dan 8:3 and *1 Enoch* 90:9, 37.

6.e. Variants: (1) ἑστηκός] A C Oecumenius[2053] 2351 Andreas Byzantine Hippolytus (*Comm. in Dan.* 4.34). (2) ἑστηκώς] ℵ 2050 Andr a[1-2428] b c[part] e[2026] f[-2023] h[-2302] n[2429] 2019; Bousset ([1906] 161, 257). Variant (1), an acc. sing. *neut.* pf. ptcp., modifies the acc. sing. neut. noun ἀρνίον, while variant (2) is a nom. sing. *masc.* pf. ptcp., which could be construed as an *ad sensum* construction (i.e., the Lamb [neut.] is Christ [masc.]) but may simply be the result of phonetic confusion between ω and o, a possibility made more probable by the following neut. ptcp. ἐσφαγμένον, which has no significant variants.

6.f. Variants: (1) ἔχον] fam 1006[1841] fam 1611[1611 1854] Oecumenius[2053] Andreas Byzantine Hippolytus (*Comm. in Dan.* 4.34). (2) ἔχων] 𝔓[24] ℵ A (lacuna in C) 046 fam 1006[1006] fam 1611[2050 2329] 2351; Tischendorf, *NT Graece;* Bousset ([1906] 258); Charles (2:268); Merk, *NT;* UBSGNT[4]; Nestle-Aland[27]. (3) ἔχοντα] Andr l[1778]. The phonetic confusion of ω/o is at least partially responsible for the alternation between ἔχον and ἔχων (Metzger, *Text,* 190); cf. similar confusion in 4:7, 8; 11:7; 13:14; 21:14 (Mussies, *Morphology,* 138). Reading (1), certainly the *lectio difficilior* because it is both *masc.* and *nom.*, is often thought to be an *ad sensum* construction similar to others found with relative frequency in Revelation (4:1; 5:2; 9:5; 11:5; 13:8, 14; 17:3, 11, 16); see Bousset (1906) 160–61. Yet it appears to function clearly as an *ad sensum* construction *only* in A and Andr e[2026], since both MSS construe the neut. accs. following καὶ εἶδον (ἀρνίον, ἑστηκός, and ἐσφαγμένον) as noms. following καὶ ἰδού (which replaces καὶ εἶδον). Since the verb εἶδον is undoubtedly original, ἀρνίον, ἑστηκός, and ἐσφαγμένον must be construed as accs. If the author used a masc. ptcp. from ἔχειν, he would in all likelihood have used the masc. sing. acc. form ἔχοντα. Since the phonetic confusion of ω/o has exacerbated the textual problem, it seems likely that ἔχον, preserved by 2053, Andreas, and Byzantine, is the original reading, although ἔχων is certainly the *lectio difficilior.*

6.g. Variants: (1) οἵ] A (lacuna in C) ℵ fam 1006[1841] fam 1611[1611] Andreas TR. (2) ἅ] 046 fam 1611[-1611] 2351 Andr f[2023-2073] in 94 2019 2351 Byzantine Hippolytus (*Comm. in Dan.* 4.34). These variants are usually congruent with the masc. pl. or neut. pl. ptcp. in *Note* 5:6.f. The attestation for variant (1) is overwhelming, making a strong case for the authenticity of the anarthrous ptcp. ἀπεσταλμένοι discussed in *Note* 5:6.i-i.

6.h. Variants: (1) omit ἑπτά] A 025 1 fam 1006 fam 1611[1611 2050] 2081 Andreas Tyconius[2] Apringius it[ar] vg eth WHort. (2) ἑπτά] 𝔓[24] (τὰ ζ πνα) ℵ 046 fam 1611[1854 2344] Oecumenius[2053] 2351 Andr f[2073] i[2042] l[2020] n[2065 2432] Byz 1[1859] Byz 2[2138]; Byzantine it[gig] Hippolytus (*Comm. in Dan.* 4.34); Primasius Tyconius[2] (MS S only); Beatus Cyprian it[gig] syr[ph,h] cop[sa,bo] arm; WHort[marg]; B. Weiss, *Johannes-Apokalypse,* 170; von Soden, *Text;* Bousset (1906) 258; Charles, 2:268; [UBSGNT[4]]; [Nestle-Aland[27]]; *TCGNT*[1], 737–38; *TCGNT*[2], 666; ASV[mg]. This variant is closely connected with the insertion of ἑπτά before λυχνίων in 1:13, where the textual support for the omission is similar, and where ἑπτά is omitted by Nestle-Aland[27] (see *Notes* on 1:13). While the omission of an original ἑπτά can be accounted for by the error of homoioteleuton (i.e., the similar ending of three words in a row, τὰ ἑπτὰ πνεύματα), the interpolation of ἑπτά is even more probable, given the occurrence of the adj. twice in the first part of 5:6.

6.i-i. Variants: (1) ἀπεσταλμένοι] A (lacuna in C) Oecumenius[2053]; all modern editions. (2) ἀπεσταλμένα] ℵ 1678 1778 fam 1611[1854 2050]. (3) τὰ ἀπεσταλμένα] fam 1006[1006 1841] fam 1611[2329] Andreas; Hippolytus (*Comm. in Dan.* 4.34). (4) ἀποστελλόμενα] 046 fam 1611[1611] 2351 Andr c d e[2026] i[1685-2042] n[2429] 94 2019 Byzantine; Bousset ([1906] 258–59). 𝔓[24] reads ἀπεσπαλ (scribal error in writing π for τ; rest of word continued on next line but not preserved). The editors of POxy 1230 (= 𝔓[24]) speculate that the second π was a slip of the pen and that ἀπεσταλμένα (ℵ) or ἀπεσταλμένοι (A) was intended. These variants, with the exception of (2), are correlated with the variant pronouns ἅ/οἵ discussed in *Note* 5:6.g. Here the issue is whether that which "is sent" modifies ὀφθαλμούς, "eyes," a masc. pl. noun, variant (1), or πνεύματα, "spirits," a neut. pl. noun., variants (2), (3), and (4). Variant (1) is a pf. pass. ptcp. masc. pl. nom., which modifies the pl. pronoun οἵ, which in turn refers to the masc. pl. acc. noun ὀφθαλμούς, "eyes." Variants (2) and (4) are all neut. pl. and represent a correction of the original text to agree with the neut. pl. relative pronoun ἅ (read instead of οἵ in many MSS), which in turn refers back to πνεύματα. Variant (3) places the article before the ptcp. in order to separate it syntactically from the relative pronoun οἵ. The original reading (1) is found only in A and 2053; the presence of reading (1) in 2053 shows that it was not simply an error in A (Schmid, *Studien* 2:238).

7.a. The conjunction καί, "and," with which this sentence begins, is left untranslated since it functions as a discourse marker indicating the beginning of a new sentence.

7.b-b. The phrase καὶ ἦλθον καὶ εἴληφεν, "then he came and took," is one of several instances in Revelation in which an aor. and a pf. are closely linked (see 7:14; 8:5; 19:3), which some regard as an aor. use of the pf. (Fanning, *Verbal Aspect,* 302–3). While the aor. ἦλθον is used as the normal tense to narrate past events, the author uses pf. εἴληφεν to highlight and dramatize the action conveyed by this verb, as in Matt 13:46 (K. L. McKay, "Syntax in Exegesis," *TynBul* 23 [1972] 54–55; id., "The Use of the Ancient Greek Perfect Down to the End of the Second Century A.D.," *Bulletin of the Institute of Classical Studies* 12 [1965] 16–17).

7.c. Variant: ἔλαβεν] Hippolytus (*Comm. in Dan.* 4.34) Byz 1[2256]; probably a harmonization with ἔλαβεν in v 8.

7.d. Variants: (1) insert τὸ βιβλίον] fam 1006[1006 1841] fam 1611[2050] Andr f[2073] g[2045] n[2429] 2019 it vg[cl] syr cop Cyprian Hippolytus (*Comm. in Dan.* 4.34); Primasius. (2) insert τήν] 046. These two modifications are intended to solve the problem that the roll is not specifically mentioned here.

7.e-e. The prep. phrase ἐκ τῆς δεξιᾶς τοῦ καθημένου ἐπὶ τοῦ θρόνου, "from the right hand of the one seated upon the throne," is a partitive gen. (intensified by the prep. ἐκ, "of/from"), functioning as the *obj.* of the verb εἴληφεν, "he took"; see BDR § 164. Though partitive gen. often occurs in Revelation as the subject or obj. of various verbs (usually intensified by ἀπό or ἐκ; see 2:7, 10, 17; 5:9; 11:9; 21:6; 22:19), this usage is different because the implied obj. is not an indefinite pl. but rather the scroll referred to in 5:1. In order to supply an explicit obj. for the verb εἴληφεν, several witnesses have inserted τὸ βιβλίον before ἐκ τῆς δεξιᾶς; see *Note* 5:7.d. The phrase ἐκ τῆς δεξιᾶς may mean either "from the right hand" (Euripides *Andromache* 812) or "from the right side" (Galen *De anat. admin.* 2.600); see Stefanovič, "Background," 153.

8.a. Though neut. pl. nouns usually take third-person sing. verbs, the author of Revelation avoids this when the neut. pl. nouns refer to living beings (BDR § 133; Charles, 1:cvli); here ζῷα, "cherubim" (neut. nom. pl.), is the subject of the verb ἔπεσαν, "they fell" (aor. ind. third-person pl.); see Rev 4:8, 9; 5:14; 19:4, 21 (Mussies, *Morphology,* 231). Variant spelling: ἔπεσον] Hippolytus (*Comm. in Dan.* 4.34).

8.b. Here the article before "lamb" is anaphoric, referring back to the introduction of the lamb in v 6.

8.c. In the phrase ἔχοντες ἕκαστος, "each with," the sing. form ἕκαστος is normally used with pl. pronouns (e.g., Rev 2:23; 6:11) and verbs (Rev 5:8; 20:13; cf. Matt 18:35; John 16:32; Acts 11:29); BDR § 305. Turner (*Syntax,* 312) observes that ἕκαστος occurs with a pl. verb eleven times in the NT, twenty-five times with a sing. verb; in the LXX ἕκαστος occurs with pl. verbs eighty-nine times and with sing. verbs fifty-six times. The pl. forms of ἕκαστοι are found rarely; see Phil 2:4, where the original reading ἕκαστοι (supported by A B F G Ψ and several cursives) was corrected to ἕκαστος (supported by 𝔓⁴⁶ ℵ C D Koine), which was syntactically more familiar (G. F. Hawthorne, *Philippians*, WBC 43 [Waco, TX: Word Books, 1983] 63).

8.d. Variants: (1) κιθάραν] A ℵ 025 fam 1006¹⁰⁰⁶ ¹⁸⁴¹ fam 1611¹⁶¹¹ ¹⁸⁵⁴ ²⁰⁵⁰ ²³²⁹ (κηθαραν) Oecumenius²⁰⁵³ Andrᶜⁱˡ Byzantine. (2) κιθάρας] Andreas. Reading (1) κιθάράν, "kithara," was corrected to reading (2), the acc. pl. form κιθάρας, in the Andreas commentary tradition to agree with the acc. pl. φιάλας that follows. The translation of κιθάρα as "kithara" requires some explanation, since it is often rendered "harp" or "lyre" (Louw-Nida, § 6.83; Bauer-Aland, 878, s.v. "Zither"; BAGD, 432). The translation "kithara" is preferred by historians of Christian music (Quasten, *Musik und Gesang*, 104, s.v. "Zithermusik"; McKinnon, *Music*, 17). The term "harp" is used of instruments with strings of graduated lengths attached at one end to a sounding board and at the other end to a neck extending from one end of the soundbox; the "lyre" and the "kithara" have strings of equal length attached to a crossbar supported by two arms attached at the far end of the neck (Maas-Snyder, *Stringed Instruments*, 219).

8.e. The definite article αἱ, "the," conforms in gender and number to the predicate αἱ προσευχαί, "the prayers"; however, αἱ probably refers to θυμιαμάτων, "incense," even though it is a neut. gen. pl., indicating that it is the incense that represents the prayers of the saints. For other NT examples, see Matt 7:12; 22:38; Mark 15:16; Acts 16:12; Gal 3:16; Col 1:27; Eph 1:14; 1 Tim 3:15; 1 John 2:8; Rev 4:5 (BDR § 132.1).

8.f. Variants: (1) αἱ before προσευχαί] ℵ* fam 1611¹⁸⁵⁴²³²⁹ 2351 Byzantine; Nestle-Aland²⁷; UBSGNT⁴. (2) omit αἱ before προσευχαί] 2351 Hippolytus (*Comm. in Dan.* 4.34).

8.g. Variant: insert ὄντων after προσευχαί] 2351.

8.h-h. The substantive οἱ ἅγιοι, lit. "holy ones," should be translated "God's people" (Louw-Nida, § 11.27).

9.a. "Chanted" here represents both the verb ᾄδουσιν (a historic present and so rendered as a past tense) and the redundant present ptcp. λέγοντες, "saying," which, like ὅτι *recitative*, can function to introduce direct discourse. The term "chant" more accurately represents the way ancients performed songs.

9.b. Variants: (1) τῷ θεῷ] A (lacuna in C) eth; WHort; Nestle-Aland²⁷; UBSGNT⁴; *TCGNT*¹, 738; *TCGNT*², 666. (2) τῷ θεῷ ἡμᾶς] ℵ fam 1006¹⁰⁰⁶ ¹⁸⁴¹ fam 1611¹⁶¹¹ ²³²⁹ Oecumenius²⁰⁵³ 2351 Andreas Byzantine; von Soden, *Text*. (3) ἡμᾶς τῷ θεῷ] fam 1611²⁰⁵⁰ ²³⁴⁴ Andr f²⁰⁷³ n²⁴²⁹ 94 598 2019 itᵃʳ ᵍⁱᵍ vg syrᵖʰ ʰ arm Hippolytus (*Comm. in Dan.* 4.34) Cyprian. (4) omit τῷ θεῷ] Andr a c. The original presence of reading (1), though poorly attested, best accounts for the origins of the other readings (*TCGNT*¹, 738; *TCGNT*², 666). ἡμᾶς in readings (2) and (3) was probably added because an obj. seemed missing (B. Weiss, *Johannes-Apokalypse*, 108).

9.c. The term αἷμα, "blood," means, by figurative extension, "death" (Louw-Nida, § 23.107).

9.d. The partitive gen. phrase ἐκ πάσης φυλῆς . . . , "people from every tribe . . . ," functions as the *obj.* of the aor. verb ἠγόρασας, "you ransomed"; see BDR § 164. For a similar use of the partitive gen., intensified by the prep. ἐκ used as the obj. of the verb, see 2:10 (obj. of the inf. φαγεῖν); 2:17 (obj. of the verbal periphrasis μέλλει βάλλειν).

10.a. Variants: (1) αὐτούς] *lectio originalis*; *TCGNT*², 666. (2) omit αὐτούς] Hippolytus (*Comm. in Dan.* 4.34). (3) ἡμᾶς (*nos*)] itᵍⁱᵍ vgᴰᶠᴼᴷᴼˢᵁⱽᵂᶻ copᵗᵃ Primasius Beatus.

10.b. Variants: (1) βασιλείαν] ℵ A (lacuna in C); fam 1611 latt syrᵖʰ cop arm. (2) βασιλεῖς] 2351 Andreas Byzantine syrʰ.

10.c-c. Variants: (1) βασιλεύουσιν] A (lacuna in C) 046 fam 1006 fam 1611¹⁶¹¹ ²³²⁹ Andr b²⁰⁵⁹* ²⁰⁸¹* h l¹⁷⁷⁸ n⁻²⁴²⁹ l Byzantine itᵃʳ syrʰ; WHort; Charles, 1:148; Allo, 65; Lohmeyer, 57; J. H. Elliott, *The Elect and the Holy: An Exegetical Examination of 1 Peter 2:4–10 and the Phrase* Basileion Hierateuma, NovTSup 12 (Leiden: Brill, 1966) 114–15. (2) βασιλεύσουσιν] ℵ 025 fam 1611⁻¹⁶¹¹⁻²³²⁹ Oecumenius²⁰⁵³ 2351 Andreas itᵍⁱᵍ vg syrᵖʰ cop arm; Cyprian; B. Weiss, *Johannes-Apocalypse*, 133; Bousset (1906) 261; von Soden, *Text*; Nestle-Aland²⁷; UBSGNT⁴; *TCGNT*¹, 736; *TCGNT*², 666–67. (3) βασιλεύσομεν] Andr n²⁴³² 296 2049 (both copies of printed TR); Primasius Beatus arm. Since A mistakenly read βασιλεύουσιν for the fut. in 20:6, some have argued that reading (2) may be correct here (Schmid, *Studien* 2:123; *TCGNT*¹, 738; *TCGNT*², 666–67).

11.a. Variants: (1) omit ὡς] A (lacuna in C) 046* fam 1611¹⁶¹¹* Oecumenius²⁰⁵³ 2351 Andreas latt copᵇᵒ; Nestle-Aland²⁷; UBSGNT⁴. (2) insert ὡς] ℵ 046ᶜᵒʳ fam 1006¹⁰⁰⁶ ¹⁸⁴¹ fam 1611⁻²³²⁹ Andr c d i¹⁶⁸⁵ ²⁰⁴² n 94 2019 Byzantine syrᵖʰ ʰ copᵇᵒ Fulgentius; Tischendorf, *NTGraece*; WHortᵐᵍ; von Soden, *Text*; Bousset (1906) 261.

11.b. See *Comment* on 4:6.

12.a. The masc. pl. nom. ptcp. λέγοντες, "chanting," is an anacolouthon (a Hebraism), since grammatically it should modify the noun φωνήν, "voice," in 5:11, and so should have the form λέγουσαν (fem. sing. acc. ptcp.); see BDR § 136.

12.b. Variant: (1) ἄξιον] ℵ Andreas Byzantine; Swete, 81; Charles, 2:270; Allo, 84; von Soden, *Text;* Nestle-Aland[27]; UBSGNT[4]. (2) ἄξιος] A; Bousset (1906) 261; Charles,1:149.

12.c. Here εὐλογία means "praise," referring to the superiority and excellence of the object of praise without reference to the subject or agent of that praise; see J. Mateos, "Analysis de un Campo Lexematico: Εὐλογία en el Nuevo Testamento," *FNT* 1 (1988) 10–12, 23; see Louw-Nida, § 33.356. Εὐλογία also occurs in 5:13; 7:12.

13.a. Variant: insert ἐστιν] fam 1611[1611 2050] Andreas vg Primasius.

13.b-b. Variant: omit καὶ ὑποκάτω τῆς γῆς] ℵ Oecumenius[2053] fam 1611[1854 2050 2329 2344] it[a] vg.

13.c. Variants: (1) ἐστίν, καί] A fam 1006[1006 1841] fam 1611[1611c 1854 2329 2344] 94 Byzantine syr[ph]; [WHort]; B. Weiss, *Johannes-Apokalypse,* 171; von Soden, *Text;* Charles, 2:271. (2) καί] ℵ fam 1611[1611] Andr i[2042] 1 n[-2429] it[gig] syr[h] cop arm eth Primasius Beatus; Tischendorf, *NT Graece;* Bousset (1906) 262; Merk, *NT;* Nestle-Aland[27]; UBSGNT[4]. (3) insert ἅ ἐστιν καί] 025 046 fam 1611[2050] Andreas. (4) ὅσα ἐστίν καί] Oecumenius[2053] 2351. It is possible that reading (1), the simplest, gave rise to the others (*TCGNT,* 737; *TCGNT*[2], 667). While reading (2) has modern support, and is certainly the *lectio difficilior* (lacking a verbal copula in the relative clause), the MS evidence is weak. The external MS evidence for reading (2) is strongest, and probably gave rise to readings (3) and (4).

13.d. Variant: πάντας] fam 1006 2351 Byzantine vg (*omnes*).

13.e. Variants: λέγοντα] A Andr a d e[2057]. λέγοντας, the masc. pl. acc. ptcp., is peculiar here because it should be congruent with the preceding noun cluster τὰ ἐν αὐτῇ πάντα, "everything in it [sc. 'the sea']," and so should have the form λέγοντα (neut. pl. acc. ptcp.), a form that is attested in some MSS but should probably be regarded as a scribal correction. While the reading λέγοντας is an anacolouthon, John's normal practice is to use the nom. masc. pl. form λέγοντες (see 5:12).

13.f-f. Variants: (1) τῷ θρόνῳ] *lectio originalis;* A Byzantine Andr l[2080]. (2) τοῦ θρόνου] ℵ fam 1006[1006 1841] fam 1611[1611] Oecumenius[2053] Andreas vg. In the phrase ἐπὶ τῷ θρόνῳ, "on the throne," the prep. is used with a dat. of place, though the author uses ἐπί with the gen., dat., and acc. without distinguishing location *in* a place or movement *to* a place. However, the ptcp. phrase καθημεν- ἐπί occurs twenty-seven times, and the author shows a tendency to use a case with ἐπί congruent with the case of the ptcp., i.e. a gen. following καθημένου ἐπί, a dat. following καθημένῳ ἐπί, and an acc. following καθήμενος οι καθήμενον ἐπί (see *Introduction,* Section 7: Syntax). Since the ptcp. here is τῷ καθημένῳ, reading (1) is certainly correct, since reading (2) violates the style of the author (Schmid, *Studien* 2:123).

13.g-g. ἡ εὐλογία καὶ ἡ τιμὴ καὶ ἡ δόξα καὶ τὸ κράτος: these four attributes are all arthrous because they denote what is due or requisite, and thus the article is found where a personal pronoun might be used in English (Winer, *Grammar,* 134–35); see 4:11. For examples elsewhere in the NT, see Rom 11:36; 16:27; Eph 3:21; Gal 1:5; 1 Pet 4:11.

13.h. See *Note* 5:12.c.

13.i. Variants: (1) omit ἀμήν] ℵ A (a lacuna in C) 025 fam 1006 fam 1611 Oecumenius[2053] 2351 latt syr cop. (2) ἀμήν] Andreas Byzantine. The tendency of copyists to insert the term ἀμήν in NT MSS at liturgically appropriate points and the strength of the MS witnesses makes it certain that the shorter text is the *lectio originalis.*

14.a. See *Comment* on 4:6.

14.b. Variant: λέγοντα τό] fam 1611[2344] Byzantine cop[sa mss bo]. The impf. ind. verb ἔλεγον is translated as a neutral past tense because this is a case in which the not-completed action characteristic of the impf. tense focuses attention on the consequences or the response to the completed action indicated by the verb, a use of the impf. with verbs involving calling, speaking, asking, requesting, etc. when the action itself is completed but the result or reaction is not yet known (see Rijksbaron, *Syntax,* 17–19). In this case the "amen" uttered by the four living creatures is complemented by the worshipful prostration of the twenty-four elders. The normal use of a third-person sing. verb with a neut. pl. subject (BDR § 133) is not followed here (see *Note* 8.a.), for the subject of ἔλεγον (third-person pl. impf. ind.) is ζῷα (neut. pl. nom.). However, in Revelation third-person pl. verbs are used with living beings such as ζῷα, "living creatures" (4:8, 9; 5:8; 19:4), and ὄρνεα, "birds," (19:21); πνεύματα is sometimes found with third-person sing. verbs (4:5), but in 16:13–14 both sing. and pl. verb forms are used (Mussies, *Morphology,* 231).

14.c. Variant: add ζῶντι εἰς τοὺς αἰῶνας τῶν αἰώνων] Andr g[2045] 296 2047 (both printed copies of the TR); scribal addition based on 4:9, 10; 10:6; 15:7.

*Form/Structure/Setting*

## I. OUTLINE

b. The investiture of the Lamb (5:1–14)
    (1) John sees and describes the scroll (v 1)
        (a) In God's right hand (v 1a)
        (b) Written on both sides (v 1a)
        (c) Sealed with seven seals (v 1b)
    (2) The quest for someone worthy to open the sealed scroll
        (vv 2–5)
        (a) The proclamation of the mighty angel (v 2a)
            [1] Who is worthy to open the scroll? (v 2b)
            [2] Who is worthy to break its seals? (v 2b)
        (b) No one found who was able to open the scroll (v 3)
            [1] No one in heaven
            [2] No one on earth
            [3] No one under the earth
        (c) Result: John wept bitterly (v 4)
            [1] Because no one was found worthy to open the book
            [2] Because no one was found worthy to look into it
        (d) The solution of one of the elders (v 5)
            [1] He tells John not to weep
            [2] Someone has conquered and can open the seals
                [a] The Lion of the tribe of Judah
                [b] The root of David
    (3) The Lamb is worthy to open the scroll (vv 6–10)
        (a) John then sees the Lamb (v 6a)
        (b) Description of the Lamb (v 6bc)
            [1] Location
                [a] In the midst of the throne and the four cherubim
                [b] In the midst of the elders
            [2] Appearance of the Lamb
                [a] Standing as though slaughtered
                [b] With seven horns and seven eyes = the seven
                    spirits of God
        (c) The Lamb acts: He takes the scroll from the right hand
            of God (v 7)
        (d) Reaction of the twenty-four elders (vv 8–10)
            [1] They prostrate themselves before the Lamb (v 8a)
            [2] The objects they hold (v 8bc)
                [a] Harps
                [b] Golden bowls of incense = the saints' prayers
            [3] They sing a new song to the Lamb (vv 9–10)
                [a] He is worthy (v 9b)
                    {1} To take the scroll
                    {2} To open its seals

        [b] Reasons for his worthiness (v 9c–10)
         {1} He was slaughtered (v 9c)
         {2} He ransomed people for God (v 9c–10)
           {a} Means: by his blood (v 9c)
           {b} Scope: people from all nations (v 9d)
           {c} Result (v 10):
              <1> They are priests
              <2> They are kings
              <3> They will reign on the earth
(4) The heavenly acclamation of God and the Lamb (vv 11–12)
    (a) The angelic participants (v 11)
        [1] Their location
           [a] Around the throne
           [b] Around the cherubim
           [c] Around the elders
         [2] Their number
           [a] Myriads of myriads
           [b] Thousands of thousands
    (b) The hymn (v 12)
        [1] Major predicate: worthiness (v 12a)
        [2] Addressee: the Lamb (v 12b)
        [3] Implied reason: he was slaughtered (v 12b)
        [4] Attributes (v 12c)
           [a] Power
           [b] Wealth
           [c] Wisdom
           [d] Might
           [e] Honor
           [f] Glory
           [g] Blessing
(5) The universal doxology addressed to God and the Lamb
    (vv 13–14)
    (a) Participants (v 13a)
        [1] Every being in heaven
        [2] Every being in earth
        [3] Every being under the earth
        [4] Every being in the sea
    (b) The double doxology (vv 13b–14)
        [1] Address in dative (v 13b)
           [a] To the enthroned one
           [b] To the Lamb
         [2] Attributes (v 13c)
           [a] Blessing
           [b] Honor
           [c] Glory
           [d] Might
        [3] Temporal formula: forever and ever (v 13c)

[4] The response (v 14)
[a] The four cherubim said, "Amen!" (v 14a)
[b] The elders fell down in worship (v 14b)

## II. LITERARY ANALYSIS

The vision report in Rev 5:1–14 is a continuation of Rev 4:1–11, framed by the vision-narrative formula καὶ εἶδον, "then I saw" (5:1; 6:1), and punctuated by the same formula in 5:2, 6, as well as the less frequent formula καὶ εἶδον καὶ ἤκουσα, "then I saw and heard" (5:11). This formula clearly functions in two ways in Revelation: it can be used to introduce a major break in the vision narration (as in 5:1; 6:1), and so frame a discrete text unit; it can also be used to mark a change in the focus of the vision report. This text unit is divided into three subunits, 5:1–5, 5:6–10, and 5:11–14; each of these sections is introduced by the formulaic καὶ εἶδον, "then I saw." The first section focuses on the inability to find anyone worthy to open the scroll (vv 1–5). The second section focuses on the worthiness of the Lamb to receive and open the scroll (vv 6–10). The third section focuses on the heavenly joy that accompanies the identification of the Lamb as the only one worthy to open the scroll (vv 11–14).

The central dramatic feature of Rev 5, the primary function of this textual unit, is the introduction of the Lamb, who will break the seals of the mysterious scroll, and the cosmic sovereignty that he is revealed to possess. Anticipating the breaking of the seven seals are seven constituent dramatic features: (1) The sealed scroll is seen in the right hand of the One seated on the throne (5:1). (2) There is the proclamation of a perplexing *aporia:* "Who is worthy to open the scroll and to break its seals?" (5:2). (3) There is a vain quest for someone able to open the scroll (5:3). (4) The seer weeps (5:4). (5) An elder announces that the Lion of the tribe of Judah is able to open the scroll (5:5). (6) The Lamb, suddenly seen standing between the throne and the cherubim, takes the scroll from the One seated on the throne (5:6–7). (7) The scene concludes with an elaborate liturgy of thankfulness and praise (5:8–14) as a prelude to the actual opening of the scroll, which begins in 6:1. The New Song in vv 9–10 (introduced by the *aporia* in v 2) is sung by the four cherubim and the twenty-four elders. The concluding "amen" in v 14 is uttered by the same heavenly beings, so that vv 8, 14 serve to frame the heavenly liturgy. The doxology, in the form of an acclamation found in v 12 (Peterson, *Von den Engeln*, 340), is sung by a larger group of heavenly beings, for it includes countless numbers of angels. Finally, a dramatic crescendo is reached in v 13, where an acclamatory doxology is sung by beings throughout the entire cosmos.

One of the closer parallels to this dramatic sequence is found in a rather strange text in *Odes Sol.* 23:5–22. As in Rev 5:1–14, the focus of the brief drama is the revelation of the Son of Truth who vanquishes all the enemies of God. The primary dramatic features are the following: (1) The thought of the Lord is compared to a heavenly letter (the Syriac term *'rt'* occurs five times in *Odes Sol.* 23:5, 7, 10, 17, 21), *Odes Sol.* 23:5–6. (2) When the letter descended, many tried to catch it and read it, but it escaped their fingers (23:7–8a). (3) They feared the seal (Syriac *ḥtm'*; cf. Dan 12:4) on the letter, for it was more powerful than they (23:8b–9); i.e., they did not think they were capable of breaking it. (4) Nevertheless, those who had seen the letter pursued it (23:10). (5) However, a wheel (Syriac *gyg'*; cf. Hebrew אוֹפָן *'wpn*) received the letter and overcame all opposition (23:11–16). (6) The letter (now apparently open) was one of great authority, and the head of all regions was the Son of Truth from the Most High Father, who inherited everything (23:17–19). (7) All seducers fled, and all persecutors were obliterated (23:20). (8) The narrative concludes with these lines (23:21–22; tr. J. H. Charlesworth, *The Odes of Solomon* [Oxford: Clarendon, 1973]):

> ²¹And the letter became a large volume [Syriac *pnqyt'*],
> Which was entirely written by the finger of God.
> ²²And the name of the Father was upon it;
> And of the Son and of the Holy Spirit,
> To rule for ever and ever.
>     Hallelujah.

In Rev 5:1–14 and *Odes Sol.* 23:5–22, the elements in each short drama are remarkably similar, and the symbolism is also close. Nevertheless, there can be no *direct* connection between the two texts because of the unique features that each exhibits. In *Odes Sol.* 23:11–16, it is apparent that the "wheel" is connected with Merkavah ("chariot") mysticism based on Ezek 1. This feature ties the two texts even closer together, since the "wheel" in Ezek 1 (which is essentially a throne vision) is closely connected to the four cherubim, and the four cherubim are also prominent in the throne vision of Rev 4–5 (Charlesworth, *Odes*, 95–96 n. 8). A comparison of similar dramatic features found in both Rev 5:1–14 and *Odes Sol.* 23:5–22 yields this result: A heavenly document that is sealed cannot be opened by anyone. Only one had the power to take the document and reveal its significance. In both scenarios, the sovereignty of a major heavenly figure is revealed, the Lamb in Rev 5:1–14 and the Son of Truth in *Odes Sol.* 23:5–22. While the conquest of the enemies of God is narrated in *Odes Sol.* 23:13–15, 19–20, that feature is not found in Rev 5 but is narrated later in Rev 6:1–8:1.

There are also some differences that must be noticed: (1) In Revelation the drama takes place within the heavenly throne room, while in *Odes of Solomon* the drama is set on the earth. (2) In Revelation the Lamb is the only one able to open the sealed scroll, while in *Odes of Solomon* the Wheel plays that role, though the act of unsealing the letter is implied, even if not specifically mentioned. (3) In *Odes of Solomon* it appears that the letter = large volume *is* the Son of Truth, while in Revelation the sealed scroll represents the eschatological events determined by the sovereign will of God.

## III. THE VERB SEQUENCE

After introducing this vision narrative with the aorist verb εἶδον, John uses four more verbs in past tenses: εἶδον, "I saw" (aorist, v 2), ἐδύνατο, "was able" (imperfect, v 3), ἔκλαιον, "I wept" (imperfect, v 4), and εὑρέθη, "was found" (aorist, v 4). Revelation contains very few imperfect verbs, and here they are used to convey continued action in past time, thus rendering the account more vivid. At this point, however, the author switches to the present tense in v 5 with the verb λέγει, "says" (instead of an expected εἶπεν, "said"). The verbs in the brief speech of the elder are all appropriate to a speech uttered in the past but reported in direct discourse. The narrator intrudes on the scene with an aorist εἶδον, "I saw," and then follows (apart from the interpretive gloss in v 6b) another series of four verbs in past tenses: ἦλθεν, "he came" (aorist, v 7); εἴληφεν, "he received" (perfect, v 7); ἔλαβεν, "he received" (aorist, v 8); and ἔπεσαν, "fell" (aorist, v 8). John then reverts to the present tense in introducing the New Song sung by the elders: ᾄδουσιν, "they chant." The present tense of ᾄδουσιν (v 9) is functionally parallel to λέγει (v 5), for both introduce verbal communications heard by John. After the hymn in direct discourse in vv 9–10, the author describes his vision with another series of verbs in the past tense: εἶδον, "I saw" (aorist, v 11), ἤκουσα, "I heard" (aorist, v 11), and ἦν, "was" (imperfect, v 11; though note that εἰμί has no aorist form, probably because it is a stative verb for which an aoristic form with its aspectual implication of completed action was thought inappropriate). After the next hymn in direct discourse (v 12), John introduces the last antiphonal segment with the aorist verb ἤκουσα, "heard" (v 13).

## IV. LITERARY FORMS

The entire chapter is dominated by the heavenly liturgy consisting of the two hymns of praise found in 5:2, 9–10; 5:12, the doxology in 5:13, and the amen in 5:14. This is confirmed by an analysis of the composition of chap. 5, for the question asked by the mighty angel in 5:2, "Who is worthy to open the scroll and break its seals?" functions as the opening part of the hymn that is concluded in 5:9–10. The content of this hymn suggests that it is an ἐπινίκεον, a "song of praise" (Peterson, *Von den Engeln*, 338). Beginning hymns with an ἀπορία, "difficulty, problem," had a long tradition in Greek hymnology (Bundy, *CSCA* 5 [1972] 57–77). In such hymnic contexts the *aporia* is expressed as a declarative question beginning with "how" (see *Odyssey* 9.12–16; *Homeric Hymn to Apollo* 19, 207, πῶς τ᾽ ἄρ σ᾽ ὑμνήσω πάντως εὔυμνον ἐόντα, "How, then, shall I sing of you, who are in all ways worthy of song?"; see Miller, *Delos*, 21–22, 70–72) or "who" (e.g., *Iliad* 2.484–93; 11.218; 14.508; Callimachus *Hymn to Zeus* 91–92). Usually the *aporia* takes the form of a rhetorical question in which the author asks either *how* he shall praise the god, in view of his *embarras de richesse* (e.g., *Homeric Hymn to Apollo* 19), or *who* should be the subject of song (e.g., *Iliad* 11.218–19, "Tell me now, Muses, with dwelling on Olympus, *who* was it that first came to face Agamemnon?"). In the introduction (*Or.* 47.1–4) to Aelius Aristides' rewritten collection of 130 dreams in his *Sacred Tales* (*Or.* 47–52), which combines dream narratives with praise for Asclepius, the god in whose honor they were written, the author begins with a lengthy *aporia* in which he emphasizes the impossibility of adequately conveying his experiences with Asclepius (Pearcy, *TAPA* 118 [1988] 377–91). In Rev 5:2 the *aporia* deals not with the problem of *how* to praise but rather with the question of *who* should be praised, and the identity of that person is the object of a verbal revelation to John by one of the elders (5:5). The *aporia* is followed by a prose *amplificatio* (αὔξησις) of the problem in vv 3–4 intended to heighten the suspense and emphasize the unique role and identity of the person in question. This is accomplished through the statement that no one in heaven, on earth, or under the earth could be found who would be able to open the scroll (for the view that the ἀπορία in *Hymn to Apollo* 19–29 is an αὔξησις in the Aristotelian sense, see B. A. van Groningen, *La composition littéraire*, 307). According to Aristotle *Rhetorica* 1.9.1368a (tr. W. R. Roberts, *Aristotle, Rhetoric* [New York: Modern Library, 1954]), "There are, also, many useful ways of heightening the effect of praise [αὐξητικῶν]. We must, for instance, point out that a man is the only one, or the first, or almost the only one who has done something, or that he has done it better than any one else; all these distinctions are honorable." In 5:3–4 the emphasis is building up to the unique role of the Lamb. The incipit of another hymn, this one addressed to the Beast in Rev 13:4, consists entirely of an *aporia:* "Who is like the Beast and who can fight against it?" Although there are lines in three OT psalms that begin "who is like" (Exod 15:11; Pss 35:10; 113:5; see 1 Sam 26:15), they are *not* placed at the beginning of hymns nor are they part of the consistent structural features of such hymns. An *aporia* is found in the introduction to the star hymn in Ign. *Eph.* 19.2: "How [πῶς] then was he revealed to the aeons?"

## V. REV 5 AS THE INVESTITURE OF THE LAMB

Rev 5 is often interpreted as depicting the *enthronement* of the Lamb, based on the assumption that the text reflects the pattern of ancient enthronement ritual (discussed below in section A). Others have argued that Rev 5 is modeled after the tradition of a *commission* in the heavenly court, sometimes combining the two patterns (discussed below in section B). The view argued in this commentary (presented below in section C) is that it is more appropriate to understand Rev 5 as depicting the *investiture* of the Lamb based not on ancient enthronement customs and procedures but rather on the literary adaptation of Dan 7 and Ezek 1–2.

### A.  *Rev 5 as the* Enthronement *of the Lamb*

Earlier this century, scholars influenced by the presuppositions of the history-of-religions school frequently expressed the view that the depiction of the Lamb in Rev 5 was based on ancient mythological models. A. Jeremias suggested a background in the ancient Near Eastern myth of the battle and victory of the "year god," perhaps in the form of the myth of Marduk who gained control of the tablets of destiny (*Babylonisches,* 13–14, 17–18). Gunkel saw the more general pattern of "the enthronement of a new god," one who could gain control of both heaven and earth through his great magical powers; the sealed scroll therefore represents a magical book (*Verständnis,* 62–63), and he was followed by Bousset, who, like Jeremias, refers to the Marduk myth ([1906] 259). Following the suggestion of Gunkel, a number of scholars have argued that Rev 5 depicts the enthronement of Christ based on the pattern of the coronation of a new ruler (Hadorn, 78; Lohmeyer, 51–52; Holtz, *Christologie,* 27–54; Sweet, 121–27; Roloff, 72–73). Lohse's views are more nuanced, for he combines two views, regarding vv 1–5 as a commission scene in the heavenly court, while considering vv 6–14 to be an enthronement scene (44). There are a number of other scholars, however, who argue against this view (van Unnik, "Worthy," 445–61; Müller, 151–52). Lohmeyer, who thought that Rev 5 reflected parallels to the enthronement of Horus, based his view that Rev 5 reflected an enthronement scene on two lines of argument, neither of which really proves the point: (1) He called attention to Rev 3:21, where the exalted Christ says that he sat down on his Father's throne after he had conquered, linking the notion of conquest with the *sessio ad dextram dei,* and combined it with Rev 7:17, which speaks ambiguously of the Lamb ἀνὰ μέσον τοῦ θρόνου, "in the midst of the throne," to claim that enthronement occurs in Rev 5. (2) He cites a number of texts that depict the enthronement of a ruler, since he is convinced that Rev 5:1–14 "recalls in the most vivid way the enthronement of a new ruler" (51).

T. Holtz begins by referring to an ancient Egyptian three-stage enthronement ritual, which he claims forms the basic structure for Rev 5 (*Christologie*, 28). The source Holtz cites for this enthronement ritual pattern is Joachim Jeremias (Jeremias-Strobel, *Briefe*, 28–29), who was himself primarily interested in applying the pattern to 1 Tim 3:16, though he also thought that it was evident in Phil 2:9–11; Matt 28:18–20; Rev 5:5–14; Heb 1:5–14. Holtz (following Jeremias) connects each of the three stages of the Egyptian enthronement ritual with a sequence of passages in Rev 5: (1) *Erhöhung*, "Elevation": the new king receives divine status through a solemn symbolic action (not actually shown, but described in the speech of the elder in v 5, who declares that the Lion of the tribe of Judah has conquered and can open the seals; here "conquer" = "elevation"); (2) *Präsentation*, "Presentation": the now deified king is presented to the assembly of gods (in v 6 John sees the slaughtered Lamb standing in the midst of the throne and the four cherubim and the elders); (3) *Inthronisation*, "Enthronement": royal power and authority are then transferred to the new king (i.e., the transfer of power is symbolized when the Lamb takes the book from the hand of God in the presence of the heavenly assembly in v 7).

Roloff agrees that there is a three-stage enthronement ritual of oriental kings reflected in Rev 5 (though he does not reveal the sources on which he is dependent), but he revises the categories in a surprisingly arbitrary way (by reversing the second and third stages and redefining them), apparently so that the three stages will more closely "fit" the events narrated in Rev 5 (72): (1) *Erhöhung*, "Exaltation": the description of the event of exaltation in the speech of the elder (v 5); (2) *Herrschaftsübertragung*, "Conferment of Ruling Power": in the taking of the scroll (vv 6–7); and (3) *Präsentation des Herrschers*, "Presentation of the Ruler": in the homage paid to the Lamb by the inhabitants of the heavenly world (vv 8–14).

This proposal, in the varying forms in which it is presented by Jeremias, Holtz, and Roloff, is extremely vulnerable to criticism on a number of fronts. First, both Jeremias and Holtz claim that this three-stage pattern is found in other early Christian texts that reflect the enthronement of Christ (Matt 28:18–20; Phil 2:9–11; 1 Tim 3:16; Heb 1:5–14). This is neither helpful nor convincing, however, for there are major differences between these hymnic texts (particularly Phil 2:5–11; 1 Tim 3:16) and Rev 5:1–14, and scholars who have analyzed these hymns have apparently not found the Exaltation-Presentation-Enthronement schema particularly useful or enlightening (see J. T. Sanders, *Hymns*, 94–95). Jeremias attributed the basic three-part scheme to E. Norden (apparently referring to *Die Geburt des Kindes* [Leipzig; Berlin: Teubner, 1924] 116–28). Norden, however, was primarily interested in applying the scheme to Vergil *Eclogues* 4, though he did mention 1 Tim 3:16 in passing (a reference that apparently caught the eye of Jeremias). Norden himself (*Geburt*, 119) derived the scheme from A. Moret, *Du Charactère religieux de la royauté Pharaonique* (Paris, 1902) 75–113. However, Moret's account of Egyptian enthronement ritual is itself a synthesis of a variety of sources (temple reliefs of the New Kingdom, Pyramid Texts, and the Ramesseum Dramatic Papyrus; on the latter see Frankfort, *Kingship*, 123–39), since *no connected account of Egyptian coronation ritual has survived*, but only partial and fragmentary accounts distributed over many centuries (Bonnet, *RÄRG*, 396; Fairman, "Kingship Rituals," 78). While tomb reliefs depict various select moments in coronation ceremonies (Bonnet, *RÄRG*, 397, 398, 399), the order of these events also remains a matter of speculation. Bonnet suggested his own synthetic list of five separate elements in Egyptian coronations but did not claim that they occurred in chronological order: (1) *Erwählung*, "election," (2) *Einführung*, "inauguration," (3) *Krönung*, "coronation," (4) *Herrschaftsantritt* or *Thronbesteigung*, "assumption of rule" or "ascent to the throne," (5) *Festzügen*, "processions" (*RÄRG*, 396–98). More recent discussions of enthronement ritual in ancient Egypt focus on two temporally and ideologically distinct enthronement rituals, *coronation* and *enthronement* (see "Königskrönung," *LexÄgypt* 3:531–33, and "Thronbesteigung," *LexÄgypt* 6:529–32), though these were probably focal moments in a much more complex series of actions (Frankfort, *Kingship*, 105–9; Fairman, "Kingship," 78–81). It is important to realize, however, that both the three-stage ritual proposed by Moret and adopted by Norden and the five-element ritual suggested by Bonnet are modern reconstructions that would not and could not have been known in the first century A.D. The idea that the author of Rev 5 had access to this reconstruction, then, is simply impossible.

Why would the author of Revelation have relied on an ancient *Egyptian* enthronement pattern (even if it were known in Ptolemaic-Roman times, as Norden erroneously claimed), particularly when there was an Israelite coronation ritual closer at hand? As we have concluded above, it is apparent that such a three-part Egyptian enthronement pattern did not exist in the first century A.D. in the form synthesized by Moret, summarized by Norden, and then simplified by Jeremias and Holtz and arbitrarily revised by Roloff. A further complication lies in the fact that, in the tradition of Israelite enthronement ritual, the central act was the *unction* of the new king, representing his election by Yahweh (Halpern, *Monarchy*, 13–19). That the term "Messiah," "anointed one," was used in some phases of late second temple Judaism to refer to the coming eschatological ruler indicates the central function of unction in Israelite kingship ideology. The term *Christos*, "anointed one," is, of course, used several times in Revelation as a messianic designation (11:15; 12:10; 20:4, 6). The ritual of anointing or unction, however, is not found in Rev 5, though unction could occur earlier than the coronation ceremony itself (as, for example, in David's anointing by Samuel in 1 Sam 16:1–13). The evidence is such that the reconstruction of a diachronic treatment of Israelite enthronement ritual is virtually impossible, since very little is known about it (see Brettler, *King*, 125–39). A completely different three-part ritual has been proposed by H.-J. Kraus, depending primarily on Ps 110 and Ps 2:7 (a precarious method; cf. Brettler, *King*, 139–41), who suggests that the Israelite coronation ritual consisted of three distinct phases, only one phase of which is also found in the Moret-Norden-Jeremias-Holtz pattern, the enthronement stage (*Psalms*, 111–19): (1) a prophetic speaker declared that the king was the "son of God" (Pss 2:7; 110:3); (2) the king was then told to ascend the throne and sit at the right hand of God (Ps 110:1); (3) after ascending the throne the king was declared the legitimate heir (Ps 110:4). R. de Vaux, focusing on Israelite enthronement ritual (note that 1 Kgs 1:32–48 and 2 Kgs 11:12–20 are the only coronation accounts in the OT), suggests a five-part structure based on a synthesis of these two narratives (*Ancient Israel*, 102–7): (1) investiture with royal insignia, (2) the anointing, (3) the acclamation (e.g., "long live the king!"), (4) the enthronement, and (5) the homage. Of course, the more detailed the ritual pattern, the more obvious it becomes that Rev 5 does not conform to such constructs.

Van Unnik has proposed the following arguments against the view that Rev 5 depicts an enthronement or coronation ritual ("Worthy," 447–48): (1) The scroll or book that is taken by the Lamb from the hand of God is understood not as a royal insignia or symbol but simply as a book that can be unrolled and read. (2) Nothing is said in Rev 5 about the elevation of the Lamb; he does not receive a new status but already possesses status. (3) Nothing is said about the accession of the Lamb to the throne, though such an accession is clear in other enthronement texts such as *1 Enoch* 69:26–29 and Phil 2:5–11. (4) The Lamb does not change status, but the sealed scroll does change status in that it can now be opened. Some further arguments can be added to those of van Unnik: (5) The "elevation" stage, said to be reflected in v 5, does not mention the reception of divine status or the reception of insignia symbolizing divine status by the Lamb. The seer is simply told that the Lamb has conquered and can open the seals. This "conquest" clearly refers to the death of Christ, as v 9 makes clear, but there is no link between this conquest by death and the acquisition of divine status, unless Rev 5 is supplemented by Rev 3:21 (the *only* place in Revelation where conquest and enthronement are linked). (6) The "presentation" of the Lamb in Rev 5:6 is not a ritual introduction to the heavenly assembly (analogous to the *Vorstellung* stage described by Norden, *Geburt*, 121–22), but simply the statement that the seer saw the Lamb in the heavenly court for the first time. (7) The sealed scroll that the Lamb takes from the hand of God might be construed as a symbol of power and authority, but it should then be understood to indicate the "elevation" stage.

## B. *Rev 5 as a* Commission *in the Heavenly Court*

The two focal aspects of the narrative in Rev 5 are the search for someone worthy to open the mysterious sealed scroll (v 2) and the identification of the Messiah as the only one worthy to take the scroll and open its seals (v 5). While much of Rev 5 must be attributed to the creativity of the author, there are certain basic traditional elements that he derived from OT and early Jewish heavenly court scenes. Müller (*ZNW* 54 [1963] 254–67) has shown that there is a lengthy tradition of heavenly court scenes, preserved in both the OT and ancient Near Eastern texts, in which the focus is on a *commission* given to someone in response to a question such as that in Rev 5:2, where the angelic herald asks, "Who is worthy to open the scroll and break its seals?" In the two heavenly court scenes in 1 Kgs 22:1–38 and Isa 6:1–13, the interrogative pronoun "who" is used to introduce a question that is directed toward identifying someone who might serve as a messenger or agent of God (Lohse, 42; Müller, *ZNW* 54 [1963] 257–60; Giesen, 57). In 1 Kgs 22:20 the Lord asks the members of the heavenly court "Who will entice Ahab, so that he may go up and fall at Ramoth-Gilead?" In Isa 6:8 it is again the Lord who says "Whom shall I send and who will go for us?" In both scenes it is the enthroned Lord who frames the question, while in Rev 5:2 the question is put by a mighty angel serving as a court herald. It is probably John himself who has decided to attribute the question to an angel rather than to God himself (God speaks in Revelation only in 1:8; 21:5–8). An analogous scene occurs in the Ugaritic Keret myth, where the god Latipan or El (the text is fragmentary), speaking in the assembly of the gods, repeatedly asks "Who among the gods will banish his [i.e., 'Keret's'] illness and drive out the plague? None among the gods did answer him." After repeating the question seven times, Latipan himself initiates magical procedures to heal Keret (KRT C v.8–29; Pritchard, *ANET*, 148; Gibson, *Canaanite Myths*, 99–100; this and the following texts were collected by Müller, *ZNW* 54 [1963] 260–67). In the Akkadian Myth of Zu, which deals with the theft of the Tablet of Destinies by Zu, Anu the god speaks in the assembly of the gods, "Which of the gods shall slay Zu?" and the assembly chooses the Irrigator (an epithet of Adad) the son of Anu to perform the deed (Pritchard, *ANET*, 111). In the Sumerian poem "Gilgamesh and Agga," in the context of a political assembly, Gilgamesh frames the question "Who has heart, let him stand up, to Agga I would have him go," and Birhurturri, one of those present, volunteers to go (Pritchard, *ANET*, 46).

## C. Rev 5 as the Investiture of the Lamb

The arguments against reading Rev 5 as the *enthronement* of the Lamb center on two central issues: (1) there is no reference in Rev 5 to the act of enthronement (or to the insignia typical of enthronement scenes), and (2) the utilization of an artificially constructed coronation ritual to make sense of the structure of Rev 5 is a useless exercise. On the other hand, the text of Rev 5 reflects features of commission scenes with many parallels in earlier biblical and extrabiblical literature. The argument that Rev 5 should be construed as the *investiture* of the Lamb is based on an analysis of the text of Rev 5 as an adaptation of Dan 7 and Ezek 1–2, and by analogy with the investiture features of other visions of the heavenly court, particularly 1 Kgs 22 and Isa 6. The term "investiture" is a more appropriate designation for the narrative in Rev 5 than "enthronement," since "investiture" refers to the act of establishing someone in office or the ratification of the office that someone already holds informally.

The narrative in Rev 5 centers on the recognition of the Lamb as the only one worthy to open the scroll sealed with seven seals. The focus of the action is the taking or reception of the scroll from the right hand of God by the Lamb, for it is this act that is immediately celebrated by the two narrative hymns in 5:9–10; 5:11–12, followed by the doxology sung by all the living beings of the cosmos in 5:13–14. It is clear that the act of "taking" or "reception" (εἴληφεν) of the scroll from the right hand of God (v 7) signifies the "reception" (λαβεῖν) of the honors mentioned in v 12: power, wealth, wisdom, might, honor, glory, and praise. Some of these qualities are ascribed elsewhere in Revelation either to God alone (power, 4:11; 7:12; 11:17; 19:1; wisdom, 7:12; might, 7:12; honor, 4:11; 7:12; glory, 4:11; 7:12; 19:1; blessing, 4:11; 7:12) or to God and the Lamb jointly (honor, 5:13; glory, 5:13). It is precisely the Lamb's reception of this scroll that symbolizes his investiture.

The investiture scene in Rev 5 appears to have been adapted from Dan 7:9–14 (Yarbro Collins, *Combat Myth*, 214–15; Beale, *Daniel*, 200–228; Krodel, 160), which centers on the *investiture* of "one like a son of man," not his enthronement. Even though enthronement is not mentioned in Dan 7, however, scholars frequently assume that it is suggested or implied (Collins, *Comm. Daniel*, 301). The author does make use of Dan 7 in Rev 5, even though there are just two clear allusions. In Rev 5:11 there is an allusion to Dan 7:10 in the phrase μυριάδες μυριάδων καὶ χιλιάδες χιλιάδων, "myriads and myriads and thousands of thousands" (LXX Dan 7:10, χίλιαι χιλιάδες *ἐθεράπευον αὐτὸν* καὶ μύριαι μυριάδες παρειστήκεισαν αὐτῷ [Theod: *ἐλειτούργουν αὐτῷ*], "a thousand thousands served him and ten thousand times ten thousand stood before him"), found in Rev 5:11 (also alluded to in *1 Enoch* 14:22; 40:1; *1 Clem.* 34:6; *Apoc. Zeph.* 4:1; 8:1). In Rev 5:9b–10 there is an allusion to Dan 7:14, 18 (where the author interprets the "one like a son of man" figure in 7:13 collectively as in Dan 7:18, 27). Here is a synoptic comparison of Rev 5:9b–10 and Dan 7:14, 18:

| *Rev 5:9b–10* | *Dan 7:14* | *Dan 7:18* |
|---|---|---|
| every tribe, tongue, people, and nation | [14b] all peoples, nations, languages | |
| and made them a | [14a] To him was given | The holy ones of the Most High shall receive the kingdom |
| kingdom and priests and they will reign on the earth | dominion and glory and kingship | |
| | his dominion is an everlasting dominion that shall not pass away | and possess the kingdom forever |
| | and his kingship shall never be destroyed | |

The author has applied the language of Dan 7:14, 18 to the redemptive death of Christ, which has "enthroned" Christians as kings and priests. The author has overlaid the existing kingship language in Dan 7:14, 18 with the "kingdom and priests" language from Exod 19:6 (which he has also used in 1:7; 20:6).

The mysterious reference in Dan 7:9 to thrones that were set in place was apparently transformed by the author into the twenty-four thrones on which the heavenly elders sit (Rev 4:4), quite independently of the rabbinic messianic speculation about the thrones of Dan 7:9 (see *Comment* on Rev 3:21).

The narrative focus in the throne theophany of Dan 7:9–14 is the enthroned Ancient of Days who judges the fourth beast and has it executed and burned with fire (v 11). In v 13, "one like a son of man" comes with the clouds and "he was presented" (Aramaic וּקְדָמוֹהִי *ûqĕdāmôhî;* Theod προσηνέχθη) before the Ancient of Days, i.e., a royal audience (Montgomery, *Daniel*, 304). This presentation is followed by an investiture, which Montgomery describes as a "viceregal investiture" (*Daniel*, 304). The character of this investiture is described in v 14, though symbols of investiture are mentioned:

To him was given *dominion* and *glory* and *kingship*,
that all peoples, nations, and languages should serve him.
His dominion is an everlasting dominion
that shall not pass away,
and his kingship is one
that shall never be destroyed

This short list of three prerogatives, two of which deal with imperial power, is greatly expanded to seven prerogatives in Rev 5:12 and four prerogatives in Rev 5:13.

The author of Rev 4–5 has taken the basic framework of Dan 7:9–18 and freely adapted it for a new purpose. The presentation of the "one like a son of man" before the enthroned Ancient of Days in Dan 7:13 results in his investiture. John has grounded that investiture on the sacrificial death of Christ, which now becomes the very basis for investiture. The motif of the sealed scroll does not occur in Dan 7 (there is only the reference to the books being opened; cf. Rev 20:12) but is imported from Ezek 2:9–10 to serve as a symbol of investiture.

*Comment*

**1a** καὶ εἶδον ἐπὶ τὴν δεξιὰν τοῦ καθημένου ἐπὶ τοῦ θρόνου βιβλίον γεγραμμένον ἔσωθεν καὶ ὄπισθεν, "Then I saw in the right hand of the One seated on the throne a scroll written both inside and on the back." This is the first occurrence of the phrase καὶ εἶδον, "and I saw," which occurs thirty-three times in Revelation (including one instance when the object of the vision is inserted between καί and εἶδον in 21:2).

> καὶ εἶδον functions in three ways: (1) It introduces a new vision narrative (8:2; 10:1; 13:1; 14:1, 6, 14; 15:1; 19:11, 17; 20:1, 4, 12; 21:1; cf. Acts 11:5; Dan 8:2; 10:5; 12:5; Ezek 1:4; 3:13; 8:2; 13:1). (2) It introduces a major scene within a continuing vision narrative (5:1; 6:1; 8:13; 13:11; 15:2; 19:19; 21:2; 21:22; cf. Ezek 2:9). (3) It is used to focus on a new or significant figure or action that occurs within a continuing vision narrative (5:2, 6, 11; 6:2, 5, 8, 12; 7:2; 9:1; 16:13; 17:3, 6; cf. Acts 11:6; Dan 12:5; Ezek 37:8; 44:4). See also μετὰ ταῦτα εἶδον in the *Comment* on 4:1a.

The sealed scroll and the Lamb constitute the narrative focus of Rev 5. It appears likely that the author assumes that the scroll was in the right hand of God in the description in Rev 4 even though it is not specifically mentioned. If God took or was given the scroll before 5:1, the moment for this action would be between 4:8 and 4:9–11 (Jörns, *Evangelium*, 32). The scroll is introduced here at the beginning of this section of text, while mention of the Lamb is intentionally delayed until v 6 (though he is referred to in v 5, anticipating v 6, under the titles "Lion of the tribe of Judah" and "Descendant of David," both of which underline the messianic character of the Lamb). The sealed scroll would look like a cylinder held in the right hand of God who is seated on the throne, perhaps with the scroll resting on his lap, an image with many parallels in Greco-Roman art (Birt, *Buchrolle*, 85–91, esp. plates 46–48).

The main interpretive problems in this passage include the determination of the precise meaning of the phrase γεγραμμένον ἔσωθεν καὶ ὄπισθεν, as well as the difficulty of deciding on the specific form, content, and function of this βιβλίον. While the phrase ἔσωθεν καὶ ὄπισθεν is almost certainly the *lectio originalis*, these two adverbs are not opposites or antonyms as one might expect (Zahn, *Introduction* 3:405), and this has led to modifications in the MS tradition (see *Note* 5:1.d.). ἔσωθεν means "within, on the inside" (Louw-Nida, § 83.16), and one of its antonyms is ἔξωθεν, "outside," "on the outside," "outside of" (Louw-Nida, § 83.21), as in Luke

11:40. ὄπισθεν, on the other hand, means "the back of," "[from] behind," or "on the back" (Louw-Nida, § 83.41), and one of its antonyms is ἔμπροσθεν, "in front," "on front" (Louw-Nida, § 83.36), as in Rev 4:6. The Greek term ὀπισθόγραφος, used of a papyrus roll written on both sides (Pliny *Ep.* 3.5.17; Lucian *Vit. auc.* 9; Ulpian *Digest* 37.11.4), indicates the appropriateness of translating ὄπισθεν as "on the back." This translation, however, presupposes that the βιβλίον was an *opistograph* rather than a doubly written document (see below). The fact that the scroll was "written both inside and on the back" would be relatively unusual, since normally a papyrus roll was used only on one side. However, this reference can be construed primarily as an allusion to the scroll in Ezek 2:9–10, which is described as having "writing on the front and on the back," i.e., "on the obverse and on the reverse" (Hebrew וְהִיא כְתוּבָה פָנִים וְאָחוֹר *wĕhîʾ kĕtûbâ pānîm wĕʾāḥîr*; LXX καὶ ἐν αὐτῇ γεγραμμένα ἦν τὰ ὄπισθεν καὶ τὰ ἔμπροσθεν [B τὰ ἔμπροσθεν καὶ τὰ ὀπίσω]), where the two Greek adverbs are in the reverse order of their counterparts in the MT, though the order of the MT is followed in MS B (Spitta, 280; Schlatter, *Apokalypse*, 61). This is an allusion to Ezek 2:9–10, although the scroll mentioned there is at first closed but then apparently unrolled before the eyes of the prophet (i.e., unrolled as is the little scroll in Rev 10:2, 8), while the scroll in Rev 5 is closed and sealed with seven seals. Taking the seer's visionary perspective seriously means that he only sees the ὄπισθεν or *back* of the closed scroll, and therefore must have inferred or assumed that there was also writing on the inside, probably on the basis of his familiarity with Ezek 2:9–10. An iconographical parallel to the scroll written on the inside and on the back is found in the portrait of a man reading a scroll found on the west wall of the Dura Europas synagogue (third century A.D.), identified variously as Moses or Ezra (Kraeling, *Synagogue*, 232–35; Goodenough, *Jewish Symbols* 9:113–15), who is reading a scroll (presumably the Torah) that is *written on the back side*, i.e., the reverse (Kraeling, *Synagogue*, 233 and plate LXXVII). Kraeling explains this as a naïve way of indicating that there was writing on the obverse. It is also possible, however, that the painter was intending to depict an *opistograph*, though late rabbinic tradition, of course, insisted that only *one* side of a parchment Torah could be written on (Str-B, 4/1, 126, 129). On the other hand, it is also legitimate to translate ὄπισθεν as "on the outside" (Louw-Nida, § 83.21), in which case the entire phrase "written both inside and outside" could refer to a doubly written document in which there was a *scriptura interior*, "inside text," and *scriptura exterior*, "outside text"; see below.

The phrase ἐπὶ τὴν δεξιάν is problematic primarily because of the preposition ἐπί (the use of ἐπί in Revelation in general is problematic; see Schmid, *Studien* 2:209–13). ἐπί + genitive, ἐπί + dative, and ἐπί + accusative can all be used, apparently interchangeably, to mean "on, upon," as 14:9 indicates: ἐπὶ τοῦ μετώπου αὐτοῦ ἢ ἐπὶ τὴν χεῖρα αὐτοῦ, "on his forehead or on his hand." ἐπὶ τὴν δεξιάν could mean (1) "in the right hand," i.e., held in the hand (an unusual meaning, but the unanimous choice of the major English versions: AV, RSV, NRSV, NEB, REB, NIV), (2) "upon the right hand," i.e., lying on the open palm of the right hand (some Latin translations of ἐπὶ τὴν δεξιάν, such as Tyconius[2] and Beatus, have *supra dexteram*, "on the right hand"; Bousset [1906] 254; Charles, 1:136; 2:399), or (3) "at the right side" (cf. LXX Ps 120:5, ἐπὶ χεῖρα δεξιάν, "at your right hand"; BAGD, 288; Bauer-Aland, 584, *auf der rechten Hand*). Evidence for these possibilities is surveyed in Stefanovič, ("Background," 145–57), who almost alone favors the third view. In the phrase ἐπὶ τὴν δεξιάν (found only here in Revelation as a *lectio originalis*), ἐπί probably means "in," just as the phrase ἐπὶ τὴν χεῖρα αὐτοῦ in 20:1 means "in his hand" (clarified by scribal alteration to read ἐν τῇ χειρί; see *Notes* on 20:1) and is analogous with ἐπὶ τῆς δεξιᾶς μου, "in my right hand," in 1:20 (as the parallel ἐν τῇ δεξιᾷ χειρὶ αὐτοῦ, "in his right hand," in 1:16 indicates). The phrase κρότησον ἐπὶ τὴν χεῖρα σου, "grasp in your hand" (LXX Ezek 21:17), is a close parallel to this use of ἐπί + accusative, since the author is probably dependent for his image of a scroll written on both sides on Ezek 2:9–10, where the phrase ἐν αὐτῇ, "in it [i.e., 'the hand']" is used for the location of the unrolled scroll handed to the prophet. While the scroll here is described as in the "right hand" of the one sitting on the throne, in Ezek 2:9 it simply says that "a hand" (the owner is not identified) was extended to Ezekiel holding a scroll. In addition, the phrase ἐπὶ τὴν δεξιάν is a variant for ἐπὶ τῆς δεξιᾶς in Rev 1:20 attested by Oecumenius[2053 2062] Andr h[2302], where it must mean "in the right hand." The less ambiguous phrase ἐν τῇ χειρί, "in the right hand," is used to describe the location of the little scroll held by the angel in Rev 10:2, 8. That the Lamb takes the scroll ἐκ τῆς δεξιᾶς τοῦ καθημένου ἐπὶ τοῦ θρόνου, "from the right hand of the one seated on the throne" (5:7), further suggests that the roll is depicted "in" the hand of God in 5:1, though ἐκ τῆς δεξιᾶς can also mean "from the right side." The "right hand" of God is of course a common metaphor frequently found in the OT and Judaism signifying his power and authority (Exod 15:6, 12; Pss 18:35; 20:6; 63:8; Isa 41:10; 48:13). The exalted Christ is depicted holding seven stars in his right hand (Rev 1:16; 2:1), but here the "right hand" probably symbolizes a place of refuge and protection (see *Comment* on 1:16). The detailed analysis of the phrase ἐπὶ τὴν δεξιάν by Stefanovič ("Background," 145–57) deserves some discussion. Stefanovič argues that the phrase ἐπὶ τὴν δεξιάν means "at the right hand" or "at the right side"; i.e., the sealed scroll is described as lying on the throne at the right side of the one enthroned. He regards this interpretation as extremely significant in light of the NT conception of the exaltation of Christ to the throne "at the right hand of God" ("Background," 156). He appears to regard the sealed scroll "at the right side" of God as a surrogate for Christ *ad dextram dei*, though he never articulates his view in this way.

There are numerous iconographical and literary parallels to the motif of a scroll held in one or both hands, though the meaning of this symbol varies (Birt, *Buchrolle*; Goodenough, *Jewish Symbols* 9:146–47; vol. 11, plates 126, 138). In a detailed study of the depiction of scrolls held by people depicted in Greco-Roman art, Birt distinguishes between depictions of *closed* book rolls and those of *open* book rolls (*Buchrolle*, 40–123, 124–96). He further divides the motif of the *closed* scroll into submotifs, including the closed scroll in the *left* hand (*Buchrolle*, 43–80) and the closed scroll in the *right* hand (*Buchrolle*, 80–123). In a relief often called the "Apotheosis of Homer" now in the British Museum (see Pollitt, *Art*, 15, plate 4), by the sculptor Archelaos of Priene, ca. 220–150 B.C. (Priene was located on the Maeander a few miles southeast of Ephesus), the lowest of three registers shows Homer (depicted as a Zeus-like figure) enthroned with a scepter in his left hand and a scroll in his right hand (obviously representing his famous epics). Several late Roman sarcophagi depict the deceased holding an open scroll (Koch-Sichtermann, *Sarkophage*, plates 119, 264–65). In a Greek translation of an aretalogy of the Egyptian god Imouthes of Ptah, a vision of the god describes him as dressed in bright linen and holding a closed scroll in his left hand (POxy 1381, lines 120–21). More directly relevant to this passage are the numerous reliefs from the period of the Roman empire that depict an emperor holding a scroll in his hand (Birt, *Buchrolle,* 68–73; Reichelt, *Buch,* 164–66). This scroll in the hands of various emperors apparently functions as a symbol of imperial power and authority.

Another set of three interpretive problems involves the *form, content,* and *function* of the scroll, which have been interpreted in an astonishing variety of ways, as the following discussion indicates.

1. *The Form of the* βιβλίον. (a) The βιβλίον as an *opistograph,* i.e., a scroll "written on both sides" (Swete, 75; Beckwith, 506; Reichelt, *Buch,* 68–72). The basic book form in antiquity was the roll or scroll, made of either parchment or papyrus, both extremely expensive materials (the codex, or page form, with each leaf written on both sides began to come into use during the late first century A.D.). Normally only one side of a scroll was written on, but sometimes the other side was also used (Birt, *Buchrolle,* 7–8). Occasionally the other side was used to finish a text longer than expected (Juvenal 1.6). The term ὀπισθόγραφος, "written on the back as well as the front," is used of papyrus rolls in Lucian *Vitarum Auctio* 9, clearly suggesting the poverty of the owner; i.e., he was forced for reasons of economy to use both sides of a papyrus roll. In Pliny *Ep.* 3.5.17 (see Ulpian *Digest* 37.11.4), the term *opisthographus* is used as a Greek loanword, meaning "written on the back [as well as the front]" (*OLD,* 1254), referring to the works of the Elder Pliny. Birt (*Buchrolle,* 349 n. 2) concludes, after comparing the passage in Pliny *Ep.* 3.5.17 to the references in *Hist. nat.* 14.121 and 30.12, that the text of Pliny *Historia naturalia* was left as an "opistograph" (see Sherwin-White, *Letters.* 219). Some of the papyrus fragments of rolls from Qumran are written on both sides. Many commentators on Revelation regard the scroll referred to in Rev 5:1 as an *opistograph* (Bousset [1906] 254; Charles, 1:136–37; Allo, 60–61; Hadorn, 74–75). There are two major arguments for regarding the βιβλίον of 5:1 as an *opistograph:* (1) the allusion to Ezek 2:9–10 (Holtz's view that the βιβλίον is a *double document* rather than an *opistograph* [see below] leads him to argue that the description of the scroll in Ezek 2:9–10 has nothing to do with Rev 5:1 [*Christologie,* 32]), and (2) the original reading ἔσωθεν καὶ ὄπισθεν (see *Note* 5:1.e-e.), "on the inside and on the back," i.e., "on the obverse and the reverse," which is appropriate for describing a closed or rolled up *opistograph,* as the formation of the Greek term ὀπισθόγραφος itself indicates.

(b) The βιβλίον as a *Doppelurkunde,* or *doubly written legal document* (Staritz, *ZNW* 30 [1931] 157–70; Roller, *ZNW* 36 [1937] 98–107; Lohse, 37–38; for a discussion of the form, see Kubitschek, "Signum," PW, 2nd series, 2:2408–30; Reichelt, *Buch,* 72–76, 92–94). The basic rationale for a "doubly written document" is to provide a sealed document that cannot be altered with an unsealed copy that can be read. It is written "within" and "without" in the sense that it consists of two copies of a legal document, one sealed (i.e., "within") and one unsealed (i.e., "without"). The earliest evidence for a "doubly written document" is Jer 32:9–15, which describes a sealed deed and an open or unsealed deed, both of which were placed in a clay jar (Fischer, *ZAW* 30 [1910] 137–39). The procedure was to write two copies of the same legal document separated by a short space; the upper document was rolled together and sealed, while the lower document was simply folded together, but could be read (Koffmann, *Doppelurkunden,* 10–11; Holladay, *Jeremiah* 1:214–15). Types of the kind of double document described in Jer 32:9–15 are also mentioned in rabbinic literature (*m. B. Bat.* 10:1–2; *t. B. Bat.* 11.1; *b. B. Bat.* 160b–61a). Early Egyptian double documents have been discovered (Bilabel, *Aegyptus* 6 [1925] 93–113), and some legal documents with this double form were found at the fifth-century B.C. Jewish colony at Elephantine (Porten, *Elephantine,* 197–99). More recently a number of such documents in Imperial Aramaic, Mishnaic Hebrew, and Greek were discovered in the deserts of Judah (Koffmahn, *Doppelurkunde,* 10–30). Both the Greeks and the Romans used a type of written legal document called a δίπτυχος or *tabella duplex,* i.e., *diptychum* (or *triptychum*), "double-fold" (or "triple-fold"), composed of two (or three) rectangular tablets of wood or bronze connected with a cord through holes in the edges (*Kleine Pauly* 2:98–99, s.v. "Diptychon"; Berger, *Roman Law,* 438; see *Iliad* 6.168–69 ["inscribing many life-destroying things in a folded tablet," the only clear reference to writing in the *Iliad;* see G. S. Kirk, *The Iliad: A Commentary* [Cambridge: Cambridge UP, 1990] 2:181]; Herodotus 7.239.3). The text was written twice, once on the inside (*scriptura interior,* "inner text") and once on the outside (*scriptura exterior,* "outer text"), which could be read without opening the document, or a synopsis of the document is written on the outside, while the official document is recorded *in extenso* within; i.e., the seals function not to *conceal* the contents of the document but rather to protect them from alteration. One type of double document was the *diplomata militaria,* i.e., "military papers," with a sealed text on the inside and a readable copy on the outside (*Kleine Pauly* 3:1300–1301). The seven seals have led some scholars to identify the scroll as a testament or will, *testamentum* or διαθήκη (e.g., Zahn, *Introduction* 3:393–94, 406 n. 8; Zahn, 1:341–42; G. Schrenk, *TDNT* 1:618; Birt, *Buchrolle,* 243–44; Hadorn, 75; Behm, 34), which is sealed by five or seven witnesses who must eventually attest to its authenticity upon the death of the testator (Kubitschek, "Signum," PW, 2nd series, 2:2400; B. Kübler, "Testament [juristisch]," PW, 2nd series, 5/1:998–99). According to Roman law, a will had to be validated by the seals of five or seven witnesses (Gaius *Institutes* 2.147 [*si septem testium signis signata sint testamenta,* "if the will bears the seal of seven witnesses"]; Justinian *Institutes* 2.10.2–3) and could be recorded on *tabula,* parchment, or other material (2.10.12). The *testamentum praetorium* in particular had to be made in the presence of seven witnesses and sealed by them (Berger, *Roman Law,* 735). However, the motif of seven seals is used in a variety of contexts and cannot be exclusively linked with the testamentary form. Roller (*ZNW* 36 [1937] 106) has objected to this interpretation, arguing that no example of a doubly written testament is known from the ancient world. A number of scholars consider the double document to be the model for the scroll in Rev 5:1, though they reject the more specific "testament" hypothesis (Staritz, *ZNW* 30 [1931] 157–70; Roller, *ZNW* 36 [1937] 100–107; Bornkamm, *ZNW* 36 [1937] 133; Holtz, *Christologie,* 31–33; Roloff, 74). Though the double-document hypothesis is widely held, there are some weighty objections to it. Koep has objected that this scroll cannot be a doubly written document since the contents of such a document are summarized on the outside and evident to all, making unsealing unnecessary (*Himmlische Buch,* 24). Prigent has similarly argued that the dramatic character of the scene is compromised if the contents of the scroll are known before it is opened (94). Of course, it is the *enactment* of the eschatological plan in the scroll (symbolized by its opening), and not just its existence, that is of central importance. While the double-document hypothesis is clever, and certainly conforms to ancient usage, there is no compelling reason to reject the notion that the βιβλίον is an *opistograph* modeled after Ezek 2:9–10, with the writing on both sides primarily representing the fullness of the prophetic message given to Ezekiel, as well as the fullness of God's eschatological plan for the world in the scroll of Rev 5:1. The statement that "no one could open the scroll or look into it" (5:3–4) does not fit well with the doubly-written-document hypothesis, since the presence of the *scriptura exterior* would reveal the essential contents of the scroll. John's inclusion of the seven-seal motif (see below) is based not on testamentary witnesses (who are these unnamed witnesses?) but rather on the notion that seven seals indicate the secrecy and inaccessibility of the contents of the scroll to all but those authorized to read it. Further, the *lectio originalis* ἔσωθεν καὶ ὄπισθεν supports the *opistograph* theory, while the secondary reading ἔσωθεν καὶ ἔξωθεν, "on the inside and on the outside," supports the double-document theory.

(c) The βιβλίον as *seven separate leaves rolled one on top of the other and sealed*. Rissi (*Babylon*, 14), reviving an older proposal of Grotius (*Annotationes* 8:284–85) and Spitta (281), speculates that the scroll with seven seals consists of seven separate leaves rolled together, each with a separate seal, but cites no ancient parallels. If the sealed scroll is thought to have this form, then the opening of each seal reveals a document that presumably involves only those eschatological events that immediately follow the opening of each seal.

(d) The βιβλίον as a *codex*. Zahn argued that the phrase γεγραμμένον ἔσωθεν, "written inside," referred to the content of the βιβλίον, while ὄπισθεν belonged with κατεσφραγισμένον σφραγῖσιν ἑπτά and translated both phrases together as "a book written within and sealed on the back side with seven seals" (Zahn, 1:327–34). For Zahn and a few other scholars, the βιβλίον is therefore not a scroll but a *codex* (i.e., a book with pages), which could be sealed in such a way that parts of it could be opened with the breaking of individual seals (Zahn, 1:333–34; id., *Introduction* 3:405; Grotius, *Annotationes* 8:284–85; E. Nestle, *Introduction to the Textual Criticism of the Greek New Testament*, tr. A. Menzies [London: Williams and Norgate; New York: Putnam, 1901] 333). Zahn also argued that the phrase ἐπὶ τὴν δεξιάν, "*upon* the right hand," suggested that there was a codex in the open hand of God, while ἐν τῇ δεξιᾷ, "*in* his right hand," would have been more appropriate for holding a closed roll (Zahn, *Introduction* 3:405). Both notions are ridiculed by Birt, *Buchrolle*, 86 n. 2. However, arguments that the βιβλίον of 5:1 could not be a codex because the codex form was developed only in the second century are problematic. Christians were quick to adopt the codex form, as the papyrus evidence from the second and third centuries indicates, and two of the foremost experts on the codex have proposed (the admittedly speculative hypothesis) that the Gospel of Mark was originally written in codex form (Roberts-Skeat, *Codex*, 38–61). 𝔓⁴⁶ is a codex containing ten Pauline letters (including Hebrews), which can be dated ca. A.D. 200.

2. *The Content of the Scroll*. Although there has been a great deal of speculation about the contents of the sealed scroll, the text of Rev 5:1–8:1 (the section dealing explicitly with the sealed scroll and the breaking of its seven seals by the Lamb) contains no explicit indication of the contents of the scroll. If the scroll of Rev 5 is regarded as identical with the open scroll of Rev 10 (which is not likely), more clues to its character are found in that chapter. An important clue for the contents of the scroll is found in Ezek 2:9–10, the model for this passage, in which the contents of the scroll shown to Ezekiel are described as "words of mourning, lamentation, and woe," i.e., the message of divine judgment that the prophet will announce. This

probably refers to the prophet's proclamation of the coming judgment on Israel (Ezek 4–24) and on the nations (Ezek 25–32). The contents of the scroll of Rev 5 have been interpreted narrowly and broadly: (a) Narrow conceptions of the significance of the scroll maintain that the author intended his audience to understand that the contents are identical with all or part of the narration of eschatological events that follow the breaking of the first seal in Rev 6:1 (perhaps even with the entire book of Revelation itself). There is a partial parallel to the sealed scroll in *1 Enoch* 93:1–15, where "Enoch" is said to know the words of the tablets of heaven and prophesies by speaking "from the books" (v 3). Similarly, another heavenly book is referred to in Hermas *Vis.* 1.2.2; 2.1.3–4; 2.4.2–3. (b) Broader conceptions of the contents of the scroll hold that it has little or nothing to do with the narrative of eschatological events in part or all of the remainder of the book. Let us consider the various options within each of these approaches.

(a) The view that there is a correlation between the content of the scroll to the eschatological events narrated in part or all of Revelation following 6:1 has been expressed in a variety of ways.

[1] At a more general level, it has been maintained that the scroll narrates the eschatological punishments inflicted on the world by the will of God (Schüssler Fiorenza, *CBQ* 30 [1968] 564), or that it is essentially identical with what John has been commissioned to write to the seven churches.

[2] If the scroll contains a narrative of eschatological events that are put in motion by the breaking of the seven seals, it has been argued that the contents of the scroll begin to be actualized with the opening of the first seal in 6:1 and extend either to 8:1 (the opening of the seventh seal) or even further into the book (Bousset [1906] 254–55; Charles, 1:135; Hadorn, 75; Lohmeyer, 53; G. Schrenk, *TDNT* 1:619; Müller, *ZNW* 54 [1963] 255).

[3] Others argue that the contents of the scroll cannot begin to be actualized until all seven seals have been broken, an event that does not occur until 8:1, so that the contents of the scroll are only revealed beginning with 8:2 (Swete, 75; Beckwith, 263–64; Bornkamm, *ZNW* 36 [1937] 132–49; Jeremias, *TDNT* 4:872 n. 250; Strobel, "Apokalypse," *TRE* 3:178–79).

[4] Views [2] and [3] have been neatly combined by Hellholm, who regards the form of the scroll as a doubly written legal document (see above), arguing that 6:1–7:17 is the *scriptura exterior* that summarizes the content of the scroll, while 8:1–22:5 is the *scriptura interior*, i.e., an account of the content of the scroll ("Genre," 48–53). The problem with this view is that this scroll is never given to the narrator to transcribe, as most heavenly books are, and the scroll is never mentioned again after 8:1.

[5] Some scholars have gone so far as to regard Rev 6:1–22:6 as essentially a transcript of the scroll (Staritz, *ZNW* 30 [1931] 166; Holtz, *Christologie*, 35).

[6] Since the author describes his composition as a prophetic βιβλίον (1:11; 22:7, 9, 18–19), some have identified the entire work as the scroll with seven seals (even though it is explicitly stated in 22:10 that John's prophetic book should *not* be sealed).

(b) There are several other ways of understanding the broader significance of the sealed scroll apart from assuming that all or part of Revelation is a transcription or enactment of the eschatological plan of God contained in the scroll.

[1] A typical broad understanding of the significance of the scroll is that it is a

"book of destiny," consisting of God's predetermined plan for human beings and the world (variously described by Swete, 75; Caird, 72; Beasley-Murray, 120; Lohse, 41–42), or the foreordained eschatological plan of God, which cannot be known until the period of fulfillment, a biblical tradition reflected in Ezek 2:9–10; Dan 8:26; 12:9; *Jub.* 32:20–22; *1 Enoch* 81:2–3. An example is the "tablets of heaven" that "Enoch" was commanded to read that contained "all the deeds of men, and all who will be born of flesh on the earth for the generations of eternity" (*1 Enoch* 81:2; cf. 106:19–107:1).

[2] The scroll is the Book of Life referred to frequently in Revelation (3:5; 13:8; 17:8; 20:12, 15; 21:27), containing the names of the saints (A. Jeremias, *Babylonisches*, 17). The opening of this book would then represent the disclosure of the names of the saints. This view is problematic, since the opening of the Book of Life is first mentioned in 20:12, while the scroll with seven seals is opened in 6:1–8:1 (Staritz, *ZNW* 30 [1931] 157–58). Further, the opening of the seals in 6:1–8:1 has nothing to do with the disclosure of the identity of the saints.

[3] The scroll is a record of the sins of humankind, or *Schulderkunde*, for which the Lamb has made atonement, and the accomplishment of this atonement or redemption is symbolized by the opening of the scroll (Roller, *ZNW* 36 [1937] 98–113; Müller, *Messias*, 163–65). The chief objection to this view is that Rev 5 is not a judgment scene.

[4] The scroll is Scripture or the Old Testament (Piper, *CH* 20 [1951] 13–15) or more specifically the Torah (Mowry, *JBL* 71 [1952] 82–83; Shepherd, *Liturgy*, 88; Sweet, 123), which is a sealed book until christologically interpreted (Luke 4:21; 28:25–27; 2 Cor 3:15; Prigent, 94–95; Harrington, *Apocalypse*, 32, 116, 148). The tables of the law are described as ἔνθεν καὶ ἔνθεν ἦσαν γεγραμμέναι, "written on both sides" (Exod 32:15). The views of Piper and Mowry are based in part on the supposition that the liturgy of Rev 4–5 is a heavenly counterpart to the worship services of early Christianity. The scene in which the Lamb takes the sealed scroll from the right hand of God has suggestive parallels in rabbinic sources, where it is supposed that Moses received the Torah from the right hand of God (*Deut. Rab.* 11.10; Freedman, *Midrash Rabbah* 7:185), and the king of Israel may have been given a copy of the Torah (Deut 17:18–20). The view that the sealed scroll of Rev 5 is all or part of the OT is very old and is found as early as Hippolytus (*Comm. in Dan.* 34.3), Origen (*Comm. in Joh.* 5.4; *Hom. in Exod.* 12.4; *Hom. in Ezek.* 14.2; *Philocalia* 2.1; 5.5), and Victorinus (*Comm. ad Apoc.* 5.1). Origen understood this book to mean the whole of Scripture, and the statement that it was written in front and in back refers to the obvious and the remote (i.e., the literal and the spiritual) meanings of Scripture. Stefanovič ("Background," 228–313) argues that the sealed scroll is analogous to "the Covenant Book [i.e., the Book of Deuteronomy] in the enthronement ceremony of the OT Israelite kings" ("Background," 301). Because of the unworthiness of the Israelite kings, this book was "sealed" but has now been given to the ideal Israelite king. He further describes the sealed scroll as "the 'book' of God's eternal covenant, the revelation of his salvific acts on behalf of man," which has been partially disclosed to John (i.e., it is in part identical with Revelation itself) but will not be finally opened until the end of history ("Background," 311).

[5] Interpreting the scroll of Rev 5 under the metaphor of a bill of divorce (Deut 24:1–3; Matt 19:7; Mark 10:4; *m. B. Bat.* 10:1–2; *b. B. Bat.* 160a), Ford understands the scroll to represent Christ's divorce of the unfaithful Jerusalem and marriage to

the New Jerusalem (Ford, *JSJ* 2 [1971] 136–43; Ford, 92–94).

3. *The Function of the Scroll.* (a) The sealed scroll clearly serves as a literary device for structuring the narrative of the six plagues that follow the opening of the first six seals, however else it may function. (b) The transfer of the sealed scroll from God to the Lamb clearly functions as a symbol of the unique role of Christ as the Lamb, the sovereignty of Christ, which he received from the Father. This is certainly the view of the author, for when the two hymnic segments of 5:9, 12 are compared, receiving the scroll in v 9 (λαβεῖν τὸ βιβλίον) is parallel to receiving power and wealth and wisdom and might and honor and glory and praise in v 12 (λαβεῖν τὴν δύναμιν κτλ). Irenaeus paraphrases Rev 5:3–7 and seems to interpret the taking of the sealed scroll from the hand of God as "receiving power over all things from the same God who made all things by the Word" (*Adv. haer.* 4.20.2); i.e., the βιβλίον is construed as a symbol of Christ's sovereignty (Stefanovič, "Background," 9–10).

**1b**  κατεσφραγισμένον σφραγῖσιν ἑπτά, "sealed with seven seals." Beyond the obvious allusion to Ezek 2:9–10, there is a possible allusion here to Isa 29:11, in which a revelatory vision of Isaiah is compared to a sealed book, which people complain that they cannot read (i.e., it is a metaphor for spiritual blindness; Kraft, 103), and perhaps to Theod Dan 12:4, 9 as well (Beale, *Daniel*, 201), though there is nothing in the context to confirm these speculations (Fekkes, *Isaiah*, 149–50). However, the extent to which the author uses Daniel may suggest that he is revealing the true meaning of that prophetic book in his own vision narrative. *1 Enoch* 89:71 refers to a book containing the deeds of the "shepherds," written by an archangel scribe covering the first historical period from 89:72–77, which God himself sealed after it was read out to him. The unsealing and reading of this book (89:76–77) involves the punishment of the "shepherds" for what they had destroyed (90:17). According to CD[a] 5:2, David had not read "the sealed book of the law" in the ark and was therefore unaware that Deut 17:17 prohibited a prince from polygamy. The purpose of so many seals was certainly to keep the contents of the scroll completely secret until it is finally opened. 3 Kgdms 20:8(MT 21:8) refers to the sealing of a letter with the king's seal (see *Vita Aesopi* 104 [Denis, *Fragmenta*, 134]). In 4Q550 = 4QProto Esther[a] 4:5 there is a reference to a scroll that Darius, the king's father, had sealed with seven seals: ספריא אשתכח מגלה <ח]כה> חתי[מה חרמי[ן] שבעה *spry ʾšhkh mglh <ḥ[kh> ḥty]mh ḥrmy[n] šbʿh*, "among the books was found a scroll [sealed with] seven seals of the ring of Darius" (Hebrew text: Eisenman, *Scrolls*, 102; translation: García Martínez, *Dead Sea Scrolls*, 291). According to *Gos. Pet.* 8.33 the tomb of Jesus was sealed with seven seals for security reasons (the motif of sealing the tomb is elsewhere mentioned only in Matt 27:66). According to *Par. Jer.* 3:10, God sealed (ὁ σφραγίσας) the earth with seven seals (ἐν ἑπτὰ σσφραγῖσιν) for seven epochs (ἐν ἑπτὰ καιροῖς). The motif of sealing with seven seals is an extremely common device in the world of Jewish magic. The Jewish Aramaic incantation bowls occasionally mention the use of "seven seals" (שבעה חתמין *šbʿh ḥtmyn*), as in text 10.2–3, "You are bound with the seven spells and sealed with the seven seals" (Isbell, *Incantation*, 40; cf. 28.3 [p. 80]; 29.3 [p. 81]; 30.3 [p. 82]; 31.3 [p. 83]). The effectiveness of the use of the divine name in such seals is attested in text 51.6–7 (Isbell, *Incantation*, 116), "with the great seal of the Lord of the Universe [whose] knot cannot be untied and whose seal cannot be broken." The significance of *seven* seals is apparently the impossibility of any unauthorized person gaining access to what has been sealed in such a manner, particularly when sealed by God or in the name of God.

**2a** καὶ εἶδον ἄγγελον ἰσχυρὸν κηρύσσοντα ἐν φωνῇ μεγάλῃ, "Then I saw a mighty angel proclaiming with a loud voice." The scene in vv 2–5 provides the entire section with a strong dramatic element, but that it can easily be omitted without interrupting the flow of the narrative in vv 1, 6–14 suggests that it has been inserted into an existing schema by the author (see Jörns, *Evangelium*, 44–47). The weeping of the seer, which is so central to the episode in vv 2–5, appears to belong to the *past*, reflecting the unfulfilled messianic expectation of the seer. That the narrative is dominated by the two imperfect verbs ἐδύνατο and ἔκλαιον (the aorist tense is the basic narrative tense) indicates that the author is intentionally foregrounding these aspects of this episode. On καὶ εἶδον, see *Comment* on 5:1. The expression, ἄγγελον ἰσχυρόν, "mighty angel," occurs three times in Revelation (5:2; 10:1; 18:21), where it seems to refer to three different angelic beings. Similar descriptions of such supernatural beings occur in the magical papyri: *PGM* III.71, ἄγγελον κραταιὸν καὶ ἰσχυρόν, "a strong and mighty angel"; cf. *PGM* I.172, ὁ κραταιὸς ἄγγελος, "the mighty angel." See *Adam and Eve* 40:2 (οἱ τρεῖς μεγάλοι ἄγγελοι); *Par. Jer.* 4:1 (ὁ μέγας ἄγγελος). The phrase "mighty angel" in Revelation seems to suggest a supernatural being relatively high in the angelic hierarchy; in 5:2 the mighty angel functions as a herald in the heavenly court; in 10:1 he brings a revelation of the nearness of the end; in 18:21 he performs a symbolic action by casting a millstone representing Babylon-Rome into the sea (though these three are not necessarily identical). The phrase ἐν φωνῇ μεγάλῃ, "with a loud voice," is a literal rendering of a Semitic idiom (in Hebrew most commonly בקול גדול *běqôl gādôl*, literally "with a great voice," but also ויצעק צעקה גדלה *wayyiṣ 'aq se 'āqâ gĕdōlâ*, literally "he cried a great cry," Gen 27:34, and תרועה גדולה *tĕrû'â gĕdôlâ*, Ezra 3:11; in Aramaic the phrase בקל עציב *běqāl 'uṣîb*, literally "with a voice of pain," occurs only in Dan 6:21). The noun phrase φωνὴ μεγάλη occurs twenty times in Revelation (1:10; 5:2, 12; 6:10; 7:2, 10; 8:13; 10:3; 11:12, 15 [the plural form φωναὶ μεγάλαι occurs only here]; 12:10; 14:7, 9, 15, 18; 16:1 [in the unusual order μεγάλης φωνῆς]; 16:17; 19:1, 17; 21:3). The same phrase occurs nearly fifty times in the LXX, usually in the dative form φωνῇ μεγάλῃ, three times in the accusative (LXX Gen 27:34; 1 Esdr 3:11; Sir 50:16), and once in the nominative (LXX Esth 1:1). In four additional instances the adjective is placed before the noun (1 Esdr 5:64; 9:10; Prov 2:3; 26:25; cf. Rev 16:1). The phrase also occurs in the Greek texts and fragments of the Pseudepigrapha (*Adam and Eve* 5:2; 29:11; *T. Abr.* 5:9; *Par. Jer.* 2:2; *2 Apoc. Bar.* 11:3; *Sib. Or.* 3.669; 5.63).

**2b** τίς ἄξιος ἀνοῖξαι τὸ βιβλίον καὶ λῦσαι τὰς σφραγῖδας αὐτοῦ, "'Who is worthy to open the book by breaking its seals?'" One must assume that the one holding the scroll has the right and the ability to open it and read it, but it is equally obvious that in this context this is abrogated. The term ἄξιος, "worthy," does not simply mean "able" (i.e., the opposite of οὐδεὶς ἐδύνατο, "no one was able," in v 3), but it means rather "qualified" in the sense of having the proper qualifications to perform this special task. The purpose for opening the scroll is not so that it can be read (nothing is said anywhere in Revelation about the *contents* of the scroll) but so that the eschatological events can begin to take place. V 2b is an instance of *hysteron-proteron* ("last-first"), i.e., the reversal of the logical sequence of events, a figure of speech that occurs several times in Revelation (3:3, 17; 5:5; 6:4; 10:4, 9; 20:4–5, 12–13; 22:14), for surely breaking the seals is the necessary prerequisite for opening the scroll.

**3** καὶ οὐδεὶς ἐδύνατο ἐν τῷ οὐρανῷ οὐδὲ ἐπὶ τῆς γῆς οὐδὲ ὑποκάτω τῆς γῆς ἀνοῖξαι τὸ βιβλίον οὔτε βλέπειν αὐτό, "No one was able, either in heaven or on earth or under the earth, to open the scroll or to look into it." The striking and disappointing conclusion of the universal search for someone worthy to open the sealed book is emphasized here. All of the achievements of all of the priests and prophets of the world do not adequately qualify them for opening this sealed book. Using this dramatic device, the author emphasizes the uniqueness of the conquest of Christ, which he mentions in v 5. Only here and in v 13 is the three-level cosmos of heaven, earth, and underworld mentioned in Revelation (in v 13 the sea is added), though in vv 3, 13 the emphasis is on the beings who populate each of these three zones. The comprehensive way of referring to each of the three major zones of the cosmos is a way of saying "nowhere in the entire universe" (cf. Houtman, *Himmel*, 36–37). The same three divisions of the cosmos are mentioned in the context of the well-known Christ hymn in Phil 2:10, "every knee will bow, in heaven and on earth and under the earth [ἐπουρανίων καὶ ἐπιγείων καὶ καταχθονίων]," and a similar conception occurs within a creedal context in Ignatius *Trall.* 9:1, "those in heaven and on earth and under the earth [τῶν ἐπουρανίων καὶ ἐπιγείων καὶ ὑποχθονίων]." Both of these passages emphasize the denizens of the three-level cosmos (primarily supernatural beings), as in Rev 5:3, 13. In the *T. Sol.* 16:3, Beelzeboul is referred to as the ruler of the spirits of the air and the earth and beneath the earth. The tendency in ancient Roman prayer to be as inclusive as possible often led to the formulation of such phrases as *dique omnes caelestes vosque, terrestres, vosque, inferni, audite,* "hear, all you gods of heaven, of earth, and you of the underworld" (Livy 1.32.10). The same cosmic structure is found throughout the ancient Near East and is reflected in the Egyptian Hymn to the Nile, which refers to "every god, be he in the underworld, in heaven, or upon earth" (*ANET*, 372–73). Though the phrase "under the earth" does not occur elsewhere in Revelation, the related conception "abyss" (which sometimes means "ocean"; cf. 13:1 with 11:7 and 17:8) is found in Rev 9:1, 2, 11; 11:7; 17:8; 20:1, 3, though it is never coordinated with the other divisions of the cosmos except implicitly in 20:1, which describes an angel who descends from heaven (to earth) with a key to the abyss. The Greek term ἄβυσσος, "abyss," is the usual way in which the Hebrew word תְּהוֹם *tĕhôm*, "deep, primeval ocean, sea" (KB³, 1557–59), is translated in the LXX (e.g., Gen 1:2; 7:11; 8:2; Deut 8:7; 33:13). A Greek fragment of *Jub.* 2:2 mentions the creation on the first day of "the spirits of his creatures which are in the heavens and on the earth, the abyss which is under the earth (Denis, *Fragmenta*, 72; however, I emend the impossible phrase τὰς ἀβύσσους, τήν τε ὑποκάτω τῆς γῆς to read τὴν ἄβυσσον τήν τε ὑποκάτω τῆς γῆς). In ancient Israel the association of the deep (תְּהוֹם *tĕhôm*) with the underworld led to the conception of Sheol as a watery abyss (2 Sam 22:5; Jonah 2:1–6; Pss 18:5–6; 42:7–8; 88:3–7; Job 26:5–6; see Stadelmann, *World*, 170). The cosmos is also conceived of as divided into heaven, earth, and abyss in *T. Levi* 3:9; *Jos. As.* 12:2; *PGM* IV.1116–21; *Corp. Herm.* 16.5. Similarly, in *1 Clem.* 28:3, three places where one cannot hide from God are mentioned: heaven, the ends of the earth, the abyss; this is an allusion to Ps 139:8–9 (LXX 138:8–9), where the three places are heaven, Sheol (LXX: Hades), and the uttermost parts of the sea (the earth is assumed). In Rom 10:6–7, heaven and the abyss are mentioned, while earth is presupposed; this is an allusion to Deut 30:12–13, where "heaven" and "beyond the sea" are mentioned. In the ancient Near Eastern and Israelite tripartite conception of the cosmos as heaven, earth, and sea, the "sea" or "ocean" is sometimes understood as the chaotic waters under the earth (Exod 20:4, 11; Deut 5:8), identical with the abyss, as in the phrase τῆς ἀβύσσου τῆς ὕδατος, "the abyss of the water" (*Jos. As.* 12:2; see *PGM* XIII.169–70, 481–84 [parallel], which mentions a god named Eschakleo [or Promsacha Aleeio] who was put in authority over the abyss, "for without him moisture neither increases or decreases"; i.e., he regulates the waters), sometimes as simply "the sea" (Jdt 9:13; *PGM* V.459–63; VII.261). Of course the tripartite world of sea, heaven, and earth also occurs without including the abyss (Gen 1:26–27). The two-level division of the cosmos into (1) heaven and (2) earth and sea occurs several times elsewhere in Revelation (10:5, 6; 12:12; 14:6; 21:1). See *Comment* on 10:6.

**4** καὶ ἔκλαιον πολύ, ὅτι οὐδεὶς ἄξιος εὑρέθη ἀνοῖξαι τὸ βιβλίον οὔτε βλέπειν αὐτό, "Then I wept profusely, because no one was found worthy to open the scroll or to look into it." This dramatic episode may have been influenced by Isa 29:11, "And the vision of all this has become to you like the words of a book that is sealed. When men give it to one who can read, saying, 'Read this,' he says, 'I cannot, for it is sealed.'"

**5a** καὶ εἷς ἐκ τῶν πρεσβυτέρων λέγει μοι, "Then one of the elders said to me." Here, as in 7:13, an elder serves as a narrator, analogous to the narrative role of particular bowl angels in 17:1; 21:9. Normally in apocalypses the seer asks one or more questions of a supernatural revealer that together with the answers form a revelatory dialogue. This apocalyptic literary technique is strikingly absent from Revelation.

**5b** μὴ κλαῖε, ἰδοὺ ἐνίκησεν ὁ λέων ὁ ἐκ τῆς φυλῆς Ἰούδα, ἡ ῥίζα Δαυίδ, ἀνοῖξαι τὸ βιβλίον καὶ τὰς ἑπτὰ σφραγῖδας αὐτοῦ, "'Stop weeping, behold the lion of the tribe of Judah, the descendant of David, he has conquered so that he is able to open the book and its seven seals.'" The weeping of the seer is probably linked with the initial promise at the beginning of this vision that he would learn about impending future events (4:1), which now appears impossible of fulfillment. On the phenomenon of *hysteron-proteron* ("last-first") in the reversed order of "open the book" and "open its seals," see *Comment* on 3:3. A prohibition with the present tense is usually taken to mean that action already in progress is being forbidden; i.e., the seer is weeping, v 4 (see Moulton, *Prolegomena*, 122–26); however, this rule has been called into serious question (Louw, *AcCl* 2 [1959] 43–57; Fanning, *Verbal Aspect*, 335–40) and does not appear to be applicable here. The fact that the verb νικᾶν, "to conquer," is used without an object limiting the scope of victory suggests that his victory is unlimited and absolute (Rissi, *Int* 22 [1968] 7). It has been pointed out by many scholars that the Aramaic term זְכָא *zĕkā'* means both "to conquer" and "to be worthy" (Levy, *Wörterbuch* 1:534–35; Dalman, *Handwörterbuch*, 128; *TDNT* 4:943 n. 6), thus linking the verb ἐνίκησεν, "he conquered," here in v 5 with the phrase ἄξιος εἶ, "you are worthy," in v 9 (Scott, *Apocalypse*, 20; Torrey, *Apocalypse*, 107–8). The use of the term νικᾶν for the salvific death of Jesus has partial parallels in Paul's allusion to Isa 25:8 in 1 Cor 15:54, "Death is swallowed up in victory [νῖκος]," and in John 16:33, where the saying is attributed to Jesus, "I have conquered [νενίκηκα] the world" (cf. Holtz, *Christologie*, 37 n. 3). The atoning death of Christ, conceptualized as conflict resulting in victory, reflects the classic idea of the atonement in which Christ fights against and triumphs over all the evil powers in the world, under whom human beings were in bondage and suffering, and decisively triumphs over them, thereby reconciling the world to himself (Aulén, *Christus Victor*, 4; cf. Cousar, *Cross*, 83–84). The background for this conflict imagery is probably that strand of early Jewish eschatological anticipation that expected the Messiah to conquer hostile forces (Rev 19:11–21; see Spitta, 74). The claim that νικᾶν is used as an eschatological technical term in Rev 5:5 is groundless (G. Reichelt, *Buch,* 131).

Of the two messianic titles in this passage, "the Lion of the tribe of Judah" is an allusion to Gen 49:9 (Str-B, 3:801) and "the Root of David" is an allusion to Isa 11:1, 10 (where the phrase ἡ ῥίζα τοῦ Ἰεσσαί, "the root of Jesse," may already be used as a messianic title; see C. Maurer, *TDNT* 6:986–87). An expanded form of this title occurs in Rev 22:16 in the self-designation "I am the Root and Descendant of David." Both Gen 49:9 ("lion of Judah") and Isa 11:1, 10 ("root of Jesse") were important messianic texts in early Judaism and early Christianity:

(1) The motif of the Messiah as a *lion* occurs in early Judaism (see the lion in 4 Ezra 11:36–46, interpreted in 12:31–34) and early Christianity (Justin *Dial.* 52.2; Ps.-Epiphanius *Test.* 71.3). Judah is called a lion in Gen 49:9 (as is the tribe of Dan in Deut 33:22). In a Jewish inscription from Sardis dating to the late second century A.D., a tribe of Jews is called Λεόντιοι, "Leontioi" (Robert, *Sardes,* 45-46; Lifshitz, *Donateurs,* no. 19), a name that Robert understands as a way of referring to the tribe of Judah (*Sardes,* 47). Here the lion of the tribe of Judah, i.e., the Davidic Messiah (who turns out to be the slain Lamb of v 6), is the subject of the verb νικᾶν; elsewhere in Revelation it is only in 17:14 (a redactional passage) that the Lamb is the subject of the verb νικᾶν. Elsewhere in the NT, in John 16:33, Jesus says "I have conquered [νενίκηκα] the world," and in 1 Cor 15:57 Paul praises God "who gives us victory [νῖκος] through our Lord Jesus Christ." In early Christian magic the νικᾷ acclamation, often expressed with the formula "Jesus Christ is victorious" (Daniel-Maltomini, *Supplementum Magicum,* no. 25), occurs frequently, often in an exorcistic context (Peterson, *Εἷς Θεός,* 152–63; H. Heinen, "Eine neue alexandrinische Inschrift und die mitteralterichen *laudes regiae,*" in *Romanitas-Christianitas,* ed. G. Wirth [Berlin; New York: de Gruyter, 1982] 683 n. 17).

(2) In the phrase "the Root of David," "root" (צֶמַח *semaḥ*) is used in a royal or messianic sense found earlier in OT prophetic literature (Maurer, *TDNT* 6:985–90). The messianic term ῥίζα, "root," is also used in Rev 22:16 in the phrase ἡ ῥίζα καὶ τὸ γένος Δαυίδ, "the root and offspring of David." The coming new king from the house of David was called צֶמַח *semaḥ,* "Branch," in Jer 23:5 (LXX ἀνατολή); 33:15 (omitted in MT); Zech 3:8 (Greek ἀνατολή); 6:12 (ἀνατολή); 4Q252 = 4QGenesis Pesher 5:3–4 (עד בוא משיח הצדק צמח דויד *'ad bōʾ māšîaḥ haṣṣedek ṣemaḥ dāwîd,* "until the messiah of righteousness, the branch of David, comes"); 4Q285 7:1–4 (Isa 11:1 is interpreted to refer to the צמח דויד *ṣemaḥ dawîd,* "Branch of David," referred to in Jeremiah and Zechariah). Two different terms for the Davidic king are used in a parallel couplet in Isa 11:1, "A shoot [חטר *ḥōṭer;* LXX ῥάβδος] shall come out from the stump of Jesse [ישי גזע *gezaʿ yišay;* LXX ἡ ῥίζα τοῦ Ἰεσσαί], and a branch [נצר *nēṣer;* ἄνθος] shall grow out of his roots." Yet another term from the same semantic field, שרש *šōreš,* "root," is used in Isa 11:10, "On that day the root of Jesse [ישי שרש *šōreš yišay;* LXX ἡ ῥίζα τοῦ Ἰεσσαί] shall stand as a signal to the peoples." This motif was derived from early Jewish messianic tradition (4Q174 = 4QFlor 1–3 i 12; 4QPatriarchal Blessings 3–4 [interpreting Gen 49:10]; 4QpIsaᵃ 3:15–22; 4Q285 7:1–4; *T. Judah* 24:4–6; Sir 47:22; 4 Ezra 12:32 ["from the offspring of David" is absent from the Latin MSS but present in the Syriac, Ethiopic, and Arabic MSS; see B. Violet, *Die Esra-Apokalypse* (Leipzig: Hinrichs, 1910–24) 1:356–

57]; *Tg. Isa* 11:1, 10), which was the source for its use in early Christianity (Rom 15:12; Justin *2 Apol.* 32.12–13; *Dial.* 52.2; 86.4; *Apost. Const.* 6.11; Hippolytus *De antichristo* 8; Ps.-Epiphanius *Test.* 5.23, 27; Victorinus *Comm. in Apoc.* 2 [ed. Haussleiter, *Victorinus,* 62–63]). The emphases on the tribe of Judah and on Davidic descent together underline one of the crucial qualifications of the Jewish royal Messiah: he must be a descendant of the royal house of David (*Pss. Sol.* 17:21; Mark 12:35–37; John 7:42), sometimes conceived as David *redivivus* (Jer 23:5; 30:9). Descent from the tribe of Judah (Heb 7:14), and more specifically the Davidic descent of Jesus, is frequently mentioned in the NT and early Christian literature (Matt 1:1, 6; Luke 1:32, 69; 2:4; 3:31; Acts 2:30–32; 13:22–23; Rom 1:3; 2 Tim 2:8; Ignatius *Eph.* 18:2; 20:2; *Rom.* 17:3; *Smyrn.* 1:1), and he is frequently called "son of David" (Matt 1:1; 9:27; 12:23; 15:22; 20:30; Mark 10:47–48; 12:35; Luke 18:38–39; *Barn.* 12:10).

The close connection between the death of Jesus (here under the metaphor of "conquest") and the sealed book that he alone is able to open has a peculiar parallel in *Gos. Truth* 19.34–20.27 (tr. Attridge-MacRae, in Attridge, *Nag Hammadi Codex I,* 87): "There was manifested in their heart the living book of the living—the one written in the thought and the mind [of the] Father, which from before the foundation of the totality was within his incomprehensibility—that (book) *which no one was able to take* [Rev 5:4–5], *since it remains for the one who will take it to be slain* [Rev 5:9] . . . . For this reason the merciful one, the faithful one, Jesus, was patient in accepting sufferings until *he took that book* [Rev 5:4] since he knows that his death is life for many. Just as there lies hidden in a will [διαθήκη], before it is opened, the fortune of the deceased master of the house, so (it is) with the totality, which lay hidden while the Father of the totality was invisible, being something which is from him, from whom every space comes forth. For this reason Jesus appeared; he put on that book; he was nailed to a tree; he published the edict of the Father on the cross." On this difficult passage, see Ménard, *Vérité,* 110–13, and Attridge-MacRae, in Attridge, *Nag Hammadi Codex I Notes,* 57–60.

**6a** καὶ εἶδον ἐν μέσῳ τοῦ θρόνου καὶ τῶν τεσσάρων ζῴων καὶ ἐν μέσῳ τῶν πρεσβυτέρων ἀρνίον ἑστηκὸς ὡς ἐσφαγμένον, "Then I saw, between the throne and the four cherubim and the elders, a lamb standing as though slaughtered." An important interpretive issue here is the problem of why the Lamb, who has not been seen by John before, suddenly appears on the scene. It could simply be for dramatic purposes, just as the scroll in the right hand of the One seated on the throne is not mentioned in Rev 4 but is suddenly the focus of attention in 5:1. It has also been suggested (less probably) that the appearance of the Lamb in the heavenly court indicates Christ's ascent to heaven as if it has just now been accomplished (1 Tim 3:16; Phil 2:9; Eph 1:22; Müller, *ZNW* 54 [1963] 256; Holtz, *Christologie,* 29–31; however, the phrase ὤφθη ἀγγέλοις in 2 Tim 3:16 probably means "seen by messengers [i.e., 'apostles']"; see R. Lülsdorff, "ΕΚΛΕΚΤΟΙ ΑΓΓΕΛΟΙ," *BZ* 36 [1992] 104–8). On καὶ εἶδον, see *Comment* on 5:1. The way in which the location of the Lamb is described as "in the midst of" the throne and the four cherubim and "in the midst of" the twenty-four elders is problematic and can be understood in two ways: (1) ἐν μέσῳ can refer to a position in the middle of an area and mean "in the middle" or "in the midst" (Louw-Nida, § 83.10). Thus BAGD, 570, suggests the translation "on the center of the throne and among the four living creatures." Therefore, if the two ἐν μέσῳ phrases are parallel, it could indicate that the Lamb is at the center of everything described, as in 7:17 (Bousset [1906] 257). This seems unlikely, however, since the narrator says that the Lamb "came and took" the scroll from the one seated on the throne (v 7), suggesting that he was somewhat removed from the throne of God. Glasson has suggested that this throne is a dais with more than one occupant, as elsewhere in Revelation (43–44; Giesen, 58). (2) ἐν μέσῳ can refer to the interval between two things, reflecting the Hebrew idiom בין ובין *bên ûbên,* found in Lev 27:12, translated ἀνὰ μέσον καὶ ἀνὰ μέσον in the LXX, and so can mean that the position of the Lamb is "between" the throne and the four cherubim, on the one hand, and the elders, on the other (Charles, 1:140; Delebecque, 182), or between the elders and the middle of the throne, i.e., the four cherubim. (3) ἐν μέσῳ can also refer to a position within an area occupied by other objects and mean "among, with" (Louw-Nida, § 83.9). According to this view, which is probably the correct one, the Lamb would be standing in close proximity to the throne.

The term ἀρνίον, "lamb," occurs twenty-nine times in Revelation (all references to Jesus with the exception of 13:11) and is the most frequent title for Jesus (for a full discussion of ἀρνίον and theories of its origin, see *Excursus 5A: Christ as the Lamb*). As a title or designation for Jesus, ἀρνίον was a contribution of the author even though he made use of a number of traditional motifs in designating this eclectic figure as the ἀρνίον. The two main constituent traditions that stand behind the figure of Christ as the Lamb are the *lamb as ruler or leader* and the *lamb as a sacrificial metaphor* (see *Excursus 5A*). The figure of the Lamb first appears in Revelation here in v 6, and vv 5–6 capture the two complementary aspects of this apocalyptic metaphor, namely, Jesus as the conquering Messiah (v 5) and Jesus as the atoning sacrificial victim (v 6). This dual presentation of the salvific function of Jesus as the crucified Messiah, i.e., in terms of a *theologia crucis,* "theology of the cross," and a *theologia gloriae,* "theology of glory," pervades various phases of early Christianity, including the Gospel of Mark, the letters of Paul, and the Fourth Gospel. While this "irony of kingship through crucifixion" (L. L. Thompson, *Revelation,* 48–40, 65) is certainly a central theological emphasis here in Rev 5, it is a marginal conception elsewhere in the book (cf. 1:7; 19:13). In 1 Cor 1:23–24, Paul emphasizes these same two antithetical features of the role of Jesus: "We proclaim Christ crucified, a stumbling block to Jews and foolishness to Gentiles, but to those who are the called, both Jews and Greeks, Christ the power of God and the wisdom of God."

That the Lamb is "standing" is a significant detail in the narrative (the Lamb is also described as "standing" on Mount Zion; see *Comment* on 14:1), which contrasts with the description of the twenty-four elders *seated* on thrones (see *Comment* on 4:4). In Revelation the heavenly beings are occasionally described as *standing* before the throne of God (7:9, 11; 8:2). This coheres with a widespread rabbinic notion (with roots in the OT) that only God was allowed to be seated in heaven and that all who entered the heavenly court or surrounded the throne had to stand (1 Kgs 22:19; 2 Chr 18:18; Isa 6:2; Jer 23:18, 22; Dan 7:10; Gk. *1 Enoch* 14:22; *2 Apoc. Bar.* 21:6; 48:10; *T. Abr.* [Rec. A] 4:5; 8:1; 9:7; 15:11; 16:3; *T. Levi* 2:10; *b. Ḥag.* 15a; *y. Ber.* 2c.23; *Pesiq. R.* 22:6; *Gen. Rab.* 65:21; *Lev. Rab.* 6:3; *3 Enoch* 18:24). Further, Israelite priests and other worshipers are often described as "standing" before the Lord (Deut 10:8; 17:12; 18:5, 7; 1 Sam 1:26; Pss 24:3; 134:1; 135:2; Jer 7:10; 15:1; 15:19; 1 Esdr 8:90; Jdt 4:14; 1 Macc 7:36). The statement that the Lamb is "standing" may be an oblique reference to the *resurrection* of Jesus, perhaps already alluded to in v 5, where it is said that "he has conquered." Rulers are often depicted as seated, while those around them are standing (1 Kgs 22:10, 19; Neh 2:6; Esth 5:1–2; Jer 36:21; Dan 1:5, 19; 2:2), and the protocol associated with the royal court was undoubtedly applied to the descriptions of priestly service and the service of angelic beings in the heavenly court.

The phrase "the slaughtered Lamb" is also found in 5:12; 13:8. Here the fact that the adjectival participle ἐσφαγμένον, "slaughtered," is introduced with the comparative particle ὡς, "as, like," does not mean that the Lamb only *appeared* to have been slaughtered but rather that the Lamb had been slaughtered and was now alive, thus combining the two theological motifs of death and resurrection. The phrase ὡς ἐσφαγμένον is also used of one of the heads of the Beast from the Sea in 13:3, perhaps intended by the author as a negative counterpart to Christ. The basic term for sacrifice in the OT is זָבַח *zābaḥ*, meaning "to slaughter" (see *TWAT* 2:509–31), though σφάζειν is only used twice in the LXX to translate זָבַח *zābaḥ* (Lev 17:5; Ezek 34:3). The slaughtered Lamb suggests a background in the Jewish Passover festival (N. Hillyer, *EvQ* 39 [1967] 228–36), while references to "the blood of the Lamb" (7:14; 12:11; see *Comment* on 7:14), to "his [Jesus'] blood" (1:5), and to "your [Jesus'] blood" (5:9) suggest a background in the blood ritual of Israelite-Jewish expiatory sacrifice (Daly, *Origins*, 25–35; id., *Christian Sacrifice*, 87–138); see the more extended discussion in *Excursus 5A: Christ as the Lamb*. The conception of the death of Jesus as analogous to the sacrifice of the Passover lamb is mentioned as early as Paul (1 Cor 5:7; see 1 Pet 1:19; Justin *Dial.* 111.3) and is a notion that achieves central significance in the theology of the Fourth Gospel, where Jesus is expressly designated "the Lamb of God" (John 1:29, 36). The Fourth Evangelist even alters the chronology of Passion week so that Jesus is crucified precisely when the Passover lambs are slaughtered in the temple on 14 Nisan (John 19:14). The reference in Isa 53:7 to the servant of the Lord who is "led like a lamb to the slaughter" (ὡς πρόβατον ἐπὶ σφαγὴν ἤχθη, which may be alluded to in the phrase ἀρνίον ἑστηκὸς ὡς ἐσφαγμένον) is frequently applied to the trial and execution of Jesus (Acts 8:32; *Barn.* 5:2; *1 Clem.* 16:7; Justin *Dial.* 72.3; 114.2). Malina has argued improbably that the vision of the Lamb was based on the constellation Aries, a lamb/ram looking backward, as if its neck were broken, i.e., as if it were "slaughtered" (*Revelation*, 78–79, citing Manilius *Astron.* 1.263–64). However, lambs or rams were not slaughtered in the ancient world by breaking their necks (like poultry), and they are perfectly capable of looking behind themselves.

**6b** ἔχων κέρατα ἑπτὰ καὶ ὀφθαλμοὺς ἑπτά, "with seven horns and seven eyes." The reference to "seven eyes" is an allusion to Zech 4:10, where the seven lamps of fire in Zech 4:2 (see Rev 4:5), located on the menorah in the temple, are identified as the "seven eyes" of the Lord (a symbol for divine omniscience), identified in Rev 5:6c as the seven spirits of God, i.e., the seven archangels before the throne (see *Comment* on 1:4). The mention of *seven* horns and *seven* eyes suggests that this is a redactional description intended to introduce the interpretation found in v 6c. The horn is frequently a symbol of power (Jer 48:25; Pss 18:1–3; 75:10[MT 75:11]; 89:17[MT 88:18]; 92:10[MT 92:11]; 132:17[MT 131:17]; Dan 7:20–21; 8:3–4, *1 Enoch* 90:37; see *RAC* 16:547, 550–51), often royal power (Ps 132:17; Dan 7:7–8, 11–12 [a succession of horns symbolizes a succession of kings]). The Messiah is never symbolized as a lamb in Judaism, and the special attributes of seven horns and seven eyes together suggest that this composite image is the creation of the author, though the elements are drawn from traditional imagery. In 1QSb 5:26, the Prince of the Congregation is addressed in a way that suggests messianic conceptions: "may he [the Lord] make your horns [קרניכה *qrnykh*] iron and your hooves bronze" (*RAC* 16:550–51). This steer imagery (perhaps derived from Deut 33:17) has a counterpart in *1 Enoch* 90:37, in which a "white bull," apparently representing the Messiah, is described as having large horns (Spitta, 72). The phrase "the horn of the Messiah" occurs with some frequency in rabbinic literature (Str-B, 1:10; 2:111). The eye is frequently a symbol of divine omniscience or omnipresence (2 Chr 16:9; Job 28:10; Pss 34:15; 139:16; Prov 15:3; Sir 11:12; 17:15, 19; 23:19; 39:19; 1 Pet 3:12; Heb 4:13; Pol. *Phil.* 6:2). Both the seven horns and the seven eyes are appropriate symbols for the "Lion of the tribe of Judah," i.e., the Davidic Messiah (v 5).

**6c** οἵ εἰσιν τὰ ἑπτὰ πνεύματα τοῦ θεοῦ ἀπεσταλμένοι εἰς πᾶσαν τὴν γῆν, "(these are the seven spirits of God sent to the entire earth)." Here the metaphorical significance of the seven eyes is explained, while the meaning of the seven horns is left unexplained. The seven spirits of God have been mentioned in various ways earlier in Revelation: they have been described as "before the throne" in the epistolary prescript in 1:4; the exalted Christ is described as the one who has the seven spirits of God and the seven stars (3:1); the seven burning torches "before the throne" (see 1:4) are allegorically interpreted as the seven spirits of God in 4:5. While this phrase has often been considered an interpretive gloss added by a redactor (Spitta, 67; Weiss-Heitmüller, 258), it seems likely that v 6b is actually part of the author's final revision of this visionary episode. The association of *eyes* with the seven spirits of God is appropriate, for there is an allusion here to Zech 4:10, "These seven [lamps; see v 2] are the eyes of the Lord, which range through the whole earth." The number seven itself is important so that the seven horns and seven eyes *both* appear to be interpreted as the seven spirits of God.

**7** καὶ ἦλθεν καὶ εἴληφεν ἐκ τῆς δεξιᾶς τοῦ καθημένου ἐπὶ τοῦ θρόνου, "He came and took the scroll from the right hand of the One seated on the throne." The center of the action is highlighted by using the perfect εἴληφεν, "took," which contrasts with the aorist, the characteristic background tense used in narratives. While the stereotypical seated figure holding a closed scroll in his right hand rests the scroll in his lap (Birt, *Buchrolle*, 86–89), probably the image in 5:1, this passage presupposes that the scroll is held in an extended right hand, for which there are also iconographical parallels (Birt, *Buchrolle*, 90). The reason for specifying the *right* hand is that the right hand had the positive cultural associations of success and fortune (Gornatowski, "Rechts," 45ff.), in contrast with the left hand, which had negative associations. Further, the right hand was the culturally accepted hand for giving and taking (Birt, *Buchrolle*, 82), a notion fossilized in the etymology of δεξίος, which is related both to δεξιόομαι, "to take with the right hand," and to δέχομαι, "to take, receive" (Frisk, *Wörterbuch* 1:366–67, 373–74). This suggests that the scroll is depicted as held in the right hand of God precisely because it is God's intention to give the scroll to another. Though there are no intentional verbal parallels, the author also depicts himself taking a scroll from the outstretched hand of the standing angel in 10:10. *Gos. Truth* 20.12 (probably not dependent on Revelation) speaks of Jesus who "took that book," which "no one was able to take" (20.4), apparently referring to the destiny of Jesus. That a four-footed creature is depicted as "taking" the sealed scroll from the hand of God indicates the perils of taking such imagery literally. *Deut. Rab.* 11.10 mentions that Moses "received the Law from the right hand of God" (Freedman, *Midrash Rabbah* 7:185).

**8a** καὶ ὅτε ἔλαβεν τὸ βιβλίον, τὰ τέσσαρα ζῷα καὶ οἱ εἴκοσι τέσσαρες πρεσβύτεροι ἔπεσαν ἐνώπιον τοῦ ἀρνίου, "And when he took the scroll, the four cherubim and the twenty-four elders fell down before the Lamb." The instantaneous adoration of the heavenly court underscores the significance of the Lamb's action in taking the scroll from God. This verse introduces a section consisting of vv 8–12, which, more than any other passage in Revelation (or in the NT generally), centers on the worship of Christ as the Lamb (Swete, 127; Bauckham, "The Worship of Jesus," 118–49; id., "Jesus, Worship of," *ADB* 3:812–19; id., *Theology*, 58–63). Two reservations, however, are in order: (1) The verb προσκυνεῖν, "worship," is conspicuous by its absence, and (2) God, as "the One who sits on the throne," and the Lamb are kept separate in v 14. It is important to note that this clause is closely parallel to one that occurred earlier in 4:10, in which the object of worship was the One seated on the throne: πεσοῦνται οἱ εἴκοσι τέσσαρες πρεσβύτεροι ἐνώπιον τοῦ καθημένου ἐπὶ τοῦ θρόνου, "the twenty-four elders prostrate themselves before the One sitting on the throne." There are several scenes of worship in which the initial action involves falling down before God and worshiping him (using the two verbs πίπτειν and προσκυνεῖν), but always varying somewhat in phraseology (4:10; 7:11; 11:16; 19:4). Rev 5:8, however, is the only scene in Revelation in which members of the heavenly court fall down before the Lamb, though the term προσκυνεῖν, as already noted above, is conspicuously absent, thus suggesting a degree of subordination (Beskow, *Rex Gloriae*, 140–41). Irenaeus paraphrases Rev 5:3–7 and seems to interpret the taking of the sealed scroll from the hand of God as "receiving power over all things from the same God who made all things by the Word" (*Adv. haer.* 4.20.2); i.e., the βιβλίον is construed as a symbol of Christ's sovereignty (Stefanovič, "Background," 9–10).

**8b** ἔχοντες ἕκαστος κιθάραν καὶ φιάλας χρυσᾶς γεμούσας θυμιαμάτων, "each with a kithara and a golden pan filled with incense." The term κιθάρα, "kithara," occurs three times in Revelation (5:8; 14:2; 15:2; elsewhere in the NT only in 1 Cor 14:7). The verb κιθαρίζειν, "to play the kithara," occurs once (14:2), and the *nomen professionis*, κιθαρῳδός, "kithara-player," twice (14:2; 18:22). Ignatius refers to the κιθάρα twice (*Eph.* 4:1–2; *Phld.* 1:2); both passages use the relationship of the kithara to its strings as a metaphor of social and religious harmony. It has been suggested that liturgical music was accompanied by the kithara at Ephesus; see J. Foster, "The Harp at Ephesus," *ExpTim* 74 [1962–63] 156.

Since each of the twenty-four elders holds both a kithara and a golden incense pan, it is difficult to imagine how the author thought that they could play the former without first disposing of the latter (see *Apoc. Mos.* 38.2, where *some* angels have censers [θυμιατήρια], while *others* have kitharas, and bowls and trumpets [κιθάρας καὶ φιάλας καὶ σάλπιγγας]). Yet the scene is not as awkward as it appears, for several Attic red-figured vases depict a libation scene with Apollo holding a kithara in his left hand and a φιάλη, or wide shallow drinking dish, in his right (Maas-Snyder, *Stringed Instruments,* 71, plate 1; 77, plate 16; 78, plate 19; 100, plate 2), suggesting that this represents a typical way in which a worship scene can be visualized.

There is a close association in the OT and early Jewish literature between hymns and the kithara or lyre, a stringed instrument commonly used to accompany songs of praise (Pss 33:2–3[LXX 32:2–3]; 43:4[LXX 42:4]; 57:7–9[LXX 56:7–9]; 71:22[LXX 70:22]; 81:1–3[LXX 80:1–3]; 92:1–3[LXX 91:1–3]; 98:4–6[LXX 97:4–

6]; 108:1–3[LXX 107:1–3]; 147:7[LXX 146:7]; 150:3–5; 1 Macc 4:54; *T. Job* 14.1–3). All the preceding texts from the Psalms used κιθάρα to translate כנור *kinnôr*, except Ps 81:2[LXX 80:2], where the Hebrew term behind κιθάρα is נבל *nēbel*. The *kinnôr* (כנור), "lyre, kithara," is the most frequently mentioned instrument in the OT (Gressmann, *Musik,* 24–26) and appears to have originated in Assyria (Gerson-Kiwi, "Musique," *DBSup* 5:1422). The noun κιννύρα and the verb κιννύρεσθαι are Phoenician loanwords in Hebrew (Gressmann, *Musik,* 24). A fragmentary text from Ras Shamra contains a Hurrian cult hymn with notations of chords to be played in accompaniment on a lyre (see Kilmer et al., *Sounds*). Several ancient lyres have been discovered in archeological excavations; see Pritchard, *ANEP,* fig. 206. Josephus claims that the κιννύρα (a Greek transliteration of כנור) has ten strings that were struck with a plectrum, while the νάβλα (a Greek transliteration of נבל) had twelve strings that were plucked with the fingers (*Ant.* 7.305–6). The harp (Syriac קיתר *qytr,* a transliteration of κιθάρα) is linked to songs of praise in *Odes Sol.* 7:17; 26:3 (see metaphorical uses of harp imagery in *Odes Sol.* 6:1; 14:8).

Though the elders are not actually depicted as singing to their own musical accompaniment in 5:8, that idea is clearly intended both here and in 14:2; 15:2 as well. According to *m. ʿArak.* 2:5, there were never less than nine lyres in the temple. In Greek tradition the kithara (κιθάρα) is a more elaborate form of the lyre (λύρα) and had strings of equal length (harps have strings of unequal length), which are played by plucking. In the Greek world, the lyre and the flute were the only instruments used in serious music. The sound box was made from the carapace of a tortoise (cf. *Hom. Hymn to Hermes* 39–61) or a wooden box of similar shape with ox hide stretched over the concave side.

The word φιάλη, usually translated "bowl" (RSV; NRSV; NEB; REB; NIV; Louw-Nida, § 6.124), must be understood in this context as a *cultic utensil* and is therefore translated "bowl used in offerings" by BAGD, 858, and *Opferschale,* "offering dish," by Bauer-Aland, 1711. The term φιάλη occurs twelve times in Revelation (5:8; 15:7; 16:1, 2, 3, 4, 8, 10, 12, 17; 17:1; 21:9). The meaning of φιάλη in 5:8, however, appears to be slightly different from the meaning of φιάλη in the other eleven references. Here the φιάλαι are filled with incense and are used in a positive, beneficial way, while in the other references the φιάλαι are said to contain the wrath of God and are used to inflict punishments on the earth and its inhabitants. The problem in understanding the significance of these "offering bowls" or "incense pans" lies in determining whether the author intentionally modeled them after Israelite cultic utensils (which presumably were also used in the second temple until its destruction in A.D. 70) or he based these "offering bowls" on more general conceptions of cultic usage and sacrificial practice common to Greeks and Romans as well as Jews. Here we are certainly dealing with the early Jewish conception that angelic beings function as the heavenly priests of God, so that cultic furnishings (e.g., the altar of incense, the ark of the covenant), cultic utensils (e.g., incense pans, censers, libation bowls), places of worship (e.g., the tabernacle, the temple), and cultic liturgies (the *sanctus,* doxologies, hymns) are all part of the heavenly worship of God presided over and accomplished by angelic beings. In OT accounts of the furnishings of the tabernacle (in most respects a back-projection to the wilderness period of the furnishings of the Solomonic temple from the period of the monarchy) and the temple, each major piece of furniture had an appropriate set of utensils. The four major pieces of furniture with such utensils included (Haran,

*Temples*, 156–57): (1) the table of the presence, resembling an altar (Ezek 41:21–22) with four types of vessels: bowls, ladles, jugs, and jars (Exod 25:29; 31:8; 35:13; 37:16; 39:36; Num 4:7; Jos. *Ant*. 3.142–43; *Ep. Arist*. 50–82 = Jos. *Ant*. 12.60–84), (2) the altar of incense, with no specific mention of utensils (Exod 30:1–10; 37:25–39; 1 Kgs 6:20–21; 7:48; 2 Chr 26:16), (3) the menorah, with tongs, trays or firepans, lamps, and oil utensils (Exod 25:37–39; 31:8; 37:23–24; 39:37; Num 4:9–10), and (4) the outer bronze altar, with pails, scrapers, basins, forks, and firepans (Exod 27:3; 31:8; 38:3; 40:10; Num 4:14; Jos. *Ant*. 3.140). Two parallel passages, Exod 25:29 and 37:16, differentiate *four* different types of cultic vessels made of gold and kept on the table of presence (a designation found only in Num 4:7; cf. Lev 24:6; 2 Chr 13:11; 28:18; 1 Kgs 7:48). According to Exod 25:29, "And you shall make its plates [קערות *qĕʿārōt*/τρυβλία] and dishes for incense [כפות *kappôt*/θυίσκας], and its flagons [קשות *qĕśāôt*/σπονδεῖα] and bowls [מנקיות *mĕnaqqiyyôt*/κυάθους] with which to pour libations; of pure gold you shall make them." Each of these four vessels apparently had a distinct function (Durham, *Exodus*, 361–62): (1) The קערה, or τρυβλίον, appears to have been a golden dish or plate for the bread of the presence, mentioned only in Exodus and Numbers (Kelso, *Ceramic*, 31, no. 77). (2) The כף *cap*, or θυίσκη, was a small cup or bowl in which frankincense was placed (Kelso, *Ceramic*, 22, no. 47; Nielsen, *Incense*, 41). The cups were important enough to be mentioned in Jer 52:18 in a list of temple vessels carried off to Babylon. There is a tendency among scholars to describe the כף as a spoon or ladle (see Nielsen, *Incense*, 41–42).

This vessel is pictured as a cup on the Arch of Titus, where there is a frieze depicting the triumphal procession of Titus in his victory over the Jews. The menorah and the table of shewbread are depicted, and on the table sits (precariously) a cup or goblet about six inches high and five inches in diameter (in proportion to the human faces nearby). Most pictures of this frieze do not clearly show the cup; see A. Bonanno, *Roman Relief Portraiture to Septimus Severus*, BARevSup 6 (Oxford: British Archaeological Reports, 1976) plate 140; F. Magi, "Ancora sull' Arco di Tito," *Mitteilungen des deutschen archaeologischen Instituts, Römische Abteilung* 84 (1977) 331–47, plate 150. Though a definitive treatment of the Arch of Titus is lacking, the most comprehensive treatment is K. Lehmann-Hartleben, "L'Arco di Tito," *Bulletino della Commissione Archeologicale Comunale di Roma* 62 (1934) 89–122.

(3) The קשוה *qaśwâ*, or σπονδεῖον, was a pitcher for pouring a libation of wine into a מנקיה *mĕnaqqiyyâ*, "bowl," both of which stood on the table of the presence (Kelso, *Ceramic*, 31, no. 78), and (4) the מנקיה *mĕnaqqiyyâ*, or κύαθος, was a bowl into which the libation was poured (Kelso, *Ceramic*, 24, no. 54). *Ep. Arist*. 33 (cf. Jos. *Ant*. 12.40) mentions *three* rather than four types of vessels: "mixing bowls, bowls, a table, and libation bowls of gold" (κρατήρων τε καὶ φιαλῶν καὶ τραπέζης καὶ σπονδείων χρυσίου). It is noteworthy that Josephus uses the Greek terminology of the *Epistle of Aristeas*, which has no relationship to the terminology of the LXX. The longer description in *Ep. Arist*. 42 (which Josephus abbreviates) reports that twenty gold and thirty silver bowls (φιάλαι) were constructed, as well as five mixing bowls (κρατῆραι), while closer descriptions of the gold and silver mixing bowls (κρατῆραι) and the golden bowls (χρυσᾶς φιάλας) are found in *Ep. Arist*. 73–79 (cf. Jos. *Ant*. 12.78–82). Josephus makes no attempt to harmonize either the number or the names of the vessels used in connection with the table of the presence he found in the *Epistle of Aristeas* with his earlier account in *Ant*. 3.143 (where he was dependent

on Exod 25:29, which mentions *four* utensils); he mentions only *two* kinds of objects on the table of the presence, the bread of the presence and two bowls of gold filled with incense (φιάλαι δύο χρύσεαι λιβάνου πλήρεις), in apparent continuity with Lev 24:5–7 and in agreement with *m. Menah.* 11:5–8. In *Ant.* 3.256, however, he speaks of "two golden plates filled with frankincense" (δύο δὲ χρυσέων . . . πινάκων λιβανωτοῦ γεμόντων). The ritual procedure was that after the old loaves of the presence and the bowls of incense were replaced, the incense was burned (on the golden altar) and the loaves were eaten by the priests (*m. Menah.* 11:7). Therefore, since the φιάλαι in Rev 5:8 are used not to pour libations but simply to contain incense, they correspond most closely to the incense pans (כפות *kappôt*) of Exod 25:29; 37:16, the only vessels used in connection with the table of the presence according to Josephus *Ant.* 3.143 and *m. Menah.* 11:5–8. Three iron incense shovels from the eighth century B.C. have been excavated at Tel Dan (pictured and described in *BARev* 15 [1989] 31). That the twenty-four elders have harps and incense pans suggests their angelic status.

The religious use of cultic utensils such as the φιάλη, however, is not restricted to ancient Israel or Judaism. The φιάλη is attested in Greek religion (Diodorus 4.49.8), where it was used primarily to pour libations of wine. The term is also used in an entirely different context in connection with revelatory magic ceremonies, where visions are reflected on the surface of a liquid contained in a bowl (*PGM* IV.224, 3210; LXII.44, 48). The equivalent Latin term is *patera,* meaning a shallow, broad dish used in libation offerings (*OLD,* 1308; see Varro *De lingua Latina* 5.122 [LCL tr.], "it is this kind of cup that the magistrate uses in sacrificing to the gods, when he gives wine to the god"). Vergil *Georgics* 2.192 mentions offering wine from golden pateras (*qualem pateris libamus et auro*). A particularly relevant use of incense took place in Roman imperial ceremonial in which officiants carried incense in *turibula* and burned it in the sacred fire in the presence of the emperor (Alföldi, *MDAIRA* 49 [1934] 111–13).

**8c** αἵ εἰσιν αἱ προσευχαὶ τῶν ἁγίων, "(which are the prayers of God's people)." This phrase, like that in v 6, is an interpretive gloss or parenthetical explanation added by the author (Spitta, 67). Although Rev 8:3–4 distinguishes between incense and prayer and does not treat the former as a metaphor for the latter, here incense is clearly understood *metaphorically.* The origin of this metaphorical interpretation is found in Ps 141:2 (MT 141:3), "Let my prayer be counted as incense before thee, and the lifting up of my hands as an evening sacrifice" (H. J. Hermisson, *Sprache und Ritus im altisraelitischen Kult: Zur "Spiritualtisierung" der Kultbegriffe im AT,* WMANT 19 [Neukirchen: Neukirchener, 1965] 154; W. Zwickel, *Der Tempelkult in Kanaan und Israel* [Tübingen: Mohr-Siebeck, 1994] 318). Here both מנחה *minhâ,* "sacrifice," and קטרת *qĕtōret,* "incense offering," are spiritualized (Rendtorff, *Opfers,* 65); for a critique of sacrifice in the OT, see Pss 40:6; 51:16–17. This spiritualization is particularly evident in Ps 51:17, "the sacrifice acceptable to God is a broken spirit," which in the context of vv 15–17 refers to *prayer* (cf. Heb 13:15; *Barn.* 2:10). The metaphorical understanding of incense and sacrifice is also reflected in Justin *Dial.* 118.2, "Do not think that Isaiah or the other prophets speak of blood sacrifices or libations being presented at the altar on the occasion of his coming again, but of true and spiritual praises and thanksgivings." Origen links the metaphorical interpretation of incense in Rev 5:8 with that found in Ps 141:2 (*Contra Cels.* 8.17; tr. H. Chadwick, *Origen: Contra Celsum* [Cambridge: Cambridge UP, 1953]):

Our altars are the mind of each righteous man, from which true and intelligible incense with a sweet savour is sent up, prayers from a pure conscience. That is why it is said by John in the Apocalypse "And the incense is the prayers of the saints," and by the Psalmist "Let my prayers be as incense before thee."

In the ritual of the second temple, prayer was increasingly used, yet was never considered equal to the sacrifices (Heinemann, *Prayer*, 123). On the rabbinic conception that prayer can take the place of sacrifice, see G. F. Moore, *Judaism* 2:217–19. According to *Tg. Neb.* Mal 1:12, "your prayer is like a pure offering before me" (tr. Cathcart-Gordon, *Targum*). Pagan Greek philosophy developed the notion of the λογικὴ θυσία, "rational or spiritual sacrifice," which rejected bloody sacrifices as well as the formal liturgical features of cultic worship and emphasized instead the inner disposition of the human spirit (Casel, *Jahrbuch für Liturgiewissenschaft* 4 [1924] 37ff.).

The term ἅγιοι, "the holy ones, saints," is used here of Christians and so should be translated "God's people," since the term emphasizes their relationship to God, not their sanctity (see Louw-Nida, § 11.27). The term occurs twelve times elsewhere in Revelation (8:3, 4; 11:18; 13:7, 10; 14:12; 16:6; 17:6; 18:20, 24; 19:8; 20:9) and frequently in early Christian literature (Acts 9:13, 32, 41; 26:10; Rom 8:27; 12:13; 15:26; 16:2, 15; 1 Cor 6:1–2; 14:33; 2 Cor 1:1; 13:12; Eph 1:15; 3:18; 4:12; 5:3; 6:18; Phil 4:22; Col 1:4; 1 Tim 5:10; Philem 5, 7; Heb 6:10; 13:24; Jude 3; Ignatius *Smyrn.* 1:2; Justin *Dial.* 139.4). The term "holy ones" or "saints" is derived from Jewish tradition, where it can refer to both the people of God and angels (Dequeker, *OTS* 18 [1973] 108–87). Ps 34:9(MT 34:10) is the only undisputed passage in the Hebrew OT in which the term קְדֹשִׁים *qĕdōšîm*, "holy ones," is used of Israelites (Deut 33:3 is problematic; the *Fragmentary Targum* interprets "holy ones" as "holy angels"; see M. L. Klein, *Fragment-Targums* 2:87, 188); in Aramaic portions of the OT, the corresponding term קַדִּישִׁין *qaddîšîn* is used of Israelites in Dan 7:21–22, 25, 27; 8:24. In early Jewish literature "holy ones" is often used of righteous Jews (*1 Enoch* 38:4, 5; 41:2; 43:4; 48:1; 50:1; 51:2; 58:3, 5; 62:8; 65:12; 99:16; 100:5; 1QM 6:6; 10:10; 12:1b; 16:1). Perhaps even more commonly, however, ἅγιοι or its equivalent is frequently used in early Jewish literature of angels (see LXX Ps 82:4; LXX Dan 7:8, 21, 22; 8:24; Wis 18:9; Tob 12:15 [MSS B A]; 1 Macc 1:46 [though here the Latin *sancta*, "holy things," may be preferable to the Greek ἅγιους, "holy ones"; see J. A. Goldstein, *1 Maccabees*, AB 41 (Garden City: Doubleday, 1976) 221–22]; *Jub.* 17:11; 31:14; *T. Levi* 18:11; *T. Iss.* 5:4; *T. Dan* 5:11–12; 3 Macc 6:9 [MS A]; *1 Enoch* 47:2; 57:2; 60:4; 61:8, 10; 69:13; 71:4; *2 Apoc. Bar.* 66:2; see *Sib. Or.* 5.161, 432; 1QM 10:12; 12:1a; 1QSb 1:5; 1QS 11:7–8; 1QH 4:25), a usage carried over into early Christianity (1 Thess 3:13; 2 Thess 1:10; Col 1:12; Eph 1:18; see Benoit, "Ἅγιοι," 83–99).

**9a** καὶ ᾄδουσιν ᾠδὴν καινήν, "Then they sang a new song." The expression "new song" occurs only here and in 14:3 in Revelation; both contexts also mention the kithara. The Hebrew phrase שִׁיר חָדָשׁ *šîr ḥādāš*, "new song," occurs seven times in the OT (Pss 33:3; 40:3; 96:1; 98:1; 144:9; 149:1; Isa 42:10) and simply refers to the introduction of a new composition for the purpose of celebrating a very special occasion, or the introduction of a new composition into a setting in which many songs have been used traditionally for a very long time. In the OT the phrase is used in formulaic clauses (R. C. Culley, *Oral Formulaic Language in the Biblical Psalms* [Toronto: University of Toronto Press, 1967] 58) and is thought by some (without convincing evidence) to have eschatological overtones (H.-J. Kraus, *Theologie der Psalmen* [Neukirchen: Neukirchener, 1979] 1:410). The Syriac phrase *tsbwhˀ hdtˀ*, "new song," occurs twice in *Odes Sol.* 31:3; 41:6. Similarly *Pss. Sol.* 15:3 speaks of "a new psalm with song in gladness of heart" (ψαλμὸν καινὸν μετὰ ᾠδῆς ἐν εὐφροσύνῃ καρδίας). Philo *Mos.* 1.255 refers to the song sung by the Israelites in Num 21:17–18 as an ᾆσμα καινόν, "new song." In all these cases the "new song" celebrates a saving action on the part of God (Deichgräber, *Gotteshymnus*, 52; Jörns, *Evangelium*, 48–49). See the references in Str-B, 3:801–2. The *Mek. de-Rabbi Ishmael, Shirata* 1 (Lauterbach, *Mekilta* 2:2–6) refers to the Song of Moses in Exod 15 as one of *ten* songs, in the tenth of which the biblical term "new song" is clearly understood eschatologically:

> The tenth song will be recited in the future, as it is said: "Sing unto the Lord a new song, and His praise from the end of the earth" (Isa 42:10). And it also says: "Sing unto the Lord a new song, and His praise in the assembly of the saints" (Ps 149:1).

In Greek literature, there is a *topos* that new songs are the best songs. Pindar praises old wine but the flowers of new songs (ἄνθεα ὕμνων νεωτέρων; Athenaeus *Deipn.* 1.25e; Pindar *Olymp.* 9.48–49). According to *Odyssey* 1.351–52, "people praise that song which comes newest to their ears," and Lucian alludes to that same passage when he observes that "a new song [τὴν νέαν ᾠδήν] is agreeable to the hearers" (*Zeuxis* 2). Plato, also quoting *Odyssey* 1.351, suggests that Homer means not "new songs [ᾄσματα νέα]" but a "new way of song [τρόπον ᾠδῆς νέον]" (*Rep.* 4.424b–c).

**9b** ἄξιος εἶ λαβεῖν τὸ βιβλίον καὶ ἀνοῖξαι τὰς σφραγίδας αὐτοῦ, "'You are worthy to receive the book / and open its seals.'" Three hymns in Revelation begin with the adjective ἄξιος, "worthy" (4:11; 5:9, 12), all within 4:1–5:14. The first ἄξιος εἶ, in the second-person singular *du-Stil*, "thou style" (Norden, *Agnostos Theos*, 143–63), introduces a hymn to God in 4:11, while the second ἄξιος εἶ introduces a hymn to the Lamb in 5:9. There is then a switch to the third person, the so-called *er-Stil*, "he style" (Norden, *Agnostos Theos*, 163–66), and the phrase ἄξιός ἐστιν in 5:12 introduces a second hymn to the Lamb. Hymns directed toward Christ in heaven are mentioned in *Ap. Jas.* 14.29–30; 15.19–22. This hymn in vv 9–10 is addressed to the Lamb, and so might appropriately be designated "the Song of the Lamb" (see *Comment* on 15:3). Van Unnik ("Worthy," 445–61) has collected numerous texts in which the ascription of worthiness is linked to divine revelations that can only be received by those who are considered "worthy" (Philo *Cher.* 42; Jos. *J.W.* 2.138; 5.378; *Barn.* 9:9; 14:1, 4; Ps.-Clement *Hom. Ep. Petri* 1.2; 3.1 [Rehm, *Pseudoklementinen* 1:1–2]; Ps.-Clement *Hom. Diamart.* 2.2 [Rehm, 1:3]; *Second Book of Jeu* 43; *Pistis Sophia* 106). He goes on to argue that the status of "worthiness" is not a quality that entitles a person to have access to divine revelation but the right inner attitude combined with right behavior (van Unnik, "Worthy," 457–58). This can be made evident by a severe test, as Wis 3:5 speaks of the righteous: ὅτι ὁ θεὸς ἐπείρασεν αὐτοὺς καὶ εὗρεν αὐτοὺς ἀξίους ἑαυτοῦ, "because God tested them and found them worthy of himself." The connection of "testing" with "worthiness" is therefore found before the first century A.D. in a context that has nothing to do with the mystery cults or with imagery drawn from such cults, as do several of the passages cited above. The conquest of the Lamb that reveals that he is worthy is the death he suffered, which became a means of redemption for people everywhere on earth, as v 9 explains.

**9c** ὅτι ἐσφάγης καὶ ἠγόρασας τῷ θεῷ ἐν τῷ αἵματί σου, "'Because you were slaughtered and you redeemed for God / by your death.'" The ὅτι clause introduces the basis for the worthiness ascribed to the Lamb in v 9b, by emphasizing three actions, all expressed with aorist verbs, that express the saving death of Christ with its salvific effects: ἐσφάγης, "you were slaughtered," ἠγόρασας, "you redeemed," and ἐποίησας, "you made." The term σφάζειν, "to slaughter," is a term with implications of violence and mercilessness (Louw-Nida, § 20.72); this term is used of the execution of Jesus only in Revelation (5:6, 9, 12; 13:8; θύειν, which belongs to the same semantic domain [Louw-Nida, § 20.72] is used of the death of Christ as a Passover lamb in 1 Cor 5:7 and of slaughtering Passover lambs in Mark 14:12; Luke 22:7) and of Christians in Rev 6:9; 18:24. The term ἀγοράζειν, literally "to buy, purchase," is used here and in 14:3 with the figurative meaning (based on the terminology of the slave market) "to cause the release of someone by paying a price." ἀγοράζειν is used in this sense in 1 Cor 6:20; 7:23, where the phrase ἠγοράσθητε τιμῆς, "you were redeemed for a price," is used, and in 2 Pet 2:1, where the subject of the verb ἀγοράζειν is δεσπότης, "master." The passive suggests that *God* is the one who did the purchasing (the passive of divine activity), though the price is not specified. In Rev 5:9c, of course, the price is "by your blood," i.e., by your death. The intensive form ἐξαγοράζειν occurs in Gal 3:13; 4:5. The parallelism between v 9 and 1 Pet 1:18–19 is clear in this comparison; note that 1 Pet 1:18 designates Christ under the metaphor of ἄμνος "lamb":

| *Rev 5:9* | *1 Pet 1:18–19* |
|---|---|
| ἐσφάγης καὶ ἠγόρασας ... <br> you were slain and ransomed | ἐλυτρώθητε ... <br> you were ransomed |
| ἐν τῷ αἵματί σου <br> by your blood | τιμίῳ αἵματι ὡς ἀμνοῦ ἀμώμου <br> with the precious blood of a blameless lamb |
| | καὶ ἀσπίλου Χριστοῦ <br> and spotless, Christ |

**9d** ἐκ πάσης φυλῆς καὶ γλώσσης καὶ λαοῦ καὶ ἔθνους, "'People from every tribe and tongue / and people and nation.'" This polysyndetic list of *four* ethnic units, which cumulatively emphasize universality, is probably based on the frequent mention of the *three* ethnic groups of "peoples, nations, and languages" in Daniel (3:4 [LXX has *four* ethnic units], 7, 29[LXX v 96]; 5:19; 6:25[LXX v 26]; 7:14; cf. Jdt 3:8, "nations, languages, and tribes"). The LXX expands the threefold Danielic phrase into a fourfold phrase in Dan 3:4, ἔθνη καὶ χῶραι, λαοὶ καὶ γλώσσαι, "nations and lands, peoples and languages." The *Tg. Esth I* 1:1 has a similar enumeration of four synonymous nouns: כל עמיא אומיא ולישניא ואפרכיא, "all peoples, nations, languages, and provinces" (see Grossfeld, *Esther*, 5, 40; id., *Two Targums*, 28), while the *Tg. Neb.* Joel 2:25 has "you were pillaged by peoples, tongues, governments, and kingdoms" (tr. Cathcart-Gordon, *Targum*). Bauckham points out that Gen 10:5, 20, 31, in the context of the table of nations, contains the only list of *four* ethnic units in the OT, e.g., v 31, "These are the sons of Shem, by their families, their languages, their lands, and their nations," while another fourfold phrase is used in 4 Ezra 3:7 to describe the descendants of Adam: "nations and tribes, peoples and clans"

("Conversion," 328). The number seventy, used in Judaism for the total number of nations of the world, is derived from the total number of nations mentioned in the Table of Nations in Gen 10. Similar lists of three or (more frequently) four ethnic groups are found in six other passages in Revelation, always in a polysyndetic list, but always in a different order (see Bauckham, "Conversion," 326–37): (1) Rev 7:9, nations, tribes, peoples, tongues; (2) Rev 10:11, peoples, nations, tongues, kings; (3) Rev 11:9, peoples, tribes, tongues, nations; (4) Rev 13:7, tribe, people, language, nation; (5) Rev 14:6, nation, tribe, tongue, people; (6) Rev 17:15, peoples, crowds, nations, tongues. The terms "people," "nation," and "tribe" are used in Josephus *Ant.* 7.356 as synonyms for Israel or parts of Israel. Isa 66:18 predicts the gathering of "all nations and languages," while Zech 8:22 expects "many peoples and strong nations . . . to seek the Lord of hosts in Jerusalem." Shorter lists are more frequent, e.g., "peoples and nations" (*Pss. Sol.* 17:29). These lists are meant to emphasize universality. The fact that Christians were drawn from many ethnic groups in the Roman empire but did not (unlike most Hellenistic religions) constitute an ethnic group themselves led early Christian authors to refer to Christianity as a new people or a *tertium genus,* "third race," in contrast to Jews and Greeks (Origen *Contra Cels.* 8.2; Justin *Dial.* 119; *Diogn.* 5–6; Tertullian *Ad nat.* 1.8). Paul referred to "Jews, Greeks, and the Church of God" (1 Cor 10:32), and Christians also regarded themselves as aliens whose true citizenship was in heaven (Phil 3:20; 1 Pet 1:17; 2:11; see Elliott, *1 Peter,* 21–58). Ignatius claimed that Christianity (Χριστιανισμος, the first use of that term) was made up of people from πᾶσα γλῶσσα, "every language" (*Magn.* 10:3). A similar series of two social groups is found in a decree of the *koinon* of Asia from the first century B.C. (Reynolds, *Aphrodisias,* document 5, line 24, τοῖς [ἐν τῇ Ἀσίᾳ π]ᾶσιν δήμοις τε καὶ ἔθνεσιν, "to every people and nation in Asia").

**10a** καὶ ἐποίησας αὐτοὺς τῷ θεῷ ἡμῶν βασιλείαν καὶ ἱερεῖς, "'and made them for our God / a kingdom and priests.'" This statement is an allusion to Exod 19:6; see *Comment* on 1:6. Here it is clear that the people of God possess two privileges: they constitute a kingdom, and they are priests. The plural noun ἱερεῖς, "priests," could be either a nominative or an accusative plural, though here it must be taken as an accusative and therefore helps to understand the more ambiguous phrase βασιλείαν ἱερεῖς, "a kingdom, priests," in 1:6 as referring to two privileges rather than one.

**10b** καὶ βασιλεύσουσιν ἐπὶ τῆς γῆς, "'And they will reign upon the earth.'" The reign of the saints in the sense of their participation in the reign of God is an apocalyptic theme emphasizing the acquisition of power by the powerless that first appears in Dan 7:18, 27 and thereafter appears here and there in early Jewish and early Christian texts (cf. 1QM 12:15; Matt 19:28 = Luke 23:30; 1 Cor 6:2; *Acts Thom.* 137; Athanasius *Vita Anth.* 16). According to *T. Dan* 5:13, the one who trusts in the Holy One of Israel "shall reign [βασιλεύσει] in truth in the heavens." In *Acts Thom.* 137, Tertia tells Misdaeus that he "will be a great king in heaven" if he fears the living God. This same theme also occurs in Rev 20:6 (the martyrs will reign a thousand years with Christ, also on the earth); 22:5 (the servants of God will reign for ever). There are several early Christian texts in which this eschatological motif is described as a possibility that can be realized in the present (1 Cor 4:8 [here the ἐβασιλεύσατε may be sarcastic]; *Acts Thom.* 136; *Gos. Thom.* 2; see Stroker, *Extracanonical,* 116–19), e.g., *Gos. Heb.* frag. 4b (tr. Hennecke-Schneemelcher, *NTA*), "He that seeks will not rest until he finds; and he that has found shall marvel;

and he that has marvelled shall reign [βασιλεύσει]; and he that has reigned [ὁ βασιλεύσας] shall rest" (from Clement of Alex. *Strom.* 5.14.96), and *Acts Thom.* 136, "And those who worthily receive the good things there rest, and resting they reign [βασιλεύσουσιν]." This apocalyptic motif occurs in Rom 5:17, where it is said that Christians shall reign (βασιλεύσουσιν; note the future tense) through the one Jesus Christ; i.e., those who receive grace shall reign.

**11a** καὶ εἶδον, καὶ ἤκουσα φωνὴν ἀγγέλων πολλῶν κύκλῳ τοῦ θρόνου καὶ τῶν ζῴων καὶ τῶν πρεσβυτέρων, "Then I saw and I heard the sound of many angels encircling the throne, and the cherubim and the elders." On καὶ εἶδον, see *Comment* on 5:1. It is unusual that the throne vision in Rev 4, unlike similar heavenly throne scenes, does not mention *angels* (1 Kgs 22:19; Dan 7:10; *1 Enoch* 47:3; see Gruenwald, *Apocalyptic*, 31); here that omission is rectified. Peterson (*Εἷς Θεός*, 148) suggests that φωνή here may be a technical term for "acclamation." The angels encircling the throne are mentioned again in 7:11, and the same feature is mentioned in *Apoc. Abr.* (Rec. B) 8:5, 7.

**11b** καὶ ἦν ὁ ἀριθμὸς αὐτῶν μυριάδες μυριάδων καὶ χιλιάδες χιλιάδων, "(their number was myriads and myriads and thousands and thousands)." This sentence interrupts the flow of thought and may therefore be either a gloss or a parenthetical statement. Here the author clearly alludes to Dan 7:10, where reference is made to the innumerable heavenly beings that surround the Ancient of Days: "a thousand thousands [אלף אלפים *'elep 'alpîm*] served him, and ten thousand ten thousands [ורבו רבון *wĕribô ribwān*] stood before him." There has been, however, a transposition of clauses since χίλιαι precedes μύριαι in both the Theodotianic and LXX version of Dan 7:10. The order μύριαι-χίλιαι in Rev 5:11 is also found in *1 Clem.* 34:6 (see D. A. Hagner, *The Use of the Old and New Testaments in Clement of Rome*, NovTSup 34 [Leiden: Brill, 1973] 62–63). While both the LXX and Theodotion translate the Aramaic phrases with χίλιαι χιλιάδες and μύριαι μυριάδες, the author of Revelation avoids using χίλιαι and μύριαι, which for him meant 1,000 and 10,000, respectively (Mussies, *Morphology*, 223; see *Notes* and *Comment* on Rev 9:16). Dan 7:10 is also alluded to in *1 Enoch* 14:22 (where the extant Greek version reads μύριαι μυριάδες, "myriads upon myriads," or "ten thousand times ten thousand") and in a longer form even more clearly from Daniel, "thousands upon thousands, and myriads upon myriads" (see *1 Enoch* 14:22; 40:1; 60:1; 71:8); see the Greek text of *1 Enoch* 1:9 (tr. Black, *Apocalypsis*, 19), ὅτι ἔρχεται σὺν ταῖς μυριάσιν αὐτοῦ, "Because he comes with his ten thousands." Aramaic fragments of this text were found at Qumran: רבו[את קדיש *[rbw]'t qdyšw*, "myriads of his holy ones" (Milik, *Enoch*, 184–85). This text is also quoted in Jude 14, ἰδοὺ ἦλθεν κύριος ἐν ἁγίαις μυριάσιν αὐτοῦ, "Behold the Lord came with his holy myriads." In *Jos. As.* 16:17c, Dan 7:10 is alluded to in a context referring to the many cells of a honeycomb (tr. Charlesworth, *OTP* 2:229–30): "And the man said to the comb, 'Come.' And bees rose from the cells of that comb, and the cells were innumerable, ten thousand (times) ten thousand and thousands upon thousands [ἀναρίθμηται μυριάδες μυριάδων καὶ χιλιάδες χιλιάδων]." *1 Clem.* 34:6 contains a conflation of quotations from Dan 7:10 and Isa 6:3 (see *Comment* on 4:11): "For the Scripture says, 'Ten thousand ten thousands stood before him, and a thousand thousands worshiped him, and they cried "Holy, Holy, Holy is the Lord Sabaoth, all creation is full of his glory."'" The quotation of Dan 7:10, however, though differing from both the LXX and the MT, is in agreement with Irenaeus *Adv. haer.* 2.7.4. Since the innumerable heavenly multitude described in Dan 7:10 has no speaking part in that text, the author of *1 Clement* has supplied them with the trisagion. Did he create this liturgical scene himself, or was he dependent on earlier traditions? Again in dependence upon Dan 7:10, the *Apoc. Zeph.*, in 4:1; 8:1, speaks of "thousands of thousands and myriads of myriads of angels." According to *2 Apoc. Bar.* 48:10, "innumerable hosts" stand before God. In the latter passage they give praise, and Zephaniah himself puts on an angelic garment. The notion of the innumerable multitude can be construed as a spiritualization of the promise to Abraham (Gen 22:17; 32:12; 2 Sam 7:11; 1 Kgs 4:2; Isa 10:22; Hos 1:10; Rom 9:27 [quoting Isa 10:22]; Pr Azar 1:13). In addition to Dan 7:10, there are several texts in the OT in which the angelic host is referred to as virtually innumerable (Deut 33:2; Job 19:11–12; 25:2–3; Ps 68:18).

**12** λέγοντες φωνῇ μεγάλῃ· ἄξιόν ἐστιν τὸ ἀρνίον τὸ ἐσφαγμένον λαβεῖν τὴν δύναμιν καὶ πλοῦτον καὶ σοφίαν καὶ ἰσχὺν καὶ τιμὴν καὶ δόξαν καὶ εὐλογίαν, "chanting with a loud voice: 'Worthy is the Lamb who was slain to receive / power and wealth and wisdom / and might and honor and glory and praise.'" The term ἄξιος, "worthy," appears to be used here in quite a different sense from the earlier occurrences of the term in vv 2, 4, and 9, where worthiness was linked with the special qualifications necessary for opening the sealed scroll. However, the taking (εἴληφεν) of the sealed scroll in v 7 (where the verb has no object) should be understood to symbolize the "taking" (λαβεῖν) of the various prerogatives listed here in v 12 (Irenaeus *Adv. haer.* 4.20.2; G. Reichelt, *Buch*, 156). Parallels to Christ's reception of prerogatives usually reserved for God alone are found in Matt 28:18 ("All authority in heaven and on earth have been given to me [by God]") and Matt 11:27 ("Everything has been given to me by my Father"); cf. A. Jeremias, *Babylonisches*, 14. Here the quality of ἄξιος is generalized as the qualification of the Lamb to be the recipient of a complex list of qualities such as those ascribed to benefactors. Josephus (*J.W.* 7.71) reports that the newly recognized emperor Vespasian was greeted upon his entrance to Rome by crowds of people calling him τὸν εὐεργέτην καὶ σωτῆρα καὶ μόνον ἄξιον ἡγεμόνα τῆς Ῥώμης, "benefactor and savior and the only worthy ruler of Rome." The seven substantives connected by καί constitute a rhetorical feature called *polysyndeton* (BDF § 460; D. E. Aune, "De esu carnium orationes I and II (Moralia 933a–999B)," in *Plutarch's Theological Writings and Early Christian Literature*, ed. H. D. Betz, SCHNT 3 [Leiden: Brill, 1975] 309). This "hymn" lacks the kind of descriptive or narrative content characteristic of hymns and is rather like a doxology in the form of an acclamation (Peterson, *Von den Engeln*, 340). The article is attached to only the first noun, indicating that all seven substantives form a single notion (Bousset [1906] 261). A similar doxology (addressed to God) is found in 1 Chr 29:11, though each attribute is articular: "To you, O Lord, is the greatness and the power and the glory and the victory and the majesty." Two similar doxologies addressed to Christ are found in *1 Clem.* 65:2, "through whom [God] be to him [Christ] glory, honor, power, and greatness and eternal sovereignty from eternity to eternity," and *Mart. Pol.* 21, "Jesus Christ reigns for ever, to whom be glory, honor, majesty, and eternal sovereignty from generation to generation." Perhaps the most relevant parallel, however, is Dan 2:37, where Daniel, in an introduction to a dream interpretation, tells Nebuchadnezzar that his kingship is from God: "You, O king, the king of kings—to whom the God of heaven has given the kingdom, the power, the might, and the glory . . . ." The LXX version is slightly expanded and has five prerogatives: τὴν ἀρχὴν καὶ τὴν βασιλείαν καὶ τὴν ἰσχὺν καὶ τὴν τιμὴν καὶ τὴν δόξαν, "the rule and the kingdom and the power and the honor and the glory" (Theod Dan 2:37, on the other hand, has reduced the list to three: ἰσχυρὰν καὶ κραταιὰν καὶ ἔντιμον, "might and power and honor"). All of these prerogatives reflect the royal investiture of the king and strongly suggest that the list of prerogatives in Rev 5:12 reflects the investiture of the Lamb. A list of four prerogatives closely parallel to this list of seven is found in Philo *Ebr.* 75 (LCL tr.), "Nothing else, neither *wealth* [πλοῦτον], nor *glory* [δόξαν], nor *honour* [τιμήν], nor office, nor beauty, nor *strength* [ἰσχύν]," deserves our service and honor but God. The similarity between this list and those discussed above suggests that these qualities are considered the highest and most significant qualities to which one could aspire. A comparison between the analogous lists of prerogatives in 1 Chr 29:11 (prerogatives of God) and Dan 2:37 (prerogatives of the king bestowed by God) with Rev 5:11 suggests that the ascription of these prerogatives to the Lamb means not that the Lamb is thereby venerated as God (similar prerogatives could also be ascribed to kings) but that these qualities are bestowed upon the Lamb by virtue of his investiture.

Each of the seven prerogatives is a metaphorical application to Christ of qualities that belong properly to God but may be bestowed on the king by God. Each deserves further comment: (1) "power" (δύναμις) and (4) "might" (ἰσχύς) are synonyms for "strength" and can be considered together (Brettler, *King*, 57–68). In other hymnic contexts in Revelation, δύναμις is used four more times of God alone, but never of the Lamb or Christ (4:11; 7:12; 11:17; 19:1); ἰσχύς is used elsewhere only of God (7:12). There is an apparent reticence in the OT to use the term עֹז *ʿaz*, "strength," for human kings, but when this prerogative is mentioned, it is a privilege given to the king by God (1 Sam 2:10; Ps 28:8). In contrast to the rare mention of this prerogative as characteristic of a king, this quality is frequently ascribed to God as part of the metaphor of kingship (Exod 15:2, 13; Isa 19:4; 45:24; 1 Chr 16:27–28; Pss 62:12; 59:18; 93:1; cf. *TWNT* 2:292–96; Brettler, *King*, 63–64). (2) "Wealth" (πλοῦτος) is frequently associated with kingship (cf. Rev 18:17), but in the OT it is never directly attributed to God as part of the kingship metaphor. "Wealth" as a prerogative attributed to the Lamb (or God) occurs only here in Revelation. (3) "Wisdom" (σοφία), used in one other hymnic context of God (7:12), is an attribute that is thought appropriate for an earthly king and is often regarded as a gift the king has received from God (see Kaligula, *The Wise King*; Brettler, *King*, 55–56). (5) "Honor" (τιμή) is used elsewhere in Revelation twice of God (4:11; 7:12) and once of both God and the Lamb (5:13). τιμή denotes the honor, respect, and status that a person enjoys when his position, wealth, and office are appropriately recognized in the community to which he belongs (*TDNT* 8:169–80; *EDNT* 3:357–59; *NIDNTT* 2:48–52). τιμή is therefore the prerogative of gods, kings, and people of relatively high social position (including parents and the elderly). τιμή is accorded to gods primarily through sacrifice, hymns of praise, and obedience and to kings through rich gifts, acclamations, and a variety of gestures symbolizing subordination, such as standing (when the king is seated), bowing, and prostration. In the LXX, however, τιμή, in contrast to δόξα, is rarely used for the honor of God. (6) "Glory" (δόξα) is used elsewhere in Revelation of God alone (4:11; 7:12; 19:1) and once of God and the Lamb together (5:13). The attributes τιμή and δόξα are frequently paired in the LXX (Pss 8:6; 28:1; 95:7; Job 40:10; 2 Chr 32:33; 1 Macc 14:21), in a few other Greco-Jewish texts (*1 Enoch* 5:1; 99:1), and in early Christian literature (1 Tim 1:17; Heb 2:7, 9; 3:3; 2 Pet 1:17; Rev 21:26; *1 Clem.* 45:8; 61:1, 2; for inscriptional evidence, see J. Schneider, *Doxa* [Gütersloh: Mohn, 1932]) or occur together in longer lists of attributes (1 Pet 1:7; Rev 4:9, 11; 5:13; *1 Clem.* 65:2; *Mart. Pol.* 20:2).(7) "Praise" (εὐλογία) is applied to God alone in Rev 4:11; 7:12. The term εὐλογία occurs about sixty times in the LXX as a translation of ברכה *bĕrākâ*, "blessing." In Revelation εὐλογία occurs three times (5:12, 13; 7:12), always as one of several predicates used of the Lamb (5:12) or God (5:13; 7:12), the last two in the context of a doxology. The term (and cognates) is used of God in a number of Greco-Jewish inscriptions: θεοῦ εὐλογία, "blessing of God" (*CIJ* 2:1537; *JIGRE*, 121); εὐλόγει τὸν θεόν, "bless God" (*CIJ* 2:1538). The LXX translated ברך *bārak* with εὐλογεῖν (e.g., Pss 102:1; 103:1). According to Dothan there is an epigraphic correspondence between εὐλογία αὐτῷ, "blessings on him," and the Aramaic phrase ברכתה לה *birkātâ lēh* (*Hammath*, 59).

**13a** καὶ πᾶν κτίσμα ὃ ἐν τῷ οὐρανῷ καὶ ἐπὶ τῆς γῆς καὶ ὑποκάτω τῆς γῆς καὶ ἐπὶ τῆς θαλάσσης καὶ τὰ ἐν αὐτοῖς πάντα ἤκουσα, "Then I heard every created being in heaven and on earth and under the earth and upon the sea and everything in them." This is a verbal repetition of 5:3, where no one in the entire universe was able to open the scroll (see *Comment* on 5:3), though here the phrase "upon the sea" is added. Here πᾶν κτίσμα, "every created being," at first sight appears to refer to intelligent creatures, since they sing a doxology; i.e., "every created being in heaven" seems to refer to angels and not to birds. However, the phrase "and everything in them" is not only redundant (Bousset [1906] 262), since it does no more than repeat the phrase "every created being," but it also indicates that all creation singing the praises of God is a metaphor simply because most creatures are not able to sing in human language. On the three-level universe in Revelation, see *Comments* on 5:3 and 10:6. A three-level cosmos with four sectors, essentially what we find here, encapsulates the ancient Israelite view of the universe: (1) heaven, (2) earth and sea, (3) underworld (Stadelmann, *World*, 37–176). This four-sectored cosmos is mentioned in Job 11:8–9 (heaven, Sheol, earth, sea) and also occurs in the Greek fragment of *Jub.* 2:16, "And he completed... everything which is in the heavens and the earth and the seas and the depths [ὅσα ἐν τοῖς οὐρανοῖς καὶ ἐν τῇ γῇ, ἐν ταῖς θαλάσσαις καὶ ἐν ταῖς ἀβύσσοις]" (Denis, *Fragmenta*, 74).

**13b** λέγοντας· τῷ καθημένῳ ἐπὶ τῷ θρόνῳ καὶ τῷ ἀρνίῳ, "responding, 'To the One who sits on the throne and to the Lamb.'" While vv 13b–14 constitute a *doxology* (Deichgräber, *Gotteshymnus*, 53; Jörns, *Evangelium*, 54), a liturgical form that has parallels elsewhere in Revelation (1:5b–6; 4:9–10; 7:12), this doxology, like those in 4:9–10; 7:12, is given a narrative setting within the liturgy of the heavenly court. The major change that has been introduced by placing such a doxology within a narrative context is that the concluding "amen" is given a responsory character, for it is attributed to the four cherubim. The two datives of indirect object also function as datives of advantage, τῷ καθημένῳ, "to the one seated," and τῷ ἀρνίῳ, "and to the Lamb." The latter has the appearance of an editorial addition by the author to the source he has used; see 4:9; 7:12, where equivalents to this phrase are not found.

**13c** ἡ εὐλογία καὶ ἡ τιμὴ καὶ ἡ δόξα καὶ τὸ κράτος εἰς τοὺς αἰῶνας τῶν αἰώνων, "'be praise and honor and glory and power for ever.'" The order of these four elements, (1) ἡ εὐλογία, "praise," (2) καὶ ἡ τιμή, "and honor," (3) καὶ ἡ δόξα, "and glory," (4) καὶ τὸ κράτος, "and power," can be compared with the order in which these and similar attributes are found in other doxological contexts in Revelation.

In 1:5b–6, the only doxology occurring in a non-narrative context, just two attributes of praise are mentioned: δόξα, "glory," and κράτος, "power." In the doxology found in indirect discourse in 4:9, three attributes of praise occur in the order δόξα, "glory," τιμή, "honor," εὐχαριστία, "thanksgiving." The longest doxology occurs in a narrative context in 7:12 and consists of seven attributes: εὐλογία, "praise," δόξα, "glory," σοφία, "wisdom," εὐχαριστία, "thanksgiving," τιμή, "honor," δύναμις, "power," and ἰσχύς, "might." These variations fit the author-editor's tendency to vary lists.

**14** καὶ τὰ τέσσαρα ζῷα ἔλεγον· ἀμήν. καὶ οἱ πρεσβύτεροι ἔπεσαν καὶ προσεκύνησαν, "And the four creatures responded, 'Amen,' and the elders prostrated themselves and worshiped." It is striking that the responsory "amen" is not uttered by those singing or chanting this hymn but by others (Jörns, *Evangelium*, 55), and therefore "amen" does not appear to function here as an acclamation (against Schlier, *TDNT* 1:336). Similar liturgical responses are regularly used by the author to conclude throne scenes (see 4:9–11; 7:11b–12; 11:16–18; 19:4–8). This reads like a dramatization of the conclusion of the hymn in Phil 2:5–11, where in v 10 it is said that "at the name of Jesus every knee should bow, in heaven and on earth and under the earth" (cf. the enumeration of these categories of creatures in v 13a).

*Excursus 5A: Christ as the Lamb*

*Bibliography*

**Anderson, G.** "Sacrifice and Sacrificial Offerings." *ABD* 5:870–86. **Barrett, C. K.** "The Lamb of God." *NTS* 1 (1954–55) 210–18. **Bokser, B.** "Unleavened Bread and Passover, Feasts of." *ABD* 6:755–65. **Burchard, C.** "Das Lamm in der Waagschale." *ZNW* 57 (1966) 219–28. **Burney, C. F.** *The Aramaic Origin of the Fourth Gospel.* Oxford: Clarendon, 1922. **Dodd, C. H.** *The Interpretation of the Fourth Gospel.* Cambridge: Cambridge UP, 1965. **D'Souza, J.** *The Lamb of God in the Johannine Writings.* Allahabad: St Paul Publications, 1968. **Gärtner, B.** "*ṭly* als Messiasbezeichnung." *SEÅ* 18–19 (1953–54) 99–108. **Griffiths, J. G.** "Apocalyptic in the Hellenistic Era." In *Apocalypticism*, ed. D. Hellholm. 273–93. **Harlé, P.-A.** "L'Agneau de l'Apocalypse et le Nouveau Testament." *ETR* 31 (1956) 26–35. **Hillyer, N.** "'The Lamb' in the Apocalypse." *EvQ* 39 (1967) 228–36. **Hohnjec, N.** "*Das Lamm*—τὸ ἀρνίον" *in der Offenbarung Johannes.* Rome: Herder, 1980. **Jeremias, Joachim.** "ἀρνίον." *TDNT* 1:340–41. ———. "Das Lamm, das aus der Jungfrau hervorging (Test Jos 19.8)." *ZNW* 57 (1966) 216–19. **Kiuchi, N.** *The Purification Offering in the Priestly Literature: Its Meaning and Function.* JSOTSup 56. Sheffield: JSOT, 1987. **Koch, K.** "Das Lamm, das Ägypten Vernichtet." *ZNW* 57 (1966) 79–93. **Läpple, A.** "Das Geheimnis des Lammes." *BK* 3 (1984) 53–59. **Lindars, B.** "A Bull, a Lamb and a Word." *NTS* 22 (1976) 483–86. **Milgrom, J.** *Studies in Cultic Theology and Terminology.* SJLA 36. Leiden: Brill, 1983. **O'Neill, J. C.** "The Lamb of God in the Testaments of the Twelve Patriarchs." *JSNT* 2 (1979) 2–30. **Seibert, I.** *Hirt-Herde-König: Zur Herausbildung des Königtums in Mesopotamien.* Berlin: Akademie, 1969. **Spitta, F.** "Christus das Lamm." In *Streitfragen der Geschichte Jesu.* Göttingen: Vandenhoeck & Ruprecht, 1907. 172–224. **Wenschkewitz, H.** *Die Spiritualisierung der Kultusbegriffe: Tempel, Priester und Opfer im Neuen Testament.* Leipzig: Pfeiffer, 1932. **Whale, P.** "The Lamb of John: Some Myths about the Vocabulary of the Johannine Literature." *JBL* 106 (1987) 289–95.

The term ἀρνίον, "lamb," occurs twenty-nine times in Revelation (only in 13:11 does the term not refer to Jesus; rather it refers there to the Beast from the Land or the False

Prophet), with the first occurrence in 5:6. The only other NT occurrence of the term is in John 21:15, where the plural form τὰ ἀρνία is a metaphor referring to the Christian community. Many commentators have observed that ἀρνίον is the term preferred in Revelation, while ἀμνός is preferred in John (though the plural ἀρνία occurs once in John 21:15 in a context in which it is used interchangeably with πρόβατα; see 21:16, 17), where it occurs just twice (1:29, 36). Two uses of a term can hardly be regarded as indicating preference, though John 21 was a later addition to the Gospel. In form, ἀρνίον is a diminutive of ἀρήν, "sheep, lamb" (which occurs once in the NT in Luke 10:3 and once in the Apostolic Fathers in *Barn.* 2:5), using the common diminutive ending -ιον (see Frisk, *Wörterbuch* 1:137–38). The nominative singular does not occur in the late Hellenistic and early Roman periods (Bauer-Aland, 217), but the noun ἀρήν does occur with some frequency in the papyri (e.g., PWash 1, 1.3–5[3x]). It has been widely argued that it is not a true diminutive; instead its semantic meaning has changed, and it became a "faded diminutive" (i.e., its diminutive meaning was lost during the late Hellenistic and early Roman periods; *TDNT* 1:340; *EDNT* 1:71). This is true for some but not all diminutives formed with -ιον. Further, it is extremely difficult to argue that ἀρνίον was consistently used as a faded diminutive (Swanson, *JBL* 77 [2958] 146–47; Moulton-Howard, *Accidence*, 344–45, are neutral). Some have argued that ἀρνίον should be translated "ram" or "sheep" in view of (1) the reference to wrath, (2) the mention of horns, which are found only on mature animals, (3) the sign of the ram in the zodiac, and (4) parallels with the apocalyptic rams of Dan 8:3 and *1 Enoch* 90:9, 37 (Charles, 1:141; Ford, 86; Böcher, 47). The usual objection to this translation, that the Greeks distinguished between the κριός and the ἀρήν/ἀρνίον/ἀμνός, falls away in light of texts where the two are used as alternate terms (Clemen, *Erklärung*, 383–84). Elsewhere in the NT the synonym ἀμνός is used of Christ: twice in the stereotypical expression "the Lamb of God" (John 1:29, 36), once in a quotation from Isa 53:7 in Acts 8:32, and once in 1 Pet 1:19, where the reference is to Christ's precious blood ὡς ἀμνοῦ ἀμώμου, "as from a spotless lamb" (the phrase ἀμνὸς ἀμώμος or ἀμνοὶ ἀμώμοι occurs some thirteen times in the LXX). The term ἀρνίον occurs four times in the LXX, where it means "lamb" or "sheep" (Jer 11:19; 27:45[MT 50:45]; Ps 113:4, 6[MT 114:4, 6]), though in the last two passages κριοί, "rams," in the first line of each couplet is paralleled by ἀρνία προβάτων, "lambs of the sheep," in the second line. The term occurs once in Aquila (Isa 40:11). In *Pss. Sol.* 5:28, the term ἀρνία is used of the people of God (cf. John 21:15). Josephus, too, distinguished between a κριός and an ἀρνίον (*Ant.* 3.221, 226, 251). In Philo, ἀρνίον occurs in *Leg.* 362. In the Apostolic Fathers, ἀρνίον occurs just three times, all in *2 Clem.* 5:2–4 (alluding to Luke 10:3 = Matt 9:16, where the former uses ἀρήᾳ, and the latter προβάτον), a brief allegory of wolves and lambs in which the latter, as in John 21:15, represent the Christian community. The synonym ἀμνός, on the other hand, occurs twice, as an allusion to Isa 53:7 in *Barn.* 5:2 and as a quotation of Isa 53:7 in *1 Clem.* 16:7.

There are two primary ways of interpreting the lamb metaphor in Revelation: as a *metaphor for a leader or ruler* and as a *sacrificial metaphor.* Each of these views will be discussed in some detail below. The major issue is whether the image of the lamb centers on its sacrificial associations (in which case John has expanded this to include other functions) or on its apocalyptic and messianic associations (in which case John has expanded this to include sacrificial imagery). However, it is not necessary to choose between these two possibilities, for it seems clear that the author of Revelation has fused *both* of these associations together in the single figure of the Lamb (Dodd, *Interpretation,* 232).

(1) *The Lamb as a Metaphor for a Leader or Ruler.* While the designation "Lamb" is in some respects synonymous with the term Messiah *in Revelation,* there is only a single disputed instance in which the figure of the lamb is used of the Messiah in early Jewish literature (*T. Jos.* 9:3; see below). Apart from this one text, there is no convincing evidence that the Messiah was symbolized by a lamb in second temple Judaism (Clemen, *Erklärung,* 383;

Burchard, *ZNW* 57 [1966] 228). The first mention of the Lamb in Revelation follows his introduction as "the lion of the tribe of Judah, the root of David" in 5:5, both clearly messianic designations. The Lamb is enthroned (7:17), or shares God's throne (22:1, 3; cf. 3:21 where the lamb metaphor is missing). He receives the same kind of praise and worship given to God (5:12–13; 7:9–10). He is the shepherd of the people of God (7:17; 14:1–5). "Shepherd" was a frequent OT and Near Eastern metaphor for a king (Jeremias, *TDNT* 6:486–87; Seibert, *Hirt*), and Yahweh is often depicted as the shepherd of the people (Keel, *Bildsymbolik*, 208–9; Korpel, *Clouds*, 448–52). The Lamb is depicted as a mighty warrior able to conquer those who make war against him (17:14). All who oppose the Lamb, regardless of station, fear his wrath (6:16). The role of the Lamb in judgment is suggested by the mention of the Lamb's book of life (13:8; 21:27). The New Jerusalem is presented as the bride of the Lamb (21:9), and the marriage of the Lamb is mentioned (19:7, 9) in an analogy reflecting a traditional metaphorical way of speaking of the relationship between Israel and God. Finally, the Lamb serves as both the temple and the light of the New Jerusalem (21:22–23). It is clear that the sacrificial associations of the lamb (discussed below) have no obvious connection with these more violent and powerful activities of the Lamb. Sheep were used throughout the ancient Near East as ways of depicting the gods or as symbols for the gods (*TWAT* 4:47–49), and in Egypt the "Chnum-Ram" and the "Amun-Ram" were ancient iconographical representations of the gods Chnum and Amun (*LexÄgypt* 6:1243–45; Kees, *Götterglaube*, 78–81). According to a widespread *interpretatio Graeca*, Zeus was identified with Amun and had the head of a ram (Herodotus 2.42). In ancient Egypt the ram was never used as a sacrificial victim (Herodotus 2.42, 46). In 4QpPs 37:3, 5–6, the term צאן *ṣō'n*, "sheep, goat," is used of the leaders of the Qumran community. Jewish apocalyptic literature contains very few references to the figure of a lamb, sheep, or ram. One important passage is found in *T. Jos.* 19:8 (Hollander-de Jonge, *Testaments*, 406 = 19:3), preserved in three Greek MSS and in the Armenian version (tr. Kee in Charlesworth, *OTP* 1:824; the underlined words are considered interpolations by Charles, *Testaments*, 210–11):

> And I saw that a *virgin was born from Judah, wearing a linen stole; and from her* was born a *spotless* lamb [ἀμνὸς ἄμωμος; see 1 Pet 1:19]. At his left there was something like a lion, and all the wild animals rushed against him, but the lamb [ὁ ἀμνός] conquered them, and destroyed them, trampling them underfoot.

While a number of scholars have argued that this section of the *Testament of Joseph* reflects Christian redaction (Jeremias, *ZNW* 57 [1966] 219), others reject this view (Koch, *ZNW* 57 [1966] 87–88; Ulrichsen, *Grundschrift*, 115). Charles (*Testaments*, 210–11) has a nuanced and convincing discussion of the passage in which he reconstructs the unredacted text as narrating the transformation of a μόσχος to an ἀμνός, the latter representing a Maccabean, a descendant of Levi, on whose right side fights a lion representing Judah, and suggests this wording for the first part of v 8: καὶ εἶδον ὅτι ἐν μέσῳ τῶν κεράτων μόσχος ἐγενήθη ἀμνός, "And I saw that in the midst of the horns a heifer became a lamb." The phrase "spotless lamb" is sacrificial language, which may allude to 1 Pet 1:19, while the role of this lamb in conquering the wild animals is similar to the Lamb's conquest of the Beast and his ten allied kings in Rev 17:14. It seems likely, however, that the title "Lamb of God [ὁ ἀμνὸς τοῦ θεοῦ]," found in *T. Jos.* 19:6 and *T. Benj.* 3:8, is a Christian interpolation based on John 1:29, 36 (Barrett, *John*, 176).

The ram and the goat are apocalyptic symbols in Dan 8:2–8, 20–21 for the kings of the Medio-Persian empire. Sheep, lambs, and other domesticated animals are used extensively as apocalyptic symbols in *1 Enoch* 85–90, the so-called Animal Apocalypse, which constitutes the greater part of the Book of Dreams (*1 Enoch* 83–90), composed during the Maccabean rebellion. The dream that constitutes *1 Enoch* 85–90 is an allegorical review of world history in which the principal players are represented in animal form. According to *1 Enoch* 89:11–12, Isaac, represented as a white bull, sires a black boar (Esau) and a white sheep (Jacob), who in turn sires twelve sheep (the twelve sons of Jacob). God is frequently called "the Lord of the sheep" (ὁ κύριος τῶν προβάτων; 89:16, 22, 26, 29, etc.). The sheep, after their Lord delivers them from the wolves (the Egyptians), often go astray or are victimized by wild animals. Eventually the Lord raises up a ram (κριός), i.e., Samuel (89:42). Then follows *1 Enoch* 89:45–46, which is extant in Greek:

> And the Lord of the sheep sent this lamb [τὸν ἄρνα = Samuel] to another lamb [ἄρνα = David], to establish him as a ram [εἰς κριόν = David as king] in rule over the sheep [τῶν προβάτων = Israel] in place of the ram [τοῦ κριοῦ = Saul] who lost his way.

Samuel then "raised him to be a ram, that is, to be ruler and leader of the sheep [εἰς κριὸν καὶ εἰς ἄρχοντα καὶ εἰς ἡγούμενον τῶν προβάτων]." F. Spitta maintained that the term ἀρνίον could indicate a *ram* as well as a lamb and was used as a messianic designation in *1 Enoch* 85–90 (Spitta, *Streitfragen*, 186). In this connection in Ps 113:4, 6 (MT 114:4, 6), the term κριοί, "rams," in the first line of each couplet is paralleled by ἀρνία προβάτων, "lambs of the sheep," in the second line. The term ἄρην, "lamb," from which the diminutive ἀρνίον, "little lamb," is formed, though it is related to the term ἀρνίον in Revelation, is problematic, for since it is applied to both Samuel and David it probably does not represent an underlying Aramaic טליא *ṭalyā'*, "lamb," but is simply an arbitrary way of rendering the Aramaic term אמרא *'immĕrā'*, "sheep" (see Black, *1 Enoch*, 268). After narrating the destruction of the first temple and the rebuilding of the second, the author comes down to the Maccabean period. According to *1 Enoch* 90:6, "lambs [= Hasidim] were born to those snow-white sheep." Eventually Judas Maccabeus arose: "Then I kept watching till one great horn sprouted on one of those sheep" (90:9). The author, nearing his own time, alludes to the killing of Onias III (90:8) and to the battle of Beth-zur (90:13–15; see 1 Macc 4:26–35; 2 Macc 11:1–15), which took place early in A.D. 164 (Milik, *Enoch*, 44). Since the author has now reached his own day, he shifts to the future and describes the intervention of the Lord of the sheep, who strikes the earth, which opens up and swallows the enemies of Israel (90:18). A sword is then given to the sheep, and all wild animals flee before them (90:19). A throne is then set up, and the Lord of the sheep sits on it, and the sealed books of judgment are opened before him (90:19–20).

Egyptian apocalyptic traditions also know the figure of the lamb. According to popular Egyptian tradition, a lamb spoke during the reign of Pharaoh Bokhoris of Saïs (ca. 715–710 B.C.). According to Aelian (*De nat. animal.* 12.3), the lamb had a bizarre appearance: it had eight legs, two tails, two heads, and four horns (n.b. that the Lamb in Rev 5:6 is described as having seven horns and seven eyes), all features appropriate for apocalyptic imagery. The extant fragments of Manetho's *Aegyptiaka*, frags. 64, 65 (ed. W. G. Waddell, LCL), preserve only the enigmatic phrase ἐφ' οὗ ἀρνίον ἐφθέγξατο, "during which [i.e., during the reign of Bokhoris] a lamb spoke" (a brief mention of a significant event connected with the reign of this twenty-fourth-dynasty pharaoh). A Demotic papyrus (from A.D. 7–8) preserves the story of a lamb who prophesied the subjugation of Egypt by Assyria and the removal of the gods of Egypt to Nineveh (see the translation in Gressmann, *Texte*, 48–49, and the summary by Griffiths, "Apocalyptic," 285–87). The lamb died immediately after concluding its prophecies. In Ps.-Plutarch *De proverbuus Alexandrinorum* 21, Manetho's cryptic remark is somewhat expanded: "The lamb [τὸ ἀρνίον] has spoken to you." Egyptians recorded it as speaking with a human voice. "It had a royal winged dragon on its head, and it predicted what would happen to one of the kings" (tr. W. C. Waddell, *Manetho*, LCL [Cambridge: Harvard UP, 1956] 164–65 n. 2).

Finally, there is the late (eleventh-century A.D.) tradition preserved in *Tg. Ps.-J.* Exod 1:15 in which Moses is depicted as a lamb who would destroy Egypt (tr. Maher, *Pseudo-Jonathan*):

And Pharaoh said (that while) he slept, he saw in his dream that all the land of Egypt was placed on one balance of a weighing-scales, and a lamb, the young (of a ewe) [וְטַלְיָא בַּר אִימְרְתָא *wĕṭalyā᾽ bar ᾽îmrātā᾽*], on the other balance of the weighing-scales; and the weighing-scales on which the lamb (was placed) weighed down. Immediately he sent and summoned all the magicians of Egypt and told them of his dream. Immediately Jannes and Jambres, the chief magicians, opened their mouths and said to Pharaoh: "A son is to be born in the assembly of Israel, through whom all the land of Egypt is destined to be destroyed."

The interpretation is facilitated by the fact that טַלְיָא *ṭalyā᾽* can mean both "lamb" and "servant," and "servant [of the Lord]" is a widespread ancient title of Moses. Koch (*ZNW* 57 [1966] 79–93) argued that this interpolation (missing from other targums of Exodus) had early independent existence as part of a lost apocalyptic historical description in Aramaic, probably from the fragmentarily preserved book of Jannes and Jambres. Pietersma (*Apocryphon*, 81–90), however, argues that the original language was Greek. Koch also pointed to the parallel in Josephus *Ant.* 2.205 (LCL tr.):

One of the sacred scribes [of Egypt]—persons with considerable skill in accurately predicting the future—announced to the king that there would be born to the Israelites at that time one who would abase the sovereignty of the Egyptians and exalt the Israelites, were he reared to manhood.

Burchard (*ZNW* 57 [1966] 220–23) points out that there are four other medieval Jewish versions of the dream story and argues persuasively that these (including *Tg. Ps.-J.* Exod 1:15) are further developments of the narrative found earliest in Josephus *Ant.* 2.205, which lacks mention of the dream and the metaphors of the scales and the lamb.

(2) *The Lamb as a Sacrificial Metaphor.* Some of the references to the Lamb in Revelation clearly point to the sacrificial death of Jesus. The Lamb, who is standing and has seven horns and seven eyes, looks as though it had been slain, ὡς ἐσφαγμένον (5:6, 12). The consequence of the slaughter of the Lamb (doubtless referring to the crucifixion of Jesus) was the redemption by means of his blood, i.e., his death (5:9; 7:14). In 12:11, it is said that the people of God conquered Satan by the blood of the Lamb. Jesus is referred to under the metaphor of a sacrificial sheep or lamb in a number of other NT and early Christian texts. The earliest reference is found in 1 Cor 5:7, καὶ γὰρ τὸ πάσχα ἡμῶν ἐτύθη Χριστός, "for Christ our Passover lamb has been sacrificed" (cf. Luke 22:7; on πάσχα as "Passover lamb," see Louw-Nida, § 4.27). In John 1:29 Jesus is referred to as "the lamb of God who takes away the sin of the world" (the phrase "the lamb of God" is applied to Jesus again in John 1:36), a title taken by most scholars to refer to the paschal lamb, even though the expiation of sins was not linked to the Passover sacrifice (Barrett, *John*, 176). Burney (*Aramaic Origin*, 107–8), followed by Jeremias (*TDNT* 1:343), observed that the Aramaic term טַלְיָא *ṭalyā᾽*, which could mean "child, servant," as well as "lamb," was interpreted in the latter sense in John 1:29, 36, based on Isa 53:7. The other meaning of טַלְיָא *ṭalyā᾽*, is reflected in the title παῖς θεοῦ, "child [or servant] of God," which was an early title of Jesus (Acts 3:13; 4:27, 30) reflecting the Servant of the Lord in Isa 53, who is referred to in v 12 as "bearing the sins of the many" (MT נשא חטא־רבים *nāśā᾽ ḥēṭĕ᾽-rabbîm;* LXX ἁμαρτίας πολλῶν ἀνήνεγκεν). Dodd (*Fourth Gospel*, 233–40) rejects the views that "the lamb of God" in John refers to the paschal lamb or to the Servant of the Lord of Isa 53 and prefers to construe "lamb of God" as a messianic title. The term ἀμνός is also used of Jesus in Acts 8:32–33 and in 1 Pet 1:18–19. In Acts 8:32–33, Isa 53:7–8 is cited where the parallel terms πρόβατον, "sheep," and ἀμνός, "lamb," originally used as a metaphor for the servant of the Lord, are applied to Jesus. 1 Pet 1:18–19 speaks of being "ransomed . . . with the precious blood of Christ, like a lamb without blemish or defect [ὡς ἀμνοῦ

ἀμώμου καὶ ἀσπίλου]." Here the adjectives "without blemish or defect" clearly refer to the perfection expected of sacrificial victims (cf. Deut 15:21; 17:1; Philo *Spec. Leg.* 1.166).

While it is likely that the figure of the Lamb in Revelation must be understood at least in part on the basis of OT sacrificial ritual, it is not at all clear *which* type of sacrifice is primarily in view, for sheep or lambs were used as sacrificial victims in several different types of sacrifice in the OT and early Judaism: (1) Two lambs were sacrificed as an עלה *'ōlâ*, "burnt offering" (see *TWAT* 6:105–24), called a תמיד *tāmîd* offering in rabbinic sources (תמיד *tāmîd* means "regularly repeated"; cf. Haran, *Temples,* 207; Schürer, *History* 2:299–301), because Exod 29:42 prescribed that it be *repeated* regularly in the morning and evening as part of the regular temple ritual that opened and closed each day (Exod 29:38–46; Num 28:3–8; Dan 8:11; cf. Ezek 46:13–15 [only the morning sacrifice is mentioned]; 11QTemple 13:8–16; Philo *Spec. Leg.* 1.169–70; Jos. *Ant.* 3.237–47; 14.65–66). Two additional lambs were offered each sabbath (Num 28:9–10), and two young bulls, one ram, and seven male lambs were sacrificed on New Moons (Num 28:11–14), on each day of the Passover (Num 28:19–24), and on the Feast of Weeks (Num 28:26–29), on the first day of the seventh month (Num 29:1–3), and on the tenth day of the seventh month, the Day of Atonement (Num 29:7–8). On the fifteenth day of the seventh month, fourteen yearling lambs are sacrificed (Num 29:12–14). The basic daily *tamid* offering may have originally been intended to attract the attention of the deity and symbolized the meal of the deity (despite such denials as that found in Ps 50:12–14; see G. A. Anderson, *Sacrifices and Offerings in Ancient Israel: Studies in Their Social and Political Importance,* HSM 41 [Atlanta: Scholars, 1987] 14–19; Korpel, *Clouds,* 414–17), which by extension symbolized the presence of the deity among the people (Anderson, *ABD* 5:878) but never had any atoning significance. The procedure for slaughtering the *tamid* lamb, where the blood was sprinkled, the number of pieces into which it was cut, and how those pieces were burned on the altar, is described in *m. Tamid* 3:1–4.3; 7:3; see Safrai, "Temple," CRINT 1/2, 887–90; Schürer, *History* 2:304–7). (2) The institution of the Passover lamb (Exod 12:1–20, 43–49; Lev 23:5; Num 9:2–5; 28:16; Deut 16:1–8; Josh 5:10–12; 2 Chr 30:1–27; 35:1–19; Ezek 45:21; Ezra 6:19–21; 11QTemple 17:6–9; Haran, *Temples,* 317–48) was a type of the שלמים *šĕlāmîm,* "peace offering." All of the various types of peace offerings, however, had nothing to do with atonement (Anderson, *ABD* 5:878). The "lamb," however, could either be a yearling sheep or a goat (Exod 12:5), since the term צאן *sō'n* can mean either (*TWAT* 6:858–68). Even oxen could be slaughtered for Passover (Deut 16:2–3; 2 Chr 35:7). A number of scholars favor the view that the Lamb of Revelation is based on the metaphor of Christ as the Passover lamb (Str-B, 2:367–70; Holtz, *Christologie,* 45–47; Comblin, *Christ,* 26; D'Souza, *Lamb,* 25–27). The sacrifice of the Passover lamb was not a means of expiation from sins in early Judaism; rather it was a memorial of the liberation from Egyptian bondage (*Jub.* 49:1–17). The lambs were killed in the temple, roasted whole, and consumed by all Israel within the same day (Exod 12:47; 34:25). (3) Sheep or lambs were also used as sacrificial victims in various forms of the חטאת *ḥaṭṭā't,* "purification offering," usually but incorrectly translated "sin offering" (Milgrom, *Studies,* 67–69; Kiuchi, *Purification Offering,* 14). In Lev 12–15, a yearling lamb was prescribed as a *burnt offering* (עלה *'ōlâ*) to purify a woman after childbirth (12:6), and two male lambs and a ewe lamb were prescribed for the purification of a leper, one to be offered as a guilt offering (אשם *'āšām*) and the blood applied to various places on the body of the former leper (Lev 14:10–14), the second as a purification offering (חטאת *ḥaṭṭā't;* 14:19a), and the third as a burnt offering (עלה *'ōlâ;* 14:19b–20). (4) A number of sacrificial victims were slaughtered in connection with the consecration of tribal leaders in Num 7, including yearling lambs as burnt offerings (עלה *'ōlâ*). (5) A yearling lamb was sacrificed as a guilt offering (אשם *'āšām*) for Nazirites (Num 6:12). (6) One yearling lamb without defect was prescribed as a burnt offering (עלה *'ōlâ*) with the first fruits (Lev 23:12). (7) The expiatory sacrifice for unintentional sins discussed in Lev 4:1–5:13 includes the possibility of offering a sheep, if the offender cannot afford a bull, as a purification offering (חַטָּאת‎ *ḥaṭṭāʾt;* Lev 4:32). (8) The behavior and innocent death of the Servant of God is described in Isa 53 under the metaphor of a sacrificial sheep, and this metaphor is applied to Jesus in Acts 8:32. While few have argued that the Lamb of Revelation should primarily be understood against this background, the most detailed argument for this position is presented by Comblin (*Christ,* 17–47; followed by D'Souza, *Lamb,* 27–32). There is a connection between this use of sacrificial metaphor and the notion that martyrdom could be viewed as a means of purification for the sins of the people (2 Macc 7:38; 4 Macc 6:29). (9) It seems apparent that the historical *realia* of the Israelite sacrificial cult examined above do not provide anything more than a general context in which the metaphor of the slaughtered Lamb whose blood somehow effects redemption can be understood. The sacrificial features of the Lamb of Revelation are primarily a *textual phenomenon* with only very loose associations with actual cultic practice (cf. Anderson, *ABD* 5:873). The metaphor of Jesus as a sacrificial lamb whose blood (i.e., death) has atoning significance is based on the confluence of two traditions: Jesus as the (Passover) lamb (1 Cor 5:7; John 1:29, 36) and the conception of the death of Jesus as atoning in a way similar to the חַטָּאת‎ *ḥaṭṭāʾt,* "purification offering" (Lev 17:11; Heb 9:13–14 [here only the blood of bulls and goats is referred to as atoning]).

One rather remarkable feature of the Lamb in Revelation is that *he never speaks* (note that the Beast who rises from the earth in 13:11 is said to have two horns like a lamb and to *speak* like a dragon, though what he says is not included in the narrative). Yet it must also be recognized that none of the major figures opposing God and the Lamb are given speaking parts in the short narrative segments in which they are featured. An "exception" occurs when Babylon-Rome reportedly speaks "in her heart" (Rev 18:7).

The Greeks knew a constellation named Κριός, the Ram, or Aries (Aratus *Phaen.* 225, 238, 357, 515–16, 549, 709, 713), which was the first sign of the Zodiac. According to Lucian *Astrol.* 12, the people of Argos linked a golden lamb (ἀρήν) to Thyestes, who purportedly discovered the constellation Κριός.

## Explanation

Following the description of the serene magnificence of the throne room of God and the worship perpetually offered to God by heavenly beings (4:1–11), John's attention is drawn to a scroll with seven seals in the right hand of God (who is neither named nor described and throughout the entire scene remains remarkably passive). A brief drama then unfolds in which someone is sought who is worthy to break the seals and open the scroll (vv 2–4). One function of the motif of the heavenly council is to commission an emissary (cf. Isa. 6:8, "Whom can we send?"; 1 Kgs 22:20, "Who will entice Ahab?"). John makes use of this motif when an angel asks "Who is worthy to open the scroll?" (v 2). John weeps when no one is found, a conscious fiction representing the past perspective of Israel awaiting the Messiah. One of the elders tells John that the Lion of the tribe of Judah (Gen 49:9), the Root of David (Isa 11:1, 10), i.e., the Messiah, has conquered and can therefore open the scroll (v 5). Yet John sees not a Lion but a Lamb, looking as though it had been slain (v 6). The striking contrast between the two images suggests the contrast between the type of warrior messiah expected by first-century Judaism and the earthly ministry of Jesus as a suffering servant of God (see Matt 11:2–6 = Luke 7:18–23). The central dramatic scene of this vision segment is the cosmic sovereignty that the Lamb is revealed to possess, and the scene focuses on his acceptance of the sealed scroll from the hand of the one seated on the throne, symbolizing the full investiture of the Lamb (v 8). This focal revelation is followed by expressions of hymnic joy chanted by the twenty-four elders (vv 9–10), by an innumerable host of angels (v 12), by all created beings throughout the cosmos (v 13), with a concluding "amen" uttered by the four cherubim.

What is the significance of the scroll, and why is the Lamb alone able to open it? The scroll represents the final and fully predetermined stage in God's redemptive purpose for the world, which will unfold between the heavenly exaltation of Christ following his death and resurrection and the final inauguration of the eternal reign of God. The scroll and its contents therefore include the entire eschatological scenario extending from 6:1 through 22:9. That extensive section of Revelation represents a transcription of the heavenly scroll written by John to provide a revelatory preview of coming eschatological events. The antiphonal hymns of 5:9–14 celebrate the worthiness of the Lamb whose death has provided salvation for people of every nation. Though the Lamb has already been exalted to the throne of God and shares his rule, God's plan remains incomplete unless the Lamb, the only qualified emissary of God, receives full power and authority (symbolized by the scroll) to achieve the final eschatological victory.